Forensic Psychology

The editors' royalties for this book are being donated to the charity User Voice.

At User Voice we're pleased and flattered at the generosity of the two distinguished academics who have edited this book. That's because, as offenders and ex-offenders, we aren't used to being included. We live at the margins of society where we look threatening on street corners. But that big, scary-looking figure may not want to be a criminal. He may not see crime as a lifestyle choice but as inevitability. Childhood poverty, parental neglect, drug use and mental illness in the family, sexual, psychological and physical abuse, special educational needs … all these are predisposing factors to crime. By the time we get to jail, many offenders want to change and are anxious to embrace any chance to start a new life. But that chance doesn't come for most of us. Our jails get bigger and reoffending rates more atrocious but the programmes and help we need to become contributing members of society just aren't there. We leave prison, there is no one who cares enough to meet us at the gate, we have nowhere to go, and we wander, straight back to the only life we know.

User Voice is formed by and for offenders who believe that everyone who wants to change should have the opportunity to do so. The government does pour millions into programmes. These are seldom successful. So now it's time for something new. What? Well, try asking us. We understand crime and why we commit it, we know where the prison system fails, we even have a good idea of the kind of help we need to escape the tyranny of our damaged selves. User Voice exists to give a voice to users of the criminal and youth justice systems so that we can play an active role in our own rehabilitation. We accept that we must be punished and that incarceration is that punishment. But we ask that the time spent behind bars is a time of change. So stop telling us what's good for us and start giving us some responsibility. Stop designing programmes for us and start asking us what works.

Only offenders can stop reoffending.

Please listen to our voice because if you continue to ignore it the numbers of marginalised people will only grow. Listen to us, share some of your power with us, accept that our experience might mean we know something you don't. By bringing us to your attention in such a generous way, the editors of this book are acknowledging that, although we may have little formal education, we have something special to offer those who do. I thank them very warmly for this.

Mark Johnson
User Voice

Forensic Psychology

Edited by

Graham J. Towl and David A. Crighton

This edition first published 2010 by the British Psychological Society and Blackwell Publishing Ltd
© 2010 Blackwell Publishing Ltd

BPS Blackwell is an imprint of Blackwell Publishing, which was acquired by John Wiley & Sons in February 2007. Blackwell's publishing program has been merged with Wiley's global Scientific, Technical, and Medical business to form Wiley-Blackwell.

Registered Office
John Wiley & Sons Ltd, The Atrium, Southern Gate, Chichester, West Sussex, PO19 8SQ, UK

Editorial Offices
350 Main Street, Malden, MA 02148-5020, USA
9600 Garsington Road, Oxford, OX4 2DQ, UK
The Atrium, Southern Gate, Chichester, West Sussex, PO19 8SQ, UK

For details of our global editorial offices, for customer services, and for information about how to apply for permission to reuse the copyright material in this book please see our website at www.wiley.com/wiley-blackwell.

The right of Graham J. Towl and David A. Crighton to be identified as the authors of the editorial material in this work has been asserted in accordance with the UK Copyright, Designs and Patents Act 1988.

Library of Congress Cataloging-in-Publication Data

Forensic psychology / edited by Graham J. Towl and David A. Crighton.
       p.   cm.
    Includes bibliographical references and index.
    ISBN 978-1-4051-8618-6 (pbk. : alk. paper)   1. Forensic psychology–Great Britain.   I. Towl, Graham J.   II. Crighton, David A., 1964–
    RA1148.F5566 2010
    614'.15–dc22

                                        2009035842

A catalogue record for this book is available from the British Library.

Set in 9.5/11.5pt Minion by SPi Publisher Services, Pondicherry, India
Printed and bound in Malaysia by Vivar Printing Sdn Bhd

The British Psychological Society's free Research Digest e-mail service rounds up the latest research and relates it to your syllabus in a user-friendly way. To subscribe go to www.researchdigest.org.uk or send a blank e-mail to subscribe-rd@lists. bps.org.uk.

2   2011

Contents

List of Contributors

Editors

Professor David A. Crighton, Ministry of Justice and Durham University

Professor Graham J. Towl, Durham University

Contributors

Kerry Baker, University of Oxford

Dr Belinda Brooks-Gordon, Birkbeck University of London

Professor Kevin Browne, University of Nottingham

Dr Shihning Chou, University of Nottingham

Professor Brian R. Clifford, University of Aberdeen

Dr Coral Dando, University of Leicester

Professor Graham Davies, University of Leicester

Professor Connor Duggan, University of Nottingham

Dr Ceri Evans, Canterbury Regional Forensic Psychiatric Service, New Zealand

Professor David P. Farrington, University of Cambridge

David Faulkner, University of Oxford

Yu Gao, University of Southern California

Andrea L. Glen, University of Southern California

Professor Michael Gossop, Bethlehem Hospital and Institute of Psychiatry London

Professor Werner Greve, University of Hildesheim

Dr Lorraine Hope, University of Portsmouth

Dr Richard Howard, University of Nottingham

Naomi Humber, University of Manchester

Professor Andreas Kapardis, University of Cyprus

Dr Cathleen Kappes, University of Hildesheim

Dr Lila Kazemian, John Jay College of Criminal Justice, City University of New York

David La Rooy, University of Abertay

Professor William R. Lindsay, Carstairs State Hospital and University of Abertay

Melissa Peskin, University of Southern California

Professor Kathy Pezdek, Claremont Graduate University

Professor David Pilgrim, University of Central Lancashire

Professor Adrian Raine, University of Pennsylvania

Professor Jenny Shaw, University of Manchester

Professor Lawrence W. Sherman, University of Cambridge

Dr Robert A. Schug, University of Southern California

Dr Heather Strang, University of Cambridge

Professor John L. Taylor, Northumberland, Tyne and Wear NHS Trust and University of Northumbria

Yaling Yang, UCLA

Note

Points of view or opinions expressed in this book are those of the authors and not of any government, governmental agency or private funding agencies that may have supported their research.

Part I
Context

1

Introduction

Graham J. Towl

In recent years there has been a growth in the availability and popularity of both undergraduate modules and taught postgraduate courses in the broad field of forensic psychology. Indeed the term 'forensic' has been increasingly juxtaposed with a range of areas of academic study e.g. analysis, anthropology, archaeology, computing, engineering, investigation, measurement, psychobiology, psychology and science (UCAS, 2008). This is also evident in much professional practice, both within the field of health (e.g. psychiatric nurses, psychiatrists, occupational therapists and social workers) and beyond (e.g. accountants and computing specialists).

The past decade has been one of boom in forensic psychological practice with record numbers of posts in health and criminal justice, although there has been somewhat of a flattening of the total numbers of psychological staff employed in prisons and probation services between 2005 and 2009. However, there has been a growth of staffing in the Higher Education sector to accommodate course growth. There has also been a concomitant expansion in the breadth and depth of academic work (see for example, Crighton & Towl, 2008; Towl et al., 2008). Regrettably, much recent work of forensic psychologists in prisons has been increasingly restricted to unduly narrow areas of practice and theoretical perspectives. In view of the above it seemed timely to draw together a forensic textbook intended chiefly, but by no means exclusively, for the above audiences. As with some of our previous works, we have been keen to reflect a range of 'voices' or perspectives in the textbook. Thus this is not, for example, simply an uncritical treatise on the demerits and merits of

cognitive-behavioural-based approaches to working with criminals. That is a very well trodden path, with some clear ethical and empirical limitations. That said, we do cover some of this territory in a spirit of inclusivity, as opposed to the exclusivity which appears prevalent in some of the forensic literature; particularly in the forensic domain of research and practice with criminals in working towards reducing their risk of reoffending.

We are keen to capture not only some of the key areas of growth and development but also to draw upon an understanding of psychology and the context of its applications in the current social and political environment. The first section of this textbook has as its focus the forensic context. Inexorably this section touches upon the social and political. The second section covers some key areas of the knowledge base from leading contributors in the field.

Justice

The justice system in England and Wales is the starting point for setting the scene for many of the activities and interests of forensic psychologists. David Faulkner helpfully begins his chapter on the justice system with a brief exploration of what justice means. And such thinking and reflection are perhaps a helpful starting point when considering the ethical basis of much of the domain of forensic psychology whether as an area of academic study or professional practice. After outlining some key developments over the past century or so in the criminal justice system he goes on to consider what a crime is. Forensic psychologists can often derive great benefit from a fuller understanding of criminological perspectives. It is often asking the most fundamental questions that can yield some of the most fruitful hypotheses. Scientifically the methods that are used to collect data on crime will clearly be important in informing our understanding of crime, for example, in understanding the prevalence rates for particular crimes. Psychologists who are professionally interested in crime will want to familiarise themselves with the different methodologies commonly used and drawn upon in reports of crime in official figures. The social construction of crime and indeed the social structures that administer the criminal justice process or processes is apparent from the chapter. One example of the social construction of crime which may be familiar particularly perhaps to student readers is the behaviour of some students in damaging property in their universities after having consumed comparatively large quantities of alcohol. If caught, they may be admonished by their university but rarely in such circumstances would they find themselves in court on charges of criminal damage. By contrast, similar levels of property damage discharged by young people in economically deprived areas may be far more readily criminalised and viewed as wanton vandalism. The same could be said for those students who, under the influence of drink, drop their trousers. Such behaviours may be interpreted by some as high spirits and by others as simply offensive and inappropriate. Outside the cosy cloisters of academia such individuals may find themselves charged with criminal offences. More topically at the time of writing, the conduct of police officers at the G20 protests in London in early 2009 raises some interesting questions about who the criminal is. The gratuitous violence of police officers was, on occasion, plain to see in the media. The wearing of a uniform or membership of a particular profession may protect one from such potentially pejorative behavioural labelling (i.e. being designated a criminal). But it can happen; police officers are, on occasion, charged with offences, some are found guilty and some of those become prisoners.

The chapter includes coverage of some of the key structures and institutions of criminal justice processes. One problem which sets part of the context for the level of access that convicted criminals are likely to have to psychological services is that of the high numbers of people accommodated within prisons and under the supervision of probation services. Prisons in the UK are largely full. Less visible is the fact that probation supervision appears to be working beyond its reasonable capacity. Such capacity problems inexorably lead to the rationing of psychological services. Many psychologists within prisons will feel grave discomfort at the number of children in prisons (about 2800 in 2008). Some may not be unduly troubled, although they should surely be concerned about this. David Faulkner is. He goes on to cover the growing and demanding area of youth justice.

This is a theme that Kerry Baker takes up in the next chapter with her main focus upon community and residential services for children and young people. She also begins with a salutary reminder that only a small proportion of young people convicted by the courts receive custodial sentences. Her chapter consists of an overview of youth justice and the types of interventions provided for young people in the community. Of course, investments in the criminal justice system to address youth crime will only ever have a marginal effect on levels of crime. This is partly because the substantive issues that need addressing are not directly about crime *per se* but rather linked to poverty and economic, educational and sometimes emotional privation. Thus political and social policy based interventions are an essential element of effectively tackling youth crime. More unequal societies are more unhealthy societies. Hence relative poverty as well as absolute poverty is important to tackle. Sadly, in recent years there has been little progress in this important area in terms of results despite the investment of a great deal of public money. Just as in the adult system, a great deal of money has been invested in various 'assessment tools' which may have served the financial and professional interests of some but have not served the public particularly well. The marketisation and manualisation of some such youth services have, at times, led to narrow notions of intervention. A parallel may be drawn with the privatisation of bus services where the market dictates that only some services are profitable irrespective of customer needs. The increasing use of manual-based interventions has led some to conclude that there is a real danger of the dumbing down of such interventions with a failure to reflect the complexities of human behaviour (Towl, 2004). But there are signs that more broadly based approaches may be becoming increasingly popular, e.g. with multi-systemic therapy (MST). Kerry Baker argues for more multi-modal treatments and also considers some topical debates around 'best practice' in this challenging area. Having considered various types of service provision for children and young people she focuses upon some key debates around issues of policy and practice. The context of much criminal-justice-based work has been a toughening up on sentencing over the past decade but with comparatively little done to address the causes of crime. We see in subsequent chapters how much may be learned from a public health based model of crime reduction. Sadly, this appears to be a lesson still to be learnt in the domain of youth justice, with an emphasis on assessment and identifying 'risks' overriding investment in interventions. Kerry Baker also touches upon the so-called 'What works?' literature in her wide-ranging chapter. She helpfully points readers in the direction of the wider debate about such modern political mantras (e.g. Merrington & Stanley, 2007; Thomas-Peter, 2006). There is a real political resonance to her comment about the importance of being seen to do 'something' in the domain of criminal justice in general and youth offender work in particular. This is a theme which resonates in areas which have comparatively high levels of public interest. Thus it is not only in work with children and young people that this interest is aroused but also, for example, in the area of sex offending. This has arguably contributed to the evaluation of interventions which have sometimes been characterised more by political expediency than by empirical rigour.

In the context-setting first section of this book, Chapter 4 covers the area of expert testimony. As Brian Clifford points out, one feature that distinguishes this as a form of evidence is that opinions are actively sought. A great premium can sometimes be put upon 'expert evidence'. Hence it is potentially important as part of the criminal and civil justice process. Interestingly, although the practice of 'expert testimony' has been around for a number of centuries, it is only comparatively recently that psychologists have been called upon in such roles. Expert witnesses, according to the British Psychological Society, are there to serve the courts rather than the parties instructing them (BPS, 2007). This is the legal basis of the relationship between expert witnesses and the courts.

Expert Controversies

One of the controversies in the area of expert evidence by psychologists, and for that matter psychiatrists too, is that the scientific basis of some of the assertions made about the evidence base may be deeply equivocal. Thus there are some major doubts about aspects of the disciplines of both psychology and psychiatry. For example, some have reported scientific concerns about the validity of psychiatric diagnoses which are derived from a series of checklists. Although some psychologists have been critical of this approach, many have warmed to it,

content to offer their views (and pick up their fee for so doing) on whether or not an individual may be deemed fit to be allocated to a particular diagnostic category. In general, such diagnostic taxonomies have been seen to have greater reliability than validity. Many requests for psychological evidence in the forensic domain can hinge upon whether or not an individual is deemed to fit in this or that diagnostic category. Similar issues are to the fore with the psychometrics industry. The heavily marketed claim is that various psychometric 'tools' may furnish us with much-coveted 'objective' information about germane psychological aspects of human functioning, using an algorithm. Of course, such information needs to be viewed in the wider context of its use. Another area of expert testimony has been in relation to memory research. A knowledge and understanding of memory research have perhaps most widely been highlighted in relation to eyewitness testimony as a particular type of expert witness testimony. Indeed this is one application of experimental psychology that is routinely referred to in undergraduate and postgraduate forensic psychology courses. Of course, the scope for applications of our understanding of memory research can potentially go much wider. For example, the application of the understanding of memory to the assessment of life-sentenced prisoners would be one area of development. Part of the standard assessment methods used for such prisoners involves the collection of interview-based data. Thus prisoners may be asked to give their recollection of their thoughts, emotions and actions during the commission of their index offence. Some of the findings from memory research would suggest that this would be likely to be a constructive process, perhaps with a recall effect of previous accounts given at various points over the period since the commission of the offence. This is an area ripe for research. But it is not just in relation to memory research that there may be forensic applications. An understanding of developmental psychology, and indeed social psychology, may be helpful in their applications to working with children, young people and adults in contact with criminal justice organisations.

But the whole area of expert testimony warrants close scrutiny on ethical grounds. Almost by definition, lay-persons are unlikely to be good at detecting errors in scientific research presented to them. It is incumbent upon the 'expert' to offer not only scientific opinion but to express it in a manner in which a jury is most likely to understand and appreciate the precise status and relevance of such views. But the ultimate ethical issue, as

Brian Clifford asserts, revolves around the quality of the science that the 'expert' draws upon.

Thinking about Ethics

The fifth and final chapter in the context-setting section of the book is about ethics. It has been observed that although the substantive ethical issues are not different to those found elsewhere, they perhaps are brought into sharper focus in the forensic field (Towl, 1994). Ethical issues underpin what we research and how we practise. It is worth exploring some of the philosophical roots to our ethical understanding. Considerations of both individual rights and a sense of the common good are key considerations which underpin many professional ethical codes of practice. Ethics and ethical thinking and reflection do not occur in a vacuum but rather in the context of power relations in particular cultures during particular times. Power differentials are pervasive across cultures. Professional cultures set the scene for both ethical and unethical behaviour. Some aspects of research and practice may change speedily over time in terms of adjustments to wider societal norms, others more slowly. One underlying concern about professionals in general has been the extent to which they are considered to be self-serving rather than serving the public interest. Professions tend to attract higher levels of pay and related benefits in comparison with the workforce in general. It is perhaps unsurprising, then, that professional ethical guidance can sometimes be seen in the same way, i.e. there to serve the self-interests of the profession. Psychology and the work of psychologists are not immune to this. Indeed, the numbers of complaints in forensic practice have grown in recent years, e.g. particularly in prisons. As indicated above, forensic practice can bring into sharper focus some fundamental ethical issues. If forensic psychologists are criticised, which they frequently are, in service user outlets (see, for example, Hanson, 2009; Rose, 2009), this can lead to defensive professional practices. These can include the avoidance of some areas of work or an unwillingness to take appropriate and just risks. There is no excuse for such practices. Indeed, such practices themselves may reasonably be deemed unethical and are by no means exclusive to the forensic psychological field. But it is important to acknowledge some of the potential dynamics that may come into play. When complained about, individuals may feel hurt or even angry. Complaints may feel as if they are rather personal, whether or not that is the intention of the complainant. There is some good guidance available for forensic psychologists (see, for example, the BPS code of conduct and also the very useful European-wide guidance produced by Lindsay et al., 2008). Responses to complaints can be an opportunity for reflection on one's own practice; there may be learning to benefit from. Of course, in forensic practice there may be more of a tendency for recipients of services to complain in relation to decision making which may have an impact on their liberty. This is perfectly understandable.

It is probably axiomatic to state that, in general, the greater the power imbalances the greater the opportunity for abuses, and thus unethical behaviour. This touches upon a tension within the growth of professions. Characteristically, professional groups tend to work towards increasing their power bases rather than decreasing them. One unintended consequence is that it becomes more likely that some will abuse such powers and a recipient of such unethical services may well eventually, and not unreasonably, complain. More power for a particular profession is not by any means necessarily a good thing, far from it. One test of a professional is the extent to which an individual is willing to 'whistle blow' about a colleague. Perhaps too often it is easier not to comment upon, let alone intervene, when a colleague is behaving in a professionally inappropriate manner. Some, of course, will cover up for the mistakes of colleagues and this can be a rarely acknowledged problem across professions and beyond. However, increased influence or power may, of course, be used positively and this is the basis of countervailing arguments. But such tensions provide us with a salutary reminder of the need always to treat others with dignity and respect, especially when dealing with differences. Compassion, understanding, justice and kindness are crucial to just, ethical decision-making processes. Another useful 'rule of thumb' test can be not to treat others how we would not wish to be treated ourselves. Again, it is also the case when applying aspects of psychological development to our understanding of criminals and crime. The second section of the book has as its focus the evidence base in forensic psychology and its applications. We begin with the evidence in the domain of neurobiological research.

Developmental Perspectives

Neurobiological research into crime and antisocial behaviour has grown considerably in recent years. Robert

Schug and his colleagues cover this exciting area of research in their detailed chapter. Brain research has moved on considerably since the days of clinical lobotomies to control aggressive or disruptive behaviour in UK psychiatric hospitals. A combination of improved technologies, ethical standards and a more rigorously scientific approach have improved the knowledge and understanding yielded in this complex area of research. Studies have been undertaken with brain-injured patients which have led to links being made between orbitofrontal cortex and experiences of rage and hostility. Frontal lobe damage has generally been equated with a greater proneness to demonstrate antisocial behaviour. Establishing causal relationships is much more challenging. Head injuries of various sorts may, for example, act as a trigger that disrupts normal functioning in terms of behavioural inhibitors. There are a range of potential hypotheses as to how the underlying biological mechanisms may impact upon behaviour in this exciting area of research. What complicates matters further is that there are likely to be a range of environmental aspects to the manifestation of underlying biological mechanisms that may be at work. The field has moved on since the intellectually vacuous debates about issues of nature vs. nurture. Such complex interactions can be difficult to study with an appropriate level of scientific rigour.

Psychometric testing provides us with one avenue of exploration in improving our understanding of specific brain functioning and links to antisocial behaviour, although some of the results in this challenging area of research are open to a range of interpretations. For example, it has been reported that antisocial behaviour is associated with comparatively lower levels of verbal intelligence. From a neurobiological perspective this may, not unreasonably, be interpreted as linked to left hemispheric dysfunction. However, the reason for comparatively higher levels of performance IQ may simply be attributable to a lack of educational opportunities. Both such explanations may, of course, be accurate. Again, it is the causal links or specific mechanisms underpinning such differences that are perhaps most challenging to demonstrate. Significant verbal deficits in children can be predictive of subsequent delinquency. Whichever of these interpretations of the data is taken to be true, it would seem that there is a compelling case for improved access to educational opportunities, especially for those young children without social and economic advantages. This is a form of social engineering very popular and actively accessed within the middle classes with such a keen focus on which schools their children go to. Unlike their middle-class counterparts, educational disadvantage tends to be a feature of (young) offender populations. It is perhaps encouraging, albeit in a relatively small way, that increasingly psychologists are taking an interest in working with children and young people in young offender institutions, i.e. prisons, although, to be most effective, such work should be undertaken earlier in the trajectory towards crime, with individual children and young people. The next chapter in the book includes coverage of the key area of 'prevention'.

The first chapter in this book by David Farrington draws upon the developmental evidence base in seeking to address the important policy and public concern of the prevention of the development of criminal behaviour. Effective prevention will result in fewer victims and also more individuals living fulfilling and productive lives. One recent trend in some of the research evaluating the efficacy of particular interventions aimed at reducing the risk of (re)offending has been the introduction of measures of 'cost effectiveness' in addition to traditional psychological methods of evaluation. This is a very positive development. It is positive because it allows us not only to focus upon the area of 'treatment impact' but also the financial cost of such impacts. Thus we have the potential to invest such public money more wisely. The idea underlying the developmental prevention of criminality is that 'risk factors' may be identified in advance and addressed early, before the 'risks' manifest themselves behaviourally. Also, 'protective factors' may be identified to further ameliorate the frequency and severity of such 'risks'. Children who have poor parental supervision are exposed to a greater risk of engaging in offending than those who do not. Even in purely financial terms some interventions can be demonstrably effective in saving the public purse. This has been revealed by a number of cost–benefit-based studies. One comparatively famous 'intensive' intervention involved home visitors giving advice about prenatal and postnatal care to young mothers. There was a focus upon appropriate nutrition and related health advice. In short, it was a general parental education intervention. Postnatal home visits resulted in decreased levels of child neglect and abuse. Children of these mothers had less than half the rate of arrests of a comparison group. These are powerful findings. The focus in Farrington's chapter is rightly on high quality evaluations. The quality of the research data is crucial. It is crucial in making evident the strengths and weaknesses of particular research methods. In public policy terms he makes the case for the development of a national prevention agency. The arguments are compelling. Such an idea has been implemented elsewhere (e.g. in Sweden and Canada). Such an enterprise would allow for a much more appropriate use of forensic psychologists who could work alongside their educational psychology counterparts. One of the key problems in the development of forensic psychological services in England and Wales is that there are far fewer such psychologists engaging in preventative work and rather more working in prisons and particularly high-security prisons which some would say are overstaffed with forensic psychologists. Even within the prison system, in terms of the potential impact upon crime reduction, there are too few psychologists working in young offender institutions. A wiser distribution of resources would target schools, pupil referral units, youth justice services in the community and residential estates and caseloads of 'high risk' offenders in the probation services.

Psychosocial research has been key in the study of offenders. Offenders tend to be versatile in their criminal activities, switching sometimes effortlessly from one offence type to another, e.g. burglary and assaults. Most convicted violent offenders will have convictions for non-violent crimes too. In his next chapter on the developmental evidence base, David Farrington reviews work on risk factors that influence the development of criminal careers. This is an area where there are a number of studies with comparatively robust research methods that have been employed. David Farrington in his review adopts a rigorous approach to the research quality of the studies that he covers.

Early signs of impulsivity can be used to predict an inflated risk of antisocial behaviour. This has perhaps found a recent manifestation in the currently fashionable diagnosis of 'attention deficit-hyperactivity disorder'. Related perhaps to this is that low school achievement is linked to an increased risk of youth violence. Indeed, there are a whole host of correlations that may be made with the prediction of subsequent crime. More recent studies in particular have begun to look, not just at correlations, but also at mediating factors in behavioural outcomes. For example, it has been proposed that the link between low school achievement and delinquency may be mediated by psychological disinhibition. The executive functioning of young brains may well be important in the prediction of future functioning. This is perhaps a good example of future research opportunities, with the need to draw upon wider learning within the expanding cognitive psychology field to help in our understanding of the developmental trajectories towards crime.

Parenting methods have also been looked at in terms of links with future potential crimes. These methods have often been categorised in terms of factors such as parental supervision, discipline and warmth (or coldness). One seminal study in this area provided evidence that poor parental supervision, harsh discipline and a rejecting attitude predicted an inflated chance of subsequent delinquency. Authoritarian parenting styles in particular have been linked to the prediction of subsequent violence. This is entirely in keeping with social learning theory. Brutalisation begets brutalisation. Attachment theory has also been drawn upon in understanding the psychosocial trajectories towards delinquency (Crighton & Towl, 2008; Crittenden, 2008).

The family can be a significant protective factor for some; however, if a child is unfortunate enough to have a father or mother who is involved in crime, then the probability is that they themselves will end up with a criminal record. Although the term 'criminal careers' is widely used in the field, it should perhaps be noted that there is no good evidence that the above finding reflects a 'career choice' that the child has moved into the family trade or profession. Far from it. Criminal parents tend to be highly critical of their child's involvement in crime. Family size is also important, with more children being equated with a higher risk of delinquency. This may well be linked to the thinner distribution of emotional, social and financial resources.

In the UK it has been amply demonstrated that poverty predicts an inflated risk of criminal conviction. Low family income and poor housing tend to characterise those with a higher risk of delinquency. Boys are at a higher risk of conviction while unemployed than when in employment. These findings present some clear moral and related social policy challenges. The potential to impact upon the design of prevention-based interventions is evident.

Every bit as important as understanding the developmental progression through 'criminal careers' is the need to understand what leads to desistence from crime. One advantage of a developmental perspective is that it lends itself to the notion that at different life stages different factors may come to the fore as the best predictors of desistence. Marriage and stable employment are two factors which have been widely researched in terms of their predictive value in desistence. Others have argued that personal resolve and determination to stop committing crime are also important. Desistence, in one sense, may be likened to 'spontaneous recovery' in medicine. Generally when we are unwell we subsequently recover. This is true of both physical and mental health. It would very often be the case without any medical intervention. A parallel can be drawn with crime. A certain number of those committing crimes (probably most) will eventually desist from committing crimes. The rate of crime by individual offenders is, in large part, age dependent. Thus it could be argued that one factor potentially important in desistence is the ageing process. The field is replete with a lack of agreement about how precisely desistence should be operationalised. Some consider deceleration of the rate or seriousness of the type of crime to be a form of desistence. Others assume that desistence means no longer committing crime. This is an under-researched area with plenty of potential and indeed promise for the future.

Offender Profiling: Smoke and Mirrors?

Offender profiling, possibly like no other topic across the forensic psychological field, generates much interest, some of which is prurient, some not. Whatever the motivation, this is an area of the forensic field which has spawned a number of films and television programmes. Much of the forensic field, well beyond the boundaries of psychology, has been booming. Some of the increased interest across the field is due to some genuine developments with clear forensic applications (e.g. DNA testing). However, much in this popular area of forensic psychology amounts merely to empirical smoke and mirrors. David Crighton, in his chapter on offender profiling, gives a more generous outline of the field, and crucially its potential. He looks afresh at some of the evidence, including the methodologies used by 'profilers'. He accurately concludes that the scientific evidence in support of offender profiling in its various guises is somewhat limited.

Witnesses

The three chapters of the book that follow are about witnesses. These are critical areas of forensic psychology. Lorraine Hope helpfully points out that eyewitnesses can play an important role in the courtroom. The accuracy, or otherwise, of such eyewitness testimony is clearly crucial. For many students of psychology this will have a real resonance with much of memory research covered during their undergraduate studies. The reconstructive functioning of memory can plausibly lead to biases and inaccuracies in eyewitness testimony. This is

an area of forensic psychological research and practice where opportunities to draw from the learning from experimental psychological studies into memory and learning abound. Of course, one feature of the field is the challenge of how results observed in the psychological laboratory may transfer to real-life events. This is largely a question of the ecological validity of such learning, which is by no means exclusive to this area of forensic study. But the models and methods developed in laboratories and lecture halls can be convincingly applied to study in real-world settings. Concepts from memory and learning research can clearly be helpful in assisting our understanding of eyewitness testimony. For example, we may wish to look at errors in encoding information or systematic biases in recall. Memory decay effects may also be an interesting area for further examination. Facial recognition studies also have had an impact, drawing from work in experimental psychology. One practical social policy area of influence drawn from these areas of research in the forensic psychological field has been in relation to the development of procedural guidance relating to the identification of suspects by the police in England and Wales.

One area of witness testimony which presents a set of its own challenges is in the area of children as witnesses. This area of study is of particular interest in the forensic field because when children are victims of crimes, especially sexual or physically assaultative crimes, they may well be the only witnesses to such events. Graham Davies and Kathy Pezdek give an account of the factors which may affect the veracity of children's memory. They also touch upon interview techniques and the presentation of child witness testimony in court. Such areas tend to hold a relatively high level of media and public interest. They are also areas where both experimental and field-based studies may be drawn upon. One key lesson is in the importance of the amount of time which has elapsed from the point of the relevant events to the recall of the events. The nature of the crimes themselves in combination with the inefficiencies built into the criminal justice process may together result in less complete accounts of events than could be the case. However, overall, children are perfectly capable of providing accurate reports of such events. In general, children are reliable witnesses. However, such reported memories may be shaped to some degree by the information-gathering process, most commonly the interviewing of the child. The memorandum of good practice in child witness interviewing includes video recording the interview. The memorandum is based on three precepts: the need to be ethical in eliciting testimony, the need to draw from the scientific literature and also the related need of operating within the relevant legal structures and systems. However, there appears to have been a difference, sometimes substantially so, between theory and practice. In practice, some interviewers have not shown an appropriate level of regard for such important procedural issues. Hence the distribution of 'Achieving Best Evidence in Criminal Proceedings' (Home Office, 2002), although the development of new guidance does not necessarily address some of the issues of managerial incompetence that may well play more of a role with such problems. Appearing as a witness in court can be a stressful event for an adult, and this is arguably even more so for a child. In view of this, special measures have been introduced to reduce the stressfulness of the role, e.g. the removal of formal court dress and the clearing of the public gallery. Live video links have also been used so that the child does not have to experience being in the courtroom. However, there is some evidence that jurors may be less likely to convict when receiving video rather than live child testimony. Arguably what is most important in this challenging field of application is that lawyers and psychologists work more closely together to try to ensure both accurate and just decision making.

Witness testimony with adults is also an area which has received a great deal of attention from, amongst others, psychologists. Again the field is characterised by both the application of findings in experimental psychology and also some field-based studies. Our understanding of memory and aids to enhance the detail and accuracy of memories for particular events are central to this area of work. An understanding of encoding, storage and the retrieval of memories is important as is, in particular, an awareness of the processes of forgetting. Cognitive interviewing is also covered in the chapter by David La Rooy and Coral Dando on witness interviewing.

Victims of crimes frequently find themselves in the uncomfortable position of having to give evidence. This can be very important if a conviction is to be secured. Of course, many, probably most, victims of crimes do not get to court. This is an important area of the study of victims. Indeed, some of the more grandiose claims made by researchers in, for example, much of the sex offender literature seem effortlessly dismissive of the full implications of low reporting rates upon what is sometimes purported to be 'what we know about sex offenders'. In addition to the area of unreported victims is the area of the consequences for victims of particular crimes,

and factors which may help alleviate or circumvent personal consequences. Offenders as a group and those who go on to become offenders often have some of the highest rates of victimhood themselves. In short, offenders and victims are by no means mutually exclusive groups; there is a great deal of overlap. Young men have some of the highest rates of victimhood for violent crime. This is perhaps contrary to the sometimes received understanding that it may be the elderly who are most likely to be victims of such crime. That is not to suggest that the elderly do not experience more fear of violent crime than many.

In terms of the criminal justice process played out in the courts, one crucial grouping is juries. Jury decision making has been the subject of much research. References to juries go back a long way in recorded history. But a commonly referred to historical reference point is that of the Magna Carta, in 1215. Juries remain prominent in our court system. This is despite evidence that many members of the jury may struggle to understand particularly complex cases. Furthermore, they can also struggle to follow the instructions of judges, e.g. when asked to ignore inadmissible evidence – although, of course, some would question whether or not the instructions of judges are always just, or on occasion simply effectively protecting existing power relationships. The legal professions have little or no incentives to change this as the confusion, in effect, serves to enhance their power bases.

Psychological Assessment

Power relationships are an important aspect of the context of much forensic work. This is very much the case in the area of the psychological assessment of offenders. For example, prisons are fundamentally coercive institutions (Towl, 2005a). Psychologists wield a great deal of influence in forensic contexts. This has been raised as a matter of concern amongst some service users. Readers may wish to thumb the pages of the publication *Inside Time*, the National Newspaper for Prisoners, to get a flavour of some of the concerns related to the power of psychologists in prisons. This is, or in some cases, perhaps, should be, a key ethical issue in everyday practice. Psychological assessments are not immune to biases, e.g. attributional errors that we may all from time to time be prone to in everyday judgements and decision making. But at the core of a good psychological assessment is a rigorously scientific approach applied with appropriate human consideration for the individual or individuals who are the subject of such assessments. A range of theoretical models may be applied but each involves, in some way or another, data collection (ideally from a good range of sources), formulation and judgement (which includes a sense of justice). It is not good enough merely to provide a scientifically accurate report in the forensic domain; there is an ethical responsibility for the psychologist to ensure that their report is also a just report. Whereas the field is replete with examples of discussion and debate over the accuracy of some psychological assessment methods, comparatively rarely is the issue of the justness or fairness of reports covered with such energy and detail. This perhaps reflects poorly upon us in the forensic psychology profession. One particularly important aspect of assessment is the ability to capture the work within a report form. The precise format of assessment reports may vary. However, all should have certain features. They should be evidence based and written in an appropriately respectful and accurate manner. Any recommendations included in such a report should be explicitly linked to the body of data/evidence that characteristically will make up the main body of the report. They need to be both accurate and just.

One area of psychological assessments, which are particularly common in forensic practice, is in the domain of risk assessments. Again, issues of the accuracy and justice of such assessments come into sharp focus (Towl, 2005b). There has been an aggressive marketing of some risk assessment tools in recent years. There are some significant financial gains to be made for psychologists involved in the development of such tools and the often compulsory training and interpretation of 'the psychometrics'. It is perhaps unsurprising that this has been a key area of the 'for profit' (or private) sector involvement in forensic psychological practice. In assessing the utility of particular structured tools it is perhaps worth reflecting upon who benefits from their use. This is an area that forensic psychologists have often tended to fight shy of, preferring instead to debate the relative empirical strengths and weaknesses of particular tools. Clearly this is very important too. But it is also important that practitioners are aware that businesses, by definition, are on the whole structured to make money and this will thus be the primary driver in the marketing of psychometrics. This can result in conflicts of interest. It is not unknown for those with financial interests in particular tools to recommend that others use them without being explicit

about their conflict of interest. This is, of course, unethical, but comparatively rarely challenged.

There is much that can be learnt about the nature of risk assessment across disciplinary boundaries. The contemporary social and political concerns about climate change, international terrorism and transnational banking systems have given rise to a number of interdisciplinary approaches to understanding 'risk'. There are a range of professions and disciplines with an interest in these challenging and fascinating areas. There are a particular set of 'risks' that tend to be focused upon within forensic practice. The relevant 'risks' tend to be about the chances of an individual committing crimes, and often violent and sexual crimes. Psychologists have contributed a great deal to improve the accuracy of such 'risk assessments'. Risk assessment reports may be used both to inform judgements about whether or not an individual is released from prison or hospital and also to inform the allocation to particular interventions. White-collar crime is much less commonly a focus of forensic psychological practice. Of course, the impacts of so-called white collar crime may well be every bit as serious as those of identified potential violent or sexual offenders. The international 'banking crisis' perhaps provides an illustrative example of this. In the modern world poverty is a moral crime which is widespread, including within the 'developed' world. This will result in heightened levels of 'risk' of unnecessary suffering and victimhood for many, and, as has been discussed above, an increased chance of ending up on a social and individual trajectory to the perpetration of crime. All violent and sexual crimes are interpersonal. Forensic psychologists tend to focus primarily upon potential perpetrators rather than potential victims. Not only is this scientifically limited as an approach, it is also questionable in terms of ethical practice. There also perhaps needs to be a wider recognition and acknowledgement that victims and perpetrators, when it comes to violent and sexual crimes, are overlapping groups. And this is a real challenge in criminal justice in that we know that many of the measures which may impact on lowering crime are linked to the remit of government departments other than those concerned with criminal justice. But forensic psychologists as a group are well placed to challenge inappropriate policies and practices. There is something of a history of this amongst some; for example, forensic psychologists have challenged aspects of racism in prisons. Some forensic psychologists have challenged the dubious practices of colleagues who, in the past, have not always given prisoners sufficiently full information about the assessments that are being undertaken. It is a healthy sign within a profession if members of that profession are (publicly) prepared to question and challenge the behaviour and conduct of colleagues. This is a sometimes uncomfortable but necessary process. It is essential if as a discipline forensic psychologists wish to enjoy the respect of all the public (including prisoners).

Critical Psychology

Although some psychologists remain critical or circumspect about the scientific credentials of psychiatric diagnoses, such categorisations are routinely used by many psychologists. There can be professional comfort in categorisation. Once such an allocation of a diagnostic label has taken place, there is, in effect, purportedly, an 'explanation' of the behaviour which may be of concern or interest. As David Pilgrim asserts in his chapter on aspects of diagnosed mental illness and offending, none of us can plausibly claim to be in perfect mental health. The area of hypothesised links between offending and mental illness is contentious. There can be tensions between psychological and psychiatric knowledge. Unlike in psychology, the focus in psychiatry is with mental disorder rather than 'mental order'; this is one of the themes that David Pilgrim explicates further in his chapter. Poverty and social exclusion play a part in informing our understanding of who is and is not diagnosed with mental disorders. Indeed, there is a parallel with recorded crime. Just as there are systematic biases in what crime gets recorded (or is designated as a crime), there are similar such biases in who does or does not get diagnosed with what. Again the issue of power inequalities raises its head.

The issue of power inequalities is arguably more salient in the area of diagnosed mentally disordered offenders with identified intellectual disabilities. This is because it is evident to most of us that intellectual disabilities may well result in a fundamental vulnerability. The term 'learning disabilities' is synonymous with 'intellectual disability' and perhaps reflects particular professional sensibilities in terms of the more or less desirable term to be used. Again, this is an area of practice where the psychometrics industry maintains a firm hold. Screening measures for intellectual disabilities abound and are vigorously marketed. This is a large and financially lucrative market for the psychometrics industry, its proponents and beneficiaries. Much of the territory which may be considered to be 'mental disorder' is subject to the effective ownership of such categories through the auspices

of DSM-IV and ICD-10, with an array of additional profitable product lines such as psychometric tests for intellectual assessment. The contempt that some of the early test makers had for those with intellectual disabilities is all too evident in the chapter by William Lindsay and John Taylor. They cite Terman's (albeit unfounded) assertions about the inexorable link between the potential for criminality and 'feeblemindedness'. This is a field characterised by a history of prejudice. This is the context in which psychological assessments and interventions take place. Psychologists themselves are also subject to the potential prejudices common in this area, but at least as a professional group we should be aware of the effects of such potential prejudices on our behaviour and judgements.

One significant area of practice for forensic psychologists is in giving an opinion on fitness to stand trial and enter a plea on behalf of the court. The extent to which the accused party understands the nature of the crime and court process needs to be assessed. Their capacity to 'instruct' their legal representatives needs assessing too. There also needs to be an understanding of the issue of responsibility in criminal law. The level of understanding of the 'wrongness' of the relevant criminal acts by the defendant may well also be a consideration for the courts. Relevant psychological assessments and evidence can lead to a defence of diminished responsibility or not guilty by reason of insanity.

Those with intellectual disabilities may have communication needs different from those of the general population. Effective communication is crucial to psychological assessments. But arguably this need is amplified when working with those with intellectual disabilities whether undertaking assessments or interventions. Arguably this is an aspect of working with offenders that needs more visibility. Such challenges sometimes remain hidden from everyday discourses about offenders.

One increasingly highly visible area of study, policy and practice is in relation to work with those diagnosed as having 'personality disorders'. Historically there has been a discussion and debate about whether or not those diagnosed with personality disorders are simply at the more extreme ends of some key identified dimensions of personality or if they are qualitatively different. In their far-ranging chapter Richard Howard and Conor Duggan make a case in favour of the 'qualitative differences' side of the debate. Whichever side of that particular debate the reader favours, this is a complex and challenging field and one that has exercised many an academic and clinician. It is an area where both fundamental questions about the putative nature (or existence) of personality disorders may be addressed and also practical clinical questions (e.g. about potentially suitable interventions) may be answered.

In recent years there has been a great deal of government investment in the 'treatment' of those categorised as having personality disorders. Some 'personality disorders' have been the subject to more study than others within forensic populations. There are some gender differences in such studies, with links between men and 'antisocial personality disorders' and women and borderline 'personality disorders'. This is one of those comparatively few areas of research and practice which has been generously funded by the public. The much-vaunted Dangerous Severe Personality Disorder (DSPD) units in prisons and hospitals have perhaps tended to be overstaffed with psychologists. There has been a massive investment of public money in research, with what appears to be very little indeed to show for it in terms of results which will be helpful in policy terms, or in clinical management and practice. This is disappointing, but not remotely surprising. Some of the problems have arisen out of a conceptual confusion regarding what precisely constitutes DSPD; it is not a clinical category, but rather a political one. Another part of the problem is that a range of behavioural disorders appear to have been captured under the muddled rubric of DSPD. In short, the term is bereft of any intellectual integrity. Of course, this reflects a more general problem when underlying personality traits are attributed to particular behavioural patterns. And it is an argument that could be used to call into question the scientific basis of the construct of personality disorders *per se*. Many, aware of some of the limitations of such terms, will simply take a pragmatic approach. As we have seen in some other areas of forensic practice, this is an area replete with financial interests from, for example, the psychometric testing industry. There have also been some large research grants available to support such work, which will tend to draw in interest and further financial, professional and intellectual investments.

Continuing along the theme of controversies, Ceri Evans covers the challenging and potentially contentious area of the trauma of being violent. The psychological impact of having committed a violent crime is rarely considered amongst those routinely dispatched to undertake risk assessments with violent offenders. Some of the work in this area has been linked to post-traumatic stress disorder (PTSD) reactions, but as Ceri Evans points out, this is only one of a range of potential diagnoses that may be employed in such cases. This is an area of study which perhaps powerfully illustrates the importance of our emotions in the reconstruction and repetition of memories of significant life events. Perhaps one reason why this can be a difficult area for some clinicians to engage with is that it is easier and more psychologically comfortable to dichotomise the world into victims and perpetrators, as 'good' or 'bad', respectively. As is discussed below in relation to a later chapter, a similar problem may occur with suicidality. Violent and sexual offenders have an increased risk of suicide, but prison staff may find it difficult to engage effectively with such offenders while they themselves put up the psychological barrier of deeming the individual dangerous rather than desperate.

Drugs

Drug and alcohol misuse has become an increasingly major problem in relation to both problems of public health and criminal justice. A compulsion to consume such products is an underlying commonality in the, oftentimes, absolutely desperate domain of the habitual drug user. Some official estimates have asserted that about half of all recorded crime is drug related, as Michael Gossop reminds us in his chapter on substance misuse. Individuals may commit crimes while under the influence of drugs. Alternatively or additionally they commit crimes to fund their drug habits. Drug addicts lie and deceive those around them, even their close friends and family, such is the power of the compulsion to access drugs. The deplorable truth is that drug addicts can often have more chance of receiving treatment if they go to prison than if they do not. This health service inadequacy contributes to the creation of a perverse incentive for addicts who want treatment to commit crime and get caught doing so, with a view to imprisonment. This cannot be right.

Drug crime is big business, and the relevant markets are vigorously policed and protected by such criminals. Thus there can be a significant difference between the supplier and the user or consumer of the particular drug. Drug overdose is a relatively common cause of death amongst regular drug users. It is frequently difficult for individual users to gauge the quality and thereby quantity of the drugs that they are intending to use. Notwithstanding the devastating impacts of drug misusage in both health and crime-related terms, one of the most dangerous drugs routinely used in prisons is nicotine. Stopping smoking in prisons must surely be the single biggest public health policy in prisons that has not happened in recent years. This is despite the very strong empirical evidence indicating that smoking is detrimental to health. It is also despite the fact that the challenges of an imposed ban on smoking, which some thought unworkable, in public houses in the UK can be overcome. Perhaps one reason that it has not been focused upon with so much vigour within a criminal justice setting is that it is not known to be linked to increased levels of criminality. This illustrates the difficulty of departments of state not being as integrated as they could be in addressing issues which cut across government departmental boundaries. The capacity to function effectively across (and outwith) central departmental boundaries is perhaps one of the biggest challenges of public service, specifically perhaps for senior civil servants, for our purposes both within and beyond the Ministry of Justice and Home Office. There has perhaps been an increasing recognition in recent years that many public policy problems warrant multidisciplinary and multi-agency partnership working to be most likely to be effective.

As a general rule it seems that earlier interventions are potentially more effective. We see from the earlier developmentally orientated chapters that those who go on to commit serious offences as adults can, as a group, be identified comparatively early in their criminal careers. Children and young people who are violent and engage in sexually harmful behaviours particularly warrant our attention. Kevin Browne and Choug Shang make a case for early intervention and support. This is especially important given the known links between those who have been abused themselves and those who go on to commit acts of abuse. A great deal of such sexually abusive behaviour may go on within the family. For example, teenage children may be trusted to care for younger siblings who then experience abuse. Often such developmental trajectories may well manifest themselves into adulthood from the perspective of both the abuser and abused.

The UK sex offender assessment and treatment industry is booming. Again this is an area where a great deal of public money has been spent. There are no UK studies for prisons over the past 14 years that have demonstrated an independent treatment effect for the statistically significant reduction of risk of reconvictions for a sexual offence, although there is evidence that convicted sex offenders will show clinical improvements on various self-report methods before and after treatment.

But some would argue that they 'would do, wouldn't they', with some clear response biases, such as the wish for parole. The elephant in the living room is that so-called sex offender treatment 'programmes' in prisons may not work. Researchers in this field seem sometimes reluctant to consider such a potentially unpalatable hypothesis. This can lead to a defensiveness which goes beyond the data. Indeed, there is sometimes a sense of desperation and exasperation at the inability of demonstrating improvements on disappointing results. Despite such empirical problems, this has not halted the industry expanding its markets in the UK, underpinned by public funding and political imperatives. The industry has been supported by legislation, with an increased number of behaviours being deemed 'sexual offences'. There are also much higher levels of bureaucratic scrutiny that have been implemented. Yet the disarming truth is that overwhelmingly, most men who rape will not be brought to trial and if they are they will have a comparatively strong chance of not being convicted and sent to prison. The same is highly likely to be true with child sexual abuse. In the unlikely event that a victim of a sexual crime reports it, the chances of a conviction being secured are very slim indeed.

One fundamental caveat to strident assertions about what we 'know about sex offenders' is that much of what is known draws upon convicted sex offender populations. It would seem highly unlikely that they would be representative of sex offenders as a whole, given the very small sampling involved relative to prevalence and incidence rates. Some sex offenders may be more difficult to detect, let alone convict. Many will enjoy a very high degree of protection. In some occupations there are increased opportunities to sexually offend, for example doctors in general practice and various specialisms such as gynaecology or paediatrics. 'Trusted' professions are thus extremely well protected. The medical profession is fiercely protective of its members and whistle-blowing about colleagues, as in a number of occupations, is difficult and for all intents and purposes discouraged. Previously victims of abuse by church leaders have had little voice, but increasingly such abuses have come out into the open. There is no convincing reason to believe that those so motivated will not be distributed across a number of walks of life and some may seek to get themselves into positions where opportunities to abuse abound.

Another problem in the sex offender assessment and treatment industry is that in the UK there is a great deal of undue manualisation. There appears to be an implicit understanding in some of the literature, and much practice, that there will some significant commonalities within particular offence types. This understanding is more persuasive in terms of the legal categories that have been assigned to the particular offence category than it is in terms of a psychological understanding of the behaviours involved. This will have implications for interventions. There are a wide range of sexual offences which, as Belinda Brooks-Gordon notes, have been added to in recent years. Within the offence types there may be a wide range of motivations and behaviours. Individual assessment is crucial. Groups (whether manualised or not) may well have their place but so does individualised treatment.

The psychometrics industry is a big and lucrative business in this field. The markets tapped into are linked not only with the promotion and marketing of particular psychometric instruments but also through sometimes mandatory training to ensure that those administering and interpreting the output data are appropriately skilled and knowledgeable. There are a relatively small number of main providers in the UK and so competition is minimal within a comparatively small research and clinical field.

Imprisoned sex offenders (including alleged sex offenders held on remand) have an inflated risk of suicide. This is a fact that can easily be forgotten in our everyday clinical practice. But by far the most powerful predictor of prisoner suicide is time in the particular prison. There is a compelling case for ensuring that prisoners have access to support early in their time in a given prison. There are some sub-groups that fall out of this general pattern. For example, although life-sentenced prisoners have an inflated risk of suicide they may, on average, complete suicide later in their sentence, possibly linked to particular milestone decisions about their progress (or lack of it) towards parole. Psychologists in prisons have tended to become less involved in this important area of practice, with a shift towards involvement with manualised interventions to reduce the risk of reoffending. This is unfortunate, because psychologists have contributed much in this important area of public health (e.g. Crighton, 2000; McHugh & Snow, 2000). There are a number of 'suicide myths' in this field, e.g. that young people or those held on remand are at a greater risk of suicide than others; the data would suggest otherwise. Also, interestingly, black prisoners are at a reduced risk of suicide. The precise and sometimes complex links between suicide and self-injury remain unclear. But both remain as significant problems in prisons. Staff attitudes towards suicidal prisoners can

be considerably less than helpful. The depersonalising practice of referring to prisoners by their surname with a number is somewhat dehumanising and unhelpful as part of any strategy to reduce suicides. Jenny Shaw and Naomi Humber put some of the data in this vital area in its broader public health context. This builds neatly on some of the more recent directions set within suicide research (see, for example, Crighton, 2000).

Justice Restored

The penultimate chapter in this book is on the area of restorative justice. Heather Strang and Lawrence Sherman have worked extensively on this area. There are a range of models of restorative justice, and the research base has recently taken a number of steps forward with some high quality evaluations supporting the efficacy of the approach. Lamentably, this is not an area where psychologists have been as active as they might have been. Yet there is huge potential for psychologists to get more involved in both evaluative research and consultancy advice. Most importantly perhaps, there is the potential to reduce the number of future victims and to help and assist existing victims.

The forensic field is broad, with a growing knowledge base. But it is a knowledge base that could be further developed with more explicit links with the experimental psychology base of much of what is most effective, useful and just in policy and practice.

References

BPS (2007). *Psychologists as expert witnesses: Guidelines and procedure for England and Wales*. Leicester: Author.

Crighton, D.A. (2000). Suicide in prisons in England and Wales 1988–1998: An empirical study. Unpublished PhD Dissertation, ARU (Cambridge).

Crighton, D.A. & Towl, G.J. (2008). *Psychology in prisons* (2nd edn). Oxford: BPS Blackwell.

Crittenden, P.M. (2008). *Raising parents: Attachment, parenting and child safety*. Cullompton, Devon: Willan.

Hanson, C. (2009). Thinking skills? Think again! *Inside Time*, Issue 119, May, p.20.

McHugh, M.J. & Snow, L. (2000). Suicide prevention: Policy and practice. In G.J. Towl, M.J. McHugh & L. Snow (Eds.) *Suicide in prisons*. Oxford: BPS Blackwell.

Home Office (2000). *Achieving best evidence in criminal proceedings*. London: Author.

Lindsay, G., Koene, C., Øvreeide, H. & Lang, F. (2008). *Ethics for European psychologists*. Göttingen, Germany: Hogrefe.

Merrington, S. & Stanley, S. (2007). Effectiveness: Who counts what? In L. Gelsthorpe & R. Morgan (Eds.) *Handbook of probation*. Cullompton, Devon: Willan.

Rose, K. (2009). Has ETS reduced your impulsivity? *Inside Time*, Issue 119, May, p.21.

Thomas-Peter, B. (2006). The modern context of psychology in corrections: Influences, limitations and values of 'what works'. In G.J. Towl (Ed.) *Psychological research in prisons*. Oxford: Blackwell.

Towl, G.J. (1994). Ethical issues in forensic psychology. *Forensic Update*, *39*, 23–26.

Towl, G.J. (2004). Applied psychological services in HM Prison Service and the National Probation Service. In A. Needs & G.J. Towl (Eds.) *Applying psychology to forensic practice*. Forensic Practice Series. Oxford: BPS Blackwell.

Towl, G.J. (2005a). National offender management services: Implications for applied psychological services in probation and prisons. *Forensic Update*, *81*, 22–26.

Towl, G.J. (2005b). Risk assessment. *Evidence Based Mental Health*, *8*, 91–93.

Towl, G.J., Farrington, D.P, Crighton, D.A. & Hughes, G. (2008). *Dictionary of forensic psychology*. Cullompton, Devon: Willan.

UCAS (2008). Website. www.ucas.com, accessed 2 September 2009.

2

The Justice System in England and Wales

David Faulkner

What Justice Means

The word 'justice' can be used in several different ways. Social reformers will speak of justice in the sense of the fair distribution of power and wealth among a country's citizens. An organisation's workforce may demand justice for themselves in terms of their pay and conditions of service. Minority groups may call for justice in the sense of equal rights and protection from discrimination. Or people may demand justice for an individual who has been unfairly treated, or for the victim of a crime. There will often be contested views about what counts as justice in the situation concerned.

At other times, the word is used – as it is in this chapter – in the context of the courts and an issue which has to be resolved through a prosecution in a criminal court, or a civil dispute to be resolved in the civil or family courts. Even then, the word can be used in two senses. It can refer to an outcome of the process, one which is accepted as fair and legitimate, as one where authority has been properly used and the relevant interests have been suitably represented and taken into account. Or it can refer to the process itself – in criminal matters, the process of arrest, trial and sentence which is centred on the courts but which also involves other agencies of the state. Those agencies include the police, prosecution, prison and probation services, which together make up what has become known as the criminal justice system, sometimes spelt with capital letters and abbreviated to CJS.

Used in the first sense, justice implies a context of moral or social values, and an expectation that they will be shared and respected. Like the rule of law, it stands above the interests of any individual or group, including those of the government. Used in the second sense, the word does not have a normative sense; justice is seen as serving a more instrumental purpose such as protection of the public or satisfaction for the victim, and it is judged by its efficiency and effectiveness in achieving that purpose. It does not have much space for mercy, compassion or forgiveness – a space which supporters of restorative justice try to fill (see below).

The Criminal Justice System

The origins of the system of justice as it now exists in England and Wales can be traced back a long way. (There are important differences but similar principles in Scotland and Northern Ireland.[1]) A single framework of law administered consistently throughout the country – the common law – began to be developed in the time of Henry II (1154–1179). Magna Carta (1215) introduced the principles of trial before a jury, proportionate punishment, and no imprisonment without trial. Justices of the Peace were appointed under the Justices of the Peace Act 1361, although their origins go back another 100 years. The offices of Secretary of State and Lord Chancellor, although of earlier origin, became powerful and prominent at the time of Henry VIII in the persons of Thomas Cromwell, Thomas Wolsey and Thomas More.

The Enlightenment, and especially the work of philosophers such as Kant and Locke, of jurists such as

Blackstone and Mansfield, and of penal reformers such as John Howard and Elizabeth Fry, brought further influences during the 18th century. A 'classical' view of justice emerged which was based on the rule of law, the independence of the judiciary, the presumption of innocence, proportionality of punishment, the adversarial system with 'equality of arms' (an equal contest between the prosecution and the defence), the rule that no one should be tried twice for the same offence (no 'double jeopardy'), and the principle that all people are born equal and are entitled to dignity and respect as human beings (although that did not apply to slaves or indigenous people until later). Those principles inspired the constitutions of the USA and the common law countries of the Commonwealth, and they later found expression in the European Convention on Human Rights. The Convention was eventually incorporated into UK domestic law by the Human Rights Act 1998.

The structure of what is now known as the criminal justice system began to take its present shape in the Victorian period, with the formation of regular police forces (1829 in London, later in the provinces), a national prison system (in 1877) and the probation service (in 1907). The pace of change gathered speed from the 1960s, and especially the 1980s, onwards. The changes included:

- the reforms of the police under the Police Act of 1966, the Police and Magistrates' Courts Act 1994 and the Police Reform Act 2002;
- the creation of a unified Crown Court under the Courts Act 1971;
- the Creation of the Crown Prosecution Service under the Prosecution of Offences Act 1985;
- the rapid expansion of the private security industry, performing policing functions alongside the statutory police forces;
- contracting out of some prisons and some prison functions (such as escorts) to the private sector;
- reforms of youth justice, including new powers for youth courts and the formation of the Youth Justice Board and youth offending teams under the Crime and Disorder Act 1998;
- new measures for preventing and dealing with terrorism;
- the creation of the Ministry of Justice in 2007.

Greater attention came to be paid to the treatment of victims of crime, to the position of minority groups, and to antisocial behaviour. The degree of interdependence between different procedures and organisations came to be more widely recognised, and increasing efforts were made to 'manage' the system as a coherent whole.

Managerial reforms in all public services brought a new emphasis on performance measurement, evidence-based practice, contracting-out, and risk assessment and risk management. The National Offender Management Service was created in 2004 following a report by Lord Carter (2003), with the intention of bringing prisons and probation closer together and of providing for a continuous process of 'offender management' throughout a person's sentence. Since April 2008 the two services have had a single director-general.

Legislation since 1991 has included between 50 and 60 Criminal Justice or other Acts of Parliament designed to make the system more effective in protecting the public. It increased maximum sentences; restricted judges' discretion to pass sentences which might be considered too lenient; created new indeterminate sentences of imprisonment for public protection (IPP); enabled the police to impose on-the-spot fines for offences of public disorder; made convictions easier to obtain by removing or modifying some of the traditional safeguards; and introduced civil orders such as the Anti-Social Behaviour Order (ASBO) for which breach carries a substantial sentence of imprisonment. Special powers were also introduced to deal with terrorism. The number of people in prison doubled between 1992 and 2009, from about 42,000 to over 84,500.

What Is a Crime?

A 'crime' can be defined for legal purposes simply as an offence against the criminal law (the word may be used more loosely in ordinary language). For nearly all offences the definition is now in statute, although for a few (murder is one example) it is still part of the common law. For some offences such as murder, assault and theft there is widespread agreement through time and across different cultures that the act is wrong, it should be treated as a crime, and the law against it should be effectively enforced. But there are many actions which people consider to be wrong without believing that they should be criminal; or which they may not regard as wrong in themselves but which are made criminal for the sake of good order or public health or safety. Outside the small area of 'obvious' crimes, actions which should and should not be treated as criminal vary over time, and reflect different social attitudes and circumstances, different economic conditions, and different political priorities on the part of the government of the day. In that sense, crime is what criminologists have called 'socially constructed' (Zedner, 2004).

No one knows exactly how many criminal offences actually exist. The law reform group JUSTICE calculated that in 1980 there were about 7200 (JUSTICE, 1980); an estimate in 2000 suggested that the number had by then grown to about 8000 (Ashworth, 2007); and it has been claimed that 3000 new offences were created between 1997 and 2007. An offence once created is hardly ever abolished, although it may cease to be enforced.

For a fuller discussion of legal and social constructions of crime, see Lacey (2007).

Measurement of Crime

Crime is measured in two ways. The *Criminal Statistics* have since the mid-19th century shown the number of crimes recorded by the police; the British Crime Survey, introduced in 1982, is a survey of households in which people are asked about their experience of crime over the previous 12 months.[2] Neither can give a complete account. Statistics of recorded crime do not include crimes which the police do not record, usually because they are not reported to them or do not otherwise come to their notice; changes in rates of recorded crime may be due to changes in police priorities or public attitudes to different types of crime or towards the police, as well as changes in the rates themselves. The Survey does not cover offences against children or very rare crimes such as murder. Taken together, the two sources do, however, give a reasonable indication of the volume of crime that is committed and especially of changes in the rate at which it is being committed.

Criminal Statistics show that recorded crime increased almost continuously during the period from the end of the First World War until 1995. The British Crime Survey uncovered, as had long been suspected, a rate of crime which was about double the rate for recorded crime. Further analysis showed that for offences in the survey, only about 2 per cent were likely to result in a conviction in court. Other research showed that about 30 per cent of young men were likely to have a conviction for a 'standard list' (roughly speaking indictable – see below) offence by the age of 30; but that about 5 per cent of known offenders were responsible for about 70 per cent of total crime.

Crime rates vary a great deal between different places, both between different parts of the country and between different types of neighbourhood. The highest rates are in the inner city areas of London, Birmingham and Manchester. So do a person's chances of becoming a victim, with young men being most at risk. Many offences are not 'cleared up' – that is to say they are not traced to an offender who admits the offence or is convicted in court. Clear up rates vary from about 20 per cent for burglary and criminal damage, to over 75 per cent for violent and sexual offences, and 90 per cent for homicide.

Since 1995 the total volume of crime has fallen sharply, especially for burglary and vehicle offences which made up about half the total. Figures for 2006–2007 show a total of 5.4 million recorded and 11.3 surveyed offences in that year. Both sources show a fall in the overall crime rate of about 40 per cent since 1995. Violent crime has not fallen significantly and for some offences there has been a small increase, so that violent crime now represents a larger proportion of the total (about 20 per cent).

For fuller discussion of crime data and statistics, see Maguire (2007).

The Criminal Justice Process

The criminal justice process normally begins when an offence is reported to the police or otherwise becomes known to them, for example if they are already on the scene when the incident takes place. The police investigate the alleged offence, interview witnesses and suspects, and may in due course make an arrest. The person is taken to a police station for further questioning under caution, and may then be detained or released on bail. If detained, the person must as soon as possible be charged and brought before a magistrates' court.

The process up to that point is regulated by the Police and Criminal Evidence Act 1984 (PACE) and codes of practice issued under the Act. There are strict time limits, and rules which cover such matters as the recording of interviews, the suspect's access to legal advice and the granting of bail. A person must normally be charged within 24 hours of being detained by the police, and brought before a court within 36 hours of being charged, with extensions up the 96 hours in certain circumstances on the authority of a senior police officer (for a further 36 hours) or a magistrates' court. A longer period of 28 days applies if the person has been charged with an offence of terrorism. The government did not pursue its controversial proposals for an even longer period of 42 days.

Alternative procedures allow the police to impose on-the-spot fines in certain cases, or the police or CPS to administer a caution instead of a charge, provided that the person admits the offence and is prepared to accept the fine or caution. If not, the case must be taken to court in the normal way.

Once a person has been charged, the case goes to the CPS which decides whether to proceed to prosecution. The decision is taken in accordance with the Code for Crown Prosecutors (www.cps.gov.uk/publications/code_for_crown_prosecutors/index.html, accessed 2 September 2009). Prosecution will normally follow unless the CPS decides that there is not enough evidence to obtain a conviction or there are compelling reasons why a prosecution would not be in the public interest. Relevant considerations are set out in the Code (for example if the person is suffering from a terminal illness).

The presumption of innocence applies until the person has admitted the offence or been found guilty by a court. The suspect must not be referred to as an offender or a criminal, and the offence must always be described as 'alleged'.

All proceedings begin with a hearing in the magistrates' court, initially to confirm the defendant's identity, to establish that he or she understands the charge and to consider whether bail should be granted or refused. Straightforward cases are then disposed of with (usually) a discharge, a fine or an acquittal; other cases are adjourned and the defendant remanded on bail or in custody. If bail is refused, the defendant is taken to a prison.

The process from then on depends on the nature of the offence. Offences are of three kinds. 'Summary only' cases can only be dealt with in the magistrates' court and include less serious road traffic offences, common assault, and criminal damage where the cost is below a certain amount (at present £5000). The maximum penalty is usually a fine.

'Either way cases' can be dealt with either in the magistrates' court or the Crown Court. They include theft, burglary, assault causing actual bodily harm (ABH) and most offences which involve the possession or supply of drugs. The magistrates' court normally decides on mode of trial with advice of the prosecution, and usually with an eye to the sentence which is likely to be appropriate if the person is found guilty and whether it is within the sentencing powers of the magistrates' court (see below). The defendant may, however, insist on trial at the Crown Court, and therefore before a jury, if he or she chooses.[3]

'Indictable only' offences are the most serious and least numerous and can only be tried in the Crown Court.[4] They include homicide, rape, robbery, assault causing grievous bodily harm with intent (GBH) and conspiracy to commit a crime.

A person convicted and sentenced at a magistrates' court can appeal to the Crown Court, and a person convicted and sentenced at the Crown Court can appeal to the Court of Appeal. An appeal can be against conviction, sentence or both. A further appeal may be made to the Supreme Court when it has been certified that a point of law of general public importance is involved and the Court of Appeal or the Supreme Court grants leave to appeal. A defendant may appeal against his or her conviction as of right on any question of law (e.g. whether the judge properly directed the jury by correctly outlining the ingredients of the offence). In cases which involve questions of fact (e.g. whether the jury should have convicted on the evidence in the case) the offender may only appeal if he or she obtains a certificate from the trial judge that the case is fit for appeal or, more usually, leave from the Court of Appeal. The rule is that an appeal against conviction should be set aside if the court thinks that the conviction is unsafe.[5]

Appeals to the Court of Appeal against sentence always require the leave of the Court of Appeal. The Court may quash a sentence imposed by the Crown Court and in its place substitute any sentence which that court could have imposed, but the effect must not be that the applicant is more severely dealt with as a result.

The Attorney General may refer a case to the Court of Appeal if he or she considers that the Crown Court has passed an over-lenient sentence. The power is restricted to certain specified (but quite numerous) serious offences. Requests to consider referring a sentence may come from the prosecution, the victim or victim's family, Members of Parliament, pressure groups or members of the public.

Complaints of wrongful conviction sometimes occur when all the normal rights of appeal have been exhausted. Until the mid-1990s, it was a function of the Home Secretary acting under the Royal Prerogative to consider those complaints and to refer them to the Court of Appeal if he or she considered it appropriate. This was normally done only where there was new evidence or some other substantial consideration which was not before the original trial court. The weakness of that arrangement became evident from a number of notorious miscarriages of justice which took place during the 1980s. The Criminal Cases Review Authority, later the Criminal Cases Review Commission (CCRC), was set up under the Criminal Appeal Act 1995 with authority to review suspected miscarriages of justice and refer them to the Court of Appeal if there is a 'real possibility' that it would not be upheld.

For more detailed accounts and fuller discussion of the criminal justice process, see the *Handbook of the Criminal Justice Process* (McConville & Wilson, 2002) and *The Criminal Process* (Ashworth with Redmayne, 2005).

The Sentencing Framework

The main sentences or 'disposals' available to criminal court (some are not strictly sentences) are imprisonment (which may be immediate or suspended) or detention in a young offender institution (YOI); a community sentence; a fine; discharges; compensation orders; and so-called ancillary orders. The maximum sentence for an offence is laid down in legislation, for example life imprisonment for manslaughter, arson or rape; 14 years for house burglary or blackmail; 10 years for obtaining by deception or indecent assault on a woman; 7 years for theft; 5 years for causing actual bodily harm; 2 years for carrying an offensive weapon (4 years for a knife). For some offences there are mandatory or minimum sentences – life imprisonment for murder, 5 years for possession of a prohibited firearm, 12 months' disqualification for drunk driving. The Criminal Justice Act 2003 introduced a new and controversial indeterminate sentence of IPP for offenders who are considered dangerous.

The previous range of community-based sentences has been consolidated into a single generic community sentence for which a court may select those requirements that are most suitable for a given offender in a particular case. The possible requirements include unpaid work; taking part in certain activities or programmes; a curfew; residence in a specified place such as an approved hostel; drug rehabilitation; and attendance at an attendance centre (up to age 25). Electronic monitoring (known as 'tagging') can also be added, especially for example if a curfew is imposed. The courts can also make a Drug Treatment and Testing Order (DTTO), an important feature of which is that it results in offenders being brought back to court so that their progress and the orders themselves are kept under review. There is now a greater emphasis on enforcement, with more offenders being sent to prison if they do not comply with the conditions of their orders.

For most offences for which the fine is commonly used, the maximum is set at one of five statutory levels – Level 1 (at present £100), Level 2 (£200), Level 3 (£1000), Level 4 (£2500) and Level 5 (£5000). The offender can also be ordered to pay compensation to the victim where appropriate, and courts are encouraged to make compensation orders wherever possible. Both fines and compensation have to take account of the offender's ability to pay. The use of the fine has been falling for many years, partly because of difficulties of enforcement, and partly because many defendants do not have the means to pay fines which the courts consider adequate for the seriousness of the offence. Ancillary orders can cover such matters as disqualification from driving, confiscation or forfeiture of property or assets and a 'Criminal Anti-Social Behaviour Order' or CRASBO.

Maximum sentences for 'either way' and 'indictable only' offences are always expressed in terms of sentences of imprisonment. Many of those convicted receive a community rather than a custodial sentence, but community sentences can only be imposed if the offence is 'imprisonable' in the sense that a prison sentence is available in law.

The Sentencing Commission issues guidance on the types of sentence to be imposed in particular types of case. It is to be replaced by a Sentencing Guidelines Commission – see below.

Mention has already been made of the changes in legislation and the new types of offence which they have created. A feature of some of those sentences, especially IPP sentences, is that a person can lose their liberty not only for what they have done but also for what it is thought they might do in the future. That situation places an expectation of certainty on the assessment of risk and beliefs about 'what works' which the present techniques may not be able to bear (Crighton & Towl, 2008). It also raises questions about the legitimacy of the punishment involved, especially where the judgement is made administratively by the executive and not judicially by a court (Zedner, 2004). Those questions may in due course be tested under the Human Rights Act 1998.

The present statutory framework for sentencing is set out in the Criminal Justice Act 2003. For a description of the Act, see Gibson (2004); for a discussion of sentencing more generally, see Ashworth (2005, 2007). Statistics on sentencing are included in the *Criminal Statistics* (note 1).

The Criminal Courts

The courts are at the centre of the justice system, but judges and magistrates are in some ways regarded as separate from it. The constitutional doctrine of the separation of powers requires that the Legislature (Parliament), the Executive (government and statutory services) and the Judiciary should be independent of one another. Neither Parliament nor Ministers can tell the courts what a particular law means or how it should be interpreted or applied in an individual case. Nor should they say what sentence should be imposed on an individual offender.

The criminal courts at present comprise magistrates' courts; youth courts; the Crown Court; and the High Court, Court of Appeal and House of Lords. The last three are known collectively as the higher courts but became the new Supreme Court in October 2009 as a result of the Constitutional Reform Act 2005.

Magistrates' courts

Magistrates' courts sit in some 360 locations in England and Wales. The number has been drastically, and controversially, reduced from about 1000 in the 1960s, and they still vary a great deal in size and the types of case which come before them. There are some 29,000 magistrates, or justices of the peace, who sit part time and are unpaid except for expenses. There are also about 100 district judges who are full-time salaried professional lawyers.

Magistrates usually sit in threes but a district judge can sit alone. Magistrates' courts are administered by a chief executive and by legally qualified court clerks and other supporting staff. Since 2005 they have formed part of HM Court Service, an executive agency of the Ministry of Justice. The maximum term of imprisonment in the magistrates' court for an individual offence is 6 months; or 12 months in aggregate where consecutive sentences are passed for two or more offences. There is power to double those terms to 12 and 24 months, but it has not so far been brought into effect.

Youth courts

Youth courts were established in 1991 when they took over the work of the former juvenile court. They consist of specially trained magistrates who are members of a statutory youth court panel.

The investigation, processing and outcome of cases involving juveniles follow a similar pattern to that in relation to adults, but with additional safeguards, procedures, and sentencing powers. There are different powers, procedures and considerations in relation to children aged from 10 (the age of criminal responsibility[6]) to 13 years, and for young persons aged from 14 to 17. Investigating police officers have a duty to ensure that

someone concerned with the welfare of the juvenile is informed about the person's arrest, and to obtain the involvement of an 'appropriate adult', usually a parent but sometimes a social worker. All first-time offenders are where possible dealt with by the police under a scheme of reprimands and warnings, or where they appear in court by way of a referral order to a youth offending panel composed of two volunteers from the local community and a member of the youth offending team. They meet the young person and their parents or guardians and agree a programme of action for putting things right. The victim is encouraged to be present (for restorative justice more generally, see below). Very serious cases can, and for most serious offences must, be committed to the Crown Court.

The Crown Court

The Crown Court is organised on the basis of six circuits and sits in some 90 locations known as Crown Court Centres, of which the Old Bailey in London is the best known. There about 100 full-time Crown Court judges, and a number of part-time recorders who are also practising lawyers. Cases are heard by a single judge and in a contested trial before a jury. The Crown Court has been administered by HM Court Service since it was formed from the old Assizes and Quarter Sessions in 1972. Crown Court judges are addressed as 'His (or Her) Honour Judge …' or as 'Your Honour' in court.

The High Court

The High Court sits in three divisions – the Queen's Bench Division (QBD), Chancery Division and Family Division – and deals predominantly with the more important civil disputes. But it also has a general supervisory jurisdiction in relation to a wide range of courts, tribunals and public bodies and their officers, including the criminal courts, the police, government departments and their ministers, local authorities, and other public authorities, exercised through the process known as 'judicial review'. There are some 30 High Court judges, who may also sit in the Crown Court to hear especially serious or complicated cases and some of whom may act as the presiding judge for a court centre of circuit. Their judicial form of address is 'His Honour Mr Justice' or 'Her Honour Lady Justice', or 'My Lord' or 'My Lady' in court. High Court judges are automatically appointed to knighthoods and are addressed in the normal way as 'Sir' or 'Dame' (followed by their first name) for non-judicial purposes.

The Court of Appeal (Criminal Division)

The Court of Appeal (Criminal Division) hears appeals from people convicted and sentenced in the Crown Court. Its senior judge is the Lord Chief Justice (LCJ) and its members comprise 30 Lords Justices of Appeal. They may be assisted by High Court judges. As well as giving judgements in particular cases, the LCJ may issue Practice Directions to be followed by other criminal courts, and Court of Appeal may give guidance on sentencing, although that function has now been largely superseded by the work of the Sentencing Guidelines Council (see below). Lords Justices of Appeal become members of the Privy Council on appointment and are addressed formally as 'The Rt. Hon. Lord/Lady Justice ...' and as 'My Lord' or 'My Lady' in court. Non-judicially they are addressed as 'Sir' or 'Dame'.

The House of Lords

The House of Lords was until 2009 the final court of appeal in the UK for both criminal and civil cases. Appeals were heard by an Appellate Committee of the House made up of Law Lords (sometimes called Lords of Appeal in Ordinary), of whom there were usually between 9 and 11. Law Lords were usually judges who became life peers when they were appointed. There was a convention that they did not participate in the general business of the House except where there was a direct legal or judicial context, for examples in debates on Criminal Justice Bills.

For many years, the High Court and Court of Appeal together were been loosely called the 'Supreme Court'. A new form of Supreme Court, in the new sense (for this country) of being the highest court in the land, was made in the Constitutional Reform Act 2005. The new Court is began its work in October 2009. It took over the judicial function of the House of Lords and became the final court of appeal for England, Wales and Northern Ireland with regard to criminal cases, and for Scotland with regard to civil cases. Members of the new Supreme Court are known as Justices of the Supreme Court.

Police and Policing

The police service in England and Wales is organised on the basis of 43 police forces, with a total (in 2008) of about 140,000 police officers, of whom about 33,000 were women and 5500 were from minority ethnic groups.

There are in addition about 14,000 community support officers, a new category of officer with more limited powers and duties which was introduced by the Police Reform Act 2002. Total police strength, including civilian support staff and various technical experts, was about 233,000. Police forces vary a great deal in size, ranging from the Metropolitan Police with over 24,000 police officers to several county forces with under 1500. The highly specialised City of London force has about 850 officers.

Under the Police Act 1964, each force is overseen by a tripartite structure comprising the chief constable who is in operational command, the police authority which has responsibility for administration and the budget, and the Home Secretary who is in charge of overall policy and sets national priorities and targets. Police authorities were originally committees of the local authority, with local councillors and magistrates as members; the Police and Magistrates' Courts Act 1994 made them freestanding bodies, reduced their size and introduced independent members.

The operational independence of the chief officer and the discretion of the constable have always been regarded as important principles of British policing, although they have not been seen as having the constitutional importance of the independence of the judiciary. Operational independence requires that the chief officer should not be subject to political direction on the way in which he or she enforces the law in a particular situation or at a particular event; the constable's discretion requires that he or she should be able to use his or her own judgement on when or whether for example to make an arrest. Managerial reforms such as the setting of objectives and targets and the publication of 'league tables' have been criticised as undermining that independence, and as distorting police practice by encouraging police to make unnecessary arrests (especially of young people) in order to improve their 'score'.

The numerous municipal police forces which existed before the Police Act 1964 were amalgamated to form the existing structure during the late 1960s and 1970s. But arguments have continued, both for a single national force and for further amalgamations to create a small number of regional forces. Those arguments have for the most part related to the greater efficiency and the economies thought to be achievable through larger units of command and administration, but also the need for specialised resources to deal with terrorism and international crime. They have not so far prevailed against the counterargument that the police need to be locally based and able to identify themselves with their local communities, and the government and the police are themselves developing 'neighbourhood policing' to provide stronger links with local communities.

The police are naturally seen as being concerned primarily with the prevention of crime and the apprehension of offenders. But the police have a number of other administrative and regulatory functions, of which the control of road traffic is the most obvious, and 'catching criminals' may be quite a small part of an individual police officer's working life. That fact has led to regular demands for 'more bobbies on the beat' and there is always pressure for police officers to be relieved of bureaucratic responsibilities so that they can spend more time on the 'front line'. A visible police presence on the street undoubtedly helps public confidence, and community support officers perform a valuable role in that respect, but it has always been open to question how having more officers on patrol, in any numbers that could be sustained over time, will have a significant effect on the level of crime, or whether it would only be displaced to other areas or types of crime.

Two important central agencies are the *Serious and Organised Crime Agency* (SOCA), and the *National Policing Improvement Agency* (NPIA). SOCA was launched in 2006 under the Serious Organised Crime and Police Act 2005 and brought together the former National Crime Squad (NCS), National Criminal Intelligence Service (NCIS) and their associated databases. Its aim is 'to reduce the harm caused to the UK by serious organized crime'. The NPIA was formed in 2007 to support police forces and improve the way in which they work. It replaced or incorporated former national policing organisations such as the Police Information Technology Organisation (PITO) and the police training organisation CENTREX, and took over certain functions that were formerly carried out by the Home Office and Association of Chief Police Officers.

The *Independent Police Complaints Commission* was established under the Police Reform Act 2002 to provide greater independence, openness and transparency in the investigation of serious complaints against the police. It replaced the former Police Complaints Authority. The Commission has an especially sensitive role in cases where a person dies in police custody or while being chased by the police.

There is an increasing range of 'policing' functions that are not carried out by police forces as so far described but by other organisations of different kinds – the British Transport Police, local authorities, private

security firms, and the Health and Safety Executive are some examples (see Crawford, 2003).

Police reform remains a live issue for government and the police themselves, with continuing debate on issues such as structure, accountability, powers and the use of new technology for investigation, surveillance and criminal records.

For a more detailed account of the police and policing, including a discussion of questions such as race, ethnicity and gender; accountability and governance; ethics; leadership; and the use of new technologies, see the *Handbook of Policing* (Newburn, 2008).

The Crown Prosecution Service

The Crown Prosecution Service (CPS) is responsible for most public prosecutions in England and Wales, usually taking over from the police at the stage when a suspect has been arrested and charged. The CPS was formed in 1985 as an independent national service – prosecutions had previously been the responsibility of the police or police solicitors – and was one outcome of the Royal Commission on Criminal Procedure set up after irregularities in police procedures had come to light during the 1970s.

The national head of the CPS is the Director of Public Prosecutions (DPP), an office which was first established with more limited functions in the 19th century. He or she is appointed by and responsible to the Attorney-General. Crown prosecutors are usually solicitors, but may be barristers by training. Prosecutors do not have a role in sentencing as they do in some other countries, but may advise the judge on any relevant guidelines if asked to do so. The Service's role is continuing to develop.

Prisons and the Prison Service

The prison system in England and Wales comprises some 143 establishments, of which 132 are run by the national Prison Service and 11 by private contractors. The Prison Service's statement of purpose says:

> Her Majesty's Prison Service serves the public by keeping in custody those committed by the courts. Our duty is to look after them with humanity and help them lead law abiding and useful lives in custody and after release.

The total population of prison establishments at the end of January 2009 was about 82,000, of whom 66,500 were adult men and 3800 were adult women; 9000 were young men and 420 were young women aged 18–20; and 2000 were boys and 50 were girls aged under 18. Of that total, about 13,000 were on remand awaiting trial or sentence; about 100 were non-criminal prisoners; and the remainder were serving sentences of various lengths.[7]

About a quarter of the prison population were from minority ethnic groups, of whom about half were black and a third were foreign nationals. Of the British population in prisons, about 11 per cent were black, compared with 2 per cent in the population as a whole, and about 5 per cent were Asian. (On questions of racial discrimination, see below.)

In 2008 the national Prison Service employed about 49,000 staff and total prisons expenditure was about £4.3bn; the cost of a new prison place was about £119,000 and the average annual cost per prisoner was about £40,000.

Britain has one of the highest rates of imprisonment in Europe – 150 per 100,000 in the population, compared with 93 in Germany and 85 in France. About 65 per cent of prisoners, and 75 per cent of young prisoners, are reconvicted within two years of release. The Prison Service has targets for bringing those figures down and claims to have some success, but reoffending is also affected by social and other factors over which the Service has no control.

Following a further report by Lord Carter (2007), the government announced controversial plans to expand the capacity of the prison system by another 10,500 places, including the construction of three 'Titan' prisons each for about 2500 prisoners, by 2014. Those are in addition to the 9500 extra places already being provided.

For fuller accounts of the issues affecting prisons and imprisonment, see Liebling (2005) and Morgan and Liebling (2007). Facts about prisons and imprisonment are conveniently brought together in *Bromley Briefing Factfile*, issued by the Prison Reform Trust and regularly updated. It is available on the Trust's website, www.prisonreformtrust.org.uk (accessed 2 September 2009).

Probation

The probation service in England and Wales was formed in 1907 to 'advise, assist and befriend' offenders whom the courts placed under its supervision. Probation orders were made as an alternative to a sentence and were not intended as a punishment. Other duties came to be added over the years, especially the after-care and supervision of prisoners who had been released from custody and the provision and supervision of community service.

In the more punitive climate of the 1990s, probation became a normal sentence of the court and the requirements of probation and community orders began to acquire a 'tougher' and more punitive content. The requirement to 'advise, assist and befriend' was replaced by an emphasis on 'enforcement, rehabilitation and public protection'. The various forms of community order were combined into a single 'community sentence' in 2003.

Probation in England and Wales is organised on the basis of 42 areas. Until 2001 each area had a separate service, with a probation committee composed mainly of local magistrates as the employing authority. In that year the separate services were combined into a single National Probation Service, with much stronger central direction from the Home Office. Probation committees became probation boards with a different, more business-orientated composition and more limited functions. In 2004, following the first Carter report (2003), the Service became part of the National Offender Management Service. Further reforms in the Offender Management Act 2007 provided for probation boards to be replaced in turn by probation trusts, with more changes in structure and functions.

In 2009, over 200,000 offenders were under the Service's supervision at any one time, 90 per cent of them men and 10 per cent women. Just over a quarter were aged under 21. About 70 per cent were serving community sentences and 30 per cent were on licence after serving the custodial part of a prison sentence. Each year the Service provides the courts with some 265,000 pre-sentence reports.

The Service also works with victims of crime, for example in connection with the arrangements for an offender's release from prison and subsequent supervision.

The Service has about 21,000 staff, of whom about 10,000 are fully qualified probation officers, about 6500 are probation service officers with more limited duties, and about 4500 are support staff of various kinds.

Youth Justice

It has been recognised since the 19th century that young people should be treated differently from adults in the criminal justice system, with the youngest children being dealt with outside the system altogether and separate arrangements for those who are older. In principle, the person's welfare should be the main concern. Policy and practice have to some extent retreated from that principle since 1997, reflecting a punitive element in public attitudes to children which does not seem to be present in other European countries.

The arrangements for young offenders were substantially reformed in 1998. Responding to a public perception that young people were 'getting away with it' and out of control, the Crime and Disorder Act 1998 established the National Youth Justice Board for England and Wales (YJB) and a network of local youth offending teams (YOTs). The YJB is an executive non-departmental public body. Its 12 board members are appointed by the Secretary of State for Justice; it oversees the youth justice system and works to prevent offending and reoffending by children and young people under the age of 18, 'ensuring that custody for them is safe, secure, and addresses their offending behaviour'. Its functions include advising ministers on the operation of the youth justice system, monitoring its performance, commissioning accommodation for children and young people remanded or sentenced to custody, identifying and promoting effective practice, and publishing information.

Youth offending teams (YOTs) coordinate youth justice services in their area – for example rehabilitation schemes, activities carried out under community sentences, measures to prevent and reduce crime, and reparation schemes for victims. The team identifies the problems that lead young people to offend, assesses the risk they present to others, and devises suitable programmes which might help to prevent them from reoffending. Each should include people from a wide range of professional backgrounds and different areas of expertise.

The YJB and the Ministry of Justice are now working more closely with the Department of Children, Schools and Families in the context of a national policy for children and young people set out in the White Paper *Every Child Matters* (Department for Education and Skills, 2004), but the number and cost of children and young people who are in custody remain matters of serious concern.

Home Office

Within central government, the main departments concerned with the administration of justice are the Home Office, the Ministry of Justice and the Law Officers' Department. Of those, the Home Office is the oldest and has traditionally been the largest and most powerful. The Office of Secretary of State is of medieval origin; it was divided in 1782 between the Home Department and Foreign Affairs and from then on the Home Department or Home Office became the department for all subjects which were not specifically allocated elsewhere. Subjects such as education, health, employment, local government and children were in due course moved to separate departments and by the late 20th century the Home Office had become more exclusively identified with maintaining the rule of law and the Queen's Peace, or in modern language crime, criminal justice, the treatment of offenders and immigration. The need to keep the proper balance between public protection and the liberty of the individual became deeply rooted in the department's traditions and culture, although opinions would differ – as they still do – on where the balance should be placed.

Suggestions for dividing the Home Office into a ministry for internal safety and a ministry of justice were been made at various times from the 1860s onwards. The arguments were sometimes about efficiency and the volume of the Home Secretary's workload, but a more important issue was whether the balance could be better maintained within a single department or by dividing the relevant functions between two departments, as they are in many other countries. The argument for a single department prevailed for many years, and when responsibility for criminal justice, prisons and probation was transferred to the newly formed Ministry of Justice in 2007, the main reasons given for the change were improved efficiency and effectiveness in the context of the increased threat from terrorism and the internal difficulties which were affecting the Home Office at that time.

The main responsibilities of the Home Office are now security, counter-terrorism, crime reduction and community safety, for which it works through the UK Border Agency, the UK Identity and Passport Service, the Criminal Records Bureau and the police service in England and Wales.

Ministry of Justice

The *Ministry of Justice* has its origins in the former Lord Chancellor's Department, which became the Department for Constitutional Affairs for a brief period between 2003 and 2007. The Office of Lord Chancellor is also of ancient origin but its supporting department was not formed until the 19th century.

For many years the department's principal concerns were civil law and matters relating to the judiciary; it had few administrative responsibilities. The situation began to change when the structure of the courts was reformed and a national Court Service was formed in 1972. The department grew in size and importance from then onwards and other functions were progressively added – the administration of the magistrates' courts in the 1990s; constitutional affairs in 2003; criminal justice, prisons and probation when it became the Ministry of Justice in 2007.[8] The department's main responsibilities are now constitutional matters; the justice system, including civil justice; criminal law; sentencing policy; and the National Offender Management Service, comprising prisons and probation and now with single director-general for both services.

Law Officers' Department

The Attorney General and the Solicitor General are together known as the Law Officers of the Crown and their department as the *Law Officers' Department*. The Attorney General is the government's principal legal adviser and certain prosecutions require his or her consent. He or she may also appear as prosecuting counsel in high profile cases or cases where the national interest is involved. The Attorney General is accountable to Parliament for the Crown Prosecution Service, appoints the Director of Public Prosecutions, and is also responsible for certain specialised legal functions within the government. The role is complex and has sometimes been controversial, for example over the nature of the advice given to the government concerning the legality of the war in Iraq and over investigations and possible prosecutions where political interests may be involved.

Other National Bodies

The *Parole Board* for England and Wales is an independent body which makes risk assessments to inform decisions on the release and recall of prisoners. It operates in accordance with statutory directions which are issued by the Secretary of State for Justice and cover subjects such as the criteria to be used and the procedures to be followed. The board comprises a chair and some 80 members of whom a small proportion are full-time. Members include judges, psychologists, psychiatrists, chief probation officers, criminologists and independent members. The work is sensitive, onerous and controversial, and the Board's quasi-judicial functions require an independence from government which is not easy to sustain.

The *Sentencing Guidelines Commission* (SGC) was established under the Coroners and Justice Act 2009. It consists of eight judicial members and six non-judicial members. Its purpose is to give authoritative guidance on sentencing to the Crown Court and magistrates' courts; to give a strong lead on the approach to sentencing issues, based on a principled approach which commands general support; and to enable sentencers to make decisions that are supported by information on the effectiveness of sentences and on the most effective use of resources. It also has a remit to raise public awareness and understanding of sentencing issues and seek to match capacity and demand.

Inspectorates have come to play an increasingly prominent role in the oversight of criminal justice services. *HM Inspectorate of Constabulary* has its origins in the 19th century; *HM Inspectorate of Probation* dates from before the Second World War. *HM Inspectorate of Prisons*, *HM Inspectorate of Court Administration* and *HM Inspectorate of the Crown Prosecution Service* are of more recent origin. They now function mainly as part of the system's mechanisms of accountability to central government, with a focus on efficiency, standards and performance. The exception is the prisons inspectorate which is primarily concerned with the treatment and experiences of prisoners, questions of decency and human rights, and the 'health' – in the broadest sense – of the institution as a whole.

The *Prisons and Probation Ombudsman* investigates complaints from those who are or have been in prison or under the supervision of the Probation Service. He or she is not able to issue directions but can make recommendations to the Prison or Probation Service or to the Ministry of Justice.

Each prison establishment has an *Independent Monitoring Board*, composed of unpaid volunteers, which oversees the activities of the prison and the treatment of prisoners. Boards have a long history, going back to visiting committees of magistrates appointed under the Prison Act 1877. They were at one time the main disciplinary authority for the prison. Members have open access to all parts of the prison and may discuss matters with prisoners out of the hearing of prison governors or prison officers. Each board reports annually to the Secretary of State for Justice.

Some Special Subjects

Victims of crime

For many years, victims of crime were largely ignored in the criminal justice process unless they were needed as witnesses, and even then they had no special treatment or status. A limited (although by international standards quite generous) scheme of compensation for criminal injuries was introduced in 1964, but otherwise victims' interests were not taken seriously until the rise of the victims' support movement in the 1980s and the publication of the first Victim's Charter in 1990. All criminal justice agencies are now expected to be sensitive and responsive to victims' experience and concerns; help from the national organisation Victim Support (www.victimsupport.org.uk, accessed 2 September 2009) is available to any victim who wants it; and the Witness Service provides information, reassurance and practical help for those who have to appear in court.

Issues involving the rights and expectations of victims are not straightforward. Victims deserve proper help, consideration and respect, and there are still instances where the system has let the victim down. It seems natural to argue that anything that could be done for victims ought to be done. But it is not a 'zero sum' where anything that is 'bad' for offenders is 'good' for victims or vice versa. Victims are able to make statements which can be used in court, but there may be a fine line between a factual statement of the victim's injury or loss, a description of their feelings about what they have experienced, and an emotional account intended to influence the court towards a severe (or occasionally lenient) sentence. There are also special difficulties about cases where intimidation may be involved, and about the investigation and prosecution of offences of rape, domestic violence and 'honour violence' against a person who has not conformed to the cultural expectations of (usually) her family.

Restorative justice

Restorative justice is a distinctive approach to crime, and to the resolution of conflicts more generally, which concentrates on putting right the harm that has been caused. In criminal justice it may take the form of a conference between the offender and the victim, together with other people who are close to them; it may be instead of or in addition the normal criminal process. The outcome may be an apology and an understanding about future behaviour, sometimes including some form of service or act of reparation. The approach can also be used as part of the management of institutions such as prisons (Edgar & Newell, 2006) or schools, in preventing antisocial behaviour, or in dealing with complaints against public authorities. It has inspired the work of two charities – Circles of Support and Accountability which works with sex offenders, and Escaping Victimhood which helps the families of victims of homicide.

Restorative justice has attracted widespread interest and support, including some support from the government, but to the frustration of its enthusiasts its influence on criminal justice is still at the margins and confined to youth offending panels (see above) and a few local schemes. It is popular with victims, but evidence of its effect on reoffending is still uncertain and it is hard to accommodate within an adversarial system that is focused on punishment.

Community justice

The term 'community justice' is sometimes used in a general sense to refer to local efforts to promote the use of community sentences, the employment of offenders to do unpaid work for the benefit to local communities, and the involvement of local communities and especially voluntary organisations in providing various kinds of support for offenders, victims and their families.

The term is also used more specifically to refer to the North Liverpool Community Justice Centre, established in 2005, and to similar, smaller schemes in other areas which began in 2007 (www.communityjustice.gov.uk, accessed 2 September 2009). Based on the Red Hook Center in New York, the Liverpool Centre is described as a community resource providing both a court function and a range of preventative and social services for the wider community. A single judge has charge of the centre, holding a joint appointment as both a district judge and Crown Court judge. Much of the work of the centre is focused on low-level offending, antisocial behaviour (ASB) and compliance with court orders, but the court is also able to deal with some non-criminal matters and the judge can try more serious criminal cases when it is convenient for him to do so. The coordination of local services and the involvement of the local community are important features of the scheme.

Race and racism

Courts and criminal justices became increasingly and sometimes painfully aware of the problems of race and racism from the late 1970s onwards. Prison psychologists were among the first to recognise racist attitudes and behaviour in prisons; the police faced criticism for what was seen as their discriminatory use of their powers of 'stop and search'; and the disproportionate number of black people in prison prompted concern about racial discrimination at the various stages of the criminal justice process and especially in sentencing. Racist behaviour was also found among the staff of the criminal justice services, and the small number of members of minority groups, especially in senior positions, also caused concern.

The Criminal Justice Act 1991 introduced a requirement for the Secretary of State to publish:

> such information as he considers expedient for the purposes of ... facilitating the performance by [persons engaged in the administration of criminal justice] of their duty to avoid discriminating against any person on the ground of race, sex or any other improper ground

and reports have been published regularly since that time. The Race Relations (Amendment) Act 2000 went further and placed a duty on all public authorities to be proactive in promoting race equality.

Policies for preventing and dealing with discrimination were in place across the system by the early 1990s, but they were not implemented as consistently or as effectively as might have been hoped. A turning point came with the failure of the investigation into the murder of Stephen Lawrence in 1994 and the subsequent report by Sir William Macpherson and its finding that the Metropolitan Police were 'institutionally racist' (Macpherson, 1999). Instances of racist behaviour were also investigated in prisons, of which the most serious was the failure of the Prison Service to prevent the racist murder of Zahid Mubarak in Feltham Young Offenders Institution in 2000. The Director General, Martin Narey, acknowledged that the Prison Service was also institutionally racist, and announced that overt racist behaviour or membership of a racist organisation would not be tolerated and would lead to dismissal. A prison officer was later dismissed for wearing Nazi insignia.

Following those events, efforts to prevent discrimination were redoubled across the criminal justice system, including measures to increase the number and proportion of members of minority groups in all the services. Even so, measures to combat discrimination are still sometimes sneered at as 'political correctness'; racist attitudes are still widespread in the media (Sveinsson, 2008); and racist incidents still occur in the system.

For a general account of race issues in criminal justice, see Phillips and Bowling (2007).

Conclusions

Crime and criminal justice became the subject of increasing political attention from the late 1970s onwards (Downes & Morgan, 2007). One reason was the increase in crime, so that more people had been victims of crime or knew people who had been victims. Another was a change towards more sensational reporting in the media. A third was the increasingly adversarial style of politics and the sense that governments had to be constantly active, with a solution to every problem.

Until the early 1990s, governments had more or less accepted the conclusion of a Home Office review (Home Office, 1977) that criminal justice measures could have only a marginal effect on the general level of crime. There was then a change of mood,[9] after which successive governments determined to bring forward criminal justice measures that they could claim would have a direct effect in restoring public confidence and reducing crime. The pace accelerated after the change of government in 1997. Ministers not only considered public services to be in desperate need of modernisation, but some of them also regarded criminal justice as an outdated system which had grown up haphazardly in a previous age (Blair, 2004). It was not capable of dealing with the problems of crime, disorder and antisocial behaviour in a modern, globalised world. Less attention should be paid to traditional principles such as those indicated earlier in this chapter.

A difficulty for criminal justice ministers and administrators is that much of the evidence is counterintuitive. Sentencing does not have much deterrent effect, and sending more people to prison does very little to reduce crime[10] (Halliday, 2001). Having more police officers on the streets reassures the public, but may not have much effect on crime itself. People do not behave better when they are publicly humiliated. A large proportion of the male population has criminal convictions or admits to having committed criminal offences, many victims are or have been offenders, and vice versa, and it is mislead-ing to talk of 'innocent victims' and the 'law-abiding majority' (Karstedt & Farrall, 2007). Crime has been fall-ing, but the figures are widely disbelieved. Despite all the reforms of the previous 15 years, there is still in 2009 a sense that the problem of crime is no better than it was.

Characteristics of the present approach to crime and criminal justice include economic rather than social ways of thinking; a belief in a 'science' of crime management and evidence-based policy; an instrumental view of jus-tice which sees its purpose as essentially one of public protection, and greater intervention (even 'micro man-agement') by government. An alternative or complemen-tary approach would pay more attention to relationships and motivation (Hough, 2008), drawing on studies of desistance and the factors that influence offenders to stop offending (McNeill *et al.*, 2005; McNeill & Weaver 2007).[11] It could be linked to more locally based and less politi-cised programmes building on existing initiatives such as neighbourhood policing and community justice.

There have been several accounts, from different per-spectives, of the transformation which has taken place over the past 25 years (Faulkner, second edition, 2006; Garland, 2001; Lacey, 2007).

Notes

1 Some of the most obvious differences in Scotland are the role of the procurator fiscal in prosecutions, the system of sheriff courts, and the arrangements for children's hearings in youth justice.

2 *Criminal Statistics* and reports from the British Crime Survey are published annually by Home Office Research, Devel-opment, Statistics (RDS) at www.homeoffice.gov.uk/rds/crimstats05.html and www.homeoffice.gov.uk/rds/bcs1.html respectively (retrieved 2 September 2009). They are sup-plemented by an annual summary *Crime in England Wales*, and by Updates which are issued as Statistical Bulletins every quarter. A useful *Digest of Information on the Criminal Justice System in England and Wales* is available at http://rds.homeoffice.gov.uk/rds/digest4/publicationsc.pdf (retrieved 2 September 2009) but it has unfortunately not been updated since 1999.

3 Various attempts have been made to restrict access to trial before a jury, either to prevent interference with the jury or for cases which were considered too complicated or likely to be too long drawn out (for example some types of fraud), and the Criminal Justice Act 2003 made provision for restrictions in those cases. Attempts to prevent 'frivo-lous' demands for jury trial, for example by well-to-do

defendants charged with minor offences for which a conviction might damage their reputations or careers, have not so far been pursued. No provision has been made in England and Wales for the equivalent of 'Diplock' courts which tried terrorist cases in Northern Ireland.

4 'Either way' and 'indictable only' offences are often grouped together and called simply 'indictable offences'. They are almost but not quite the same as 'notifiable offences' which form the basis of statistics of recorded crime: the classification of 'indictable' and summary or non-indictable offences has changed from time to time but the same definition has been kept for statistical pur-poses so that figures can remain comparable.

5 There have been suggestions that the Court of Appeal should nonetheless be required to uphold a conviction where it is satisfied that there has been no injustice.

6 One of the lowest in Europe and often criticised by chil-dren's charities and others. The Crime and Disorder Act 1998 removed the presumption of *doli incapax* under which it had been necessary to prove that a child under 14 knew that what they were doing was wrong.

7 Ministry of Justice *Population in Custody, Monthly Tables (England and Wales)* January 2009.

8 The full title of the ministerial head of the Ministry is 'Secretary of State for Justice and Lord Chancellor', the title of Lord Chancellor still being needed for certain spe-cial functions which cannot be transferred without legis-lation or other special authority. The title in normal use is 'Secretary of State for Justice' or 'Justice Secretary', and 'Justice Minister' for less senior ministers appointed to the Ministry or department.

9 The change coincided with the murder of two-year-old Jamie Bulger by two older children in Liverpool in 1993 – a shocking crime of the kind which arouses an exceptional degree of public feeling and which seems to take place about once in five years. It also coincided with the political weakness of the then Conservative government after the UK's expulsion from the European Exchange rate Mechanism, the divisions within the Conservative Party over the Maastricht Treaty, and the appointment of Tony Blair as shadow Home Secretary and later as Leader of the Opposition with a newly aggressive stance on 'crime and the causes of crime'.

10 It is thought that a 15 per cent increase in the prison population would reduce crime by 1 per cent.

11 Mike Hough (2008). For studies of desistence, see for example McNeill *et al.* (2005); McNeill & Weaver (2007).

Further Reading

Suggestions for further reading on particular aspects of criminal justice have been included at various points in the text.

The *Oxford Handbook of Criminology*, edited by Mike Maguire, Rod Morgan and Robert Reiner, third edition 2007, is the most comprehensive source of information and discussion on criminology and criminal justice and its 32 chapters, nearly 1200 pages, its index and the references included in its text provide a good starting point for serious further study of almost any of the subject's various aspects. Many of the references noted above are to chapters in the *Handbook*. It also contains material on specialised subjects such as mental health, drugs and alcohol, white-collar crime or organised crime and terrorism which have not been dealt with here – see the chapters by Jill Peay, Nigel South, David Nelken and Micheal Levi, respectively. The *Handbook* also includes a chapter by Clive Hollin on criminological psychology. References are given below.

Bryan Gibson's *The Criminal Justice System – An Introduction*, third edition 2008, provides a useful source for more detailed information on most of the aspects covered in this chapter. Its 15 chapters (239 pages) give an authoritative and easy-to-read account of the main features of the system and their latest developments, and the book includes a useful glossary. Companion volumes on the Home Office and the Ministry of Justice deal similarly with those two departments.

Criminal Justice by Lucia Zedner (2004) provides a more reflective commentary on criminal justice, its concepts, structures and processes, the central themes and debates, and the historical and cultural contexts in which those debates are now taking place.

References

Ashworth, A. (1980). Is the criminal law a lost cause? *Law Quarterly Review, 116*, 225–256.

Ashworth, A., with Redmayne, M. (2005). *The criminal process* (3rd edn). Oxford: Oxford University Press.

Ashworth, A. (2007). Sentencing. In M. Maguire, R. Morgan & R. Reiner (Eds.) *Oxford handbook of criminology* (pp.990–1023). Oxford: Oxford University Press.

Blair, T. (2004). Speech on the government's 5-year strategy for crime. Available at www.pm.gov.uk/output/Page6129.asp, accessed 2 September 2009.

Carter, P. (2003). *Managing offenders, reducing crime*. London: Prime Minister's Strategy Unit.

Carter, P. (2007). *Securing the future: Proposals for the efficient and sustainable use of custody in England and Wales*. London: Ministry of Justice.

Crawford, A. (2003). The pattern of policing in the United Kingdom: Policing beyond the police. In T. Newburn (Ed.) *Handbook of policing*. Cullompton, Devon: Willan.

Crighton, D. & Towl, G. (2008). *Psychology in prisons* (2nd edn). Oxford: BPS Blackwell.

Department for Education and Skills (2004). *Every child matters: Change for children*. CM 5860. London: Stationery Office.

Downes, D. & Morgan, R. (2007). No turning back: The politics of law and order into the millennium. In M. Maguire, R. Morgan & R. Reiner (Eds.) *Oxford handbook of criminology* (pp.201–240). Oxford: Oxford University Press.

Edgar, K. & Newell, T. (2006). *Restorative justice in prisons: A guide to making it happen*. Winchester, UK: Waterside Press.

Faulkner, D. (2006). *Crime, state and citizen: A field full of folk* (2nd edn). Winchester: Waterside Press.

Garland, D. (2001). *The culture of control: Crime and social order in contemporary society*. Oxford: Oxford University Press.

Gibson, B. (2004). *The Criminal Justice Act, 2003: A guide to the new procedures and sentencing*. Winchester: Waterside Press.

Gibson, B. (2008). *The criminal justice system: An introduction* (3rd edn). Winchester: Waterside Press.

Halliday, J. (2001). *Making punishments work: Report of a review of the sentencing framework for England and Wales* (pp.130–132). London: Home Office.

Hollin, C. (2007). Criminological psychology. In M. Maguire, R. Morgan & R. Reiner (Eds.) *Oxford handbook of criminology* (pp.43–77). Oxford: Oxford University Press.

Home Office (1977). *A review of criminal justice policy 1976*. London: HMSO.

Hough, M. (2008). *Reducing reoffending: Getting off the treadmill*. Paper prepared for the National Audit Office. London: Institute for Criminal Policy Research, King's College, London.

JUSTICE (1980). *Breaking the rules*. London: JUSTICE.

Karstedt, S. & Farrall, G. (2007). *Law-abiding majority? The everyday crimes of the middle classes*. London: Centre for Crime and Justice Studies.

Lacey, N. (2007). Legal constructions of crime. In M. Maguire, R. Morgan & R. Reiner (Eds.) *Oxford handbook of criminology* (pp.179–200). Oxford: Oxford University Press.

Levi, M. (2007). Organised crime and terrorism. In M. Maguire, R. Morgan & R. Reiner (Eds.) *Oxford handbook of criminology* (pp.771–809). Oxford: Oxford University Press.

Liebling, A. (2005). *Prisons and their moral performance: A study of values, quality and prison life*. Oxford: Clarendon Press.

Macpherson, W. (1999). *The Stephen Lawrence Inquiry*. CM4262. London: Stationery Office.

McNeill, F., Batchelor, S., Burnett, R. & Knox, J. (2005). *21st century social work: Reducing re-offending: Key practice skills*. Edinburgh: Scottish Executive.

McNeill, F. & Weaver, B. (2007). *Giving up crime: Directions for policy*. Glasgow: Scottish Centre for Crime and Justice Research.

McConville, M. & Wilson, G. (Eds.) (2002). *Handbook of the criminal justice process*. Oxford: Oxford University Press.

Maguire, M. (2007). Crime data and statistics. In M. Maguire, R. Morgan & R. Reiner (Eds.) *Oxford handbook of criminology* (pp.241–301). Oxford: Oxford University Press.

Morgan, R. & Liebling, W. (2007). Imprisonment: An expanding scene. In M. Maguire, R. Morgan & R. Reiner (Eds.).

Oxford handbook of criminology (pp.1100–1138). Oxford: Oxford University Press.

Nelken, D. (2007). White-collar and corporate crime. In M. Maguire, R. Morgan & R. Reiner (Eds.) *Oxford handbook of criminology* (pp.733–770). Oxford: Oxford University Press.

Newburn, T. (Ed.) (2008). *Handbook of policing* (2nd edn). Cullompton, Devon: Willan.

Peay, J. (2007). Mentally disordered offenders, mental health, and crime. In M. Maguire, R. Morgan & R. Reiner (Eds.) *Oxford handbook of criminology* (pp.496–527). Oxford: Oxford University Press.

Phillips, C. & Bowling, B. (2007). Ethnicities, racism, crime and criminal justice. In M. Maguire, R. Morgan & R. Reiner (Eds.) *Oxford handbook of criminology* (pp.421–460). Oxford: Oxford University Press.

South, N. (2007). Drugs, alcohol and crime. In M. Maguire, R. Morgan & R. Reiner (Eds.) *Oxford handbook of criminology* (pp.810–840). Oxford: Oxford University Press.

Sveinsson, K. (2008). *A tale of two Englands – 'race' and violent crime in the press.* London: Runnymede Trust.

Zedner, L. (2004). *Criminal justice* (pp.39–47). Oxford: Clarendon Press.

3

Community Services for Children and Young People

Kerry Baker

Only a small proportion of young people convicted by the courts receive custodial sentences – the majority remain in the community under the supervision of youth justice services who provide and/or broker access to a wide range of services. Children and young people who offend typically have a complex range of needs (relating, for example, to mental health, substance misuse, poor cognitive skills or disengagement from education) and comprehensive assessment of young people involved in the criminal justice system should form the basis for individually tailored and targeted interventions to address factors such as these that may contribute to offending behaviour. Evidence on the effectiveness of different types of community services is mixed and there remain some significant gaps in the knowledge base (for example with regard to specific types of offending or the effectiveness of interventions with particular groups such as female offenders). The provision of services to children and young people in the community occurs within a context of ongoing debate on topics as diverse as: the purpose and values of youth justice; the balance between care and control; the intersection of risk, welfare and rights; methods of assessment; multi-agency working; and how best to engage young people.

Introduction

Few would disagree that concern about offending by young people is high in the eyes of the public, media and politicians. The vexed question of how to respond to this problem remains a matter of debate, and starkly highlights society's conflicting views about children and young people. On the one hand, children can be seen as vulnerable and in need of protection while, on the other, there is an expectation that they can be morally held to account for their actions. The intersection between risk, welfare and rights in youth justice is complex (Jones & Baker, 2009) and the balance between these different elements fluctuates over time and also varies considerably between jurisdictions (Muncie & Goldson, 2006).

Only a small proportion of young people convicted by the courts receive custodial sentences – the majority remain in the community under the supervision of youth justice services who provide and/or broker access to a wide range of services and interventions. This chapter provides an overview of youth justice and the types of interventions provided for young people in the community. Given the wide range of services available it is not possible to go into extensive detail but the aim is rather to illustrate the variety and complexity of work with this group of young people. The second half of the chapter uses examples of specific interventions to highlight some of the debates and tensions inherent in current youth justice practice.

Youth Justice in the UK

Within the UK there are significant differences in the organisation and operation of youth justice services and, since it would be difficult to examine them all within the scope of one chapter, the focus here is on youth justice provision in England and Wales. However, some examples from Scotland and Northern Ireland are included to illustrate different types of service provision and because the contrast in these approaches to youth justice throws into relief some of the fundamental questions about working in community or residential settings with young people who offend.

Although the origins of the youth justice system in England and Wales can be traced back over a century or more, major reforms were introduced by the 1998 Crime and Disorder Act, leading to what some have described as the 'new youth justice' (Goldson, 2000). The 1998 Act (section 37) stated that: '[i]t shall be the principal aim of the youth justice system to prevent offending by children and young people' and all those who work within youth justice are required to have regard to that statutory aim. The Act also introduced new multi-agency youth offending teams (YOTs) which bring together professionals from a range of disciplines. Statutory involvement is required from local authority social services and education departments (now children's services), the police, probation service and health authorities. Other agencies, such as housing, and specialist services around substance misuse or mental health also work in partnership with YOTs. Youth justice is not a national service but each YOT is accountable to the Local Authority in its area and there are three stages at which community-based services are provided:

- Pre-conviction: prevention services. For young people deemed to be 'at risk' of becoming involved in offending, there are initiatives such as Youth Inclusion and Support Panels (YISPs), Youth Inclusion Programmes (YIPs) and Parenting Programmes and Safer Schools Partnerships (SSPs) (see Morgan & Newburn, 2007 for a more detailed review of these provisions).
- Post-conviction: community sentences. For young people aged 10–17 who are convicted but not sentenced to custody, the previous range of community sentences (NACRO, 2006) has now been replaced by the generic Youth Rehabilitation Order (YRO) introduced as a result of the 2008 Criminal Justice and Immigration Act. This provides a 'menu' of intervention options that courts can attach to an Order.[1]
- Post-custody: resettlement. All young people released from custody will be on licence and subject to YOT supervision. The duration of supervision will vary according to the type and length of custodial sentence imposed but, in contrast to the adult criminal justice system where some offenders can be released from custody without any licence period, all young people will be supervised for a time to help promote resettlement into the community.

The nature and direction of youth justice in England and Wales has been much debated. For example, it has been argued that there is a trend towards the 'adulteration' (Muncie, 2007) of youth justice, particularly in relation to sentencing provisions (Easton & Piper, 2005), which erodes the long-standing principle that the criminal justice system should treat adults and young people differently. On the other hand, recent developments such as the emergence of Children's Trusts (Youth Justice Board, 2004), the Every Child Matters agenda in England (HM Government, 2004) and the equivalent Seven Core Aims initiative in Wales (Welsh Assembly Government, 2004) suggest a possible shift towards a greater focus on responding to 'needs' as well as 'deeds'. Further changes in service provision are likely in the light of recent government policy announcements (HM Government, 2008), although it is too early to be clear on the details of what this might mean in practice.

The Scottish approach is noticeably different. The system of 'children's hearings' reflects a 'belief in the welfare principle in relation to offending behaviour – that meeting the child's needs will, in itself, lead to the reduction or, indeed, ideally the elimination of his/ her criminality' (McDiarmid, 2005, p.33). Young people can be referred to a hearing on either offence or non-offence grounds and a panel of lay members will decide on what action needs to be taken, with promoting a young person's welfare seen as the primary obligation. Recent policy initiatives may suggest a move towards a more punitive approach, but even though the system may now be 'underpinned by a more complex set of penal rationales' (McAra, 2006, p.142) than previously there is undoubtedly still a stronger emphasis on welfare than in England and Wales.

In Northern Ireland, the Justice (NI) Act of 2002 introduced a range of new measures for dealing with children who offend, the most significant being *youth conferencing* which is based upon restorative justice principles. This operates both as an alternative to prosecution or as a court-ordered process and is intended to allow children to take responsibility for their actions and to give victims an opportunity to say how they have been affected. This emphasis on diverting young people from the criminal justice system where possible is a significant difference from current practice in England and Wales.

Debate about youth justice has traditionally focused on the tension between justice and welfare but the current picture is more complex. Two other significant factors to take into account are the rise of 'risk' in criminal justice (Kemshall, 2007) and also now the increasing emphasis on children's rights. Understanding the way in which systems – and practitioners within those systems – balance these competing demands is important because it sets the context in which interventions and services are provided.

Characteristics and Needs of Young People Who Offend

In 2006/07, the number of offences by young people aged 10–17 in England and Wales that resulted in a pre-court or court disposal was 295,129. The most common types of offence were theft and handling, violence against the person, criminal damage and motoring offences. Although there was a noticeable rise in offending by young women, young males were responsible for 80 per cent of the offences committed by this age group (Youth Justice Board, 2007). Eighty-five percent of these offences were committed by white young people (with the other 15 per cent comprised of 6 per cent Black, 3 per cent Asian, 3 per cent mixed and 3 per cent 'other' or not known). Seventy per cent of the offences were committed by 15–17-year-olds and 30 per cent by the 10–14 age group.

Young people coming into contact with the criminal justice system typically have multiple needs. In relation to housing, the Audit Commission (2004) has previously estimated that 9000 young people under YOT supervision were in unsuitable accommodation. Substance misuse is regularly reported as being higher amongst young people who offend than those not involved in the criminal justice system (Matrix and the Institute for Criminal Policy Research, 2007). A study commissioned by the Youth Justice Board (YJB) found that 31 per cent of young people serving custodial or community sentences had mental health problems; for example, 9 per cent

reported self-harming in the previous month and 9 per cent were diagnosed as suffering from post-traumatic stress disorder (Harrington & Bailey, 2005). There is also increasing evidence of communication and language difficulties amongst young offenders (Bryan et al., 2007). Many young people who offend have also been the victims of crime (Smith, 2004). This can be particularly acute in those who commit serious violent and sexual offences where there is evidence to indicate a higher prevalence of experiences of abuse (Boswell, 1996). These examples begin to show the complexity of services required for young people who offend.

Framework for Practice

This section considers the overall 'end-to-end' case management framework for young people who offend.

Core practice model

Community supervision of young offenders in England and Wales is based on a core practice model of 'Assessment, Planning Interventions and Supervision' (Youth Justice Board, 2008) which includes the following key elements.

Assessment
- Collecting relevant information
- Analysis of relevant information
- Prediction of possible future behaviour(s)

Classification and planning interventions
- Identifying the level, intensity, content and types of interventions required
- Defining relevant, clear targets for action

Supervision
- Relationship between worker and young person
- Ways of working/staff effectiveness
- Specific interventions
- Enforcement/compliance.

This approach of assessment → planning → action → review is neither new nor specific to England and Wales. Similar models could be used in other parts of the UK, although there would, for example, be differences in the focus of assessment, with practitioners in Scotland likely to give more attention to welfare needs. Another difference is that in England and Wales the model is applied in a way that more explicitly reflects the Risk, Need and

Responsivity framework (RNR) (Andrews *et al.*, 1990: Ogloff & Davis, 2004). This is built on three key principles that reflect general personality and social psychological theories of crime:

1. *The risk principle:* more intensive interventions are best reserved for cases assessed as at higher risk of recidivism.
2. *The need principle:* interventions should be focused on needs or problems most closely associated with offending.
3. *The responsivity principle:* interventions need to take account of factors such as an offender's age, gender, ethnicity, personality, motivation and ability.

Assessment

Currently, assessment focuses on the following three key outcomes (Youth Justice Board, 2008a):

i)   offending/reoffending: the likelihood that a young person will become involved in offending or commit further offences;
ii) serious harm to others: the risk that a young person might inflict serious harm on other people (e.g. serious violent or sexual offences);
iii) vulnerability: the possibility that a young person might be harmed, either because of their own behaviour or through the actions or omissions of others.

There has been an increase in the use of standardised assessment tools within youth justice, including *Asset* (used in England and Wales and some parts of Scotland) and the Youth Level of Service/Case Management Inventory (YLS/CM-I) (also used in parts of Scotland). Other tools are available for particular types of offence such as the Structured Assessment of Violence Risk in Youth (SAVRY) for violent offending and the Assessment, Intervention and Moving On assessment (AIM2), the Juvenile Sex Offender Assessment Protocol (J-SOAP) or the Estimate of Risk of Adolescent Sexual Offence Recidivism (ERASOR) for young people who commit sexual offences.[2] Use of these more specialist tools varies considerably between services. Notwithstanding the growth in the use of assessment tools, however, the application of professional judgement and discretion remains a critical feature of decision making in relation to young people who offend (Baker, 2005, 2007).

Classification and planning interventions

Currently the frequency of contact between a YOT and young person is determined by the type of order a young person receives. This has meant that young people with potentially significant differences in needs/risks were receiving similar intensity of service. For example, the Audit Commission (2004) found that persistent young offenders were receiving on average only 1.8 hours' contact in the first three months of supervision compared to 1.1 hours for other young people. The obvious exception to this has been the Intensive Supervision and Surveillance Programme (ISSP) aimed at serious and/ or persistent offenders. For the first three months of the programme young people should receive a structured programme of activities for at least five hours each day during the week and access to support during the evenings and weekends. There has thus been a disparity between provision for this group and others, with very few gradations in between.

However, the youth justice system is now adopting a practice model based much more explicitly on the risk principle outlined earlier, i.e. that more intensive interventions are best reserved for cases assessed as at higher risk of recidivism. This is intended to allow for greater differentiation in the level of intervention and the frequency of contact as determined by the outcome of a risk assessment (Youth Justice Board, 2009).

Supervision

Core supervision of young people who offend will include direct provision of interventions and brokering/ enabling access to both mainstream service provision and specialist resources where required. YOT practitioners also need to manage referrals to Local Safeguarding Children Boards (LSCBs) in cases where there are serious concerns about a young person's welfare and/or to Multi-Agency Public Protection Arrangements (MAPPA) where there are concerns regarding a risk that the young person presents to others.

A young person may require multiple services and a YOT worker will need to coordinate this effectively in a way that encourages a young person to engage positively. For example, a young person may benefit more from a particular groupwork programme if it is delivered in a context where staff try to engage him/her in a positive relationship and also demonstrate a consistent approach to compliance and enforcement. This reflects the 'case management' literature which highlights the importance of the four Cs, namely consistency, continuity, commitment and consolidation in shaping the way offenders view and experience the services they receive (Holt, 2002).

Interventions and Services

It has been suggested that 'there are two fundamental ways to change a young person's behaviour; by changing the individual or by changing the environment in which he/she operates or both' (Wikström & Treiber, 2008, p.28). In practice it may be difficult to maintain such a clear demarcation as some interventions try to change both elements but it is a useful conceptual device and so this section considers, firstly, interventions which centre primarily on the individual young person and, secondly, programmes which also focus on the wider social context.

Interventions focused on the individual

Some interventions will be provided in the form of groupwork programmes (although this is less common than in the adult criminal justice system which places more emphasis on such groupwork-based interventions) while others, generally the majority (Morgan Harris Burrows, 2006), are more likely to be based around one-to-one contact.

Offending behaviour work

'Offending behaviour work' in YOTs can encompass a wide range of activities, although much of it is likely to reflect – to varying degrees – the principles of cognitive behavioural therapy (CBT). CBT is based on the idea that 'if you can change the way an individual perceives and thinks about the social settings he/she encounters and his/her actions, you can change his/her behaviour' (Wikström & Treiber, 2008, p.28). There are different types of cognitive behavioural interventions but the areas most commonly addressed are: anger management, behaviour modification, cognitive restructuring, cognitive skills training, moral reasoning, relapse prevention, social skills training and victim impact/empathy work. CBT can also be used in addressing specific behaviours such as arson (Bailey & Kerslake, 2008).

One very specific type of offending behaviour work is that which relates to young people who sexually abuse. While sexual offences account for only a very small proportion of the offences committed by children and young people (0.6 per cent for 2006/7; see Youth Justice Board, 2007), there is some evidence to suggest a steady increase in the number of such offences dealt with by the criminal justice system (Grimshaw, 2008). YOTs will often either 'buy in' expertise or refer young people to specialist service providers (such as the Lucy Faithfull Foundation), some of whom may adopt a CBT-based model while others may focus more on family therapy approaches.[3] Most such interventions will be delivered to young people living in the community, although there are a small number of places available in residential therapeutic facilities (Grimshaw, 2008). Young people can also be placed in either non-specialist or specialist therapeutic foster care (Farmer, 2004).

Restorative justice

Restorative justice is defined as 'a process whereby parties with a stake in a specific offence resolve collectively how to deal with the aftermath of the offence and its implications for the future' (Marshall, 1999, p.5). This is distinct from the more widely defined term 'restorative practice' which encompasses approaches that attempt to increase offender awareness of the harm they have caused, or enable offenders to make reparation for that harm, but which may not involve engagement with victims. There has been a significant increase in the application of restorative principles in youth justice, although this includes practices which vary significantly, particularly with regard to the extent to which they involve victims (Wilcox et al., 2004).

Mentoring

Mentoring is not exclusive to youth justice and is used with other groups of disaffected young people but has become more widespread in work with young offenders. The one-to-one relationship at the heart of mentoring can have a positive impact in terms of helping young people to develop positive life goals, although its impact on reducing reoffending is less clear (Jolliffe & Farrington, 2007; Newburn & Shiner, 2005).

Accommodation

YOTs do not directly provide housing but can help young people gain access to other services. However, there is a shortage of suitable accommodation for this age group (Arnull et al., 2007), particularly for young people on their release from custody into the community (HMI Probation, 2007). There have been a number of legal challenges in cases where Children's Services have failed to meet the accommodation needs of young offenders to whom they had statutory obligations under the Children Act 2004 and/or the Children (Leaving Care) Act 2000,[4] and this remains a contentious issue.

Education, training and employment (ETE)

Although there is some evidence of YOTs providing educational services themselves (Moore et al., 2004) their major role is in brokering access to provision from other agencies. Interventions under this umbrella heading of ETE can have a variety of objectives, which include: improving basic literacy and numeracy skills; keeping young people engaged in ETE (Cooper et al., 2007) and facilitating entry to employment (Foster, 2006). Any such interventions have to take account of the fact that young people who offend often have poor previous experiences of education and consequently little confidence in their abilities to achieve. The content of ETE programmes and the style of delivery need to be matched to the literacy and skill levels of the young people involved.

Health and substance misuse

YOTs normally have a designated health specialist who can assess health-related needs and make referrals to external services where required (Pitcher et al., 2004). The National Service Framework for Children and Young People (Department of Health, 2004) clearly states (in Standard 9) that all young people should have access to multidisciplinary mental health services and some YOTs will have specialist Child and Adolescent Mental Health Services (CAMHS) workers (Bailey & Kerslake, 2008). Overall, there has been an improvement in the provision of CAMHS services to YOTs, although some teams still report difficulties in obtaining the necessary support (Commission for Healthcare Audit and Inspection, 2006).

All YOTs should now have dedicated substance misuse workers (Pitcher et al., 2004)[5] who can undertake additional screening and assessment of young people. This is an area of intervention where YOTs may be more likely to try groupwork activities, although there can be difficulties in implementation if the focus is too specific. For practical reasons it can sometimes be better to incorporate work on substance misuse into more generic offending behaviour programmes (Hammersley et al., 2003). For those with more complex problems, some residential treatment services are available, although the evidence regarding their suitability for young people is mixed (Britton & Farrant, 2008).

Surveillance

Although surveillance would not typically be described as an intervention, it is included here because it can be a significant feature of community-based work with young people who offend. Surveillance is a core feature of the ISSP in which teams are required to use one or more of the following:

- tagging;
- voice verification;
- tracking;
- intelligence-led policing.

Some young people referred to MAPPA might also be subject to surveillance. Use of surveillance has been controversial (Smith, 2007) but it is worth noting that not all young people were hostile to it. The evaluation of ISSP found that some young people thought being tagged was helpful because it gave them a way to avoid peer pressure and an excuse to stay away from places or situations where offending was likely to occur (Moore et al., 2004).

Interventions with a wider focus

Youth justice services engage with young people's familial and social contexts in a variety of ways. For example, YOTs provide programmes for parents on a voluntary basis but there are also statutory Parenting Orders which mean that parents can be legally required to attend. In addition, there are other more specific and/or intensive services as described below.

Multi-systemic therapy

Unlike CBT which focuses primarily on changing a young person's attitudes, thinking patterns and views, multi-systemic therapy (MST) has a wider scope which attempts to alter a young person's social context as well. It is generally used for more serious offenders and is based on the premise that offending results from the interaction of individual and external factors in a young person's life. The primary goals of MST are to: improve parenting and family relationships, decrease associations with pro-criminal peers and increase interaction with pro-social friends, improve educational or vocational performance through increasing parental monitoring/

involvement, modify social perceptual problem-solving skills and develop a support network to help sustain the changes achieved during intervention (Wikström & Treiber, 2008). MST is used in the UK with, for example, young people who sexually abuse (Hackett *et al.*, 2003), those with substance misuse problems (Hengeller *et al.*, 2006) and one of the ISSP projects also adopted this model (Moore *et al.*, 2004).

Intensive fostering
The intensive fostering programme, funded by the YJB, is an alternative to custody for children and young people whose home life is felt to have contributed significantly to their offending behaviour. Foster care can be specified as a requirement of a Youth Rehabilitation Order and the programme provides highly intensive care for up to 12 months for each individual, as well as a comprehensive programme of support for their family. The scheme is based on the Multi-dimensional Treatment Foster Care (MTFC) model initially developed in Oregon and its implementation in the UK is currently being evaluated.

Summary

As this overview has shown, there are a wide variety of interventions and services available in the community for young people who offend. For many, particularly those with more complex problems, multidimensional and multimodal treatments are likely to be required. This raises a number of challenges for youth justice services, such as the practical issue of sequencing the interventions appropriately so as not to overload a young person with too many expectations or requirements. Another example would be the difficulty of balancing competing 'needs', e.g. finding appropriate educational provision for a young person who has committed sexual offences that would not put either him/her or other children at a high risk of harm.

Critical Debates

Having considered the different types of service provision currently available, this section moves on to explore some of the current debates about practice.

Foundations and values

Firstly, there are some 'core' questions concerning the purpose, scope and values of youth justice.

Individual vs. social perspectives
One recurrent criticism of current government policy is that it has focused too much on individual or personal factors and ignored the wider socioeconomic structures that may contribute to offending behaviour (Webster *et al.*, 2006). That is to say, government has been 'tough on crime' (or on individual offenders) but not so 'tough on the causes of crime'. This macro-level debate on the relative importance of social context versus individual responsibility will no doubt continue, but what can, and should, front-line practitioners do when working with young people?

The limited evidence currently available on the congruence between assessments and intervention plans produced by YOT workers shows that, in a significant proportion of cases where assessments identify offending-related problems associated with wider contextual factors (such as a young person's family or peer group), there are few if any interventions proposed to address these difficulties (Baker *et al.*, 2005; Sutherland, 2009). It is not entirely clear why this is the case but it could be a combination of workers not feeling sufficiently skilled to address these problems and/or a lack of appropriate services.

Even where programmes which deal with the individual plus their family and social context are available, the impact may still be limited. 'There are, for example, limits to how much even the most effectively implemented and delivered MST programme can influence relevant aspects of the wider social environment in which a young person who offends takes part (e.g. high levels of disadvantage and poor collective efficacy), and criminogenic factors arising from individual characteristics that have emerged during the offender's early development (e.g. reversing or counteracting serious early developmental cognitive deficiencies)' (Wikström & Treiber, 2008, p.38). Thus, there is a need for realism about what practitioners can achieve, but wider consideration of the impact of social and economic circumstances cannot be ignored just because of the difficulties associated with producing positive change in a young person's environment.

Too much 'risk'?
While there is continued debate about the extent to which risk is the dominant paradigm in current criminal justice policy and practice (Kemshall, 2007; O'Malley, 2004), there is no doubt that it has assumed significant importance in recent years. Scepticism about the value of risk is perhaps more evident in relation to work with

young people than with adults. Some would argue that it is inappropriate and the focus should be more on welfare. Particular applications of the risk concept – such as the 'risk and protective factors paradigm' (Farrington, 2007) and the RNR model – have been criticised for lacking a value base and ignoring wider social contexts (Case, 2007; Ward & Maruna, 2007). Others suggest that it still has value but that our conceptualisation of risk needs to become more sophisticated, for example through developing greater understanding of the ways in which young people themselves perceive and navigate risks (Sharland, 2006).

The expanding literature on desistance from offending (Farrall, 2002) and the growing interest in the 'good lives model' (Ward & Maruna, 2007), which focuses on helping people to adopt long-term positive goals for the future, suggest some alternative approaches for practice, although much of the discussion has centred on adult offenders and more consideration needs to be given to how these approaches might work with young people. In a review of these developments, McNeill (2009) suggests that the concept of risk need not be disregarded because addressing risk may be a necessary part of effective offender supervision, but it may not be sufficient on its own to promote change. Given the current climate of penal populism and the political prioritisation given to public protection it is likely that 'risk' will continue to be a significant feature of youth justice, so the challenge will be to find ways of making this effective for young people rather than just replicating adult-focused models of practice.

Care vs. control

The balance of care and control in interventions with young offenders is another long-debated topic (Muncie, 2004; Whyte, 2008) and the tensions become particularly acute in complex interventions such as ISSP. Remand fostering for young people awaiting trial or sentence provides another striking example as 'these foster-carers have to bridge the divide between providing the care of the welfare system and the control of the criminal justice system' (Lipscombe, 2007, p.974). Care and control are not mutually exclusive (Dunbar, 1995) but questions arise about whether the balance between the two is appropriate – this may vary depending on the type of intervention, the seriousness of the offending or the age of the young people involved.

The care/control question is related to the earlier discussion about risk in that a preoccupation with risk is more likely to lead to restrictive or controlling interventions. This can be particularly evident in responses to more serious offenders and there are some anecdotal but recurring indications emerging of, for example, MAPPA being reluctant to agree to reintegrative measures (Baker, 2009). Although this might directly affect only a small number of young people, the language of risk and control permeates other aspects of criminal justice services and thus has a much wider impact.

Research, evaluation and evidence

On balance, evidence suggests that interventions delivered in the community are more likely to produce positive outcomes than those provided in institutions (McGuire & Priestley, 1995), but this finding on its own doesn't help services to know which interventions to provide. It has recently been argued that youth justice practitioners should 'make sure they only use programmes and interventions that have proven effective or promising' (Wikström & Treiber, 2008, p.6), but this presents a number of challenges.

'What works?'[6]

The findings from research in relation to the effectiveness of different interventions – where this is defined as reducing the occurrence, frequency or seriousness of offending – are still rather mixed. There is evidence to show that CBT can be effective in reducing recidivism, although effect sizes tend to be small to medium. Evidence also suggests that CBT is more effective for older young people (e.g. aged 13–17) whereas for younger ones, parent-focused interventions may be more appropriate (McCart et al., 2006). Also, CBT is most likely to be effective for those whose offending is shaped primarily by cognitive distortion. In other areas, however, there are significant gaps in the literature, for example in relation to interventions with young people who commit violent offences (Burman et al., 2007). With regard to some of the more specialist interventions for serious offenders, such as therapeutic foster care, there is a small amount of evidence on factors that may be associated with positive outcomes and progress (Farmer, 2004) but there is a continued need for more and better designed research.

Systematic reviews examining the effectiveness of interventions report recurring methodological problems. These include:

- small sample sizes – for example this has been a problem in relation to evaluation of MST programmes (Wikström & Treiber, 2008);

- a significant difference in effect between demonstration projects and programmes run as part of ordinary practice (Farrington & Welsh, 2002);
- implementation failure (Feilzer *et al.*, 2004).

Grimshaw's summary of the current knowledge base, although written specifically about work with young people who sexually abuse, could also be applied more widely across the field of youth justice interventions: 'the evidence does not support firm conclusions about the effectiveness of particular treatment approaches, though some young people show reductions in recidivism and other benefits after going through some programmes' (Grimshaw, 2008, p.37).

Evaluation: what and how?

The New Labour embrace of evidence-based policy and practice (EBPP) has been welcomed in some quarters for introducing more methodological rigour to evaluations of project effectiveness but criticised on other grounds, for example its emphasis on a hierarchy of evidence which prioritises randomised control trials (RCTs) and the question of whether it allows government to have too much control of the research agenda (Davies *et al.*, 2000). It is not possible to explore the issue in depth here but two brief points can be made. Firstly, if young people are subject to a range of different interventions, it is difficult to identify which of them, if any, produced an impact on recidivism. In addition to specific programme evaluations, therefore, there is a need for studies which look at multimodal and sequential interventions. Secondly, there is a need to understand *how* things work and this requires a different methodological approach. Factors such as the quality of practitioner/young person relationships cannot fully be explored through quantitative approaches and thus there remains a need for qualitative studies to help understand the reality of how services are provided for, and perceived by, young people.

Working with young people

This section considers some of the key challenges that arise in frontline day-to-day practice with young people.

Assessment, identification and targeting

If assessment is at the heart of the core practice model described earlier, then it is important to consider questions about the methods and tools used. There is firstly a question about the predictive validity of assessment frameworks and while there is some positive evidence on this in relation to tools such as *Asset*, there are other gaps (for example, there is little information on the use of the Structured Assessment of Violence Risk in Youth assessment (SAVRY) with UK populations). Secondly, there is a question with regard to the appropriateness of such tools. *Asset*, for example, has been criticised by some for deprofessionalising practice (Smith, 2007), although these claims are challenged by others who note that, if used appropriately, *Asset* can help to improve assessment quality (Baker, 2005).

The use of structured tools may lead to the potential danger of staff and sentencers 'inferring greater certainty about reoffending calculations than actually exists' but also of the opposite situation in which they respond 'to the uncertainty of prediction by becoming more cautious' (Kemshall, 1996, p.19). Assessment frameworks should therefore be seen not as a panacea but rather as tools which can provide useful indicators about possible future behaviour. Practitioners also have a responsibility to use such tools in 'professionally ethical ways' (Crighton & Towl, 2008, p.110) which will require the application of knowledge, practice, wisdom and professional discretion.

Diversity

There are some examples of programmes designed for particular groups, for example in the mental health field there are examples of projects working specifically with young women or black and minority ethnic (BME) groups (Perry *et al.*, 2008), although more research is required into their effectiveness. When addressing particular types of offending there may be particular difficulties in arranging provision if there are only a few cases involved, one example being the lack of services for the small number of young women who commit sexual offences (Hackett *et al.*, 2003). Service provision also needs to take account of differences in offending patterns so that, for example, interventions targeting substance misuse will need to reflect the prevalence of different drugs in different locations (Britton & Farrant, 2008). Young people who sexually abuse are not a homogeneous group and service provision needs to reflect the differing needs of, for example, those with learning difficulties, BME groups and those with comorbid conditions such post-traumatic stress disorder (PTSD) or attention deficit hyperactivity disorder (ADHD). To achieve this diversity of provision, youth justice services need to know and understand the characteristics and needs of the young people they are working with and to be familiar with research evidence regarding provision for particular groups (where this is available).

Engagement and participation

Encouraging young people to engage with interventions in the community is essential yet often difficult and one reason for this could be young people's (mis)understandings of what the services may be like. To take interventions relating to substance misuse as an example, White *et al.* (2004) found that young people did not really know what to expect or thought that programmes would be authoritarian in style. In such a context staff will need to be skilled in explaining the nature of services and encouraging participation. There are also dilemmas in engaging parents/carers. There is some evidence to suggest that involving them in substance misuse interventions can be helpful (McIntosh *et al.*, 2006) but on the other hand their involvement in the assessment process can inhibit a young person from providing information. Service providers therefore need to operate a balanced approach and use professional discretion when involving family members.

A recent review of literature on effective techniques for engaging young people who offend highlighted the importance of relationships between practitioners and young people (Mason & Prior, 2008) and noted the relevance of practice approaches such as motivational interviewing. It is encouraging that the YJB are now giving more explicit attention to the importance of relationships but this needs to be strengthened by further research in this area and accompanied by ongoing organisational commitment to retain this emphasis rather than revert to a more technical 'tick box' approach which might appear easier to implement.

Transitions

Young people are often most vulnerable at the point of transition from one service to another; for example, a need has been identified for more facilities to help young people who have been in residential treatment (in this case to address sexually abusive behaviour) make the transition back into the community (Whittle *et al.*, 2006). Data from the USA suggest that 'assertive continuing care' following residential treatment for adolescents with substance use disorders can have a positive impact in terms of promoting change, although again further research is needed (Godley *et al.*, 2007). Release from custody back to the community is clearly a critical

point and it is therefore of concern that many YOT workers considered the continuity of health care provision from custody to community to be poor (Pitcher *et al.*, 2004). Since that research was conducted, however, the YJB has produced a strategic action plan on resettlement (Youth Justice Board, 2006) and also provided funding for Resettlement and Aftercare Provision (RAP) in 50 YOT areas[7] so it is to be hoped that the situation has now improved.

Resources and Multi-Agency Working

The final theme in this discussion of current practice relates to organisational issues.

Partnership working

Partnerships and multi-agency working are a key feature of the reformed youth justice system and are particularly significant when dealing with young people requiring complex and/or specialist provision (Bailey & Kerslake, 2008). Significant progress has been made in this area, although there are still some difficulties regarding confidentiality and information sharing (HMI Probation, 2007).

There is also an unresolved question regarding YOTs' role in providing interventions directly versus their role in brokering access for young people to services provided by other agencies. This can be illustrated by considering the role of healthcare workers in YOTs – it was intended that this role would primarily be one of negotiating access to relevant services but in reality many staff provide interventions themselves. While this may have the benefit of some young people receiving advice or a service that they might not otherwise obtain, a disadvantage is that they need to be involved with the YOT on an ongoing basis to receive help and may not be able to continue this once their orders come to an end (Commission for Healthcare Audit and Inspection, 2006). The multi-agency nature of YOTs, and the fact that they *can* provide some services, does not mean that they *should* do so if responsibility rests with other (mainstream or specialist) organisations.

Resources

Finally, it would be remiss not to mention the matter of resources. There will always be demands for additional funds and there continue to be examples of gaps in provision, particularly in relation to residential or therapeutic placements (Hackett *et al.*, 2003). One key issue concerns the criteria through which resources are allocated. For example, there are reports of YOTs using MAPPA as a means of leverage to gain access to resources that would not otherwise be provided (Sutherland & Jones, 2008). In some cases, it will clearly be appropriate for such cases to be under MAPPA supervision but there are concerns about the potential for the risk that a young person presents to be inflated for the purpose of obtaining services. Another critical question relates to who pays for services. The YJB is currently responsible for funding custodial placements but there are proposals set out in the Youth Crime Action Plan (HM Government, 2008) for local authorities to be made responsible for the full cost of court-ordered secure remands. If this were to occur, it is possible that local authorities may divert more of their resources into community provision that could help to keep young people out of custody.

Conclusions

Community and residential services for young people who offend have to be delivered in a context of limited resources alongside rising public concern about youth violence and a political imperative for the government to be seen to be 'doing something' to reduce crime. In addition, the purpose and values of youth justice services are themselves contested, resulting in varying, and sometimes conflicting, developments in policy and practice. This review has also highlighted some of the gaps in the knowledge base about interventions and ways of working effectively with young people and highlighted areas for further research.

In thinking about future service provision, perhaps the key is to balance optimism with realism. This applies both to practitioners working with individual young people and at the wider policy/government level. The complexity of the needs and problems of this group of young people are well known and for staff working with them every day there is a challenge to believe in the possibility of positive change while being realistic about the fact that progress in changing a young person's behaviour might be slow. For policy makers, there is a similar challenge to adopt a balanced approach. There has been a tendency to over-promote new initiatives and to underestimate the difficulties in obtaining reductions in reoffending. Consequently, there may be negative publicity when evaluation findings fail to live up to the

expectations that have been created (as was the case with ISSP, for example; Moore *et al.*, 2004). A transparent and sanguine approach to developing policy and practice is thus required, but having a realistic view of the difficulties need not mean adopting a pessimistic 'nothing works' approach: community interventions can have a positive impact and the challenge for the future is to improve them still further.

Notes

1 Further information about the YRO can be found at: www.yjb.gov.uk/en-gb/practitioners/CourtsAndOrders/CriminalJusticeandImmigrationAct/#YRO, accessed 2 September 2009.
2 For a useful summary of these and other risk assessment tools see Risk Management Authority (2007).
3 For an interesting study of the current level of consensus in the UK on appropriate interventions with children and young people who sexually abuse see Hackett *et al.* (2006).
4 For example, *R (on application of M)* v *London Borough of Hammersmith and Fulham* [2008] UKHL 14.
5 The term 'substance' here includes tobacco, alcohol, volatile substances and illegal drugs.
6 The emphasis here is on the quantity and strength of evidence currently available in relation to interventions for young offenders. For wider debate on the 'What Works?' literature see, for example, Thomas-Peter (2006) or Merrington and Stanley (2007).
7 RAP provides up to 25 hours of planned support and activities each week (on a voluntary basis) to young people after they leave custody, including work to address substance misuse.

Further Reading

Morgan, R. & Newburn, T. (2007). Youth justice. In M. Maguire, R. Morgan & R. Reiner (Eds.) *The Oxford handbook of criminology* (4th edn). Oxford: Oxford University Press.
This chapter provides a comprehensive overview of, and introduction to, the youth justice system in England and Wales, summarising its recent development and the impact of the New Labour reforms. It gives details of current sentences for children and young people and discusses the most common interventions provided. The authors set this account within the context of wider social and political developments such as the rise of managerialism and the rebirth of populist punitiveness while also raising important questions about the criminalisation of young people, the current trend towards

intensifying community interventions and the future direction of services for children who offend.

Wikström, P-O. & Treiber, K. (2008). *Offending behaviour programmes: Source document*. London: Youth Justice Board.

This systematic review provides an in-depth overview of research findings about offending behaviour programmes for young people who offend, with a particular focus on cognitive behavioural treatment (CBT) and multi-systemic therapy (MST). Wikström and Treiber summarise the evidence regarding the effectiveness of CBT and MST and then consider a range of practice-related issues, such as identifying factors that can influence how well these therapies work in routine practice and whether there are particular groups of young people for whom these types of interventions are more (or less) effective. In addition, the authors also address wider debates concerning the significance of the distinction between causation and prevention of offending, the difficulties encountered when trying to determine whether an intervention has been effective and the practical challenges of ensuring proper programme intervention and delivery.

Whyte, B. (2008). *Youth justice in practice: Making a difference*. Bristol: The Policy Press.

In this practice-focused text, Bill Whyte explores the challenges of delivering services in the community for young people who offend. The discussion is framed by consideration of the broader political context and the complex task of maintaining an appropriate balance between welfare and justice, although the main emphasis is on the application of evidence to service delivery. The areas of practice covered include early intervention, restorative justice, assessment needs and risks, principles of effective practice, intensive supervision, and maintaining and evaluating change over time. With its very clear focus on practice, the book provides a useful introduction for students or practitioners working in services which address offending by children and young people.

References

Andrews, D.A., Bonta, J. & Hoge, R. (1990). Classification for effective rehabilitation: Rediscovering psychology. *Criminal Justice and Behavior*, 17(1), 19–52.

Arnull, E., Eagle, S., Gammampila, A., Patel, S., Sadler, J., Thomas, S. *et al.* (2007). *Housing needs and experiences*. London: Youth Justice Board.

Audit Commission (2004). *Youth justice 2004: A review of the reformed youth justice system*. London: Audit Commission.

Bailey, S. & Kerslake, B. (2008). The process and systems for juveniles and young persons. In K. Soothill, P. Rogers & M. Dolan (Eds.) *Handbook of forensic mental health*. Cullompton, Devon: Willan.

Baker, K. (2005). Assessment in youth justice: Professional discretion and the use of Asset. *Youth Justice*, 5(2), 106–122.

Baker, K. (2008). Risk, uncertainty and public protection: Assessment of young people who offend. *British Journal of Social Work*, 36(8), 1463–1480.

Baker, K. (forthcoming). MAPPA as 'risk in action': Discretion and decision-making. In K. Baker & A. Sutherland (Eds.) *Multi-agency public protection arrangements and youth justice*. Bristol: Policy Press.

Baker, K., Jones, S., Merrington, S. & Roberts, C. (2005). *Further development of* Asset. London: Youth Justice Board.

Boswell, G. (1996). *Young and dangerous: The backgrounds and careers of Section 53 offenders*. Aldershot: Avebury.

Britton, J. & Farrant, F. (2008). *Substance misuse: Source document*. London: Youth Justice Board.

Bryan, K., Freer, J. & Furlong, C. (2007). Language and communication difficulties in juvenile offenders. *International Journal of Language and Communication Disorders*, 42(5), 505–520.

Burman, M., Armstrong, S., Batchelor, S., McNeill, F. & Nicholson, J. (2007). *Research and practice in risk assessment and risk management of children and young people engaging in offending behaviours*. Paisley: Risk Management Authority.

Case, S. (2007). Questioning the 'evidence' of risk that underpins evidence-led youth justice interventions. *Youth Justice*, 7(2), 91–105.

Commission for Healthcare Audit and Inspection (2006). *Let's talk about it: A review of healthcare in the community for young people who offend*. London: Commission for Healthcare Audit and Inspection.

Cooper, K., Sutherland, A. & Roberts, C. (2007). *Keeping young people engaged (KYPE)*. London: Youth Justice Board.

Crighton, D. & Towl, G. (2008). *Psychology in prisons* (2nd edn). Malden, MA: Blackwell.

Davies, T., Nutley, S. & Smith, P. (2000). *What works? Evidence based policy and practice in public service*. Bristol: Policy Press.

Department of Health (2004). *National service framework for children, young people and maternity services*. London: Department of Health.

Dunbar, I. (1995). *A sense of direction*. London: Home Office.

Easton, S. & Piper, C. (2005). *Sentencing and punishment: The quest for justice*. Oxford: Oxford University Press.

Farmer, E. (2004). Patterns of placement, management and outcome for sexually abused and/or abusing children in substitute care. *British Journal of Social Work*, 34(3), 375–393.

Farrall, S. (2002). *Rethinking what works with offenders: Probation, social context and desistance from crime*. Cullompton, Devon: Willan.

Farrington, D. (2007). Childhood risk factors and risk-focused prevention. In M. Maguire, R. Morgan & R. Reiner (Eds.)

The Oxford handbook of criminology (4th edn). Oxford: Oxford University Press.

Farrington, D. & Welsh, B. (2002). Developmental prevention programmes: Effectiveness and cost-benefit analysis. In J. McGuire (Ed.) *Offender rehabilitation and treatment: Effective programmes and policies to reduce reoffending*. Chichester: Wiley.

Feilzer, M., Appleton, C., Roberts, C. & Hoyle, C. (2004). *National evaluation of the Youth Justice Board's cognitive behaviour projects*. London: Youth Justice Board.

Foster, J. (2006). *Entry to employment*. London: Youth Justice Board.

Godley, M., Godley, S., Dennis, M., Funk, R. & Passetti, L. (2007). The effect of assertive continuing care on continuing care linkage, adherence and abstinence following residential treatment for adolescents with substance use disorders. *Addiction, 102*(1), 81–93.

Goldson, B. (Ed.) (2000). *The new youth justice*. Lyme Regis: Russell House.

Grimshaw, R. with Malek, M., Oldfield, M. & Smith, R. (2008). *Young people who sexually abuse (source document)*. London: Youth Justice Board.

Hackett, S., Masson, H. & Phillips, S. (2003). *Mapping and exploring services for young people who have sexually abused others*. London: Youth Justice Board.

Hackett, S., Masson, H. & Phillips, S. (2006). Exploring consensus in practice with youth who are sexually abusive: Findings from a Delphi study of practitioner views in the United Kingdom and the Republic of Ireland. *Child Maltreatment, 11*(2), 146–156.

Hammersley R., Marsland, L. & Reid, M. (2003). *Substance use by young offenders: The impact of the normalization of drug use in the early years of the 21st century*. London: Home Office.

Harrington, R. & Bailey, S. (2005). *Mental health needs and effectiveness of provision for young offenders in custody and in the community*. London: Youth Justice Board.

Hengeller, S., Halliday-Boykins, C., Cunningham, P., Randall, J., Shapiro, S. & Chapman, J. (2006). Juvenile drug court: Enhancing outcomes by integrating evidence-based treatments. *Journal of Consulting and Clinical Psychology, 74*(1), 42–54.

HM Government (2004). *Every child matters: Change for children*. London: Stationery Office.

HM Government (2008). *Youth crime action plan*. London: Stationery Office.

HMI Probation (2007). *Joint inspection of youth offending teams annual report 2006/2007*. London: HMIP.

Holt, P. (2002). Case management evaluation: Pathways to progress. *VISTA, 7*(1), 16–25.

Jolliffe, D. & Farrington, D. (2007). *A rapid evidence assessment of the impact of mentoring on re-offending: A summary*. Home Office Online Report 11/07. London: Home Office.

Jones, S. & Baker, K. (2009). Setting the scene: Risk, welfare and rights. In K. Baker & A. Sutherland (Eds.) *Multi-agency public protection arrangements and youth justice*. Bristol: Policy Press.

Kemshall, H. (1996). *Reviewing risk: A review of research on the assessment and management of risk and dangerousness, implications for policy and practice in the Probation Service*. Croydon: Home Office.

Kemshall, H. (2007). Risk assessment and risk management: The right approach? In M. Blyth, E. Solomon & K. Baker (Eds.) *Young people and 'risk'*. Bristol: The Policy Press.

Lipscombe, J. (2007). Fostering children and young people on remand: Care or control? *British Journal of Social Work, 37*(6), 973–986.

Marshall, T. (1999). *Restorative justice: An overview*. London: Home Office.

Mason, P. & Prior, D. (2008). *Engaging young people who offend: Source document*. London: Youth Justice Board.

Matrix Research and Consultancy & Institute for Criminal Policy Research (2007). *Evaluation of drug intervention programme pilots*. London: Home Office.

McAra, L. (2006). Welfare in crisis? Key developments in Scottish youth justice. In J. Muncie & B. Goldson (Eds.) *Comparative youth justice*. London: Sage.

McCart, M., Priester, P., Hobart Davies, W. & Azen, R. (2006). Differential effectiveness of behavioural parent-training and cognitive-behavioral therapy for anti-social youth: A meta-analysis. *Journal of Abnormal Child Psychology, 34*(4), 527–543.

McDiarmid, C. (2005). Welfare, offending and the Scottish children's hearings system. *Journal of Social Welfare and Family Law, 27*(1), 31–42.

McGuire, J. & Priestley, P. (1995). Reviewing what works: Past, present and future. In J. McGuire (Ed.) *What works: Reducing reoffending*. Chichester: Wiley.

McIntosh, J., MacAskill, S., Eadie, D., Curtice, J., McKeganey, N., Hastings, G. *et al.* (2006). *Evaluation and description of drug projects working with young people and families*. Edinburgh: Scottish Executive.

McNeill, F. (2009). Young people, serious offending and managing risk: A Scottish perspective. In K. Baker & A. Sutherland (Eds.) *Multi-agency public protection arrangements and youth justice*. Bristol: Policy Press.

Merrington, S. & Stanley, S. (2007). Effectiveness: Who counts what? In L. Gelsthorpe & R. Morgan (Eds.) *Handbook of probation*. Cullompton, Devon: Willan.

Moore, R., Gray, E., Roberts, C., Merrington, S., Waters, I., Fernandez, R. *et al.* (2004). *National evaluation of the Intensive Supervision and Surveillance Programme: Interim report to the Youth Justice Board*. London: Youth Justice Board.

Morgan Harris Burrows (2006). *Juvenile cohort study: Feasibility study for the Home Office and Youth Justice Board*. London: Unpublished.

Morgan, R. & Newburn, T. (2007). Youth justice. In M. Maguire, R. Morgan & R. Reiner (Eds.) *The Oxford handbook of criminology* (4th edn). Oxford: Oxford University Press.

Muncie, J. (2004). *Youth and crime*. London: Sage.

Muncie, J. (2007). Adulteration. In B. Goldson (Ed.) *Dictionary of youth justice*. Cullompton, Devon: Willan.

Muncie, J. & Goldson, B. (2006). *Comparative youth justice*. London: Sage.

NACRO (2006). *Guide to the youth justice system in England and Wales*. London: NACRO.

Newburn, T. & Shiner, M. (Eds.) (2005). *Dealing with disaffection: Young people, mentoring and social inclusion*. Cullompton, Devon: Willan.

Ogloff, J., & Davis, M. (2004). Advances in offender assessment and rehabilitation: Contributions of the risks–needs–responsivity approach. *Psychology, Crime and Law*, 10(3), 229–242.

O'Malley, P. (2004). *Risk, uncertainty and government*. London: Cavendish Press/Glasshouse.

Perry, A., Gilbody, S., Akers, J. & Light, K. (2008). *Mental health: Source document*. London: Youth Justice Board.

Pitcher, J., Bateman, T. Johnston, V. & Cadman, S. (2004). *The provision of health, education and substance misuse workers in youth offending teams*. London: Youth Justice Board.

Risk Management Authority (2007). *Risk Assessment Tools Evaluation Directory (RATED)*. Paisley: RMA.

Sharland, E. (2006). Young people, risk taking and risk making: Some thoughts for social work. *British Journal of Social Work*, 36(2), 247–265.

Smith, D. (2004). *The links between victimization and offending*. Edinburgh: Centre for Law and Society.

Smith, R. (2007). *Youth justice: Ideas, policy and practice* (2nd edn). Cullompton, Devon: Willan.

Sutherland, A. (2009). The scaled approach in youth justice: Fools rush in … *Youth Justice*, 9(1), 44–60.

Sutherland, A. & Jones, S. (2008). *MAPPA and youth justice: An exploration of youth offending team engagement with multi-agency public protection arrangements*. London: Youth Justice Board.

Thomas-Peter, B. (2006). The modern context of psychology in corrections: Influences, limitations and values of 'what works'. In G. Towl (Ed.) *Psychological research in prisons*. Malden, MA: Blackwell Publishing.

Ward, T. & Maruna, S. (2007). *Rehabilitation: Beyond the risk paradigm*. London: Routledge.

Webster, C., MacDonald, R. & Simpson, M. (2006). Predicting criminality: Risk factors, neighbourhood influence and desistance. *Youth Justice*, 6(1), 7–22.

Welsh Assembly Government (2004). *Children and young people: Rights to action*. Cardiff: Welsh Assembly Government.

White, M., Godley, S. & Passetti, L. (2004). Adolescent and parent perceptions of outpatient substance abuse treatment: A qualitative study. *Journal of Psychoactive Drugs*, 36(1), 65–74.

Whittle, N., Bailey, S. & Kurtz, Z. (2006). *The needs and effective treatment of young people who sexually abuse: Current evidence*. London: Department of Health and National Institute for Mental Health in England.

Whyte, B. (2008). *Youth justice in practice: Making a difference*. Bristol: Policy Press.

Wikström, P-O. & Treiber, K. (2008). *Offending behaviour programmes: Source document*. London: Youth Justice Board.

Wilcox, A., Young, R. & Hoyle, C. (2004). *National evaluation of the Youth Justice Board's restorative justice projects*. London: Youth Justice Board.

Youth Justice Board (2004). *Sustaining the success*. London: Youth Justice Board.

Youth Justice Board (2006). *Youth resettlement: A framework for action*. London: Youth Justice Board.

Youth Justice Board (2007). *Youth justice annual workload data 2006/07*. London: Youth Justice Board.

Youth Justice Board (2008). *Assessment, planning interventions and supervision (source document)*. London: Youth Justice Board.

Youth Justice Board (2009). *Youth justice: The scaled approach*. London: Youth Justice Board.

4

Expert Testimony

Brian R. Clifford

Expert testimony is a form of evidence that differs from ordinary witness testimony by allowing the expression of opinion and the drawing of inferences. This chapter makes clear what giving such testimony involves and why psychological expert testimony is problematic both to the law and to many psychologists. It identifies and discusses certain key issues in the debate about the propriety of such testimony: the integrity of the knowledge base that psychiatrists, clinicians and experimental psychologists would draw upon in testifying; trespassing on the ultimate issue; possible 'battle of experts', and the consequent 'side-lining' of baffled juries. It then discusses proposed alternatives and antidotes to expert testimony. It is concluded that, on balance, with appropriate safeguards, circumspect testimony and a strong ethical stance, expert testimony of a psychological nature can benefit justice.

Introduction

Expert testimony has been employed by the court since at least the 14th century (Wigmore, 1978), and experts appearing for the rival parties to a dispute since about the 18th century (Miller & Allen, 1998). While the legal purpose of engaging such witnesses has always been the same – to provide expertise that the triers of fact do not possess – the ground rules for their admissibility have undergone constant revision.

Historically it can be seen that courts initially preferred experts who testified about physical factors rather than human factors; then later, experts who testified about human physical states rather than human mental states. When experts concerning mental states were accepted, the courts preferred experts who testified about abnormal mental states rather than normal mental states. Within this, courts preferred psychiatric experts over clinical psychology experts because the former were grounded in medical science. Only lately have the courts come to accept experts whose expertise lies in experimental investigations of normal states of mind, who study memory, perception and language. Until fairly recently such normal human processes were held to be within the knowledge and experience of the jury, the triers of fact, thus requiring no expert opinion to clarify or inform their rational decision-making roles (see Clifford, 2003a, 2008; Mackay *et al.*, 1999).

This evolution of the type of expert acceptable to the court can be traced in both the adversarial and inquisitorial court systems, although, historically, the inquisitorial system has employed experts for longer than the adversarial system (Spencer, 1998). It can also be seen in both civil and criminal proceedings.

This overall trend of increased scope of expert witnessing hides quite substantial differences as between countries, jurisdictions and type of legal proceedings. While the USA, UK, Australia, New Zealand and Canada all employ the adversarial method of trial, the use of normal-mental-state experts varies quite markedly among these countries (see Kapardis, 1997). Today, experts who offer testimony in areas of abnormality such as brain damage and mental impairment are generally welcome in civil and criminal courts because the nature and sequelae of, for example, closed-head injuries do not fall within the common knowledge and experience of the jury. Likewise, mental impairment leading to heightened suggestibility, and post-traumatic stress disorder (PTSD) (now recognised by the DSM-IV Revision) with its well-documented syndromal characteristics, fall outside juries' competence. Thus such expert evidence has been admitted by the courts within the UK and other Western common law countries as well as in the USA, as it is recognised that such testimony can educate and sensitise the jury or the court as to the likely outcomes of such conditions and thus guide their decision making.

These areas are, in general, non-contentious in most jurisdictions. However, the latest acceptance of expert testimony, concerning what I call normal-mental-state cases, has traditionally been regarded as falling within the purview of the jury, particularly in the UK. Such testimony is designed to sensitise jurors to matters they may not have considered, to disabuse them of long-held but perhaps erroneous assumptions, preconceptions and lay theories, thus allowing them to reach better decisions and thus serve justice better. As we will see, this is still a very contentious area of admissibility.

Who and What Is an Expert?

An expert witness is so designated by the court system, not by one's profession. The BPS's *Psychologists as expert witnesses: Guidelines and procedures for England and Wales* (2007) define an expert witness as 'a person who through special training, study or experience, is able to furnish the Court, tribunal, or oral hearing with scientific or technical information which is likely to be outside the experience and knowledge of a judge, magistrate, convenor or jury'. The *Guidelines* stress that the expert's role is to assist the court and not the parties instructing them. It goes on to point out that the main difference between an expert witness and an ordinary witness, i.e. a witness to fact, is that the former type of witness is able to give an opinion whereas the latter can only give factual statements or evidence.

An expert will most frequently be instructed by a solicitor acting for either the prosecution or the defence but the expert's evidence will be allowed only if it is deemed relevant and admissible, where relevance is determined by the probative value of the evidence in the particular case, by the judge hearing the case. The use of experts in the USA is much more formalised and codified than in the UK. In the former the admissibility of

experts is governed by landmark cases such as *Frye* (1923) and later *Daubert* (1993) which specify the conditions that must be met to allow an expert to testify. However, the judge in both the UK and the US jurisdictions is the ultimate 'gatekeeper' of whether or not expert testimony is allowable.

To give best evidence, therefore, the expert must be qualified by education, training, experience, skill and knowledge. The area of the expert's expertise must fit with the issue at trial. The database to which they make recourse must be sufficiently valid and reliable to allow definitive statements, opinions, conclusions and assertions under both direct and cross-examination, or in the face of counter-experts. Lastly, the expert must be prepared to get involved in the adversarial process in which their scientific credentials, objectivity and expertise can be attacked by counsel less concerned with either truth or justice than with asserting his or her client's position and using any and all means – fair or foul – to have it prevail. The courtroom is the arena of choice of the barrister, not the expert. The barrister knows the rules of the game, what the game is, and how best to play that game; the expert does not. The BPS *Guidelines* (2007) offer some useful suggestions on how to manage several of the practical, ethical and legal issues that can arise while serving as an expert witness.

Haward (1981) lists the main roles an expert may perform as (a) clinician, (b) experimentalist, (c) actuary or (d) adviser. Within these classifications an expert witness can give testimony in open court, or they may provide expert reports or opinions to be presented in court, or after trial, but before sentencing, but not actually appear as a witness. Experts may also act as adviser to counsel faced with the other side's expert. Clearly then, there are gradations of 'being an expert'.

The nature, scope and practices of experts in the UK have been surveyed in three separate questionnaires by Gudjonsson (1985, 1996, 2007/8). The latest survey involved members of the BPS Directory of Expert Witnesses, the earlier report sampled all psychologists who had prepared a court or tribunal report during the last five years, while the earliest survey involved only those psychologists who had given oral testimony in court. While the response rates were very low in all the surveys, and the questionnaires differed somewhat in each sweep, nonetheless some interesting commonalities appeared across the three surveys. More written reports were prepared than oral testimony was given. The ratio varied as between civil and criminal proceedings, with oral testimony being much more prevalent in criminal cases. Most referrals were from solicitors. Most reports were written for civil proceedings, followed by family, marital and juvenile proceedings, followed by criminal proceedings, and finally tribunals. Most topics of written reports involved personal injury and compensation claims, followed by child and other care proceedings. Oral evidence was sought most often in criminal and magistrates' courts followed by family court and tribunals. Appearance in civil proceedings was very low.

Some 45 per cent of all respondents who had given oral evidence said they were extensively cross-examined while, in the 1995 survey, 44 per cent said they had faced an opposing expert, compared to the earliest, 1985, report where only 22 per cent experienced an opposing expert. Pleasingly, between 95 and 97 per cent of those experts proffering expert testimony reported that they found the court positively disposed towards their testimony. There were, however, certain issues that required attention – training in giving oral testimony was requested. This chimes with the BPS *Psychologists as expert witnesses: Guidelines and procedures for England and Wales* (2007) which talks of experts being qualified in content *and* process, that is, skilled in the delivery of evidence, because poor court performance can undo excellent prior work.

Depending upon the type of case: criminal or civil; the legal system: adversarial or inquisitional; and their area of expertise: clinical or experimental, an expert may be called upon to talk (a) directly to a fact or consideration at issue, such as competence to stand trial, hyper suggestibility, 'of sound mind', that is, proffer what has been referred to as 'substantive testimony' (Walker & Monahan, 1987), or (b) perform an educative function such as discussing factors that could cause a witness to be unreliable, a victim to succumb to suggestion, or explain why an abused child could be asymptomatic, i.e. show no signs of abuse, delay disclosing the abuse, or recant the allegation on one or more occasions. This type of testimony has been referred to as 'Social Framework testimony' (Walker & Monahan, 1987). If experts are asked to perform the first type of role they almost certainly will have examined the defendant, and, as such, the expertise will be that of a psychologist, psychiatrist, clinician or therapist. If asked to perform the latter role, the expert will not have interacted with the defendant, victim or witness, and the expertise will be that of a researcher or experimental psychologist. This type of testimony does not concern the particular party directly but rather indirectly in the sense that a particular party is viewed as a specific case of generally observed findings. As Clifford (2008) has pointed out, the epistemological, or knowledge, base of these two types of testimony is held to be quite conflicting and antithetical.

The Controversial Nature of Expert Evidence

Why has there been a reluctance to admit testimony concerning human behaviour generally and psychological testimony specifically? If courts have to deal with matters beyond the knowledge of the ordinary citizen, the use of experts is a necessary contribution. However, this simple proposition conceals a multitude of difficulties when it is proposed to cover, and render permissible, psychological expert testimony. For example, what does the ordinary citizen know? Will the contribution of psychological knowledge necessarily help the jury in its final determination? This last question raises the issue of quality, consistency and coherence of the data which an expert would draw upon, and ultimately the quality of its scientific base. Let us look at three cases that will illustrate these problems. The first involves psychiatric experts, the second psychometric experts, and the third eyewitness testimony experts.

In November 1990 in the Australian state of New South Wales (see McSherry, 2001), Andre Chayna invited her sister-in-law to her house A few hours later she made a frenzied attack upon her, attempting to strangle her before cutting her throat and stabbing her until she died. Later that day Chayna killed her daughter Sandy. Three days later she stabbed her second daughter Suzanne who had been at camp when the first two killings occurred. Seven psychiatrists were called to give evidence at the trial. All had examined Chayna. The psychiatric testimony as to her state of mind at the time of the killing differed markedly. Having been asked to state an opinion on Chayna's condition at the time of the killing, the applicability of the defence of insanity and of diminished responsibility, three psychiatrists testified that Chayna was in a psychotic state at the time of the killing such that she did not know what she was doing was wrong for the purpose of the insanity defence. Another said she was suffering from a dissociative state that could support a defence of either insanity or diminished responsibility. Two others said she was suffering from a depressive illness that could support diminished responsibility, but not insanity. Chayna's treating psychiatrist who was called by the prosecution said that

Chayna had not been suffering from a mental illness at all at the time of the killing. The jury convicted.

The second case occurred in the UK. The case concerned the creation of a bogus bank that was used to conduct fraudulent financial transactions. The defendant's defence was that he had been deceived by his co-defendants and had acted only on their instructions. Several psychologists, based upon a battery of tests, testified that the defendant's intelligence was abnormally low so he could not have played an active role in the fraud. The co-defendant called an opposing expert who observed the defendant in the witness box over a period of nine days. She stated that from this observation she could see that the defendant's intelligence was average. The defendant and the co-defendant were found guilty. The *Bulletin of the British Psychological Society* later published the views of the opposing experts. The group who used the empirical psychometric material (Tunstall *et al.*, 1982) felt that the opposing expert (Heim, 1982) had brought psychometrics into disrepute and had led to a miscarriage of justice. Dr Heim's final reply was that her attackers were indignant because their side had lost the case.

The third case comes from the USA, *People of California* v. *Joseph J. Pacely* in 1994. A Mexican woman, Mrs M, reported that a stranger came into her house via an open window and attempted to sexually assault her while she was asleep. The attacker was frightened off when children and guests sleeping in the house woke up. Mrs M described her attacker as a black man, about five foot seven to five foot nine, 170 pounds, medium build. He had braids and wore a blue baseball cap. One block north of the assault, police saw Joseph Pacely standing by his car. He was a black male, five foot nine and 140 pounds. He claimed he knew nothing about the assault. He was identified by Mrs M and charged with attempted rape. Professor Loftus proffered testimony for the defence concerning the effect of stress and fright upon memory and cited empirical evidence to demonstrate the effect. The prosecution presented Dr Ebbesen as an opposition expert. Ebbesen denied there was any known relationship between stress and memory. He attacked both the general theory and the specific applicable empirical studies cited by Loftus. In addition to stress, Loftus also gave testimony on the cross-race effect in identification, arguing that the overall pattern of results in this area justifies the conclusion that people of one race find it more difficult to identify people of another race than they do people of their own race. Ebbesen denied this was the case and singled out

one study that did not fit the overall pattern of studies. The jury acquitted Pacely.

These three studies encapsulate many, but not all, of the issues that render the admission of expert psychological testimony problematic, both to law and to psychology. We will now consider these various issues.

Junk Science

As Bermant (1986) pointed out, the controversy over the propriety of psychological and psychiatric expert testimony camouflages arguments about the strength of psychological knowledge. Proponents and opponents of such testimony are really arguing about the state of psychological knowledge and its certainty.

Rogers (2004) notes that over the past 20 years a growing suspicion of psychiatric expert evidence has been expressed by legal practitioners, the judiciary and even mental health professionals themselves (e.g. Coles & Veiel, 2001). Mossman (1999) carried out a computer search of US court decisions that made reference to derogatory statements concerning mental health experts. He found 567 such cases. In 35 judicial opinions such professionals were termed or compared to 'hired guns', 5 cases described testifying experts with the word 'whore', and 5 cases used variations of the term 'prostitute'. Brinded (1998) canvassed all crown prosecutors in New Zealand and concluded that the credibility of psychiatrists was being damaged by poor quality expert evidence and partial (biased) testimony.

As Rogers (2004) points out, however, operating outside their area of core competence, usurping the function of juries, proffering one-sided evidence to benefit the client, and labouring under irreconcilable role conflicts of therapist and forensic expert does not amount to a fundamental critique of psychiatric knowledge *per se*. There is, however, one other critique that does amount to a fundamental attack on the profession at the scientific level.

Kenny (1983, 1984) proposes four criteria which he believes to be necessary conditions for a discipline to be scientific. It must be consistent, methodological, cumulative and predictive, thus falsifiable.

Frequent contradictory diagnoses (see case illustration one above), doubts about the major concepts of the discipline, frequent changes of mind about key concepts such as homosexuality being a mental illness, and conceptions of 'the psychopath' all point to a flaw at the deepest level of epistemic knowledge within psychiatry.

Rogers (2004) traces this to problems of validity. He points out that validity has several forms – face, descriptive, predictive and construct validity – with construct validity being the most important. He goes on to say that the construct validity of most of psychiatry's diagnoses is extremely low. There are too few externally validating criteria to allow us to establish whether the major diagnoses are real or fictional. The apparent reliability of diagnoses must not blind us to the problem of validity. Thus, while a large international study of reliability of ICD-10 diagnosis in 32 countries (Sartorius et al., 1995) found the inter-rater reliability to be typically .8–1.0 (i.e. 80–100 per cent probability that any two independent clinicians would reach the same diagnosis), the Introduction to the DSM-IV should be noted. The DSM-IV is a comparable manual to the ICD-10. Here the compilers specifically write 'When the DSM-IV categories, criteria and textual descriptions are employed for forensic purposes, there are significant risks that diagnostic information will be misused or misunderstood …'.

In short, the ease of making a clinical diagnosis of a DSM-IV mental disorder is not sufficient to establish the existence, for legal purposes, of a mental disorder, mental disability, mental disease or mental defect. Rogers (2004) concludes by stating that if psychiatrists ignore the low construct validity of their diagnoses or worse still deny it, they bring themselves and their profession into disrepute.

These arguments reflect those of Coles and Veiel (2001) who aver that expert witnesses are obliged to present testimony that is based on a generally accepted scientific theory. To Kenny's (1984) four criteria, Coles and Veiel (2001) add the requirements of objectivity and open-mindedness. The testimony of many mental health experts frequently fails to meet these standards by presenting idiosyncratic theories, making inappropriate conceptualizations, quantifying data inappropriately, selectively collecting, presenting or interpreting data, and thus lacking the prime requirement of an open sceptical mind. He contrasts the tendency of psychiatrists and psychologists (psychometricians) to describe individuals in terms of fundamental, unitary characteristics with the law's conception of many of the conditions with which psychiatrists deal, which is situation-dependent, synthetic and heterogeneous.

Coles and Veiel (2001) illustrate the problems perceived in psychiatric testimony by the distinction between 'possible' and 'probable'. Psychology and psychiatry are probabilistic sciences. When one refers to 'consistent with', this is frequently taken to mean that the condition being discussed is more likely. In fact it does not mean that. An event that is consistent with another event only raises the possibility of the second event, not its probability. Thus, an unsubstantiated possibility is an impermissible speculation. Clifford (2008) raised this same 'consistent with' problem in the case of expert substantive testimony concerning child sexual abuse.

In terms of psychometric expert testimony (see illustrative case two above) the tests which are relied upon in these cases are designed to allow objective decisions based upon a fixed and explicit algorithm. However, behaviour is the result of an individual–environmental interaction. What is missing with most psychometric instruments is consideration of the environmental triggers, sustainers and accelerators of the behaviour being measured. As Coles and Veiel (2001) point out, we need to identify, measure and control the relevant characteristics of the environment and then insert these into the algorithm.

This holistic approach is seen in the work of Gudjonsson (1994, p.243) where he states that he will not accept instruction which limits his freedom to examine all the surrounding contextual and situational factors of an alleged false confession. Clear indications from a psychometric test (e.g. Gudjonsson Suggestibility Scale), in and of itself, are insufficient in a forensic situation to offer expert evidence of falsity in confessions.

When we move to the case of research testimony (Loftus, 1986) or social framework testimony (Walker & Monahan, 1987) issues of, inter alia, ecological validity, generalisability, internal and external validity, replicability, etc., keep appearing. The proponents of expert experimental psychologist testimony would contend that a great many factors (see Clifford, 1979) and estimator and system variables (Wells, 1978) are unknown to the layperson (jurors) and should be brought to their attention to ensure that justice is done.

Opponents of expert psychological testimony would concede that (a) we can agree that memory comprises encoding, storage and retrieval components, and (b) various system and estimator variables can impinge on one or more of these stages to reduce the veracity of memory. However, just what phases, and to what degree, we can never know, and certainly not in the case of a particular witness/victim in a particular case that is being tried. By offering expert testimony against this background of uncertainty, such testimony may unjustifiably increase scepticism on the part of jurors where it is not merited.

In addition, to what extent do controlled laboratory studies generalise to real-life crimes? How often should a finding replicate before it is regarded as a 'fact'? What if a finding replicates but in one case the variable's effect size (magnitude) is large (.8 or above), in another medium (.6) and in a third only small (.2)? And how do we weigh all the known (and possibly larger unknown) studies that have not replicated the effect?

Over and above factors that may or may not have been operational, and effects that may or may not be present in a particular case, there is another consideration. Experimental psychology is largely predicated upon group means, with overlap between the distributions. What this means in practice is that while an experimental group as a whole may perform 'better' than a control group, any one member of the experimental group may, in fact, perform more poorly than any one member of the 'poorer' group. More concretely, if we find that 70 per cent of an experimental group give an incorrect identification under condition x, how do we know that the particular witness in the particular case currently being tried, which involves condition x, falls into the 70 per cent category and not the 30 per cent category? We just cannot possibly know. How, then, can we possibly seek to educate the jury when what we may be doing is rendering them more sceptical than they need to be in the particular case at hand? If this line of reasoning is adopted then expert testimony may be more prejudicial than probative (see Ebbesen & Konecni, 1996).

This internal debate concerning the state of psychological knowledge has surfaced periodically in several special issues of leading journals, for example, *Law and Human Behavior* (1986), *American Psychologist* (1983/84) and *Expert Evidence* (1996/7). However, they have not settled the issue of whether, or how, experimental psychologists should appear as expert witnesses.

Opponents of experimentally based psychological expert testimony frequently argue that such testimony is little better than common sense, dressed up as scientific fact. However, it is much more than this. Several studies have shown that the knowledge eyewitness experts agree upon differs markedly from the views held by legal personnel and jury-eligible respondents. This has been demonstrated in, for example, Canada (Yarmey & Jones, 1983), the USA (Benton *et al.*, 2006; Kassin *et al.*, 1989, 2001), Australia (McConkey & Roche, 1989), and in the UK (Noon & Hollin, 1987). Thus there is a prima facie case that the knowledge that experts in the field would bring to the court differs from the knowledge (beliefs) that they would find there.

However, there are a number of strident and dissenting voices to this conclusion. Ebbesen and Konecni (1996) make the point that in all the cited surveys of experts, and non-expert but legally relevant participants, the apparent homogeneity of the experts' views, and their discrepancy with non-experts, would likely be eliminated if the surveys had given a response option of 'don't know'. This is Ebbesen and Konecni's main point: most findings are inconsistent, inapplicable or invalid because either experimental procedures or measures used to study various relationships are not well tied to legal procedures, or particular findings are not well substantiated. In addition, they argue that knowledge about, for example, memory is so complex that any honest presentation of this knowledge to a court would serve only to confuse rather than improve the jury decision-making process. These authors argue that where expert evidence has been admitted it is because the courts have been misled about the validity, consistency and generalisability of the research in the area due to the legal system's lack of understanding about the nature of science, and partly because researchers have been overconfident in their own expertise.

While Clifford (1997) broadly agreed with the basic tenets of this view, but argued that they overstated their case, Yarmey (1997, 2001) disagreed with their assertions, pointing out that a great number of findings upon which experts would be prepared to offer testimony are reliable and consistent.

The Problem of the Ultimate Issue

There are many evidential rules governing the admissibility, use and scope of expert evidence in both criminal and civil trials. As a general rule, expert psychological and psychiatric evidence is accepted in court only where the issue to be determined goes beyond the experience of members of the jury. The 'ultimate issue' rule has traditionally prevented the use of expert evidence in relation to the question that falls to be determined by the judge or jury. However, in some trials, particularly involving psychiatric evidence, this rule may prove very difficult. The expert evidence may be led in relation to the issue as to whether the accused was suffering a recognised mental impairment at the time of committing an offence because a determination of mental impairment requires a level of special knowledge that goes beyond the realm of experience of members of the jury.

There have been various conceptions of the ultimate issue rule, the rule itself has been modified or abandoned in many jurisdictions, and a wide gap exists between the theory and the practical application of the rule. Under the McNaughton Rules (1843) the defence must show that at the time of the crime the accused was labouring under a defect of reason from disease of the mind so as not to know the nature and quality of the act or that what he or she was doing was wrong. Similarly, the defence of diminished responsibility has traditionally concerned the question as to whether abnormality of mind substantially affects the accused's mental responsibility for his or her act. Here the court is ignoring the ultimate issue in allowing medical evidence as to not only the existence of an abnormality of mind but also its effect on the accused's mental responsibility (Dell, 1982). Thus, where psychiatric evidence is involved the ultimate issue rule is extremely difficult to apply.

In the light of this, calls for the abolition of the ultimate issue rule have been made (Goldstein, 1989; Jackson, 1984) and several jurisdictions have responded – Canada, New Zealand, Australia, Scotland, and England and Wales. Australia has argued that evidence of an opinion is not inadmissible only because it is about a fact in issue or an ultimate issue, and in the USA the Federal Rules of Evidence 704 (1975) stated that testimony in the form of an opinion or inference otherwise admissible is not objectionable because it embraces an ultimate issue to be decided by the trier of fact. This was felt to widen the circumstances in which expert evidence could be proffered. However, in 1984 Congress reinstated the ultimate issue rules, specifically for psychiatric testimony.

From the expert witness point of view there seems to be two issues as to why the ultimate issue rule is important. Firstly, such evidence, presented in scientific language which the jury does not easily understand and submitted by an expert with impressive credentials, is apt to be accepted by the jury as being infallible and as having more weight than it perhaps deserves. Secondly, allowing expert evidence on the ultimate issue usurps the role of the jury – a contest of experts with the triers of fact acting as referees in deciding which expert to accept (see, for example, *R* v. *Mohan*, 1994).

On the first point the jury has the discretion to accept or reject expert testimony on, for example, the effects of mental impairment, and Rogers *et al.* (1992) examined the question of whether jurors are uncritical consumers of psychological and psychiatric testimony and found that they were not. Looking at the effect of psychiatric evidence on decision making in 460 adults, they concluded that juries appear astute in weighing evidence, not convinced by overconfidence and unmoved by ultimate opinion. Freckelton (1994) concluded that the claim that juries give undue weight to expert testimony rests on anecdote, observation and intuition rather than empirical evidence.

The issue of expert testimony and ultimate issue can be resolved by accepting that criminal responsibility is a moral not a medical issue. Thus the jury's role in criminal trials in which, for example, mental impairment is raised is to decide the question of the accused's criminal responsibility – essentially a moral question. As McSherry (2001) points out, it is only when expert evidence as to the effect of the mental impairment on the accused's criminal responsibility is allowed that usurpation is likely. McSherry argues that defences of mental impairment and/or diminished responsibility involve a two-stage process: identifying whether or not the accused was suffering from a form of mental impairment, and whether or not that mental impairment has an effect on the accused's knowledge of wrongdoing or mental responsibility. If the expert evidence is confined to the first step then the juries' function in deciding the second is left intact.

Trials focusing upon the mental state of the accused raise particular difficulties, which are not necessarily seen in the other types of evidence given in the cases illustrated above, where psychometric or social framework testimony is given. However, where psychiatric or psychometric assessments are involved, the ultimate issue concern can be avoided if the psychiatrist or clinician is not asked, nor attempts, to go beyond the clinical assessment of mental impairment or mental status.

Battle of the Experts

A frequently heard argument is that with the introduction of expert testimony within an adversarial system, justice will not be served because juries will simply be confused, and the profession itself will fall into disrepute.

Research suggests that laypersons may not be successful in detecting errors in scientific research (Clifford, 2003b; Nisbett, 1993). For example, people do not recognise that results obtained from small samples are less reliable than those obtained from larger samples (Tversky & Kahneman, 1974). The layperson has difficulty with concepts of chance and probability information (e.g. Gilovich *et al.*, 1985). This suggests that laypersons would have difficulty evaluating statistical or methodological issues that could be presented by expert witnesses.

Kovera et al. (1999) manipulated the construct validity, general acceptance and ecological validity of research presented by the plaintiff's expert in a sexual harassment case. It was found that construct validity was not considered in the jury's deliberations and decision making but the other two factors were. That is, tests were taken to be valid if the evidence was generally accepted (by the relevant scientific community) and the methods producing the data were ecologically valid. Additional research suggests that jurors are insensitive to internal validity threats such as confounds and non-blind experimenters (McAuliff & Kovera, 2008).

In the light of these inadequacies, opposing experts should, at least in principle, aid the juror in coming to more rational decisions in the face of scientific evidence. As the surveys by Gudjonsson (1985, 1996, 2007/8) show, when an expert witness knows that their testimony will be challenged by an opposing expert, that expert (in 39 per cent of cases) will give more technical information about test scores and findings (Gudjonsson, 1985, p.329). This, however, may be a double-edged sword.

Several studies have looked at the influence of opposing experts on juries' decisions (Cutler & Penrod, 1995; Devenport & Cutler, 2004; Greene et al., 1999; Griffith et al., 1998; Levett & Kovera, 2008) and concluded that opposing expert testimony may not effectively counter the testimony offered by the initial expert. Griffith et al. (1998) and Raitz et al. (1990) have studied the influence of opposing expert witnesses compared to no opposing testimony on juror decisions concerning verdicts. Unfortunately, this research suggests that an opposing expert does not effectively counter the testimony offered by the initial expert. Such opposing testimony can, however, influence the credibility ratings of the first expert (e.g. Devenport & Cutler, 2004; Greene et al., 1999).

Certain studies have varied both the presence and absence of an opposing expert and the quality of the evidence presented by them. In one study Cutler and Penrod (1995) presented mock jurors with an eyewitness case in which eyewitnesses viewed a crime under good and poor viewing conditions. The jurors heard either a defence expert only, both a defence and a prosecution expert, or no expert testimony at all. The defence expert testified about the reliability of eyewitnessing under different viewing conditions while the prosecution expert discussed limitations of this research. Adding the opposition expert caused jurors to become more sceptical of the eyewitness identification than jurors who heard no

opposing expert, regardless of the conditions under which the witness viewed the crime.

In a study by Devenport et al. (2002), 800 mock jurors viewed a videotaped trial that included information about a line-up identification procedure. Suggestiveness of the identification procedure varied in terms of foil selection bias, instruction bias (being told that the perpetrator may or may not be present, or not being told this) and presentation bias (simultaneous line-ups being categorised as biased, sequential line-ups as unbiased). The researchers were interested in the degree to which expert testimony would sensitise mock jurors to these three separate factors affecting line-up suggestiveness. They found that initially jurors were sensitive to foil selection bias, but not to instruction bias or presentation bias. The presentation of expert testimony served to enhance sensitivity to instruction bias. Importantly, there was little evidence for expert testimony creating an overall sceptical attitude to identification evidence as indicated by culpability and verdict measures.

However, in a later study, Devenport and Cutler (2004), using the same foil and instruction bias manipulations in expert testimony, introduced an opposing expert's testimony. In this study they found that the defence expert's testimony did not influence jurors' judgements about the evidence but the introduction of an opposing expert caused jurors to evaluate the defence expert's credibility more negatively.

Levett and Kovera (2008) presented jurors with a written summary of a child sexual abuse case in which a defence expert testified about research she had conducted demonstrating the effects of suggestive interviewing techniques on children's reports of sexual abuse. They manipulated the defence expert's testimony such that it was either valid, lacked control groups or lacked required counterbalancing of questions. The opposing expert's testimony either addressed these methodological shortcomings, did not address these specific issues, offering only generalised rebuttal critiques of the research in general, or no opposing expert testimony was presented. Participants were asked to render a verdict and rate their perceptions of the trial testimony on a variety of dimensions. Levett and Kovera (2008) found strong scepticism effects. When an opposing expert was present, verdicts and ratings were affected, irrespective of the nature of the opposing expert's testimony. There was little evidence of sensitisation effects concerning the flawed methodology of the defence expert's testimony. Thus there was no evidence that opposing expert testimony helped jurors distinguish between flawed and valid scientific testimony. These researchers conclude that it is unlikely that opposing experts will prevent junk science entering the court.

A less pessimistic view can be found in Vidmar (2005). He does not believe that jurors are confused by expert opinion or that opposing experts have the effect of neutralising the respective perspectives with the net result being scepticism. He argues that a large body of empirical research over the past 50 years into jury behaviour in the face of expert evidence is positive and that claims that juries defer to experts is without empirical foundation. To substantiate his argument he looks at systematic jury interviews, jury simulation studies and actual videotaped jury deliberation (which would not be possible in the UK).

Schuman et al. (1994) interviewed lawyers, testifying experts and jurors about how jurors responded to expert testimony presented in a large number of cases. They found little evidence of superficial responses to experts (messenger rather than message; credibility rather than the validity of their testimony). The jurists were focused on the experts' tendency to draw firm conclusions, their familiarity with the facts of the case, and their appearance of impartiality. Thus there was little evidence of the 'white coat syndrome' (Vidmar, 2005). Vidmar (1995) likewise found that in medical malpractice cases jurors could identify the main medical issues in the case and identify the basic points made by the opposing experts. They actively and critically evaluated the expert and the expert's testimony – considering both the absence of evidence and the incompleteness of the testimony. Kutnjak-Ivkovich and Hans (2003) interviewed in depth 55 of 269 jurors who had served in a range of cases and found that they critically evaluated expert testimony by looking at its completeness, consistency and complexity. Presentational style was evaluated in terms of its coherence.

Much the same story appears in jury simulation research. Finkel (1995) has indicated that legal concepts such as insanity are often at variance with laypersons' understanding of mental states and abnormal behaviour. Expert testimony on such matters is frequently interpreted in the light of the juror's own social and cognitive conceptions about what constitutes abnormal behaviour. Indeed, several studies have shown that while jurors do try to evaluate testimony concerning mental states objectively, beliefs about mental states held before the trial often override or modify interpretations of that evidence (e.g. Ellsworth et al., 1984; Roberts & Golding, 1991; Vidmar & Diamond, 2001). Sundby (1997) actually found, in interviewing jurors who decided death penalty cases, that they ignored the testimony of mental health experts when it differed substantially from their own preconceived notions of abnormal mental or emotional behaviour.

Diamond et al. (2003) and Diamond & Vidmar, (2001) discuss the unique Arizona Jury Project which videotaped the jury room discussions and deliberations in 50 actual civil cases. It was found that during the trials jurists had many questions about the expert evidence. Of all the juries, 94 per cent asked at least one question, with the range of questions asked being 0–110. This project clearly indicates that real juries attend to the content of expert testimony and interactively review, interpret and evaluate such testimony.

Vidmar (2005) concludes that the claims of incompetent, irresponsible and biased juries in responding to expert evidence are not consistent with the research literature. In addition, such critics tend to ignore explicit instructions to juries from the judge on how to evaluate expert evidence, the rules of evidence constraining expert testimony, opposing experts (but see above), cross-examination, and final arguments from the advocates that can address such testimony and its meaning, interpretation and force.

Alternatives and Antidotes to Adversarial Expert Testimony

All nations and legal jurisdictions have had to confront the increased complexity of the modern world. This complexity has led to the increased use of experts in the courts of law. This complexity involves not only physical and technological areas but also societal domains. This is why the human sciences in general and psychology specifically are the 'new boys on the block' in terms of admissible testimony. However, the reaction of the courts to this new social science evidence is frequently an uneasy one. What social science tells us is often too closely related to what we are presumed to already know. If congruent, the evidence appears to serve little purpose: if incongruent, it is regarded as suspicious. In addition, the 'truths' of social science can seldom be demonstrated with the precision or elegance of the physical science's 'truths'. To offset the ever-increasing involvement of experts, especially social science experts, several extant legal procedures have been stressed as adequate to handle the complexity.

Judges

The courts have been very wary of 'junk science' (*Frye* v. *United States*, 1923). Thus, in the USA, in a series of landmark cases – *Daubert* v. *Merrill Dow Pharmaceuticals Inc.*, 1993; *General Electric Co.* v. *Joiner*, 1997; and *Kumho Tire Co.* v. *Carmichael*, 1999 – the Supreme Court ruled that judges were responsible for evaluating the quality of scientific evidence and with admitting only evidence they deemed to be relevant and reliable. This 'gatekeeper' function of the judge is common to all countries throughout the world. As evidentiary gatekeepers, judges have to evaluate the methodology, the error rate and the general acceptance of the research being offered to the court by any prospective expert witness. As Clifford (2008) argued, this may be an impossible role to fulfil on purely logistical and practical grounds. Research supports this argument. Several studies suggest that judges may not be up to this task (e.g. Kovera & McAuliff, 2000; Wingate & Thornton, 2004). Gatowski *et al.* (2001) surveyed 400 State trial court judges about their understanding of the basic scientific criteria outlined in Daubert. Only 4 per cent of judges could give clear explanation of 'falsifiability' and 35 per cent gave answers that were unequivocally wrong. Only 4 per cent could explain 'error rate' and 86 per cent gave answers that were unequivocally wrong.

Thus it is unlikely that pre-trial judges' discretion concerning proper scientific subject matter will prevent either junk science or valid science getting into the courtroom. However, it is argued, even if unacceptable science gets past the 'gatekeepers' there are further procedural safeguards that will help jurors evaluate the validity of the science: cross-examination, judicial instruction, and final summing up.

Cross-examination

Kovera *et al.* (1999) suggest that cross-examination may not be effective in assisting jurors in making sound decisions concerning scientific evidence because, according to Brodsky (1977), the aim of cross-examination is to portray the expert as ignorant, irresponsible or biased.

Judicial warnings and instructions

Following the *Neil* v. *Biggers* (1972) case in the USA and *R.* v. *Turnbull* (1976) in England, whenever identification evidence is disputed, a trial judge must advise (warn) the jury to consider carefully the circumstances of witnessing or identification. The relevant factors are such things as the amount of time for which the perpetrator was in view, distance of the witness from the perpetrator, visibility of the perpetrator, obstruction of the witness's view, whether the perpetrator was known to the witness, any reasons for remembering the perpetrator, time delay between the incident and identification, and discrepancies in description-giving and the appearance of the suspect. The problem with these warnings is that empirical research casts doubt on their validity as indicants of testimony veracity (e.g. Brigham *et al.*, 1999; Wells & Murray, 1983). In addition, when it comes to judges' instruction to juries, we know that juries often fail to understand such instruction, and when they do understand them, they fail to apply them (e.g. Cutler *et al.*, 1990).

Amicus curiae briefs

This 'friend of the court' approach to expert evidence consists of a grouping of experts proffering a consensus view on a topic in dispute that they feel may be helpful to the court. These briefs are presented as simple, objective statements of findings, and conclusions and inferences that follow from the data. The presenters see themselves as responsible to the court, not to any one side in the dispute. This position, however, is no different from the hired expert who is both *de jure* and *de facto* responsible to the court, not the hiring agent. In addition, several objections can be raised against it (e.g. Konecni & Ebbesen, 1986). An amicus brief that would appear as a neutral, objective, scientifically unimpeachable document could, in reality, be nothing more than the entrenched views of a few recognised authorities, which would then be the only voice heard, and if the underlying science was weak or flawed, then it would be letting junk science into court by the back door. Inviting a series of oppositional briefs would once again simply result in a battle of experts, albeit at one remove, and hence, once again leave the triers of fact possibly bemused and confused.

Court vs. party-appointed experts

This solution to the 'expert witness problem' is suggested in the light of the belief that experts too often become advocates rather than educators because of the all-too-human failing of identifying with the side that hires them. It would also at a stroke obviate the presumed problem of the battle of the experts which, it is argued, leaves the jury befuddled and bemused. There is a clear historical precedent for this suggestion. In the inquisitorial system of justice found in most continental countries, experts are appointed by the courts. They are questioned by the judge and frequently by the parties to the dispute, but their allegiance is undoubtedly to the court and the interests of justice. Or so it is believed. But who exactly would that expert be? Would he or she be value-free; disinterested enough in the question of whether eyewitness testimony research is sufficiently mature as to give unequivocal, parameter-based assertions and opinions on matters of witness credibility and reliability given the facts of the case? Would he or she have a sufficiently settled view on whether psychometric tools are situation-specific, context-free, or only partially scientific in the way they are currently used, as to serve as a court-appointed expert?

Whatever the deep theoretical, philosophical and scientific questions that underpin this suggested answer to the problem of the expert witness, the law is not waiting for their resolution. It is moving ahead. The Woolf Reforms in the Civil Procedure Rules (1999), especially Part 35, stress that expert reports rather than court appearance should become the norm, and further, and most importantly, 'where two or more parties wish to submit expert evidence on a particular issue, the court may direct that the evidence on that issue is to be given by one expert only' (Part 35.7). In terms of criminal cases the Criminal Procedure Rule Committee was established in 2004 to formulate rules of procedure for all criminal courts in England and Wales. In 2005 the committee proposed procedural rules for experts (Part 33) designed to follow the Civil Procedure Rules, Part 35. Part 33 is almost identical with Part 35. In 2005 the rules concerning expert witnesses and single joint expert were imported into the Criminal Procedure Rules 2005 (Part 33.7) but in these Procedures the Rule refers to 'co-defendants' or 'more than one defendant' (whereas the Civil Procedure Rules uses the term 'where two or more parties'). This seems to leave open the possibility of the two parties in criminal cases (defence and prosecution) still fielding their respective experts. The notes to the guide to the second amendment to these Rules (No. 2, 2006) make it clear that a single joint expert applies only to the defence. Thus, not a court-appointed agent as such.

In the consultation document sent out by the Committee they pointed out that the initial intention was to refer to both prosecution and defence, that is, a single joint expert that would be a court-appointed expert. They also, however, countenanced the possibility that it should apply only to parties whose interests did not conflict – co-defendants. As the Rules currently stand, this is what is meant.

The UK Register of Expert Witnesses (2008) responded to the consultation by talking about the no-man's land of the single joint expert in civil cases and suggested the alternative of the court-appointed expert assessor, who would be the judge's expert, and if required, the court's evidence provider if such evidence was required.

How these changes and proposed changes work out in terms of rendering better justice rather than merely more rapid and less costly proceedings remains to be seen.

Conclusions

The ultimate question is whether expert witnesses are beneficial to the court system. There is no doubt that in certain areas the jury must be aided because of a known *a priori* ignorance on the part of jurists – in most matters dealt with by the physical sciences. This same assumed ignorance must be granted in most areas of medical science. The problem arises when we come to human abnormal behaviour and human normal behaviour. Here we are confronted with the court's belief that jurors have either individual or collective wisdom which negates the need for expert testimony in these fields.

Allied to this redundancy argument is the reliability argument of the opponents of expert testimony in those domains. These opponents argue that the scientific base underlying psychiatric, psychometric and psychological evidence is not sufficiently reliable, valid, generalisable or applicable as to justify appearing as an expert in these various domains. This scientific debate is the most important consideration that a would-be expert must consider. All the other anecdotal 'problems' of expert witnesses, such as over-believing juries, usurping the juries' function, negative perception of 'battles of experts', being a 'hired gun', 'lap dog' or 'whore' can all be answered by either empirical refutation or strong ethical stances in the face of unreasonable demands. There is no reason for the psychologist to be a knowing instrument of injustice. What remains is the quality of the underlying science – this is the ultimate ethical choice.

Science will always be provisional, tentative and probabilistic. The issue is whether an expert should 'take the stand' in the face of the 'stand off' between opponents and proponents of expert witnessing. Lempert (1986) points out that in discussions of the generalisability of laboratory research, theory is frequently missing, with only external and ecological validity being focused upon. He argues that the key to generalisation is through theory. What is critical is that a body of research, whatever the external validity of the constituent studies, fits consistently into a more encompassing theory. If a well-grounded theory applies, in principle, to situations that arise in trials, there is a basis for expert psychological testimony. However, this just shifts the argument. Proponents of witnessing will argue that we can bring to bear a reasonably broad body of well-grounded theory. The opponents will argue that research is so ambiguous and inconsistent that it is premature to even suggest that we are approaching theoretical closure. While we do not have a general theory of memory that everyone subscribes to, nonetheless the BPS has just published *Guidelines on Memory and the Law* (2008) as a basis for future law–psychology interaction.

Malpass *et al.* (2008) argue that two central positions have emerged concerning the adequacy of an empirical literature: the best available, or best practice (BP) model, and the well-established knowledge (WEK) model. While their concern is with adequacy in terms of policy recommendations, the distinction is equally applicable to expert witnessing. The WEK stance suggests that studies forming the research base should be scientifically well established and have scientific respectability (Yarmey, 1986) and be based on settled science (Kargon, 1986). By drawing upon theories and findings from both situation-specific studies and the larger research literature of experimental psychology, expert witnesses can explain particular inquiries for the judge and jury that are beyond commonsense understandings.

None of the law's currently held misconceptions about human nature and behaviour will be significantly altered unless research continues to produce strong evidence that the legal system's current assumptions are wrong, and produces this evidence as expert testimony. We have only to consider 'battered woman syndrome', child testimony in child sexual abuse cases, and false confessions to see the value that legal education via expert psychological testimony can have. Clifford (2008) concluded that provided the expert witness and his or her testimony are ethical, moral, reliable, relevant and admissible, then the quality of justice will be enhanced by such testimony.

Further Reading

British Psychological Society (2007) *Psychologists as expert witnesses: Guidelines and procedures for England and Wales.* Leicester: Author.
These guidelines are the official view of the BPS on how psychologists should conduct themselves as expert witnesses. It gives clear guidance on ethical, practical and professional conduct from instruction to delivery of testimony in court. All experts and would-be experts must be familiar with its contents.

Bruck, M. (1998). The trials and tribulations of a novice witness. In S.J. Ceci & H. Hembrooke (Eds.) *Expert witnesses in child abuse cases* (pp.85–104). Washington, DC: American Psychological Association.
This is a salutary account by an American fledgling expert witness proffering testimony and undergoing cross-examination in a child sexual abuse case. Her experiences are somewhat extreme but the lessons she draws have universal application in terms of the content and process of giving testimony.

Clifford, B.R. (2008). Role of the expert witness. In G. Davies, C. Hollin & R. Bull (Eds.) *Forensic psychology* (pp.235–261). Chichester: John Wiley & Sons.
This chapter explores the possible roles of expert testimony in the contentious areas of mistaken identification, child testimony generally and in child sexual abuse cases specifically, and the recovered/false memory debate. It points out the strengths and weaknesses of the knowledge bases drawn upon in giving legal testimony in court cases involving these issues as points of disputation.

References

American Psychologist. (1983/84). Issues 38 and 39.
Benton, T.R., Ross, D.F., Bradshaw, E., Thomas, W.N. & Bradshaw, G.S. (2006). Eyewitness memory is still not common sense: Comparing jurors, judges and law enforcement to eyewitness experts. *Applied Cognitive Psychology, 20,* 115–129.
Bermant, G. (1986). Two conjectures about the issue of expert testimony. *Law and Human Behavior, 10,* 97–100.
Brigham, J.C., Wasserman, A.W. & Meissner, C.A. (1999). Disputed eyewitness identification evidence: Important legal and scientific issues. *Court Review, 36,* 12–25.
Brinded, P. (1998). Crown prosecutors' views of psychiatric evidence in New Zealand. *Psychiatry, Psychology and Law, 5,* 231–235.
British Psychological Society (2007). *Psychologists as expert witnesses: Guidelines and procedures for England and Wales.* Leicester: Author.
British Psychological Society (2008). *Guidelines on memory and the law: Recommendations from the scientific study of human memory.* A report from the research board. Leicester: Author.

Brodsky, S.L. (1977). The mental health professional on the witness stand: A survival guide. In B.D. Sales (Ed.) *Psychology in the legal process*. New York: Spectrum.

Civil Procedure Rules (1999). Retrieved 9 September 2009 from www.opsi.gov.uk/si/si1999/19991008.htm

Clifford, B.R. (1979). The relevance of psychological investigation to legal issues in testimony and identification. *Criminal Law Review, March*, 153–163.

Clifford, B.R. (1997). A commentary on Ebbesen and Konecni's eyewitness memory research: Probative v prejudicial value. *Expert Evidence*, 6, 140–143.

Clifford, B.R. (2003a). Forensic psychology. In R. Bayne & I. Horton (Eds.) *Applied psychology* (pp.67–78). London: Sage.

Clifford, B.R. (2003b). Methodology: Law's adopting and adapting to psychology's methods and findings. In D. Carson & R. Bull (Eds.) *Handbook of psychology in legal contexts* (pp.605–624). Chichester: John Wiley & Sons.

Clifford, B.R. (2008). Role of the expert witness. In G. Davies, C. Hollin & R. Bull (Eds.) *Forensic psychology* (pp.235–261). Chichester: John Wiley & Sons.

Coles, E.M. & Veiel, H.O.F. (2001). Expert evidence and pseudoscience: How mental health professionals are taking over the courtroom. *International Journal of Law and Psychiatry*, 24, 607–625.

Criminal Procedure Rules (2005). Retrieved 9 September 2009 from www.opsi.gov.uk/si/si2005/20050384.htm

Criminal Procedure Rules (2006). Retrieved 1 August 2009 from www.dca.gov.uk/criminal/procrules_fin/rulesmenu.htm

Cutler, B.L., Dexter, H.R. & Penrod, S.D. (1990). Non adversarial methods for sensitising jurors to eyewitness evidence. *Journal of Applied Social Psychology*, 20, 1197–1207.

Cutler, B.L. & Penrod, S.D. (1995). *Mistaken identification: The eyewitness: Psychology and the law*. New York: Cambridge University Press.

Daubert (1993). *Daubert v Merrell Dow Pharmaceuticals Inc.* 509 U.S., 113 S.Ct. 2786.

Dell, S. (1982). Diminished responsibility reconsidered. *Criminal Law Review*, 809–818.

Devenport, J.L. & Cutler, B.L. (2004). Impact of defense-only and opposing eyewitness experts on juror judgments. *Law and Human Behavior*, 28, 569–576.

Devenport, J.L., Stinson, V., Cutler, B.L. & Kravitz, D.A. (2002). How effective are the cross examination and expert testimony safeguards? Juror's perceptions of the suggestiveness and fairness of biased lineup procedures. *Journal of Applied Psychology*, 87(6), 1042–1054.

Diamond, S. & Vidmar, N. (2001). Jury room ruminations on forbidden topics. *Virginia Law Review*, 87, 1857–1915.

Diamond, S., Vidmar, N., Rose, M., Ellis, L. & Murphy, B. (2003). Juror discussion during civil trials: Studying an Arizona innovation. *Arizona Law Review*, 45, 1–81.

Ebbesen, E.B. & Konecni, V.J. (1996). Eyewitness memory research: Probative v prejudicial value. *Expert Evidence*, 5(1–2), 2–28.

Ellsworth, P., Bukaty, R., Cowan, C. & Thompson, W. (1984). The death-qualified jury and the defense of insanity. *Law and Human Behavior*, 8, 81–94.

Expert Evidence (1996/7). Issues 5 and 6.

Finkel, N. (1995). *Common sense justice: Jurors' notions of the law*. Washington, DC: APA Books.

Freckelton, I. (1994). Expert evidence and the role of the jury. *Australian Bar Review*, 12, 73–106.

Frye (1923). *Frye v United States 293 F.1013* (D.C. Cir. 1023).

Gatowski, S., Dobbins, S., Richardson, J., Ginsburg, G., Merlino, M. & Dahir, V. (2001). Asking the gatekeepers: A national survey of judges in judging expert evidence in a post-Daubert world. *Law and Human Behavior*, 25, 433–458.

General Electric Co. v. Joiner (1997). 552 U.S. 136.

Gilovich, T., Vallone, R. & Tversky, A. (1985). The hot hand in basketball: On the misperception of random sequences. *Cognitive Psychology*, 17, 295–314.

Goldstein, R.L. (1989). The psychiatrist's guide to right and wrong: Part IV. The insanity defence and the ultimate issue rule. *Bulletin of the American Academy of Psychiatry and Law*, 17(3), 269–281.

Greene, E., Downey, C. & Goodman-Delahunty, J. (1999). Juror decisions about damages in employment discrimination cases. *Behavioral Sciences and the Law*, 17(1), 107–121.

Griffith, J.D., Libkuman, T.M. & Poole, D.A. (1998). Repressed memories: The effects of expert testimony on mock jurors' decision making. *American Journal of Forensic Psychology*, 16(1), 5–23.

Gudjonsson, G.H. (1985). Psychological evidence in court: Results from the BPS survey. *Bulletin of the British Psychological Society*, 38, 327–330.

Gudjonsson, G.H. (1994). Confessions made to the expert witness: Some professional issues. *Journal of Forensic Psychiatry*, 5(2), 237–247.

Gudjonsson, G.H. (1996). Psychological evidence in court: Results from the 1985 survey. *The Psychologist*, May, 213–217.

Gudjonsson, G.H. (2007/8). Psychologists as expert witnesses: The 2007 BPS survey. *Forensic Update*, 92(Winter), 23–29.

Haward, L.R.C. (1981). *Forensic psychology*. London: Batsford.

Heim, A. (1982). Professional issues arising from psychological evidence presented in court: A reply. *Bulletin of the British Psychological Society*, 35, 332–333.

Jackson, J.D. (1984). The ultimate issue rule – one rule too many. *Criminal Law Review*, 75–86.

Kapardis, A. (1997). *Psychology and law: A critical introduction*. Cambridge: Cambridge University Press.

Kargon, R. (1986). Expert testimony in historical perspective. *Law and Human Behavior*, 10, 15–27.

Kassin, S.M., Ellsworth, P.C. & Smith, V.L. (1989). The general acceptance of psychological research on eyewitness testimony: A survey of the experts. *American Psychologist*, 44, 1089–1098.

Kassin, S.M., Tubb, V.A., Hosch, H.M. & Memon, A. (2001). On the general acceptance of eyewitness testimony research:

A new survey of the experts. *American Psychologist, 56*(5), 405–416.

Kenny, A. (1983). The expert in court. *Law Quarterly Review, 99*, 197–216.

Kenny, A. (1984). The psychiatric expert in court. *Psychological Medicine, 14*, 291–302.

Konecni, V.J. & Ebbesen, E.B. (1986). Courtroom testimony by psychologists on witness identification issues. *Law and Human Behavior, 10*(1/2), 117–126.

Kovera, M.B. & McAuliff, B.D. (2000). The effects of peer review and evidence quality on judge evaluations of psychological science: Are judges effective gatekeepers? *Journal of Applied Psychology, 85*(4), 574–586.

Kovera, M.B., McAuliff, B.D. & Herbert, K.S. (1999). Reasoning about scientific evidence: Effects of juror gender and evidence quality on juror decisions in a hostile work environment case. *Journal of Applied Psychology, 84*(3), 362–375.

Kumho Tire Co v. Carmichael (1999). 526 U.S. 137.

Kutnjak-Ivkovich, S. & Hans, V. (2003). Jurors' evaluation of expert testimony: Judging the messenger and the message. *Law and Social Inquiry, 28*, 441–482.

Law and Human Behavior (1986). Issue *10*(3), 1–181.

Lempert, R.O. (1986). Social science in court: On 'eyewitness experts' and other issues. *Law and Human Behavior, 10*(1/2), 167–181.

Levett, L.M. & Kovera, M.B. (2008). The effectiveness of opposing expert witnesses for educating jurors about unreliable expert evidence. *Law and Human Behavior, 32*, 363–374.

Loftus, E.F. (1986). Ten years in the life of an expert witness. *Law and Human Behavior, 10*(3), 241–263.

Mackay, R.D., Colman, A.M. & Thornton, P. (1999). The admissibility of expert psychological and psychiatric testimony. In A. Heaton-Armstrong, E. Shepherd & D. Wolchover (Eds.) *Analysing witness testimony: A guide for legal practitioners and other professionals.* London: Blackstone Press.

Malpass, R.S., Tredoux, C.G., Schreiber Compo, N., McQuiston-Surrett, D.E., MacLin, O.H., Zimmerman, L.A. *et al.* (2008). Study space analysis for policy development. *Applied Cognitive Psychology, 22*(6), 789–801.

McAuliff, B.D. & Kovera, M.B. (2008). Juror need for cognition and sensitivity to methodological flaws in expert evidence. *Journal of Applied Social Psychology, 38*, 385–408 .

McConkey, K.M. & Roche, S.M. (1989). Knowledge of eyewitness testimony. *Australian Psychologist, 24*, 337–384.

McSherry, B. (2001). Expert testimony and the effects of mental impairment: Reviving the ultimate issue rule. *International Journal of Law and Psychiatry, 24*, 13–21.

Miller, J.S. & Allen, R.J. (1998). The expert as an educator. In S.J. Ceci & H. Hembrooke (Eds.) *Expert witnesses in child abuse cases* (pp.137–155). Washington, DC: American Psychological Association.

Mossman, D. (1999). Hired guns, whores and prostitutes. Case law references to clinicians of ill repute. *Journal of the American Academy of Psychiatry and the Law, 27*, 414–425.

Neil v *Biggers* (1972). 409 U.S. 188.

Nisbett, R.E. (1993). *Rules for reasoning.* Hillsdale, NJ: Lawrence Erlbaum.

Noon, E. & Hollin, C.R. (1987). Lay knowledge of eyewitness behaviour: A British survey. *Applied Cognitive Psychology, 1*(2), 143–153.

People v. *Pacely* (1984). Superior Court, San Diego, California, No CR 70541. Cited in Loftus, E.F. (1986). Ten years in the life of an expert witness. *Law and Human Behavior, 10*(3), 241–263.

R v *Mohan* (1994). 89 CCC (3d), 402 at 414.

R v. *Turnbull* (1976). 3 All ER 549.

Raitz, A., Greene, E., Goodman, J. & Loftus, E.F. (1990). Determining damages: The influence of expert testimony on jurors' decision making. *Law and Human Behavior, 14*(4), 385–395.

Roberts, C. & Golding, S. (1991). The social construction of criminal responsibility and insanity. *Law and Human Behavior, 15*, 349–376.

Rogers, R., Bagby, R.M. & Chow, M.K. (1992). Psychiatrists and the parameters of expert testimony. *International Journal of Law and Psychiatry, 15*, 387–396.

Rogers, T. (2004). Diagnostic validity and psychiatric expert testimony. *Law and Psychiatry, 27*, 281–290.

Sartorius, N., Ustan, T.B., Korten, A., Cooper, J.E. & von Drimmelen, J. (1995). Progress towards achieving a common language in psychiatry: II Results from an international field trial of the ICD-10 diagnostic criteria for research for mental and behavioural disorders. *American Journal of Psychiatry, 152*, 1427–1437.

Schuman, D., Whitaker, E. & Champagne, A. (1994). An empirical examination of the use of expert witnesses in the courts – part II: A three city study. *Jurimetrics Journal, 34*, 193–208.

Spencer, J.R. (1998). The role of experts in the common law and the civil law: A comparison. In S.J. Ceci & H. Hembrooke (Eds.) *Expert witnesses in child abuse cases* (pp.29–59). Washington, DC: American Psychological Association.

Sundby, S. (1997). The jury as critic: An empirical look at how capital juries perceive expert and law testimony. *Virginia Law Review, 83*, 1108–1109.

Tunstall, O., Gudjonsson, G. H., Eysenck, H. & Haward, L. (1982). Professional issues arising from psychological evidence presented in court. *Bulletin of the British Psychological Society, 35*, 329–331.

Tversky, A. & Kahneman, D. (1974). Judgment under uncertainty: Heuristics and biases. *Science, 185*, 1124–1131.

UK Register of Expert Witnesses (2008). Criminal procedure rules part 33: Expert evidence. The Register's proposed submission. Retrieved 9 September 2009 from www.jspubs.com/Surveys/CrimPR0512/Part33.cfm

Vidmar, N. (1995). *Medical malpractice and the American jury.* Ann Arbor, MI: University of Michigan Press.

Vidmar, N. (2005). Expert evidence, the adversary system, and the jury. *American Journal of Public Health, 95*(S1), 137–143.

Vidmar, N. & Diamond, S. (2001). Juries and expert evidence. *Brooklyn Law Review, 66*, 1121–1180.

Walker, L.E. & Monahan, J. (1987). Social frameworks: A new use of social science in law. *Virginia Law Review, 73*, 559–98.

Wells, G.L. (1978). Applied eyewitness testimony research: System variables and estimator variables. *Journal of Personality and Social Psychology, 36*(12), 1546–1557.

Wells, G.L. & Murray, D.M. (1983). What can psychology say about the *Neil v. Biggers* criteria for judging eyewitness accuracy? *Journal of Applied Psychology, 68*, 347–362.

Wigmore, J.H. (1978). *Evidence in trials at common law.* Boston, MA: Little Brown.

Wingate, P.H. & Thornton, G.C. (2004). Industrial/organisational psychology and the federal judiciary: Expert witness testimony and the Daubert standards. *Law and Human Behavior, 28*, 97–114.

Yarmey, A.D. (1986). Ethical responsibilities governing the statements experimental psychologists make in expert testimony. *Law and Human Behavior, 10*, 101–115.

Yarmey, A.D. (1997). Probative v prejudicial value of eyewitness memory research. *Expert Evidence, 5*, 89–97.

Yarmey, A.D. (2001). Expert testimony: Does eyewitness memory research have probative value for the courts? *Canadian Psychology, 42*(2), 92–100.

Yarmey, A.D. & Jones, H.P.T. (1983). Is the psychology of eyewitness identification a matter of common sense? In S. Lloyd-Bostock & B.R. Clifford (Eds.) *Evaluating witness evidence* (pp.18–40). Chichester: John Wiley & Sons.

5

Ethical Issues in Forensic Psychological Policy and Practice

Graham J. Towl

This chapter begins with an outline of some of the philosophical roots which underpin much of what is deemed morally acceptable behaviour in Western societies. In one sense ethics may be seen as an application of moral philosophic principles which are sometimes explicit but more often implicit.

One distinguishing characteristic of reasonably well-developed professions is that they have sets of ethical guidance. I include a brief review of some germane guidance, drawing upon international and inter-professional sets of guidance.

The focus of the chapter is primarily on psychologists and especially those undertaking work in 'forensic' settings, for example those working with prisoners. However, the discussion is not intended to be restricted by the work of forensic psychologists, but will be taken to include the work of psychologists from applied areas where there is work with forensic populations. Indeed, a number of the issues raised could be seen to have some application in a number of professions and not just in a prison or forensic psychiatric service context, but rather in a broader social welfare and health context too. However, although there may well be relevant learning from other such broader areas, our focus will remain in the forensic domain.

In setting the focus for understanding ethics in forensic practice a key underpinning theme is the contested area of power relationships. A basic conceptual framework is outlined as an heuristic device into understanding and reflecting upon the broader context of ethical decision making in forensic policy and practice.

The chapter will draw to a close with some ideas and reflections upon the development and maintenance of an ethical understanding in everyday forensic policy and practice.

Philosophical Roots

Just as with many other areas of study there is a particular language to philosophical ideas in relation to ethics and it is worth perhaps briefly outlining some of the relevant terms. Familiarity with such terms will hopefully help in informing some of our thinking, ultimately in relation to decision making on ethical matters.

Two key types of theory which we need to consider in philosophical thinking are those referred to as teleological and deontological theories (see, for example, Mendonca & Kanungo, 2007). Teleological or, as they are sometimes described, 'consequentialist' theories are characterised by a focus on outcomes. Thus the notion of 'intent' or motivation may be seen to take a philosophical backseat in such theories. A focus on consequences takes primacy with such theories.

Two major, highly pertinent manifestations of the consequentialist perspective may be seen in what is termed 'egoistic hedonism' and the more commonly known 'utilitarianism'.

Egoistic hedonism may broadly be viewed as self-interest, a commonly used implicit philosophical model in much work attempting to understand or predict human behaviour. It is, for example, a popular implicit philosophical model used across a range of professional disciplines, including psychology and economics. Egoistic hedonism has its roots in early Greek philosophical thinking (Mothershead Jr, 1955) and has been, and remains, a powerful implicit theory in informing our understanding of much human behaviour. Indeed it may often inform much of the behaviour of many individual professionals. However, sometimes professionals may be a little defensive about such possibilities in *their* practice.

Utilitarianism, which is underpinned by the principle of 'utility', has historically had a number of influential proponents such as Hume, Bentham and Mill (Mendonca & Kanungo, 2007). One key difference between egoistic hedonism and utilitarianism is that the latter has as its focus the maximum utility or benefit for the majority. Both theories appear to have at least an implicit disregard for the means, or indeed the motives, to achieve a particular end or consequence. A consideration of 'utility' has underpinned much of the recent deliberations of those engaged in deciding which drugs may or may not be prescribed through the National Health Service in England and Wales. In such cases the notion of 'utility' is considered in relation to the cost of specified likely benefits. Such 'cost utility' considerations may be compared with other actions or inactions in terms of their cost benefits too. Indeed, it is perhaps worth noting here that inactions are sometimes erroneously conflated with neutrality. In power terms, apparently neutral acts may simply maintain existing power inequalities. An illustrative application of the potential problems which may result from the proposition that inaction means being 'neutral' follows. Many prison staff still struggle to refer to individual prisoners by using the suffix 'Mr'. This is often a term proudly reserved for staff. The defence of such an approach by many prison staff is that it is important to distinguish between the status of the prisoner and staff. It is, of course, incumbent upon psychologists working in prisons to challenge such institutionalised abuses of power. I would not wish to suggest that this is a problem exclusive to prisons. Fundamentally, the same sorts of problems arise in hospitals too, but may manifest themselves in different ways, but as institutions dominated by professional power they can be potentially every bit as abusive in terms of the basic dignity and worth (implicitly and explicitly) with which patients are sometimes treated.

In marked contrast with the above teleological approaches is the deontological perspective. This perspective is about the notion of duties or obligations. In terms of European philosophical thought, one of its leading proponents was Immanuel Kant. Indeed, it is Kant's 'categorical imperative' which is explicitly referred to in the British Psychological Society's most recent set of ethical guidance for practitioner psychologists (British Psychological Society, 2006) as being central to the underpinning moral philosophy of the code. Kant contended that an act was only morally correct if we would be happy to see all (including ourselves) being treated in a particular manner. This does not necessarily sit well with the teleological or consequentialist position that it is the end rather than the means that matters. However, it does sit well with much Eastern and religious thinking. For example, the Far Eastern philosopher Confucius exhorts his students '… Do not impose on others what you yourself do not desire' (*The Analects*, 15:24 (Confucius, 1979)). There are parallels in Islamic, Christian, Jewish and Buddhist traditions too amongst other organised religions. On a practical level, whenever working with a patient, prisoner or client, one useful discipline and 'test' may be when considering particular 'assessments' or 'interventions' to ask ourselves how we would feel about the interaction if the particular recipient of services was someone we loved. The ability to honestly explore and understand one's own motivations in psychological practice is a very challenging area to teach effectively. But it remains an important habit of professional reflection (Koocher & Keith-Spiegel, 1998).

So, we have noted the respective perspectives of teleological and deontological thinking and we will return to these ideas when looking in more detail at professional policies and practices.

The popular media and political discourse on public service has it that the notion of altruism is important in understanding the motivations and behaviours of a number of professionals, perhaps especially so, purportedly, with health professionals such as nurses and doctors. Prejudices tend to come to the fore in such discourses. Nurses are assumed to be attracted to their work on a vocational basis; in short, they want to help the sick. Similarly, doctors are commonly perceived to have similarly noble motivations to their work, although this reputation has perhaps been somewhat called into question more recently with the substantial pay rises that general practitioners have received in recent years (*Sunday Times*, 2008). Professional hospital managers are not afforded the same level of generosity of presumed motivation, nor for that matter are they necessarily assumed to be as competent, unless, of course, they are doctors or nurses themselves. Often the analysis underlying such arguments is somewhat thin. For example, 'Managers who have been doctors and nurses know how to stop simple conditions becoming expensive illnesses because they have medical training as well as MBAs. Executives from the business schools do not because they only have MBAs' (Cohen, 2008). The key ethical point here is that whatever the background of the individual they need to be competent in the tasks that they are required to undertake whether it is in the domain of management or clinical practice.

Despite professional self-interests, the notion of altruism remains important to our understanding of the motivations and behaviour associated with much ethical practice. Psychological definitions of altruism have tended to focus upon individual dispositions to help others to meet internal nurturance needs (Krebs, 1982). The selfless helping of others remains widely regarded as a moral virtue, if not always described explicitly in such terms.

Most modern professional ethical guidance appears to draw primarily on deontological perspectives but they by no means ignore the importance of teleological considerations. Below we go on to consider some of the implications and further applications arising from our brief introduction to some of the more relevant philosophical positions underpinning, explicitly or implicitly, many such professional codes of conduct.

Ethical Guidance for Professionals

The widely cited four principles of medical ethics are: respect for autonomy, doing good (or beneficence), doing no harm (non-maleficence) and acting with fairness/equality (Baxter et al., 2005). Many other professions would make similar explicit demands on their members. Indeed, as mentioned above, one important defining characteristic of an occupation with professional status is that there will be an ethical code. Ethical codes are designed to benefit both recipients of professional services and also the particular professionals themselves. But it is important to remember that although ethical guidance can be very useful in guiding behaviour or expectations about behaviour, it does not provide 'answers' in a categorical and case-specific manner. Nor will it or should it ever be so. When drawing on such guidance it is important that professionals possess a range of skills, including critical reasoning skills, as well as drawing upon a clear 'moral compass'. Ethical

decision making needs to be both well reasoned and fair-minded (Thomson, 2006).

After two world wars which included some truly appalling and well-documented atrocities (including by professionals on all 'sides') in and beyond Europe, the General Assembly of the United Nations made a universal declaration of Human Rights (United Nations, 1948). This has provided a useful source document from which professional ethical guidance has drawn. The Declaration is essentially deontological in its approach; it contains both human rights and responsibilities (or duties).

Professional ethical guidance is thus informed by the need to protect human rights while also providing professionals and those in receipt of professional services with guidance about the principles underpinning behavioural expectations. Whereas it is tempting for any professional grouping to concern themselves exclusively with their own professional guidance for ethical practice, it is perhaps fruitful to consider other relevant sets of guidance which might further inform our understanding. The ethical issues of policy and practice are by no means exclusive to the forensic field, although, of course, some matters may come into sharper focus (Towl, 1994). Indeed, similar sorts of critical and often contested considerations have been the subject of a growing literature within social-welfare-based disciplines such as social work (see, for example, Banks, 2008; Banks & Williams, 2005). Below, for illustrative purposes, are some international perspectives within the general discipline of professional psychology and also guidance from the British Association for Counselling and Psychotherapy (BACP). The BACP guidance is used as an example because, in terms of the processes of interaction with clients and its psychological basis, there is much in common with the professional work of many psychologists. Before going further with this line of reasoning and exploration it is perhaps worth mentioning some caveats. First, a number of modern moral philosophers have called into question whether or not such codes of 'ethical practice' are actually about ethics *per se*. Some have argued that they diminish the level of engagement with ethical issues as a result of the thinking having been pre-prepared for the practitioner (see, for example, Dawson, 1994). Second, some have noted that a number of moral philosophers question whether or not the codes may confuse ethics with what amounts to 'law or rule making' rather than reflection, argument and understanding (Banks, 2003). There are, of course, other criticisms which may be considered in relation to the development of ethical guidance, but hopefully the reader has a flavour of some of the potential problems from a philosophical and ultimately policy and practice-based perspective. Some of these concerns are perhaps reflected in the development of a European-wide meta-code of ethics. The legal status and organisation of professional psychology throughout Europe is somewhat varied. In 1990 the European Federation of Psychologists Associations (EFPA) set up a task force on ethics. The meta-code set out what areas each ethical code should process without being prescriptive about how such areas should be addressed (Lindsay *et al.*, 2008). This approach reflected recognition of the political, cultural and professional diversity within Europe. But arguably, most importantly it reflected recognition of the importance of reflection, argument and understanding over simple behavioural prescription. The meta-code does, of course, include a significant degree of exhortation in terms of the areas it advocates being covered in individual national codes.

Next we take a brief look at the American Psychological Society ethical guidance. This has been influential in the development of such guidance in the UK. The first set of ethical guidance prepared for the Division of Criminological and Legal Psychology (DCLP) of the British Psychological Society (BPS) drew heavily upon the work of the APA in its structure and content (DCLP, 1997). Guidance from Ireland is also considered because of its geographical propinquity and most importantly its practical utility. Such practical utility can help meet some of the criticism and concerns raised by some about the everyday usefulness of such guidance in improving ethical practice.

APA ethical guidance

The APA set of ethical principles and code of conduct has two key sections, one on general ethical principles and the other on ethical standards (APA, 2002). The five general underlying ethical principles are: beneficence and non-maleficence, fidelity and responsibility, integrity, justice, and respect for people's rights and dignity. These are aspirational goals rather than specific rules of behaviour or conduct. However, the ethical standards that follow from these principles are rules which are enforceable through the rules and procedures of the APA. Unsurprisingly, in the event of a complaint, it is not deemed to be a good defence that an individual claims simply not to be aware of specific rules. It is not my intention to go through the details of the code, but rather to give the reader a flavour of the territory covered.

The standards are split into 10 sections which include standards for: Resolving Ethical Issues, Competence, Human Relations, Privacy and Confidentiality, Advertising and Other Public Statements, Record Keeping and Fees, Education and Training, Research and Publication, Assessment, and finally Therapy. The full details of the code are available at http://www.apa.org/ethics for those readers with an interest in examining the American code further.

The Psychological Society of Ireland (PSI) Code of Professional Ethics

Similar to the APA code, the PSI code is split into two sections, one on four overall ethical principles and the other on specific ethical standards. The PSI principles are: Respect for the rights and dignity of the person, competence, responsibility and integrity. These principles are used as the headings for all the ethical standards listed. The code also contains two appendices which are informative and worth bringing to the reader's attention.

Appendix A of the code is entitled 'Recommended Procedure for Ethical Decision-Making', which consists of a useful set of seven points to guide the process of an informed ethical decision-making process. It may well be a useful aide-memoire for policy makers and practitioners alike. The advice is unsurprising but helpful in its focus. It includes the need for defining the relevant issues for parties affected by the decision making, a scanning of the code for key issues and a careful evaluation of the rights and responsibilities of all concerned. The useful practical suggestion is made that it may be helpful to generate as many alternative decisions as possible while carefully examining likely and possible outcomes. The importance of the effective communication of ethical decision making is also helpfully addressed. The key and final point in the seven-point structure is that the individual is personally accountable for their decision making. In other words, although contextual information may be taken into account as possible mitigation, fundamentally psychologists must take personal responsibility for their ethical decision making. In forensic practice psychologists have a particular responsibility to ensure that the needs of the individual are given due weight. Sometimes it will be most ethical to decline to provide some services. Just because an organisational policy is legal does not mean that it is necessarily morally correct, or ethical. This is why the importance of individual decision making and personal responsibility and accountability is difficult to overstate. In this respect the planned statutory regulation of forensic psychologists in the UK as health professionals under the umbrella regulatory body of the Health Professions Council (HPC) may well provide helpful professional support for those concerned with challenging particular organisational policies which may be at odds with ethical practice.

Appendix B of the code usefully lists potential parties who may be affected by ethical decision making. Again this may well be a useful aide-memoire for policy makers and practitioners. When the general public are referred to as a party affected by ethical decision making it is perhaps culturally interesting that the example given as a potentially controversial issue is that of abortion. This perhaps serves to illustrate the importance of an appreciation of the cultural context of any such code.

On a final point about the PSI code it is perhaps worth noting that it explicitly excludes a consideration of any wider social concerns. This has been a point for debate within psychological policy and practice within England and Wales, with some arguing that social concerns and inequalities underpin many ethical issues for psychologists (see, for example, Gale, 1994; Towl, 1994). Arguably, nowhere is this more so than in forensic psychological practice with a patient/client group characterised by social inequality.

Above, two sets of contrasting ethical guidance have been drawn on for international comparative purposes. Below, I move on to looking at ethical guidance provided for those undertaking counselling and psychotherapeutic work in the UK. This is done with the aim of considering what we have to learn from practice in a closely related profession to that of professional psychology.

British Association for Counselling and Psychotherapy – Ethical Framework for Good Practice in Counselling & Psychotherapy

One distinctive feature of this guidance is that it is not structured merely with principles and standards, but from the outset contains an explicit set of values (BACP, 2009). Stress is given to the importance of practising with a high degree of cultural sensitivity to the needs of clients. A consideration of the importance of human rights tops the list of values. Again, distinctively, there is an emphasis on a value base which appreciates the value bases of human experiences and culture. Values inform principles.

The principles listed have a resonance elsewhere in the other ethical codes we have touched upon, with the possible exception of the emphasis which is given to the importance of self-respect, defined as fostering the practitioners' self-knowledge and care for the self. Unusually for a code of professional ethics there is a section, albeit aspirational, on personal moral qualities. Moral qualities include: empathy, sincerity, integrity, resilience, respect, humility, competence, fairness, wisdom and courage. Emphasis is given to practitioners continually engaging with the challenge of coming to ethical decisions in practice. I will not list the full range of standards here. Suffice to observe that the standards are derived from the underlying principles mentioned above, and also reflect the moral qualities needed to ensure that the counselling and psychotherapeutic values which underpin the guidance are manifest.

What seems clear about the world of counselling and psychotherapy is that there appears to be a greater acknowledgement about the wider context of any psychotherapeutic services when compared with codes for psychologists.

Having briefly considered both some international codes and that of a profession with close theoretical and sometimes practical links with psychology, I will now focus upon the code of ethics and conduct for psychologists in the UK and then on some of the specific guidance for forensic psychologists. But it is perhaps worth reiterating at this point the need for an emphasis on both underpinning 'values' and the socioeconomic context in understanding the potential application of such ethical codes.

The British Psychological Society (BPS) Code of Ethics and Conduct (2006)

In 1985 the BPS adopted a code of conduct which has been periodically updated, with some relatively minor revisions over the years. However, the 2006 guidance was, and remains, a marked improvement upon the quality of guidance previously available under the auspices of the BPS.

The introduction to the guidelines explains the rationale and context of the guidance. One fundamental observation which is brought to the reader's attention early on in the document is that ethics are inextricably linked to power relationships. Related to this is the importance of individual responsibility and personal accountability for one's actions. The guidance is there to help inform and not to replace professional decision making and accountabilities. This may, in part, be seen as having taken account of some of the philosophical criticisms cited above about the problems with ethical codes.

On a practical level practitioners may well find the concise section on decision making useful for informing the development of local policies and practices. There are similarities with the appendix provided by the Irish code, but there are some additions too. The section concludes with ideas for further reading.

The code is underpinned by four ethical principles: respect, competence, responsibility and integrity. Each of these principles is reflected in a statement of relevant values and a set of specific standards. All this is potentially helpful when trying to make sometimes difficult judgements about ethical decision making. However, it is lacking in some conceptual clarity. Respect is referred to as a principle rather than a value; some may find this inconsistent, and perhaps somewhat confused. Putting aside this relatively minor beef, essentially the code provides some of the key parameters of professional decision making while ensuring that individual practitioners are exhorted to retain their accountabilities for their practice.

In sum, the BPS guidance has been improved in recent years and has much in common with not only international codes for psychologists but also those of other related professions.

Specialist BPS forensic guidance

In the late 20th century and early in the 21st century the Division of Criminological and Legal Psychology (DCLP), which was subsequently renamed the Division of Forensic Psychology (DFP), began to formulate its own specialist guidance (British Psychological Society, 1997, 2002). This guidance was informed by previous APA and BPS guidance and also a number of relevant papers which reflected Divisional activity in this important area (see, for example, Gale, 1994; Towl, 1994, 1995). More recently, with the advent of the relatively new set of BPS ethical guidance, the specialist guidance has received less attention. This reflects, in part, an acknowledgement that the fundamental concerns associated with ethical guidance are generic to a range of areas of professional practice. In one important sense, then, the forensic domain is no different to anywhere else where issues of power imbalances are to the fore.

In the next section I will move on to an examination of how we may glean guidance to inform good practice

from a consideration of the power imbalances embedded in professional relationships with clients across many professions involved in health or social care. These are the general domains within which forensic policy and practice is situated. All the work of forensic psychologists in courts, police stations, prisons, hospitals and community settings may arguably be construed within this broader health and social care context.

Power Relationships

All professional relationships beget power relationships. Such relationships may be helpfully conceptualised at three levels: socio-political, organisational and individual. The context of these may be viewed through the lenses of 'the state' and 'societal status'.

A similar framework could be used with a range of professional groups in a range of settings. The key point is that to understand what ethical conduct may look like in particular cases and everyday practice, it is important to have an understanding of the power relationships between the professional and the recipient of services. In the forensic context (as is often the case in health more generally in practice) the recipient of services often has limited 'choices' that they may exercise. A limited choice (if any are tangible) serves to augment the already markedly skewed existing power relationships. Clearly forensic psychologists need to be mindful of this in their everyday practice, and so do policy makers.

The framework is not intended to capture every aspect of the layers of the complex power relationships between, in this case, forensic psychologist and offender. However, it does serve as an anchor point in looking at some key characteristics which have a potential impact upon the power relationships in such relationships.

If we look at the socio-political domain, the state positively supports the work of forensic psychologists. Evidence in support of this can be seen in the large organisational growth in the numbers of posts over recent years (Crighton & Towl, 2008). Also, there have been some significant improvements in pay and conditions for forensic psychologists in England and Wales. The Parole Board also appears to heavily weight psychological and psychologically based reports when considering whether or not a prisoner may be released.

By marked contrast, prisoners are not allowed to vote in UK state-sponsored elections and are contained within the confines of a prison. At an organisational or institutional level they tend not to have benefited from educational opportunities (which many have not experienced in real terms).

At an organisational level, psychologists benefit from both the strong support of their employers and the support of professional bodies such as the British Psychological Society and Health Professions Council (HPC). Offenders enjoy no similar such support.

At an individual level, psychologists are state 'successes' with hopefully high levels of verbal intelligence and all the trappings or benefits of professional status. For example, they enjoy the benefits of professional supervision and continuing professional development (CPD) and have access to ethical guidance. By, again, marked contrast, prisoners may be construed, in effect, as 'state failures'. They do not have a ready-made infrastructure for support.

In short, the power inequalities in the relationship start from a position of marked inequality. If we are concerned with the rights of 'another' then we perhaps need to be especially concerned when, as professionals, we hold such power. Many will feel discomfort at the extent of the power differential in such relationships. This may be particularly so amongst forensic psychologists who will be all too well aware of the potential dangers in such relationships. As a general rule, the wider the power differential the higher the risk of power abuses. This is amply illustrated elsewhere in, for example, cases of child abuse and patient abuses by medical doctors. The child has relatively little power in such circumstances and the same, in practice, can be said for a patient experiencing the potential vulnerabilities associated with illness (whether physical or mental health related). By marked contrast, the doctor will enjoy the trappings of their professional status and firm power base. Thus the gulf in the power relationship is further amplified. Psychologists need to learn from such problems.

Increasingly within psychological practice there has been a growth in awareness about the wider context of the application of ethical guidance. This is illustrated with the more recent BPS guidance cited above, the hallmark of which is the importance of our individual responsibility and accountability. The defence of a professional practice on the basis that 'I was only following my organisational (or professional) guidelines' is not in itself good enough in terms of the extent of one's individual accountability. There is an expectation that a professional will make an informed decision, taking account of guidance but retaining *their* accountability for *their* actions and inactions. Sometimes this can be difficult. This may be even more so on occasions when doing the right thing means experiencing a personal or professional disbenefit.

Conclusions

It is important to have some understanding of the philosophical basis of our ethical practice. I have argued that one key underpinning of what is deemed ethical in terms of policy and practice is an understanding of the power relationship between the professional psychologist and offender. These relationships need to be set within their wider social context. Offenders tend to come from socially disadvantaged backgrounds. Psychologists tend to come from socially advantaged backgrounds. A consideration of such factors, in combination with the reading of ethical guidance not just for one's own profession, can clearly be helpful. But arguably most important is the need to engage in discussion and reflection with colleagues about both current and future policy and practices in terms of their potential ethical implications. We have seen how a consideration of one's own values and beliefs is important in such discussions. From these discussions will come, on occasion, the need to decide what to do next to challenge such policies and practices. Active engagement in discussions and actions in relation to ethical practice is sometimes a difficult process. We need to routinely reflect upon who benefits from some areas of our decision making. There can sometimes be a broad range of potential stakeholders. Self-reflection is an important element of informing ethical decision making, particularly in relation to a reflection upon one's own values and how they impact upon decision making. In short, we need to periodically challenge our own ethical practice and its basis. I hope that there is food for thought within this chapter which will be helpful in such reflections, discussions, deliberations and, most importantly, actions in this intellectually and emotionally challenging field.

Further Reading

Banks, S. (2003). From oaths to rulebooks: A critical examination of codes of ethics for social professions. *European Journal of Social Work*, 6(2).
In this paper a reflective approach is taken to the nature of ethical codes. Criticisms of the formulation of ethical codes are

covered. Some of the key lenses through which ethical codes may be considered in terms of their utility and impact are examined. In particular, the functions of ethical codes as rhetorical, educational and regulatory devices are considered.

British Psychological Society (2006). *Code of ethics and conduct*. Leicester: Author.
The context, values and principles outlined in the code are essential reading for all practising forensic psychologists. Although forensic settings may beget a sharper focus to some of the ethical tensions and challenges in the field, the fundamental values and principles remain the same. So do many of the required good professional practices. The code provides a highly readable and useful structure (the parameters within which professional judgements may be made) which will be helpful in informing ethical decision making.

Lindsay, G., Koene, C., Overeedide, H. & Lang, F. (2008). *Ethics for European psychologists*. Gottingen, Germany: Hogrefe.
In this recent and stimulating book the European Federation of Psychologists Associations (EFPA) meta-code of ethics (2nd edition) is detailed, with a number of chapters on key themes in professional practice. Although designed with individual psychological associations primarily in mind, the code can be drawn upon to inform individual practice too. The book contains much material which may be of practical help to forensic practitioners. For example, appendix 4 covers the potentially uncomfortable professional territory of behavioural expectations of the psychologist when responding to a complaint that has been made. The advice has been taken from a Norwegian source but clearly has a resonance across Europe. The advice is clear, specific and helpful. Complaints about forensic psychologists have increased over the years. In sum, this book will be potentially of much practical help as a resource for the trainee or qualified forensic psychologist.

References

American Psychological Association (APA) (2002). *Ethical principles of psychologists and code of conduct*. Washington, DC: Author.

BACP (2009). *Ethical framework for good practice in counselling and psychotherapy*. London: Author.

Banks, S. (2003). From oaths to rule books: A critical examination of codes of ethics for the social professions. *European Journal of Social Work, 6*(2), 133–144.

Banks, S. (2008). Critical commentary: Social work ethics. *British Journal of Social Work, 38*, 1238–1249.

Banks, S. & Williams, R. (2005). Accounting for ethical difficulties in social welfare work: Issues, problems and dilemmas. *British Journal of Social Work, 35*, 1005–1022.

Baxter, C., Brennan, M.G., Coldicott, Y. & Moller, M. (Eds.) (2005). *The practical guide to medical ethics and law* (2nd edn). Pastest. Bodmin: MPG Books.

British Psychological Society, Division of Criminological and Legal Psychology (DCLP) (1997). *Ethical guidelines on forensic psychology*. Leicester: Author.

British Psychological Society, Division of Forensic Psychology (DFP) (2002). *Ethical guidelines on forensic psychology*. August. Leicester: Author.

British Psychological Society (2006). *Code of ethics and conduct*. March. Leicester: Author.

Cohen, N. (2008). Let the PM be the best-paid public servant. Comment. *The Observer*, 23 November.

Confucius (1979). *The analects* (translated with an introduction by D.C. Lau). London: Penguin.

Crighton, D.A. & Towl, G.J. (2008). *Psychology in prisons* (2nd edn). Oxford: BPS Blackwell.

Dawson, A. (1994). Professional codes of practice and ethical conduct. *Journal of Applied Philosophy, 11*(2) 125–133.

Gale, A. (1994). Do we need to think a bit more about ethical issues? *Division of Criminological and Legal Psychology, Newsletter, 37*, 16–22.

Koocher, G.P. & Keith-Spiegel, P. (1998). *Ethics in psychology; Professional standards and cases* (2nd edn). Oxford Textbooks in Clinical Psychology. Oxford: Oxford University Press.

Krebs, D. (1982). Altruism: A rational approach. In H. Eizenberg (Ed.) *The development of prosocial behaviour*. New York: Academic Press.

Lindsay, G., Koene, C., Halder O. & Lang, F. (2008). *Ethics for European psychologists*. Gottinggen, Germany: Hogrefe.

Mendonca, M. & Kanungo, R.N. (2007). Ethical leadership. C. Brotherton, Series Editor. *Work and organisational psychology*. Maidenhead: Open University Press.

Mothershead, J.R., Jr (1955). *Ethics: Modern conceptions of the principles of right*. New York: Henry Holt and Company.

Sunday Times (2008). NHS staff earnings, NHS information centre. *Sunday Times*, 30 November, under Freedom of Information Act.

Thomson, A. (2006). *Critical reasoning in ethics: A practical introduction*. London: Routledge.

Towl, G.J. (1994). Ethical issues in forensic psychology. *Forensic Update, 39*(October). Leicester: DCLP, BPS.

Towl, G.J. (1995). Ethics: A framework for forensic psychologists. *Forensic Update, 42*(July). Leicester: DCLP, BPS.

United Nations (1948). *Universal Declaration of Human Rights, adopted and proclaimed by General Assembly Resolution 217 A (III) of 10 Dec, 1948*. Geneva: Author.

Part II

Evidence-based Practice

6

The Developmental Evidence Base
Neurobiological Research and Forensic Applications

Robert A. Schug, Yu Gao, Andrea L. Glenn,
Melissa Peskin, Yaling Yang and Adrian Raine

A significant empirical base for the lifespan development of crime and antisocial behaviour has accumulated through key areas of neurobiological research. Genetic studies indicate significant heritability estimates of antisocial behaviour; and candidate genes for antisociality are becoming identified along with important gene–environment interactions. Neuroimaging research has found structural and functional deficits in frontal, temporal and subcortical regions in antisocial children and adults, and these findings are largely supported by neurological studies of brain trauma in antisocial populations. Neuropsychological studies have reported deficits in verbal, spatial and executive abilities in antisocial adults and children, and risk factors early in childhood appear to predict later forms of antisocial behaviour. Psychophysiological research has focused upon cardiovascular and electrodermal activity, electroencephalogram and event-related potentials, while studies in endocrinology have focused upon hormones such as cortisol and testosterone. Important contributions have also been made from research in areas of moral development and nutrition. This developmental neurobiological evidence base has to date begun to impact various facets of criminal justice systems, including lie detection and judicial process applications; and may enhance forensic psychological assessment and inform policies and procedures regarding the identification, management and treatment of various forms of adult and juvenile offending.

The Developmental Evidence Base: Neurobiological Research

Essential to forensic psychology is an empirical understanding of the initiation, maintenance and potential desistance from criminal behaviour. Developmental perspectives of crime – emphasising lifespan continuities/discontinuities of criminality rather than general causes or correlates – have contributed significantly to this understanding; especially as the neurobiological roots and sociological origins of crime are often present in the earliest years of life. Prominent developmental theories of antisocial behaviour have incorporated both elements. For example, Patterson's (1982) coercion model uses social learning to explain early-onset persistent offending, while Moffitt's (1993) developmental theory of life-course persistent offending emphasises an additional interactive role of biological factors (i.e. prenatal and perinatal disruptions in neural development which lead to specific neurobiological deficits) in the early-onset trajectory. Both models have received impressive empirical support from studies of childhood antisocial behaviour, aggression and delinquency (Brennan *et al.*, 2003).

As developmental theories may be ideal for informing future intervention and public policy directions (Brennan *et al.*, 2003), criminal justice systems in general and forensic psychology in particular stand to benefit tremendously from their application. Moreover, neurobiological research – with its extensive contributions to criminological study dating back more than a century (i.e. Lombroso, 1876) – has offered a unique understanding of the aetiological mechanisms underlying antisocial behaviour, and provided a sizeable evidence base for developmental criminological perspectives. This chapter will serve as an integrative review of findings from key areas of neurobiological research on antisocial behaviour, with particular focus upon developmental perspectives and associated theories. Additionally, it will provide an overview of current and potential application of this research within forensic arenas – which may be of value in informing the clinical practitioner.

Genetics

Genetic predispositions towards antisocial behaviour provide an ideal starting point for a discussion of developmental neurobiological crime research. Twin studies, adoptive studies, studies in twins reared apart and molecular genetic studies have provided substantial evidence for genetic influences on antisocial and aggressive behaviour (Popma & Raine, 2006); and though published estimates of heritability vary widely among studies (Waldman & Rhee, 2006), the genetic contribution is thought overall to be 40–50 per cent (Moffitt, 2005). Variability may be due in part to the use of a variety of semi-overlapping phenotypes (i.e. the detectable expression of an individual's genotype interacting with their environment; Walsh & Ellis, 2007) – including dimensional personality traits (e.g. impulsivity, aggressiveness), psychiatric diagnoses (e.g. antisocial personality disorder [ASPD], conduct disorder [CD]) and behaviour (e.g. crime, delinquency) related to antisociality – which are considered less than ideal (Goldman & Ducci, 2007). Some genetic determinants of antisociality are common to other externalising disorders (i.e. the aforementioned disorders, along with attention-deficit/hyperactivity disorder [ADHD], alcoholism and other addictions; Goldman & Ducci, 2007), and may be explained by intermediate endophenotypic expressions (Waldman & Rhee, 2006). Additionally, several monoamine neurotransmitter genes have demonstrated a genetic association with antisocial behaviour (Goldman & Ducci, 2007); including those coding for precursor, receptor, transporter, metabolite or conversion elements in the serotonin and catecholamine (i.e. dopamine and norepinephrine) neurotransmitter systems (e.g. 5-hydroxy-tryptamine receptor 1B [HTR1B], tryptophan hydroxylase [TPH2], 5-hydroxytryptamin transporter [HTT], monoamine oxidase A [MAOA], and catechol-O-methyltransferase [COMT]; Goldman & Ducci, 2007; Waldman & Rhee, 2006) – systems thought to modulate aggressive and impulsive behaviour. None of these candidate genes, however, accounts for a large amount of phenotypic variance in antisociality (Goldman & Ducci, 2007). This suggests both that many individual genes are involved in coding the neurobiological risk factors for crime, and also that gene–environment interactions are likely important in the developmental progression and expression of antisocial behaviour.

Developmental psychopathology researchers have begun to seek evidence for these interactions. For example, Caspi and colleagues (2002) found maltreated children with a genotype conferring high levels of monoamine oxidase A (a neurotransmitter-metabolising enzyme) expression to be less likely to become antisocial and violent in adolescence than maltreated children having a genotype conferring low levels of monoamine oxidase A expression. Twin data have also contributed to a developmental neurobiological perspective, demonstrating: (1) most genetic effects upon antisocial behaviour increase with age while shared environmental effects decrease; (2) early-onset persistent antisocial behaviour is more heritable than (later-onset) conduct disorder; (3) family environment is relevant for the initiation and early maintenance of aggression (particularly in men), but its effect fades; and (4) some genes influence antisocial behaviour across the entire lifespan, and others only in adolescence and adulthood (Goldman & Ducci, 2007). The effect of gene–environment interactions is embedded in the social-push theory, which states that biological factors may more likely explain antisocial behaviour in the absence of predispositional social factors (Popma & Raine, 2006). In total, there remains little doubt regarding the role of genetic influences in the developmental progression of antisocial behaviour.

Neuroimaging

With the increase in neuroimaging research over the past decade, evidence has accumulated supporting a plausible relationship between brain impairments and antisocial behaviour. The strongest evidence implicates the prefrontal cortex, a result not surprising considering the key multiple functions of this region, which include inhibiting behavioural impulses and regulating emotion generated by subcortical structures such as the amygdala. Structurally, several imaging studies have found significant grey matter volume reduction in the prefrontal cortex in antisocial aggressive individuals. For example, Raine and colleagues (2000) reported an 11 per cent volume reduction in prefrontal grey matter in individuals with antisocial personality disorder. Functionally, earlier studies found antisocial individuals to show decreased functioning such as glucose metabolism and regional blood flow (rCBF) in this region (Volkow & Tancredi, 1987; Volkow et al., 1995).

The orbitofrontal cortex (OFC) and dorsolateral prefrontal cortex (DLPFC) are the two prefrontal sub-regions most consistently found to be impaired in antisocial, violent individuals. The orbitofrontal cortex is critical in ethical decision making and emotion regulation, whereas the dorsolateral prefrontal cortex plays an important role in behavioural control and executive functioning. The only structural imaging study to date that examined prefrontal sub-regions showed significant reduced volume in the orbitofrontal and dorsolateral prefrontal cortex in patients with antisocial personality disorder (Laakso et al., 2002); which is consistent with functional imaging studies that revealed abnormal orbitofrontal and dorsolateral prefrontal functioning during cognitive and emotional tasks in antisocials. For example, Raine et al. (1994) found reduced glucose metabolism in the orbitofrontal and dorsolateral prefrontal cortex in murderers during a continuous performance task. Alternatively, antisocial, violent individuals were found more recently to show heightened neural activation in the orbitofrontal and dorsolateral prefrontal areas during emotional processes (e.g. the viewing of affective pictures) compared to controls (Müller et al., 2003; Schneider et al., 2000). Overall, these findings suggest that impairments in the prefrontal cortex, particularly the orbitofrontal and the dorsolateral prefrontal regions, may contribute crucially to the neurobiological pathology in antisocial individuals.

The prefrontal cortex, however, is not the only structure to be linked to violent criminal behaviour. It has long been known that damage to the temporal lobe may result in blunted emotional responses (Klüver & Bucy, 1939), similar to what has been observed in antisocial violent individuals. Indeed, several studies that found prefrontal dysfunction in their antisocial violent subjects also found reduced temporal functioning. For example, Soderstrom et al. (2000) revealed reduced rCBF in the frontal cortex as well as the temporal cortex in violent perpetrators compared to controls. Hirono et al. (2000) also found rCBF reduction in the left anterior temporal cortex in addition to the bilateral dorsofrontal cortex in individuals convicted of impulsive violent offences. Within the temporal region, antisocial and violent behaviour is particularly associated with deficits in the amygdala–hippocampal complex. The amygdala is crucial not only in the reception and production of emotion, but also the processing of fear conditioning, while the hippocampus is involved in emotional memory. Functional abnormalities in the amygdala–hippocampal complex in antisocial aggressive individuals have been reported in several studies. For example, criminal psychopaths have demonstrated decreased amygdala–hippocampal activations during the viewing of negative affective pictures (Kiehl et al., 2001). Another study (Soderstrom et al., 2000) found reduced hippocampal rCBF in violent perpetrators compared to controls. Together, these findings suggest that deficits in the temporal lobe, particularly the amygdala and hippocampus, may predispose one to a lack of fear of punishment and result in the disruption of normal moral development (see below).

Although these studies provide strong evidence for a link between brain impairments and antisocial violent behaviour, the causal effect remains unclear. Studies on children with antisocial personalities have reported brain abnormalities similar to those found in antisocial personality-disordered or aggressive adults. For example, Kruesi et al. (2004) report significant temporal lobe and non-significant prefrontal lobe volume reductions in early-onset conduct-disordered children; and a trend towards corpus callosum but not prefrontal white matter volume/ratio reductions in youth liars (compared to antisocial controls and healthy volunteers; Kruesi & Casanova, 2006). In aggressive children with epilepsy, Juhasz et al. (2001) found a significant correlation between a higher severity of aggression and lower metabolism in the bilateral medial prefrontal and left temporal cortex. Furthermore, Sterzer et al. (2005) found decreased activation in the right dorsal anterior cingulate cortex in aggressive children with conduct disorders during the viewing of negative affective pictures. Though prospective imaging studies of antisocial behaviour in children remain largely unreported, these results – along with those above – highlight the importance of neuroimaging data in elucidating the developmental neurobiological basis to antisocial behaviour.

Neurology

Neurological studies of brain trauma in antisocial populations have provided important contributions to the understanding of the pathogenesis of antisocial behaviour. Interestingly, age groups at highest risk for traumatic brain injury (adolescents, young adults, those over age 75, males; Ehrenreich *et al.*, 2007) largely overlap with those associated with increased antisociality (see Moffitt, 1993). Some adult antisocial populations are characterised by an unusually high prevalence of adult and childhood brain injury (e.g. Blake *et al.*, 1995; Lewis *et al.*, 1986). More-striking evidence comes from case descriptions of frontally damaged patients who subsequently developed marked antisociality (e.g. Phineus Gage [Harlow, 1848] and patient E.V.R. [Saver & Damasio, 1991]; see also Damasio, 1994, and Damasio *et al.*, 1990) – a condition known as 'acquired psychopathy' (Granacher & Fozdar, 2007).

Although damage to different brain areas may result in a variety of emotional and cognitive impairments, studies have shown that individuals are more likely to display aggression when the damage involves the frontal and temporal regions. Grafman *et al.* (1996) found that aggressive and violent attitudes were heightened in Vietnam War veterans who had suffered orbitofrontal lesions when compared to those with lesions in other brain regions. Specifically, patients with temporal injuries reported more feelings of rage and hostility, whereas patients with injuries to the prefrontal cortex, particularly the orbitofrontal cortex, reported a much higher level of violent and aggressive behaviour. These findings are consistent with imaging studies on antisocial violent individuals, and suggests that individuals who suffer brain damage to these two regions may not have sufficient cognitive and emotion-regulation capability to satisfy their desires through socially acceptable channels (e.g. negotiation), thus resorting to aggressive and violent behaviour to achieve their goals (León-Carrión & Ramos, 2003).

Studies examining juvenile criminals and delinquents also report a high prevalence of brain injury history (Andrews *et al.*, 1998; Lewis *et al.*, 1988; Pincus & Lewis, 1991), at higher rates than non-delinquents (Lewis *et al.*, 1987), and with head injuries largely pre-dating violence and law-enforcement contact (Lewis *et al.*, 1986; Sarapata *et al.*, 2008); while other studies in children report antisocial and externalising behavioural sequelae commonly following head injury (Raine, 2002a). Additionally, Anderson *et al.* (1999) have found that patients who incur damage very early in life (i.e. before age 16 months)

develop antisocial tendencies very similar to those observed in individuals who incur damage as adults, but the tendencies are often more severe and persist throughout development. In aggregate, these findings suggest that the occurrence of brain injury, particularly at an early age, could be a risk factor for developing aggression and other behavioural problems.

It is worth mentioning that head injury, even when resulting in frontal or temporal damage, does not automatically predispose one to delinquency. Criminal behaviour, particularly violent crime, likely results from the complex interaction of risk factors including genetic predisposition, emotional distress, poverty, substance abuse, child abuse and academic underachievement (Filley *et al.*, 2001). For example, for those individuals who suffered from learning disabilities and school behavioural problems, adding a head injury greatly increases the possibility of criminal and violent behaviour later on in life (León-Carrión & Ramos, 2003). In other words, head injuries may act as a trigger that disrupts the neural mechanisms that normally mediate and control behaviour in individuals with sociobiological predispositions to aggression and crime.

These neurological studies support neuroimaging evidence suggesting that impairments in frontal lobe functioning may be involved in the development of antisocial behaviour. However, in some cases, brain damage has not produced behavioural changes, and even reduced aggression in previously aggressive individuals (e.g. Bigler, 2001; Ellenbogen *et al.*, 2005; Mataró *et al.*, 2001), though this may be the result of concomitant dorsolateral prefrontal damage (an area spared in the cases of Gage and E.V.R.; Mataró *et al.*, 2001). Alternatively, this may suggest that frontal lobe impairment, particularly in the orbitofrontal cortex, is merely a *risk factor* for antisocial behaviour, but does not *necessarily* result in antisocial behaviour in all cases. Additionally, brain trauma in general and acquired psychopathy in particular may be risk factors for later development of neurodegenerative disorders (Granacher & Fozdar, 2007) which may exacerbate antisocial tendencies. In any event, the literature to date demonstrates that neurological factors can be key contributors to the developmental progression of crime.

Neuropsychology

Several decades of research have highlighted a growing interest in relating neuropsychological performance to forensic aspects of behaviour (Rasmussen *et al.*, 2001). Neuropsychological investigations of violent, aggressive and antisocial behaviour have largely focused on specific domains of cognitive functioning such as verbal and spatial intelligence and executive abilities.

Verbal and spatial intelligence

While general intelligence (e.g. IQ or Full Scale IQ) deficits are the best-replicated cognitive correlate of antisocial, violent and criminal behaviour among non-mentally ill individuals (Wilson & Herrnstein, 1985), identifying component verbal versus spatial/performance intelligence deficits has demonstrated utility in the understanding of the aetiological mechanisms underlying antisociality. Reduced verbal as opposed to spatial/performance IQ – possibly indicating left hemispheric dysfunction – is widely reported in adult antisocial populations (Raine, 1993). However, general intellectual performance or verbal intelligence deficits have not been reported in individuals with antisocial personality disorder and psychopathy (Barkataki *et al.*, 2006; Kosson *et al.*, 2007), though some specific psychopathic traits (i.e. criminal versatility and violence) may be related to verbal dysfunction (Rasmussen *et al.*, 2001). Thus, while global and/or verbal IQ deficits may characterise adult antisocials in general, they may not characterise specific subsets of antisocial trait constellations.

Lowered verbal IQ appears largely characteristic of antisocial children and adolescents (Barker *et al.*, 2007; Brennan *et al.*, 2003; Raine, 1993; Teichner & Golden, 2000; Vermeiren *et al.*, 2002). Moffitt *et al.* (1994), in a study of children from a New Zealand birth cohort, found that verbal deficits at age 13 predicted delinquency at age 18 for persistent, high-level offending beginning in pre-adolescence – longitudinal neuropsychological evidence which supports Moffitt's (1993) proposed theory. Verbal deficits may affect the development of language-based self-control mechanisms (Luria, 1980), leading ultimately to socialisation failure (Eriksson *et al.*, 2005), although the verbally deficient juvenile offender is thought to have a more positive prognosis, with environmental modifications and therapy (Teichner & Golden, 2000). Additionally, there is a paucity of literature related to global verbal intelligence in juvenile psychopathy (itself a largely unexplored and controversial topic; Salekin, 2006) – though Loney *et al.* (1998) found no verbal deficits in children with conduct problems characterised by callous-unemotional traits (CU traits – related to adult psychopathy; Frick *et al.*, 2003); and Salekin *et al.* (2004) recently found verbal intelligence to be related positively with the superficial and deceitful interpersonal style traits and inversely with the affective processing-disturbance traits of psychopathy in juvenile prisoners. In all, verbal deficits in antisocial youth populations overall appear relatively consistent, though future investigations of psychopathic youth may help clarify heterogeneity in verbal IQ findings among antisocial juveniles as in adults.

Evidence from longitudinal community-based studies may call into question the classic view (derived primarily from institutionalised samples) of verbal but not performance intelligence impairments in antisocial individuals. Raine *et al.* (2005) identified both spatial and verbal impairments in a Pittsburgh youth sample including childhood-limited, adolescent-limited and life-course persistent offenders. In a Mauritius sample, Raine *et al.* (2002) found spatial but not verbal deficits at age 3 and both spatial and verbal deficits at age 11 in persistently antisocial individuals – suggesting that early spatial deficits contribute to persistent antisocial behaviour, while verbal deficits may be developmentally acquired. These authors proposed an early starter spatial impairment model of antisocial behaviour, in which early visuospatial deficits potentially interfere with mother–infant bonding, and may reflect right hemisphere dysfunction that disrupts the processing and regulation of emotions, in turn contributing to life-course antisociality.

Executive functioning

Executive functioning refers to the cognitive processes that allow for goal-orientated, contextually appropriate behaviour and effective self-serving conduct (Lezak *et al.*, 2004; Luria, 1980). Executive dysfunction is thought to represent frontal lobe impairment, and is indicated by performance errors on neuropsychological measures of strategy formation, cognitive flexibility or impulsivity (i.e. category, maze-tracing, Stroop interference, card sorting, verbal fluency and tower tests; and go/no-go and gambling tasks). Neuropsychological investigations of executive functioning deficits and antisocial behaviour have traditionally focused on categorical clinical syndromes (i.e. antisocial personality disorder, conduct disorder, psychopathy) and legal/judicial concepts (criminality and delinquency). Morgan and Lilienfeld's (2000) quantitative review of 39 studies found overall executive functioning deficits in antisocials compared to controls, and strongest effects for the Porteus Mazes test and antisociality defined by judicial status. More recently, executive functioning deficits have been associated with aggressive (e.g. male batterers) and antisocial personality-disordered populations (Dolan & Park, 2002; Stanford et al., 2007a; Teichner et al., 2001), property crimes (Barker et al., 2007) and reactive versus instrumental violent offenders (Broomhall, 2005). Adult psychopathy has not consistently been associated with general executive functioning deficits (Blair & Frith, 2000; Dinn & Harris, 2000; Hiatt & Newman, 2006; Kosson et al., 2007), and recent neuropsychological evidence indicates that psychopathy may be characterised more by orbitofrontal dysfunction (Blair et al., 2006). Additionally, better dorsolateral prefrontal task performance has been demonstrated in successful, uncaught psychopaths relative to unsuccessful psychopaths and controls (Ishikawa et al., 2001).

Evidence for executive dysfunction in delinquent children and conduct-disordered adolescents has historically varied depending upon sample characteristics, control groups, assessment measures, executive functioning operationalisations, and methodology (Moffitt & Henry, 1989; Teichner & Golden, 2000). Recent findings are mixed, with executive functioning deficits characterising some antisocial youths (Nigg et al., 2004; Raine et al., 2005; White et al., 1994) and not others (Moffitt et al., 1994; Nigg et al., 2004). Important to consider, however, is the development of executive functioning along with the ongoing myelination of the frontal cortex into adolescence and beyond (Nigg et al., 2004; Raine, 2002b), which may explain differential patterns of executive functioning deficits among children and adults. Some findings may reflect this phenomenon. Nestor (1992), for example, found executive functioning impairments in older (i.e. middle-aged) but not younger (i.e. early adulthood) maximum security hospital patients. Blair (2006) found impairments on an orbitofrontal neuropsychological task to be more pronounced in psychopathic adults than psychopathic children. Furthermore, the influences of comorbid hyperactivity and aggression may affect neuropsychological performance (Raine, 2002b; Séguin et al., 2004).

Biological versus social influences

Earlier prospective neuropsychological studies have found interactions of neuropsychological/neurobiological dysfunction and adverse social/environmental influences to significantly increase levels of later antisocial behaviour over each factor individually (Raine, 2002b). Recent longitudinal evidence supports these findings, highlights the relative importance of social risk factors and may clarify the nature of these biosocial interactions. For example, progressive cognitive dysfunction affected by adverse psychosocial experience may explain early-onset antisociality (Aguilar et al., 2000); and lifetime, cumulative biosocial risk interactions may be stronger predictors of persistent aggression than risks specific to childhood or adolescence (Brennan et al., 2003). Alternatively, an overload of the late-developing prefrontal cortex by the social and executive functioning demands of late adolescence may lead to prefrontal dysfunction, behavioural inhibition failure and significantly increased antisocial behaviour (Raine, 2002b). Clearly, these neuropsychological studies underscore the need for considering biosocial interactions in the lifespan progression of criminality.

In sum, the neuropsychological literature demonstrates how the study of behavioural expressions of brain dysfunction – particularly in verbal, spatial and executive abilities – has informed developmental neurobiological perspectives of crime.

Psychophysiology

Lykken's (1957) seminal work involving psychophysiological processes in psychopaths largely marks the beginnings of the modern neurobiological investigation of crime. Psychophysiological studies have since focused upon the cardiovascular, electrodermal and electrocortical concomitants of antisocial behaviour.

Heart rate

Heart rate reflects both sympathetic and parasympathetic nervous system activity, and heart rate factors demonstrate an interesting developmental relationship with antisocial behaviour. While heart rate findings in adult antisocials are variable and inconsistent (Herpertz, 2007; Stanford et al., 2007b) – with low resting heart rate (an indicator of low autonomic arousal) and heart rate reactivity correlating with aggression but not psychopathy in adults (Lorber, 2004) – low resting heart rate is the best-replicated biological correlate of antisocial behaviour in children and adolescents (Herpertz, 2007; Stanford et al., 2007b), and greater heart rate reactivity appears characteristic of conduct-disordered children (Lorber, 2004). Low heart rate is diagnostically specific of conduct disorder, and has demonstrated predictive value – being a childhood predictor of adolescent aggression (Raine, 1996) and LCP offending (Moffitt & Caspi, 2001). Additionally, *high* heart rate appears to protect against the development of criminality, characterising antisocial boys who later desist from adult criminal offending (Raine *et al.*, 1995).

Prospective studies indicate that the developmental relationship between heart rate factors and antisocial behaviour may be moderated by social influences. For example, age 3 low resting heart rate was shown to be related to age 11 aggression in high but not low social class individuals (Raine *et al.*, 1997). Furthermore, increased heart rate variability has shown a positive relationship with aggression in young adults who have not been violently victimised, but not in those who have (Scarpa *et al.*, 1999).

Skin conductance

Skin conductance is controlled exclusively by the sympathetic nervous system, and reflects both arousal (e.g. skin conductance response frequency, level and fluctuations at rest) and responsivity (e.g. skin conductance orientating responses to novel stimuli and task responses to emotionally valenced stimuli). Strongest findings in this area are reduced skin conductance classical conditioning in psychopaths, criminals, delinquents and other antisocials (Raine, 1997). In adults, psychopaths demonstrate fewer skin conductance fluctuations (Raine, 1996), and Lorber's (2004) meta-analysis indicates negative relationships between skin conductance reactivity and both adult aggression and psychopathy. Attenuated task skin conductance responsivity has overall been associated with adult psychopathy, but only for negative stimuli (Lorber, 2004). Finally, antisocial personality-disordered adults have demonstrated reduced skin conductance orientating responses when comorbid for schizophrenia-spectrum personality disorders (Schug *et al.*, 2007), as do antisocial adolescents when additional schizoid features are present (Raine & Venables, 1984).

In children, low skin conductance arousal has been associated with conduct problems (Lorber, 2004), and reduced skin conductance fluctuations have been reported in conduct-disordered boys (Herpertz *et al.*, 2005) – in fact, together these may be a risk factor for adult criminality (Raine, 2002b). Reduced skin conductance arousal at age 15 has been associated with

criminal offending at age 24 years (Raine *et al.*, 1990b). Orientating deficits have also been reported in conduct-disordered boys (Herpertz *et al.*, 2003); and childhood conduct problems (in contrast to adult psychopathy) have overall been associated with reduced task skin conductance responsivity only for non-negative stimuli (Lorber, 2004). However, skin conductance hyporesponsivity during anticipation of aversive stimuli has since been reported in psychopathy-prone adolescents (Fung *et al.*, 2005), similar to that observed in adult psychopaths.

Cardiovascular and electrodermal underarousal have been interpreted in different ways. Fearlessness theory argues that lack of fear, represented by low heart rate or skin conductance arousal, leads in childhood to poor socialisation as low fear of punishment reduces the effectiveness of conditioning. Stimulation-seeking theory argues that underarousal represents an aversive state that is compensated for by stimulation/thrill-seeking and by risk-taking behaviour. In this context, 3-year-old children who show temperamentally high stimulation seeking and reduced fearlessness have been found to show increased aggression at age 11 (Raine *et al.*, 1998). Finally, prefrontal dysfunction theory argues that reduced skin conductance orientating is a marker for abnormalities in the prefrontal–cortical–subcortical circuitry involved in arousal regulation and stress responsivity – abnormalities associated with attentional and executive deficiencies (Herpertz, 2007). While both fearlessness and stimulation-seeking theories may be complementary in nature (Raine, 2002b), they could also represent independent risk factors as childhood fearlessness and stimulation-seeking have been found to be independent predictors of later aggression (Raine *et al.*, 1998).

Developmental relationships between skin conductance indices and antisociality have been reported, and multiple studies have found that skin conductance deficits show stronger relationships to antisocial behaviour in those from benign childhood social backgrounds that lack classic psychosocial risk factors for crime (Raine, 2002b). For example, reduced age 3 skin conductance orientating is related to age 11 aggression, but only for children from high social class backgrounds (Raine *et al.*, 1997). Additionally, higher heart rate and skin conductance arousal, high orientating, and increased conditioning responses distinguished adolescents who desisted from crime by age 29 from those that did not (Raine *et al.*, 1995, 1996), suggesting a protective role of these mechanisms against antisociality. Similar psychophysiological protective factors have also been found in the offspring of criminal fathers who desist from adult criminality (Brennan *et al.*, 1997).

Electroencephalogram and event-related potentials

The electroencephalogram (EEG) reflects regional electrical activity of the brain. Extensive reviews indicate that many studies have assessed EEG in antisocial populations such as criminals, delinquents, psychopaths, murderers and violent offenders (Raine, 1993). While a large number of studies have implicated varied EEG abnormalities in violent recidivistic offenders, results from EEG studies of psychopathic individuals are more inconsistent (see Raine, 1993; Herpertz, 2007). Commonly reported are slow-wave (i.e. theta and delta) abnormalities – reflecting underarousal – within frontal and temporal regions (Blake *et al.*, 1995; Evans & Park, 1997; Gatzke-Kopp *et al.*, 2001; Green *et al.*, 2001; Herpertz, 2007; Lindberg *et al.*, 2005), although other regional cortical abnormalities have also been noted (Lindberg *et al.*, 2005).

Key developmental findings have also been reported. For example, alpha wave slowing among children and adolescents has been associated with later delinquency, particularly with thefts (Lindberg *et al.*, 2005). Also, increased age 15 slow-wave EEG activity and decreased autonomic reactivity predicted age 24 criminality in a prospective longitudinal study of 101 male schoolchildren (Raine *et al.*, 1990a, 1990b). EEG abnormalities may reflect cortical immaturity – a developmental lag in those prone to recidivistic crime (Herpertz, 2007). Additionally, emotion regulation deficits, indexed by abnormal frontal EEG asymmetry, may contribute to antisociality as atypical right > left hemispheric frontal EEG activation has been associated with antisocial/externalising behaviour problems in children and adults (Ishikawa & Raine, 2002).

The event-related potential (ERP) refers to averaged changes in the electrical activity of the brain in response to specific stimuli. Several ERP components appear to be biological markers for antisociality. For example, the P300 (a positive-going waveform occurring approximately 300 milliseconds after a stimulus; Ishikawa & Raine, 2002) is thought to represent deployment of neural resources to task-relevant information, and reductions in P300 amplitude have been traditionally associated with forms of antisocial behaviour in both adolescents and adults (Bernat *et al.*, 2007; Herpertz, 2007). In a recent meta-analysis, Gao and Raine (2009)

also found longer P300 latencies to be associated with general antisocial behaviour, although amplitude effects appeared less prominent in psychopaths. Indeed, overall *increased* P300 amplitude was observed in psychopaths on complex tasks, possibly reflecting increased callosal volume (Polich & Hoffman, 1998; Raine *et al.*, 2003a). Additionally, violent but not non-violent offending has been negatively associated with P300 amplitude (Bernat *et al.*, 2007). Reduced P300 evoked potentials also appear to characterise impulsive but not premeditated aggression (Barratt *et al.*, 1997).

Developmentally, P300 amplitude decreases from childhood through adolescence, and its sensitivity as a putative marker for antisociality may vary with age (Gao & Raine, 2009). For example, Polich *et al.* (1994) found reduced P300 amplitudes only in males with a pre-adulthood family history of alcoholism, while Bauer and Hesselbrock (1999) found reduced P300 amplitudes in conduct-disordered adolescents younger than 16.5 years. Prospective studies of P300-antisocial relationships are rare. In one such study increased N1 amplitudes and faster P300 latencies to warning stimuli at age 15 predicted criminality at age 24 (Raine *et al.*, 1990c). Iacono *et al.* (2002) similarly observed that reduced P300 amplitude at age 17 predicted the development of substance use disorders at age 20. Though these findings appear somewhat mixed, Gao and Raine's (2009) meta-analysis found a trend for younger antisocials to have twice as large a deficit in P300 amplitudes compared to older antisocials.

Other ERP components have demonstrated relationships with antisociality. Adult psychopaths have shown reduced frontal N275 amplitudes (thought to reflect response inhibition) during the Go/NoGo task (Kiehl *et al.*, 2000) and reduced N300 amplitudes (thought to be particularly sensitive to affective features of stimuli) while processing positively and negatively valenced emotional faces (Campalla *et al.*, 2005). In aggregate, psychophysiological contributions to the understanding of crime have been noteworthy, although much remains to be learned about developmental progressions of antisociality by examining the dynamic interface between psychological and physiological processes.

Endocrinology

Neurobiological research has also explored associations between antisocial behaviour and common hormones such as cortisol (a glucocorticoid stress reactivity hormone) and testosterone (a sex hormone that is part of the hypothalamic–pituitary–gonadal [HPG] axis). In adults, reduced cortisol levels have characterised violent adults (Virkkunen, 1985) and psychopathic offenders (Cima et al., 2008; Holi et al., 2006). In children and adolescents, low cortisol levels have been associated with aggression (McBurnett et al., 2000), externalising behaviour and low anxiety (van Goozen et al., 1998), conduct disorder symptomatology (McBurnett et al., 2000; Oosterlaan et al., 2005; Pajer et al., 2001) and callous-unemotional traits (Loney et al., 2006). In one five-year longitudinal study, Shoal and colleagues (2003) found reduced cortisol in pre-adolescent boys (age 10–12 years) to be associated with low harm-avoidance, low self-control and increased aggression later in adolescence (age 15–17 years). Lower levels of cortisol may suggest reduced responsivity to stressors which in turn leads to decreased fear of negative consequences such as potential punishment.

Evidence for an association between testosterone and aggressive behaviour has also been reported, a line of inquiry largely based upon the higher male-to-female ratios of antisocial behaviour (e.g. about 4:1 for antisocial personality disorder and as large as 10:1 for violent crimes; van Honk & Schutter, 2007), along with the several-fold increase in testosterone levels in men compared to women. In adults, elevated testosterone levels have been linked to antisocial behaviour and violent crime (Banks & Dabbs, 1996; Dabbs et al., 1987); however, studies of aggressive children and adolescents have yielded mixed results (Loney et al., 2006; Maras et al., 2003; Pajer et al., 2006). It has been suggested that testosterone may not be linked specifically to aggression, but rather to social dominance (Archer, 2006), which may account for discrepant findings. Either way, antisocial behavioural studies based in endocrinology form an important sector of neurobiological research into crime development.

Moral Development

Neurobiological research has increasingly focused upon moral development – which emphasises the role of emotion in moral socialisation (Kochanska, 1994) – as an alternative theoretical framework for understanding the initiation and progression of antisocial behaviour over the lifespan. Impaired moral development may result from neurobiological dysfunction, which – when beginning in early childhood – prevents some individuals from successfully passing through critical moral developmental stages. It has been hypothesised that it is the *emotional* component of moral decision making that is impaired in antisocial individuals (Raine & Yang, 2006). Whereas basic cognitive processes involved in moral decision making may be intact, it may be the *feeling* of what is moral that is deficient in antisocial groups.

Many of the regions involved in moral decision making – including the medial and ventromedial prefrontal cortex (VMPFC – also known as the orbitofrontal cortex), posterior cingulate, angular gyrus and amygdala – have been found to be impaired in adult antisocial groups (Raine & Yang, 2006), suggesting that antisocial individuals may have deficits in the online processing of moral stimuli. The medial and ventromedial prefrontal cortex have been implicated in moral tasks, including the viewing of pictures depicting moral violations (Harenski & Hamann, 2006; Moll et al., 2002b), morally disgusting statements (Moll et al., 2005), making judgements about auditory moral sentences (Oliveira-Sousa & Moll, 2000), moral decision making versus semantic decision making (Heekeren et al., 2003), judgement on moral actions (Borg et al., 2006), sensitivity to moral issues (Robertson et al., 2007), difficult versus easy moral dilemmas, personal versus impersonal moral dilemmas, and utilitarian moral decision making (e.g. sacrificing life for the greater good) versus 'non-utilitarian' decision making (e.g. prohibiting a loss of life even though more lives could be saved) (Greene et al., 2004). It has been hypothesised that the medial prefrontal cortex is important in moral judgement because it may be involved in processing the emotional and social component of moral stimuli, and assessing the perspectives of the self and others (Ochsner et al., 2005). The ventromedial prefrontal region may be important in integrating moral knowledge with emotional cues, understanding the emotional states of others and inhibiting antisocial impulses. In addition to its role in moral development, the ventromedial prefrontal cortex appears to be involved in the process of moral decision making, as patients who incur damage to this region as adults exhibit impairments in moral decision making (Koenigs et al., 2007).

The angular gyrus, posterior cingulate and amygdala are also commonly activated in moral judgement tasks. The angular gyrus may be important in complex social cognition and linking emotional experiences to moral appraisals (Moll et al., 2005); the posterior cingulate in the recall of emotional memories (Maratos et al., 2001), the experience of emotion (Mayberg *et al.*, 1999) and self-referencing (Johnson *et al.*, 2006). The amygdala is important in generating an emotional response to aversive stimuli (LeDoux, 2000). As reviewed above, these and other regions have been found to be impaired in antisocial groups. Furthermore, individuals with frontotemporal dementia, a progressive neurodegenerative disorder affecting the frontal and temporal lobes, demonstrate disrupted moral behaviour – suggesting that impairments in these regions can also result in immoral behaviour (Mendez, 2006).

Neurobiological research of moral judgement in children and adults has led to the formulation of three hypothesised pathways to impaired moral development, involving key components to proper moral socialisation. The first is fear conditioning (Lykken, 1995). Psychopaths demonstrate impairments in this process (Patrick, 1994), indicated by reduced skin conductance responses in anticipation of shock (Lykken, 1957) and reduced fear potentiated startle (Patrick *et al.*, 1993). Birbaumer *et al.* (2005), using functional magnetic resonance imaging (fMRI), found that criminal psychopaths failed to show normal activations in the amygdala, ventromedial prefrontal cortex, insula and anterior cingulate during fear conditioning, and exhibited no skin conductance responses – suggesting deficits in the fear conditioning neural circuitry critical to moral development.

A second component is empathy, or the affective response to another's distress (Blair, 1995), which develops as the mental representation of a moral transgression (i.e. causing another harm) – through stimulus-reinforcement learning – generates an aversive emotional response. Children with callous-unemotional traits have demonstrated reduced recognition of distress cues in others, such as sad and fearful facial expressions (Blair, 1997; Blair *et al.*, 2001, 1997) and fearful vocalisations (Blair *et al.*, 2002), and show autonomic impairments in responsiveness to these cues (Aniskiewicz, 1979; Blair, 1999). Children with callous-unemotional traits have also demonstrated reduced amygdala activity to fearful facial expressions and amygdala/orbitofrontal connectivity reductions associated with callous-unemotional trait severity (Marsh *et al.*, 2008). Blair (2007) argues that the integrative functioning of the amygdala and orbitofrontal cortex enables the basics of care-based morality.

The third component is somatic marker generation. Somatic markers, or bodily signals, are argued to critically guide emotional decision making (Damasio, 1994). The somatic marker reflects the previous reward/punishment history associated with a behavioural act

(e.g. individuals will develop an anticipatory skin conductance response when contemplating a previously risky or disadvantageous action), and is thought to be generated with orbitofrontal cortex involvement. Impaired somatic marker generation is evidenced by individuals with orbitofrontal lesions who choose disadvantageously on the gambling task (a paradigm which simulates real-life decisions in terms of uncertainty, reward, and punishment), and fail to develop anticipatory skin conductance responses before selecting disadvantageous responses (Bechara *et al.*, 1999). In all, these studies demonstrate how the alternative theoretical framework of moral development may be particularly useful in understanding antisocial behavioural development.

Nutrition

There is growing recognition that along with other neurobiological risk factors, poor nutrition represents a potentially important risk factor for the development of antisocial behaviour in children and adults. Longitudinal studies have shown that increased aggression and attention deficits in childhood are related to malnutrition during infancy (Galler & Ramsey, 1989; Galler *et al.*, 1983a, 1983b). Vitamin and mineral deficiencies appear to be related to increased aggression, as evidenced by epidemiological studies (Breakey, 1997; Werbach, 1992) and investigations of individuals with histories of aggressive behaviour. For instance, Rosen *et al.* (1985) reported that one-third of incarcerated juvenile delinquents suffered from iron-deficient anaemia, while others have found violence-prone, assaultive young males to have elevated copper/zinc blood ratios (indicating zinc deficiencies; Cunnane, 1988) compared with individuals with no history of assaultive behaviour (Walsh *et al.*, 1997). Furthermore, Neugebauer *et al.* (1999) found male offspring of women nutritionally deprived during the first and second trimesters of pregnancy (the period of most rapid fetal brain growth) to have 2.5 times the normal rate of antisocial personality disorder in adulthood.

Studies have also implicated low levels of omega-3 long chain essential fatty acid in antisocial behaviour. For instance, Corrigan *et al.* (1994) found reduced blood levels of omega-3 essential fatty acids in violent offenders compared to non-criminals. This is consistent with other reports suggesting that violent offenders have abnormalities in essential fatty acid metabolism (Hibbeln *et al.*, 1998; Virkkunen *et al.*, 1987). Other studies have examined whether increased consumption of fish rich in omega-3 essential fatty acids is related to lower levels of violent and aggressive behaviour. For instance, Iribarren *et al.* (2004) reported an association between greater intake of seafood high in omega-3 fatty acids and lower hostility scores in 3381 male and female adults. In a larger sample of 14,541 pregnant women, mothers who ate more fish during pregnancy had off-spring who showed significantly higher levels of proso-cial behaviour at age 7 years (Hallahan *et al.*, 2007). In addition, a cross-national study of 26 counties observed a correlation of −0.63 between homicide rates and sea-food consumption; countries with higher fish consump-tion had lower homicide rates (Hibbeln, 2001).

Experimental studies have provided more compelling evidence. A recent longitudinal prospective investigation (Liu *et al.*, 2004) demonstrated that children with iron, zinc or protein deficiencies at age 3 had greater external-ising behaviour problems at ages 8, 11 and 17, even after controlling for multiple indicators of psychosocial adversity. In comparison to controls, malnourished chil-dren at age 3 were more aggressive or hyperactive at age 8 and had more externalising behaviour at age 11 and greater conduct disorder and excessive motor activity at age 17. Moreover, a dose-response relationship was found between the extent of malnutrition at age 3 and behaviour problems at ages 8 and 17.

Additionally, research is converging on the idea that malnutrition predisposes to brain dysfunction, and in turn to antisocial behaviour throughout childhood and adolescence (Liu & Raine, 2006; Liu *et al.*, 2004, 2005), an idea which has received support from several studies (Gallagher *et al.*, 2005; Liu *et al.*, 2004, 2006; Nakagawasai *et al.*, 2006; Young & Leyton, 2002). For example, in one study poor nutrition was found to impair cognitive functioning (IQ) which in turn was found to predispose to later antisocial behaviour (Liu *et al.*, 2004). Clearly, nutrition research – along with other key neuro-biological approaches – has a significant role to play in elucidating the important aetiological mechanisms of criminality, and potentially in reducing criminal offending.

Forensic Applications of Developmental Neurobiological Research

The potential importance within criminal justice systems of developmental neurobiological crime research is sig-nificant. Although technological advances have allowed for new and exciting neurobiological approaches to antisocial behavioural research, forensic applications of biological risk factors for crime are not a novel idea and have their roots in the writings of early positivist crimi-nology (Lombroso, 1876). Thus, of importance to the clinical practitioner is an understanding of how neuro-biological research has to date impacted various facets of criminal justice systems, and how future forensic prac-tice may rely more and more heavily upon neurobio-logical assessment – which can inform policies and procedures regarding the identification, management and treatment of various forms of adult and juvenile offending. More crucial, however, is a thorough under-standing of its limitations and of the philosophical, ethical and political dilemmas surrounding its use in the service of justice.

Lie detection

The detection of deception is among the first practical applications of neurobiological measures to the crimi-nal justice system. The polygraph ('lie detector') is the earliest and most well-known physiological measure of lie detection (Trovillo, 1939) and is based upon the assumption that autonomic responses (e.g. increased heart rate, blood pressure, respiration rate and skin con-ductance response) during questioning indicate anxiety and therefore lying. Polygraph techniques include the control question technique (CQT), directed lie tech-nique (DLT) and guilty knowledge test (GKT). Despite the presumably unfalsifiable nature of psychophysio-logical indicators of deception, and vehement propo-nents for its use among law enforcement and national security policy makers, polygraph lie-detection is gener-ally considered by scientists to be fraught with concep-tual and methodological weaknesses, and polygraph evidence has generally been excluded from the courts (Iacono, 2007; Iacono & Patrick, 2006).

More recently, an interest in brain-based methods for detecting deception has developed. The most promising line of inquiry has focused on ERP components – particularly the P300 response to significant, infrequent (i.e. 'oddball') stimuli. In a P300-based GKT procedure, crime-relevant information keys constitute the oddball stimuli. Several validation studies of the ERP-GKT appear to indicate its effectiveness, and potential utility within the court system has been noted (Iacono & Patrick, 2006). Neuroimaging approaches to lie detection have also generated recent interest, although the complexities of the structural and functional correlates of deception must be considered. For example, while the first evidence for structural brain abnormalities in pathological liars (i.e. prefrontal grey matter reductions and *increased* inferior, middle and orbitofrontal white matter) has been reported (Yang *et al.*, 2005, 2007), a recent review of 15 functional imaging studies (Sip *et al.*, 2007) indicates multiple areas of cortical and subcortical activation during deception – although dorsolateral prefrontal activation appeared most common across studies (i.e. in 9 out of 15). This, along with the conceptual and methodological issues that bedevilled the old technology, must still be resolved before neuroimaging may become a viable approach to lie detection (Sip *et al.*, 2007).

Neuropsychological tests have demonstrated utility in the detection of another form of deception – malingering. On intelligence tests, malingering can be detected by an unusual scatter of scores, failing/passing items that legitimate responders would tend to pass/fail, and 'approximately correct' answers. Malingerers appear unable to mimic the performance of brain-injured patients on memory assessments, and often score well below the level of chance on 'forced-choice' tests. Also, malingering may be detected via the evaluation of consistency across measures of common constructs and/or across repetitions of administrations (Ackerman, 1999). Together, these methods demonstrate how neurobiological approaches may soon have much to offer in the way of deception-detection for forensic purposes.

Legal and judicial process

Structural and functional brain imaging have already begun to impact the legal system (Yang *et al.*, 2008). Feigenson (2006) reports that approximately 130 court cases have admitted brain imaging data into evidence, a large number considering that the technique has only become more accessible in the past few years – possibly reflecting the belief that brain imaging represents an objective assessment of a defendant's mental functioning. Generally speaking, brain abnormalities as indicated by imaging data have been used to argue for reduced criminal responsibility, and outcomes of homicide cases incorporating this approach have varied, from successful NGRI defences, to sentencing mitigation (i.e. life imprisonment versus death penalty), to failure resulting in guilty verdicts and death sentencing. Though the potential implications of brain imaging within the legal system may seem significant, numerous limitations remain – including the inability of this technique to provide retrospective functional information (i.e. brain

functioning at the time of the crime), and the subjectivity of structural interpretations (Yang *et al.*, 2008).

Neuropsychological measures may also have utility in the legal system. For example, a diagnosis of mental retardation (MR) – determined largely by sub-average intellectual functioning (i.e. IQ < 70) can significantly mitigate sentencing outcomes for murder defendants (specifically death penalty candidates), and may now become a key component of pre-trial competency to stand trial evaluations (Dwyer & Frierson, 2006). Additionally, neurotransmitter functioning has been introduced as evidence to support an insanity defence (Berman & Coccaro, 1998). In sum, the practical application of developmental neurobiological crime research in informing legal and judicial processes is still in its incipient stages and while replication of current findings is needed to allow for more widespread acceptance and implementation, it nonetheless demonstrates significant potential.

Assessment

Initial evidence suggests that neurobiological measures may enhance specificity and effectiveness in key areas of future forensic assessment (Popma & Raine, 2006).

Diagnostic identification

Biological factors may help extend the available range of diagnostic possibilities, assist in identifying difficult-to-assess psychobiological deficits (e.g. using blunted heart rate reactivity rather than self-report measures to identify psychopathic traits, or brain imaging to identify pathological lying or malingering), and increase diagnostic specificity by reducing group heterogeneity within forensic-related psychopathologies. For example, researchers are attempting to identify differential neurobiological profiles of aggression subtypes (e.g. reactive versus proactive; Popma & Raine, 2006). Effective diagnostic identification is crucial within forensic arenas, and developmental neurobiological crime research may soon contribute to increased diagnostic capabilities.

Treatment

Neurobiological assessment approaches which reduce diagnostic heterogeneity may also contribute to improved forensic pharmacological interventions. For example, certain biological types of clinical aggression (i.e. impulsive, as opposed to premeditated) may be more amenable to pharmacological treatment (Moeller & Swann, 2007), whereas a biological subset of disruptive behaviour-disordered children (i.e. with low cortisol stress responsivity) have been associated with poor treatment outcome (Van de Wiel *et al.*, 2004). Additionally, certain stimulants (e.g. methylphenidate), which increase arousal and reduce aggressive behaviour (Connor, 2002), may have direct applications within forensic settings.

Furthermore, given the limited financial and staffing resources within correctional settings, clinical decisions must be made regarding the allocation of these resources to those offenders who will most benefit. Developmental neurobiological research may assist in determining the most viable treatment candidates. For example, Moffitt's (1993) theory differentiates life-course persistent from *adolescence-limited* offending – a normative, late-onset and largely desisting form of antisocial behaviour originating in social mimicry. As such, cognitive-behavioural strategies targeting desistence-related needs (Gendreau *et al.*, 2006) may be ideal for adolescence-limited but not life-course persistent offenders; and knowledge of characteristic adolescence-limited or life-course persistent developmental histories in juveniles may help forensic practitioners identify those with a potentially better prognosis within criminal justice systems. Alternatively, some offenders with characteristic neurobiological profiles (i.e. psychopaths) may not benefit from non-pharmacological programmes such as therapeutic communities. In fact, these programmes have led to increased violent recidivism in psychopaths (essentially making them worse), although recent views are more optimistic (McGauley *et al.*, 2007). Nonetheless, knowledge of treatment-resistant psychopathologies may contribute to more efficient use of limited criminal justice system time and monies.

Other non-pharmacological approaches such as nutritional interventions may be more suitable for reducing antisocial behaviour within incarcerated populations. For example, Schoenthaler *et al.* (1997) found that vitamin and mineral supplementation significantly reduced antisocial behaviour by 28 per cent among incarcerated juvenile delinquents (in 16 of 26 subjects, violent acts were reduced by over 90 per cent), along with improving brain function and reducing electrocortical abnormalities – success which prompted the State of California legislature to amend the Health and Welfare Code to determine if replication was possible among adult male prisoners. In another randomised, double-blind, placebo-controlled trial of 231 English prisoners (Gesch *et al.*, 2002), omega-3 essential fatty acid and multivitamin/mineral treatment for 142 days

produced a significant 26.3 per cent reduction in antisocial and aggressive behaviour, and a 37 per cent decrease in serious (including violent) offences. While many interventions for criminal behaviour are time, labour and cost intensive, nutritional interventions may offer a successful, easily implemented, and cost-effective approach for reducing antisocial behaviour in violent populations.

Intervention

Novel non-pharmacological interventions which consider and even alter biological vulnerabilities to juvenile antisocial behaviour also appear promising. For example, biofeedback may be an effective method for increasing physiological arousal in children with attention deficit hyperactivity disorder (Monastra, 2008); and non-pharmacological foster care interventions which normalise abnormally flattened diurnal cortisol-level patterns (Fisher *et al.*, 2007) may reduce aggression associated with these patterns in juveniles (Murray-Close *et al.*, 2008). Additionally, child studies have shown that daily vitamin, mineral and omega-3 essential fatty acid supplementation can reduce antisocial behaviour as much as 47 per cent in four months (Schoenthaler & Bier, 2000; Stevens *et al.*, 2003), though results have not always been consistent (e.g. Hirayama *et al.*, 2004). Early nutritional guidance (Olds *et al.* 1998) and enrichment programmes have also successfully reduced crime and antisocial behaviour. One randomised controlled trial (Raine *et al.*, 2003b) demonstrated that environmental enrichment consisting of better nutrition, cognitive stimulation and increased physical exercise from ages 3 to 5 years significantly reduced antisociality at age 17 years and criminality at age 23 years. The fact that the prevention programme was more effective in children with poor nutritional status prior to study entry suggests that better nutrition was an active ingredient in the programme. This environmental enrichment was also shown to produce long-term improvements in arousal and psychophysiological information processing (Raine *et al.*, 2003b). In fact, biological parameters – useful in devising forensic treatment/intervention approaches – may also be useful in evaluating these approaches (i.e. assessing a certain biological profile that is correlated with behavioural problems before and after treatment/intervention as a measure of outcome; Popma & Raine, 2006). In all, developmental neurobiological research has potentially much to offer in the way of informing the treatment and prevention of crime.

Dangerousness and risk prediction

Biological parameters may also be useful in predicting the risk of future antisocial behaviour (Popma & Raine, 2006). For example, low IQ and high antisociality have been described as components of dangerousness, and these factors have differentiated death-row from life-sentence male murderers (Heilbrun, 1990). Other neuropsychological deficits associated with psychopathy (Hiatt & Newman, 2006) could be used as indices of risk, as elevated psychopathy ratings (i.e. *Psychopathy Checklist – Revised*; Hare, 2003) are the strongest known actuarial predictors of criminal recidivism (Quinsey *et al.*, 1999). Low levels of cerebrospinal 5-HIAA (a serotonin metabolite) have differentiated recidivistic violent offenders from non-recidivists (Virkkunen *et al.*, 1989), while other neurobiological measures, such as penile plethysmography, have shown some promise in differentiating child molesters from other sex offenders and non-offenders, non-familial child molesters from incest offenders, and homicidal child molesters from non-homicidal child molesters and non-offenders – though this technique has drawn criticism from the scientific community (Bourget & Bradford, 2008). The prediction of dangerousness and assessment of risk is among the gravest and most imperative roles of the forensic practitioner, and developmental neurobiological research may soon help to increase the capabilities of those called upon to do so.

Though the contributions of neurobiological research to forensic assessment remain largely hypothetical, first evidence appears promising, and further research is both feasible and warranted. Enormous efforts must, however, be undertaken to understand and address the significant philosophical, ethical and political issues – largely centred in arguments of biological determinism versus free will – inherent to neurobiological applications within criminal justice systems (Popma & Raine, 2006; Yang *et al.*, 2008), particularly as forensic psychology may one day be faced with issues such as state-sponsored pre-emptive interventions which deny individual civil liberties, and even implanted behaviour-controlling neurotechnologies. However, underlying these very real and legitimate concerns is perhaps an antiquated notion of the biological nature of crime. For while Lombroso's legacy continues, its foundation has been shaken – we have since learned through developmental neurobiological crime research that biology is not destiny, and that physical properties of mind and body in the criminal can in fact be alterable.

Conclusions

Key areas of neurobiological research have contributed to a greater empirical understanding of the initiation, maintenance and potential desistance from criminal behaviour. This body of research has also served to inform prominent developmental perspectives of crime. In turn, applications of neurobiological crime research and developmental theories of crime have both become essential to the field of forensic psychology. As such, the three – developmental theories of crime, neurobiological research and forensic applications – are inextricably bound, each serving both to inform and benefit from the other. It is hoped that this interdependence of theory, research and practice will contribute to a growing base of evidence from which the causes and cures of criminality will eventually be revealed.

Further Reading

Lorber, M.F. (2004). Psychophysiology of aggression, psychopathy, and conduct problems: A meta-analysis. *Psychological Bulletin, 130*(4), 531–552.

A meta-analysis of 95 studies was conducted to examine the relationships between three measures of heart rate (HR) and electrodermal activity (EDA) – resting, task and reactivity – and three types of antisocial spectrum behaviour – aggression, psychopathy and conduct problems. Results indicated multiple interactive effects, with an inability in some cases to generalise across antisocial spectrum behaviours. Low resting and task EDA were both associated with psychopathy and conduct problems, though EDA reactivity was positively associated with aggression and negatively associated with psychopathy. Both low resting HR and high HR reactivity were associated with aggression and conduct problems. In some cases, physiology–behaviour relationships varied with age and stimulus valence. Results are considered to have important empirical and clinical implications.

Moffitt, T.E., Lynam, D.R. & Silva, P.A. (1994). Neuropsychological tests predicting persistent male delinquency. *Criminology, 32*(2), 277–300.

This longitudinal study examined data from a birth cohort of several hundred New Zealand males, ages 13–18, to see if prospective measures of neuropsychological status predict antisocial outcomes. Subjects were administered an extensive neuropsychological battery at age 13 which included verbal, visuospatial and executive function measures. Results indicated that neuropsychological performance at age 13 predicted delinquency at age 18 (measured by official police and court records and self-report inventories) for persistent, high-level offending beginning in pre-adolescence. Findings were strongest for verbal measures, and visuospatial and mental flexibility executive function tasks did not demonstrate these relationships. In contrast, however, age 13 neuropsychological performance appeared unrelated to adolescent-onset offending. Results are considered the first longitudinal neuropsychological evidence for a previously proposed developmental taxon of antisocial behaviour in children and adolescents.

Raine, A., Mellingen, K., Liu, J.H., Venables, P.H. & Mednick, S.A. (2003). Effects of environmental enrichment at 3–5 years on schizotypal personality and antisocial behavior at ages 17 and 23 years. *American Journal of Psychiatry, 160,* 1627–1635.
In this study, the authors evaluated whether a 2-year nutritional, educational and physical exercise programme for children at ages 3 to 5 reduced rates of schizotypal personality and antisocial behaviour when subjects were 17 and 23 years of age. Children who participated in the enrichment programme were matched on temperament, nutritional, cognitive, autonomic and demographic variables with a control group of children who experienced standard community conditions. Schizotypal personality and antisocial behaviour were assessed through both self-report and objective measures (e.g. court records) when subjects were 17 and 23 years of age. Subjects assigned to the enrichment programme at ages 3 to 5 had significantly lower scores for both schizotypal personality and antisocial behaviour at age 17, and for criminal behaviour at age 23. Children who were malnourished at age 3 benefited more from the enrichment, especially in relation to scores for schizotypal personality and conduct disorder at age 17, and schizotypal personality at age 23. Results add to the growing literature on the beneficial effects of an enriched environment on psychological and behavioural outcomes, and have implications for prevention efforts for schizophrenia and criminal behaviour.

References

Ackerman, M.J. (1999). *Essentials of forensic psychological assessment.* New York: John Wiley & Sons.

Aguilar, B., Sroufe, A., Egeland, B. & Carlson, E. (2000). Distinguishing the early-onset/persistent and adolescent-onset antisocial behavior types: From birth to 16 years. *Development and Psychopathology, 12,* 109–132.

Anderson, S.W., Bechara, A., Damasio, H., Tranel, D. & Damasio, A.R. (1999). Impairment of social and moral behavior related to early damage in human prefrontal cortex. *Nature Neuroscience, 2,* 1031–1037.

Andrews, T.K., Rose, F.D. & Johnson, D.A. (1998). Social and behavioural effects of traumatic brain injury in children. *Brain Injury, 12,* 133–138.

Aniskiewicz, A.S. (1979). Autonomic components of vicarious conditioning and psychopathy. *Journal of Clinical Psychology, 35,* 60–67.

Archer, J. (2006). Testosterone and human aggression: An evaluation of the challenge hypothesis. *Neuroscience and Biobehavioral Reviews, 30,* 319–345.

Banks, T. & Dabbs, J.J.M. (1996). Salivary testosterone and cortisol in a delinquent and violent urban subculture. *Journal of Social Psychology, 136,* 49–56.

Barkataki, I., Kumari, V., Das, M., Taylor, P. & Sharma, T. (2006). Volumetric structural brain abnormalities in men with schizophrenia or antisocial personality disorder. *Behavioural Brain Research, 169,* 239–247.

Barratt, E.S., Stanford, M.S., Felthous, A.R. & Kent, T.A. (1997). The effects of phenytoin on impulsive and premeditated aggression: A controlled study. *Journal of Clinical Psychopharmacology, 17,* 341–349.

Barker, E.D., Séguin, J.R., White, H.R., Bates, M.E., Lacourse, E., Carbonneau, R. *et al.* (2007). Developmental trajectories of male physical violence and theft: Relations to neurocognitive performance. *Archives of General Psychiatry, 64,* 592–599.

Bauer, L.O. & Hesselbrock, V.M. (1999). P300 decrements in teenagers with conduct problems: Implications for substance abuse risk and brain development. *Biological Psychiatry, 46,* 263–272.

Bechara, A., Damasio, H., Damasio, A.R. & Lee, G.P. (1999). Different contributions of the human amygdala and ventromedial prefrontal cortex to decision-making. *Journal of Neuroscience, 19,* 5473–5481.

Berman, M.E. & Coccaro, E.F. (1998). Neurobiologic correlates of violence: Relevance to criminal responsibility. *Behavioral Sciences and the Law, 16,* 303–318.

Bernat, E.M., Hall, J.R., Steffen, B.V. & Patrick, C.J. (2007). Violent offending predicts P300 amplitude. *International Journal of Psychophysiology, 66,* 161–167.

Bigler, E.D. (2001). Frontal lobe pathology and antisocial personality disorder. *Archives of General Psychiatry, 58,* 609–611.

Birbaumer, N., Viet, R., Lotze, M., Erb, M., Hermann, C., Grodd, W., *et al.* (2005). Deficient fear conditioning in psychopathy: A functional magnetic resonance imaging study. *Archives of General Psychiatry, 62,* 799–805.

Blair, R.J. (1995). A cognitive developmental approach to morality: Investigating the psychopath. *Cognition, 57,* 1–29.

Blair, R.J. (1997). Moral reasoning in the child with psychopathic tendencies. *Personality and Individual Differences, 22,* 731–739.

Blair, R.J. (1999). Responsiveness to distress cues in children with psychopathic tendencies. *Personality and Individual Differences, 27,* 135–145.

Blair, R.J.R. (2006). The emergence of psychopathy: Implications for the neuropsychological approach to developmental disorders. *Cognition, 101,* 414–442.

Blair, R.J. (2007). The amygdala and ventromedial prefrontal cortex in morality and psychopathy. *Trends in Cognitive Science, 11,* 387–392.

Blair, R.J., Colledge, E., Murray, L. & Mitchell, D.G.V. (2001). A selective impairment in the processing of sad and fearful facial expressions in children with psychopathic tendencies. *Journal of Abnormal Child Psychology, 29,* 491–498.

Blair, R.J. & Frith, U. (2000). Neurocognitive explanations of the antisocial personality disorders. *Criminal Behaviour and Mental Health, 10,* S66–S81.

Blair, R.J., Jones, L., Clark, F. & Smith, M. (1997). The psychopathic individual: A lack of responsiveness to distress cues. *Psychophysiology, 34,* 192–198.

Blair, R.J., Mitchell, D.G.V., Richell, R.A., Kelly, S., Leonard, A., Newman, C., *et al.* (2002). Turning a deaf ear to fear: Impaired recognition of vocal affect in psychopathic individuals. *Journal of Abnormal Psychology, 111,* 682–686.

Blair, K.S., Newman, C., Mitchell, D.G.V., Richell, R.A., Leonard, A., Morton, J. *et al.* (2006). Differentiating among prefrontal substrates in psychopathy: Neuropsychological test findings. *Neuropsychology, 20,* 153–165.

Blake, P.Y., Pincus, J.H. & Buckner, C. (1995). Neurologic abnormalities in murderers. *Neurology, 45,* 1641–1647.

Borg, J.S., Hynes, C., Van Horn, J., Grafton, S. & Sinnott-Armstrong, W. (2006). Consequences, action, and intention as factors in moral judgments: An fMRI investigation. *Journal of Cognitive Neuroscience, 18,* 803–817.

Bourget, D. & Bradford, J.M.W. (2008). Evidential basis for the assessment and treatment of sex offenders. *Brief Treatment and Crisis Intervention, 8,* 130–146.

Breakey, J. (1997). The role of diet and behaviour in childhood. *Journal of Paediatrics and Child Health, 33,* 190–194.

Brennan, P.A., Hall, J., Bor, W., Najman, J.M. & Williams, G. (2003). Integrating biological and social processes in relation to early-onset persistent aggression in boys and girls. *Developmental Psychology, 39,* 309–323.

Brennan, P.A., Raine, A., Schulsinger, F., Kirkegaard-Sorense, L., Knop, J., Hutchings, B. *et al.* (1997). Psychophysiological protective factors for male subjects at high risk for criminal behavior. *American Journal of Psychiatry, 154,* 853–855.

Broomhall, L. (2005). Acquired sociopathy: A neuropsychological study of executive dysfunction in violent offenders. *Psychiatry, Psychology, and Law, 12,* 367–387.

Campalla, S., Vanhoolandt, M.E. & Philippot, P. (2005). Emotional deficit in subjects with psychopathic tendencies as assessed by the Minnesota Multiphasic Personality Inventory-2, an event-related potentials study. *Neuroscience Letters, 373,* 26–31.

Caspi, A., McClay, J., Moffitt, T. E., Mill, J., Martin, J., Craig, I.W. *et al.* (2002). Role of genotype in the cycle of violence in maltreated children. *Science, 297,* 851–854.

Cima, M., Smeets, T. & Jelicic, M. (2008). Self-reported trauma, cortisol levels, and aggression in psychopathic and non-psychoathic prison inmates. *Biological Psychiatry, 78,* 75–86.

Connor, D.F. (2002). *Aggression and antisocial behavior in children and adolescents.* New York: Guilford Press.

Corrigan, F., Gray, R., Strathdee, A., Skinner, R., Van Rhijn, A., Horrobin, D. (1994). Fatty acid analysis of blood from violent offenders. *Journal of Forensic Psychiatry, 5,* 83–92.

Cunnane, S.C. (1988). *Zinc: Clinical and biochemical significance.* Boca Raton, FL: CRC Press, Inc.

Dabbs, J.M., Frady, R.L. & Carr, T.S. (1987). Saliva testosterone and criminal violence in young adult prison inmates. *Psychosomatic Medicine, 49,* 174–182.

Damasio, A.R. (1994). *Descartes' error: Emotion, reason, and the human brain.* New York: GP Putnam's Sons.

Damasio, A.R., Tranel, D., & Damasio, H. (1990). Individuals with sociopathic behavior caused by frontal damage fail to respond autonomically to social stimuli. *Behavioural Brain Research, 41,* 81–94.

Dinn, W.M. & Harris, C.L. (2000). Neurocognitive function in antisocial personality disorder. *Psychiatry Research, 97,* 173–190.

Dolan, M. & Park, I. (2002). The neuropsychology of antisocial personality disorder. *Psychological Medicine, 32,* 417–427.

Dwyer, R.G. & Frierson, R.L. (2006). The presence of low IQ and mental retardation among murder defendants referred for pretrial evaluation. *Journal of Forensic Sciences, 51,* 678–682.

Ehrenreich, H., Krampe, H. & Sirén, A.L. (2007). Brain trauma. In A.R. Felthous & H. Saß (Eds.) *International handbook of psychopathic disorders and the law: Vol. 1* (pp.217–236). Chichester: John Wiley & Sons.

Ellenbogen, J.M., Hurford, M.O., Liebskind, D.S., Neimark, G.B. & Weiss, D. (2005). Ventromedial frontal lobe trauma. *Neurology, 64,* 757.

Eriksson, Å, Hodgins, S. & Tengström, A. (2005). Verbal intelligence and criminal offending among men with schizophrenia. *International Journal of Forensic Mental Health, 4,* 191–200.

Evans, J.R. & Park, N.S. (1997). Quantitative EEG findings among men convicted of murder. *Journal of Neurotherapy, 2,* 31–37.

Feigenson, N. (2006). Brain imaging and courtroom evidence; on the admissibility and persuasiveness of fMRI. *International Journal of Law in Context, 2,* 233–255.

Filley, C.M., Price, B.H., Nell, V., Antoinette, T., Morgan, A.S. Bresnahan, J.F. *et al.* (2001). Toward an understanding of violence: Neurobehavioral aspects of unwarranted physical aggression: Aspen Neurobehavioral Conference consensus statement. *Neuropsychiatry, Neuropsychology, and Behavioral Neurology, 14,* 1–14.

Fisher, P.A., Stoolmiller, M., Gunnar, M.R. & Burraston, B.O. (2007). Effects of a therapeutic intervention for foster preschoolers on diurnal cortisol activity. *Psychoneuroendocrinology, 32,* 892–905.

Frick, P.J., Cornell, A.H., Bodin, S.D., Dane, H.E., Barry, C.T. & Loney, B.R. (2003). Callous-unemotional traits and developmental pathways to severe conduct problems. *Developmental Psychology, 39*, 372–378.

Fung, M.T., Raine, A., Loeber, R., Lynam, D.R., Steinhauer, S.R., Venables, P.H. *et al.* (2005). Reduced electrodermal activity in psychopathy-prone adolescents. *Journal of Abnormal Psychology, 114*(2), 187–196.

Gallagher, E.A., Newman, J.P., Green, L.R. & Hanson, M.A. (2005). The effect of low protein diet in pregnancy on the development of brain metabolism in rat offspring. *Journal of Physiology, 568*, 553–558.

Galler, J.R. & Ramsey, F. (1989). A follow-up study of the influence of early malnutrition on development. *Journal of the American Academy of Child and Adolescent Psychiatry, 26*, 23–27.

Galler, J.R., Ramsey, F., Solimano, G. & Lowell, W. (1983b). The influence of early malnutrition on subsequent behavioral development. II. Classroom behavior. *Journal of the American Academy of Child and Adolescent Psychiatry, 22*, 16–22.

Galler, J.R., Ramsey, F., Solimano, G., Lowell, W. & Mason, E. (1983a). The influence of early malnutrition on subsequent behavioural development. I. Degree of impairment of intellectual performance. *Journal of the American Academy of Child and Adolescent Psychiatry, 22*, 8–15.

Gao, Y. & Raine, A. (2009). P3 event-related potential impairments in antisocial and psychopathic individuals: A meta-analysis. *Biological Psychology, 82*, 199–210.

Gatzke-Kopp, L.M., Raine, A., Buchsbaum, M. & LaCasse, L. (2001). Temporal lobe deficits in murderers: EEG findings undetected by PET. *Journal of Neuropsychiatry and Clinical Neuroscience, 13*, 486–491.

Gendreau, P., Goggin, C., French, S. & Smith, P. (2006). Practicing psychology in correctional settings. In I.B. Weiner & A.K. Hess (Eds.) *The handbook of forensic psychology* (3rd edn, pp.722–750). Hoboken, NJ: John Wiley & Sons.

Gesch, C.B., Hammond, S.M., Hampson, S.E., Eves, A. & Crowder, M.J. (2002). Influence of supplementary vitamins, minerals and essential fatty acids on the antisocial behaviour of young adult prisoners: Randomised, placebo-controlled trial. *British Journal of Psychiatry, 181*, 22–28.

Goldman, D. & Ducci, F. (2007). The genetics of psychopathic disorders. In A.R. Felthous & H. Saß (Eds.) *International handbook on psychopathic disorders and the law: Vol. 1* (pp.149–169). Chichester: John Wiley & Sons.

Grafman, J., Schwab, K., Warden, D., Pridgen, A., Brown, H.R. & Salazar, A.M. (1996). Frontal lobe injuries, violence, and aggression: A report of the Vietnam Head Injury Study. *Neurology, 46*, 1231–1238.

Granacher, R.P. & Fozdar, M.A. (2007). Acquired psychopathy and the assessment of traumatic brain injury. In A.R. Felthous & H. Saß (Eds.) *International handbook of psychopathic disorders and the law: Vol. 1* (pp.237–250). Chichester: John Wiley & Sons.

Green, J., Leon-Barth, C., Venus, S. & Lucey, T. (2001). Murder and the EEG. *The Forensic Examiner, 10*, 32–34.

Greene, J.D., Nystrom, L.E., Engell, A.D., Darley, J.M. & Cohen, J. (2004). The neural bases of cognitive conflict and control in moral judgment. *Neuron, 44*, 389–400.

Hallahan, B., Hibbeln, J.R., Davis, J.M. & Garland, M.R. (2007). Omega-3 fatty acid supplementation in patients with recurrent self-harm – single-centre double-blind randomised controlled trial. *British Journal of Psychiatry, 190*, 118–122.

Hare, R.D. (2003). *The Hare Psychopathy Checklist – Revised* (2nd edn). Toronto, ON: Multi-Health Systems.

Harenski, C.L. & Hamann, S. (2006). Neural correlates of regulating negative emotions related to moral violations. *NeuroImage, 30*, 313–324.

Harlow, J.M. (1848). Passage of an iron bar through the head. *Boston Medical Surgery Journal, 13*, 389–393.

Heekeren, H.R., Wartenburger, I., Schmidt, H., Schwintowski, H.P. & Villringer, A. (2003). An fMRI investigation of emotional engagement in moral judgment. *Neuroreport, 14*, 1215–1219.

Heilbrun, A.B. (1990). Differentiation of death-row murderers and life-sentence murderers by antisociality and intelligence measures. *Journal of Personality Assessment, 54*, 617–627.

Herpertz, S.C. (2007). Electrophysiology. In A.R. Felthous & H. Saß (Eds.) *International handbook of psychopathic disorders and the law: Vol. 1* (pp.187–198). Chichester: John Wiley & Sons.

Herpertz, S.C., Mueller, B., Wenning, B. *et al.* (2003). Autonomic responses in boys with externalizing disorders. *Journal of Neural Transmission, 110*, 1181–1195.

Herpertz, S.C., Mueller, B., Qunaibi, M. *et al.* (2005). Emotional responses in boys with conduct disorder. *American Journal of Psychiatry, 162*, 1100–1107.

Hiatt, K.D. & Newman, J.P. (2006). Understanding psychopathy: The cognitive side. In C.J. Patrick (Ed.) *Handbook of psychopathy* (pp.334–352). New York: Guilford Press.

Hibbeln, J.R. (2001). Seafood consumption and homicide mortality: A cross-national ecological analysis. *World Review of Nutrition and Dietetics, 88*, 41–46.

Hibbeln, J.R., Umhau, J.C., Linnoila, M., George, D.T., Ragan, P.W., Shoaf, S.E. *et al.* (1998). A replication study of violent and nonviolent subjects: Cerebrospinal fluid metabolites of serotonin and dopamine are predicted by plasma essential fatty acids. *Biological Psychiatry, 44*, 243–249.

Hirayama, S., Hamazaki, T. & Terasawa, K. (2004). Effect of docosahexaenoic acid-containing food administration on symptoms of attention-deficit/hyperactivity disorder – a placebo-controlled double-blind study. *European Journal of Clinical Nutrition, 58*, 467–473.

Hirono, N., Mega, M.S., Dinov, I.D., Mishkin, F. & Cummings, J.L. (2000). Left frontaltemporal hypoperfusion is associated with aggression in patient with dementia. *Archives Neurology, 57*, 861–866.

Holi, M., Auvinen-Lintunen, L., Lindberg, N., Tani, P. & Virkkunen, M. (2006). Inverse correlation between severity of psychopathic traits and serum cortisol levels in young adult violent male offenders. *Psychopathology, 39,* 102–104.

Iacono, W.G. (2007). Detection of deception. In J.T. Cacioppo, L.G. Tassinary & G.G. Berntson (Eds.) *Handbook of psychophysiology* (3rd edn, pp.688–703), Cambridge: Cambridge University Press.

Iacono, W.G., Carlson, S.R., Malone, S.M. & McGue, M. (2002). P3 event-related potential amplitude and the risk for disinhibitory disorders in adolescent boys. *Archives of General Psychiatry, 59,* 750–757.

Iacono, W.G. & Patrick, C. (2006). Polygraph ('lie detector') testing: Current status and emerging trends. In I.B. Weiner & A.K. Hess (Eds.) *Handbook of forensic psychology* (3rd edn, pp.552–588). Hoboken, NJ: John Wiley & Sons.

Iribarren, C., Markovitz, J.H., Jacobs, D.R., Schreiner, P.J., Daviglus, M. & Hibbeln, J.R. (2004). Dietary intake of n-3, n-6 fatty acids and fish: Relationship with hostility in young adults – the CARDIA study. *European Journal of Clinical Nutrition, 58,* 24–31.

Ishikawa, S.S. & Raine, A. (2002). Psychophysiological correlates of antisocial behavior: A central control hypothesis. In J. Glicksohn (Ed.) *The neurobiology of criminal behavior* (pp.187–229). Norwell, MA: Kluwer Academic.

Ishikawa, S.S., Raine, A., Lencz, T., Bihrle, S. & Lacasse, L. (2001). Autonomic stress reactivity and executive functions in successful and unsuccessful criminal psychopaths from the community. *Journal of Abnormal Psychology, 110,* 423–432.

Johnson, M.K., Raye, C.R., Mitchell, K.J., Touryan, S.R., Greene, E.J. & Nolen-Hoeksema, S. (2006). Dissociating the medial frontal and posterior cingulate activity during self-reflection. *Social, Cognitive, and Affective Neuroscience, 1,* 64.

Juhasz, C., Behen, M.E., Muzik, O., Chugani, D.C. & Chugani, H.T. (2001). Bilateral medial prefrontal and temporal neocortical hypometabolism in children with epilepsy and aggression. *Epilepsia, 42,* 991–1001.

Kiehl, K.A., Smith, A.M., Hare, R.D. & Liddle, P.F. (2000). An event-related potential investigation of response inhibition in schizophrenia and psychopathy. *Biological Psychiatry, 48,* 210–221.

Kiehl, K.A., Smith, A.M., Hare, R.D., Mendrek, A., Forster, B.B., Brink, J. *et al.* (2001). Limbic abnormalities in affective processing by criminal psychopaths as revealed by functional magnetic resonance imaging. *Biological Psychiatry, 50,* 677–684.

Klüver, H. & Bucy, P.C. (1939). Preliminary analysis of functions of the temporal lobes in monkeys. *Archive of Neurological Psychiatry, 42,* 979–100.

Kochanska, G. (1994). Beyond cognition: Expanding the search for the early roots of internalization and conscience. *Developmental Psychology, 30,* 20–22.

Koenigs, M., Young, L., Adolphs, R., Tranel, D., Cushman, F., Hauser, M., *et al.* (2007). Damage to the prefrontal cortex increases utilitarian moral judgements. *Nature, 446,* 908–911.

Kosson, D.H., Miller, S.K., Byrnes, K.A. & Leveroni, C.L. (2007). Testing neuropsychological hypotheses for cognitive deficits in psychopathic criminals: A study of global-local processing. *Journal of the International Neuropsychological Society, 13,* 267–276.

Kruesi, M.J.P. & Casanova, M.V. (2006). White matter in liars. *British Journal of Psychiatry, 188,* 293–294.

Kruesi, M.J.P., Casanova, M.F., Mannheim, G. & Jonson-Bilder, A. (2004). Reduced temporal lobe volume in early onset conduct disorder. *Psychiatry Research: Neuroimaging, 132,* 1–11.

Laakso, M.P., Gunning-Dixon, F., Vaurio, O., Repo, E., Soininen, H. & Tiihonen, J. (2002). Prefrontal volume in habitually violent subjects with antisocial personality disorder and type 2 alcoholism. *Psychiatry Research Neuroimaging, 114,* 95–102.

LeDoux, J.E. (2000). Emotion circuits in the brain. *Annual Review of Neuroscience, 23,* 155–184.

León-Carrión, J. & Ramos, F.J. (2003). Blows to the head during development can predispose to violent criminal behaviour: Rehabilitation of consequences of head injury is a measure for crime prevention. *Brain Injury, 17,* 207–216.

Lewis, D.O., Pincus, J.H., Bard, B., Richardson, E., Prichep, L.S., Feldman, M. *et al.* (1988). Neuropsychiatric, psychoeducational, and family characteristics of 14 juveniles condemned to death in the United States. *American Journal of Psychiatry, 145,* 584–589.

Lewis, D.O., Pincus, J.H., Feldman, M., Jackson, L. & Bard, B. (1986). Psychiatric, neurological, and psychoeducational characteristics of 15 death row inmates in the United States. *American Journal of Psychiatry, 143,* 838–845.

Lewis, D.O., Pincus, J.H., Lovely, R., Spitzer, E. & Moy, E. (1987). Biopsychosocial characteristics of matched samples of delinquents and nondelinquents. *Journal of the American Academy of Child and Adolescent Psychiatry, 26,* 744–752.

Lezak, M.D., Howieson, D.B., Loring, D.W., Hannay, H.J. & Fischer, J.S. (2004). *Neuropsychological assessment* (4th edn). New York: Oxford University Press.

Lindberg, N., Tani, P., Virkkunen, M., Porkka-Heiskanen, T., Appelberg, B., Naukkarinen, H. *et al.* (2005). Quantitative electroencephalographic measures in homicidal men with antisocial personality disorder. *Psychiatry Research, 136,* 7–15.

Liu, J. & Raine, A. (2006). The effect of childhood malnutrition on externalizing behavior. *Current Opinion in Pediatrics, 18,* 565–570.

Liu, J., Raine, A., Venables, P. & Mednick, S.A. (2004). Malnutrition at age 3 years predisposes to externalizing behavior problems at ages 8, 11 and 17 years. *American Journal of Psychiatry, 161,* 2005–2013.

Liu, J., Raine, A., Venables, P. & Mednick, S.A. (2005). Behavioral effects of childhood malnutrition. Reply to Galler *et al.* *American Journal of Psychiatry*, 1629–1761.

Liu, J., Raine, A., Venables, P. & Mednick, S.A. (2006). Malnutrition, brain dysfunction, and antisocial criminal behavior. In A. Raine (Ed.) *Crime and schizophrenia: Causes and cures* (pp.109–128). New York: Nova Science Publishers.

Lombroso, C. (1876). *Criminal man*. Milan: Hoepli.

Loney, B.R., Butler, M.A., Lima, E.N., Counts, C.A. & Eckel, L.A. (2006). The relation between salivary cortisol, callous-unemotional traits, and conduct problems in an adolescent non-referred sample. *Journal of Child Psychology and Psychiatry*, 47, 30–36.

Loney, B.R., Frick, P.J., Ellis, M.L. & McCoy, M.G. (1998). Intelligence, psychopathy, and antisocial behavior. *Journal of Psychopathology and Behavioural Assessment*, 20, 231–247.

Lorber, M.F. (2004). Psychophysiology of aggression, psychopathy, and conduct problems: A meta-analysis. *Psychological Bulletin*, 130, 531–552.

Luria, A. (1980). *Higher cortical functions in man* (2nd edn). New York: Basic Books.

Lykken, D. (1957). A study of anxiety in the sociopathic personality. *Journal of Abnormal and Social Psychology*, 55, 6–10.

Lykken, D. (1995). *The antisocial personalities*. Hillsdale, NJ: Erlbaum.

Maras, A., Laucht, M., Gerdes, D., Wilhelm, C., Lewicka, S., Haack, D., *et al.* (2003). Association of testosterone and dihydrotestosterone with externalizing behavior in adolescent boys and girls. *Psychoneuroendocrinology*, 28, 932–940.

Maratos, E.J., Dolan, R.J., Morris, J.S., Henson, R.N.A. & Rugg, M.D. (2001). Neural activity associated with episodic memory for emotional context. *Neuropsychologia*, 39, 910–920.

Marsh, A.A., Finger, E.C., Mitchell, D.G.V., Reid, M.E., Sims, C., Kosson, D.S. *et al.* (2008). Reduced amygdala response to fearful expressions in children and adolescents with callous-unemotional traits and disruptive behavior disorders. *American Journal of Psychiatry*, 165, 712–720.

Mataró, M., Jurado, M.A., García-Sánchez, C., Barraquer, L., Costa-Jussá, F.R. & Junqué, C. (2001). Long-term effects of bilateral frontal brain lesion: 60 years after injury with an iron bar. *Archives of Neurology*, 58, 1139–1142.

Mayberg, H.S., Liotti, M., Brannan, S.K., McGinnis, S., Mahurin, R.K. & Jerabek, P.A. (1999). Reciprocal limbic-cortical function and negative mood: Converging PET findings in depression and normal sadness. *American Journal of Psychiatry*, 156, 675–682.

McBurnett, K., Lahey, B.B., Rathouz, P.J. & Loeber, R. (2000). Low salivary cortisol and persistent aggression in boys referred for disruptive behavior. *Archives of General Psychiatry*, 57, 38–43.

McGauley, G., Adshead, G. & Sarkar, S.P. (2007). Psychotherapy of psychopathic disorders. In A.R. Felthous & H. Saß (Eds.) *International handbook of psychopathic disorders and the law: Vol. 1* (pp.449–466). Chichester: John Wiley & Sons.

Mendez, M.F. (2006). What frontotemporal dementia reveals about the neurobiological basis of morality. *Medical Hypotheses*, 67, 411–418.

Moeller, F.G. & Swann, A.C. (2007). Pharmacotherapy of clinical aggression in individuals with psychopathic disorders. In A.R. Felthous & H. Saß? (Eds.) *International handbook on psychopathic disorders and the law* (pp.397–416). Chichester: John Wiley & Sons.

Moffitt, T.E. (1993). Adolescence-limited and life-course-persistent antisocial behavior: A developmental taxonomy. *Psychological Review*, 100, 674–701.

Moffitt, T.E. (2005). The new look of behavioral genetics in developmental psychopathology: Gene–environment interplay in antisocial behavior. *Psychological Bulletin*, 131, 533–554.

Moffitt, T.E. & Caspi, A. (2001). Childhood predictors differentiate life-course persistent and adolescence-limited antisocial pathways among males and females. *Developmental Psychopathology*, 13, 355–375.

Moffitt, T.E. & Henry, B. (1989). Neuropsychological assessment of executive functions in self-reported delinquents. *Development and Psychopathology*, 1, 105–118.

Moffitt, T.E., Lynam, D.R. & Silva, P.A. (1994). Neuropsychological tests predicting persistent male delinquency. *Criminology*, 32, 277–300.

Moll, J., Oliveira-Sousa, R., Bramati, I.E. & Grafman, J. (2002a). Functional networks in emotional moral and nonmoral social judgments. *NeuroImage*, 16, 696–703.

Moll, J., Oliveira-Sousa, R., Eslinger, P.J., Bramati, I.E., Mourao-Miranda, J., Andreiuolo, P.A., *et al.* (2002b). The neural correlates of moral sensitivity: A functional magnetic resonance imaging investigation of basic and moral emotions. *The Journal of Neuroscience: The Official Journal of the Society for Neuroscience*, 22, 2730–2736.

Moll, J., Oliveira-Sousa, R., Moll, F.T., Ignacio, F.A., Bramati, I.E., Caparelli-Daquer, E.M., *et al.* (2005). The moral affiliations of disgust: A functional MRI study. *Cognitive Behavioral Neurology*, 18, 68–78.

Monastra, V.J. (2008). Electroencephalographic feedback in the treatment of ADHD: A model for clinical practice. In V.J. Monastra (Ed.) *Unlocking the potential of patients with ADHD: A model for clinical practice* (pp.147–159). Washington, DC: American Psychological Association.

Morgan, A.B. & Lilienfeld, S.O. (2000). A meta-analytic review of the relationship between antisocial behavior and neuropsychological measures of executive function. *Clinical Psychology Review*, 20, 113–136.

Müller, J.L., Sommer, M., Wagner, V., Lange, K., Taschler, H., Roder, C.H. *et al.* (2003). Abnormalities in emotion processing within cortical and subcortical regions in criminal psychopaths: Evidence from a functional magnetic resonance imaging study using pictures with emotional content. *Psychiatry Research Neuroimaging, 54,* 152–162.

Murray-Close, D., Han, G., Cicchetti, D., Crick, N.R. & Rogosch, F.A. (2008). Neuroendocrine regulation and physical and relational aggression: The moderating roles of child maltreatment and gender. *Developmental Psychology, 44,* 1160–1176.

Nakagawasai O., Mamadera, F., Sato, S., Taniguchi, R., Hiraga, H., Arai, Y. *et al.* (2006). Alterations in cognitive function in prepubertal mice with protein malnutrition: Relationship to changes in choline acetyltransferase. *Behavioural Brain Research, 167,* 111–117.

Nestor, P.G. (1992). Neuropsychological and clinical correlates of murder and other forms of extreme violence in a forensic psychiatric population. *Journal of Nervous and Mental Disease, 180,* 418–423.

Neugebauer, R., Hoek, H.W. & Susser, E. (1999). Prenatal exposure to wartime famine and development of antisocial personality disorder in early adulthood. *Journal of the American Medical Association, 4,* 479–481.

Nigg, J.T., Glass, J.M., Wong, M.M., Poon, E., Jester, J., Fitzgerald, H.E. *et al.* (2004). Neuropsychological executive functioning in children at elevated risk for alcoholism: Findings in early adolescence. *Journal of Abnormal Psychology, 113,* 302–314.

Ochsner, K.N., Beer, J.S., Robertson, E.R., Cooper, J.C., Gabrieli, J.D.E., Kihsltrom, J.F., *et al.* (2005). The neural correlates of direct and reflected self-knowledge. *NeuroImage, 28,* 797–814.

Olds, D., Henderson, C.R.J., Cole, R., Eckenrode, J., Kitzman, H., Luckey, D. *et al.* (1998). Long-term effects of nurse home visitation on children's criminal and antisocial behavior: 15-year follow-up of a randomized controlled trial. *Journal of the American Medical Association, 280,* 1238–1244.

Oliveira-Sousa, R. & Moll, J. (2000). The moral brain: Functional MRI correlates of moral judgment in normal adults. *Neurology, 54,* 252.

Oosterlaan, J., Geurts, H.M. & Sergeant, J.A. (2005). Low basal salivary cortisol is associated with teacher-reported symptoms of conduct disorder. *Psychiatry Research, 134,* 1–10.

Pajer, K., Gardner, W., Rubin, R.T., Perel, J. & Neal, S. (2001). Decreased cortisol levels in adolescent girls with conduct disorder. *Archives of General Psychiatry, 58,* 297–302.

Pajer, K., Tabbah, R., Gardner, W., Rubin, R.T., Czambel, R.K. & Wang, Y. (2006). Adrenal androgen and gonadal hormone levels in adolescent girls with conduct disorder. *Psychoneuroendocrinology, 31,* 1245–1256.

Patrick, C.J. (1994). Emotion and psychopathy: Startling new insights. *Psychophysiology, 31,* 319–330.

Patrick, C.J., Bradley, M.M. & Lang, P.J. (1993). Emotion in the criminal psychopath: Startle reflex modulation. *Journal of Abnormal Psychology, 102,* 82–92.

Patterson, G.R. (1982). *A social learning approach: Vol. 3. Coercive family processes.* Eugene, Oregon: Castalia.

Pincus, H.J. & Lewis, O.D. (1991). Episodic violence. *Seminars in Neurology, 11,* 146–154.

Polich, J. & Hoffman, L.D. (1998). P300 and handedness: On the possible contribution of corpus callosal size to ERPs. *Psychophysiology, 35,* 497–507.

Polich, J., Pollock, V.E. & Bloom, F.E. (1994). Meta-analysis of P300 amplitude from males at risk for alcoholism. *Psychological Bulletin, 115,* 55–73.

Popma, A. & Raine, A. (2006). Will future forensic assessment be neurobiologic? *Child and Adolescent Psychiatric Clinics of North America, 15,* 429–444.

Quinsey, V.L., Harris, G.T., Rice, M.E. & Cormier, C.A. (1999). *Violent offenders: Appraising and managing risk.* Washington, DC: American Psychological Association.

Raine, A. (1993). *The psychopathology of crime: Criminal behavior as a clinical disorder.* San Diego, CA: Academic Press.

Raine, A. (1996). Autonomic nervous system factors underlying disinhibited, antisocial, and violent behavior. *Annals of the New York Academy of Science, 794,* 46–59.

Raine, A. (1997). Classical conditioning, arousal, and crime: A biosocial perspective. In H. Nyborg (Ed.) *The scientific study of human nature: Tribute to Hans J. Eysenck at eighty* (pp.122–141). New York: Elsevier Science.

Raine, A. (2002a). Annotation: The role of prefrontal deficits, low autonomic arousal, and early health factors in the development of antisocial and aggressive behavior in children. *Journal of Child Psychology and Psychiatry, 43,* 417–434.

Raine, A. (2002b). Biosocial studies of antisocial and violent behavior in children and adults: A review. *Journal of Abnormal Child Psychology, 30,* 311–326.

Raine, A., Buchsbaum, M., Stanley, J., Lottenberg, S., Abel, L. & Stoddard, J. (1994). Selective reductions in prefrontal glucose metabolism in murderers. *Biological Psychiatry, 36,* 365–373.

Raine, A., Lencz, T., Bihrle, S., LaCasse, L. & Colletti, P. (2000). Reduced prefrontal gray matter volume and reduced autonomic activity in antisocial personality disorder. *Archives of General Psychiatry, 57,* 119–127.

Raine, A., Lencz, T., Taylor, K., Hellige, J.B., Bihrle, S., LaCasse, L., *et al.* (2003a). Corpus callosum abnormalities in psychopathic antisocial individuals. *Archives of General Psychiatry, 60,* 1134–1142.

Raine, A., Liu, J.H., Venables, P.H. & Mednick, S.A. (2006). Preventing crime and schizophrenia using early environmental enrichment. In A. Raine (Ed.) *Crime and schizophrenia: Causes and cures* (pp.249–266). New York: Nova Science Publishers.

Raine, A., Mellingen, K., Liu, J.H., Venables, P.H. & Mednick, S.A. (2003b). Effects of environmental enrichment at 3–5 years on schizotypal personality and antisocial behavior at ages 17 and 23 years. *American Journal of Psychiatry, 160,* 1627–1635.

Raine, A., Moffitt, T.E., Caspi, A., Loeber, R., Stouthamer-Loeber, M. & Lynam, D. (2005). Neurocognitive impairments in boys on the life-course persistent antisocial path. *Journal of Abnormal Psychology, 114*, 38–49.

Raine, A., Reynolds, C., Venables, P.H. & Mednick, S.A. (1997). Biosocial bases of aggressive behavior in childhood. In A. Raine, P.A. Brennan, D.P. Farrington & S.A. Mednick (Eds.) *Biosocial bases of violence* (pp.107–126). New York: Plenum.

Raine, A., Reynolds, C., Venables, P.H., Mednick, S.A. & Farrington, D.P. (1998). Fearlessness, stimulation-seeking, and large body size at age 3 years as early predispositions to childhood aggression at age 11 years. *Archives of General Psychiatry, 55*, 745–751.

Raine, A. & Venables, P.H. (1984). Electrodermal responding, antisocial behavior, and schizoid tendencies in adolescence. *Psychophysiology, 21*, 424–433.

Raine, A., Venables, P.H. & Williams, M. (1990a). Autonomic orienting responses in 15-year-old male subjects and criminal behavior at age 24. *American Journal of Psychiatry, 147*, 933–937.

Raine, A., Venables, P.H. & Williams, M. (1990b). Relationship between central and autonomic measures of arousal at age 15 and criminality at age 24 years. *Archives of General Psychiatry, 47*, 1003–1007.

Raine, A., Venables, P.H. & Williams, M. (1990c). Relationships between N1, P300, and contingent negative variation recorded at age 15 and criminal behavior at age 24. *Psychophysiology, 27*, 567–574.

Raine, A., Venables, P.H. & Williams, M. (1995). High autonomic arousal and electrodermal orienting at age 15 years as protective factors against criminal behavior at age 29 years. *American Journal of Psychiatry, 152*, 1595–1600.

Raine, A., Venables, P.H. & Williams, M. (1996). Better autonomic conditioning and faster electrodermal half-recovery time at age 15 years as possible protective factors against crime at age 29 years. *Developmental Psychology, 32*, 624–630.

Raine, A. & Yang, Y. (2006). Neural foundations to moral reasoning and antisocial behavior. *Social, Cognitive, and Affective Neuroscience, 1*, 203–213.

Raine, A., Yaralian, P.S., Reynolds, C., Venables, P.H. & Mednick, S.A. (2002). Spatial but not verbal cognitive deficits at age 3 in persistently antisocial individuals. *Development and Psychopathology, 14*, 25–44.

Rasmussen, K., Almvik, R. & Levander, S. (2001). Performance and strategy indices of neuropsychological tests: Relations with personality, criminality and violence. *Journal of Forensic Neuropsychology, 2*(2), 29–43.

Robertson, D., Snarey, J., Ousley, O., Harenski, K., Bowman, F.D., Gilkey, R., *et al.* (2007). The neural processing of moral sensitivity to issues of justice and care. *Neuropsychologia, 45*, 755–766.

Rosen, G.M., Deinard, A.S., Schwartz, S., Smith, C., Stephenson, B. & Grabenstein, B. (1985). Iron deficiency among incarcerated juvenile delinquents. *Journal of Adolescent Health Care, 6*, 419–423.

Salekin, R.T. (2006). Psychopathy in children and adults: Key issues in conceptualization and assessment. In C. J. Patrick (Ed.) *Handbook of psychopathy* (pp.389–414). New York: Guilford Press.

Salekin, R.T., Neumann, C.S., Leistico, A.R. & Zalot, A.A. (2004). Psychopathy in youth and intelligence: An investigation of Cleckley's hypothesis. *Journal of Clinical Child and Adolescent Psychology, 33*, 731–742.

Sarapata, M., Hermann, D., Johnson, T. & Aycock, R. (2008). The role of head injury in cognitive functioning, emotional adjustment and criminal behavior. *Brain Injury, 12*, 821–842.

Saver, J.L. & Damasio, A.R. (1991). Preserved access and processing of social knowledge in a patient with acquired sociopathy due to ventromedial frontal damage. *Neuropsychologia, 29*, 1241–1249.

Scarpa, A., Romero, N., Fikretoglu, D., Bowser, F.M. & Wilson, J.W. (1999). *Community violence exposure and aggression: Biosocial interactions.* Paper presented at the meeting of the American Society of Criminology, Toronto, Canada.

Schneider, F., Habel, U., Kessler, C., Posse, S., Grodd, W. & Müller-Gartner, H. (2000). functional imaging of conditioned aversive emotional responses in antisocial personality disorder. *Neuropsychobiology, 42*, 192–201.

Schoenthaler, S.J., Amos, S.P., Doraz, W.E., Kelly M.A., Muedeking G.D. & Wakefield J.A. (1997). The effect of randomised vitamin-mineral supplementation on violent and non-violent antisocial behavior among incarcerated juveniles. *Journal of Nutritional and Environmental Medicine, 7*, 343–352.

Schoenthaler, S.J. & Bier, I.D. (2000). The effect of vitamin-mineral supplementation on juvenile delinquency among American schoolchildren: A randomized, doubleblind placebo-controlled trial. *The Journal of Alternative and Complementary Medicine, 6*, 19–29.

Schug, R.A., Raine, A. & Wilcox, R.R. (2007). Psychophysiological and behavioural characteristics of individuals comorbid for antisocial personality disorder and schizophrenia-spectrum personality disorder. *British Journal of Psychiatry, 190*, 408–414.

Séguin, J.R., Nagin, D., Assad, J.M. & Tremblay, R. (2004). Cognitive-neuropsychological function in chronic physical aggression and hyperactivity. *Journal of Abnormal Psychology, 113*, 603–613.

Shoal, G.D., Giancola, P.R. & Kilrillova, G.P. (2003). Salivary cortisol, personality, and aggressive behavior in adolescent boys: A 5-year longitudinal study. *Child and Adolescent Psychiatry and Mental Health, 42*, 1101–1107.

Sip, K.E., Roepstorff, A., McGregor, W. & Frith, C.D. (2007). Detecting deception: The scope and limits. *Trends in Cognitive Sciences, 12*, 48–53.

Soderstrom, H., Tullberg, M., Wikkelsoe, C., Ekholm, S. & Forsman, A. (2000). Reduced regional cerebral blood flow in non-psychotic violent offenders. *Psychiatry Research: Neuroimaging, 98,* 29–41.

Stanford, M.S., Conklin, S.M., Helfritz, L.E. & Kockler, T.R. (2007a). P3 amplitude reduction and executive function deficits in men convicted of spousal/partner abuse. *Personality and Individual Differences, 43,* 365–375.

Stanford, M.S., Houston, R.J. & Barratt, E.S. (2007b). Psychophysiological correlates of psychopathic disorders. In A.R. Felthous & H. Saß (Eds.) *International handbook of psychopathic disorders and the law: Vol. 1* (pp.83–101). Chichester: John Wiley & Sons.

Sterzer, P., Stadler, C., Krebs, A., Kleinschmidt, A. & Poustka, F. (2005). Abnormal neural responses to emotional visual stimuli in adolescents with conduct disorder. *Biological Psychiatry, 57,* 7–15.

Stevens, L., Zhang, W., Peck, L., Kuczek, T., Grevstad, N., Mahon, A. *et al.* (2003). EFA supplementation in children with inattention, hyperactivity, and other disruptive behaviors. *Lipids, 38,* 1007–1021.

Teichner, G. & Golden, C.J. (2000). The relationship of neuropsychological impairment to conduct disorder in adolescence: A conceptual review. *Aggression and Violent Behavior, 5,* 509–528.

Teichner, G., Golden, C.J., Van Hasselt, V.B. & Peterson, A. (2001). Assessment of cognitive functioning in men who batter. *International Journal of Neuroscience, 111,* 241–253.

Trovillo, P.V. (1939). A history in lie detection. *Journal of Criminal Law and Criminology, 29,* 848–881.

Van de Wiel, N.M.H., Van Goozen, S.M.H., Matthys, W., Snoek, H. & Van Engeland, H. (2004). Cortisol and treatment effect in children with disruptive behavior disorders: A preliminary study. *Journal of the American Academy of Child and Adolescent Psychiatry, 43,* 1011–1018.

van Goozen, S.H.M., Matthys, W., Cohen-Hettenis, P.T., Wied, C.G., Wiegant, V.M. & van Engeland, H. (1998). Salivary cortisol and cardiovascular activity during stress in oppositional defiant disorder boys and normal controls. *Biological Psychiatry, 43,* 531–539.

van Honk, J. & Schutter, D.J.L.G. (2007). Testosterone reduces conscious detection of signals serving social correction: Implications for antisocial behavior. *Psychological Science, 18,* 663–667.

Vermeiren, R., De Clippele, A., Schwab-Stone, M., Ruchkin, V. & Deboutte, D. (2002). Neuropsychological characteristics of three subgroups of Flemish delinquent adolescents. *Neuropsychology, 16,* 49–55.

Virkkunen, M. (1985). Urinary free cortisol secretion in habitually violent offenders. *Acta Psychiatrica Scandinavica, 72,* 40–44.

Virkkunen, M.E., DeJong, J., Bartko, J., Goodwin, F.K. & Linnoila, M. (1989). Relationship of psychological variables to recidivism in violent offenders and impulsive fire setters. *Archives of General Psychiatry, 46,* 600–603.

Virkkunen, M.E., Horrobin, D.F., Jenkins, D.K. & Manku, M.S. (1987). Plasma phospholipid essential fatty acids and prostaglandins in alcoholic, habitually violent, and impulsive offenders. *Biological Psychiatry, 22,* 1087–1096.

Volkow, N.D. & Tancredi, L.R. (1987). Neural substrates of violent behavior. A preliminary study with positron emission tomography. *British Journal of Psychiatry, 151,* 668–673.

Volkow, N.D., Tancredi, L.R., Grant, C., Gillespie, H., Valentine, A., Mullani, N. *et al.* (1995). Brain glucose metabolism in violent psychiatric patients: A preliminary study. *Psychiatry Research, 61,* 243–253.

Waldman, I.D. & Rhee, S.H. (2006). Genetic and environmental influences on psychopathy and antisocial behavior. In C.J. Patrick (Ed.) *Handbook of psychopathy* (pp.205–228). New York: Guilford Press.

Walsh, A. & Ellis, L. (2007). *Criminology: An interdisciplinary approach.* Thousand Oaks, CA: Sage Publications.

Walsh, W.J., Isaacson, H.R., Rehman, F. & Hall, A. (1997). Elevated blood copper/zinc ratios in assaultive young males. *Physiology and Behavior, 62,* 327–329.

Werbach, M.R. (1992). Nutritional influences on aggressive behavior. *Journal of Orthomolecular Medicine, 7,* 45–51.

White, J.L., Moffitt, T.E., Caspi, A., Jeglum, D., Needles, D.J. & Stouthamer-Loeber, M. (1994). Measuring impulsivity and examining its relationship to delinquency. *Journal of Abnormal Psychology, 103,* 192–205.

Wilson, J.Q. & Herrnstein, R. (1985). *Crime and human nature.* New York: Simon & Schuster.

Yang, Y., Glenn, A.L. & Raine, A. (2008). Brain abnormalities in antisocial individuals: Implications for the law. *Behavioral Sciences and the Law, 26,* 65–83.

Yang, Y., Raine, A., Lencz, T., Bihrle, S., Lacasse, L. & Colletti, P. (2005). Prefrontal white matter in pathological liars. *British Journal of Psychiatry, 187,* 320–325.

Yang, Y., Raine, A., Narr, K.L., Lencz, T., LaCasse, L., Colletti, P. *et al.* (2007). Localisation of increased prefrontal white matter in pathological liars. *British Journal of Psychiatry, 190,* 174–175.

Young, S.N. & Leyton, M. (2002). The role of serotonin in human mood and social interaction – Insight from altered tryptophan levels. *Pharmacology, Biochemistry and Behavior, 71,* 857–865.

7

The Developmental Evidence Base
Prevention

David P. Farrington

This chapter aims to review effective prevention programmes that tackle key risk factors for delinquency. It focuses especially on programmes that have been evaluated in randomised experiments that have included a cost–benefit analysis. The chapter reviews family-based programmes, including home visiting by nurses, parent training, functional family therapy, treatment foster care and multi-systematic therapy. It reviews school-based programmes, including preschool intellectual enrichment, teacher training, after-school programmes and anti-bullying projects. It reviews programmes targeted on peer influence, including peer tutoring and mentoring programmes. It reviews cognitive-behavioural skills training programmes targeted on children and adults, and the 'Communities That Care' programme. Recent UK developments are discussed, including the government's action plan for social exclusion and Sure Start. It is concluded that a national agency for early prevention is needed.

Introduction

The main aim of this chapter is to summarise briefly some of the most effective programmes for preventing delinquency and antisocial behaviour whose effectiveness has been demonstrated in high-quality evaluation research. My focus is especially on programmes evaluated in randomised experiments with reasonably large samples, since the effect of any intervention on delinquency can be demonstrated most convincingly in such experiments (Farrington & Welsh, 2005, 2006). The

major methods of reducing crime can be classified as developmental, community, situational and criminal justice prevention (Tonry & Farrington, 1995).

Criminal justice prevention refers to traditional deterrent, incapacitative and rehabilitative strategies operated by law enforcement and criminal justice system agencies. Community prevention refers to interventions designed to change the social conditions and institutions (e.g. families, peers, social norms, clubs, organisations) that influence offending in residential communities (Hope, 1995). These interventions target community risk factors and social conditions such as cohesiveness or disorganisation. Situational prevention refers to interventions designed to prevent the occurrence of crimes by reducing opportunities and increasing the risk and difficulty of offending (Clarke, 1995). Developmental prevention refers to interventions designed to prevent the development of criminal potential in individuals, especially those targeting risk and protective factors discovered in studies of human development (Tremblay & Craig, 1995). My focus in this chapter is on developmental or risk-focused prevention.

Risk-focused prevention

The basic idea of developmental or risk-focused prevention is very simple: Identify the key risk factors for offending and implement prevention techniques designed to counteract them. There is often a related attempt to identify key protective factors against offending and to implement prevention techniques designed to enhance or strengthen them (Catalano *et al.*, 2002).

Longitudinal surveys are used to advance knowledge about risk and protective factors, and experimental and quasi-experimental methods are used to evaluate the impact of prevention and intervention programmes.

Risk-focused prevention was imported into criminology from medicine and public health by pioneers such as David Hawkins and Richard Catalano (1992). This approach has been used successfully for many years to tackle illnesses such as cancer and heart disease. For example, the identified risk factors for heart disease include smoking, a fatty diet and lack of exercise. These can be tackled by encouraging people to stop smoking, to have a more healthy low-fat diet and to take more exercise.

Risk-focused prevention links explanation and prevention, links fundamental and applied research, and links scholars, policy makers and practitioners. The book *Saving Children from a Life of Crime: Early Risk Factors and Effective Interventions* (Farrington & Welsh, 2007) contains a detailed exposition of this approach. Importantly, risk-focused prevention is easy to understand and to communicate, and it is readily accepted by policy makers, practitioners and the general public. Both risk factors and interventions are based on empirical research rather than on theories. This approach avoids difficult theoretical questions about which risk factors have causal effects.

What is a risk factor?

By definition, a risk factor predicts an increased probability of later offending (Kazdin *et al.*, 1997). For example, children who experience poor parental supervision have an increased risk of committing criminal acts later on. In the Cambridge Study in Delinquent Development, which is a prospective longitudinal survey of 400 London males from age 8 to age 48, 61 per cent of those experiencing poor parental supervision at age 8 were convicted up to age 50, compared with 36 per cent of the remainder, a significant difference (Farrington *et al.*, 2006). Since risk factors are defined by their ability to predict later offending, it follows that longitudinal studies are needed to establish them.

The most important risk factors for delinquency are well known (Farrington, 2007). They include individual factors such as high impulsiveness and low intelligence; family factors such as poor parental supervision and harsh or erratic parental discipline; peer factors such as hanging around with delinquent friends; school factors such as attending a high-delinquency-rate school;

socio-economic factors such as low income and poor housing; and neighbourhood or community factors such as living in a high-crime neighbourhood. My focus is on risk factors that can be changed by interventions. There is also a focus on protective or promotive factors that predict a low probability of offending, but less is known about them (see Lösel & Bender, 2003).

Risk factors tend to be similar for many different outcomes, including delinquency, violence, drug use, school failure and unemployment. This is good news, because a programme that is successful in reducing one of these outcomes is likely to be successful in reducing the others as well. In this chapter, I will review family programmes, then school programmes, then peer-based programmes, and finally, skills training programmes.

Cost–benefit analysis

I will describe some of the most important and best-evaluated programmes, with special reference to programmes that have carried out a cost–benefit analysis. The conclusion from the Perry project (discussed later) that, for every $1 spent on the programme, $7 were saved in the long term (Schweinhart *et al.*, 1993), proved particularly convincing to policy makers. The monetary costs of crime are enormous. For example, Sam Brand and Richard Price (2000) estimated that they totalled £60 billion in England and Wales in 1999. Mark Cohen (1998) estimated that a high-risk youth in the USA cost society about $2 million. There are tangible costs to victims, such as replacing stolen goods and repairing damage, and intangible costs that are harder to quantify, such as pain, suffering and a reduced quality of life. There are costs to the government or taxpayer for police, courts, prisons, crime prevention activities and so on. There are also costs to offenders – for example, those associated with being in prison or losing a job.

To the extent that crime prevention programmes are successful in reducing crime, they will have benefits. These benefits can be quantified in monetary terms according to the reduction in the monetary costs of crime. Other benefits may accrue from reducing the costs of associated social problems such as unemployment, divorce, educational failure, drug addiction, welfare dependency and so on. The fact that offending is part of a larger syndrome of antisocial behaviour (West & Farrington, 1977) is good news, because the benefits of a crime prevention programme can be many and varied. The monetary benefits of a programme can be compared with its monetary costs to determine the benefit:cost ratio. Surprisingly few cost–benefit analyses of crime prevention programmes have ever been carried out (Welsh & Farrington, 2000; Welsh *et al.*, 2001).

Family-based Prevention

Family programmes are usually targeted on risk factors such as poor parental supervision and inconsistent discipline. The behavioural parent management training developed by Gerald Patterson (1982) in Oregon is one of the most influential approaches. His careful observations of parent–child interaction showed that parents of antisocial children were deficient in their methods of child-rearing. These parents failed to tell their children how they were expected to behave, failed to monitor their behaviour to ensure that it was desirable, and failed to enforce rules promptly and unambiguously with appropriate rewards and penalties. The parents of antisocial children used more punishment (such as scolding, shouting or threatening), but failed to use it consistently or make it contingent on the child's behaviour.

Patterson's method involved linking antecedents, behaviours and consequences. He attempted to train parents in effective child-rearing methods, namely noticing what a child is doing, monitoring the child's behaviour over long periods, clearly stating house rules, making rewards and punishments consistent and contingent on the child's behaviour, and negotiating disagreements so that conflicts and crises did not escalate.

His treatment was shown to be effective in reducing child stealing and antisocial behaviour over short periods in small-scale studies (Dishion *et al.*, 1992; Patterson *et al.*, 1992). However, the treatment worked best with children aged 3–10 and less well with adolescents. Also, there were problems of achieving cooperation from the families experiencing the worst problems. In particular, single mothers on welfare were experiencing so many different stresses that they found it difficult to use consistent and contingent child-rearing methods. (For a recent review of parent training programmes, see Piquero *et al.*, 2008.)

I will now review the most important types of family-based programmes that have been evaluated. These are home visiting programmes (and especially the work of David Olds), parent training programmes (especially those used by Carolyn Webster-Stratton, Stephen Scott, Frances Gardner and Matthew Sanders), home or community programmes with older children (especially those implemented by James Alexander and Patricia Chamberlain) and multi-systemic therapy or MST (used by Scott Henggeler and Alison Cunningham).

Home visiting programmes

In the most famous intensive home visiting programme, David Olds and his colleagues (1986) in Elmira (New York State) randomly allocated 400 mothers either to receive home visits from nurses during pregnancy, or to receive visits both during pregnancy and during the first two years of life, or to a control group who received no visits. Each visit lasted about one and a quarter hours, and the mothers were visited on average every two weeks. The home visitors gave advice about prenatal and postnatal care of the child, about infant development, and about the importance of proper nutrition and avoiding smoking and drinking during pregnancy. Hence, this was a general parent education programme. The results of this experiment showed that the postnatal home visits caused a decrease in recorded child physical abuse and neglect during the first two years of life, especially by poor unmarried teenage mothers; 4 per cent of visited versus 19 per cent of non-visited mothers of this type were guilty of child abuse or neglect. This last result is important because children who are physically abused or neglected tend to become violent offenders later in life (Widom, 1989). In a 15-year follow-up, the main focus was on lower-class unmarried mothers. Among these mothers, those who received prenatal and postnatal home visits had fewer arrests than those who received prenatal visits or no visits (Olds *et al.*, 1997). Also, children of these mothers who received prenatal and/or postnatal home visits had less than half as many arrests as children of mothers who received no visits (Olds *et al.*, 1998). According to Steve Aos and his colleagues (2001), $3 were saved for every $1 expended on high-risk mothers in this programme. (For a recent review of home visiting programmes, see Olds *et al.*, 2007.)

Parent management training

One of the most famous parent training programmes was developed by Carolyn Webster-Stratton (1998) in Seattle. She evaluated its success by randomly allocating 426 children aged 4 (most with single mothers on welfare) either to an experimental group which received parent training or to a control group which did not. The experimental mothers met in groups every week for eight or nine weeks, watched videotapes demonstrating parenting skills, and then took part in focused group discussions. The topics included how to play with your child, helping your child learn, using praise and encouragement to bring out the best in your child, effective setting of limits, handling misbehaviour, how to teach your child to solve problems, and how to give and get support. Observations in the home showed that the experimental children behaved better than the control children.

Carolyn Webster-Stratton and Mary Hammond (1997) also evaluated the effectiveness of parent training and child skills training with about 100 Seattle children (average age 5) referred to a clinic because of conduct problems. The children and their parents were randomly allocated to receive either (a) parent training, (b) child skills training, (c) both parent and child training, or (d) to a control group. The skills training aimed to foster prosocial behaviour and interpersonal skills using video modelling, while the parent training involved weekly meetings between parents and therapists for 22 to 24 weeks. Parent reports and home observations showed that children in all three experimental conditions had fewer behaviour problems than control children, in both an immediate and a one-year follow-up. There was little difference between the three experimental conditions, although the combined parent and child training condition produced the most significant improvements in child behaviour at the one-year follow-up. It is generally true that combined parent and child interventions are more effective than either one alone.

Stephen Scott and his colleagues (2001) evaluated the Webster-Stratton parent training programme in London and Chichester. About 140 mainly poor, disadvantaged children aged 3–8 who were referred for antisocial behaviour were randomly assigned to receive parent training or to be in a waiting-list control group. The parent training programme, based on videotapes, covered praise and rewards, setting limits, and handling misbehaviour. Follow-up parent interviews and observations showed that the antisocial behaviour of the experimental children decreased significantly compared to that of the controls. Furthermore, after the intervention, experimental parents gave their children more praise to encourage desirable behaviour, and used more effective commands to obtain compliance.

Frances Gardner and her colleagues (2006) evaluated the success of the Webster-Stratton programme in Oxfordshire. Over 70 children, aged 2–9, referred for conduct problems, were randomly assigned to receive parent training or to be in a waiting-list control group. Follow-up parent reports and observations again showed that the antisocial behaviour of the experimental children decreased compared with the controls.

Matthew Sanders and his colleagues (2000) in Brisbane, Australia, developed the Triple-P parenting programme. This programme either can be delivered to the whole community in primary prevention using the mass media or can be used in secondary prevention with high-risk or clinic samples. Sanders evaluated the success of Triple-P with high-risk children aged 3 by randomly allocating them either to receive Triple-P or to be in a control group. The Triple-P programme involves teaching parents 17 child management strategies, including talking with children, giving physical affection, praising, giving attention, setting a good example, setting rules, giving clear instructions, and using appropriate penalties for misbehaviour ('time-out', or sending the child to his or her room). The evaluation showed that the Triple-P programme was successful in reducing children's antisocial behaviour.

Other parenting interventions

Another parenting intervention, termed functional family therapy, was developed by James Alexander in Utah (Alexander & Parsons, 1973). This aimed to modify patterns of family interaction by modelling, prompting and reinforcement, to encourage clear communication between family members of requests and solutions, and to minimise conflict. Essentially, all family members were trained to negotiate effectively, to set clear rules about privileges and responsibilities, and to use techniques of reciprocal reinforcement with each other. The programme was evaluated by randomly allocating 86 delinquents to experimental or control conditions. The results showed that this technique halved the recidivism rate of minor delinquents in comparison with other approaches (client-centred or psychodynamic therapy). Its effectiveness with more serious offenders was confirmed in a replication study using matched groups (Barton *et al.*, 1985; see also Sexton & Alexander, 2000).

Patricia Chamberlain and John Reid (1998) in Oregon evaluated treatment foster care (TFC), which was used as an alternative to custody for delinquents. Custodial sentences for delinquents were thought to have undesirable effects especially because of the bad influence of delinquent peers. In treatment foster care, families in the community were recruited and trained to provide a placement for delinquent youths. The TFC youths were closely supervised at home, in the community and in the school, and their contacts with delinquent peers were minimised. The foster parents provided a structured daily living environment, with clear rules and limits, consistent discipline for rule violations and one-to-one monitoring. The youths were encouraged to develop academic skills and desirable work habits.

In the evaluation, 79 chronic male delinquents were randomly assigned to treatment foster care or to regular group homes where they lived with other delinquents. A one-year follow-up showed that the TFC boys had fewer criminal referrals and lower self-reported delinquency. Hence, this programme seemed to be an effective treatment for delinquency. Similarly encouraging results were obtained in an evaluation of TFC for delinquent girls (Leve *et al.*, 2005).

Multi-systemic therapy

Multi-systemic therapy (MST) is an important multiple-component family preservation programme that was developed by Scott Henggeler and his colleagues (1998) in South Carolina. The particular type of treatment is chosen according to the particular needs of the youth. Therefore, the nature of the treatment is different for each person. MST is delivered in the youth's home, school and community settings. The treatment typically includes family intervention to promote the parent's ability to monitor and discipline the adolescent, peer intervention to encourage the choice of prosocial friends, and school intervention to enhance competence and school achievement.

In an evaluation by Scott Henggeler and his colleagues (1993), 84 serious delinquents (with an average age of 15) were randomly assigned either to receive MST or the usual treatment (which mostly involved placing the juvenile outside home). The results showed that the MST group had fewer arrests and fewer self-reported crimes in a one-year follow-up. In another evaluation in Missouri, Charles Borduin and his colleagues (1995) randomly assigned 176 juvenile offenders (with an average age of 14) either to MST or to individual therapy focusing on personal, family and academic issues. Four years later, only 29 per cent of the MST offenders had been rearrested, compared with 74 per cent of the individual therapy group. Other evaluations by Henggeler and his colleagues (1997, 1999, 2002) have also produced impressive results. According to Steve Aos and his colleagues (2001), MST had one of

the highest benefit:cost ratios of any programme. For every $1 spent on it, $13 were saved in victim and criminal justice costs.

Unfortunately, disappointing results were obtained in a large-scale independent evaluation of MST in Canada by Alan Leschied and Alison Cunningham (2002). Over 400 youths who were either offenders or at risk of offending were randomly assigned to receive either MST or the usual services (typically probation supervision). Six months after treatment, 28 per cent of the MST group had been reconvicted, compared with 31 per cent of the control group, a non-significant difference. Therefore, it is not totally clear how effective MST is when it is implemented independently, although it was successful in a Norwegian evaluation (Ogden & Hagen, 2006). Unfortunately, two recent meta-analyses of the effectiveness of MST reached contradictory conclusions. Nicola Curtis and her colleagues (2004) found that it was effective, but Julia Littell (2005) found that it was not. Nevertheless, MST is a promising intervention technique, and it is being used in the UK (Jefford & Squire, 2004).

Is family-based intervention effective?

Evaluations of the effectiveness of family-based intervention programmes have produced both encouraging and discouraging results. In order to assess effectiveness according to a large number of evaluations, Brandon Welsh and I reviewed 40 evaluations of family-based programmes each involving at least 50 persons in experimental and control groups combined (Farrington & Welsh, 2003). All of these had outcome measures of delinquency or antisocial child behaviour. Of the 19 studies with outcome measures of delinquency, 10 found significantly beneficial effects of the intervention and 9 found no significant effect. Happily, no study found a significantly harmful effect of family-based treatment.

Over all 19 studies, the average effect size (d, the standardised mean difference) was 0.32. This was significantly greater than zero. When we converted it into the percentage reconvicted, a d value of 0.32 corresponds to a decrease in the percentage reconvicted from 50 per cent to 34 per cent. Therefore, we concluded that, taking all 19 studies together, they showed that family-based intervention had substantial desirable effects. Also, there is evidence that some programmes (e.g. home visiting) have financial benefits that greatly exceed the programme costs.

School-based Prevention

I now turn to school-based prevention programmes, most of which also had a family-based component. I will first of all review the Perry preschool programme, which is perhaps the most influential early prevention project, because it concluded that $7 were saved for every $1 expended. Then I will review some famous school-based programmes implemented in Seattle by David Hawkins, in Newcastle-upon-Tyne by Israel Kolvin, and in Baltimore by Sheppard Kellam. I will also review anti-bullying programmes by Dan Olweus in Norway and Peter Smith in England.

Preschool programmes

The most famous preschool intellectual enrichment programme is the Perry project carried out in Ypsilanti (Michigan) by Lawrence Schweinhart and David Weikart (1980). This was essentially a 'Head Start' programme targeted on disadvantaged African American children. A small sample of 123 children were allocated (approximately at random) to experimental and control groups. The experimental children attended a daily preschool programme, backed up by weekly home visits, usually lasting two years (covering ages 3–4). The aim of the 'plan–do–review' programme was to provide intellectual stimulation, to increase thinking and reasoning abilities, and to increase later school achievement.

This programme had long-term benefits. John Berrueta-Clement and his colleagues (1984) showed that, at age 19, the experimental group was more likely to be employed, more likely to have graduated from high school, more likely to have received college or vocational training, and less likely to have been arrested. By age 27, the experimental group had accumulated only half as many arrests on average as the controls (Schweinhart et al., 1993). Also, they had significantly higher earnings and were more likely to be home-owners. More of the experimental women were married, and fewer of their children were born to unmarried mothers.

The most recent follow-up of this programme at age 40 found that it continued to make an important difference in the lives of the participants (Schweinhart et al., 2005). Compared to the control group, those who received the programme had significantly fewer lifetime arrests for violent crimes (32 per cent vs. 48 per cent), property crimes (36 per cent vs. 56 per cent) and drug crimes (14 per cent vs. 34 per cent), and they were

significantly less likely to be arrested five or more times (36 per cent vs. 55 per cent). Improvements were also recorded in many other important life-course outcomes. For example, significantly higher levels of schooling (77 per cent vs. 60 per cent graduating from high school), better records of employment (76 per cent vs. 62 per cent), and higher annual incomes were reported by the programme group compared to the controls.

Several economic analyses show that the financial benefits of this programme outweighed its costs. The Perry project's own calculation (Barnett, 1993) included crime and non-crime benefits, intangible costs to victims, and even projected benefits beyond age 27. This generated the famous benefit-to-cost ratio of 7 to 1. Most of the benefits (65 per cent) were derived from savings to crime victims. The most recent cost–benefit analysis at age 40 found that the programme produced $17 in benefits per $1 of cost.

Like the Perry project, the Child Parent Centre (CPC) in Chicago provided disadvantaged children with a high-quality, active-learning preschool supplemented by family support (Reynolds et al., 2001). However, unlike Perry, CPC continued to provide the children with the educational enrichment component into elementary school, up to age 9. Focusing on the effect of the preschool intervention, it was found that, compared to a control group, those who received the programme were less likely to be arrested for both non-violent and violent offences by the time they were 18. The CPC programme also produced other benefits for those in the experimental compared to the control group, such as a higher rate of high-school completion.

Desirable results were also obtained in evaluations of other preschool programmes (e.g. Campbell et al., 2002). Also, a large-scale study by Eliana Garces and her colleagues (2002) found that children who attended Head Start programmes (at ages 3 to 5) were significantly less likely to report being arrested or referred to court for a crime by ages 18 to 30 compared to their siblings who did not attend these programmes.

School programmes

One of the most important school-based prevention experiments was carried out in Seattle by David Hawkins and his colleagues (1991). They implemented a multiple-component programme combining parent training, teacher training and child skills training. About 500 first-grade children (aged 6) in 21 classes in 8 schools were randomly assigned to be in experimental or control classes. The children in the experimental classes received special treatment at home and school which was designed to increase their attachment to their parents and their bonding to the school. Also, they were trained in interpersonal cognitive problem-solving. Their parents were trained to notice and reinforce socially desirable behaviour in a programme called 'Catch them being good'. Their teachers were trained in classroom management, for example to provide clear instructions and expectations to children, to reward children for participation in desired behaviour, and to teach children prosocial (socially desirable) methods of solving problems.

This programme had long-term benefits. By the sixth grade (age 12), experimental boys were less likely to have initiated delinquency, while experimental girls were less likely to have initiated drug use (O'Donnell et al., 1995). In a later follow-up, David Hawkins and his colleagues (1999) found that, at age 18, the full intervention group (those who received the intervention from grades 1 to 6) admitted less violence, less alcohol abuse and fewer sexual partners than the late intervention group (grades 5–6 only) or the control group. According to Steve Aos and his colleagues (2001), over $4 were saved for every $1 spent on this programme.

Another important school-based prevention experiment was carried out by Israel Kolvin and his colleagues (1981) in Newcastle-upon-Tyne. They randomly allocated 270 junior school children (aged 7–8) and 322 secondary school children (aged 11–12) to experimental or control groups. All children had been identified as showing some kind of social or psychiatric disturbance or learning problems (according to teacher and peer ratings). There were three types of experimental programmes: (a) behaviour modification-reinforcement with the seniors, 'nurture work' teaching healthy interactions with the juniors; (b) parent counselling–teacher consultations with both; and (c) group therapy with the seniors, play groups with the juniors.

The programmes were evaluated after 18 months and after three years using clinical ratings of conduct disturbance. Generally, the experimental and control groups were not significantly different for the juniors, although there was some tendency for the nurture work and play group conditions to be better behaved than the controls at the three-year follow-up. For the seniors, those who received group therapy showed significantly less conduct disturbance at both follow-ups, and there was some tendency for the other two programmes also to be effective at the three-year follow-up.

In Baltimore, Hanno Petras, Sheppard Kellam, and their colleagues (2008) evaluated the 'Good Behaviour Game' (GBG) which aimed to reduce aggressive and disruptive child conduct through contingent reinforcement of interdependent team behaviour. First-grade classrooms and teachers were randomly assigned either to the GBG condition or to a control condition, and the GBG was played repeatedly over two years. In trajectory analyses, the researchers found that the GBG decreased aggressive/disruptive behaviour (according to teacher reports) up to grade 7 among the most aggressive boys, and also caused a decrease in antisocial personality disorder at age 19–21. However, effects on girls and on a second cohort of children were less marked.

There have been a number of comprehensive, evidence-based reviews of the effectiveness of school-based programmes (Gottfredson et al., 2006; Wilson et al., 2001; Wilson & Lipsey, 2007). Meta-analyses identified four types of school-based programmes that were effective in preventing delinquency: school and discipline management, classroom or instructional management, reorganisation of grades or classes, and increasing self-control or social competency using cognitive-behavioural instruction methods. Reorganisation of grades or classes had the largest average effect size ($d = 0.34$), corresponding to a significant 17 per cent reduction in delinquency.

After-school programmes (e.g. recreation-based, drop-in clubs, dance groups and tutoring services) are based on the belief that providing prosocial opportunities for young people in the after-school hours can reduce their involvement in delinquent behaviour in the community. After-school programmes target a range of risk factors for delinquency, including association with delinquent peers. Brandon Welsh and Akemi Hoshi (2002) identified three high-quality after-school programmes with an evaluated impact on delinquency. Each had desirable effects on delinquency, and one programme also reported lower rates of drug use for participants compared to controls.

Anti-bullying programmes

School bullying, of course, is a risk factor for offending (Farrington, 1993). Several school-based programmes have been effective in reducing bullying. The most famous of these was implemented by Dan Olweus (1994) in Norway. The general principles of the programme were: to create an environment characterised by adult warmth, interest in children, and involvement with children; to use authoritative child-rearing, includ-ing warmth, firm guidance, and close supervision, since authoritarian child-rearing is related to child bullying (Baldry & Farrington, 1998); to set firm limits on what is unacceptable bullying; to consistently apply non-physical sanctions for rule violations; to improve moni-toring and surveillance of child behaviour, especially in the playground; and to decrease opportunities and rewards for bullying.

The Olweus programme aimed to increase awareness and knowledge of teachers, parents and children about bullying and to dispel myths about it. A 30-page booklet was distributed to all schools in Norway describing what was known about bullying and recommending what steps schools and teachers could take to reduce it. Also, a 25-minute video about bullying was made available to schools. Simultaneously, the schools distributed to all parents a four-page folder containing information and advice about bullying. In addition, anonymous self-report questionnaires about bullying were completed by all children.

Each school received feedback information from the questionnaire, about the prevalence of bullies and vic-tims, in a specially arranged school conference day. Also, teachers were encouraged to develop explicit rules about bullying (e.g. do not bully, tell someone when bullying happens, bullying will not be tolerated, try to help vic-tims, try to include children who are being left out) and to discuss bullying in class, using the video and role-playing exercises. Also, teachers were encouraged to improve monitoring and supervision of children, espe-cially in the playground.

The effects of this anti-bullying programme were evaluated in 42 Bergen schools. Dan Olweus measured the prevalence of bullying before and after the pro-gramme using self-report questionnaires completed by the children. Since all schools received the programme, there were no control schools. However, Olweus com-pared children of a certain age (e.g. 13) before the pro-gramme with different children of the same age after the programme. Overall, the programme was very success-ful, because bullying decreased by half.

A similar programme was implemented in 23 Sheffield schools by Peter Smith and Sonia Sharp (1994). The core programme involved establishing a 'whole-school' anti-bullying policy, raising awareness of bully-ing and clearly defining roles and responsibilities of teachers and students, so that everyone knew what bul-lying was and what they should do about it. In addition, there were optional interventions tailored to particular

schools: curriculum work (e.g. reading books, watching videos), direct work with students (e.g. assertiveness training for those who were bullied) and playground work (e.g. training lunch-time supervisors). This pro-gramme was successful in reducing bullying (by 15 per cent) in primary schools, but had relatively small effects (a 5 per cent reduction) in secondary schools.

Maria Ttofi and her colleagues (2008) completed a systematic review of the effectiveness of anti-bullying programmes in schools. They found 59 high-quality evaluations of 30 different programmes. Overall, anti-bullying programmes were effective. The results showed that bullying and victimisation were reduced by about 17 to 23 per cent in experimental schools compared with control schools.

Peer Programmes

There are few outstanding examples of effective inter-vention programmes for antisocial behaviour targeted on peer risk factors. The most hopeful programmes involve using high-status conventional peers to teach children ways of resisting peer pressure; this is effective in reducing drug use (Tobler et al., 1999). Also, in a ran-domised experiment in St Louis, Ronald Feldman and his colleagues (1983) showed that placing antisocial adolescents in activity groups dominated by prosocial adolescents led to a reduction in their antisocial behav-iour (compared with antisocial adolescents placed in antisocial groups). This suggests that the influence of prosocial peers can be harnessed to reduce antisocial behaviour. However, putting antisocial peers together can have harmful effects (Dishion et al., 1999).

The most important intervention programme whose success seems to be based mainly on reducing peer risk factors is the Children at Risk programme (Harrell et al., 1997), which targeted high-risk adolescents (average age 12) in poor neighbourhoods of five cities across the United States. Eligible youths were identified in schools, and randomly assigned to experimental or control groups. The programme was a comprehensive commu-nity-based prevention strategy targeting risk factors for delinquency, including case management and family counselling, family skills training, tutoring, mentoring, after-school activities and community policing. The programme was different in each neighbourhood.

The initial results of the programme were disappoint-ing, but a one-year follow-up showed that (according to self-reports) experimental youths were less likely to have committed violent crimes and used or sold drugs (Harrell *et al.*, 1999). The process evaluation showed that the greatest change was in peer risk factors. Experimental youths associated less often with delinquent peers, felt less peer pressure to engage in delinquency and had more positive peer support. In contrast, there were few changes in individual, family or community risk factors, possibly linked to the low participation of parents in parent training and of youths in mentoring and tutoring. In other words, there were problems of implementation of the programme, linked to the serious and multiple needs and problems of the families.

Peer tutoring was also involved in the Quantum Opportunities Programme, which was implemented in five sites across the United States (Hahn, 1994, 1999). It aimed to improve the life-course opportunities of disadvantaged, at-risk youth during the high-school years and included peer tutoring for educational development and adult assistance with life skills, career planning and community service. Participants received cash incentives to stay in the programme, and staff received cash incentives for keeping youth in the programme.

Fifty adolescents aged about 14 were randomly assigned to experimental or control conditions in each site, making an initial sample size of 250. The programme was successful. Experimental adolescents were more likely to graduate from high school (63 per cent vs. 42 per cent) and were less likely to be arrested (17 per cent versus 58 per cent). During the 6-month follow-up period, experimental adolescents were more likely to have volunteered as a mentor or tutor themselves (28 per cent versus 8 per cent) and were less likely to have claimed welfare benefits.

A cost–benefit analysis of the Quantum Opportunities Programme (Hahn, 1994) revealed substantial benefits for both the participants and taxpayers. There was a desirable benefit: cost ratio of 3.7 to 1. Monetary benefits were limited to gains from education and fewer children, with the benefits from fewer children accruing from reduced costs for health and welfare services for teenage mothers. The calculations by Steve Aos and his colleagues (2001) yielded a more conservative benefit: cost ratio of 1.9 to 1.

Community-based mentoring programmes usually involve non-professional adult volunteers spending time with young people at risk of delinquency, dropping out of school, school failure, or other social problems. Mentors behave in a supportive, non-judgemental manner while acting as role models (Howell, 1995, p.90). Brandon Welsh and Akemi Hoshi (2002) identified seven mentoring programmes (of which six were of high quality) that evaluated the impact on delinquency. Since most programmes found desirable effects, Welsh and Hoshi concluded that community-based mentoring was a promising approach in preventing delinquency.

A systematic review and meta-analysis of 18 mentoring programmes by Darrick Jolliffe and myself (2008) found that this was an effective approach to preventing delinquency. The weighted mean effect size was $d = 0.21$, corresponding to a significant 10 per cent reduction in delinquency. Mentoring was more effective in reducing offending when the average duration of each contact between mentor and mentee was greater, in smaller-scale studies, and when mentoring was combined with other interventions.

Skills Training

The most important prevention techniques that target the risk factors of impulsiveness and low empathy are cognitive-behavioural skills training programmes. For example, Robert and Rosslyn Ross (1995) devised a programme that aimed to teach people to stop and think before acting, to consider the consequences of their behaviour, to conceptualise alternative ways of solving interpersonal problems, and to consider the impact of their behaviour on other people, especially victims. It included social skills training, lateral thinking (to teach creative problem solving), critical thinking (to teach logical reasoning), values education (to teach values and concern for others), assertiveness training (to teach non-aggressive, socially appropriate ways to obtain desired outcomes), negotiation skills training, interpersonal cognitive problem-solving (to teach thinking skills for solving interpersonal problems), social perspective training (to teach how to recognise and understand other people's feelings), role-playing and modelling (demonstration and practice of effective and acceptable interpersonal behaviour).

Robert and Bambi Ross (1988) implemented this 'Reasoning and Rehabilitation' programme in Ottawa, and found (in a randomised experiment) that it led to a large decrease in reoffending for a small sample of adult offenders in a short 9-month follow-up period. Their training was carried out by probation officers, but they believed that it could be carried out by parents or teachers. This programme has been implemented widely in several different countries, and forms the basis of many accredited cognitive-behavioural programmes used in the UK prison and probation services, including the Pathfinder projects (McGuire, 2001).

A similar programme, entitled 'Straight thinking on Probation' was implemented in Glamorgan by Peter Raynor and Maurice Vanstone (2001). Offenders who received skills training were compared with similar offenders who received custodial sentences. After one year, offenders who completed the programme had a lower reconviction rate than control offenders (35 per cent as opposed to 49 per cent), although both had the same predicted reconviction rate of 42 per cent. The benefits of the programme had worn off at the two-year follow-up point, when reconviction rates of experimentals (63 per cent) and controls (65 per cent) were similar to reach other and to predicted rates. However, the reconvicted experimentals committed less serious crimes than the reconvicted controls.

Joy Tong and I (2008) completed a systematic review of the effectiveness of 'Reasoning and Rehabilitation' in reducing offending. We located 32 comparisons of experimental and control groups in four countries. Our meta-analysis showed that, overall, there was a significant 14 per cent decrease in offending for programme participants compared with controls.

Marshall Jones and Dan Offord (1989) implemented a skills training programme in an experimental public housing complex in Ottawa and compared it with a control complex. The programme centred on non-school skills, both athletic (e.g. swimming and hockey) and non-athletic (e.g. guitar and ballet). The aim of developing skills was to increase self-esteem, to encourage children to use time constructively and to provide desirable role models. Participation rates were high; about three-quarters of age-eligible children in the experimental complex took at least one course in the first year. The programme was successful; delinquency rates decreased significantly in the experimental complex compared to the control complex. The benefit:cost ratio, based on savings to taxpayers, was 2.5 to 1.

The Montreal longitudinal-experimental study combined child skills training and parent training. Richard Tremblay and his colleagues (1995) identified disruptive (aggressive or hyperactive) boys at age 6, and randomly allocated over 300 of these to experimental or control conditions. Between ages 7 and 9, the experimental group received training designed to foster social skills and self-control. Coaching, peer modelling, role playing and reinforcement contingencies were used in small group sessions on such topics as 'how to help', 'what to do when you are angry' and 'how to react to teasing'. Also, their parents were trained using the parent management training techniques developed by Gerald Patterson (1982).

This prevention programme was successful. By age 12, the experimental boys committed less burglary and theft, were less likely to get drunk, and were less likely to be involved in fights than the controls (according to self-reports). Also, the experimental boys had higher school achievement. At every age from 10 to 15, the experimental boys had lower self-reported delinquency scores than the control boys. Interestingly, the differences in antisocial behaviour between experimental and control boys increased as the follow-up progressed. A later follow-up showed that fewer experimental boys had a criminal record by age 24 (Boisjoli et al., 2007).

Friedrich Lösel and Andreas Beelman (2006) completed a systematic review of the effectiveness of skills training with children and adolescents. They located 89 comparisons of experimental and control groups. Their meta-analysis showed that, overall, there was a significant 10 per cent decrease in delinquency in follow-up studies for children who received skills training compared with controls. The greatest effect was for cognitive-behavioural skills training, where there was an average 25 per cent decrease in delinquency in seven follow-up studies. The most effective programmes targeted children aged 13 or older and high-risk groups who were already exhibiting behaviour problems.

Communities That Care

In the interests of maximising effectiveness, what is needed is a multiple-component community-based programme including several of the successful interventions listed above. Many of the programmes reviewed in this chapter are of this type. However, Communities That Care (CTC) has many attractions (Farrington, 1996). Perhaps more than any other programme, it is evidence-based and systematic: the choice of interventions depends on empirical evidence about what are the important risk and protective factors in a particular community and on empirical evidence about 'What works' (Sherman et al., 2006). It has been implemented in at least 35 sites in England, Scotland and Wales, and also in the Netherlands and Australia (Communities That Care, 1997). Unfortunately, it is difficult to draw any conclusion from the evaluation of three UK CTC projects (Crow et al., 2004) because of implementation problems. While the effectiveness of the overall CTC strategy has not yet been demonstrated, the effectiveness of its individual components is clear (Harachi et al., 2003).

CTC was developed as a risk-focused prevention strategy by David Hawkins and Richard Catalano (1992), and it is a core component of the US Office of Juvenile Justice and Delinquency Prevention's (OJJDP's) Comprehensive Strategy for Serious, Violent and Chronic Juvenile Offenders (Wilson & Howell, 1993). CTC is based on a theory (the social development model) that organises risk and protective factors. The intervention techniques are tailored to the needs of each particular community. The 'community' could be a city, a county, a small town, or even a neighbourhood or a housing estate. This programme aims to reduce delinquency and drug use by implementing particular prevention strategies that have demonstrated effectiveness in reducing risk factors or enhancing protective factors. It is modelled on large-scale community-wide public health programmes designed to reduce illnesses such as coronary heart disease by tackling key risk factors. There is great emphasis in CTC on enhancing protective factors and building on strengths, partly because this is more attractive to communities than tackling risk factors. However, it is generally true that health promotion is more effective than disease prevention (Kaplan, 2000).

CTC programmes begin with community mobilisation. Key community leaders (e.g. elected representatives, education officials, police chiefs, business leaders) are brought together, with the aim of getting them to agree on the goals of the prevention programme and to implement CTC. The key leaders then set up a Community Board that is accountable to them, consisting of neighbourhood residents and representatives from various agencies (e.g. school, police, social services, probation, health, parents, youth groups, business, church, media). The Community Board takes charge of prevention on behalf of the community.

The Community Board then carries out a risk and protective factor assessment, identifying key risk factors in that particular community that need to be tackled and key protective factors that need enhancing. This risk assessment might involve the use of police, school, social or census records or local neighbourhood or school surveys. After identifying key risk and protective factors, the Community Board assesses existing resources and develops a plan of intervention strategies. With specialist technical assistance and guidance, they choose programmes from a menu of strategies that have been shown to be effective in well-designed evaluation research.

The menu of strategies listed by Hawkins and Catalano (1992) includes prenatal and postnatal home visiting programmes, preschool intellectual enrichment programmes, parent training, school organisation and curriculum development, teacher training and media campaigns. Other strategies include child skills training, anti-bullying programmes in schools, situational prevention, and policing strategies. The choice of prevention strategies is based on empirical evidence about effective methods of tackling each particular risk factor, but it also depends on what are identified as the biggest problems in the community. While this approach is not without its challenges and complexities (e.g. cost, implementation, establishing partnerships among diverse agencies), an evidence-based approach that brings together the most effective prevention programmes across multiple domains offers the greatest promise for reducing crime and building safer communities.

Recent UK Developments

In September 2006, the UK government announced an action plan for 'social exclusion', which is a general concept including antisocial behaviour, teenage pregnancy, educational failure and mental health problems (Cabinet Office, 2006). This action plan emphasised early intervention, better coordination of agencies, and evidence-based practice (systematically identifying what works and rating evaluations according to methodological quality: see Farrington, 2003). It proposed home visiting programmes targeting at-risk children from birth to age 2, implemented by midwives and health visitors, inspired by the work of David Olds (Olds et al., 1998). It proposed that teenage pregnancy 'hot spots' would be targeted with enhanced social and relationship education and better access to contraceptives. It proposed multi-agency and family-based approaches to tackle behavioural and mental health problems in childhood, including treatment foster care (Chamberlain & Reid, 1998) and multisystemic therapy (Henggeler et al., 1998). It also proposed interventions for adults with chaotic lives, mental health problems and multiple needs, to try to get more of them into employment.

Since the mid-1990s, there has been increasing emphasis on early intervention and evidence-based practice in the UK (Sutton et al., 2004, 2006). In 1995,

Child and Adolescent Mental Health Services (CAMHS) teams were established in every part of the country to provide support for children and young people who were experiencing a range of emotional and behavioural difficulties. The services fall within the remit of the Department of Health and practitioners typically employ a wide range of theoretical approaches.

The major government initiative for preschool children is called *Sure Start* (www.dcsf.gov.uk/every-childmatters/earlyyears/surestart/whatsurestartdoes/). The first Sure Start centres were established in 1999 in disadvantaged areas, and there are now over 800 Sure Start programmes in the UK. These centres provide early education and parenting programmes, integrated with extended child care, health and family support services. The services are supposed to be evidence-based. Widely used parenting programmes include *The Incredible Years* (Webster-Stratton, 2000), *Triple-P* (Sanders *et al.*, 2000) and *Strengthening Families, Strengthening Communities* (Steele *et al.*, 1999). A National Academy for Parenting Professionals has been established.

It is very difficult to evaluate large-scale national programmes such as Sure Start. The main evaluation so far compared outcomes for 150 Sure Start areas and 50 non-Sure Start areas (Sure Start-to-be) by assessing a random sample of families with a 9-month-old child or with a 3-year-old child in each locality (Melhuish *et al.*, 2005). The results showed that, for 3-year-old children, with non-teenage mothers (86 per cent of the sample), the children showed greater social competence and had fewer behaviour problems, and there was less negative parenting in the Sure Start areas than in the control group areas. However, among teenage mothers (14 per cent of the sample), in the Sure Start areas the children showed less social competence, had lower verbal ability and had more behaviour problems than in the control areas.

Sure Start programmes are currently being developed into Children's Centres, to cover every part of the UK. Typically, these will be service hubs, offering and coordinating information to support children and their parents. One of their implicit objectives is to reduce conduct disorder and aggressiveness among young children through the provision of parenting programmes. The Centres also contribute to the strategic objectives of *Every Child Matters*, the major government policy document (Chief Secretary to the Treasury, 2003; www.dcsf.gov.uk/everychildmatters/). This applies to all children from birth to age 19 and aims to improve educational achievement and reduce the levels of ill health, teenage pregnancy, abuse and neglect, crime and antisocial behaviour.

In 1999 the Home Office supported a national initiative intended to prevent children's future antisocial or criminal behaviour by working with children aged 8–13, together with their families. Projects entitled *On Track* were set up in 24 local authorities and practitioners were required to employ a limited number of approaches to supporting families, including behaviour management, promoting home–school liaison, play therapy and parenting packages. The Department for Children, Schools and Families has now assumed responsibility for taking forward all work with children aged 0–19. It has invited bids from 15 local authorities to provide parenting support focusing on children aged 8–13, requiring that those bidding for funding shall use one of the three parenting packages mentioned above.

Parenting orders can be given by courts to the parents or carers of young people who offend or truant, or who have received a Child Safety Order, Antisocial Behaviour Order or Sex Offender Order. The parenting order can be extended to 12 months. Parents or carers who receive Parenting Orders are required to attend counselling or guidance sessions to enable them to communicate better with their children and to manage their behaviour more effectively. The approaches taught to parents are typically based on social learning theory, but there does not yet seem to be any wholesale adoption of specific evidence-based parenting programmes.

Conclusions

High-quality evaluation research shows that many programmes are effective in reducing delinquency and antisocial behaviour, and that in many cases the financial benefits of these programmes outweigh their financial costs. The best programmes include general parent education, parent management training, preschool intellectual enrichment programmes, child skills training, teacher training, anti-bullying programmes, mentoring and MST. While most is known about programmes for boys, there are also effective interventions designed specifically for girls (Hipwell & Loeber, 2006).

High-quality experimental and quasi-experimental evaluations of the effectiveness of crime reduction programmes are needed in the UK. Most knowledge about the effectiveness of prevention programmes, such as cognitive-behavioural skills training, parent training and preschool intellectual enrichment programmes, is based on American research. Ideally, prevention programmes should aim not only to tackle risk factors but also to strengthen protective factors, and both risk and protective factors should be measured and targeted. An important development in recent years has been the increasing use of cost–benefit analysis in evaluating prevention programmes. Cost–benefit analyses of the effectiveness of prevention programmes should be given some priority, and a standard how-to-do-it manual should be developed.

Experiments and quasi-experiments should have large samples, long follow-up periods, and follow-up interviews. Sample size is particularly important for both individual- and area-based studies. Many interventions have proved effective in small-scale demonstration programmes but less effective in large-scale implementation. More research is needed on the transportability of programmes. Long-term follow-ups are needed to establish the persistence of effects. This information may indicate the need for booster sessions. Long follow-ups are rare after criminological interventions and should be a top priority of funding agencies. Research is also needed to identify the active ingredients of successful early prevention programmes. Many programmes are multimodal, which makes it difficult to isolate the independent or interactive effects of the different components. Future experiments are needed that attempt to disentangle the different elements of the most successful programmes.

It is difficult to evaluate large-scale crime reduction strategies, and to answer questions about whether it is better (in terms of crimes saved per £ spent, for example) to invest in risk-focused early prevention, in physical or situational prevention, in more police officers or in more prison cells. Nevertheless, this question is of vital importance to government policy makers and to the general population. Therefore, research is needed to investigate the cost-effectiveness of risk-focused prevention in comparison with other general crime reduction strategies.

Turning to policy implications, consideration should be given to implementing a multiple-component risk-focused prevention programme such as CTC more widely throughout the UK. This programme could be implemented by existing Crime and Disorder Partnerships. However, they would need resources and technical assistance to conduct youth surveys and household surveys to identify key risk and protective factors for both people and places. They would also need resources and technical assistance to measure risk

and protective factors, to choose effective intervention methods, and to carry out high-quality evaluations of the effectiveness of programmes in reducing crime and disorder.

The focus should be on primary prevention – offering the programme to all families living in specified areas – not on secondary prevention – targeting the programme on individuals identified as at risk. Ideally, the programme should be presented positively, as fostering safe and healthy communities by strengthening protective factors, rather than as a crime prevention programme targeting risk factors.

Nationally and locally, there is no agency whose main mandate is the primary prevention of crime. A national prevention agency could provide technical assistance, skills and knowledge to local agencies in implementing prevention programmes, could provide funding for such programmes, and could ensure continuity, coordination and monitoring of local programmes. It could provide training in prevention science for people in local agencies, and could maintain high standards for evaluation research. It could also act as a centre for the discussion of how policy initiatives of different government agencies influence crime and associated social problems. It could set a national and local agenda for research and practice in the prevention of crime, drug and alcohol abuse, mental health problems and associated social problems.

National crime prevention agencies have been established in other countries, such as Sweden (Andersson, 2005) and Canada (Sansfaçon & Waller, 2001). These agencies have emphasised three main mechanisms: collaboration with other government departments, development of local problem-solving partnerships, and involvement of citizens (Waller & Welsh, 1999). These points specify how evidence-based results can be translated into local practice. Each point specifies concrete actions that a national agency can influence at the local level, but programme success ultimately will depend on local persons. A national agency can influence these implementation issues in a number of ways; for example, by developing guidelines on effective practice and making project funding conditional on the use of evidence-based programmes.

A national agency could also maintain a computerised register of evaluation research and, like the National Institute for Health and Clinical Excellence, advise the government about effective and cost-effective crime prevention programmes. Medical advice is often based on systematic reviews of the effectiveness of healthcare interventions organised by the Cochrane Collaboration and funded by the National Health Service. Systematic reviews of the evaluation literature on the effectiveness of criminological interventions, possibly organised by the Campbell Collaboration (Farrington & Petrosino, 2001), should be commissioned and funded by government agencies.

Crime prevention also needs to be organised locally. In each area, a local agency should be established to take the lead in organising risk-focused crime prevention. In Sweden, 80 per cent of municipalities had local crime prevention councils in 2005 (Andersson, 2005). The local prevention agency could take the lead in measuring risk factors and social problems in local areas, using archival records and local household and school surveys. It could then assess available resources and develop a plan of prevention strategies. With specialist technical assistance, prevention programmes could be chosen from a menu of strategies that have been proved to be effective in reducing crime in well-designed evaluation research. This would be a good example of evidence-based practice.

Recent promising developments in the UK, such as Sure Start and *Every Child Matters* (Chief Secretary to the Treasury, 2003) have clearly been influenced by recent research on childhood risk factors and risk-focused intervention strategies. The time is ripe to expand these experimental programmes into a large-scale evidence-based integrated national strategy for the reduction of crime and associated social problems, including rigorous evaluation requirements.

Further Reading

Farrington, D.P. & Welsh, B.C. (2007). *Saving children from a life of crime: Early risk factors and effective interventions.* Oxford: Oxford University Press.
This book reviews knowledge about individual, family, socio-economic, peer, school and community risk factors. It then reviews intervention programmes targeted on the individual (e.g. child skills training and preschool intellectual enrichment programmes), family (e.g. home visiting and parent training programmes), peer, school and community. The final chapter sets out the need for a national strategy for early intervention.

McCord, J. & Tremblay, R.E. (Eds.) (1992). *Preventing antisocial behavior: Interventions from birth through adolescence.* New York: Guilford Press.

This book contains chapters describing many of the most important developmental prevention programmes, including those by Lawrence Schweinhart, Richard Tremblay, David Hawkins, Sheppard Kellam, Ronald Feldman and Gerald Patterson.

Greenwood, P.W. (2006). *Changing lives: Delinquency prevention as crime-control policy.* Chicago, IL: University of Chicago Press.
This book reviews programmes designed to prevent delinquency in children and adolescents, highlighting both effective and ineffective programmes. It is particularly strong in its discussions of cost–benefit analyses, and it includes recommendations about the large-scale national implementation of delinquency prevention programmes.

References

Alexander, J.F. & Parsons, B.V. (1973). Short-term behavioral intervention with delinquent families: Impact on family process and recidivism. *Journal of Abnormal Psychology, 81,* 219–225.

Andersson, J. (2005). The Swedish National Council for Crime Prevention: A short presentation. *Journal of Scandinavian Studies in Criminology and Crime Prevention,* 6, 74–88.

Aos, S., Phipps, P., Barnoski, R. & Lieb, R. (2001). The comparative costs and benefits of programs to reduce crime: A review of research findings with implications for Washington State. In B.C. Welsh, D.P. Farrington & L.W. Sherman (Eds.) *Costs and benefits of preventing crime* (pp.149–175). Boulder, CO: Westview Press.

Baldry, A.C. & Farrington, D.P. (1998). Parenting influences on bullying and victimization. *Legal and Criminological Psychology,* 3, 237–254.

Barnett, W.S. (1993). Cost–benefit analysis. In L.J. Schweinhart, H.V. Barnes & D.P. Weikart (Eds.) *Significant benefits: The High/Scope Perry Preschool Study through age 27* (pp.142–173). Ypsilanti, MI: High/Scope Press.

Barton, C., Alexander, J.F., Waldron, H., Turner, C.W. & Warburton, J. (1985). Generalizing treatment effects of functional family therapy: Three replications. *American Journal of Family Therapy,* 13, 16–26.

Berrueta-Clement, J.R., Schweinhart, L.J., Barnett, W.S., Epstein, A.S. & Weikart, D.P. (1984). *Changed lives: The effects of the Perry Preschool Program on youths through age 19.* Ypsilanti, MI: High/Scope Press.

Boisjoli, R., Vitaro, F., Lacourse, E., Barker, E.D. & Tremblay, R.E. (2007). Impact and clinical significance of a preventive intervention for disruptive boys. *British Journal of Psychiatry,* 191, 415–419.

Borduin, C.M., Mann, B.J., Cone, L.T., Henggeler, S.W., Fucci, B.R., Blaske, D.M. *et al.* (1995). Multisystemic treatment of serious juvenile offenders: Long-term prevention of criminality and violence. *Journal of Consulting and Clinical Psychology*, 63, 569–587.

Brand, S. & Price, R. (2000). *The economic and social costs of crime*. London: Home Office (Research Study No. 217).

Cabinet Office (2006). *Reaching out: An action plan for social exclusion*. London: Cabinet Office.

Campbell, F.A., Ramey, C.T., Pungello, E., Sparling, J. & Miller-Johnson, S. (2002). Early childhood education: Young adult outcomes from the Abercedarian Project. *Applied Developmental Science*, 6, 42–57.

Catalano, R.F., Hawkins, J.D., Berglund, L., Pollard, J.A. & Arthur, M.W. (2002). Prevention science and positive youth development: Competitive or cooperative frameworks? *Journal of Adolescent Health*, 31, 230–239.

Chamberlain, P. & Reid, J.B. (1998). Comparison of two community alternatives to incarceration for chronic juvenile offenders. *Journal of Consulting and Clinical Psychology*, 66, 624–633.

Chief Secretary to the Treasury (2003). *Every child matters*. London: The Stationery Office.

Clarke, R.V. (1995). Situational crime prevention. In M. Tonry & D.P. Farrington (Eds.) *Building a safer society: Strategic approaches to crime prevention* (pp.91–150). Chicago, IL: University of Chicago Press.

Cohen, M.A. (1998). The monetary value of saving a high-risk youth. *Journal of Quantitative Criminology*, 14, 5–33.

Communities that Care (1997). *Communities that Care (UK): A new kind of prevention programme*. London: Communities that Care.

Crow, I., France, A., Hacking, S. & Hart, M. (2004). *Does Communities That Care work? An evaluation of a community-based risk prevention programme in three neighbourhoods*. York: Joseph Rowntree Foundation.

Curtis, N.M., Ronan, K.R. & Borduin, C.M. (2004). Multisystemic treatment: A meta-analysis of outcome studies. *Journal of Family Psychology*, 18, 411–419.

Dishion, T.J., McCord, J. & Poulin, F. (1999). When interventions harm: Peer groups and problem behavior. *American Psychologist*, 54, 755–764.

Dishion, T.J., Patterson, G.R. & Kavanagh, K.A. (1992). An experimental test of the coercion model: Linking theory, measurement and intervention. In J. McCord & R.E. Tremblay (Eds.) *Preventing antisocial behavior: Interventions from birth through adolescence* (pp.253–282). New York: Guilford Press.

Farrington, D.P. (1993). Understanding and preventing bullying. In M. Tonry & N. Morris (Eds.) *Crime and justice* (vol. 17, pp.381–458). Chicago, IL: University of Chicago Press.

Farrington, D.P. (1996). *Understanding and preventing youth crime*. York: Joseph Rowntree Foundation.

Farrington, D.P. (2003). Methodological quality standards for evaluation research. *Annals of the American Academy of Political and Social Science*, 587, 49–68.

Farrington, D.P. (2007). Childhood risk factors and risk-focussed prevention. In M. Maguire, R. Morgan & R. Reiner (Eds.) *The Oxford handbook of criminology* (4th edn, pp.602–640). Oxford: Oxford University Press.

Farrington, D.P., Coid, J.W., Harnett, L., Jolliffe, D., Soteriou, N., Turner, R. *et al.* (2006). *Criminal careers up to age 50 and life success up to age 48: New findings from the Cambridge Study in Delinquent Development*. London: Home Office (Research Study No. 299).

Farrington, D.P. & Petrosino, A. (2001). The Campbell Collaboration Crime and Justice Group. *Annals of the American Academy of Political and Social Science, 578*, 35–49.

Farrington, D.P. & Welsh, B.C. (2003). Family-based prevention of offending: A meta-analysis. *Australian and New Zealand Journal of Criminology*, 36, 127–151.

Farrington, D.P. & Welsh, B.C. (2005). Randomized experiments in criminology: What have we learned in the last two decades? *Journal of Experimental Criminology*, 1, 9–38.

Farrington, D.P. & Welsh, B.C. (2006). A half-century of randomized experiments on crime and justice. In M. Tonry (Ed.) *Crime and justice* (vol. 34, pp.55–132). Chicago, IL: University of Chicago Press.

Farrington, D.P. & Welsh, B.C. (2007). *Saving children from a life of crime: Early risk factors and effective interventions*. Oxford: Oxford University Press.

Feldman, R.A., Caplinger, T.E. & Wodarski, J.S. (1983). *The St. Louis conundrum*. Englewood Cliffs, NJ: Prentice-Hall.

Garces, E., Thomas, D. & Currie, J. (2002). Longer-term effects of Head Start. *American Economic Review*, 92, 999–1012.

Gardner, F., Burton, J. & Klimes, I. (2006). Randomized controlled trial of a parenting intervention in the voluntary sector for reducing child conduct problems: Outcomes and mechanisms of change. *Journal of Child Psychology and Psychiatry*, 47, 1123–1132.

Gottfredson, D.C., Wilson, D.B. & Najaka, S.S. (2006). School-based crime prevention. In L.W. Sherman, D.P. Farrington, B.C. Welsh & D.L. MacKenzie (Eds.) *Evidence-based crime prevention* (rev. edn, pp.56–164). London: Routledge.

Hahn, A. (1994). *Evaluation of the Quantum Opportunities Program (QOP): Did the program work?* Waltham, MA: Brandeis University.

Hahn, A. (1999). Extending the time of learning. In D.J. Besharov (Ed.) *America's disconnected youth: Toward a preventive strategy* (pp.233–265). Washington, DC: Child Welfare League of America Press.

Harachi, T.W., Hawkins, J.D., Catalano, R.F., Lafazia, A.M., Smith, B.H. & Arthur, M.W. (2003). Evidence-based community decision making for prevention: Two case studies of Communities That Care. *Japanese Journal of Sociological Criminology*, 28, 26–37.

Harrell, A.V., Cavanagh, S.E., Harmon, M.A., Koper, C.S. & Sridharan, S. (1997). *Impact of the Children at Risk program: Comprehensive final report* (vol. 2). Washington, DC: The Urban Institute.

Harrell, A.V., Cavanagh, S.E. & Sridharan, S. (1999). *Evaluation of the Children at Risk program: Results one year after the program*. Washington, DC: US National Institute of Justice.

Hawkins, J.D. & Catalano, R.F. (1992). *Communities that Care*. San Francisco, CA: Jossey-Bass.

Hawkins, J.D., Catalano, R.F., Kosterman, R., Abbott, R. & Hill, K.G. (1999). Preventing adolescent health risk behaviors by strengthening protection during childhood. *Archives of Pediatrics and Adolescent Medicine, 153*, 226–234.

Hawkins, J.D., von Cleve, E. & Catalano, R.F. (1991). Reducing early childhood aggression: Results of a primary prevention program. *Journal of the American Academy of Child and Adolescent Psychiatry, 30*, 208–217.

Henggeler, S.W., Clingempeel, W.G., Brondino, M.J. & Pickrel, S.G. (2002). Four-year follow-up of multisystemic therapy with substance-abusing and substance-dependent juvenile offenders. *Journal of the American Academy of Child and Adolescent Psychiatry, 41*, 868–874.

Henggeler, S.W., Melton, G.B., Brondino, M.J., Scherer, D.G. & Hanley, J.H. (1997). Multisystemic therapy with violent and chronic juvenile offenders and their families: The role of treatment fidelity in successful dissemination. *Journal of Consulting and Clinical Psychology, 65*, 821–833.

Henggeler, S.W., Melton, G.B., Smith, L.A., Schoenwald, S.K. & Hanley, J.H. (1993). Family preservation using multisystematic treatment: Long-term follow-up to a clinical trial with serious juvenile offenders. *Journal of Child and Family Studies, 2*, 283–293.

Henggeler, S.W., Rowland, M.D., Randall, J., Ward, D.M., Pickrel, S.G., Cunningham, P.B. *et al.* (1999). Home-based multisystemic therapy as an alternative to the hospitalization of youths in psychiatric crisis: Clinical outcomes. *Journal of the American Academy of Child and Adolescent Psychiatry, 38*, 1331–1339.

Henggeler, S.W., Schoenwald, S.K., Borduin, C.M., Rowland, M.D. & Cunningham, P.B. (1998). *Multisystemic treatment of antisocial behavior in children and adolescents*. New York: Guilford Press.

Hipwell, A.E. & Loeber, R. (2006). Do we know which interventions are effective for disruptive and delinquent girls? *Clinical Child and Family Psychology Review, 9*, 221–255.

Hope, T. (1995). Community crime prevention. In M. Tonry & D.P. Farrington (Eds.) *Building a safer society: Strategic approaches to crime prevention* (pp.21–89). Chicago, IL: University of Chicago Press.

Howell, J.C. (Ed.) (1995). *Guide for implementing the comprehensive strategy for serious, violent, and chronic juvenile offenders*. Washington, DC: Office of Juvenile Justice and Delinquency Prevention, US Department of Justice.

Jefford, T. & Squire, B. (2004). Multi-systemic therapy: Model practice. *Young Minds, 71*, 20–21.

Jolliffe, D. & Farrington, D.P. (2008). *The influence of mentoring on reoffending*. Stockholm, Sweden: National Council for Crime Prevention.

Jones, M.B. & Offord, D.R. (1989). Reduction of antisocial behaviour in poor children by non-school skill development. *Journal of Child Psychology and Psychiatry, 30*, 737–750.

Kaplan, R.M. (2000). Two pathways to prevention. *American Psychologist, 55*, 382–396.

Kazdin, A.E., Kraemer, H.C., Kessler, R.C., Kupfer, D.J. & Offord, D.R. (1997). Contributions of risk-factor research to developmental psychopathology. *Clinical Psychology Review, 17*, 375–406.

Kolvin, I., Garside, R.F., Nicol, A.R., MacMillan, A., Wolstenholme, F. & Leith, I.M. (1981). *Help starts here: The maladjusted child in the ordinary school*. London: Tavistock.

Leschied, A. & Cunningham, A. (2002). *Seeking effective interventions for serious young offenders: Interim results of a four-year randomized study of multisystemic therapy in Ontario, Canada*. London, ON: London Family Court Clinic.

Leve, L.D., Chamberlain, P. & Reid, J.B. (2005). Intervention outcomes for girls referred from juvenile justice: Effects on delinquency. *Journal of Consulting and Clinical Psychology, 73*, 1181–1185.

Littell, J.H. (2005). Lessons from a systematic review of effects of multisystemic therapy. *Children and Youth Services Review, 27*, 445–463.

Lösel, F. & Beelmann, A. (2006). Child social skills training. In B.C. Welsh & D.P. Farrington (Eds.) *Preventing crime: What works for children, offenders, victims, and places* (pp.33–54). Dordrecht, Netherlands: Springer.

Lösel, F. & Bender, D. (2003). Protective factors and resilience. In D.P. Farrington & J.W. Coid (Eds.) *Early prevention of adult antisocial behaviour* (pp.130–204). Cambridge: Cambridge University Press.

McGuire, J. (2001). What works in correctional intervention? Evidence and practical implications. In G.A. Bernfeld, D.P. Farrington & A.W. Leschied (Eds.) *Offender rehabilitation in practice: Implementing and evaluating effective programmes* (pp.25–43). Chichester: Wiley.

Melhuish, E., Belsky, J. & Leyland, A. (2005). *Early impacts of Sure Start local programmes on children and families: Report of the cross-sectional study of 9 and 36 months old children and their families*. London: The Stationery Office.

O'Donnell, J., Hawkins, J.D., Catalano, R.F., Abbott, R.D. & Day, L.E. (1995). Preventing school failure, drug use, and delinquency among low-income children: Long-term intervention in elementary schools. *American Journal of Orthopsychiatry, 65*, 87–100.

Ogden, T. & Hagen, K.A. (2006). Multisystemic treatment of serious behaviour problems in youth: Sustainability of effectiveness two years after intake. *Child and Adolescent Mental Health, 11*, 142–149.

Olds, D.L., Eckenrode, J., Henderson, C.R., Kitzman, H., Powers, J., Cole, R. *et al.* (1997). Long-term effects of home visitation on maternal life course and child abuse and neglect: Fifteen-year follow-up of a randomized trial. *Journal of the American Medical Association, 278*, 637–643.

Olds, D.L., Henderson, C.R., Chamberlin, R. & Tatelbaum, R. (1986). Preventing child abuse and neglect: A randomized trial of nurse home visitation. *Pediatrics, 78,* 65–78.

Olds, D.L., Henderson, C.R., Cole, R., Eckenrode, J., Kitzman, H., Luckey, D. *et al.* (1998). Long-term effects of nurse home visitation on children's criminal and antisocial behavior: 15-year follow-up of a randomized controlled trial. *Journal of the American Medical Association, 280,* 1238–1244.

Olds, D.L., Sadler, L. & Kitzman, H. (2007). Programs for parents of infants and toddlers: Recent evidence from randomized trials. *Journal of Child Psychology and Psychiatry, 48,* 355–391.

Olweus, D. (1994). Bullying at school: Basic facts and effects of a school based intervention programme. *Journal of Child Psychology and Psychiatry, 35,* 1171–1190.

Patterson, G.R. (1982). *Coercive family process.* Eugene, OR: Castalia.

Patterson, G.R., Reid, J.B. & Dishion, T.J. (1992). *Antisocial boys.* Eugene, OR: Castalia.

Petras, H., Kellam, S.G., Brown, C.H., Muthen, B.O., Ialongo, N.S. & Poduska, J.M. (2008). Developmental epidemiological courses leading to antisocial personality disorder and violent and criminal behaviour: Effects by young adulthood of a universal preventive intervention in first and second grade classrooms. *Drugs and Alcohol Dependence, 95S,* S45–S59.

Piquero, A.R., Farrington, D.P., Welsh, B.C., Tremblay, R.E. & Jennings, W. (2008). *Effects of early family/parent training programs on antisocial behavior and delinquency: A systematic review.* Stockholm, Sweden: National Council for Crime Prevention.

Raynor, P. & Vanstone, M. (2001). 'Straight thinking on probation': Evidence-based practice and the culture of curiosity. In G.A. Bernfeld, D.P. Farrington & A.W. Leschied (Eds.) *Offender rehabilitation in practice: Implementing and evaluating effective programmes* (pp.189–203). Chichester: Wiley.

Reynolds, A.J., Temple, J.A., Robertson, D.L. & Mann, E.A. (2001). Long-term effects of an early childhood intervention on educational achievement and juvenile arrest: A 15-year follow-up of low-income children in public schools. *Journal of the American Medical Association, 285,* 2339–2346.

Ross, R.R. & Ross, B.D. (1988). Delinquency prevention through cognitive training. *New Education, 10,* 70–75.

Ross, R.R. & Ross, R.D. (Eds.) (1995). *Thinking straight: The Reasoning and Rehabilitation programme for delinquency prevention and offender rehabilitation.* Ottawa, Canada: Air Training and Publications.

Sanders, M.R., Markie-Dadds, C., Tully, L.A. & Bor, W. (2000). The Triple P-Positive Parenting Program: A comparison of enhanced, standard and self-directed behavioral family intervention for parents of children with early onset conduct problems. *Journal of Consulting and Clinical Psychology, 68,* 624–640.

Sansfaçon, D. & Waller. I. (2001). Recent evolution of governmental crime prevention strategies and implications for evaluation and economic analysis. In B.C. Welsh, D.P. Farrington & L.W. Sherman (Eds.) *Costs and benefits of preventing crime* (pp.225–247). Boulder, CO: Westview Press.

Schweinhart, L.J., Barnes, H.V. & Weikart, D.P. (1993). *Significant benefits: The High/Scope Perry Preschool Study through age 27.* Ypsilanti, MI: High/Scope Press.

Schweinhart, L.J., Montie, J., Zongping, X., Barnett, W.S., Belfield, C.R. & Nores, M. (2005). *Lifetime effects: The High/Scope Perry Preschool Study through age 40.* Ypsilanti, MI: High/Scope Press.

Schweinhart, L.J. & Weikart, D.P. (1980). *Young children grow up: The effects of the Perry Preschool Program on youths through age 15.* Ypsilanti, MI: High/Scope Press.

Scott, S., Spender, Q., Doolan, M., Jacobs, B. & Aspland, H. (2001). Multicentre controlled trial of parenting groups for child antisocial behaviour in clinical practice. *British Medical Journal, 323,* 194–196.

Sexton, T.L. & Alexander, J. F. (2000). *Functional family therapy.* Washington, DC: US Office of Juvenile Justice and Delinquency Prevention.

Sherman, L.W., Farrington, D.P., Welsh, B.C. & MacKenzie, D.L. (Eds.) (2006). *Evidence-based crime prevention* (rev. edn). London: Routledge.

Smith, P.K. & Sharp, S. (1994). *School bullying.* London: Routledge.

Steele, M., Marigna, M.K., Tello, J. & Johnson, R. (1999). *Strengthening multi-ethnic families and communities: A violence prevention parent training program.* Los Angeles, CA: Consulting and Clinical Services.

Sutton, C., Utting, D. & Farrington, D.P. (Eds.) (2004). *Support from the start: Working with young children and their families to reduce the risks of crime and antisocial behaviour.* London: Department for Education and Skills (Research Report 524).

Sutton, C., Utting, D. & Farrington, D.P. (2006). Nipping criminality in the bud. *The Psychologist, 19,* 470–475.

Tobler, N.S., Lessard, T., Marshall, D., Ochshorn, P. & Roona, M. (1999). Effectiveness of school-based drug prevention programs for marijuana use. *School Psychology International, 20,* 105–137.

Tong, L.S.J. & Farrington, D.P. (2008). Effectiveness of 'Reasoning and Rehabilitation' in reducing offending. *Psicothema, 20,* 20–28.

Tonry, M. & Farrington, D.P. (1995). Strategic approaches to crime prevention. In M. Tonry & D.P. Farrington (Eds.) *Building a safer society: Strategic approaches to crime prevention* (pp.1–20). Chicago, IL: University of Chicago Press.

Tremblay, R.E. & Craig, W.M. (1995). Developmental crime prevention. In M. Tonry & D.P. Farrington (Eds.) *Building a safer society: Strategic approaches to crime prevention* (pp.151–236). Chicago, IL: University of Chicago Press.

Tremblay, R.E., Pagani-Kurtz, L., Masse, L.C., Vitaro, F. & Pihl, R.O. (1995). A bimodal preventive intervention for disruptive kindergarten boys: Its impact through mid-adolescence. *Journal of Consulting and Clinical Psychology, 63,* 560–568.

Ttofi, M.M., Farrington, D.P. & Baldry, A.C. (2008). *Effectiveness of programmes to reduce school bullying.* Stockholm, Sweden: National Council for Crime Prevention.

Waller, I. & Welsh, B.C. (1999). International trends in crime prevention: Cost-effective ways to reduce victimization. In G. Newman (Ed.) *Global report on crime and justice* (pp.191–220). New York: Oxford University Press.

Webster-Stratton, C. (1998). Preventing conduct problems in Head Start children: Strengthening parenting competencies. *Journal of Consulting and Clinical Psychology, 66,* 715–730.

Webster-Stratton, C. (2000). *The Incredible Years training series.* Washington, DC: Office of Juvenile Justice and Delinquency Prevention.

Webster-Stratton, C. & Hammond, M. (1997). Treating children with early-onset conduct problems: A comparison of child and parent training interventions. *Journal of Consulting and Clinical Psychology, 65,* 93–109.

Welsh, B.C. & Farrington, D.P. (2000). Monetary costs and benefits of crime prevention programs. In M. Tonry (Ed.) *Crime and justice,* vol. 27 (pp.305–361). Chicago, IL: University of Chicago Press.

Welsh, B.C., Farrington, D.P. & Sherman, L.W. (Eds.) (2001). *Costs and benefits of preventing crime.* Boulder, CO: Westview Press.

Welsh, B.C. & Hoshi, A. (2002). Communities and crime prevention. In L.W. Sherman, D.P. Farrington, B.C. Welsh & D.L. MacKenzie (Eds.) *Evidence-based crime prevention.* New York: Routledge.

West, D.J. & Farrington, D.P. (1977). *The delinquent way of life.* London: Heinemann.

Widom, C.S. (1989). The cycle of violence. *Science, 244,* 160–166.

Wilson, D.B., Gottfredson, D.C. & Najaka, S.S. (2001). School-based prevention of problem behaviors: A meta-analysis. *Journal of Quantitative Criminology, 17,* 247–272.

Wilson, J.J. & Howell, J.C. (1993). *A comprehensive strategy for serious, violent, and chronic juvenile offenders.* Washington, DC: US Office of Juvenile Justice and Delinquency Prevention.

Wilson, S.J. & Lipsey, M.W. (2007). School based interventions for aggressive and disruptive behavior: Update of a meta-analysis. *American Journal of Preventive Medicine, 33*(2S), 130–143.

8

The Developmental Evidence Base
Psychosocial Research

David P. Farrington

Introduction

It is plausible to suggest that criminal behaviour results from the interaction between a person (with a certain degree of criminal potential or antisocial tendency) and the environment (which provides criminal opportunities). Given the same environment, some people will be more likely to commit offences than others, and conversely the same person will be more likely to commit offences in some environments than in others (see Farrington, 2005).

Criminological research typically concentrates on either the development of criminal persons or the occurrence of criminal events, but rarely on both. The focus in this chapter is primarily on offenders rather than offences. An advantage of studying offenders is that they are predominantly versatile rather than specialised. The typical offender who commits violence, vandalism or drug abuse also tends to commit theft or burglary. For example, in the Cambridge Study (described later) 86 per cent of violent offenders had convictions for non-violent offences up to age 32 (Farrington, 1991). Also, violent and non-violent but equally frequent offenders were very similar in their childhood and adolescent features in the Cambridge Study, in the Oregon Youth Study (Capaldi & Patterson, 1996) and in the Philadelphia Collaborative Perinatal project (Piquero, 2000). Therefore, in studying offenders, it is unnecessary to develop a different theory for each different type of offence. In contrast, in trying to explain why offences occur, the situations are so diverse and specific to particular crimes that it probably is

necessary to have different explanations for different types of offences.

In an attempt to identify possible causes of offending, this chapter reviews risk factors that influence the development of criminal careers. Fortunately or unfortunately, literally thousands of variables differentiate significantly between official offenders and non-offenders and correlate significantly with reports of offending behaviour by young people. In this chapter, it is only possible to review briefly some of the most important risk factors for offending: individual difference factors such as high impulsivity and low intelligence, family influences such as poor child-rearing and criminal parents, and social influences: socio-economic deprivation, peer, school and community factors.

Within a single chapter, it is obviously impossible to review everything that is known about psychosocial influences on offending. I will be very selective in focusing on some of the more important and replicable findings obtained in some of the projects with the strongest methodology, namely prospective longitudinal follow-up studies of large community samples. The better projects are defined here according to their possession of as many as possible of the following criteria:

(a) a large sample size of at least several hundreds;
(b) repeated personal interviews;
(c) a large number of different types of variables measured from different data sources (which makes it possible to study the effect of one independently of others, or interactive effects);

(d) a longitudinal design spanning at least five years (which makes it possible to establish causal order, to study the strength of effects at different ages, and to control extraneous variables better by investigating changes within individuals; see Farrington, 1988);

(e) a prospectively chosen, community sample (as opposed to retrospective comparisons between prisoners and controls, for example); and

(f) self-reported and official measures of offending (since results replicated with both methods probably provide information about offending rather than about any measurement biases).

Very few projects fulfil all or nearly all of these criteria, and abbreviated details of the most important 20 are listed in Table 8.1. This specifies the principal investigator(s), the sample initially studied, the length of the follow-up period, the most important types of data collected, and a representative publication. I will review results obtained in these projects in this chapter.

I will refer especially to knowledge gained in the Cambridge Study in Delinquent Development, which is a prospective longitudinal survey of over 400 London males from age 8 to age 48 (Farrington *et al.*, 2006). Fortunately, results obtained in British longitudinal surveys of delinquency are highly concordant with those obtained in comparable surveys in North America, the Scandinavian countries and New Zealand and indeed with results obtained in British cross-sectional surveys. For example, a systematic comparison of the Cambridge Study and the Pittsburgh Youth Study showed numerous replicable predictors of offending over time and place, including impulsivity, attention problems, low school attainment, poor parental supervision, parental conflict, an antisocial parent, a young mother, large family size, low family income, and coming from a broken family (Farrington & Loeber, 1999).

Individual Factors

Temperament and personality

Personality traits such as sociability or impulsiveness describe broad predispositions to respond in certain ways, and temperament is basically the childhood equivalent of personality. The modern study of child temperament

began with the New York longitudinal study of Stella Chess and Alexander Thomas (1984). Children in their first five years of life were rated on temperamental dimensions by their parents, and these dimensions were combined into three broad categories of easy, difficult and 'slow to warm up' temperament. Having a difficult temperament at age 3–4 (frequent irritability, low amenability and adaptability, irregular habits) predicted poor psychiatric adjustment at age 17–24.

Unfortunately, it was not very clear exactly what a 'difficult' temperament meant in practice, and there was the danger of tautological conclusions (e.g. because the criteria for difficult temperament and 'oppositional defiant disorder' were overlapping). Later researchers have used more specific dimensions of temperament. For example, Jerome Kagan (1989) in Boston classified children as inhibited (shy or fearful) or uninhibited at age 21 months, and found that they remained significantly stable on this classification up to age 7 years. Furthermore, the uninhibited children at age 21 months significantly tended to be identified as aggressive at age 13 years, according to self and parent reports (Schwartz *et al.*, 1996).

Important results on the link between childhood temperament and later offending have been obtained in the Dunedin longitudinal study in New Zealand (Caspi, 2000). Temperament at age 3 years was rated by observing the child's behaviour during a testing session. The most important dimension of temperament was being under-controlled (restless, impulsive, with poor attention), and this predicted aggression, self-reported delinquency and convictions at age 18–21.

Studies using classic personality inventories such as the MMPI and CPI (Wilson & Herrnstein, 1985, pp.186–198) often seem to produce essentially tautological results, such as that delinquents are low on socialisation. The Eysenck personality questionnaire has yielded more promising results (Eysenck, 1996). In the Cambridge Study, those high on both Extraversion and Neuroticism tended to be juvenile self-reported delinquents, adult official offenders and adult self-reported offenders, but not juvenile official delinquents (Farrington *et al.*, 1982). Furthermore, these relationships held independently of other variables such as low family income, low intelligence and poor parental child-rearing behaviour. However, when individual items of the personality questionnaire were studied, it was clear that the significant relationships were caused by the items measuring impulsiveness (e.g. doing things quickly without stopping to think).

Table 8.1 Twenty prospective longitudinal surveys of offending

Authors	Study	Description
Elliott, Huizinga	National Youth Survey, US	Nationally representative US sample of 1725 adolescents aged 11–17 in 1976. Interviewed in 5 successive years (1977–81) and subsequently at 3-year intervals up to 1993, and in 2002–03. Focus on self-reported delinquency, but arrest records collected (Elliott, 1994).
Eron, Huesmann	Columbia County Study, US	All 876 third-grade children (aged 8) in Columbia County in New York State first assessed in 1960. Focus on aggressive behaviour. Interviewed 10, 22, and 40 years later. Criminal records searched up to age 48 (Huesmann *et al.*, 2009).
Farrington, West	Cambridge Study in Delinquent Development, UK	411 boys aged 8–9 in 1961–62; all of that age in 6 London schools. Boys interviewed 9 times up to age 48. Information also from parents, teachers, and peers. Boys and all biological relatives searched in criminal records up to 2004 (Farrington, 2003).
Fergusson, Horwood	Christchurch Health Development Study, New Zealand	All 1365 children born in Christchurch in mid-1977. Studied at birth, 4 months, 1 year, annually to age 16, and at ages 18, 21, and 25. Data collected in parental interviews and self-reports, psychometric tests, teacher reports, and official records (Fergusson *et al.*, 1994).
Hawkins, Catalano	Seattle Social Development Project, US	808 grade 5 students (age 10) in 18 elementary schools in Seattle in 1985. Also intervention study. Followed up annually to age 16 and then every 2–3 years at least to age 27, with interviews and criminal records (Hawkins *et al.*, 2003).
Huizinga, Esbensen	Denver Youth Survey, US	1528 children aged 7, 9, 11, 13 or 15 in high-risk neighbourhoods of Denver, Colorado, in 1988. Children and parents assessed at yearly intervals up to 1998. Youngest two cohorts assessed in 2002. Focus on self-reported delinquency; criminal record data collected up to 1992 (Huizinga *et al.*, 2003).
Janson, Wikström	Project Metropolitan, Sweden	All 15,117 children born in Stockholm in 1953, and living there in 1963. Tested in schools in 1966. Subsample of mothers interviewed in 1968. Followed up in police records to 1983 (Wikström, 1990).
Kolvin, Miller	Newcastle Thousand Family Study, UK	1142 children born in Newcastle-upon-Tyne in mid-1947. Studied between birth and age 5 and followed up to age 15. Criminal records searched at age 33, and subsamples interviewed (Kolvin *et al.*, 1990).
LeBlanc	Montreal Longitudinal Study Two-Samples, Canada	Representative sample of 3070 French-speaking Montreal adolescents. Completed self-report questionnaires in 1974 at age 12–16 and again in 1976. Followed in criminal records to age 40. Males interviewed at ages 30 and 40 (LeBlanc and Frechette, 1989).
Loeber, Stouthamer-Loeber, Farrington	Pittsburgh Youth Study, US	1517 boys in first, fourth, or seventh grades of Pittsburgh public schools in 1987–88 (ages 7, 10, 13). Information from boys, parents, and teachers every 6 months for 3 years, and then every year up to age 19 (youngest) and 25 (oldest). Focus on delinquency, substance use, and mental health problems (Loeber *et al.*, 2003).
Magnusson, Stattin, Klinteberg, Bergman	Orebro Project, Sweden	1027 children age 10 (all those in third grade) in Orebro in 1965. School follow-up data between ages 13 and 15. Questionnaire and record data up to age 43–45 (Bergman & Andershed, 2009).

Table 8.1   (cont'd)

Authors	Study	Description
McCord	Cambridge-Somerville Youth Study, US	650 boys (average age 10) nominated as difficult or average by Cambridge-Somerville (Boston) public schools in 1937–39. Randomly assigned to treated or control groups. Treated group visited by counsellors for an average of 5 years, and all followed up in 1975–80 by interviews, mail questionnaires, and criminal records (McCord, 1991).
Moffitt, Caspi	Dunedin Multidisciplinary Health and Development Self-reported Study, New Zealand	1037 children born in 1972–73 in Dunedin and first assessed at age 3. Assessed every 2–3 years on health, psychological, education, and family factors up to age 32. Delinquency measured from age 13. Convictions collected up to age 32 (Moffitt et al., 2001).
Patterson, Dishion, Capaldi	Oregon Youth Study, US	206 fourth-grade boys (age 10) in Eugene/Springfield (Oregon) in 1983–85. Assessed at yearly intervals, with data from boys, parents, teachers, and peers, at least to age 30. Followed up in criminal records at least to age 30 (Capaldi & Patterson, 1996).
Pulkkinen	Jyvaskyla Longitudinal Study of Personality and Social Development, Finland	369 children aged 8–9 in Jyvaskyla in 1968. Peer, teacher, and self-ratings collected. Followed up five times to age 42 with interviews and questionnaires and in criminal records (Pulkkinen et al., 2009).
Thornberry, Lizotte, Krohn	Rochester Youth Development Study, US	1000 seventh and eighth graders (age 13–14) in Rochester (New York State) public schools, first assessed in 1988. Disproportionally sampled from high-crime neighbourhoods. Followed up initially every 6 months, then every year, then at intervals to age 32. Self-reports and criminal records collected (Thornberry et al., 2003).
Tremblay	Montreal Longitudinal-Experimental Study, Canada	1037 French-speaking kindergarten boys (age 6) from poor areas of Montreal assessed by teachers in 1984. Boys randomly allocated to treatment (parent training plus skills training) or control groups. All boys followed up each year from age 10 to age 26, including self-reported delinquency and aggression (Tremblay et al., 2003).
Wadsworth, Douglas	National Survey of Health and Development, UK	5362 children selected from all legitimate single births in England, Scotland, and Wales during one week of March 1946. Followed in criminal records to age 21. Mainly medical and school data collected, but samples were interviewed at ages 26, 36, 43, and 50 (Wadsworth, 1991).
Werner, Smith	Kauai Longitudinal Study, US	698 children born in 1955 in Kauai (Hawaii) assessed at birth and ages 2, 10, 18, 30, and 40. Criminal records up to age 40. Focus on resilience (Werner & Smith, 2001).
Wolfgang, Figlio, Thornberry, Tracy	Philadelphia Birth Cohort Studies, US	(1) 9945 boys born in Philadelphia in 1945 and living there at least from 10 to 17. Sample interviewed at age 26 and followed up in police records to age 30 (Wolfgang et al., 1987). (2) 27,160 children born in Philadelphia in 1958 and living there at least from 10 to 17. Followed up in police records to age 26 (Tracy & Kempf-Leonard, 1996).

Since 1990, the most widely accepted personality system has been the 'Big Five' or five-factor model (McCrae & Costa, 2003). This suggests that there are five key dimensions of personality: Neuroticism (N), Extraversion (E), Openness (O), Agreeableness (A) and Conscientiousness (C). Openness means originality and openness to new ideas, Agreeableness includes nurturance and altruism, and Conscientiousness includes planning and the will to achieve. It is commonly found that low levels of agree-ableness and conscientiousness are related to offending (Heaven, 1996; John *et al.*, 1994).

Hyperactivity and impulsivity

Impulsiveness is the most crucial personality dimension that predicts antisocial behaviour (Lipsey & Derzon, 1998). Unfortunately, there are a bewildering number of constructs referring to a poor ability to control behaviour. These include impulsiveness, hyperactivity, restlessness, clumsiness, not considering consequences before acting, a poor ability to plan ahead, short time horizons, low self-control, sensation-seeking, risk-taking, and a poor ability to delay gratification. Travis Pratt and his colleagues (2002) carried out a meta-analysis of research on ADHD and delinquency, and concluded that they were strongly associated. Similar conclusions about impulsiveness were drawn by Darrick Jolliffe and me (2009).

Many studies show that hyperactivity or 'attention deficit hyperactivity disorder' predicts later offending. In the Copenhagen Perinatal project, hyperactivity (restlessness and poor concentration) at age 11–13 significantly predicted arrests for violence up to age 22, especially among boys whose mothers experienced delivery complications (Brennan *et al.*, 1993). Similarly, in the Orebro longitudinal study in Sweden, hyperactivity at age 13 predicted police-recorded violence up to age 26. The highest rate of violence was among males with both motor restlessness and concentration difficulties (15 per cent), compared to 3 per cent of the remainder (Klinteberg *et al.*, 1993). In the Seattle Social Development Project, hyperactivity and risk-taking in adolescence predicted violence in young adulthood (Herrenkohl *et al.*, 2000).

In the Cambridge Study, boys nominated by teachers as lacking in concentration or restless, those nominated by parents, peers or teachers as the most daring or taking most risks, and those who were the most impulsive on psychomotor tests at age 8–10 all tended to become offenders later in life. Daring, poor concentration and restlessness all predicted both official convictions and self-reported delinquency, and daring was consistently one of the best independent predictors (Farrington, 1992b). Interestingly, hyperactivity predicted juvenile offending independently of conduct problems (Farrington *et al.*, 1990). Donald Lynam (1996) proposed that boys with both hyperactivity and conduct disorder were most at risk of chronic offending and psychopathy, and Lynam (1998)

presented evidence in favour of this hypothesis from the Pittsburgh Youth Study.

The most extensive research on different measures of impulsiveness was carried out in the Pittsburgh Youth Study by Jennifer White and her colleagues (1994). The measures that were most strongly related to self-reported delinquency at ages 10 and 13 were teacher-rated impulsiveness (e.g. acts without thinking), self-reported impulsiveness, self-reported under-control (e.g. unable to delay gratification), motor restlessness (from videotaped observations) and psychomotor impulsiveness (on the Trail Making Test). Generally, the verbal behaviour rating tests produced stronger relationships with offending than the psychomotor performance tests, suggesting that cognitive impulsiveness (e.g. admitting impulsive behaviour) was more relevant than behavioural impulsiveness (based on test performance).

Low intelligence and attainment

Low IQ and low school achievement also predict youth violence. In the Philadelphia Biosocial project (Denno, 1990), low verbal and performance IQ at ages 4 and 7, and low scores on the California Achievement test at age 13–14 (vocabulary, comprehension, maths, language, spelling), all predicted arrests for violence up to age 22. In Project Metropolitan in Copenhagen, low IQ at age 12 significantly predicted police-recorded violence between ages 15 and 22. The link between low IQ and violence was strongest among lower-class boys (Hogh & Wolf, 1983).

Low IQ measured in the first few years of life predicts later delinquency. In a prospective longitudinal survey of about 120 Stockholm males, low IQ measured at age 3 significantly predicted officially recorded offending up to age 30 (Stattin & Klackenberg-Larsson, 1993). Frequent offenders (with four or more offences) had an average IQ of 88 at age 3, whereas non-offenders had an average IQ of 101. All of these results held up after controlling for social class. Similarly, low IQ at age 4 predicted arrests up to age 27 in the Perry preschool project (Schweinhart *et al.*, 1993) and court delinquency up to age 17 in the Collaborative Perinatal Project (Lipsitt *et al.*, 1990).

In the Cambridge Study, twice as many of the boys scoring 90 or less on a nonverbal IQ test (Raven's Progressive Matrices) at age 8–10 were convicted as juveniles as of the remainder (West & Farrington, 1973). However, it was difficult to disentangle low IQ from low school achievement, because they were highly intercorrelated and both predicted delinquency. Low-nonverbal

IQ predicted juvenile self-reported delinquency to almost exactly the same degree as juvenile convictions (Farrington, 1992b), suggesting that the link between low IQ and delinquency was not caused by the less intelligent boys having a greater probability of being caught. Also, low IQ and low school achievement predicted offending independently of other variables such as low family income and large family size (Farrington, 1990).

Low IQ may lead to delinquency through the intervening factor of school failure. The association between school failure and delinquency has been demonstrated repeatedly in longitudinal surveys (Maguin & Loeber, 1996). In the Pittsburgh Youth Study, Donald Lynam and his colleagues (1993) concluded that low verbal IQ led to school failure and subsequently to self-reported delinquency, but only for African American boys. An alternative theory is that the link between low IQ and delinquency is mediated by disinhibition (impulsiveness, ADHD, low guilt, low empathy), and this was also tested in the Pittsburgh Youth Study (Koolhof et al., 2007).

A plausible explanatory factor underlying the link between low IQ and delinquency is the ability to manipulate abstract concepts. Children who are poor at this tend to do badly in IQ tests and in school achievement, and they also tend to commit offences, mainly because of their poor ability to foresee the consequences of their offending. Delinquents often do better on nonverbal performance IQ tests, such as object assembly and block design, than on verbal IQ tests (Moffitt, 1993), suggesting that they find it easier to deal with concrete objects than with abstract concepts.

Impulsiveness, attention problems, low IQ and low school achievement could all be linked to deficits in the executive functions of the brain, located in the frontal lobes. These executive functions include sustaining attention and concentration, abstract reasoning, concept formation, goal formulation, anticipation and planning, programming and initiation of purposive sequences of motor behaviour, effective self-monitoring and self-awareness of behaviour, and inhibition of inappropriate or impulsive behaviours (Moffitt & Henry, 1991; Morgan & Lilienfeld, 2000). Interestingly, in the Montreal longitudinal-experimental study, a measure of executive functioning based on tests at age 14 was the strongest neuropsychological discriminator between violent and non-violent boys (Seguin et al., 1995). This relationship held independently of a measure of family adversity (based on parental age at first birth, parental education level, broken family and low social class). In

the Pittsburgh Youth Study, the life-course-persistent offenders had marked neurocognitive impairments (Raine et al., 2005).

Low empathy

Numerous other individual factors have been related to delinquency, including depression (Burke et al., 2005), moral judgement (Stams et al., 2006) and social information processing (Lösel et al., 2007). I will focus on empathy, which is related to other concepts such as having callous-unemotional traits (Frick & White, 2008) and being cold, manipulative and Machiavellian (Sutton et al., 1999).

A distinction has often been made between cognitive empathy (understanding or appreciating other people's feelings) and emotional empathy (actually experiencing other people's feelings). Darrick Jolliffe and myself (2004) carried out a systematic review of 35 studies comparing questionnaire measures of empathy with official record measures of delinquent or criminal behaviour. We found that low cognitive empathy was strongly related to offending, but low affective empathy was only weakly related. Most importantly, the relationship between low empathy and offending was greatly reduced after controlling for IQ or socio-economic status, suggesting that they might be more important risk factors or that low empathy might mediate the relationship between these risk factors and offending.

Empathy has rarely been investigated in prospective longitudinal studies but there have been important large-scale cross-sectional surveys. In Australia, Anita Mak (1991) found that delinquent females had lower emotional empathy than non-delinquent females, but that there were no significant differences for males. In Finland, Ari Kaukiainen and his colleagues (1999) reported that empathy (cognitive and emotional combined) was negatively correlated with aggression (both measured by peer ratings). In Spain, Maria Luengo and her colleagues (1994) carried out the first project that related cognitive and emotional empathy separately to (self-reported) offending, and found that both were negatively correlated.

Darrick Jolliffe and I (2006) developed a new measure of empathy called the Basic Empathy Scale. An example of a cognitive item is 'It is hard for me to understand when my friends are sad,' and an example of an emotional item is 'I usually feel calm when other people are scared.' In a study of 720 British adolescents aged about 15, we found that low emotional empathy was related to self-reported offending and violence for both males and females, and to an official record for offending by females (Jolliffe & Farrington, 2007).

Family Factors

Child-rearing

Many different types of child-rearing methods predict offending. The most important dimensions of child-rearing are supervision or monitoring of children, discipline or parental reinforcement, warmth or coldness of emotional relationships, and parental involvement with children. Parental supervision refers to the degree of monitoring by parents of the child's activities, and their degree of watchfulness or vigilance. Of all these child-rearing methods, poor parental supervision is usually the strongest and most replicable predictor of offending (Smith & Stern, 1997). Many studies show that parents who do not know where their children are when they are out, and parents who let their children roam the streets unsupervised from an early age, tend to have delinquent children. For example, in Joan McCord's (1979) classic Cambridge-Somerville study in Boston, poor parental supervision in childhood was the best predictor of both violent and property crimes up to age 45.

Parental discipline refers to how parents react to a child's behaviour. It is clear that harsh or punitive discipline (involving physical punishment) predicts offending (Haapasalo & Pokela, 1999). In their follow-up study of nearly 700 Nottingham children, John and Elizabeth Newson (1989) found that physical punishment at ages 7 and 11 predicted later convictions; 40 per cent of offenders had been smacked or beaten at age 11, compared with 14 per cent of non-offenders. Erratic or inconsistent discipline also predicts delinquency. This can involve either erratic discipline by one parent, sometimes turning a blind eye to bad behaviour and sometimes punishing it severely, or inconsistency between two parents, with one parent being tolerant or indulgent and the other being harshly punitive.

Cold, rejecting parents tend to have delinquent children, as Joan McCord (1979) found in the Cambridge-Somerville study. More recently, she concluded that parental warmth could act as a protective factor against the effects of physical punishment (McCord, 1997). Whereas 51 per cent of boys with cold physically punishing mothers were convicted in her study, only 21 per cent of boys with warm physically punishing mothers

were convicted, similar to the 23 per cent of boys with warm non-punitive mothers who were convicted. The father's warmth was also a protective factor against the father's physical punishment.

The classic longitudinal study by Lee Robins (1979) in St. Louis shows that poor parental supervision, harsh discipline and a rejecting attitude all predict delinquency. Also, in the Seattle Social Development Project, poor family management (poor supervision, inconsistent rules and harsh discipline) in adolescence predicted violence in young adulthood (Herrenkohl et al., 2000). Similar results were obtained in the Cambridge Study. Harsh or erratic parental discipline, cruel, passive or neglecting parental attitudes, and poor parental supervision, all measured at age 8, all predicted later juvenile convictions and self-reported delinquency (West & Farrington, 1973). Generally, the presence of any of these adverse family background features doubled the risk of a later juvenile conviction.

Laurence Steinberg and his colleagues (1992) distinguished an authoritarian style of parenting (punitively emphasising obedience) from an authoritative style (granting autonomy with good supervision). In the Cambridge Study (Farrington, 1994), having authoritarian parents was the second most important predictor of convictions for violence (after hyperactivity/poor concentration). Interestingly, having authoritarian parents was the most important childhood risk factor that discriminated between violent offenders and frequently convicted non-violent offenders (Farrington, 1991).

Most explanations of the link between child-rearing methods and delinquency focus on attachment or social learning theories. Attachment theory was inspired by the work of John Bowlby (1951), and suggests that children who are not emotionally attached to warm, loving and law-abiding parents tend to become offenders. Social learning theories suggest that children's behaviour depends on parental rewards and punishments and on the models of behaviour that parents represent (Patterson, 1995). Children will tend to become offenders if parents do not respond consistently and contingently to their antisocial behaviour and if parents themselves behave in an antisocial manner.

Teenage mothers and child abuse

At least in Western industrialised countries, early childbearing, or teenage pregnancy, predicts many undesirable outcomes for the children, including low school attainment, antisocial school behaviour, substance use and early sexual intercourse. The children of teenage mothers are also more likely to become offenders. For example, Merry Morash and Lila Rucker (1989) analysed results from four surveys in the US and UK (including the Cambridge Study) and found that teenage mothers were associated with low-income families, welfare support and absent biological fathers, that they used poor child-rearing methods, and that their children were characterised by low school attainment and delinquency. However, the presence of the biological father mitigated many of these adverse factors and generally seemed to have a protective effect. In the Cambridge Study, teenage mothers who went on to have large numbers of children were especially likely to have convicted children (Nagin *et al.*, 1997). In the Newcastle Thousand Family study mothers who married as teenagers (a factor strongly related to teenage childbearing) were twice as likely as others to have sons who became offenders by age 32 (Kolvin *et al.*, 1990).

There is considerable intergenerational transmission of aggressive and violent behaviour from parents to children, as Michael Maxfield and Cathy Widom (1996) found in a retrospective study of 908 abused children and 667 matched controls in Indianapolis. Children who were physically abused up to age 11 were significantly likely to become violent offenders in the next 15 years. In the Cambridge-Somerville study in Boston, Joan McCord (1983) found that about half of the abused or neglected boys were convicted for serious crimes, became alcoholics or mentally ill, or died before age 35. In the Rochester Youth Development Study, child maltreatment under age 12 (physical, sexual or emotional abuse or neglect) predicted later self-reported and official offending (Smith & Thornberry, 1995). Furthermore, these results held up after controlling for gender, race, socio-economic status and family structure. Margaret Keiley and her colleagues (2001) reported that maltreatment under age 5 was more damaging than maltreatment between ages 6 and 9. The extensive review by Robin Malinosky-Rummell and David Hansen (1993) confirms that being physically abused as a child predicts later violent and non-violent offending.

Possible causal mechanisms linking childhood victimisation and adolescent offending have been reviewed by Cathy Widom (1994). First, childhood victimisation may have immediate but long-lasting consequences (e.g. shaking may cause brain injury). Second, childhood victimisation may cause bodily changes (e.g. desensitisation to pain) that encourage later aggression. Third, child abuse may lead to impulsive or dissociative coping styles that, in turn, lead to poor problem-solving skills or poor school performance. Fourth, victimisation may cause changes in self-esteem or in social information-processing patterns that encourage later aggression. Fifth, child abuse may lead to changed family environments (e.g. being placed in foster care) that have harmful effects. Sixth, juvenile justice practices may label victims, isolate them from prosocial peers and encourage them to associate with delinquent peers.

Parental conflict and disrupted families

There is no doubt that parental conflict and interparental violence predict adolescent antisocial behaviour, as the meta-analysis of Cheryl Buehler and her colleagues (1997) shows. In the Cambridge Study, parental conflict predicted delinquency (West & Farrington, 1973). In the Christchurch Study in New Zealand, children who witnessed violence between their parents were more likely to commit both violent and property offences according to their self-reports (Fergusson & Horwood, 1998). Witnessing father-initiated violence was still predictive after controlling for other risk factors such as parental criminality, parental substance abuse, parental physical punishment, a young mother and low family income.

Many studies show that broken homes or disrupted families predict delinquency. In the Newcastle Thousand Family Study, Israel Kolvin and his colleagues (1988) reported that marital disruption (divorce or separation) in a boy's first five years predicted his later convictions up to age 32. Similarly, in the Dunedin study in New Zealand, Bill Henry and his colleagues (1993) found that children who were exposed to parental discord and many changes of the primary caretaker tended to become antisocial and delinquent.

The importance of the cause of the broken home was demonstrated by Michael Wadsworth (1979) in the UK National Survey of Health and Development. Boys from homes broken by divorce or separation had an increased likelihood of being convicted or officially cautioned up to age 21, in comparison with those from homes broken by death or from unbroken homes. Homes broken while the boy was under age 5 especially predicted offending, while homes broken while the boy was between ages 11 and 15 were not particularly criminogenic. Remarriage (which happened more often after divorce or separation than after death) was also associated with an increased risk of offending, suggesting a possible negative effect of step-parents. The meta-analysis by Edward Wells and

Joseph Rankin (1991) also indicates that broken homes are more strongly related to delinquency when they are caused by parental separation or divorce rather than by death.

Most studies of broken homes have focused on the loss of the father rather than the mother, simply because the loss of a father is much more common. Joan McCord (1982) in Boston carried out an interesting study of the relationship between homes broken by loss of the natural father and later serious offending of the children. She found that the prevalence of offending was high for boys reared in broken homes without affectionate mothers (62 per cent) and for those reared in united homes characterised by parental conflict (52 per cent), irrespective of whether they had affectionate mothers. The prevalence of offending was low for those reared in united homes without conflict (26 per cent) and – importantly – equally low for boys from broken homes with affectionate mothers (22 per cent). These results suggest that it is not so much the broken home which is criminogenic as the parental conflict which often causes it, and that a loving mother might in some sense be able to compensate for the loss of a father.

In the Cambridge Study, both permanent and temporary separations from a biological parent before age 10 (usually from the father) predicted convictions and self-reported delinquency, providing that they were not caused by death or hospitalisation (Farrington, 1992b). However, homes broken at an early age (under age 5) were not unusually criminogenic (West & Farrington, 1973). Separation before age 10 predicted both juvenile and adult convictions (Farrington, 1992a), and it predicted adult convictions independently of other factors such as low family income or poor school attainment.

Explanations of the relationship between disrupted families and delinquency fall into three major classes. Trauma theories suggest that the loss of a parent has a damaging effect on a child, most commonly because of the effect on attachment to the parent. Life-course theories focus on separation as a sequence of stressful experiences, and on the effects of multiple stressors such as parental conflict, parental loss, reduced economic circumstances, changes in parent figures and poor child-rearing methods. Selection theories argue that disrupted families produce delinquent children because of pre-existing differences from other families in risk factors such as parental conflict, criminal or antisocial parents, low family income or poor child-rearing methods.

Hypotheses derived from the three theories were tested in the Cambridge Study (Juby & Farrington, 2001). While boys from broken homes (permanently disrupted families) were more delinquent than boys from intact homes, they were not more delinquent than boys from intact high-conflict families. Overall, the most important factor was the post-disruption trajectory. Boys who remained with their mother after the separation had the same delinquency rate as boys from intact low-conflict families. Boys who stayed with their father, with relatives or with others (e.g. foster parents) had high delinquency rates. These living arrangements were more unstable, and other research shows that frequent changes of parent figures predict offending. It was concluded that the results favoured life-course theories rather than trauma or selection theories.

Criminal parents

Lee Robins and her colleagues (1975) showed that criminal, antisocial and alcoholic parents tend to have delinquent sons. Robins followed up over 200 males in St. Louis and found that arrested parents tended to have arrested children, and that the juvenile records of the parents and children had similar rates and types of offences. Joan McCord (1977) also reported that convicted fathers tended to have convicted sons. She found that 29 per cent of fathers convicted for violence had sons convicted for violence, in comparison with 12 per cent of other fathers, but this may reflect the general tendency for convicted fathers to have convicted sons rather than any specific tendency for violent fathers to have violent sons.

In the Cambridge Study, the concentration of offending in a small number of families was remarkable (Farrington et al., 1996). Less than 6 per cent of the families were responsible for half of the criminal convictions of all members (fathers, mothers, sons and daughters) of all 400 families. Having a convicted mother, father, brother or sister significantly predicted a boy's own convictions. As many as 63 per cent of boys with a convicted parent were themselves convicted up to age 40. Furthermore, convicted parents and delinquent siblings predicted self-reported as well as official offending (Farrington, 1979). Same-sex relationships were stronger than opposite-sex relationships, and older siblings were stronger predictors than younger siblings. Therefore, there is intergenerational continuity in offending.

Similar results were obtained in the Pittsburgh Youth Study. Arrests of fathers, mothers, brothers, sisters, uncles, aunts, grandfathers and grandmothers all predicted the boy's own delinquency (Farrington et al.,

2001). The most important relative was the father; arrests of the father predicted the boy's delinquency independently of all other arrested relatives. Only 8 per cent of families accounted for 43 per cent of arrested family members. Similarly, in the Dunedin study in New Zealand, the antisocial behaviour of grandparents, parents and siblings predicted the antisocial behaviour of boys (Odgers *et al.*, 2007).

While arrests and convictions of fathers predicted antisocial behaviour of boys, imprisonment of fathers before boys were aged 10 further increased the risk of later antisocial and delinquent outcomes in the Cambridge Study (Murray & Farrington, 2005). Interestingly, the effect of parental imprisonment in Sweden (in Project Metropolitan) disappeared after controlling for parental criminality (Murray *et al.*, 2007). This cross-national difference may have been the result of shorter prison sentences in Sweden, more family-friendly prison policies, a welfare-orientated juvenile justice system, an extended social welfare system, or more sympathetic public attitudes towards prisoners.

It is not entirely clear why criminal parents tend to have delinquent children. In the Cambridge Study, there was no evidence that criminal parents directly encouraged their children to commit crimes or taught them criminal techniques. On the contrary, criminal parents were highly critical of their children's offending; for example, 89 per cent of convicted men at age 32 disagreed with the statement that 'I would not mind if my son/daughter committed a criminal offence'. Also, it was extremely rare for a parent and a child to be convicted for an offence committed together. The main link in the chain between criminal parents and delinquent sons seemed to be poor parental supervision (West & Farrington, 1977).

There are several possible explanations (which are not mutually exclusive) for why offending tends to be concentrated in certain families and transmitted from one generation to the next. First, there may be intergenerational continuities in exposure to multiple risk factors. For example, each successive generation may be entrapped in poverty, disrupted families, single and/or teenage parenting, and living in the most deprived neighbourhoods. Second, the effect of a criminal parent on a child's offending may be mediated by environmental mechanisms such as poor parental supervision. Third, this effect may be mediated by genetic mechanisms.

Fourth, criminal parents may tend to have delinquent children because of official (police and court) bias against criminal families, who also tend to be known to official agencies because of other social problems. At all levels of self-reported delinquency in the Cambridge

Study, boys with convicted fathers were more likely to be convicted themselves than were boys with unconvicted fathers (West & Farrington, 1977). However, this was not the only explanation for the link between criminal fathers and delinquent sons, because boys with criminal fathers had higher self-reported delinquency scores and higher teacher and peer ratings of bad behaviour.

Large family size

Large family size (a large number of children in the family) is a relatively strong and highly replicable predictor of offending (Ellis, 1988). It was similarly important in the Cambridge and Pittsburgh studies, even though families were on average smaller in Pittsburgh in the 1990s than in London in the 1960s (Farrington & Loeber, 1999). In the Cambridge Study, if a boy had four or more siblings by his 10th birthday, this doubled his risk of being convicted as a juvenile, and large family size predicted self-reported offending as well as convictions (Farrington, 1992b). It was the most important independent predictor of convictions up to age 32 in a logistic regression analysis (Farrington, 1993).

In the National Survey of Health and Development, Michael Wadsworth (1979) found that the percentage of boys who were convicted increased from 9 per cent for families containing one child to 24 per cent for families containing four or more children. John Newson and his colleagues (1993), in their Nottingham study, also concluded that large family size was one of the most important predictors of offending. A similar link between family size and antisocial behaviour was reported by Israel Kolvin and his colleagues (1990) in their follow-up of Newcastle children from birth to age 33.

There are many possible reasons why a large number of siblings might increase the risk of a child's offending. Generally, as the number of children in a family increases, the amount of parental attention that can be given to each child decreases. Also, as the number of children increases, the household tends to become more overcrowded, possibly leading to increases in frustration, irritation and conflict. In the Cambridge Study, large family size did not predict delinquency for boys living in the least crowded conditions (West & Farrington, 1973). This suggests that household overcrowding might be an important intervening factor between large family size and delinquency.

David Brownfield and Ann Sorenson (1994) reviewed several possible explanations for the link between large families and delinquency, including those focusing on features of the parents (e.g. criminal parents, teenage parents), those focusing on parenting (e.g. poor supervision, disrupted families) and those focusing on economic deprivation or family stress. Another interesting theory suggested that the key factor was birth order: large families include more later-born children, who tend to be more delinquent. Based on an analysis of self-reported delinquency in a Seattle survey, they concluded that the most plausible intervening causal mechanism was exposure to delinquent siblings. In the Cambridge Study, co-offending by brothers was surprisingly common; about 20 per cent of boys who had brothers close to them in age were convicted for a crime committed with their brother (Reiss & Farrington, 1991).

Social Factors

Socio-economic deprivation

The voluminous literature on the relationship between socio-economic status (SES) and offending is characterised by inconsistencies and contradictions, and some reviewers (e.g. Thornberry & Farnworth, 1982) have concluded that there is no relationship between SES and either self-reported or official offending. British studies have reported more consistent links between low social class and offending. In the UK National Survey of Health and Development, Michael Wadsworth (1979) found that the prevalence of official juvenile delinquency in males varied considerably according to the occupational prestige and educational background of their parents, from 3 per cent in the highest category to 19 per cent in the lowest.

Numerous indicators of SES were measured in the Cambridge Study, both for the boy's family of origin and for the boy himself as an adult, including occupational prestige, family income, housing, and employment instability. Most of the measures of occupational prestige (based on the Registrar General's scale) were not significantly related to offending. Low SES of the family when the boy was aged 8–10 significantly predicted his later self-reported but not his official delinquency. More consistently, low family income and poor housing predicted official and self-reported, juvenile and adult, offending (Farrington, 1992a, 1992b).

It was interesting that the peak age of offending, at 17–18, coincided with the peak age of affluence for many convicted males. In the Cambridge Study, convicted males tended to come from low-income families at age 8 and later tended to have low incomes themselves at age 32. However, at age 18, they were relatively well paid in comparison with non-delinquents (West & Farrington,

1977). Whereas convicted delinquents might be working as unskilled labourers on building sites and getting the full adult wage for this job, non-delinquents might be in poorly paid jobs with prospects, such as bank clerks, or might still be students. These results show that the link between income and offending is quite complex.

Socio-economic deprivation of parents is usually compared to offending by children. However, when the children grow up, their own socio-economic deprivation can be related to their own offending. In the Cambridge Study, official and self-reported delinquents tended to have unskilled manual jobs and an unstable job record at age 18. Just as an erratic work record of his father predicted the later offending of the study boy, an unstable job record of the boy at age 18 was one of the best independent predictors of his own convictions between ages 21 and 25 (Farrington, 1986). Between ages 15 and 18, the study boys were convicted at a higher rate when they were unemployed than when they were employed (Farrington et al., 1986), suggesting that unemployment in some way causes crime, and conversely that employment may lead to desistance from offending. Since crimes involving material gain (e.g. theft, burglary, robbery) especially increased during periods of unemployment, it seems likely that financial need is an important link in the causal chain between unemployment and crime.

Several researchers have suggested that the link between a low-SES family and antisocial behaviour is mediated by family socialisation practices. For example, Richard Larzelere and Gerald Patterson (1990) in the Oregon Youth Study concluded that the effect of SES on delinquency was entirely mediated by parent management skills. In other words, low SES predicted delinquency because low-SES families used poor child-rearing practices. In the Christchurch Health and Development Study, David Fergusson and his colleagues (2004) reported that living in a low-SES family between birth and age 6 predicted self-reported and official delinquency between ages 15 and 21. However, this association disappeared after controlling for family factors (physical punishment, maternal care and parental changes), conduct problems, truancy and deviant peers, suggesting that these may have been mediating factors.

Peer influences

Having delinquent friends is an important predictor of later offending. Sara Battin and her colleagues (1998) showed that peer delinquency predicted self-reported violence in the Seattle Social Development Project. Delinquent acts tend to be committed in small groups (of two or three people, usually) rather than alone. Large gangs are comparatively unusual. In the Cambridge Study, the probability of committing offences with others decreased steadily with age. Before age 17, boys tended to commit their crimes with other boys similar in age and living close by. After age 17, co-offending became less common (Reiss & Farrington, 1991).

The major problem of interpretation is whether young people are more likely to commit offences while they are in groups than while they are alone, or whether the high prevalence of co-offending merely reflects the fact that, whenever young people go out, they tend to go out in groups. Do peers tend to encourage and facilitate offending, or is it just that most kinds of activities out of the home (both delinquent and non-delinquent) tend to be committed in groups? Another possibility is that the commission of offences encourages association with other delinquents, perhaps because 'birds of a feather flock together' or because of the stigmatising and isolating effects of court appearances and institutionalisation. Terence Thornberry and his colleagues (1994) in the Rochester Youth Development Study concluded that there were reciprocal effects, with delinquent peers causing delinquency and delinquency causing association with delinquent peers.

In the Pittsburgh Youth Study, the relationship between peer delinquency and a boy's offending was studied both between individuals (e.g. comparing peer delinquency and offending over all boys at a particular age and then aggregating these correlations over all ages) and within individuals (e.g. comparing peer delinquency and offending of a boy at all his ages and then aggregating these correlations over all boys). Peer delinquency was the strongest correlate of offending in between-individual correlations but did not predict offending within individuals (Farrington et al., 2002). In contrast, poor parental supervision, low parental reinforcement and low involvement of the boy in family activities predicted offending both between and within individuals. It was concluded that these three family variables were the most likely to be causes, whereas having delinquent peers was most likely to be an indicator of the boy's offending.

It is clear that young people increase their offending after joining a gang. In the Seattle Social Development Project, Sara Battin and her colleagues (1998) found this, and also showed that gang membership predicted delinquency above and beyond having delinquent friends. In the Pittsburgh Youth Study, Rachel Gordon and her colleagues (2004) reported not only a substantial increase in drug selling, drug use, violence and property crime after a boy joined a gang, but also that the frequency of offending decreased to pre-gang levels after a boy left a gang. Terence Thornberry and his colleagues (2003) in the Rochester Youth Development Study and Uberto Gatti and his colleagues (2005) in the Montreal longitudinal-experimental study also found that young people offended more after joining a gang. Several of these studies contrasted the 'selection' and 'facilitation' hypotheses and concluded that future gang members were more delinquent to start with but became even more delinquent after joining a gang. Gang membership in adolescence is a risk factor for later violence (Herrenkohl et al., 2000), but this may be because both are measuring the same underlying construct.

Associating with delinquent friends at age 14 was an important independent predictor of convictions at the young adult ages in the Cambridge Study (Farrington, 1986). Also, the recidivists at age 19 who ceased offending differed from those who persisted, in that the desisters were more likely to have stopped going round in a group of male friends. Furthermore, spontaneous comments by the youths indicated that withdrawal from the delinquent peer group was an important influence on ceasing to offend (West & Farrington, 1977). Therefore, continuing to associate with delinquent friends may be a key factor in determining whether juvenile delinquents persist in offending as young adults or desist.

School influences

The prevalence of delinquency among students varies dramatically between different secondary schools, as Michael Power and his colleagues (1967) showed many years ago in London. Characteristics of high-delinquency-rate schools are well known (Graham, 1988). For example, such schools have high levels of distrust between teachers and students, low commitment to the school by the students, and unclear and inconsistently enforced rules. However, what is much less clear is how much of the variation between schools should be attributed to differences in school organisation, climate and practices, and how much to differences in the composition of the student body.

In the Cambridge Study, attending a high-delinquency-rate school at age 11 significantly predicted a boy's later juvenile delinquency (Farrington, 1992b). The effects of secondary schools on delinquency were investigated by following boys from their primary schools to their secondary schools (Farrington, 1972). The best primary school predictor of juvenile delinquency was the rating of the boy's troublesomeness at age 8–10 by peers and teachers, showing the continuity in antisocial behaviour.

The secondary schools differed dramatically in their official delinquency rates, from one school with 21 court appearances per 100 boys per year to another where the corresponding figure was only 0.3. Moreover, going to a high-delinquency-rate secondary school was a significant predictor of later convictions.

It was, however, very noticeable that the most troublesome boys tended to go to the high-delinquency-rate schools, while the least troublesome boys tended to go to the low-delinquency-rate schools. Most of the variation between schools in their delinquency rates could be explained by differences in their intakes of troublesome boys. The secondary schools themselves had only a very small effect on the boys' offending. However, reviews of American research show that schools with clear, fair and consistently enforced rules tend to have low rates of student misbehaviour (Gottfredson, 2001; Herrenkohl et al., 2001).

The most famous study of school effects on delinquency was also carried out in London, by Michael Rutter and his colleagues (1979). They studied 12 comprehensive schools, and again found big differences in official delinquency rates between them. High-delinquency-rate schools tended to have high truancy rates, low-ability pupils, and low-social-class parents. However, the differences between the schools in delinquency rates could not be entirely explained by differences in the social class and verbal reasoning scores of the pupils at intake (age 11). Therefore, they must have been caused by some aspect of the schools themselves or by other unmeasured factors.

In trying to discover which aspects of schools might be encouraging or inhibiting offending, Rutter and his colleagues found that the main school factors that were associated with delinquency were a high amount of punishment and a low amount of praise given by teachers in class. Unfortunately, it is difficult to know whether much punishment and little praise are causes or consequences of antisocial school behaviour, which in turn may be linked to offending outside school. In regard to other outcome measures, they argued that an academic emphasis, good classroom management, the careful use of praise and punishment, and student participation were important features of successful schools.

Community influences

Many studies show that boys living in urban areas are more violent than those living in rural ones. In the US National Youth Survey, the prevalence of self-reported assault and robbery was considerably higher among urban youth (Elliott et al., 1989). Within urban areas, boys living in high-crime neighbourhoods are more violent than those living in low-crime neighbourhoods. In the Rochester Youth Development Study, living in a high-crime neighbourhood significantly predicted self-reported violence (Thornberry et al., 1995). Similarly, in the Pittsburgh Youth Study, living in a bad neighbourhood (either as rated by the mother or based on census measures of poverty, unemployment, and female-headed households) significantly predicted official and reported violence (Farrington, 1998).

Robert Sampson and his colleagues (1997) studied community influences on violence in the Project on Human Development in Chicago Neighbourhoods. The most important community predictors were concentrated economic disadvantage (as indexed by poverty, the proportion of female-headed families, and the proportion of African Americans), immigrant concentration (the proportions of Latinos or foreign-born persons), residential instability, and low levels of informal social control and social cohesion. They suggested that the 'collective efficacy' of a neighbourhood, or the willingness of residents to intervene to prevent antisocial behaviour, might act as a protective factor against crime. In the same project, Sampson and his colleagues (2005) concluded that most of the difference between African Americans and Caucasians in violence could be explained by racial differences in exposure to risk factors, especially living in a bad neighbourhood. Similar conclusions were drawn in the Pittsburgh Youth Study (Farrington et al., 2003).

It is clear that offenders disproportionately live in inner-city areas characterised by physical deterioration, neighbourhood disorganisation and high residential mobility (Shaw & McKay, 1969). However, again, it is difficult to determine to what extent the areas themselves influence antisocial behaviour and to what extent it is merely the case that antisocial people tend to live in deprived areas (e.g. because of their poverty or public housing allocation policies). Interestingly, both neighbourhood researchers such as Denise Gottfredson and her colleagues (1991) and developmental researchers such as Michael Rutter (1981) have argued that neighbourhoods have only indirect effects on antisocial behaviour through their effects on individuals and families. In the Chicago Youth Development Study, Patrick Tolan and his colleagues (2003) concluded that the relationship between community structural characteristics (concentrated poverty, racial heterogeneity, economic resources, violent crime rate) and individual violence was mediated by parenting practices, gang membership and peer violence.

In the Pittsburgh Youth Study, Per-Olof Wikström and Rolf Loeber (2000) found an interesting interaction between types of people and types of areas. Six individual, family, peer and school variables were trichotomised into risk, middle, or protective scores and added up. Boys with the highest risk scores tended to be delinquent irrespective of the type of area in which they were living. However, boys with high protective scores or balanced risk and protective scores were more likely to be delinquent if they were living in disadvantaged public housing areas. Hence, the area risk was most important when other risks were not high.

One key question is why crime rates of communities change over time, and to what extent this is a function of changes in the communities or in the individuals living in them. Answering this question requires longitudinal research in which both communities and individuals are followed up. The best way of establishing the impact of the environment is to follow people who move from one area to another. For example, in the Cambridge Study, moving out of London led to a significant decrease in convictions and self-reported offending (Osborn, 1980). This decrease may have occurred because moving out led to a breaking up of co-offending groups, or because there were fewer opportunities for crime outside London.

Clearly, there is an interaction between individuals and the communities in which they live. Some aspects of an inner-city neighbourhood may be conducive to offending, perhaps because the inner city leads to a breakdown of community ties or neighbourhood patterns of mutual support, or perhaps because the high population density produces tension, frustration or anonymity. There may be many interrelated factors. As Albert Reiss (1986) argued, high-crime-rate areas often have a high concentration of single-parent female-headed households with low incomes, living in low-cost, poor housing. The weakened parental control in these families – partly caused by the fact that the mother had to work and left her children largely unsupervised – meant that the children tended to congregate on the streets. In consequence, they were influenced by a peer subculture that often encouraged and reinforced offending. This interaction of individual, family, peer and neighbourhood factors may be the rule rather than the exception.

Conclusions

A great deal has been learned in the past 20 years, particularly from longitudinal surveys, about risk factors for offending and other types of antisocial behaviour. Offenders differ significantly from non-offenders in many respects, including impulsiveness, empathy, low IQ and low school achievement, poor parental supervision, child physical abuse, punitive or erratic parental discipline, cold parental attitude, parental conflict, disrupted families, antisocial parents, large family size, low family income, antisocial peers, high-delinquency-rate schools, and high-crime neighbourhoods. These differences are present before, during and after criminal careers. While the precise causal chains that link these factors with antisocial behaviour, and the ways in which these factors have independent, interactive or sequential effects, are not well understood, it is clear that individuals at risk can be identified with reasonable accuracy.

The comorbidity and versatility of antisocial behaviour pose a major challenge to scientific understanding. It is important to investigate to what extent research findings are driven by a minority of multiple problem adolescents or chronic delinquents. Often, multiple risk factors lead to multiple problem boys (Farrington, 2002; Loeber et al., 1998). To what extent any given risk factor generally predicts a variety of different outcomes (as opposed to specifically predicting one or two outcomes) and to what extent each outcome is generally predicted by a variety of different risk factors (as opposed to being specifically predicted by only one or two risk factors) is unclear. An increasing number of risk factors leads to an increasing probability of antisocial outcomes, almost irrespective of the particular risk factors included in the prediction measure, but more research is needed on this. There was insufficient space in this chapter to review theories explaining the links between risk factors and antisocial outcomes, but these have to be based on knowledge about the additive, independent, interactive and sequential effects of risk factors (see Farrington, 2005).

In order to advance knowledge about development and risk factors for offending, new multiple-cohort longitudinal studies are needed in all countries. Also, the time is ripe to mount a large-scale evidence-based integrated national strategy for the reduction of crime and associated social problems, including rigorous evaluation requirements, in all countries. This should implement effective programmes to tackle risk factors and strengthen protective factors.

Further Reading

Farrington, D.P. & Welsh, B.C. (2007). *Saving children from a life of crime: Early risk factors and effective interventions.* Oxford: Oxford University Press.

This book discusses the meaning of risk and protective factors, key issues in risk factor research, and major prospective longitudinal surveys of offending. It then reviews individual factors (low intelligence and attainment, personality, temperament, empathy, impulsiveness and social cognitive skills), family factors (criminal parents, large family size, child-rearing methods, child abuse and neglect, parental conflict and disrupted families, teenage pregnancy) and socio-economic, peer, school and community risk factors for offending.

Thornberry, T.P. & Krohn, M.D. (Eds.) (2003). *Taking stock of delinquency: An overview of findings from contemporary longitudinal studies.* New York: Kluwer/Plenum.

This book contains detailed descriptions of key results obtained in several of the major prospective longitudinal studies of offending summarised in Table 1, including the Cambridge Study, the Pittsburgh Youth Study, the Seattle Social Development Project, the Rochester Youth Development Study, the Denver Youth Survey, and the Montreal Longitudinal-Experimental Study. There is a great deal of information about psychosocial factors in the development of offending.

Rutter, M., Giller, H. & Hagell, A. (1998). *Antisocial behaviour by young people.* Cambridge: Cambridge University Press.

This is a very useful textbook on antisocial behaviour and delinquency. It contains chapters on individual factors (including genetic and biological influences, intelligence, temperament, personality and hyperactivity), psychosocial features (including family factors, peer groups, gangs, poverty and social disadvantage) and societal influences (including the mass media, area differences, school effects and ethnic variations). It also reviews gender differences, historical trends, criminal careers, and the prevention and treatment of offending.

References

Battin, S.R., Hill, K.G., Abbott, R.D., Catalano, R.F. & Hawkins, J.D. (1998). The contribution of gang membership to delinquency beyond delinquent friends. *Criminology, 36*, 93–115.

Bergman, L.R. & Andershed, A-K. (2009). Predictors and outcomes of persistent or age-limited registered criminal behavior: A 30-year longitudinal study of a Swedish urban population. *Aggressive Behavior, 35*, 164–178.

Bowlby, J. (1951). *Maternal care and mental health.* Geneva, Switzerland: World Health Organization.

Brennan, P.A., Mednick, B.R. & Mednick, S.A. (1993). Parental psychopathology, congenital factors, and violence. In S. Hodgins (Ed.) *Mental disorder and crime* (pp.244–261). Newbury Park, CA: Sage.

Brownfield, D. & Sorenson, A.M. (1994). Sibship size and sibling delinquency. *Deviant Behavior, 15*, 45–61.

Buehler, C., Anthony, C., Krishnakumar, A., Stone, G., Gerard, J. & Pemberton, S. (1997). Interparental conflict and youth problem behaviors: A meta-analysis. *Journal of Child and Family Studies, 6*, 233–247.

Burke, J.D., Loeber, R., Lahey, B.B., & Rathouz, P.J. (2005). Developmental transitions among affective and behavioural disorders in adolescent boys. *Journal of Child Psychology and Psychiatry, 46*, 1200–1210.

Capaldi, D.M. & Patterson, G.R. (1996). Can violent offenders be distinguished from frequent offenders? Prediction from childhood to adolescence. *Journal of Research in Crime and Delinquency, 33*, 206–231.

Caspi, A. (2000). The child is father of the man: Personality continuities from childhood to adulthood. *Journal of Personality and Social Psychology, 78*, 158–172.

Chess, S. & Thomas, A. (1984). *Origins and evolution of behavior disorders: From infancy to early adult life.* New York: Brunner/Mazel.

Denno, D.W. (1990). *Biology and violence: From birth to adulthood.* Cambridge: Cambridge University Press.

Elliott, D.S. (1994). Serious violent offenders: Onset, developmental course, and termination. *Criminology, 32*, 1–21.

Elliott, D.S., Huizinga, D. & Menard, S. (1989). *Multiple problem youth: Delinquency, substance use, and mental health problems.* New York: Springer-Verlag.

Ellis, L. (1988). The victimful–victimless crime distinction, and seven universal demographic correlates of victimful criminal behaviour. *Personality and Individual Differences, 3*, 525–548.

Eysenck, H.J. (1996). Personality and crime: Where do we stand? *Psychology, Crime and Law, 2*, 143–152.

Farrington, D.P. (1972). Delinquency begins at home. *New Society, 21*, 495–497.

Farrington, D.P. (1979). Environmental stress, delinquent behavior, and convictions. In I.G. Sarason & C.D. Spielberger (Eds.) *Stress and anxiety* (vol. 6, pp.93–107). Washington, DC: Hemisphere.

Farrington, D.P. (1986). Stepping stones to adult criminal careers. In D. Olweus, J. Block & M.R. Yarrow (Eds.) *Development of antisocial and prosocial behavior* (pp.359–384). New York: Academic Press.

Farrington, D.P. (1988). Studying changes within individuals: The causes of offending. In M. Rutter (Ed.) *Studies of psychosocial risk: The power of longitudinal data* (pp.158–183). Cambridge: Cambridge University Press.

Farrington, D.P. (1990). Implications of criminal career research for the prevention of offending. *Journal of Adolescence, 13*, 93–113.

Farrington, D.P. (1991). Childhood aggression and adult violence: Early precursors and later life outcomes. In D.J. Pepler & K.H. Rubin (Eds.) *The development and treatment of childhood aggression* (pp.5–29). Hillsdale, NJ: Lawrence Erlbaum.

Farrington, D.P. (1992a). Explaining the beginning, progress and ending of antisocial behaviour from birth to adulthood. In J. McCord (Ed.) *Facts, frameworks and forecasts: Advances in criminological theory* (vol. 3, pp.253–286). New Brunswick, NJ: Transaction.

Farrington, D.P. (1992b). Juvenile delinquency. In J.C. Coleman (Ed.) *The school years* (2nd edn, pp.123–163). London: Routledge.

Farrington, D.P. (1993). Childhood origins of teenage antisocial behaviour and adult social dysfunction. *Journal of the Royal Society of Medicine, 86*, 13–17.

Farrington, D.P. (1994). Childhood, adolescent and adult features of violent males. In L.R. Huesmann (Ed.) *Aggressive behavior: Current perspectives* (pp.215–240). New York: Plenum.

Farrington, D.P. (1998). Predictors, causes and correlates of male youth violence. In M. Tonry & M.H. Moore (Eds.) *Youth violence* (pp.421–475). Chicago, IL: University of Chicago Press.

Farrington, D.P. (2002). Multiple risk factors for multiple problem violent boys. In R.R. Corrado, R. Roesch, S.D. Hart & J.K. Gierowski (Eds.) *Multi-problem violent youth: A foundation for comparative research on needs, interventions and outcomes* (pp.23–34). Amsterdam: IOS Press.

Farrington, D.P. (2003). Key results from the first 40 years of the Cambridge Study in Delinquent Development. In T.P. Thornberry & M.D. Krohn (Eds.) *Taking stock of delinquency: An overview of findings from contemporary longitudinal studies* (pp.137–183). New York: Kluwer/Plenum.

Farrington, D.P. (2005). The Integrated Cognitive Antisocial Potential (ICAP) theory. In D.P. Farrington (Ed.) *Integrated developmental and life-course theories of offending* (pp.73–92). New Brunswick, NJ: Transaction.

Farrington, D.P., Barnes, G. & Lambert, S. (1996). The concentration of offending in families. *Legal and Criminological Psychology, 1*, 47–63.

Farrington, D.P., Biron, L. & LeBlanc, M. (1982). Personality and delinquency in London and Montreal. In J. Gunn & D.P. Farrington (Eds.) *Abnormal offenders, delinquency, and the criminal justice system* (pp.153–201). Chichester: Wiley.

Farrington, D.P., Coid, J.W., Harnett, L., Jolliffe, D., Soteriou, N., Turner, R. *et al.* (2006). *Criminal careers up to age 50 and life success up to age 48: New findings from the Cambridge Study in Delinquent Development.* London: Home Office (Research Study No. 299).

Farrington, D.P., Gallagher, B., Morley, L., St. Ledger, R.J. & West, D.J. (1986). Unemployment, school leaving, and crime. *British Journal of Criminology, 26*, 335–356.

Farrington, D.P., Jolliffe, D., Loeber, R., Stouthamer-Loeber, M. & Kalb, L.M. (2001). The concentration of offenders in families, and family criminality in the prediction of boys' delinquency. *Journal of Adolescence, 24*, 579–596.

Farrington, D.P. & Loeber, R. (1999). Transatlantic replicability of risk factors in the development of delinquency. In P. Cohen, C. Slomkowski & L.N. Robins (Eds.) *Historical and geographical influences on psychopathology* (pp.299–329). Mahwah, NJ: Lawrence Erlbaum.

Farrington, D.P., Loeber, R. & van Kammen, W.B. (1990). Long-term criminal outcomes of hyperactivity-impulsivity-attention deficit and conduct problems in childhood. In L.N. Robins & M. Rutter (Eds.) *Straight and devious pathways from childhood to adulthood* (pp.62–81). Cambridge: Cambridge University Press.

Farrington, D.P., Loeber, R., & Stouthamer-Loeber, M. (2003). How can the relationship between race and violence be explained? In D.F. Hawkins (Ed.) *Violent crime: Assessing race and ethnic differences* (pp.213–237). Cambridge: Cambridge University Press.

Farrington, D.P., Loeber, R., Yin, Y. & Anderson, S. (2002). Are within-individual causes of delinquency the same as between-individual causes? *Criminal Behaviour and Mental Health, 12*, 53–68.

Farrington, D.P. & Welsh, B.C. (2007). *Saving children from a life of crime: Early risk factors and effective interventions.* Oxford: Oxford University Press.

Fergusson, D.M. & Horwood, L.J. (1998). Exposure to interparental violence in childhood and psychosocial adjustment in young adulthood. *Child Abuse and Neglect, 22*, 339–357.

Fergusson, D.M., Horwood, L.J. & Lynskey, M.T. (1994). The childhoods of multiple problem adolescents: A 15 year longitudinal study. *Journal of Child Psychology and Psychiatry, 35*, 1123–1140.

Fergusson, D., Swain-Campbell, N., & Horwood, J. (2004). How does childhood economic disadvantage lead to crime? *Journal of Child Psychology and Psychiatry, 45*, 956–966.

Frick, P.J. & White, S.F. (2008). The importance of callous-unemotional traits for developmental models of aggressive and antisocial behaviour. *Journal of Child Psychology and Psychiatry, 49*, 359–375.

Gatti, U., Tremblay, R.E., Vitaro, F., & McDuff, P. (2005). Youth gangs, delinquency and drug use: A test of the selection, facilitation, and enhancement hypotheses. *Journal of Child Psychology and Psychiatry, 46*, 1178–1190.

Gordon, R.A., Lahey, B.B., Kawai, E., Loeber, R., Stouthamer-Loeber, M., & Farrington, D.P. (2004). Antisocial behavior and youth gang membership: Selection and socialization. *Criminology, 42*, 55–87.

Gottfredson, D.C. (2001). *Schools and delinquency.* Cambridge: Cambridge University Press.

Gottfredson, D.C., McNeil, R.J. & Gottfredson, G.D. (1991). Social area influences on delinquency: A multilevel analyses. *Journal of Research in Crime and Delinquency, 28*, 197–226.

Graham, J. (1988). *Schools, disruptive behaviour and delinquency.* London: Her Majesty's Stationery Office.

Haapasalo, J. & Pokela, E. (1999). Child-rearing and child abuse antecedents of criminality. *Aggression and Violent Behavior, 1*, 107–127.

Hawkins, J.D., Smith, B.H., Hill, K.G., Kosterman, R., Catalano, R.F. & Abbott, R.D. (2003). Understanding and preventing crime and violence: Findings from the Seattle Social Development Project. In T.P. Thornberry & M.D. Krohn (Eds.) *Taking stock of delinquency: An overview of findings from contemporary longitudinal studies* (pp.255–312). New York: Kluwer/Plenum.

Heaven, P.C.L. (1996). Personality and self-reported delinquency: Analysis of the 'Big Five' personality dimensions. *Personality and Individual Differences*, 20, 47–54.

Henry, B., Moffitt, T., Robins, L., Earls, F. & Silva, P. (1993). Early family predictors of child and adolescent antisocial behaviour: Who are the mothers of delinquents? *Criminal Behaviour and Mental Health*, 2, 97–118.

Herrenkohl, T.I., Hawkins, J.D., Chung, I-J., Hill, K.G. & Battin-Pearson, S. (2001). School and community risk factors and interventions. In R. Loeber & D.P. Farrington (Eds.) *Child delinquents: Development, intervention and service needs* (pp.211–246). Thousand Oaks, CA: Sage.

Herrenkohl, T.I., Maguin, E., Hill, K.G., Hawkins, J.D., Abbott, R.D., & Catalano, R F. (2000). Developmental risk factors for youth violence. *Journal of Adolescent Health*, 26, 176–186.

Hogh, E. & Wolf, P. (1983). Violent crime in a birth cohort: Copenhagen 1953–1977. In K.T. van Dusen & S.A. Mednick (Eds.) *Prospective studies of crime and delinquency* (pp.249–267). Boston, MA: Kluwer-Nijhoff.

Huesmann, L.R., Dubow, E.F. & Boxer, P. (2009). Continuity of aggression from childhood to early adulthood as a predictor of adult criminality and life outcomes: Implications for the adolescent-limited and life-course-persistent models. *Aggressive Behavior*, 35, 136–149.

Huizinga, D., Weiher, A.W., Espiritu, R. & Esbensen, F. (2003). Delinquency and crime: Some highlights from the Denver Youth Survey. In T.P. Thornberry & M.D. Krohn (Eds.) *Taking stock of delinquency: An overview of findings from contemporary longitudinal studies* (pp.47–91). New York: Kluwer/Plenum.

John, O.P., Caspi, A., Robins, R.W., Moffitt, T.E., & Stouthamer-Loeber, M. (1994). The 'Little Five': Exploring the nomological network of the Five-Factor Model of personality in adolescent boys. *Child Development*, 65, 160–178.

Jolliffe, D. & Farrington, D.P. (2004). Empathy and offending: A systematic review and meta-analysis. *Aggression and Violent Behavior*, 9, 441–476.

Jolliffe, D. & Farrington, D.P. (2006). Development and validation of the Basic Empathy Scale. *Journal of Adolescence*, 29, 589–611.

Jolliffe, D. & Farrington, D.P. (2007). Examining the relationship between low empathy and self-reported offending. *Legal and Criminological Psychology*, 12, 265–286.

Jolliffe, D. & Farrington, D.P. (2009). A systematic review of the relationship between childhood impulsiveness and later violence. In M. McMurran & R. Howard (Eds.), *Personality, personality disorder, and violence* (pp. 41–61) Chichester: Wiley.

Juby, H. & Farrington, D.P. (2001). Disentangling the link between disrupted families and delinquency. *British Journal of Criminology*, 41, 22–40.

Kagan, J. (1989). Temperamental contributions to social behavior. *American Psychologist*, 44, 668–674.

Kaukiainen, A., Bjorkvist, K., Lagerspetz, K., Osterman, K., Salmivalli, C., Rothberg, S. *et al.* (1999). The relationships between social intelligence, empathy, and three types of aggression. *Aggressive Behavior*, 25, 81–89.

Keiley, M.K., Howe, T.R., Dodge, K.A., Bates, J.E., & Pettit, G.S. (2001). The timing of child physical maltreatment: A cross-domain growth analysis of impact on adolescent externalizing and internalizing problems. *Development and Psychopathology*, 13, 891–912.

Klinteberg, B.A., Andersson, T., Magnusson, D. & Stattin, H. (1993). Hyperactive behaviour in childhood as related to subsequent alcohol problems and violent offending: A longitudinal study of male subjects. *Personality and Individual Differences*, 15, 381–388.

Kolvin, I., Miller, F.J.W., Fleeting, M. & Kolvin, P.A. (1988). Social and parenting factors affecting criminal-offence rates: Findings from the Newcastle Thousand Family Study (1947–1980). *British Journal of Psychiatry*, 152, 80–90.

Kolvin, I., Miller, F.J.W., Scott, D.M., Gatzanis, S.R.M. & Fleeting, M. (1990). *Continuities of deprivation? The Newcastle 1000 Family Study*. Aldershot: Avebury.

Koolhof, R., Loeber, R., Wei, E.H., Pardini, D., & D'Escury, A.C. (2007). Inhibition deficits of serious delinquent boys of low intelligence. *Criminal Behaviour and Mental Health*, 17, 274–292.

Larzelere, R.E. & Patterson, G.R. (1990). Parental management: Mediator of the effect of socioeconomic status on early delinquency. *Criminology*, 28, 301–324.

LeBlanc, M. & Frechette, M. (1989). *Male criminal activity from childhood through youth*. New York: Springer-Verlag.

Lipsey, M.W. & Derzon, J. H. (1998). Predictors of violent or serious delinquency in adolescence and early adulthood: A synthesis of longitudinal research. In R. Loeber & D.P. Farrington (Eds.) *Serious and violent juvenile offenders: Risk factors and successful interventions* (pp.86–105). Thousand Oaks, CA: Sage.

Lipsitt, P.D., Buka, S.L. & Lipsitt, L.P. (1990). Early intelligence scores and subsequent delinquency: A prospective study. *American Journal of Family Therapy*, 18, 197–208.

Loeber, R., Farrington, D.P., Stouthamer-Loeber, M. & van Kammen, W.B. (1998). Multiple risk factors for multiproblem boys: Co-occurrence of delinquency, substance use, attention deficit, conduct problems, physical aggression, covert behavior, depressed mood and shy/withdrawn behavior. In R. Jessor (Ed.) *New perspectives on adolescent risk behavior* (pp.90–149). New York: Cambridge University Press.

Loeber, R., Farrington, D.P., Stouthamer-Loeber, M., Moffitt, T.E., Caspi, A., White, H.R. *et al.* (2003). The development of male offending: Key findings from 14 years of the Pittsburgh Youth Study. In T.P. Thornberry & M.D. Krohn (Eds.) *Taking stock of delinquency: An overview of findings from contemporary longitudinal studies* (pp.93–136). New York: Kluwer/Plenum.

Lösel, F., Bliesener, T., & Bender, D. (2007). Social information processing, experiences of aggression in social contexts, and aggressive behaviour in adolescents. *Criminal Justice and Behavior, 34*, 330–347.

Luengo, M.A., Otero, J.M., Carrillo-de-la-Pena, M.T., & Miron, L. (1994). Dimensions of antisocial behaviour in juvenile delinquency: A study of personality variables. *Psychology, Crime and Law, 1*, 27–37.

Lynam, D. (1996). Early identification of chronic offenders: Who is the fledgling psychopath? *Psychological Bulletin, 120*, 209–234.

Lynam, D.R. (1998). Early identification of the fledgling psychopath: Locating the psychopathic child in the current nomenclature. *Journal of Abnormal Psychology, 107*, 566–575.

Lynam, D., Moffitt, T.E. & Stouthamer-Loeber, M. (1993). Explaining the relation between IQ and delinquency: Class, race, test motivation, school failure or self-control? *Journal of Abnormal Psychology, 102*, 187–196.

McCord, J. (1977). A comparative study of two generations of native Americans. In R.F. Meier (Ed.) *Theory in criminology* (pp.83–92). Beverly Hills, CA: Sage.

McCord, J. (1979). Some child-rearing antecedents of criminal behavior in adult men. *Journal of Personality and Social Psychology, 37*, 1477–1486.

McCord, J. (1982). A longitudinal view of the relationship between paternal absence and crime. In J. Gunn & D.P. Farrington (Eds.) *Abnormal offenders, delinquency, and the criminal justice system* (pp.113–128). Chichester: Wiley.

McCord, J. (1983). A forty year perspective on effects of child abuse and neglect. *Child Abuse and Neglect, 7*, 265–270.

McCord, J. (1991). Family relationships, juvenile delinquency, and adult criminality. *Criminology, 29*, 397–417.

McCord, J. (1997). On discipline. *Psychological Inquiry, 8*, 215–217.

McCrae, R.R. & Costa, P.T. (2003). *Personality in adulthood: A five-factor theory perspective.* New York: Guilford Press.

Maguin, E. & Loeber, R. (1996). Academic performance and delinquency. In M. Tonry (Ed.), *Crime and justice* (vol. 20, pp.145–264). Chicago, IL: University of Chicago Press.

Mak, A.S. (1991). Psychosocial control characteristics of delinquents and non-delinquents. *Criminal Justice and Behavior, 18*, 287–303.

Malinosky-Rummell, R. & Hansen, D.J. (1993). Long-term consequences of childhood physical abuse. *Psychological Bulletin, 114*, 68–79.

Maxfield, M.G. & Widom, C.S. (1996). The cycle of violence revisited 6 years later. *Archives of Pediatrics and Adolescent Medicine, 150*, 390–395.

Moffitt, T.E. (1993). The neuropsychology of conduct disorder. *Development and Psychopathology, 5*, 135–151.

Moffitt, T.E., Caspi, A., Rutter, M. & Silva, P.A. (2001). *Sex differences in antisocial behaviour.* Cambridge: Cambridge University Press.

Moffitt, T.E. & Henry, B. (1991). Neuropsychological studies of juvenile delinquency and juvenile violence. In J. S. Milner (Ed.) *Neuropsychology of aggression* (pp.131–146). Boston, MA: Kluwer.

Morash, M. & Rucker, L. (1989). An exploratory study of the connection of mother's age at childbearing to her children's delinquency in four data sets. *Crime and Delinquency, 35*, 45–93.

Morgan, A.B. & Lilienfeld, S.O. (2000). A meta-analytic review of the relation between antisocial behavior and neuro-psychological measures of executive function. *Clinical Psychology Review, 20*, 113–136.

Murray, J. & Farrington, D.P. (2005). Parental imprisonment: Effects on boys' antisocial behaviour and delinquency through the life-course. *Journal of Child Psychology and Psychiatry, 46*, 1269–1278.

Murray, J., Janson, C-G., & Farrington, D.P. (2007). Crime in adult offspring of prisoners: A cross-national comparison of two longitudinal samples. *Criminal Justice and Behavior, 34*, 133–149.

Nagin, D.S., Pogarsky, G. & Farrington, D.P. (1997). Adolescent mothers and the criminal behavior of their children. *Law and Society Review, 31*, 137–162.

Newson, J. & Newson, E. (1989). *The extent of parental physical punishment in the UK.* London: Approach.

Newson, J., Newson, E. & Adams, M. (1993). The social origins of delinquency. *Criminal Behaviour and Mental Health, 3*, 19–29.

Odgers, C.L., Milne, B.J., Caspi, A., Crump, R., Poulton, R., & Moffitt, T.E. (2007). Predicting prognosis for the conduct-problem boy: Can family history help? *Journal of the American Academy of Child and Adolescent Psychiatry, 46*, 1240–1249.

Osborn, S.G. (1980). Moving home, leaving London, and delinquent trends. *British Journal of Criminology, 20*, 54–61.

Patterson, G.R. (1995). Coercion as a basis for early age of onset for arrest. In J. McCord (Ed.) *Coercion and punishment in long-term perspectives* (pp.81–105). Cambridge: Cambridge University Press.

Piquero, A.R. (2000). Frequency, specialization, and violence in offending careers. *Journal of Research in Crime and Delinquency, 37*, 392–418.

Power, M.J., Alderson, M.R., Phillipson, C.M., Shoenberg, E. & Morris, J.N. (1967). Delinquent schools? *New Society, 10*, 542–543.

Pratt, T.C., Cullen, F.T., Blevins, K.R., Daigle, L. & Unnever, J.D. (2002). The relationship of attention deficit hyperactivity disorder to crime and delinquency: A meta-analysis. *International Journal of Police Science and Management, 4*, 344–360.

Pulkkinen, L., Lyyra, A-L. & Kokko, K. (2009). Life success of males on non-offender, adolescence-limited, persistent, and adult-onset antisocial pathways: Follow-up from age 8 to 42. *Aggressive Behavior, 35*, 117–135.

Raine, A., Moffitt, T.E., Caspi, A., Loeber, R., Stouthamer-Loeber, M. & Lynam, D. (2005). Neurocognitive impairments in boys on the life-course-persistent antisocial path. *Journal of Abnormal Psychology, 114*, 38–49.

Reiss, A.J. (1986). Why are communities important in understanding crime? In A.J. Reiss & M. Tonry (Eds.), *Communities and crime* (pp.1–33). Chicago, IL: University of Chicago Press.

Reiss, A.J. & Farrington, D.P. (1991). Advancing knowledge about co-offending: Results from a prospective longitudinal survey of London males. *Journal of Criminal Law and Criminology, 82,* 360–395.

Robins, L.N. (1979). Sturdy childhood predictors of adult outcomes: Replications from longitudinal studies. In J.E. Barrett, R.M. Rose & G.L. Klerman (Eds.) *Stress and mental disorder* (pp.219–235). New York: Raven Press.

Robins, L.N., West, P.J. & Herjanic, B.L. (1975). Arrests and delinquency in two generations: A study of black urban families and their children. *Journal of Child Psychology and Psychiatry, 16,* 125–140.

Rutter, M. (1981). The city and the child. *American Journal of Orthopsychiatry, 51,* 610–625.

Rutter, M., Giller, H. & Hagell, A. (1998). *Antisocial behaviour by young people.* Cambridge: Cambridge University Press.

Rutter, M., Maughan, B., Mortimore, P., Ouston, J. & Smith, A. (1979). *Fifteen thousand hours: Secondary schools and their effects on children.* London: Open Books.

Sampson, R.J., Morenoff, J.D., & Raudenbush, S. (2005). Social anatomy of racial and ethnic disparities in violence. *American Journal of Public Health, 95,* 224–232.

Sampson, R.J., Raudenbush, S.W. & Earls, F. (1997). Neighborhoods and violent crime: A multilevel study of collective efficacy. *Science, 277,* 918–924.

Schwartz, C.E., Snidman, N. & Kagan, J. (1996). Early childhood temperament as a determinant of externalizing behavior in adolescence. *Development and Psychopathology, 8,* 527–537.

Schweinhart, L.J., Barnes, H.V. & Weikart, D.P. (1993). *Significant benefits.* Ypsilanti, MI: High/Scope.

Seguin, J., Pihl, R.O., Harden, P.W., Tremblay, R.E. & Boulerice, B. (1995). Cognitive and neuropsychological characteristics of physically aggressive boys. *Journal of Abnormal Psychology, 104,* 614–624.

Shaw, C.R. & McKay, H.D. (1969). *Juvenile delinquency and urban areas* (rev. ed.). Chicago, IL: University of Chicago Press.

Smith, C.A. & Stern, S.B. (1997). Delinquency and antisocial behavior: A review of family processes and intervention research. *Social Service Review, 71,* 382–420.

Smith, C.A. & Thornberry, T.P. (1995). The relationship between childhood maltreatment and adolescent involvement in delinquency. *Criminology, 33,* 451–481.

Stams, G. J., Brugman, D., Dekovic, M., van Rosmalen, L., van der Laan, P., & Gibbs, J. C. (2006). The moral judgment of juvenile delinquents: A meta-analysis. *Journal of Abnormal Child Psychology, 34,* 697–713.

Stattin, H. & Klackenberg-Larsson, I. (1993). Early language and intelligence development and their relationship to future criminal behavior. *Journal of Abnormal Psychology, 102,* 369–378.

Steinberg, L., Lamborn, S.D., Dornbusch, S.M. & Darling, N. (1992). Impact of parenting practices on adolescent achievement: Authoritative parenting, school involvement and encouragement to succeed. *Child Development, 63,* 1266–1281.

Sutton, J., Smith, P.K., & Swettenham, J. (1999). Social cognition and bullying: Social inadequacy or skilled manipulation? *British Journal of Developmental Psychology, 17,* 435–450.

Thornberry, T.P. & Farnworth, M. (1982). Social correlates of criminal involvement: Further evidence on the relationship between social status and criminal behavior. *American Sociological Review, 47,* 505–518.

Thornberry, T.P., Huizinga, D. & Loeber, R. (1995). The prevention of serious delinquency and violence: Implications from the program of research on the causes and correlates of delinquency. In J.C. Howell, B. Krisberg, J.D. Hawkins & J.J. Wilson (Eds.) *Sourcebook on serious, violent and chronic juvenile offenders* (pp.213–237). Thousand Oaks, CA: Sage.

Thornberry, T.P. & Krohn, M. (Eds.) (2003). *Taking stock of delinquency: An overview of findings from contemporary longitudinal studies.* New York: Kluwer/Plenum.

Thornberry, T.P., Krohn, M.D., Lizotte, A.J., Smith, C.A. & Tobin, K. (2003). *Gangs and delinquency in developmental perspective.* New York: Cambridge University Press.

Thornberry, T.P., Lizotte, A.J., Krohn, M.D., Farnworth M. & Jang, S.J. (1994). Delinquent peers, beliefs and delinquent behavior: A longitudinal test of interactional theory. *Criminology, 32,* 47–83.

Thornberry, T.P., Lizotte, A.J., Krohn, M.D., Smith, C.A. & Porter, P.K. (2003). Causes and consequences of delinquency: Findings from the Rochester Youth Development Study. In T.P. Thornberry & M.D. Krohn (Eds.) *Taking stock of delinquency: An overview of findings from contemporary longitudinal studies* (pp.11–46). New York: Kluwer/Plenum.

Tolan, P.H., Gorman-Smith, D., & Henry, D.B. (2003). The developmental ecology of urban males' youth violence. *Developmental Psychology, 39,* 274–291.

Tracy, P.E. & Kempf-Leonard, K. (1996). *Continuity and discontinuity in criminal careers.* New York: Plenum.

Tremblay, R.E., Vitaro, F., Nagin, D., Pagani, L. & Seguin, J.R. (2003). The Montreal Longitudinal and Experimental Study: Rediscovering the power of descriptions. In T.P. Thornberry & M.D. Krohn (Eds.) *Taking stock of delinquency: An overview of findings from contemporary longitudinal studies* (pp.205–254). New York: Kluwer/Plenum.

Wadsworth, M.E.J. (1979). *Roots of delinquency: Infancy, adolescence and crime.* London: Martin Robertson.

Wadsworth, M.E.J. (1991). *The imprint of time.* Oxford: Clarendon Press.

Wells, L.E. & Rankin, J.H. (1991). Families and delinquency: A meta-analysis of the impact of broken homes. *Social Problems, 38,* 71–93.

Werner, E.E. & Smith, R.S. (2001). *Journeys from childhood to midlife.* Ithaca, NY: Cornell University Press.

West, D.J. & Farrington, D.P. (1973). *Who becomes delinquent?* London: Heinemann.

West, D.J. & Farrington, D.P. (1977). *The delinquent way of life.* London: Heinemann.

White, J.L., Moffitt, T.E., Caspi, A., Bartusch, D.J., Needles, D.J. & Stouthamer-Loeber, M. (1994). Measuring impulsivity and examining its relationship to delinquency. *Journal of Abnormal Psychology*, *103*, 192–205.

Widom, C.S. (1994). Childhood victimization and adolescent problem behaviors. In R.D. Ketterlinus & M.E. Lamb (Eds.) *Adolescent problem behaviors* (pp.127–164). Hillsdale, NJ: Lawrence Erlbaum.

Wikström, P-O.H. (1990). Age and crime in a Stockholm cohort. *Journal of Quantitative Criminology*, *6*, 61–84.

Wikström, P-O.H. & Loeber, R. (2000). Do disadvantaged neighborhoods cause well-adjusted children to become adolescent delinquents? A study of male juvenile serious offending, individual risk and protective factors, and neighborhood context. *Criminology*, *38*, 1109–1142.

Wilson, J.Q. & Herrnstein, R.J. (1985). *Crime and human nature*. New York: Simon & Schuster.

Wolfgang, M.E., Thornberry, T.P. & Figlio, R.M. (1987). *From boy to man, from delinquency to crime*. Chicago, IL: University of Chicago Press.

9

The Developmental Evidence Base
Desistance

Lila Kazemian and David P. Farrington

In recent years, the growing literature on the topic of desistance from crime has generated a large body of knowledge on this dimension of the criminal career. Despite these efforts, it has been suggested that our understanding of the processes underlying desistance remains limited. In particular, very little is known about the causal processes underlying desistance. The objective of this chapter is to offer an overview of the state of knowledge on desistance, and to highlight some unresolved issues in this area of study. It reviews social and cognitive predictors of desistance, as well as the shortcomings of past desistance research. The chapter also offers recommendations for future research.

Current State of Knowledge on Desistance

This first section aims to provide a brief summary of some of the key findings from influential studies on desistance research with regard to social and cognitive factors associated with desistance from crime. Desistance may be viewed either as a gradual process or as a sharp termination of offending.

Social predictors of desistance

Although Gottfredson and Hirschi (1990) have argued that associations between life events and desistance from crime are spurious (also see Hirschi & Gottfredson, 1995), a large body of research on desistance has drawn attention to the importance of social bonds in the process of desistance. Desistance from crime is said to be gradual, resulting from an accumulation of social bonds (see Horney *et al.*, 1995). Irwin (1970) identified three key factors in the explanation of desistance from crime: a good job, a good relationship with a woman, and involvement in extracurricular activities. Giordano *et al.* (2002) made reference to the 'respectability package', and argued that marriage and job stability exert a more substantial impact on desistance if they occur jointly. In this respect, turning points (marriage, employment, etc.) are likely to be interdependent.

Horney *et al.* (1995, p.658) explored the association between crime and local life circumstances, which they defined as '… conditions in an individual's life that can fluctuate relatively frequently'. According to the authors, variables explaining short-term variations in criminal behaviour are similar to variables explaining long-term variations (i.e. strength of bonds to conventional social institutions). Horney *et al.* (1995, p.669) found that individuals were '… less likely to commit crimes when living with a wife' (see also Farrington & West, 1995; Laub & Sampson, 2003; Rand, 1987; Sampson & Laub, 1993). The authors argued that time invested in conventional social institutions was time away from sources of temptation (bars, delinquent peers, etc.). Horney *et al.* (1995, p.670) did however admit that local life circumstances may not have been randomly distributed, and that '… local life circumstances can change criminal careers by modifying the likelihood of offending *at particular times*'. Since their analyses were limited to a short period of the life course, it is difficult to assess whether these changes were permanent, and whether they reflected stable changes in life-course trajectories.

Farrington and Hawkins (1991) argued that predictors of desistance may vary across different periods of the life course. Similarly, Sampson and Laub's (1993, p.17; see also Sampson & Laub, 1997) age-graded theory of informal social control emphasises the idea that '... the important institutions of both formal and informal social control vary across the life span'. Sampson and Laub's (1993) argument relies on the premise that changes in social bonds across the life course can explain offending behaviour, even after accounting for different degrees of self-control. In childhood and adolescence, delinquency is explained by the strength of bonds (or lack thereof) to family and school. In adulthood, variations in offending behaviour are explained by job stability and marital attachment, which are recognised as triggers of the desistance process. How individuals adapt to life-course transitions and turning points may mould the decision to engage in criminal (or non-criminal) behaviour. Thus, life events can either be positive or negative, depending on the 'quality, strength, and interdependence of social ties' (Sampson & Laub, 1993, p.21). In this respect, adult crime would largely result from weak bonds to social institutions, and desistance from crime would entail some 'social investment' in conventional institutions.

Employment

Using data from the National Supported Work Demonstration Project, Uggen (2000) explored the effect of employment on recidivism. This project recruited participants from underprivileged neighbourhoods and randomly assigned them to control or experimental groups. Offenders, drug users and dropouts were targeted. Individuals in the treatment group were given minimum-wage employment opportunities. Results showed that the programme had a more substantial impact on older individuals (over 26 years of age). Furthermore, 'Offenders who are provided even marginal employment opportunities are less likely to reoffend than those not provided such opportunities' (Uggen, 2000, p.542). Although the general consensus in the literature is that job stability does exert an impact on desistance, some studies have found that employment did not have an impact on the likelihood of desistance from crime (Giordano et al., 2002; Rhodes, 1989).

The life narratives explored in Laub and Sampson's (2003, p.129) study suggested that '... stable work may not trigger a change in an antisocial trajectory in the way that marriage or serving in the military does, even

though employment may play an important role in sustaining the process of desistance'. In their explanation of the impact of employment on desistance, Laub and Sampson (2003) continue to emphasise the important role of routine activities. The authors argued that the processes underlying the relationship between work and desistance are similar to those underlying the relationship between marriage and desistance. Employment promotes desistance through four main processes: a reciprocal exchange of social capital between employer and employee, reduced criminal opportunities and the '... probability that criminal propensities will be translated into action', direct informal social control, and the development of a '... sense of identity and meaning' to one's life' (Laub & Sampson, 2003, p.47). The latter factor leads us to a discussion of the individual factors contributing to the process of desistance from crime.

Marriage

Farrington and West (1995, p.265) found that '... individuals who had married and never separated were the least antisocial at age 32 while those who had married and separated and were now living alone were the most antisocial'. They studied rates of offending before and after marriage, and concluded that getting married led to a decrease in offending compared with staying single. They also discovered that separation from a wife led to an increase in offending compared with staying married. However, they argued that 'It is not clear from these results how far marriage and separation may be causes, consequences, or symptoms' (1995, p.265). They considered that the effect of marriage may have been dependent on '... the reasons for getting married (e.g. pregnancy), on the happiness of the marriage, and on the extent to which the wife is conventional and prosocial' (1995, p.278). They concluded that 'Marriage may have a cumulative rather than a sharply-delimited effect' (1995, p.278).

Laub et al. (1998) also found that high-rate offenders had weaker marital bonds than other offenders. In agreement with Farrington and West's results, Laub et al. (1998) argued that the timing and quality of marriage were important (see also Rutter, 1996), with stable marriages having an increased preventive effect (see also Sampson & Laub, 1993). Also in agreement with Farrington and West's study, Laub et al. (1998) argued that the inhibiting effect of marriage on crime is gradual rather than abrupt. Laub and

Sampson (2003) defined the effect of marriage on crime as an 'investment process'; the more that individuals invest in social bonds (e.g. marriage), the less likely they are to engage in criminal activities because they have more to lose. Laub and Sampson (2003, p.33) rejected the idea that the effect of marriage on crime is merely a result of self-selection (i.e. people who decide to reform are more likely to get married), and claimed that marital effects remained strong despite selection effects.

Laub and Sampson (2003) summarised the key processes involved in the effect of marriage on desistance from crime, many of which revolve around shifts in routine activities. Marriage leads to reduced deviant peer associations, new friends and extended family, as well as overall changes in routine activities. Spouses also constitute an extra source of social control, and an effective means of monitoring routine activities. Residential changes and children may also promote changes in routine activities. Laub and Sampson (2003, p.43) also argued that '... marriage can change one's sense of self'.

In contrast to these results, Knight et al. (1977) found that early marriage (under age 21) had little effect on self-reported delinquency, although it was followed by a reduction in drinking and drug use. Kruttschnitt et al. (2000) explored the predictors of desistance among a sample of sex offenders placed on probation in Minnesota in 1992. They found that '... job stability significantly reduces the probability of reoffending among convicted sex offenders, although marital status exerts virtually no effect' (2000, p.80; see also Giordano et al., 2002). Kruttschnitt et al. (2000) added that this lack of association between marriage and reoffending may be a result of the fact that they did not possess any information about the quality of the marital relationship.

Consistent with the hypothesis that turning points are interdependent, Sampson and Laub's (1993) results revealed interaction effects between various social institutions and desistance from crime. For example, they found that the impact of job stability on desistance was not as significant for married men. Whereas their perspective is more consistent with Hirschi's (1969) control theory, others have adopted a social learning or differential association position, which stipulates that the effect of marriage on crime is mediated by peer associations (see Akers, 1990). This perspective attributes desistance to associations with conventional peers, increased noncriminal routine activities, and reduced exposure to definitions favourable to crime.

Peers

Using a sample from the National Youth Survey (NYS), Warr (1993) found that changes in offending behaviour with age were related to changes in peer associations. The author concluded that, when controlling for peer associations, '... the association between age and crime is substantially weakened and, for some offences, disappears entirely' (1993, p.35). In a later study, Warr (1998) found that married people tend to spend less time with their friends than unmarried people, and that married individuals tend to have fewer delinquent friends than unmarried individuals. According to his argument, the effect of marriage on desistance is mediated by peer influences and more particularly by the reduced involvement with delinquent friends and lower exposure to criminal opportunities.

Wright and Cullen (2004) replicated Warr's (1998) study and also used data from the National Youth Survey (NYS), but focused on work rather than marriage. The authors studied the predictors of changes in rates of offending (using delinquency and drug scales already constructed as part of the NYS). They found that employment increased the interactions with prosocial co-workers, which '... restructure friendship networks by diminishing contact with delinquent peers' (2004, p.185). Work was said to promote desistance not through the development of increased social capital, but rather through increased associations with prosocial co-workers. In other words, relationships with prosocial co-workers minimised interactions with delinquent peers and promoted desistance from crime. Wright and Cullen (2004, p.185) did not dismiss Sampson and Laub's position, nor did they deny the important role of adult employment in the process of desistance from crime, but they also suggest that '... the workplace is a social domain in which learning can take place'. Like Sampson and Laub, they also found that adult employment reduces misbehaviour. However, Wright and Cullen (2004, p.200) argued that the effects of unemployment on desistance were not dependent on the quality of the job (as argued by Sampson and Laub), but rather on the '*quality of peer associations* that occur within the context of work'. Wilson and Herrnstein (1985, p.285) put forth a similar idea regarding the role of school in the development of criminal behaviour, maintaining that '... the school may contribute to criminality because of the peer groups that form there'.

In agreement with these results, Cromwell et al. (1991, p.83) found that for some offenders, '... desistance was a gradual process that appeared to be associated with the disintegration of the adolescent peer group, and with employment and the ability to earn money legitimately' (see also Warr, 1998). Rand (1987) also found a positive correlation between gang membership and offending. Similarly, in his explanation of desistance from family violence offences, Fagan (1989) underlined the importance of replacing old social networks by new prosocial networks that would disapprove of violent behaviour and promote prosocial behaviour. In the debate concerning the relative influences of sibling and peer delinquency on an individual's offending habits, Robins (1966) maintained that associations with delinquent peers were the result of a choice. In this perspective, delinquent peers would exert a more substantial influence on criminal behaviour, since individuals choose their friends but not their siblings.

It is clear that the association with delinquent friends decreases at the same time as a person's own offending decreases. However, it is less clear whether decreasing peer delinquency has a causal effect on a person's offending (in encouraging desistance) or whether it is merely a risk marker (e.g. because many offences are committed in groups, delinquency and delinquent peers could both reflect the same underlying construct). In the Pittsburgh Youth Study, Farrington et al. (2002) found that, while delinquent peers were strongly correlated with delinquency between individuals, delinquent peers did not predict delinquency in within-individual analyses where boys were followed up over time, suggesting that peer delinquency may not have had a causal effect on offending.

Cognitive predictors of desistance

The study of subjective changes that promote desistance from crime has generally been addressed in ethnographic studies and qualitative analyses of crime. Maruna (2001, p.8) argued that 'Subjective aspects of human life (emotions, thoughts, motivations, and goals) have largely been neglected in the study of crime, because the data are presumed to be either unscientific or too unwieldy for empirical analysis'.

According to Gove (1985), desistance from crime is a result of five key internal changes: shifting from self-centredness to consideration for others, developing prosocial values and behaviour, increasing ease in social interactions, greater consideration for other members of the community, and a growing concern for the 'meaning of life'. Through life history narratives, Giordano et al. (2002) discussed the theory of cognitive transforma-

tion, which is defined as *cognitive shifts* that promote the process of desistance. The authors described four processes of cognitive transformations. First, the offender must be open to change. Second, through a process of self-selection, the individual exposes himself/herself to prosocial experiences that will further promote desistance (e.g. employment, etc.). Third, the individual adheres to a new prosocial and noncriminal identity. Finally, there is a shift in the perception of the criminal lifestyle, i.e. the negative consequences of offending become obvious. As such, desistance is perceived to be a gradual process. Haggard et al. (2001, p.1056) claimed that 'The decision to change one's life seemed only to be the beginning of a long pathway to actual behavioural alterations'.

Shover and Thompson (1992) found that the relationship between age and desistance was mediated by *optimism for achieving success via legitimate pursuits* and *expectations of criminal success*. In this respect, the individual's optimism and genuine desire to adopt a prosocial lifestyle may play an important role in the desistance process. Burnett (2004) also found that pre-release self-assessments of optimism about desistance were positively associated with actual desistance outcomes after release (see Farrall, 2002, for similar results). Maruna (2001, p.9) concluded that desisting ex-offenders '... displayed an exaggerated sense of control over the future and an inflated, almost missionary, sense of purpose in life'. The individuals' motivation and determination to cease offending is also a key component in the desistance process (Burnett, 2004; Moffitt, 1993a; Pezzin, 1995; Shover, 1983; Shover & Thompson, 1992; Sommers et al., 1994).

Through interviews with a sample of incarcerated burglars, Shover (1996) highlighted the importance of *resolve and determination*, which are also essential to the desistance process. He argued that '... men who are most determined to avoid crime are more successful in doing so than their equivocating peers, even allowing for the possible influences of other factors' (1996, p.130). Some of the interviewees expressed increasing concern with getting caught as they got older, fearing that they might spend the rest of their lives in prison and therefore miss out on the opportunity to make something of their lives (see also Cromwell et al., 1991). Furthermore, with age, some offenders gave less importance to material gain, which reduced the appeal of crime. Overall, crime (and all the pitfalls attached to it) has a cumulative effect on offenders and sooner or later, they get 'worn down' by a life in crime.

These findings suggest that it may not be age in itself that causes a decline in offending (Gottfredson & Hirschi, 1990), but rather the accumulation, over time, of failures, contacts with the criminal justice system, betrayals and other problems associated with crime. Shover (1996, p.138) suggested that '... aging makes offenders more interested in the rewards of conventional lifestyles and also more rational in decision making'. Individuals will be more willing to shift from crime to non-crime if the perceived benefits of non-crime are greater than those of crime. It is important to highlight here that the perceived benefits may be quite different from the *actual* benefits, and that this assessment is dependent on the offender's perception of reality. These findings suggest that desistance requires both internal and external changes.

The role of identity change in the desistance process

Some authors have highlighted the importance of identity transformation in the process of desistance (Bottoms *et al.*, 2004; Burnett, 2004; Gartner & Piliavin, 1988; Giordano *et al.*, 2002; Laub & Sampson, 2003; Maruna, 2001; Meisenhelder, 1977; Shover, 1983). Maruna (2001, p.7) argued that '... to desist from crime, ex-offenders need to develop a coherent, prosocial identity for themselves' (see also Shover, 1983). In his sample, Maruna identified a need for desisting offenders to separate their past self from their current self (see also Mischkowitz, 1994). *Making good* refers to a process of 'self-reconstruction' (Maruna, 2001). *Making good* entails an understanding of why past offences were committed, and of the reasons supporting the decision to stop. Additionally, it also involves an ability to see the link between past mistakes and current accomplishments, to make the best of past experiences and to discover one's 'true self'.

Laub and Sampson (2003) argued that desistance does not necessarily require cognitive transformation. The authors maintained that '... offenders can and do desist without a conscious decision to 'make good' ... and offenders can and do desist without a "cognitive transformation"' (p.279). According to the authors, most offenders desist as a result of changes in adult social bonds. *Desistance by default* refers to the idea that all offenders naturally desist sooner or later (Laub & Sampson, 2003, p.278). This idea is similar to the notion of 'spontaneous remission' developed by Stall and Biernacki (1986), which suggests that desistance occurs naturally, without the assistance of external forces. Although desistance does eventually occur for all offenders, it occurs earlier for some individuals than others. Evidence from the studies presented in this chapter seems to suggest that, rather than being a process that occurs 'naturally', desistance needs to be prompted and supported by strong social networks and an individual resolve to change.

The role of cognitive deficits in the desistance process

The large body of research that has explored the role of cognitive distortions in the offending process has often been limited to sex offenders (Abel *et al.*, 1984; Marshall & Barbaree, 1990; Murphy, 1990; Segal & Stermac, 1990; Ward *et al.*, 1998, 1995), and these studies have generally found that cognitive deficits promote sex offending (Ward *et al.*, 1997, 2000). Cognitive distortions have also been said to promote aggressive behaviour (Abel *et al.*, 1989; Bumby, 1996; Murphy, 1990). It is acknowledged that the term *cognitive deficits* may encompass a wide range of cognitive traits, although there tends to be some redundancy in the literature with regard to some of these traits.

Barriga *et al.* (2000, p.37) offer a more general definition of cognitive distortions, defining them as '... inaccurate ways of attending to or conferring meaning on experience'. The authors made the distinction between *self-serving* and *self-debasing* cognitive distortions. Self-serving cognitive distortions protect the 'self' from developing a negative self-image, push the blame away from oneself, and promote harmful acts towards others. In contrast, self-debasing cognitive distortions promote self-harm, with individuals being more likely to blame themselves when negative events occur. Self-debasing cognitive distortions include four dimensions: *catastrophising* (assuming that every situation will turn into a catastrophe), *overgeneralising* (believing that the same outcome will apply to all future experiences), *personalising* (blaming oneself when negative events occur and 'interpreting such events as having a personal meaning', Barriga *et al.*, 2000, p.39), and *selective abstraction* (selectively focusing on the negative elements of a given experience). The four dimensions used to describe self-serving cognitive distortions are drawn from the Gibbs *et al.* (1995) typology. These dimensions include self-centredness (giving central importance to one's own views, needs, rights, etc., and minimal importance to those of others), placing the blame on others (with regard to harmful actions or victimisations), minimising the harm caused (see also Bandura, 1991) or labelling others with demeaning titles, and *assuming the worst.*

Barriga *et al.* (2000, p.50) found that 'Self-serving cognitive distortions were specifically associated with externalising behaviour problems, whereas self-debasing cognitive distortions were specifically associated with internalising behaviour problems. However, these cognitive distortions are not necessarily mutually exclusive. In other words, it was possible for these youths to drift from one type of cognitive distortion to another. For instance, they may blame their victims, but also blame themselves if they have been victimised. The authors concluded that the processes linking cognition and behaviour are "reciprocal, interactive, and mutually reinforcing"' (2000, p.54).

One of the major cognitive-behavioural programmes developed in offending therapy is the Reasoning and Rehabilitation Program (see Ross, 1995; Ross *et al.*, 1995), which is a '... multifaceted, cognitive-behavioural program designed to teach offenders social cognitive skills and values which are essential for prosocial competence' (Ross, 1995, p.195). This programme was designed to develop skills in eight key cognitive areas: impulsivity, concrete thinking, cognitive rigidity, externality, interpersonal problem-solving skills, egocentricity, a self-centred value system, and critical reasoning.

There is still little consensus in the literature as to whether cognitive distortions occur after the act (in which case they would contribute to maintaining offending behaviour and hampering desistance efforts) or whether they occur before the act, which would imply a causal link to the onset and persistence of crime (see Mann & Beech, 2003, for a detailed literature review; see Ward *et al.*, 1997). Indeed, Ward *et al.* (1998, p.147) argued that 'A major problem with most existing research on the cognitions of sex offenders is that it focusses primarily on postoffence cognitions and neglects the possibility that cognitive processes influence all phases of the offending cycle' (see also Ward *et al.*, 1997, for a similar comment). *Post-offence cognitive distortions* '... refer to self-statements made by offenders that allow them to deny, minimise, justify, and rationalise their behaviour' (Murphy, 1990, p. 332). This definition is similar to the concept of *techniques of neutralisation* developed by Sykes and Matza (1957), which refer to post-offence rationalisations that allow offenders to divert the blame away from themselves.

Techniques of neutralisation have been regarded as a category of 'thinking errors' that may promote offending behaviour. According to Sykes and Matza (1957), delinquents are bound by law like conventional individuals, but occasionally they engage in illegal behaviours that are justified through *techniques of neutralisation.* Sykes and Matza described five techniques used to rationalise criminal acts. The *denial of responsibility* makes reference to the tendency to adopt a victim stance, to attribute one's behaviour to external forces, and to refuse to assume responsibility for one's actions. The *denial of injury* minimises the harm caused by the act. The *denial of the victim* can occur either when there is the absence of a known and evident victim, or by claiming that some victims deserve to be treated in the way that they were (see Minor, 1981, for an explanation of the limitations associated with this dual definition). The *condemnation of the condemner* involves criticism directed towards those who express disapproval of one's actions. Finally, the *appeal to higher loyalties* refers to the justification of acts through the claim that actions were a response to the '... demands of the smaller social groups to which the delinquent belongs such as the sibling pair, the gang, or the friendship clique' (Sykes & Matza, 1957, p.669). Attempts to deny, justify or rationalise one's criminal behaviour or lifestyle have been noted in various studies (Abel *et al.*, 1984; Bandura, 1991; Covell & Scalora, 2002; Herman, 1990; Laub & Sampson, 2003; Nugent & Kroner, 1996; Stermac *et al.*, 1990; Ward *et al.*, 1995). It should be noted that although Sykes and Matza have received much recognition for their techniques of neutralisation, other researchers had previously explored this question (Festinger, 1957; Redl & Wineman, 1951).

Maruna and Copes (2004) argued that neutralisation theory may not be relevant to criminal aetiology (i.e. 'primary deviations', see Lemert, 1951), but may contribute to the maintenance of offending behaviour. In other words, neutralisation theory is better suited to explain criminal persistence or desistance from crime rather than onset. Similarly, Minor (1981, p.313) argued that '... neutralising excuses may not only *allow* deviance, but also *encourage* it'. Maruna and Copes (2004) further argued that longitudinal data are necessary to determine the sequence of neutralisation and offending.

In summary, Laub and Sampson (2001, p.3) summarised the main elements involved in the process of desistance, '... aging; a good marriage; securing legal, stable work; and deciding to "go straight", including a reorientation of the costs and benefits of crime'. Shover (1985) found that, with age, offenders developed an

increased interest in employment and prosocial relationships. What remains less understood, however, is
how the cognitive and social processes interact to cause
a shift towards desistance.

The interaction between social and cognitive factors

One of the most interesting dimensions of the desistance process refers to the way individual predispositions
and life events converge to promote this process. Piquero
and Pogarsky (2002, pp.207–208) argued that '… any
explanation of crime must address both the person and
the person's social situation, and in this sense, the study
of crime is intrinsically social-psychological'. Farrington
et al. (1990, pp.285–286) suggested that '… criminal
behavior results from the interaction between a *person*
(with a certain degree of criminal potential or antisocial
potential) and the *environment* (which provides criminal opportunities)' (see also Bottoms *et al.*, 2004).
Farrington *et al.* (1990) argued that a given environment can promote offending only for certain individuals, whereas others are likely to offend regardless of the
environment. Giordano *et al.* (2002, p.1026) discussed
the link between cognitive processes and situational circumstances, and argued that 'Given a relatively "advantaged" set of circumstances, the cognitive transformations
and agentic moves we describe are hardly necessary;
under conditions of sufficiently extreme disadvantage,
they are unlikely to be nearly enough' (see Warr, 2001
for a similar comment on the link between motivation
and opportunity). In this perspective, both individual
and environmental components should be taken into
account in order to better understand the processes
underlying desistance.

Giordano *et al.* (2002) supported the idea that permanent desistance from crime may be a result of both
cognitive changes and turning points ('hooks for
change'). Through a process of self-selection, life
events promote shifts in identity and act as *catalysts*
for permanent changes in offending. Some of the main
hooks for change identified in the narratives were the
links to formal institutions (prison and religion) and
intimate or informal networks (spouse and/or children), which is consistent with Sampson and Laub's
(1993) theory of formal and informal social control.
Various other studies have emphasised the important
roles of internal and external factors in the explanation of desistance (Fagan, 1989; Farrall & Bowling,
1999; Laub & Sampson, 2003; Sommers *et al.*, 1994;
Stall & Biernacki, 1986).

LeBel *et al.* (2008) made the distinction between
social (i.e. life events, situational factors, 'objective'
changes) and *subjective* (cognitive factors, internal
changes) components in the explanation of desistance.
The authors explain that these two categories of factors
are not necessarily independent of each other. The
authors discussed three models explaining the interaction between social and subjective factors. First, the
strong subjective model stipulates that it is the individual's motivation and desire to change that increases the
likelihood that bonds will be strengthened by conventional social sources (marriage, legitimate employment,
etc.). In this respect, turning points that promote desistance would be the result of a process of self-selection
and would not cause a change in behaviour. Second, the
strong social model asserts that life events occur randomly among individuals, and that these turning points
are directly responsible for desistance from crime. Thus,
from this viewpoint, subjective characteristics are not
essential to desistance from crime. Finally, the third
model, the *subjective-social model*, supports the idea
that life events may contribute to the desistance process, but that the impact of these events will be dependent on the *mindset* of the individuals. As argued above,
although motivation is a crucial component of change,
it still requires support from conventional social networks to maintain desistance efforts. This last model
thus integrates both objective and subjective factors
(external and internal changes) in its explanation of
desistance.

LeBel *et al.*'s (2008) findings suggested that the desistance process is a system in which various internal and
external factors interact in different ways. On one hand,
the authors suggested that some social problems occur
independently of the optimistic views of the offender.
On the other, they also concluded that individuals dis-
playing the greatest motivation to change were also the
least likely to recidivate. Individuals who had the right
mindset and the social networks to support them were
better equipped to face problems, resist temptations and
avoid setbacks, provided that the problems faced were
not tremendous. However, the authors also concluded
that the desire to change may be insufficient when social
problems are overwhelming and excessive (see also
Bottoms *et al.*, 2004; Farrall & Bowling, 1999; Maruna,
2001). Maruna (2001) explained that the decision and
desire to desist from crime is often put to the test by
situational factors, such as temptations and frustrations,
and in such scenarios the desire to desist from crime
may not always be sufficient.

Ross and Ross (1995) found that cognitive deficits are related to offending. They also argued, however, that some offenders have highly developed cognitive skills, to the extent that they manage to escape detection and labelling by the criminal justice system. On the other end of the spectrum, some well-adapted individuals may display some of these cognitive deficits. Some environments may provide better opportunities for education, employment, and interactions with prosocial others, and these factors are likely to neutralise the effects of cognitive deficits. Ross and Ross (1995, p.66) argued that 'Crime is much too complex a phenomenon to allow one to think that a single factor such as faulty thinking could be a useful *explanatory* concept'. Although cognitive deficits may not be the sole cause of offending behaviour, they may contribute to its explanation. By creating academic, employment and social disadvantages, these cognitive deficits put individuals '… at risk of behaving in illegal ways, but they do not cause them to do so' (Ross & Ross, 1995, p.66).

Summary

Laub and Sampson (2001, p.38) summarised the key components promoting the desistance process: 'The significant elements to date are the decision or motivation to change, cognitive restructuring, coping skills, continued monitoring, social support, and general lifestyle change, especially new social networks'. This section has shown that a large body of research has suggested the need to integrate both objective and subjective levels of explanation in the analysis of desistance from crime (Bottoms *et al.*, 2004; LeBel *et al.*, 2008; Le Blanc, 2004; Shover, 1983, 1985, 1996). Despite the substantial developments in desistance research in recent years, some important issues remain unresolved. These will be addressed in the following sections.

Unresolved Issues in Desistance Research[1]

Defining and measuring desistance

In an extensive review of the desistance literature, Laub and Sampson (2001) argued that few studies have offered an operational definition of desistance, and that there is currently no consensus in the literature on this issue (see also Maruna, 2001; Piquero *et al.*, 2003). For example, 'Can desistance occur after one act of

crime?' (Laub & Sampson, 2001, p.6). Is the desistance process characterised by a reduction in offending frequency or seriousness of crime (Bushway *et al.*, 2001)? How many years of non-offending are required to be sure that desistance has occurred (Bushway *et al.*, 2001; Laub & Sampson, 2001, 2003; Maruna, 2001; Piquero *et al.*, 2003)? Uggen and Massoglia (2003, pp.316–317) argued that 'Because conceptual and operational definitions of desistance vary across existing studies, it is difficult to draw empirical generalisations from the growing literature on desistance from crime'. The disparity in definitions inevitably raises the question as to whether it would be useful to reach a consensus on how to define the concept of desistance, in order to reach some degree of generalisability regarding its predictors.

False desistance

Desistance is often identified at the last officially recorded or self-reported offence. Since most longitudinal studies have followed up individuals over a relatively limited period of the life course, the issue of false desistance is an important limitation of desistance studies (Blumstein *et al.*, 1982, 1985; Brame *et al.*, 2003; Bushway *et al.*, 2004, 2001, 2003; Greenberg, 1991; Laub & Sampson, 2001). Many have argued that definite desistance only occurs when individuals have died (Blumstein *et al.*, 1982; Elliott *et al.*, 1989; Farrington & Wikström, 1994). Patterns of intermittency may be misinterpreted as 'desistance'. This issue of 'temporary' versus 'permanent' desistance from crime (or 'zig zag', see Laub & Sampson, 2003; Piquero, 2004) has been highlighted by criminal career researchers (Barnett *et al.*, 1989; Bushway *et al.*, 2004, 2001; Laub & Sampson, 2001; Piquero *et al.*, 2003), although very few studies have explored this question in depth (Piquero, 2004; Piquero *et al.*, 2003).

Desistance as a process

Most studies on desistance have adopted a dichotomous measure of desistance (static) rather than a process view of the phenomenon (dynamic). As a result, these studies do not account for *changes* in rates of offending, nor for the progression along the desistance process. In recent years, an increasing number of researchers have acknowledged the relevance of perceiving desistance as a gradual process rather than an event that occurs abruptly (Bottoms *et al.*, 2004; Bushway *et al.*, 2001,

2003; Fagan, 1989; Greenberg, 1975; Haggard *et al.*, 2001; Laub *et al.*, 1998; Laub & Sampson, 2001, 2003; Le Blanc, 1993; Loeber & Le Blanc, 1990; Maruna, 2001; Shover, 1983). Since complete desistance is difficult to attain (at least in a sudden manner), the definition of desistance as a concrete state (i.e. the absence of offending) may mask the progress made by individuals across various stages of this process (see Bushway *et al.*, 2001 for a similar discussion). Although different individuals may cease offending at the same age, their criminal careers may be distinguished by very different desistance processes (in terms of frequency, seriousness and length).

In summary, in cases where prospective longitudinal data are not available, where observation periods are short and where dichotomous measures of desistance are used, 'desistance' is more likely to refer to a state of 'temporary nonoffending' (Bushway *et al.*, 2001).

Within- versus between-individual predictors of desistance

Gottfredson and Hirschi (1990) claimed that, since criminal potential remains stable across time, it is not useful to follow up individuals over long periods. Sampson and Laub (1993, p.16) responded to this comment by arguing that 'The continuity to which they [Gottfredson and Hirschi, 1990] refer is relative stability, which does not mean that individuals remain constant in their behavior over time'. Relative stability refers to differences observed between individuals rather than within individuals. In a previous study, Huesmann *et al.* (1984) argued a similar point. They found continuity in the level of aggression displayed in childhood and adulthood, but referred to it as a stability in the relative rank within a group, rather than within-individual stability in the behavioural manifestation.

One interesting paradox in the field of criminology relates to the fact that, although most adult offenders displayed antisocial behaviour as children, most antisocial children do not become adult offenders (Gove, 1985; Robins, 1978); this observation highlights the importance of change in offending behaviour across the life course. Though studies have shown that the causes of long-term involvement in offending can be traced back to early ages, and that there is a substantial level of stability in offending behaviour across the life-course (Farrington & Hawkins, 1991; Gottfredson & Hirschi, 1990; Huesmann *et al.*, 1984; Le Blanc & Fréchette, 1989; Loeber & Le Blanc, 1990; Nagin & Farrington, 1992;

Sampson & Laub, 1993; Wilson & Herrnstein, 1985), it has also been suggested that adult life events can potentially influence these offending pathways (Farrington & West, 1995; Laub & Sampson, 2003; Sampson & Laub, 1993). An increasing number of researchers seem to agree that there are both stability and change in offending across the life-course (Farrington & West, 1995; Horney *et al.*, 1995; Moffitt, 1993a; Sampson & Laub, 1993). Sampson and Laub (2003, p.584) recently argued that '... life-course-persistent offenders are difficult, if not impossible, to identify prospectively using a wide variety of childhood and adolescent risk factors', and that '... adult trajectories of offending among former delinquents cannot be reduced to the past' (p.588). The idea that variables measured in childhood cannot always predict desistance from crime in adulthood has been addressed in previous studies (Laub *et al.*, 1998; Nagin *et al.*, 1995).

Some authors have stressed that little attention has been given to within-individual change in offending patterns across the life-course (Farrington, 1988; Farrington *et al.*, 2002; Horney *et al.*, 1995; Le Blanc & Loeber, 1998; Sampson & Laub, 1992). In their discussion on within-individual change, Le Blanc and Loeber (1998, p.116) stated that 'An important feature of this approach is that individuals serve as their own controls'. Past research has focused more on differences in offending patterns between offenders, in contrast to changes within individuals. It has been argued that it is more relevant to demonstrate that offending decreases within individuals after getting married, getting a job or moving house than to demonstrate lower offending rates of married compared with unmarried people, employed versus unemployed people, and so on (Farrington, 2007). Unsurprisingly, between-individual analyses tend to show that individuals with higher self and social control are more likely to desist from crime when compared to those with lower self and social control, and this finding has been demonstrated abundantly in the literature. What is lacking in desistance research is not a contrast of desisting versus persisting offenders, but rather a description of the internal and external factors that promote the desistance process for individuals over time.

Self-selection and sequencing

The issue of self-selection has been addressed by various researchers (Farrington & West, 1995; Gottfredson & Hirschi, 1990; Horney *et al.*, 1995; Laub & Sampson,

2001, 2003; McCord, 1994; Moffitt, 1993a; Pallone & Hennessy, 1993; Sampson & Laub, 1993, 1997; Uggen, 2000; Uggen & Massoglia, 2003; Warr, 1998). Since turning points and life events are not randomly assigned among individuals, it is difficult to assess whether these events are *causes or correlates* of desistance. Just as children with neuropsychological and other temperamental deficits are not randomly assigned to supportive or non-supportive environments (Moffitt, 1993b), life-course events may not be coincidental; these may occur as the result of a process of self-selection and reflect underlying criminal propensities. Moffitt (1993b) refers to *proactive* interactions, which occur when individuals select environments or situations that support their lifestyle. Laub and Sampson (2001, p.23) concluded that 'Selection is thus a threat to the interpretation of any desistance study'. This issue highlights the limited state of knowledge regarding the mechanisms underlying desistance from crime.

Many authors have discussed the complexity of establishing temporal or causal order between cognitive processes, situational circumstances and desistance from crime (Bottoms *et al.*, 2004; Laub & Sampson, 2001; Maruna, 2001; Maruna *et al.*, 2002; Mischkowitz, 1994; Shover, 1983; Walters, 2002). The unravelling of these sequences is thorny, mainly because external and internal changes are often interdependent and occur simultaneously (Maruna, 2001; Shover, 1983). Le Blanc (1993, p.56) summarised this idea:

> Some potential variables may occur in such close proximity to desistance that, for all practical purposes, it is impossible to measure which comes first; moreover, they may have reciprocal influences ... For example, delinquency can be caused by a weak parental attachment and it may also weaken that bond.

Le Blanc (2004) discussed the interactions between self-control, social control and offending, and argued that these two 'general mechanisms of control' interact through various dynamic processes. These cyclical interactions generate criminal behaviour. According to the author, 'chaos' may occur when an individual offends regularly, and displays weak social bonds and self-control. The key postulate in this theory is that dimensions of self and social control are interdependent and interact in complex ways to produce offending behaviour. In short, cognitive and situational processes often occur simultaneously, which makes it difficult to unravel causal sequences.

Conclusions

Policy relevance of desistance research

It is important to provide information about predicted future criminal careers (e.g. the probability of persistence vs. desistance, predicted residual career length) to sentencers, parole decision makers, and policy makers. If offenders are about to desist, it is a waste of scarce prison space to lock them up (from the viewpoint of incapacitation). Risk assessment instruments could be developed on the basis of knowledge about the predictors of termination, deceleration, and residual career length. It has been suggested that incapacitation could be used more selectively for those offenders who are predicted to be the most frequent and serious (Greenwood & Abrahamse, 1982). It is also important to investigate when (if ever) an ex-offender becomes indistinguishable from a non-offender in the probability of future offending (Kurlycheck *et al.*, 2006). This probability would obviously depend on criminal career features such as the time since the last offence and the previous frequency of offending. To the extent that ex-offenders are indistinguishable from non-offenders, ex-offenders should not be discriminated against (e.g. in jobs).

Information about protective factors that foster or accelerate desistance would be important in informing interventions after the onset of criminal careers. Information about the desistance process after release from prison or jail could indicate which offenders need particular types of supervision or support. Ideally, implications about effective interventions to foster desistance at different ages or stages of criminal careers should be drawn from knowledge about the predictors and causes of desistance.

The topic of desistance is also particularly relevant to issues relating to the reintegration process among formerly incarcerated individuals. In his interviews with ex-offenders, Maruna (2001) found that individuals who expressed the will to desist from crime were given little support when they tried to reintegrate into the community after their release from prison. Issues relating to prisoner reintegration are now more pressing than ever. Various authors have reported the staggering increase in prison populations in the United States over the past few decades, despite relatively steady crime rates (Maruna *et al.*, 2004; Petersilia, 2003; Travis & Petersilia, 2001). This 'mass incarceration' phenomenon has resulted in critical implications for post-release re-entry efforts (Petersilia, 2003; Travis, 2005). Petersilia (2003, p.139) reported that 'Recent data tracking inmates released from prison in 1994 show that two-thirds are rearrested, and nearly one-quarter are returned to prison for a new crime within three years of their release'; the author also added that these statistics have been relatively stable since the mid-1960s. These figures illustrate the urgent need to facilitate the transition from prison to the community among individuals who have been formerly incarcerated.

As such, there is a genuine need to invest more efforts in offender reintegration and to provide individuals with tools that will allow them to maintain desistance efforts and resist temptations to engage in criminal behaviour (Haggard *et al.*, 2001; Laub & Sampson, 2003; Maruna, 2001). Laub and Sampson (2001, p.58) argued that '... it is critical that individuals are given the opportunity to reconnect to institutions like family, school, and work after a long period of incarceration or any criminal justice contact for that matter'.

Next steps in desistance research

To conclude, although desistance research has greatly contributed to the advancement of knowledge in the past few years, some important shortcomings remain in this area. Considering all the diverse methodologies that can be used in the analysis of desistance from crime, it comes as no surprise that researchers cannot reach a consensus on this question. Farrington (2007) summarised some of the priority questions that need to be addressed in desistance research:

i) How can desistance (defined as either termination or deceleration) be measured?

ii) How do self-report and official measures of offending and desistance compare?

iii) Could there be desistance from one criminal career followed by reinitiation of another?

iv) Do individuals decelerate in offending before they terminate?

v) What factors predict desistance (or residual career length)? Which features of the past criminal career predict the future criminal career?

vi) Are predictors of desistance similar to predictors of late onset and low continuity?

vii) Are there different predictors of early versus later desistance?

viii) What factors cause desistance according to analyses of within-individual changes?

ix) What protective factors encourage or accelerate desistance?

x) What is the relative importance of later life events and earlier risk factors?

xi) Are life events causes or correlates of desistance?

xii) How accurate are predictions about desistance from developmental and life-course theories?

xiii) Is it useful to distinguish types of individuals who differ in their probability of desistance?

xiv) What interventions foster or accelerate desistance?

xv) What are the effects of criminal justice sanctions on desistance?

xvi) Can a risk assessment instrument for desistance be developed, and would it be valuable for criminal justice decisions and reducing crime?

Farrington (2007) further argued that these questions should be addressed for different ages, times and places, ethnic groups and cultures, offence types and types of antisocial behaviour, and for males versus females.

Much previous research on desistance has been based on official records. Future research should focus on self-reports of offending as well. Ideally, a new accelerated longitudinal design should be mounted with at least four age cohorts (10, 20, 30 and 40), drawn from the same area to be as comparable as possible, each followed up for 10 years with annual or biannual interviews. At least at ages 20 and 30, offender samples drawn from the same area should be chosen and also followed up for 10 years. All samples should be drawn from the same large city and should consist of at least 500 persons.

There should be repeated measures of offending; individual, family, peer, school and neighbourhood risk factors; life events (e.g. marriage or cohabitation, jobs, joining or leaving gangs, substance use); situational or opportunity factors; cognitive or decision-making processes; and death, disability or emigration. Special efforts should be made to carry out within-individual analyses. The effects of interventions should be investigated, using either experimental designs or quasi-experimental analyses. In summary, despite the substantial progress and advancement of knowledge in desistance research, much remains unknown about this dimension of the criminal career, and a better understanding of the processes underlying desistance is likely to offer valuable insight for post-onset intervention and prevention efforts.

Note

1 This section draws heavily from Kazemian (2007).

Further Reading

Kazemian, L. and Farrington, D.P. (Eds.) (2007). Special issue on desistance from crime. *Journal of Contemporary Criminal Justice*, 23(1).
The articles included in this special issue are revised versions of papers presented at a workshop on desistance held in Washington, DC, on 3–4 May, 2006. The workshop was funded by the National Consortium on Violence Research (NCOVR). The workshop was organised by ourselves and attended by the authors of the articles. The special issue includes a variety of papers that address the topic of desistance, from both theoretical and policy viewpoints. The papers emphasise the need to further develop desistance research in order to address essential questions about this key dimension of the criminal career.

Laub, J.H. & Sampson, R.J. (2001). Understanding desistance from crime. In M. Tonry (Ed.) *Crime and justice* (vol. 28, pp.1–69). Chicago, IL: University of Chicago Press.
This chapter offers a comprehensive review of the desistance literature (up to 2001). The authors address issues of measurement and operationalisation of desistance, and present an overview of the predictors of desistance. Laub and Sampson also make the parallel between desistance from criminal behaviour and from other forms of antisocial behaviour, discuss relevant theoretical frameworks, and offer insights for future research and policy implications as it relates to desistance from crime.

Maruna, S. (2001). *Making good: How ex-convicts reform and rebuild their lives*. Washington, DC: American Psychological Association.
This book offers an in-depth analysis of the desistance process among a sample of desisting ex-inmates. Using concepts deriving from the field of narrative psychology, Maruna uses the narratives of ex-offenders to study the process of change and desistance from crime.

References

Abel, G.G., Becker, J.V. & Cunningham-Rathner, J. (1984). Complications, consent and cognitions in sex between children and adults. *International Journal of Law and Psychiatry*, 7, 89–103.

Abel, G.G., Gore, D.K., Holland, C., Camp, N., Becker, J.V. & Rathner, J. (1989). The measurement of the cognitive distortions of child molesters. *Annals of Sex Research*, 2, 135–152.

Akers, R. (1990). Rational choice, deterrence, and social learning theory in criminology: The path not taken. *Journal of Criminal Law and Criminology*, 81, 653–676.

Bandura, A. (1991). Social cognitive theory of moral thought and action. In W.M. Kurtines & J.L. Gewirtz (Eds.) *Handbook of moral behavior and development: Vol. 1. Theory* (pp.45–103). Hillsdale, NJ: Lawrence Erlbaum.

Barnett, A., Blumstein, A. & Farrington, D.P. (1989). A prospective test of a criminal career model. *Criminology*, 27(2), 373–387.

Barriga, A.Q., Landau, J.R., Stinson, B.L., Liau, A.K. & Gibbs, J.C. (2000). Cognitive distortions and problem behaviors in adolescents. *Criminal Justice and Behavior*, 27(1), 36–56.

Blumstein, A., Cohen, J. & Hsieh, P. (1982). *The duration of adult criminal careers: Final report to the National Institute of Justice*. Pittsburgh, PA: Carnegie-Mellon University.

Blumstein, A., Farrington, D.P. & Moitra, S.D. (1985). Delinquency careers: Innocents, desisters, and persisters. In M. Tonry & N. Morris (Eds.) *Crime and Justice* (vol. 6, pp.187–219). Chicago, IL: University of Chicago Press.

Bottoms, A., Shapland, J., Costello, A., Holmes, D. & Muir, G. (2004). Towards desistance: Theoretical underpinnings for an empirical study. *The Howard Journal of Criminal Justice*, 43(4), 368–389.

Brame, R., Bushway, S.D. & Paternoster, R. (2003). Examining the prevalence of criminal desistance. *Criminology*, 41(2), 423–448.

Bumby, K.M. (1996). Assessing the cognitive distortions of child molesters and rapists: Development and validation of the MOLEST and RAPE scales. *Sexual Abuse: A Journal of Research and Treatment*, 8, 37–53.

Burnett, R. (2004). To reoffend or not to reoffend? The ambivalence of convicted property offenders. In S. Maruna & R. Immarigeon (Eds.) *After crime and punishment: Pathways to offender reintegration* (pp.152–180). Cullompton, Devon: Willan.

Bushway, S.D., Brame, R. & Paternoster, R. (2004). Connecting desistance and recidivism: Measuring changes in criminality over the life span. In S. Maruna & R. Immarigeon (Eds.) *After crime and punishment: Pathways to offender reintegration* (pp.85–101). Cullompton, Devon: Willan.

Bushway, S.D., Piquero, A.R., Broidy, L.M., Cauffman, E. & Mazerolle, P. (2001). An empirical framework for studying desistance as a process. *Criminology*, 39(2), 491–515.

Bushway, S.D., Thornberry, T.P. & Krohn, M.D. (2003). Desistance as a developmental process: A comparison of static and dynamic approaches. *Journal of Quantitative Criminology*, 19(2), 129–153.

Covell, C.N. & Scalora, M.J. (2002). Empathic deficits in sexual offenders: An integration of affective, social, and cognitive constructs. *Aggression and Violent Behavior*, 7, 251–270.

Cromwell, P.F., Olson, J.N. & Wester Avary, D.A. (1991). *Breaking and entering: An ethnographic analysis of burglary*. Newbury Park, CA: Sage.

Elliott, D.S., Huizinga, D. & Menard, S. (1989). *Multiple problem youth: Delinquency, substance use, and mental health problems.* New York: Springer-Verlag.

Fagan, J. (1989). Cessation of family violence: Deterrence and dissuasion. In L. Ohlin & M. Tonry (Eds.) *Family violence* (pp.377–425). Chicago, IL: University of Chicago Press.

Farrall, S. (2002). *Rethinking what works with offenders: Probation, social context and desistance from crime.* Cullompton, Devon: Willan.

Farrall, S. & Bowling, B. (1999). Structuration, human development and desistance from crime. *British Journal of Criminology, 39*(2), 253–268.

Farrington, D.P. (1988). Studying changes within individuals: The causes of offending. In M. Rutter (Ed.) *Studies of psychosocial risk* (pp.158–183). Cambridge: Cambridge University Press.

Farrington, D.P. (2007). Advancing knowledge about desistance. *Journal of Contemporary Criminal Justice, 23,* 125–134.

Farrington, D.P. & Hawkins, J.D. (1991). Predicting participation, early onset, and later persistence in officially recorded offending. *Criminal Behavior and Mental Health, 1,* 1–33.

Farrington, D.P., Loeber, R., Elliott, D.S., Hawkins, J.D., Kandel, D.B., Klein, M.W. *et al.* (1990). Advancing knowledge about the onset of delinquency and crime. In B.B. Lahey & A.E. Kazdin (Eds.) *Advances in clinical and child psychology* (vol. 13, pp.283–342). New York: Plenum.

Farrington, D.P., Loeber, R., Yin, Y. & Anderson, S.J. (2002). Are within-individual causes of delinquency the same as between-individual causes? *Criminal Behavior and Mental Health, 12*(1), 53–68.

Farrington, D.P. & West, D.J. (1995). Effects of marriage, separation, and children on offending by adult males. In Z.S. Blau & J. Hagan (Eds.) *Current perspectives on aging and the life cycle* (vol. 4, pp.249–281). Greenwich, CT: JAI Press.

Farrington, D.P. & Wikström, P.-O.H. (1994). Criminal careers in London and Stockholm: A cross-national comparative study. In E.G.M. Weitekamp & H.-J. Kerner (Eds.) *Cross-national longitudinal research on human development and criminal behavior* (pp.65–89). Dordrecht, The Netherlands: Kluwer Academic.

Festinger, L. (1957). *A theory of cognitive dissonance.* Evanston, IL: Row, Peterson and Company.

Gartner, R. & Piliavin, I. (1988). The aging offender and the aged offender. In P.B. Baltes, D.L. Featherman & R.M. Lerner (Eds.) *Life-span development and behavior* (vol. 9). Hillside, NJ: Lawrence Erlbaum.

Gibbs, J.C., Potter, G. & Goldstein, A.P. (1995). *The EQUIP program: Teaching youth to think and act responsibly through a peer-helping approach.* Champaign, IL: Research Press.

Giordano, P.C., Cernkovich, S.A. & Rudolph, J.L. (2002). Gender, crime, and desistance: Toward a theory of cognitive transformation. *American Journal of Sociology, 107*(4), 990–1064.

Gottfredson, M.R. & Hirschi, T. (1990). *A general theory of crime.* Stanford, CA: Stanford University Press.

Gove, W. (1985). The effect of age and gender on deviant behavior: A biopsychological perspective. In A.S. Rossi (Ed.) *Gender and the life course* (pp.115–144). New York: Aldine.

Greenberg, D.F. (1975). The incapacitative effect of imprisonment: Some estimates. *Law and Society Review, 9*(4), 541–580.

Greenberg, D.F. (1991). Modelling criminal careers. *Criminology, 29,* 17–46.

Greenwood, P.W. & Abrahamse, A. (1982). *Selective incapacitation.* Santa Monica, CA: RAND Corporation.

Haggard, U., Gumpert, C.H. & Grann, M. (2001). Against all odds: A qualitative follow-up study of high-risk violent offenders who were not reconvicted. *Journal of Interpersonal Violence, 16*(10), 1048–1065.

Herman, J.L. (1990). Sex offenders: A feminist perspective. In W.L. Marshall, D.R. Laws & H.E. Barbaree (Eds.) *Handbook of sexual assault: Issues, theories, and treatment of the offender* (pp.177–193). New York: Plenum.

Hirschi, T. (1969). *Causes of delinquency.* Berkeley, CA: University of California Press.

Hirschi, T. & Gottfredson, M.R. (1995). Control theory and the life-course perspective. *Studies on Crime and Crime Prevention, 4*(2), 131–142.

Horney, J., Osgood, D.W. & Marshall, I.H. (1995). Criminal careers in the short-term: Intra-individual variability in crime and its relation to local life circumstances. *American Sociological Review, 60,* 655–673.

Huesmann, L.R., Eron, L.D., Lefkowitz, M.M. & Walder, L.O. (1984). Stability of aggression over time and generations. *Developmental Psychology, 20*(6), 1120–1134.

Irwin, J. (1970). *The felon.* Englewood Cliffs, NJ: Prentice Hall.

Kazemian, L. (2007). Desistance from crime: Theoretical, empirical, methodological, and policy considerations. *Journal of Contemporary Criminal Justice, 23*(1), 28–49.

Knight, B.J., Osborn, S.G. & West, D.J. (1977). Early marriage and criminal tendencies in males. *British Journal of Criminology, 17,* 348–360.

Kruttschnitt, C., Uggen, C. & Shelton, K. (2000). Predictors of desistance among sex offenders: The interaction of formal and informal social controls. *Justice Quarterly, 17*(1), 61–87.

Kurlycheck, M.C., Brame, R. & Bushway, S.D. (2006). Scarlet letters and recidivism: Does an old criminal record predict future offending? *Criminology and Public Policy, 5,* 483–503.

Laub, J.H., Nagin, D.S. & Sampson, R.J. (1998). Trajectories of change in criminal offending: Good marriages and the desistance process. *American Sociological Review, 63,* 225–238.

Laub, J.H. & Sampson, R.J. (2001). Understanding desistance from crime. In M. Tonry (Ed.) *Crime and justice* (vol. 28, pp.1–69). Chicago, IL: University of Chicago Press.

Laub, J.H. & Sampson, R.J. (2003). *Shared beginnings, divergent lives: Delinquent boys to age 70.* Cambridge, MA: Harvard University Press.

LeBel, T.P., Burnett, R., Maruna, S. & Bushway, S. (2008). The 'chicken and egg' of subjective and social factors in desistance from crime. *European Journal of Criminology, 5*(2), 130–158.

Le Blanc, M. (1993). Late adolescence deceleration of criminal activity and development of self- and social control. *Studies on Crime and Crime Prevention*, 2, 51–68.

Le Blanc, M. (2004). *Self-control and social control in the explanation of deviant behavior: Their development and interactions along the life course.* Paper presented at the Conference on the social contexts of pathways in crime: Development, context, and mechanisms, Cambridge, England (December).

Le Blanc, M. & Fréchette, M. (1989). *Male criminal activity from childhood through youth: Multilevel and developmental perspectives.* New York: Springer-Verlag.

Le Blanc, M. & Loeber, R. (1998). Developmental criminology updated. In M. Tonry (Ed.) *Crime and justice* (vol. 23, pp.115–198). Chicago, IL: University of Chicago Press.

Lemert, E.M. (1951). *Social pathology.* New York: McGraw-Hill.

Loeber, R. & Le Blanc, M. (1990). Toward a developmental criminology. In M. Tonry & N. Morris (Eds.) *Crime and justice* (vol. 12, pp.375–473). Chicago, IL: University of Chicago Press.

Mann, R.E. & Beech, A.R. (2003). Cognitive distortions, schemas, and implicit theories. In T. Ward, D.R. Laws & S.M. Hudson (Eds.) *Sexual deviance: Issues and controversies* (pp.135–153). Thousand Oaks, CA: Sage.

Marshall, W.L. & Barbaree, H.E. (1990). An integrated theory of the etiology of sexual offending. In W.L. Marshall, D.R. Laws & H.E. Barbaree (Eds.) *Handbook of sexual assault: Issues, theories, and treatment of the offender* (pp.257–275). New York: Plenum Press.

Maruna, S. (2001). *Making good: How ex-convicts reform and rebuild their lives.* Washington, DC: American Psychological Association.

Maruna, S. & Copes, H. (2004). Excuses, excuses: What have we learned from five decades of neutralization research? In M. Tonry (Ed.) *Crime and justice* (vol. 32, pp.221–320). Chicago, IL: University of Chicago Press.

Maruna, S., Immarigeon, R. & LeBel, T.P. (2004). Ex-offender reintegration: Theory and practice. In S. Maruna & R. Immarigeon (Eds.) *After crime and punishment: Pathways to offender reintegration* (pp.3–26). Cullompton, Devon: Willan.

Maruna, S., LeBel, T.P., Burnett, R., Bushway, S. & Kierkus, C. (2002). *The dynamics of desistance and prisoner reentry: Findings from a 10-year follow-up of the Oxford University 'Dynamics of Recidivism' study.* Paper presented at the American Society of Criminology Annual Meeting, Chicago, Illinois (November).

McCord, J. (1994). Crimes through time. *Contemporary Sociology*, 23(3), 414–415.

Meisenhelder, T. (1977). An explanatory study of exiting from criminal careers. *Criminology*, 15(3), 319–334.

Minor, W.W. (1981). Techniques of neutralization: A reconceptualization and empirical examination. *Journal of Research in Crime and Delinquency*, 18, 295–318.

Mischkowitz, R. (1994). Desistance from a delinquent way of life? In E.G.M. Weitekamp & H.-J. Kerner (Eds.) *Cross-national longitudinal research on human development and criminal behavior* (pp.303–327). Dordrecht, The Netherlands: Kluwer Academic.

Moffitt, T.E. (1993a). 'Life-course persistent' and 'adolescence-limited' antisocial behavior: A developmental taxonomy. *Psychological Review*, 100, 674–701.

Moffitt, T.E. (1993b). The neuropsychology of conduct disorder. *Development and Psychopathology*, 5, 133–151.

Murphy, W.D. (1990). Assessment and modifications of cognitive distortions in sex offenders. In W.L. Marshall, D.R. Laws & H.E. Barbaree (Eds.) *Handbook of sexual assault: Issues, theories, and treatment of the offender* (pp.331–342). New York: Plenum Press.

Nagin, D.S. & Farrington, D.P. (1992). The stability of criminal potential from childhood to adulthood. *Criminology*, 30(2), 235–260.

Nagin, D.S., Farrington, D.P. & Moffitt, T.E. (1995). Life-course trajectories of different types of offenders. *Criminology*, 33(1), 111–139.

Nugent, P.M. & Kroner, D.G. (1996). Denial, response styles, and admittance of offenses among child molesters and rapists. *Journal of Interpersonal Violence*, 11, 475–486.

Pallone, N.J. & Hennessy, J.J. (1993). Tinderbox criminal violence: Neurogenic impulsivity, risk-taking, and the phenomenology of rational choice. In R.V. Clarke & M. Felson (Eds.) *Routine activity and rational choice* (Crime Prevention Studies, vol. 5, pp.127–157). New Brunswick, NJ: Transaction.

Petersilia, J. (2003). *When prisoners come home: Parole and prisoner reentry.* New York: Oxford University Press.

Pezzin, L.E. (1995). Earning prospects, matching effects, and the decision to terminate a criminal career. *Journal of Quantitative Criminology*, 11(1), 29–50.

Piquero, A. (2004). Somewhere between persistence and desistance: The intermittency of criminal careers. In S. Maruna & R. Immarigeon (Eds.) *After crime and punishment: Pathways to offender reintegration* (pp.102–125): Cullompton, Devon: Willan.

Piquero, A., Farrington, D.P. & Blumstein, A. (2003). The criminal career paradigm. In M. Tonry (Ed.) *Crime and justice* (vol. 30, pp.359–506). Chicago, IL: University of Chicago Press.

Piquero, A. & Pogarsky, G. (2002). Beyond Stafford and Warr's reconceptualization of deterrence: Personal and vicarious experiences, impulsivity, and offending behavior. *Journal of Research in Crime and Delinquency*, 39, 153–186.

Rand, A. (1987). Transitional life events and desistance from delinquency and crime. In M.E. Wolfgang, T.P. Thornberry & R.M. Figlio (Eds.) *From boy to man, from delinquency to crime* (pp.134–162). Chicago, IL: University of Chicago Press.

Redl, F. & Wineman, D. (1951). *Children who hate: The disorganization and breakdown of behavior controls.* Glencoe, IL: Free Press.

Rhodes, W.M. (1989). The criminal career: Estimates of the duration and frequency of crime commission. *Journal of Quantitative Criminology*, 5(1), 3–32.

Robins, L.N. (1966). *Deviant children grown up*. Baltimore, MD: Williams and Wilkins.

Robins, L.N. (1978). Sturdy childhood predictors of adult anti-social behavior: Replications from longitudinal studies. *Psychological Medicine*, 8, 611–622.

Ross, R.R. (1995). The Reasoning and Rehabilitation program for high-risk probationers and prisoners. In R.R. Ross, D.H. Antonowicz & G.K. Dhaliwal (Eds.) *Going straight: Effective delinquency prevention and offender rehabilitation* (pp.195–222). Ottawa: Air Training and Publications.

Ross, R.R., Antonowicz, D.H. & Dhaliwal, G.K. (Eds.) (1995). *Going straight: Effective delinquency prevention and offender rehabilitation*. Ottawa: Air Training and Publications.

Ross, R.R. & Ross, R.D. (1995). *Thinking straight: The Reasoning and Rehabilitation program for delinquency prevention and offender rehabilitation*. Ottawa: Air Training and Publications.

Rutter, M. (1996). Transitions and turning points in developmental psychopathology: As applied to the age span between childhood and mid-adulthood. *Journal of Behavioral Development*, 19, 603–626.

Sampson, R.J. & Laub, J.H. (1992). Crime and deviance in the life course. *Annual Review of Sociology*, 18, 63–84.

Sampson, R.J. & Laub, J.H. (1993). *Crime in the making: Pathways and turning points through life*. Cambridge, MA: Harvard University Press.

Sampson, R.J. & Laub, J.H. (1997). A life-course theory of cumulative disadvantage and the stability of delinquency. In T.P. Thornberry (Ed.) *Developmental theories of crime and delinquency* (Advances in Criminological Theory, vol. 7, pp.133–161). New Brunswick, NJ: Transaction.

Sampson, R.J. & Laub, J.H. (2003). Life-course desisters: Trajectories of crime among delinquent boys followed to age 70. *Criminology*, 41(3), 555–592.

Segal, Z.V. & Stermac, L.E. (1990). The role of cognition in sexual assault. In W.L. Marshall, D.R. Laws & H.E. Barbaree (Eds.) *Handbook of sexual assault: Issues, theories, and treatment of the offender* (pp.161–172). New York: Plenum.

Shover, N. (1983). The later stages of ordinary property offender careers. *Social Problems*, 31(2), 208–218.

Shover, N. (1985). *Aging Criminals*. Beverly Hills, CA: Sage.

Shover, N. (1996). *Great Pretenders*. Boulder, CO: Westview Press.

Shover, N. & Thompson, C.Y. (1992). Age, differential expectations, and crime desistance. *Criminology*, 30(1), 89–104.

Sommers, I., Baskin, D.R. & Fagan, J. (1994). Getting out of the life: Crime desistance by female street offenders. *Deviant Behavior*, 15, 125–149.

Stall, R. & Biernacki, P. (1986). Spontaneous remission from the problematic use of substances. *International Journal of the Addictions*, 21, 1–23.

Stermac, L.E., Segal, Z.V. & Gillis, R. (1990). Social and cultural factors in sexual assault. In W.L. Marshall, D.R. Laws & H.E. Barbaree (Eds.) *Handbook of sexual assault: Issues, theories, and treatment of the offender* (pp.143–156). New York: Plenum.

Sykes, G. & Matza, D. (1957). Techniques of neutralization: A theory of delinquency. *American Sociological Review*, 22, 664–670.

Travis, J. (2005). *But they all come back: Facing the challenges of prisoner reentry*. Washington, DC: The Urban Institute Press.

Travis, J. & Petersilia, J. (2001). Reentry reconsidered: A new look at an old question. *Crime and Delinquency*, 47(3), 291–313.

Uggen, C. (2000). Work as a turning point in the life course of criminals: A duration model of age, employment, and recidivism. *American Sociological Review*, 67, 529–546.

Uggen, C. & Massoglia, M. (2003). Desistance from crime and deviance as a turning point in the life course. In J.T. Mortimer & M.J. Shanahan (Eds.) *Handbook of the life course* (pp.311–329). New York: Kluwer Academic/Plenum.

Walters, G.D. (2002). Developmental trajectories, transitions, and nonlinear dynamical systems: A model of crime deceleration and desistance. *International Journal of Offender Therapy and Comparative Criminology*, 46(1), 30–44.

Ward, T., Fon, C., Hudson, S.M. & McCormack, J. (1998). A descriptive model of dysfunctional cognitions in child molesters. *Journal of Interpersonal Violence*, 13(1), 129–155.

Ward, T., Hudson, S.M., Johnston, L. & Marshall, W.L. (1997). Cognitive distortions in sex offenders: An integrative review. *Clinical Psychology Review*, 17(5), 479–507.

Ward, T., Hudson, S.M. & Marshall, W.L. (1995). Cognitive distortions and affective deficits in sex offenders: A cognitive deconstruction interpretation. *Sexual Abuse: A Journal of Research and Treatment*, 7, 67–83.

Ward, T., Keenan, T. & Hudson, S.M. (2000). Understanding cognitive, affective, and intimacy deficits in sexual offenders: A developmental perspective. *Aggression and Violent Behavior*, 5(1), 41–62.

Warr, M. (1993). Age, peers, and delinquency. *Criminology*, 31, 17–40.

Warr, M. (1998). Life-course transitions and desistance from crime. *Criminology*, 36(2), 183–216.

Warr, M. (2001). Crime and opportunity: A theoretical essay. In R.F. Meier, L.W. Kennedy & V.F. Sacco (Eds.) *The process and structure of crime: Criminal events and crime analysis* (Advances in Criminological Theory, vol. 9, pp.65–94). New Brunswick, NJ: Transaction.

Wilson, J.Q. & Herrnstein, R.J. (1985). *Crime and human nature*. New York: Simon & Schuster.

Wright, J.P. & Cullen, F.T. (2004). Employment, peers, and life-course transitions. *Justice Quarterly*, 21(1), 183–205.

10

Offender Profiling

David A. Crighton

Offender profiling involves the use of behavioural data to inform the process of investigating crimes by seeking to predict the likely characteristics of perpetrators of crimes. In doing this, it involves the logical process of working backwards from available data in the form of crime scene data and witness accounts, to arrive at useful profiles designed to reduce the extent of search required of investigating agencies. Historically, such profiling grew out of routine practice in psychology and psychiatry drawing from the evidence base in these areas. Such practice expanded rapidly to become part of investigative procedure and also popular culture. Such development, though, was on the basis of a relatively weak evidence base and poorly developed practice. In recent years there have been clear trends to challenge the historical underpinning and poorly developed evidence base, and profiling has increasingly become part of mainstream forensic psychology practice in terms of regulation, methodology and research. It is now seen as a developing and largely experimental area of practice, where there is a pressing need to move towards scientifically validated methods.

Introduction

Offender profiling has been described as the process of observation, reflection and construction using available data to predict the likely characteristics of an offender (Kocsis, 2007). This activity has attracted a number of labels, including Criminal Investigative Analysis (CIA) (Ressler *et al.*, 1986; Tenten, 1989), Investigative Psychology (IP) (Canter, 1989), Profile Analysis (PA)

(Jackson & Bekerian, 1997) and Crime Action Profiling (CAP) (Kocsis, 2003). While each of these labels may reflect differences in emphasis, they are all substantively similar, since they involve common logic and using similar techniques. Behaviour exhibited at a crime scene or series of crime scenes is used as the basis for drawing inferences about the likely characteristics of criminal offenders. In turn these inferences are used to produce psychosocial composites to assist investigators: based on the fundamental assumption that there will be high levels of consistency shown in behaviour and personality (Ressler *et al.*, 1986).

Historical Development

The notion that crime scenes can provide valid and useful information about offenders has a significant history and many of the elements of offender profiling have been reflected in fictional detectives such as Sherlock Holmes (Conan Doyle, 1897/2001) and Hercule Poirot (Christie, 1934) and more recently in books such as *Red Dragon* (Harris, 1981). As early as the 1880s Thomas Bond, a physician, tried to develop a profile of the personality characteristics of the perpetrator of a series of sexual homicides in the East End of London. The perpetrator was never identified in these cases but went on to become notorious as 'Jack the Ripper'. The profiler in this case was a police surgeon and he assisted in the autopsy on one of the victims. He noted the sexual aspects of the murders and made inferences about the apparent rage and hatred of women shown by the offender, as demonstrated by severe pre- and post-mortem injuries. Based on the limited information then available he went on to reconstruct the murder, providing an assessment of the behaviour and personality characteristics of the offender. From his analysis of the available evidence he suggested that five out of seven murders committed in that part of London had been perpetrated by a single man acting alone. It was also suggested that the offender was physically strong, composed, and willing to take significant risks. It was also suggested that the perpetrator was likely to be a relatively quiet and unassuming individual, socially isolated and without regular employment: someone who would generally draw little public attention. Dr Bond went on to suggest a possible diagnosis of satyriasis – what would now probably be termed promiscuity. Contrary to much mythology at the time, and subsequently, he also believed that the offender had no specialist knowledge as either a surgeon or butcher (Petherick, 2005).

Another key milestone in the development of profiling of criminal offenders followed a series of explosions in New York between 1940 and 1956.[1] A serial offender carried out a campaign of terror by planting explosives in public settings such as cinemas, telephone boxes and railway stations. In 1956, the police commissioned Dr James Brussel, then New York State's assistant commissioner of mental hygiene, to complete a profile of the offender. In this profile it was suggested that the offender would be a heavily built middle-aged man. It was also suggested that he would be single, perhaps living with a sibling, have some basic mechanical skills, come from Connecticut, be a Roman Catholic immigrant and harbour an obsessional love for his mother and hatred for his father. Brussel also noted that the offender appeared to have a grudge against the city's power company, on the basis that the first bomb had targeted its headquarters. Curiously, the profile also went on to mention a high probability that the offender would be wearing a 'buttoned' double-breasted suit when arrested. Brussel went on to assist the New York police as a profiler until 1972 and published a popular account of his work (Brussel, 1968).

Based on this profile the police began looking at unhappy former employees of the power company and this helped them to identify the offender, George Metesky, who lived in Connecticut. In line with the profile the offender was reported to be heavily built, single, Roman Catholic and foreign-born. It was also reported that when told to get dressed by the police, the offender returned wearing a fully buttoned double-breasted suit as Brussel had predicted. This case is perhaps largely responsible for some of the mythical status that has attended profiling

through much of its subsequent history. In fact, Brussel's work was probably less impressive than the earlier work of Bond in the 1890s. Subsequent reviews have suggested that the profile developed did not, in reality, show much understanding of the offender. Rather it involved the generation of a large number of predictions, many of which turned out to be inaccurate or misleading. However, with a high number of predictions, some with high base rates, it was inevitably the case that some would turn out to be accurate. Subsequently these accurate predictions were recalled as positive evidence of accuracy, while inaccurate predictions were forgotten (Gladwell, 2007).

In 1972 the FBI formed a Behavioural Science Unit (BSU) with a remit for developing methods for identifying unknown offenders in unsolved cases. The early work of the unit was greatly shaped by the work of Howard Teten, a Californian police officer who had worked for the FBI since the 1960s. Teten was strongly influenced by the work of Brussel and, with colleagues at the BSU, went on to develop a methodology which they called Criminal Investigative Analysis (CIA). The BSU went on to build progressively on these early methods which had, to an extent, been influenced by the work of Brussel in New York (Geberth, 1981; Tenten, 1989). The unit, though, went on to conduct a series of systematic studies, particularly in relation to serial homicides. These initially involved the intensive study of a group of sexual homicide offenders using semi-structured interview methods to produce systematic descriptions of these offenders (Ressler et al., 1986). The work is described as involving four stages: data assimilation; crime classification; crime reconstruction; and profile generation. The final stage of profile generation tended to follow a consistent format covering a range of sociodemographic and psychosocial descriptors along with suggestions for interview techniques that might be applicable. Such descriptions were drawn from known offenders, based on the assumption that unknown offenders would show significant similarities. A number of offence types were felt to be particularly suited to such an approach. These included arson and sexual offences, in addition to sexual homicides.

An alternative approach, developed in parallel to the work of the BSU, was undertaken by Keppel and Walter (1999). The methods developed gained wide coverage when they were used to aid in the capture of notorious serial killers Ted Bundy and Gary Ridgway. Walter has worked as a psychologist within the Michigan prison system. Based on his clinical experience, he suggested that all killings and sex crimes could be categorised into four subtypes: power-assertive, power-reassurance, anger-retaliatory, and anger-excitation or sadism.

The development of profiling in Europe occurred somewhat later than in North America and began with attempts to apply a range of techniques to a number of high-profile cases (Britton, 1998; Canter, 1994). Practice in Europe tended to develop along two distinct lines, which have often been misleadingly summarised as 'clinical' and actuarial approaches. This probably relates to the fact that many early profiles were constructed by NHS-based psychologists and followed a similar pattern to the work of Brussel, with a focus on attempts to identify known patterns of psychopathology. Such approaches were often what was requested by police services and were initially greeted with great enthusiasm. Such efforts, though, have increasingly attracted concern and dissatisfaction from the researchers and the courts (Copson, 1995; R v. Stagg [1994]). The alternative 'empirical' approach has involved the use of statistical methods such as multidimensional scaling as a means of identifying consistent patterns in offending (Alison et al., 2002).

Current Approaches to Offender Profiling

It has been suggested by some that there is a relatively high level of agreement that, theoretically at least, it ought to be possible to evaluate criminal behaviours on the basis of available data from crime scenes and witnesses and in turn go on to use these to derive some impression of the offender (Kocsis, 2007). A number of competing schools of thought have emerged over how this may be achieved, with four major approaches being widely advocated: diagnostic evaluation (DE); criminal investigation analysis (CIA); crime action profiling (CAP); and investigative psychology (IP).

Diagnostic evaluation

This approach differs substantively from the three other widely advocated approaches to profiling and is in many respects more akin to the approach to profiling pioneered by Brussel (1968). It essentially involves the use of what might broadly be termed clinical models and methods. These are used to deliver a series of predictions about offenders based on a practitioner's analysis of the crime scene and, often, a mental-health-related diagnosis. The prediction of characteristics is generated in an idiographic manner and appears to be based on prior experience, for example from work with a series of mental

health patients. In many respects this method is similar to that seen in mental health practice where information from a number of sources may be used to allocate individuals into psychopathological categories which are claimed to have prognostic value, although in the context of offender profiling such methods are being applied in a markedly different context and for different purposes (Copson et al., 2006).

Criminal investigation analysis

The use of criminal investigation analysis (CIA) is the method largely developed by the FBI BSU in North America (Tenten, 1989). The method sought to take a markedly different approach from diagnostic evaluation methods by developing an evidence base on offenders. The method replaced the use of diagnostic terminology with terms commonly in use in forensic science and criminology. These included terms such as 'crime scene analysis' to describe the systematic analysis of the site of the crime, or crimes, and terms such as 'staging' and 'signature' to describe aspects of the scenes. The method was initially directed at crimes which had proved particularly difficult to solve using conventional methods of investigation and detection, such as serial stranger homicides. CIA involves the generation of empirically grounded profiles or typologies of likely offenders based on an analysis primarily of crime scene data. One of the earliest and probably the best known and most influential of these distinctions has been that between 'organised' and 'disorganised' homicide perpetrators. The method has subsequently been expanded to consider other types of offenders, including rapists and arsonists (Kocsis, 2007). The approach has also gone on to be codified into manual form as the Crime Classification Manual (Douglas et al., 1997), which provides templates of types of offender for use by investigative teams.

Crime action profiling

Crime action profiling (CAP) is largely similar to CIA but has been described as working within the boundaries of forensic psychology and psychiatry (Kocsis, 2007). As with CIA, the focus has tended to be on specific types of offence which have proved difficult to solve using conventional methods. The approach has developed to include the study of other factors surrounding the production of profiles, including such things as logistical factors surrounding profiling, such as data collection and accuracy. CAP has also drawn heavily on the use of a statistical technique called multidimensional scaling (MDS). It is suggested that CAP uses MDS in combination with other statistical tools as a means of developing conceptual models which are, in turn, used to generate predictors contained in profiles (Kocsis, 2003, 2007).

Investigative psychology

The term investigative psychology (IP) is most closely associated with researchers and practitioners at the University of Liverpool in the UK (Alison & Kebbel, 2006). The approach involves an empirical approach to profiling crimes. IP has been extended to a broad range of crimes beyond the historical focus of profiling, including burglary and domestic violence. It is characterised by the use of ideographic analysis of crime-related behaviours and offender characteristics using empirical methods. In particular, the approach has relied heavily on MDS, leading to the approach often being described, somewhat misleadingly, as an 'empirical' or sometimes a 'statistical' approach. MDS is generally used in this context to analyse both crime-related behaviours and offender characteristics. A concrete example here might be the use of MDS to study domestic violence offenders: separating this group into 'instrumental' and 'expressive' types and defining the characteristics that are more common to each type (Kocsis, 2007).

Current Developments

Since the 1980s the development of profiling has moved on from initial pioneering techniques towards the development of more evidence-based approaches. This has been generally associated with two major developments in this area of practice. Firstly, in both practice and research it has moved to become a part of mainstream forensic psychology. Secondly, in common with other areas of forensic psychology, there have been clear efforts to develop evidence-based practice. Scientific research and practice in this area has in recent years been primarily concerned with three central questions arising from crime scenes. Firstly, what happened at the crime scene? Secondly, what sociodemographic characteristics is the person who carried out the activities observed at the crime scene likely to have? Thirdly, what are the most likely psychological characteristics of the person concerned (Read & Oldfield, 1995)?

Current scientific practice has also been described as resting on two major assumptions: behavioural consistency and homology. Behavioural consistency refers to the notion that the variance shown by serial offenders will be less than that shown in comparison to a random series of other offenders. Homology in evolutionary biology refers to similarities that reflect shared ancestry. In profiling the term refers to the assumption that the degree of similarity in two offenders, from any given category of crime, will be reflected by similarity in their characteristics (Alison & Kebbel, 2006).

Efforts at evidence-based profiling as a means of identifying and giving investigative priority to offenders has tended, as outlined above, to focus on serious violent and sexual crimes. The example used below for illustrative purposes is work on sexual offences, where around half of reported sexual offences are perpetrated by strangers. The use of profiling in such offences has been attractive to police services, since this group of offences is particularly difficult to solve. Investigating officers in such offences are deprived of many of the normal lines of inquiry in what may appear to be random offences, so the appeal of any methods that reduce uncertainty is not difficult to see. The challenge, though, is significant. One of the most widely reported and generally accepted characteristics of sexual offenders is their heterogeneity as a group (Prentky & Burgess, 2000). This has led to numerous attempts to develop valid typologies of sexual offenders, as a means of managing this heterogeneity as an aid to investigation and also to assessment and intervention. Many attempts have been made at such typologies. For example, Cohen et al. (1969) suggested dividing rapists into four sub-types: compensatory; impulsive; sex-aggression diffused; and displaced aggressive. They also suggested dividing child molesters into regressed, aggressive, fixated and exploitative subgroups.

The use of such categories went on to gain wide currency amongst practitioners and it is still common to see reference to such categories as regressed or fixated paedophiles. It is also easy to see how, if valid, such categories might have significant value within the processes of criminal investigation. While many of the categories have an intuitive appeal, there is little evidence of a firm empirical base. Nor is there much good evidence favouring one model of categorisation over another. Such typologies have repeatedly been criticised for the failure to collect data on the reliability and validity of types (Prentky et al., 1988). It is therefore perhaps not surprising that subsequent research has generally failed to provide support for the utility of such typologies.

There have been subsequent efforts to develop empirically valid categorical systems, such as the Massachusetts Treatment Center (MTC) classification system, currently in its third revision (Prentky *et al.*, 1989). While this system has potential clinical utility, it has proved less useful for investigative purposes, since it draws heavily on issues of motivation. In turn these can generally not be discerned from crime scenes (Alison, 2006; Alison *et al.*, 2006).

Profiling Databases

The development of systematic structured databases relating to offender characteristics followed on from the twin developments of profiling and the availability of relatively cheap computers and relational database software. A number of such databases now exist as tools for police and investigative authorities to draw upon.

Child Abduction and Serial Murder Investigative Resources Center (CASMIRC)

CASMIRC is a US centre established in order to improve the quality of investigation into violent crimes, by coordinating the work of US federal, state and local authorities. It also acts as a central database for case data on child abductions, disappearances, homicides, and serial homicides. In this manner CASMIRC is described as a means to improve operational support from behavioural services provided by the FBI to investigative authorities.

Violent Criminal Apprehension Program (ViCAP)

ViCAP is a US system introduced by the US Department of Justice in 1985 and run by the FBI. It serves as a database for homicides, sexual assaults, missing persons, and unidentified human remains. The database includes a wide range of case information submitted by investigative authorities. This includes information about the victim, information about offenders and suspects, offence details such as the modus operandi, dates and locations of offences, crime scene details, offence details and what is termed 'holdback' information concerning specific details of offences to be kept confidential. This national database is used to compare incoming cases with the database of past cases to seek out similarities. In addition, incoming cases are reviewed by analysts in an effort to identify any similarities missed by automated searches.

Violent and Sexual Offender Register (ViSOR)

ViSOR is a UK database designed to facilitate the work of Multi Agency Public Protection Arrangements (MAPPA) (National Probation Service, 2007). It contains detailed confidential information on convicted violent and sexual offenders collated by police, probation and prison services. ViSOR is currently used by all police forces in England, Wales, Scotland and Northern Ireland, along with HM Forces and other specialist police units such as the Child Exploitation and Online Protection (CEOP) centre. ViSOR provides a searchable database against which new cases can be compared.

The Evidence Base for Profiling

The evidence base in relation to offender profiling is remarkably limited. There is a general lack of good-quality evidence available and that which does exist is often methodologically weak. Early FBI internal research into the effectiveness of criminal investigative analysis methods reported some areas as showing 80 per cent accuracy (Alison, 2006). The reporting of these studies, though, is incomplete and it is unclear how such accuracy ratings were arrived at from the published data. Claims of the accuracy of diagnostic evaluation have also been made. However, such claims often came from the profilers using these methods, often in the absence of empirical data to support these.

A number of criticisms have been made of early approaches to profiling, suggesting that there was a lack of any firm scientific basis to much of the practice in the area, while early efforts drawing on environmental psychology often produced results of limited value (Gladwell, 2007; Towl & Crighton, 1996). Much of the early work of the FBI BSU and its equivalents in Europe and Australasia, it was suggested, lacked credibility. Gladwell (2007) notes that such profiles have a great deal in common with the 'cold reading' techniques used by many psychics, in that they make a reasonably large number of vague and unspecific predictions, of a kind that people will generally agree to. Similarly, they also make a number of predictions that are not testable and that are therefore not falsifiable. Finally, even where the predictions are demonstrably wide of the mark, some of the vague and general comments will be applicable and may therefore be used to search retrospectively for accurate predictions.

Concerns that practice in this area of forensic psychology has at times run well ahead of the evidence base have been repeatedly raised (Alison, 2006; Copson, 1995; *R v. Stagg* [1994];[2] West & Alison, 2006). This has also resulted in serious failings within this area of forensic psychology practice, with the potential (sometimes clearly realised) for significant harm. Much of the work in this area of practice has also been popularised through the press and media in a manner that takes little account of scientific weaknesses.

Efforts to look at the accuracy of profilers empirically have yielded mixed results. A study by Pinizzotto and Finkel (1990) sought to compare the accuracy of profilers comparing experienced profilers with a group of non-profilers. A series of closed murder and closed rape cases were used as the basis for the study. Participants were required to construct profiles using a series of multiple choice questions. The authors reported that experienced profilers were significantly better at predicting the characteristics of the group of closed rapist cases but that the groups did not differ for the closed murder cases. A similar method was used by Kocsis (2003) to look at rape and arson cases, where profilers performed better but with two specific limitations. Firstly, the study was based on a small number of profilers, and secondly, there was a high degree of statistical variance amongst profilers. These findings echo those found in other areas of clinical or expert decision making where some practitioners appear to perform well, while others perform at chance levels and others perform at markedly below chance levels. Such studies can, though, be criticised on a number of grounds. As already noted, they have tended to be small-sample studies involving only a few practitioners. They also present material in a very artificial manner, quite distinct from what profilers would actually do in practice when seeking to aid an investigation. While this makes for a convenient experimental method and analysis, it does reduce the extent to which such evidence can be generalised to actual practice.

The notion of behavioural consistency that underpins profiling has received some degree of support. It can draw from a considerable evidence base into the development of criminal behaviour where a high level of consistency in behaviour emerges early and persists over long periods of time (Farrington *et al.*, 2006). Such research suggests the development of often quite stable and enduring patterns of criminal behaviour. There has also been some evidence to support notions of behavioural consistency at crime scenes (Grubin *et al.*, 2001). A number of studies of sexual offenders have also provided support for the notion that offenders may share characteristics at a group level. For example, amongst convicted rapists the more violent offenders have been reported to show higher levels of various forms of personality difficulty: showing higher levels on paranoid, narcissistic, histrionic and paranoid sub-scales than less violent rapists (Proulx *et al.*, 1994). Following on from this work, a study was conducted which divided convicted rapists into three groups: 'sadistic', 'opportunistic' and 'anger' rapists. Allocation to these groups was based on their mode of offending. The authors reported significant differences between the sadistic and opportunistic groups on structured measures of personality disorder (Proulx *et al.*, 1999).

Support for notions of homology is weaker and a number of studies have failed to support this hypothesis. In one study an attempt was made to integrate crime scene data felt to be predictive, using logistic regression. This failed to show any substantive improvement over base rates for most of the predictors considered (Davies *et al.*, 1998). Another study of 50 convicted rapists suggested that they were relatively homogeneous in terms of criminal history, independent of the observed offence characteristics (House, 1997). A larger study of 100 convicted males who raped strangers considered a sample of 28 dichotomous variables. This study found no clear links between crime scene behaviours and background (Mokros & Alison, 2002).

It has been suggested that much of the early work in profiling bears a striking resemblance to naive personality theories (Alison, 2006). These approaches tended to be nomothetic in nature, making group-based predictions. Like naive personality theories, they have also been extensively criticised as being deterministic and failing to adequately consider and address situational effects. Research into personality suggests that these are general trends in our naive efforts to explain personality characteristics (Mischel *et al.*, 2004). There is also the possibility of what have been termed 'Barnum' effects in psychology. This is where people routinely accept vague and ambiguous descriptions as accurate descriptions about themselves, even though they are universally applicable (Forer, 1949). This has led to the suspicion that many areas of profiling may bear more than a passing resemblance to the kind of 'cold reading' practised by many psychics (Gladwell, 2007). A clear concrete example of this effect is in newspaper horoscopes. These are widely read and believed by many, but cannot logically be accurate given that each will cover large numbers of people. The way horoscopes get around this is by remaining vague and making multiple predictions: leading individuals to interpret these in the context of their lives and focus on the more accurate assertions while neglecting those that do not apply. Much of what has historically constituted profiling may therefore be legitimately criticised as being a sophisticated example of 'cold reading' based on a series of ambiguous and contradictory statements. The investigator receiving such a 'reading' is then faced with the task of making sense of this material and how it might fit the case. In turn this raises issues of utility in profiling and again there is little good-quality evidence in this area. There have been a number of what might be termed 'consumer' satisfaction surveys. These generally involve asking investigative officers how useful they have found profiles to be (Pinizzotto & Finkel, 1990). In general, the results from such surveys are moderately positive, with investigating officers generally saying they have appreciated and valued such inputs. Yet it has been noted that this methodology provides little in the way of meaningful utility analysis (Copson, 1995).

A study by Alison et al. (2003) looked at this suggestion empirically. Participants in the study were presented with a questionnaire regarding a sequence of events in a real murder case, an offender profile and the characteristics of either offender, A or B. Offender A was genuine while offender B was a set of fabricated characteristics designed to be quite distinct from profile A. The results suggested that both groups rated the profile as 'generally accurate', with no participant rating the profile as 'generally' or 'very inaccurate'. The findings from this study tend to support the notion that people are seeking to make sense and achieve a fit between profiles and characteristics, largely independent of accuracy.

There is also little good-quality evidence concerned with how profiles and advice from profilers are interpreted and used. There has been some small research into this question which suggests that nearly half the profiles considered included advice that could not be confirmed post conviction, while around a fifth contained information that was vague or open to wide interpretation. In over 80 per cent of profilers' reports they note that the basis for the advice given was not made clear; although it is perhaps worth noting that this poor practice has been widespread in many areas of psychological reporting (Alison, 2006; Alison et al., 2003). Alison suggests the use of a structured analysis technique developed to systematically consider legal rhetoric (Toulmin, 1958) as a means of assessing offender profiles. This framework suggests the use of six interrelated components for analysis: the claim; the strength of the claim; the grounds supporting the claim; the warrant that authorises the grounds for a claim; the backing; and the rebuttal (Alison, 2006; Alison et al., 2006; West & Alison, 2006). It is suggested that there are a number of reasons why such a framework might be useful. These include the fact that there are few formal models available for analysis of offender profiles and, in turn, how, why or indeed if they are effective. There are also increasing pressures on investigating officers to consider the legal basis for their actions and the framework provides a systematic means of considering many of these. The framework is also posited as a useful mechanism for the self-reflective practice that applied psychologists are encouraged to engage in.

It has been astutely observed that many of those most involved in forensic psychology have been the most resistant to developing a critically evaluative approach to profiling (Alison, 2006). The conclusions drawn from profiling approaches and the public and popular claims have also often run well ahead of the very limited evidence base – what Kocsis (2007) evocatively described, with considerable veracity, as 'mountains of conclusions from molehills of evidence'. There has certainly been a tendency to extrapolate from initial research into areas without an evidence base, as in the expansion of methods to new types of crime. There has also been a general failure to consider diversity and cultural issues. An example given here has been the use of profiles developed in North America for serial rapists in other cultures such as Australasia. Such profiles suggest African descent as a marker in such offences but, when used in Australia where the population with African descent is less than 1 per cent, such a 'marker' is not only unhelpful but is misleading (Kocsis, 2007). Surprisingly perhaps, there has been little consideration given to cases where crime scene data are limited or absent. While profiling has been used widely in cases of serial homicide, it has contributed little to cases where offenders retain and hide the body of victims, as in the case of Jeffrey Dahmer.

Some more recent developments in profiling have also faced criticism on the grounds of being irrelevant or obvious. While more scientific in approach, such studies have focused on offences where issues of detection and investigation are generally not significant, for example studies of offenders perpetrating criminal violence within families (Burgess et al., 1997). Such research appears to overlap with other, perhaps better developed, areas of forensic psychology practice which have approached such characteristics from the direction of clinical assessment and treatment of offenders.

The reliability of profiling data has also been to focus on study as it is, effectively, a form of retrospective classification. Typologies are developed after the event or events have taken place and these are used to provide some understanding of more recent crimes. For this process to be effective requires a number of elements. Most obviously perhaps, it requires that the information used is accurate. In fact this is somewhat problematic as it often rests on information contained in written records and also the reliability of information elicited from offenders themselves. Both sources are likely to be less than perfect and this, in turn, will impact on the validity of profiling. In addition, there is a lack of uniform definitions within this field, when compared to other areas of practice. Within mental health, for example, there are agreed frameworks for discussing mental health – most notably DSM-IV (American Psychiatric Association, 2000) and ICD-10 (World Health Organization, 1990). While such frameworks are imperfect, it can be suggested that they do at least serve the function of providing a common frame of reference.

Despite the generally poor state of scientific development within profiling, issues of who 'owns' the subject area have been the focus of discussions. A review by the Association of Chief Police Officers (2000) in the UK concluded that the area should be 'owned' by the police. This perhaps largely reflects justified concerns about the release of sensitive investigative materials and the leakage of such material to offenders and potential offenders. There is here a potential conflict between the needs of science and those of policing services; where the former depends on a high degree of openness and transparency for peer review of material. Such distinctions are, though, easy to overstate and it is not impossible for good science to take place within such sensitive contexts. Certainly discussions of issues of ownership seem premature.

Practice Issues

The early development of profiling has been characterised as a largely unregulated free market. This has served to drive up the public profile of the methods and availability from a number of practitioners. This free market approach has also been extensively criticised on a number of grounds. These include the fact that there is little in the way of quality control in terms of what investigative authorities might reasonably expect from such work. It has also proved difficult to gather adequate empirical data on the accuracy and utility of profiles. This is in marked contrast to other areas of forensic practice such as pathology. Here there is a well-established protocol agreement between the central government department overseeing such work (the Home Office) and practitioners undertaking such work (Home Office, 2005a, 2005b). It has been widely suggested that a similar process of registration and protocol for practice might usefully be applied within psychology, analogous to that used for forensic pathologists.

It is an open question whether offender profiling as an area of forensic psychology has reached a stage of development where separate accreditation would be appropriate, desirable or achievable in a credible manner. What is largely agreed, though, is the need for more effective professional regulation of such activities and it seems likely that the advent of statutory regulation may effectively drive this process. In addition, there seems to be a broad consensus that future practice in such areas needs to become much more clearly evidence based (Crighton & Towl, 2008).

In moving to more evidence-based practice it seems clear that the current research base is generally of poor quality. Alison (2006) suggests that the current evidence base available to practitioners can be broken down into research into:

- the type of victim information used;
- how this information is used;
- what information is of particular value;
- provision of reliable and valid systems of profiling.

Historically, it appears that crime scene information and the modus operandi (MO) have been the sources of information most relied upon. Indeed, the MO and what have been termed 'signature' behaviours have been stressed by many engaged in profiling. It has also been suggested that there is a logical distinction here between MO and the 'psychological signature' of an offence (Ressler *et al.*, 1986). The MO is thought to be functionally relevant to the perpetration of the offence but psychologically irrelevant. The psychological signature is felt to be the reverse of this: being psychologically relevant but functionally irrelevant. As such, it has been suggested that the MO will be context dependent and will change with circumstances. The psychological signature by contrast will be context independent. It is, though, unclear how this distinction between MO and psychological signature is drawn in practice (Alison, 2006).

The use of discrete offender behaviours is also potentially problematic given the high degree to which investigators often depend on victim or witness reports. The extent to which these may be unreliable and are subject to systematic biases has been well documented. Additionally, it seems likely that the two areas of MO and psychological signatures will overlap and, in some cases, the latter will be context dependent. An example cited here is sexual behaviours, which may have high base rates, where the meaning may be context dependent (Alison, 2006).

A key aspect of linking offences relates to the consistent use of reliable variables for assigning crimes to a single offender. The decision to link two crimes is a diagnostic question, similar to those addressed in other areas of forensic psychology. It will rest on two key factors:

- setting a decision threshold for the point at which evidence is sufficient to define two cases as similar;
- identifying information that the decision should be based upon in order to make the most accurate decisions.

Setting accurate decision thresholds has been described as requiring:

- base rates;
- analysis of costs and benefits.

Indeed, the use of base rate information for various forms of crime scene behaviours forms an important part of profiling. For example, behaviours with low base rates and high costs to the offender will generally lower the threshold for linking two or more offences. However, the establishment of accurate base rates for such behaviours is far from straightforward and the estimation of costs and benefits is often difficult. There are other means of establishing decision thresholds but these are generally less powerful than the optimal method described.

Swets *et al.* (2000) describe diagnostic decision making as a process of repetitive choices between two competing alternatives. This process may involve the use of a variety of data such as self-report information, behavioural observation and tests of performance. In the case of OP the question facing a psychologist is the probability that two or more offences were committed by a single person. In doing this they need to establish a threshold criterion for linking offences and these will vary, at least

in part, depending on the context of the decision making.

Conclusions

Profiling of offenders in order to assist investigations has developed rapidly from its early origins in psychiatric and psychological diagnosis. Such growth occurred in light of rising violent crime rates and concerns surrounding serial homicides and other forms of serial offence. Greater publicity surrounding these comparatively rare offences has been associated with greater public anxiety, although the question of whether such behaviours are new is at best questionable. Early efforts at profiling represented efforts to assist investigators with some of the most difficult crimes to solve, such as stranger homicides. Here investigators were often deprived of the normal means of investigation and left with few avenues to pursue.

It can, though, be convincingly argued that from its inception the development of profiling has tended to quickly outstrip its scientific foundations. It can also be argued that profiling has at times crossed the border between providing scientifically grounded advice towards the realms of pseudo-science. Profiling has also at times crossed the dividing line between scientific advice and criminal investigation. In doing this profiling has strayed into areas that are the legitimate role of police and prosecutors rather than scientific advisers. There is pleasingly now evidence of a rowing back from such practices as profilers are more effectively regulated and as police services develop a clearer understanding of the methodological uses and misuses of profiling.

The field of profiling suffers from a plethora of terminology and acronyms. Yet these differing terms refer to a common process of seeking to use the information available to investigators, in order to try to predict the likely characteristics of offenders. The use of multiple terms to describe this may well have been as much about marketing (commercial, professional or personal) as it is about the scientific development of this area of forensic practice. Indeed, it can be argued that such marketing has served to limit and sometimes distort the development of both research and practice. As noted above, many of the forensic psychologists most involved in profiling have sometimes appeared to be resistant to developing evidence-based practice. The conclusions drawn by forensic psychologists in this area of practice have often run very far ahead of a very limited and tentative evidence base. Consideration of issues such as culture and diversity often received scant or cursory consideration. Early and necessarily tentative research findings were often built on with little consideration for limitations and caveats. More worryingly, research into one type of criminal behaviour was often extrapolated, with limited consideration of the implications, to other types of crime and then applied in practice. Such developments were clearly inappropriate and highlight the dangers of rushing to uncritical application of methods and models that have not been adequately tested.

Profiling has until recently given little consideration to cases where crime scene data are limited or absent. While profiling has been used widely in cases of serial homicide, it has contributed little to cases where offenders retain and hide the body of victims or systematically avoid leaving evidence in other ways. More recent developments in profiling can also be criticised for researching offences where issues of detection and investigation are generally not significant, for example studies of domestic homicide offenders (Salfati, 2000). It has been suggested that the value of such research in aiding investigators is at best unclear (Alison, 2006; Alison *et al.*, 2006).

The reliability of profiling data has also been the focus of attention as it is, effectively, a form of retrospective classification. Typologies are developed after the event or events have taken place and these are used to provide some understanding of more recent crimes. For this process to be effective a number of elements are required. Information on past crimes needs to be accurate. In fact this is somewhat problematic and rests on the reliability of information contained in written records and also the reliability of information elicited from offenders themselves. Both sources are notably unreliable and this, in turn, will impact on the validity of profiles. The development of centralised and high-quality relational databases offers the promise of improving this situation, although such datasets raise significant ethical and human rights issues. As yet, in the UK these have received little consideration.

Despite the generally poor state of scientific development within profiling, the issue of who 'owns' profiling has quickly become the focus of discussion. Given the 'free market' manner in which profiling has developed this is disappointing but perhaps not a complete surprise. Much of current practice has been developed in haste and for profit. The limited number and expertise of practitioners in the area has meant that investigating authorities may have found impartial information and advice difficult to come by. If profiling becomes more

clearly an area of mainstream forensic psychology research and practice, this is something that should improve. Indeed, overall there are grounds for optimism. Profiling is becoming increasingly evidence based, as the scientific foundations improve. It is also seen increasingly (and in common with many other areas of forensic practice) as a largely experimental field. Such developments bode well for the more effective and ethical support of investigative authorities in Europe and beyond.

Notes

1 During the Second World War the United States Office of Strategic Services (OSS) commissioned Dr Walter Langer to provide a psychological profile of Adolf Hitler. Langer was psychoanalytically trained and used this as the basis for much of the profile. However, in other respects, the profile was similar to the offender profiles that followed. The profile was, though, far more detailed, arguably because Langer had access to a much richer dataset, including observation of the behaviour of the person being profiled.

2 Unreported, but see Central Criminal Court, 14 September 1994. See F. Gibb, 'Judge attacks police over "murder trap"'. *The Times*, 15 September 1994; M. Doherty, 'Watching the Detectives' (1994) *New Law Journal*, 1525.

Further Reading

Copson, G. (1995). *Coals to Newcastle? Part 1: A study of offender profiling.* London: Home Office.

A seminal paper in the development of evidence-based profiling, this is probably still the single most important paper for postgraduate students to read. At the time of publication and for some years, the paper was sadly neglected by practitioners and researchers. Yet it identified many of the concerns about offender profiling before they began to have adverse impacts on the investigation and prosecution of crime. Despite the passage of time the paper is still well worth reading, providing a clear, concise and well-written analysis of profiling. In the way in which it raised detailed concerns about the poor evidence base for practice it can be seen as being ahead of its time. Written from a UK perspective, the paper also raised issues of international relevance.

Alison, L. (Ed.) (2006). *The forensic psychologists casebook: Psychological profiling and criminal investigation.* Cullompton, Devon: Willan.

This is an edited text of 19 chapters covering both offender profiling and aspects of psychological research and practice into criminal investigation. As with all edited texts, there is a degree of variation across chapters. However, Chapters 1, 5, 10 and 16 provide a detailed, clear and well-written summary of current practice in profiling. These chapters adopt a strongly evidence-based approach to the area and there is a high degree of critical bite in relation to much of the practice within the field.

Jackson, J.L. & Bekerian, D.A. (Eds.) (1997). *Offender profiling theory research and practice*. Chichester: John Wiley.
This is an edited text of 12 chapters. Here the contributions vary markedly in terms of style and content. Chapters 1, 4, 7, 8, 11 and 12 provide useful reviews of key findings in relation to offender profiling. Chapter 6 also provides a helpful and informative account of what investigators may need and value in profiling. The text is now somewhat dated and coverage ends around the mid-1990s.

References

Alison, L. (2006). From trait-based profiling to psychological contributions to apprehension methods. In L. Alison (Ed.) *The forensic psychologists casebook: Psychological profiling and criminal investigation*. Cullompton, Devon: Willan.

Alison, L., Bennett, C., Mokros, A. & Ormrod, D. (2002). The personality paradox in offender profiling. A theoretical review of the processes involved in deriving background characteristics from crime scene actions. *Psychology, Public Policy and Law, 8*, 115–135.

Alison, L., Goodwill, A. & Allison, E. (2006). Guidelines for profilers. In L. Alison (Ed.) *The forensic psychologists casebook: Psychological profiling and criminal investigation*. Cullompton, Devon: Willan.

Alison, L. & Kebbell, M. (2006). Offender profiling: Limits and potential. In M. Kebbell & G. Davies (Eds.) *Practical psychology for forensic investigations and prosecutions*. Chichester: John Wiley.

Alison, L.J., Smith, M.D. & Morgan, K. (2003). Interpreting the accuracy of offender profiles. *Psychology, Crime and Law, 9*(2), 185–195.

American Psychiatric Association (2000). *Diagnostic and statistical manual of mental disorders: DSM-IV-TR*. Washington, DC: Author.

Association of Chief Police Officers (2000). *ACPO Crime Committee, Behavioural Science Sub Committee, internal report*. London: Association of Chief Police Officers.

Britton, P. (1998). *The jigsaw man*. London: Corgi Books.

Brussel, J. (1968). *Case book of a crime psychiatrist*. New York: Bernard Geis.

Burgess, A.W., Baker, T., Greening, D. *et al.* (1997). Stalking behaviours within domestic violence. *Journal of Family Violence, 12*(4), 389–403.

Canter, D. (1989). Offender profiles. *The Psychologist, 2*(1), 12–16.

Canter, D. (1994). *Criminal shadows*. London: HarperCollins.

Christie, A. (1934). *Murder on the Orient Express*. London: Collins Crime Club.

Cohen, M., Seghorn, T. & Calmas, W. (1969). Sociometric study of the sex offender. *Journal of Abnormal Psychology, 74*(2), 249–255.

Conan Doyle, A. (2001). *A study in scarlet*. Contributor Iain Sinclair (Ed.) London: Penguin Classics. First published 1897.

Copson, G. (1995). *Coals to Newcastle? Part 1: A study of offender profiling*. London: Home Office.

Copson, G., Badcock, R., Boon, J. & Britton, P. (2006). Editorial: Articulating a systematic approach to clinical crime profiling. *Criminal Behaviour and Mental Health, 7*(1), 13–17.

Crighton, D.A. & Towl, G.J. (2008). *Psychology in prisons* (2nd edn). Oxford: BPS Blackwell.

Davies, A., Wittebrood, K. & Jackson, J.L. (1998). *Predicting the criminal record of a stranger rapist*. Special interest series paper 12. London: Home Office Policing and Reducing Crime Unit.

Douglas, J.E., Burgess, A.W., Burgess, A.G., *et al.* (1997). *Crime classification manual: A standard system for investigating and classifying violent crimes*. San Francisco, CA: Jossey-Bass.

Farrington, D.P., Coid, J.W., Harnett, L.M. *et al.* (2006). Criminal careers up to age 50 and life success up to age 48: New findings from the Cambridge Study in Delinquent Development, 2nd edition. *Home Office Research Study 299*. London: Home Office Research, Development and Statistics Directorate.

Forer, B. (1949). The fallacy of personal validation: A classroom demonstration of gullibility. *Journal of Abnormal and Social Psychology, 44*, 118–123.

Geberth, V. (1981). Psychological profiling. *Law and Order, 29*(2), 46–52.

Gladwell, M. (2007). Dangerous minds: Criminal profiling made easy. *New Yorker November 12*. Available from www.newyorker.com/reporting/2007/11/12/071112fa_fact_gladwell, retrieved 8 May 2009.

Grubin, D., Kelly, P. & Brunsdon, C. (2001). Linking serious sexual assaults through behaviour. *Home Office Research Study 215*. London: Home Office Research, Development and Statistics Directorate.

Harris, T. (1981). *Red dragon*. New York: Random House.

Home Office (2005a). *Protocol for Home Office registered pathologist* (rev. 12 August 2005). Available from: www.homeoffice.gov.uk/documents/PDB-protocol-registration-fp.pdf?view=Binary, retrieved 1 June 2009.

Home Office (2005b). *Register of forensic pathologists disciplinary guidance*. Available from: www.homeoffice.gov.uk/documents/Disciplinary-Guidance-Issue1.pdf?view=Binary, retrieved 1 June 2009.

House, J.C. (1997). Towards a practical application of offender profiling: The RNC's criminal suspect prioritization system. In J.L. Jackson & D.A. Bekerian (Eds.) *Offender profiling: Theory, research and practice* (pp.177–190). Chichester: Wiley.

Jackson, L. & Bekerian, D.A. (Eds.) (1997). *Offender profiling theory research and practice*. Chichester: John Wiley.

Keppel, R.D. & Walter, R. (1999). Profiling killers: A revised classification model for understanding sexual murder. *International Journal of Offender Therapy and Comparative Criminology, 43*(4), 417–437.

Kocsis, R.N. (2003). Criminal psychological profiling: An outcome and process study. *Law and Human Behaviour, 14*, 215–233.

Kocsis, R.N. (Ed.) (2007). *Criminal profiling international theory, research, and practice*. Totowa, NJ: Humana Press.

Mischel, W., Shoda, Y. & Smith, R.E. (2004). *Introduction to personality: Toward an integration* (7th edn). New York: Wiley.

Mokros, A. & Alison, L. (2002). Is profiling possible? Testing the predicted homology of crime scene actions and background characteristics in a sample of rapists. *Legal and Criminological Psychology, 7*, 25–43.

National Probation Service (2007). *The Violent and Sex Offender Register (ViSOR)*. National Probation Service Briefing Issue 37 (August). London: Author.

Petherick, W. (2005). *Serial crime: Theoretical and practical issues in behavioral profiling*. Burlington, MA: Academic Press.

Pinizzotto, A.J. & Finkel, N.J. (1990). Criminal personality profiling an outcome and process study. *Law and Human Behavior, 14*(3), 215–233.

Prentky, R.A. & Burgess, A. W. (2000). *Forensic management of sexual offenders*. New York: Kiuwer Academic/Plenum.

Prentky, R.A., Knight, R.A. & Rosenberg, R. (1988). Validation analyses on a taxonomic system for rapists: Disconfirmation and reconceptualization. *Annals of the New York Academy of Sciences, 528*, 21–40.

Prentky, R.A., Knight, R.A., Rosenberg, R. & Lee, A. (1989). A path analytic approach to the validation of a taxonomic system for classifying child molesters. *Journal of Quantitative Criminology, 5*(3), 231–257.

Proulx, J., Aubut, J., Perron, L. *et al.* (1994). Troubles de la personalité et viol: Implications théoriques et cliniques [Personality disorders and violence: Theoretical and clinical implications]. *Criminologie, 27*, 33–53.

Proulx, J., St-Yves, M., Guay, J.P. *et al.* (1999). Les aggresseurs sexuels de femmes: Scénarios délictuels et troubles de la per-sonalitié [Sexual aggressors of women: Offence scenarios and personality disorders]. In J. Proulx, M. Cusson & M. Ouimet (Eds.) *Les violences criminelles*. Quebec: Les Presses de L'Université Laval.

Read, T. & Oldfield, D. (1995). Local crime analysis. *Police Research Group Paper 65*. London: Home Office. Available from: www.homeoffice.gov.uk/rds/prgpdfs/fcdps65.pdf, retrieved 1 June 2009.

Ressler, R.K., Burgess, A.W., Douglas, J.E. *et al.* (1986). Serial killers and their victims: Identifying patterns through crime scene analysis. *Journal of Interpersonal Violence, 1*, 288–308.

Salfati, G. (2000). The nature of expressiveness and instrumentality in homicide implications for offender profiling. *Homicide Studies, 4*(3), 265–293.

Swets, J.A., Dawes, R.M. & Monahan, J. (2000). Psychological science can improve diagnostic decisions. *Psychological Science in the Public Interest, 1*(1), 1–26.

Tenten, H.D. (1989). Offender profiling. In W.G. Bailey (Ed.) *The encyclopaedia of police science*. New York: Garland.

Toulmin, S. (1958). *The uses of argument*. Cambridge: Cambridge University Press.

Towl, G.J. & Crighton, D.A. (1996). *The handbook of psychology for forensic practitioners*. London: Routledge.

West, A. & Alison, L. (2006). Conclusions: Personal reflections on the last decade. In L. Alison (Ed.) *The forensic psychologists casebook: Psychological profiling and criminal investigation*. Cullompton, Devon: Willan.

World Health Organization (1990). *International statistical classification of diseases and related health problems, tenth revision*. Available from: www.who.int/classifications/icd/en/index.html, retrieved 1 June 2009.

11

Eyewitness Testimony

Lorraine Hope

Eyewitness testimony plays an important role within the criminal justice system and has, over the past four decades, emerged as a significant research area for psychologists and other social scientists. This chapter aims to provide a comprehensive overview of the key findings of an extensive literature on eyewitness identification performance, signposting both classic studies and emergent research strands. Taking the reader through the witnessing experience, from the initial encoding of the perpetrator to the final stage of delivering testimony in court, this chapter identifies the factors likely to lead to mistaken identifications. Theoretical implications and methodological difficulties associated with eyewitness research are also considered. In the second half of the chapter, the difficulties associated with identifications from closed-circuit television (CCTV) are examined and a full overview of the current UK guidelines for the conduct of identifications is provided.

Information obtained from eyewitnesses plays an important role in many forensic investigations. For instance, the positive identification of a suspect can provide major advances in an investigation (Coupe & Griffiths, 1996; Kebbell & Milne, 1998). Eyewitness testimony is also extremely influential in the courtroom where 'few kinds of evidence are as compelling, or as damning, as eyewitness testimony' (Overbeck, 2005, p.1895). Yet identifications are often disputed – and inaccurate. A review of DNA exoneration cases suggests that eyewitness errors have played some part in over 75 per cent of the convictions overturned by DNA testing in the United States (Innocence Project, 2007; see Scheck *et al.*, 2000). That erroneous eyewitness testimony is a

leading cause of wrongful convictions suggests that jurors fail to take into account factors which may have influenced or biased the eyewitness and led to a mistaken identification (Boyce *et al.*, 2007; Huff *et al.*, 1996). In this chapter, we examine the performance of eyewitness and consider some of the key factors underpinning mistaken identifications.

Eyewitness Identification Performance: Experimental Research and the Real World

The scientific study of eyewitness identification, which emerged in a programmatic fashion during the 1970s, has mainly been conducted by cognitive or social psychologists and typically adopts a standard scientific experimental model. In the mock witness paradigm, volunteers and/or unsuspecting members of the public are exposed to a selected target (perpetrator) as part of a staged event (or simulated crime) and become eyewitnesses. As the events and target individuals are stipulated by the researcher, the nature of witness errors can be documented and systematic manipulations can be made to establish which recall and recognition errors are most likely under particular, forensically relevant conditions. Thus, the primary purpose of such experiments has been to establish cause-effect relations among variables (Wells & Quinlivan, 2008).

An important question for applied researchers and the legal fraternity concerns the extent to which the findings obtained in laboratory research can be generalised to the experience of actual witnesses. There are, of course, a number of important differences between the experience of (some) witnesses and unsuspecting participants in research. For instance, witnesses to 'real' crimes rarely receive a warning – or may not even be aware they have witnessed something important until after the event. A further concern frequently expressed by those in the legal system is that many of the 'witnesses' in such experiments are drawn from rather homogeneous samples of college students. In fact, many studies of eyewitness memory have included community-based samples (e.g. Gabbert et al., 2009; Lindsay et al., in press) while a significant body of research has examined the identification performance of different age groups, including young children (e.g. Pozzulo & Dempsey, 2006) and the elderly (e.g. Dodson & Krueger, 2006). Importantly, research consistently demonstrates that college-age students outperform other age populations. Thus, as noted by Wells and Quinlivan (2008), college-age participants may in fact underestimate the magnitude of eyewitness fallibility.

Witnesses to 'real' crime events may experience a higher level of emotional arousal, particularly if the witnessed incident involves weapons or violence and the witnesses feel threatened. For sound ethical reasons, researchers are typically not permitted to induce stress in experimental participants and are, therefore, unable to replicate violent crime scenarios in any meaningful way. Of course, it is also worth noting that the nature of the stress evoked in a controlled experimental setting may differ qualitatively from the stress associated with involvement in an actual criminal event. In brief, the effects of stress and enhanced emotion on memory are complicated, but the results of research conducted in ecologically sound settings suggest that memory is more likely to be impaired than enhanced in a stressful or arousing situation (e.g. Morgan et al., 2004; Valentine & Mesout, 2008).

Perhaps foremost on the minds of those reluctant to embrace scientific findings on eyewitness performance is the fact that the consequences of an identification decision diverge significantly when that decision is made in a laboratory as opposed to a police identification suite. It is difficult to demonstrate whether or not legal consequences have any actual bearing on witness identification accuracy. However, archival studies of actual witnesses to serious crimes indicate that witnesses taking part in identification parades, where they are presented with a suspect and a number of innocent 'stand-ins', select a foil (i.e. an innocent 'stand-in' or filler) up to 30 per cent on average (Slater, 1994; Wright &

McDaid, 1996; Wright & Skagerberg, 2007). These archival data suggest that witnesses can be highly prone to error and do not necessarily become extremely cautious when faced with a high-stake identification decision (see Memon et al., 2003b).

Many factors may affect the accuracy of an eyewitness and the research literature examining these factors is extensive (Wells & Olson, 2003). A useful distinction between these factors was introduced by Wells (1978) who differentiated between *estimator variables* and *system variables*. System variables are factors which are (or could be) under the control of the criminal justice system, specifically identification test factors such as pre-lineup instructions, lineup composition, structure and presentation method. By contrast, estimator variables are not under control of the criminal justice system and, while these are factors which can be manipulated in research (such as exposure duration, age or race of witness, or presence of a weapon), they cannot be controlled in the actual witnessed incident. Therefore, the impact of such factors on witness accuracy has to be estimated, or taken into account, in a *post-hoc* manner.

Working systematically through the witnessing experience, from the encoding of the original incident to eyewitness testimony in court, this chapter examines several important estimator and system factors which have been shown to impair eyewitness identification accuracy. This is not intended to be an exhaustive review of all possible factors but rather a consideration of the more well-researched witness, perpetrator and contextual factors which provide some insight into subsequent witness identification behaviour and accuracy.

The Witnessed Event

Witness factors

Stable witness characteristics are not, on the whole, useful predictors of identification performance. Research examining factors such as gender, race or intelligence has not revealed any particularly robust effects indicating that members of some groups are better witnesses than others. Nor has research documented any strong relationship between eyewitness accuracy and personality factors. While a small number of studies have examined certain personality characteristics such as self-monitoring (Hosch & Platz, 1984) and trait anxiety (Shapiro & Penrod, 1986), 'no strong theory relating

personality to eyewitness identification has emerged'
(Wells & Olson, 2003, p.281).

However, the age of the witness has been consistently
associated with identification accuracy, with findings
for young children mapping onto the performance of
older witnesses under certain test conditions. Specifically,
when the originally encoded perpetrator is present in
the lineup (a culprit present lineup), both young children and the elderly do not differ significantly from
young adults in their ability to correctly identify the
perpetrator. However, when the perpetrator is not
present in the lineup (a culprit absent lineup), both
young children and elderly witnesses are more likely
than young adults to make a false identification of an
innocent foil (see meta-analysis by Pozzulo & Lindsay,
1998). More recent research demonstrates that older
eyewitnesses (e.g. 60 to 80 years) tend to make more
false identifications than younger adults in both target
present and target absent lineups (Memon et al., 2003a,
2002). No unifying theory has emerged to fully account
for this finding across both age groups. For instance, it
appears that young children's identification performance is hampered by a 'choosing problem' (Brewer et al.,
2005). Keast et al. (2007) also noted a marked overconfidence in children's judgements relating to their identification decisions which suggests that children may be
poor at monitoring their own memory, a conclusion
consistent with the developmental literature (Howie &
Roebers, 2007). The mechanisms underlying higher
false identification rates for older witnesses are less well
explored. Ageing is typically associated with reduced
cognitive capacity (such as a decline in attentional
resources, see Craik & Byrd, 1982; Salthouse 1982) and
an increased reliance on a more 'automatic' feeling of
familiarity rather than a more effortful recollection
process (Jacoby, 1999; Mandler, 1980). Thus, it seems
unlikely that the explanations for difficulties experienced by younger witnesses will also apply to older
witnesses.

A more malleable witness factor at the time of encoding is blood alcohol level. If the witness has been
drinking and is intoxicated, both encoding and storage
may be impaired (Cutler & Penrod, 1995). In terms of
identification performance, Dysart et al. (2002) found
that participants with high blood alcohol readings were
more likely to make a false identification when faced
with a culprit absent identification task. While a number
of explanations have been proposed to account for these
findings, such as a tendency to focus on salient cues
when intoxicated (alcohol myopia hypothesis), research

on the performance of intoxicated witnesses is limited
due to the associated methodological and ethical
difficulties.

Perpetrator factors

Stable factors (such as gender or age of the culprit) have
little or no impact on witness ability to correctly identify
the perpetrator. However, there are a number of well-
documented factors that can serve to either impair or
enhance recognition ability. For instance, distinctive
faces are far more likely to be correctly identified than
non-distinctive faces. Similarly, and perhaps due to their
distinctiveness, attractive faces are also more easily identified than less attractive or more typical faces. The psychological mechanisms underlying these findings are
relatively straightforward. When an encoded face is distinctive or atypical in some way, it will not only attract
more attention and greater processing resources but the
distinctive feature is also more likely to benefit from an
enhanced representation in memory (Ryu & Chaudhuri,
2007; see Brewer et al., 2005 for an interesting examination of the role of distinctiveness).

Unsurprisingly, disguises usually have a negative
impact on identification ability (Cutler et al., 1987; but
see O'Rourke et al., 1989). Simple changes, such as covering the head, wearing glasses, growing facial hair or
even altering hair style slightly, can significantly impair
face recognition (Narby et al., 1996; Shapiro & Penrod,
1986). Furthermore, changes in appearance over time
(such as ageing, changes in weight, etc.) also have a
negative impact on identification performance. In one
study, Read et al. (1990) found that photographs of a
target face taken after a two-year delay were less likely to
be recognised than photographs taken nearing the time
of original encoding.

An extensive literature has documented the identification impairment that occurs when the perpetrator is
from a different race or ethnic group to the witness.
Research on own-race (also known as cross-race) bias
typically demonstrates that witnesses are less accurate
when attempting to identify a target from another race
or ethnic group than when tasked with identifying
a member of their own race (see meta-analysis by
Meissner & Brigham, 2001). Specifically, research docu-
ments a higher correct identification rate from target
present lineups and a lower false identification rate
from target absent lineups when the witness and perpetrator are from the same race. This bias has been
demonstrated in both laboratory and field studies

(e.g. Wright *et al.*, 2001) and has been observed across various combinations of ethnic groups (e.g. whites identifying blacks, blacks identifying whites, etc.). Work by Chiroro and Valentine (1995) exploring a basic contact hypothesis suggested that everyday interactions with people of different races may reduce the effect – but not consistently. Other evidence suggests that the quality rather than the quantity of cross-racial interactions may be more important in reducing own-race bias (Lavrakas *et al.*, 1976). Interestingly, a similar pattern of results has been demonstrated for gender and age such that a match between witness and target age and gender can promote recognition accuracy (e.g. Wright & Sladden, 2003; Wright & Stroud, 2002). Taken together, these findings suggest a somewhat preferential processing mechanism for familiar stimuli. In this vein, McClelland and Chappell (1998) have argued that own-race faces may benefit from more accurate and efficient processing due to their familiarity.

Situational factors

In any witnessed incident, there may be a number of situational factors which impinge on subsequent eyewitness performance. An important factor which has received surprisingly little attention from researchers is the nature of the exposure duration (i.e. the opportunity, or length of time, the witness had to observe the perpetrator). In their meta-analysis of face recognition studies, Shapiro and Penrod (1986) found the predicted linear relationship between exposure duration and hit rates (i.e. as the amount of time spent viewing the target increases so does the likelihood of a correct recognition decision). Only a handful of studies have systematically manipulated exposure duration in an eyewitness context. These studies have typically demonstrated the expected beneficial effect of longer exposure duration on subsequent identification accuracy (e.g. Memon *et al.*, 2003a; Read, 1995). However, inconsistent choosing patterns in target absent conditions require further experimental examination. Similarly, relatively little research attention has been paid to the effect of distance on identification and the ability of eyewitnesses to correctly estimate distances from an incident or perpetrator. Obviously, a correct identification is somewhat unlikely if the witness was unable to *see* the perpetrator so research has tended to focus on identifying a useful 'rule of thumb' with respect to distance. For instance, Wagenaar and van der Schrier (1996) suggested that identification performance was optimal when the viewing distance was less than 15 metres from the target. However, recent work by Lindsay *et al.* (2008) reveals that the 15-metre rule may not be useful – or accurate – for two reasons. Firstly, if witnesses are unable to estimate distance reliably then they are unlikely to be able to report accurately whether they were less than 15 metres from the target. Secondly, it seems rather unlikely that all identifications made when the viewing distance was less than 15 metres will be correct – or vice versa. In Lindsay *et al.* (2008), over 1300 participants observed a target person at various distances, estimated the distance to the target, generated a description and attempted an identification of the target from either a target present or target absent lineup. Participants were poor at accurately estimating the distance between themselves and the target (particularly when required to make this estimate from memory). While the reliability of target descriptions was unimpaired up to distances of approximately 50 metres, a decline in identification performance occurred for both target present and target absent lineups as distance between the witness and target at encoding increased. Although this finding is broadly consistent with those of Wagenaar and van der Schrier (1996), Lindsay *et al.* (2008) did not observe any dramatic drop-off in identification accuracy at 15 metres, noting that many participants made correct identifications beyond this distance, suggesting that a 15-metre rule is not a particularly useful diagnostic for the courts.

Another variable aspect of a criminal incident is the amount of stress or fear a witness may experience. Research inducing realistic levels of stress is, for obvious methodological and ethical reasons, difficult to conduct. However, in a field training scenario, Morgan *et al.* (2004) subjected soldiers to either a high- or low-stress interrogation in a mock prisoner of war camp over a 12-hour period. After a 24-hour delay, soldiers who had experienced a high-stress interrogation were significantly less likely to correctly identify their interrogator than those who had experienced the low-stress interrogation. A more recent study conducted on civilian participants in an arousing context (the London Dungeon) demonstrated that high-state anxiety was associated with fewer correct identifications of a target (Valentine & Mesout, 2008).

Other researchers have focused on the forensically relevant problem of witnesses to crimes involving weapons. Although some field research suggests that the emotional arousal associated with violent witnessing conditions may actually serve to benefit memory (e.g. Yuille & Cutshall, 1986; but see Wright, 2006), eyewitness experts have tended to favour the view that incidents involving the presence of a weapon will have a negative impact on eyewitness performance (Kassin *et al.*, 2001). This phenomenon has become known as the *weapon focus effect* (Loftus *et al.*, 1987) and occurs when the presence of a weapon adversely affects subsequent eye-witness recall performance such that memory for details such as the perpetrator's facial characteristics and cloth-ing is impaired (e.g. Cutler *et al.*, 1987; Hope & Wright, 2007; Loftus *et al.*, 1987; Maas & Kohnken, 1989; Pickel *et al.*, 2003; Steblay, 1992). One explanation is that increased arousal (or stress) due to the presence of a weapon reduces attentional capacity as increased atten-tion is paid to the weapon while peripheral cues are ignored or filtered (Hope & Wright, 2007; Loftus, 1980; Macleod & Mathews, 1991). A meta-analytic review of the effects of stress on eyewitness memory by Deffenbacher *et al.* (2004) concluded that high levels of stress impair the accuracy of eyewitness recall and iden-tification but that the detriment depends on the response mode elicited by the stress manipulation. The authors propose that some emotion manipulations generate an 'orientating' response while others generate a 'defensive' response (Deffenbacher, 1994; Deffenbacher *et al.*, 2004; see also Klorman *et al.*, 1977; Sokolov, 1963). Deffenbacher *et al.* (2004) argue that the orientating response leads to enhanced memory for 'informative aspects' of a scene but that the defensive response can lead to either enhanced memory or significant memory impairment depending on other cognitive and physio-logical factors.

Between the Witnessed Event and Identification Task

Retention interval

In the delay between an individual witnessing a crime and making an identification attempt, the witness's memory is not only prone to decay, but it is also vulnerable to the influence of post-event information from numerous sources. Both delay and post-event information have been shown to compromise recall completeness and accuracy (see Anderson, 1983; Ayers & Reder, 1998; Ellis *et al.*, 1980; Gabbert *et al.*, 2003; Loftus *et al.*, 1978; McCloskey & Zaragoza, 1985; Meissner, 2002; Tuckey & Brewer, 2003).

Delay systematically decreases the amount of infor-mation that can be recalled (Ebbinghaus, 1885; Kassin *et al.*, 2001; Rubin & Wenzel, 1996; see also Tuckey &

Brewer, 2003). Furthermore, a meta-analysis of 128 studies of face recognition suggests that there is a decline in the correct identification of previously seen faces after a delay (Shapiro & Penrod, 1986). Sporer (1992) found a decrease in correct identifications and an increase in false alarms over various intervals up to three weeks. Importantly, the field work by Valentine *et al.* (2003b) examining performance of real witnesses sug-gests that the greatest decline in performance occurs when the delay exceeds one week.

Post-event misinformation

Research conducted by Elizabeth Loftus in the 1970s demonstrated the misinformation effect – a powerful phenomenon resulting in memory distortion (for a review see Loftus, 2005). In a now classic experiment, Loftus and Palmer (1974) presented participants a short film of a car accident and subsequently tested participant recall for details of the incident. Importantly, they found that simply changing one word in a question pertaining to the speed the car was travelling when the accident occurred resulted in significantly different estimates of speed. Specifically, participants asked to estimate what speed the car was travelling at when it *contacted* the other vehicle provided slower speed estimates (31.8 mph) than those asked to estimate the speed of the car when it *smashed* into the other vehicle (40.5 mph). Including the verb 'smashed' in the question also led to increased false reports of witnessing broken glass at the scene of the accident (no broken glass was ever shown). Several hundred experiments since have demonstrated the mis-information phenomenon, explored boundary condi-tions of the effect and served the development of theoretical explanations. More pertinent to eyewitness identification accuracy is an emerging body of work on the impact of co-witness influence on memory. In a recent survey 86 per cent of real eyewitnesses discussed their memory with a co-witness who was present at the witnessed event (Paterson & Kemp, 2006). Witnesses to an event may share the same experience but their indi-vidual recall of the event may differ for many reasons, including naturally occurring differences in attention paid to various details of the event, differences in spatial or temporal location at the scene or perceived differences in ability to recall those details (Gabbert *et al.*, 2006). Research amply demonstrates that the most likely out-come when two witnesses discuss their memories is that their accounts of the witnessed event become more simi-lar and, hence, seemingly corroborative (Gabbert *et al.*,

2004; Wright *et al.*, 2000). A witness is also more likely to be influenced by a co-witness with whom they have a prior acquaintance, such as a friend or partner (Hope *et al.*, 2008). However, very few studies have explored the impact of misleading information on subsequent identifications. A recent study conducted by Gabbert *et al.* (2007) which manipulated co-witness confidence and accuracy across both target present and target absent lineups found that participants were more likely than controls to reject the lineup incorrectly when they were aware that the co-witness had rejected the lineup. However, participants were no more likely than controls to identify the perpetrator correctly after seeing the co-witness make an accurate identification, and the pre-lineup confidence expressed by the confederate did not appear to influence the witness.

While unbiased lineup procedures may ensure that identification decisions themselves are unlikely to be shared with other witnesses, misinformation concerning descriptive details or pertaining to the general appearance of the target may have a negative impact on eyewitness accuracy, and this hypothesis is worthy of further experimental scrutiny.

Intermediate Recognition Tasks

Mugshots

In the course of an investigation, witnesses may be asked to search through a set of mugshots (usually photographs of potential suspects). Unsurprisingly, a number of studies have shown that previous exposure to the suspect increases the likelihood that the suspect will be identified in a subsequent lineup. In other words, repeated exposure to a suspect can increase mistaken identifications of an innocent suspect (Brigham & Cairns, 1988; Dysart *et al.*, 2001; Gorenstein & Ellsworth, 1980; Memon *et al.*, 2002).

Composite production

In an investigation where no suspect has emerged, the police may work with a witness to produce a facial composite of the perpetrator. Previously, this composite might have been produced by a sketch artist but technological advances have led to the use of computerised systems for composite production (such as the E-Fit or Profit identification systems). While research demonstrates that the quality of composites is often rather poor, with little likeness to the appearance of the actual

perpetrator (see Wells & Hasel, 2007, for a review), a more important question concerns the extent to which generating a composite might impair identification accuracy. In two studies, Wells *et al.* (2005) examined whether building a face composite had a negative effect on memory for the target face. Results indicated that building a composite resulted in significantly lower identifications for the original target face (Experiment 1), while a second experiment revealed that the results might be generalised to a standard witness paradigm (Experiment 2). In light of these results, Wells *et al.* (2005) suggest that where multiple witnesses are available 'it might be possible to use one witness to build a composite and save the other witnesses for any later lineup identification attempts' (p.155).

The Identification Task

In this section, we consider several important system variables which can have a significant impact on eyewitness identification performance. These variables are ultimately under the control of the criminal justice system and, to date, research has focused on demonstrating the identification errors resulting from poor practice in the production and administration of identification tests (i.e. lineups) while delivering recommendations for improved procedures.

Pre-lineup instructions

Often witnesses assume that the suspect apprehended by the police and presented to them in the formal setting of a lineup must have a high probability of being the actual perpetrator. In other words, witnesses assume that they would not have been invited to make an identification if there was not a good reason for the police to believe the suspect was the actual perpetrator and their role is to make a positive identification (i.e. choose someone from the array). This bias may be further exacerbated if the witnesses are presented with the task in a misleading manner (i.e. 'Take a good look at the lineup and see if you can identify the offender'). In fact, Memon *et al.* (2003a) found that over 90 per cent of mock witnesses indicated that they expected the perpetrator to be present in a lineup even under unbiased conditions. Therefore, it is extremely important that witnesses are informed that the person they saw 'may or may not be present in the lineup'. Incorrect identifications from target absent lineups are significantly lower when witnesses are given this simple cautionary instruction (see meta-analyses by Steblay, 1997; Clark, 2005).

Lineup composition

When a suspect disputes his involvement in an incident or claims an identification error, a lineup must be conducted. Here the police face a number of challenges as there are (at least) two important dilemmas with respect to lineup composition, namely, the number of lineup members (or foils) present in addition to the suspect, and how those foils are selected. The requisite number of lineup members is typically specified in law. For instance, in the UK a lineup must contain at least eight foils, while in the US lineups containing five (or more) foils are common. However, researchers have drawn a sharp distinction between the *nominal size* of a lineup (i.e. the number of people appearing in the lineup) and what has been described as the *functional size* of a lineup (Wells *et al.*, 1979). Functional size refers to the number of plausible lineup members. If an eyewitness describes a perpetrator as a male, in his early twenties with long, dark hair, but then views a lineup in which two of the foils have short dark hair and one other foil is in his 40s, then the functional size of the lineup is reduced by three members, as these foils will be automatically discarded by the witness as they do not match the original description provided. The purpose of the lineup is to provide a fair identification task in which the suspect does not 'stand out' inappropriately from the other foils. Reducing the functional size of the lineup – particularly when the suspect is not the actual perpetrator – significantly increases the chance of a false identification (Lindsay & Wells, 1980; Tredoux, 2002). Thus, the selection of appropriate foils is critical for the production of a fair lineup and has been the focus of a good deal of debate. In the UK, police are required to select foils that resemble the suspect in what might be described as a 'match to suspect' strategy. In other words, foils are selected on the grounds that they match the appearance of the suspect (rather than the description of the perpetrator). This strategy is problematic as research has documented that foils who do not coincide with a witness's prior verbal description are likely to be disregarded, resulting in a biased lineup and an increased likelihood that an innocent suspect may be mistakenly identified (e.g. Clark & Tunnicliff, 2001). Thus, a 'match to description' strategy (i.e. where foils are selected based on their match to descriptions of the perpetrator provided by the witness) may be preferable (Luus &

Wells, 1991). However, more recent research by Darling *et al.* (2008) did not identify any differences in either correct or incorrect identifications as a function of these lineup composition strategies. Clearly, further research is necessary to identify specifically how alterations to the composition of a lineup affect choosing behaviour.

Investigator bias

Ideally, lineups should take place under double-blind administration where both the witness and lineup administrator are unaware of the identity of the suspect. Where the person conducting the lineup knows which lineup member is the suspect, there is a possibility that they will unintentionally transmit this knowledge to the witness (Harris & Rosenthal, 1985), resulting in increased rates of false identification (Phillips *et al.*, 1999). More recently, Greathouse and Kovera (2008) noted that administrators displayed more biasing behaviours (such as inviting the witness to 'take another look', providing overt cues as to the identity of the suspect, and exerting greater pressure on witnesses to choose) during single-blind administration procedures (i.e. when they knew the identity of the suspect) than under double-blind procedures.

Lineup procedure: Comparing absolute and relative judgements

The lineup task has probably received greater research attention than any other topic relating to eyewitness testimony. In the traditional lineup (which may involve photographs or live participants, depending on the jurisdiction), the suspect and foils are presented simultaneously. Given witnesses tendency to assume that the perpetrator will be present in the lineup, the opportunity to examine all lineup members at once can lead witnesses to compare the lineup members with each other and select the lineup member who best matches their original memory. This has been described as a relative judgement strategy (Wells, 1984; Wells & Seelau, 1995). An alternative method of lineup presentation, known as the sequential lineup, was proposed by Lindsay and Wells (1985). Unlike the traditional simultaneous lineup where all lineup members are viewed at once, in the sequential lineup method each lineup member is presented sequentially, one member at a time. The witness is required to make an absolute identification decision for each lineup member (Is this the perpetrator you saw? Yes or No) prior to seeing the next person in the lineup. In the optimal version of the lineup, the witness does not know how many faces will be presented and the lineup terminates when a choice is made, with witnesses not permitted to see any further photos, review previously presented photos or change their identification decision. This lineup method promotes an absolute identification decision as, unlike the simultaneous lineup, witnesses cannot engage in relative comparisons between lineup members but instead have to compare the face presented with their memory for the perpetrator. Many studies have demonstrated that the sequential lineup method significantly reduces false identifications (see Steblay et al., 2001 for a meta-analysis) as a consequence of promoting a more conservative response criterion than the simultaneous lineup procedure (Meissner et al., 2005). However, a number of recent studies, while typically observing the predicted improvements in the false identification rate, have also noted a reduction in correct identifications under sequential procedures (Ebbesen & Flowe, 2002; Memon & Gabbert, 2003). Interestingly, in their meta-analysis, Clark et al. (2008) noted that only biased lineups produced the sequential lineup advantage with respect to false identifications. Further research is necessary to better understand the mechanisms driving choosing behaviour in order to develop accuracy-promoting lineup formats.

Post-identification feedback

Witness confidence is, perhaps, the most influential cue used by juries when evaluating the credibility and reliability of eyewitness testimony (Cutler et al., 1990; Lindsay et al., 1981). However, mistaken eyewitnesses can be overconfident (Shaw & McClure, 1996; Wells & Bradfield, 1999) and eyewitness confidence can be highly malleable in the period after making an identification (Luus & Wells, 1994a, 1994b; Wells & Bradfield, 1998). For instance, Wells and Bradfield (1998) found that witnesses who were given positive feedback (e.g. 'Good, you identified the suspect') reported higher confidence and better viewing conditions than those who received no feedback. Conversely, witnesses given negative feedback were less confident and reported worse witnessing conditions. The effects of feedback have also been shown to occur for both target present and target absent lineups (Bradfield et al., 2002), when there are long delays between identification and feedback (Wells et al., 2002), and even extend to witness willingness to

testify (Wells & Bradfield, 1998, 1999). Post-identification effects may be reduced (but not eliminated) by means of warnings (e.g. Lampinen et al., 2007).

Is confidence ever related to accuracy?

Police, lawyers, judges and other legal practitioners, in addition to lay jurors, typically consider confidence as a useful indicator of likely eyewitness accuracy (Deffenbacher & Loftus, 1982; Noon & Hollin, 1987; Potter & Brewer, 1999). As we have seen, however, eyewitness confidence is malleable and susceptible to bias which can, in the worst-case scenario, produce highly confident mistaken identifications. But can witness confidence actually tell us anything useful about identification accuracy? Until recently, researchers have tended to take the view that confidence is not reliably associated with accuracy and, in particular, is not a reliable predictor of accuracy given low or non-significant confidence–accuracy correlations (e.g. Bothwell et al., 1987; Sporer et al., 1995; see also Kassin et al., 2001). However, in an extensive programme of research focusing on confidence and adapting alternative analyses, Brewer and his colleagues have challenged this conclusion (Brewer, 2006; Brewer & Wells, 2006; Weber & Brewer, 2004). Using a calibration approach, these authors have documented substantial confidence–accuracy relations for lineup choosers (i.e. witnesses who make positive identifications) across various stimuli materials (for extended discussion of this method and the relationship between confidence and accuracy, see Brewer, 2006; Brewer et al., 2005).

Identifications from CCTV

Intuitively, one might expect that identification performance might improve significantly when the 'witness', be that the original witness, a CCTV operator or police officer reviewing the evidence, has access to a video recording of the (alleged) target and, possibly, still photographs of the suspect. With video footage of the incident available, the task would no longer rely so heavily on memory (or prior familiarity with the perpetrator) and would simply require the witness to engage in an apparently simple matching task. However, the identification of individuals from CCTV footage is not necessarily a simple identification task and, like other identification tasks, is prone to error – even under optimal conditions.

There are two quite distinct circumstances where an attempt may be made to identify a face from a video image (Bruce *et al.*, 1999). In the first situation, a spontaneous identification may be made by a member of the public (or perhaps, a CCTV operator or police officer) who claims that the target appearing in the CCTV image is personally known to them. In the second situation, the target appearing in the CCTV footage is compared to an apprehended suspect to establish whether, in fact, the suspect was recorded at the scene of the incident under investigation. Identification accuracy varies under these circumstances with respect to whether the face is previously known or previously unknown to the witness.

In one of the early studies on spontaneous identifications based on prior exposure, Logie *et al.* (1987) examined the ability of the general public to identify a live target in a town centre from a previously presented photograph. The photograph had been published in a local newspaper. Despite circulating details of the precise location of the target, the spontaneous detection (i.e. identification) rate for the general public was very low and this was coupled with a high false recognition rate (i.e. false identifications of other 'innocent' passers-by).

These low recognition rates in dynamic interactions where the target face is continually available to the witness have been documented elsewhere. In a field study, Kemp *et al.* (1997) examined whether credit cards bearing a photograph of the cardholder might serve to reduce credit card fraud. Including a photograph of the legal cardholder on a credit card (or indeed, other identity document) would seem to be a relatively foolproof method of ensuring that the card is used only by the person entitled to use it. In their study, shoppers presented a credit card bearing a photograph of themselves to pay for half the transactions while for other transactions they presented a card bearing the photograph of another individual. Experienced checkout cashiers were required to either accept or decline the card depending on their verification of the cardholder's identity, and rate their confidence that the photograph appearing on the card was, in fact, that of the shopper. More than 50 per cent of the fraudulent cards were accepted by the cashiers – despite the fact that cashiers were aware that a study was under way and indicated that they both spent longer examining cards and had been more cautious than usual.

High error rates in the ability to match a target from CCTV footage have also been documented. Typically, it has been assumed that difficulties in identifying faces from video recordings are largely due to the frequently poor-quality nature of the recording and that were high-quality recordings available such difficulties would be reduced. While it is true that many CCTV images may be of poor quality for a number of technical reasons (such as unsuitable lighting conditions, intermittent image sampling, etc.), the assumption that this alone underpins low accuracy rates in face matching from CCTV has been challenged by research findings.

Bruce and her colleagues (1999) examined how well people were able to match faces extracted from a high-quality video-recording against high-quality photographic images. The results revealed that overall accuracy was relatively poor (averaging only 70 per cent across trials) even under these optimal conditions. Performance was further degraded when the target expression or viewpoint was altered. Furthermore, the use of colour target images (as opposed to black-and-white images) did not appear to lend any particular advantage (or disadvantage) to performance on the matching task. Thus, it would appear that our ability to identify an unfamiliar face – even in the presence of a reference image (such as a CCTV still or a photograph) is surprisingly error-prone (Davies & Thasen, 2000; Henderson *et al.*, 2001).

In contrast, identification accuracy for known or familiar faces can be very accurate – even when the target images are of poor quality. To examine the impact of familiarity on face recognition, Burton *et al.* (1999) showed study participants surveillance video footage of a target who was known to some participants but not others. Results indicated a marked advantage for people who were personally familiar with the target – 73 per cent of the poor-quality image targets were recognised *when they were familiar*. In a series of studies exploring the role of familiarity, Bruce *et al.* (2001) found that participants were able to correctly verify (or reject) a familiar target with a high degree of accuracy (over 90 per cent) despite the use of poor-quality video images. When participants were unfamiliar with the targets, the accuracy rate was significantly lower (56 per cent). Subsequent experiments revealed that brief periods of exposure to the target do not necessarily generate sufficient familiarity to improve the recognition or matching of unfamiliar faces – unless some 'deep' or social processing has taken place (i.e. discussing the faces with another person).

Face recognition is of central importance to investigative police work (Scott-Brown & Cronin, 2007). CCTV has the benefit of providing investigators with a permanent record of an event and, importantly, who may have been involved in it. The availability of CCTV footage – and the speed at which it was analysed – facilitated the rapid identification of the 7/7 and 21/7 bombers from thousands of hours of recordings (Metropolitan Police, 2005). Furthermore, actual CCTV footage is generally considered powerful evidence in court (NACRO, 2002; Scott-Brown & Cronin, 2007; Thomas, 1993). However, relying on CCTV for the recognition and identification of suspects may foster a false sense of security and a potentially dangerous over-reliance on such evidence. We expect to be able to do this task with a high degree of accuracy. However, the research consistently demonstrates that people are poor at this task – even under optimal conditions.

Is eyewitness identification evidence reliable?

Experimental psychological research on eyewitness identification has flourished over the past 30 years, producing hundreds of articles and thousands of identification data-points. Given the size of the literature and the many different designs and research hypotheses deployed, it is often difficult to compare between studies and reach an overall conclusion with respect to our ability to identify correctly a previously seen individual. As Clark *et al.* (2008) note, correct identification rates often vary widely across experiments, for instance from as high as 80 per cent to as low as 8 per cent. To establish what the results of eyewitness experiments can tell us, Clark *et al.* (2008) conducted a meta-analysis of 94 comparisons between target present and target absent lineups. The most important conclusions to emerge from this analysis were as follows: 1. correct identifications (from target present lineups) and correct non-identifications (target absent lineups) were not correlated; 2. an identification of the suspect is diagnostic of the suspect's guilt but the identification may be less informative if any of the identification procedures are in any way biased (such as lineup composition); and 3. non-identifications were diagnostic of the suspect's innocence while 'don't know' responses were, unsurprisingly, non-diagnostic with respect to guilt or innocence. Based on these and earlier analyses (e.g. Clark, 2005), Clark *et al.* (2008) suggest as a basic principle that 'a suspect identification has greater probative value to the extent that it is based on the witness's memory, and less probative value to the extent that it is due to lineup composition or an increase in the witness's conformity, willingness, or desire to make an identification' (p.211). Thus, when assessing the reliability and likely accuracy of an identification, legal practitioners and juries alike need to consider the extent to which these factors might have played a role in the identification process.

Procedural Guidelines Relating to Suspect Identification in the UK

In England and Wales, Code D of the Police and Criminal Evidence Act (PACE) 1984 sets out guidelines, or Codes of Practice, for the conduct of identification procedures by police officers. The main purpose of Code D is to prevent mistaken identifications and the Code sets broad provisions relating to the circumstances and manner in which identification procedures should be conducted and the hierarchy among those procedures. The Code embodies many of the recommendations of the Devlin Report (1976) which was prepared following a number of criminal cases in which biased identification procedures and erroneous witnesses led to the misidentification, and in several instances the wrongful conviction, of the suspect. One such case was that of Laszlo Virag who was convicted of stealing and using a firearm when attempting to escape from police officers in Liverpool in 1969. Despite an alibi and several other evidential contradictions, Virag was identified by eight witnesses as the man who committed the crime. One witness claimed that Virag's face was 'imprinted' on his brain while another had spent some time with him at a hotel bar, yet these identifications were incorrect. Subsequently, another individual confessed to the crime and Virag was pardoned. Cases such as this one led to the conclusion that eyewitness identification evidence could be unreliable and that convictions should not generally rely on such evidence alone.

Under PACE, the Code initially required that a live lineup, otherwise known as an identity parade, must be held when the suspect disputes an identification and holding the lineup is practicable. Unlike in the USA and other international jurisdictions, the presentation of still photographs is not a permitted identification procedure in England and Wales when a suspect has been detained. The Code stipulates the following key requirements for a live identification procedure: the lineup must contain at least eight foils (i.e. volunteers who are known to be innocent) in addition to the suspect and these foils should resemble the suspect in 'age, height, general appearance and position in life'. Unusual or distinctive features (scars, tattoos, etc.) which cannot be replicated across foils may be concealed by means of a plaster or hat so that all members of the lineup resemble each other in general appearance. The suspect may choose their own position in the lineup and their legal representative may also be present during the identification procedure. Importantly, witnesses must be informed that the perpetrator may or may not be present in the lineup, and if they cannot make a positive identification they should say so. Lineup members may be requested to comply with a witness's request to hear them speak, move or adopt a particular pose. Despite these provisions, analyses of archival identification data indicate that witnesses attending a formal police identification parade mistakenly identify a foil over one-fifth of the time. Slater (1994) reported that of 843 witnesses (302 lineups), 36 per cent identified the suspect and 22 per cent identified an innocent foil as the perpetrator while 42 per cent made no positive identification decision. Similarly, Wright and McDaid (1996) reviewed identification decisions for 1561 witnesses (616 lineups) where 39 per cent of witnesses identified the suspect, 20 per cent identified a foil and the remainder made no identification. The most recent substantive revision of Code D was made in 2005 (with a very minor revision issued in 2008). The most important feature of the 2005 revision is that it made provision for the conduct of a video identification procedure. Specifically, the Code requires that the suspect will be initially offered a video identification unless this procedure is not practicable or an identification parade would be 'more suitable'.

Video identification lineups present a video clip of the head and shoulders of each lineup member. Each film clip lasts approximately 15 seconds and follows the following movement sequence: firstly, the lineup member looks at the camera directly for a full-frontal shot of the face and shoulders, then they are required to slowly turn their head to first the left and then the right to present both profile views. Finally, a full-face view is presented once more. Video lineups must comprise at least eight foils who are drawn from over 20,000 foils available from the National Video Identification Database. The database is made up of video clips of volunteers drawn from the general public and, as with the live lineup, suitable foils are selected which resemble the suspect in 'age, height, general appearance and position in life'. In the UK, two main systems are used for producing video lineups: VIPER (Video Identity Parade Electronic Recording) and PROMAT (Profile Matching). For both systems, a single clip of the suspect performing the movement sequence described is prepared. The witness views at least nine clips presented sequentially on a screen, with each clip identified by a number. As in the earlier code for live lineups, witnesses receive unbiased lineup instructions stating that the perpetrator may not be present. Witnesses are also informed that they may see a particular part of the set of images again, or may have a particular image 'frozen'. There is no limit on the number of times they can view the whole set of images (or any part of the images). The Code also indicates that witnesses should be asked not to make an identification decision until they have viewed the whole set of images at least twice.

Video identification has a number of important advantages over live lineups. Research on actual VIPER video lineups has shown that the lineups produced using this system are fairer to suspects than live lineups (Valentine & Heaton, 1999). Valentine and his colleagues also found that VIPER lineups were fair for both white European and African Caribbean suspects (Valentine et al., 2003a). Of course, this is likely due to the availability of a large database of images from which to select foils. The availability of a database of foils has also reduced the delay typically involved in organising a live identification parade – video lineups can typically be produced within two hours (Valentine et al., 2003b). Lineups are also far less likely to be cancelled (Pike et al., 2000). Finally, the use of video lineups is less threatening for victims, who are not required to be in the physical presence of their attacker at the identification suite. Furthermore, the video lineup can be taken to a victim who may be unable to attend the police station (Valentine et al., 2006).

While research on photograph arrays suggests that sequential presentation can reduce mistaken identifications when an absolute decision on each lineup member is required (Lindsay & Wells, 1985), the video lineup instructions stipulated under Code D are incompatible with the strict sequential administration procedure discussed earlier in this chapter in that they require the witness to review the entire lineup image set at least twice before making a decision. However, recent research by Valentine et al. (2007) suggests that strict instructions did not result in a reliably reduced rate of mistaken identification when compared with the existing view-twice procedure used in the UK. With respect to the benefit of moving lineup images (over still lineup images), combined data from recent research suggests that moving images may yield fewer false identifications in perpetratror absent lineups (Valentine et al., 2007).

The Code also provides for two other forms of identification under certain circumstances: group identification and witness confrontation. Group identification occurs when the witness sees the suspect in an informal group of people and may take place overtly (with the suspect's cooperation) or covertly. In a witness confrontation, under the provision of the Code, the witness is shown the suspect, provided with unbiased instructions and asked 'Is this the person?' Compared with lineup identification procedures, the group identification and witness confrontation procedures may be more susceptible to bias (e.g. due to reduced functional size), thus caution should be exercised when evaluating the reliability of such identifications.

The Eyewitness in Court

The final stage of the eyewitness's role within the legal process takes place in court. Courts in many jurisdictions acknowledge that there is a risk that eyewitness evidence may be unreliable and jurors are typically instructed to scrutinise the circumstances under which the witness encountered the suspect (Memon, 2008). For instance, in England and Wales trial judges are required to 'protect against unsafe convictions in cases involving disputed identification' (Roberts & Ormerod, 2008, p.74). The Turnbull guidelines (*R* v. *Turnbull*) stipulate that if a prosecution case is heavily based on eyewitness identification evidence, where the judge considers that evidence to be weak, of poor or questionable quality, the case must not proceed. When a case involving eyewitness identification evidence does proceed before a jury, the judge is required to provide both a general warning regarding the risks associated with eyewitness evidence and a more specific warning tailored to the nature of the potential weaknesses of the eyewitness evidence in that particular case.

The admissibility of expert testimony concerning eyewitness testimony remains a topic for some debate in legal circles (see Benton *et al.*, 2006 for a review), In most adversarial systems, including North America and the UK, the judge decides whether expert testimony is admissible against certain criteria (Benton *et al.*, 2006; Kovera *et al.*, 2002; Read & Desmarais, in press). The one criterion common across most jurisdictions concerns the extent to which issues pertaining to eyewitness memory are considered to be a matter of juror common sense. In the UK this means that the jurors are usually expected to make a sound decision about the quality of eyewitness evidence unaided by testimony from an expert. The judicial conclusion that eyewitness memory is indeed a matter of common sense is one of the most frequently cited reasons for the rejection of eyewitness expert testimony (Benton *et al.*, 2006; Leippe, 1995; Yarmey, 2001), and legal experts are often in agreement (e.g. Benton *et al.*, 2006; Stuesser, 2005).

However, jurors are not particularly sensitive to potential eyewitness error – or responsive to judicial instructions on the matter (Kassin & Sommers, 1997). In fact, over a quarter of a century of research has demonstrated that lay understanding of eyewitness psychology is limited – and often mistaken (e.g. Benton *et al.*, 2006; Brigham & WolfsKeil, 1983; Deffenbacher & Loftus, 1982; McConkey & Roche, 1989; Noon & Hollin, 1987; for a comprehensive review see Benton *et al.*, 2006). Jurors tend to be unaware of the implications of biased procedures used by law enforcement, such as poorly constructed lineups, misleading feedback or biased instructions (Shaw *et al.*, 1999). Potential jurors also find it difficult to distinguish between accurate and inaccurate witnesses (e.g. Lindsay *et al.*, 1989, 1981). Even legal professionals are typically rather limited in their understanding of factors affecting eyewitness accuracy (Granhag *et al.*, 2005; Wise & Safer, 2004). Furthermore, convictions which originally relied heavily on eyewitness testimony, but are now known to have been in error, illustrate quite clearly that jurors are often unable to either generate or apply the common sense expected of them by the courts.

Conclusions

Eyewitnesses serve an important function in the delivery of justice and can, under the right circumstances, correctly confirm the identity of a criminal. However, caution needs to be exercised with respect to identifications as the leading cause of mistaken convictions is erroneous eyewitness testimony. In particular, consideration must be paid to the conditions under which the witness encoded the perpetrator, the presence of any intervening misleading information, the nature and fairness of the identification procedures and whether the witness received feedback – unwittingly or otherwise.

Further Reading

Brewer, N., Weber, N. & Semmler, C. (2005). Eyewitness identification. In N. Brewer & K.D. Williams (Eds.) *Psychology and law: An empirical perspective* (pp.177–221). New York: Guilford Press.

An excellent and thoughtful overview of key issues in eyewitness research, Specifically, this chapter examines the various stages of the identification process that occur in the real world, from features of the event which may impede the witness to the impact of exposure to inaccurate post-event information and, finally, the identification task. Brewer and his colleagues also critically examine other factors which research suggests may be diagnostic of identification accuracy (e.g. confidence and latency). Throughout the chapter, the authors highlight several important methodological shortcomings which beset the extant research literature, such as underpowered experiments, a limited stimulus set and inadequate lineup conditions. Not only does this chapter provide a comprehensive review of the eyewitness literature and consider some of the problematic methodological issues faced by researchers but, importantly, it also focuses on the need to further develop our theoretical understanding of eyewitness identification behaviour.

Valentine, T. & Heaton, P. (1999). An evaluation of the fairness of police lineups and video identifications. *Applied Cognitive Psychology*, *13*, S59–S72.

Valentine's work evaluating the fairness of VIPER lineups makes an important contribution to our understanding of current UK identification procedures. In this initial study of video identifications, Valentine and Heaton compared the 'fairness' (in terms of non-biased lineup selections) of photo versus video identification stimuli. In a fair lineup the suspect should be chosen, by chance, by 11 per cent of the mock witnesses (i.e. each lineup member should have an equal chance of being selected if the actual perpetrator is not present and correctly identified). However, in this study, 25 per cent of mock witnesses selected the suspect from the photographs of live lineups while only 15 per cent of mock witnesses selected the suspect from video lineups. The authors concluded that the video lineups were fairer than the live lineups. Given that mistaken eyewitness identifications are a significant source of miscarriages of justice, Valentine and Heaton argue that the more widespread use of video identification may actually improve the reliability of identification evidence.

Weber, N. & Brewer, N. (2004). Confidence–accuracy calibration in absolute and relative face recognition judgments. *Journal of Experimental Psychology: Applied*, *10*, 156–172.

This paper introduces an important new conceptual and analytical approach to eyewitness confidence which continues to show promise in determining the likely diagnosticity of eyewitness identification decisions. Confidence–accuracy calibration was analysed for both absolute and relative face recognition judgements. The most interesting finding is that recognition judgements for 'old' (i.e. previously viewed) stimuli demonstrated a strong confidence–accuracy calibration. In other words, there was an association between accuracy and the level of confidence expressed. This finding suggests that there was a meaningful relationship between subjective and objective probabilities of judgement accuracy for previously seen items. However, for 'new' judgements there was little or no association between confidence and accuracy using the calibration approach. See also: Brewer, N. (2006). Uses and abuses of eyewitness identification confidence. *Legal and Criminological Psychology*, *11*, 3–23.

Wells, G.L., Memon, A. & Penrod, S. (2006). Eyewitness evidence. Improving its probative value. *Psychological Science in the Public Interest*, *7*, 45–75.

A thorough review of the eyewitness literature and its role within the legal system. In this article, both estimator and system variables are examined and, in particular, the authors focus on how procedures based on scientific research findings can be developed to improve the probative value of eyewitness evidence. Other important questions are addressed, including the frequently occurring tension in applied research between scientific rigour and external validity when moving from the laboratory to real-world contexts. Specifically, the authors consider issues of base rates, multicollinearity, selection effects, subject populations and psychological realism and note how a combination of critical theory and field data can work together to improve the generalisability of eyewitness research.

References

Anderson, J.R. (1983). A spreading activation theory of memory. *Journal of Verbal Learning and Verbal Behavior*, *22*, 261–295.

Ayers, M.S. & Reder, L.M. (1998). A theoretical review of the misinformation effect: Predictions from an activation-based memory model. *Psychonomic Bulletin and Review*, *5*, 1–21.

Benton, T.R., Ross, D.F., Bradshaw, E., Thomas, W.N. & Bradshaw, G.S. (2006). Eyewitness memory is still not common sense: Comparing jurors, judges and law enforcement to eyewitness experts. *Applied Cognitive Psychology 20*, 115–129.

Bothwell, R.K., Brigham, J.C. & Deffenbacher, K.A. (1987). Correlation of eyewitnesses accuracy and confidence: Optimality hypothesis revisited. *Journal of Applied Psychology*, *72*, 691–695.

Boyce, M., Beaudry, J.L. & Lindsay, R.C.L. (2007). Belief of eyewitness identification evidence. In R.C.L. Lindsay, D.F. Ross, J.D. Read & M.P. Toglia (Vol. Eds.), *The handbook of eyewitness psychology: Vol. 2. Memory for people* (pp.501–529). Mahwah, NJ: Lawrence Erlbaum.

Bradfield, A.L., Wells, G.L & Olson, E.A. (2002). The damaging effect of confirming feedback on the relation between eyewitness certainty and identification accuracy. *Journal of Applied Psychology*, *87*, 112–120.

Brewer, N. (2006). Uses and abuses of eyewitness identification confidence. *Legal and criminological psychology*, *11*, 3–21.

Brewer, N. & Weber, N. (in press). Eyewitness confidence and latency: Indices of memory processes not just markers of accuracy. *Applied Cognitive Psychology*.

Brewer, N., Weber, N. & Semmler, C. (2005). Eyewitness identification. In N. Brewer & K.D. Williams (Eds.) *Psychology and law: An empirical perspective* (pp.177–221). New York: Guilford Press.

Brewer, N. & Wells, G.L. (2006). The confidence–accuracy relationship in eyewitness identification: Effects of lineup instructions, foil similarity and target-absent base rates. *Journal of Experimental Psychology: Applied, 12*, 11–30.

Brigham, J.C. & Cairns, D.L. (1988). The effect of mug shot inspections on eyewitness identification accuracy. *Journal of Applied Social Psychology, 18*, 1394–1410.

Brigham, J.C. & WolfsKeil, M.P. (1983). Opinions of attorney's and law enforcement personnel on the accuracy of eyewitness identifications. *Law and Human Behavior, 7*, 337–349.

Bruce, V., Henderson, Z., Greenwood, K., Hancock, P., Burton, A.M. & Miller, P. (1999). Verification of face identities from images captured on video. *Journal of Experimental Psychology: Applied, 5*, 339–360.

Bruce, V., Henderson, Z., Newman, C. & Burton, A.M. (2001). Matching identities of familiar and unfamiliar faces caught on CCTV images. *Journal of Experimental Psychology: Applied, 7*, 207–218.

Burton, A.M, Wilson, S., Cowan, M & Bruce, V. (1999). Face recognition in poor quality video: Evidence from security surveillance. *Psychological Science, 10*, 243–248.

Chiroro, P. & Valentine, T. (1995). An investigation of the contact hypothesis of the own race bias in face recognition. *Quarterly Journal of Experimental Psychology A: Human Experimental Psychology, 48A*, 897–894.

Clark, S.E. (2005). A re-examination of the effects of biased lineup instructions in eyewitness identification. *Law and Human Behaviour, 29*, 395–424.

Clark, S.E., Howell, R.T. & Davey, S.L. (2008). Regularities in eyewitness identification. *Law and Human Behavior, 32*, 187–218.

Clark, S.E. & Tunnicliff, J.L. (2001). Selecting lineup foils in eyewitness identification: Experimental control and real-world simulation. *Law and Human Behavior, 25*, 199–216.

Coupe, T. & Griffiths, M. (1996). *Solving residential burglary*. Crime Detection and Prevention Series No. 77. London: Home Office.

Craik, F.I.M. & Byrd, M. (1982). Aging and cognitive deficits: The role of attentional resources. In F.I.M. Craik & S. Trehub (Eds.) *Aging and cognitive processes* (pp.191–211). New York: Plenum.

Cutler, B.L. & Penrod, S.D. (1995). *Mistaken identifications: The eyewitness, psychology, and the law*. New York: Cambridge University Press.

Cutler, B.L., Penrod, S.D. & Dexter, H.R. (1990). Juror sensitivity to eyewitness identification evidence. *Law and Human Behavior, 14*, 185–192.

Cutler, B.L., Penrod, S.D. & Martens, T.K. (1987). The reliability of eyewitness identification: The role of system and estimator variables. *Law and Human Behavior, 11*, 233–258.

Darling, S., Valentine, T. & Memon, A. (2008). Selection of lineup foils in operational contexts. *Applied Cognitive Psychology, 22*, 159–169.

Davies, G. & Thasen, S. (2000). Closed circuit television: How effective an identification aid? *British Journal of Psychology, 91*, 411–426.

Deffenbacher, K.A. (1994). Effects of arousal on everyday memory. *Human Performance, 7*, 141–161.

Deffenbacher, K.A., Bornstein, B.H., Penrod, S.D. & McGorty, E.K. (2004). A meta-analytic review of the effects of high stress on eyewitness memory. *Law and Human Behavior, 28*, 687–706.

Deffenbacher, K.A. & Loftus, E.F. (1982). Do jurors share a common understanding concerning eyewitness behavior? *Law and Human Behavior, 6*, 15–30.

Devlin Committee Report: *Report of the Committee on Evidence of Identification in Criminal Cases*, 1976. Cmnd 338 134/135, 42.

Dodson, C.S. & Krueger, L.E. (2006). I misremember it well: Why older adults are unreliable eyewitnesses. *Psychonomic Bulletin and Review, 13*, 770–775.

Dysart, J.E., Lindsay, R.C.L., Hammond, R. & DuPuis, P.R. (2001). Mug shot exposure prior to lineup identification: Interference, transference, and commitment effects. *Journal of Applied Psychology, 86*, 1280–1284.

Dysart, J.E., Lindsay, R.C.L., MacDonald, T.K. & Wicke, C. (2002). The intoxicated witness: Effects of alcohol on identification accuracy from show-ups. *Journal of Applied Psychology, 87*, 170–175.

Ebbesen, E.B. & Flowe, H.D. (2002). *Simultaneous v. sequential lineups: What do we really know?* Retrieved 12 July 2008 from www-psy.ucsd.edu/ per cent7eeebbesen/SimSeq.htm

Ebbinghaus, H. (1885). *Memory: A contribution to experimental psychology*. Leipzig: Duncker and Humblot.

Ellis, H.D., Shepherd, J.W. & Davies, G.M. (1980). The deterioration of verbal descriptions of faces over different delay intervals. *Journal of Police Science and Administration, 8*, 101–106.

Gabbert, F., Brewer, N. & Hope, L. (2007, July). *Effects of co-witness confidence on identification decisions.* Seventh Biennial Conference of the Society for Applied Research in Memory and Cognition, Lewiston.

Gabbert, F., Hope, L. & Fisher, R. (2009). Protecting eyewitness evidence: Examining the efficacy of a self-administered interview tool. *Law and Human Behavior, 33*(4), 298–307.

Gabbert, F., Memon, A. & Allan, K. (2003). Memory conformity: Can eyewitnesses influence each other's memories for an event? *Applied Cognitive Psychology, 17*, 533–543.

Gabbert, F., Memon, A., Allan, K. & Wright, D.B. (2004). Say it to my face: Examining the effects of socially encountered misinformation. *Legal and Criminological Psychology, 9*, 215–227.

Gabbert, F., Memon, A. & Wright, D.B. (2006). Memory conformity: Disentangling the steps towards influence during a discussion. *Psychonomic Bulletin and Review, 13*, 480–485.

Gorenstein, G.W. & Ellsworth, P.C. (1980). Effect of choosing an incorrect photograph on a later identification by an eyewitness. *Journal of Applied Psychology, 65*, 616–622.

Granhag P.A., Strömwall, L.A. & Hartwig, M. (2005). Eyewitness testimony: Tracing the beliefs of Swedish legal professionals. *Behavioral Sciences and the Law, 23*, 709–727.

Greathouse, S.M. & Kovera, M.B. (2008). Instruction bias and lineup presentation moderate the effects of administrator knowledge on eyewitness identification. *Law and Human Behavior.* DOI 10.1007/s10979-008-9133-0. Retrieved 7 July 2008 from www.springerlink.com/content/653110767808kt43/fulltext.pdf

Harris, M.J. & Rosenthal, R. (1985). Mediation of interpersonal expectancy effects: 31 meta-analyses. *Psychological Bulletin, 97*, 363–386.

Henderson, Z., Bruce, V. & Burton, A.M. (2001). Matching the faces of robbers captured on video. *Applied Cognitive Psychology, 15*, 445–464.

Hope, L., Ost, J., Gabbert, F., Healey, S. & Lenton, E. (2008). 'With a little help from my friends …': The role of co-witness relationship in susceptibility to misinformation. *Acta Psychologica, 127*, 476–484.

Hope, L. & Wright, D. (2007). Beyond unusual? Examining the role of attention in the weapon focus effect. *Applied Cognitive Psychology, 21*, 951–961.

Hosch, H.M. & Platz, S.J. (1984). Self-monitoring and eyewitness identification. *Personality and Social Psychology Bulletin, 10*, 289–292.

Howie, P. & Roebers, C.M. (2007). Developmental progression in the confidence–accuracy relationship in event recall: Insights provided by a calibration perspective. *Applied Cognitive Psychology, 21*, 871–893.

Huff, C.R., Rattner, A. & Sagarin, E. (1996). *Convicted but innocent: Wrongful conviction and public policy.* Thousand Oaks, CA: Sage.

Innocence Project (2007). Available from http://innocence-project.org/docs/newsletter_0607.html, retrieved 9 September 2009.

Jacoby, L.L. (1999). Ironic effects of repetition: Measuring age-related differences in memory. *Journal of Experimental Psychology: Learning, Memory, and Cognition, 25*, 3–22.

Kassin, S.M. & Sommers, S.R. (1997). Inadmissible testimony, instructions to disregard, and the jury: Substantive versus procedural considerations. *Personality and Social Psychology Bulletin, 23*, 1046–1054.

Kassin, S.M., Tubb, V.A., Hosch, H.M. & Memon, A. (2001). On the 'general acceptance' of eyewitness memory research. *American Psychologist, 56*, 405–416.

Keast, A., Brewer, N. & Wells, G.L. (2007). Children's metacognitive judgments in an eyewitness identification task. *Journal of Experimental Child Psychology, 97*, 286–314.

Kebbell, M.R. & Milne, R. (1998). Police officers' perceptions of eyewitness performance in forensic investigations. *Journal of Social Psychology, 138*, 323–330.

Kemp, R., Towell, N. & Pike, G. (1997). When seeing should not be believing: Photographs, credit cards and fraud. *Applied Cognitive Psychology, 11*, 211–222.

Klorman, R., Weissberg, R.P. & Wiesenfeld, A.R. (1977). Individual differences in fear and autonomic reactions to affective stimuli. *Psychophysiology, 14*, 45–51.

Kovera, M.B., Russano, M.B. & McAuliff, B.D. (2002). Assessment of the commonsense psychology underlying Daubert – legal decision makers' abilities to evaluate expert evidence in hostile work environment cases. *Psychology Public Policy and Law, 8*, 180–200.

Kramer, T.H., Buckhout, R. & Eugenio, P. (1990). Weapon focus, arousal and eyewitness memory – attention must be paid. *Law and Human Behavior, 14*, 167–184.

Lampinen, J.M., Scott, J., Leding, J.K., Pratt, D. & Arnal, J.D. (2007). 'Good, you identified the suspect … but please ignore this feedback': Can warnings eliminate the effects of post-identification feedback? *Applied Cognitive Psychology, 21*(8), 1037–1056.

Lavrakas, P.J., Buri, J.R. & Mayzner, M.S. (1976). A perspective of the recognition of other race faces. *Perception and Psychophysics, 20*, 475–481.

Leippe, M.R. (1995). The case for expert testimony about eyewitness memory. *Psychology Public Policy and Law, 1*, 909–959.

Lindsay, R.C.L., Semmler, C., Weber, N., Brewer, N. & Lindsay, M.R. (2008). How variations in distance affect eyewitness reports and identification accuracy. *Law and Human Behavior, 32*, 526–535.

Lindsay, R.C.L. & Wells, G.L. (1980). What price justice? Exploring the relationship between lineup fairness and identification accuracy. *Law and Human Behavior, 4*, 303–314.

Lindsay, R.C.L. & Wells, G.L. (1985). Improving eyewitness identifications from lineups: Simultaneous versus sequential lineup presentation. *Journal of Applied Psychology, 70*(3), 556–564.

Lindsay, R.C.L., Wells, G.L. & O'Connor, F. (1989). Mock juror belief of accurate and inaccurate eyewitnesses: A replication. *Law and Human Behavior, 13*, 333–340.

Lindsay, R.C.L, Wells, G.L. & Rumpel, C.M. (1981). Can people detect eyewitness-identification accuracy within and across situations? *Journal of Applied Psychology, 66*, 79–89.

Loftus, E.F. (1980). *Memory.* Reading, MA: Addison-Wesley.

Loftus, E.F. (2005). Planting misinformation in the human mind: A 30-year investigation of the malleability of memory. *Learning and Memory, 12*, 361–366.

Loftus, E.F., Loftus, G.R. & Messo, J. (1987). Some facts about 'weapon focus'. *Law and Human Behavior, 11*, 55–62.

Loftus, E.F., Miller, D.G. & Burns, H.J. (1978). Semantic integration of verbal information into a visual memory. *Journal of Experimental Psychology: Human Learning and Memory, 4*, 19–31.

Loftus, E.F. & Palmer, J.C. (1974). Reconstruction of automobile destruction: An example of the interaction between language and memory. *Journal of Verbal Learning and Verbal Behaviour*, 13, 585–589.

Logie, R.H., Baddeley, A.D. & Woodhead, M.M. (1987). Face recognition, pose and ecological validity. *Applied Cognitive Psychology*, 1, 53–69.

Luus, C.A.E. & Wells, G.L. (1991). Eyewitness identification and the selection of distracters for lineups. *Law and Human Behavior*, 15(1), 43–57.

Luus, C.A.E. & Wells, G.L. (1994a). The malleability of eyewitness confidence: Co-witness and perseverance effects. *Journal of Applied Psychology*, 79(5), 714–723.

Luus, C.A.E. & Wells, G.L. (1994b). Determinants of eyewitness confidence. In D.F. Ross, J.D. Read & M.P. Toglia (Eds.) *Adult eyewitness testimony: Current trends and developments* (pp.348–362). New York: Cambridge University Press.

Maas, A. & Kohnken, G. (1989). Eyewitness identification: Simulating the 'weapon effect'. *Law and Human Behavior*, 13, 397–408.

Macleod, C. & Mathews, A. (1991). Biased cognitive operations in anxiety – accessibility of information or assignment of processing priorities. *Behavior Research and Therapy*, 29, 599–610.

Mandler, G. (1980). Recognizing: The judgment of previous occurrence. *Psychological Review*, 87, 252–271.

McClelland, J.L. & Chappell, M. (1998). Familiarity breeds differentiation: A subjective-likelihood approach to the effects of experience in recognition memory. *Psychological Review*, 105, 724–760.

McCloskey, M. & Zaragoza, M. (1985). Misleading postevent information and memory for events – Arguments and evidence against memory impairment hypotheses. *Journal of Experimental Psychology – General*, 114, 1–16.

McConkey, K.M. & Roche, S.M. (1989). Knowledge of eyewitness memory. *Australian Psychologist*, 24, 377–384.

Meissner, C.A. (2002). Applied aspects of the instructional bias effect in verbal overshadowing. *Applied Cognitive Psychology*, 16, 911–928.

Meissner, C.A. & Brigham, J.C. (2001). A meta-analysis of the verbal overshadowing effect in face identification. *Applied Cognitive Psychology*, 15, 603–616.

Meissner, C.A., Tredoux, C.G., Parker, J.F. & MacLin, O.H. (2005). Eyewitness decisions in simultaneous and sequential lineups: A dual-process signal detection theory analysis. *Memory and Cognition*, 33, 783–792.

Memon, A. (2008). Eye witness research: Theory and practice. In D.V. Canter & R. Žukauskienė (Eds.) *Psychology and law*. Aldershot: Ashgate.

Memon, A. & Gabbert, F. (2003). Unraveling the effects of sequential presentation in culprit present lineups. *Applied Cognitive Psychology*, 17, 703–714.

Memon, A., Hope, L., Bartlett, J. & Bull, R. (2002). Eyewitness recognition errors: The effects of mugshot viewing and choosing in young and old adults. *Memory and Cognition*, 30, 1219–1227.

Memon, A., Hope, L. & Bull, R.H.C. (2003a). Exposure duration: Effects on eyewitness accuracy and confidence. *British Journal of Psychology*, 94, 339–354.

Memon, A., Vrij, A. & Bull, R. (2003b). *Psychology and law: Truthfulness, accuracy and credibility of victims, witnesses and suspects* (2nd edn). Chichester: Wiley.

Metropolitan Police (2005). 'Police investigation continues into the 7/7 bombings'. *Metropolitan Police Bulletin* 222, 18 July 2005. Available from: http://cms.met.police.uk/news/major_operational_announcements/terrorist_attacks/police_investigation_continues_into_the_7_7_bombings, retrieved 12 March 2008.

Morgan, C.A., Hazlett, G., Doran, A., Garrett, S., Hoyt, G., Thomas, P. *et al.* (2004). Accuracy of eyewitness memory for persons encountered during exposure to highly intense stress. *International Journal of Law and Psychiatry*, 27, 265–279.

NACRO (2002). *To CCTV or not to CCTV? A review of current research into the effectiveness of CCTV systems in reducing crime.* Publication Number 2002062800. London: Author.

Narby, D.J., Cutler, B.L. & Penrod, S.D. (1996). The effects of witness, target, and situational factors on eyewitness identifications. In S.L. Sporer, R.S. Malpass & G. Koehnken (Eds.) *Psychological issues in eyewitness identification* (pp.23–52). Mahwah, NJ: Lawrence Erlbaum.

Noon, E. & Hollin, C.R. (1987). Lay knowledge of eyewitness behaviour: A British survey. *Applied Cognitive Psychology*, 1, 143–153.

O'Rourke, T.E., Penrod, S.D., Cutler, B.L. & Stuve, T.E. (1989). The external validity of eyewitness identification research: Generalizing across subject populations. *Law and Human Behavior*, 13, 385–395.

Overbeck, J.L. (2005). Beyond admissibility: A practical look at the use of eyewitness expert testimony in the Federal courts. *New York University Law Review*, 80(6), 1895–1920.

Paterson, H.M. & Kemp, R.I. (2006). Co-witnesses talk: A survey of eyewitness discussion. *Psychology Crime and Law*, 12, 181–191.

Phillips, M.R., McAuliff, B.D., Kovera, M.B. & Cutler, B.L. (1999). Double-blind photoarray administration as a safeguard against investigator bias. *Journal of Applied Psychology*, 84, 940–951.

Pickel, K.L., French, T.A. & Betts, J.M. (2003). A cross-modal weapon focus effect: The influence of a weapon's presence on memory for auditory information. *Memory*, 11, 277–292.

Pike, G., Kemp, R., Brace, N., Allen, J. & Rowlands, G. (2000). The effectiveness of video identification parades. *Proceedings of The British Psychological Society*, 8, 44.

Potter, R. & Brewer, N. (1999). Perceptions of witness behaviour–accuracy relationships held by police, lawyers and jurors. *Psychiatry, Psychology and Law*, 6, 97–103.

Pozzulo, J.D. & Dempsey, J. (2006). Biased lineup instructions: Examining the effect of pressure on children's and adults' eyewitness identification accuracy. *Journal of Applied Social Psychology*, 36, 1381–1394.

Pozzulo, J.D. & Lindsay, R.C.L. (1998). Identification accuracy of children versus adults: A meta-analysis. *Law and Human Behavior*, 22, 549–570.

Read, J.D. (1995). The availability heuristic in person identification – the sometimes misleading consequences of enhanced contextual information. *Applied Cognitive Psychology*, 9, 91–121.

Read, J.D. & Desmarais, S.L. (in press). Lay knowledge of eyewitness issues: A Canadian survey. *Applied Cognitive Psychology*.

Read, J.D., Vokey, J.R. & Hammersley, R. (1990). Changing photos of faces: Effects of exposure duration and photo similarity on recognition and the accuracy–confidence relationship. *Journal of Experimental Psychology: Learning, Memory and Cognition*, 16, 870–882.

Roberts, A. & Ormerod, D. (2008). Identification in court. In D. Canter & R. Zukauskien (Eds.) *Bridging the gap between psychology and law: International perspectives*. Aldershot: Ashgate.

Rubin, D.C. & Wenzel, A.E. (1996). One hundred years of forgetting: A quantitative description of retention. *Psychological Review*, 103, 743–760.

Ryu, J.J. & Chaudhuri, A. (2007). Differences in attentional involvement underlying the perception of distinctive and typical faces. *Perception*, 36, 1057–1065.

Salthouse, T.A. (1982). *Adult cognition: An experimental psychology of human aging*. New York: Springer-Verlag.

Scheck, B., Neufeld, P. & Dwyer, J. (2000). *Actual innocence*. New York: Doubleday.

Scott-Brown, K.C. & Cronin, P.D. (2007). An instinct for detection: Psychological perspectives on CCTV surveillance. *The Police Journal*, 80, 287–305.

Shapiro, P.N. & Penrod, S. (1986). Meta-analysis of facial identification studies. *Psychological Bulletin*, 100, 139–156.

Shaw, J.S., III & McClure K.A. (1996). Repeated postevent questioning can lead to elevated levels of eyewitness confidence. *Law and Human Behavior*, 20, 629–654.

Shaw, J.S., III, Garcia, L.A. & McClure, K.A. (1999). A lay perspective on the accuracy of eyewitness testimony. *Journal of Applied Social Psychology*, 29, 52–71.

Slater, A. (1994). *Identification parades: A scientific evaluation*. London: Police Research Group. Home Office.

Sokolov, E.N. (1963). *Perception and the conditioned reflex*. Oxford: Pergamon Press.

Sporer, S.L. (1992). *Das Wiedererkennen von Gesichtern* [Recognizing faces]. Weinheim: Beltz/Psychologie Verlags Union.

Sporer, S.L., Penrod, S., Read, D. & Cutler, B. (1995). Choosing, confidence, and accuracy: A meta-analysis of the confidence–accuracy relation in eyewitness identification studies. *Psychological Bulletin*, 118, 315–327.

Steblay, N.M. (1992). A meta-analytic review of the weapon focus effect. *Law and Human Behavior*, 16, 413–424.

Steblay, N. (1997). Social influence in eyewitness recall: A meta-analytic review of lineup instruction effects. *Law and Human Behavior*, 21, 283–297.

Steblay, N., Dysart, J., Fulero, S. & Lindsay, R.C.L. (2001). Eyewitness accuracy rates in sequential and simultaneous lineup presentations: A meta-analytic comparison. *Law and Human Behavior*, 25, 459–473.

Stuesser, L. (2005). Experts on eyewitness identification: I don't just see it. *International Commentary on Evidence*, 3(1), Article 2.

Thomas, M. (1993). *Every mother's nightmare: The killing of James Bulger*. London: Pan.

Tredoux, C.G. (2002). A direct measure of facial similarity and its relation to human similarity perceptions. *Journal of Experimental Psychology: Applied*, 8(3), 180–193.

Tuckey, M.R. & Brewer, N. (2003). The influence of schemas, stimulus ambiguity, and interview schedule on eyewitness memory over time. *Journal of Experimental Psychology: Applied*, 9, 101–118.

Valentine, T., Darling, S. & Memon, A. (2006). How can psychological science enhance the effectiveness of identification procedures? An international comparison. *Public Interest Law Reporter*, 11, 21–39.

Valentine, T, Darling, S. & Memon, A. (2007). Do strict rules and moving images increase the reliability of sequential identification procedures? *Applied Cognitive Psychology*, 21, 933–949.

Valentine, T., Harris, N., Colom Piera, A. & Darling, S. (2003a). Are police video identifications fair to African-Caribbean suspects? *Applied Cognitive Psychology*, 17, 459–476.

Valentine, T. & Heaton, P. (1999). An evaluation of the fairness of police line-ups and video identifications. *Applied Cognitive Psychology*, 13, S59–S72.

Valentine, T. & Mesout, J. (2008). Eyewitness identification under stress in the London Dungeon. *Applied Cognitive Psychology*, 23(2), 151–161.

Valentine, T., Pickering, A. & Darling, S. (2003b). Characteristics of eyewitness identification that predict the outcome of real lineups. *Applied Cognitive Psychology*, 17, 969–993.

Wagenaar, W.A. & van der Schrier, J.H. (1996). Face recognition as a function of distance and illumination: A practical tool for use in the courtroom. *Psychology, Crime and Law*, 2, 321–332.

Weber, N. & Brewer, N. (2004). Confidence–accuracy calibration in absolute and relative face recognition judgments. *Journal of Experimental Psychology: Applied*, 10, 156–172.

Wells, G.L. (1978). Applied eyewitness-testimony research: System variables and estimator variables. *Journal of Personality and Social Psychology*, 36, 1546–1557.

Wells, G.L. (1984). The psychology of lineup identifications. *Journal of Applied Social Psychology*, 14, 89–103.

Wells, G.L. & Bradfield, A.L. (1998). 'Good, you identified the suspect': Feedback to eyewitnesses distorts their reports of the witnessing experience. *Journal of Applied Psychology*, 83, 360–376.

Wells, G.L. & Bradfield, A.L. (1999). Measuring the goodness of lineups: Parameter estimation, question effects, and limits to the mock witness paradigm. *Journal of Applied Psychology, 13,* S27–S39.

Wells, G.L., Charman, S.D. & Olson, E.A. (2005). Building face composites can harm lineup identification performance. *Journal of Experimental Psychology: Applied, 11,* 147–157.

Wells, G.L. & Hasel, L.E. (2007). Facial composite production by eyewitnesses. *Current Directions in Psychological Science, 16,* 6–16.

Wells, G.L., Leippe, M.R. & Ostrom, T.M. (1979). Guidelines for empirically assessing the fairness of a lineup. *Law and Human Behavior, 3,* 285–293.

Wells, G.L. & Olson, E. (2003). Eyewitness identification. *Annual Review of Psychology, 54,* 277–295.

Wells, G.L., Olson, E. & Charman, S. (2002). Eyewitness identification confidence. *Current Directions in Psychological Science, 11,* 151–154.

Wells, G.L. & Quinlivan, D.S. (2008). Suggestive eyewitness identification procedures and the Supreme Court's reliability test in light of eyewitness science: 30 years later. *Law and Human Behavior, 33*(1), 1–24.

Wells, G.L. & Seelau, E.P. (1995). Eyewitness identification: Psychological research and legal policy on lineups. *Psychology, Public Policy, and Law, 1,* 765–791.

Wise, R.A. & Safer, M.A. (2004). What US judges know and believe about eyewitness testimony. *Applied Cognitive Psychology, 18,* 427–443.

Wright, D.B. (2006). Causal and associative hypothesis in psychology: Examples from eyewitness testimony research. *Psychology, Public Policy and Law, 12,* 190–213.

Wright, D.B., Boyd, C.E. & Tredoux, C.G. (2001). A field study of own-race bias in South Africa and England. *Psychology, Public Policy, and Law, 7,* 119–132.

Wright, D.B. & McDaid, A.T. (1996). Comparing system and estimator variables using data from real line-ups. *Applied Cognitive Psychology, 10,* 75–84.

Wright, D.B., Self, G. & Justice, C. (2000). Memory conformity: Exploring misinformation effects when presented by another person. *British Journal of Psychology, 91,* 189–202.

Wright, D.B. & Skagerberg, E.M. (2007). Post-identification feedback affects real eyewitnesses. *Psychological Science, 18,* 172–178.

Wright, D.B. & Sladden, B. (2003). An own gender bias and the importance of hair in face recognition. *Acta Psychologica, 114,* 101–114.

Wright, D.B. & Stroud, J.N. (2002). Age differences in lineup identification accuracy: People are better with their own age. *Law and Human Behavior, 26,* 641–654.

Yarmey, A.D. (2001). Expert testimony: Does eyewitness memory research have probative value for the courts? *Canadian Psychology–Psychologie Canadienne, 42,* 92–100.

Yuille, J.C. & Cutshall, J.L. (1986). A case study of eyewitness memory of a crime. *Journal of Applied Psychology, 71,* 291–301.

12

Children as Witnesses

Graham Davies and Kathy Pezdek

When children are victims of a crime, frequently their testimony is the only prosecution evidence in the case. This is because crimes against children – particularly crimes of child abuse – typically occur in situations that are unlikely to involve other evidence or other witnesses. It is thus especially important that child witness evidence be collected, documented and evaluated carefully. Elsewhere, Pezdek (1994) has argued about the costs and benefits of weighing children's eyewitness accounts too lightly or too heavily. Suffice it to say here, that weighing children's eyewitness accounts too lightly can result in the perpetuation of child victimisation; weighing children's eyewitness accounts too heavily can result in false charges that can permanently destroy families. In light of the dire consequences at both ends of this criterion, it is critical for forensic investigators and the courts to understand the factors that affect children's memory for traumatic events, and to follow procedures that are most likely to maximise the veracity of children's accounts.

In this chapter we first present what is known from the scientific research about factors that affect the veracity of children's memory, with the focus on the topics of the suggestibility of children's memory and false memories for childhood events. Second, we review research on interview procedures and the special measures that have been suggested for interviewing children and presenting their evidence at court and discuss the experimental and field research on the utility of these procedures. Together, these two sections of this chapter provide the reader with a solid understanding of how best to interview children and present their evidence at court and the sci-

entific basis for these recommendations. We believe that professionals are more likely to follow the suggested procedures if they understand the rationale for them.

Definition of 'Memory Suggestibility' and 'False Memory'

Following Quas *et al.* (1997) and Pezdek and Lam (2007) we distinguish between the terms 'suggestibility' and 'false memory'. Suggestibility refers to children's susceptibility to suggestions about non-existent details of events that were actually witnessed. False memory refers to children's development of a memory for an entirely new event that never occurred. In a typical suggestibility study, children first experience an entire event (e.g. a magic show staged in the classroom or laboratory) and after a short or long delay, a target detail of the event is suggested to have occurred even though it did not (e.g. 'When the magician touched you on the arm …'). In this line of research, the suggested details are typically presented in the questions asked by the interviewer. Accuracy and suggestibility are then assessed by analysing children's responses to free-recall questions (e.g. 'What happened on the day that you saw the magic show?'), or specific non-leading questions (e.g. 'Which magic trick did you like best?') or misleading questions (e.g. 'The magician touched you on the arm, didn't he?'). If the child recalls the suggested detail or assents to the occurrence of the target detail, we say that their memory has been suggestively influenced. In a typical false memory study, children are first asked about true events that are documented by parents to have occurred. Then, once the interviewer's credibility is established, the child is questioned about a target false event that did not happen to the child. If the child assents to a target false event or actually reports details of the false event beyond that conveyed by the interviewer, we say that the child has a false memory for the event.

Inappropriate or insensitive interview procedures can produce both suggested memories and false memories. However, given what we know about the cognitive processes that underlie the formation of suggested memories and false memories, it is easier to suggestively plant memories for (a) details of an event that did occur than (b) an entirely new event that did not occur. This is because memories for events are schematically organised. That is, when we remember an event, we form a structured schema for what occurred. The schema includes details of the event that actually occurred along with generic details of that event that typically occur. For example, children do not retain an accurate memory for every birthday party that they ever attended; memory is just not that precise a process. Rather, they retain a schema for what they have learned typically occurs at a birthday party, and related to this, they retain some specific details for what occurred at a specific birthday party. This effect was also reported in a study on memory for crimes by Holst and Pezdek (1992). In this study they found that people have schemata for typical crimes and there is a high rate of agreement regarding the actions that comprise these crimes. Further, when participants in this study were presented a mock trial that activated these schemata, they incorporated into their memory schema-relevant information not presented, along with the information that was presented.

Whereas memories for specific details of events typically fade over time relatively quickly, the schema for an event is more likely to persist in memory over time and actually becomes more intractable with repeated exposure to instances of that event. People are familiar with this aspect of their memory and are not surprised if they forget a detail of an event but are disturbed if they forget the occurrence of a whole event. Thus, if an interviewer questions a child about an event that the child remembers, but a detail of the event that the child cannot remember is suggested by the interviewer, the child is likely to infer that that detail probably occurred but they just forgot it. On the other hand, if an interviewer questions a child about an event that he or she has no memory of, the child is not likely to infer that they just forgot that this

occurred; rather, the more likely conclusion is that the interviewer is wrong, the event did not happen. This explains why it is easier to suggestively plant memories for (a) details of an event that did occur than (b) an entirely new event that did not occur. This general disbelief is also evidenced by the lower assent rates to false events that usually occur during initial interviews compared to subsequent interviews.

Factors that Affect the Suggestibility of Children's Memory

From childhood to middle adulthood, memory improves with age. When children experience an event – whether in a laboratory or a real-world setting – their recall and recognition memory for the event increase with age. When children are asked to free recall an interaction with a stranger (Leippe et al., 1991), a story (Saywitz, 1987), or even a list of words (Flavell et al., 1966), there is a linear increase in the completeness of recall across the age span from preschool to early adolescence. However, it is important to note that although younger children typically free recall 'less' than older children, their recall is not less accurate; that is, omission errors (i.e. leaving something out) are more common with younger children but commission errors (i.e. recalling something erroneous) are generally rare and do not reliably differ with age. Thus, if a child is asked a direct question about 'what happened?' the content of their response is likely to be accurate but incomplete.

There are a number of explanations for the increase in memory with age. One leading hypothesis relates these increases to differences in the way information is encoded by children and adults. According to this view, when people encode information, they form two different types of memory representations, verbatim and gist (Brainerd & Reyna, 2004). Verbatim memories preserve the literal details of what was experienced; gist memories preserve the essence of what was experienced. Whereas adults utilise relatively more gist than verbatim memory encoding, children's memory is better characterised as more verbatim than gist. Because gist memories persist longer than verbatim memories, children's memories tend to be less enduring than those of adults. Further, weak memories are more vulnerable to suggestibility than strong memories; this finding is known as the *memory trace strength theory of suggestibility* (Pezdek & Roe, 1995). This theory explains why young children's memory is generally more vulnerable to suggestibility than that of older children and adults. However, under some conditions children's memory is quite accurate and not likely to be suggestively influenced. In this section we will explore six factors that affect the suggestibility of children's memory. In general, as suggested by the memory trace strength theory of suggestibility, stronger memories are more resistant to suggestibility than weaker memories. As each of the six factors is discussed, it will be seen that the conditions that produce stronger memories are associated with less memory suggestibility than those that produce weaker memories.

Event knowledge

It is a general characteristic of memory that individuals remember an event better if they have prior knowledge about the event. This is true for children as well. Prior knowledge aids memory because it helps people attend to, encode and integrate relevant details of events into a well-organised interconnected structure that is more resistant to forgetting and more accessible during retrieval attempts. Ornstein *et al.* (2006) tested 4- to 7-year-old children on their memory for a paediatric exam. The children were tested multiple times over six months. Prior to the exam, half of the children were also tested on their prior knowledge about routine doctor visits. At each age, children with more prior knowledge recalled more information about the target paediatric exam. Although as predicted, prior knowledge increased with age, the association between prior knowledge and recall of the target event was significant even with the effect of age removed.

Similar results were reported by Goodman *et al.* (1997) with 3- to 10-year-old children who were tested on their memory for a medical procedure called voiding cystourethrogram fluoroscopy (VCUG). This is an invasive, stressful and embarrassing medical procedure for which the child is awake. One relationship that Goodman and her colleagues assessed in this research is the extent to which prior knowledge of the VCUG affected memory for the target incidence of the procedure. The amount of correct information recalled about the target event was significantly associated with prior knowledge as well as age. Interestingly, memory accuracy was not predicted by the number of prior VCUG procedures *per se*. Rather, prior knowledge in this study came from parents' explanations to their child prior to the procedure. It is important to note, however, that when children recalled the target event, they were not simply recalling the information provided in advance by their parent. The detailed memory required to answer the questions

posed by Goodman and her colleagues went far beyond what was provided by parents.

How does prior knowledge specifically affect the suggestibility of memory? Ceci *et al.* (1981) presented 7- and 10-year-old children with a story that included familiar television characters. The story presented some information that was inconsistent with children's prior knowledge of the characters. Three weeks later, when asked to recall what they had been presented in the target event, the children recalled information that was consistent with their prior knowledge but inconsistent with what they actually heard in the story. This is similar to the results reported above by Holst and Pezdek (1992), that when individuals recalled a mock trial for a robbery, they recalled a high percentage of information that was relevant to their schema for a robbery even though this information was not presented in the mock trial. Together, these results suggest that in recall of an experienced event, prior knowledge often trumps the information that was actually experienced. Further, in this latter study, most participants did not distinguish between information that was presented in the mock trial by the eyewitness versus the attorney. This finding, along with results from a number of other studies, suggests that interviewers should be cautious how they word their questions as information in the questions themselves can become incorporated into memory along with the information that was actually presented, especially if the wording of the question includes schema-consistent information.

It is also important to note that experts have difficulty assessing the veracity of children's accounts if the children are describing a familiar event about which they have prior knowledge. Blandon-Gitlin *et al.* (2005) had children describe a true or a fabricated event. Half described a familiar event; half described an unfamiliar event. Two judges trained on the Criterion Based Content Analysis (CBCA) rated transcripts of these descriptions. The CBCA is worldwide, the most commonly used deception detection technique (for a discussion see Vrij, 2008). CBCA scores were more strongly influenced by the event familiarity than the actual veracity of the event, and CBCA scores were significantly correlated with age. Thus, prior knowledge produced accounts that appeared to be true, even if they were not.

Repeated experience

As would be predicted from the research on prior knowledge, it is also the case that repeated experience with an event produces a stronger memory for the event and more resistance to suggestibility. This is important to know because some criminal acts against children, particularly sexual abuse, are typically repeated experiences that do not occur in isolation. Pezdek and Roe (1995) presented 4- and 10-year-old children with a slide sequence of an event in which four target slides were presented one or two times each. Afterwards, a narrative was read to the children which misled them about two target items. On a subsequent recognition memory test, for both age groups, stronger memories (those viewed twice) were more resistant to suggestibility than weaker memories (those viewed once). Powell et al. (1999, Experiment 1) extended these findings to an event that children experienced once or six times over several weeks. They too reported that repetition increased memory for the event and resistance to suggestibility. In this study, repetition had a powerful effect of attenuating the detrimental effects of suggestibility, age and delay on memory. However, if the event was repeatedly experienced with some details varying across repetitions, when children were subsequently asked about specific details of an event that varied across repetitions, the accuracy of their memory was less reliable and they were more vulnerable to suggestively worded questions. These findings suggest that children's memories of repeated experiences involving fixed details will be strong, and accounts based on those memories are likely to be accurate.

However, caution must be taken because experts in the field may not be able to make accurate veracity assessments of children's accounts of events that were experienced once versus multiple times. Pezdek et al. (2004) conducted a CBCA analysis of accounts of the children who had received a VCUG procedure in several previously published studies, including the Goodman et al. (1994) study discussed above. The CBCA scores were significantly lower for accounts of children who had experienced the VCUG procedure only once, than for those who had experienced the procedure multiple times. This finding suggests that true accounts of an event experienced only once are less likely to be judged as true than true accounts of an event experienced multiple times.

Time delay

The time delay between when a child observes an event and when he or she recalls the event is a forensically important factor that affects the quantity and accuracy of information in memory. This is because it is common that children will not provide testimony about criminal acts until months or even years after the original event. Hershkowitz (2006) reported that in a sample of about 26,000 children suspected of abuse in Israel, 73.7 per cent delayed disclosures at least a month after the alleged crime. The effect of delayed disclosure is compounded by typically very lengthy criminal proceedings.

In an early study on this factor, Flin et al. (1992) tested adults and children 6 and 9 years of age on their memory for a target event, an argument among adults. One day after observing the event, the mean number of accurate responses to interview questions did not significantly differ among the three age groups. However, at the five-month interview, the number of accurate responses was significantly reduced for both age groups of children, but not for adults, and the decline in memory over time was greater for the 6-year-olds than the 9-year-olds. This finding is consistent with the results of a field study conducted by Lamb et al. (2000). In this study, the accounts of children involved in 145 cases of alleged sexual abuse were examined. Long delays between each event and the child's reporting (5 to 14 months) were associated with significantly less information reported by children than short delays (less than a month).

How does time delay specifically affect the suggestibility of memory? Consistent with the memory trace strength theory of suggestibility (Pezdek & Roe, 1995), as memory decreases with time delay, the vulnerability to suggestibility increases. This finding has been reported in a number of studies, including that by Burgwyn-Bailes et al. (2001). In this study, 3- to 7-year-old children were interviewed three times (after a few days, six weeks, and one year) following treatment at a plastic surgeon's office for facial lacerations. The interview protocols included questions about the procedure that did occur as well as suggestive questions about events that did not occur (e.g. 'Dr. Hanna played some music for you, didn't he?', 'Did Dr. Hanna put something cold on the hurt place?'). Although the recall of accurate information was high and the decline in recall of accurate information over time was not significant (78 per cent, 73 per cent and 72 per cent respectively), the false alarm rates to misleading questions significantly increased over time (12 per cent, 18 per cent and 22 per cent respectively).

Similar results were reported by Bruck et al. (1995) who tested 5-year-old children's memory for an inoculation from a paediatrician. Immediately after the inoculation, the children were given misleading information about how much the inoculation had hurt (e.g. some children were told that it did not hurt very much when in fact it did). When this suggestive information was presented one week after the inoculation, the children were not misled by the suggestion. However, when they were presented this information one year later, their responses were suggestively influenced and they were more likely to underestimate the level of pain they had actually experienced. Together the findings are clear that children's vulnerability to suggestibility increases over time.

Multiple interviews

In forensic settings, it is common in many countries for children to be repeatedly interviewed, often over long time periods. Malloy *et al.* (2007) recently reported that in a sample of sexual abuse cases in Los Angeles, children participated in formal interviews on average 4.26 times, with the range being 1 to 25 times – and this did not include informal interviews with family members or therapists. What is the effect of multiple interviews on children's memory and suggestibility?

Although, as discussed above, memory generally declines with time, some of the deleterious effects of time delay can be offset by reinstating memory for an experienced event with repeated questioning. Tizzard-Drover and Peterson (2004) assessed the reliability of children's reports at various delay intervals after an emergency visit to the hospital for treatment of a traumatic injury (e.g. a bone fracture). Children ages 3 to 9 were either interviewed immediately after the visit and at various intervals over one year, or for the first time at the one-year mark. Although memory declined over the one-year duration, the early interview had a beneficial effect on subsequent memory; children reported more information in the one-year interview if they had also been interviewed immediately following the hospital visit than if they had not. Similar results were reported by Peterson *et al.* (2004).

In a related study, Peterson *et al.* (2001) interviewed children 2–13 years of age about an injury they received that required emergency room treatment. The children were interviewed at one week, six months, one year and two years. The focus of this study was on the relationship between the consistency of recall over time and the accuracy of memory. They found that information that was recalled consistently by a child at all four interviews was virtually always correct. However, information that

was sometimes omitted was less likely to be accurately recalled. Further, although new information that was recalled for the first time at the six-month interview was more likely to be accurate than inaccurate, new information that was recalled for the first time at the one-year or two-year interviews was equally likely to be wrong as right for all but the 12–13-year-old children.

A very different story emerges when we examine the effect of repeated questions about a fictitious event. Erdmann *et al.* (2004) interviewed first-grade children four times about one real and one fictitious event. The interviews included various suggestive techniques such as inviting speculation, selectively reinforcing desired information recalled, and offering possible details of the alleged fictitious event. Over the course of multiple interviews, there was a significant increase in the assents to the fictitious event. Further, by the fifth interview, experts could not discriminate between the children's accounts of the true and suggested events on the basis of the CBCA scores rated by experts. The finding that repeated exposure increases assents to fictitious suggestions was reported with adults by Zaragoza and Mitchell (1996).

How do multiple interviews specifically affect the suggestibility of memory? Consistent with the memory trace strength theory of suggestibility, these findings show that multiple interviews, especially soon after an event, when performed in a non-suggestive manner, reactivate event memory, keeping it strong and more resistant to misleading suggestions. However, the repeated use of direct and leading questions across interviews can significantly distort children's accounts.

Stress and emotions

The effects of stress and emotions on event memory are not straightforward. Whereas it seems clear that the occurrence of emotional events is highly memorable, memory for the details of these same events appears to be impaired. For example, although few people will ever forget the occurrence of the events of 9/11, their memory for exactly what transpired that day is less than impressive and, in fact, is comparable to memory for non-emotional events (Pezdek, 2003). Also, Morgan *et al.* (2004) recently tested active-duty military personnel in military survival school on their ability to identify the individual who interrogated them for almost 40 minutes after only a 24-hour delay. Recognition memory was significantly lower in a high-stress than low-stress interrogation condition (hit rates in the photospread condition were 34 per cent and 76 per cent respectively). They attributed this effect to stress-induced elevation of hormones such as cortisol that are known to impair declarative memory. Findings consistent with these have been reported in a number of other studies as well.

However, in a forensic setting, when an interviewer is assessing a child's memory for a traumatic event, the question of interest is rarely whether traumatic events are remembered better than non-traumatic events. Rather, what is important is knowing whether the factors that apply to memory for non-traumatic events apply as well to memory for traumatic events. Pezdek and Taylor (2002) recently reviewed the research on children's and adults' memories for a range of traumatic events (i.e. medical procedures, natural disasters, violent events, sexual abuse). The conclusion from this extensive review was that the cognitive factors that affect memories for non-traumatic events also apply to memories for traumatic events, and although memories for traumatic experiences are generally correct, they appear to be no more accurate than other memories. Similar to memories of non-traumatic experiences, memories for traumatic events (a) are not impervious to forgetting, (b) show an age-related pattern whereby accuracy and amount of details increases with age during childhood, (c) are likely to be accurately remembered in gist but not veridical form, and (d) are susceptible to distortion by suggestive influences. It seems clear that traumatic memories are subject to the same laws that govern memory for everyday experiences. It is possible, however, that traumatic memories may survive longer and in greater detail than everyday memories if they are repeatedly and accurately rehearsed either mentally or in recounting to others.

Parental support

Two important conditions that foster accurate and complete event memory by children are the nature of the parent–child conversations that occur about experienced events and the quality of the parent–child relationship. A number of researchers have documented that memory for events experienced by a young child and his or her mother is affected by the mother's style of discourse about the shared event. Tessler and Nelson (1996) observed mothers and their 3- to 3½-year-old children as they visited a natural history museum; their conversations were recorded. One week later, the children were interviewed about the visit, without the mothers present. An open-ended interview format was used first, followed by a standard set of questions that probed for recall of specific objects and scenes in the museum. No child recalled any of the information about their visit to the museum that they had not talked about with their mother. Child-only conversation or mother-only conversation was not sufficient for recall; all recalled information had been part of a joint conversation with the child and the mother. Further, children's accounts were more detailed and more accurate if their mother had conversed with them in a dynamic narrative style rather than a static paradigmatic style. These findings are consistent with the notion developed by Nelson (1993) and Fivush (1998) that autobiographical memory is socially constructed.

Regarding the effect of parental attachment style on the accuracy and completeness of children's memory, this relationship has been reported in a number of studies by Goodman and her colleagues (see, for example, Alexander et al., 2002; Edelstein et al., 2004; Goodman et al., 1997). Specifically, mothers' attachment patterns have been reported to be strongly associated with the accuracy and completeness of children's event memory. The interpretation given for this association is that mothers who show secure attachment with their child – defined by lower levels of anxiety and less discomfort with close relationships – are more likely to discuss negative events that their child may experience. These conversations help the child encode and store coherent, well-elaborated representations of events that are more likely to persist in memory. And, consistent with the memory trace strength theory of suggestibility, these memories are more resistant to suggestibility. In Bruck and Ceci's (1999) review of the research on the suggestibility of children's memory, five of the six studies on this topic reported that children of securely attached mothers were less likely to acquiesce to misleading suggestions than children of insecurely attached mothers. In addition, Clarke-Stewart et al. (2004) reported that fathers' positive support of their child as well as mothers' healthy attachment style were related to reduced suggestibility in children.

It is important to note that there are conditions that can reduce the suggestibility of children who have insecurely attached parents. Bottoms et al. (2007) had a supportive or an unsupportive interviewer question 6- to 7-year-old children about an event that they had experienced. Each child was categorised as having parents with a secure or insecure attachment style. When interviewed about their memory for the event, children of securely attached parents were not affected by interview style, but children of insecurely attached parents were more accurate when interviewed by the supportive than the unsupportive interviewer. The supportive interview style reduced the deleterious effect of insecure parental attachment on the suggestibility of children's event memory.

Children's True and False Autobiographical Memories

In general, children's autobiographical memory is remarkably accurate. Across a number of studies, Peterson and her colleagues assessed the recall of 2- to 13-year-old children for a traumatic event that they had experienced – an injury that had required emergency treatment (see, for example, Peterson & Bell, 1996; Peterson et al., 2001). The children were interviewed immediately, or after six months, one year or two years, about components of their injury experience and components of their hospital treatment. Memories for components of their injury were recalled impressively well (75 per cent of these components were accurately recalled in the initial interview), and this information was recalled more accurately and in more detail than were components of their hospital treatment (initially only 57 per cent of these components were accurately recalled). Over the two-year delay, there was a modest but significant increase in the number of inaccurate details recalled by the children about components of their injury; these proportions increased from 7 per cent of all details recalled initially to 16 per cent of all details recalled after two years. These results are typical of findings from other studies that have also examined children's memory for autobiographical events. Although children's memory inaccuracies are more likely to occur under some conditions than others, overall, even young children's accounts of traumatic life events are remarkably accurate.

However, under some conditions, children as well as adults can and do construct false memories for events that they never experienced. It has been demonstrated that false events can be implanted in memory under specific conditions that are now beginning to be understood. Loftus and Pickrell (1995) had 24 volunteers suggest to offspring or younger siblings that they had been lost in a shopping mall when they were about 5 years old. Later, six of the 24 subjects reported either full or partial memory for the false event. Ceci et al. (1996) read preschool children a list of true and false events and asked them to 'think real hard about each' and 'try to remember if it really happened.' In the initial session, 44 per cent of the children

age 3 to 4 years and 25 per cent of the children age 5 to 6 years remembered at least one of the false events. However, children's false memories did not tend to persist over time. Huffman et al. (1997) tested 22 of the children in the study by Ceci et al. (1996) two years later when they were 71–89 months of age. Each child was re-interviewed at the site of their original interview. They were shown cards describing the same true and false events included in the original study and for each were asked to think really hard about the event and to indicate whether the event had ever happened. Of the 37 true events recalled by these children in the original study, 29 (78 per cent) were recalled two years later. However, of the 39 false events assented to in the original study, only 9 (23 per cent) were assented to two years later; 77 per cent of the initial false assents were recanted two years later. These results raise serious doubts about whether the original 'assents to false events' reflect true false memories or simply compliance with authority.

A number of procedures have been used to suggestively plant false events in memory. Two of the most effective procedures – and they are important because of their forensic relevance – are imagining the suggested event and presenting the individual with a photograph related to the suggested event. Mazzoni and Memon (2003), for example, reported that after imagining a target event, 40 per cent of participants reported having a memory for the event, in comparison with only 23 per cent of those in the exposure-only condition. The effect of imagination on memory has also been assessed using the imagination inflation procedure in which imagined events on the Life Events Inventory increased belief that the events occurred in one's childhood (Garry et al., 1996; Garry & Polaschek, 2000).

In terms of presenting photographs to suggestively plant false events in memory, Wade et al. (2002) presented individuals with photographs of themselves as children and asked them to think about and remember the depicted event. Most of the photographs presented true events. One photograph depicted a false event; the photo was created by digitally inserting an image of the child into the basket of a hot-air balloon. Of the 20 participants, 50 per cent were classified as reporting partial or complete false memories of the hot-air balloon ride. In a more subtle manipulation, Lindsay et al. (2004) asked college-age participants to think hard and try to remember two true events and one false event from their childhood. Half of the participants were presented with the group photograph of their school class from the year that the false event was reported to have occurred. Simply presenting the class photograph, not even a photograph of the suggested event, significantly increased the reported rate of false memory. In terms of forensic interview techniques, these results suggest that although providing children with old photographs might be useful to cue long-forgotten memories, it might also serve to contribute to the construction of false memories.

This research should be considered with caution, however, in light of recent studies in which it has been reported that false memories are significantly less likely to be suggestively planted for events that are relatively implausible. Pezdek et al. (1997, Experiment 2) had 20 confederates read descriptions of one true event and two false events to a younger sibling or close relative. One false event was plausible and the other was implausible. The more plausible false event described the relative being lost in a mall while shopping; the less plausible false event described the relative receiving an enema. One week later, only three participants recalled a false event, and all three of the false events were the more plausible: being lost in a shopping mall. This finding was replicated in an additional experiment, in which a suggested description of a Catholic ritual was more likely to be accepted as a true memory for Catholics than for Jews; the result was reversed when the false memory concerned a Jewish ritual. Similar results were reported with children by Pezdek and Hodge (1999). Further, although, as reported above, imagination can induce false autobiographical memories, Pezdek et al. (2006) reported that this finding is restricted to imagining plausible events. In their study, imagining plausible events increased individuals' beliefs that the event had occurred to them, but imagining implausible events had no effect on occurrence ratings.

Together, these results raise questions about the relative ease of suggestively planting false memories for traumatic events such as childhood sexual abuse. These findings suggest that it should be easier to plant false memories of childhood sexual abuse with individuals for whom sexual contact with an adult during their childhood is more plausible than with those for whom sexual contact with an adult during their childhood is less plausible.

Guidelines for Effective Child Witness Interviewing

The preceding review of research on children's memory demonstrates that children can provide reliable accounts of events which they have observed or experienced, but immaturities in their processing and recall of events make them vulnerable to specific types of error. If justice is to be done to both victims and the accused, care must be taken not only in eliciting accounts from children in the investigative phase. Based on laboratory findings and on field research with actual child witnesses, a range of procedures have been developed for interviewing child witnesses with the minimum of suggestion, but there are no accepted international guidelines for how children should be interviewed (Lamb et al., 2008). However, the evidence-based procedures developed in England and Wales and first published as the *Memorandum of Good Practice on Video Recorded Interviews with Child Witnesses for Criminal Proceedings* (Home Office, 1992) and later revised and updated as *Achieving Best Evidence in Criminal Proceedings* (Home Office, 2002) have been highly influential in shaping procedures both in the United Kingdom and elsewhere (Bull, 1995).

Memorandum of Good Practice

The original *Memorandum* guidelines were derived from an examination of existing research and best practice and were drafted by a forensic psychologist (Professor Ray Bull) working with a lawyer (Professor Diane Birch). The guidelines were introduced in conjunction with a statutory requirement that, in future, all investigative interviews with children by police officers and social workers should be videotaped and these videotapes would form the basis of the Evidence in Chief offered by the prosecution at trial. Thus, rather than the child being interviewed in court, the judge and jury would view the videotaped interview. The tape would also be made available to the defence who would have the opportunity to examine the interview for suggestive questioning techniques and adherence to *Memorandum* guidelines. While the guidelines are not enforceable in law, serious departures can be brought to the attention of the court and may lead to the judge requiring the interview to be edited or in more extreme cases, ruling that an interview is inadmissible with the consequent collapse of the case.

The *Memorandum* interview uses a phased approach: all interviews should contain four distinct and distinguishable phases, with a different function for each phase. The initial *rapport building phase* was designed to have two functions: first, to break down social barriers between the interviewer and child by discussing age-appropriate topics such as sport, television or popular music and second, to impart the *ground rules* for the interview. This would include exploring the child's understanding of (a) truth and lies and the social importance of telling the truth, (b) communicating to the interviewer when they do not know or do not understand a question, and (c) the fact that they and they alone know what did and did not occur. For most children, being closely questioned by an adult who does not actually know the 'right' answer will be a novel situation.

Only after the rapport building phase should the purpose of the interview be broached via an open prompt designed to trigger free narrative from the child (such as 'Why have we asked you to come here today?'). This *free narrative phase* enables the child to provide an account of the events under investigation in their own words. Interviewers are encouraged to tolerate pauses and to sustain the child's narrative through 'active listening' techniques, including verbal ('what happened next?') and non-verbal (eye-contact; head nodding) signs of attention. The accounts provided by free narrative are then elaborated through the *questioning phase*. In the questioning phase, interviewers are encouraged to employ open-ended questions which elicit extended answers from the child. Only when open questions are ineffective are interviewers advised to use *specific, yet non-leading* ('What colour were his eyes') or *closed* questions ('Were his eyes blue or brown?'). The dangers of the use of *leading* questions are stressed ('I take it his eyes were blue?'), and they are only recommended when other forms of questioning fail to engage the child in the topic of the interview. When the interviewer is satisfied that the child has nothing further to say or if the child is showing signs of fatigue or distress (the *Memorandum* advised a limit of one hour on the length of any interview), the interviewer can move to the final *closure phase*. In this phase, the interviewer is advised to summarise what the child has said about the events under investigation, using, as far as possible, the child's own words. In closing, it is suggested that the interview refer to some of the rapport topics and then thank the child.

The original *Memorandum* interview became a popular and widely used device in trials involving child complainants and witnesses. No official figures are available, but it is estimated that around 20,000 such interviews have been conducted per annum in England and Wales and many of these have figured as evidence in civil and criminal cases involving allegations of physical or sexual abuse (Westcott & Jones, 2003). But how effective were the guidelines in shaping interviewer behaviour? With

the permission of the children and interviewers involved, Sternberg *et al.* (2001) analysed the content of 119 interviews conducted by officers from 13 different regional police forces in England and Wales and found substantial departures from recommended practice. In the rapport stage, elements of the ground rules were frequently omitted – 86 per cent failed to emphasise that 'don't know' was an acceptable response. In the narrative phase, only a bare majority (52 per cent) began with an open question (the children themselves spontaneously raised the issue of concern in a further 17 per cent of cases). In the questioning phase, only 6 per cent of questions were open-ended, compared to 47 per cent which were specific and non-leading and 29 per cent closed. Guidance on the use of leading questions was more effective, with only 5 per cent of questions being categorised as leading. Later surveys (Westcott & Kynan 2006; Westcott *et al.*, 2006) produced similar findings regarding non-compliance with the *Memorandum* guidelines; in addition, Westcott and Kynan (2006) reported that around half of all interviews contained at least one instance of an inaccurate or inappropriate précis of what the child had actually said, which could have had serious consequences for their subsequent evidence at court.

Achieving Best Evidence

These discrepancies between recommendations and interviewer performance influenced the revised and updated guidance, *Achieving Best Evidence in Criminal Proceedings* (Home Office, 2002). This document retained the four-phase interview structure, but sought to assist interviewer compliance with guidelines in the rapport phase by providing checklists of issues to be covered and explicit interviewer scripts for raising the focus of the interview and probing the child's understanding of truth and lies. In the interview phase, there was an even greater emphasis on the need for open-ended questions and an explicit recognition that interview techniques needed to be geared to the developmental age of the child. A revision of this document published in 2007 further increased the proscriptive and checklist element in an effort to increase compliance from interviewers.

NICHD Investigative Protocol

The problems of encouraging free narrative from children and the avoidance of other, more suggestive questioning techniques were also the theme of the

NICHD Investigative Protocol developed by Lamb, Sternberg and others at the National Institute for Mental Health in the USA (Lamb *et al.*, 2008). This style of interview also employs the four-phased approach of the *Memorandum*, but seeks to encourage an extended narrative from the child by utilising a *practice interview* where children are encouraged to describe in detail a familiar neutral event from their own lives, such as recent birthday party. Interviewers are taught scripted prompts designed to elicit extended narrative from the child and how to rephrase questions in an open form; specific questions are very much a last option. Research in Israel and the USA confirms that the introduction of the NICHD Protocol and the intensive training associated with it significantly increased the average amount of useful information derived from the free narrative phase of investigative interviews. The amount of such information secured in this phase rose from 16 to 49 per cent and the number of open-ended questions employed from 10 to 35 per cent.

How do guidelines accommodate to the characteristics of children's memory?

Do guidelines take sufficient account of what is known about the strengths and vulnerabilities of children's memory? It is instructive to take each of the areas of concern described earlier in the chapter and to see how existing guidelines accommodate these issues, beginning with *event knowledge*. The great majority of children testifying in the courts will be doing so about alleged sexual or physical abuse by a perpetrator known to the child within a familiar context (such as the family home) and which has occurred repeatedly (Myers, 1998). Children certainly do testify to one-off, unfamiliar events, such as road accidents or crimes they have witnessed as a bystander. In these situations, it is important that the child interviews are conducted by officers experienced in interviewing children (Chapman & Perry, 1995). Much testimony will be concerned with *repeated experience*, where events follow a regular pattern (as in inter-familial child sexual abuse). This will give rise to a robust gist memory of what normally occurs, which according to trace strength theory, will be resistant to suggestion. To gather further detail, *Achieving Best Evidence* advises interviewers to elicit an initial account and then to ask about the first and most recent assaults or those which were different or distinctive in some way. Difficulties may arise in those legislatures which require the defendant to be charged with an offence committed on a specific day at a given location, when confusions may arise as to the specific features of that event and so detract from the general credibility of the allegation; again specialised techniques may be required to reduce such confusions (Powell & Thomson, 2003).

As the earlier review confirms, *time delay* is clearly an important factor in determining quality of recall and may interact with suggestibility, such that weaker memories may be more prone to suggestible responding. Delay can be a particular problem with intra-familial sex abuse cases, where a delayed disclosure can raise issues of the extent to which the child's narrative has been influenced by discussions with siblings or the non-accused parent. In a recent case the English courts took the view that a delay of 9 weeks between disclosure and interview was too long for the consequent investigative interview to be reliable (*R v. Powell (Michael John)* [2006]). It would be unfortunate if this decision were applied arbitrarily to future cases, without any consideration of the age of the child, the duration of the alleged abuse or the potential opportunities for contamination.

As noted earlier, *multiple interviews* are very much a feature of US investigations, but are much rarer in England and Wales subsequent to the introduction of video-recorded interviews. The taped interview is the evidence in chief and the only reason for further interviews prior to trial would be the emergence of further allegations or the introduction of a line of defence by the accused which required questions to be raised with the child. As the review emphasises, multiple interviews can have positive as well as negative effects. In the absence of further interviews, it is important that trials take place in a timely manner to ensure that children's evidence remains as fresh and detailed as possible. In England and Wales, a recent survey reported an average delay of 11.6 months between committal and trial for child witnesses in abuse cases (Plotnikoff & Woolfson, 2004). As reported in the first half of this chapter, the presence of *parental support* can also be a significant factor, both in maintaining an accurate memory of events and sustaining children emotionally over the long delays that frequently occur in the resolution of legal issues.

Adhering to guidelines

As has been demonstrated, the guidance described in *Achieving Best Evidence* and the *NICHD Investigative Protocol* incorporates important safeguards designed to deal with the strengths and vulnerabilities of children's memory. However, as shown by the Sternberg *et al.* (2001) study with the original *Memorandum*, there is often a yawning gulf between recommendations and actual practice. It is necessary for interviewers to apply guidelines consistently. Lamb *et al.* (2008) highlighted the need for intensive training to instil a style of questioning that is inconsistent with normal everyday discourse with children. To maintain these interview skills, it is also important to periodically refresh and review this training. Westcott *et al.* (2006) have also demonstrated the value of intensive training in improving and entrenching *Memorandum* interview skills for the English police. Currently, officers in the UK typically receive only a one-week training course in interviewing children, which is not formally assessed or accredited, and there is no national standard or provision for continuing performance appraisal (Davies *et al.*, 1998). Until such procedures are instituted, the likelihood of false allegations by children against adults is increased. Equally, the number of cases coming to court based on good evidence from child victims sufficient to convict guilty adults may continue to disappoint child protection agencies. But an informative interview in itself is insufficient to ensure convictions. Child witnesses must not only provide sound evidence prior to trial, they must also survive presenting this evidence in the often alien and intimidating atmosphere of the courtroom.

Child Witnesses in Court

Witnesses giving evidence under the adversarial system of justice practised in the UK and the USA normally appear for one or other 'side' in a criminal case – the prosecution or the defence. Witnesses are first taken through their evidence by the advocate for their own side (Examination in Chief) before being cross-examined by the advocate for the other side. The aim of cross-examination is to identify gaps and inconsistencies in the witness's evidence and generally to undermine the credibility of the witness. Most witnesses find being examined and cross-examined at court to be a taxing and stressful experience, and this is even more the case for child witnesses. Indeed, concerns about appearing in court account for part of the high rates of attrition observed in court cases involving children. Some estimates suggest as few as 10 per cent of all allegations initially reported by children lead to prosecution at trial (Spencer & Flin, 1993).

Special Measures

Surveys of child witnesses scheduled to make court appearances reveal that children have widespread apprehensions about appearing in court (Goodman *et al.*, 1992). In recent years, legislatures have introduced a range of Special Measures designed to make the giving of evidence by children a less gruelling and traumatic experience (Hill & Sales, 2008). Since 1999, advocates in England and Wales have had access to such a range of Special Measures, which can be granted at the discretion of the presiding judge.

Some Special Measures, such as *the removal of court dress* during the hearing of children's evidence and *the clearing of public galleries* when evidence is given by witnesses in sexual assault cases, have always been available at the discretion of the presiding judges but are now promoted as good practice in all cases involving children. The *use of an intermediary* is a recent innovation which provides young or learning-disabled witnesses access to a qualified adult to assist in the communication of questions and interpretation of answers during pre-trial investigation and court appearance. Intermediaries initially assess witnesses for communication deficits and brief investigators and courtroom personnel accordingly. Despite some initial resistance from advocates and judges, intermediaries have been successfully introduced into courts in England and Wales and a national scheme is now in operation (Plotnikoff & Woolfson, 2007a). By contrast, the provision of *support persons* for vulnerable witnesses is a responsibility shared by a number of different organisations and national provision is patchy. The best schemes provide support to child witnesses on the progress of their case, teach relaxation strategies, familiarise witnesses with the court and court procedures and accompany the child to court (Plotnikoff & Woolfson, 2007b).

One final Special Measure, the *use of the video link or the 'Live Link'* as it is known in the UK, has been available in the English courts since 1989. The Live Link allows the child to give evidence from a small room away from the main courtroom and to have that evidence relayed via video to the courtroom for viewing by judge, advocates and jury. This procedure obviates the need for the child to enter the courtroom or see the accused during testimony. Its use is currently mandatory for child witnesses in the English courts, a decision that has attracted considerable controversy and a great deal of research.

Video links for child witnesses were pioneered in the USA, but are not routinely used there because of concerns that it may violate the Sixth Amendment to the US

Constitution which enshrines the right of the accused to confront his or her accuser (Hill & Sales, 2008). In American courts, the judge and the advocates are sequestered with the child and the whole proceeding is broadcast to the courtroom. In England and Wales, the child alone is out of court and the cameras are interactive, allowing questions to be asked by the judge and advocates from court and the child's response to be relayed to the court. In terms of video image, the child sees whosoever is speaking from the court, while the court always sees the child. This same arrangement is also available in Australia, New Zealand and Scotland (Davies, 1999). In England and Wales, there is currently a presumption that all child witnesses (defined as those under 17 years of age) will give evidence via the Live Link rather than in open court, though in some other legislatures access to the Live Link is granted by the judge only to children who have a proven fear of the accused (Hill & Sales, 2008).

The Live Link on trial

Does the availability of the Live Link permit children to give more complete, accurate and credible evidence than testifying in open court? A number of field studies have been conducted assessing the evidence of children using the Live Link and the reaction of court professionals to this innovation. Davies and Noon (1991) reported observations of 100 trials where the Live Link was employed by children during its first two years of use in the English courts. Compared to a sample of Scottish children giving evidence in open court, the Live Link children were rated as significantly less unhappy, more forthcoming in the their evidence and more audible, a finding supported by the comments from advocates with experience of both the traditional and new system. Overall, the majority of judges and defence and prosecution advocates who had familiarity with the new system favoured its continuing employment in child witness trials. Positive effects on evidence quality were not observed by Murray (1995) in a study when the Live Link was introduced in Scotland. Whatever differences emerged between the two methods favoured the children giving evidence in open court. However, differences in legal procedure between the two legislatures may explain this contradiction. Judges in Scotland have discretion over the granting of the use of the Live Link and at the time of the study, these were exercised conservatively, such that the Live Link group comprised much younger witnesses, giving evidence in more serious cases and who were more likely to be testifying against a parent. Murray

found widespread support for the Live Link among users and their parents, such that 73 per cent of the Live Link sample said they would have found difficulty in testifying in open court, and 92 per cent were glad to have had the opportunity to testify this way. Similar positive views from users on the value of the Live Link were reported by Cashmore and De Haas (1992) in a study in Australia. Live Link users were judged more relaxed than open-court witnesses, but no other differences emerged. However, among the in-court witnesses, those who had applied for the Live Link and been refused were rated as significantly less competent and more stressed than any other group. In summary, these field studies demonstrate that children value the Live Link and the protection it provides from the court and from sight of the accused, with consequent positive effects on the child's confidence and demeanour. But, how is video-mediated testimony received by the jury?

Impact of video-mediated testimony on jurors

Davies and Noon (1991) reported that a major concern for both judges and advocates was that video-mediated evidence might not have the same impact on a jury as in-court testimony and that concern has continued to influence attitudes among lawyers in all legislatures that give discretion over ways of testifying (Cashmore, 2002). It colours debate not merely on the use of the Live Link, but also the playing of pre-recorded interviews as a substitute for the child's live examination at court (Davies, 1999). A number of experiments have explored this issue, of which the most impressive are a pair of studies by Goodman and colleagues (Goodman et al., 1998; Orcutt et al., 2001). These studies were marked by a high degree of realism, with children being exposed to an incident involving a confederate who was later 'tried' in a mock trial. The mock trials were conducted in a real courtroom, using actual courtroom personnel. Children were examined and cross-examined by advocates about the incident either live in court, or in a room outside court with their testimony relayed via a video link. The children either told the truth regarding the incident or were coached to lie.

In accord with earlier findings, children giving evidence via video showed less pre-trial anxiety and were more relaxed when examined at court than children giving their evidence live and they were able to provide more complete and detailed accounts than those testifying live (Goodman et al., 1998). However, the perceptions of the citizen jurors taken prior to deliberation favoured live over video testimony. Children giving evidence on the witness stand were rated more positively on a range of factors, including attractiveness, believability and honesty, compared to those on video and jurors were less likely to convict when testimony was given via video link. However, following deliberation, there was an overall drop in the likelihood of a guilty verdict from 48 to 32 per cent and any differences in guilty verdicts based on live as opposed to video evidence disappeared. Jurors were as likely to return a guilty verdict when the child was telling the truth concerning the allegation (42 per cent) as when the child was lying (38 per cent) and once again these figures were unaffected by whether jurors saw the evidence given live or on video This latter finding is of significance to the debate among lawyers regarding whether seeing a child on the video link denies lawyers and jurors vital cues to deception which would be available to them when the child takes the stand (Montoya, 1993). Extensive research by psychologists has demonstrated that lay observers are actually very poor at detecting deception from non-verbal cues and frequently confuse signs of stress with indicators of deception (Vrij, 2008). Landstrom (2008) recently confirmed Goodman's findings that jurors generally perceive video evidence less positively than live evidence, but also that live evidence does not lead to any more accurate decisions than video, regardless of whether the British or US versions of the video link are employed.

In summary, there is now considerable evidence that video-mediated evidence does lack some of the immediacy of evidence from the stand and that this influences juror perceptions of the child. However, there is no evidence that live evidence leads to any more accurate decisions by jurors. Any loss of immediacy needs to be balanced against the advantages for the child witness, both in terms of the quality of their evidence and the reduced impact of testifying on their future well-being (Davies, 1994).

Are these Special Measures enough?

Are these Special Measures sufficient to address the concerns of children at court? Unfortunately they do not address another area of concern mentioned by child witnesses – cross-examination. In contrast to investigative interviews, where leading questions are discouraged, advocates in court are free to use leading questions repeatedly with children. If lawyers are unable to undermine their testimony through such questions, they are free to imply that the child is not merely mistaken but a liar, an allegation

which can damage a child's self-esteem, particularly where the defendant is found not guilty, but the child has told the truth (Henderson, 2002). The great American jurist Wigmore (1974) described cross-examination as 'beyond any doubt, the greatest legal engine ever invented for the discovery of truth' (p.1367). Research has demonstrated that this does not appear to apply to children.

Zajac and Hayne (2003) demonstrated that this adage does not apply to children. Children aged 5–6 years visited their local police station where they took part in four key events, including having their mugshots and fingerprints taken. A few weeks later, some of the children were exposed to misinformation about two events which had not occurred on their visit and six weeks afterward they underwent a brief investigative interview concerning the visit, which included both a free narrative and specific questions about what had and had not happened. Consistent with laboratory findings reviewed earlier, the children showed some impact of the misleading information, but their accuracy for the real events remained high. Some nine months after the visit, after viewing a video recording of their interview, they were 'cross-examined' by a confederate on both the real and misleading events, using styles of questioning derived from actual cross-examinations at court. Some 85 per cent of the children changed their statements from those given in the investigative interview under cross-examination. Moreover, children were as likely to change their testimony away from their earlier true accounts as to correct an item on which they had been misled.

A later study using the same paradigm demonstrated that 9–10-year-old children were less vulnerable to leading questions in cross-examination, but they still changed over 40 per cent of their statements and again cross-examination led to significantly greater inaccuracy relative to the children's original statements (Zajac & Hayne, 2006). It could be argued that this disturbing result could have been mitigated by Special Measures provisions, such as the intervention of an intermediary or a judge to request that the advocate rephrase questions. However, given that the questions were derived from actual trials, such an intervention would be unlikely to be successful.

Conclusions

Research reviewed in the opening section of this chapter has consistently demonstrated that children are capable of observing events and testifying with sufficient accuracy as to assist triers of fact in establishing whether these events occurred. This same research has highlighted the strengths and weaknesses of children's testimony and how these are modulated by the age of the child and the circumstances surrounding the events. The movement to develop new guidelines for interviewing children aimed at maximising truth and minimising suggestion in children's evidence has also been research-led. Studies in the concluding section have highlighted the additional difficulties that face children when they recount a witnessed event, not to a friendly interviewer, but to an advocate in the adversarial cauldron of the courtroom. Special Measures such as the video link can assist children in being heard in court. However, these measures do not assist children with coping with cross-examination, which emerging research suggests may often have a destructive, rather than constructive role in establishing the truth of children's allegations.

The challenge for psychologists is to come up with an alternative method of assessing the veracity of children's allegations. In countries that employ the European inquisitorial system of justice, the veracity of children's evidence is often assessed by examining their statements for the presence of features believed to be associated with truthfulness. The most commonly employed technique involves the CBCA. However, research suggests that the CBCA is in need of further development as the presence and number of key 'truth' features present can be influenced by the developmental age of the child and their familiarity with events, quite independent of the truth or falsity of the statement (Blandon-Gitlin *et al.*, 2005). Major problems still remain in developing techniques for effectively collecting and assessing children's evidence within an adversarial system of justice. Solutions to these problems will require greater understanding and unprecedented cooperation between lawyers and psychologists.

References

Alexander, K.W., Goodman, G.S., Schaaf, J.M., Edelstein, R.S., Quas, J.A. & Shaver, P.R. (2002). The role of attachment and cognitive inhibition in children's memory and suggestibility for a stressful event. *Journal of Experimental Child Psychology*, 83, 262–290.

Blandon-Gitlin, I., Pezdek, K., Rogers, M. & Brodie, L. (2005). Detecting deception in children: An experimental study of the effect of event familiarity on CBCA ratings. *Law and Human Behavior*, 29, 187–197.

Bottoms, B.L., Quas, J.A. & Davis, S.L. (2007). The influence of the interviewer-provided social support on children's suggestibility, memory, and disclosures. In M. Pipe, M.E. Lamb, Y. Orbach & A. Cederborg (Eds.) *Child sexual abuse: Disclosure, delay, and denial* (pp.135–157). Mahwah, NJ: Lawrence Erlbaum.

Brainerd, C.J. & Reyna, V.F. (2004). Fuzzy-trace theory and memory development. *Developmental Review*, 24, 396–439.

Bruck, M. & Ceci, S.J. (1999). The suggestibility of children's memory. *Annual Review of Psychology*, 50, 419–439.

Bruck, M., Ceci, S.J., Francoeur, E. & Barr, R.J. (1995). 'I hardly cried when I got my shot!': Influencing children's reports about a visit to their pediatrician. *Child Development*, 66, 193–208.

Bull, R. (1995). Interviewing children in legal contexts. In R. Bull & D. Carson (Eds.) *Handbook of psychology in legal contexts* (pp.235–246). Chichester: Wiley.

Burgwyn-Bailes, E., Baker-Ward, L., Gordon, B.N. & Ornstein, P.A. (2001). Children's memory for emergency medical treatment after one year: The impact of individual difference variables on recall and suggestibility. *Applied Cognitive Psychology*, 15, 25–48.

Cashmore, J. (2002). Innovative procedures for child witnesses. In H. Westcott, G.M. Davies & R. Bull (Eds.) *Children's testimony: A handbook of psychological research and forensic practice* (pp.203–218). Chichester: Wiley.

Cashmore, J. & De Haas, N. (1992). *The use of closed-circuit television for child witnesses in the ACT*. Sydney: Australian Law Reform Commission Research Paper.

Ceci, S.J., Caves, R.D. & Howe, M.J.A. (1981). Children's long term memory for information that is incongruous with their prior knowledge. *British Journal of Psychology*, 72, 443–450.

Ceci, S.J., Huffman, M.L.C., Smith, E. & Loftus, E.F. (1996). Repeatedly thinking about a non-event: Source of misattributions among preschoolers. In K. Pezdek & W.P. Banks (Eds.) *The recovered memory/false memory debate* (pp. 225–244). San Diego, CA: Academic Press.

Chapman, A.J. & Perry, D.J. (1995). Applying the cognitive interview procedure to child and adult eyewitnesses of road accidents. *Applied Psychology: An International Review*, 44, 283–294.

Clarke-Stewart, K.A., Malloy, L.C. & Allhusen, V.D. (2004). Verbal ability, self-control, and close relationships with parents protect children against misleading suggestions. *Applied Cognitive Psychology*, 18, 1037–1058.

Davies, G.M. (1994). Editorial. Live Live Links: Understanding the message of the medium. *Journal of Forensic Psychiatry*, 5, 225–227.

Davies, G.M. (1999). The impact of television on the presentation and reception of children's evidence. *International Journal of Law and Psychiatry*, 22, 241–256.

Davies, G.M., Marshall, E. & Robertson, N. (1998). *Child abuse: Training investigative officers*. Police Research Series Paper No. 94. London: Home Office.

Davies, G.M. & Noon, E. (1991). *An evaluation of the Live Live Link for child witnesses.* London: The Home Office.

Edelstein, R.S., Alexander, K.W., Shaver, P.R., Schaaf, J.M., Quas, J.A., Lovas, G.S. *et al.* (2004). Adult attachment style and parental responsiveness during a stressful event. *Attachment and Human Development, 6,* 31–52.

Erdmann, K., Volbert, R. & Böhm, C. (2004). Children report suggested events even when interviewed in a non-suggestive manner: What are its implications for credibility assessment? *Applied Cognitive Psychology, 18,* 589–611.

Fivush, R. (1998). The stories we tell: How language shapes autobiography. *Applied Cognitive Psychology, 12,* 483–487.

Flavell, J.H., Beach, D.H. & Chinsky, J.M. (1966). Spontaneous verbal rehearsal in a memory task as a function of age. *Child Development, 37,* 283–299.

Flin, R., Boon, J., Knox, A. & Bull, R. (1992). The effect of a five-month delay on children's and adults' eyewitness memory. *British Journal of Psychology, 83,* 323–336.

Garry, M., Manning, C.G., Loftus, E.F. & Sherman, S.J. (1996). Imagination inflation: Imagining a childhood event inflates confidence that it occurred. *Psychonomic Bulletin and Review, 3,* 208–214.

Garry, M. & Polaschek, D.L.L. (2000). Imagination and memory. *Current Directions in Psychological Science, 9,* 6–10.

Goodman, G.S., Pyle-Taub, E., Jones, D.R.H, England, P., Port, L.P., Rudy, L. *et al.* (1992). Emotional effects of criminal court testimony on child sexual assault victims. *Monographs of the Society for Research in Child Development, 57* (Serial No. 229).

Goodman, G.S., Quas, J.A., Batterman-Faunce, J.M., Riddlesbergger, M. & Kuhn, J. (1994). Predictors of accurate and inaccurate memories of traumatic events experienced in childhood. *Consciousness and Cognition, 3,* 269–294.

Goodman, G.S., Quas, J.A., Batterman-Faunce, J.M., Riddlesberger, M.M. & Kuhn, J. (1997). Children's reactions to and memory for a stressful event: Influences of age, anatomical dolls, knowledge, and parental attachment. *Applied Developmental Science, 1,* 54–75.

Goodman, G.S., Toby, A.E., Batterman-Faunce, J.M., Orcutt, H., Thomas, S., Shapiro, C. *et al.* (1998). Face to face confrontation: Effects of closed circuit technology on children's eyewitness testimony and juror's decision, *Law and Human Behavior, 22,* 165–203.

Henderson, E. (2002). Persuading and controlling: The theory of cross-examination in relation to children. In H.L. Westcott, G.M. Davies & R.H.C. Bull (Eds.) *Children's testimony: A handbook of psychological research and forensic practice* (pp.279–294). Chichester: Wiley.

Hershkowitz, I. (2006). Delayed disclosure of alleged child abuse victims in Israel. *American Journal of Orthopsychiatry, 76,* 444–450.

Hill, S.R. & Sales, B.D. (2008). *Courtroom modifications for child witnesses.* Washington, DC: American Psychological Association.

Holst, V.F. & Pezdek, K. (1992). Scripts for typical crimes and their effects on memory for eyewitness testimony. *Applied Cognitive Psychology, 6,* 573–587.

Home Office (1992). *The memorandum of good practice on video recorded interviews with child witnesses for criminal proceedings.* London: Home Office. Available at www.homeoffice.gov.uk/rds/prgpdfs/brf115.pdf, retrieved 20 August 2008.

Home Office (2002). *Achieving best evidence in criminal proceedings: Guidance for vulnerable or intimidated witnesses, including children.* London: Home Office Communication Directorate. Available at www.homeoffice.gov.uk/documents/achieving-best evidence/guidance-witnesses.pdf?view=Binary, retrieved 20 August 2008.

Huffman, M.L., Crossman, A.M. & Ceci, S.J. (1997). 'Are false memories permanent?': An investigation of the long-term effects of source misattributions. *Consciousness and Cognition, 6,* 482–490.

Lamb, M.E., Hershkowitz, I., Orbach, Y. & Esplin, P.W. (2008). *Tell me what happened: Structured investigative interviews of child victims and witnesses.* Chichester: Wiley.

Lamb, M.E., Sternberg, K.J. & Esplin, P.W. (2000). Effects of age and delay on the amount of information provided by alleged sex abuse victims in investigative interviews. *Child Development, 71,* 1586–1596.

Landstrom, S. (2008). *CCTV, Live and videotapes.* Gothenburg, Sweden: University of Gothenburg.

Leippe, M.R., Romanczyk, A. & Manion, A.P. (1991). Eyewitness memory for a touching experience: Accuracy differences between child and adult witnesses. *Journal of Applied Psychology, 76,* 367–379.

Lindsay, D.S., Hagen, L., Read, J.D., Wade, K.A. & Garry, M. (2004). True photographs and false memories. *Psychological Science, 15,* 149–154.

Loftus, E.F. & Pickrell, J.E. (1995). The formation of false memories. *Psychiatric Annals, 25,* 720–725.

Malloy, L.C., Lyon, T.D. & Quas, J.A. (2007). Filial dependency and recantation of child sexual abuse allegations. *Journal of the American Academy of Child and Adolescent Psychiatry, 46,* 162–170.

Mazzoni, G.[A.L.] & Memon, A. (2003). Imagination can create false autobiographical memories. *Psychological Science, 14,* 186–188.

Montoya, J. (1993). Something not so funny happened on the way to conviction: The pretrial interrogation of child witnesses. *Arizona Law Review, 35,* 927–987.

Morgan, C.A., Hazlett, G., Baranosk, M., Doran, A., Southwick, S. & Loftus, E.F. (2004). Accuracy of eyewitness memory for persons encountered during exposure to highly intense stress. *International Journal of Law and Psychiatry, 27,* 265–279.

Murray, K. (1995). *Live television Live Link: An evaluation of its use by child witnesses in Scottish criminal trials.* Edinburgh: HMSO.

Myers, J.O.B. (1998). *Legal issues in child abuse and neglect practice*. Thousand Oaks, CA: Sage.

Nelson, K. (1993). The psychological and social origins of autobiographical memory. *Psychological Science, 4,* 1–8.

Orcutt, H.K., Goodman, G.S., Tobey, A.E., Batterman-Faunce, J.M. & Thomas, S. (2001). Detecting deception in children's testimony: Fact finders' abilities to reach the truth in open court and closed circuit trials, *Law and Human Behavior, 25,* 339–372.

Ornstein, P.A., Baker-Ward, L., Gordon, B.N., Pelphrey, K.A., Tyler, C.S. & Gramzow, E. (2006). The influence of prior knowledge and repeated questioning on children's long-term retention of the details of a pediatric examination. *Developmental Psychology, 42,* 332–344.

Peterson, C. & Bell, M. (1996). Children's memory for traumatic injury. *Child Development, 67,* 3045–3070.

Peterson, C., Moores, L. & White, G. (2001). Recounting the same events again and again: Children's consistency across multiple interviews. *Applied Cognitive Psychology, 15,* 353–371.

Peterson, C., Parsons, T. & Dean, M. (2004). Providing misleading and reinstatement information a year after it happened: Effects on long-term memory. *Memory, 12,* 1–13.

Pezdek, K. (1994). Avoiding false claims of child sexual abuse: Empty promises. *Family Relations, 43,* 258–260.

Pezdek, K. (2003). Event memory and autobiographical memory for the events of September 11, 2001. *Applied Cognitive Psychology, 17,* 1033–1045.

Pezdek, K., Blandon-Gitlin, I. & Gabbay, P. (2006). Imagination and memory: Does imagining implausible events lead to false autobiographical memories? *Psychonomic Bulletin and Review, 13,* 764–769.

Pezdek, K., Finger, K. & Hodge, D. (1997). Planting false childhood memories: The role of event plausibility. *Psychological Science, 8,* 437–441.

Pezdek, K. & Hodge, D. (1999). Planting false childhood memories in children: The role of event plausibility. *Child Development, 70,* 887–895.

Pezdek, K. & Lam, S. (2007). What research paradigms have cognitive psychologists used to study 'false memory,' and what are the implications of these choices? *Consciousness and Cognition, 16,* 2–17.

Pezdek, K., Morrow, A., Blandon-Gitlin, I., Goodman, G.S., Quas, J.A., Saywitz, K.J. *et al.* (2004). Detecting deception in children: Event familiarity affects criterion-based content analysis ratings. *Journal of Applied Psychology, 89,* 119–126.

Pezdek, K. & Roe, C. (1995). The effect of memory trace strength on suggestibility. *Journal of Experimental Child Psychology, 60,* 116–128.

Pezdek, K. & Taylor, J. (2002). Memory for traumatic events. In M.L. Eisen, G.S. Goodman & J.A. Quas (Eds.) *Memory and suggestibility in the forensic interview.* Mahwah, NJ: Lawrence Erlbaum.

Plotnikoff, J. & Woolfson, R. (2004). *In their own words: The experiences of 50 young witnesses in criminal proceedings.* London: NSPCC.

Plotnikoff, J. & Woolfson, R. (2007a). *The 'go between': Evaluation of intermediary pathfinder projects.* London: Home Office. Available at: www.justice.gov.uk/publications/research120607a.htm, retrieved 20 August 2008.

Plotnikoff, J. & Woolfson, R. (2007b). *Evaluation of young witness support: examining the impact on witnesses and the criminal justice system.* London: Home Office. Available at: http://lexiconlimited.co.uk/PDF per cent20files/Young_Witness_Study_Report.pdf, retrieved 20 August 2008.

Powell, M.B., Roberts, K.P., Ceci, S.J. & Hembrooke, H. (1999). The effects of repeated experience on children's suggestibility. *Developmental Psychology, 35,* 1462–1477.

Powell, M.B. & Thomson, D.M. (2003). Improving children's recall of an occurrence of a repeated event: Is it a matter of helping them to generate options? *Law and Human Behavior, 27,* 365–384.

Quas, J.A., Qin, J., Schaaf, J. & Goodman, G.S. (1997). Individual differences in children's and adults' suggestibility and false event memory. *Learning and Individual Differences, 9,* 359–390.

R v. Powell (Michael John) [2006] EWCA Crim 3.

Saywitz, K.J. (1987). Children's testimony: Age-related patterns of memory errors. In S.J. Ceci, M.P. Toglia & D.F. Ross (Eds.) *Children's eyewitness memory* (pp.36–52). New York: Springer-Verlag.

Spencer, J.R. & Flin, R.H. (1993). *The evidence of children: The law and the psychology* (2nd edn). London: Blackstone.

Sternberg, K.J., Lamb, M.E., Davies, G.M. & Westcott, H.L. (2001). The memorandum of good practice: Theory versus application. *Child Abuse and Neglect, 25,* 669–681.

Tessler, M. & Nelson, K. (1996). Making memories: The influence of joint encoding on later recall by young children. In K. Pezdek & W.P. Banks (Eds.) *The recovered memory/false memory debate.* San Diego, CA: Academic Press.

Tizzard-Drover, T. & Peterson, C. (2004). The influence of an early interview on long-term recall: A comparative analysis. *Applied Cognitive Psychology, 18,* 727–743.

Vrij, A. (2008). *Detecting lies and deceit: Pitfalls and opportunities.* Chichester: Wiley.

Wade, K.A., Garry, M., Read, J.D. & Lindsay, D.S. (2002). A picture is worth a thousand lies: Using false photographs to create false childhood memories. *Psychonomic Bulletin and Review, 9,* 597–603.

Westcott, H.L. & Jones, D.P.H. (2003). Are children reliable witnesses to their experiences? In P. Reder, S. Duncan & C. Lucey (Eds.) *Studies in the assessment of parenting* (pp.105–123). Hove: Brunner-Routledge.

Westcott, H.L. & Kynan, S. (2006). Interviewer practice in investigative interviews for suspected child sexual abuse. *Psychology, Crime and Law, 12,* 367–382.

Westcott, H.L., Kynan, S. & Few, C. (2006). Improving the quality of investigative interviews for suspected child abuse: A case study. *Psychology, Crime and Law, 12,* 77–96.

Wigmore, J.J. (1974). *Wigmore on evidence* (revised by J.H. Chadbourne). Vol. 5. Boston, MA: Little Brown.

Zajac, R. & Hayne, H. (2003). I don't think that's what really happened: The effect of cross examination on the accuracy of children's reports. *Journal of Experimental Psychology: Applied, 9,* 187–195.

Zajac, R. & Hayne, H. (2006). The negative effect of cross-examination on children's accuracy: Older children are not immune. *Applied Cognitive Psychology, 20,* 3–16.

Zaragoza, M.S. & Mitchell, K.J. (1996). Repeated exposure to suggestion and the creation of false memories. *Psychological Science, 7,* 294–300.

13

Witness Interviewing

David La Rooy and Coral Dando

In order to bring the perpetrators of crime to justice, investigators need to interview witnesses to find out what has occurred. Witness testimony helps provide the necessary leads in the early stages of an investigation and is also used in court to help in coming to decisions as to guilt or innocence. When witnesses are interviewed it is important that they are interviewed in a way that is likely to produce the most accurate and detailed accounts of what happened. In this chapter the contribution of psychology to furthering our understanding of witness interviewing is examined. Important concepts of memory will be explored using key empirical, applied and field studies, to show the conditions under which witness memory can be maximised as well as the conditions in which witness memory is most likely to be unreliable. The practical implications of psychological research for the area of witness interviewing are explained. The chapter concludes with an overview of the Cognitive Interview technique. This procedure is based on many of the principles discussed in this chapter, and is currently taught to all police officers in the England, Wales and Northern Ireland.

Introduction

When investigating crime, police investigators strive to answer two primary questions, namely what has occurred and who is responsible (Milne & Bull, 2006). When attempting to answer these questions, and in order to bring the perpetrators of crime to justice, investigators require information about what has happened.

Such information is generally provided by witnesses (who can also be victims). Not only do witnesses generally provide the central leads (Kebbell & Milne, 1998), but the information they supply often directs the entire investigatory process from the very outset (Milne & Bull, 2001; Milne & Shaw, 1999). For example, in the initial stages, witnesses report what has occurred and frequently provide a description of the perpetrator. Further, they often signal additional lines of inquiry and even indicate other potential sources of information. As an investigation progresses, witnesses can be asked to identify perpetrators, objects or places, and in the final stages of bringing an offender to justice, witness evidence is central to most court cases (Kebbell & Milne, 1998; Zander & Henderson, 1993). Certainly, when presented at a court of law, witness testimony is extremely powerful, with jurors relying heavily on witness accounts when coming to decisions as to guilt or innocence (e.g. Cutler *et al.*, 1990).

Witness information is generally gathered by way of an interview (a conversation with a purpose) during which a police officer asks a witness to explain what they can remember about a previously experienced event, the primary objective being to obtain a full and accurate account from each witness. Remembering a crime event, such as a robbery or an assault, is essentially a (re)constructive process. It is generally accepted that witnesses do not store the literal input stimulus of an experienced event but, instead, store a series of coded representations (Bower, 1967). Therefore, remembering is not simply a case of rewinding and playing back a video-recording of what has been experienced but involves the reactivation and construction of the appropriate coded representations prior to vocalisation. Consequently, the manner in which a witness's memory is accessed and (re)constructed can be a significant determinant, not only of the amount of information they recall, but also the accuracy of that information. The types of questions asked, the manner in which they are asked, and the structure of the retrieval process (in this case the interview) have all been found to impact upon witness memorial performance in terms of both the *quantity* (amount) and the *quality* (accuracy) of the information recalled (e.g. see Loftus, 1975, 1979; Milne & Bull, 2001; Tulving, 1991).

Owing to the importance of witness interviewing to the criminal justice system, and because the reliability of witness evidence can be directly called into question in legal contexts, psychologists have long sought to clarify the conditions under which witness memory is likely to be most accurate in an effort to inform the legal system as to how justice is best served. Consequently, there now exists a large body of psychological research that has informed the current approach to witness interviewing, not only in the UK but worldwide. In this chapter, laboratory, applied and field research will be reviewed, showing how the basic concepts of memory inform our understanding of witness interviewing. Throughout this chapter attention will be drawn to important developmental differences that must be considered when evaluating the reliability of witness testimony, and as such, the interviewing of adults and children will sometimes be considered separately. We will conclude by describing the development and application of the Cognitive Interview procedure which is taught to police officers in the UK (excluding Scotland). The Cognitive Interview incorporates many of the psychological principles that will be discussed in this chapter and provides an excellent example of how psychological research can be successfully translated into best practice in the real world.

Encoding, Storage and Retrieval

When witnesses are interviewed concerning what they can remember about a past event, irrespective of its complexity, the cognitive processes underlying memory can be divided into a three-stage process of *encoding*, *storage* and *retrieval* (Melton, 1963). Employing an analogy between human memory and computer processor (Atkinson & Shiffrin, 1971; Bower, 2000; Brown & Craik, 2000), information is described as moving through the three stages sequentially. Encoding involves the initial

uptake of information in our environment by our sensory systems (Atkinson & Shiffrin, 1971). The newly acquired 'raw' information is then briefly retained in the appropriate sensory store, where, if attended to, it initially proceeds to short-term memory, which has a limited capacity and a brief duration. From here the information progresses to long-term memory, which is believed to have a virtually unlimited capacity and is further subdivided into a number of memory systems, each of which is concerned with specific types of information (Tulving, 1972). Information that has been encoded and stored can then be retrieved, thus bringing about the conscious recollection of past events and experiences (e.g. Atkinson & Shiffrin, 1968, 1971). The ability to recall specific past events and experiences is referred to by different scholars as episodic memory, autobiographical memory, event memory and witness memory. These terms are largely interchangeable and we refer to witness memory in the current chapter.

This three-stage conceptualisation of memory also provides some indication as to how interdependent each of the memorial processes is. From an information processing perspective, attention is vital for the successful encoding of memory. Encoding is a necessary prerequisite for storage, and retrieval is, in turn, dependent upon the preceding encoding and storage processes (Tulving, 1974). Thus, the efficacy of all three of the aforementioned cognitive processes is crucial for the accurate memories of events. However, despite the simplicity of the three-stage conception of memory, these processes are complex and multifaceted (Baddeley, 2001). Memory can fail at each and/or all of these stages (Brainerd *et al.*, 1990). For example, information can be forgotten, recovered, distorted and reinstated at each stage, thereby impacting on both the amount of information recalled about experienced events and the accuracy of that information.

Forgetting

Witnesses rarely remember as much information about an experienced event as police investigators would like. It is not at all unusual for a witness to say to an interviewer 'I don't know, can't remember. I am sure I saw him but I have forgotten what he looked like.' Forgetting has long been of interest to psychologists and it was empirical research conducted by Ebbinghaus (1964/1885) that first indicated that the rate of forgetting (also sometimes referred to as decay) is not uniform and that memories are not forgotten gradually at a constant rate, little by little, over time. Ebbinghaus memorised lists of nonsense syllables (for example 'gar' and 'hep'), of varying lengths, and measured the number of times that it took to learn them. When he was able to learn the lists completely he then tested himself at varying delays to see how long it took to re-learn the word list. The results of numerous highly controlled studies of this type indicated that forgetting from memory is negatively exponential in nature. That is, forgetting is at its most rapid soon after the lists of nonsense syllables have been successfully encoded and then tapers off (or flattens) as time passes. Since then researchers have also examined whether there are developmental differences in how quickly memories are forgotten. When children of different ages are required to learn lists of words until they can recall them without error, later recall tests clearly show that younger children forget more quickly than older children (Brainerd et al., 1990).

Given that much of the early research was conducted in highly controlled experiments it is no surprise that memory researchers have also examined forgetting in applied settings that are more typical of everyday recall. Typically, such research involves participants trying to recall events depicted in video presentations, live presentations, or interactive events. Researchers then return at various delays to test how much information is accurately recalled, using various structured interview procedures and recall techniques specifically designed for use in experiments. For example, Jones and Pipe (2002) interviewed 5- and 6-year-old children concerning what they could remember about a school-based pirate show either immediately afterwards, or after a delay of one day, one week, one month, and six months. These delays allowed the rapid forgetting at short recall delays to be measured and, thus, to be compared to recall performance at the comparatively longer delay of six months. The results did not reveal any significant decreases in recall performance, employing conventional statistical tests, until the six-month delay interviews. However, when a forgetting function was calculated of the type proposed by Ebbinghaus (1964/1885) and fitted to these data, it was clear that the largest decreases in recall were occurring soon after the event and that the rate of forgetting decreased (flattened out) at the longer delays.

Although the results of applied research do confirm the basic prediction of Ebbinghaus, that over time the greatest decreases in what is remembered about an event occur soon after the event in question (Jones & Pipe, 2002; Pipe et al., 2004), sometimes applied studies do not show the effects of forgetting, and it is important to be aware that alternative explanations are sometimes needed, especially when attempting to understand witness memory. Gee and Pipe (1995) studied both 6- and 9-year-old children and followed their memory across a 10-week period. They found evidence that the 9-year-old children forgot stored information across the 10-week delay, but that the 6-year-old children did not. The reason for this inconsistency with the findings of controlled experiments using lists of words (e.g. Brainerd et al., 1990) may be due to the amount of information that was initially encoded. Younger children may have actually encoded fewer details about the event in the first instance so that they had less to forget over time, thereby making their rate of forgetting appear less dramatic. The older children encoded much more of what had happened and, thus, had more to forget. Consequently their forgetting appeared to be more rapid.

Another instance where the findings of applied studies provide findings that are seemingly inconsistent to those of controlled experiments of forgetting is illustrated by Fivush et al. (2004). They interviewed children shortly after they had experienced Hurricane Andrew, which struck the coast of Florida in 1992. Six years later, the same children were interviewed again about what they could remember and it was found that they now reported twice as much as they had done originally. In this case the most likely reason for the increase in the amount recalled (the opposite of forgetting) could be attributed to the fact that during the intervening six years between interviews the children experienced many reminders of the hurricane, for example anniversaries, conversations with friends, and a protracted clean-up operation. They may have developed their stories accordingly and added details that they learned after the event to what they had previously recalled. Moreover, across the six-year delay, the children obviously underwent significant developmental changes in their abilities to recall, communicate, and elaborate their ideas, which may have also contributed to the increase in recall.

Field studies of real interviews have also examined whether witnesses recall progressively fewer details as the time between witnessing a crime and recalling it increases (Lamb et al., 2008). Van Koppen and Lochun (1997) researched archival data from police records to investigate both the quantity of the information recalled about robbery suspects and the accuracy of that information. Not surprisingly, the most complete descriptions were associated with a short delay between the crime event and providing a description. Lamb *et al.* (2000) examined interviews with 4- to 12-year-old children after delays of three days, one month, up to three months, and between 5 and 14 months. These data clearly show evidence of a change in the rate of forgetting, there having been a 7 per cent drop in recall between the shortest delays of up to a month and a further 9 per cent drop in recall up to 14 months.

These basic findings of research on forgetting suggest that, in theory, the best time to conduct a witness interview is as soon as possible after a witness has experienced the event in question, as over time critical evidence may well be forgotten. Furthermore, this is especially important for younger children because research has indicated that they are likely to forget more quickly. However, in the 'real world' of witness interviewing it is often neither appropriate nor practicable to interview a witness immediately. Sometimes it can often be hours, weeks or even months, post experiencing a crime, that a witness comes forward and makes themselves known to police: they may be intimidated, frightened, or in many cases are unaware that they have actually witnessed a crime until it has been publicised. Equally, even when a police investigator is in a position whereby he/she can conduct a witness interview quickly, the quality of witness memorial performance can also be affected by many other important incidental factors which must be taken into consideration. Witnesses are often stressed and anxious as a result of their experiences, and this may affect their ability to communicate. In laboratory studies, stress has been found to reduce the quantity of information recalled by mock witnesses (e.g. Yuille & Cutshall, 1986; Yuille *et al.*, 1994), although the information that was recalled was found to be mostly accurate. Witness interviewers often find themselves in a 'trade off' situation whereby both immediacy and witness anxiety/stress levels have to be considered. It may be that an interview conducted immediately post an event, with a stressed/anxious witness, may elicit less (albeit accurate) information than one conducted some time later when a witness is more composed. Therefore, although interviewing witnesses immediately after a crime is desirable, from an information processing perspective, it may not always be in the best interests of an investigation.

Reminiscence

Other studies have been conducted that show that sometimes memory is *recovered* (the opposite of forgetting), a phenomenon known as *reminiscence*.

Ballard (1913) first investigated the reminiscence effect in 12-year-old boys. They were asked to memorise a poem in a short space of time and then to recall it. Only one of the 19 boys was able to recall all the lines of poetry when they were first asked. Two days later a second test was administered and it was unexpectedly found that eight of the boys were now able to recall all the lines of poetry. On average, the number of lines of poetry recalled increased from 27.6 to 30.6 in the second test, clear evidence of reminiscence of previously unrecalled information. More recently, Erdelyi and Becker (1974) asked participants to remember sets of pictures and lists of words and then asked them to write down what they could remember three times in a row with a seven-minute break separating each memory test. The results showed that progressively more new correct details were recalled from the first to third tests, clearly demonstrating the reminiscence effect. Subsequent experiments showed that the reminiscence effect was stronger when the participants thought about what it was they were trying to remember between memory tests, thus suggesting that reminiscence may be facilitated by actively trying to retrieve memories. There have been many more highly controlled laboratory experiments also showing the reminiscence effect (for reviews see Erdelyi, 1996; Payne, 1987).

Applied witness-interviewing studies have examined whether it would also be possible for witnesses to reminisce meaningful information, and whether there would be any advantage to re-interviewing witnesses to find out more information about a crime (Bluck *et al.*, 1999; Bornstien *et al.*, 1998; Dunning & Stern, 1992; Gilbert & Fisher, 2006; La Rooy *et al.*, 2005; Scrivner & Safer, 1988; Turtle & Yuille, 1994). A typical applied study of the reminiscence effect surrounded the events of the O.J. Simpson trial verdict which was televised live across the USA and watched by millions of viewers (Bluck *et al.*, 1999). Eight months after the verdict announcement, adult participants were interviewed concerning what they could remember about the details of the trial verdict, three times in a row within the space of an hour. They found that the amount recalled by the participants actually increased between the first and the third interviews, demonstrating the reminiscence of new information. Importantly, from a witness-interviewing perspective, there was no increase in errors suggesting advantages of repeated interviewing.

Research by Gilbert and Fisher (2006) directly examined the accuracy of the newly reminisced information and found that the recall of new information can be facilitated by changing retrieval cues between recall tests. Adults were asked to watch a three-minute eyewitness video of a bank robbery in progress, after which they were asked to write down everything that they could remember. Two days later they returned to recall what they could remember from the video clip using different recall cues. For example, if they had originally recalled the clip in chronological order they were asked to recall what happened in reverse order in the follow-up test, and vice versa. The results showed that the greatest amount of reminiscence occurred when the retrieval cues were different in the second test. However, what was most striking was that the accuracy of the reminiscence was 87 per cent.

Similarly, high accuracy of reminiscence has also been observed in studies with children. La Rooy et al. (2005) had 5- and 6-year-olds engage in a 15-minute interaction with a friendly pirate who led them through a sequence of hands-on pirate activities. Immediately after the interaction with the pirate the children were interviewed about what they could remember and 24 hours later they were asked again to recall everything they could remember. As with Gilbert and Fisher (2006), the second interview contained new details and a very similar accuracy rate of 92 per cent was found for the newly reminisced details. However, a series of further experiments that explored whether such results could be achieved with children after a long delay, as in the case of Bluck et al. (1999), did not reveal comparable results for children (La Rooy et al., 2005, 2007). Hence, it would appear that for children the most reliable reminiscence effects occur when they are asked about what happened shortly after the event in question, whereas the benefits of repeated interviews are still evident even after long delays for adults.

Very few studies have examined reminiscence in real witness interviews. Hershkowitz and Terner (2007) examined the details reported by children in forensic interviews. After an initial interview the children were re-interviewed after a 30-minute 'rest'. Most of the details reported were provided in the initial interview, but the repeated interview was still a useful means of obtaining more information. Fourteen per cent of the details, which were central to the allegations in question, were only provided in the second interview, adding further clarity to the allegations that had been made. Collectively, the findings discussed above suggest that witnesses can provide more information about crimes when they are re-interviewed.

Witness interviewers, therefore, need to be aware that recall of events and experiences is not always complete and exhaustive. Interviewers should take particular care to probe memory fully on the one hand, but also know that it may be useful to return and re-interview witnesses at a later date to see if they can remember more information about a crime. Indeed, the social context of being re-questioned about something may encourage a witness to work harder to retrieve more information and not simply repeat what they may have already told the interviewer (Bluck et al., 1999). However, the research on reminiscence does not dovetail well with the legal and forensic process of interviewing witnesses in terms of creating a strong legal case. The criminal justice system generally values information offered early in an investigation more highly than information offered later. For example, consider the situation whereby, when initially questioned by the police, a witness is unable to remember exactly what has occurred, or is unable to describe a perpetrator, but sometime later says, 'oh yes now I remember where I was that night, I remember what he was wearing. . .' Such testimony is often viewed with scepticism by legal experts, it being assumed that a witness who changes their initial story may be doing so to fit with facts learned about the case sometime later, for example from media sources, conversations with friends, or even other witnesses. Adding new details can also raise doubts as to the overall reliability of a witness's memory and whether *all* their evidence should, thus, be considered less valuable. Research has, however, indicated that outright scepticism as to the validity of the information obtained from multiple witness interviews is unjustified. What remains is for researchers to further investigate the conditions under which witness memorial performance, across multiple interviews, is likely to be accurate (La Rooy et al., 2008).

Encoding Specificity

The principle of encoding specificity (Thomson & Tulving, 1970; Tulving & Thomson, 1973) provides an indication as to how witness memorial performance might be enhanced during an interview by providing a theoretical framework for understanding the importance of contextual information and how it can affect memory. The encoding specificity principle was initially illustrated in a series of word association experiments. For example, participants were presented with pairs of common words whereby the first word acted as a cue to a second target word. The cues were either strongly associated to the target word e.g. *white – BLACK* (black being the target word) or weakly associated, e.g. *train – BLACK*. When participants' recall of the target word was tested, recall was greatest when the cues presented at recall were the same as those when they were first presented, irrespective of whether they were strongly or weakly associated with the target word. The results of this series of experiments were such that Tulving and Thomson (1973) concluded that remembering was the result of an interaction between both the encoding and retrieval environments. A retrieval cue will be effective only if the information in that cue was encoded in the original memory trace. Memory is, thus, improved when information present at encoding is then presented at retrieval because it facilitates conscious recall of aspects of the original event.

This was further illustrated by Godden and Baddeley (1975) who demonstrated just how powerful *physical* reinstatement of context can be. Scuba divers learned word lists either underwater or on land. Later the divers were asked to recall the word lists, either in the same or a different learning environment (some of the participants who learned the word lists on land were tested on land, while others who learned word lists on land were asked to recall the word lists underwater). The basic finding was that divers who learned the word lists underwater recalled more words (approximately 50 per cent) underwater than they did on land – recall of the word lists was enhanced when the encoding and retrieval environment were the same. The encoding context, however, need not necessarily always be part of the external environment, and an internal subjective state, such as mood, at the time of encoding may also act as a powerful retrieval cue (Eich *et al.*, 1994; Schacter, 1996).

From an applied perspective these findings suggest that returning a witness to the scene of a crime may be a useful means of obtaining more information about what happened. In applied research Wilkinson (1988) asked 3- and 4-year-old children to participate in a number of activities during a walk in a park. The following day the children were asked to recall everything that they could remember either in a quiet room, or in the park that they had visited the day before. The results showed the effects of context reinstatement, with children retrieving more about what happened when they were interviewed in the park. At longer delays, Pipe and Wilson (1994) interviewed children about a visit to a 'magician' that had occurred either 10 days or 10 weeks earlier. The interviews occurred in either the same or a different room from that in which they had seen the

magic show. As expected, the results showed that the children who were interviewed in context, with all the original items from the magic show present, recalled the most information. Moreover, one group that was exposed to an incorrect context reinstatement, where items that were not originally present had been added, did not differ in their recall compared to children who received the true context reinstatement. La Rooy *et al.* (2007) also examined the effects of inaccurate context reinstatement in 5- and 6-year-old children after a delay of six months. As with Wilson and Pipe (1989), children who were interviewed with context reinstatement recalled more information than those interviewed without context reinstatement, irrespective of whether the context reinstatement contained incorrect items. However, the results also showed that children interviewed in the true context, which matched exactly what they had seen six months earlier, were more accurate in their recall.

That said, returning to a crime scene is generally viewed as inappropriate in many real-life cases. Owing to the passage of time, the crime scene may have changed and, thus, will be of limited value in terms of being a useful retrieval cue. Moreover, returning to the scene may prove so upsetting that a witness's memorial performance may suffer as a result of increased levels of anxiety and stress. Therefore, given that it may not be possible or appropriate to use 'physical' context reinstatement, researchers have investigated whether 'mental' context reinstatement would be sufficient to improve the amount of correct information recalled by witnesses. That is, would asking witnesses to clearly imagine the environment in which they saw the crime, before they are questioned about what they remember, be as effective at improving recall as returning to the scene?

Milne and Bull (2002) investigated this possibility. Adult participants viewed a video-taped mock crime event and were interviewed two days later employing a number of interview procedures, one of which incorporated the mental context reinstatement. Results revealed that the interview procedure that comprised mental context reinstatement instructions elicited the greatest number of correct details. Further, there was no associated increase in the number of errors reported by witnesses when this technique was used. More recently, Dando *et al.* (2009a) have also found that an interview procedure which incorporates the mental context reinstatement combined with an instruction for witnesses to 'report everything' elicits more correct information from mock witnesses compared to a similarly structured procedure that excludes mental context reinstatement. However, it is, nonetheless, important to be aware that mentally reinstating the context of a crime may also be anxiety inducing, and as such, may limit memorial performance rather than having the desired effect.

In sum, according to the theory of encoding specificity, context reinstatement may be a means of enhancing witness recall. Indeed, the beneficial effect of mentally reinstating the psychological and physical context within which an event was encoded is generally well established in eyewitness memory research with both children and adults (e.g. Clifford & Gwyer, 1999; Geiselman et al., 1984; La Rooy et al., 2007; Memon & Bruce, 1985; Milne & Bull, 2002; Smith, 1988). However, while the increases in participants' memorial performance in the aforementioned experiments (believed to be attributed to context reinstatement) are often technically 'statistically significant', it is important to be aware that improvements in the amount of information recalled is, in real terms, very modest; typically, the benefits of context reinstatement lead to the recall of only a few extra details. Although context reinstatement does not lead to complete recall, any interview procedure that increases the amount and quality of the information recalled by a witness has merit. Indeed, recent research has indicated that mentally reinstating the context, within a witness interview procedure, does improve the accuracy of the information recalled compared to a procedure that excludes the technique altogether (e.g. Dando et al., in press, 2009b; Milne & Bull, 2002). Moreover, in real-life investigations even one single extra detail elicited from a witness may prove vital in terms of its forensic/investigative importance.

Suggestibility and False Memory

It is essential to consider *false memory* and *suggestibility* in relation to witness interviewing. Numerous real-world cases have demonstrated that witness recollection in interviews can be entirely false, and the tragic consequences include false imprisonment for serious crimes (e.g. see Savage & Milne, 2006). What is striking from the perspective of a witness interviewer is that it is almost impossible to distinguish false memories, seemingly confidently and clearly held by an interviewee, from true memories. What is possible, however, is an understanding of the conditions in which false memories can be created and, therefore, the conditions in which the veracity of witness statements could be

justifiability questioned. Moreover, false memory and suggestibility research also provides clear insights into to what interviewers should *not* be doing when they are interviewing witnesses.

False memories can be created because memory is (re)constructive. Bartlett (1932) asked English university students to read a North American folktale called 'The War of the Ghosts'. When the participants were asked to recall the story, Bartlett found that not only was information forgotten, but also that there were frequent distortions to the story. The participants' recollections became shorter, more concise, simplified, disordered, and they rationalised parts of the story that were ambiguous by adding completely false details consistent with their own cultural and individual perspectives. For example, a 'canoe' in the story was remembered as a 'boat'. The very reconstructive nature of memory as demonstrated by Bartlett (1932) means that it is vulnerable to distortion. Subsequent research has shown that there are numerous ways in which memory can be distorted and this has highlighted many areas of concern.

False memories are also comparatively easy to create. Wade et al. (2002) obtained four childhood photos of their adult participants. One of the four photos was digitally re-edited, such that the photo of the participant was pasted into a photo of a hot-air balloon. The participants discussed the photos a number of times for two weeks, at which point half were claiming to have remembered 'something' about taking a ride in a hot air balloon in their childhood. Garry and Wade (2005) used this basic procedure to compare whether images of false events were more, or less, powerful at creating false memories than simply talking about false events. Eighty per cent of participants reading a false narrative about a childhood trip in a hot air balloon came to remember 'something' about the ride by the third discussion session. The reason that the narrative was actually a more powerful means of creating false memory than the photo was that it left greater scope for participants to build up their own individual mental picture, thus making the false memory seem more real and unique. These demonstrations of how easily false memory can be created are a sober reminder of the fallibility of memory and it is easy to see how people could be 'talked into' recovering memories of events that didn't happen. There are many historical cases where people have 'recovered' memories of physical and sexual abuse in therapy sessions when they have been specifically asked to 'dig up' hidden memories that have ended with miscarriages of justice. The lesson is that what is reported in witness interviews may sometimes seem plausible, but it is not until the circumstances in which the memory came to light are known that investigators can judge whether what has been reported is likely to be true or not.

The paradigm that has been most commonly used for demonstrating that people can have false memories has been the Deese–Roediger–McDermott paradigm (DRM; Pezdek & Lam, 2007). This paradigm involves participants studying lists of words that they will later be required to recall or recognise. The words in the lists come from the same category, for example they could all be items of furniture (e.g. table, couch, seat, stool, etc.). An obvious member of the category is deliberately not included in the list (e.g. chair) and is called the false memory 'target word'. When the participant recalls what they remember from the lists they typically recall the false target word that wasn't presented in the original list. This is taken as evidence of false memory (Roediger et al., 2001).

What is interesting about the DRM paradigm is that it provides counterintuitive results when the question of developmental differences between children and adults is considered. Typically, children are viewed within the legal system as being less reliable witnesses than adults because they are prone to memory errors and false memory owing to their less well-developed cognitive abilities. As we get older we expect to be less susceptible to false memory, and, as such, the witness evidence of children is more heavily scrutinised compared to that of adults. However, when Brainerd et al. (2002) involved 5- and 11-year-old children and adults in a typical study using the DRM paradigm they found that the 5-year-old children were the least likely to make the critical word recall error. The likelihood of making the false memory error actually increased with age, with adults showing the greatest susceptibility to false memory. The explanation of these findings is put down to a lack of understanding of 'gist' by younger children. When they encode the word lists they do not recognise as quickly as adults that the words are all coming from the same category, whereas adults are very quick to pick up the gist. When recalling the words, adults depend on their knowledge of gist to help them recall more correct responses. However, this strategy also results in them falsely recalling the false target word. By contrast, because children are not relying so heavily on category or gist information as a cue to recall, they concentrate on trying to recall the list 'verbatim' and consequently make fewer false memory errors.

Despite these intriguing findings, applied studies of false memory and suggestibility involving children do show powerful effects of suggestibility. Leichtman and Ceci (1995) organised a day-care visit by a stranger called 'Sam Stone' who entered children's classrooms, greeted the teacher, and then told the children that a story they were being read was one of his favourites. Before the children were interviewed about what they could remember about the brief encounter, the researchers stereotyped Sam Stone by returning to the children's classrooms a number of times to read stories that depicted him as a very clumsy person. Some of the children were also interviewed in a highly suggestive manner about Sam Stone's visit and were asked questions implying that he had ripped a book and soiled a teddy bear. To maximise the suggestion, in two of the interviews children were actually shown a ripped book and a soiled teddy bear as evidence of Sam Stone's clumsy misdeeds. In a final interview children were asked to tell about what had happened during the day-care visit and were directly asked whether they saw the book getting ripped and the teddy bear being soiled. Almost half of the 3- and 4-year-olds who had received the stereotype and were then interviewed in a highly suggestive manner made false claims about Sam Stone. When they were asked direct questions 72 per cent of children agreed that Sam Stone had some part in ripping the book and soiling the teddy. This clearly shows that children can create false memories and report false information about events that did not happen. However, it is interesting to note that when these children were confronted about Sam Stone's misdeeds 'you didn't really see him … [rip book/soil teddy] … did you?' the agreements that the false event had actually taken place dropped to 21 per cent, further suggesting how easily led they are.

While false memory and suggestibility clearly involve distortions of memory, social factors may also play a role in encouraging false reports. Jones and Pipe (2002) asked children who had visited a 'friendly pirate' misleading questions about what happened, for example 'was the pirate wearing red and white trousers?' when the pirate's trousers were actually blue and white. They found that children could answer the misleading questions correctly only 60 per cent of the time. Because the children were questioned about what happened immediately after the event in question, the incorrect responses couldn't be entirely attributed to a failing of memory. Children very likely acquiesced (agreed) and simply went along with what the interviewer suggested happened, perhaps not willing to disagree with an adult they perceive as a more knowledgeable interlocutor.

When evaluating the accuracy of information reported by witnesses in interviews it is, therefore, important to be aware that there is always a possibility that a witness may be recollecting a false memory. While not all individuals are equally likely to be susceptible to suggestibility and the effects of post-event information (Eisen *et al.*, 2002), witnesses may generally be more susceptible to post-event information generated by a police officer than when generated by a member of the public (Dodd & Bradshaw, 1980). As both a 'credible' and 'knowledgeable' source, when combined with the situational demands of the interview process, witnesses may be particularly susceptible to cues given by the officer during the interview (be they correct or incorrect). This may be even more pronounced when memory of the original event is poor (Schooler & Loftus, 1993) as is often the case with eyewitnesses due to less than optimal perception and encoding environments.

Interviewers should, therefore, approach interviews with an open mind and seek corroborating evidence to support witnesses' claims whenever possible. It is also vital that interviewers consider the types of questions they ask and pay particular attention to the wording of questions. Police officers often interview several witnesses of the same crime; thus, as their knowledge of the event in question increases they should ensure that event information (learned from prior interviews) is not subsumed into any subsequent questioning. This is especially important when interviewing children. That said, professionals, throughout the criminal justice system, are now aware of the effects of asking leading questions to a far greater extent than has previously been the case. Research conducted by suggestibility researchers has informed and guided those whose job it is to collect witness information.

Witness Interviewing in the UK

The problems associated with witness memorial performance, discussed above, provide an indication as to just how difficult it can be to elicit a detailed and accurate account when interviewing a witness. Conducting such an interview is a complex skill, a process of conversational exchange (Shepherd, 1991) in which both the witnesses and interviewers play an integral role. However, the onus is on the interviewer to optimise witness memorial performance in terms of both the amount and accuracy of information reported about a crime (Koriat & Goldsmith, 1994). It should be clear from the preceding discussion that the two primary problems encountered by police officers during an interview, which negatively impact both the quantity and quality of witness recall, are errors of omission (forgetting) and errors of commission (false memories). Owing to the importance placed on witness testimony by the criminal justice system, it is clear that incomplete, erroneous and distorted witness information can have serious ramifications.

In the early 1990s, following well-publicised criticisms of police interviewing techniques (e.g. Baldwin, 1992), the Home Office in conjunction with the Association of Chief Police Officers developed and introduced the PEACE investigative interview model. The PEACE model (a mnemonic for the stages of an investigative interview; *Planning and preparation, Engage and explain, Account, Closure* and *Evaluation*) was designed to equip interviewers with the skills necessary to conduct ethical and effective investigative interviews in any situation. Introduced across England and Wales in 1992, PEACE not only standardised investigative interview training for the first time, but also introduced the notion that interviewing was an investigatory process whereby the officers' role was to gather evidence and obtain information (NCF, 1996). Prior to this, the prevailing approach for obtaining information about crimes was to focus on suspect interviews during which police investigators generally aimed to obtain a confession and to confirm what was 'believed' to have happened rather than searching for the truth by interviewing all those involved (Baldwin, 1992).

With respect to witness interviewing, PEACE advocates that the cognitive interview procedure should be employed when conducting such interviews. The Cognitive Interview is a multidisciplinary interview technique that was initially developed in the early 1980s, in response to many requests by American investigators and other legal professionals for clear guidelines as to how witness memory could be improved. The cognitive interview is one of the most well-researched and widely acknowledged interview procedures for enhancing information obtained in witness interviews and has been described by those in the field as 'one of the most exciting developments in psychology in the last ten years' (Memon, 2000, p.343). Devised as a practical forensic tool, the cognitive interview is concerned exclusively with the retrieval of information from memory, specifically with how the retrieval (remembering) process might be optimised during an interview situation.

Initially presented in 1984 (Geiselman *et al.*, 1984), the procedure evolved over several ensuing years with a number of refinements and enhancements being made (Fisher *et al.*, 1989). This development process is well documented and falls into two fairly distinct phases, with the initial procedure being referred to as the original cognitive interview and the latter as the enhanced cognitive interview. In its current enhanced form (see Fisher & Geiselman, 1992) the procedure comprises four retrieval components, generally referred to as the 'cognitive' components, namely (i) *mental context reinstatement*, (ii) *report everything*, (iii) *recall in a variety of temporal orders*, and (iv) *change perspective*.

The *mental context reinstatement* technique emanates from the principle of encoding specificity. It is one of the principal components of the cognitive interview whereby the interviewer encourages the witness to mentally reinstate both the psychological and physical environment that existed at the time of the event in question (for example their thoughts, emotions and smells) in order that they might act as retrieval cues for that event. The mental context reinstatement procedure comprises a series of 'mini' instructions in that the witness is encouraged to re-create the context one step at a time. For example, an interviewer will ask a witness to:

> Reinstate in your mind the context surrounding the incident. Think about what the room looked like … where you were sitting … how you were feeling at the time, and think about your reactions to the incident. (Geiselman *et al.*, 1984, p.76)

The *report everything* instruction aims to lower witnesses' subjective criterion for reporting information by instructing them not to edit any details about the event of interest because even those details they believe to be insignificant or irrelevant may actually be important. Hence, the interviewer should take time to explain to witnesses just how important it is that they explain absolutely everything they remember.

The assumption here is that even partial or apparently insignificant features of an event can act as retrieval cues by 'triggering' the recall of associated information, thus increasing the total amount reported. By obtaining as much information as possible the first time a witness is questioned the need for repeated interviews is reduced, thereby avoiding associated problems discussed. Interestingly, the *report everything* instruction is also

viewed as a useful method for increasing the overall amount of information collected from several witnesses to the same crime, because lots of small apparently insignificant pieces of information collected from several witness accounts can become important clues when aggregated together.

The *recall in a variety of temporal orders* component is viewed as an additional method of accessing information that may have been previously irretrievable. The theoretical rationale here is that the retrieval of information from memory can be influenced by gist-related (schemata) information (see Schank & Abelson, 1977) that acts as an organising structure for knowledge that 'fills in' aspects of an event according to previous experience/knowledge. New information is, therefore, understood in terms of old information, and gist- or script-guided retrieval can result in limited retrieval due to the filtering of recalled information that does not fit the usual script, and/or the filling in of 'gaps in memory' with script information when a witness's memory for an event is incomplete. Encouraging a witness to recall details of an event from the end, or even the middle, is therefore aimed at limiting script-consistent recall by interfering with forward-only recall.

Finally, the *change perspective* retrieval method aims to access information that may have been irretrievable using the previous three techniques (Bower, 1967). Witnesses have a tendency to report events from their own psychological perspective. Asking a witness to try to adopt the perspective of another person, who may have been involved in the event, may help 'jog' witnesses' memory, thereby increasing the amount of information recalled (Fisher & Geiselman, 1992).

In addition to the aforementioned components, the importance of the social and communication aspects of the investigative interview situation is also considered. Thus, the enhanced cognitive interview also includes several techniques that aim to ensure that the four cognitive components are implemented to best effect. It is recommended that, before the cognitive components described above are used, interviewers take time to establish rapport with the interviewee, so reducing their anxiety about the interview process by commencing the interview with innocuous and easily answered questions.

Furthermore, several straightforward interviewer behaviours are included in the enhanced cognitive interview, which aim to further encourage *focused retrieval*. First, the interviewer should explain/convey to the interviewee that it is their effort that will affect the outcome of the interview, and that ultimately the success of the interview will depend on the interviewee's mental effort. Second, the interviewer should encourage the interviewee both to concentrate and to actively participate by allowing the interviewee to do the majority of the talking by using open-ended questions, wherever possible, and the strategic use of pauses. Finally, *witness-compatible questioning* advocates that interviewers should tailor their questioning according to the witness's pattern of recall rather than the interviewer adhering to a rigid sequencing of requests for information that imposes a 'police report' style of organisation on the retrieval process which, in turn, may limit witness recall. To that end, witness-compatible questioning dictates that the interviewer should actively listen to each interviewee's account of what they have experienced and ask questions in the same order as they have initially recounted the event (see Fisher & Geiselman, 1992; Memon & Bull, 2000; Milne & Bull, 1999 for a more comprehensive description of the enhanced cognitive interview).

All police officers (police recruits and expert interviewers alike) in England, Wales, and Northern Ireland are now taught to employ many of the enhanced cognitive interview components when interviewing witnesses. Currently, the enhanced cognitive interview procedure is taught to police officers using a building-block approach within a tiered interview training framework ranging from tier 1 to tier 5 (see Griffiths & Milne, 2005 for an introduction to the tiered approach to interview training in the UK). All police officers commence their police career as a tier 1 interviewer. They are taught a basic cognitive interview procedure (comprising a limited number of techniques) that is commensurate, not only with their limited experience and training, but also with the types of witness interviews they conduct (i.e. with the witnesses of less serious crime). Should their duties and interviewing competency warrant it, officers are then able to undertake further training and can progress through the tiers, ultimately becoming a tier 5 interview adviser, the most well-trained and skilled interview strategists.

It can be seen that psychological research has, undoubtedly, not only informed the criminal justice system as to the problems associated with witness memory, but it also underpins the current approach to witness interviewing in the UK. Police officers are now being trained to apply interview procedures/protocols that take account of the complexities of the retrieval process in terms of guiding them how best to assist each witness to recall as much accurate information as possible during an interview, thereby maximising this important information gathering opportunity. As previously introduced, witnesses are a fundamental part of the criminal justice system and obtaining witness information is a complex skill and one which has, only relatively recently, begun to be afforded the status it deserves. Historically, witness interviewing was viewed as a low-status police activity, when compared to the interviewing of suspects, a situation that was borne of a lack both of training and knowledge.

Post the introduction of PEACE, witness interviewing has, without doubt, improved. However, that said, there are some well-documented problems associated with the application of the cognitive interview procedure in forensic settings. For example, police officers consistently report that they apply some of the individual cognitive interview components they are taught far more frequently than others, and that some of the techniques are not applied at all (e.g. Dando *et al.*, 2008; Kebbell *et al.*, 1999; Wright & Holliday, 2005). Field studies carried out in the early 1990s (Clifford & George, 1996; George, 1991) found that no officers applied the cognitive interview procedure in full. More recently, a national evaluation of investigative interviewing in England and Wales (Clarke & Milne, 2001) reviewed 75 'real life' witness interviews. No evidence, at all, was found of the cognitive interview procedure having been used in 83 per cent of these witness interviews, which is somewhat alarming.

Practical reasons as to why the cognitive interview is not implemented in many real-life witness interviews may be that it takes longer to conduct and police officers experience considerable time constraints while on duty. Furthermore, not only is the cognitive interview viewed by some police interviewers as time consuming, it is also viewed as inappropriate in some situations, especially when interviewing witnesses about less serious crime. Equally, it is acknowledged that the cognitive interview places extensive cognitive demands on the interviewer (e.g. Fisher *et al.*, 1987). Consequently, it may be that psychologists now need to concentrate on modifying the procedure with a view to increasing its forensic application, especially in time-critical and complex situations, while at the same time retaining the well-demonstrated cognitive interview superiority effect.

Equally, however, the type of training provided may also account, in part, for the apparently patchy application of the cognitive interview. Despite the introduction of the new tiered approach to training, police officers are initially taught how to interview witnesses during a one-week interview training course. This course combines the teaching of both suspect and witness interview techniques. Thus, the average amount of time spent teaching novice officers to apply the cognitive interview when interviewing witnesses is only two days! This timeframe does not allow police officers to become highly familiar with the cognitive interview or any of the principles of memory discussed in this chapter. Recent research shows that police officers agree that the training they are receiving is not sufficient to equip them with the skills necessary to confidently apply the cognitive interview procedure as it is taught (Dando et al., 2008). Indeed, research has long indicated that cognitive interview training should be separate from suspect interview training (rather than combined as it is currently; e.g. Clifford & George, 1996), as this has been found to be more effective in terms of officers' application of the procedure in real witness interviews.

In summary, there has been a great deal of empirical, applied and field research that has informed and continues to inform the forensic community as to how witnesses should and should not be interviewed. These advances in our understanding have undoubtedly resulted in justice being better served. Increasing the quality of witness evidence in an investigation increases the chances of ensuring that the correct decisions are made as to guilt or innocence. A success story for the field of psychology has been seeing the development of the cognitive interview and its uptake into the system of police training in the UK. With an eye to the future, the new frontier for researchers of witness interviewing will, undoubtedly, be to improve training and interviewer skills, as well as further honing interview techniques/procedures towards the great variety of situations in which they are called into use.

have been developed in accordance with scientific principles that have become the 'gold standards' in the world of witness interviewing today.

Lamb, M.E., Hershkowitz, I., Orbach, Y. & Esplin, P.W. (2008). *Tell me what happened: Structured investigative interviews of child victims and witnesses*. Chichester: Wiley.
This book reviews the development of a purpose-designed interview protocol for interviewing children about sexual and physical abuse. Acknowledging that the greatest difficulty in applying the principles of memory and communication to witness interviewing is actually getting interviewers to follow scientific and government guidelines, Lamb and collaborators have developed a 'structured' interview protocol that leads the investigator through each stage of a forensic interview. Using the protocol has been proven to result in interviewers eliciting a larger number of relevant details from witnesses compared to interviewers who are not trained in the use of the protocol. The guidelines outlined in the book are based on analysis of 30,000 forensic interviews with children in Israel, Sweden, the UK and the USA. It is the largest research database of this type in the world. The protocol is consistent with the interviewing approach recommended by the Home Office in *Achieving Best Evidence*.

Milne, R. & Bull, R. (2001). *Investigative interviewing: Psychology and practice*. Chichester: John Wiley & Sons.
Milne and Bull provide a comprehensive, concise, and clearly written overview of investigative interviewing that introduces the reader to both the psychological theory and empirical research that underpin the current approach to conducting interviews with suspects, witnesses and victims. Further, they describe good investigative interview practice, explain how investigative interviewing has evolved and the practical problems faced by those tasked with conducting interviews in applied settings, and draw attention to the difficulties associated with interviewing children and other vulnerable people. Without doubt, this book is highly relevant for all those who have an interest in investigative interviewing, whether that be from an applied or a research perspective.

Further Reading

Brainerd, C.J. & Reyna, V.F. (2005). *The science of false memory: An integrative approach*. Oxford: Oxford University Press.
Brainerd and Reyna compile the most comprehensive review of false memory theory, research and debate. This book begins by reviewing the history of false memory research before tackling theoretical explanations and associated research. Throughout the book there is detailed consideration of developmental differences important to understanding false memory. Applied research is also reviewed and issues to do with witness interviewing and suspect identification are explored. The book concludes by reviewing the interview protocols that

References

Atkinson, R.C. & Shiffrin, R.M. (1968). A proposed system and its control processes. In K.W. Spence & J.T. Spence (Eds.) *The psychology of learning and motivation: Advances in research and theory* (vol. 2, pp.89–195). New York: Academic Press.

Atkinson, R.C. & Shiffrin, R.M. (1971). The control of short term memory. *Scientific American, 225*, 80–92.

Baddeley, A. (2001). *Human memory theory and practice*. Hove: Psychology Press.

Baldwin, J. (1992). *Video-taping police interviews with suspects – an evaluation*. London: Home Office.

Ballard, P.B. (1913). Oblivescence and reminiscence. *British Journal of Psychology*, 1, 1–82.

Bartlett, F.C. (1932). *Remembering: A study in experimental and social psychology*. Cambridge: Cambridge University Press.

Bluck, S., Levine, L.J. & Laulhere, T.M. (1999). Autobiographical remembering and hypermnesia: A comparison of older and younger adults. *Psychology and Aging*, 14, 671–682.

Bornstien, B.H., Liebel, L.M. & Scarberry, N.C. (1998). Repeated testing in eyewitness memory: A means to improve recall of a negative emotional event. *Applied Cognitive Psychology*, 12, 119–131.

Bower, G. (1967). A multicomponent theory of a memory trace. *Psychology of Learning and Motivation*, 1, 230–325.

Bower, G. (2000). A brief history of memory research. In E. Tulving & F.I.M. Craik (Eds.) *The Oxford handbook of memory*. Oxford: Oxford University Press.

Brainerd, C.J. & Reyna, V.F. (2005). *The science of false memory: An integrative approach*. Oxford: Oxford University Press.

Brainerd, C.J., Reyna, V.F. & Forrest, T.J. (2002). Are young children susceptible to the false-memory illusion? *Child Development*, 73, 1363–1377.

Brainerd, C.J., Reyna, V.F., Howe, M.L. & Kingma, J. (1990). The development of forgetting and reminiscence. *Monographs for the Society of Research in Child Development*, 55, 3–4.

Brown, S.C. & Craik, F.I.M. (2000). Encoding and retrieval of information. In E. Tulving & F.I.M. Craik (Eds.) *The Oxford book of memory*. Oxford: Oxford University Press.

Clarke, C. & Milne, R. (2001). *National evaluation of the PEACE investigative interviewing course*. London: Home Office.

Clifford, B.R. & George, R. (1996). A field evaluation of training in three methods of witness/victim investigative interviewing. *Psychology, Crime and Law*, 2, 231–248.

Clifford, B.R. & Gwyer, P. (1999). The effects of the cognitive interview and other methods of context reinstatement on identification. *Psychology, Crime and Law*, 5, 61–80.

Cutler, B.L., Penrod, S.D. & Dexter, H.R. (1990). Juror sensitivity to eyewitness identification evidence. *Law and Human Behaviour*, 14, 185–191.

Dando, C.J., Wilcock, R. & Milne, R. (2009a). The cognitive interview: The efficacy of a modified mental reinstatement of context procedure for frontline police investigators. *Applied Cognitive Psychology*, 23, 138–147.

Dando, C.J., Wilcock, R. & Milne, R. (2008). The cognitive interview: Inexperienced police officers' perceptions of their witness interviewing behaviour. *Legal and Criminological Psychology*, 13, 59–70.

Dando, C.J., Wilcock, R. & Milne, R. (in press). The cognitive interview: The efficacy of a modified mental reinstatement of context procedure for frontline police investigators. *Applied Cognitive Psychology*.

Dando, C.J., Wilcock, R., Milne, R. & Henry, L. (2009b). An adapted cognitive interview procedure for frontline police investigators. *Applied Cognitive Psychology*, 23, 698–716.

Dodd, D.H. & Bradshaw, J.M. (1980). Leading questions and memory: Pragmatic constraints. *Journal of Verbal Learning, and Verbal Behaviour*, 6, 695–704.

Dunning, D. & Stern, L.B. (1992). Examining the generality of eyewitness hypermnesia: A close look at time delay and question type. *Applied Cognitive Psychology*, 6, 643–657.

Ebbinghaus, H. (1964/1885). *Memory: A contribution to experimental psychology*. New York: Dover.

Eich, E., Macauley, D. & Ryan, L. (1994). Mood dependant memory for events of the personal past. *Journal of Experimental Psychology: General*, 123, 201–215.

Eisen, M.L., Winograd, E. & Qin, J. (2002). Individual differences in adults' suggestibility and memory performance. In M.L. Elsin, J.A. Quas & G.S. Goodman. (Eds.) *Memory and suggestibility in the forensic interview*. Mahwah, NJ: Lawrence Erlbaum.

Erdelyi, M.H. (1996). *The recovery of unconscious memories: Hypermnesia and reminiscence*. Chicago, IL: University of Chicago Press.

Erdelyi, M.H. & Becker, J. (1974). Hypermnesia for pictures: Incremental memory for pictures but not words in multiple recall trials. *Cognitive Psychology*, 6, 159–171.

Fisher, R. & Geiselman, R. (1992). *Memory-enhancing techniques for investigative Interviewing: The cognitive interview*. Springfield, IL: Charles Thomas.

Fisher, R.P., Geiselman, R.E. & Amador, M. (1989). Field test of the cognitive interview: Enhancing recollection of actual victims and witnesses of crime. *Journal of Applied Psychology*, 74, 722–727.

Fisher, R.P., Geiselman, R.E., Raymond, D.S., Jurkevich, L. & Warhaftig, M.L. (1987). Enhancing enhanced eyewitness memory: Refining the cognitive interview. *Journal of Police Science and Administration*, 15, 291–297.

Fivush, R., McDermott Sales, J., Goldberg, A., Bahrick, L. & Parker, J. (2004). Weathering the storm: Children's long-term recall of Hurricane Andrew. *Memory*, 12, 104–118.

Garry, M. & Wade, K.A. (2005). Actually, a picture is worth less than 45 words: Narratives produce more false memories than photographs. *Psychonomic Bulletin and Review*, 12, 359–366.

Gee, S. & Pipe, M-E. (1995). Helping children to remember: The influence of object cues on children's accounts of a real event. *Developmental Psychology*, 31, 746–758.

Geiselman, R.E., Fisher, R.P., Firstenberg, I., Hutton, L., Sullivan, S.J., Avetissian, I.V. *et al.* (1984). Enhancement of eyewitness memory: An empirical evaluation of the cognitive interview. *Journal of Police and Science*, 12, 74–79.

George, R. (1991). *A field evaluation of the cognitive interview*. Unpublished master's thesis, Polytechnic of East London.

Gilbert, J.A.E. & Fisher, R.P. (2006). The effects of varied retrieval cues on reminiscence in eyewitness memory. *Applied Cognitive Psychology*, 20, 723–739.

Godden, D. & Baddeley, A.D. (1975). Context-dependent memory in two natural environments: On land and under water. *British Journal of Psychology*, 66, 325–331.

Griffiths, A. & Milne, R. (2005). Will it all end in tiers? Police interviews with suspects. In T. Williamson (Ed.) *Investigative interviewing. Rights, research, regulation.* Cullompton, Devon: Willan.

Hershkowitz, I. & Terner, A. (2007). The effects of repeated interviewing on children's forensic statements of sexual abuse. *Applied Cognitive Psychology, 21,* 1131–1143.

Jones, C.H. & Pipe, M-E. (2002). How quickly do children forget events? A systematic study of children's event reports as a function of delay. *Applied Cognitive Psychology, 16,* 755–768.

Kebbell, M. & Milne, R. (1998). Police officers' perceptions of eyewitness factors in forensic investigations. *Journal of Social Psychology, 138,* 323–330.

Kebbell, M., Milne, R. & Wagstaff, G. (1999). The cognitive interview: A survey of its forensic effectiveness. *Psychology, Crime and Law, 5,* 101–115.

Koriat, A. & Goldsmith, M. (1994). Memory in naturalistic and laboratory contexts: Distinguishing accuracy-orientated and quantity orientated approaches to memory assessment. *Journal of Experimental Psychology, 123,* 297–316.

Lamb, M.E., Hershkowitz, I., Orbach, Y. & Esplin, P.W. (2008). *Tell me what happened: Structured investigative interviews of child victims and witnesses.* Chichester: Wiley.

Lamb, M.E., Sternberg, K.J. & Esplin, P.W. (2000). Effects of age and delay on the amount of information provided by alleged sex abuse victims in investigative interviews. *Child Development, 71,* 1586–1596.

La Rooy, D., Lamb, M.E. & Pipe, M-E. (2008). Repeated interviewing: A critical evaluation of the risks and potential benefits. In K. Kuehnle & M. Connell (Eds.) *The evaluation of child sexual abuse allegations: A comprehensive guide to assessment and testimony.* Chichester: Wiley.

La Rooy, D., Pipe, M.-E. & Murray, J.E. (2005). Reminiscence and hypermnesia in children's eyewitness memory. *Journal of Experimental Child Psychology, 90,* 235–254.

La Rooy, D., Pipe, M.-E. & Murray, J.E. (2007). Enhancing children's event recall after long delays. *Applied Cognitive Psychology, 21,* 1–17.

Leichtman, M.D. & Ceci, S.J. (1995). The effects of stereotypes and suggestions on preschoolers' reports. *Developmental Psychology, 31,* 568–578.

Loftus, E.F. (1975). Leading questions and eyewitness reports. *Cognitive Psychology, 7,* 560–572.

Loftus, E.F. (1979). *Eyewitness testimony.* Cambridge, MA: Harvard University Press.

Melton, A.W. (1963). Implications of short-term memory for a general theory of memory. *Journal of Verbal Learning and Verbal behaviour, 2,* 1–21.

Memon, A. (2000). Interviewing witnesses: The cognitive interview. In A. Memon & R. Bull (Eds.) *The handbook of the psychology of interviewing.* Chichester: Wiley.

Memon, A. & Bruce, V. (1985). Context effects in episodic studies of verbal and facial memory: A review. *Current Psychological Research and Reviews, Winter,* 349–369.

Memon, A. & Bull, R. (2000). *The handbook of the psychology of interviewing.* Chichester: Wiley.

Milne, R. & Bull, R. (1999). *Investigative interviewing: Psychology and practice.* Wiley series in the psychology of crime, policing, and law. Chichester: Wiley.

Milne, R. & Bull, R. (2001). *Investigative interviewing: Psychology and practice.* Chichester: John Wiley & Sons.

Milne, R. & Bull, R. (2002). Back to basics: A componential analysis of the original cognitive interview mnemonics with three age groups. *Applied Cognitive Psychology, 16,* 743–753.

Milne, R. & Bull, R. (2006). Interviewing victims of crime, including children and people with intellectual disabilities. In M.R. Kebbell & G. Davies (Eds.) *Practical psychology for forensic investigations and prosecutions.* Chichester: Wiley.

Milne, R. & Shaw, G. (1999). Obtaining witness statements: Best practice and proposals for innovation. *Medicine, Science, and the Law, 39,* 127–138.

NCF (1996). *Investigative interviewing: A practical guide.* Bramshill, UK: National Crime Faculty and National Police Training.

Payne, D.G. (1987). Hypermnesia and reminiscence in recall: A historical and empirical review. *Psychological Bulletin, 101,* 5–27.

Pezdek, K. & Lam, S. (2007). What research paradigms have cognitive psychologists used to study 'false memory', and what are the implications of these choices? *Consciousness and Cognition, 16,* 2–17.

Pipe, M.-E., Sutherland, R., Webster, N., Jones, C.H. & La Rooy, D. (2004). Do early interviews affect children's long-term recall? *Applied Cognitive Psychology, 18,* 1–17.

Pipe, M.-E. & Wilson, J.C. (1994). Cues and secrets: Influences on children's event reports. *Developmental Psychology, 30*(4), 515.

Roediger, H.L. III., Watson, J.M., McDermott, K.B. & Gallo, D.A. (2001). Factors that determine false recall: A multiple regression analysis. *Psychonomic Bulletin and Review, 8,* 385–407.

Savage, S. & Milne, R. (2006). Miscarriages of justice – the role of the investigative process. In T. Newburn, T. Williamson & A. Wright (Eds.) *Handbook of criminal investigation.* Cullompton, Devon: Willan.

Schacter, D.L. (1996). *Searching for memory: The brain the mind and the past.* New York: Basic Books.

Schank, R.C. & Abelson, R.P. (1977). *Scripts, plans, goals, and understanding: An enquiry into human knowledge structures.* Hillsdale, NJ: Lawrence Erlbaum.

Schooler, J.W. & Loftus, E.F. (1993). Multiple mechanisms mediate individual differences in eyewitness accuracy and suggestibility. In J.M. Pucket & H.W. Reese (Eds.) *Mechanisms of everyday cognition.* Hillsdale, NJ: Lawrence Erlbaum.

Scrivner, E. & Safer, M.A. (1988). Eyewitnesses show hypermnesia for details about a violent event. *Journal of Applied Psychology, 73,* 371–377.

Shepherd, E. (1991). Ethical interviewing. *Policing, 7,* 42–60.

Smith, S.M. (1988). Environmental context-dependent memory. In G. Davies & D. Thomson (Eds.) *Memory in context: Context in memory.* London: John Wiley & Sons.

Thomson, D.M. & Tulving, E. (1970). Associative encoding and retrieval: Weak and strong cues. *Journal of Experimental Psychology*, 86, 255–262.

Tulving, E. (1972). Episodic and semantic memory. In E. Tulving & W. Donaldson (Eds.) *Organisation of memory*. London: Academic Press.

Tulving, E. (1974). Cue-dependent forgetting. *American Scientist*, 62, 74–82.

Tulving, E. (1991). Concepts of human memory. In L.R. Squire, N.M. Weinberger, G. Lynch & J.L. McGaugh (Eds.) *Memory: Organization and locus of change*. New York: Oxford University Press.

Tulving, E. & Thomson, D.M. (1973). Encoding specificity and retrieval processes in episodic memory. *Psychological Review*, 80, 352–373.

Turtle, J.W. & Yuille, J.C. (1994). Lost but not forgotten details: Repeated eyewitness recall leads to reminiscence but not hypermnesia. *Journal of Applied Psychology*, 79, 260–271.

van Koppen, P.J. & Lochun, S.K. (1997). Portraying perpetrators: The validity of offender descriptions by witnesses. *Law and Human Behavior*, 21(6), 661–685.

Wade, K.A., Garry, M., Read, J.D. & Lindsay, D.S. (2002). A picture is worth a thousand lies: Using false photographs to create false childhood memories. *Psychonomic Bulletin and Review*, 9, 597–603.

Wilkinson, J. (1988). Context effects in children's event memory. In M.M. Gruneberg, P.E. Morris & R.N. Sykes (Eds.) *Practical aspects of memory: Current research issues* (Vol. 1, pp.107–111). New York: Wiley.

Wilson, J.C. & Pipe, M-E. (1989). The effects of cues on young children's recall of real events. *New Zealand Journal of Psychology*, 18, 65–70.

Wright, A.M. & Holliday, R.E. (2005). Police officers' perceptions of older eyewitnesses. *Legal and Criminological Psychology*, 10, 211–223.

Yuille, J.C. & Cutshall, J.L. (1986). A case study of eyewitness's memory for a crime. *Journal of Applied Psychology*, 71, 291–301.

Yuille, J.C., Davies, G., Gibling, F., Marxsen, D. & Porter, S. (1994). Eyewitness memory of police trainees for realistic role plays. *Journal of Applied Psychology*, 79, 931–936.

Zander, M. & Henderson, P. (1993). *Crown court study*. Royal Commission on Criminal Justice Research Study, 19. London: HMSO.

14

Victims of Crime: Towards a Psychological Perspective

Werner Greve and Cathleen Kappes

Investigating the sufferings of a victim of crime, even from a scientific point of view, is a delicate task. In particular, it must not be forgotten that victims of crime have rights. Amongst these are acknowledgement that they have been subject to an injustice and not simply misfortune. Accordingly, it is important that the suffering of victims of crime is not seen simply as a voyeur (Sontag, 2003). This is certainly not the intention of scientists, although it may sometimes be a hidden epiphenomenon: it is not always an easy task to change one's own ambivalent fascination by the harm experienced by others and adopt an entirely prosocial stance. As quick as we are to claim our innocence in this respect, it is as difficult to prove our truly altruistic intent. Perhaps partly as a consequence of this difficult balance, the scientific interest in victims of crime has been, throughout the past century, subject to significant switches in focus.

Indeed, the scientific examination of victims of crime can serve various goals, three of which we will discuss in greater detail in this chapter. First, victimology can be seen as a complementary addition to official crime records, being one important way to investigate the 'dark figure' of true crime behind recorded crime rates. In order to successfully prevent crimes it is important to know as much as possible about the true frequencies and conditions surrounding criminal victimisation. Second, the consequences of such victimisation for individuals are investigated. In order to help victims of crime we have to know which offences produce what consequences, for whom and under what conditions. Certainly, this has to be done in a broader, developmental perspective: beyond immediate clinical symptoms

and sufferings, it is the long-term (developmental) consequences for an individual that make victimisation a critical life event. Third, it is of profound importance to learn more about the social and individual adaptive resources that may buffer or alleviate the impact of certain forms of victimisation or that can contribute to healing. Since this latter perspective is particularly in need of an integrative theoretical approach, we argue that this is where scientific victimology truly begins.

Brightening the Dark Figure: Descriptive Victimology

Certainly one of the main purposes of victimology is the investigation of frequencies of victimisation (prevalence) and delicts (legal incidence of wrongs). Both for practical and theoretical reasons, we want to know how high the (statistical) risk of victimisation for various delict types (e.g. burglary vs. pickpocketing vs. rape) is and which subgroups of a given population are especially affected by specific crime types (e.g. purse snatching vs. assault).

Limitations of official data

Effective criminal policies, especially concerning prevention, need a realistic assessment of the underlying magnitude of crime figures. However, official recordings are constrained by several limitations, especially with regard to their longitudinal comparability of crime rates. This is due to fluctuating definitions and applications of the criminal law, differing recording practices, and their dependence on the reporting of crime incidents (Goudriaan *et al.*, 2006; Levitt, 1998; Warner, 1997). Since crimes, as a rule, only come to the attention of the police because people report an incident which they consider to be criminal, victims themselves (and, sometimes, relatives and observers) have an essential role in the process of recording victimisation: first, they need to decide what they consider to be a criminal act or not (Goodey, 2005).

Nevertheless, trends in officially recorded 'criminality' have some value. For example, officially recorded data from the German Police Crime Statistics (PCS) show that an enormous increase in the victimisation rate over time (victims per 100,000 inhabitants per year) has occurred with regard to dangerous and serious violent crime (Figure 14.1). This increase is particularly significant for male juveniles and young adults. However, as Baier (2008) shows, this tendency is not evident in victim surveys (questionnaire studies with representative samples asking for certain events in the past; we will return to this approach shortly). This discrepancy between official data and victim surveys suggests that official crime trends may simply reflect, sometimes to a large degree, changes in the reporting behaviour of the population or recording practices of police services. Indeed, Baier (2008) demonstrates that an enhanced willingness to report crime events produces higher rates in official statistics (for a further discussion of reporting behaviour see Levitt, 1998).

Hence, official records of crime, owing to their dependence on reporting rates, provide an inadequate estimate of criminal behaviour. Moreover, there are more decisions to be made in the process of official crime recording. The police have to decide whether the reported incident should be noted as a crime or not. If the police are investigating the case, further legal institutions, such as the Crown Prosecution Service in England and Wales, will review the evidence and determine whether the case should be brought to court. Since sometimes the answer will be no, the number of victims counted will decrease at each step of the decision-making sequence. An even lower estimate of the number of victims is found if only offences resulting in conviction are counted. Temkin and Krahé (2008) showed that an increase in reporting a rape incident since 1979 was accompanied by a relative decrease in conviction rates, which declined from 32 per cent of the cases in 1979 to 5.3 per cent in 2004/2005. Moreover, they point out that of the rape cases which were actually brought to the

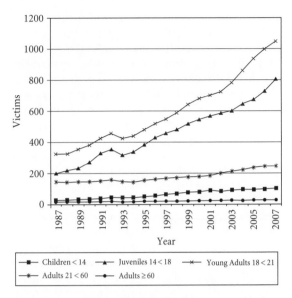

Figure 14.1   Victimization rates for dangerous and serious bodily harm (per 100,000 inhabitants per age group). *Source*: Data taken from German Police Crime Statistics (table 91); 1987–1990: West Germany, 1991–1992: West Germany and the whole of Berlin, from 1993: entire territory of the Federal Republic of Germany.

court, 43 per cent were convicted, whereas, for example, the conviction rate for 'wounding or other act endangering life' was 56 per cent. This illustrates that, depending on which source is used, one could get entirely different figures for what could be counted as victimisation. Unfortunately, the question of which factors influence these attrition rates and how and why they differ with respect to different crime types has received little attention from researchers.

Limitations of victimisation surveys

Victimisation surveys with large and representative samples may help to contrast and, thus, to complete data from official figures. By asking for certain events (e.g. 'being slapped by your partner') instead of legal categories (e.g. 'personal injury'), experiences of victimisation may get reported at higher rates than in official recordings. Moreover, by asking the participants whether they reported these experiences to the police or not, it is possible not only to estimate the extent of the 'dark figure' of crime, but also partly to explain the gap between reported crime incidents and actual crimes. However, while police-recorded data suffer from several limitations in their informative value, it has long been recognised that crime survey data are not without drawbacks themselves (e.g. Bilsky *et al.*, 1993; Block & Block, 1984; Fattah, 1991; Fattah & Sacco, 1989; Sparks, 1981). Lavrakas (1993) distinguishes four types of error: sampling error, coverage error, non-response error, and measurement error. *Sampling error* refers to the degree of imprecision of the data in reflecting the whole population. Since the sample is only a fragment of the population, smaller samples are more likely to be biased by extremes, especially if the population is highly heterogeneous, or they run the risk of being insensitive to aspects that have a low occurrence probability in the whole population. An enlargement of sample size is the most direct way to decrease this kind of error.

The generalisability of results is also endangered by the *coverage error* which refers to the overrepresentation of certain members of a group where others are underrepresented or neglected altogether. This problem stems, to a notable degree, from the methodological advantages and disadvantages of different survey methods (e.g. personal interview, telephone interview, mail, and internet). For example, telephone surveys of private households exclude the experiences of people without phones (for instance, the homeless or illegal immigrants). Surveys through the internet not only require access to the equipment but are also less controllable with respect to the identity of the reporting person. As a rule, certain social groups tend to be ignored by any method, with serious consequences for the validity of the resulting figures and rates. For instance, many if not most 'white collar crimes' (e.g. fraudulent bankruptcy, defalcation) will not be registered by victimisation surveys since they most often do not have a concrete victim (or they have victims that have not even recognised that they have been victimised). Another important example of a certain 'blindness' of victim surveys is the delicate area of family violence, which is not only underreported officially but is also oftentimes not reported in victim surveys (Wetzels, 1993; Wetzels & Bilsky, 1997). Therefore, thorough planning of who shall be included in the survey and which instrument is suited best for which sample is needed.

Even if these essentials are taken into account, the *non-response error* can intrude insofar as individuals who deny participation are potentially different in certain characteristics from those agreeing to participate, which is why their specific experiences would possibly not be reflected in the data. For example, individuals disapproving of the police could be more willing to answer questions regarding their attitudes towards the police (if a survey is conducted by other institutions), whereas individuals satisfied with the police may see little value in such a survey and decline to answer it. A lower average value of satisfaction with the police could be the result. Likewise, crimes in certain social ('criminal') milieus (e.g. red light districts) will remain underreported because these persons, whether victims or not, neither participate in victimisation surveys nor report their experiences to the police. Unfortunately, the size of systematic influence by selection effects of this kind is hard to estimate.

Finally, the *measurement error* refers to the extent of inaccurate assessment of the phenomenon of interest. This error can occur, for example, because of poor question wording, interviewer bias, bias due to the method of survey-administration (e.g. face-to-face vs. mail), or question formats. For instance, Ramirez and Straus (2006) showed that the order of the survey items led to a different disclosure rate for violent behaviour in the domestic sphere.

Besides the question of who is asked, several intricacies are connected with the question of how to ask. First of all, several general effects concerning the reliability of the memory have to be considered. For example, individuals often show the tendency to place prominent memories closer to the present, termed 'telescoping' (Gottfredson & Hindelang, 1977; Schneider & Sumi, 1981). Even where everything has been validly remembered, individual memories are biased with several evaluations, starting with the very question of whether a person perceives him- or herself as a *victim*; which certainly depends on individually varying processes of attribution, appraisal and coping (Greve *et al.*, 1997). Finally, it is plausible to assume individually varying tendencies to remember burdensome and critical life events in detail, only partly or not at all depending on the way that an individual copes with these experiences.

Risks of victimisation

However, keeping these potential restrictions and biases in mind, regularly repeated victim surveys (with unchanging methods) may still offer insightful perspectives with respect to our knowledge about crime trends and understanding of the emerging interests of perpetrators. The first victim surveys were carried out in the USA (National Crime Victim Survey, NCVS) from 1972 on and underwent a major redesign in 1992. Other countries were to follow their example. In England and Wales the British

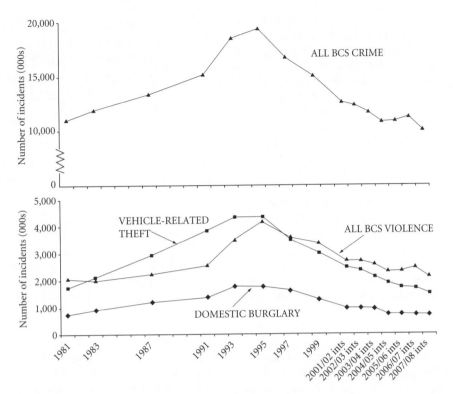

Figure 14.2 Trends in crime, 1981 to 2007/2008. *Source*: Kershaw *et al.*, 2008, p.2.

Crime Survey (BCS) was carried out in 1981 for the first time. Since then it has undergone various adjustments. By now, the BCS is conducted continuously as a face-to-face interview with those aged 16 or older living in private households and is publicised annually. The sample is designed to be representative of private households. The respondents are asked about their experiences of crime-related incidents in the 12 months prior to the interview. Moreover, they are posed questions about their attitudes towards different crime-related issues such as the police, the criminal justice system, perceptions of crime and antisocial behaviour. Scotland and Northern Ireland collect and publish crime data separately with largely similar crime surveys (Scottish Crime and Justice Survey and Northern Ireland Crime Survey).

Looking at the recent publication of the BCS by the Home Office for 2007/2008 based on almost 47,000 interviews, the overall crime indicator has decreased by 10 per cent in comparison with the results of the last BCS from 2006/2007, while simultaneously being at the lowest level since the first BCS was conducted in 1981 (Kershaw *et al.*, 2008).

While the dark figure of crime showed an overall increase since its first estimation, with a peak in 1995, it has fallen since then (Figure 14.2). Though this trend is reflected in the development of different crime types, there is some diversity in the course of the increase and decrease observable. Domestic burglary, for instance, had a lower curve progression than violence.[1]

Results cannot simply be compared cross-nationally since they differ with respect to various factors, such as included age group (e.g. the NCVS includes people aged 12 and older, the BCS has people aged 16 and older), included crimes and the specific way of recording them, or aggregation of those crimes. In order to enable cross-national comparisons, a group of European criminologists started an international victimisation study in 1989 (Van Dijk *et al.*, 1990). Since then, the International Crime Victim Survey (ICVS) has been conducted in 1992, 1996, 2000 and 2004/2005 (e.g. Mayhew & Van Dijk, 1997; Nieuwbeerta, 2002; Van Dijk & Mayhew, 1992; Van Kesteren, 2007) Though it offers the chance of comparison independent from differing methodologies used in the national crime surveys, only a fragment of potential countries can be included and, of those, not all are incorporated longitudinally. Still, what can be observed generally is the decline of overall crime and specific crime types. Results of the NCVS concur with the BCS in the decline of violent crime rates. For overall violent crime (encompassing rape, robbery, aggravated assault and simple assault), the rate per 1000 persons per year began at 47.7 in 1973 and increased to 52.3 in 1981. After this time, the rate decreased, reaching a low of 21.0 in 2005. Since Germany does not carry out a nation-wide crime victim survey, there is no possibility for a direct national comparison in this respect. Yet, some studies support the conclusion that also in Germany the overall crime rate is on the decrease (e.g. Baier & Windzio, 2008; Greve & Bilsky, 1997; Wetzels *et al.*, 1995).

This general trend is also mirrored in the police data, though at a lower level of recorded crimes. Overall, less than half of BCS crime is reported to the police. However, this statement is an overt oversimplification for it blurs the differences in the relationship between the dark figure and police-recorded data dependent on crime type, as, for example, more serious violent crime comes to the attention of the police with higher probability than theft with relatively low property value (however, theft of higher property value has a bigger chance of being reported because of insurance issues).

Explaining Victimisation: Between Probabilities and Blame

Beyond simply depicting the incidence of various categories of crime and comparing them with police-recorded data, the statistical risk of victimisation can be estimated from the frequency of occurrence. For example, the risk of becoming a victim for all BCS crime at least once in 12 months averages 22.1 per cent for the year 2007/2008, which is a decrease of 2.3 per cent compared with the survey period 2006/2007. However, this figure conceals the differential distribution of victimisation dependent on crime type, demographic variables, and their interaction. The victimisation risk for domestic burglary, for example, is 2.4 per cent whereas it is 6.4 per cent for vehicle theft. Considering the risk of becoming a victim of violent crime for various groups shows pronounced differences. Risk is highest for men aged 16 to 24 (13.4 per cent, Figure 14.3), decreasing with age. The same pattern is observable for women, though at a lower average risk level. Beyond these basic figures, risk factors can be identified which contribute to the statisti-

Figure 14.3 Groups most at risk of violence, prevalence in BCS 2007/2008. *Source*: Kershaw *et al.*, 2008, p.6.

cal prediction of victimisation. Though some of these factors (e.g. gender, age, marital status, employment status and profession, lifestyle, and area of living) proved to be reliable predictors, these categories are interrelated, so for example young people have a higher probability of living alone and not being married.

Nevertheless, even reliable predictions lead to the question of why some groups are at greater risk than others, and, hence, the quest for predictors of individual victimisation; and also predictors for those who belong to groups with lower statistical risk. Here, one possible and prominent approach is the search for the causal significance of certain attributes and behaviours of the victim in relation to the victimising event. Since the reception and interpretation of the victim's attributes by the offender will, at least in the majority of cases, be the decisive point, this kind of research will be, though in the victim's interest, not specifically victim research. Yet, the attempt at identifying typologies of victims by descriptive studies marks the beginning of the modern criminological research of the victim (e.g. Shafer, 1968/1977; see also Fattah, 1991, for a discussion). Over a relatively long period of time victimological studies were dedicated to the question of whether individual victimisation could be explained, predicted and eventually prevented by referring to characteristics of the victims themselves (Jung, 1993). These considerations were based on the contentious assumption that the victim is to a certain extent involved in the process of getting victimised (Schneider, 1994, 2007; detailed discussion: Karmen, 1991 or 2006, pp.95–127).

Blaming the victim: Ruthless or a mode of coping?

However, this perspective is problematic in multiple respects, even if a causal contribution from the victim, developed in the interaction with the perpetrator and leading to the victimisation, could be identified in most cases. First of all, any perspective looking at the causal contribution of the victimised to their victimisation not only neglects that most people are not victimised by serious crime, it also ignores situational factors. Moreover, it has ethically problematic connotations, which in the worst case could support an attitude that, beyond the mere causal involvement, attributes a part of the moral guilt to the victim ('blaming the victim', Ryan, 1971; see also Sank & Caplan, 1991).[2] This can entail quite negative consequences in juridical and social reactions for the victim (e.g. Herbert & Dunkel-Schetter, 1992; Krahé et al., 2008). In this way, victims of rape, for example, often have to suffer in many ways under what have become termed 'rape myths', for example that 'women who get raped while hitchhiking get what they deserve', or 'in the majority of rapes, the victim is promiscuous or has a bad reputation' (Burt, 1980). Such myths have been shown to be influential in partly blaming the victim, possibly resulting in a 'secondary victimisation'[3] (Campbell et al., 1999; Kiefl & Sieger, 1993; Montada, 1988; Williams, 1984; for a summary see Krahé & Scheinberger-Olwig, 2002).

Although such blaming is factually wrong and has to be morally criticised, examining the tendency of witnesses or bystanders to attribute some guilt to the victim from a psychological point of view may provide interesting insights. Specifically it could be a hint at a coping reaction in people which helps to see an event as controllable, explainable and, hence, innocuous when it otherwise could have had threatening impacts for one's trust in the world (Montada, 1988). In this context, the so-called 'just-world-motive' (Lerner, 1977) has gained considerable attention as a responsible factor (e.g. Correia et al., 2001; overview: Montada & Lerner, 1998). There is some evidence that this could be an explanation for the tendency for even some victims to attribute part of the guilt for the crime to themselves, even if uninvolved persons deny this or there are strong objective reasons arguing against it (Janoff-Bulman, 1982). Particularly, this tendency of 'self-blaming' is presumably only explicable against the backcloth of a theory of coping; i.e. self-attribution could be a potential *coping* mechanism for victim experiences whose functionality consists in sustaining a sense of controllability of potential future replications of this event (Janoff-Bulman, 1982).

Risk markers are not risk factors

Yet beyond this moral perspective, folk psychology is inclined to believe that some attributes of the victim may have attracted the offender. For example, it seems reasonable to assume that older persons are more vulnerable to robbery owing to their reduced capabilities to defend or escape (Yin, 1985). It seems dubious, however, that there is potential for framing a coherent and complete theory of a 'victim-prone person' (Von Hentig, 1948, quoted in Fattah, 1989, p.44) that would go significantly beyond a sheer accumulation of individual and social statistical risk factors. As demonstrated above, there is ample evidence, given a large dataset, that risk factors can be empirically identified, e.g. the gender of a person (men are more frequently the victim of physical violence; see e.g. Daly & Wilson, 1988), the age of a person (the statistical risk of becoming a victim decreases with age, e.g. Greve, 1998a, 1998b), or a person in a certain living area (as stated by the 'broken windows' theory; e.g. O'Shea, 2006; Skogan, 1990). On closer inspection, though, these factors constitute barely more than risk markers, contributing no substantial explanation but a mere statistical prognosis. This is best comprehended in relation to the most prominent risk factor for physical violence. Data here consistently show that (especially young) men are the most frequent victims (and perpetrators) of physical violence (Daly & Wilson, 1988; Farrington, 1996; Farrington & Painter, 2004; Gannon & Mihorean, 2005; Moffitt et al., 2001). Nonetheless, one cannot draw the conclusion that the majority of men are violent or become victims of violence, nor does it explain which of the numerous aspects that are connected to the descriptive feature 'male' plays a causal role in victimisation and offending; explanatory approaches vary from social stereotypes (e.g. gender role expectations and socialisation, cf., Eagly & Wood, 1999; Fagot & Hagan, 1985; Reidy et al., 2009) to behavioural, genetic and evolutionary approaches (e.g. Baschetti, 2008; Daly & Wilson, 1988; Hilton et al., 2000). At any rate, this 'predictive' perspective entails a shift in the theoretical focus: these victimisation theories become, at least to some extent, theories of the behaviour or decision processes of the perpetrator (e.g. Birkbeck & LaFree, 1993).

Understanding interactions: Towards a prevention focus

Such considerations should not be misunderstood as arguing against a closer investigation of social interaction processes between victims and their perpetrators. At least in certain circumstances, there is a lot to be learned from closely examining the social interaction at the outset of the victimisation and possible communication problems abetting the escalation (Krahé & Scheinberger-Olwig, 2002). The focus on critical elements and sequences in the interaction not only avoids a moral undertone but also establishes the chance for a psychological explanation of victimisation (and thus also prevention) while at the same time shifting the focus away from the victim as a *person*. Yet there may exist significant inter-individual differences, for example with respect to lacking social competences on the side of the victim due to development that can still play a role in the explanatory model. A special problem here, however, is the arbitrariness of the categorising and segmenting of the event in question. One and the same event can be viewed completely differently depending on the scope of coverage of the context of the event's genesis. By way of example, a woman who assaults her husband could have been humiliated and tortured by him for years. The respective interest of research is ultimately decisive at this point. Whenever the *consequences* of victimisation are the focus, objective 'validations' of the individual's experience and evaluation will be of less interest. In contrast, this may be considered differently, for instance in court, with respect to interventional aspects (e.g. in therapeutic settings), or from a crime-policy perspective: here we need (additional) information about where reality ends and biases of perception begin.

From a developmental psychology viewpoint, however, the question of which causal part is held by the victim of a criminal event has some additional insights to offer. Especially with regard to domestic and sexual violence there are various findings supporting the risk of a biographic dynamic of revictimisation ('intergenerational transmission of family violence'; Carroll, 1977; Cole *et al.*, 2008; Ehrensaft *et al.*, 2003; Hosser *et al.*, 2007; Krahé, 2000). The different approaches for explaining this dynamic have not yet been sufficiently tested empirically due to factors such as the necessity of long-term prospective longitudinal studies. Hence, the question of which aspects of biographical processes play a role for the widely documented continuity of violence needs to be considered as open and important. How can it be explained that experiences of violence do not always lead to special *avoidance* of violence, but occasionally downright heighten the probability of seeking out or remaining in social situations that are tightly related to violence (for a review see Stith *et al.*, 2004)? A central problem with such research projects will remain in the unresolved base rate problem: is the proportion of persons with serious experiences of violence in childhood

and youth (quantitatively and/or qualitatively), who experience this also in young and middle adulthood, significantly increased compared to other deviations of the developmental course (e.g. own delinquency; see e.g. Enzmann & Greve, 2001; Enzmann *et al.*, 1999)? At least different studies point out that the continuity of such biographical experiences is not exceptional. This could be seen as an indicator of life courses that seem maladaptive at first glance and could follow an inherent logic of development against the background of potential functionalities for behavioural patterns (e.g. familiarity of the situation – even with aversive constellations – increases continuity and sense of control). Coping – as with development in general – naturally does not always follow the best imaginable path but rather at best the individually possible (i.e. available) path. We will return to this perspective shortly.

Recognising the Suffering: Consequences of Victimisation

The obvious beginning of research into victims perhaps really lies in the significance of critical life events focusing on the clinical outcomes of single or even continuing experiences of (deliberate) physical or psychic violence by others. Not least this has to do with concrete practical reasons, since the knowledge about the circumstances that condition the occurrence of different psychic and physical consequences often entails the directions for possible and effective reactions. Naturally, bodily consequences of physical violence are dependent on the instruments of violence (e.g. weaponry, fists and other instruments); frequently there are haematoma, bone fractures, head injuries and lacerations. Long-term effects may include scars, damages to the auditory and visual system, gastrointestinal complaints, and chronic pain (e.g. Natvig *et al.*, 2001; Ruback & Thompson, 2001; Shapland & Hall, 2007). An important focus of research on the consequences of serious criminal, in particular violent, experiences has been the prevalence and symptomatic profiles of posttraumatic stress disorder (PTSD; e.g. Maercker *et al.*, 1998; Saigh, 1995; for an introduction: Friedman, 2006 or Schiraldi, 2000). The symptoms encompass a state of heightened fear with panic attacks, extreme startle responses, phobic fears (e.g. fear of the dark), avoidance behaviour, nightmares and increased arousal (e.g. difficulty falling or staying asleep, anger and hypervigilance). Typical cognitive and psychic symptoms are difficulties with concentration and performance, and depressed mood. Spontaneous memories (so-called flashbacks) of the traumatic situation, psychically caused lapses of memory (psychogenic amnesia) and a higher rate of suicide have been reported (e.g. Ben-Ya'acov & Amir, 2004; Tarrier & Gregg, 2004). Psychic accessory symptoms and subsequent damage, however, cannot easily be distinguished from comparable cases, in which the damage has been caused differently (e.g. accident, illness, etc.). Yet, different consequences can be observed in the wake of specific forms of violence compared to non-violent or non-criminal critical experiences; for instance, with rape, results may include considerable fears, depression and distrust for a longer time period (Feldmann, 1992; Resnick, 1987; Riggs et al., 1992; Shapland et al., 1985). Violent crime victims have also been shown to suffer more immediate psychological distress than property crime victims and non-victims (Denkers & Winkel, 1998; Norris & Kaniasty, 1994). Unfortunately, most of the longitudinal studies are not prospectively designed, which is why it is not possible to control for prior differences in the level of psychological distress. Moreover, those studies often do not possess a matched control group, further complicating comparison (for a review of longitudinal studies see Shapland & Hall, 2007). However, from these studies it can be tentatively concluded that – despite the differences in the consequences between delict types – there are also differences in the reaction to the same criminal incidence in the immediate response as well as in the long run. We will return to this point below.

Aside from focusing unilaterally on clinical aspects of victimisation of (supposedly) serious delict forms, specific 'vulnerable' groups have been at the centre of attention in victimology: in particular, women (Burgess & Holmstrom, 1979a; Krahé & Scheinberger-Olwig, 2002; Löbmann et al., 2003; Ruch & Leon, 1983), children (Finkelhor, 2008; Widom, 2000; Widom et al., 2008) and the elderly (e.g. Bachman et al., 1998; Bennett & Kingston, 1995; Biggs et al., 1995; Fattah & Sacco, 1989; Greve, 1998b; Hosser & Greve, 1998; Klaus, 2000; Payne, 2000).[4] There are several reasons for this focus, of course. For instance, in accordance with myths on rape referred to above, it proved necessary to investigate the psychological consequences of sexual violence against women (e.g. Burgess & Holmstrom, 1979a, 1979b; Feldmann, 1992; Krahé, 1992; Lurigio & Resick, 1990). With respect to older victims of crime, the fact that older people are found to suffer longer from their experiences

of victimisation has implications for support services (Greve & Niederfranke, 1998).

In contrast, the consequences of violence against people who are also more likely to be offenders have been researched less frequently. As pointed out above, young people (especially males from lower socio-economic groups) have a higher victimisation rate pertaining to violent crime relative to other age groups. Though, as in every age group, criminally less serious cases predominate here (e.g. theft of clothes or mobile phone), psychic consequences such as social withdrawal, heightened anxiety or damage to self-esteem, which can be detected in every victim group, can have especially sustainable detrimental consequences for development if experienced in earlier stages of life (Wilmers et al., 2002).

With regard to specific crime-based psychic consequences of criminal victimisation, two topics have been central to research: fear of crime (e.g. Arnold, 1991; Farrall & Gadd, 2004; Gray et al., 2008; Hale, 1996; Jackson, 2004; Kury & Würger, 1993) and punitive responses to perpetrators of crime (e.g. Orth et al., 2006; Sprott & Doob, 1997). With respect to fear of crime, which has been a topic of research for over a century (Ditton & Farrall, 2000; Hale, 1996), the results are somewhat mixed. Contrary to the plausible assumption of an increased fear of crime as a result of victimisation, the evidence is not that conclusive. The heterogeneous effects rather allude to the notion that specific outcomes of coping (e.g. attribution, fear) are not only dependent on the victimisation experience itself but also on the individual's response to it (Greve, 2004): Fear generally seems only to develop if the victimisation experience and its consequences are perceived as largely uncontrollable, and if the individual wasn't able to cope successfully with this experience. If the person is even able to benefit (in certain respect) from the victimisation experience in the sense of a subjective (developmental) gain (e.g. 'friends in need are friends indeed'), the victimisation, which has been perceived as serious and personally uncontrollable, might even strengthen confidence instead of fear. In a similar manner, the evidence for cognitive consequences of victimisation shows a differentiated pattern as well. Accordingly, no results can be found demonstrating that victims demand more severe punishments than non-victims. On the contrary, restitution often has a high priority for victims (Kury & Ferdinand, 2008; Oswald et al., 2009).

Overall, these studies offer a rich description of psychological and physical consequences of victimisation (for a detailed overview see Ruback & Thompson, 2001).

Even though it is not possible to deduce a general theory of victims on the grounds of these studies, they point out severe and long-term consequences of victimisation for further psychological and physical development. For practical purposes such research can serve as an important base (for an overview of victim policy see: Goodey, 2005, pp.183–216 or Spalek, 2006). However, for a scientific study of victimisation processes, these approaches remain insufficient as they are essentially descriptive and inductive. The fact that in many areas of research the findings are so heterogeneous points also to the moderating role of individual and situational conditions and especially intra-individual coping processes. Results from research into coping suggest that the externally estimated seriousness of violence or other crime experiences can only insufficiently predict the differential reactions to victimisation – the individual gravity will fundamentally depend on the available and activated coping processes. Furthermore, the focus on severe experiences of crime, especially violent crime, narrows the research to a clinical perspective and leaves the coping with experiences of crime on an allegedly lower scale (e.g. purse snatching) or delicts aside from violence (e.g. burglary with little property damage, fraud) outside the scope of examination. Moreover, there has been little research so far that deals with the question of the extent of psychic consequences differing between crime experiences and other critical life events (e.g. accident, illness, etc.), for instance due to different attributional patterns with respect to the (assumed) intention of impairment ('why me?', see above) that may leading to different coping reactions.

Coping with Criminal Victimisation: Towards a Theoretical Integration

We have mentioned already that even the very question of whether or not a person who was treated violently perceives (evaluates) him- or herself as a *victim* may depend on individual emotional and cognitive processes. The burden of a victimisation experience certainly has to refer to the *subjectively perceived* burden which can only be estimated by the victim. Biases in memory or attribution (e.g. towards self-incrimination) are not sources of *errors* from this perspective but part of the phenomenon in question. As well as other kinds of reaction they are of special interest in relation to the processes of the psychological and social coping following victimisation. Certainly, such a subjective notion of the term 'victim' cannot altogether operate without intersubjective determinations; the subjective perspective can reach too far as well as be too narrow.

In a first approximation – provided that the underlying experience of the victimisation as an event is chronologically identifiable – four conceptual constitutive aspects of such a victim term can be distinguished. We speak of a *victimisational* experience if an event is (1) perceived or evaluated as aversive, (2) experienced as uncontrollable, (3) attributed to one or more persons as an offender, and (4) perceived as violating a normative expectation (e.g. the formal law) (Greve *et al.*, 1994).

Differences between subjective and objective perspectives may arise with respect to each of these criteria. Accordingly, as mentioned above, it has to be considered with regard to the criterion of controllability that self-attribution could be a potential coping mechanism, whose purpose consists in the perception of controllability of future repetitions of victimisation (Janoff-Bulman, 1979, 1982, 1985; Montada, 1988). This has to be acknowledged in the assessment of the victims' witness accounts: Beyond the psychological memory effects, retrospective evaluations of the event by personally affected people will be systematically biased in multiple ways because of coping processes, without having an impact on the credibility of their accounts (in terms of an *experience-based* account).

Furthermore, the criterion of norm violation is especially problematic. For a criminal victimisation it is doubtless indispensable that the victimising act has been in some sense 'prohibited', 'unfair', and thus 'criminal' in the broadest (juridical or moral) sense; insofar as the victim status is necessarily relative to existing *norms*. However, it is not as straightforward as it seems to qualify those prescriptive norms in terms of the content because it can be unacceptable to take mere subjective standards as a basis. On the other hand, the obvious pragmatic resort to explicitly agreed norms (such as the penal law) equally evokes problems since reference systems can differ considerably between, as well as within, societies (at different points in time). In short: the theoretical clarification of the normative components poses a challenge for criminological victim research that has been hardly dealt with so far; correspondingly, German judicial discussions have made too little effort at developing precise terms in relation to victims (for the German discussion see Höynck, 2002, 2005; Patsourakou, 1994). Here, too, additional difficulties arise from the circumstance that an important coping response to a threat that is perceived as uncontrollable consists in justification, apology, or also belittlement, i.e. in an adjustment of normative standards and frames of judgement (Brandtstädter & Greve, 1994). This will especially frequently be the case if complex social and psychological relations prevail (sexual abuse of spouse may serve as only one example here) that cannot or can only be eluded under extensive psychic 'costs'. The respective subjective criteria finally also fail in those cases in which the victimisation experience is *denied* (repressed).

Notwithstanding, mostly these indicated intricacies can be regarded as methodological challenges rather than obstacles in principle and are therefore translatable into specific research questions. In this sense, it is the task of an ambitious victimology to identify those processes and situations that initiate or promote the devaluation of a threat or the self-attribution of responsibility as a *reaction* to victimisation. As a matter of fact, objective conditions thereby need to be kept in mind; otherwise, research would run the risk, as mentioned above, of eliding the difference between illusion and memories. Even with an intensive anamnesis not only biases can result but also pseudo-biographical memories (Loftus, 1993). Nonetheless, the social scientist will be also interested in the kinds of reaction and processing mechanisms of those cases as though the victim had really experienced these (alleged) events.

After all that has been said so far, it is clear that subjective coping processes of threatening experiences and information play a key role in the explanation of emotional reactions to individually experienced or even only anticipated crime (Agnew, 1985; Lurigio & Resick, 1990; Tov, 1993). Coping with an experience of criminal victimisation will be especially dependent on how far it is perceived as a threat to personal identity (Bard & Sangrey, 1980). The question is – to put it differently – by means of which strategies and mechanisms does an individual succeed in 'neutralising' the consequences of a direct or indirect victimisation experience (Agnew, 1985)? Surprisingly, criminological victimology to date has done relatively little research on coping with anticipated or experienced crime and mainly has not integrated it in more comprehensible theoretical models (Agnew, 1985; Burgess & Holmstrom, 1979a; Tov, 1993). The reason why this is startling is that on the basis of existing studies it is evident that even persons who have been victims of 'serious' events do *not remain* constantly burdened. Psychological research into so-called resilience (e.g. Luthar, 2006; see also Greve & Staudinger, 2006) has only latterly recognised this (Bonanno, 2004;

Masten, 2001) and speaks in the light of these typical results of 'ordinary magic'.

This shortage of systematic coping research with respect to victims of crime is observable even in the better studied fields such as, for example, violence against women (Frazier *et al.*, 2005; Löbmann *et al.*, 2003). An exception in the German language area can be seen in the study of Richter (1997) which explicitly refers to a psychological coping theory (Lazarus, 1991). Yet, classical coping models such as Lazarus's do not account for the particularity of criminal victimisation; in particular, the intentional harming of the victim by the offender is hardly considered. Moreover, subsequent integration with developmental psychology is lacking. For example, one could ask whether the influence of such severe incisions in the development differs for different developmental situations (life phases). Furthermore, coping reactions should not only vary in dependence on the experience of victimisation but also be dependent on individual experiences and resources (see e.g. Hosser & Greve, 1998). With regard to other, better studied stressful events such as, for example, diseases or accidents, numerous studies point out that coping reactions do not only differ between people but also to a large extent between situations within the same person (e.g. Montada *et al.*, 1992). Unfortunately, there is a shortage of longitudinal studies spanning a considerable time in the field of criminal victimisation, and an integrative theoretical frame is still missing.

The central thesis of this chapter claims that a developmental psychological perspective could possibly offer an integrative frame for research on victims dealing with the victimisation experience. According to this perspective, coping reactions can be seen as being dependent on development on the one hand and regulating development (and its consequences) on the other (Brandtstädter, 2006; Brandtstädter & Greve, 1994). The psychological significance of such an event in life (apart from the already addressed direct clinical effect in the sense of a trauma) should be visible in a life-changing impact (Greve & Wilmers, 2003) – only then can one speak meaningfully about a 'critical life event'.

The starting point of such an approach lies in the observation that the majority of the currently discussed theories in the psychological coping research share the basic assumption that burdensome and threatening events create a discrepancy between the perceived and the aspired individual situation, which can be solved either through changing the threatening problem or through adjusting the individual's evaluation of it.

'Defensive' strategies such as e.g. complete perceptive ignorance, denegation or context avoidance (Brandtstädter & Greve, 1994) come logically prior to the described kinds of reactions. This notion of two possible modes of reaction to a *perceived and accepted* aversive experience or situation results in a two-process model, the basic assumptions of which are shared by several of the current approaches to developmental regulation (Brandtstädter, 2001; Brandtstädter & Rothermund, 2002; Brandtstädter et al., 1999; Freund et al., 1999; Heckhausen & Mayr, 1998; for a summary: Börner & Jopp, 2007; Greve & Wentura 2007).

With regard to the experienced victimisation, the affected people are only able to respond in compensatory or restitutive ways. Nevertheless, pertaining to their further development, they can actively try to avoid additional consequences and especially repetitions of criminal victimisation through their behaviour, for example by moving from a (subjectively) dangerous area, participating in self-defence classes, or changing their social behaviour in order to prevent a suspected crime (e.g. Skogan, 1981; Yin, 1985). Such 'assimilative' coping (Brandtstädter & Rothermund, 2002) will not only represent a current reparation but also a development of the person if subsequently the life course, the competence profile of the person or the social constellation is changed substantially and sustainably. Besides, these (possibly enforced) changes of the life situation may produce new conditions for development that again mean a change of the life course.

Beyond individual resources of resilience, the effects of social support for victims of crime have also been studied. Often, however, social support for victims of crime is low and, even worse, ambivalent in its influence (Hosser, 1997). On the one hand, helpers often are not sensitive enough at recognising the needs of victims, or not adequately competent to fulfil them. Furthermore, helpers sometimes feel threatened by the victim's violence experience, for example in their feeling of security or trust in other people. That could be a reason why they may behave in additionally burdening ways towards the victim, for instance through imputing a special need for help to the victim. The support and treatment of victims – beyond the generally warranted health care and principally accessible judicial counselling – is mostly only systematically available for specific crimes (e.g. violence against women). Frequently, institutional resources are neither known nor are they drawn on (Wetzels et al., 1995). On the other hand, victims are, for several reasons, not in every case able or willing to accept help offered by others. The individual search for professional support frequently fails because of psychological obstacles: shame and fear of secondary victimisation and stigmatisation inhibit the utilisation of therapeutic support in a multitude of cases and have effects on the willingness to report the criminal event (Campbell, 2006; Kühnle & Sullivan, 2003; Lurigio & Mechanic, 2000; Singer, 1988; for further discussion of victims' needs and rights and balancing of offenders' rights see Goodey, 2005, pp.121–177).

Individual coping resources may thus become the key factor in explaining successful coping responses. As mentioned previously, coping with criminal victimisation will aim at adjusting the self-image and the personal goals and values ('readjustment of the self'; Bard & Sangrey, 1980, p.29). Only such adaptations can help to permanently overcome the victimisation and its associated consequences. Hence, in such an 'accommodative' mode (Brandtstädter & Rothermund, 2002) the palliative integration of threatening experiences is accomplished by, for example, flexible adjustment of goals, standards of evaluation and preferences. These modifications not only denote a development in themselves but ultimately also influence the ongoing shaping of the life course.

If crime victimisations are considered as prototypes of a critical (developmental) life event, then the individual meaning of such an experience has not only to be studied with regard to acute emotional (e.g. fear of crime) or clinical consequences (e.g. PTSD), but also with respect to long-term shifts and adjustments of developmental characteristics (e.g. concerning the self and personality). Accordingly, if our claim that accommodative ways of development regulation are especially important in the individual coping with an experience of crime victimisation (as a prototype of a threatening and damaging event that is perceived as unalterable) is not to fail, then it should be possible to show empirically that the individual's tendency to respond to stressful events with accommodative reactions also predicts adaptive ways of dealing with crime victimisation with respect to psychic health and personal well-being. The assumption that people, who tend towards 'accommodative' coping in this sense, show significantly less fear or other indicators of burdening could be confirmed in initial studies (e.g. Greve et al., 1996; Greve & Wilmers, 2003). These results also suggest differentiating the individual responses more thoroughly. For instance, fear reactions need in no way to be strictly considered as dysfunctional. On the contrary, it frequently implies protective, respectively preventive (and in this sense adaptive) behaviour. Fear is often measured on a behavioural level which not only may result in a reduction of the risk of victimisation (Greve, 1998a, 2004) but also offers options for the individual's positive framing of the necessity to behave cautiously. Admittedly, the findings available so far merely prove the plausibility of such a train of thought. Particularly with respect to the cross-sectional design of existing studies, it cannot be spoken about as a strict testing of the developmental psychological arguments thus far.

Perspectives for Intervention and Research

Victimological research is indeed in need of extension pertaining to this line of reasoning in multiple respects. For instance, it would be interesting to examine the consequences of victimisation for other facets of the self (e.g. self-efficacy) rather than for self-esteem which has been the main focus of attention until now. Moreover, experiences of victimisation influence different aspects of the mental state (well-being, general life-quality, depression and mental health). Apart from the regular recording of post-traumatic stress disorders, psychosomatic or physical consequences could be systematically included as well. This is especially true for ostensibly less serious crimes (e.g. burglary, theft, harassment).

Furthermore, an important aspect lies in the question of the operationalisation of victimisation. Especially from a developmental psychology perspective, not only the point in time, duration and the quality of the victimisation have to be accounted for but also the possible (biographical) history. Moreover, after all that has been said above, it can be deduced that it may sometimes be more reasonable to analyse delicts separately, instead of using an overall indicator for some research questions: the question then becomes which experiences of victimisation have what consequences. Accordingly, some findings indicate that different delicts (e.g. with familiar offenders vs. strangers) have markedly differential effects.

The question about resources of transformation would be a valid continuation with respect to developmental psychology, going beyond a deeper understanding of coping with experiences of victimisation. Which individual and social resources support adjustment perhaps depends on delict type and also individual preconditions. Conversely, which individual and social resources are developed in reaction to victimisation and

which are the individual and social aiding conditions therefore are important issues. The finding that flexible resources of coping occur along with especially high rates of fear raises the question of in what way fear itself could be an adaptive resource in coping with crime. It also remains to be investigated – on the grounds of the previously outlined perspective of escalation risks – to what extent resources of coping and developmental processes contribute to the occurrence of victimisation. This could have significant practical importance, specifically for preventive purposes.

Altogether, the current state of affairs is barely more than the beginning of a mosaic. Research into coping with criminal victimisation experiences is only now beginning to be seriously addressed. All mentioned aspects show convergently that longitudinal studies over a long span of time are a central desideratum of victimology. Moreover, there is a lack of research that concentrates on the noteworthy characteristic of crime victimisation (in contrast to diseases, accidents or catastrophes with respect to deliberately or recklessly harming). Particularly, there is a scarcity of attempts at integrating a multitude of specific findings and considerations into a theoretical framework which makes the meaning of an experience with serious crime for the life of the directly or indirectly affected persons comprehensible.

Notes

1 *All* BCS violence includes common assault, wounding, robbery and snatch theft.
2 Special circumstances such as the case with self-defence (the 'victim' of the self-defending victim) or dynamics of escalation where the involved could expect or accept violence (e.g. fights between rival gangs or hooligans) are not part of the scope of this chapter. In these cases the description of the persons concerned as 'victims' would not be prototypical any more in an important way, if appropriate at all.
3 The term 'secondary victimisation' denotes the victim's stressing social experiences following a criminal victimisation experience in contact with, e.g. the criminal justice system, family, friends, and co-workers, hospital personnel, or social service workers. The victimisation results, for example, due to the already mentioned blaming of the victim, but also by the lack of or incompetent help service provision or the inadequately perceived social response to the criminal victimisation (e.g. disbelieving, making fun of, and seeing distress as a personal problem).

4   We do not discuss the literature on the consequences of victimisation in war or torture here (for a review see, e.g. Butterfield *et al.*, 2005; Fairbank *et al.*, 1991), although these experiences, of course, result in serious psychic damages and impairment (sleep disorder, panic attacks, flashbacks) despite the physical damages produced by such immoral practices.

References

Agnew, R.S. (1985). Neutralizing the impact of crime. *Criminal Justice and Behavior, 12*, 221–239.

Arnold, H. (1991). Fear of crime and its relationship to directly and indirectly experienced victimization: A binational comparison of models. In K. Sessar & H.-J. Kerner (Eds.) *Development in crime and crime control research* (pp.87–125). New York: Springer.

Bachman, R., Dillaway, H. & Lachs, M.S. (1998). Violence against the elderly: A comparative analysis of robbery and assault across age and gender groups. *Research on Ageing, 20*(2), 183–198.

Baier, D. (2008). *Entwicklung der Jugenddelinquenz und ausgewählter Bedingungsfaktoren seit 1998 in den Städten Hannover, München, Stuttgart und Schwäbisch Gmünd* [Development of youth delinquency and selected causal factors in the cities Hannover, Munich, Stuttgart, and Schwäbisch Gmünd since 1998]. KFN: Forschungsberichte Nr. 104.

Baier, D. & Windzio, M. (2008). Zur Entwicklung der Jugendgewalt seit 1998 in den Städten München, Stuttgart und Schwäbisch Gmünd [About the development of youth violence in the cities Munich, Stuttgart & Schwäbisch Gmünd since 1998]. In Rehberg, K.-S. (Ed.) *Die Natur der Gesellschaft. Verhandlungen des 33. Kongresses der Deutschen Gesellschaft für Soziologie in Kassel 2006.* Frankfurt/Main: Campus.

Bard, M. & Sangrey, D. (1980). Things fall apart: Victims in crisis. *Evaluation and Change (Special Issue)*, 28–35.

Baschetti, R. (2008). Genetic evidence that Darwin was right about criminality: Nature not nurture. *Medical Hypotheses, 70*, 1092–1102.

Ben-Ya'acov, Y. & Amir, M. (2004). Posttraumatic symptoms and suicide risk. *Personality and Individual Differences, 36*, 1257–1264.

Bennett, G. & Kingston, P. (1995). *Elder abuse: Concepts, theories and interventions.* London: Chapman & Hall.

Biggs, S., Phillipson, C. & Kingston, P. (1995). *Elder abuse in perspective.* Buckingham: Open University Press.

Bilsky, W., Pfeiffer, C. & Wetzels, P. (Eds.) (1993). *Fear of crime and criminal victimization.* Stuttgart: Enke.

Birkbeck, C. & LaFree, G. (1993). The situational analysis of crime and deviance. *Annual Review of Sociology, 19*, 113–137.

Block, C.R. & Block, R.L. (1984). Crime definition, crime measurement, and victim surveys. *Journal of Social Issues, 40*, 137–160.

Börner, K. & Jopp, D. (2007). A review and comparison of three major life-span theories: Common and unique feature. *Human Development, 50*, 171–195.

Bonanno, G.A. (2004). Loss, trauma, and human resilience. Have we underestimated the human capacity to thrive after extremely aversive events? *American Psychologist, 59*, 20–28.

Brandtstädter, J. (2001). *Entwicklung – Intentionalität – Handeln* [Development – intentionality – action]. Stuttgart: Kohlhammer.

Brandtstädter, J. (2006). Action perspectives on human development. In R.M. Lerner (Ed.) *Handbook of child psychology: Vol. 1. Theoretical models of human development* (6th edn, pp.516–568). New York: Wiley.

Brandtstädter, J. & Greve, W. (1994). The aging self: Stabilizing and protective processes. *Developmental Review, 14*, 52–80.

Brandtstädter, J. & Rothermund, K. (2002). The life course dynamics of goal pursuit and goal adjustment: A two-process framework. *Developmental Review, 22*, 117–150.

Brandtstädter, J., Wentura, D. & Rothermund, K. (1999). Intentional self-development through adulthood and later life: Tenacious pursuit and flexible adjustment of goals. In J. Brandtstädter & R.M. Lerner (Eds.) *Action and self-development: Theory and research through the life span* (pp.373–400). Thousand Oaks, CA: Sage.

Bundeskriminalamt. *Polizeiliche Kriminalstatistik* [Police Crime Statistics] [Data file]. Retrieved 2 September 2009 from www.bka.de/pks/zeitreihen/pdf/t91_opfer_insg.pdf

Burgess, A.W. & Holmstrom, L.L. (1979a). Adaptive strategies and recovery from rape. *American Journal of Psychiatry, 136*, 1278–1282.

Burgess, A.W. & Holmstrom, L.L. (1979b). *Rape: Crisis and recovery.* Bowie, MD: Brady.

Burt, M.R. (1980). Cultural myths and supports for rape. *Journal of Personality and Social Psychology, 38*(2), 217–230.

Butterfield, M.I., Lapp, K.G., Bosworth, H.B., Strauss, J.L., Stechuchak, K.M., Horner, R.D. *et al.* (2005). Lifetime sexual and physical victimization among male veterans with combat-related post-traumatic stress disorder. *Military Medicine, 170*(9), 787–790.

Campbell, R. (2006). Rape survivors' experiences with the legal and medical systems: Do rape victim advocates make a difference? *Violence Against Women, 12*, 30–45.

Campbell, R., Sefl, T., Barnes, H.E., Ahrens, C.E., Wasco, S.M. & Zaragoza-Diesfeld, Y. (1999). Community services for rape survivors: Enhancing psychological well-being or increasing trauma? *Journal of Consulting and Clinical Psychology, 67*(6), 847–858.

Carroll, J.C. (1977). The intergenerational transmission of family violence: The long-term effects of aggressive behavior. *Aggressive Behavior, 3*, 289–299.

Cole, J., Logan, T. & Shannon, L. (2008). Women's risk for revictimization by a new abusive partner: For what should we be looking? *Violence and Victims*, 23(3), 315–330.

Correia, I., Vala, J. & Aguiar, P. (2001). The effects of belief in a just world and victim's innocence on secondary victimization, judgements of justice and deservingness. *Social Justice Research*, 14(3), 327–342.

Daly, M. & Wilson, M. (1988). *Homicide*. New York: Aldine de Gruyter.

Denkers, A. & Winkel, F. (1998). Crime victims' well being and fear in a prospective and longitudinal study. *International Review of Victimology*, 5, 93–140.

Ditton, D. & Farrall, S. (2000). *The fear of crime*. Aldershot: Ashgate.

Eagly, A.H. & Wood, W. (1999). The origins of sex differences in human behavior: Evolved dispositions versus social roles. *American Psychologist*, 54, 408–423.

Ehrensaft, M.K., Cohen, P., Brown, J., Smailes, E., Chen, H. & Johnson, J.G. (2003). Intergenerational transmission of partner violence: A 20-year prospective study. *Journal of Consulting and Clinical Psychology*, 71, 741–753.

Enzmann, D. & Greve, W. (2001). Jugend im Gefängnis: Soziale und individuelle Bedingungen von Delinquenz und Sanktionierung [Youth in prison: Social and individual conditions of delinquency and sanction]. In M. Bereswill & W. Greve (Hrsg.) *Forschungsthema Strafvollzug* [Research topic penal system] (S.109–145). Baden-Baden: Nomos.

Enzmann, D., Wetzels, P. & Pfeiffer, C. (1999). Youth violence in Germany: A study of victimisation and delinquency in four major cities. In G.J.N. Bruinsma & C.D. van der Vijver (Eds.) *Public Safety in Europe* (pp.93–109). Enschede: International Police Institute Twente, University of Twente.

Fagot, B.I. & Hagan, R. (1985). Aggression in toddlers: Responses to the assertive acts of boys and girls. *Sex Roles*, 12, 241–351.

Fairbank, J.A., Hansen, D.J. & Fitterling, J.M. (1991). Patterns of appraisal and coping across different stressor conditions among former prisoners of war with and without posttraumatic stress disorder. *Journal of Consulting and Clinical Psychology*, 59(2), 274–281.

Farrall, S. & Gadd, D. (2004). The frequency of the fear of crime. *British Journal of Criminology*, 44, 127–132.

Farrington, D.P. (1996). *Understanding and preventing youth crime*. New York: Joseph Rowntree Foundation.

Farrington, D.P. & Painter, K. A. (2004). *Gender differences in risk factors for offending*. London: Home Office.

Fattah, E.A. (1989). Victims and victimology: The facts and the rhetoric. *International Review of Victimology*, 1(1), 43–66.

Fattah, E.A. (1991). *Understanding criminal victimization*. Scarborough, ON: Prentice Hall.

Fattah, E.A. & Sacco, V.F. (1989). *Crime and victimization of the elderly*. New York: Springer.

Feldmann, H. (unter Mitarbeit von J. Westenhöfer) (1992). *Vergewaltigung und ihre psychischen Folgen* [Rape and its psychological consequences]. Stuttgart: Enke.

Finkelhor, D. (2008). *Childhood victimization: Violence, crime, and abuse in the lives of young people*. New York: Oxford University Press.

Frazier, P.A., Mortensen, H. & Steward, J. (2005). Coping strategies as mediators of the relations among perceived control and distress in sexual assault survivors. *Journal of Counseling Psychology*, 52(3), 267–278.

Freund, A., Li, K. & Baltes, P. (1999). Successful development and aging: The role of selection, optimization, and compensation. In J. Brandtstädter & R.M. Lerner (Eds.) *Action and selfdevelopment: Theory and research through the life span* (pp.401–434). Thousand Oaks, CA: Sage.

Friedman, M. (2006). *Post-traumatic and acute stress disorders: The latest assessment and treatment strategies* (4th edn). Kansas City, MO: Compact Clinicals.

Gannon, M. & Mihorean, K. (2005). Criminal victimization in Canada, 2004. *Juristat*, 25(7), 1–27.

Germany's Federal Criminal Police Office (n.d.). Retrieved 16 February 2009, from www.bka.de/pks/zeitreihen/pdf/t91_opfer_insg.pdf.

Goodey, J. (2005). *Victims and victimology: Research, policy and practice*. London: Longman.

Gottfredson, M.R. & Hindelang, M.J. (1977). A consideration of telescoping and memory decay biases in victimization surveys. *Journal of Criminal Justice*, 5(3), 205–216.

Goudriaan, H., Wittebrood, K. & Nieuwbeerta, P. (2006). Neighborhood characteristics and reporting crime. Effects of social cohesion, confidence in police effectiveness and socio-economic disadvantage. *British Journal of Criminology*, 46, 719–742.

Gray, E., Jackson, J. & Farrall, S. (2008). Reassessing the fear of crime. *European Journal of Criminology*, 5(3), 363–380.

Greve, W. (1998a). Fear of crime among the elderly: Foresight, not fright. *International Review of Victimology*, 5, 277–309.

Greve, W. (1998b). The threat of violence and criminality in old age: Findings and open questions. In M. Oehmichen (Ed.) *Maltreatment and torture* (pp.115–133). Lübeck: Schmidt-Römhild.

Greve, W. (2004). Fear of crime among older and younger adults: Paradoxes and other misconceptions. In H.-J. Albrecht, T. Serassis & H. Kania (Eds.) *Images of crime II* (pp.167–186). Freiburg: Max-Planck-Institut für Internationales und vergleichendes Strafrecht.

Greve, W. & Bilsky, W. (1997). Viktimologie. Opfererfahrungen und Prozesse der Bewältigung [Victimology. Victimization experiences and processes of coping]. In M. Steller & R. Volbert (Hrsg.) *Psychologie im Strafverfahren* [Psychology in the criminal proceeding] (S. 206–223). Bern: Huber.

Greve, W., Hosser, D. & Wetzels, P. (1996). *Bedrohung durch Kriminalität im Alter. Kriminalitätsfurcht älterer Menschen als Brennpunkt einer Gerontoviktimologie* [Threat through criminality in old age. Fear of crime of the elderly as focus of gerontovictimology]. Baden-Baden: Nomos.

Greve, W. & Niederfranke, A. (1998). Bedrohung durch Gewalt und Kriminalität im Alter [Threat through violence and crime in old age]. *Zeitschrift für Klinische Psychologie, 27,* 130–135.

Greve, W. & Staudinger, U.M. (2006). Resilience in later adulthood and old age: Resources and potentials for successful aging. In D. Cichetti & D. Cohen (Eds.) *Developmental psychopathology* (2nd edn, vol. 3, pp.796–840). New York: Wiley.

Greve, W., Strobl, R. & Wetzels, P. (1994). *Das Opfer kriminellen Handelns: Flüchtig und nicht zu fassen. Konzeptuelle Probleme und methodische Implikationen eines sozialwissenschaftlichen Opferbegriffes* [The victim of criminal actions: Elusive and not to grasp. Conceptual problems and methodological implications of a social scientific victim term]. KFN-Forschungsberichte, Nr. 33. Hannover: KFN.

Greve, W., Strobl, R. & Wetzels, P. (1997). Opferforschung und Zeugenpsychologie: Opferzeugen in der viktimologischen Forschung [Victimology and psychology of the witness: Victim witnesses in the victimological research]. In L. Greuel, T. Fabian & M. Stadler (Hrsg.) *Psychologie der Zeugenaussage. Ergebnisse der rechtspsychologischen Forschung* [Psychology of the victim account. Results of a law psychological research] (S. 247–260). Weinheim: PVU.

Greve, W. & Wentura, D. (2007). Personal and subpersonal regulation of human development: Beyond complementary categories (Commentary on Boerner and Jopp). *Human Development, 50,* 201–207.

Greve, W. & Wilmers, N. (2003). Schulgewalt und Selbstwertempfinden. Zum moderierenden Einfluss von Bewältigungsressourcen bei Tätern und Opfern [School violence and self-esteem. About the moderating role of coping resources of perpetrators and victims]. *Psychologie in Erziehung und Unterricht, 50,* 353–368.

Hale, C. (1996). Fear of crime: A review of the literature. *International Review of Victimology, 4,* 79–150.

Heckhausen, J. & Mayr, U. (1998). Entwicklungsregulation und Kontrolle im Erwachsenenalter und Alter: Lebenslaufpsychologische Perspektiven [Developmental regulation and control in adulthood and old age: Life-span psychological perspectives]. In H. Keller (Hrsg.) *Lehrbuch der Entwicklungspsychologie* [Textbook of developmental psychology] (pp.399–422). Bern: Huber.

Herbert, T.B. & Dunkel-Schetter, C. (1992). Negative social reactions to victims: An overwiew of responses and their determinants. In L. Monada, S.-H. Filipp & M.J. Lerner (Eds.) *Life crises and experiences of loss in adulthood* (pp.497–518). Hillsdale, NJ: Lawrence Erlbaum.

Hilton, N.Z., Harris, G.T. & Rice, M.E. (2000). The functions of aggression by male teenagers. *Journal of Personality and Social, 79*(6), 988–994.

Hosser, D. (1997). Hilfe oder Hindernis? Die Bedeutung sozialer Unterstützung für Opfer krimineller Gewalt [Help or obstacle? The meaning of social support for victims of criminal violence]. *Monatsschrift für Kriminologie und Strafrechtsreform, 80*(6), 389–403.

Hosser, D. & Greve, W. (1998). Victimization in old age: Consequences for mental health and protective conditions. In A. Maercker, Z. Solomon & M. Schützwohl (Eds.) *Posttraumatic stress disorder: Life-span developmental perspective* (pp.177–198). Seattle/Göttingen: Hogrefe & Huber.

Hosser, D., Raddatz, S. & Windzio, M. (2007). Child maltreatment, revictimization and violent behavior. *Violence and Victims, 22,* 318–333.

Höynck, T. (2002). Viktimologische Forderungen an Rechtspflege und Strafrechtswissenschaft [Victimological demands on judicature and penology]. In Barton, S. (Hrsg.) *Verfahrensgerechtigkeit und Zeugenbeweis: Fairness für Opfer und Beschuldigte* [Procedual justice and evidence of a witness: Fairness for the victim and the defendant]. Reihe Interdisziplinäre Studien zu Recht und Staat. Baden-Baden: Nomos.

Höynck, T. (2005). *Das Opfer zwischen Parteirechten und Zeugenpflichten. Eine rechtsvergleichende Untersuchung zur Rolle des Opfers im Strafverfahren in Deutschland, der Schweiz und England* [The victim between rights and obligations. A comparative law study about the role of the victim in the criminal proceeding in Germany, Switzerland, and England]. Baden-Baden: Nomos.

Jackson, J. (2004). Experience and expression: Social and cultural significance in the fear of crime. *British Journal of Criminology, 44*(6), 946–966.

Janoff-Bulman, R. (1979). Characterological versus behavioral self-blame: Inquiries into depression and rape. *Journal of Personality and Social Psychology, 37,* 1798–1809.

Janoff-Bulman, R. (1982). Esteem and control bases of blame: 'Adaptive' strategies for victims versus observers. *Journal of Personality, 50,* 180–192.

Janoff-Bulman, R. (1985). Criminal vs. non-criminal victimization: Victims' reactions. *Victimology, 10,* 498–511.

Jung, H. (1993). Viktimologie [Victimology]. In G. Kaiser, H.-J. Kerner, F. Sack & H. Schellhoss (Hrsg.) *Kleines Kriminologische Wörterbuch* [Small criminological dictionary] (3. Aufl., S. 582–588). Heidelberg: C.F. Müller.

Karmen, A. (1991). The controversy over shared responsibility. Is victim-blaming ever justified? In D. Sank & D.I. Caplan (Eds.) *To be a victim. Encounters with crime and justice* (pp.395–408). New York: Plenum.

Karmen, A. (2006). *Crime victims: An introduction to victimology* (6th edn). Belmont, CA: Wadsworth.

Kershaw, C., Nicholas, S. & Walker, A. (Eds.) (2008). *Crime in England and Wales. Findings from the British Crime Survey and police recorded crime 2007/2008.* Home Office Statistical Bulletin, 07/08. London: Home Office. Retrieved 2 September 2009 from www.homeoffice.gov.uk/rds/pdfs08/hosb0708.pdf

Kiefl, W. & Sieger, M. (1993). Kein Ausweg für Karin? Anmerkungen zur Opferkarriere [No back door for Karin? Notes on a victim career]. *Kriminalistik, 4*(93), 261–267.

Klaus, P.A. (2000). *Crimes against persons age 65 or older, 1992–97*. Washington, DC: Bureau of Justice Statistics.

Krahé, B. (1992). Coping with rape: A social psychological perspective. In L. Montada, S.-H. Filipp & M.R. Lerner (Eds.) *Life crises and experiences of loss in adulthood* (pp.477–496). Hillsdale, NJ: Lawrence Erlbaum.

Krahé, B. (2000). Childhood sexual abuse and revictimization in adolescence and adulthood. *Journal of Personal and Interpersonal Loss, 5*, 149–165.

Krahé, B. & Scheinberger-Olwig, R. (2002). *Sexuelle Agression: Verbreitungsgrad und Risikofaktoren bei Jugendlichen und jungen Erwachsenen* [Sexual aggression: Prevalence and risk factors of juveniles and young adults]. Göttingen: Hogrefe.

Krahé, B., Temkin, J., Bieneck, S. & Berger, A. (2008). Prospective lawyers' rape stereotypes and schematic decision-making about rape cases. *Psychology, Crime and Law, 14*, 461–479.

Kühnle, K. & Sullivan, A. (2003). Gay and lesbian victimization. *Criminal Justice and Behavior, 30*(1), 85–96.

Kury, H. & Ferdinand, T. (Eds.) (2008). *International perspectives on punitivity*. Bochum: Universitätsverlag Brockmeyer.

Kury, H. & Würger, M. (1993). Opfererfahrung und Kriminalitätsfurcht. Ein Beitrag zur Viktimisierungsperspektive [Victimization and fear of crime. A contribution to the victimization perspective]. In G. Kaiser & H. Kury (Hrsg.) *Kriminologische Forschung in den 90er Jahren* [Criminological research of the 90ies] (S. 411–462). Freiburg: Max-Planck-Institut für ausländisches und internationales Strafrecht.

Lavrakas, P. (1993). *Telephone survey methods: Sampling, selection, and supervision (Applied social research methods)* (2nd edn). Thousand Oaks, CA: Sage.

Lazarus, R.S. (1991). *Emotion and adaption*. New York: Oxford University Press.

Lerner, M.J. (1977). The justice motive: Some hypotheses as to its origins and forms. *Journal of Personality, 45*, 1–52.

Levitt, S.D. (1998). The relationship between crime reporting and police: Implications for the use of uniform crime reports. *Journal of Quantitative Criminology, 14*(1), 61–81.

Löbmann, R., Greve, W., Wetzels, P. & Bosold, C. (2003). Violence against women: Conditions, consequences, and coping. *Psychology, Crime and Law, 9*(4), 309–331.

Loftus, E.F. (1993). The reality of repressed memories. *American Psychologist, 48*, 518–537.

Lurigio, A.J. & Mechanic, M.B. (2000). The importance of being sensitive and responsive to crime victims. *Police Magazine, 24*, 22–28.

Lurigio, A.J. & Resick, P.A. (1990). Healing the psychological wounds of criminal victimization. Predicting postcrime distress and recovery. In A.J. Lurigio, W.G. Skogan & R.C. Davis (Eds.) *Victims of crime. Problems, policies, and programs* (pp.50–68). Beverly Hills, CA: Sage.

Luthar, S.S. (2006). Resilience in development: A synthesis of research across five decades. In D. Cicchetti & D.J. Cohen (Eds.) *Developmental psychopathology: Risk, disorder, and adaptation* (pp.740–795). New York: Wiley.

Maercker, A., Solomon, Z. & Schützwohl, M. (Eds.) (1999). *Post-traumatic stress disorder: A life-span developmental perspective*. Seattle/Göttingen: Hogrefe & Huber.

Masten, A.S. (2001). Resilienz in der Entwicklung. Wunder des Alltags [Resilience in development. Magic of the everyday life]. In G. Röper, C. von Hagen & G. Noam (Hrsg.) *Entwicklung und Risiko. Perspektiven einer klinischen Entwicklungspsychologie* [Development and risk. Perspectives of a clinical developmental psychology] (S. 192–219). Stuttgart: Kohlhammer.

Mayhew, P. & Van Dijk, J.J.M. (1997). *Criminal victimisation in eleven industrialised countries. Key findings from the 1996 International Crime Victims Survey*. The Hague: Ministry of Justice, WODC.

Moffitt, T.E., Caspi, A., Rutter, M. & Silva, P.A. (2001). *Sex differences in antisocial behavior: Conduct disorder, delinquency, and violence in the Dunedin Longitudinal Study*. Cambridge: Cambridge University Press.

Montada, L. (1988). Bewältigung von 'Schicksalsschlägen' – erlebte Ungerechtigkeit und wahrgenommene Verantwortlichkeit [Coping with 'strokes of fate' – experienced injustice and perceived responsibility]. *Schweizerische Zeitschrift für Psychologie, 47*, 203–216.

Montada, L., Filipp, S.-H. & Lerner, M.J. (Eds.) (1992). *Life crises and the experience of loss in adulthood*. Hillsdale, NJ: Lawrence Erlbaum.

Montada, L. & Lerner, M.J. (Eds.) (1998). *Responses to victimizations and belief in a just world*. New York: Plenum.

Natvig, G.K., Albrektsen, G. & Qvarnstrom, U. (2001). Psychosomatic symptoms among victims of school bullying. *Journal of Health Psychology, 6*(4), 365–377.

Nieuwbeerta. P. (Ed.) (2002). *Crime victimization in comparative perspective. Results from the International Crime Victims Survey, 1989–2000*. The Hague: Boom Legal Publishers.

Norris, F.H. & Kaniasty, K. (1994). Psychological distress following criminal victimization in the general population: Cross-sectional, longitudinal and prospective analyses. *Journal of Consulting and Clinical Psychology, 62*, 111–123.

Oehmichen, M. (Ed.) (1998). *Maltreatment and torture*. Lübeck: Schmidt-Römhild.

Orth, U., Montada, L. & Maerker, A. (2006). Feelings of revenge, retaliation motive, and posttraumatic stress reactions in crime victims. *Journal of Interpersonal Violence, 21*, 229–243.

O'Shea, T. (2006). Physical deterioration, disorder, and crime. *Criminal Justice Policy Review, 17*(2), 173–187.

Oswald, M.E., Bieneck, S. & Hupfeld-Heinemann, J. (Eds.) (2009). *Social psychology of punishment of crime*. Chichester: Wiley.

Patsourakou, S.N. (1994). *Die Stellung des Verletzten im Strafrechtssystem: Eine rechtsdogmatische, rechtsphilosophische und rechtspolitische Analyse* [The status of the victimized in the penal system: An analysis according to legal doctrine, philosophy, and politics]. Bonn: Forum-Verlag Godesberg.

Payne, B.K. (2000). *Crime and elder abuse: An integrated perspective.* Springfield, IL: Charles Thomas.

Ramirez, I.L. & Straus, M.A. (2006). The effect of question order on disclosure of intimate partner violence: An experimental test using the Conflict Tactics Scales. *Journal of Family Violence, 21,* 1–9.

Reidy, D.E., Sloan, C.A. & Zeichner, A. (2009). Gender role conformity and aggression: The influence of perpetrator and victim conformity on direct physical aggression in women. *Personality & Individual Differences, 46,* 231–235.

Resick, P.A. (1987). Psychological effects of victimization: Implications for the criminal justice system. *Crime and Delinquency, 33,* 468–478.

Richter, H. (1997). *Opfer krimineller Gewalttaten: Individuelle Folgen und ihre Verarbeitung; Ergebnisse einer Untersuchung* [Victims of violent crime: Individual consequences and their prevalence; results of a study]. Mainz: Weißer Ring.

Riggs, D.S., Kilpatrick, D.G. & Resnick, H.S. (1992). Long-term psychological distress associated with marital rape and aggravated assault: A comparison to other crime victims. *Journal of Family Violence, 7,* 783–296.

Ruback, R.B. & Thompson, M.P. (2001). *Social and psychological consequences of violent victimization.* Thousand Oaks, CA: Sage.

Ruch, L.O. & Leon, J.L. (1983). Type of sexual assault trauma: A multidimensional analysis of a short-term panel. *Victimology, 8*(3–4), 237–250.

Ryan, W. (1971). *Blaming the victim.* New York: Pantheon Books.

Saigh, A.P. (1995). *Posttraumatische Belastungsstörung. Diagnose und Behandlung psychischer Störungen bei Opfern von Gewalttaten und Katastrophen* [Post-traumatic stress disorder. Diagnosis and treatment of psychic disorders of victims of violence or catastrophes]. Bern: Huber.

Sank, D. & Caplan, D.I. (Eds.) (1991). *To be a victim. Encounters with crime and justice.* New York: Plenum.

Schneider, H.J. (1994). *Kriminologie der Gewalt* [Criminology of violence]. Stuttgart: Hirzel.

Schneider, H.J. (Hrsg.). (2007). *Internationales Handbuch der Kriminologie 1. Grundlagen der Kriminologie* [International handbook of criminology 1. Basics of criminology]. Berlin: de Gruyter Recht.

Schneider, A.L. & Sumi, D. (1981). Patterns of forgetting and telescoping. *Criminology, 19*(3), 400–410.

Schiraldi, G.R. (2000). *The post-traumatic stress disorder source book: A guide to healing, recovery, and growth.* Lincolnwood, IL: Lowell House.

Shafer, S. (1968/1977). *Victimology: The victim and his criminal.* Reston, VA: Reston.

Shapland, J. & Hall, M. (2007). What do we know about the effects of crime on victims? *International Review of Victimology, 14,* 175–217.

Shapland, J., Willmore, J. & Duff, P. (1985). *Victims in the criminal justice system.* Aldershot: Gower.

Singer, S.I. (1988). The fear of reprisal and the failure of victims to report a personal crime. *Journal of Quantitative Criminology, 4*(3), 289–302.

Skogan, W.G. (1981). On attitudes and behaviors. In D.A. Lewis (Ed.) *Reactions to crime* (pp.19–45). Beverly Hills, CA: Sage.

Skogan, W.G. (1990). *Disorder and decline: Crime and the spiral of decay in American neighbourhoods.* New York: Free Press.

Sontag, S. (2003). *Regarding the pain of others.* London: Hamish Hamilton.

Spalek, B. (2006). *Crime victims: Theory, policy and practice.* Basingstoke: Palgrave Macmillan.

Sparks, R.F. (1981). Surveys of victimization – an optimistic assessment. In M. Tonry & N. Morris (Eds.) *Crime and justice. An annual review of research* (vol. 3, pp.1–60). Chicago, IL: University of Chicago Press.

Sprott, J.B. & Doob, A.N. (1997). Fear, victimization and attitudes to sentencing, the courts and the police. *Canadian Journal of Criminology, 39,* 275–292.

Stith, S.M., Rosen, K.H., Middleton, K.A., Busch, A.L., Lundeberg, K. & Carlton, R.P. (2004). The intergenerational transmission of spouse abuse: A meta-analysis. *Journal of Marriage and Family, 62*(3), 640–654.

Tarrier, N. & Gregg, L. (2004). Suicide risk in civilian PTSD patients. Predictors of suicidal ideation, planning and attempts. *Social Psychiatry and Psychiatric Epidemiology, 39*(8), 655–661.

Temkin, J. & Krahé, B. (2008). *Sexual assault and the justice gap: A question of attitude.* Oxford: Hart.

Tov, E. (1993). Verbrechensverarbeitung bei Opfern schwerster Kriminalität [Coping with crime by victims of serious crime]. In G. Kaiser & H. Kury (Hrsg.) *Kriminologische Forschung in den 90er Jahren* [Criminological research in the 90ies] (S. 255–285). Freiburg: Max-Planck-Institut für ausländisches und internationales Strafrecht.

Van Dijk, J.J.M. & Mayhew, P. (1992). *Criminal victimization in the industrialized world: Key findings of the 1989 and 1992 International Crime Surveys.* The Hague: Ministry of Justice, Department of Crime Prevention.

Van Dijk, J.J.M., Mayhew, P. & Killias, M. (1990). *Experiences of crime across the world: Key findings from the 1989 International Crime Survey.* Deventer: Kluwer Law and Taxation.

Van Kesteren, J.N. (2007). *Integrated Database from the International Crime Victims Survey (ICVS) 1989–2005, codebook and data.* Tilburg: Intervict.

von Hentig, H. (1948/1967). *The criminal and his victim. Studies in the sociobiology of crime.* Hamden, CT: Archon Books.

Warner, B. D. (1997). Community characteristics and the recording of crime: Police recording of citizens' complaints of burglary and assault. *Justice Quarterly, 14*(4), 631–650.

Wetzels, P. (1993). Victimization experiences in close relationships: Another blank in victim surveys. In W. Bilsky,

C. Pfeiffer & P. Wetzels (Eds.) *Fear of crime and criminal victimization* (pp.21–41). Stuttgart: Enke.

Wetzels, P. & Bilsky, W. (1997). Victimization in close relationships: On the darkness of 'dark figures'. In S. Redondo, V. Garrido, J. Pérez, J. Bajet & R.M. Martínez (Eds.) *Psychology and law*. Berlin: deGruyter.

Wetzels, P., Greve, W., Mecklenburg, E., Bilsky, W. & Pfeiffer, C. (1995). *Kriminalität im Leben alter Menschen. Eine altersvergleichende Untersuchung von Opfererfahrungen, persönlichem Sicherheitsgefühl und Kriminalitätsfurcht* [Criminality in the life of the elderly. An age comparative study of victimization experiences, personal safety feelings, and fear of crime]. (Schriftenreihe des Bundesministerium für Familie, Senioren, Frauen und Jugend, Bd. 105). Stuttgart: Kohlhammer.

Widom, C.S. (2000). Childhood victimization: Early adversity, later psychopathology. *National Institute of Justice Journal, 242*, 3–9.

Widom, C.S., Czaja, S.J. & Dutton, M.A. (2008). Childhood victimization and lifetime revictimization. *Child Abuse and Neglect, 32*(8), 785–96.

Williams, J.E. (1984). Secondary victimization – confronting public attitudes about rape. *Victimology, 9*(1), 66–81.

Wilmers, N. Enzmann, D., Schaefer, D., Herbers, K., Greve, W. & Wetzels, P. (2002). *Jugendliche in Deutschland zur Jahrtausendwende: Gefährlich oder gefährdet? Ergebnisse wiederholter, repräsentativer Dunkelfelduntersuchungen zu Gewalt und Kriminalität im Leben junger Menschen 1998–2000* [Adolescents in Germany at the turn of the millenium: Dangerous or in danger? Results of repeated, representative studies of the dark figure of violence and criminality in the life of young people 1998–2000]. Baden-Baden: Nomos.

Yin, P. (1985). *Victimization and the aged*. Springfield, IL: Charles Thomas.

15

Jury Decision Making

Andreas Kapardis

You must not suppose from all this that trial by jury has remained unchanged. It has been altered beyond recognition. It has been whittled away. It no longer subsists on civil cases in England save for libel. It is still retained in criminal cases of any consequence, but it has defects which cause concern.

Lord Denning, 1982, in *What Next in the Law*, p.35

Introduction: The Jury Idea

The origins of a jury system, of a trial by one's peers, are lost in the mist of time. An early documented example of a jury system existed in ancient Egypt 4000 years ago (Moore, 1973) but the idea and the right to trial by a jury of laypersons was invented in Athens (McDowell, 1978, p.34) where a representative stratified sample of Athenian citizens was drawn by lottery to be the jury in a trial. From ancient Greece the concept of a jury was adopted across Europe in various forms and the Normans introduced it to Britain in the middle of the 11th century (Kerr, 1987, p.64). Generally speaking, considering jury systems around the world today (see Kaplan & Martin, 2006a), we can distinguish between mixed juries on continental Europe and the jury to be found in western English-speaking common law countries, namely the UK, USA, Australia, New Zealand and Canada. The latter can be traced to the following clause in the Magna Carta,[1] which dates back to 1215:

> No freeman shall be seized, or imprisoned, or disposed or outlawed, or in any way destroyed; nor will we condemn him, nor will we commit him to prison, excepting by the lawful judgement of his peers, or by the law of the land. (Clause 39, Magna Carta, 1215)

The idea of a jury of 12 (it is 15 in Scotland) has been an essential feature of English common law and was passed on to the Anglo-Saxons by the Vikings.

Unanimous verdicts were introduced in 1367 and abolished in 1978. Unanimity of jury verdicts was reiterated by the US Supreme Court in *Patton* v. *United States* [1930] 231 US 276, as a basic requirement of the American jury. However, four decades later, the decision in *Johnson* v. *Louisiana* [1972] 32 L.Ed.2d 152 introduced majority verdicts in non-capital felony cases and in *Burch* v. *Louisiana* [1979] 441 US 130 it was stated that six-person juries must be unanimous. Regarding jury eligibility, there have always been qualifications required of every man to serve on a jury: originally, the requirement was to be a freeholder, but it became a householder in the 19th century. In England, the *Juries Act* (1974) changed the qualification for jury service to eligibility to vote at an election of a Member of Parliament, thus making possible 'jury vetting' of persons with a criminal record. The 1970s saw an unprecedented onslaught on the jury in the UK and a number of serious restrictions were imposed (see below), resulting in the proportion of criminal cases tried by jury being drastically reduced.

The Notion of an Impartial and Fair Jury: A Critical Appraisal

Those common law and civil law countries that have a jury system differ regarding various aspects of their jury system, including: the number of possible verdicts is two ('guilty', 'not guilty') or three, as in Scotland[2] ('guilty', 'not guilty' and 'not proven'); whether the jury comprises 12 members (as is the case in England and Wales, the USA, New Zealand, Australia and Canada) or more; its composition – just laypersons, as in England and Wales, the USA, New Zealand, Australia and Canada, or a combination of laypersons and judges as in Denmark, Belgium, France, Italy, Germany, Sweden, Poland and Russia;[3] who is disqualified from or is ineligible for jury service; whether peremptory challenges are allowed and how many, and the categories of individuals who can be excused from service as of right; the permissible age for jurors (it is 18–65 in England but 20–65 in New Zealand while in Australia there is no upper age-limit); and, finally, how many peremptory challenges (5–20 in the US, not available in England, 3–5 for both sides in Australia) and how many challenges for cause are allowed each side at a trial. In contrast to the US, in England, Scotland, Australia and New Zealand opposing counsels have little opportunity to affect the composition of the jury and, consequently, 'scientific jury selection' is not a lucrative business for trial consultants. Such differences between jurisdictions mean that one should not unquestionably generalise findings about juror decision making across jurisdictions. Of course, the methods by which people eligible for jury service are summoned and the criteria used to excuse some of them affect their representativeness. Airs and Shaw (1999), for example, reported that in England and Wales, members of ethnic minorities, those aged 20–24 years and those living in rented accommodation were less likely to be registered voters. They also found that a significant proportion (38 per cent) of potential jurors was excused for various reasons and, at the end of the day, only 34 per cent were available to serve on a jury.

The very concept of the jury itself is problematic (Darbyshire, 1991). The view that it is desirable to be tried by one's 'peers' is based on the argument that: (a) it is good to be tried by a group of individuals who are representative of one's community, and (b) that 'representativeness' makes for impartial, objective, just and fair jury verdicts. Marshall (1975) pointed out that 'the right to trial by an impartial jury' is not an ideal that can be achieved because trial by one's 'peers', 'representativeness' and 'impartiality' do not go together and, even if they did, they would not guarantee that a jury's verdict would be a fair one. Before examining empirical studies of juror and jury decision making, let us first consider some of the arguments put forward against and in favour of the jury (see Kapardis, 2003, p.130–133 for more such arguments).

Arguments against jury trials

- In England, Scotland, Australia and New Zealand the right to trial by jury is not enshrined in a constitution.[4]
- Trial by jury is not the cornerstone of the criminal justice system.[5]
- Juries are not representative of the wider community.[6]
- In some jurisdictions jury trial has declined drastically.[7]
- A jury does not give reasons and is not accountable for its verdict.[8]
- Jury deliberation is secret.
- No precedent is established by a jury's verdict.[9]
- Juries are unpredictable.
- In a significant number of trials there is a hung jury.[10]
- Trials by a judge are speedier and less costly.[11]
- A jury can be interfered with.[12]
- Jury verdicts are influenced by non-legal factors.[13]
- Jurors often lack the ability to understand and judge a legal case adequately.[14]
- Juries acquit too readily.[15]
- Perverse jury verdicts are not uncommon.[16]
- Any form of *voir dire* is incompatible with both randomness and representativeness.[17]
- In many jurisdictions there is no longer a need for perverse jury verdicts to counter the death penalty.
- Jury verdicts are not significantly different from a judge deciding alone.[18]
- The jury's function is not for amateurs but for professionals.[19]

In response to one of the criticisms of the jury system mentioned above, in England and Wales it was proposed by the Auld Report (2001) that juries should move more towards reasoned verdicts, using case summaries and a list of questions they must answer. The judge could require the jury to give a verdict on each question. Such reasoned verdicts are provided for in Spain and Russia, for example (see Kaplan & Martin, 2006a, for details), while judges in New Zealand have been providing juries with guidance on how to reach a reasoned verdict.

Arguments in favour of jury trials[20]

- The jury is an antidote to tyranny.[21]
- Twelve heads are better than one.

- Unlike an experienced judge, a jury brings a fresh perception to each trial.
- Jurors' common sense and experience compensates for their lack of professional knowledge and training.
- Undesirable idiosyncrasies of individual jurors are minimised by jury deliberations.
- Jurors are suitable to decide complex legal cases.[22]
- Unlike a judge, a jury can choose to ignore strict and unfair legal rules and return a verdict that reflects its own social and ethical standards.
- A significant proportion of people who have served on juries have confidence in the jury system and are satisfied with the experience.[23]

The arguments in favour of and against the jury listed above make it clear that there are two contrasting views of what the function of the jury ought to be: (a) to return a 'correct verdict' applying the law and on the basis of the facts as presented during the trial; and (b) to go beyond the law and the facts of the case and to mediate 'between the law and community values' (Jackson, 1996, p.327). No amount of juror/jury research will resolve the jury controversy and, in the end, value judgements remain to be made. What is certain is that the jury trial on both sides of the Atlantic and in the Antipodes will undergo further reforms (see below) but its very existence is not seriously threatened.

Since the Chicago Jury Project of the 1950s (Kalven & Zeisel, 1966), the jury has been a very popular research topic for psychologists, especially in the USA. Kaplan and Martin (2006b, p.2) remind their readers, however, that differences in cultural norms and trial procedures mean that 'large gaps' remain in extrapolating empirical findings from jury research in North America. Of course, as Hastie (1993b, pp.6–10) and Hans (1992, pp.56–58) point out, there are very good reasons for the popularity of jury studies for psychologists keen on experimental simulation. Some mock juror researchers have claimed since the 1970s that they can predict juror verdict preference with such accuracy as to be able to talk about 'scientific jury selection', raising serious ethical issues irrespective of whether their claim is valid (Brigham, 2006). Furthermore, as argued in this chapter, scientific jury selection, a 'high-tech way of jury-rigging' (Brigham, 2006), is incompatible with and erodes the very concept of a fair trial by a jury that is a microcosm of the community at large.

Methods for Studying Juries/Jurors

We need to understand the strengths and weaknesses of different research methodologies in order to be able to interpret the validity and usefulness of psycholegal research. Let us next take a look at six methods used to study juror/jury decision making.

Archival research

Two limitations of archival research are that important information of interest to a researcher may well be missing, and it is not possible to draw causal inferences on the basis of such data. Nineteen per cent of the empirical studies identified by Devine et al. (2001) involved analysis of archival data.

Questionnaire surveys

The best-known jury questionnaire survey is Chicago Law School's Kalven and Zeisel's (1966) pioneering study The American Jury. They sent a questionnaire to 3500 judges in the United States of whom 15.8 per cent cooperated, providing data on 3576 trials. This frequently cited study, which provided the basis for a great deal of the subsequent jury/juror research, however, suffers a number of very serious limitations (Law Reform Commission of Victoria (LRCV), 1985; Pennington & Hastie, 1990; Stephenson, 1992). To illustrate, the sample of cases surveyed comprised 3 per cent out of the total number of jury trials (60,000) during the two-year period in question in the 1950s; half of the 3576 cases were provided by only 15 per cent of the judges; the researchers changed their questionnaire midway after obtaining data for two-thirds of the cases and lumped the findings from both questionnaires together, thus undermining the reliability and validity of their survey (LRCV, 1985, p.82). Furthermore, it was judges and not jurors themselves who were asked to assess the jurors' competence in understanding the content of a trial and the quality of the judge–juror communication.

Kalven and Zeisel (1966) found that: (a) the judge agreed with the jury's verdict in 75 per cent of the cases; (b) most jurors decided on their verdict before they retire to deliberate; and, finally, (c) the majority view prevailed. If accepted, (b) and (c) emphasise the importance of screening potential jurors during voir dire so as to have as many jurors as possible who will favour one's client (see below). The same findings have also led many juror researchers (see Hastie, 1993a) to investigate how jurors behave before they retire to deliberate. Stephenson

(1992, pp.180–2) analysed the figures on judge–jury agreement provided by the Chicago researchers and showed convincingly that the conclusion that jurors' verdicts are not significantly different from what trial judges themselves would decide is not justified.

Unlike the USA, in the UK, Australia, New Zealand and Canada, the function of the jury in criminal trials is confined to deciding whether a defendant is guilty and the judge decides sentence. British researchers have also reported questionnaire surveys: the Oxford survey by McCabe and Purves (1974) of judges, counsel and solicitors involved in 266 contested trials found a rate of 12.5 per cent 'perverse acquittals', i.e. cases where the jury verdict is against the weight of the evidence; Zander's (1974) study of jury trials at the Old Bailey and the Inner London Crown Court reported that perverse acquittals comprised 6 per cent of the total. The well-known Birmingham jury study of 500 trials by Baldwin and McConville (1979) surveyed defence solicitors and judges (with a response rate of 84 and 94 per cent respectively) as well as police and found that about one in four of the prosecuting solicitors and one-third of the judges were dissatisfied with the jury's verdict, with 12 per cent of such verdicts being considered as 'perverse'. Finally, the questionnaire survey of jurors and other trial protagonists in Britain by Zander and Henderson (1994) found that the percentage of verdict acquittals considered 'surprising' varied depending on the category of respondents.

Contrary to what the majority of mock jury researchers have reported (see below), Baldwin and McConville (1979, p.104) found no relationship between the social composition of juries in terms of age, social class, gender and race and their verdicts, indicating that real jury verdicts are perhaps largely unpredictable. A similar conclusion was reached by Dunstan, Paulin and Atkinson's (1995, p.55) assessment of the relevant literature concerning jurors' sex, age and occupation and jury deliberations. Negative results from studies of actual juries (see also below) challenge the external validity of a lot of mock juror/jury studies. Young (2003, 2004) and Ogloff et al. (2006) reported surveys[24] of 131 judges in New Zealand and 136 in Australia, respectively, as far as their communications with jurors were concerned. It was found that more judges in New Zealand than in Australia in their opening remarks provide jurors with some discussion about the elements of the relevant substantial law and tell them of their right to ask questions during the trial. Of the 206 empirical studies surveyed by Devine et al. (2001), very few indeed used retrospective surveys.

Mock juries

Mock juror/jury studies have been the most commonly used method (Nietzel et al., 1999), especially in the USA, and have attracted a great deal of criticism. In the literature review by Devine et al. (2001), two-thirds of the 206 studies involved mock juries. Experimental simulation allows one to (a) investigate a number of significant variables while controlling for extraneous influences, and (b) have direct access to the deliberation process. However, the external validity of a great deal of experimental simulation juror research has been repeatedly seriously questioned (see Kerr & Bray, 2005, for detailed discussion of the issue). As McEwan (2000) points out, since we cannot interview real jurors, 'laboratory experiments and mock trials appear to be the best alternative psychologists can adopt' but 'It would be dangerous to make too much of their findings' (p. 111).

Mock juror/jury studies have reported a significant amount of experimental evidence suggesting that characteristics of both the defendant and the jurors impact on jury decisions about verdict and (in the USA) severity of sentence (see Levett et al., 2005, for a review). Since the early 1980s, the quality of mock jury studies has improved in terms of its sensitivity to the social and legal context of jury decision making, methodological subtlety and legal sophistication (Hans, 1992, p.60). Such improvement has come about in the wake of criticism of jury simulation research by both psychologists and judges such as Chief Justice Rehnquist in the USA in the case of Lockhart v. McCree [1986] 106 S.Ct. 1758 who rejected on methodological grounds the American Association's amicus brief provided in that case. This is not to suggest that the types of variables examined in such studies are irrelevant; rather, that actual jury decision-making processes are more complex than laboratory studies low on ecological validity would seem to suggest. On the basis of their in-depth and critical evaluation of the experimental jury research, Kerr and Bray (2006) have argued convincingly that authors of unrealistic jury simulations should qualify their findings and should refrain from putting them forward as the basis for policy changes (p.358).

Shadow juries

This is the closest one can get to simulating a real jury. McCabe and Purves (1974) studied 30 'shadow juries' (recruited utilising the electoral roll) sitting in on actual trials. Their deliberations were recorded and transcribed, and shadow jurors were interviewed subsequently. It was found that the verdicts of the real and shadow juries were very similar indeed. While field studies of jury behaviour are more realistic than experimental ones, their findings are difficult to interpret due to possible confounding variables.

Post-trial juror interviews

Post-trial interviews have been used, for example, to ascertain jurors' experience and understanding of judges' instructions (see Bowers, 1995; Costanzo & Costanzo, 1994; Horan, 2004; Ryan, 2003; Tinsley, 2001),[25] and judges' communications with jurors (Ogloff et al., 2006; Young, 2003, 2004). Limitations of the interview method include, for example, the fact that verbal reports of mental events are often incomplete (Nisbett & Wilson, 1977) and, furthermore, people generally find it difficult to determine the effect different factors have had on their thinking processes; jurors' memories of what was said in the retiring room is bound to be limited and, consequently, different jurors may well disagree about the content of the deliberation. Despite their limitations, post-trial juror interviews can yield very significant findings. Lengthy face-to-face interviews with capital jurors carried out by university students is the chief source of data in the national Capital Jury Project (CJP) in the USA.[26]

Books by ex-jurors

Some jurors have published their experiences (see Barber & Gordon, 1976; Burnett, 2001; Zerman, 1977). The major limitation of such books is that they are about the experience of one or a few individuals in isolated cases. Nevertheless, such books can still provide an insight into the jury experience.

Selecting Jurors

In England, Wales and Scotland potential jurors aged 18–65 are randomly selected from the electoral roll. A prospective juror must have lived in the UK for at least five years after the age of 13. People who are suffering from a serious mental disorder or have been sentenced to a term of imprisonment of five years or more are disqualified. As already mentioned, the scope for selecting jurors is very limited in the UK, Australia and New Zealand and there is no voir dire equivalent to that in the USA.

Lawyers and trial consultants in the USA use one or more of three approaches to select jurors (Brigham, 2006, pp.18–19): (a) focusing on general attitudes or personality characteristics such as legal authoritarianism; (b) case-specific attitudes; and (c) supplemental juror questionnaires. By using the juror challenge procedure and supplemental juror questionnaires which are reviewed by the lawyers on both sides, such as the 'Juror Bias Scale' (see Kassin & Wrightsman, 1983), an accused in the USA, especially one with a lot of money, can influence significantly the composition of the jury who will try the case and pass sentence.[27] If the evidence against the defendant is weak, such 'jury packing' can make the difference to the verdict. The whole voir dire process is predicated on the assumption that jurors give honest answers. There is evidence that between 25 and 30 per cent of real ex-jurors conceal relevant information about themselves when questioned in court (Seltzer et al., 1991), casting doubt on a basic assumption that underlies the whole voir dire.

The question, therefore, arises of whether 'scientific', systematic jury selection is as possible and successful in influencing trial outcome as some psychologists and jury selection experts claim. As Lloyd-Bostock (1988, p.52) pointed out, 'Systematic jury selection has coincided with winning in a growing number of cases. However, there are good reasons to remain sceptical about some of the more extravagant claims made for it'. The use of the term 'scientific jury selection' has been criticised by Hans and Vidmar (1986) on the basis that it conveys an impression of accuracy and precision not justified by existing knowledge and methods. As a number of juror/jury decision-making literature reviews testify (Brigham, 2006; Devine et al., 2001; Levett et al., 2005), the same criticism applies more than two decades later.

A lot of juror research has concerned itself with how individual jurors in serious criminal cases behave before they retire to deliberate (see Hastie, 1993b and below). This focus stems from a belief that: (a) most jurors have decided on a verdict before they retire to deliberate; and (b) that the pre-deliberation distribution of individual jurors' verdict preferences is the best predictor of the final jury verdict (Kalven & Zeisel, 1966; McCabe & Purves, 1974). However, it is the strength of the evidence against the defendant that impacts on the trial result. For mock jurors' personality, physical attractiveness, attitudes and so forth correlate significantly with trial outcome if the evidence against the defendant is weak (Reskin & Visher, 1986).

Individual differences among mock jurors are not very good predictors of jury decision making (Ellsworth, 1993, p.42; Wrightsman et al., 2002). This is further supported by studies of real juries such as Baldwin and McConville's (1979, p.104) Birmingham study. Close examination of jury literature shows that: (a) some enduring characteristics of jurors (e.g. authoritarianism) are useful in understanding the jury verdict (see below); and (b) that it is the interaction of juror and case characteristics that should be the focus of the jury researcher since neither set of variables can be said to be operating alone. In the absence of sufficient such research, a certain amount of scepticism is therefore warranted when considering research findings on the relationship between juror characteristics and verdict. At the same time, it needs to be remembered that juries are supposed to be representative of the broader community and such features of jurors as authoritarianism and racial prejudice reflect the same characteristics in society. To minimise their undesirable impact on juries, one must first and foremost reduce their presence among the public at large. In the final analysis, a society gets the juries and the justice it deserves.

Pre-trial publicity

Different kinds of prejudice can influence a juror (see Vidmar, 2002, for details). It is the courts' role to ensure a fair trial by, *inter alia*, enforcing legal restrictions on pre-trial publicity. In the USA, fundamental fairness in prosecuting federal crimes is provided in Article III of the Constitution, the Sixth Amendment, the Due Process Clause of the Fifth Amendment, and the *Federal Rules of Civil Procedure* (FRCP). In fact, Rule 21(a) of the FRCP provides for the trial to be held elsewhere to protect an accused from prejudice. Recognising the real threat posed by prejudicial publicity, restrictions have been imposed on trial publicity by the courts in Britain by the *Contempt of Court Act 1981*. Section 2(3) of the said Act provides that publicity before or during a trial is only a contempt when there is 'a substantial risk that the course of justice in the proceedings in question will be seriously impeded or prejudiced'. This restriction is supported by the weight of the evidence in the empirical literature (see the meta-analysis of 44 studies by Steblay et al., 1999) showing that case-specific pre-trial publicity in both civil and criminal cases impacts adversely on prosecution verdicts (i.e. makes a guilty verdict significantly more likely) by potential jurors who are presented with negative pre-trial information about the defendant

(Bornstein et al., 2002; Honess et al., 2003; Hope et al., 2004). It should also be noted in this context, however, that some judiciaries are reluctant to accept that pre- and mid-trial publicity may prejudice a trial (Studebaker & Penrod, 1997). As far as the impact of pre-trial publicity on actual jurors is concerned, post-trial interviews of judges, lawyers and ex-jurors in criminal cases during 1997–2000 by Chesterman et al. (2001) in New South Wales, Australia, found that 8 per cent of the verdicts were believed to have been influenced more by publicity than by the evidence. Their finding, however, should be treated with caution owing to serious methodological flaws of the study (Goodman-Delahunty & Tait, 2006, p.58). Finally, Vidmar's (2002) research indicates that pre-trial publicity will not impact on jurors with polarised attitudes towards a particular crime or defendant.

The reported importance of juror characteristics

A number of studies have reported that mock jurors are less likely to find a defendant guilty if he or she is similar to them in terms of beliefs, ethnicity or background (Amato, 1979; Griffitt & Jackson, 1973; Kerr et al., 1995; Stephan & Stephan, 1986). However, if a defendant who is similar to mock jurors is said to have acted in such a way as to bring shame on those similar to him, they are more likely to treat him more harshly (Kerr et al., 1995). Concerning the importance of jurors' *gender*, women are minimised on juries in England and Wales (Lloyd-Bostock & Thomas, 1999). Studies have reported conflicting findings regarding the relationship between jurors' gender and verdict (Arce, 1995, p.566). A follow-up study of jurors in Florida by Moran and Comfort (1982) found no gender differences as far as attitudes prior to deliberation or final verdicts were concerned. However, the weight of the research evidence shows that *female* jurors are more likely to convict a defendant charged with rape or child sexual abuse and especially if there had been no eye-contact between the rape victim and the offender during the attack (see Kapardis, 2003). Interestingly, Brekke and Borgida (1988) reported that juror deliberation narrows such gender verdict differences. Conflicting findings have been reported concerning the importance of having jurors of a higher *educational standard* (Hans & Vidmar, 1986; Mills & Bohannon, 1980).

As far as *race* is concerned, a number of authors (e.g. Lloyd-Bostock & Thomas, 1999; Zander & Henderson, 1993) have drawn attention to the fact that in England non-whites/ethnic minorities are under-represented on juries. The US Supreme Court has stated that peremptory challenges (i.e. rejecting a juror during *voir dire* without giving the court any reason) on the basis of a juror's race are unconstitutional. Baldwin and McConville (1979) found that the racial composition of a jury was not important in explaining the verdict. It was the race of the defendant that emerged as significant – even when a jury was predominantly black, a black defendant was more likely to feature among perverse convictions than acquittals. The meta-analysis of 37 studies by Mazzella and Feingold (1994) found that, perhaps due to jurors' stereotypes, African Americans were given harsher sentences for negligent homicide, in contrast to whites who were given harsher penalties for economic crimes such as fraud and embezzlement. Evidence for juror prejudice and racial discrimination has also been reported in Canada (Avio, 1988; Bagby *et al.*, 1994). The literature review by Devine *et al.* (2001) of the racial composition of the jury concluded that, 'Jury-defendant bias has thus been observed across a number of studies and contexts and appears to be a robust phenomenon'. Kemmelmeier (2005) maintains that race is a significant factor in white mock jurors' decision making.

According to social psychologists, people scoring high on an authoritarianism scale think in terms of absolutes, are intolerant of others who are different, are hostile towards deviants in society, are pro-death penalty and, finally, accept and do not question the authority of officials (including judges) and institutions. The meta-analysis of 20 studies by Narby *et al.* (1993) distinguished between 'legal' and 'traditional' authoritarianism and concluded that the latter was a better predictor of verdict preference and that *high authoritarians* are more likely than low authoritarians to convict and impose harsh sanctions. The same conclusion was reached by Devine *et al.* (2001) on the basis of their literature review. Finally, there is evidence that high-authoritarian mock jurors decide on their verdicts early in the trial (Boehm, 1968) but conflicting findings have been reported concerning their susceptibility to influence. A juror's *previous jury experience* correlates with a greater likelihood of a guilty verdict (Dillehay & Nietzel, 1985) and severer sentences in both criminal and civil trials (Himelein *et al.*, 1991).

According to Brigham (2006), approximately three-quarters of the states and the federal government in the USA authorise the death penalty. Utilising an in-depth standard protocol to interview ex-jurors in capital cases in 14 states that have the most variation in death-penalty

sentencing, the Capital Jury Project[28] (CJP) has been an attempt by a consortium of university-based research studies (founded in 1991) to improve on mock jury research with student subjects and to resolve the debate concerning arbitrary or racist death penalties in the USA. By October 2007, a total of 1198 jurors from 353 capital juries in the 14 states had been interviewed. CJP researchers have found that a defendant's race is a significant factor in understanding jury decisions; more specifically, if the defendant is white, the jury is more likely to assess him as mentally unstable (a mitigating factor) than if he were black. In turn, this mitigating factor influences a jury's penalty decision, resulting in a sentence that is less harsh than the death penalty.

Conflicting views have been expressed about whether death-qualified juries are conviction prone (Bowers, 1995; Elliott, 1991; Mauro, 1991; Nietzel *et al.*, 1999). The American Psychological Association's (APA's) *amicus* brief, submitted on behalf of the defendant McCree in *Lockhart* v. *McCree* [1986] 106 S.Ct. 1758, concluded, on the basis of existing experimental evidence, that: (a) such juries are conviction prone; (b) by being under-representative death-qualified juries violate a defendant's right to a trial by a representative jury; and, finally, (c) death qualification interferes with the proper functioning of the jury. On the basis of data from 916 actual jurors from 257 capital juries in 11 states, Bowers (1995) concluded that a juror's attitude to the death penalty is crucial in understanding how he or she processes trial information and behaves when the jury retires to deliberate. More specifically, jurors with pro-death penalty attitudes were more likely to make up their minds about the defendant's guilt and the appropriateness of the death penalty very early in the trial process and, consequently, were significantly more likely to want to impose the death penalty even when the jury was deliberating whether to find the defendant guilty or innocent.

Juror competence

Comprehending evidence

In support of Heuer and Penrod's (1994b) finding with real jurors, there is overwhelming evidence from mock juror studies (Cutler *et al.*, 1990; Horowitz *et al.*, 1996) that as case-complexity increases, juror comprehension of the evidence decreases and that mock jurors find it difficult to discount a defendant's confession made under pressure (i.e. involuntary) when instructed to do so and proceed to convict (Kassin & Sukel, 1997). Mixed results have been reported by mock jury studies concerning whether jurors are able to ignore inadmissible evidence when instructed to do so by the judge (London & Nunez, 2000). The finding reported by Zander and Henderson (1994) that most of the jurors in their national Crown Court study had been able to understand and remember the evidence is questionable because they did not actually test for jurors' competence.

Rather alarming in this context is the finding from the Capital Jury Project that, while capital jurors could remember well details about the defendant, they admitted to having hardly understood and could barely recall the legal rules relevant to their decision to impose the death penalty (Luginbuhl & Howe, 1995; Sarat, 1995). The available evidence[29] (Kovera et al., 1999; McAuliff & Kovera, 2003) shows that some jurors are not able to evaluate scientific evidence proffered by an expert but do so better if judicial instructions to the jury are revised to make them more comprehensible (Grosscup & Penrod, 2002).[30]

Understanding and following the judge's instructions/ the jury charge

Inadequacies of the judicial instructions/charges to the jury are a ground for appeal. Drawing on Ogloff and Rose (2005), studies in Canada have reported jury verdict reversal rates by appellate courts ranging from 34 to 74 per cent. Ogloff and Rose concluded, on the basis of their extensive literature review, that, whatever the method used, 'jurors appear largely incapable of understanding judicial instructions as they are traditionally delivered by the judge' (p.425). Similarly, the meta-analysis of 48 published studies by Nietzel et al. (1999) concluded that 'when instructions are not psychologically well crafted, they are minimally effective'.

Suggestions to ameliorate this problem have included rewriting and standardising judges' instructions to juries (Hans, 1992), allowing jurors to take notes in order to assist their memory of important trial details (see Heuer & Penrod, 1994a; Horowitz & ForsterLee, 2001) and to ask questions during the trial in order to clarify issues (Hollin, 1989), and, finally, to facilitate juror compliance with judicial instruction by presenting that instruction early in the evidence-processing task (Goodman-Delahunty & Tait, 2006, p.64).

The US Supreme Court in *Gregg* stated a requirement that capital jurors must decide guilt and punishment separately. However, Sandys (1995, p.1221) found in interviews with 67 capital jurors in Kentucky that they made the decision concurrently, before the penalty stage of the trial, thus rendering irrelevant any subsequent evaluation of information about the defendant's mitigating and aggravating factors in order to decide on the right sentence. Such findings are a cause for concern and call for effective juror guidance by the judge.

The Jury Foreperson

The juror characteristics that predict foreperson election are: male sex, high socio-economic status, sitting at the end of the jury table and initiating discussion (Baldwin & McConville, 1980, pp.40–1). The forepersons in the study by Saks and Hastie (1978, p.190) were disproportionately male, 40 years or older and in managerial, professional and intermediate occupations. Similar findings were reported by Deosoran (1993).

The foreperson can, of course, influence the deliberation result by directing discussion, timing poll votes and influencing whether poll votes will be public or secret (see below). The Spanish mock jury study by Arce et al. (1999) reported that in hung juries the foreperson: (a) failed to control the deliberation in order to guide it to evaluate the evidence; (b) did not avoid destructive interventions; (c) failed to be persuasive; and (d) did not inspire either authority or respect (p.269). Similarly, the New Zealand study of post-deliberation interviews of jurors found that if the foreperson was weak in performing his or her role and the deliberation process was unstructured, some jurors would dominate the deliberation and some would feel intimidated by them (Tinsley, 2001). In the light of their findings, Arce et al. (1999) recommended that the foreperson should be trained in order to perform his or her role effectively. A follow-up survey of judicial practices in New Zealand reported that as a result of the juror survey, more judges provided guidance to jurors as far as selection of a foreperson is concerned (Ogloff et al., 2006).

Jury Deliberation

What we know today about jury deliberation is from mock and shadow jury studies as well as from a small number of post-trial surveys of real jurors. None of the researchers in this area has observed real juries at their task. Most of the mock research into jury decision making (see Devine et al., 2001; Levett et al., 2005; Memon et al., 2003, for reviews)[31] focuses on juror behaviour at the pre-deliberation stage in the belief (which can be traced back to Kalven and Zeisel's 'liberation hypothesis') that most jurors have already decided on a verdict before they retire to deliberate and that first-ballot majority verdict preferences predict the final verdict reliably. The said prediction has been borne out by some studies (Meyers et al., 2001; Sandys & Dillehay, 1995) but not by others (Ellsworth, 1993; Hastie et al., 1983; Kerr & MacCoun, 1985). On the basis of their own work, the well-known American researchers Pennington and Hastie (1990, p.102) concluded that the relationship between individual jurors' initial verdicts and the final jury verdict is more complex than the simple one proposed by Kalven and Zeisel (1966).

Available empirical evidence (Hastie et al., 1983) indicates that we need to distinguish between: (a) deliberations where jurors announce their verdict preferences before discussion begins in the jury room (known as 'verdict-driven' deliberations); and (b) deliberations in which jurors' verdict preferences are expressed later in the deliberation process (known as 'evidence-driven' deliberations).

If a majority verdict is required, it has been reported by Hastie et al. (1983) that minority jurors will participate less and will be paid less attention by the rest of the jury and that taking a vote very early on speeds up the deliberation process. Also, jury deliberation will take longer if the jury is evidence rather than verdict driven (Hastie et al., 1983) but this will not necessarily result in a different verdict. Real jury studies have found that the longer the retirement, the more likely it will lead to an acquittal (Baldwin & McConville, 1980, p.42). Multiple charges against the defendant are associated with a greater likelihood of a guilty verdict (Tanford et al., 1985), as is knowledge that the defendant has a prior conviction (Greene & Dodge, 1995). Jurors are more likely to acquit if a reasonable doubt standard of proof is emphasised (McCabe & Purves, 1974). Finally, Osborne et al. (1986) found that, following deliberation, jurors shift to a severer decision if the jury is heterogeneous rather than homogeneous. In this sense, the composition of a jury can be said to be related to its verdict.

In the 1970s the US Supreme Court upheld the use of six-person juries in criminal (Williams v. Florida [1970] 399 US 78, 86) and civil (Colgrove v. Battin [1973] 413 US 149, 156) cases (Cammack, 1995, p.435). Smaller juries such as six-member ones can only be less representative of the broader community than the conventional 12-member jury, and their verdicts are likely to be different (Hans & Vidmar, 1986; Zeisel & Diamond, 1987). In fact, a meta-analysis by Saks and Marti (1997) of studies that investigated six- vs. 12-member juries found that juries of 12 are more representative of the community; contain a range of opinion and experience; and deliberate longer because twice as many people are present but, on average, each juror contributes the same to the deliberation (Hastie et al., 1983). The finding that each juror on average contributes the same to the deliberation in six- and in 12-member juries may well be an artefact of the homogeneity of the mock jurors (psychology students) used extensively in US studies. Also, juries of 12 recall more evidence accurately; generate more arguments; and minority views are more likely to be represented. However, while jury size influences deliberation, the evidence indicates it does not make any significant difference to the verdict. Small juries are less likely to recall evidence accurately, to examine the evidence thoroughly or to result in a hung jury (Saks, 1977) and are more likely to hold secret ballots and to convict (Hans & Vidmar, 1986).[32] There are conflicting views on whether jurors in a smaller jury participate less (Saks, 1977) or more (Arce, 1995, p.567). It becomes clear that the real reason for introducing small-size juries has been economic concerns (Zeisel & Diamond, 1987, p.204).

Defendant characteristics

A number of studies have reported that a defendant's *attractiveness* is a good predictor of defendant guilt in mock jury studies (Bagby et al., 1994)[33] and whether mock jurors will apply the reasonable doubt standard (MacCoun, 1990). Interestingly, jurors have been shown to be harsher on an attractive defendant whose good looks enabled them to commit a deception offence (Sigall & Ostrove, 1975). Regarding a defendant's display of *remorse* in the courtroom, Devine et al. (2001) concluded that, on the basis of the review of the relevant studies, no conclusions are possible due to conflicting findings reported.

Victim/plaintiff characteristics

Barnett (1985) found that juries in Georgia were more likely to impose the death penalty when the victim was a *stranger* to the defendant, and Daudistel et al. (1999) reported that longer sentences were imposed when the victim and the defendant were of the same race. One of the worrying findings yielded by the Capital Jury Project in the USA is that jurors see the defendant as more dangerous if the victim is white, and that the race of the victim plays a significant role in whether they find mitigating factors that would lead them to decide on a lesser sentence than the death penalty, Thus, in the case of a defendant charged with killing a white victim, jurors would be unlikely to find mitigating factors and would decide on the death penalty. Regarding the importance of plaintiff characteristics in civil trials, an interaction effect between a victim's *age* and *race* has been reported by Foley and Pigott (1997) who found that when the plaintiff was young, jurors considered black plaintiffs as less responsible and awarded them more damages than white plaintiffs in a sexual assault case. However, the reverse was found when the plaintiff was older.

Interaction of defendant and victim characteristics

There is overwhelming evidence that blacks in the USA are disproportionately sentenced to death by juries (Kapardis, 2003, pp.172–177). Furthermore, African-American defendants who kill white victims are significantly more likely to be sentenced to death than white defendants and African-American defendants guilty of killing black victims.

Lawyer and judge characteristics

The importance of lawyer and judge characteristics as far as trial outcome is concerned has been neglected by psycholegal researchers. Blanck (1985) had observers rate judges' verbal and non-verbal behaviour using videotaped parts of their instruction to the jury and found that the defendant was more likely to be found guilty if the trial judge was rated as less dogmatic, less wise, less dominant and less professional. Regarding the importance of lawyer characteristics, McGuire and Bermant (1977) reported that a higher acquittal rate was associated with the defence lawyer being a male. Lawyers' behaviour in court can sometimes be annoying and even offensive. Kaplan and Miller (1978) found that jury deliberation eliminated any adverse effect (e.g. bias) the annoying or offensive behaviour of lawyers or judges might have for or against the annoying party.

Hung juries

The meta-analysis of 17 studies by Saks and Marti (1999) found that in real jury trials a hung verdict occurred in only 1 per cent of the instances. The study of criminal cases involving state offences in New South Wales in Australia during the period 1997–2000 by

Baker *et al.* (2002) reported that out of 2771 jury cases for this period, 81.8 per cent reached a verdict, 9.8 per cent were aborted and 8.3 per cent were hung. Thus, it appears that significantly more jury trials fail to reach a verdict in Australia than in the USA. The weight of the empirical evidence[34] indicates that larger juries deliberate for longer (Saks & Marti, 1999) and the number of hung juries increases with jury size when a unanimous verdict is required and when case complexity is high.

Models of Jury Decision Making[35]

According to Hastie (1993b), there are basically four descriptive models of jury decision making (see Levett *et al.*, 2005, pp.370–375 for a discussion): (a) the Bayesian probability theory model (see Hastie, 1993b, pp.11–17); (b) the algebraic weighted average model (Hastie, 1993b); (c) the stochastic Poisson process model (Kerr, 1993); and (d) the cognitive story model (see Pennington & Hastie, 1993). Thus, we have two broad categories of models of jury decision making: the mathematical approach ones and the explanation-based/cognitive approach model.

In contrast to mathematical models, the story model (see Hastie *et al.*, 1983; Pennington & Hastie, 1986) assumes that jurors actively construct explanations for the evidence presented to them and decide on a verdict accordingly. In constructing a story, jurors use three types of knowledge, namely: (a) personal knowledge about the offence; (b) knowledge acquired through the evidence presented during the trial; and (c) jurors' own knowledge or expectation about what constitutes a complete story. Pennington and Hastie (1992) used the story model successfully in three experiments to explain juror decision making.

Reforming the Jury to Remedy Some of Its Problems

In support of mock juror research (Horowitz & ForsterLee, 2001), the New Zealand juror survey by Young *et al.* (1999) found that note-taking during the trial helped jurors during their deliberations. Support for allowing jurors to ask questions during the trial has been provided by Penrod and Heuer (1998) who found in their study that jurors felt better informed and in a better position to reach a verdict as a result of having been allowed to ask questions. However, Penrod and Heuer also found that judges and lawyers were not positive about jurors being allowed to ask questions.

The 2001 Auld Committee's *Review of the Criminal Courts of England and Wales*, chaired by Lord Justice Auld, has made a number of recommendations to make juries more representative. The findings reported about New Zealand judges by Ogloff *et al.* (2006) and Young (2004) show that New Zealand is good example of a country where increasingly more judges aid jurors in their difficult task by better introduction to the task at hand, written aids, allowing access to transcripts of testimony, guidance on foreperson selection and on how to avoid impasses in deliberations, requiring juries to reason their verdict and, finally, providing jurors with a special verdict form to help in the process.

The well-known English judge Lord Denning (1982, p.77) argued for a new way of selecting jurors in England on the basis that the ordinary man is no longer suitable to sit on the jury. He has also argued that there should be a qualification for service as a juror so that a jury would be 'composed of sensible and responsible members of the community. It should be representative of the best of them of whatever sex or colour and of whatever age or occupation … Those on the jury list should be selected in much the same way as magistrates are now'. He also proposed that people could apply or be recommended to go on the jury list, should need to provide references and, finally, be interviewed for suitability. Lord Denning's radical proposal for jury reform seems to have gone largely unheeded.

Alternatives to Trial by Jury

In the light of some of the arguments against the jury mentioned above, an obvious alternative to trial by jury is trial by a single judge. A second alternative is a combination of judge and jury (laypersons) as it exists in Germany or as the one to be introduced in Japan in 2009 (see Ohtsubo, 2006). Lord Denning (1982, pp.72–73) was a strong advocate of a mixed jury for fraud trials in England, comprising a High Court judge and two lay assessors. Some commentators have questioned whether in a mixed jury the laypersons would outvote the judge often enough (Knittel & Seiler, 1972). Research cited by Antonio and Hans (2001, p.69) shows that mixed courts limit the impact of lay participation on decision making because lay judges are often marginalised when they hear

and decide cases with professional judges (Kutnjak Ivkovich, 1999; Machura, 1999).[36]

Conclusions

The concept of the jury in western English-speaking common law countries has been eroded (e.g. with the introduction of majority verdicts, six-member juries) and the use of juries has declined drastically in some jurisdictions. Despite the problem of low ecological validity of many mock juror/jury research as well as conflicting findings reported by experimental simulation and real juror/jury studies, as far as juror competence is concerned, the evidence discussed in this chapter shows that: as trial complexity increases, juror comprehension of the evidence decreases; both mock and real jurors are generally unable to comprehend and apply the law or to evaluate scientific evidence proffered by an expert witness, thus negating the very notion of a fair trial; there is overwhelming evidence that jurors find it difficult to comply with judges' instructions, for example to discount a defendant's involuntary confession or to ignore inadmissible evidence. 'Scientific jury selection', in itself a controversial practice, is not as possible nor as successful in influencing trial outcome as some mock jury researchers and trial consultants have claimed. Inconsistent findings have been reported by experimental studies on the one hand and research into actual jurors on the other. A certain degree of scepticism is warranted in considering research findings about the relationship between juror characteristics and sentence due to the fact that simulation studies often lack deliberation and conflicting findings have been reported by mock and real juror studies. Juror/jury research should focus more on the interaction between juror and case characteristics. The empirical evidence casts doubt on the wisdom of having six-member juries and, finally, the 'cognitive story model' of jury decision making has been shown to be very useful in focusing on juror characteristics, the deliberation process and features of the case under consideration. Juridical decision making is an area where psychologists have contributed and will continue to contribute useful knowledge to a vital debate in society. A number of reforms mentioned above will make the jury both more representative of the community and more competent.

It is unlikely that we shall see judges and laypersons deciding criminal cases together in the US, English, Australian or New Zealand courts in the near future. The notion of the jury has miraculously survived thus far despite its inherent contradictions and an onslaught since the 1960s in western English-speaking common law countries. Psychologists still have a lot to contribute to improving our understanding of juror and jury decision making as well as improving juror competence.

Notes

1   See Darbyshire (1991) concerning the controversy surrounding the content and interpretations of this clause in the Magna Carta.

2   See Hope and Memon (2006, p.35–37) for a detailed discussion of 'Not Proven Verdict' that made up 21 per cent of Scottish acquittals in 2002 (*Criminal Proceedings of Scottish Courts, 2002*).

3   See Kaplan, Martin and Hertel (2006) for an overview of European mixed (lay and professional) juries.

4   Lloyd-Bostock (1996, p.350).

5   Darbyshire (1991, p.751).

6   Due to persons who are disqualified, excused from jury service, or are rejected when the jury is empanelled in court.

7   The onslaught on the jury in England can be seen, for example, in restrictions of the right to question jurors (1973), restriction on the cases to be tried by the jury (1977), restricting the right of defence counsel to challenge jurors (1977), the abolition of unanimous verdicts (1978) and, finally, the legitimisation of jury vetting (1978). Also, only 1–2 per cent of all trials in England are heard by a jury (Hope & Memon, 2006, p.31) while reforms in New Zealand have drastically reduced the use of civil juries (Horan, 2004).

8   Blom-Cooper (1974).

9   Blom-Cooper (1974).

10 Willis (1983).

11 Blom-Cooper (1974).

12 Denning (1982, p.61); Queensland Criminal Justice Commission (1991).

13 Kapardis, 2003; Memon, Vrij and Bull (2003), Nathanson (1995), Studebaker and Penrod (1997).

14 Thompson (2002).

15 Mark (1973) but see Zander (1974) for a rebuttal.

16 Baldwin and McConville (1979,1980), Kalven and Zeisel (1966), McCabe and Purvis (1974), Zander and Henderson (1994).

17 Darbyshire (1991, p.744), Dunstan, Paulin and Atkinson (1995, p.33).

18 See Levett *et al.* (2005, p.394–5) for discussion of this point.

19 Roskill Committee (1986).

20 Russell (2004) – cited by Goodman-Delahunty and Tait (2006).

21 Devlin (1974).

22 Thompson (2002). The mode of presentation of instructions is to the jury is crucial in this context (Brewer, Harvey and Semmler, 2004).

23 Jackson (1996, p.331); Cutler and Hughes (2001); Boatright (2001), Ryan (2003).

24 The surveys are cited in Cited by Goodman-Delahunty and Tait (2006).

25 Horan (2004), Ryan (2003) and Tinsley (2001) are cited in Goodman-Delahunty and Tait (2006).

26 See issues of *Indiana Law Review*, 1995, vol.70 (3,4).

27 In the much-publicised O.J. Simpson trial, for example, prospective jurors had to respond to a 61-page questionnaire comprising 294 questions (Gordon, 1997).

28 See http://en.wikipedia.org/wiki/Capital_Jury_Project

29 Cited by Levett *et al.* (2005)

30 Cited by Levett *et al.* (2005).

31 See Hastie (1993a), Levine (1992) and Nietzel *et al.* (1999), for earlier reviews.

32 Cited in Hollin (1989, p.168).

33 See also Izzett and Leginski (1974), Landy and Aronson (1969), Ostrom, Werner and Saks (1978).

34 Kalven and Zeisel (1966), Zeisel (1971), Saks (1977), Kerr and MacCoun (1985), Foss (1981).

35 See Hastie (1993b) and Levett *et al.* (2005) for a discussion.

36 Both studies are cited by Antonio and Hans (200169).

References

Airs, J. & Shaw, A. (1999). *Jury excusal and deferral*. Home Office Research Development and Statistics Directorate Report No.102. London: Home Office.

Amato, P.R. (1979). Juror–defendant similarity and the assessment of guilt in politically-motivated crimes. *Australian Journal of Psychology*, *31*, 79–88.

Antonio, M.E. & Hans, V.P. (2001). Race and the civil jury: How does a juror's race shape the jury experience? In R. Roesch *et al.* (Eds.) *Psychology in the courts: International advances in knowledge* (pp.69–81). London: Routledge.

Arce, R (1995). Evidence evaluation in jury decision making. In R. Bull & D. Carson (Eds.) *Handbook of psychology in legal contexts* (pp.565–580). Chichester: Wiley.

Arce, R., Fariña, F., Novo, M. & Seijo, D. (1999). In search of causes of hung juries. *Expert Evidence*, *6*, 243–260.

Auld, Lord Justice (2001). *Review of the Criminal Courts of England and Wales* [The Auld Report]. London: HMSO.

Avio, K.L. (1988). Capital punishment in Canada: Statistical evidence and constitutional issues. *Canadian Journal of Criminology*, *30*, 331–345.

Bagby, R.M., Parker, J.D., Rector, N.A. & Kalemba, V. (1994). Racial prejudice in the Canadian legal system: Juror decisions in a simulated rape trial. *Law and Human Behavior*, *18*, 339–50.

Baker, J., Allan, A. & Weatherburn, D. (2002). Hung juries and aborted trials: An analysis of their prevalence, predictors and effects. *Crime and Justice Bulletin, 66*, 1–19.

Baldwin, J. & McConville, M. (1979). *Jury trials.* Oxford: Clarendon Press.

Baldwin, J. & McConville, M. (1980). Juries, foremen and verdicts. *British Journal of Criminology, 20*, 35–44.

Barber, D. & Gordon, G. (Eds.) (1976). *Members of the jury.* London: Wildwood House.

Barnett, A. (1985). Some distribution patterns for the Georgia death sentence. *U.C. Davis Law Review, 18*, 1327–1374.

Blanck, P.D. (1985). The appearance of justice: Judges' and verbal and nonverbal behavior in criminal jury trials. *Stanford Law Review, 38*, 89–164.

Blom-Cooper, L. (1974). The jury on trial. *The Guardian,* 10 June, p.9.

Boatright, R.G. (2001). Generational and age-based differences in attitudes towards jury service. *Behavioral Science and the Law, 19*, 285–304.

Boehm, V.R. (1968). Mr Prejudice, Miss Sympathy, and the authoritarian personality: An application of psychological measuring techniques to the problem of jury bias. *Wisconsin Law Review, 3*, 734–750.

Bornstein, B.H., Wisehunt, B., Nemeth, R.J. & Dunaway, D. (2002). Pretrial effects in a civil trial: A two-way street? *Law and Human Behavior, 26*, 3–17.

Bowers, W. (1995). The capital jury project: Rationale, design, and preview of early findings. *Indiana Law Review, 70*, 1043–1068.

Brekke, N.J. & Borgida, E. (1988). Expert psychological testimony in rape trials: A social cognitive analysis. *Journal of Personality and Social Psychology, 55*, 372–386.

Brewer, N., Harvey, S. & Semmler, C. (2004). Improving comprehension of jury instructions with audio-visual presentation. *Applied Cognitive Psychology, 18*, 765–776.

Brigham, J.C. (2006). The jury system in the United States of America. In M.F. Kaplan & A.M. Martin (Eds.) *Understanding world systems through social psychological research* (pp.11–29). New York: Psychology Press.

Burnett, D.G. (2001). *A trial by jury.* New York: Knopf.

Cammack, M. (1995). In search of the post-positivist jury. *Indiana Law Journal, 70*(2), 405–489.

Chesterman, M., Chan, J. & Hampton, S. (2001). *Managing prejudicial publicity: An empirical study of criminal jury trials in New South Wales.* Sydney, Australia: Justice Research Center, Law and Justice Foundation of New South Wales.

Costanzo, S. & Costanzo, M. (1994). Life or death decisions: An analysis of capital jury decision making under the special issues sentencing framework. *Law and Human Behavior, 18*, 151–170.

Cutler, B.L. & Hughes, D.M. (2001). Judging jury service: Results of the North Carolina administrative office of the courts survey. *Behavioral Science and the Law, 19*, 305–320.

Cutler, B.L., Penrod, S.D. & Dexter, H.R. (1990). Juror sensitivity to eyewitness identification evidence. *Law and Human Behavior, 14*, 185–191.

Darbyshire, P. (1991). The lamp that shows that freedom lives – is it worth the candle? *Criminal Law Review,* 740–752.

Daudistel, H., Hosch, H., Holmes, M. & Graves, J.B. (1999). Effect of defendant ethnicity on juries' disposition of felony cases. *Journal of Applied Social Psychology, 29*, 317–336.

Davies, G.M., Lloyd-Bostock, S. McMurran, & Wilson, C. (Eds.) (1996). *Psychology, law and criminal justice: International developments in research and practice.* New York: de Gruyter.

Denning, Lord. (1982). *What next in the law?* London: Butterworths.

Deosoran, R. (1993). The social psychology of selecting jury forepersons. *British Journal of Psychology, 33*, 70–80.

Devine, D.J., Clayton, L.D., Dunford, B.B., Seying, R.P., & Pryce, J. (2001). Jury decision making: 45 years on deliberating groups. *Psychology, Public Police and Law, 7*(3), 622–727.

Devlin, P.A., Sir. (1974). Trial by jury. *The Guardian,* 10 June, p.9.

Dillehay, R.C. & Nietzel, M.T. (1985). Juror experience and jury verdicts. *Law and Human Behavior, 9*, 179–191.

Dunstan, S., Paulin, J. & Atkinson, K.A. (1995). *Trial by peers? The composition of New Zealand juries.* Wellington, New Zealand: Department of Justice.

Elliott, R. (1991). On the alleged prosecution-proneness of death-qualified juries and jurors. In P.J. Suedfeld & P.E. Terlock (Eds.) *Psychology and social policy* (pp.255–265). New York: Hemisphere.

Ellsworth, P.C. (1993). Some steps between attitudes and verdicts. In R. Hastie (Ed.) *Inside the jury: The psychology of juror decision making* (pp.42–64). New York: Cambridge University Press.

Foley, L.A. & Pigott, M.A. (1997). Race, age and jury decisions in a civil rape trial. *American Journal of Forensic Psychology, 15*, 37–55.

Foss, R.D. (1981). Interactions between jurors as a function of majority vs. unanimity decision rules. *Journal of Applied Psychology, 7*, 38–56.

Goodman-Delahunty, J. & Tait, D. (2006). Lay participation in legal decision-making in Australia and New Zealand: Jury trials and administrative tribunals. In M.F. Kaplan & A.M. Martin (Eds.) *Understanding world systems through social psychological research* (pp.147–170). New York: Psychology Press.

Gordon, W.L. III. (1997). Reflections of a criminal defence lawyer on the Simpson trial. *Journal of Social Issues, 53*, 615–622.

Greene, E. & Dodge, M. (1995). The influence of prior record evidence on juror decision making. *Law and Human Behavior, 19*, 67–78.

Griffitt, W. & Jackson, T. (1973). Simulated jury decisions: The influence of jury defendant attitude similarity dissimilarity. *Social Behavior and Personality, 1*, 1–7.

Grosscup, J. & Penrod, S.D. (2002, March). *Limiting instructions' effects on juror assessment of scientific validity and reliability.* Paper session presented at the biennial meeting of the American Psychology-Law Society, Austin, Texas.

Hans, V.P. (1992). Jury decision making. In D.K. Kagehiro & W.S. Laufer (Eds.) *Handbook of psychology and law* (pp.56–76). New York: Springer.

Hans, V.P. & Vidmar, N. (1986). *Judging the jury*. New York: Plenum.

Hastie, R. (Ed.) (1993a). *Inside the jury: The psychology of juror decision making*. New York: Cambridge University Press.

Hastie, R. (1993b). Introduction. In R. Hastie (Ed.) *Inside the jury: The psychology of juror decision making* (pp.3–41). New York: Cambridge University Press.

Hastie, R., Penrod, S.D. & Pennington, N. (1983). *Inside the jury*. Cambridge, MA: Harvard University Press.

Heuer, L. & Penrod, S. (1994a). Juror note taking and question asking during trials: A national field experiment. *Law and Human Behavior, 18*, 121–150.

Heuer, L. & Penrod, S. (1994b). Trial complexity its meaning and effects. *Law and Human Behavior, 18*, 29–51.

Himelein, M., Nietzel, M.T. & Dillehay, R.C. (1991). Effects of prior juror experience on jury sentence. *Behavioral Sciences and the Law, 9*, 97–106.

Hollin, C.R. (1989). *Psychology and crime: An introduction to criminological psychology*. London: Routledge.

Honess, T.M., Charman, E.A. & Levi, M. (2003). Factual and affective/evaluative recall of pretrial publicity: Their relative influence on juror reasoning and verdict in a simulated fraud trial. *Journal of Applied Social Psychology, 30*, 1404–1416.

Hope, L. & Memon, A. (2006). Cross-border diversity: Trial by jury in England and in Scotland. In M.F. Kaplan & A.M. Martin (Eds.) *Understanding world systems through social psychological research* (pp.31–46). New York: Psychology Press.

Hope, L., Memon, A. & McGeorge, P. (2004). Understanding pretrial publicity: Predecisional distortion of evidence in mock jurors. *Journal of Experimental Psychology: Applied, 10*, 111–119.

Horan, J. (2004). *The civil jury system: An empirical study*. Unpublished Doctoral Dissertation, University of Melbourne School of Law, Victoria, Australia.

Horowitz, I.A. & ForsterLee, L. (2001). The effects of note-taking and trial transcript access on mock jury decisions in a complex civil trial. *Law and Human Behavior, 25*(4), 371–389.

Horowitz, I.A., ForsterLee, L. & Brolly, I. (1996). Effects of trial complexity on decision making. *Journal of Applied Psychology, 81*, 757–768.

Izzett, R. & Leginski, W. (1974). Group discussion and the influence of defendant characteristics in a simulated jury setting. *Journal of Social Psychology, 93*, 271–279.

Jackson, J. (1996). Jury decision-making in the trial process. In G. Davis, S. Lloyd-Bostock, M. McMurran & C. Wilson (Eds.) *Psychology, law and criminal justice* (pp.327–336). Berlin: de Gruyter.

Kalven, H. & Zeisel, H. (1966). *The American jury*. Chicago, IL: University of Chicago Press.

Kapardis, A. (2003). *Psychology and law: A critical introduction*. Melbourne: Cambridge University Press.

Kaplan, M.F. & Martin, A.M. (Eds.) (2006a). *Understanding world systems through social psychological research*. New York: Psychology Press.

Kaplan, M.F. & Martin, A.M. (2006b). Introduction and overview. In M.F. Kaplan & A.M. Martin (Eds.) *Understanding world systems through social psychological research* (pp.1–8). New York: Psychology Press.

Kaplan, M.F., Martin, A.M. & Hertel, J. (2006). Issues and prospects in European juries: An overview. In M.F. Kaplan & A.M. Martin (Eds.) *Understanding world systems through social psychological research* (pp.111–124). New York: Psychology Press.

Kaplan, M.F. & Miller, L.E. (1978). Reducing the effects of juror bias. *Journal of Personality and Social Psychology, 36*, 1443–1455.

Kassin, S.M. & Sukel, H. (1997). Coerced confessions and the jury: An experimental test of the 'harmless error' rule. *Law and Human Behavior, 21*, 27–46.

Kassin, S.M. & Wrightsman, L.S. (1983). The construction and validation of juror bias scale. *Journal of Research in Personality, 17*, 423–442.

Kemmelmeier, M. (2005). The effects of race and social dominance orientation in simulated juror decision making. *Journal of Applied Social Psychology, 35*, 1030–1045.

Kerr, J.F. (1987). *A presumption of wisdom: An expose of the jury system of injustice*. Sydney: Angus & Robertson.

Kerr, N.L. (1993). Stochastic models of juror decision making. In R. Hastie (Ed.) *Inside the jury: The psychology of juror decision making* (pp.116–135). New York: Cambridge University Press.

Kerr, N.L. & Bray, R.M. (2005). Simulation, realism, and the study of the jury. In N. Brewer & K.D. Wilson (Eds.) *Psychology and law: An empirical perspective* (pp.322–364). New York: Guilford Press.

Kerr, N.L. & MacCoun, R. (1985). The effects of jury size and polling method on the process and product of jury deliberation. *Journal of Personality and Social Psychology, 48*, 349–363.

Kerr, N.L., Hymes, R.W., Anderson, A.B. & Weathers, J.E. (1995). Defendant–juror similarity and mock-juror judgments. *Law and Human Behavior, 19*, 545–567.

Knittel, E. & Seiler, D. (1972). The merits of trial by jury. *Cambridge Law Journal, 56*, 223–228.

Kovera, M.B., McAuliff, B.D. & Hebert, K.S. (1999). Reasoning about scientific evidence: Effects of juror gender and evidence quality on juror decisions in a hostile work environment case. *Journal of Applied Psychology, 84*, 362–375.

Kutnjak Ivkovich, S. (1999). *Lay participation in criminal trials: The case of Croatia*. San Francisco, CA: Austin and Winfield.

Landy, D. & Aronson, E. (1969). The influence of the character of the criminal and his victim on decisions of simulated jurors. *Journal of Experimental Social Psychology, 5*, 141–152.

Law Reform Commission of Victoria (LRCV) (1985). *The jury in a criminal trial*. Melbourne, Australia.

Levett, L.M., Danielsen, E.M., Kovera, M.B. & Cutler, B.L. (2005). The psychology of jury and juror decision making. In N. Brewer & K.D. Wilson (Eds.) *Psychology and law: An empirical perspective* (pp.365–406). New York: Guilford Press.

Levine, J.P. (1992). *Juries and politics*. Pacific Grove, CA: Brooks/Cole Publishing.

Lloyd-Bostock, S.M.A. (1988). *Law in practice: Applications of psychology to legal decision making and legal skills*. London: Routledge/British Psychological Society.

Lloyd-Bostock, S. (1996). Juries and jury research in context. In G. Davies, S. Lloyd-Bostock, M. McMurran & C. Wilson (Eds.) *Psychology, law and criminal justice: International developments in research and practice* (pp.349–359). New York: de Gruyter.

Lloyd-Bostock, S. & Thomas, C. (1999). Decline of the little parliament: Juries and jury reform in England and Wales. *Law and Contemporary Problems, 7*, 21.

London, K. & Nunez, N. (2000). The effect of jury deliberation on jurors' propensity to disregard inadmissible evidence. *Journal of Applied Psychology, 85*, 932–939.

Luginbuhl, J. & Howe, J. (1995). Discretion in capital sentencing: Guided or misguided? *Indiana Law Journal, 70*, 1161–1185.

MacCoun, R. (1990). The emergence of extralegal bias during jury deliberation. *Criminal Justice and Behavior, 17*, 303–314.

Machura, S. (1999). *Interaction between lay assessors and professional judges in German mixed courts*. Paper presented at the conference, Lay participation in the criminal trial in the 21st century, at the International Institute for Higher Studies in the Criminal sciences, Siracuse, Italy.

Mark, R. Sir (1973). *Minority verdict* (pp.8–14). Dimbleby Lecture. London: British Broadcasting Corporation.

Marshall, G. (1975). The judgement of one's peers: Some aims and ideals of jury trial. In N.D. Walker & A. Pearson (Eds.) *The British jury system: Papers presented at the Cropwood Round-Table Conference*, December 1974. Cambridge: Institute of Criminology.

Mauro, R. (1991). Tipping the scales toward death: The biasing effects of death qualification. In P. Suedfeld & P. E. Tetlock (Eds.) *Psychology and social policy* (pp.243–54). New York: New York Publishing Corporation.

Mazzella, R. & Feingold, A. (1994). The effects of physical attractiveness, race, socioeconomic status, and gender of defendants and victims on judgments of mock jurors: A meta-analysis. *Applied Social Psychology, 24*, 1315–1344.

McAuliff, B.D. & Kovera, M.B. (2003). *Need for cognition and juror sensitivity to methodological flaws in psychological science*. Unpublished manuscript, Florida International University, Miami, FL.

McCabe, S. & Purves, R. (1974). *The jury at work*. Oxford: Blackwell.

McDowell, D.M. (1978). *The law in classical Athens*. London: Thames and Hudson.

McEwan, J. (2000). Decision making in legal settings. In J. Maguire, T. Mason & A. O'Kane (Eds.) *Behaviour, crime and legal processes* (pp.111–131). Chichester: Wiley.

McGuire, M. & Bermant, G. (1977). Individual and group decisions in response to a mock trial: A methodological note. *Journal of Applied Social Psychology, 3*, 200–226.

Memon, A., Vrij, A. & Bull, R. (2003). *Psychology and law* (2nd edn). Chichester: Wiley.

Meyers, R.A., Brashers, D.E. & Hanner, J. (2001). Majority/minority influence: Identifying argumentative patterns and predicting argument-outcome links. *Journal of Communication, 50*, 3–30.

Mills, C.J. & Bohannon, W.E. (1980). Juror characteristics: To what extent are they related to jury verdicts? *Judicature, 64*, 23–31.

Moore, L.E. (1973). *Tool of kings, palladium of liberty*. Cincinnati, OH: W.H. Anderson.

Moran, G. & Comfort, J.C. (1982). Scientific jury selection: Sex as a moderator of demographic and personality predictors of impaneled felony jury behaviour. *Journal of Personality and Social Psychology, 47*, 1052–1063.

Narby, D.J., Cutler, B.L. & Moran, G. (1993). A meta-analysis of the association between authoritarianism on jurors' perceptions of defendant's culpability. *Journal of Applied Psychology, 78*, 34–42.

Nathanson, H.S. (1995). Strengthening the criminal jury: Long overdue. *Criminal Law Quarterly, 38*, 217–248.

Nietzel, M.T., McCarthy, D.M. & Kery, M. (1999). Juries: The current state of the empirical literature. In R. Roesch, S.D. Hart & J.R. Ogloff (Eds.) *Psychology and law: The state of the discipline* (pp.23–52). New York: Kluwer Academic/Plenum.

Nisbett, R.E. & Wilson, T.D. (1977). Telling more than we can know: Verbal reports of mental processes. *Psychological Review, 84*, 231–259.

Ogloff, R.P. & Rose, G. (2005). The comprehension of judicial instructions. In N. Brewer & K.D. Wilson (Eds.) *Psychology and law: An empirical perspective* (pp.407–444). New York: Guilford Press.

Ogloff, J.R.P., Clough, J., Goodman-Delahunty, J. & Young, W. (2006). *The jury project: Stage I – A survey of Australian and New Zealand judges*. Melbourne, Australia: Australian Institute of Judicial Administration Incorporated.

Ohtsubo, Y. (2006). On designing a mixed jury system in Japan. In M.F. Kaplan & A.M. Martin (Eds.) *Understanding world systems through social psychological research* (pp.199–214). New York: Psychology Press.

Osborne, Y.H., Rappaport, N.B. & Meyer, R.G. (1986). An investigation of persuasion and sentencing severity with mock juries. *Behavioral Sciences and the Law, 4*, 339–349.

Ostrom, T.M., Werner, C. & Saks, M. (1978). An integration theory analysis of jurors' presumption of guilt or innocence. *Journal of Personality and Social Psychology, 36*, 436–450.

Pennington, N. & Hastie, R. (1986). Evidence evaluation in complex decision making. *Journal of Personality and Social Psychology, 51*, 242–258.

Pennington, N. & Hastie, R. (1990). Practical implications of psychological research on juror and jury decision making. *Personality and Social Psychology Bulletin, 16*(1), 90–105.

Pennington, N. & Hastie, R. (1992). Explaining the evidence: Tests of the story model for juror decision making. *Journal of Personality and Social Psychology, 62*, 189–206.

Pennington, N. & Hastie, R. (1993). The story model for juror decision making. In R. Hastie (Ed.) *Inside the jury: The psychology of juror decision making* (pp.192–221). New York: Cambridge University Press.

Penrod, S.D. & Heuer, L. (1998). Improving group performance; the case of the jury. In R.S. Tindale (Ed.) *Theory and research on small groups* (pp.127–151). New York: Plenum.

Queensland Criminal Justice Commission (1991). *Report of an investigative hearing into alleged jury interference*. Brisbane, Australia.

Reskin, B.F. & Visher, C.A. (1986). The impacts of evidence and extralegal factors in jurors' decisions. *Law and Society Review, 20*, 423–438.

Roskill, Lord P.C. (1986). *Fraud Trials Committee Report*. London: HMSO.

Russell, J. (Executive producer) (2004, July 15). Secrets of the jury room [Television broadcast] Sydney, Australia: Special Broadcasting Service. Retrieved 15 September 2009 from www.afc.gov.au/filmsandawards/filmdbsearch.aspx?view=title&title=WITHOP

Ryan, S. (2003, October). *Jury debriefing and stress*. Paper presented at the Second Annual Jury Research Conference, Sydney, Australia. Cited by Goodman-Delahunty and Tait (2006).

Saks, M. (1977). *Jury verdicts: The role of group size and social decision rule*. Lexington, MA: Heath.

Saks, M. & Hastie, R. (1978). *Social psychology in court*. London: Van Nostrand.

Saks, M.J. & Marti, M.W. (1997/2006). A meta-analysis of the effects of jury size. *Law and Human Behavior, 21*, 451–467. Reprinted in Hans, V. (Ed.) (2006). *The jury system: Contemporary scholarship*. The International Library of Essays in Law and Society. Aldershot: Ashgate.

Sandys, M. (1995). Crossovers – capital jurors who change their minds about the punishment: A litmus test for sentencing guidelines. *Indiana Law Journal, 70*, 1183–1221.

Sandys, M. & Dillehay, R.C. (1995). First-ballot votes, predeliberation dispositions, and final verdicts in jury trials. *Law and Human Behavior, 19*, 175–195.

Sarat, A. (1995). Violence, representation, and responsibility in capital trials: The view from the jury. *Indiana Law Journal, 70*, 1103–1139.

Seltzer, R., Venuti, M.A. & Lopes, G.M. (1991). Juror honesty during voir dire. *Journal of Criminal Justice, 19*(5), 451–462.

Sigall, H. & Ostrove, N. (1975). Beautiful but dangerous: Effects of offender attractiveness and nature of the crime on juridic judgements. *Journal of Personality and Social Psychology, 31*, 410–414.

Steblay, N.M., Besirevic, J., Fulero, S.M. & Jimenez-Lorente, B. (1999). The effects of pretrial publicity on juror verdicts: A meta-analytic review. *Law and Human Behavior, 23*, 219–235.

Stephan, C.W. & Stephan, W.G. (1986). Habla Ingles? The effects of language translation on simulated juror decisions. *Journal of Applied Social Psychology, 16*, 577–589.

Stephenson, G.M. (1992). *The psychology of criminal justice*. Oxford: Blackwell.

Studebaker, C.A. & Penrod, S.D. (1997). Pretrial publicity: The media, the law and common sense. *Psychology, Public Policy, and Law, 3*, 428–460.

Tanford, S., Penrod, S. & Collins, R. (1985). Decision making in joined criminal trials: The influence of charge similarity, evidence similarity and limiting instructions. *Law and Human Behavior, 9*, 319–337.

Thompson, D. (2002). *A comparison of jury understanding of self-defence instructions in Viro, McManus and Zekevic*. Presentation at the Australian Jury research Conference, Melbourne, Victoria. Cited by Goodman-Delahunty & Tait (2006).

Tinsley, Y. (2001). Juror decision-making: A look inside the jury room. In R. Tarling (Ed.) *Selected proceedings: Papers from the British Society of Criminology Conference*, Leicester 2000 (Vol.4).

Vidmar, N. (2002). Case studies of pre- and midtrial prejudice in criminal and civil litigation. *Law and Human Behavior, 26*, 73–105.

Willis, J. (1983). Jury disagreements in criminal trials – some Victorian evidence. *Australian and New Zealand Journal of Criminology, 20*, 20–30.

Wrightsman, L.S., Greene, E., Nietzel, M.T. & Fortune, W.H. (2002). *Psychology and the legal system* (2nd edn). Belmont, CA: Wadsworth.

Young, W. (2003). Summing up to juries in criminal cases – what jury research says about current rules and practice. *Criminal Law Review*, 665–689.

Young, W. (2004, November). *Judges' assistance to jurors*. Paper presented at the Third Australasian Jury Conference, Victoria, Australia.

Young, W., Cameron, N. & Tinsley, Y. (1999). *Juries in criminal trials*. Law Commission, Preliminary Paper no. 37, New Zealand.

Zander, M. (1974). Why I disagree with Sir Robert mark. *Police*, 16 April.

Zander, M. & Henderson, P. (1993). *Crown Court study*. The Royal Commission on Criminal Justice, Research Study No. 19. London: HMSO.

Zander, M. & Henderson, P. (1994). The Crown Court study. Royal Commission on Criminal Justice Study No. 19. *Research Bulletin*, No.35, pp.46–48. London: Home Office Research and Statistics Department.

Zeisel, H. (1971). '… And then there were none': The diminution of federal jury. *University of Chicago Law Review, 35*, 35–54.

Zeisel, H. & Diamond, S.S. (1987). Convincing empirical evidence on the six-member jury. In, L.S. Wrightsman, S.M. Kassin & C.E. Willis (Eds.) *In the jury box: Controversies in the courtroom* (pp.193–208). Newbury Park, CA: Sage.

Zerman, M. (1977). *Call the final witness: The People vs. Mather as seen by the 11th juror*. New York: Harper & Row.

16

Assessment

David A. Crighton

Assessment is a fundamental aspect of forensic psychology and serves to underpin a range of activities, including categorisation, formulation and treatment. Psychological assessment is characterised by attempts to apply scientific approaches ethically to human functioning both individually and in social contexts. The use of scientific approaches is characterised by a number of core aspects. These include the use of theory to derive hypotheses, the use of careful observation and measurement as a means of testing such falsifiable hypotheses leading to rejection and reformulation, and the development and refining of more valid theoretical understanding.

Effective psychological assessment requires a clear understanding of relevant theory, along with the principles that apply to accurate measurement and the appropriate application of measures. Assessment methods can be understood in terms of a range of psychometric qualities, including reliability, validly, specificity, sensitivity and power. Ethical and competent forensic psychological assessments need to be individually tailored in order to produce change most effectively. In order to be ethical, assessment also needs to actively address the issues of bias that apply to all practitioners.

Conceptual Issues in Assessment

Forensic psychological assessment can be operationally defined as the use of scientific methods to systematically evaluate a person (or persons) in relation to specific legal purposes. Most of the processes involved in conducting such assessments are common across psychology. Hence assessments conducted by clinical, counselling and educational psychologists are all fundamentally the same. What separates such assessments is the context in which assessments are undertaken, and for forensic psychology this context is ultimately a legal one.

There are several fundamental conceptual and methodological components to psychological assessment and these are interrelated. These include the need to draw on credible theories of human behaviour along with the need to make valid observations and measurements, both quantitative and qualitative, as part of the process of testing and reformulating theory-based explanations. It also involves attempts to systematically evaluate the information and data gathered. The emphasis on a scientific approach to psychological assessment is based on the assumption that using scientific methods to assess people will facilitate the ability to identify and manipulate sources of variance relating to psychological problems. It forms the basis of the dominant 'scientist-practitioner' model which predominates across all areas of applied psychology (Haynes & O'Brien, 2000).

Figure 16.1 provides an idealised and simplified outline of the process of psychological assessment.

Within a framework of scientific practice, it is critical to recognise that the beliefs and values of the assessor will strongly influence both the process and what is measured. This is inevitable and is both a technical and an ethical point, in that it is essential to recognise the impacts of such processes on assessment and make appropriate efforts to address them and mitigate any inappropriate effects (Crighton & Towl, 2008). Such efforts are perhaps

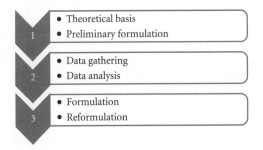

1
- Theoretical basis
- Preliminary formulation

2
- Data gathering
- Data analysis

3
- Formulation
- Reformulation

Figure 16.1 A structure outline of psychological assessment.

brought into sharpest relief in forensic practice, where assessments may have a range of legal consequences for those being assessed. This fact also implies that restricted notions of the 'objectivity' of any assessment are misplaced.

A scientific approach to assessment will generally rest, initially, on a basis of careful and detailed observation. This in turn will be associated with processes of hypothesis generation, formulation and reformulation, based on a clear theory base. It will also generally involve an emphasis on careful measurement, the use of multivariate measurements and sometimes efforts to manipulate variables. Measurement in turn can be defined as the process of trying to assign values to specific attributes of a person or variable (Haynes & O'Brien, 2000). Accurate measurement is an essential aid to clinical[1] judgements and more accurate measurement is associated with better ability to estimate covariance and describe causal relationships. An example here might be the suggested association between childhood trauma and adult depression: testing such covariance clearly rests in very large part on the ability to accurately measure 'childhood trauma' and 'adult depression' (Persons & Fresco, 1998).

One of the major functions of assessment often has particular salience in forensic practice and is that of prediction. This relates to efforts to establish links between assessment findings and future outcomes (often called prognosis in other applied sciences such as medicine). Efforts at prediction are self-evidently limited by our ability to accurately measure predictor variables (PVs). Hence any suggested association between, for example, lack of empathy and subsequent violence depends on being able to measure 'lack of empathy' reliably and validly.

Psychological assessment may also be concerned with attempts at categorisation or classification (sometimes termed diagnosis). This can be seen as an aspect of accurate measurement, where meaningful categories can be used to aid clinical judgements.

Classification

The use of classification is extensive within science and serves a number of useful functions. Most obvious of these perhaps is that it can support communication about something by ensuring a high degree of consistency between observers. Classification as a concept has made a substantial contribution to a number of sciences in this way, with biological sciences such as botany providing an archetypal example, with the development of detailed taxonomic approaches. Classification, though, may also serve as an aid to thinking about complex problems as in the case of disease categories, or diagnoses, in medicine and surgery.

The virtues of good scientific classification systems include their clarity, with explicit transparent decision rules for inclusion and exclusion. They are comprehensive in that they serve to categorise a population of things, events or behaviours. They have a high degree of acceptability to users, because they are functional and have good utility. Finally they have good levels of fidelity to nature. It is, though, noteworthy that even optimal classification systems yield categories that are concepts and not things, a fact that is often poorly recognised and integrated in practice, where there is often a tendency to reify categories (Rutter & Taylor, 2002).

The best-known and most influential categorical systems within applied sciences are medicine and surgery, which are primarily concerned with the categorisation of forms of dysfunction or diseases. In relation to mental health the best-known and most widely used categorical frameworks in Western practice are DSM-IV (American Psychiatric Association, 2000) and ICD-10 (World Health Organization, 1990). These seek to provide operationally defined categories applicable to psychological dysfunction. This approach has been described by some as the 'medical model', where assessment is concerned with description and categorisation (diagnosis), based on an analysis of observable factors (signs) and self-reported factors(symptoms), leading to the estimation of likely outcomes (prognosis) and interventions (treatment). This description is problematic in a number of ways. Whatever the successes of this model within applied biological sciences such as medicine and surgery, it is misleading to suggest that this model is in any way exclusively 'medical'. It might be more accurate to describe this as a 'categorisation' model and it is clearly one that has wide application across science (Crighton & Towl, 2008). It is similarly inaccurate to suggest that the appropriate practice of applied sciences such as medicine and surgery merely involves biological categorisation (Clare, 2003; Rutter & Taylor, 2002).

Effective categorisation of function and dysfunction may have utility in a number of respects. It potentially creates relatively homogeneous groups which are replicable for research purposes. This has clear advantages in producing testable predictions derived from classification. Practitioners will also need to know how to apply research findings to individuals, and classification systems may be helpful in doing this. However, there are clear areas of difficulty with classification systems which may also serve to mask significant differences within categories and between individuals. This may impact on the relative value of categories across settings. For example, the needs of researchers and practitioners in this respect may be quite different. A classification system that leaves many cases unallocated is not, necessarily, problematic for researchers. Yet it is likely to have much less utility for practitioners.

Classification approaches have been subject to several critiques. The most fundamental of these, already touched upon, is that classification approaches both exaggerate and reify the power of concepts. This is evident in clinical practice within psychology and psychiatry where 'diagnoses' are normally descriptive rather than explanatory. Antisocial personality disorder (APD) is a description of a person who may be impulsive and aggressive but as a concept it does not explains these behaviours. This can result in entirely circular thinking where a concept such as APD, defined in terms of aggressive and antisocial behaviour, can be misused as an apparent 'explanation' of why an individual behaves in antisocial and aggressive ways. The use of classification approaches in this way serves no useful function.

Diagnostic categories may also serve to obscure assumptions that are being made, such as the dysfunctional nature of behaviours, when in the context of an individual's social circumstances these may be adaptive. Diagnostic categories certainly serve to mask considerable heterogeneity within groupings. Those with Down's syndrome show wide variation in IQ, similar to the non-Down's syndrome population, yet the category may serve to effectively mask this fact.

The implications of such aspects of categorical approaches are the subject of considerable debate and disagreement. It is certainly the case that categories have been misused in the past. Psychological and psychiatric categories have certainly been used to justify a range of abuses, ranging from incarceration in closed institutions through to enforced sterilisation and killing of those with mental disorders. The existence of abuses alone though is, of course, not sufficient to justify the absolute rejection of categorical approaches. Categories can have considerable scientific value but their misuse within science underlines the need for a cautious approach to their use, along with a clear appreciation of the strengths and weaknesses of categorisation as one form of scientific approach.

Dimensional approaches

The choice between categorical and dimensional approaches has been a significant area of debate within science. There are, though, a number of constraints that have favoured categorical models in clinical practice. Most obvious of these is that there is often a need to make dichotomous decisions during assessment and intervention: either to undertake a particular assessment or not; either to intervene or not; and so on. This becomes a significant difficulty, though, where categories come to be used to dominate assessment and intervention, an approach which is generally inappropriate.

Categorical thinking also appears to be something which is firmly ingrained in human cognition (Macrae & Bodenhausen, 2000) and it is therefore perhaps not entirely surprising that it has tended to result in concepts which develop a life of their own. Dimensional thinking, by contrast, is less natural and has been slower to gain ground. It has, though, become increasingly attractive to researchers and has also had marked impacts in areas of practice such as neuropsychology and behavioural genetics. It is also a poorly recognised fact that, even when using good categorical models, dimensional risk and protective factors will be the norm rather than the exception.

At a more fundamental level it is also easy to exaggerate the differences between dimensional and categorical models and explanations. Generally it is possible to translate between categorical model and dimensions and vice versa. A category can often be described in terms of a set of dimensions or dimensional scores, while dimensions may reciprocally be grouped into categories.

This has a number of significant implications. These include the fact that discrete causes can be associated with problems that are distributed across a continuum. It is, for example, not unusual for genetic disorders to show a range of physical changes across one or more dimensions. It is thus inappropriate to assume that because effects are continuously distributed causal factors must also be, or indeed vice versa. To illustrate this, a child's emotional attachment to its caregivers may be assessed categorically but the effects may be seen and assessed across a number of dimensions.

Overall, the choice between dimensional and categorical approaches within biological sciences (and elsewhere) is not simple, nor is it a straightforward either/or issue. In practice the choice will be complex and challenging and dependent on the assessment context and purpose. Mixed classification patterns are likely to be the norm in psychological assessment, which may involve dimensional data and outcomes but the need to make categorical decisions.

Diagnosis and formulation

The term diagnosis is often used in clinical practice to refer to a specific form of categorisation involving the identification of signs and symptoms, and the use of these to allocate to categories which, in turn, are associated with specific outcomes or prognoses and interventions or treatments.

Formulation refers to approaches concerned with analysing specific cases to produce a plausible explanation of one or more specific problems and a prescription of interventions likely to address these. Case formulation includes an analysis of the problems to be addressed and organisation of information within a conceptual explanatory schema. This in turn is associated with intervention decisions that lead to specific procedures (Bruch, 1998).

The differences between diagnosis and case formulation are easy to exaggerate. To a large extent they can be seen as differing descriptions of similar analytic processes, with the former being traditionally dominated by medicine and the latter by psychology. Efforts to stress the differences between these could be cynically seen as reflecting demarcation disputes, rather than representing more substantive process differences. In fact, the use of scientific approaches to assessment in this way cannot reasonably be seen as the exclusive province of any professional group (Towl, 2005).

Psychological Assessment

Hypothesis formulation

Clinical case assessment and subsequent formulation (or the integration and interpretation of assessment data) involves the application of scientific method to individual cases (Shapiro, 1985). It is fundamental to the scientist-practitioner approach common across the various specialist areas of applied psychology (Lane & Corrie, 2006).

The first step within this is the adoption of a theoretical orientation as the basis for generating hypotheses. Each theoretical orientation has its own core assumptions and hypotheses. So, for example, cognitive orientations are based on an assumption of the central role of cognitive processes in behaviour. In contrast, radical behaviourist theory would stress the importance of not attempting to address such processes. While every theory will have its core assumptions and hypotheses, it is noteworthy that there may be significant overlap between these. Apparent differences may simply involve different descriptive jargon or 'packaging' of similar concepts. As an example, cognitive behavioural therapy (CBT) and narrative therapy (NT) both stress the importance of 'family cognitions', but describe this concept using quite different language.

There is clearly a wide range of theoretical orientations that might be drawn on explicitly or implicitly to inform assessments, and these will influence the entire process. Ingram (2006), though, suggests seven dominant types within clinical practice:

   i)   biological models;
  ii)   crisis and stressful situational transitions;
 iii)   behavioural and learning models;
 iv)   cognitive models;
  v)   existential and spiritual models;
 vi)   psychodynamic models;
vii)   social, cultural and environmental models.

Psychological assessment requires efforts to generate provisional explanations and hypotheses, followed by processes intended to test and refine these initial explanations. This can be further broken down into a number of activities paralleling those seen in other areas of science (Crighton & Towl, 2008). These would include:

   i)   problem definition;
  ii)   theoretical formulation;
 iii)   hypothesis generation;
 iv)   data gathering;
  v)   data analysis;
 vi)   specification of outcome goals;
vii)   intervention planning;

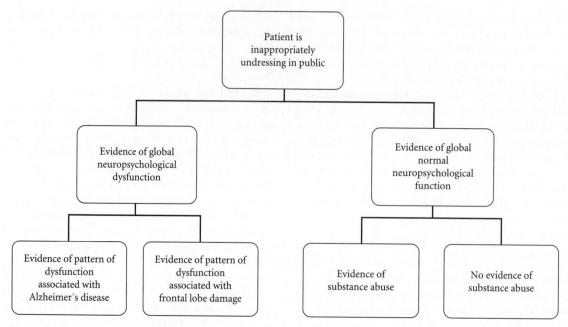

Figure 16.2   Example of an iterative assessment approach.

viii)   monitoring of intervention effects;

ix)   use of monitoring data to adapt interventions.

These processes provide the foundations of psychological assessment. The process of psychological assessment is also one which can be seen as integrative and iterative in nature. In this context the notion of integration refers to the fact that the process can involve gathering and evaluating information at different times or rates, with integration and reformulation taking place at a later time. Iterative refers to the use of incremental strategies, where the assessor will use learning from earlier stages to inform the overall assessment. This can be illustrated with an example from forensic neuropsychology as in Figure 16.2. A key aspect of such approaches is that they involve revision and reformulation in the light of information emerging from pervious iterations.

The validity and utility of any assessment can be seen to involve a number of generic activities. These include:

i)   initial theory development;

ii)   consideration of ethical issues;

iii)   clarification of hypotheses;

iv)   development of an overall 'formulation';

v)   priority setting;

vi)   planning of intervention strategies;

vii)   prediction of responses to interventions;

viii)   definition of operational criteria for successful outcomes;

ix)   assessment and revisions following failure to respond or blocks to progress;

x)   addressing and overcoming individual biases.

This outline of assessment leads on sensibly to a discussion of the role of theory, since this can be seen as underpinning the entire process. This is perhaps best illustrated not by an abstract discussion but, rather, by a practical consideration of some major theoretical orientations used in conducting psychological assessments.

Psychodynamic theory

There is no single psychodynamic approach, although all can be traced back to the work of Sigmund Freud (1999). Different schools of thought have, though, developed over the subsequent century. All of these can, however, be seen as sharing a number of common themes:

i) a focus on individual psychological pain and struggle;

ii) the existence of an internally constructed world that differs from the external world;

iii) the existence of unconscious elements of this internally constructed world which have profound impacts on behaviour;

iv) a concern with processes of adaptation to emotional pain and difficulties (Leiper, 2006).

Psychodynamic approaches can be seen as having four main perspectives. They are dynamic in nature, suggesting that all behaviour, however apparently irrational, is purposeful and motivated and explicable as such. The psychological conflicts present in a person will always be unique and are generally too complex for any formulation to fully capture.

They are developmental in nature, suggesting a need to explain the past in order to account for the present and, within psychodynamic approaches, this has often involved stage models of development. The best known of these is perhaps the oral, anal and phallic stages suggested by Freud (1999). However, other psychodynamic theorists have subsequently suggested different stage models of development and often substantive changes to the initial model developed by Freud. Erikson (1966), for example, went on to postulate eight stages of psychosexual development rather than five, suggesting that each person will goes through these in an effort to reach their full developmental potential. He also placed greater stress on the role of the ego as more than a servant of the id. Erikson also placed greater emphasis on the effects of the environment during development in enabling growth, adjustment, self-awareness and the development of a positive 'identity' (Erikson, 1980).

They are structural theories, which suggest the existence of differing conscious and unconscious psychological 'structures' (e.g. the Id, Ego and Super Ego). Importantly, it is generally assumed that the unconscious mind works in a different manner from the conscious. Thus it has no concept of negation, which allows contradictory propositions to coexist, and it lacks a clear subject–object division, so that one thing might stand for another or many others.

They are also adaptive theories, suggesting that relationships between 'internal' and 'external' worlds are influenced by behaviour and systemic influences. So individual experience will affect the way an individual intersects with the world, through both adaptive and maladaptive processes (Johnstone & Dallos, 2006).

Psychodynamic theories suggest a number of key aspects to assessment that differ from the approaches outlined so far. These would include:

i) the need to go beyond the surface presenting problems however carefully defined and described;

ii) the need to focus on the intersection between underlying internal psychodynamic processes and current interpersonal and social situation;

iii) the need to focus on early disruption in adjustment and parental relationships in order to address current difficulties in adjustment;

iv) that the internal world is the dominant force in structuring perceptions of the world;

v) that adjustment to psychological pain and challenges is relative and involves a balance between health and unhealthy approaches.

Cognitive behavioural theory (CBT)

CBT represents a fusion of two key theoretical traditions within psychology: behavioural and cognitive psychology. It is perhaps best seen as a broad church of related approaches. In application to specific issues and difficulties it involves a number of fundamental assumptions. It does, though, draw on an extensive, largely empirical, evidence base.

The approach is predicated on the assumption that any assessment needs to be framed in terms of a 'biopsychosocial' context (Beck, 2005). This involves recognition that simply focusing on psychological factors such as cognitions and behaviours is wholly inadequate. Each individual is part of a much broader and unique matrix of social and biological influences, which are fundamental to effective assessment and subsequent formulation and interventions. This is a notion that, in day-to-day practice, can be poorly recognised and at times marginalised. In addition, CBT approaches take as their starting point the assumption that the person being assessed is central to the process. More precisely, their perspective and agency are stressed as central.

Johnstone and Dallos (2006) suggest that the approach involves seven key principles:

i) that it draws on cognitive and behavioural psychological theory to inform a better understanding of others;

ii) that 'collaborative empiricism' is the basis of the approach;

iii) that CBT formulations are provisional and require adapting over the course of interventions;

iv) that the approach acts as a framework for assessment, formulation and intervention;

v) that a good therapeutic relationship is a necessary but not sufficient condition for a collaborative approach;

vi) that the focus should be on current problems and mutually agreed goals;

vii) that the approach is complementary to diagnostic categories used in mental health but that such categories are probably only marginal to the course of interventions.

There are a range of methods to assist in the process of assessment, which begins with careful identification and description of the presenting issues. This is common to good practice across psychological assessment, with its stress on the importance of careful observation, clear and agreed definitions and accurate measurement. In CBT approaches, such agreement needs to be between the practitioner and the person they are assessing. Building on such agreement, the process then involves the identification of predisposing factors, precipitating factors, perpetuating factors and protective factors (Towl & Crighton, 1996).

CBT approaches provide a variety of methods to assist in this process of assessment, including 'functional analysis', which attempts to establish functional relationships between covariates (Haynes, 1998). While there are multiple ways of completing a functional analysis, all rest on careful observation and data gathering as the basis for interpretation of complex patterns (Daffern et al., 2007; Owens & Ashcroft, 1982).

Systemic theory

Systemic approaches were initially developed in the 1920s, emerging out of the various schools of Gestalt psychology that were then popular. It suggested that individual psychological functioning tended to operate using holistic and self-organising. From the 1950s general systems theory emerged from work within both social and biological sciences and was concerned to offer an explanatory framework for complex social 'systems'. Within clinical practice in psychology this often involved the assessment of family 'systems', on the basis that these were the most powerful systems for shaping the development of psychological functioning (Ford & Lerner,

1992; Lerner *et al.*, 2000). At a theoretical level the approach can still be seen as stressing the role of group social psychological processes to a larger extent than approaches such as CBT which, notwithstanding its own theoretical basis, can often be criticised in practice for often undervaluing these.

Early systemic approaches tended to stress the external analysis of systems interactions but in recent years this has changed. Current systemic approaches stress the need to see therapists themselves as part of the 'system' and at a fundamental level the approach is seen to be based on collaborative interaction between 'helpers' and 'helped' (Dallos & Steadman, 2006).

Systemic assessment can be characterised as involving seven stages:

i) definition of the problems;

ii) deconstruction of the developmental course of the problems;

iii) establishing links between the problems and 'ordinary difficulties';

iv) exploration of attempted solutions;

v) beliefs about difficulties and responses to these;

vi) discussion and evaluation of what worked in the past and what did not;

vii) discussion about decisions to persist with some attempted solutions and not to persist with others.

A number of clear observations emerge in relation to these stages. The first is perhaps to stress areas of clear overlap between theoretical approaches. As noted above, while the language differs from that used in CBT, aspects of the logical basis are clearly very similar. What does perhaps differ is the greater influence of constructivist approaches advocated by a number of early (and later) social psychologists (e.g. Kelly, 1955). Because of this influence there is probably a greater tendency within systemic approaches to see case formulations as constructions and propositions than in some other approaches.

Social inequalities theory

Such approaches are, in many respects, similar to systemic theories but differ in drawing more from social psychology research and sociological research addressing group differences associated with economic and social inequality. As such they are perhaps especially relevant to forensic practice. Social inequality can be defined as structured differences or hierarchies of power that limit and constrain some and privilege others (Dallos & Steadman, 2006). At a theoretical level the approach is a social constructionist one with clear links to the work of Max Weber and Karl Marx, predicated on the notion of conflicts of interest between groups. The approach can also be seen as a wider challenge to dominant thinking with Western cultures, with their stress on individualism (Miller & McCleland, 2006; Rose, 1989).

There is a substantial evidence base which establishes clear links between social and economic inequality and poor health, both physical and mental (Crighton & Towl, 2008; Social Exclusion Unit, 2002). Despite this clear evidence base, issues of social inequality remain largely peripheral in the current practice of applied psychology (Smail, 2004). This is despite the fact that 'low status' groups in society tend to experience the most negative and disempowering contacts with psychologists and psychological therapists (Department of Health, 2003).

The approach differs from many other systemic approaches in stressing the centrality of social, economic and explicit political factors in mental health. The approach sees social agency as inextricably linked to such things as social class, race and gender. The approach also clearly overlaps with systemic family approaches in stressing the importance of family systems in mediating the effects of these factors.

Assessment within this model can be characterised as involving five interrelated stages:

i)   definition of difficulties;
ii)   analysis of the broad systemic forces that have operated across the person's developmental history;
iii) analysis of the manner in which they have sought to deal with these forces;
iv)   analysis of the ways in which the person has gained power and agency in their life;
v)   analysis of the ways in which changes to the broader context can contribute to positive changes.

This approach to formulation is relatively unusual in often seeing professional psychology (and indeed other professions) as being part of the problem rather than part of the solution. It suggests that there is a need in any society to create ideologies and dialogues that serve to legitimise the status quo, and hence avoid disrupting social and economic inequalities and vested interests.

Within this framework mental health professions may be central to legitimising inequality, by defining excluded groups as 'sick' or 'disordered', setting up a co-dependence between marginalised social groups and professionals (Smail, 2004).

Integrative theories

The term integrative theories refers to systematic efforts to draw from and 'integrate' more than one theoretical approach. These can be in the form of pre-structured approaches or the use of assessment and intervention mixes based on the likelihood of response (Roth et al., 2006).

An example of the former is cognitive analytic therapy (CAT) which, in essence, draws on psychodynamic theory and concepts but integrates this with theory based on cognitive psychology. The posited advantages of this are that it manages to incorporate notions from psychodynamic approaches that are felt to be of value, while also being able to draw on notions and the evidence base from cognitive psychology (Ryle, 1997).

The use of assessment and intervention mixes based on likely response is often justified by analogy with treatment in medicine. Here it is at times appropriate, indeed good practice, to use different drug formulations to address different problems. Such an analogy, though, is open to criticism as something of an intellectual sleight of hand. The use of different drugs in medicine does not necessarily imply the use of different theoretical bases at all. Such approaches also assume an ability to identify evidence on effective treatment components, something which is often far less applicable to psychological interventions than physiological.

Data Gathering

As outlined above, the use of theory serves to direct the collection of information, or data. Data gathering, though, presents a range of issues which need to be addressed, as well as a number of significant challenges. Most obvious of these is perhaps the high degree of dependence within psychology on self-report data. This has a number of implications. Psychological assessment will generally involve the use of at least some self-report data generated via semi-structured and structured interview. It will also frequently involve self-report data derived from psychometric assessments. It may also involve psychometric assessment of behaviours and, more rarely, may involve physical measures associated with psychological functioning.

Another significant challenge is addressing issues of diversity within any assessment. This includes the need to recognise social, economic and political differences as well as issues such as ethnicity, disability, social class and culture. At the most obvious level it is clear that developmental history will differ across individuals based on their social experience. There is also a substantial body of evidence addressing response biases. This refers to the cognitive biases shown when individuals respond to questions in the manner that they believe the person asking them either expects or wants them to answer, as opposed to answering in line with their true behaviour or beliefs. This can result from obvious weaknesses in the approach to assessment, such as the poor use of leading questions. Such biases may also result, though, from the person being assessed seeking to give 'socially acceptable' answers. This is likely to be a factor across many areas of forensic practice where, for example, questions about levels of violence are likely to be affected by such considerations. In turn this will influence the manner in which self-report data may be most usefully gathered. At a more profound level it will open up questions of the need, desirability or ethical basis of assessment. There are, of course, no easy answers to these challenges. First steps, though, suggest a need for explicit reflection on such issues throughout any assessment and a need to genuinely value the experiences of those with problems.[2]

Whatever the theoretical basis used to conduct an assessment, good data gathering will depend on the development of an empathic and trusting relationship. It seems self-evident that few of us would disclose often difficult, generally sensitive, personal information to someone we felt unable to like or trust. This is crucial within psychology, given the extent to which self-report data dominates many assessments. The development of such relationships is also likely to impact markedly on assessment of behaviour and psycho-physiological measures.

Within assessment it is also important to use initial hypotheses as a basis for exploratory work. This needs to be underpinned by a commitment to exploring the individual's problems with them using exploratory questioning. It also requires a fundamental commitment to such hypotheses being provisional and open to revisions or replacement where they do not fit emergent data. This also suggests a need to avoid premature moves to 'fixing' problems and a willingness to use 'trial' interventions as a means of improving the quality of assessment data.

Interviews

The use of interviews is likely to be a key part of any psychological assessment for a number of reasons. These include the fact that this is, generally, a relatively accessible source of self-report information. More fundamentally, for theories such as CBT built on collaborative approaches, it is the main way to establish a positive therapeutic rapport necessary for positive change. Within this model there is no sense that assessment and treatment are mutually exclusive and, in fact, the process of assessment may become a form of treatment. Interviews also have the advantage that they are highly flexible and so can be adapted to address themes and issues as they emerge with individuals. The idiographic nature of interviews, though, also has less positive sides. As an assessment method they tend to have poor reliability. In turn this may be seen to impact on issues of validity and utility. The extent to which interviews are used will also clearly depend on the theoretical basis for the assessment. Thus in an assessment based on purely behavioural theory, interviews would be seen as having a more limited role than, for example, in cognitive or psychodynamic approaches (Towl, 2005).

Traditional clinical interviews have a number of significant weaknesses. Most obviously the approach has been shown to have relatively low levels of reliability. In terms of categorisation, even experienced practitioners have been shown to agree at little better than chance levels (Beck et al., 1962). In turn this had adverse impacts on validity and also the specificity and sensitivity of assessments. Such findings led to efforts to improve the psychometric properties of interviews as an assessment method. This generally involved increasing the level of structure within interviews. Any interview can be seen as resting on a continuum between low and high levels of structure. At the most structured end of the continuum, such 'interviews' provide an inflexible structure in terms of the questions asked, the order of questions and the ways in which responses are coded. More common has been the development of semi-structured interviews which allow potential for varying degrees of flexibility.

As with all assessments, interviews will have particular psychometric properties, as well as degree of structure, breadth of structure and context of use. The choice of interview approach therefore needs to be tailored to the needs and priorities for any assessment. This means that careful evaluation of the approach adopted is needed. For example, while increasing the structure of an interview may increase reliability, this in turn can also adversely impact on validity. As an interview becomes more structured and reliable, it may involve questions that are irrelevant to the person being assessed, as well as missing information that is important to inform an accurate and ethical assessment (Towl, 2006).

Choice of assessment here requires consideration of the reliability of the assessment approach used in terms of inter-rater and test–retest reliability and this will be defined by multiple factors. These include the:

i) clarity and nature of questions used;
ii) degree of understanding of the questions by the person being assessed and the practitioner conducting the assessment;
iii) training, experience and values of the practitioner;
iv) interview conditions;
v) range of complexity of problems being assessed;
vi) prevalence base rates for what is being assessed;
vii) characteristics of the interviewer.

The validity of an interview will similarly be influenced by these factors, all of which need to be considered in clinical decision making. The validity of an interview might be seen as its ability to accurately evaluate an operationally defined construct, for example the capacity of a structured interview to identify an Axis I diagnostic category as defined by DSM-IV (American Psychiatric Association, 2000). An example of an Axis I category here might be a major depressive disorder. A moment's reflection, though, suggests a problem with this, in that it can simply become a tautological exercise. It can simply refer to the ability of the interview to accurately identify a collection of factors with varying degrees of association. It does not follow logically that these factors have any theoretical coherence or clinical utility and it is of course possible for an interview to achieve a high degree of reliability and some forms of validity while identifying a clinically meaningless construct (Widiger & Clark, 2000). In the example given above of the DSM IV Axis I category of major depression, the value of allocation to such a diagnostic group depends essentially on the construct validity for this category.

Psychometric assessments

Psychometrics is a specific area within psychological assessment which involves assigning numerical labels to one or more properties of an event, using fixed rules. It involves a number of key general considerations and these include the fact that such assessments are seeking to measure psychological attributes which cannot be directly measured. In this respect such assessments are quite different from superficially similar but logically quite different physical measures, concerned with attributes which can be directly measured.

Linked to this point, it is the case that psychological attributes such as 'IQ', 'extraversion' and so on are hypothetical constructs. They cannot be confirmed absolutely. There is also no universal agreement on how to measure such psychological constructs. In reality the degree or extent to which such psychological constructs can be said to be characteristic of a person can only be inferred from limited samples of the individual's behaviour (McKinnon et al., 2008).

It is also important to note that any measurement of a psychological construct depends on the use of operational definitions. In essence this requires the use of explicit rules of correspondence between the theoretical construct and a sample of observable behaviours. Axiomatically this will always be subject to error. The size of such errors will in turn depend on the accuracy of measurement. Units of measurement in psychological assessments present a range of general problems and are often not well defined. Such measurements need to be based on a clear theoretical basis and may be inter-correlated with other constructs within a theoretical system. Yet, unlike many of the physical and biological sciences, they frequently lack any physical measures.

Within psychology a 'test' can be defined as a standard procedure for obtaining a sample of behaviour from a specific domain. It is possible to further subdivide these into:

i) aptitude, achievement and proficiency tests which comprise a behavioural sample of optimal performance (e.g. IQ tests);
ii) questionnaires and inventories which comprise a behavioural sample of typical performance (e.g. assessments of personality);
iii) sampling of typical performance in naturalistic settings (e.g. assessments of response following parent–child separation).

Test theory

Most psychological tests have been constructed along the lines of classical test theory (CTT) (Wasserman & Bracken, 2003). This is concerned with the extent to which the specifics of assessment influence the measurements made in a given situation and the methods used to minimise these.

Within classical test theory any observed performance (X) is thought to be composed of the true performance (T) and random error (E). In the population E is assumed to sum to zero and the correlation between T and E is assumed to be zero.

An alternative to classical test theory is item response theory (IRT), which uses more sophisticated forms of data modelling. It is based on the notion that the probability of discrete outcomes on tests is a function of both individual and test item parameters. Within the theory, individual parameters are often termed the 'latent trait', referring essentially to the theoretical construct the test seeks to measure, for example individual 'intelligence'. IRT provides a logical framework for the estimation of tests. IRT and CTT are sometimes presented as being in opposition to each other but this is potentially misleading. IRT can be seen as a more current and evidence-based theory which serves the functions of allowing greater flexibility in evaluating assessments and achieving higher levels of reliability by extracting greater detail for individual items (Embretson & Reise, 2000).

Data Analysis

Reliability

Reliability has a specific statistical meaning within psychological assessment, quite distinct from its day-to-day usage. It is defined as the ratio of the variance in the true score (T) to the variance in the observed score (X) in the population. There are a number of approaches to estimating the reliability of a test. The most frequently used within psychology are:

i) parallel forms, where parallel versions of a test are used to estimate reliability;
ii) split-half reliability, where the correlations between item totals for two halves of a test are calculated;

iii) test–retest reliability, where the correlations between repeat administrations of a test are calculated;
iv) standardised item alpha reliability coefficient, where the average correlation of pairs of parallel items is scaled according to test length.

It is important to note that reliability, while it may be a useful measure, is not a goal to be pursued in isolation. It is entirely possible to have high degrees of reliability but little or no validity to an assessment. Clearly low levels of reliability in any assessment are problematic but, in some contexts, increasing reliability may serve to decrease validity (Summerfeldt & Anthony, 2002). It is also important to recognise that reliability is highly context dependent. Assessed levels of reliability will only be applicable across similar conditions. Hence practitioners will always be faced with making clinical judgements of how applicable reliability data (and other psychometric properties) are in the specific context of an assessment.

Validity

Validity can be defined as the potential of the true score (T) to reflect what a test intends to assess (McKinnon et al., 2008). This is the most important and fundamental property of any psychological assessment and it is always a relative property, which needs to be considered in relation to the purpose of any assessment. As such, it is an overall evaluative judgement founded on theoretical rationale and empirical evidence.

As already noted above, validity can simply become a tautological exercise where the ability of an assessment to identify a meaningless construct is calculated. Therefore, for validity to be meaningful the core concept being assessed needs to be meaningful. This in turn depends on a mix of a sound theoretical base and inductive and deductive thinking. A number of practical methods have been suggested to improve validity in this respect. For example, in the context of diagnostic categories Spitzer (1983) suggested the Longitudinal observation by Experts using All available Data (LEAD) method, as a means of ensuring that core categories are meaningful. As a method this aims to increase the levels of intersubjective agreement across a pool of expert observers (Towl, 2005). The method has also been, less charitably, described as the 'best guess' approach (Summerfeldt & Anthony, 2002).

There are three[3] main approaches to estimating the validity of an assessment.

Criterion-related validity

This refers to the extent that one measure correlates with another measure such as a 'gold standard' assessment or subsequent behavioural sample. Criterion-related validity may be further subdivided into concurrent validity, which is concerned with temporally current relationships, and predictive validity, which is concerned with temporally distal relationships. An example here would be the ability of an assessment to predict subsequent violence.

Content validity

This refers to the ability to draw inferences from a test score to a larger item domain similar to those within the test instrument and is often based on expert ratings. An example here would be the extent to which an assessment of depression assessed the relevant dimensions of depression such as the effective aspects and behavioural aspects.

Construct validity

This refers to the extent that an instrument and the theoretical basis of the construct it seeks to measure are mutually verified by way of testable hypotheses. This form of validity generally refers to theoretical constructs that would not be observable directly. An example here might be the extent to which an assessment could measure the hypothetical construct of 'psychopathic personality disorder'.

Specificity, sensitivity and power

Specificity and sensitivity are both statistical concepts with important applications in relation to psychological assessment. Yet, curiously, they are often very poorly integrated into practice and are frequently the focus of confused thinking (Gigerenzer & Selten, 2001).

Specificity refers to the probability that a person without a particular attribute will be correctly identified as not having that attribute, or alternatively the proportion of negative cases correctly identified (true negatives). Sensitivity mirrors this in that it is the probability that a person with a particular attribute will be correctly identified as having it, or alternatively the proportion of positive cases correctly identified (true positives).

The term power here refers to the predictive accuracy of an assessment instrument or the overall proportion of people correctly classified. This is logically related to specificity and sensitivity and can be described in terms of positive or negative predictive power. Negative predictive power is the proportion of those not having a characteristic correctly identified as not having it. Positive predictive power is the proportion having a characteristic correctly identified as having it.

These relationships are often set out algebraically and this perhaps explains the poor application of these concepts to assessment, since there is considerable evidence that people (including those trained in statistics) find such thinking unnatural and difficult to apply. Much easier to understand are examples using natural frequencies, and one example of this in psychological assessment might be efforts to assess the risk of suicide in a forensic setting. Here it is relatively easy to devise a test with good specificity since this involves identifying true negatives. As suicide, even in forensic settings, is a low-frequency event, this can be achieved simply by a decision rule that states that all cases will not complete suicide. The sensitivity of such as assessment, though, would be low as it would miss all the true positives, those who complete suicide. It is therefore critical that as part of any assessment the specificity, sensitivity and power of any assessment is carefully considered (Crighton & Towl, 2008).

Base rates

The term base rate (also sometimes termed prior probabilities) refers to the relative frequency of occurrence of an event being studied within the population of interest; one example being the level of violence within a population of adolescent boys. Base rates are a key issue in assessing the psychometric properties of any assessment, since they will markedly impact on the validity of assessments. A key practice implication is that statistical prediction models will not be valid when applied to populations with markedly different base rates from the population for which they were developed.

Normality judgements

Ideas of 'normality' can be approached in a number of ways in relation to psychological tests. These include an approach in terms of mastery, where performance is assessed in relation to a test standard.

Alternatively, it may be approached in terms of statistical normality. This may involve evaluating performance in relation to a specific population or populations. It might alternatively involve evaluation in relation to tolerance limits (e.g. a 95 per cent limit). In turn this might refer to outer tolerance limits (where a score falls outside the limits) and inner tolerance limits (where a score falls within the limits).

Such tolerance limits may be parametric or nonparametric in nature. The former require that the true distribution of original scores be known or can be estimated from a large sample. Non-parametric tolerance limits are those that specify a score as falling at a particular rank in relation to a standardisation sample.

Deficit measurement

Deficit measurement presupposes an ideal or normal level of performance which can be used for comparison. For example, within forensic neuropsychological assessments it many involve attempts to compare current and pre-morbid functioning.

Such measurement can involve the use of both normative standards and individual comparison standards using direct and indirect assessment methods. Direct methods involve the use of pre- and postmorbid test scores, such as IQ test scores before and after a specific head injury. Indirect methods involve efforts to estimate this on the basis of estimates based on historical data. Unsurprisingly perhaps, direct measures are rarely available. Indirect measures, though, provide only relatively weak data, leading to efforts to develop tests with good hold properties to facilitate comparisons. An example here has been the efforts to identify tests that are less influenced by neurological damage to provide estimates of pre-morbid functioning (Lezak, 2008).

Single case analysis

Zubin (1967) outlined a number of central issues involved in the analysis of intra-individual observations. Firstly, he suggested that it was essential that individuals should not be prematurely classified into 'patient' groups. Secondly, he noted that individuals will each be characterised by a given level and degree of variability in performance on any given assessment. Thirdly, he stressed that any assessment result will be the joint product of internal and external causes, which might include such things as spontaneous improvements, impacts of therapeutic interventions and impacts of many other factors. These may also affect the level and scatter of results as well.

In seeking to reach an assessment and formulation for any one person it is important that these issues are addressed. There is often a tendency in practice to reify the results of psychological 'tests' and, regrettably, this is common in both psychologists and non-psychologists alike. In reality, tests in this sense simply contribute to the scientist-practitioner process concerned with theory development, hypothesis generation, testing and reformulation. Tests may contribute to this by providing data to inform hypothesis formulation or reformulation or both.

Clinical Judgements and Biases

Clinical judgement will generally involve making predictions, inferences or decisions. As outlined above, good judgements in psychological assessment will be informed and influenced by good qualitative and quantitative data. Such judgements in forensic practice will often have important consequences for whether a child becomes a ward of court or returns to their family, or whether a child goes on to be assaulted or killed. The primary purpose of a forensic psychological assessment is to maximise the validity of such judgements. This is likely to be achieved to the extent that they are based on strategies and measurements that are relevant to that specific client.

Such judgement processes are, though, open to a range of biases (Garb, 1998). These include biases due to such things as the values held by the practitioner, their 'intuitions', training and theoretical orientation. This suggests a clear need for practitioners to reflect on these factors as part of the process of ethical and evidence-based assessment. It also suggests a clear need to develop a willingness to reflect on practice and be willing to reformulate hypotheses and judgements in the light of this.

This cuts against idealised but unduly simplistic views of psychological assessment as a process of careful definition, observation, testing using well-validated methods and refining, rejecting and reforming hypotheses to reach a balanced judgement. Faced with complex datasets, practitioners use strategies that oversimplify this, often drawing on a handful of variables, or even worse, depending simply on diagnostic categories or single variables thought to have a causal role (Gigerenzer & Selten, 2001; Kahneman *et al.*, 1986). Concrete examples here include efforts to look for the single cause of suicide (e.g. depression) or the single cause of violence (e.g. psychopathic personality disorder).

Another approach to oversimplify complex data is to rely on a standardised assessment 'battery'. Such approaches may appear superficially attractive to practitioners as providing reliable, valid and cost-effective assessments, but this is almost entirely misplaced. Such standardisation may appear to be more cost-effective than more complex and individualised assessments, although such appeal is misplaced. Such mechanistic approaches will tend to increase, not reduce, biases in assessment and will tend to result in less accurate formulations and decreased efficacy and utility of interventions (Haynes & O'Brien, 2000).

The use of such simplification strategies is also not restricted to new or inexperienced practitioners. Indeed, there is some evidence to suggest that the use of these may explain the finding that, while confidence in judgements increases with experience, validity does not (Garb, 1998).

Overall, there is a need in conducting psychological assessments to treat it as an iterative scientific process. This involves the need to reflect critically on practice and use this to adapt and improve data gathering, formulation and judgement. There are a number of clear practical ways in which the validity of assessments can be increased and biases reduced. These would include:

i) the use of multiple methods and multiple informants to supply data;

ii) the use of broadly focused and systems-level multivariate assessment strategies;

iii) active consideration of base rates;

iv) the tailoring of assessments to the individual or individual situation;

v) the collection of data at multiple points over time (time series analysis);

vi) the use of direct and minimally inferential strategies in assessment;

vii) the use of clear and transparent procedures for decision making;

viii) the use of evidence-based assessment strategies;

ix) avoidance of quick judgements;

x) treating judgements as both provisional and modifiable in the light of evidence;

xi) avoiding the selection of data that supports pre-conceptions;

xii) examination of the costs and benefits of judgement errors;

xiii) actively seeking alternative viewpoints from colleagues, supervisors, and other professionals;

xiv) keeping data on the accuracy of clinical judgements;

xv) using transparent procedures to test hypotheses wherever possible (Garb, 1998; Haynes & O'Brien, 2000).

Conclusions

Assessments within forensic psychology share common logical and scientific underpinnings with those undertaken in other areas of applied psychology. They are, though, often thrown into particularly sharp relief in the context of forensic practice by the legal context of such work. Such contextual factors mean that assessments may have serious consequences and, as a result, are likely to be subject to rigorous and indeed 'forensic' scrutiny.

It is therefore critical that in conducting assessments and subsequently formulating treatment or intervention approaches, appropriate professional practices are followed. This will generally involve the application of scientific method to individual cases in an ethical and evidence-based manner. This presupposes the use of credible theoretical models as the basis for assessment, along with a clear understanding of the models' core assumptions and hypotheses. Assessments also need to actively address issues of diversity, response biases and the biases that any psychologist will bring to their practice and reflect on the process.

Psychological assessment benefits from being seen as a clearly iterative scientific process. This involves the need for earlier steps in an assessment to inform subsequent steps. This involves a process of critical reflection on practice throughout and the use of such reflection to adapt and improve the process: including data gathering, formulation, judgements and approaches. In seeking to do this it is essential that the work is ethically grounded and that the theory base of the work is clear. It is also important that multiple sources of data are drawn upon and that these are dealt with in a manner that credibly fits with the available evidence base.

Notes

1 The term clinical in literal translation means pertaining to the bedside. In practice, its usage is much wider than this and it is used here, and throughout, to signify structured and systematic approaches to assessment and interventions with an individual or groups of people designed to deliver positive change in relation to their psychosocial functioning. Clearly, clinical activity is a fundamental core competency across applied psychology. Likewise, the term forensic in literal translation is derived from forensic meaning before the forum. In practice, its usage is much wider than simply activities that take place within the context of the judicial tribunals which are the modern equivalent of the forum.

2 This is an area where forensic psychology faces significant difficulties and has, arguably, gone backwards from 2005 to date, with a less diverse workforce increasingly made up of young, white, upper-middle-class, privately educated and heterosexual women. It is difficult to think of a social group more different from that seen in forensic practice.

3 Another form of validity sometimes referred to is face validity. This falls outside the definition of validity given in this chapter since it refers to the extent that a test seems relevant to what it seeks to measure. Sometimes seen as a relatively trivial form of validity, it is nonetheless important since it may significantly impact on the acceptability of a test to those completing it.

Further Reading

Graham, J.R. & Naglieri, J.A. (Vol. Eds.) (2003). *Handbook of psychology. Assessment psychology.* Irving B. Weiner (Editor in Chief). New York: John Wiley & Sons.

Part of an encyclopaedic *Handbook of Psychology*, this volume covers assessment issues over the course of 25 edited chapters. The text is written to exacting academic standards and covers everything likely to be needed for training up to taught doctoral level. The text is generally written in a clear and lucid style, although some chapters involve technical treatments of the subject matter. A critically balanced and evidence-based approach is taken throughout.

Johnstone, L. & Dallos, R. (Eds.) (2006). *Formulation in psychology and psychotherapy.* London: Routledge.

This is a relatively short introductory text of nine chapters. Clearly written and edited, the text covers the interactive nature of assessment and intervention well. It is particularly strong at making clear the essential role of theoretical approaches in delivering ethical and effective psychological approaches. Commendably, the book also covers a broad range of theoretical approaches beyond those that are currently dominant.

Lezak, M.D. (2008). *Neuropsychological assessment.* New York: Oxford University Press.

This is an exceptionally detailed and thorough review of the key principles of psychological assessment from a neuropsychological perspective. Written to high academic standards, it has become something of a standard in the field and is essential reading for those engaged in forensic neuropsychology. The text includes a thorough compendium of relevant tests across a broad range of psychological functioning.

References

American Psychiatric Association (2000). *Diagnostic and statistical manual of mental disorders: DSM-IV-TR.* Washington, DC: Author.

Beck, A.T. (2005). The current state of cognitive therapy: A 40-year retrospective. Aaron T. Beck. *Archives of General Psychiatry, 62,* 953–959.

Beck, A.T., Ward, C.H., Mendelson, M.D. *et al.* (1962). Reliability of psychiatric diagnoses: 2. A study of consistency of clinical judgments and ratings. *American Journal of Psychiatry, 119,* 351–357.

Bruch, M. (1998). The development of case formulation approaches. In M. Bruch & F.W. Bond (Eds.) *Beyond diagnosis: Case formulation approaches in CBT.* Chichester: John Wiley.

Clare, A. (2003). *Psychiatry in dissent.* London: Routledge.

Crighton, D.A. & Towl, G.J. (2008). *Psychology in prisons* (2nd edn). Oxford: BPS Blackwell.

Daffern, M., Howells, K. & Ogloff, J. (2007). What's the point? Towards a methodology for assessing the function of psychiatric inpatient aggression. *Behaviour Research and Therapy, 45*(1), 101–111.

Dallos, R. & Steadman, J. (2006). Systemic formulation. In L. Johnstone & R. Dallos (Eds.) *Formulation in psychology and psychotherapy.* London: Routledge.

Department of Health (2003). *Tackling health inequalities: A programme for action.* London: Author.

Embretson, S.E. & Reise, S (2000). *Item response theory for psychologists.* Mahwah, NJ: Lawrence Erlbaum.

Erikson, E.H. (1966). Eight ages of man. *International Journal of Psychiatry, 2,* 291–300.

Erikson, E.H. (1980). *Identity and the life cycle.* London: W.W. Norton.

Ford, D.H. & Lerner, R.M. (1992). *Developmental systems theory: An integrative approach.* Newbury Park, CA: Sage.

Freud, S. (1999). *The interpretation of dreams: A new translation by Joyce Crick.* Oxford: Oxford University Press.

Garb, H.N. (1998). *Studying the clinician: Judgment research and psychological assessment.* Washington, DC: American Psychological Association.

Gigerenzer, G. & Selten, R. (2001). Rethinking rationality. In G. Gigerenzer & R. Selten (Eds.) *Bounded rationality: The adaptive toolbox.* Cambridge, MA: MIT Press.

Haynes, S.N. (1998). The principles and practice of behavioral assessment with adults. In A.P. Goldstein & M. Hersen (Eds.) *Comprehensive clinical psychology: Assessment volume 4.* Amsterdam: Elsevier Science.

Haynes, S.N. & O'Brien, W.H. (2000). *Principles and practice of behavioral assessment.* New York: Kluwer Academic/ Plenum Publishers.

Ingram, B.L. (2006). *Clinical case formulation matching the integrative treatment plan to the client.* Hoboken, NJ: John Wiley & Sons.

Johnstone, L. & Dallos, R. (2006). Introduction to formulation. In L. Johnstone & R. Dallos (Eds.) *Formulation in psychology and psychotherapy.* London: Routledge.

Kahneman, D., Slovic, P. & Tversky, A. (1986). *Judgement under uncertainty.* New York: Cambridge University Press.

Kelly, G.A. (1955). *The psychology of personal constructs* (vols. 1 and 2). New York: Norton.

Lane, D. & Corrie, S. (2006). *The modern scientist-practitioner.* London: Routledge.

Leiper, R. (2006). Psychodynamic formulation: A prince betrayed and disinherited. In L. Johnstone & R. Dallos (Eds.) *Formulation in psychology and psychotherapy.* London: Routledge.

Lerner, R.M., Fisher, C.B. & Weinberg, R.A. (2000). Toward a science for and of the people: Promoting civil society through the application of developmental science. *Child Development, 71*(1), 11–20.

Lezak, M.D. (2008). *Neuropsychological assessment.* New York: Oxford University Press.

Macrae, C.N. & Bodenhausen, G.V. (2000). Social cognition: Thinking categorically about others. *Annual Review of Psychology, 51,* 93–120.

McKinnon, A.C., Nixon, R.D.V. & Brewer, N. (2008). The influence of data-driven processing on perceptions of memory quality and intrusive symptoms in children following traumatic events. *Behaviour Research and Therapy, 46*(6), 766–775.

Miller, J. & McClelland, L. (2006). Social inequalities formulation – Mad, bad and dangerous to know. In L. Johnstone & R. Dallos (Eds.) *Formulation in psychology and psychotherapy.* London: Routledge.

Owens, R.G. & Ashcroft, J.B. (1982). Functional analysis in applied psychology. *The British Journal of Clinical Psychology, 21*(3), 181–189.

Persons, J.B. & Fresco, D.M. (1998). Assessment of depression. In A.S. Bellack & M. Hersen (Eds.) *Behavioral assessment – A practical handbook* (4th edn). Boston, MA: Allyn & Bacon.

Rose, N. (1989). *Governing the soul: The shaping of the private self.* London: Routledge.

Roth, A., Fonagy, P., Parry, G. *et al.* (Eds.) (2006). *What works for whom? A critical review of psychotherapy research.* New York: Guilford Press.

Rutter, M.J. & Taylor, E.A. (2002). *Child and adolescent psychiatry* (4th edn). Oxford: Blackwell.

Ryle, A. (1997). *Cognitive analytic therapy for borderline personality disorder. The model and the method.* Chichester: John Wiley.

Shapiro, M.B. (1985). A reassessment of clinical psychology as an applied science. *British Journal of Clinical Psychology, 24,* 1–11.

Smail, D. (2004). Therapeutic psychology and the ideology of privilege. *Clinical Psychology, 38,* 9–14.

Social Exclusion Unit (2002). *Reducing re-offending by ex-prisoners.* London: The Stationery Office.

Spitzer, R.L. (1983). Psychiatric diagnosis: Are clinicians still necessary? *Comprehensive Psychiatry, 24,* 399–411.

Summerfeldt, L.J. & Anthony, M.M. (2002). Structured and semi-structured diagnostic interviews. In M.M. Anthony & D.H. Barlow (Eds.) *Handbook of assessment and treatment planning for psychological disorders.* New York: Guilford Press.

Towl, G. (2005). Risk assessment. *Evidence-Based Mental Health, 8,* 91–93.

Towl, G.J. (Ed.) (2006). *Psychological research in prisons.* Oxford: BPS Blackwell.

Towl, G.J. & Crighton, D.A. (1996). *The handbook of psychology for forensic practitioners.* London: Routledge.

Wasserman, J.D. & Bracken, B.A. (2003). Psychometric characteristics of assessment procedures. In J.R. Graham & J.A. Naglieri (Vol. Eds.) *Handbook of psychology: Assessment psychology.* Irving B. Weiner (Editor in Chief). New York: John Wiley & Sons.

Widiger, T.A. & Clark, L.A. (2000). Toward DSM-V and the classification of psychopathology. *Psychological Bulletin, 126,* 946–963.

World Health Organization (1990). *International statistical classification of diseases and related health problems: ICD-10.* Geneva: Author.

Zubin, J. (1967). Classification of the behavior disorders. *Annual Review of Psychology, 18,* 373–406.

17

Risk Assessment

David A. Crighton

Risk assessment involves systematic efforts to estimate and evaluate adverse outcomes. Seeking to achieve this involves making explicit the process involved and any underlying assumptions. While the logic behind risk assessment is straightforward, it is an area that is often technically complex for a number of reasons. These include the difficulty of defining adverse outcomes and the difficulty of measurement across the process.

Notions of risk are very broad and cover many areas of the natural, biological and social sciences. Risk assessment involves areas as diverse as economics, public health, engineering and meteorology. In some respects this has been a major strength of the field, in that it has led to a great deal of diversity in the evidence base. It has also led to the intellectual strength of the field being greatly enhanced, leading in turn to greater advances than would have been achieved otherwise. Yet such breadth has also raised problems. Different fields have tended to use differing language, models and methods to address risk. Not unrelated to this perhaps, the interchange between fields has often been limited. It is certainly the case that in risk assessment, the wheel has been reinvented many times. Within forensic psychology, learning from other fields has, until recently at least, been slow and patchy.

Attempts to describe and quantify risk and, in turn, present such information intelligibly present ongoing challenges. There has traditionally been a strong emphasis on making empirical estimates of risk and this has led to efforts to establish 'metrics'. Within social sciences such as economics these have, unsurprisingly, involved money or resource values. Such measures have, though, come to be increasingly used in areas such as health, where health outcomes have increasingly been assessed in economic terms: for example, in terms of the financial costs of such things as Quality Adjusted Life Years (QUALYs) (Drummond *et al.*, 2005). Such efforts raise a number of scientific and ethical issues. It is not clear that placing monetary values on such outcomes is appropriate. The transparency of such methods can be questioned and they can simply be seen as a means of justifying rationing, or preferences for one social group over another, clothed within apparently complex mathematics. For some risks it is also unclear whether numerical values can ever be appropriate. In areas such as global warming and climate change, what monetary or numeric value should be put on the potential devastation of the entire planet? Within forensic psychology, can the perpetration of a murder be quantified in terms of a financial value placed on the number of years of life a victim loses?

Whatever the difficulties, though, risk assessment is and will remain a fundamental part of forensic psychology. Unlike many other fora, legal systems require that decisions are made. Unlike other areas of life, it is not possible to argue that it is too difficult to make such decisions. Many of the questions asked of forensic psychologists will therefore implicitly and explicitly involve the likelihood of adverse outcomes, in the light of incomplete information. They involve trying to quantify the probability of harms and the effects of these on individuals or populations based on the best information available.

Definitional Issues

Definitional issues in risk assessment apply similarly across disciplines. Efforts at risk assessment in forensic psychology, though, have generally suffered from the inconsistent use of often poorly defined terms. Risk assessment at its simplest involves efforts to estimate both the probability of an event and its consequences (Towl & Crighton, 1996). Such broad definitions still provide a good starting point for thinking about risk assessment. Yet there is a need to go beyond this, with more tightly defined terms.

One customary term used in forensic psychology and psychiatry has been the notion of 'dangerousness' and this draws largely from the term's day-to-day use and its somewhat different use in legal practice. Legal notions of dangerousness might be seen as involving two dimensions, adverse outcomes and how undesirable those may be. The term is, though, also sometimes loosely used to address concern with issues of the probability of the outcomes and so might be seen as an overlapping yet distinct concept from risk. In the context of risk assessment the concept is generally unhelpful, since it serves to conflate issues of probabilities and outcomes in an unsystematic manner. Thus it is possible to talk about the danger of 'economic disaster' without knowing the extent to which the danger is concerned with the probability of the events, or the severely negative consequences. Similarly, it is possible for an offender to be labelled 'dangerous' on the basis of a high probability of committing many offences, or because of the potential to perpetrate a small number of very serious offences or, most commonly, an unknown mix of the two.

As in other areas where scientific method has been usefully applied, risk assessment has progressed through the use of more precisely defined language and systematic analysis of available information. In seeking to do this an initial distinction has been made between hazards and risks. A hazard refers to anything that might result in harm but does not address issues of the probability of adverse outcomes. Risk, by contrast, is concerned with the probability of adverse outcomes associated with exposure to one or more hazards. Somewhat problematically, the notion of risk has come to be used interchangeably with the term hazard in day-to-day usage. It is therefore common to talk about people being exposed to daily risks, when, in the context of risk assessment, it would be more accurate to talk about being exposed to daily hazards (Reason, 1990).

Throughout this chapter the convention used is that the term harm is used to refer to any adverse outcome, the term hazard to refer to anything which has the potential to result in harm, and the term risk specifically to refer to estimates of the likelihood of harm resulting from exposure to hazards.

Key Principles in Risk Assessment

A major area of contention within risk assessment has been the question of how harm is determined. It has been convincingly argued that the desirability or otherwise of an outcome is not always self-evident. Harms are in reality social constructs. They will range from social constructs that enjoy almost total agreement, such as the notion that children should be protected from sexual activity with adults, to those where agreement is much less universal, for example, in the case of terrorist activity.[1] Notions of harm can thus be seen as a product of social negotiation (Douglas, 1986). When such ideas were first put forward they were seen as both radical and contentious and subject to extensive but ultimately unconvincing criticism. Such notions, though, have increasingly come to be seen as mainstream (Towl, 2005).

Another key distinction in the field is between risk assessment and risk perception. The former refers to the technical process of formally estimating risk. Notions of risk perception, by contrast, refer to the ways that individuals might assess risk without use of formal processes.

Risk assessment itself can in turn be further subdivided into risk estimation and risk evaluation. Risk estimation refers to the identification of the possible outcomes of an adverse event, combined with the probability of the event and the specified outcomes. Risk evaluation, by contrast, refers to the process of identifying the significance or 'value' of the hazard in the context of a risk estimate. Put very simply, it relates to the process of trading potential benefits and costs.

Approaches to risk assessment

There have been three main approaches to assessing risk that cut across subject boundaries:

- the expression of all possible outcomes as probabilities;
- the expression of particular future outcomes as probabilities on the basis of samples of past events;

• the estimation of the likelihood of future events based on the widest range of experience, knowledge and care that can reasonably be applied to the context in question.

The first of these is typified by statistical studies of groups of events such as the results of the roll of dice, where the *a priori* probability of outcomes is known. The second example would include such things as actuarial estimates based on populations. Here the *a priori* probabilities are generally not known but are estimated on the basis of large samples, and this would include areas such as insurance and health outcomes. Here the risk ascribed to an individual case is based on historical data drawn from an ostensibly similar population. The third approach is the one that typifies most of the risk assessments undertaken within forensic psychology. Here, in order to produce the most accurate result possible, a mix of available methods is used to produce what might reasonably be seen as a best estimate.

Risk assessment can be seen to involve a number of central methodological principles. These would include:

i) efforts to precisely specify the hazards being assessed;
ii) efforts to precisely specify possible outcomes;
iii) efforts to assess the likelihood of adverse outcomes;
iv) efforts to assess the severity of specific outcomes.

From this it can be seen that even simple examples of risk assessment will involve complex levels of analysis (Breakwell, 2007). This perhaps explains the oft-reported (and misreported) general finding that people are poor at making unaided assessments of risk (Gigerenzer & Selten, 2001; Kahneman *et al.*, 1982).

This is perhaps not entirely surprising and a number of factors make unaided accurate risk assessment a difficult task. The first obvious factor is that such assessment will involve the use of imperfect information. Hazards may also be correlated, they may interact and they may indeed do so synergistically. Additionally, professional and scientific opinion may be genuinely divided and the hazards may be poorly understood. This implies that even relatively simple areas of risk assessment will involve complex analysis. A frequently used example here has been the failure of aerospace components. Such hazards are relatively well understood. In addition, the characteristics of engine components can be precisely defined and subject to controlled testing and analysis. Yet even here, within well understood and relatively constrained systems, it is evident that components can interact with other components – often in unanticipated ways. In turn, failures may result from such interactions, as well as resulting from the component itself (Reason, 1990; Towl & Crighton, 1997).

The situation in relation to risk assessment involving people is also complex. The ability to measure and specify in this context is, though, far weaker than in the example above. It is also evident that human behaviour is part of a relatively unconstrained system. Behaviour is largely interactional in nature and the nature of these interactions, and the social and cultural context of behaviour, is not well understood. In addition, the role of random events, an issue in any area of risk assessment, is likely to present escalating challenges over time (Towl, 2005).

In common with other efforts at risk assessment, the aim within forensic psychology has been to use scientific method to improve the accuracy and utility of the risk assessments produced. This can be seen as involving a number of definable and logical steps and it is important that these are well understood. In doing this a variety of structures have been suggested to inform the process of risk assessment. Figure 17.1 outlines the Cambridge Model for Risk Assessment (CAMRA), a public domain framework for doing this.

The methodology involved in completing the stages outlined within the CAMRA framework is in many respects similar to other forms of psychological assessment. It involves a number of elements that are fundamental to efforts to apply scientific method to individual cases. These include:

• experimentation, including the use of diagnostic testing, to generate data and/or the use of data from previous experimentation;
• the use of simulation based on prior analysis of systems;
• modelling to replicate larger and more complex systems;
• the analysis of databases that reflect patterns of previous related incidents;
• the use of expert opinion data (itself a form of database).

The CAMRA framework was developed and disseminated as an aid to forensic psychologists trying to logically sequence their approach to risk assessment and using

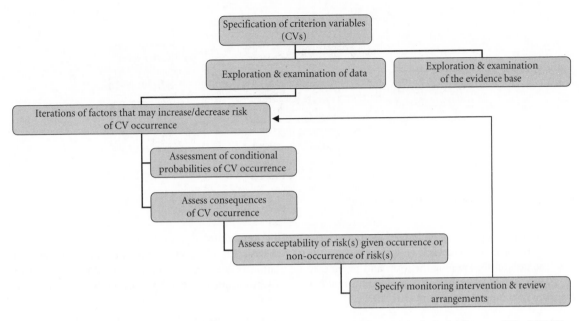

Figure 17.1 Cambridge Model for Risk Assessment (CAMRA). *Source*: Public domain from Crighton and Towl (2008).

specific methods, such as experimentation, diagnostic testing, simulation, modelling and drawing on expert databases where appropriate. The aims of such analyses are to increase the accuracy of the probability associated with given outcomes and produce more specific and accurate descriptions of likely outcomes (Towl, 2005).

Limitations of Risk Assessment

The key principles outlined above suggest a number of limitations inherent in efforts to assess risk. The most striking of these is that the hazards being assessed will generally interact in ways that are, at best, poorly understood. In addition, any evaluation will only be as good as the data, experiments and simulations used (Ansell, 1992). This presents significant difficulty across the field of risk assessment where, frequently, these sources of information will be very limited.

There are two broad systemic approaches to addressing this: 'top down' and 'bottom up'. Top-down approaches involve efforts to look holistically at risk, while bottom-up methods involve efforts to look at the basic components of a given risk. The latter method is characterised by decision tree methods. Such methods have been used extensively in engineering (as fault trees)

and areas such as medicine and surgery (decision trees). Curiously, they have been little used in forensic psychology in the past, but have enjoyed significant growth and development in recent years in North America (Crighton & Towl, 2008; Monahan *et al.*, 2001, 2005).

Such approaches serve to provide a simplified model of the hazard being assessed based on a number of logical premises. The first of these is the precise definition of elements within the tree. This is followed by the logical specification of the relationship between these elements. The third stage is the qualitative evaluation of their properties and the final stage may involve efforts to quantify these (see Figure 17.2).

The use of a systematic framework and methods such as decision trees is simply a means of ensuring more systematic approaches to risk assessment. They are not, of themselves, a panacea. Indeed the use of decision trees presents a number of challenges. These have been summarised as:

i)   the question of how to treat multiple failures that arise from a common cause;

ii) the problem of allowing for the way that uncertainty propagates in the primary inputs;

iii) the difficulty of ensuring a sufficiently comprehensive definition of the system;

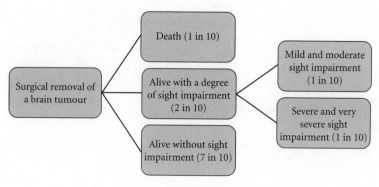

Figure 17.2   Simplified hypothetical decision tree.

iv)   the issue of specifying bounds to the fault tree so the problem is tractable;

v)   the task of determining the form and parameters of probability distribution to incorporate into failure-data inputs. (Crossland *et al.*, 1992)

The use of event trees to assist with this initial stage of risk assessment (stage 3 in CAMRA) has a clear advantage in that it requires the assessor at least to think in a systematic and logical manner about the hazard being assessed and its functional and logical relationships with other recognised hazards. Many hazards, though, will not be amenable to this method of simplification. Complex hazards will be difficult to specify precisely in the manner required, as will complex outcomes. In such cases the method is unlikely to produce simple or usable mathematical models when applied to complex systems. This means that it will generally be the case that risk assessment in forensic psychology will be based on a translation of such complex systems into discrete components. Efforts will also need to be made to simplify the system by, for example, discarding variables considered to be of marginal relevance. Such efforts will inevitably affect the sensitivity of any assessment and the basis for such decisions needs to be carefully considered.

It has been noted that:

> … This emphasises that building an understanding of risk in complex systems is an iterative business. (Breakwell, 2007)

Yet within forensic psychology this key point has been poorly integrated into practice, as has the observation that risk assessments should also be accompanied by a statement of the level of uncertainty associated with estimates (Towl, 2005). This involves an expression of the limitations of available data, the model used and analysis. These are often poorly understood so quantification may often be poor, but this doesn't excuse the assessor from a duty of openness in this respect.

Acceptable risk and rare catastrophic failures

The issue of what is an acceptable risk is contentious and not one that can be exclusively addressed in empirical terms, involving as it does moral and ethical judgements. Efforts to deal with this have varied across disciplines and contexts. In public health they may be based on standards such as protecting those most at risk, or alternatively may be framed in terms of the maximum number of 'acceptable' deaths. Here measures of lifetime risk have been widely used and it has become common to refer to this in terms of hazards which increase deaths or injury per million people. There is, of course, no logical reason why a figure of a million should be chosen or, indeed, why a risk of one in a million is deemed acceptable. In reality, such benchmarks seem to be chosen largely for convenience and in this case because it represents a very low level of perceived risk.

In addition, the question of the cut-off point for a decision arises. This may differ between groups within a population. For example, the risk from a given hazard may be very low for 99.9 per cent of the population but very high for the minority group. Response to this in turn is likely to differ on the basis of the characteristics of the sub-population concerned. If the 0.1 per cent refers to premature infants, the response is likely to be quite different from that for criminal amphetamine abusers. Issues of choice also enter into the equation and in public health the threshold for risks associated with chosen activities (e.g. liver damage following exposure to alcohol) is likely to differ from that for risks associated with hazards in the absence of choice (e.g. exposure to radioactive substances).

A major concern with much of current practice in risk assessment concerns the question of rare events. It has long been recognised that these present a serious difficulty for statistical measures of risk (Meehl, 1959). So while statistical methods can deal well with regularly occurring events, they work poorly when faced with rare events (Crighton & Towl, 2008; Gigerenzer & Selten, 2001). This issue has perhaps been most carefully examined in relation to risk within economic systems, where the statistical methods employed to assess and manage risks have seen the greatest development – and indeed, where until 2007 the greatest confidence had been expressed in such approaches (Fischer & Scholes, 1973). In fact, such methods and models showed themselves to be highly vulnerable to rare events, as could be seen from the banking crisis and collapse of other financial institutions (Peston, 2007; Taleb, 2007).

A number of cogent criticisms have been made of statistical models of risk. Perhaps the most persuasive of these is the notion that there is a tendency to overestimate the value of rational explanations of past data, and underestimate the prevalence of random factors within the data (Taleb, 2007). This analysis suggests that the knowledge of the world available to us is far more incomplete than we pretend and that, because of this, it is inappropriate to naively use the past to predict the future. Taleb (2007) stresses the role of uncertainty and randomness in science and particularly the role of high-impact low frequency events, which he calls 'black swans', in determining the course of history.

He argues that these 'black swans' are ignored because of our desire to see greater structure and predictability in the world than is there. He describes this as *the Platonic fallacy*, noting that it results in a tendency to distort the world in three key ways:

i)   the *narrative fallacy*, which refers to our creating *post hoc* stories that suggest events have an identifiable cause;
ii) the *ludic fallacy*, which refers to the assumption that the randomness found in life resembles the randomness found in statistical paradigms such as card and dice games, which underpin much of modern probability theory;
iii) the *statistical regress fallacy*, which refers to the belief that the structure of probability can be delivered from a set of data.

He also suggests that people are subject to what he terms the *triplet of opacity*. This consists of:

i)   an illusion of understanding of current events;
ii) a retrospective distortion of historical events;
iii) an overestimation of factual information, combined with an overvaluing of the intellectual elite.

Taleb (2007) has gone further in his critique, suggesting that a large degree of pseudo-science has been involved in risk assessment. In common with psychologists such as Gigerenzer and Selten (2001), he notes that human beings are not designed to understand such things as abstract statistics and that we need context to deal with such information effectively. This is far from an abstract academic critique. Within economics, globalisation created a closely interlinked and fragile system, described as reducing volatility and improving stability. The risks within this system were managed using complex mathematical and statistical models which were used to assure that the analysis was accurate, despite 'common sense' appearances to the contrary. In reality, though, such conditions contributed to the creation of circumstances in which rare events (black swans) could have devastating consequences (Derman & Taleb, 2005; Taleb, 2007).

Such suggestions that statisticians and economists have often acted as pseudo-scientists in addressing risks within financial systems and that they have hidden this incompetence behind complicated equations have, unsurprisingly, attracted a strident response. Yet the analysis has also received support from statisticians who have noted that efforts to refute Taleb's central point, that rare events with severe consequences are poorly dealt with by conventional statistics, had been unconvincing (Freedman, 2008).

There is a clear relevance here for forensic psychology where similar, though much less sophisticated, statistical models of risk have been developed and extensively marketed. The extent to which these methods are used to assess behaviour that is not understood by those who develop and use them is rarely acknowledged. Many are also surrounded by similar intellectual trappings of infallibility (e.g. Mills *et al.*, 2005). Yet just like the more mathematically sophisticated econometric methods which failed so seriously, the weaknesses and potential for catastrophic failure in such methods are evident. Such methods suggest a degree of understanding of the world that we simply do not possess and they are likely to fail to deal with rare events, with potentially catastrophic consequences. Yet, perversely, this often appears to be a key reason for their use (Crighton & Towl, 2008; Monahan *et al.*, 2001; Towl, 2005).

Communicating Risk Assessments Effectively

The ways in which risk is communicated has also often been poorly addressed. It is in fact a very difficult thing to do well, but is crucial if assessments are to influence decisions appropriately. The difficulty can be seen as arising from a number of sources, and these include the fact that it often involves trying to convey information to others that they find incomprehensible, unbelievable, irrelevant and unacceptable (Gigerenzer & Selten, 2001).

The approach of scientists to this difficulty is summarised by Fischoff (1998) as quoted in Breakwell (2007):

All we have to do is get the numbers right.
All we have to do is tell them the numbers.
All we have to do is explain what we mean by the numbers.
All we have to do is show them that they've accepted similar risks in the past.
All we have to do is show them that it is a good deal for them.
All we have to do is treat them nice.
All we have to do is make them partners.
All of the above.

There is in fact a substantial evidence base in relation to effective communication, yet this has generally been poorly used in informing risk communications. In relation to medical risks it has been suggested that there are three central factors:

i)   the certainty of risk;
ii) the level of risk;
iii) the effects of the risk on individuals or populations (Calman, 2002).

There has been a widespread and longstanding view amongst experts that the public would generally be unable to understand risk assessment and particularly issues of probability. Indeed, there is an extensive evidence base which shows how poor people are at understanding and interpreting probability-based data (Kahneman *et al.*, 1982). Interestingly, this also extends to scientific experts who often deal poorly with data presented in terms of Baysian probabilities. In contrast, people are much better at dealing with the kinds of uncertainty and probabilities involved in risk when data are presented in terms of natural frequencies (Gigerenzer & Hoffrage, 1995).

Unsurprisingly perhaps, communications about risk generally appear to be more positively viewed where they come from trusted or high-status sources. It has also been noted that trust is something which is very difficult to create but very easy to undermine (Slovic, 1993). Levels of trust, though, will certainly be influenced by the ways in which the recipients of messages about risk perceive and interpret subsequent events.

Decision Making about Risks

There is a substantial body of research which suggests that 'empirical' approaches to risk assessment perform better than unsupported 'clinical' assessments (Meehl, 1954, 1967, 1973; Swets, 1988; Swets, Dawes & Monahan, 2000). From research looking at purely empirical approaches in forensic psychology it is clear that the combination of a relatively small number of variables can yield relatively good predictors of future outcomes on a group basis (Klassen & O'Connor, 1988). This has been done by a number of researchers to develop what have come to be rather curiously termed risk assessment 'tools' and parallels work in other fields such as economics and public health. There are numerous examples of this approach to risk assessment in psychology with the development and marketing of such methods. The Violence Risk Assessment Guide (VRAG) (MHCP Research, 2008) is based on 12 predictor variables, shown to correlate with violent behaviour. The Historical and Clinical Risk 20 (HCR-20) (Webster *et al.*, 2003), using a similar approach, is based on 20 risk factors. Both these assessments and many others yield results that are better than those achieved by chance. For example, when data from the VRAG were dichotomised into high- and low-risk groups it was found that 55 per cent of the high-risk group had a record of going on to behave violently compared to 18 per cent of the low-risk group (Harris *et al.*, 1993). A 2-year follow-up study using the HCR-20 looked at patients who scored above the median, who were significantly more likely to have a record of being violent than patients scoring below the median (Douglas *et al.*, 1999). Such findings compare favourably with studies of unstructured 'clinical' assessments, which suggest poorer levels of performance. In one study of defendants in court, 39 per cent of those rated as 'medium' or 'high' risk went on to commit a violent act within 2 years, compared to 26 per cent of those rated as low risk (Sepejak *et al.*, 1983). In another study with acute psychiatric patients 53 per cent of those who aroused professional concern committed a violent act within six months compared to 36 per cent amongst those who did not elicit concern (Lidz *et al.*, 1993). These results, though, hide additional complexity in that data collected on 'clinical' assessments pooled the performance of assessors. It has been demonstrated that in reality some assessors perform relatively well, some do little better than chance and some make predictions that are negatively correlated with outcomes. Such complexity is often neglected when, at times, glib assertions are made about the fallibility of expert judgement compared to statistical methods (Arkes *et al.*, 2000).

The current use of actuarial approaches in forensic psychology raises a number of significant issues. Many of the assessments used draw on a restricted range of risk factors. This is not wholly surprising given the lack of understanding of many of the areas of concern. Even so, this limits the ability to identify relevant risk and protective factors. Such measures are also often focused on easily measured variables, in order that they can be reliably used by a wide range of potential users. In turn, though, such a focus is likely to limit accuracy. Another feature has been the use of weak criterion measures. In the context of forensic practice re-arrest rates have frequently been used, despite it being well known that detection and conviction rates for many offences are very low. In addition, actuarial approaches have often involved narrow sampling, raising questions over the extent to which findings may be generalised. These aspects are important, but perhaps more important than these is the lack of knowledge about base rates. Few actuarial risk assessment 'tools' have included the consideration of this fundamental aspect of risk assessment and the likely accruing effects.

The importance of base rate information is vividly illustrated in findings from the MacArthur risk assessment study in North America (Monahan *et al.*, 2001). This study looked in detail at base rates and also the nature and context of the violence identified. Based on officially recorded incidents, the base rate for violent acts was reported to be 4.5 per cent of the patients studied: when multiple sources of information were used this increased to 27.5 per cent (Monahan *et al.*, 2001).[2] Clearly the implications of these two figures are very different, yet many currently fashionable approaches to risk assessment have been using assumptions based on official rates of recorded violence or, less accurately still, official reconviction records. Such an approach seems at best limited.

The development of risk assessment 'tools' in forensic psychology has generally involved the use of groups of potential risk factors selected on the basis of likely association with the criterion variable. These variables have been subject to statistical analysis to identify the combination of factors most closely correlated with criteria, such as receiving a reconviction within two years. This standard main effect approach has a number of significant and often unacknowledged weaknesses. These include the fact that the selection of risk factors underpinning such methods is largely atheoretical. What is produced from this are a series of inter-correlations with limited explanatory power, with many potential risk factors being discarded from the analysis. The approach also requires that every individual be assessed on every risk factor included in the 'tool', even though, for a number, some risk factors will not be relevant, while for others risk factors not included may be critical. This is something rather counterintuitive for many forensic psychologists. Advocates of such approaches are unmoved by such objections, suggesting that such main-effects statistical approaches are the single best method for predicting risk and arguing that their use should replace clinical judgement. Such an analysis appears unduly confident about the qualities of such approaches.

Alternative approaches used extensively in biological sciences and engineering, such as classification and iterative classification tree methods, have existed for many years but have received relatively little attention with forensic psychology until recently. This is perhaps linked to the fact that such models are less easily marketed in the form of standardised assessments, suitable for administration by less professionally skilled staff. Such approaches seek to classify individuals into subgroups as the risk assessment progresses and the next area addressed is contingent on the assessment of the previous area (Crighton, 2006). Such methods are widely used in medicine and surgery where, for example, a clinician would be likely to identify high blood pressure and then conduct further assessments related to this, but would generally not conduct these same assessments for someone with normal or low blood pressure. This has the logical appeal that it is more in line with what experienced and competent forensic psychologists naturally seek to do.

There has been recent development of interest in such classification tree approaches in psychology (Applebaum *et al.*, 2000; Crighton, 2005). Analyses of simple classification tree approaches have been conducted in relation to a large sample of civil psychiatric patients discharged into the community but have yielded disappointing results, with performance slightly poorer than for a logistic regression approach. In seeking to improve on this level of performance, the curious but common approach of categorising risk using a single cut-off point (violent versus non-violent) was looked at afresh (Monahan *et al*, 2001). An approach using two cut-off points was tested. This created three groups, one where the level of risk appears indistinguishable from the population base rate on the basis of the available risk factors, one where it is lower and one higher (Applebaum *et al.*, 2000; Monahan *et al.*, 2001). It was hypothesised that by focusing on the two extreme ends of the distribution the accuracy of estimates of risk could be improved.

Drawing on the base rates for violence in their sample, high risk was defined operationally as twice the base rate (>37 per cent over 12 months) and low risk as half the base rate (<9 per cent over 12 months).[3] They found that, using these cut points, 42.9 per cent of the sample were unclassified using the logistic regression main effects approach and 49.2 per cent using the simple classification tree approach (Monahan *et al.*, 2001). In practice, this highlights a major weakness of both models. Even with the addition of a low-risk cut-off point, only slightly over half of those assessed were classified as high or low risk. The remainder were not differentiated from the base rate for violence group, providing little in the way of added utility from the risk assessment.

The researchers went on to look at the use of repeated iterations within a classification tree approach (an iterative classification tree [ICT] model) in an effort to improve on this. This involved conducting repeated iterative analyses on the remaining 'unclassified' group. A second iteration allocated 119 of these individuals to either high- or low-risk groups; a third iteration 63 and a fourth iteration 60, at which point the researchers stopped. Using this form of recursive partitioning the researchers found that 77 per cent of the sample could be allocated to high- or low-risk groups, representing a significant improvement. As a result of the analysis they had identified six low-risk subgroups (49 per cent), four high-risk subgroups (27 per cent) and two average-risk subgroups (23 per cent).[4] The approach was found to be comparable in terms of accuracy to the non-recursive model but was able to classify a significantly greater proportion of cases into high- and low-risk groups.[5] The

authors went on to test the model statistically using a technique called 'bootstrapping', which involves mathematically increasing the sample size by randomly duplicating cases. This larger hypothetical 'sample' is then randomly sampled and tested to see how effectively repeated samples fit the new model (Mooney & Duval, 1993). Although open to criticism, the results from this suggested that the model continued to work effectively.

Of the risk factors included in this analysis, the single factor which performed best was the PCL-SV (Odds Ratio (OR) 2.40), followed by grandiose delusions (OR 2.28), father's drug use (OR 2.18) and drug abuse diagnosis (OR 1.58). The researchers noted that a number of the risk factors included in the initial analysis raised both clinical and economic issues. The use of psychological assessments such as the PCL is labour intensive and expensive, raising the question of whether they have additional utility and, if so, whether this is cost-effective. This was tested by re-conducting the analysis, removing the 28 risk factors that would be most difficult to obtain in a civil mental health context. This included detailed psychological assessments such as the PCL and also details of criminal history. The model was then tested using the remaining 106 risk factors that were relatively easy to obtain. This analysis achieved three iterations allocating 72.6 per cent of individuals to high- or low-risk subgroups and yielding four low-risk subgroups (51 per cent), three high-risk subgroups (22 per cent) and four average-risk subgroups (27 per cent), and performed at a similar level in terms of accuracy (Monahan *et al.*, 2001).

This analysis suggested that the performance of the ICT model was comparable in terms of efficacy using 106 risk factors or using 134.[6] The use of expensive assessments, such as the PCL, appeared to have at best marginal utility. Equally good accuracy in risk assessment was achieved using relatively straightforwardly obtained clinical risk factors, when analysed appropriately (Applebaum *et al.*, 2000; Monahan *et al.*, 2001, 2005; Towl, 2005; Towl & Crighton, 1997).

While this model achieved comparable levels of accuracy, it did result in a degree of differential allocation, with 57 per cent of cases being similarly allocated under both approaches (*r* 0.52, *p* < 0.001). This is, of course, a general characteristic of any actuarial risk assessments, where approaches will generally be imperfectly correlated with each other. In order to address this issue an analysis was conducted repeating the ICT approach and combining two models. Interestingly, of those classified as low risk in both models, 3 per cent were violent during the 20-week follow-up period; of those classified as high risk by both models, 64 per cent were violent during the 20-week follow-up period (Monahan *et al.*, 2001).

From the emerging evidence base it can be argued that risk assessment 'tools' based on logistic regression models have some rarely highlighted limitations and should now be replaced by more evidence-based approaches. There are a number of significant potential advantages in doing this. The use of such models may enable greater confidence that the allocation of individuals to groups is accurate. In turn, it can be suggested that efforts to identify those at the extreme ends of the continuum of risk and also allocating individuals to subgroups will have greater utility (Crighton, 2005; Monahan *et al.*, 2001; Towl, 2005). Allocating individuals to subgroups is likely to help by doing empirically what individuals seek to do naturally. As such, the approach is both more easily understood and more transparent in its operation. It is likely to have greater utility as a means of identifying needs and directing individually tailored interventions to manage risk (Crighton, 2009; Crighton & Towl, 2008).

Managing Risk

Risk management was defined by the US Presidential and Congressional Committee in 1997 as the process of identification evaluation, selection and implementation of actions to reduce risk (Moteff, 2005). This is a working definition that continues to be widely used and the conservative approach to risk assessment adopted by the committee continues to dominate risk management in many settings. The committee suggested that risk management could be divided into four logical approaches:

  i) risk avoidance;
 ii) risk reduction;
iii) risk retention;
 iv) risk transfer.

Risk avoidance

In fact, this might more accurately be described as hazard avoidance, since it involves finding ways to ensure that the hazards likely to lead to adverse outcomes are avoided. An example here might be not granting parole to prisoners, where contact with the community has been associated with previous violence. At one level this provides an effective means of managing risks but, as a strategy, it is problematic on a number of levels. These include the fact that avoiding hazards itself has costs. It means losing out on the potential gain from accepting risk. It also means exposure to other risks. In the examples given above, keeping offenders in prison indefinitely imposes considerable economic costs and means that money spent on prisons cannot be spent on health or education.

Risk reduction

This involves efforts to reduce the probability of a risk occurring and/or reducing the impact should it occur. An often-used example here is the use of fire suppression technology such as fire doors, fire alarms, sprinkler systems and so on. These are used in order to reduce the risk of fire and, where fire starts, to mitigate its impact (Reason, 1990). This serves as a useful analogy for forensic psychology, where interventions may be used to try to stop specific adverse events, to warn about possible occurrence or to suppress behaviour where it occurs.

Risk retention

Risk retention refers to the acceptance of risk and the losses associated with it. Risks that cannot be avoided or transferred fall into this category.

Risk transfer

This term is used to refer to efforts to move risks to other people or other organisations. An example here might be the transfer of mentally disordered offenders between health and criminal justice settings. Here the associated risks will, at least partially, move with the patient. In fact the term can be seen as something of a misnomer, since the risks do not go away and each agency will retain a degree of risk in such cases.

Risk management frameworks

A wide range of frameworks and methods of risk assessment have been devised. At the most basic level these include managerial approaches such as risk mapping and the use of risk registers. Risk mapping refers simply to efforts to produce representations of risk in terms of the probability of occurrence and the severity of impacts. They may often be combined with risk registers which list identified risks and seek to attribute likely costs as well as probability to these.

Such methods have become widespread within organisations but are wholly inadequate for risk management within forensic psychology for a number of reasons. Firstly, they are often based on highly questionable data, with probabilities of outcomes often based on little more than guesses. Within forensic practice there is a clear requirement for estimates to be based on meaningful estimates of the probability of given outcomes.

Within forensic psychology effective risk management will follow on from effective assessment. Where risks have been identified it will require the identification of appropriate interventions to address and minimise these. Such efforts at mitigation also need to be appropriate to the individual and the context. Risk management should also involve a process of monitoring and review, so that the plan can be amended and refined in response to events and changes to the ecosystem over time (Towl, 2005; Towl & Crighton, 1996).

Notes

1   An example here might be the actions of the Norwegian resistance in the Second World War in destroying industrial and transport capacity within Norway associated with the production of materials for the development of nuclear weapons by Germany. This involved the deaths of German combatants and Norwegian civilians. At the time, such actions were clearly illegal and viewed by the German authorities as such, carrying the death penalty for those involved and often for others. The view of the Allied forces at the time and of the vast majority subsequently was that such actions were heroic.

2   The study concerned drew on official records, self-reported violent and aggressive behaviour and collateral reports from family members. The study was designed to maximise willingness to report violence, with no penalties for disclosure. It seems unlikely that such high levels of self-report would be achieved in criminal justice settings, where there are powerful disincentives for honest accounts of such behaviour.

3   Here the definition of 'high'- and 'low'-risk groups is, as with main effects approaches, arbitrary. The inclusion of base rate data does, though, make the basis for the assumptions clear. Unfortunately, in a number of areas of risk assessment such clear base rate data are largely missing and the definition of concepts such as high and low risk becomes less clear as a result.

4   The percentages here have been rounded so do not total to 100.

5   The researchers also conducted this iterative analysis for a logistic regression model. This proved significantly less effective, allocating 62.3 per cent of cases to high- or low-risk groups.

6   This performance is all the more impressive because of the elimination of criminal history factors.

Further Reading

Monahan, J., Steadman, H., Silver, E. *et al.* (2001). *Rethinking risk assessment: The MacArthur study of mental disorder and violence*. New York: Oxford University Press.
This text provides detailed analysis of a major multi-site study into risk funded by the MacArthur Foundation. The study is focused primarily on mental health services in a number of large North American centres but the value of the text goes well beyond this. Detailed coverage is given of major definitional and practice issues in conducting risk assessments and the manner in which these impact on efforts at managing the risk of violence. The book also represents a step change in approaches to risk assessment, moving away from simple models of risk in favour of more sophisticated iterative and clinical approaches.

Breakwell, G. (2007). *The psychology of risk*. Cambridge: Cambridge University Press.
This is a key text and essential reading. It covers the broad area of risk, including the foundations of risk assessment, through to the ways in which risk responses might be changed. The book provides extensive coverage of the experimental evidence base from psychology and also from related disciplines. The text also includes learning aids in the form of a number of text boxes designed to encourage thinking about related questions, or practical examples of risk assessment.

Towl, G. (2005) Risk assessment. *Evidence-Based Mental Health, 8*, 91–93.
This paper provides a thematic review of the current state of play in the area of risk assessment, with particular reference to forensic mental health. The paper adopts a conceptual approach to risk assessment and considers commonalities across areas of research and practice. The main focus is on the social construction of risk in forensic mental health and the ethical implications for the public, policy makers, and practitioners. The paper critiques the development of simple models and risk assessment tools for profit, going on to consider the appeal of these to both policy makers and practitioners. The notion of seeking ever better 'tools', in the absence of theoretical understanding, is critically evaluated.

References

Ansell, J. (1992). Reliability, industrial risk assessment. In J. Ansell & F. Wharton (Eds.) *Risk analysis, assessment and management*. Chichester: John Wiley & Sons.

Applebaum, P.S., Clark Robbins, P. & Monahan, J. (2000). Violence and delusions: Data from the MacArthur Violence Risk Assessment Study. *American Journal of Psychiatry*, 157(4), 566–572.

Arkes, H.R., Hammond, K.R. & Connolly, T. (Eds.) (2000). *Judgment and decision making: An interdisciplinary reader*. Cambridge: Cambridge University Press.

Breakwell, G.M. (2007). *The psychology of risk*. Cambridge: Cambridge University Press.

Calman, K.C. (2002). Communication of risk: Choice, consent and trust. *Lancet, 360*, 166–168.

Crighton, D.A. (2005). Risk assessment. In D.A. Crighton & G.J. Towl (Eds.) *Psychology in probation services*. Oxford: Blackwell.

Crighton, D.A. (2006). Methodological issues in psychological research in prisons. In G.J. Towl (Ed.) *Psychological research in prisons*. Oxford: Blackwell.

Crighton, D.A. (2009). Uses and abuses of the Hare Psychopathy Checklist. *Evidence-Based Mental Health, 12*, 33–36.

Crighton, D.A. & Towl, G.J. (2008). *Psychology in prisons* (2nd edn). Oxford: Blackwell.

Crossland, B., Bennett, P.A., Ellis, A.F. *et al.* (1992). *Estimating engineering risk*. London: Royal Society.

Derman, E. & Taleb, N.N. (2005). The illusions of dynamic replication. *Quantitative Finance, 5*(4), 323–326.

Douglas, K., Ogloff, J., Nichols, T. *et al.* (1999). Assessing risk for violence among psychiatric patients: The HCR-20 Violence Risk Assessment Scheme and Psychopathy Checklist: Screening Version. *Journal of Consulting and Clinical Psychology, 67*, 917–930.

Douglas, M. (1986). *Risk acceptability according to the social sciences*. London: Routledge & Kegan Paul.

Drummond, M.F., Sculper, M.J., Torrance, G.W. *et al.* (2005). *Methods for the economic evaluation of health care programmes*. Oxford: Oxford University Press.

Fischer, B. & Scholes, M. (1973). The pricing of options and corporate liabilities. *Journal of Political Economy, 81*(3), 637–654.

Fischoff, B. (1998). Risk communication. In R. Löfstedt & L. Frewer (Eds.) *Risk and modern society*. London: Earthscan.

Freedman, D.A. (2008). On types of scientific enquiry: The role of qualitative reasoning. In J.M. Box-Steffensmeier, H.E. Brady & D. Collier (Eds.) *Oxford handbook of political methodology*. New York: Oxford University Press.

Gigerenzer, G. (2002). *Reckoning with risk: Learning to live with uncertainty*. Harmondsworth: Penguin.

Gigerenzer, G. & Hoffrage, U. (1995). How to improve Bayesian reasoning without instructions. Frequency formats. *Psychological Review, 102*, 684–704.

Gigerenzer, G. & Selten, R. (2001). Rethinking rationality. In G. Gigerenzer & R. Selten (Eds.) *Bounded rationality: The adaptive toolbox*. Cambridge, MA: MIT Press.

Harris, G., Rice, M. & Quinsey, V. (1993). Violent recidivism of mentally disordered offenders: The development of a statistical prediction instrument. *Criminal Justice and Behaviour, 20*, 315.

Kahneman, D., Slovic, P. & Tversky, A. (1982). *Judgment under uncertainty: Heuristics and biases*. Cambridge: Cambridge University Press,

Klassen, D. & O'Connor, W. (1988). Crime, inpatient admissions, and violence among male mental patients. *International Journal of Law and Psychiatry, 11*, 305–312.

Lidz, C., Mulvey, E. & Gardner, W. (1993). The accuracy of predictions of violence to others. *Journal of the American Medical Association, 269*, 1007–1011.

Meehl, P.E. (1954). *Clinical versus statistical prediction: A theoretical analysis and a review of the evidence*. Minneapolis, MN: University of Minnesota.

Meehl, P. (1959). Some ruminations on the validation of clinical procedures. *Canadian Journal of Psychology, 13*, 106–128.

Meehl, P.E. (1967). Theory-testing in psychology and physics: A methodological paradox. *Philosophy of Science, 34*, 103–115.

Meehl, P.E. (1973). Why I do not attend case conferences. In P.E. Meehl (1973) *Psychodiagnosis: Selected papers*. Minneapolis, MN: University of Minnesota Press.

MHCP Research (2008). Retrieved 14 June 2009 from www.mhcp-research.com/index.htm,

Mills, J.F., Jones, M.N. & Kroner, D.G. (2005). An examination of the generalizability of the LSI-R and Vrag probability bins. *Criminal Justice and Behavior, 32*(5), 565–585.

Monahan, J., Steadman, H., Clark Robbins, P. *et al.* (2005). An actuarial model of violence risk assessment for persons with mental disorders. *Psychiatric Services, 56*, 810–815.

Monahan, J., Steadman, H., Silver, E., *et al.* (2001). *Rethinking risk assessment: The MacArthur Study of Mental Disorder and Violence*. New York: Oxford University Press.

Mooney, C. & Duval, R. (1993). *Bootstrapping: A nonparametric approach to statistical inference*. Newbury Park, CA: Sage.

Moteff, J. (2005). *Risk management and critical infrastructure protection: Assessing, integrating, and managing threats, vulnerabilities and consequences*. Washington, DC: Congressional Research Service.

Peston, R. (2007). The Citi Tsunami. Retrieved 8 September 2009 from www.bbc.co.uk/blogs/thereporters/robertpeston/2007/11/the_citi_tsunami.html

Reason, J. (1990). *Human error*. New York: Cambridge University Press.

Sepejak, D., Menzies, R., Webster, C. *et al.* (1983). Clinical prediction of dangerousness: Two-year follow-up of 408 pretrial forensic cases. *Bulletin of the American Academy of Psychiatry and Law, 11*, 171–181.

Slovic, P. (1993). Perceived risk trust and democracy. *Risk Analysis, 13*, 675–682.

Swets, J. (1988). Measuring the accuracy of diagnostic systems. *Science, 240*, 1285–1293.

272   DAVID A. CRIGHTON

Swets, J., Dawes, R. & Monahan, J. (2000). Psychological science can improve diagnostic decisions. *Psychological Science in the Public Interest, 1*, 1–26.

Taleb, N.N. (2007). *The black swan: The impact of the highly improbable*. London: Allen Lane.

Towl, G.J. (2005). Risk assessment. *Evidence Based Mental Health, 8*, 91–93.

Towl, G.J. & Crighton, D.A. (1996). *The handbook of psychology for forensic practitioners*. London: Routledge.

Towl, G. & Crighton, D. (1997). Risk assessment with offenders. *International Review of Psychiatry, 9*, 187–193.

Webster, C.D., Douglas, C.D., Eaves, D. *et al.* (2003). HCR-20. Retrieved 14 June 2009 from www.psychcorp.co.uk/product.aspx?n=1316&s=1322&cat=2020&skey=3946

18

Aspects of Diagnosed Mental Illness and Offending

David Pilgrim

The psychological assessment of people considered to be both criminal and mentally ill brings particular challenges for practitioners. What balance of criminogenic and psychopathological factors should be invoked when attempting a psychological formulation and to what degree are they relevant separately and together? Does a psychological formulation complement or challenge a psychiatric diagnosis? To what extent might the cultural norms of the offender-patient account for what, at first glance, might be seen as individual pathology, if and when we explore their actions in their context of origin? If they are incarcerated when being assessed, which is the commonest scenario, how valid are our assessments and our predictions now that the patient is outside of their normal life setting; they are in a closed system but their offending took place in an open system? To what extent might the symptoms of mental illness be relevant (or irrelevant) to understanding and predicting particular risky action?

These questions apply, by the way, to an extent to *all* criminals, because none of us, including criminals, can ever claim to be perfectly mentally healthy. Psychodynamic psychology in particular emphasises that we are all, to some degree, mentally ill and so the psychosocial transgressions of all offenders could invite forms of pathologisation and psychological expertise. Offenders break the law and few crimes are victimless, so the exploitation of others and the betrayal of mutual trust are ever present. These interpersonal and personal features are the very stuff of psychological interest. Even outside of the psychodynamic tradition, existential, behavioural and cognitive approaches to psychological functioning can be applied to criminal action.

The ambiguities implied by these opening remarks will be explored further in this chapter, via four aims:

1. Mentally disordered offenders and our response to them will be considered in their social context.
2. A summary will be provided of the overlaps and tensions between psychiatric and psychological knowledge.
3. A psychological rather than a psychiatric approach to those with a diagnosis of mental illness in forensic settings will be explored.
4. The evidence about the problematic relationship between diagnosed mental illness and risk will be examined.

The Social Context of Rule Transgressions: Normal and Abnormal Offenders

It is worth noting at the outset that because both criminality and mental health problems are always about rule transgression and frequently about social exclusion, then others, such as criminologists and sociologists, also have had much to say legitimately on this chapter's topic (Prins, 2005 – see Further Reading). Criminality and mental health are social as well as psychological matters. Prison and secure hospital populations are not representative of wider society. Men are overrepresented, as are black people, and of course poverty predicts both law breaking and the 'residual deviance' of mental disorder (Rogers & Pilgrim, 2005). The mentally abnormal offender is thus doubly deviant and more than likely to have origins in deprivation and exclusion.

Those conditions of poverty and social exclusion and their relevance for understanding the uneven social distribution of mental illness were demonstrated around the time of the Second World War by the 'ecological wing' of the Chicago School of Sociology (Rogers & Pilgrim, 2003). These poor social conditions are also the likely fate of mentally disordered offenders when, and if, they leave detention. In this context, the chances of risk reduction or minimisation cannot be predicted by individual factors alone but rely heavily also on living conditions (neighbourhood and social network characteristics). This point is returned to at the end of the chapter.

Thus, sociology has much to tell us about the social nature of individuals we assess in terms of deviance identification and amplification, in both the lay and professional arenas. This point became apparent during the 1960s from a series of studies from the other wing of the Chicago School of Sociology – symbolic interactionism (Coulter, 1973; Scheff, 1966). A sociological approach also provides us with insights into the organisational apparatus of social regulation used by the State *both* to control offenders being psychologically assessed *and* to employ those, like forensic psychologists, making those assessments (Cohen & Scull, 1985).

It is important, then, that pertinent criticisms, from our disciplinary perspective of psychiatry, do not lead to an overvaluation of psychological accounts of deviance. Replacing medical reductionism with psychological reductionism may not be a great step forward. Psychological formulation certainly has defensible advantages over psychiatric diagnosis but psychologists can learn much from bodies of knowledge outwith their discipline.

Penal and psychiatric jurisdiction of mentally abnormal offenders

With these cautions about the social context of criminal action and psychological expertise in forensic settings in mind, let us now return to psychiatry. If 'mental illness' is the discourse of psychiatry, then what features characterise this medical speciality in the shared organisational setting of forensic work? Psychiatrists, because they are medical practitioners, are happy, indeed obliged, to split off 'mental disorder', 'descriptive psychopathology' and 'morbid psychology' from normal psychological functioning. As a consequence, they have a poorly developed lexicon for ordinary thoughts, feelings and actions and have little to say about people who do not fulfil criteria for mental disorder. (Postgraduate students I teach sometimes complain that psychiatrists have a restricted and restrictive medical model. I usually reply that this is not surprising, as they are medical practitioners.)

Psychiatrists are not alone in their ignorance about ordinary experience and behaviour. Most people, medical or otherwise, have little to say about 'mental order'; the strangeness of the term to the ear tells the tale. This is because, outside of contrived psychological research, most of us tend only to become extra-attentive when things go wrong. Life would be tedious and highly disrupted if this were not the case. When things go 'right' (people comply with role–rule expectations) then this is unremarkable and so invites little or no reactive interest.

Thus conformity to role and rule expectations does not demand accountability but, by implication, transgression demands accountability. As Goffman (1971) pointed out, a meta-rule in most societies is that of social intelligibility; we are expected to account for why we break rules if asked by others. The exposed cheat or the detected criminal can disavow or excuse their actions without breaking this meta-rule because they are offering an account of sorts. By contrast, the 'mentally ill' patient breaks rules and is then unable or unwilling to account for their transgressions; they 'lack insight' into their unintelligible actions. Thereby the 'mentally ill' patient, unlike the excuse-making cheat or crook, breaks the social contract about our obligation to account for actions to others when the circumstances require.

To be unable or unwilling to be accountable can be dealt with or reacted to by others as a more serious transgression than other forms of rule breaking. For this reason, those with a diagnosis of mental illness are one of the few social groups of adults who can be detained lawfully without trial; the other obvious group are suspected terrorists. 'Mental health law' (a misnomer, because it is about the coercive social control of mental disorder, not the promotion of mental health) and terrorist legislation are rare statutes. Moreover, detention without trial is applied to 'civil patients' who have committed no crime – so judgements about prospective risk are not only about offender-patients.

Thus, the confluence of two sorts of deviance – criminal and psychological transgressions – means that two frameworks of sanction might operate together or apart. The first is the normal penal disposal of a defined sentence determined by *past actions*. The other is the organisational peculiarity of secure psychiatric detention, where the patient is detained indefinitely and assessed episodically about their *prospective actions*. It is not unusual for mentally abnormal prisoners to be moved from the first to the second organisational jurisdiction (from a prison to a secure hospital) in order to manage their prospective risk. In the latter setting, mental health professions spend much of their time evaluating risk in conditions of uncertainty and so tend to default to 'false negative' decision making. These professionals tend not to be sanctioned for detaining a patient unnecessarily, whereas the reoffending discharged patient provokes fierce criticism.

Overlaps and Tensions between Psychiatric and Psychological Knowledge

Outside of medicine, in the human sciences it has been the task of psychologists, anthropologists and sociologists deliberately to pursue the unremarkable and build up pictures of normality – the 'norms and mores', thoughts, feelings and motivations of ordinary people doing ordinary things in their everyday lives. These versions of human science start from this position about ordinary functioning and then might occasionally look to transgressions in order to define normality.

By contrast, psychiatrists start at the other end of the telescope when looking at psychological morbidity – and tend to get stuck there. Consequently, they have little or nothing to say about normal life and so lack a professional capacity to connect their field of interest with wider human functioning. This is an intellectual limitation of the medical model. It also has an important psychosocial consequence of splitting off patients from non-patients, an oppressive process increasingly called 'othering'. If psychologists find themselves too close to that medical model they risk the same problems.

However, the medical model has found some of its most robust critics not within psychology but within psychiatry itself (e.g. Kleinman, 1988; Szasz, 1961). These medical dissenters notwithstanding, most doctors live in a world of digital logic of present or absent ('no abnormality detected', 'no symptoms of mental illness could be elicited', 'the person is not mentally ill', 'the person is fit to plead', etc.). This logic, by the way, is in many ways compatible with a legal context, where questions of insanity and diminished responsibility are deemed to be present or absent by judges and juries.

By contrast, psychologists are socialised differently and so have been encouraged to think in terms of continua rather than categories. In line with their training, psychologists' assessments *ought* to be based on analogue, not digital, reasoning. People are more or less: suspicious; mindful of others; rigid in their thinking; impulsive; moral; egocentric; lacking in insight; prone to idiosyncratic thoughts and perceptions; emotionally labile, etc.

Take the example of 'paranoia'. In psychiatry this tends to be seen as a morbid condition suffered by individuals are who suspicious, rigid in their thought processes about some matters but not others and express certainty in that rigidity in a way that others do not understand and fail to challenge successfully. The patient suffers from 'delusions' and these peculiarly morbid ways of thinking are pathognomic of 'paranoid schizophrenia'. All of this suggests that those suffering the latter are, in some sense, *categorically different* from the rest of humanity. But all of us can be suspicious and feel got at (with or without good reason). All of us have beliefs not shared by others. All of us can refuse to accept the reasoning of others. All of us can quickly jump to conclusions, rightly or wrongly. So rather than viewing mentally ill people as categorically different from those who are not, psychologists might be better exploring common psychological processes in all people.

Psychological encounters with 'mental illness' in forensic settings

Psychologists working with offenders will recurrently encounter those who have a pre-existing psychiatric diagnosis. Sometimes they might be involved in assessing the presence and nature of mental health problems in offenders, when a diagnosis is being mooted for the first time. Although both penal and secure mental health settings are places of employment for forensic psychologists, they are more likely to encounter psychiatrists (and clinical psychologists) in the latter. With that engagement come presuppositions about the preferred constructs of these professionals.

The broad points below are relevant to both penal and health settings but the psychiatric discourse is more powerful in the latter because of medical dominance and its traditional enshrinement in law. In the case of Britain there has been a tradition of psychiatrists being central to decision making as Responsible Medical Officers (RMOs). The admission and discharge of patients (note that name itself is a symbolic marker of jurisdiction rather than 'offender' or 'prisoner') are under their control. Moreover, the viewpoint of the psychiatrist in reports for the Home Office or for Mental Health Review Tribunals tends to have more immediate and automatic authority than views from the members of the multidisciplinary team, such as psychologists.

At the time of writing, the role of the RMO is about to disappear under the new conditions of the 2007 Mental Health Act. A new role of 'Responsible Clinician' is to be introduced, which will permit non-psychiatrists (in the case of psychologists only at 'Consultant' grade) to enter the role previously inhabited solely by the RMO. However, the circumstances of psychologists being cast in that role, rather than a psychiatrist, will probably be limited to those with a diagnosis of personality disorder.

This is relevant for this chapter because it is much less likely, though not out of the question, that a psychologist in the role of Responsible Clinician would lead decision making about discharge for those deemed to be mentally ill. Moreover, because of successful last-minute lobbying from the Royal College of Psychiatrists, under the new Act psychiatrists will retain jurisdiction over the *admission* of patients on a compulsory basis (for both offending and non-offending patients). Any shift from a psychiatrist to a non-psychiatrist, with the latter taking over the role of Responsible Clinician, will take place only after admission.

The traditions of psychiatric and psychological knowledge

With the above organisational and administrative context in mind, the tradition of diagnosing mental illness can be examined. A good starting point is the work of Emil Kraepelin who is attributed with the leading role in developing our current psychiatric theory and practice. Kraepelin (1883) offered his colleagues three axioms about mental illness:

1   They are genetically determined.
2   They are separate, naturally occurring, categories.
3   They are fixed and deteriorating conditions.

Kraepelinian psychiatry elaborated a classification of mental illness, with these emphatic axioms. Kraepelin's focus was on lunacy: 'manic-depressive psychosis' (later 'bipolar disorder') and 'dementia praecox' (later 'schizophrenia'). Since then, the categorisation of mental disorder has expanded massively. For example, the current *Diagnostic and Statistical Manual* of the American Psychiatric Association contains nearly 400 categories

(when it is revised again in 2010 it is likely to exceed that figure). A century of growth has ensured that the acorn logic of three axioms applied to two main disorders has produced a large tree with many thick branches.

When Kraepelin offered his version of biodeterminism, it was not limited to medicine at the end of the 19th century. At that time, eugenics was commonplace and so shaped psychological knowledge as well. In the British, context Francis Galton led the intellectual rationale for a 'tainted gene' pool and its role in undermining the racial stock of the country. A range of relevant disruptive deviance was identified – the prevalence of criminality, lunacy, idiocy, inebriation and prostitution in the underclass of Victorian society was explained by their genetic defectiveness. The eugenic movement sought a range of measures to limit the fecundity of this class and to increase the birth rate in those further up the class pyramid (Pilgrim, 2008).

Thus, while Kraepelin and others were leading forms of psychiatric diagnosis within a eugenic framework, the latter was also the inspiration for the development of an important form of proto-psychology at University College London led by Galton's protégés (Pearson, Spearman and Burt). They developed the early rationale for 'biometrics' – now 'psychometrics' or 'differential psychology' – and the statistical paraphernalia to support the demonstration of the psychological, rather than psychiatric expression of eugenics. The latter, with its diagnostic emphasis, simply assumed the genetic basis for mental illness – with or without empirical evidence to support that view.

By contrast, the psychological expression of eugenics encountered an early logical challenge to genetic explanations, which was that behavioural characteristics very rarely seemed to follow simple Mendelian rules of inheritance. As a consequence, a polygenetic-plus-environmental interaction was postulated to account for the tendency towards the normal distribution of these characteristics in any population (Fisher, 1930). This type of explanation was also to be invoked later by biological psychiatrists to account for the tendency of mental illness to run in families but without following neat genetic rules. However, the mathematical assumption (note that it is an assumption) about the normal distribution of psychological characteristics was stronger and earlier.

Early in the 20th century, psychological and psychiatric expressions of eugenics encountered some setbacks. The shellshock problem of the First World War was prevalent in 'England's finest blood' (officers and gentlemen and working-class *volunteers*). As a consequence, the eugenic discourse of asylum psychiatry was tantamount to treason. As a result, a space opened up for environmentalist explanations for mental abnormality and formulations about presenting mental health crises (Stone, 1985). Also, Kraepelin's assumption about inevitable degeneration was not evident in practice, with recovery rates in asylum populations being around 25 per cent by the 1920s (Hinsie, 1931). Added to which, the great economic depression of the 1930s was reflected palpably in its individual victims and raised levels of mental distress in civil society during peacetime (Dohrenwend, 1998).

The political and humanitarian catastrophe of the Nazi period confirmed confidence in *environmental* explanations of psychological functioning in the first half of the 20th century, as well as seriously discrediting the conventional wisdom of eugenics. To complement this period of shame for eugenics, behaviourists showed how to create psychological dysfunction in the laboratory by the simple manipulation of environmental stimuli – the demonstration of 'experimental neurosis' (Watson & Rayner, 1920). Moreover, it is noteworthy, in the context of this chapter, that Pavlov (1941) made his cruelly treated dogs not just miserable but catatonic by manipulating stimuli in the closed system of the psychological laboratory.

Here we begin to see the first pieces of evidence that mammals (not humans alone) can be rendered confused, helpless and crazy by being manipulated, deprived and punished under conditions of no escape. The latter, now called 'entrapment', has been used as a conceptual springboard to explain depression (Brown *et al.*, 1995; Seligman, 1975) and psychosis (Bateson *et al.*, 1956; Laing & Esterson, 1964). Given that forensic settings permit no escape, this body of knowledge has an additional salience, especially if the institutional regime is not benign and supportive. This point about inherent entrapment applies much more to health settings than prisons because there is no estimated date for discharge – a point made earlier about the difference between a penal and a hospital disposal.

A final point to note about doubts from non-medical mental health workers about psychiatric theory and practice is that diagnosis is vulnerable to both pre-empirical and empirical attacks. Diagnoses such as 'schizophrenia' or 'depression' have poor conceptual and predictive validity (Bentall *et al.*, 1988; Pilgrim & Bentall, 1999). Functional mental illnesses *ipso facto* lack aetiological specificity and treatment specificity (usual validating criteria expected for good medical diagnoses).

Moreover, although symptom checklists, like those derived from DSM, increase the probability of reliability, a reliable concept is not necessarily a valid one. This has led some psychologists to argue for a complete abandonment of the medical categorisation of mental illness in the Kraepelinian tradition, and for new models based in 'normal' psychology to be used instead, when offering formulations for particular patient presentations (Bentall, 2003 – see annotated reference in Further Reading).

The emergence of the biopsychosocial model and neo-Kraepelinian retrenchment

By the middle of the 20th century, the Nazi stain had discredited but not eliminated a genetic emphasis in the mental health industry. Psychiatric genetics remained strong and was predicated on research in the Nazi period – exemplified by the work of Franz Kallmann in the USA and Eliot Slater in Britain. In psychology, psychometrics remained rooted in eugenic assumptions about genetic determination (Pilgrim, 2008).

At the same time, there was a strong web of environmentalist criticism to contain and even negate this biological enthusiasm. The impact of behaviourism in academic psychology has already been noted. In addition, after the Second World War, concerns about war orphans invited an examination of childhood adversity and its short- and long-term impact on mental health. The conditions of possibility were there to develop attachment theory – a hybrid of psychodynamic and behaviourist ideas (Bowlby, 1951). This theory became a springboard for understanding both mental health problems and delinquency.

Moreover, although the Kraepelinian view remained dominant in peacetime institutional psychiatry, its limits were exposed by the challenges of military psychiatry which, instead, cultivated more environmentalist and psychodynamic ways of understanding mental health. From this tension emerged both social psychiatry and the biopsychosocial model. The first was an interdisciplinary project of socially orientated psychiatrists, clinical psychologists and medical sociologists. The second informed the first and emerged from the work of Adolf Meyer and his 'psychobiology' and the use of General Systems Theory which provides an anti-reductionist and holistic paradigm in the biological and human sciences (Engel, 1980).

Meyer, a Swiss psychiatrist, who spent most of his career in the USA, unlike Kraepelin, did not force patients, Procrustean style, into pre-set, professionally preferred categories. He asked versions of the question 'Why does this patient present with these particular problems at this time in his or her life?' Meyer was proposing the need for formulation to take precedence over diagnosis.

This web of opposition to the Kraepelinian orthodoxy did not displace the latter but it did create a pressure within psychiatry to move towards a compromise in relation to mental illness. That compromise involved a more cautious interactionism about psychological and social, not just biological, causal reasoning, hence the attraction of the biopsychosocial model (Pilgrim *et al.*, 2008). It also softened the eugenic logic in psychology. Thus leaders in clinical psychology such as Hans Eysenck began to ride two horses. One was the eugenic legacy of differential psychology (hence his psychometric devices) and the other was the acceptance of behaviourism to formulate and treat neurotic problems.

However, an outcome of that ambivalence was that Eysenck offered a compromise about jurisdiction for mental illness. He suggested a simple division of labour, between psychologists treating environmentally determined neurotic symptoms with behaviour therapy and psychiatrists treating psychoses using medication, on the grounds that the latter were biologically determined (Eysenck, 1975). For many years up to the present, clinical psychology has been dominated by psychometric routines and the modified legacy of behaviour therapy (cognitive behaviour therapy). That compromise and division of labour was to have a profound effect on the ability of psychologists to think psychologically about psychosis – a point to return to later.

Another compromise across the channel soon emerged in the American Psychiatric Association (APA). The system of classification, the *Diagnostic and Statistical Manual* (DSM), which it had been developing over many years, came into crisis in the run-up to its revision in 1980. Two power blocs in the APA, one of biological psychiatrists and the other of psychoanalysts, were at loggerheads over aetiology.

Psychoanalysts have always been ambivalent about diagnosis. On the one hand, psychoanalysis is a form of biographical psychology and there is the fetish of the illustrative individual case in the 'scientific meetings' of psychoanalytical societies (an idiographic or hermeneutic way of understanding people). On the other hand, analysts have been content to use diagnosis, and even the language of pathology, when describing normal mental processes and development ('the paranoid position', 'schizoid defences', etc). The psychoanalytical insistence on *developmental* aetiology was at odds with biological psychiatry with its own genetic presuppositions.

Another factor in this internal power struggle about DSM-III was that the psychoanalytical position was a threat for the very reason that it was not limited to medical practitioners. This left the door open to the non-medical influence of 'lay analysts' in the APA. Also, at that time, scientific attacks on the tenets of psychoanalysis were beginning to bite and it was suffering a major credibility problem in American culture. As such, it had become a liability to the credibility of psychiatry (Hale, 1995).

The resolution of the political tension within the APA was to drop aetiological claims and emphasise only current and reported *descriptive* criteria for settling on a categorical diagnosis. At first glance the Kraepelinian professional project, with its three medical axioms, looked seriously compromised. As was noted above, one of them, about fixed deteriorating prognoses, had been discredited early in the 20th century (Hinsie, 1931).

And a second axiom was being discounted or at least queried – the assertion about genetic determination. However, and this is why DSM can be quite properly called 'neo-Kraeplinian', there was now the strong reassertion that mental disorders were *naturally occurring categories*. This was crucial to re-establish medical authority about the professional jurisdiction of mental disorder. This had the effect of bringing diagnosis firmly back into the medical model, to the professional relief of psychiatrists (Blacker & Tsuang, 1998). The compromise thus still strongly bolstered a medical view of mental abnormality (Wilson, 1993).

What DSM insisted on and what clinicians then did in practice is worth noting. Biological psychiatrists have not ceased to use diagnoses of mental illness that exclude assumptions of aetiology. For example, since 1980 they have still distinguished between endogenous and reactive depression (McPherson & Armstrong, 2006). Equally though, the stricture about neutrality in relation to aetiology in DSM has been flouted by psychoanalysts in the USA (McWilliams, 1994). The wide-ranging problems associated with psychiatric diagnosis in general, and the DSM system in particular, are reviewed by Horwitz (2002) – see annotated reference in Further Reading.

Psychological and Psychiatric Approaches to Mental Illness in Forensic Settings

In the light of the above discussion, psychologists can take three broad positions in relation to people with a diagnosis of mental illness in forensic settings. The first, following Eysenck's offer of the division of labour, can argue that mental illness is a biological condition to be diagnosed and treated medically – which literally means medicinally, with drugs with the grandiose name of 'anti-psychotics'. This leaves no role for the psychologist (except maybe as a psychometrician to offer additional information about the patient's intelligence or personality).

The second position can be found in those psychologists who emphasise that mental illness is a biologically driven condition but that relapse is affected by personal factors. This stance adheres to the 'stress-vulnerability' hypothesis and the emphasis on 'high expressed emotion' and 'communication deviance' in the family of origin or maybe even a ward in a hospital or the wing of a prison. Here the psychologist might offer advice about minimising the risk of relapse or might offer interventions, such as family therapy or 'psycho-education'. This might be seen as a 'peripheralist' position – the psychologist accepts the primacy of biology and then offers to deal with some of the peripheral fallout of that biological disease.

The third position is more radical and entails adopting an explicitly psychological approach to assessment and intervention. In particular, it means refusing to accept the evasion of a developmental approach to formulation found in the DSM. It is here that the psychologists can be highly challenged. Collectively, psychologists can be fairly accused of 'having their cake and eating it' about diagnosis. DSM is seductive to psychologists for a number of reasons.

Its most superficial instrumental advantage is for psychologists to enjoy the dubious and quasi-medical status of actually making a diagnosis. Another advantage is pragmatic. Most mental health professions, but especially psychiatrists and nurses, are socialised to take for granted the conceptual validity of categorical labels, such as 'schizophrenia'. To refuse to take these labels seriously isolates psychologists when communicating with colleagues in multidisciplinary settings. As far as research is concerned, most grant-giving bodies are dominated by medical practitioners and diagnostic-related groups are taken-for-granted targets for both clinical and health policy research. This locks all-comers into a diagnostic discourse if they want to access research money. Finally, in some countries such as the USA and Australia, community-based psychologists only get payments for treatment if they record a diagnostic code. These interdisciplinary and financial considerations

lock psychologists into the continued use of diagnosis (whether or not they do so willingly or resentfully).

The Problematic Relationship between Diagnosed Mental Illness and Risk

Historically the regulation of criminal lunatics preceded the strong biological programme about madness described earlier in the work of Emil Kraepelin, when eugenics was in the political ascendancy (Cohen & Scull, 1985). Accounts of the early Victorian period emphasise two aspects of this regulation. The first is that the co-existence of madness and criminality warranted separate institutional care. The second was that two groups were discernible within this incarcerated population. One seemed to be detached from their original crime and easily managed in the institution but had acute episodes of anger. The other was permanently aggressive and oppositional but less mad. Some conceptual differentiation seemed to be present, then, about those we might now think of as being 'mentally ill' (lunacy) and those that we might now think of as being 'personality disordered' (then, suffering from 'moral insanity').

In more recent times these distinctions have been retained but in practice have shown considerable overlap. Indeed, in forensic settings there are those (considered in Chapter 8) whose main psychological functioning is dominated by egocentric and antisocial action ('antisocial personality disorder' 'dissocial personality disorder' or 'psychopathy') and those whose idiosyncrasies relate more to mood, perceptions and thought processes (what psychiatrists lump together as the functional psychoses of bipolar disorder and the schizophrenias).

'Dual diagnosis' or 'comorbidity'

However, there are problems with these hard-and-fast distinctions between 'mental illness' and 'personality disorder (PD)' as obvious and separate administrative and clinical categories, just as there are problems about neatly separating normal and abnormal behaviour. Habitual criminals often fulfil criteria for ('antisocial' or 'dissocial') personality disorder in a tautological sense, so are they all mentally disordered? And arguably the non-criminal expression of 'personality disorder' can be found in opportunistic politicians, careerists of all types, office bullies, power-obsessed managers in all organisations, shallow light entertainers, boxers and mercenaries.

Thus distinctions between normal and abnormal personalities are not easily made. Self-seeking behaviour at the expense of others is sometimes rewarded and even glorified in some social contexts but not others. Thus selfish exploitative action does not always lead to criminal sanctions (Pilgrim, 2001). As for dangerous behaviour, this is sometimes positively socially valued and idolised (in racing-car drivers, mountaineers, boxers and astronauts). Thus it is not dangerousness in itself that is the issue, but the way that people are dangerous; the latter may be condemned or glorified depending on the context.

Turning to the merging of personality and psychosis, imagine this scenario (witnessed by the author). In a case review the psychiatrists and nurses present in a medium secure unit argued that the mentally disordered offender being considered must still be detained because they are still showing symptoms of 'schizophrenia'. I argued (to some sceptical looks) something like – 'yes, but why are so many with the very same diagnosis safely in the community or residing in open wards in another part of the NHS down the road from here? Why is *this particular* "sufferer" of "schizophrenia" in a secure setting?' The discussion soon revealed that the answer to this had to be that, like all other offenders, his detention ultimately related to the way he had behaved, been detected and judged by others.

What is obvious, when working with offenders who are diagnosed as being mentally ill, is that they often have much in common with dangerous criminals, whatever their mental state. They are often young, male, poor and poorly educated, with an oppositional attitude to others, which easily tips into defensive aggression or pre-emptive strikes against others. On the outside they may mix in circles in which reckless behaviour is commonplace and substance misuse is the norm.

Thus some clear risk factors are not about symptoms of mental illness but are bound up with the *life context* anticipated, if the patient I was recalling were to be discharged. He would go back to a poor environment and reconnect with a social network that drinks excessively and smokes cannabis or crack cocaine regularly. Thus it is not symptoms but the whole behavioural context of open systems that has to be considered for this patient. If this wider context is ignored then the presence of active symptoms of 'mental illness' can too readily become the rationale for detention in conditions of security and become a dubious proxy for dangerousness.

The psychiatric riposte to this observation might be that these patients have a 'dual diagnosis' or suffer from 'comorbidity'. The argument is that this particular patient also 'has' a 'personality disorder' or that they also abuse substances so they have more than one disorder (like having diabetes and arthritis). Indeed, it was common in the nomenclature of the old Mental Health Act for detained patients to be categorised as suffering from *both* 'mental illness' *and* 'psychopathic disorder'. But this social administrative contortion arises because of the reified concepts provided by the Kraepelinian tradition and the questionable assumption that these concepts are valid and separate.

It is only because the neo-Kraepelinian position starts from the unproven assumption that categories are natural and *separately occurring* that it then has to deal with behavioural and experiential complexity by forcing offender-patients onto the Procrustean (double) bed of 'comorbidity'. By contrast, a psychological approach is not obliged to begin with these assumptions about categories. In open systems, with people with particular current and past circumstances, and attributing meanings to these circumstances in particular ways, unique formulations are more likely to be descriptively richer.

A bonus might be that explanatory insights are more robust than those offered by diagnoses. For example, a fragile defensive young man who had been physically and sexually abused in younger days starts to smoke crack and becomes paranoid in his outlook when outdoors. He carries a knife in anticipation of being attacked and believes that street gangs are out to get him. He lives in a very poor area. In streets with gangs on most corners, one day he reacts to a common and apparently inconsequential taunt by using the blade with fatal consequences.

Mental illness and risk to others

The relationship between a diagnosis of mental illness and risk remains controversial. A number of points can be made to summarise this controversy:

- Those with a diagnosis of mental illness are predominantly described in the mass media as a risk to others. However, collectively psychiatric patients are at far greater risk from others and to themselves, as victims of crime and exploitation and from self-harm and suicide. Indeed, the selective media attention to mentally disordered offenders ('schizophrenic kills in frenzied knife attack') then distorts the public imagination about the risk posed by psychiatric patients in general (Pilgrim & Rogers, 2003).

- Correlational studies, which argue for the raised link between diagnosed mental illness and violence, have to invoke 'dual diagnosis' to justify the relationship persuasively. As a single variable, diagnosed mental illness is a very poor predictor of violence (Monahan, 1992). Some studies suggest raised rates (Laajasalo & Hakkanen, 2005; Shaw *et al.*, 2006; Swanson, 1994) but others note that it is only the co-presence of substance misuse or personality problems that raises the risk of those with a diagnosed mental illness compared to those without (Steadman *et al.*, 1998).

- It is important to note that substance misuse is a predictor of violent offending *independent* of mental state. However, given that substance misuse is relatively common in psychiatric patients living in the community, with prevalence rates recorded of between 20 and 30 per cent, then it is hardly surprising that this is an important matter for both risk assessment and risk management (Hambrecht & Hafner, 1996; Regier *et al.*, 1990). Given that substance misuse is a predictor of violence in both psychiatric and non-psychiatric populations, it is ironic that when the English Mental Health Act was reformed in 2007, substance misuse was *excluded* as a criterion for judging the actions of those with a mental disorder. If we need a clear behavioural criterion to justify preventative social control, then evidence of substance misuse, not mental illness, should be put at the top of the list rather than being excluded from it (Pilgrim, 2007).

- A version of these correlational studies has focused on specific symptoms rather than diagnosis of mental illness *per se* or on treatment compliance as predictors, to some advantage. For example, the risk of violence increases with the presence of positive not negative symptoms (Soyka, 2000). The latter entail social withdrawal, therefore limiting contact with potential victims. Command hallucinations with violent content unsurprisingly predict violence and so need to be taken seriously in any assessment (Junginger, 1995). Similarly, delusions with hostile content, for example an obsessive grudge about a targeted victim, predict violent action (Taylor, 1985), though the presence of delusions without this focus do not (Appelbaum *et al.*, 1999). Treatment compliance in psychotic patients (with medication) reduces but does not eliminate risk (Swartz *et al.*, 1998).

- Just as substance misuse is a good predictor of violence in psychiatric and non-psychiatric populations alike, so too with intimacy. Most victims of violent crimes are known to the perpetrator (Estroff & Zimmer, 1994; Lindqvist & Allebeck, 1989). Thus, in risk assessment the anticipated interpersonal field of the patient in the community needs to be mapped out carefully and is more important than the diagnosis given to them. In the light of the previous point, grudges and old scores need particular attention, whether they are delusional or simply bound up with the micro-politics of the patient's social and family network.

- The majority of articles in specialist journals, which focus on mentally abnormal offenders (such as the *Journal of Forensic Psychiatry and Psychology*), report studies of factors other than mental illness, such as types of offending (stalking, paedophilia, etc.) and they focus more on other diagnoses of mental disorder, especially personality disorder, rather than mental illness. This balance of articles in dedicated forensic publications is an indication that researchers of offending consider that 'mental illness' *per se* is a poor source of pickings for their inquiries.

- Even when correlational studies show raised levels of risk in those with a diagnosis of mental illness, their practical utility for risk assessment and management is undermined by the large presence of non-patients in the relevant offending category. For example, it has been estimated that between 40 and 50 per cent of stalkers are suffering from some form of mental disorder (and note that this includes diagnoses, such as personality disorder, not just mental illness). This means that between 50 and 60 per cent of stalkers *do not* warrant a diagnosis of mental disorder (Zona *et al.*, 1998). Take another example, from researchers who argue that mental illness is a worthy focus of prediction. Laajasalo and Hakkanen (2005) point out that 11 per cent of homicides are carried out by those with a diagnosis of mental illness and again, for emphasis, note that these data are dominated by those with a 'dual diagnosis'. Even this relatively high estimate means that nine out of ten homicides are carried out by people who *are not* mentally ill. What predictive use, then, is a diagnosis of mental illness in itself, given these sorts of data?

- As with any psychiatric diagnosis (even the circular notion of personality disorder), aggregate data tell practitioners faced with individual risk assessment very little. Certainly a diagnosis such as 'schizophrenia' tells us virtually nothing about risk to others. It is only by using multifactorial formulations specific to the offender that we move towards improved risk assessment and, even then, as I noted at the start of this chapter, those estimates are often being made in the closed system of confinement, not the open system of past or prospective offending. Within that shift from diagnosis to formulation, clinical variables are marginal in two senses. First, aggregate data about other social group membership, such as male gender, membership of violent subculture or low social class, are a better predictor than being in the social group of psychiatric patients. In other words, if we do use actuarial variables for predicting risk (and their practical utility remains in constant doubt), logically we would not start with 'mental illness' but with one or more other variables. Second, for those offenders with a diagnosis of mental illness, just like offenders without, detailed understandings of past-conduct-in-context are more valid ways of predicting risk than focusing on the presence of a diagnosis of mental illness.

- Best-practice guidelines about risk assessment for mentally abnormal offenders suggest that unstructured clinical assessments (where the salience of clinical variables tend to get overvalued or narrowly considered) or actuarial assessments (which are evidenced based but tell us little about individuals) need to be superseded by careful professional formulations of offender-patients and their anticipated contexts after discharge. These formulations should utilise research, detailed knowledge of the patient and the patient's own views in combination to assess risk (DH, 2007). Moreover, risk management is not the same as risk assessment. The more the latter shifts to the former, the more it is important to maintain a collaborative relationship with the patient. Thus risk assessment can be 'done to' patients – even then inefficiently if their views are not taken into account – whereas risk management can only be done with any confidence in collaboration with patients.

- Finally, and elaborating on the previous point, context is all-important. Offender variables alone are only one aspect of calculating and preventing risk to others. A good formulation should attend to contextual factors. These are what Hiday (1995) calls 'violence inducing social forces' in the life world of the individual. For example, the offender-patient's particular symptoms, personality and personal history need to be understood in the anticipated context of cultural factors, like local base rates of substance misuse and violence, and the family and social networks likely to support, reject or even attack the person. Psychiatric patients and prisoners are often released into localities of 'concentrated poverty', where they are disproportionately exposed to both substance misuse and criminality. Accordingly they are disproportionately at prospective risk, as both victims and perpetrators. Thus a wise emphasis is implied here about an *ecological* approach to risk assessment and management (Silver *et al.*, 1999).

Conclusions

This chapter has placed psychiatric diagnosis into a social and historical context in order that forensic psychologists might reflect critically on their work when dealing with people with a diagnosis of mental illness. Psychologists, like psychiatrists, are agents of social control with divided loyalties between their clients, their employers and wider society. Psychologists, unlike psychiatrists, have the educational background to move, if they choose, from digital to analogue reasoning about the mentally abnormal offenders they encounter in their work. This provides an opportunity to challenge common assumptions about diagnosed 'mental illness' on a number of fronts.

'Mental illness' does not have to be seen as a biological condition, which psychologists either avoid cautiously and deferentially or deal with in terms of its peripheral behavioural fallout, when acting as handmaidens to psychiatry. As for risk assessment and management, psychologists, being less invested than medicine in Kraepelinian assumptions about categories, can ask more straightforward but sophisticated questions about the individual in their life context. They can more readily resist the seduction of diagnosis as a reductionist focus of explanation and prediction. In other words, the experience and behaviour of a mentally abnormal offender might be understood psychologically in the way that the experience and behaviour of any other person might.

Further Reading

Prins, H. (2005). *Offenders, deviants or patients?* London: Routledge.
One way of protecting ourselves against the risks of psychological as well as psychiatric reductionism is to read the work

of an experienced student of criminality and mental health from outside both disciplines. This book, in its third edition, is an excellent source in this regard. Prins is not particularly critical of psychiatric theory and practice (compared to some sources and arguments used in this chapter). However, the book is a very good transdisciplinary exploration of our topic of interest.

Bentall, R.P. (2003). *Madness explained: Psychosis and human nature*. London: Penguin.

This is a very comprehensive and clearly written account of psychosis from a psychological rather than psychiatric viewpoint. The author has spent his whole academic career investigating his topic in this way and this is reflected in the clarity and confidence of the text. Although readers from many backgrounds read this book and find it useful, it speaks most readily to psychologists working with those with a diagnosis of mental illness.

Horwitz, A.V. (2002). *Creating mental illness*. London: University of Chicago Press.

Given that psychiatric diagnosis has been controversial for so long, it is useful to review that contention in its social and historical context. This book provides such a review in a very accessible style. It also provides a book-length examination of a topic (disputes about mental illness) that, for reasons of space, can be offered only in summary form in this chapter.

References

Appelbaum, P.S., Robbins, P.C. & Roth, L.H. (1999). A dimensional approach to delusions: A comparison across delusional type and diagnosis. *American Journal of Psychiatry*, 156, 1938–1943.

Bateson, G., Jackson, D.D., Haley, J. & Weakland, J. (1956). Toward a theory of schizophrenia. *Behavioral Science*, 1, 251–264.

Bentall, R.P., Jackson, H., & Pilgrim, D. (1988). Abandoning the concept of schizophrenia: Some implications of validity arguments for psychological research into psychotic phenomena. *British Journal of Clinical Psychology*, 27, 303–324.

Blacker, D. & Tsuang, M.T. (1998). Classification and DSM-IV. In A.M. Nicholi Jr. (Ed.) *The Harvard guide to psychiatry*. London: Harvard University Press.

Bowlby, J. (1951). Maternal care and mental health. *Bulletin of the World Health Organization* (Monograph), 3, 355–534.

Brown, G.W., Harris, T.O. & Hepworth, C. (1995). Loss, humiliation and entrapment among women developing depression: A patient and non-patient comparison. *Psychological Medicine*, 25, 7–21.

Cohen, S. & Scull, A. (Eds.) (1985). *Social control and the state*. Oxford: Basil Blackwell.

Coulter, J. (1973). *Approaches to insanity*. London: Martin Robertson.

DH (2007). *Best practice in managing risk*. London: Department of Health.

Dohrenwend, B.P. (1998). A psychosocial perspective on the past and future of psychiatric epidemiology. *American Journal of Epidemiology*, 147(3), 222–229.

Engel, G.L. (1980). The clinical application of the biopsychosocial model. *American Journal of Psychiatry*, 137, 535–544.

Estroff, A. & Zimmer, C. (1994). Social networks, social support, and violence among persons with severe, persistent mental illness. In J. Monahan & H.E. Steadman (Eds.) *Violence and mental disorder: Developments in risk assessment*. Chicago, IL: University of Chicago Press.

Eysenck, H.J. (1975). *The future of psychiatry* London: Methuen.

Fisher, R.A. (1930). *The genetical theory of natural selection*. Oxford: Clarendon Press.

Goffman, E. (1971). *Relations in public: Microstudies of the public order*. New York: Harper.

Hale, N.G. (1995). *The rise and crisis of psychoanalysis in the United States: Freud and the Americans, 1917–1985*. New York: Oxford University Press.

Hambrecht, M. & Hafner, H. (1996). Substance abuse and the onset of schizophrenia. *Biological Psychiatry*, 40, 1155–1163.

Hiday, V. (1995). The social context of mental illness and violence. *Journal of Health and Social Behavior*, 36, 911–914.

Hinsie, L.E. (1931). Criticism of treatment and recovery in schizophrenia. *Proceedings of the Association for Research in Nervous and Mental Disease for 1928. Schizophrenia (dementia praecox)*. Baltimore, MD: Williams & Wilkins.

Junginger, J. (1995). Command hallucinations and the prediction of dangerousness. *Psychiatric Services*, 46, 911–914.

Kleinman, A. (1988). *Rethinking psychiatry*. New York: Free Press.

Kraepelin, E. (1883). *Compendium der Psychiatrie*. Leipzig.

Laajasalo, T. & Hakkanen, H. (2005). Offence and offender characteristics among two groups of Finnish homicide offenders with schizophrenia. *Journal of Forensic Psychiatry and Psychology*, 16(1), 41–50.

Laing, R.D. & Esterson, A. (1964). *Sanity, madness and the family*. Harmondsworth: Penguin.

Lindqvist, P. & Allebeck, P. (1989). Criminal homicide in North West Sweden 1970–1981. Alcohol intoxication, alcohol abuse and mental disease. *International Journal of Law and Psychiatry*, 8, 19–37.

Monahan, J. (1992). Mental disorder and violent behavior: Perceptions and evidence. *American Psychologist*, 47, 511–521.

McPherson, S. & Armstrong, D. (2006). Social determinants of diagnostic labels in depression. *Social Science and Medicine*, 62(1), 50–58.

McWilliams, N. (1994). *Psychoanalytic diagnosis: Understanding personality structure in the clinical process*. New York: Guilford Press.

Pavlov, I.P. (1941). *Lectures on conditioned reflexes: Vol. II. Conditioned reflexes and psychiatry* (trans. W.H. Gantt). London: Lawrence & Wishart.

Pilgrim, D. (2001). Disordered personalities and disordered concepts. *Journal of Mental Health, 10*(3), 253–265.

Pilgrim, D. (2007). New 'mental health' legislation for England and Wales: Some aspects of consensus and conflict. *Journal of Social Policy, 36*(1), 1–17.

Pilgrim, D. (2008). The legacy of eugenics in modern psychology and psychiatry. *International Journal of Social Psychiatry, 54*(3), 272–284.

Pilgrim, D. & Bentall, R.P. (1999). The medicalisation of misery: A critical realist analysis of the concept of depression. *Journal of Mental Health, 8*(3), 261–274.

Pilgrim, D., Kinderman, P. & Tai, S. (2008). Taking stock of the biopsychosocial model in the field of 'mental health care'. *Journal of Social and Psychological Sciences* (in press).

Pilgrim, D. & Rogers, D. (2003). Mental disorder and violence: An empirical picture in context. *Journal of Mental Health* 12, 1, 7–18.

Regier, D.A., Farmer, M.E., Rae, D.S., Locke, B.J., Keith, S.L., Judd, L.L. *et al.* (1990). Comorbidity of mental disorders with alcohol and other drug abuse: Results from the epidemiologic catchment area (ECA) study. *Journal of the American Medical Association, 264*, 2511–2518.

Rogers, A. & Pilgrim, D. (2003). *Mental health and inequality*. Basingstoke: Palgrave.

Rogers, A. & Pilgrim, D. (2005). *A sociology of mental health and illness*. Buckingham: Open University Press.

Scheff, T.J. (1966). *Being mentally ill: A sociological theory*. Chicago, IL: Chicago University Press.

Seligman, M.E.P. (1975). *Helplessness: On depression, development and death*. San Francisco, CA: Freeman.

Shaw, J., Hunt, I.M., Flynn, S., Meehan, J., Robinson, J., Bickley, H. *et al.* (2006). Rates of mental disorder in people convicted of homicide: National clinical survey. *British Journal of Psychiatry, 188*, 143–147.

Silver, E., Mulvey, E.P. & Monahan, J. (1999). Assessing violence among discharged psychiatric patients. Towards an ecological approach. *Law and Human Behavior, 23*, 237–255.

Soyka, M. (2000). Substance misuse, psychiatric disorder and violent and disturbed behaviour. *British Journal of Psychiatry, 176*, 345–350.

Steadman, H.J., Mulvey, E.P., Monahan, J., Robbins, P.C., Appelbaum P.S., Grisso, T. *et al.* (1998). Violence by people discharged from acute psychiatric inpatient facilities and by others in the same neighbourhood. *Archives of General Psychiatry, 55*, 109.

Stone, M. (1985). Shellshock and the psychologists. In W.F. Bynum, R. Porter & M. Shepherd (Eds.) *The anatomy of madness*. London: Tavistock.

Swanson, J.W. (1994). Mental disorder, substance abuse, and community violence: An epidemiological approach. In J. Monahan & H.J. Steadman (Eds.) *Violence and mental disorder: Developments in risk assessment*. Chicago, IL: University of Chicago Press.

Swartz, M.S., Swanson, J.W., Hiday, V.A., Borum, R., Wagner, H.R. & Burns, B.J. (1998). Violence and severe mental illness: The effects of drug abuse and non-adherence to medication. *American Journal of Psychiatry, 155*, 226–231.

Szasz, T.S. (1961). The use of naming and the origin of the myth of mental illness. *American Psychologist, 16*, 59–65.

Taylor, P.J. (1985). Motives for offending among violent psychotic men. *British Journal of Psychiatry, 147*, 491–498.

Watson, J.B. & Rayner, R. (1920). Conditioned emotional reactions. *Journal of Experimental Psychology, 10*, 421–428.

Wilson, M. (1993). DSM-III and the transformation of American psychiatry: A history. *American Journal of Psychiatry, 150*(3), 399–410.

Zona, M.A., Palarea, R.E. & Lane, J. (1998). Psychiatric diagnosis and the offender–victim typology of stalking. In J. Reid Meloy (Ed.) *The psychology of stalking: Clinical and forensic perspectives*. San Diego, CA: Academic Press.

19

Mentally Disordered Offenders
Intellectual Disability

William R. Lindsay and John L. Taylor

In developing this chapter, we have considered the postgraduate training requirements for forensic psychology published by The British Psychological Society. In stage one, these include four knowledge dimensions of the context of practice in forensic psychology, applications of psychology to processes within the justice system, working with specific client groups, and using and communicating information in practice. There are four core roles in which these knowledge dimensions are applied, and a theme stressed through all of the guidelines is the importance of research and the research base to the profession. We shall outline the main aspects of our knowledge in the field of forensic learning disabilities according to these dimensions and throughout we will emphasise the importance and reliance on research and its crucial underpinning of practice in the field.

We have used the term 'intellectual disabilities' (ID) to refer to the population of individuals studied. 'Learning disability' is a term synonymous with ID but used only in the UK and Ireland. Until recently, the term 'mental retardation' was used in the USA and widely across English-speaking countries. The American Association for Intellectual and Developmental Disabilities recently changed its title from Mental Retardation with an intention to change terms referring to the population more generally. However, workers and researchers in the field should know that these various terms are synonymous. We have used intellectual disability since it has gained international recognition with reference to the population.

The Context of Practice in Forensic Learning Disabilities

The British Psychological Society, along with other major international diagnostic classification systems such as ICD-10 (World Health Organization, 1992), DSM-IV (American Psychiatric Association, 1994) and the American Association on Intellectual and Developmental Disabilities (1992), includes the following three core criteria for ID.

Significant impairment of intellectual functioning

Assessment of intellectual functioning, particularly in forensic contexts, should be obtained using an individually administered, reliable and valid standardised test, such as the third edition of the Wechsler Adult Intelligence Scale (WAIS-III[UK]: Wechsler, 1999). Using such tests as the WAIS-III[UK], based on a normal distribution of general intelligence, a significant impairment of intellectual functioning is conventionally understood to be a score more than two standard deviations below the population mean. Therefore, significant impairment of intellectual functioning is generally defined as an IQ less than 70. Importantly, one must take into account the standard error of the test and psychologists should always consider the range of two standard errors as an appropriately cautious finding. One should be cautious about using shorter, less time-consuming assessments of cognitive functioning which estimate or screen for intellectual ability. There are a number of screening measures available to services, such as the Quick Test (Ammons & Ammons, 1958) or the Hayes Ability Screening Index (Hayes, 2000). Screening measures are designed to be over-inclusive in relation to the population and although they will generally have a high correlation with a more comprehensive measure of intellectual ability such as the WAIS, where there are errors they are likely to be overwhelmingly in one direction. Therefore they are more likely to misclassify individuals without ID as falling within the population.

Significant associated impairment of adaptive or social functioning

Adaptive functioning is a broad concept that is concerned with an individual's ability to cope with the day-to-day demands of their environment. It will include the skills necessary for independent functioning, domestic tasks and self-care skills in addition to a range of community integration abilities such as the use of public transport, shopping skills and the ability to use services such as banking, social services, leisure services and health services. As with cognitive assessments, there are a range of assessments of adaptive behaviour. The two in most common usage are the Vineland Adaptive Behaviour Scale (Doll, 1935) and the Adaptive Behaviour Scale – Residential and Community (2nd Edition) (ABS-RC:2) developed by the American Association on Intellectual and Developmental Disabilities (2008). Depending on the classification system, an individual must have at least two or three significant deficits in adaptive behaviour. The VABS has norms which allow the assessor to review an individual's adaptive behaviour in relation to the general population, while the ABS-RC:2 has norms which enable the assessor to gauge an individual's adaptive behaviour in relation to their peers in residential and community settings. An assessment of adaptive behaviour is considered essential in any classification of ID.

Age of onset within the developmental period before adulthood

There is general international consensus that the 'age of onset' criterion means below the age of 18 (e.g. American Psychiatric Association, 1994; British Psychological Society, 2000), although ICD-10 does not specify a criterion age. The important aspect is that the assessor should partial out intellectual deterioration that may be caused by traumatic injury or disease which has occurred in adulthood. The latter would be classified as acquired

impairment rather than developmental impairment. Therefore, an assessment of ID is not confined to current abilities but is also concerned with developmental experience and developmental skills.

Because ID is defined by intellectual ability, adaptive skills and age of onset, the population is by definition heterogeneous. This can be seen if one takes as an analogy individuals whose cognitive functioning is two standard deviations above the mean rather than below the mean – individuals who have an IQ of greater than 130 with a corresponding range of adaptive skills and developmental experiences and abilities; it seems fairly obvious that these classifications represent a cross-section of the population at a certain level of ability. Therefore, all of the fields of psychological inquiry are relevant, as they would be to any cross-section of the population. It follows that work on the range of offence categories, the range of witness and victim investigations and indeed the range of diagnostic categories are all relevant to people with ID.

Mental Health Legislation

Mental health legislation in the various jurisdictions of the UK has sections that concern detention for the assessment and treatment of people with ID who have offended or engaged in offending-like behaviour. The Mental Health Act (MHA) 1983 for England and Wales and the MHA 2006 for Scotland both contain categories of mental disorder termed 'mental impairment' and 'severe mental impairment'. The acts use the terms 'severe impairment' and 'significant impairment'. These legal categories are not synonymous with the clinical definition of ID, and while they contain two of the three core clinical criteria, they also include a criterion for 'abnormally aggressive or seriously irresponsible conduct'. The Acts do not operationally define 'significant' and 'severe' mental impairment, stating that the assessment of the degree of impairment is a matter for clinical judgement. However, the level of impairment (significant or severe) is important, as under the Acts different legal sanctions apply to respective classifications. For this reason, The British Psychological Society (2000) recommends that this judgement is based on a full assessment using a reliable and valid test such as the WAIS-III [UK] along with an appropriate assessment of adaptive behaviour. Significant impairment of intellectual function is represented by an IQ score between two and three standard deviations below the population mean and severe impairment is represented by a score of more than three standard deviations below the population mean.

During 2005–2006, there were a total of 25,740 admissions to NHS facilities (including high security hospitals) under the England and Wales MHA 1983 (The Information Centre, 2007). Of the 8435 detentions under civil sections of the Act during this period for which the category of mental disorder was recorded, less than 1 per cent were categorised as mental or severe mental impairment. However of the 1304 criminal detentions under court and prison disposals during the corresponding period, just over 4 per cent were categorised as mental or severe mental impairment. Assuming a normal distribution, the proportion of people in the general population with IQ scores under 70 is approximately 2.5 per cent. Thus it appears that around more than double the expected number of people with impaired intellectual functioning are being detained in NHS facilities under sections of the England and Wales MHA 1983. It should be remembered that these are generally secure facilities and, as we pointed out earlier, the evidence that people with ID commit more crime is highly equivocal.

Learning Disability and Crime

For almost two centuries, crime and learning disability have been linked with devastating effects on the population. Until the mid to late 19th century, people with ID were generally considered as a burden on society. Living conditions for people with ID were harsh, especially in urban areas, and in rural areas they tended to work long hours in poverty. Perception changed towards the end of the century and the population began to be viewed as a menace to society. Scheerenberger (1983) notes that 'By the 1880s, mentally retarded persons were no longer viewed as unfortunates or innocents who, with proper training, could fill a positive role in the home and/or community. As a class they had become undesirable, frequently viewed as a great evil of humanity, the social parasite, criminal, prostitute and pauper' (p.116). Terman (1911), an author of one of the earliest IQ tests, wrote that 'There is no investigator who denies the fearful role of mental deficiency in the production of vice, crime and delinquency … not all criminals are feebleminded but all feebleminded are at least potential criminals' (p.11). This cultural prejudice, coming from such an authoritative and, presumably, for the time, enlightened source (Terman), gives us today a flavour of the extent of these views that ID was a cause of crime.

Despite the long association between delinquency and low intellectual functioning, it is not clear whether people with ID commit more crime than those without ID (Lindsay et al., 2004e), or in fact whether the nature and frequency of offending by people with ID differs from that committed by offenders in the general population (Holland, 2004). In relation to the prevalence of offending, there are several methodological difficulties resulting in disparity across various studies (Lindsay et al., 2007a). One of the first problems is that studies have been conducted in a variety of settings, including prisons (MacEachron, 1979), high secure hospitals (Walker & McCabe, 1973), appearance at court (Messinger & Apfelberg, 1961), probation services (Mason & Murphy, 2002) and appearance at police stations (Lyall et al., 1995). In some settings, it has been reported that particular types of offences are overrepresented among offenders with ID. For example, in their classic study of secure hospitals in England, Walker and McCabe (1973) reviewed 331 men with ID who had committed offences and had been detained under hospital orders to secure provision in England and Wales. They found high rates of fire raising (15 per cent) and sexual offences (28 per cent) when compared with other groups in their secure hospital sample. In a more recent study, Hogue et al. (2006) reviewed a number of characteristics of offenders with ID across community, medium/low secure and high secure settings. They found that rates of arson in the index offence depended on the setting with low rates in the community setting (2.9 per cent) and higher rates in the medium/low secure setting (21.4 per cent). This is a clear example of the fact that the setting in which the data are collected is very likely to influence the results and subsequent conclusions about the population.

MacEachron (1979) noted a second source of influence on prevalence rates. She reviewed the literature for prevalence of offenders with ID in prisons and found a range of 2.6–9.6 per cent. She noted that these previous studies had used a variety of methods to identify intellectual disability and concluded that the methodological variation between studies might produce the highly diverse prevalence rates. In her own more carefully controlled study, employing recognised intelligence tests, she investigated 436 adult male offenders in Maine and Massachusetts State Penal Institutions and found prevalence rates of ID of 0.6–2.3 per cent. A third source of variation is inclusion criteria, particularly if those considered to be functioning in the borderline intelligence range are included. Hayes and McIlwain (1988) conducted a review of the prevalence of ID in the prison population of New South Wales, Australia. At the time, they noted that ID is associated with significant deficits in social and adaptive skills which may make these individuals vulnerable to risks and exploitations within the prison setting. Hayes (1991) commented on this study and others which revealed that approximately 2 per cent of the prison population in New South Wales had a measured IQ lower than 70. She also noted that approximately 10 per cent of individuals were placed in the borderline range of IQ between 70 and 80. Clearly, the inclusion of individuals with borderline intelligence significantly increases the prevalence rates and several studies have used an IQ of 80 or even 85 as a cut-off for intellectual disability (Noble & Conley, 1992).

The influence of social policy changes was demonstrated by Lund (1990) in a follow-up study of 91 offenders with ID on Statutory Care Orders in Denmark. He reported a doubling of the incidence of sex offending when comparing sentencing in 1973–1983 and suggested that this rise may have been a result of policies of deinstitutionalisation whereby people with ID are no longer detained in hospital for indeterminate lengths of time. He concluded that those with propensities towards offending would be more likely to be living in the community and, as a result, were likely to be subject to normal legal processes should they engage in offending behaviour. Since 1990, there has been an increase in the amount of research related to offenders with ID and especially related to those living in community settings. This increase in the knowledge base reflects similar changes in social policy, with widespread deinstitutionalisation policies throughout the developed world.

The methodological differences between studies continue, with two recent pieces of research finding markedly different rates of offenders with ID in prison settings. Crocker et al. (2007) attempted to assess 749 offenders in a pre-trial holding centre in Montreal. For a number of reasons, including refusal to participate, administrative difficulties and technical problems, they were only able to assess 281 participants with three subscales of a locally standardised mental ability scale. They reported that 18.9 per cent were in the probable ID range with a further 29.9 per cent in the borderline range. On the other hand, in a study of prisoners in Victoria, Australia, Holland et al. (2007) found a prevalence rate of less than 1.3 per cent using the Wechsler Adult Intelligence Scale. In the latter study, all prisoners were assessed routinely by trained forensic psychologists while, in the former study, only around one-third

of potential participants were included in the study. In the former study, three subscales of an intelligence test were used while, in the latter, a full WAIS was used for all participants. It is difficult to reconcile these two pieces of work but it is likely that the difference in assessment methods and comprehensiveness of the sample were significant contributors to the disparity and results.

Studies of recidivism rates for offenders with ID suffer from the same methodological and social policy influences. However, they do indicate that the contemporary scientific interest in the field extends back to the 1940s. Wildenskov (1962) reported a 20-year follow-up of offenders with ID and found a reoffending rate of around 50 per cent. While the sophistication of studies has improved considerably since this time, it does point out that a 20-year follow-up reported in 1962 requires data going back to at least 1942. Linhorst et al. (2003) followed up 252 convicted offenders with ID who had completed a case management community programme and found that 25 per cent who had completed the programme were re-arrested within six months while 43 per cent of those who dropped out were re-arrested during the same period. Klimecki et al. (1994) reported reoffending rates in previous prison inmates with ID, two years after their release. They found that overall, reoffending rates were 41.3 per cent, with higher rates for less serious offences. However, the lower reoffending rates (around 31 per cent) for sex offences, murder and violent offences were artificially reduced because a number of those individuals were still in prison and therefore unable to reoffend.

Owing to a lack of controlled studies involving ID and mainstream offenders, it is difficult to make direct comparisons of recidivism rates. However, it would appear that recidivism rates for offenders with ID are consistent with those for populations of mainstream offenders. In one recent study, Gray et al. (2007) conducted a two-year follow-up of 145 offenders with ID and 996 offenders without ID all discharged from independent sector hospitals in the UK. The ID group had a lower rate of reconviction for violent offences after two years (4.8 per cent) than the non-ID group (11.2 per cent). This trend also held true for general offences (9.7 per cent for the ID group and 18.7 per cent for the non-ID group).

While there is an established relationship between low IQ and offending (Farrington, 1995, 2004), most of the studies done in this area are investigating the predictive value or differences between groups at one or two standard deviations below the mean (IQ < 85). It is interesting to note the small amount of information which specifically reviews individuals with an IQ less than two standard deviations below the mean. McCord and McCord (1959) evaluated an interesting early intervention study with 650 underprivileged boys in Massachusetts. The Cambridge-Sommerville Youth Study was set up 'To prevent delinquency and to develop stable elements in the characters of children' (McCord & McCord, 1959, p.2). The boys were divided into 325 matched pairs and assigned to treatment and control conditions. There was a relationship between IQ and rates of conviction in that for the treatment group, 44 per cent of those in the IQ band 81–90 had a conviction while 26 per cent of those with an IQ above 110 had a conviction. However, the 10 per cent of individuals in the lowest IQ group (less than 80) had an intermediate rate of conviction at 35 per cent, that is, lower than that recorded in the IQ band 81–90. Furthermore, of those in the higher IQ band who were convicted of crime, none went to penal institutions, while the highest percentage going to penal institutions, 19 per cent, were in the lowest IQ band. The results were similar in the control group, with 50 per cent in the IQ band 81–90 convicted of crime and 25 per cent in the IQ band less than 80 convicted. Maughan et al. (1996) and Rutter et al. (1997) followed up children who had shown severe reading difficulties at school. It might be considered that a significant proportion of children with severe reading difficulties had developmental and intellectual disabilities. They found that the rate of adult crime among boys who had had significant reading difficulties was slightly lower than the rate of adult crime in the general population comparison group. This finding held true independent of psychopathology or social functioning. Similarly, antisocial behaviour in childhood was less likely to persist into adult life when it was accompanied by reading difficulties. Therefore, while the relationship between IQ and delinquency seems firmly established, there is some evidence that this relationship may not hold when considering individuals 1.5 or more standard deviations below the mean.

Applications of Psychology to Processes within the Justice System

People with ID are vulnerable within the criminal justice system at every stage since the degree of their disability can affect their ability to understand their rights on arrest, to deal with police questioning and interrogation,

to provide valid statements or confessions, to enter a plea, to understand court proceedings and to instruct their counsel. Therefore they are likely to be at considerable disadvantage from stages of apprehension through arrest, indictment and trial to conviction and sentencing. Responsibility and competence are key concepts in criminal justice systems around the world and are particularly pertinent in relation to offenders with ID. In the pre-trial phase, the issue of competence in relation to ID defendants is relevant to the individual's susceptibility to provide self-incriminatory statements or confessions and to enter a plea of guilty or not guilty. In England and Wales, the Police and Criminal Evidence Act (PACE) 1984 provides protection to people detained by the police for questioning. PACE and its accompanying codes of practice have particular provisions for people with ID with regard to police questioning and confessional evidence (Sanders & Young, 2000). It is now the practice across the UK that for those individuals with ID, or those who appear to have ID, police interviews require the presence of 'an appropriate adult'. An appropriate adult is different from a solicitor or legal adviser and can be a relative or guardian of the interviewee, someone with experience of working with the population such as a social worker, or, in Scotland, a member of the Appropriate Adult Service. These individuals are not employed by the police service.

The process of police interview

The issue of suggestibility of accused persons with ID during police interviews has received a significant amount of attention. Gudjonnson (1992) wrote that certain categories of people with ID were more susceptible to yielding to leading questions and shifting their answers under interrogation by police and, as such, were more suggestible and liable to give false information and a false confession. Clare and Gudjonnson (1993), in a study of 20 participants with ID compared with 20 participants of average intellectual ability, found that those with ID confabulated more and tended towards greater acquiescence. Everington and Fulero (1999) also found the participants with ID were more likely to alter their answers in response to negative feedback. Both studies concluded that people with mild ID were more suggestible under conditions of interrogative interview. However, Beail (2002) reviewed a number of studies which led him to question the link between the test situation and the real-life situation. He pointed out that the Gudjonnson Suggestibility Scales (GSS; Gudjonnson,

1997), which assessed suggestibility through memory of a narrative story, may be limited in their applicability to criminal justice proceedings because 'the results are based on an examination of semantic memory, whereas police interviews are more concerned with episodic or autobiographical event memory. Also, experienced events usually involve multi-modal sensory input, resulting in a more elaborate trace in associative memory' (p.135).

White and Willner (2004) tested this hypothesis with 20 individuals with ID by comparing their ability to recall information from a standard passage when compared to a further 20 who are asked to recall an actual experienced event. They found that participants recalled greater amounts of information and they were significantly less suggestible, in relation to the experienced situation when compared to the standard verbally presented passage. Willner (2008) also demonstrated a reduction in suggestibility when events were familiar to the individual being questioned. Willner (2009) summarises some of the research and also reviews The British Psychological Society guidelines on the assessment of mental capacity (BPS, 2006), which includes discussions of both capacity to appear as a witness and fitness to plead. He cleverly uses the illustrations in the BPS guidelines to undermine the assessor's reliance on the Gudjonnson Suggestibility Scales, pointing out that although the individual in the vignette is unable to retain much of the spoken passage, the individual displays an ability not to acquiesce to questions. We would not go so far as Willner in recommending that use of the GSS should be discontinued with people with ID. However, we would advise caution because of the effects reviewed by Willner (2009) and Beail (2002).

The legal process and offenders with ID

Having made these points with regard to suggestibility, there remain concerns regarding competency of people with ID in court proceedings because confessional evidence should be considered to be valid only if it is voluntary, knowing and intelligent (Baroff et al., 2004). People with ID can be vulnerable to coercion, threats and promises of leniency, thus raising concerns about the voluntary nature of their confessions. The understanding that one has a right to silence and to other rights to protect oneself is rarely tested in ID suspects and such interviewees may be more likely to answer questions in the manner and direction they believe they are expected to. Baroff (1996) has called this 'sociable

desirability bias'. In the stressful and confusing context of arrest and interrogation, it may be difficult for suspects with ID to make a reasoned choice concerning the information they will volunteer or withhold and such interviewees are perhaps unlikely to grasp fully the implications of their responses to police questions (Baroff et al., 2004). With regard to valid confessions, the suspect with ID may have difficulty understanding that in waiving rights, such as a right to silence, they are placing themselves in jeopardy.

In assessing competence or fitness to stand trial and enter a plea, a defendant's abilities in the following areas should be considered: (a) understanding of the crime of which they are accused; (b) knowledge of the purpose of the trial and the roles of the principal officers; and (c) ability to instruct one's counsel (Baroff et al., 2004). In England and Wales, if a defendant claims at trial to be unfit to stand trial because, as a result of their ID, they are unable to comprehend the trial or its processes, then a jury will consider the matter by hearing expert medical evidence. If it is decided that the defendant is not fit to stand trial then a 'trial of the facts' takes place in which the case against the defendant is tested. The outcome of this process cannot result in a conviction; however, one consequence might be that the defendant with ID is considered to have committed the offence without having had the opportunity to raise a defence. In this event, the court can make one of several orders, including an absolute discharge or admission to hospital under mental health legislation.

Research in the USA has indicated that the issue of competence to stand trial is introduced in just 5–7 per cent of cases, with only 16 per cent of those defendants being deemed as incompetent to stand trial (Hurley, 2003). There are a number of assessments for testing a defendant's understanding of court proceedings, all based on the criminal justice procedures in the USA. The Competence Assessment to Stand Trial – Mental Retardation (CAST-MR: Everington & Luckasson, 1992) assesses competence in three areas related to court systems – basic legal concepts, skills to assist the defence counsel and understanding of court procedures. The CAST-MR was used by 45 per cent of psychologists surveyed about practices used when evaluating juvenile competence to stand trial (Ryba et al., 2003). However, this and similar assessments have a number of limitations, including the lack of an underlying conceptual structure, no standardised administration procedures, no criterion-based scoring and limited normative data (Otto et al., 1998).

In addition to the issue of competence to stand trial is the issue of responsibility in criminal law. The commission of a criminal act (*actus reus*) is distinguished from the intent to commit a crime (*mens rea*) and historically, people with severe ID were considered incapable of forming such intent and were thus not responsible for their actions (Fitch, 1992). Traditionally, in the English criminal justice system the judgement on responsibility for a person with ID was made in terms of their ability to distinguish right from wrong. However, more recently the courts have moved away from this dichotomous approach to 'moral understanding' in favour of case-by-case considerations (Baroff *et al.*, 2004).

In the legal system in England and Wales, *mens rea* is considered only in relation to serious crimes of murder, rape and violence. A lack of *mens rea* means that the person's powers of reasoning have been affected by a disease of the mind (including ID). It must be established that the defective reason resulted in either the defendant not knowing what they were doing, or not knowing that what they did was legally wrong (as opposed to morally wrong). Usually an attempt to claim a lack of *mens rea* in effect results in a defence of not guilty by reason of insanity (Baroff *et al.*, 2004). A defence of diminished responsibility is pertinent only to the charge of murder and, if accepted, results in a conviction of manslaughter. Diminished responsibility requires impaired mental responsibility for one's acts as a result of an 'abnormality of the mind' (Homicide Act, 1957). Intellectual disability can be considered as an abnormality of the mind causing diminished responsibility that results in a person's involvement in a killing. If, on the balance of probabilities, diminished responsibility is proven, a range of sentencing options for manslaughter are available to the court, as opposed to the mandatory penalty of life imprisonment for murder. In both the defences of insanity and diminished responsibility, the courts will seek expert evidence to assist them in determining if there was, in individual cases, defective reasoning or impaired mental responsibility.

In summary, there have been a number of important developments in relation to the criminal justice system concerning the assessment of responsibility and competency that acknowledge that defendants with ID require accommodation and special consideration in order to participate in legal procedures in a valid and just manner. Psychologists have been involved in the assessment of such competence through the use of cognitive assessments, the use of assessments concerning understanding of criminal justice processes and through assessments of ability to cope with the police investigative system.

Working with Offenders with ID

Assessment issues

The guidelines for the Diploma in Forensic Psychology indicate that candidates should be able to deal with assessment and intervention within the justice system as well as assessment and intervention with offenders themselves. We have already dealt with assessment related to the justice system in previous sections on the way that psychology is applied to the legal process. In this section, we will confine ourselves to assessment of offenders and the way in which assessment has been developed to inform on strengths and deficits and monitor and guide the treatment process. There have been several significant developments in assessment related to people with ID in general and offenders in particular. These fall into two broad categories, both of which have the same aims.

Firstly, it is important that any assessment can be understood by the clients completing it. Since this client group is typified by significant deficits in literary and comprehension skills, all assessments must be suitably adapted to simplify the language and concepts employed. Lindsay and Skene (2007) give an example of the way in which an assessment can be extremely complex in its conceptual structure and requires adaptation. One item on the Beck Depression Inventory (BDI; Beck *et al.*, 1995) deals with the extent to which the respondent feels guilty. As with all the questions, it is arranged on a four-point Likert scale indicating increased levels of emotion, in this case 'guilt'. However, as the response increases from 0 to 3, the concept of guilt and responsibility shifts from feeling guilty about one's actions to feeling guilty for everything bad that happens in the world. Lindsay and Skene (2007) found that the concept required simplification to deal in a straightforward fashion with personal feelings of guilt, from feeling no guilt to feeling extremely guilty, without the complicating aspect of feeling responsible for all human disasters and atrocities. A more obvious simplification is that of language. The Bumby Rape and Molest Scales have been shown to be reliable and valid with mainstream sex offenders (Bumby, 1996). However, they are difficult to use with sex offenders with ID because of the linguistic complexity of the items. Therefore, simplification of language and conceptual structure is crucial so that the assessment is basically usable in the context of forensic ID.

The second consideration, and an important one in the context of lengthy forensic assessments, is that, because of literacy deficits, all material will have to be read and explained to respondents. Therefore both the item and the response categories require to be explained. These issues have been dealt with extensively elsewhere (e.g. Lindsay, 2008; Taylor & Novaco, 2005) and it is not our intention to review them in detail here. However, this has two consequences. Assessment will take much longer as it is impossible to give the respondent a series of questionnaires and receive them back the following week. Secondly, because the assessor has to read the item and explain the responses, all such assessments take the form of a structured interview. The respondent's reactions to questions, their tangential comments and their emotional response will all be available to the assessor as part of the process. This is an enormous strength of conducting assessments with this client group and it is information that can add to the richness of any assessment process and report.

It is now clear that the adaptations required for assessment of offenders with ID are extensive. Both the assessment instrument and the process require a different approach. Following on from this, it is extremely important that the psychometric properties of the assessment remain intact and that the integrity of the process is not undermined or reduced by these adaptations. One of the first studies in this regard was conducted by Lindsay *et al.* (1994) when they investigated the psychometric properties of several psychological assessments with 73 participants with intellectual disability. All participants were taking part in a study on community living and community integration and, as such, were representative of a heterogeneous population of people with mild ID. They found that adapted versions of the Zung Anxiety Scale, the Zung Depression Inventory and the Goldberg Health Questionnaire could be used reliably by participants. In addition, there was a highly significant degree of convergent validity among the tests. As a further indication of validity, the assessments of emotion had a significant, orderly relationship with the Eysenk–Withers Personality Test in that they correlated positively with the neuroticism factor but not at all with the extraversion factor. This was an early indication that suitably adapted assessments could be used effectively with this client group.

Finlay and Lyons (2001) reviewed the available literature on the assessment of emotion and other psychotherapeutic issues in people with ID and concluded that there was ample evidence that suitably adapted assessments could be understood and used appropriately by the client group. In addition, there was a lesser amount of emerging evidence that these assessments retained their psychometric properties during these studies.

Since the publication of these studies, there have been a few further pieces of work on generic populations of people with ID, strengthening the conclusions. Kellet *et al.* (2004) conducted a factor analytic study of the Brief Symptom Inventory (BSI). The BSI screens for symptoms related to somatisation, interpersonal sensitivity, anxiety, depression, phobia, paranoid ideation, hostility, psychoticism and obsessive compulsive disorders. They had previously established the usability and reliability of the BSI (Kellet *et al.*, 2003) and in this subsequent study, in addition to further evidence on reliability, they found that the factor structure when used with this client group was essentially similar to the original studies on mainstream populations. Lindsay and Skene (2007), in a study of 108 individuals with ID, reported that the Beck Anxiety Inventory and Beck Depression Inventory both had similar factor structures when used with this client group in comparison to mainstream populations. Therefore, there is a significant amount of emerging evidence that when assessments are suitably adapted to aid understanding in people with ID, they can be used effectively to reflect emotional states and other issues relevant to therapeutic input and their psychometric integrity remains broadly intact. In fact, the BSI is an extremely useful assessment to screen for a range of problems in offenders with ID. Any indications of difficulty can be followed up with other, offence-specific assessments discussed later in this chapter.

Assessment of anger and aggression

Aggression and anger in individuals with ID are areas which have attracted a reasonable amount of research when compared with other areas of socio-affective functioning. Studies by Benson and Ivins (1992) and Rose and West (1999) have indicated that a modified self-assessment measure of anger reactivity ('the anger inventory') has some limited reliability and validity with people with ID. Oliver *et al.* (2007) reported that the Modified Overt Aggression Scale (MOAS; Sorgi et al., 1991), an informant-rated measure of the frequency and severity of aggression, had high levels of inter-rater reliability when administered for a small number of people with ID as part of a treatment outcome research study.

Novaco and Taylor (2004) evaluated the reliability and validity of several specially modified anger assessment measures with detained male offenders with ID. The Novaco Anger Scale (NAS; Novaco, 2003), the Spielberger State-Trait Anger Expression Inventory (STAXI; Spielberger, 1996), both self-report measures of anger disposition, and the Provocation Inventory (PI; Novaco, 2003), a self-report anger reactivity scale, along with the Ward Anger Rating Scale and the informant-related anger attributes measure (WARS; Novaco, 1994) were evaluated. The modified anger self-report measures were found to have high internal consistency and less robust, but reasonable, test–retest reliability. The STAXI and NAS showed substantial inter-correlation, providing evidence for the concurrent validity of these instruments. WARS staff ratings of patient anger were found to have high internal consistency and to correlate significantly with patient anger self-reports. Anger, self-reported by the patients, was significantly related to their record of assault behaviour in hospital. The NAS was found to be significantly predictive of whether the patient has physically assaulted others following admission to hospital and total number of physical assaults carried out.

In a further development, Taylor et al. (2004a) developed the Imaginal Provocation Test (IPT) as an additional idiographic anger assessment procedure with people with ID that taps key elements of the experience and expression of anger, is sensitive to change associated with anger treatment and is easily modifiable for idiographic uses. The IPT produces four indices relevant to the individual client's experience of anger: anger reaction, behavioural reaction, a composite of anger and behavioural reaction, and anger regulation. They administered the IPT to 48 patients prior to beginning an anger treatment and showed that the indices had respectable internal reliabilities and reasonable concurrent validity when correlated with the STAXI and NAS. Therefore it would appear that there are rapid, flexible and sensitive idiographic assessments of anger among people with ID and that these assessments have reasonable psychometric properties.

Alder and Lindsay (2007) also produced a Provocation Inventory (Dundee Provocation Inventory, DPI) which is easily accessible and easy to use. It is based on Novaco's

(1975, 1994) analysis and construction of anger as an emotional problem. One of the facets of Novaco's analysis is that the individual may misconstrue internal and external stimuli and respond to a perception of threat rather than a more appropriate, less aggressive response. The DPI was administered to 114 referrals with ID and Alder and Lindsay (2007) found good reliability and convergent validity. The DPI correlated significantly with the NAS ($r = .57$) and highly significantly with the PI ($r = .75$), indicating that the DPI and PI have good convergence. They also found a five-factor structure consisting of threat to self-esteem, external locus of control, disappointment, frustration and resentment. The strongest factor was threat to self-esteem, and this certainly accords with Novaco's analysis of anger and its relationship with threat. The factors can also be considered as basic self-schemata, and self-esteem has been considered a major dynamic risk factor in sex offenders by several authors (Beech et al., 2002; Boer et al., 2004). Therefore, the DPI may provide a quick assessment of provocation in relation to a range of relevant factors in offenders with ID.

Willner et al. (2005) developed the Profile of Anger Coping Skills (PACS) to assess the use by people with ID of specific skills in managing angry situations. Informants are asked to rate client's use of eight anger management strategies in specific anger coping situations salient to that individual. The strategies assessed include use of relaxation skills, counting to 10, walking away calmly, requesting help, use of distraction activities, cognitive reframing and being assertive. The PACS was found to have acceptable test, retest and inter-rater reliability coefficients. The PACS was also shown to be sensitive to change associated with an anger intervention. Following involvement in a community-based anger management group, informants reported that clients' PACS scores were significantly improved compared with scores for clients in a no-treatment control group. The treatment group participants' coping skills had improved significantly in terms of cognitive reframing, assertiveness, walking away and asking for help. These latter two areas of skill improvement were maintained at six-month follow-up. One of the most important aspects of this study and its method of assessment is that it attests to the importance of anger management treatment and the concepts employed. For many individuals, counting to 10 and relaxing (calming down) are the most common pieces of advice given to clients. It may also be thought that the relaxation component is the most important in anger management treatment.

However, by these reports, these two skills were used least frequently in the range of anger coping skills developed during treatment.

Assessment for sexual offenders

Some work has been completed on knowledge and beliefs in relation to sexual interaction with sex offenders with ID. With this client group, it is important not only to review cognitive distortions but also to consider the level of sexual knowledge an individual may have. Indeed, one of the first hypotheses put forward to account for inappropriate sexual behaviour in this group was that lack of sexual knowledge may lead the individual to attempt inappropriate sexual contact precisely because they are unaware of the means to establish appropriate interpersonal and sexual relationships. This hypothesis of 'counterfeit deviance' was first mentioned by Hingsburger *et al.* (1991) and has been recently reviewed and revised to account for more recent research findings by Lindsay (2008). The term refers to behaviour which is undoubtedly deviant but may be precipitated by factors such as lack of sexual knowledge, poor social and heterosexual skills, limited opportunities to establish sexual relationships and sexual naivety rather than a preference or sexual drive towards inappropriate objects. Following this, remediation should focus on educational issues and developmental maturation rather than inappropriate sexuality. Griffiths *et al.* (1989) gave a number of examples illustrating the concept of counterfeit deviance and developed a treatment programme, part of which was based significantly on sexual and social education.

In a review of variables associated with the perpetration of sexual offences in men with ID, Lindsay (2005) noted that, surprisingly, there were no controlled tests on this hypothesis. Counterfeit deviance would suggest that some men with ID commit sexual offences because they have poorer social and sexual knowledge, do not understand the rules and conventions of society and are unaware of taboos relating to sexuality. Therefore, men with ID who have committed sexual offences should have poorer social and sexual knowledge than those who do not.

There have now been two tests of this hypothesis. Michie *et al.* (2006) completed a test of counterfeit deviance by comparing the sexual knowledge of groups of sex offenders with ID and control participants using the Socio-Sexual Knowledge and Attitudes Test (SSKAT; Griffiths & Lunsky 2003; Wish *et al.*, 1979). In the first study comparing 17 sex offenders with 20 controls, they found that of 13 subscales in the SSKAT, three comparisons, birth control, masturbation and sexually transmitted diseases, showed significant differences between the groups and in each case the sex offenders had higher levels of sexual knowledge. There were no differences between the groups on age or IQ. In a second comparison, 16 sex offenders were compared with 15 controls. There were significant differences between the groups on seven scales and in each case the sex offenders showed a higher level of sexual knowledge. These authors then pooled the data for all 33 sex offenders and 35 control participants. They found a significant positive correlation between IQ and SSKAT total score for the control group ($r = .71$) but no significant relationship between IQ and SSKAT total score for the sex offender cohort ($r = .17$). They presented two possible reasons for this finding. The first was that, by definition, all of the sex offender cohort have some experience of sexual interaction. It is unlikely that these experiences of sexual interaction are random and one might therefore conclude that these sex offenders have given some thought and attention to sexuality at least in the period prior to the perpetration of the inappropriate sexual behaviour or sexual abuse. Therefore, we can be sure that they have at least some experience of sexual activity, which is not the case for the control participants. The second possible explanation was that these individuals might have a developmental history of increased sexual arousal. This in turn may have led to selective attention and interest in sexual information gained from informal sources. Such persistence of attention would lead to greater retention of information through rehearsal and perhaps to a higher level of associated appropriate sexual activity such as masturbation. These behavioural and informal educational experiences would lead to a higher level of sexual knowledge. This latter hypothesis, sexual arousal and sexual preference, is hypothesised to have an interactive effect with knowledge acquisition and, perhaps, attitudes and beliefs.

In the second, more sensitive comparison, Lunsky *et al.* (2007) once again compared sexual offenders with controls but divided the sexual offenders into deviant persistent offenders (those who committed contact sexual offences and offences against children) and naive offenders (public masturbation, indecent exposure). They found that the naive offenders did indeed have a lower level of sexual knowledge than the deviant offenders, although the naive offenders did not have poorer knowledge than the control group, as might be expected from the counterfeit deviance hypothesis. However, the fact that they found differences in these subgroups of sexual offenders with ID underlines the importance of assessment of sexual knowledge.

Although a number of assessments have been developed to assess cognitive distortions in sex offenders, as has been pointed out earlier, the language requires to be simplified considerably in order to be understood by individuals with ID. Kolton et al. (2001) employed the Abel and Becker Cognitions Scale and found that the response options of the test needed to be changed from a four choice system (1 = agree, 4 = strongly disagree) to a dichotomous system (agree/disagree) to reduce extremity bias in the sample. The revised assessment provided 'adequate' total score to item correlations and test–retest reliability, and internal consistency was 'acceptable' (values not reported) and preserved the psychometric integrity of the assessment. As has been pointed out, other tests such as the Bumby Rape and Molest Scales have not been used with this client group but have the drawbacks of having contained in their syntax, complex concepts, difficult words and complex response choices.

There have been a number of more recent developments specific to the assessment of sex offenders with ID. Keeling et al. (2007a) investigated the psychometric properties of adapted versions of a number of assessments relevant to this population. One of the difficulties of their study was that it was a population of convenience and in the Australian Correctional System, the population of 'special needs offenders' had been identified. This population was more diverse than offenders with ID and included significant literacy deficits, the presence of an acquired brain injury and poor communication skills. Although their population was predominantly individuals with ID, it also included men with borderline intelligence and even low average IQ and they had access to only a small sample of 16 men with special needs. In order to assess the validity and integrity of their adaptations, they compared these individuals with 53 mainstream sexual offenders. They found that the Social Intimacy Scale, the Criminal Sentiment Scale and the Victim Empathy Distortion Scale broadly retained their psychometric integrity after adaptation and simplification. Their least successful adaptation was in the Relationship Scale Questionnaire which had low internal consistency. Test–retest reliability was high and there were good correlations between the original and adapted versions, especially for the Social Intimacy Scale and the Victim Empathy Scale.

Williams et al. (2007) also assessed the psychometric properties of six self-report measures with sex offenders with ID. Their population was 211 men who had undertaken HM Prison Services' adapted sex offender treatment programme. Average IQ was 71.9 and the accepted participants had an IQ up to 80, well outside the range of ID. However, the literacy skills seem similar in that they were required to read all the questionnaires to participants and aid them with their answers. Three assessments had good internal consistency and the other three were reasonable. Factor analyses revealed interesting structures but accounted for a low 30–40 per cent of the common variance. Unfortunately, because of time constraints, test–retest reliability was not conducted.

Lindsay et al. (2007b) reported on the development of the Questionnaire on Attitudes Consistent with Sexual Offences (QACSO) which is designed to be suitable for offenders with ID. The QACSO contains a series of scales which evaluate attitudes across a range of different types of offence, including rape and attitudes to women, voyeurism, exhibitionism, dating abuse, homosexual assault, offences against children and stalking. They compared 41 sex offenders with ID, 34 non-sexual offenders with ID, 30 non-offenders with ID and 31 non-ID controls who had not committed sexual offences. They ensured that all items had an appropriate reading-ease score and the response choices were dichotomous. The assessment was revised following tests of reliability, discriminant validity and internal consistency in order to ensure that all three psychometric properties were robust. They found that six of the seven scales in the QACSO were valid and reliable measures of cognitive distortions held by sex offenders with ID (the exception was homosexual assault). Lindsay et al. (2006a) also found that the rape and offences against children scale in particular discriminated between offenders against adults and offenders against children in the hypothesised direction, with offenders against adults having higher scores on the rape scale and lower scores on the offences against children scale than child molesters. Therefore, it would appear that cognitive distortions in sex offenders with ID can be assessed with some reliability and validity. However, these authors were cautious when considering the relationship of cognitive distortions to risk. They wrote that changes in attitudes may reflect a number of processes such as suppression, influence by social desirability and even lying. They recommended that the results from the QACSO should be considered in relation to a range of risk assessment variables, including actuarial risk, socio-affective functioning and self-regulation abilities.

Assessment of fire raising

Despite the importance of this issue in societal terms, there are relatively few published studies concerning the assessment and treatment of adult fire setters, and the literature concerning clinical practice with fire setters with ID is even more limited. Murphy and Clare (1996) interviewed 10 fire setters with ID concerning their cognitions and feelings prior to, and after setting fires using a newly developed Fire Setting Assessment Schedule (FSAS). Participants were also asked to rate their feelings in relation to a series of fire-related situations described in a new 14-item Fire Interest Rating Scale (FIRS). The construction of the FSAS was guided by the functional analytical approach to fire setting proposed by Jackson et al. (1987) in which it is proposed that fire setting is associated with a number of psychological functions, including the need for peer approval, need for excitement, a need to alleviate or express sadness, mental illness, a wish for retribution and a need to reduce anxiety.

Murphy and Clare (1996) found that the participants in their study identified antecedents to fire setting with more reliability than consequences. The most frequently endorsed antecedents were anger, followed by being ignored and then feelings of depression. This assessment has proven to be clinically useful since its inception, but there had been little further research on its reliability and validity until Taylor et al. (2002b) used the FSAS in the assessment and treatment of a group of 14 people with ID to review the effectiveness of a fire-setting programme for this client group. Consistent with the results of Murphy and Clare (1996), Taylor et al. (2002) found that anger, being ignored and depression (in rank order) were the most frequently endorsed items on the FSAS in terms of antecedents to and consequences of participants' fire-setting behaviour. In a further study on women with ID who had set fires, Taylor et al. (2006) also found that anger and depression were the most frequently endorsed items in participants prior to fire-raising incidents.

Risk assessment

Assessment of risk for future offences has emerged as one of the most important fields in forensic psychology over the past 20 years. In one of the original studies,

Harris et al. (1993) assessed a range of variables for their utility in differentiating between a large group of released offenders who had not reoffended and another large group who had reoffended. After they identified a number of candidate variables, they constructed a regression model which was extremely powerful in predicting recidivists and non-recidivists. In turn, from this they developed the Violence Risk Appraisal Guide (Quinsey et al., 1998, 2005), which is one of the most frequently employed risk assessments based on actuarial variables. In fact, the variables outlined by Harris et al. (1993) have essentially formed the basis of most subsequent risk assessments, comprising as they do items related to childhood adjustment, adult adjustment, diagnostic information and criminal history. Lindsay and Beail (2004) reviewed this literature, noting that there had not been a great deal of application in the field of forensic ID. They suggested a number of ways in which it might be relevant and applied to this client group.

Studies have now emerged which suggest that risk prediction in this population, with suitably tailored risk assessments, may be as valid as prediction for mainstream offenders. Lindsay et al. (2004b) conducted a study to review the predictive value of a range of previously identified variables in relation to recidivism for 52 male sex offenders with ID. The significant variables to emerge from the regression models were generally similar to those variables which had been identified in mainstream studies. However, employment history, criminal lifestyle, criminal companions, diverse sexual crimes and deviant victim choice, which had been highly associated with recidivism in studies on mainstream offenders, did not emerge as predictor variables. On the other hand, variables related to staff behaviour and attitudes did emerge as strong predictors. These authors considered that this may be an indication of the way in which professionals making up assessments in this field should adjust their perceptions. For example, while few individuals with ID have an employment history, they are likely to have alternative regimes of special educational placement, occupational placement and the like, which make up a weekly routine of engagement with society. Non-compliance with this regime did emerge as a significant variable, suggesting that individuals with ID should be judged in relation to their peers. It may be that probation officers, used to mainstream offenders and their employment histories, may consider the occupational placement of an ID offender as tedious or boring or they may make allowances for the individual on the basis of their disability. Lindsay (2005, 2008) has written of the theoretical and practical importance of engaging offenders with ID with society in the form of interpersonal contacts, occupational/educational placements and so on. Therefore, to excuse an offender on the basis of their intellectual disability may be precisely the wrong thing to do. In another early report on sexual offenders, Tough (2001) found that the Rapid Risk Assessment for Sex Offender Recidivism (RRASOR; Hanson, 1997) had a medium effect size in predicting recidivism for a cohort of 81 participants. Subsequently, Harris and Tough (2004) reported that they employed the RRASOR as a means of allocating sex offender referrals to their service and, by accepting referrals of only low or medium risk, they targeted limited resources on appropriate individuals.

Quinsey et al. (2004) conducted a rigorous assessment of the Violence Risk Appraisal Guide (VRAG; Quinsey et al., 1998) in a 16-month follow-up of 58 participants with ID. They found a significant predictive value with a medium effect size and that staff ratings of client behaviour significantly predicted antisocial incidents. Gray et al. (2007) conducted a more extensive investigation into the VRAG, HCR-20 (Webster et al., 1997) and the Psychopathy Checklist – Revised (PCL-R: Hare, 1991). They compared 145 patients with ID and 996 mainstream patients all discharged from hospital having been admitted with serious mental illness, ID or personality disorder; and having been convicted of a criminal offence or having exhibited behaviour that might have led to a conviction in different circumstances. They found that all of the assessments predicted reconviction rates in the ID sample with an effect size as large or larger than the mainstream sample. All of the predictions for the VRAG, HCR-20 and Psychopathy Checklist – Screening Version were in excess of Receiver Operator Characteristics auc (area under curve) of .73 (medium to large effect size). For the HCR-20, the effect size was large (auc = .79).

In a further risk assessment comparison study, Lindsay et al. (2008b) employed a mixed group of 212 violent and sexual offenders with ID. They followed up participants for one year and found that the VRAG was a reasonable predictor for future violent incidents (auc = .72), the Static-99 was a reasonable predictor for future sexual incidents (auc = .71) and the RM2000 predicted somewhat less well for violent (auc = .61) and sexual (auc = .62) incidents. Since the RM2000 is relatively simple to use, these authors wrote that research should not be discouraged on this instrument because it has

considerable potential utility if it can be found to have similar predictive ability to other assessments. The study did give further validation to both the VRAG and Static-99 for use with this client group. Employing the same samples, Taylor et al. (2007) have reviewed the psychometric properties and predictive validity of the HCR-20. They found that inter-rater reliability was acceptable at over 80 per cent agreement for all scales and Cronbach's Alpha was acceptable for the H Scale (.75) but low for the C and R Scales (.59 and .39 respectively). Exploratory factor analysis found that the H Scale constituted three factors (delinquency, interpersonal functioning and personality disorder) while the C and R Scales made up distinct separate factors. They also found that the R Scale had the highest predictive value in relation to recorded incidents over a period of a year. They concluded that the HCR-20 was a robust instrument for guiding clinical judgement which would help clinicians to reach clinically consistent and defendable decisions.

All of these risk assessments have focused on static/actuarial variables which are either immutable or difficult to change in the person's history. Quinsey et al. (2004) also assessed the value of dynamic/proximal risk indicators. They found that in the month prior to a violent or sexual incident, dynamic indicators of antisociality were significantly higher than values recorded six months prior to the incident. This, they concluded, provided persuasive evidence of the value of dynamic assessment since the increase in dynamic risk factors one month prior to the offence could not be attributed to any bias in the light of an offence occurring. Employing a similar design, Lindsay et al. (2004c) tested the Dynamic Risk Assessment and Management System (DRAMS) on which staff made daily ratings of clients' mood, antisocial behaviour, aberrant thoughts, psychotic symptoms, self-regulation, therapeutic alliance, compliance with routine and renewal of emotional relationships. Ratings were compared between those taken on the day of the incident, the day prior to the incident and a further control day at least seven days distant from an incident. Although there were only five clients with full datasets on appropriate days, there were significant increases in ratings for the day prior to the incident for mood, antisocial behaviour, aberrant thoughts and DRAMS total score. Steptoe et al. (2008) conducted a larger study on the predictive utility of the DRAMS with 23 forensic patients in a high secure setting. Predictions were made against independently collected incident data and concurrent validity was assessed against the Ward Anger

Rating Scale (WARS; Novaco & Taylor, 2004). The sections of mood, antisocial behaviour and intolerance/agreeableness had significant predictive values with incidents (auc > .70) and there were highly significant differences, with large effect sizes, between assessments taken one or two days prior to an incident and control assessments conducted at least seven days from an incident. Therefore, dynamic risk assessment appears to perform well in both concurrent and predictive validity in relation to offenders with ID.

Further developments have been conducted using other assessments. Hogue et al. (2007) evaluated the utility of the Emotional Problem Scale (EPS; Prout & Strohmer, 1991) with 172 offenders with ID from a range of security settings. The EPS is generally considered to be a dynamic assessment of emotion and self-concept and these authors, using the assessment on only a single occasion, found that the derived scores successfully predicted recorded incidents over a period of a year with a medium to large effect size. Morrissey and her colleagues (Morrissey et al., 2005, 2007a, 2007b) have investigated the utility, discriminative validity and predictive validity of the PCL-R and found that it predicts both good response to treatment and positive moves from high to medium secure conditions, both within two years of assessment. However, it did not predict institutional violence at a better level than chance. Therefore, there are a number of studies, using a range of assessments, some of which are developed for this client group, which are promising in terms of the utility and validity of risk prediction for offenders with ID.

Conclusions on assessment

There have been recent important developments in research related to a number of assessments for offence-related issues in populations with ID. The most notable of these are assessments on anger and assessments on cognitive distortions related to sexual offending. Both of these groups of assessments are framed in terms of a cognitive approach which will inform on and monitor cognitive behaviour therapy for these offence-related problems. Our knowledge on static risk factors has begun to develop considerably and there have now been a few studies on the validity of risk assessments for this client group. These studies have found predictive results that are broadly consistent with the literature on mainstream offending. Studies on dynamic risk factors have confirmed their relevance in the prediction of incidents.

Intervention with Offenders with ID

There is a reasonable research base for intervention in two main areas of offender treatment: violence and sexual offending. The best developed of these are treatments for violent and aggressive behaviour and the most extensive literature concerning treatment of aggression is in the Applied Behavioural Analysis (ABA) field. Taylor and Novaco (2005) summarised the literature in this area, describing several extensive reviews, and concluding that the ABA-type behavioural interventions that are generally applied to low-functioning individuals in institutional settings may not be as effective for anger and aggression problems observed in forensic ID populations. These populations are relatively high functioning in intellectual terms, display low frequency but very serious aggression and violence, and live in relatively uncontrolled environments. The majority of research on interventions for aggression with offenders with ID has evaluated the anger management treatment approach of Novaco (1975, 1994). In contrast to ABA-type treatments, anger management is a 'self-actualising' treatment that promotes generalised self-regulation of anger and aggression. The approach employs cognitive restructuring, arousal reduction and behavioural skills training. Importantly, anger management treatment incorporates Meichenbaum's (1985) stress inoculation paradigm.

Taylor (2002) and Taylor and Novaco (2005) reviewed a number of case series studies and uncontrolled group anger treatment studies involving individual and group therapy formats, incorporating combinations of cognitive behavioural techniques including relaxation and arousal reduction, skills training and self-monitoring. Generally they produced good outcomes in reducing anger and aggression and these were maintained at follow-up. Several case studies have reported successful outcomes in people with histories of aggressive behaviour in hospital and community settings (Black & Novaco, 1993; Murphy & Clare, 1991; Rose & West, 1999). There have also been a small number of studies of cognitive behavioural anger treatment involving offenders with ID that have yielded positive outcomes. Allan et al. (2001b) and Lindsay et al. (2003) reported on group behavioural anger interventions for a series of five women and six men with ID respectively. The participants in these studies were living in community settings and they had all been referred following violent assaults resulting in criminal justice system involvement.

In both studies, improvements were reported for all participants at the end of treatment that were maintained at 15-month follow-up. Burns *et al.* (2003) reported on the results of a CBT-framed group anger management intervention for three offenders with ID residing in a specialist NHS medium secure unit. Using multiple assessment points to carry out time series analyses, the results for the participants were mixed in terms of self-reported anger and informant-related aggression measures. The authors suggested that the relatively short length of the modified intervention and unstable baseline measures contributed to limited treatment effects observed.

More recently, there have been a number of treatment trials that have shown the effectiveness of group cognitive behavioural anger treatment over waiting list/no-treatment control conditions with clients with ID living in community settings (Rose *et al.*, 2000; Willner *et al.*, 2005, 2002). Lindsay *et al.* (2004) reported a controlled study of cognitive behavioural anger treatment for individuals living in the community and referred by the court or criminal justice services. Several outcome measures were used, including the DPI, provocation role plays and self-report diaries over a follow-up period of 15 months. Aggressive incidents and reoffences were also recorded for both the treatment group and the waiting list control group. There were significant improvements in anger control on all measures, with significant differences between the treatment and control groups. In addition, the treatment group recorded significantly fewer incidents of assault and violence at the post-treatment assessment point (14 vs. 45 per cent). There was evidence that anger management treatment had a significant impact on the number of aggressive incidents recorded in these participants in addition to improvements in the assessed psychological variables.

Taylor *et al.* (2002a, 2004a, 2005) have evaluated individual cognitive behavioural anger treatment with detained male patients with mild–borderline ID and significant violent, sexual and fire-raising histories in a series of waiting list controlled studies. The 18-session treatment package included a 6-session broadly psycho-educational and motivational preparatory phase, followed by a 12-session treatment phase, based on individual formulation of each participant's anger problems and needs, that follows the classical cognitive behavioural stages of cognitive preparation, skills acquisition, skills rehearsal and then practice *in vivo*. These studies showed significant improvements on self-reported measures of anger disposition, anger reactivity and behavioural reaction indices following intervention in the treatment groups compared with scores for the control groups, and these differences were maintained for up to four months following treatment. Staff ratings of study participants' anger disposition concurred with patients' reports but did not reach statistical significance.

In summary, a building research evidence suggests that cognitive behavioural interventions can be effective for this population with regard to its self-report and informant anger measures and socially valid indices of the number of incidents carried out by offenders with ID following treatment.

Sexual offending

Until relatively recently, behavioural management approaches dominated the field of intellectual disability and, as with interventions for aggression, the most common psychological treatments for management of sexual offending have been ABA-type approaches (Plaud *et al.*, 2000). These authors noted that the purpose of a behavioural treatment programme is to improve patients' behavioural competency in daily living skills, general interpersonal and educational skills and specialised behavioural skills related to sexuality and offending. Griffiths *et al.* (1989) developed a comprehensive behavioural management regime for sex offenders with ID. Their programme included addressing deviant sexual behaviour through education, training social competence and improving relationship skills, reviewing relapse prevention through alerting support staff and training on issues of responsibility. In a review of 30 cases, they reported no reoffending and described a number of successful case studies to illustrate their methods. Others have also described similar positive outcomes with behavioural management approaches (Grubb-Blubaugh *et al.*, 1994; Haaven *et al.*, 1990). In their review, Plaud *et al.* (2000) describe aversion therapy techniques and masturbatory retraining techniques in some detail. Although there are few reports on the use of these methods with offenders with ID, Lindsay (2004, 2008) has described the successful employment of imagined aversive events to control deviant sexual arousal and routines.

A major recent development in the use of psychological treatment for sex offenders with ID has been the employment of cognitive and problem-solving techniques within therapy. These methods have been developed to a sophisticated degree with mainstream offenders. Hanson *et al.* (2002) reported in a meta-analytic study that those treatments that employed cognitive techniques showed greater reductions in recidivism rates compared to treatments employing other techniques, including behavioural treatments. The essential assumption in cognitive therapy is that sex offenders may hold a number of cognitive distortions regarding sexuality which support the perpetration of sexual offences. These cognitive distortions include mitigation of responsibility, denial of harm to the victim, thoughts of entitlement, mitigation through the claim of an altered state, denial of any intent to offend and complete denial that an offence occurred. Assessments already described represent attempts to review the extent to which each sex offender holds a range of cognitive distortions and the QACSO is specifically designed for this purpose in offenders with ID.

Support for the centrality of cognitive distortions in the offence process came from a qualitative study of nine male sex offenders with ID by Courtney *et al.* (2006), using grounded theory techniques. In the analysis of interviews with participants they concluded that all aspects of the offence process were linked to offender attitudes and beliefs such as denial of the offence, blaming others and seeing themselves as the victim. Therefore a crucial aspect of treatment is to explore these issues of denial and other cognitive distortions. Lindsay *et al.* (1998a, 1998b, 1998c) reported on a series of case studies with offenders with ID using a cognitive behavioural intervention in which various forms of denial and mitigation of the offence were challenged over treatment periods of up to three years. Strategies for relapse prevention and the promotion of self-regulation were also component parts of the treatment. Across these studies, participants consistently reported positive changes in cognitions during treatment. Each of these reports provides examples of how cognitive distortions are elicited and challenged during treatment. This component of the intervention was evaluated using the QACSO (Lindsay *et al.*, 2007b). Reductions in the number of endorsements given to cognitive distortions were found following extended treatment periods and these improvements were maintained for at least one year following cessation of treatment. More importantly, lengthy follow-up of these cases (4–7 years) showed that none had reoffended following initial conviction.

Rose *et al.* (2002) reported on a 16-week group treatment for five men with ID who had perpetrated sexual abuse. The group treatment included self-control procedures, consideration of the effects of offences on victims, emotional recognition and strategies for avoiding risky situations. Individuals were assessed using the QACSO attitudes scale, a measure of locus of control, a sexual behaviour and the law measure and a victim empathy scale. Significant differences from pre- to post-treatment were found only on the locus of control scale. The authors noted that the length of treatment was somewhat short in comparison to the majority of sex offender treatment programmes, which usually last from between 12 and 18 months. However, they reported that participants had not reoffended at one-year follow-up. Rose *et al.* (2007) reported on a further six-month treatment group for sex offenders who were living in the community. Basing part of their programme on the theoretical writing of Lindsay (2005), they made efforts to involve aspects of the offender's broader social life into treatment by inviting carers to accompany participants. They found significant improvements on the QACSO scale, changes in a locus of control measure towards more external locus of control and no reoffending at one-year follow-up.

Although there are a number of treatment comparison studies evaluating the effects of sex offender treatment, they tend to fall well short of adequate experimental standards and it is important to consider the results in light of their methodological shortcomings. Lindsay and Smith (1998) compared seven individuals who had been in treatment for two or more years with another group of seven clients who had been in treatment for less than one year. Therefore, the numbers were low and the comparison was serendipitous in that time and treatment reflected the length of the probation orders made by the court. There were no significant differences between the groups in terms of severity or type of offence. The group that had been in treatment for less than one year showed significantly poorer progress, and those in this group were more likely to reoffend than those treated for at least two years. Therefore it seemed that shorter treatment periods might be of limited value for this client group. In another comparison of convenience, Keeling *et al.* (2007b) compared 11 'special needs' offenders and 11 mainstream offenders matched on level of risk, victim choice, offence type and age. The authors noted a number of limitations, including the fact that 'special needs' was not synonymous with ID and as a result they were unable to verify the intellectual differences between the mainstream and special needs populations, the fact that the treatments were not directly comparable and the fact that assessments for the special needs population were modified. There were few differences between groups post-treatment but follow-up data identified that none of the offenders (neither completers nor non-completers) in either group committed further sexual offences, although completers had a longer average post-release period.

In a further series of comparisons, Lindsay and colleagues have compared individuals with ID who have committed sexual offences with those who have committed other types of offences. Lindsay *et al.* (2004b) compared 106 men who had committed sexual offences with 78 men who had committed other types of offences or serious incidents. There was a significantly higher rate of reoffending in the non-sexual offender cohort (51 per cent) when compared to the sex offender cohort (19 per cent). In a subsequent more comprehensive evaluation Lindsay *et al.* (2006b) compared 121 sex offenders with 105 other types of male offenders and 21 female offenders. Reoffending rates were reported for up to 12 years after the index offence. There were no significant differences between the groups on IQ, and the sex offender cohort tended to be older than the other two cohorts. Female offenders had higher rates of mental illness, although rates for male cohorts were generally high at around 31 per cent. These high rates of mental illness in sex offender cohorts have been found by other researchers (Day, 1994). The differences in reoffending rates between the three groups were highly significant, with rates of 23.9 per cent for male sex offenders, 19 per cent for female offenders and 59 per cent for other types of male offenders. The significant differences were evident for every year of follow-up except Year 1. These authors also investigated harm reduction by following up the number of offences committed by recidivists and found that for those who reoffended, the number of offences following treatment, up to 12 years, was a quarter to a third of those recorded before treatment, indicating a considerable amount of harm reduction as a result of intervention. Therefore, although these treatment comparisons have been less than satisfactory in terms of their experimental design, there are some indications that treatment interventions may significantly reduce recidivism rates in sex offenders with ID. Where recidivism does occur, treatment may result in fewer abusive incidents.

Based on the limited evidence available, it is possible to conclude tentatively that in terms of treatment of sex offenders with ID, psychologically informed and structured interventions appear to yield reasonable outcomes. Cognitive behavioural treatment may have a positive effect on offence-related attitudes and cognitions

and longer periods of treatment result in better outcomes that are maintained for longer periods.

Interventions for other offence-related problems

A number of case studies have been reported on the treatment of fire setters with ID. In an early study, Rice and Chaplin (1979) conducted a study that involved the delivery of a social skills training intervention to two groups of five fire setters in a high security psychiatric facility in North America. One of the groups was reported to be functioning in the mild–borderline ID range. Following treatment, both groups improved significantly on a reliable observation scale of role-played assertive behaviour. At the time of reporting, eight out of the ten patients treated in the study had been discharged for around 12 months, with no reconviction or suspected fire setting. Clare *et al.* (1992) reported a case study involving a man with mild ID who had been admitted to a secure hospital following convictions for two offences of arson. He had a prior history of arson and making hoax calls to the fire service. Following his transfer to a specialist in-patient unit, using a comprehensive treatment package, including social skills and assertiveness training, development of coping strategies, covert sensitisation and facial surgery (for a significant facial disfigurement), significant clinical improvements were observed in targeted areas. Clearly, it is difficult to partial out the impact of various components, especially the psychological treatment against facial surgery, but the client was discharged to a community setting and had not engaged in any fire-related offending behaviour at the 30-month follow-up.

Taylor *et al.* (2004b) reported a case series of four detained men with ID and convictions for arson offences. They received a cognitive behavioural, 40-session group-based intervention that involved work on offence cycles, education about the costs associated with setting fires, training skills to enhance future coping with emotional problems associated with previous fire-setting behaviour and work on personalised plans to prevent relapse. The treatment successfully engaged these patients, all of whom completed the programme delivered over a period of four months. Despite their intellectual and cognitive limitations, all participants showed high levels of motivation and commitment that were reflected in generally improved attitudes with regard to personal responsibility, victim issues and awareness of risk factors associated with their fire-setting behaviour. In a further series of case studies on six women with mild–borderline ID and histories of fire setting, Taylor *et al.* (2006) also employed a group intervention. The intervention successfully engaged participants in the therapy process, all completed the programme, and scores on measures related to fire treatment targets generally improved following the intervention. All but one of the treatment group participants had been discharged to community placements at two-year follow-up and there had been no reports of participants setting any fires or engaging in fire-risk-related behaviour. The results of these small and methodologically weak pilot studies do provide some limited encouragement and guidance to practitioners concerning the utility of group-based, cognitive-behavioural interventions for fire-setting behaviour in people with ID.

One of the main developments in offender rehabilitation over the past 15 years has been the introduction of programmes to improve cognitive skills in relation to social and offence-related problem situations such as those involving violence, theft and fire-raising offences. These cognitive skills programmes aim to change beliefs and attitudes that support offending. The purpose of cognitive skills programmes is to equip offenders with thinking skills which will promote alternative, prosocial means of approaching social situations, including high-risk situations in which the person is at risk of offending. In a wider context, these alternative thinking skills will allow the individual to move out of the habits of an offending lifestyle which may have been reinforced by inadequate and criminal thinking styles.

Several criminal thinking programmes have emerged and the two most dominant approaches have been Moral Reconation Therapy (MRT; Little & Robinson, 1988) and Reasoning and Rehabilitation (R&R; Ross & Fabiano, 1985). A number of reviewers have considered the effectiveness of up to 20 evaluation studies and have concluded that there is reasonable evidence for significant reductions in offending for programme participants (Allan *et al.*, 2001a; Joy Tong & Farrington, 2006; Wilson *et al.*, 2005). Given the difficulties that offenders with ID are likely to have with intellectual and moral development, it is surprising that these programmes have not spread to this field other than some pilot investigations (Doyle & Hamilton, 2006). Recently, Lindsay *et al.* (2008a) have conducted a study reviewing the effectiveness of an adapted cognitive skills programme for offenders with ID. The programme is based on the theoretical work of D'Zurilla and Nezu (1999), drawing heavily on the 'Stop and Think' programme (McMurran *et al.*, 2001) which is an offence-related problem-solving

programme for offenders with personality disorder. In an evaluation of 10 participants who had completed the programme, they found reductions in measured impulsiveness and increases in positive style and orientation towards social problem solving. Therefore, there was some limited evidence that assessment and treatment of criminal thinking styles may be a suitable addition to general work on offenders with ID.

Summary and Conclusions

Broadly we have attempted to present this review of offenders with intellectual disability within the framework for the Diploma in Forensic Psychology. We have presented information on the context for the practice of forensic psychology, on the applications within the justice system and, of course, on work with the specific client group of offenders with ID. The policy of deinstitutionalisation on services for people with ID has had an enormous impact on offenders with ID, who are now more visible in the wider community than before. Larger numbers of people with ID who engage in offending, or offending-type behaviour, are being dealt with through regular criminal justice system channels and courts are mandating more people with ID to forensic mental health programmes for access to offence-related interventions. Research and practice concerning this offender group and services and interventions developed to meet their needs have been growing significantly during the past 15 years (Lindsay *et al.*, 2004f). We have presented some research concerning the prevalence and nature of offending by people with ID and have noted the lack of consistency between these studies. Some progress has been made in helping offenders with ID to engage with the criminal justice process and we have noted approaches and assessments which will aid the forensic examiner.

A number of assessments have been adapted or developed to aid forensic psychologists in their work with the population of offenders with ID. Assessments include screening measures and general measures of psychological and psychiatric problems in the population as well as offence-specific assessments for fire raising, anger and aggression and cognitive distortions related to sexual offending. From the evidence of published reports, it would seem that these adaptations of relevant assessments began in the early 1990s and have continued with increasing pace until the present day. There have also been significant advances in the identification of risk factors for the client group and investigation into the effectiveness of risk assessments for violence and sexual offending. In general, the data from these predictive studies suggest that risk assessments are generally as effective for this client group as they are for mainstream offenders.

There have been a number of significant advances and developments in the treatment of offenders with ID. Treatment methods have been based on cognitive behaviour therapy and have also employed specific methods to adapt procedures for the client group. The most significant treatment innovations have been in the field of anger management where structured programmes have been published and these programmes have been evaluated by a number of controlled comparisons. Although the comparisons have employed waiting list controls rather than random allocation, there have been no systematic pre-treatment differences reported between experimental and control groups. As a result, the positive outcomes can be regarded with some confidence and suggest that anger management treatment programmes should be incorporated into the general management of violence and aggressive offenders with ID. The second main development to treatment has been in cognitive behavioural approaches for sexual offenders. There have been a number of single case reports producing encouraging results and, more importantly, employing lengthy follow-up periods of up to seven years. Controlled comparisons have produced positive outcomes, although their methodological integrity has not been particularly sound and results should be treated with critical caution. For other offence-related programmes, the evidence is more piecemeal. There have been several treatment case studies for fire raisers with ID, all of which have provided promising outcomes. Controlled evaluation of these treatment techniques is certainly required. In relation to social problem solving and offence-related thinking, one study has been conducted on the development of a suitably adapted programme for offenders with ID. The results were positive, suggesting improvements in cognitive skills for participants.

The upshot of the past 15 years of clinical and research work in the field is that appropriate assessments are now available for a range of criminal justice issues and offence-related difficulties, and many of these assessments have been applied to this population with appropriate reliability, validity and factor analytic studies. A number of treatments have been adapted and may be employed for a range of relevant difficulties, although some of these have not been subjected to controlled experimental trials.

References

Alder, L. & Lindsay, W.R. (2007). Exploratory factor analysis and convergent validity of the Dundee Provocation Inventory. *Journal of Intellectual and Developmental Disabilities*, 32, 179–188.

Allan, L.C., MacKenzie, D.L. & Hickman, L.J. (2001a). The effectiveness of cognitive behavioral treatment for adult offenders: A methodological, quality-based review. *International Journal of Offender Therapy and Comparative Criminology*, 45(4), 498–514.

Allan, R., Lindsay, W.R., Macleod, F. & Smith, A.H.W. (2001b). Treatment of women with intellectual disabilities who have been involved with the criminal justice system for reasons of aggression. *Journal of Applied Research in Intellectual Disabilities*, 14, 340–347.

American Association on Intellectual and Developmental Disabilities (2008). *Adaptive Behavior Scales*. Retrieved 11 September 2009 from www.assessmentpsychology.com/adaptivebehavior.htm

American Psychiatric Association (1994). *Diagnostic and statistical manual of mental disorders* (4th edn). Washington, DC: Author.

Ammons, R.B. & Ammons, C.H. (1958). *The Quick Test manual*. Missoula, MT: Southern Universities Press.

Baroff, G.S. (1996). The mentally retarded offender. In J. Jacobsen & J. Mulick (Eds.) *Manual of diagnosis and professional practice in mental retardation*. Washington, DC: American Psychological Association.

Baroff, G.S., Gunn, M. & Hayes, S. (2004). Legal issues. In W.R. Lindsay, J.L. Taylor & P. Sturmey (Eds.) *Offenders with developmental disabilities* (pp.37–66). Chichester: John Wiley.

Beail, N. (2002). Interrogative suggestibility, memory and intellectual disability. *Journal of Applied Research in Intellectual Disabilities*, 15, 129–137.

Beck, A.T., Steer, R.A. & Brown, G.K. (1995). *Beck Depression Inventory* (2nd edn). New York: Psychological Corporation.

Beech, A., Friendship, C., Erikson, M. & Hanson, R.K. (2002). The relationship between static and dynamic risk factors and reconviction in a sample of UK child abusers. *Sexual Abuse: A Journal of Research and Treatment*, 14, 155–167.

Benson, D.A. & Ivins, J. (1992). Anger, depression and self-concept in adults with mental retardation. *Journal of Intellectual Disability Research*, 36, 169–175.

Black, L. & Novaco, R.W. (1993). Treatment of anger with a developmentally disabled man. In R.A. Wells & V.J. Giannetti (Eds.) *Casebook of the brief psychotherapies*. New York: Plenum Press.

Boer, D.P., Tough, S. & Haaven, J. (2004). Assessment of risk manageability of developmentally disabled sex offenders. *Journal of Applied Research in Intellectual Disabilities*, 17, 275–284.

BPS (2000). Learning disabilities: Definitions and contexts. Retrieved 11 September 2009 from www.bps.org.uk/

downloadfile.cfm?file_uuid=1B299259-7E96-C67F-D897734
F7251D757&ext=pdf

BPS (2006). *Assessment of capacity in adults: Interim guidance for psychologists*. Leicester: Author.

Bumby, K.M. (1996). Assessing the cognitive distortions of child molesters and rapists: Development and validation of the MOLEST and RAPE scales. *Sexual Abuse: A Journal of Research and Treatment, 8*, 37–54.

Burns, M., Bird, D., Leach, C. & Higgins, K. (2003). Anger management training: The effects of a structured programme on the self-reported anger experience of forensic inpatients with learning disability. *Journal of Psychiatric and Mental Health Nursing, 10*, 569–577.

Clare, I.C.H. & Gudjonsson, G.H. (1993). Interrogative suggestibility, confabulation and acquiescence in people with mild learning disabilities (mental handicap): Implications for reliability during police interrogations. *British Journal of Clinical Psychology, 37*, 295–301.

Clare, I.C.H., Murphy, G.H., Cox, D. & Chaplain, E.H. (1992). Assessment and treatment of fire setting: A single case investigation using a cognitive behavioural model. *Criminal Behaviour and Mental Health, 2*, 253–268.

Courtney, J., Rose, J. & Mason, O. (2006). The offence process of sex offenders with intellectual disabilities: A qualitative study. *Sexual Abuse: A Journal of Research and Treatment, 18*, 169–191.

Crocker, A.G., Côté, G., Toupin, J. & St-Onge, B. (2007). Rate and characteristics of men with an intellectual disability in pre-trial detention. *Journal of Intellectual and Developmental Disability, 32*(2), 143–152.

Day, K. (1994). Male mentally handicapped sex offenders. *British Journal of Psychiatry, 165*, 630–639.

Doll, E.A. (1935). A genetic scale of social maturity. *American Journal of Orthopsychiatry, 5*, 180–190.

Doyle, M.C. & Hamilton, C. (2006). An evaluation of a social problem solving group work programme for offenders with ID. *Journal of Applied Research in Intellectual Disabilities, 19*, 257.

D'Zurilla, T.J. & Nezu, A.M. (1999). *Problem solving therapy: A social competence approach to clinical interventions* (2nd edn). New York: Springer

Everington, C. & Fulero, S. (1999). Competence to confess: Measuring understanding and suggestibility in defendants with mental retardation. *Mental Retardation, 37*, 212–220.

Everington, C.T. & Luckasson, R. (1992). *Competence assessment for standing trial for defendants with mental retardation*. Worthington: International Diagnostic Systems, Inc.

Farrington, D.P. (1995). The development of offending and antisocial behaviour from childhood: Key findings from the Cambridge study in delinquent development. *Journal of Child Psychology and Psychiatry, 36*, 929–964.

Finlay, W.M. & Lyons, E. (2001). Methodological issues in interviewing and using self-report questionnaires with people with mental retardation. *Psychological Assessment, 13*, 319–335.

Fitch, W.L. (1992). *The criminal justice system and mental retardation*. Baltimore, MD: Paul H. Brookes.

Gray, N.S., Fitzgerald, S., Taylor, J., MacCulloch, M.J. & Snowden, R.J. (2007). Predicting future reconviction in offenders with intellectual disabilities: The predictive efficacy of VRAG, PCL-SV and the HCR-20. *Psychological Assessment, 19*, 474–479.

Griffiths, D. & Lunsky, Y. (2003). Sociosexual Knowledge and Attitudes Assessment Tool (SSKAAT-R). Wood Dale, IL: Stoelting.

Griffiths, D.M., Quinsey, V.L. & Hingsburger, D. (1989). *Changing inappropriate sexual behaviour: A community based approach for persons with developmental disabilities*. Baltimore, MD: Paul H. Brookes.

Grubb-Blubaugh, V., Shire, B.J. & Baulser, M.L. (1994). Behaviour management and offenders with mental retardation: The jury system. *Mental Retardation, 32*, 213–217.

Gudjonsson, G.H. (1992). *The psychology of interrogations, confessions and testimony*. Chichester: Wiley.

Gudjonsson, G.H. (1997). *Gudjonsson Suggestibility Scales*. Hove, Sussex: Psychology Press.

Haaven, J., Little, R. & Petre-Miller, D. (1990). *Treating intellectually disabled sex offenders: A model residential programme*. Orwell, VT: Safer Society Press.

Hanson, R.K. (1997). *The development of a brief actuarial risk scale for sexual offence recidivism. (User report 1997–2004)*. Ottawa: Development of the Solicitor General of Canada.

Hanson, R.K., Gordon, A., Harris, A.J.R., Marques, J.K., Murphy, W., Quinsey, V.L. *et al.* (2002). First report of the collaborative outcome data project on the effectiveness of psychological treatment for sex offenders. *Sexual Abuse: A Journal of Research and Treatment, 14*, 169–194.

Hare, R.D. (1991). *The Hare Psychopathy Checklist – revised*. Toronto, ON: Multi Health Systems.

Harris, A.J.R. & Tough, S. (2004). Should actuarial risk assessments be used with sex offenders who are intellectually disabled. *Journal of Applied Research in Intellectual Disabilities, 17*, 235–242.

Harris, G.T., Rice, M.E. & Quinsey, V.L. (1993). Violent recidivism of mentally disordered offenders: The development of a statistical prediction instrument. *Criminal Justice and Behaviour, 20*, 315–335.

Hayes, S. (1991). Sex offenders. *Australia and New Zealand Journal of Developmental Disabilities (Journal of Intellectual and Developmental Disabilities), 17*, 220–227.

Hayes, S. & McIlwain, D. (1988). *The prevalence of intellectual disability in the New South Wales prison population – an empirical study*. Report to the Criminology Research Council, Canberra.

Hayes, S.C. (2000). *Hayes Ability Screening Index (HASI) Manual*. University of Sydney, Sydney: Behavioural Sciences in Medicine.

Hingsburger, D., Griffiths, D. & Quinsey, V. (1991). Detecting counterfeit deviance: Differentiating sexual deviance from sexual inappropriateness. *Habilitation Mental Health Care Newsletter*, 10, 51–54.

Hogue, T.E., Mooney, P., Morrissey, C., Steptoe, L., Johnston, S., Lindsay, W.R. *et al.* (2007). Emotional and behavioural problems in offenders with intellectual disability: Comparative data from three forensic services. *Journal of Intellectual Disability Research*, 51(10), 778–785.

Hogue, T.E., Steptoe, L., Taylor, J.L., Lindsay, W.R., Mooney, P., Pinkney, L. *et al.* (2006). A comparison of offenders with intellectual disability across three levels of security. *Criminal Behaviour and Mental Health*, 16, 13–28.

Holland, A.J. (2004). Criminal behaviour and developmental disability: An epidemiological perspective. In W.R. Lindsay, J.L. Taylor & P. Sturmey (Eds.) *Offenders with developmental disabilities* (pp.23–34). Chichester: John Wiley.

Holland, S., Persson, P., McClelland, M. & Berends, R. (2007). *Intellectual disability in the Victorian prison system: Characteristics of prisoners with an intellectual disability released from prison in 2003–2006*. Corrections Research Paper Series Paper No. 02 September 2007. State of Victoria, Australia: Department of Justice.

Hurley, J. (2003). *Missouri Institute of Mental Health Policy Brief: Competency to Stand Trial*. School of Medicine, University of Missouri, Columbia.

Jackson, H.F., Glass, C. & Hope, S. (1987). A functional analysis of recidivistic arson. *British Journal of Clinical Psychology*, 26, 175–185.

Joy Tong, L.S. & Farrington, D.P. (2006). How effective is the 'Reasoning and Rehabilitation' Programme in reducing offending? A meta-analysis of evaluations in four countries. *Psychology, Crime and Law*, 12, 3–24.

Keeling, J.A., Rose, J.L. & Beech, A.R. (2007a). A preliminary evaluation of the adaptation of four assessments for offenders with special needs. *Journal of Intellectual and Developmental Disability*, 32(2), 62–73.

Keeling, J.A., Rose, J.L. & Beech, A.R. (2007b). Comparing sexual offender treatment efficacy: Mainstream sexual offenders and sexual offenders with special needs. *Journal of Intellectual and Developmental Disability*, 32(2), 117–124.

Kellet, S.C., Beail, N., Newman, D.W. & Frankish, P. (2003). Utility of the Brief Symptom Inventory (BSI) in the assessment of psychological distress. *Journal of Applied Research in Intellectual Disabilities*, 16, 127–135.

Kellet, S., Beail, N., Newman, D.W. & Hawes, A. (2004). The factor structure of the Brief Symptom Inventory: Intellectual disability evidence. *Clinical Psychology and Psychotherapy*, 1, 275–281.

Klimecki, M.R., Jenkinson, J. & Wilson, L. (1994). A study of recidivism among offenders with intellectual disability. *Australia and New Zealand Journal of Developmental Disabilities (Journal of Intellectual and Developmental Disabilities)*, 19, 209–219.

Kolton, D.J.C., Boer, A. & Boer, D.P. (2001). A revision of the Abel and Becker Cognition Scale for intellectually disabled sexual offenders. *Sexual Abuse: A Journal of Research and Treatment*, 13, 217–219.

Lindsay, W.R. (2004). Sex offenders: Conceptualisation of the issues, services, treatment and management. In W.R. Lindsay, J.L. Taylor & P. Sturmey (Eds.) *Offenders with developmental disabilities* (pp.163–186). Chichester: John Wiley.

Lindsay, W.R. (2005). Model underpinning treatment for sex offenders with mild intellectual disability: Current theories of sex offending. *Mental Retardation*, 43, 428–441.

Lindsay, W.R. (2008). *The treatment of sex offenders with intellectual disability*. Chichester: John Wiley.

Lindsay, W.R., Allan, R., Macleod, F., Smart, N. & Smith, A.H.W. (2003). Long term treatment and management of violent tendencies of men with intellectual disabilities convicted of assault. *Mental Retardation*, 41, 47–56.

Lindsay, W.R., Allan, R., Parry, C., Macleod, F., Cottrell, J., Overend, H. *et al.*, (2004a). Anger and aggression in people with intellectual disabilities: Treatment and follow-up of consecutive referrals and a waiting list comparison. *Clinical Psychology and Psychotherapy*, 11, 255–264.

Lindsay, W.R. & Beail, N. (2004). Risk assessment: Actuarial prediction and clinical judgement of offending incidents and behaviour for intellectual disability services. *Journal of Applied Research in Intellectual Disabilities*, 17, 229–234.

Lindsay, W.R., Elliot, S.F. & Astell, A. (2004b). Predictors of sexual offence recidivism in offenders with intellectual disabilities. *Journal of Applied Research in Intellectual Disabilities*, 17, 299–305.

Lindsay, W.R., Hamilton, C., Moulton, S., Scott, S., Doyle, M. & McMurran, M. (2008a). Assessment and treatment of social problem solving in offenders with intellectual disability. Manuscript submitted for publication.

Lindsay, W.R., Hastings, R.P., Griffiths, D.M. & Hayes, S.C. (2007a). Trends and challenges in forensic research on offenders with intellectual disability. *Journal of Intellectual and Developmental Disability*, 32, 55–61.

Lindsay, W.R., Hogue, T., Taylor, J.L., Steptoe, L., Mooney, P., Johnston, S. *et al.* (2008b). Risk assessment in offenders with intellectual disabilities: A comparison across three levels of security. *International Journal of Offender Therapy and Comparative Criminology*, 52, 90–111.

Lindsay, W.R., Marshall, I., Neilson, C.Q., Quinn, K. & Smith, A.H.W. (1998a). The treatment of men with a learning disability convicted of exhibitionism. *Research on Developmental Disabilities*, 19, 295–316.

Lindsay, W.R., Michie, A.M., Baty, F.J., Smith, A.H.W. & Miller, S. (1994). The consistency of reports about feelings and emotions from people with intellectual disability. *Journal of Intellectual Disability Research*, 38, 61–66.

Lindsay, W.R., Michie, A.M., Whitefield, E., Martin, V., Grieve, A. & Carson, D. (2006a). Response patterns on the Questionnaire on Attitudes Consistent with Sexual Offending in groups of sex offenders with intellectual disability. *Journal of Applied Research in Intellectual Disabilities*, 19, 47–54.

Lindsay, W.R., Murphy, L., Smith, G., Murphy, D., Edwards, Z., Grieve, A. et al. (2004c). The Dynamic Risk Assessment and Management System: An assessment of immediate risk of violence for individuals with intellectual disabilities, and offending and challenging behaviour. *Journal of Applied Research in Intellectual Disabilities*, 17, 267–274.

Lindsay, W.R., Neilson, C.Q., Morrison, F. & Smith, A.H.W. (1998b). The treatment of six men with a learning disability convicted of sex offences with children. *British Journal of Clinical Psychology*, 37, 83–98.

Lindsay, W.R., Olley, S., Jack, C., Morrison, F. & Smith, A.H.W. (1998c). The treatment of two stalkers with intellectual disabilities using a cognitive approach. *Journal of Applied Research in Intellectual Disabilities*, 11, 333–344.

Lindsay, W.R. & Skene, D.D. (2007). The Beck Depression Inventory II and The Beck Anxiety Inventory in people with intellectual disabilities: Factor analyses and group data. *Journal of Applied Research in Intellectual Disability*, 20(5), 401–408.

Lindsay, W.R. & Smith, A.H.W. (1998). Responses to treatment for sex offenders with intellectual disability: A comparison of men with 1 and 2 year probation sentences. *Journal of Intellectual Disability Research*, 42, 346–353.

Lindsay, W.R., Smith, A.H.W., Law, J., Quinn, K., Anderson, A., Smith, A. et al. (2004d). Sexual and non-sexual offenders with intellectual and learning disabilities: A comparison of characteristics, referral patterns and outcome. *Journal of Interpersonal Violence*, 19, 875–890.

Lindsay, W.R., Steele, L., Smith, A.H.W., Quinn, K. & Allan, R. (2006b). A community forensic intellectual disability service: Twelve year follow-up of referrals, analysis of referral patterns and assessment of harm reduction. *Legal and Criminological Psychology*, 11, 113–130.

Lindsay, W.R., Sturmey, P. & Taylor, J.L. (2004e). Natural history and theories of offending in people with developmental disabilities. In W.R. Lindsay, J.L. Taylor & P. Sturmey (Eds.) *Offenders with developmental disabilities* (pp.3–22). Chichester: John Wiley.

Lindsay, W.R., Taylor, J.L. & Sturmey, P. (2004f). *Offenders with developmental disabilities*. Chichester: John Wiley.

Lindsay, W.R., Whitefield, E. & Carson, D. (2007b). An assessment for attitudes consistent with sexual offending for use with offenders with intellectual disability. *Legal and Criminological Psychology*, 12, 55–68.

Linhorst, D.M., McCutchen, T.A. & Bennett, L. (2003). Recidivism among offenders with developmental disabilities participating in a case management programme. *Research in Developmental Disabilities*, 24, 210–230.

Little, G.L., & Robinson, K.D. (1988). Moral Reconation Therapy. A systematic step-by-step treatment system for treatment resistant clients. *Psychological Reports*, 62, 135–151.

Lund, J. (1990). Mentally retarded criminal offenders in Denmark. *British Journal of Psychiatry*, 156, 726–731.

Lunsky, Y., Frijters, J., Griffiths, D.M., Watson, S.L. & Williston, S. (2007). Sexual knowledge and attitudes of men with intellectual disabilities who sexually offend. *Journal of Intellectual and Developmental Disability*, 32, 74–81.

Lyall, I., Holland, A.J., Collins, S. & Styles, P. (1995). Incidence of persons with a learning disability detained in police custody. *Medicine, Science and the Law*, 35, 61–71.

MacEachron, A.E. (1979). Mentally retarded offenders prevalence and characteristics. *American Journal of Mental Deficiency*, 84, 165–176.

Mason, J. & Murphy, G. (2002). Intellectual disability amongst people on probation: Prevalence and outcome. *Journal of Intellectual Disability Research*, 46, 230–238.

Maughan, B., Pickles, A., Hagell, A., Rutter, M. & Yule, W. (1996). Reading problems and antisocial behaviour: Developmental trends in comorbidity. *Journal of Child Psychology and Psychiatry*, 37, 405–418.

McCord, W. & McCord, J. (1959). *Origins of crime: A new evaluation of the Cambridge-Somerville*. New York: Columbia Press.

McMurran, M., Fyffe, S., McCarthy, L., Duggan, C. & Latham, A. (2001). Stop and think!: Social problem solving therapy with personality disordered offenders. *Criminal Behaviour and Mental Health*, 11, 273–285.

Meichenbaum, D. (1985). *Stress inoculation training*. New York: Pergamon Press.

Messinger, E. & Apfelberg, B. (1961). A quarter century of court psychiatry. *Crime and Delinquency*, 7, 343–362.

Michie, A.M., Lindsay, W.R., Martin, V. & Grieve, A. (2006). A test of counterfeit deviance: A comparison of sexual knowledge in groups of sex offenders with intellectual disability and controls. *Sexual Abuse: A Journal of Research and Treatment*, 18, 271–279.

Morrissey, C., Hogue, T., Mooney, P., Allen, C., Johnston, S., Hollin, C. et al. (2007a). Predictive validity of the PCL-R in offenders with intellectual disabilities in a high secure setting: Institutional aggression. *Journal of Forensic Psychology and Psychiatry*, 18, 1–15.

Morrissey, C., Hogue, T., Mooney, P., Lindsay, W.R., Steptoe, L., Taylor, J. et al. (2005). Applicability, reliability and validity of the Psychopathy Checklist – Revised in offenders with intellectual disabilities: Some initial findings. *International Journal of Forensic Mental Health*, 4, 207–220.

Morrissey, C., Mooney, P., Hogue, T., Lindsay, W.R. & Taylor, J.L. (2007b). Predictive validity of psychopathy in offenders with intellectual disabilities in a high security hospital: Treatment progress. *Journal of Intellectual and Developmental Disabilities*, 32, 125–133.

Murphy, G. & Clare, I. (1991). MIETS: A service option for people with mild mental handicaps and challenging behaviour or psychiatric problems. *Mental Handicap Research*, 4, 180–206.

Murphy, G.H. & Clare, I.C.H. (1996). Analysis of motivation in people with mild learning disabilities (mental handicap) who set fires. *Psychology, Crime and Law, 2*, 153–164.

Noble, J.H. & Conley, R.W. (1992). Toward an epidemiology of relevant attributes. In R.W. Conley, R. Luckasson & G. Bouthilet (Eds.) *The criminal justice system and mental retardation* (pp.17–54). Baltimore, MD: Paul H. Brookes.

Novaco, R.W. (1975). *Anger control: The development and evaluation of an experimental treatment*. Lexington, MA: Heath.

Novaco, R.W. (1994). Anger as a risk factor for violence among the mentally disordered. In J. Monahan & H.J. Steadman (Eds.) *Violence in mental disorder: Developments in risk assessment*. Chicago, IL: University of Chicago Press.

Novaco, R.W. (2003). *The Novaco Anger Scale and Provocation Inventory Manual (NAS-PI)*. Los Angeles: Western Psychological Services.

Novaco, R.W. & Taylor, J.L. (2004). Assessment of anger and aggression in offenders with developmental disabilities. *Psychological Assessment, 16*, 42–50.

Oliver P.C. *et al.* (2007). Modified Overt Aggression Scale (MOAS) for people with intellectual disability and aggressive challenging behaviour: A reliability study. *Journal of Applied Research in Intellectual Disabilities, 20*(4), 368–372.

Otto, R.K., Poythress, N.G., Nicholson, R.A., Edens, J.F., Monahan, J., Bonnie, R.J. *et al.* (1998). Psychometric properties of the MacArthur Competence Assessment Tool – Criminal Adjudication. *Psychological Assessment, 10*, 435–443.

Plaud, J.J., Plaud, D.M., Colstoe, P.D. & Orvedal, L. (2000). Behavioural treatment of sexually offending behaviour. *Mental Health Aspects of Developmental Disabilities, 3*, 54–61.

Prout, H.T. & Strohmer, D.C. (1991). *Emotional problem scales: Professional manual for the behaviour rating scales and the self-report inventory*. Psychological Assessment Resources Inc.

Quinsey, V.L., Book, A. & Skilling, T.A. (2004). A follow-up of deinstitutionalised men with intellectual disabilities and histories of antisocial behaviour. *Journal of Applied Research in Intellectual Disabilities, 17*, 243–254.

Quinsey, V.L., Harris, G.T., Rice, M.E. & Cormier, C.A. (1998). *Violent offenders: Appraising and managing risk*. Washington, DC: American Psychological Association.

Quinsey, V.L., Harris, G.T., Rice, M.E. & Cormier, C.A. (2005). *Violent offenders, appraising and managing risk*: (2nd edn). Washington, DC: American Psychological Association.

Rice, M.E. & Chaplin, T.C. (1979). Social skills training for hospitalised male arsonists. *Journal of Behaviour Therapy and Experimental Psychiatry, 10*, 105–108.

Rose, J., Anderson, C., Hawkins, C. & Rose, D. (2007). *A community based sex offender treatment group for adults with intellectual disabilities*. Paper presented to The World Congress on Behavioural and Cognitive Psychotherapy, Barcelona.

Rose, J., Jenkins, R., O'Conner, C., Jones, C. & Felce, D. (2002). A group treatment for men with intellectual disabilities who sexually offend or abuse. *Journal of Applied Research in Intellectual Disabilities, 15*, 138–150.

Rose, J. & West, C. (1999). Assessment of anger in people with intellectual disabilities. *Journal of Applied Research in Intellectual Disabilities, 12*, 211–224.

Rose, J., West, C. & Clifford, D. (2000). Group interventions for anger and people with intellectual disabilities. *Research in Developmental Disabilities, 21*, 171–181.

Ross, R.R. & Fabiano, E.A. (1985). *Time to think: A cognitive model on delinquency prevention and offender rehabilitation*. Tennessee: Institute of Social Sciences and Arts.

Rutter, M., Maughan, B., Meyer, J., Pickles, A., Silberg, J., Simonoff, E. *et al.* (1997). Heterogeneity of antisocial behaviour: Causes, continuities and consequences. In D.W. Osgood (Ed.) *Motivation and delinquency* (pp.45–118). Lincoln, NE: University of Nabraska Press.

Ryba, N.L., Cooper, V.G. & Zapf, P.A. (2003). Juvenile competence to stand trial evaluations: A survey of current practices and test usage among psychologists. *Professional Psychology: Research in Practice, 34*, 499–507.

Sanders, A. & Young, R. (2000). *Criminal justice* (2nd edn). London: Butterworths.

Scheerenberger, R.C. (1983). *A history of mental retardation*. London, UK: Brooks.

Sorgi, P., Ratey, J., Knoedler, D.W., Markert, R.J. & Reichman, M. (1991). Rating aggression in the clinical setting. A retrospective adaptation of the Overt Aggression Scale: Preliminary results. *Journal of Neuropsychiatry and Clinical Neuroscience, 3*(2), S52–S56.

Spielberger, C.D. (1996). *State-Trait Anger Expression Inventory Professional Manual*. Florida: Psychological Assessment Resources.

Steptoe, L., Lindsay, W.R., Murphy, L. & Young, S.J. (2008). Construct validity, reliability and predictive validity of the Dynamic Risk Assessment and Management System (DRAMS) in offenders with intellectual disability. *Legal and Criminological Psychology*, in press.

Taylor, J.L. (2002). A review of the assessment and treatment of anger and aggression in offenders with intellectual disability. *Journal of Intellectual Disability Research, 46* (Suppl. 1), 57–73.

Taylor, J.L., Lindsay, W.R., Hogue, T.E., Mooney, P., Steptoe, L., Johnston, S. *et al.* (2007). Use of the HCR-20 in offenders with intellectual disability. *Submitted for publication.*

Taylor, J.L. & Novaco, R.W. (2005). *Anger treatment for people with developmental disabilities: A theory, evidence and manual based approach*. Chichester: Wiley.

Taylor, J.L., Novaco, R.W., Gillmer, B.T., Robertson, A. & Thorne, I. (2005). Individual cognitive behavioural anger treatment for people with mild–borderline intellectual disabilities and histories of aggression: A controlled trial. *British Journal of Clinical Psychology, 44*, 367–382.

Taylor, J.L., Novaco, R.W., Gillmer, B. & Thorne, I. (2002a). Cognitive behavioural treatment of anger intensity among offenders with intellectual disabilities. *Journal of Applied Research in Intellectual Disabilities, 15*, 151–165.

Taylor, J.L., Novaco, R.W., Guinan, C. & Street, N. (2004a). Development of an imaginal provocation test to evaluate treatment for anger problems in people with intellectual disabilities. *Clinical Psychology and Psychotherapy, 11*, 233–246.

Taylor, J.L., Robertson, A., Thorne, I., Belshaw, T. & Watson, A. (2006). Responses of female fire-setters with mild and borderline intellectual disabilities to a group based intervention. *Journal of Applied Research in Intellectual Disabilities, 19*, 179–190.

Taylor, J.L., Thorne, I., Robertson, A. & Avery, G. (2002b). Evaluation of a group intervention for convicted arsonists with mild and borderline intellectual disabilities. *Criminal Behaviour and Mental Health, 12*, 282–293.

Taylor, J.L., Thorne, I. & Slavkin, M.L. (2004b). Treatment of fire setting behaviour. In W.R. Lindsay, J.L. Taylor & P. Sturmey (Eds.) *Offenders with developmental disabilities* (pp.221–240). Chichester: John Wiley.

Terman, L. (1911). *The measurement of intelligence*. Boston, MA: Houghton Mifflin Co.

The Information Centre (2007). In-patients formally detained in hospitals under the Mental Health Act 1983 and other legislation, NHS Trusts, Care Trusts, Primary Care Trusts and Independent Hospitals, England; 1996–97 to 2006–07. London: Government Statistical Service.

Tough, S.E. (2001). *Validation of two standard risk assessments (RRASOR, 1997; Static-99, 1999) on a sample of adult males who are developmentally disabled with significant cognitive deficits*. Unpublished Master's Thesis, University of Toronto, Toronto, Ontario, Canada.

Walker, N. & McCabe, S. (1973). *Crime and insanity in England*. Edinburgh: University Press.

Webster, C.D., Douglas, K.S., Eaves, D. & Hart, S.D. (1997). *HCR-20: Assessing risk for violence*, version 2. Burnaby, British Columbia: Mental Health, Law, and Policy Institute, Simon Fraser University.

Wechsler, D. (1999). *Manual for the Wechsler Adult Intelligence Scale – Third Edition*. Sanantonio, TX: Psychological Corporation.

White, R. & Willner, P. (2004). Suggestibility and salience in people with intellectual disabilities: An experimental critique of the Gudjonsson Suggestibility Scale. *Journal of Forensic Psychiatry and Psychology, 16*, 638–650.

Wierzbicki, M. & Pekarik, G. (1993). A meta-analysis of psychotherapy drop out. *Professional Psychology: Research and Practice, 24*, 190–195.

Wildenskov, H.O.T. (1962). A long term follow-up of subnormals originally exhibiting severe behaviour disorders or criminality. *Proceedings of the London Conference on the Scientific Study of Mental Deficiency* (pp.217–222). London: May & Baker.

Williams, F., Wakeling, H. & Webster, S. (2007). A psychometric study of six self-report measures for use with sexual offenders with cognitive and social functioning deficits. *Psychology, Crime and Law, 13*(5), 505–522.

Willner, P. (2008). Clarification of the memory artefact in the assessment of suggestibility. *Journal of Intellectual Disability Research, 52*(4), 318–326.

Willner, P. (2009). *Assessment of capacity to participate in court proceedings, with particular reference to the assessment of suggestibility*. Retrieved 11 September 2009 from www.bps.org.uk/document-download-area/document-download$.cfm?file_uuid=A1818FBC-C406-52A9-60E6-C88DE6317865&ext=ppt

Willner, P., Brace, N. & Phillips, J. (2005). Assessment of anger coping skills in individuals with intellectual disabilities. *Journal of Intellectual Disability Research, 49*, 329–339.

Willner, P., Jones, J., Tams, R. & Green, G. (2002). A randomised controlled trial of the efficacy of a cognitive behavioural anger management group for clients with learning disabilities. *Journal of Applied Research in Intellectual Disabilities, 15*, 224–253.

Wilson, D.B., Bouffard, L.A. & MacKenzie, D.L. (2005). A quantitative review of structured group orientated cognitive behavioural programmes for offenders. *Criminal Justice and Behaviour, 32*, 172–204.

Wish, J.R., McCombs, K.F. & Edmonson, B. (1979). *The sociosexual knowledge and attitudes test*. Wood Dale, IL: Stoelting Company.

World Health Organization (1992). *Tenth revision of the international classification of diseases and related health problems (ICD-10)*. Geneva: Author.

20

Mentally Disordered Offenders
Personality Disorders

Richard Howard and Conor Duggan

This chapter divides into three main sections. In the first, we address some broad questions regarding the nature of personality disorder, and argue that personality disorder can only properly be understood with reference to normal personality functioning. In the second section we turn to more practical issues regarding how personality disorder can be assessed and treated in a forensic context. In the third section we raise questions about whether, and how, personality is linked to offending, particularly to violent offending, ending with the outline of a model of how personality disorder might be linked to violent offending. In addressing these and other questions we draw heavily on the work of John Livesley, who has made a major contribution to placing the field on a sound scientific footing (Livesley, 2003, 2007a, 2007b).

Issues Surrounding the Concept of Personality Disorder

What is 'personality disorder'?

We concur with Livesley (2007a) in believing that the study of personality disorder needs to take normal personality functioning as its starting point. The question, then, is whether personality disorders are simply extreme variations of normal personality, or whether there is a discontinuity between normal and abnormal personality traits.

Differently stated: is it possible to derive personality disorders from scores on conventional measures of normal personality variation such as the 'Big Five' from the Five Factor Model (FFM) of Costa and McCrae (1992)? In short, is there something qualitatively different about personality disorder that distinguishes it from the normal range of personality variation, or is there merely a quantitative difference, with disorder representing an extreme position on some traits or dimensions? Livesley and others (e.g. Blackburn, 2000) have argued that the latter position confuses extreme scores on a trait or dimension with disorder – high or low levels on a given trait such as agreeableness or conscientiousness are neither necessary nor sufficient to indicate disordered functioning (Parker & Barrett, 2000; Wakefield, 1992). Blackburn points out that there is an important difference between the extreme of normal conscientiousness – striving for excellence in everything – and the maladaptive conscientiousness associated with obsessive compulsive personality disorder. The same point is made by Livesley (2007a) when he states: 'With personality disorder, it is difficult to see how an extreme position on dimensions such as agreeableness, sociability, or conscientiousness is necessarily pathological. Some additional factor needs to be present to warrant the diagnosis' (p.203).

What is this additional factor? Livesley (1998) appeals to evolutionary biology in suggesting that personality disorder can be said to be present when 'the structure of personality prevents the person from achieving adaptive solutions to universal life tasks' (p.141). More specifically, from this evolutionary perspective personality disorder can be seen as a failure to solve adaptive life tasks relating to three areas: identity or self, intimacy and

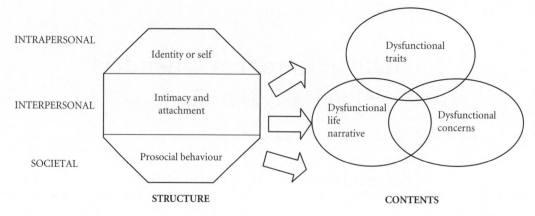

Figure 20.1   A schematic representation of Livesley's conception of personality disorder.

attachment, and prosocial behaviour. Livesley suggests that personality disorders can be expressed at three different levels: intrapersonal, interpersonal and societal: see Figure 20.1. At the intrapersonal level, personality disorder involves poorly developed or fragmented representations of self and others. At the interpersonal level, it involves difficulties resolving attachment problems and developing the capacity for sustained intimacy. At the group level, it involves problems with prosocial behaviour, altruism, and maintaining the cooperativeness needed for effective social functioning. Problems with prosocial behaviour are of particular concern to forensic psychologists who are confronted with personality disordered individuals, of whom it is often said that they are difficult, unpleasant and troublesome, and (sometimes) given to breaking social rules, laws and codes of conduct. Like normal personality theorists, clinical classification systems adopt, either explicitly or implicitly, the trait as the basic taxonomic unit. The ICD-10, for example, defines personality disorder as '... deeply ingrained and enduring behaviour patterns, manifesting themselves as inflexible responses to a broad range of personal and social situations. They represent either extreme or significant deviations from the way the average individual in a given culture perceives, thinks, feels, and particularly relates to others.' (ICD-10; World Health Organization, 1992, p.200).

i. Do the traits of personality disorder overlap with the traits that reflect normal personality variation?
To some extent the traits of personality disorder are certainly continuous with normal traits. Livesley (2003) points out that it is possible to see a correspondence or

continuity between the Big Five factors – Neuroticism, Agreeableness, Extraversion, Conscientiousness, and Openness – and major dimensions of personality disorder derived from multivariate analysis of PD traits. Four broad dimensions of PD identified in this way – Emotional Dysregulation, Dissocial Behaviour, Inhibitedness and Compulsivity[1] – correspond broadly to Neuroticism, low Agreeableness, low Extraversion and high Conscientiousness (the 'Big Five') in the Five Factor Model of Costa and McCrae (1992) (see Table 20.1). If one looks, for example, at the primary traits of personality disorder in Table 20.1, derived from phenotypic and behavioural genetic analyses of the Dimensional Assessment of Personality Pathology (DAPP) questionnaire, one sees some examples of overlap. Anxiousness overlaps with Neuroticism, for example, and Stimulus Seeking with Impulsivity. However, most of the primary traits listed in Table 20.1 describe traits that are dysfunctional in the sense that they are inimical to the attainment of major life tasks, and as such they represent 'the dark side' of normal personality. Another instrument that was developed to capture the range of dysfunctional traits found in personality disorders is the MMPI-based PSY-5 which identifies five major domains: Neuroticism, Disconstraint, Introversion/Low Positive Emotionality, Aggressiveness and Psychoticism (Harkness & McNulty, 1994). A recent comparison of the PSY-5 with the Five Factor Model conducted by Bagby *et al.* (2008) found the PSY-5 to be superior in capturing four of the PDs most associated with externalising and disturbance of thought, namely: paranoid, schizotypal, antisocial and narcissistic PDs. The Neuroticism, Disconstraint, and

Table 20.1 Thirty primary traits organised into four secondary domains (Livesley, 2007). The four secondary domains are said to be aetiologically distinct insofar as all traits in a domain are influenced by the same general genetic module which has minimal effect on other domains (Livesley, 2008, p.46)

Secondary domain	Primary trait
Emotional Dysregulation	Anxiousness
	Emotional reactivity
	Emotional intensity
	Pessimistic anhedonia
	Submissiveness
	Insecure attachment
	Social apprehensiveness
	Need for approval
	Cognitive dysregulation
	Oppositional
	Self-harming acts
	Self-harming ideas
Dissocial Behaviour	Narcissism
	Exploitativeness
	Sadism
	Conduct problems
	Hostile-dominance
	Sensation seeking
	Impulsivity
	Suspiciousness
	Egocentrism
Inhibitedness	Low affiliation
	Avoidant attachment
	Attachment need
	Inhibited sexuality
	Self-containment
	Inhibited emotional expression
	Lack of empathy
Compulsivity	Orderliness
	Conscientiousness

Introversion/Low Positive Emotionality domains identified in the PSY-5 correspond rather closely to the domains of Emotional Dysregulation, Dissocial Behaviour and Inhibitedness, respectively, in Livesley's schema shown in Table 20.1. We can conclude, in answering the question raised at the beginning of this section, that while there is some continuity between normal and abnormal traits, nonetheless personality disordered individuals show a range of dysfunctional traits that are not well captured by instruments designed to measure normal personality variation.

This is illustrated by considering a global trait like impulsivity. It is particular facets of this trait that appear to be dysfunctional in personality disorder, in particular the sensation-seeking and risk-taking aspects captured by some (e.g. Blackburn's (1971) MMPI derived measure) but by no means all impulsivity measures. Derivation of the primary traits shown in Table 20.1 was informed by behavioural genetic analyses which indicated that the genetic factor that explained most of the variance in sensation seeking and recklessness did not explain the genetic variance in impulsivity, which was influenced by a genetic factor specific to itself. Therefore stimulus seeking, originally a primary trait, was split into the separate primary traits of Impulsivity and Sensation Seeking, shown in Table 20.1. A recent review of longitudinal studies linking childhood impulsivity to adult violence (Jolliffe & Farrington, 2008) concluded that the sensation-seeking/risk-taking aspect of impulsivity best predicts violent offending in later life. A neurophysiological correlate of Blackburn's Impulsivity measure, capturing the sensation-seeking aspect of impulsivity, has been found to predict with reasonable accuracy both general and violent reoffending in mentally disordered offenders released into the community (Howard & Lumsden, 1996, 1997). It can be concluded from these findings that it is the sensation-seeking and affective dyscontrol aspects of impulsivity, representing its 'dark side', that predispose to antisocial behaviour.

ii. Is personality disorder no more than a set of dysfunctional traits?

Livesley (2007b) argues cogently that there is much more to personality disorder than simply a set of dysfunctional traits:

> The pathology associated with personality disorder includes not only problems with the contents of personality – regulatory problems, maladaptive behaviours and cognitions, and dysfunctional traits – but also severe disturbances in the structure or organisation of personality. These disturbances range at the most global level from the failure to forge a cohesive self-structure capable of integrating cognitions and affects and connecting different aspects of self-experience. Such focal problems are illustrated by the failure of many patients to recognise the situational and experiential factors that trigger a variety of problematic behaviours such as deliberate self-harm or interpersonal violence. (p.30)

Thus Livesley suggests two levels of construct in addition to the trait level: *personal concerns*, including motives, roles, goals and coping strategies; and *the life narrative* which provides an integrated account of past, present and future.

A curious feature of trait-based theories of personality, and accounts of personality disorder, is that they assume temporal and situational stability. Yet, as pointed out by some personality theorists (e.g. Apter, 2005), what characterises normal human behaviour and experience is precisely a *lack* of stability, evidenced by a tendency for people to switch rapidly between opponent modes of experiencing the world and their actions in it, for example between a playful, hedonistic state and a serious-minded, future-orientated state. According to this view, stability, rather than instability, is dysfunctional and characterises the experience and behaviour of personality disordered individuals, who often appear 'stuck' in a particular experiential mode. Someone who is 'stuck' in a playful state, for example, would be constantly striving to avoid boredom by seeking high-arousal situations, and would lack any focus on the future. This accords with Livesley's description of personality disordered patients, most of whom '… live in the present and have difficulty formulating and working towards long-term goals' (Livesley, 2007b, p.40). This lack of changeability is acknowledged by DSM when it refers to the traits of personality disordered individuals as *rigid and inflexible*.

What is the implication of this for the assessment of personality disorder, to which we turn next? First, it would be as mistaken to classify personality disorders just in terms of normal personality variation as it would be to classify language disorders simply in terms of normal language. To do so, in either case, would be to ignore the discontinuity that exists between the normal and the abnormal, albeit the boundary between the two is sometimes unclear. Second, while an assessment of dysfunctional traits is a necessary component in an assessment of personality disorder, particularly for an assessment of what Livesley (2007a) refers to as the *contents* of personality, it is not sufficient. Also required is an assessment of the disturbance in the structure or organisation of personality. In particular, one needs to address the question, firstly, of whether a personality disorder is present. Livesley (2003) points out that a set of criteria needs to be worked out to assess this in terms of global disturbance in the three domains outlined above: intrapersonal, interpersonal and societal. Then, in addition to an assessment of dysfunctional traits, one ideally would

like an assessment of the individual's motives, roles, goals and coping strategies as he or she experiences them, as well as the experienced life narrative. In the next section, we will review briefly the assessments that are currently available for an evaluation of personality disorders, particularly in forensic contexts. To a large extent these are confined to an assessment of dysfunctional traits. The development of assessment tools to tap the other two levels mentioned above has largely been neglected.

Assessment and Treatment of Personality Disorder

Problems with assessing personality disorder

There are major problems with the current classification of personality disorder, especially as conceived by DSM-1V (for a review, see Tyrer *et al.*, 2007). These difficulties include poor reliability between differing instruments and a problem of overlap between the differing personality disorder diagnoses (Benjamin, 1993). Additional criticisms are that it fails to capture much of the personality psychopathology that is relevant to clinicians and, perhaps most importantly of all, that it does not provide clear guidance on treatment interventions (Clark, 2007; Clark *et al.*, 1997; Westen & Arkowitz-Westen, 1998). While it is tempting therefore to dismiss the current classification in the assessment of personality disorder and start again, this approach is unhelpful for the student who will be faced with personality disordered individuals to assess and manage. Many of these will be familiar to the practitioner and it seems pointless to adopt a completely new system, however flawed the old system may be. This section will therefore critically examine some of the approaches to the assessment of personality disorder before indicating an approach that is practical and has a sound theoretical basis. Among the key questions in assessment are the following: Which is the best method for assessing personality disorder? Who should be the informant? What level of training is required to conduct the assessment?

Methods of assessing personality disorder

Methods of assessment can be conveniently grouped into: (a) unstructured clinical interview; (b) self-report inventories and semi-structured interviews; and (c) observer-rated measures.

Unstructured clinical interviews

The main problem in using unstructured clinical interviews is their poor reliability (Zimmerman, 1994). For instance, Mellsop *et al.* (1982) found a kappa coefficient of .41 for the presence of any personality disorder, with the coefficient for specific disorders ranging from .01 to .49, when they assessed the reliability of clinical assessment of personality disorder. Thus, the reliability of unstructured clinical interview is so low that it ought to be discouraged.

Self-report questionnaires

The main advantages of self-report questionnaires are: (a) their ease and low cost of administration; (b) their freedom from systematic interviewer bias; and (c) their results can be compared to normative data. There are a number of self-report instruments available to assess personality disorder, including: the Millon Clinical Multiaxial Inventory, now in its third version (MCMI-III; Millon *et al.*, 1994); the Personality Diagnostic Questionnaire – Revised (PDQ-R; Hyler & Rieder, 1987); the Personality Assessment Inventory (PAI; Morey, 1991) and the Antisocial Personality Questionnaire (APQ; Blackburn & Fawcett, 1999). Despite their advantages, the evidence is that questionnaires tend to over-diagnose personality disorders when compared to semi-structured interviews, and that they do so by a significant order of magnitude (e.g. Hunt & Andrews, 1992; Hyler *et al.*, 1990, 1992). The MCMI in particular has been criticised for yielding excessive prevalence rates (Zimmerman, 1994). Although questionnaires tend to yield higher prevalence rates of disorder, they tend, as Blackburn (2000) points out, to have high specificity, i.e. they detect most patients without disorder. On these grounds it has been suggested that questionnaires may be more useful as screening tools, with detailed interviews being reserved for those who screen positive (Zimmerman, 1994). Some believe that the MCMI in particular may have only limited utility even as a screening instrument because of its high false positive rate (Cantrell & Dana, 1987).

The APQ (Blackburn & Fawcett, 1999) has the advantage that it focuses on personality deviations relevant to offenders, having been developed originally using data acquired in the UK Special Hospitals (its precursor was the Special Hospitals Assessment of Personality and Socialization [SHAPS; Blackburn, 1982]). It is a short (125 items, answered in a 'yes/no' format), multi-trait, self-report inventory that measures intrapersonal and interpersonal dispositions of relevance to antisocial populations (Blackburn & Fawcett, 1999). Its advantages are firstly, its brevity; secondly, its focus on traits associated with social deviance; and thirdly, its validity in discriminating both within offenders and between offenders and non-offenders. There are eight scales (self-control, self-esteem, avoidance, paranoid suspicion, resentment, aggression, deviance and extraversion), all having acceptable reliabilities (Cronbach's alphas between .79 and .88 in patients). Two higher-order factors emerged from principal components analysis: one, labelled 'hostile impulsivity', contrasts aggression, resentment, deviance and paranoid beliefs with self-control; the other, labelled 'social withdrawal', contrasts avoidance and poor self-esteem (neurotic introversion) with stable extraversion. A two-dimensional space defined by these factors has been used to define a useful typology of personality disordered offenders (reviewed in Blackburn, 2009: see Figure 20.2). The impulsivity factor, incorporating elements of emotional dyscontrol (anger, irritability, loss of temper), loads highly on a higher-order IPDE 'antisocial' or 'psychopathy' factor (Blackburn *et al.*, 2005) and correlates highly with hostile dominance as measured using the CIRCLE (see below) (Blackburn *et al.*, 2005).

Semi-structured interviews

A number of semi-structured interviews have been developed to address the problem of the low reliability of unstructured clinical interviews. Some of these (the IPDE and SCID-II) also have self-report versions that can be used as a screening instrument to give some guidance to the subsequent interview. Unique to the SCID-II (First *et al.*, 1994) is that the interviewer inquires only about criteria that are endorsed on the questionnaire, thereby reducing the length of the interview.

An advantage of semi-structured interviews is their flexibility. In addition to standard questions, optional probes and unstructured questions are used to elicit relevant information. When using the International Personality Disorder Examination (IPDE; Loranger *et al.*, 1994) to assess 99 DSM-defined traits, there are three phases to the assessment of each trait: (a) is it present or absent? (b) if the answer to (a) is 'yes', is the severity of the trait sufficient to have a significant clinical impact on the individual's level of functioning? (c) if the answers to (a) and (b) are in the affirmative, does the motivation behind the behaviour satisfy the relevant DSM criteria? An example is the following question to elicit an avoidant personality trait: Q. Do you usually try to avoid jobs or things you have to do at work (school)

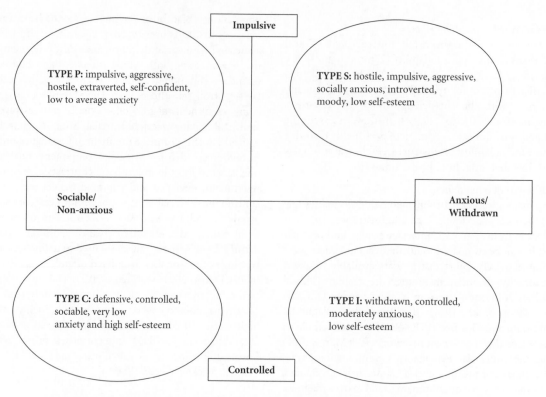

Type P: Primary psychopaths; Type S: Secondary psychopaths; Type I: Inhibited; Type C: Controlled

Figure 20.2   The two-dimensional space defined by Impulsivity and Social Withdrawal. *Source*: after Blackburn (2009).

that bring you into contact with other people? (This is the structured question and must be asked in this format.) If the answer is 'yes', the individual is then asked to provide examples to provide the interviewer with convincing evidence that the patient's avoidant behaviour satisfies the three 'Ps' of personality disorder (i.e. that it is persistent, pervasive and pathological). Finally, the interviewee is asked: 'Why do you do that?' Here the interviewer is inquiring about the motivation in the mind of the interviewee for this behaviour, since according to the DSM manual, the reason for the avoidance must be fear of criticism, disapproval or rejection.

The inter-rater reliability of these semi-structured instruments is moderate to good. In his review, Zimmerman (1994) found that 80 per cent of the 15 joint interview studies reported a kappa of .6 or above and 60 per cent had a kappa of .70 and above. The temporal stability of the IPDE has been assessed at six months by Loranger *et al.* (1994) who found a low moderate consistency for categorical diagnoses (median k = .48) but a superior rating for the dimensional diagnoses

(median ICC = .79 for DSM-111-R). Of special relevance for the forensic practitioner, the antisocial personality disorder rating has the greatest temporal stability as it is largely based on antisocial, including criminal, behaviour (Grilo *et al.*, 1998).

Despite their reasonable reliability, the convergent validity between different interview-based instruments, and between these and questionnaire measures, is only poor to fair (Zimmerman, 1994). In the largest study comparing the SCID-II with the PDE, Skodol *et al.* (1991) found that the mean kappa for the 11 DSM-111-R personality disorders was .45, only dependent PD achieving a kappa greater than .6. When similar comparisons are made for Axis I conditions, the agreement is no better (Hasin & Grant, 1987a, 1987b).

Assessment of Psychopathy

A number of self-report and interview-based measures have been developed to assess psychopathy, the best known of which is the Psychopathy Checklist (PCL), originally developed in the early 1980s as a research scale for the assessment of psychopathy (Hare, 1980). This exists in various forms for different purposes, e.g. the PCL-SV (Hart et al., 1995) was developed for screening purposes and was originally entirely interview based. The PCL is loosely based on Cleckley's psychopathy criteria, although it should be noted that there is not complete overlap between PCL criteria and Cleckley's (1988) checklist. Loss of insight, for example, is not captured by the PCL, and by including items related to criminal behaviour, the PCL goes beyond Cleckley's criteria (Blackburn, 2007). The most recent revision of the PCL (Hare, 2003) yields, as well as a total score, scores on two factors – selfish, callous and remorseless use of others (F1), and chronically unstable and antisocial lifestyle (F2). Each factor subsumes two facets, so that F1 subsumes the facets Interpersonal and Affective, while F2 subsumes the facets Lifestyle and Antisocial. Most relevant to the present context is the PCL's increasing use as a measure of risk within the criminal justice system. Its early promise in this regard led Blackburn (2000) to conclude: 'There is a compelling case for including the PCL-R routinely in the assessment of personality disorder among mentally disordered offenders' (p.S10). Unfortunately, more recent research has cast doubt on the PCL's accuracy in predicting both violent and non-violent recidivism. Two large meta-analyses of recidivism data (Leistico et al., 2008; Walters, 2003) both reported significantly better predictive accuracy for Factor 2 than for Factor 1. The UK Prisoner Cohort Study (Coid et al., 2008) recently compared the ability of a range of possible risk measures, including the PCL, to predict violent and non-violent reoffending in high-risk prisoners. PCL performed relatively poorly as a predictor of reoffending in comparison with a measure – the Offender Group Reconviction Scale – that relied solely on past offending. PCL items that predicted reoffending mainly reflected antisociality and impulsivity. A recent study that examined PCL's predictive accuracy using a very large database across six separate samples showed that only facet 4 (Antisocial) displayed incremental validity in predicting recidivism relative to facets 1, 2 and 3. In contrast, facets 1, 2 and 3 failed to attain a consistent level of incremental validity relative to facet 4 (Walters et al., 2008). Thus it appears to be the combination of criminal behaviour and poor behavioural control (irritability, aggression and inadequate control of anger) that, among traits tapped by the PCL, accurately predicts future violent and non-violent offending. This combination seems very similar to the traits subsumed under the IPDE Antisocial Dyscontrol factor that appear to be particularly criminogenic (Howard et al., 2008). Given that both IPDE and PCL are interview based and therefore time consuming (1–3 hours), and PCL requires additional reading of casenotes, it seems unnecessary to use both PCL and IPDE to assess antisocial traits. Moreover, since those DSM PDs measured with IPDE that contribute to the Dissocial factor (antisocial, borderline narcissistic/histrionic and paranoid) correlate highly with PCL F2 (Blackburn, 2007), it seems that PCL can be dropped in favour of IPDE which covers a much wider range of dysfunctional traits than does PCL.

Moreover, recent research by Blackburn (2009) indicates that several sub-types of PCL psychopath exist, who differ in important ways such as their offending histories and DSM Axis I and Axis II correlates. Type S in Figure 20.2, originally labelled 'secondary psychopaths', show a high rate of comorbid Axis I disorders, a high rate of post-traumatic stress disorder, a high rate of sexual abuse, and the most severe personality pathology measured by IPDE, with paranoid and schizoid traits particularly prominent. Type P in Figure 20.2 show high rates of conviction for violence and early onset of antisocial disorder; they appear similar to McCord psychopaths. Borderline, histrionic, narcissistic, and adult/child antisocial traits are prominent in both Type P and Type S. Type C show a high rate of sexual offending, higher IQ and the least severe personality pathology measured using IPDE; of all four types they approximate most closely to Cleckley psychopaths. The implication of these findings is that if PCL psychopaths are so heterogeneous, a high score on the PCL may tell us little more about the individual than that he or she is a high PCL scorer.

Measures of Interpersonal Style

As disordered interpersonal functioning is a crucial aspect of personality disorder, another approach to consider in personality disorder assessment stems from interpersonal theory and the interpersonal circle (IPC; Leary, 1957). The latter represents interpersonal styles as a circular array or circumplex, around two dimensions of power or control (dominance versus submission) and affiliation (hostile versus friendly: see Blackburn, 2000 for a fuller description). The IPC is of particular relevance to mentally disordered offenders because, as Blackburn (2000) points out, hostile-dominant styles are associated with interpersonal conflict and aggression. Blackburn and colleagues have developed a nurse rating measure for use with forensic psychiatric inpatients, the Chart of Interpersonal Reactions in Closed Living Environments (CIRCLE: Blackburn & Renwick, 1996). It contains 49 statements describing discrete social behaviours, for example 'Joins in group activities', that are independently rated by two members of staff who know the patient well and the scores are combined and used to calculate the individual's relative position in the eight octants of the IPC (Dominant, Coercive, Hostile, Withdrawn, Submissive, Compliant, Nurturant, Gregarious). A single point that characterises a particular individual can be plotted within the IPC. There is evidence that the categories of personality disorder in DSM can be mapped on to the IPC, for example antisocial, narcissistic and histrionic PDs show hostile-dominant styles, and hostile dominance as measured by CIRCLE loads strongly on the higher-order IPDE Antisocial factor described above. Hostile dominance correlates significantly (.46) with PCL-R total score (Blackburn *et al.*, 2005) and with APQ scales contributing to the higher-order APQ Impulsivity factor (Blackburn & Fawcett, 1999). Despite the superior theoretical and empirical underpinnings of this approach, this has not as yet become a mainstream evaluation among forensic psychologists.

Practical Considerations

An important (and unanswered) question is: who should provide the information when assessing personality disorder – the individual concerned or someone who knows him or her well? Allied to this is if (and how) collateral information (e.g. from files) should be used. It could be argued that since PD patients usually see their disorder as ego-syntonic (i.e. an inevitable or natural part of the person's life), an informant interview would be a more accurate indication of the psychopathology. On the other hand, several of the questions in personality assessment refer to internal mental states (e.g. a feeling of emptiness) or to unusual perceptual and cognitive experiences. It is difficult to see how an informant would be able to provide useful information in these areas. Again, as with the comparison between different instruments, when the two sources are compared, there is often poor agreement between them. For example, Zimmerman *et al.* (1988) compared the views of patients and informants using the Structured Interview for DSM-III personality disorders (SIDP) in 66 depressed patients and found poor agreement (k = .13 for any PD and for all individual PDs k < .35. What this tells us is that there is likely to be poor agreement when more than one source of information is provided. What it does not tell us, however, is which of the sources is the more valid. While many suggest that two sources of information ought to be collected and then combined, it is unclear how this is to be done if the information is discrepant. This is of particular relevance in a forensic context where there may be a considerable incentive for individuals to downplay their psychopathology in order to minimise the length of a custodial sentence or to avoid admission to a secure hospital. Unfortunately, these instruments were not designed to detect this degree of denial or deception and hence have to be used very cautiously in such a context.

Another practical issue is that of the experience, training and qualifications deemed necessary in order to administer the interviews. The degree of training required and clinical experience expected varies between the various semi-structured interview instruments. For instance, the Personality Interview Questionnaire was designed deliberately to avoid preconceived clinical biases so that it used lay interviewers. Conversely, the Personality Disorder Examination (PDE; Loranger, 1988) and IPDE were designed for use by experienced practitioners and the manual for the latter explicitly states that it should *not* be used by '… research assistants, nurses, students and other clinicians early in their training …'. Other instruments (e.g. the Structured Interview for Personality Disorders (SIPD; Stangl *et al.*, 1985) recommend a more intermediate level of experience. In the UK, PCL requires three days' expensive basic training, and additional advanced training to receive the PCL manual. Its use is restricted to those with a degree in behavioural or social science. Clearly, a minimum level of training is necessary for administering any instrument, but beyond this, experience in the interpretation of responses is required to arrive at a valid assessment when using and interpreting additional probes to clarify answers.

Summary: Assessment of Personality Disorder

Our review of the evidence on the assessment of personality disorder shows that, while there is agreement in certain areas, there remain significant uncertainties. Nonetheless, we believe that the following conclusions may be drawn:

(a) The reliability of unstructured clinical interviews is only poor to fair and hence ought not to be recommended.

(b) Judicious and selective use of self-report inventories is required since some over-diagnose, making their interpretation difficult and the planning of interventions near impossible. However, we have pointed to particular merits attaching to one self-report inventory, the Antisocial Personality Questionnaire (Blackburn & Fawcett, 1999), which has the additional merit of tapping not just dysfunctional traits relevant to mentally disordered offenders, but also traits related to normal personality variation such as Neuroticism, Extraversion and possibly Agreeableness from the Big Five.

(c) Semi-structured assessments have reasonable reliability but the convergent validity between the instruments is only poor to fair. Thus, it is unclear as to which (of any of these) ought to be recommended, but research using the International Personality Disorder Examination has yielded consistent evidence for a higher-order Antisocial factor (we prefer the label 'Antisocial Dyscontrol') that correlates highly with PCL psychopathy and a coercive interpersonal style on the CIRCLE.

(d) Patients and informants do not agree on the patients' personality evaluation and it is unclear as to which of these is the more valid.

(e) The training and experience required by the differing semi-structured instruments varies considerably and this will have an effect on the cost and accuracy of the assessment.

Procedural Recommendations in Assessing Personality Disorder

We endorse Livesley's suggestion that an initial focus should be on assessing whether the general criteria for personality disorder are met, in terms of intrapersonal, interpersonal and societal dysfunction as described above in the first section. A set of specific criteria remain to be articulated, but as Livesley (2003, p.172) points out, 'The definition of personality disorder could be developed through a conceptual analysis of the functions of normal personality and the way these functions are disturbed in personality disorder'. Only then should one proceed to assessment of individual differences in

personality, using a variety of assessment instruments. We would suggest that a basic assessment of dysfunctional traits should be carried out using measures from all three domains: self-report, interview-based, and observer-rated. Based on the considerations outlined earlier, including economy of time and cost, we would suggest a triad of APQ, IPDE and CIRCLE. If thought appropriate, e.g. for delineating specific treatment targets, more specific areas of dysfunction could then be explored using instruments designed for their measurement. If, for example, emotional dysregulation needed to be assessed, the General Emotional Dysregulation Measure (GEDM; Newhill et al., 2004) could be administered.

Given, firstly, the high proportion of mentally ill offenders who also suffer from a personality disorder (some 60 per cent), and secondly, the high comorbidity between DSM Axis I and Axis II disorders (e.g. McGlashan et al., 2000), an assessment of personality disorder should be carried out on all individuals undergoing a routine psychiatric assessment. Indeed, Livesley (2003) suggests that personality disorder should be included together with other psychiatric disorders on a single Axis I in any future reformulation of the DSM nosology. This raises the issue of how to interpret measures of PD that may be inflated by comorbid Axis I disorders (Zimmerman, 1994). While it has been argued that this reflects over-diagnosis of PD, Blackburn (2000) points out that the reduction in personality pathology following remission of acute symptoms of mental illness may reflect genuine personality change. Nevertheless, he points out that assessing PD in acutely disturbed patients remains an unresolved problem.

Treatment of Personality Disorder: Some caveats

There are a number of general issues to discuss before considering some of the specifics in the treatment of personality disorder. First, does personality disorder change, and if so *what* changes? Considering that one of the defining features of personality, and hence of personality disorder, is its long-term stability, does it make sense to attempt to treat that which, by definition, is unchanging?

This issue can be addressed at two levels. First, there is recent evidence from naturalistic follow-up studies – and this especially applies to those with borderline personality disorder – that change is indeed possible, with a significant reduction in key symptoms over the medium term (Skodol *et al.*, 2007: Zanarini *et al.*, 2005). For example, about 74 per cent failed to meet criteria for the disorder at six years' follow-up, and once remission occurred, recurrences were uncommon (about 6 per cent). While a number of acute symptoms in borderline personality disorder (BPD) such as self-mutilation, help-seeking behaviour and suicidal threats resolve rapidly, regardless of intervention, other symptoms that are not specific to BPD, such as chronic feelings of intense anger, resolve much more slowly, if at all (Zanarini *et al.*, 2005). All studies concur in suggesting that, over time, BPD patients improve psychosocially, that the prognosis for patients with BPD is better than previously recognised, and that while some aspects of BPD change, others are more resistant to change. Similarly, in the case of men with antisocial PD, while impulsivity, and hence also rates of reoffending, declines over time, major problems in interpersonal relationships persist (Black *et al.*, 1995; Grilo *et al.*, 1998; Weissman, 1993).

Secondly, an important implication of this is that caution is required when interpreting results of clinical trials purporting to show changes in behaviours such as self-harm which are likely to remit spontaneously over time. Such results beg the question of whether the intervention has achieved a greater reduction in the target behaviour compared with the mere passage of time, and highlight the importance of properly designed trials, a feature that unfortunately does not characterise research in personality disorder. With regard to treatment, relatively brief interventions may augment changes in those more malleable aspects of personality that are likely to change spontaneously with the passage of time, while other, less malleable aspects are more resistant to change and therefore require a longer and more sophisticated intervention.

Treatment Issues

In his review of treatments for personality disordered offenders, Livesley (2007b) notes that a wide spectrum of treatments, from psychodynamic psychotherapy at one end to antipsychotic medication at the other, has been used to treat personality disorder; while there is evidence of limited success for all, this also suggests that none is especially effective. There have been recent reviews of the efficacy of treatments for personality

disorders in general (Duggan *et al.*, 2007, 2008; Oldham, 2007; Soloff, 1998) as well as more specific reviews of particular PDs, e.g. reviews supporting NICE Guidelines for borderline and antisocial personality disorder and Cochrane reviews of borderline (Binks *et al.*, 2006) and antisocial (Gibbon *et al.*, 2009) PDs. The main conclusion from these is that if one considers only those studies that adopt as standard a high level of evidence, i.e. well-conducted randomised controlled trials (RCTs), then the evidence base is very thin. Duggan *et al.* (2007, 2008), for example, reviewed RCT evidence for both psychological and pharmacological interventions for any personality disorder. Only 49 trials up to December 2006 could be included that met their inclusion criteria, and of these, almost half focused on borderline PD and only five involved antisocial PD. The reason why this evidence base is so thin is not difficult to identify given the difficulties that we have identified above. First, since many of the assessment instruments have such poor convergent validity, one cannot be certain that individuals entering the trial with the same diagnosis but assessed with differing instruments are the same. Second, as a result of frequent disagreement between studies concerning relevant outcome measures, there is considerable variability in those chosen, making cross-study comparisons very difficult. Finally, most of the trials are underpowered, with a very brief follow-up period, making findings difficult to interpret. In summary, relying on this evidence base will not take the practitioner very far; as it is unlikely to change in the near future, an alternative approach is necessary.

Livesley (2007b) makes the important point that, contrary to what many of the proponents of specific interventions might claim, there is very good evidence that it is the common factors shared between therapies, rather than their specific aspects, that lead to a successful outcome. Treatment should, therefore, optimise the non-specific effects that are common to all types of treatment. Livesley advocates an eclectic approach, based on what works, requiring an array of interventions selected systematically from different treatment models – psychotherapeutic, cognitive-behavioural, pharmacological, etc. – to target specific problems. He goes further in suggesting that such a comprehensive treatment for personality disordered offenders requires not only interventions aimed at bringing about changes in the *contents* of personality, but at promoting more cohesive personality functioning, for example to foster integration and to construct a more adaptive and prosocial life script. A systematic treatment approach should

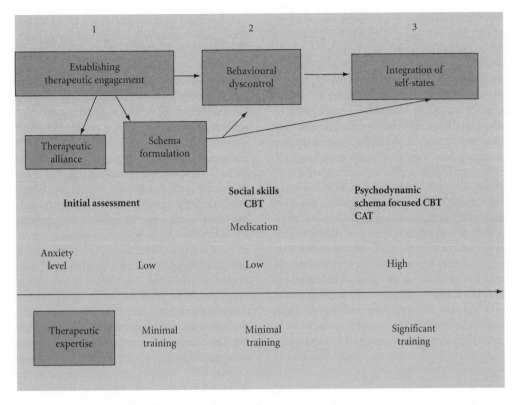

Figure 20.3 A stepped care model of therapeutic intervention.

progressively target: first, those aspects of personality disorder that are most susceptible to change (e.g. symptoms and states); then those aspects that are less changeable, such as affective impulse control and maladaptive modes of thinking; and finally those aspects that are least susceptible to change, such as core schemata central to self and identity.

An outline of a possible approach is provided in Figure 20.3. This identifies three therapeutic tasks: (a) establishing therapeutic engagement; (b) reducing behavioural dyscontrol; (c) integration of self-states. Establishing therapeutic engagement is best achieved, in our view, by focusing on the individual's difficulties in functioning and relating these to the content of the personality assessment. Thus the processes of assessment and treatment are connected. We have found that providing information on the individual's personality difficulties through a process of psychoeducation strengthens therapeutic engagement (Banerjee *et al.*, 2006; Huband *et al.*, 2007). It is the case, however, that specific PD diagnoses have limited value in deciding on

specific treatments or indicating prognosis. After conducting one of the semi-structured interviews described above, one often finds that the individual assessed meets criteria for more than one, and sometimes several, personality disorders, so that the practitioner is then faced with making a choice as to which of these ought to be prioritised. In addition, psychological and pharmacological interventions are used to treat specific behaviours (e.g. self-harming behaviour) or dimensions such as cognitive-perceptual symptoms – not specific disorders. This is a limitation of our current assessment process but one that Livesley's approach as discussed would overcome.

If this process identifies difficulties in behavioural control then this becomes the second target of treatment. This can be effected by either psychological interventions (e.g. social problem solving) or medication to reduce impulsive behaviour so that the individual thinks before he or she acts. In both phases, building up a therapeutic relationship and dealing with behavioural dyscontrol, the therapy is relatively directive so that the level of anxiety experienced by the patient/client is low. In addition, the skill level demanded is relatively modest.

However, as has been pointed out, there is more to personality disorder than improving behaviour: the third stage in Figure 20.3 involves tackling core schemata that are central to the individual's identity and is a major task of treatment. This is a much more challenging task and requires a greater level of sophistication and training. As core issues concerning the patient's identity are confronted, a greater level of anxiety is evoked so that there is greater resistance to change.

Thus, as in many other areas of therapeutic intervention, a stepped care approach is adopted. This ranges from relatively simple interventions that can be offered to many, to more sophisticated interventions that, because of both the degree of time involved and the level of expertise demanded, are likely to be offered to very few. This is important, as there are significant shortfalls in expertise in programme delivery for those with personality disorder. Hence, it is important to be able to match expectations with available resources.

Dealing with drop-outs from treatment

Prevention of treatment drop-out is an important component of service delivery for the following reasons. First, high drop-out rates are seen in PD patients undergoing treatment, particularly in borderline patients undergoing psychodynamic therapy (Gunderson et al., 1989; Skodol et al., 1983; Waldinger & Gunderson, 1984), although lower rates have been reported for other approaches (e.g. Bateman & Fonagy, 1999; Linehan et al., 1991; Stevenson & Meares, 1992).

Second, a high drop-out rate is an uneconomical use of a resource that, as already noted, is very limited. Third, drop-outs have a detrimental effect on both patient and therapist. For example, those offered treatment who then drop out are more likely to reoffend compared with those left untreated (McMurran & Theodosi, 2007).

Predicting and preventing drop-out

Factors found to be associated with dropping out of treatment include: low educational attainment and poor social support; young age; more symptoms and a high PCL-R score; high levels of anger; and a low capacity to work collaboratively (Huband et al., 2007). These characteristics are common in those who come to the attention of forensic psychologists.

In the light of these findings, it is not surprising that attention is increasingly being given to reducing the likelihood of drop-out. While improving the motivation for treatment has always been a preoccupation of service providers, this has recently been extended to assessing 'readiness' for treatment. Readiness denotes more than just the individual's motivation to engage in treatment; it involves consideration of the match between the individual's capacity to engage with the treatment and the provider's capacity to meet that individual's needs. The correctional literature indicates that the closer the fit between these, the more likely is the intervention offered to be effective (Andrews & Bonta, 2003). A final aspect of 'readiness' is the organisation's commitment and structure to deliver the programme. All too often the impact of programmes introduced with enthusiasm by practitioners is severely curtailed because they are not supported by the larger organisation. An example is the introduction of programmes for individuals in prison that require a stable period of placement. All too often the authorities ignore this and move inmates around the prison estate due to other pressures. This, more comprehensive, matching of the therapeutic need with the organisation's capacity to respond to it is well captured in the 'MORM' concept of Ward et al. (2004).

Managing ruptures in the therapeutic relationship

An important consideration in those with personality disorder is the active management of the therapeutic rupture, defined as a breakdown in the emotional relationship between patient and therapist. This is evidenced by the individual arriving late or missing sessions, not complying with home work or medication, and so on. When faced with this type of change, instead of ignoring the rupture or confronting the patient, it is suggested that, rather than being seen as a problem stemming from the patient, the rupture should be explored as an exchange between co-equal partners. This kind of dialogue may then model a kind of non-value-laden exploratory activity that the patient might internalise (Safran & Muran, 2000).

Personality Disorder and Offending

Is personality disorder linked to offending?

There is no doubt that the prevalence of personality disorder, which is around 4 per cent of the general

UK population (Coid *et al.*, 2006), is markedly raised in criminal populations. In a systematic review of 62 surveys of prisoners in 12 countries, Fazel and Danesh (2002) reported that of 18,530 men, 65 per cent had a personality disorder and 47 per cent had an antisocial personality disorder (ASPD). The equivalent figures for women were 42 and 21 per cent. In the five studies that measured it, borderline personality disorder (BPD) showed a moderately high prevalence among women prisoners (25 per cent).

A proportion of offenders transferred from prison, the courts and other psychiatric hospitals to high secure forensic hospital under the various sections of the UK Mental Health Act (1983, revised 2008[2]) are admitted under the 'Psychopathic Disorder' (PD) category. The precise figure has fluctuated over the past 30 years, but it averages about 20–25 per cent of high-secure hospital admissions. 'PD' is a catch-all label which comprises patients with a variety of personality disorders, most commonly borderline, antisocial, narcissistic and paranoid personality disorder (Coid, 1992). This is not to say that patients admitted under the Mental Illness (MI) category are *not* personality disordered: roughly 60 per cent of MI patients meet clinical criteria for personality disorder (Blackburn, 2000), and some patients are admitted with a dual (MI + PD) legal classification. The co-occurrence of personality disorders, both with other personality disorders and with Axis I mental disorders, is very high in forensic psychiatric samples, yet systematic study of patterns of comorbidity found in mentally disordered offenders has been lacking. Coid (1992) noted in passing that a proportion of his forensic sample had both antisocial and borderline PD 'in devastating combination' (p.89), and this combination was said by Mullen (1992, p.238) to represent '… a very particular constellation of abnormalities of mental state with a wide range of disorderly conduct', abnormalities said to be developmental in origin. The co-occurrence of antisocial and borderline personality disorders varies with level of security, being most common in very high security samples, and least common in the general community (see Duggan & Howard, 2009, figure 2). It is a combination that appears strongly linked to the risk of violence, to be considered next, and that contributes to the higher-level Dissocial dimension mentioned previously.

The question of the nature of the relationship between personality disorder and violence, and more importantly, of how they are they linked together (see following section), has been systematically explored in a recent volume (McMurran & Howard, 2009). The personality disorder most often found to associate with violence is antisocial PD (e.g. Coid *et al.*, 1999). In forensic psychiatric samples, antisocial PD has been found to correlate, albeit very modestly ($r = .23$), with a history of violence (Blackburn, 2007). Blackburn pointed out that the correlation between ASPD and violent offending was inflated by criterion contamination, and interpreted his results as suggesting that '… none of the personality disorders is strongly associated with persistent offending' (Blackburn, 2007, p.155). However, recent results from the UK Prisoner Cohort Study (Coid *et al.*, 2008) confirm that antisocial PD predicts violent reoffending in prisoners followed up after their release, even in the absence of a high (>/= 30) PCL psychopathy score.

How is personality disorder linked to violence?

It is important to note that an association between personality disorder and violence does not necessarily imply a causal link between them, and evidence for such a link in the case of antisocial PD is lacking (Duggan & Howard, 2009). It appears that it is the comorbidity, both between different personality disorders (e.g. borderline and antisocial) and between personality disorders and DSM Axis I disorders, that is key to understanding this relationship and the mechanisms that mediate it. Comorbid substance (including alcohol) abuse is very high in those personality disordered individuals who act violently, particularly when it is combined with another Axis I mental disorder. The striking co-occurrence of substance misuse, mental illness and antisocial personality disorder in violent men is well illustrated by results of a study of 90 male mentally ill homicides by Putkonen *et al.* (2004). Men showing this diagnostic triad were responsible for two-thirds of all homicidal acts committed by those who, comprising 50 per cent of the sample, received a double diagnosis of mental illness (mostly schizophrenia) and substance abuse. The critical question, then, is: what is the mechanism through which mental disorder *in general* becomes linked to violence? DeBrito and Hodgins (2009) suggested comorbid childhood conduct disorder as the critical intervening variable, while Howard *et al.* (2008) suggested a developmental/neurobiological mechanism, early-onset alcohol/substance abuse, as the critical mediating mechanism. An answer to this question must await results of longitudinal studies.

Furthermore, when addressing this question it must be borne in mind that different types of violence exist, and that particular personality disorders may be differentially linked to the various types. A typology of violence, suggested by Howard (2009), expands upon the instrumental vs. affective distinction, which is considered too simplistic. The revised typology suggests a distinction between appetitively and aversively motivated violence, the former associated with positive affect, the latter with negative affect. Within each of these, violence may be impulsive or controlled, yielding a 2 × 2 matrix (see table 1 in Howard, 2009), with four distinct types of violence: Appetitive/Impulsive, Appetitive/Controlled, Aversive/Impulsive and Aversive/Controlled. It will be a task for future research to attempt to map different types of personality disorder onto this typology. Howard (2009) argued that antisocial PD may be particularly associated with the impulsive type of appetitively motivated violence, while borderline PD may be associated with the impulsive type of aversively motivated violence.

To conclude this section, it is perhaps appropriate to warn the reader against the naive assumption that all violent people are personality disordered, and all personality disordered people are violent. Both the strength and the nature of the relationship between personality disorder and violence are far from clear, and will only become apparent when further longitudinal studies are conducted.

Towards a model of personality disorder and violence

We will use a clinical example (case 4 from Coid, 1998) to illustrate a model of how personality disorder might play a role in instigating an act of violence.[3] The patient, who suffered from narcissistic personality disorder, became increasingly angry and jealous in the course of a telephone conversation with his ex-girlfriend, whom he had telephoned regarding the collection of some of his personal belongings, including a pullover which, he suggested, her new boyfriend might make use of. His girlfriend's mother then interrupted the telephone conversation to suggest that the pullover would be too small for the new boyfriend. This was taken by the narcissistic patient as a demeaning comment about his physique, triggering a rage reaction that resulted in the violent killing of his ex-girlfriend's new partner. Prior to the final murderous act he had travelled by bus to his ex-girlfriend's house, and had interrupted his journey to buy the weapon, a butcher's knife, used to commit the murder. The trigger factor that precipitated the act of violence (the ex-girlfriend's mother's comment) acted in tandem with his narcissism, a significant predisposing factor. The act of violence can be interpreted as directed at the goal of removing a significant threat to his self-esteem, motivated by revenge. It illustrates the 'aversive/controlled' type of violence in Howard's (2009) typology, which is accompanied by ruminative anger.

In the model, outlined in Figure 20.4, the brain mediates the effects of triggering events and predisposing factors, producing, as outputs, cognitions (e.g. ruminative thoughts of revenge), affective/somatic reactions (e.g. a fight/flight reaction, with sympathetic autonomic arousal), and motor behaviour (including the actions involved in committing the act of murder). Since there was a considerable delay between formation of the intention to commit the murder and the consummation of the act, we need to distinguish between a preparatory phase of the act, comprising actions in preparation for its consummation – walking to the bus-stop, buying a bus ticket, getting on the bus, breaking the journey to buy a knife in a hardware store, locating the address of the person to be attacked – and the final consummation of the act. Contextual factors can also influence the final output. For example, if the phone conversation triggering the act had occurred at night, the buses might not have been running, the shops might have been closed, and so on, so that the act of violence might have been delayed or even aborted.

Also shown in Figure 20.4 is the feedback (sometimes called 'reafference') from the cognitive, affective and motor outputs from the brain. Only the cognitive feedback gains direct access to consciousness, but feedback from affective and motor outputs can, by accessing the cognitive processing stream in the brain, gain access to consciousness. In this way we normally have coherent, conscious representations of our acts, and of ourselves as authors of those acts, allowing us to monitor our own thoughts, affects and behaviours and to consciously reflect on them. This self-monitoring is thought to be defective in people with personality disorder, particularly in psychopaths where it can manifest as a 'specific loss of insight' (Cleckley, 1941). Cleckley remarks that the psychopath 'has absolutely no capacity to see himself as others see him' (p.350) and shows 'a total absence of self-appraisal as a real and moving experience' (p.351). Livesley (2007a) also remarks on the absence of the evaluative aspect of self-observation in personality disordered people. This deficit in the ability to monitor the feedback from cognitive, affective and motor outputs appears to have a neural basis, since individuals

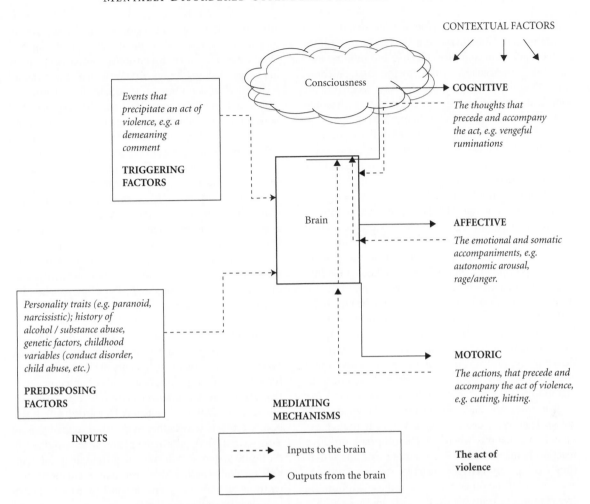

Figure 20.4   A schematic model of how personality disorder may result in violence. Dysfunctional personality traits, in conjunction with a variety of other **predisposing factors**, bias motivational neural circuits such that they respond to particular **triggering events**, leading to the initiation of an act of violence. This may be impulsive or controlled, appetitive or defensive. Once having initiated an act of violence, which would include actions preparatory to the act as well as its consummation, personality disordered individuals fail to adequately process the feedback (indicated by dashed arrows) from the motor, cognitive and affective outputs from the brain (indicated by solid arrows). Consequently, their brains fail to register 'errors' which would normally act to inhibit or abort the violent act.

('externalizers') having a propensity to act out impulsively show a deficit in a brain-wave, the error-related negativity (ERN) that is evoked when behavioural errors are made (Hall *et al.*, 2007). This brain-wave is thought to be generated in the anterior cingulate cortex (Dehaene *et al.*, 1994). A similar brain mechanism would putatively evaluate errors in the cognitive and affective outputs, so that these can be corrected. A 'crazy' thought or an inappropriate affective reaction such as jealous rage, for example, could be monitored in this way and corrected.

Despite its apparently static appearance, the model shown is in fact a highly dynamic one – the only static elements are the predisposing influences that set the thresholds for detecting and responding to inputs (triggering factors and feedback from outputs, shown as dashed lines in Figure 20.4). Thus in our example of the narcissistic patient, several successive triggers would have operated subsequent to the initial trigger of the demeaning comment. For example, having arrived at his ex-girlfriend's house and rung the doorbell, the appearance of the new boyfriend triggered the final murderous act. Nonetheless, it is the failure to monitor the feedback from cognitive, affective and motoric outputs that was arguably critical to the fatal outcome. Normally, these outputs would, via feedback, be appraised and an error message registered which would lead to interruption or inhibition of the behaviour. It is, we argue, a characteristic of the personality disordered individual that these error messages fail to get detected in the relevant neural mechanism, so that maladaptive thoughts, affects and behaviours are not inhibited.

The traits of impulsivity and compulsivity will doubtless play a key role here. To the extent that individuals are impulsive *cognitively* (their acts lack premeditation and forethought), *affectively* (their emotional impulses are poorly controlled) and *motorically* (their actions are rash and precipitate), they will be more liable to failure in detecting an error message. In short, the brains of impulsive individuals will putatively be deficient in the ability to detect error messages contained in the feedback from their cognitive, motor and affective outputs. Those who are affectively impulsive, whose offending is driven by negative affective states such as reactive anger and boredom, are particularly likely to have criminal, including violent, histories and to manifest a combination of borderline and antisocial traits (Howard *et al.*, 2008). Their error-detection deficit is likely to be most salient in situations where an inappropriate affective reaction is manifested in, for example, extreme sensation-seeking or extreme reactive (threat-induced) aggression. At the other extreme are those with obsessive compulsive traits, which correlate inversely with a history of criminal and violent offending (Howard *et al.*, 2008) and are inversely related to a broad PD dimension of antisocial dyscontrol (Fossati *et al.*, 2007). In their case the error message is likely to be too sensitively detected (the threshold for error detection is set too low), so that any action performed is flagged with an error message. Having detected the error message, the brain 'instructs' that the action be repeated, which again throws up an error message leading to further, compulsive repetition of the action.

Conclusions and Implications for the Future

It is clear from our review of the current 'state of play' regarding personality disorders in a forensic context that issues persist regarding how they are to be defined, assessed, and treated. As we move towards DSM-V in

2012, there is a need to develop a classificatory system that achieves a rapprochement between the current DSM categories and a dimensional approach, along the lines suggested by Livesley (2003). Such a system should include a clear definition of personality disorder in general, specifying its essential features that distinguish it both from other categories of mental disorder, and from normal personality functioning. In assessment there is a need to move beyond a simple trait-based approach to one that acknowledges other domains of dysfunction, such as dysfunctional *concerns* – motives, roles and goals – and dysfunctions in the *life narrative*, as these are experienced by the individual, i.e. a structural phenomenology of personality disorder. There is a need also for innovative treatment approaches, including those that target the neurobiological substrates of antisocial dyscontrol, since, as our review shows, this has emerged as an important criminogenic dimension of personality disorder. One of the current authors has made specific suggestions in this regard (Howard, 2009).

Particular interest currently focuses on the programme initiated by the UK government to pilot the assessment and treatment of patients with severe personality disorders supposedly linked functionally to their dangerousness ('dangerous and severe personality disorder' [DSPD]: see Duggan & Howard, 2009). It will be interesting to see whether they survive in their present form – two DSPD units in the prison system, and two in the health system – in the face of current financial stringencies; and whether the treatment evaluations currently being undertaken enable conclusions to be drawn regarding treatment outcomes.

Notes

1 While studies vary in terms of three versus four higher-order factors and the labels attached to them (see Tyrer *et al.*, 2007), nonetheless there is consensus across studies for a higher-order factor comprising antisocial, narcissistic-histrionic, paranoid and borderline traits, in forensic psychiatric patients (Blackburn *et al.*, 2005), prison inmates (Ullrich & Marneros, 2004, 2007) and in a community sample (Howard *et al.*, 2008). While Livesley uses the term 'Dissocial' to describe this factor, we prefer to use the term 'Antisocial Dyscontrol' to describe this dimension.

2 Note that under the proposed revision of the Mental Health Act currently going through Parliament, the distinction between Psychopathic Disorder and Mental Illness is abolished in favour of the generic term 'mental disorder',

defined (in an entirely circular fashion) as 'any disorder of disability of the mind'.

3 Care should be taken to distinguish between an *act*, defined by an outcome (in the case of a violent act, the infliction of harm and suffering), and the *actions* taken to achieve the outcome.

Further Reading

Hall, J.R., Bernat, E.M. & Patrick, C.J. (2007). Externalizing psychopathology and the error-related negativity. *Psychological Science*, *18*, 326–333.

This study examined the error-related negativity (ERN) in high and low 'externalisers', selected using the Externalizing Inventory developed by Krueger *et al.* (2007). Externalising is a higher-order, highly heritable trait that resembles the Antisocial Dyscontrol factor mentioned in the text (see Figure 20.2) and reflects a general vulnerability towards the development of impulse control problems. ERN was recorded in a Go/No Go task in which target letters (S, H) displayed on a computer screen must be responded to, while responses to a non-target (X) must be inhibited. The large ERN normally recorded frontally on error trials was present in low externalisers, but was significantly diminished in high externalisers. Note that the sample used in this study was drawn from a student population. Studies are required that investigate ERN in personality disordered populations, particularly those that score high on the Dissocial factor.

Coid, J. (1998). Axis II disorders and motivation for serious criminal behaviour. In A.E. Skodol (Ed.) *Psychopathology and violent crime. Review of psychiatry, Vol. 17* (pp.53–97). Washington, DC: American Psychiatric Association.

This was one of the first studies to systematically explore the relationship between personality disorder in criminal offenders and violent crime. It was unique in also exploring the motivations behind the criminal offending in the personality disordered, and attempted to draw up a taxonomy of motivations. The study samples were male and female psychopaths from three maximum security hospitals, and male inmates of three special units for dangerous prisoners, a total sample of 243. All underwent detailed psychiatric assessment to ascertain personality disorder diagnoses and level of psychopathy using the Psychopathy Checklist. The text is illustrated with several interesting case studies, including Case 4, the narcissistic offender referred to in this chapter (p. 322). A drawback of the study is that it is correlational, so that no causal inferences can be drawn regarding the relationship between personality disorder and violent offending.

Livesley, W.J. (2007). A framework for integrating dimensional and categorical classifications of personality disorder. *Journal of Personality Disorders*, *21*, 199–224.

This paper is a good introduction to the views of John Livesley on personality disorder, summarised here in Figure 20.1. Livesley outlines his attempt to combine categorical and dimensional diagnoses of personality disorder in an integrated framework. He adopts a two-component classification, summarised here in Figure 20.4, that distinguishes between the diagnosis of personality disorder in general (a breakdown in the structure of personality), and individual differences in the form the disorder takes, assessed in terms of a set of empirically derived primary traits. The strength of his approach is that it introduces an aetiological perspective, derived from behavioural genetic studies, to the classification of personality disorders. It also points to the need to develop instruments for the assessment of areas of content, such as concerns and the life narrative, other than dysfunctional traits. Implicit in Livesley's account is the idea that a breakdown in the structure of personality gives rise to measurable changes in the content of personality, as shown by the arrows in Figure 20.1. However, it is not clear from his account whether the structure of personality disorder has some kind of neurobiological substrate, nor how deformations of the structure give rise to dysfunctional traits, abnormal concerns, and a lack of coherence in the life narrative.

References

Andrews, D.A. & Bonta, J. (2003). *The psychology of criminal conduct* (3rd edn). Cincinnati, OH: Anderson.

Apter, M.J. (2005). *Personality dynamics. Key concepts in reversal theory*. Loughborough: Apter International.

Bagby, R.M., Sellbom, M., Costa, P.T. & Widiger, T.A. (2008). Predicting diagnostic and statistical manual of mental disorders-IV personality disorders with the five-factor model of personality and the personality psychopathology five. *Personality and Mental Health*, *2*, 55–69.

Banerjee, P., Duggan, C. Huband, N. & Watson, N. (2006). Brief psycho-education for people with personality disorder – a pilot study. *Psychology and Psychotherapy; Theory, Research and Practice*, *79*, 385–394.

Bateman, A. & Fonagy, P. (1999). Effectiveness of partial hospitalization in the treatment of borderline personality disorder: A randomized controlled trial. *American Journal of Psychiatry*, *156*(10), 1563–9.

Benjamin, L.S. (1993). *Interpersonal diagnosis and treatment of personality disorder*. New York: Guilford Press.

Binks, C., Fenton, M., McCarthy, L., Lee, T., Adams, C.E. & Duggan, C. (2006). Psychological therapies for people with borderline personality disorder. *Cochrane Database of Systematic Reviews*, Issue 1. Art. No.: CD005652. DOI: 10.1002/14651858.CD005652.

Black, D.W., Baumgard, C.H. & Bell, S.E. (1995). A 16 to 45 year follow-up of 71 men with antisocial personality disorder. *Comprehensive Psychiatry*, *36*, 130–140.

Blackburn, R. (1971). MMPI dimensions of sociability and impulse control. *Journal of Consulting and Clinical Psychology*, 37, 166.

Blackburn, R. (1982). *The special hospitals assessment of personality and socialization.* Unpublished manuscript, Park Lane Hospital, Liverpool.

Blackburn, R. (2000). Classification and assessment of personality disorders in mentally disordered offenders: A psychological perspective. *Criminal Behaviour and Mental Health*, 10, S8–S32.

Blackburn, R. (2007). Personality disorder and antisocial deviance: Comments on the debate on the structure of the Psychopathy Checklist-Revised. *Journal of Personality Disorders*, 21, 142–159.

Blackburn, R. (2009). Subtypes of psychopath. In M. McMurran & R. Howard (Eds.) *Personality, personality disorder and violence.* Chichester: John Wiley & Sons.

Blackburn, R. & Fawcett, D. (1999). The antisocial personality questionnaire: An inventory for assessing personality deviation in offender populations. *European Journal of Psychological Assessment*, 15, 14–24.

Blackburn, R., Logan, C., Renwick, S.J.D. & Donnelly, J.P. (2005). Higher-order dimensions of personality disorder: Hierarchical structure and relationships with the five factor model, the interpersonal circle, and psychopathy. *Journal of Personality Disorders*, 19(6), 597–623.

Blackburn, R. & Renwick, S.J. (1996). Rating scales for measuring the interpersonal circle in forensic psychiatric inpatients. *Psychological Assessment*, 8, 76–84.

Cantrell, J.D. & Dana, R.D. (1987). Use of the Millon Clinical Multiaxial Inventory (MCMI) as a screening instrument at a community mental health center. *Journal of Clinical Psychology*, 43, 366–375.

Clark, L.A. (2007). Assessment and diagnosis of personality disorder: Perennial issues and an emerging reconceptualization. *Annual Review of Psychology*, 58, 227–257.

Clark, L.A., Livesley, J.W. & Morey, L. (1997). Personality disorder assessment: The challenge of construct validity. *Journal of Personality Disorders*, 11, 205–231.

Cleckley, H. (1941). *The mask of sanity.* Oxford: Mosby.

Cleckley, H. (1988). *The mask of sanity* (5th edn). St. Louis, MO: Mosby. Retrieved 14 September 2009 from http://www.cassiopaea.org/cass/sanity_1.PdF

Coid, J. (1992). DSM-III diagnosis in criminal psychopaths: A way forward. *Criminal Behaviour and Mental Health*, 2, 78–94.

Coid, J. (1998). Axis II disorders and motivation for serious criminal behaviour. In A.E. Skodol (Ed.) *Psychopathology and violent crime. Review of Psychiatry, Vol. 17* (pp.53–97). Washington, DC: American Psychiatric Association.

Coid, J., Kahtan, N., Gault, S. & Jarman, B. (1999). Patients with personality disorder admitted to secure forensic psychiatry services. *British Journal of Psychiatry*, 175, 528–536.

Coid, J., Yang, M., Tyrer, P., Roberts, A. & Ullrich, S. (2006). Prevalence and correlates of personality disorder in Great Britain. *British Journal of Psychiatry*, 188, 423–431.

Coid, J., Yang, M., Ullrich, S., Zhang, T. & Roberts, A. (2008). *Predicting and understanding risk of re-offending: The Prisoner Cohort Study. Final report.* London: Home Office/Department of Health.

Costa, P.T. & McCrae, R.R. (1992). *Revised NEO personality inventory: Professional manual.* Odessa, FL: Psychological Assessment Resources.

DeBrito, S.A. & Hodgins, S. (2009). Antisocial personality disorder. In M. McMurran & R. Howard (Eds.) *Personality, personality disorder and violence.* Chichester: John Wiley & Sons.

Dehaene, S., Posner, M.I. & Tucker, D.M. (1994). Localization of a neural system for error detection and compensation. *Psychological Science*, 5, 303–305.

Duggan, C. & Howard, R.C. (2009). The 'functional link' between personality disorder and violence: A critical appraisal. In M. McMurran & R. Howard (Eds.) *Personality, personality disorder and violence.* Chichester: John Wiley & Sons.

Duggan, C., Huband, N., Smailagic, N. *et al.* (2007). The use of psychological treatments for people with personality disorder: A systematic review of randomized controlled trials. *Personality and Mental Health*, 1, 95–125.

Duggan, C., Huband, N., Smailagic, N. *et al.* (2008). The use of pharmacological treatments for people with personality disorder: A systematic review of randomized controlled trials. *Personality and Mental Health*, 2, 119–170.

Fazel, S. & Danesh, J. (2002). Serious mental disorder in 23 000 prisoners: A systematic review of 62 surveys. *The Lancet*, 359, 545–550.

First, M.B., Spitzer, R.I., Gibbon, M., Williams, J.B.W. & Benjamin, L (1994). *The Structured Clinical Interview for DSM-1V Axis II Personality Disorders (SCID-11) (Version 2.0).* New York: Biometrics Research, New York State Psychiatric Institute.

Fossati, A., Barratt, E.S., Borroni, S., Villa, D., Grazioli, F. & Maffei, C. (2007). Impulsivity, aggressiveness, and DSM-IV personality disorders. *Psychiatry Research*, 149, 157–167.

Gibbon, S., Duggan, C., Stoffers, J.M., Huband, N., Völlm, B.A., Ferriter, M. *et al.* (2009). Psychological interventions for antisocial personality disorder (Protocol). *Cochrane Database of Systematic Reviews* 2009, Issue 1. Art. No.: CD007668. DOI: 10.1002/14651858.CD007668.

Grilo, C.M., McGlashan, T.H. & Oldham, J.M. (1998). Course and stability of personality disorders. *Journal of Practical Psychiatry and Behavioral Health*, 4, 61–75.

Gunderson, J.G., Frank, A.F., Ronningstam, E.F. *et al* (1989). Early discontinuance of borderline patients from psychotherapy. *Journal of Nervous and Mental Disease*, 177(1), 38–42.

Hall, J.R., Bernat, E.M. & Patrick, C.J. (2007). Externalizing psychopathology and the error-related negativity. *Psychological Science*, 18, 326–333.

Hare, R.D. (1980). A research scale for the assessment of psychopathy in criminal populations. *Personality and Individual Differences*, 1, 111–119.

Hare, R.D. (2003). *The Hare Psychopathy Checklist-Revised* (2nd edn). Toronto: Multi-Health Systems.

Harkness, A.R. & McNulty, J.L. (1994). The personality psychopathology five (PSY-5): Issues from the pages of a diagnostic manual instead of a dictionary. In S. Strack & M. Lorr (Eds.) *Differentiating normal and abnormal personality* (pp.291–315). New York: Springer.

Hart, S.D., Cox, D.N. & Hare, R.D. (1995). *Manual for the Psychopathy Checklist: Screening Version (PCL:SV)*. Toronto: Multi-Health Systems.

Hasin, D.S. & Grant, B.F. (1987a). Psychiatric diagnosis of patients with substance abuse problems: A comparison of two procedures, the DIS and the SADS-L. *Journal of Psychiatric Research, 21,* 7–22.

Hasin, D.S. & Grant, B.F. (1987b). Diagnosing depressive disorders in patients with alcohol and drug problems: A comparison of the SADS-L and the DIS. *Journal of Psychiatric Research, 21,* 301–311.

Howard, R.C. (2009). The neurobiology of affective dyscontrol: Implications for understanding 'dangerous and severe personality disorder'. In M. McMurran & R. Howard (Eds.) *Personality, personality disorder and violence*. Chichester: John Wiley & Sons.

Howard, R.C., Huband, N., Duggan, C. & Mannion, A. (2008). Exploring the link between personality disorder and criminality in a community sample. *Journal of Personality Disorders, 22*(6), 589–603.

Howard, R.C. & Lumsden, J. (1996). A neurophysiological predictor of re-offending in Special Hospital patients. *Criminal Behaviour and Mental Health, 6,* 147–156.

Howard, R.C. & Lumsden, J. (1997). CNV predicts violent outcomes in patients released from special hospital. *Criminal Behaviour and Mental Health, 7,* 237–240.

Huband, N., McMurran, M., Evans, C. & Duggan, C. (2007). Social problem-solving plus psychoeducation for adults with personality disorder: A pragmatic randomised clinical trial. *British Journal of Psychiatry, 190,* 307–313.

Hunt, C. & Andrews, G. (1992). Measuring personality disorder: The use of self-report questionnaires. *Journal of Personality Disorders, 6,* 125–133.

Hyler, S.E. & Rieder, R.O. (1987). *PDQ-R: Personality diagnostic questionnaire- revised*. New York: New York State Psychiatric Institute.

Hyler, S.E., Skodol, A.E., Kellman, D., Oldham, J.M. & Rosnick, L. (1990). Validity of the Personality Diagnostic Questionnaire-Revised: Comparison with two structured interviews. *American Journal of Psychiatry, 147,* 1043–1048.

Hyler, S.E., Skodol, A.E., Oldham, J.M., Kellman, D. & Doidge, N. (1992). Validity of the Personality Diagnostic Questionnaire-Revised: A replication in an outpatient sample. *Comprehensive Psychiatry, 33,* 73–77.

Krueger, R.F., Markon, K.E., Patrick, C.J., Benning, S.D. & Kramer, M.D. (2007). Linking antisocial behaviour, substance use and personality: An integrative quantitative model of the adult externalizing spectrum. *Journal of Abnormal Psychology, 116,* 645–666.

Jolliffe, D. & Farrington, D.P. (2008). A systematic review of the relationship between childhood impulsiveness and later violence. In M. McMurran & R. Howard (Eds.) *Personality, personality disorder and violence*. Chichester: John Wiley & Sons.

Leary, T. (1957). *Interpersonal diagnosis of personality*. New York: Ronald Press.

Leistico, A.-M., Salekin, R.T., DeCosta, J. & Rogers, R. (2008). A large-scale meta-analysis relating the hare measure of psychopathy to antisocial conduct. *Law and Human Behavior, 32,* 28–45.

Linehan, M.M., Armstrong, H.E., Suarez, A., Allmon, D. & Heard, H.L. (1991). Cognitive-behavioral treatment of chronically parasuicidal borderline patients. *Archives of General Psychiatry, 48,* 1060–1064.

Livesley, W.J. (1998). Suggestions for a framework for an empirically based classification of personality disorder. *Canadian Journal of Psychiatry, 43.* Retrieved 11 September 2009 from http://server03.cpa-apc.org:8080/Publications/Archives/CJP/1998/Mar/mar98_rev1.htm

Livesley, W.J. (2003). Diagnostic dilemmas in the classification of personality disorders. In K. Phillips, M. First MB & H.A. Pincus (Eds.) *Advancing DSM: Dilemmas in psychiatric diagnosis*. Washington, DC: American Psychiatric Press.

Livesley, W.J. (2007a). A framework for integrating dimensional and categorical classifications of personality disorder. *Journal of Personality Disorders, 21,* 199–224.

Livesley, W.J. (2007b). The relevance of an integrated approach to the treatment of personality disordered offenders, *Psychology, Crime and Law, 13,* 27–46.

Livesley, W.J. (2008). Toward a genetically-informed model of borderline personality disorder. *Journal of Personality Disorders, 22,* 42–71.

Loranger, A.W. (1988). *Personality Disorder Examination (PDE) manual*. Yonkers, NY: DV Communications.

Loranger, A.W., Sartorius, N., Andreoli, A., Berger, P., Buchheim, P., Channabasavanna, S.M. *et al.* (1994). The International Personality Disorder Examination: The World Health Organization and Alcohol, Drug Abuse and Mental Health Administration international pilot study of personality disorders. *Archives of General Psychiatry, 551,* 215–224.

McGlashan, T.H., Grilo, C.M., Skodol, A.E., Gunderson, J.G., Shea, M.T., Morey, L.C. *et al.* (2000). The Collaborative Longitudinal Personality Disorders Study: Baseline Axis I/II and II/II diagnostic co-occurrence. *Acta Psychiatrica Scandinavica, 102,* 256–264.

McMurran, M. & Howard, R.C. (2009). *Personality, personality disorder and violence*. Chichester: John Wiley & Sons.

McMurran, M. & Theodosi, E. (2007). Is treatment non-completion associated with increased reconviction over no treatment? *Psychology, Crime and Law, 13,* 333–343.

Mellsop, G., Varghese, F., Joshua, S. & Hicks, A. (1982). The reliability of Axis II of DSM-III. *American Journal of Psychiatry, 139,* 1360–1361.

Millon, T., Millon, C. & Davis, R.D. (1994). *Millon Clinical Multiaxial Inventory-III*. Minneapolis, MN: National Computer Systems.

Morey, L.C. (1991). *Personality Assessment Inventory*. Lutz, FL: Psychological Assessment Resources.

Mullen, P.E. (1992). Psychopathy: A developmental disorder of ethical action. *Criminal Behaviour and Mental Health, 2*, 234–244.

Newhill, C.E., Mulvey, E.P. & Pilkonis, P.A. (2004). Initial development of a measure of emotional dysregulation for individuals with Cluster B personality disorders. *Research on Social Work Practice, 14*, 443–449.

Oldham, J.M. (2007). Psychodynamic psychotherapy for personality disorders. *American Journal of Psychiatry, 164*, 1465–1467.

Parker, G. & Barrett, E. (2000). Personality and personality disorder: Current issues and directions. *Psychological Medicine, 30*, 1–9.

Putkonen, A., Kotilainen, I., Joyal, C.C. & Tühonen, J. (2004). Comorbid personality disorders and substance use disorders of mentally ill homicide offenders: A structured clinical study on dual and triple diagnoses. *Schizophrenia Bulletin, 30*, 59–72.

Safran, J.D. & Muran, J.C. (2000). *Negotiating the therapeutic alliance: A relational treatment guide*. New York: Guilford Press.

Skodol, A.E., Buckley, P. & Charles, E. (1983). Is there a characteristic pattern to the treatment history of clinic outpatients with borderline personality? *Journal of Nervous and Mental Disease, 171*, 405–410.

Skodol, A.E., Johnson, J.G., Cohen, P. et al. (2007). Personality disorder and impaired functioning from adolescent to adulthood. *British Journal of Psychiatry, 190*, 415–420.

Skodol, A.E., Oldham, J.M., Rosnick, L., Kellman, H.D. & Hyler, S.E. (1991). Diagnosis of DSM-III-R personality disorders: A comparison of two structured interviews. *International Journal of Methods in Psychiatric Research, 1*, 13–26.

Soloff, P. (1998). Symptom-orientated psychopharmacology for personality disorders. *Journal of Practical Psychiatry and Behavioral Health, 4*(1), 3–11.

Stangl, D., Pfohl, B., Zimmerman, M., Bowers, W. & Corenthal, C. (1985). A structured interview for the DSM-III personality disorders. A preliminary report. *Archives of General Psychiatry, 42*, 591–596.

Stevenson, J. & Meares, R. (1992). An outcome study of psychotherapy for patients with borderline personality disorder. *American Journal of Psychiatry, 149*, 358–362.

Tyrer, P., Coombs, N., Ibrahimi, F., Mathilakath, A., Bajaj, P., Ranger, M. et al. (2007). Critical developments in the assessment of personality disorder. *British Journal of Psychiatry, 190*(Suppl. 49), s51–s59. doi: 10.1192/bjp.190.5.s51.

Ullrich, S. & Marneros, A. (2004). Dimensions of personality disorders in offenders. *Criminal Behaviour and Mental Health, 14*, 202–213.

Ullrich, S. & Marneros, A. (2007). Underlying dimensions of ICD-10 personality disorders: Risk factors, childhood antecedents, and adverse outcomes in adulthood. *Journal of Forensic Psychiatry and Psychology, 18*(1), 44–58.

Wakefield, J.C. (1992). The concept of mental disorder: On the boundary between biological facts and social values. *American Psychologist, 47*, 373–388.

Waldinger, R.J. & Gunderson, J.G. (1984). Completed psychotherapies with borderline patients. *American Journal of Psychotherapy, 38*, 190–202.

Walters, G.D. (2003). Predicting institutional adjustment and recidivism with Psychopathy Checklist factor scores: A meta-analysis. *Law and Human Behavior, 27*, 541–558.

Walters, G.D., Knight, R.A., Grann, M. & Dahle, K.-P. (2008). Incremental validity of the Psychopathy Checklist facet scores: Predicting release outcome in six samples. *Journal of Abnormal Psychology, 117*, 396–405.

Ward T., Day, A. & Howells, K. (2004). The Multifactor Offender Readiness Model. *Aggression and Violent Behaviour, 9*, 645–673.

Weissman, M.M. (1993). The epidemiology of personality disorders: A 1990 update. *Journal of Personality Disorders*, Suppl., 44–62.

Westen, D. & Arkowitz-Westen, L. (1998). Limitations of Axis II in diagnosing personality pathology in clinical practice. *American Journal of Psychiatry, 155*, 1767–1771.

World Health Organization (1992). *10th revision of the International Classification of Diseases (ICD-10)*. Geneva: WHO.

Zanarini, M.C., Frankenberg, F.R., Hennen, J., Reich, B. & Silk, K. (2005). The Mclean Study of Adult Development (MSAD): Overview of the first six years of prospective follow-up. *Journal of Personality Disorders, 19*, 505–523.

Zimmerman, M. (1994). Diagnosing personality disorders: A review of issues and research methods. *Archives of General Psychiatry, 51*, 225–245.

Zimmerman, M., Pfohl, B., Coryell, W., Stangl, D. & Corenthal, C. (1988). Diagnosing personality disorder in depressed patients: A comparison of patient and informant interviews. *Archives of General Psychiatry, 45*, 733–737.

21

The Trauma of Being Violent

Ceri Evans

Violent offenders can develop persistent intrusive memories and post-traumatic stress disorder (PTSD) in relation to their violent crime. Initial case reports have been followed by several prevalence studies, which have established that crime-related PTSD occurs in forensic settings, including prison and secure hospital populations.

One limitation of the body of research as a whole is that the predominant focus has been on the presence or absence of the diagnosis of PTSD, and most studies have failed to report information about the specific content and nature of the intrusive memories. However, there is preliminary evidence that the phenomenological detail of the intrusive memories experienced by violent offenders is reminiscent of victims of violent crime, in that the intrusions appear to be predominantly sensory-based visual fragments, which are stereotyped, resistant to change and distressing.

Recent studies have investigated the emotional and cognitive correlates of PTSD in forensic samples, as the focus has turned to addressing the question of which individuals are more likely to develop intrusive memories and PTSD in relation to their offending behaviour.

The possibility of traumatic responses to be violent has important legal and clinical implications. In particular, the question of the appropriateness of treatment of crime-related PTSD in violent offenders is likely to be controversial.

Introduction

Although extreme violence, and murder in particular, has fascinated the public and researchers alike, in general,

the focus has been on addressing the 'who does it?' and 'why did they do it?' questions. Much less attention has been placed on the aftermath of violence, especially the psychological impact of committing an act of serious violence on the perpetrator (Curle, 1989). It is striking that very little is known about how perpetrators remember and think about their violent acts, particularly as the idea that violent perpetrators can be distressed and even traumatised by their own offending behaviour was reported over two decades ago (Harry & Resnick, 1986). However, the literature related to the nature of memory of violence is significantly more developed with respect to victims of violence than for those who perpetrated it.

The idea that offenders can be literally traumatised by their own violent actions has mainly been pursued empirically through investigations into the prevalence of PTSD in clinical or criminal populations. It must be acknowledged that PTSD represents only one of a range of diagnoses linked to traumatic responses. Further, PTSD, the archetypal response to trauma, is uncommonly found alone, even in community samples, with around 80 per cent of people meeting diagnostic criteria for another mental disorder (Breslau et al., 1997; Kessler et al., 1995). However, studies into PTSD predominate and therefore this forms the focus for this chapter.

Our knowledge about the *risk factors* for, and what might contribute to, the development of distressing memories or PTSD in perpetrators of violence is even more limited than our knowledge about the phenomenology of memories of violent crime in offenders. While the studies that are available about perpetrators' memories of violence often discuss the risk factors that *might* be associated with the kinds of memory under investigation, most studies are descriptive and do not include measures of purported mechanisms in their design. This represents a clinically relevant gap in our knowledge base in forensic psychiatry and psychology.

Whether the perpetrators of violence should be seen as potentially traumatised by their own behaviour is controversial, particularly when there might be self-serving reasons why offenders might claim that it is (Kruppa et al., 1995). According to DSM-IV (American Psychiatric Association, 1994), for an event to constitute a trauma, it must satisfy both objective and subjective criteria. PTSD can follow traumatic events in which individuals experience (1) a threat to their own life or the lives of others, or a threat to their own or other's physical integrity, and (2) the person's response involved intense fear, helplessness, or horror. The extent to which perpetrators of violence experience these intense emotions has not been examined systematically. It has also been argued that the DSM-IV criteria for a traumatic stressor are too narrowly focused on intense fear, and do not allow for the traumatising effect of guilt or shame, which might be more relevant to perpetrators of violence (McNally, 2003).

The study of intrusive memories and the study of PTSD are intimately related because theoretical approaches to PTSD obviously have to account for the clinical features, especially *intrusive memories*, for some *the hallmark of PTSD* (Brewin et al., 1996; Krystal et al., 1995; McNally, 1988). Intrusive memories have been defined as memories of a traumatic event that are recurrent, distressing and involuntarily triggered (diagnostic criteria of Post Traumatic Stress Disorder (PTSD[1]), (DSM-IV; American Psychiatric Association, 1994). These recollections tend to be vivid, sensory, and experienced as relatively uncontrollable, unwanted, and extremely distressing (Halligan et al., 2003). Therefore, many of the empirical data that are relevant to intrusive memories are to be found in studies of PTSD, particularly those of assault victims.

Surprisingly little is known about the *phenomenological form* of intrusive re-experiences related to violence, even in the victims of traumatic events (Briere & Conte, 1993; De Silva & Marks, 1999; Ehlers et al., in press; Falsetti et al., 2002; Reynolds & Brewin, 1998, 1999). Issues such as which aspects of the trauma memory are typically re-experienced, whether individuals experience different parts of the memory at different times, whether they experience parts of the event or the whole

event, and how the intrusive memories are experienced have yet to be systematically studied (Hackmann et al., 2004). However, some recent advances have been made in understanding the phenomenology of intrusive memories in trauma victims, which helps to highlight corresponding gaps in our knowledge about intrusive memories in violent offenders:

1. Preliminary research suggests that intrusive memories mainly consist of *sensory impressions*, rather than thoughts (Ehlers & Steil, 1995; Mellman & Davis, 1985; van der Kolk & Fisler, 1995), particularly visual intrusions (Ehlers et al., 2002; Mellman & Davis, 1985; van der Kolk & Fisler, 1995).

2. It has been argued that traumatic memories are *fragmented*, without a coherent semantic component, but that a narrative can be formed over time as the individual becomes more and more aware of elements of the traumatic experience (van der Kolk & Fisler, 1995).

3. The sensory impressions and the emotions accompanying them are experienced as if they are occurring in the '*here and now*' rather than being related to past events (Brewin et al., 1996; Ehlers & Clark, 2000; Foa & Rothbaum, 1998). This 'lack of time perspective' contrasts with other autobiographical memories that are characterised by an awareness that the content of memory relates to the past (Tulving, 2002; Wheeler, 2000).

4. It has been suggested that intrusive memories for trauma are relatively *resistant to change* (van der Kolk & van der Hart, 1991). This idea has been supported by observations that trauma survivors with PTSD continue to experience their original sensory impressions and emotions in a repetitive, *stereotyped* way, even if this is inconsistent with, or even contradicted by, later information learned (Ehlers & Clark, 2000; Halligan et al., 2003).

Little is also known about the *content* of intrusive memories, even in trauma victims (Ehlers et al., 2002; Reynolds & Brewin, 1998, 1999). As indicated, there is preliminary evidence that intrusive cognitions consist of sensory impressions rather than thoughts; however, it is not clear *which* of the sensory impressions from a traumatic experience will be re-experienced (Ehlers et al., 2002; Ehlers & Steil, 1995; Mellman & Davis, 1985; van der Kolk & Fisler, 1995). There are some empirical data from laboratory studies on eyewitness testimony that central information from the event is well remembered while peripheral information is poorly remembered (Christianson, 1992). This would suggest that the strongest memories would be for the most traumatic or emotional aspects of the event, in line with a narrowing of attention in conditions of high arousal (Easterbrook, 1959). An example of this would be so-called 'weapon focus', a phenomenon whereby a witness's attention is narrowly focused on the assailant's weapon during the commission of a crime (Kramer et al., 1990).

The related category of cognition is *ruminations*. Patients with PTSD have reported that dwelling on intrusive questions such as 'Why did this event happen to me?', 'How could the event have been prevented?', dwelling on how one's life has been ruined by the event, or plans for revenge, are more frequent than intrusive images or flashbacks (Reynolds & Brewin, 1998, 1999). These are *non-memory* intrusive cognitions, which should be distinguished from intrusive *memory* phenomena, as these are possibly functionally distinct (Ehlers & Clark, 2000; Joseph et al., 1997). Such intrusive *thoughts* can be linked to preoccupations with appraisal of the traumatic event rather than representing trauma memories, *per se*. This cognitive elaboration was recognised by Reynolds and Brewin who used the term '*elaborative cognitions*' to describe this type of intrusive thought (Reynolds & Brewin, 1998).

With this background about the nature of intrusive memories in victims of trauma in mind, the general purpose of this chapter is: (1) to systematically describe the empirical evidence about the general nature of the traumatic responses of violent offenders to their own acts of violence; (2) to discuss some of the mechanisms and risk factors that might contribute to these traumatic responses; and (3) to summarise the potential clinical and legal implications of violent offenders developing PTSD in relation to their violent crime. Table 21.1 provides a summary of relevant research studies in this area.

Empirical Evidence

Combat samples

The traumatic effect of killing has mainly been investigated in those who have killed within the context of their roles as *soldiers*, typically in studies designed to identify PTSD. Studies of Vietnam War veterans have shown that although the development of PTSD is multi-determined and related to a wide array of pre-military, military and post-military variables, the evidence suggests that the primary aetiological factor is combat exposure (Foy et al., 1987). More specifically, even though different studies have used different measures to delineate and quantify the degree of combat exposure in Vietnam veteran 'cases' and 'controls' (e.g. The Combat Exposure Scale) (Foy et al., 1984), a consistent finding has been that those who develop PTSD are more likely to report greater personal involvement in the killing (Foy et al., 1987; Gallers et al., 1985; Solkoff et al., 1986). This is particularly so if the deliberate harming and killing was perpetrated on non-military subjects in the context of an 'atrocity'; epidemiologic data from the National Vietnam Readjustment Study confirmed that involvement in atrocities strongly predicts PTSD (King et al., 1995). Even among veterans qualifying for a PTSD diagnosis, commission of atrocities (or having witnessed them) predicted PTSD over and above that predicted by extent of combat exposure (King et al., 1995).

The studies on PTSD in Vietnam veterans have mainly been diagnostic in nature, but they are still relevant to our understanding of intrusive memories in perpetrators of violence. Although they did not typically report breakdown details about the nature of the psychopathology reported by the individual veterans, the measures for PTSD invariably included one criterion requiring re-experiencing of the trauma in the form of vivid memories, nightmares or flashbacks. This makes it likely that at least some of the Veterans had intrusive re-experiences of personal violence.

Intrusive memories and PTSD (with the diagnostic implication of intrusive re-experiencing symptoms) related to killing others have also been reported in non-military occupations. The development of PTSD was reported in 3 out of 25 UK police firearm officers, as a consequence of wounding or killing members of the public during the course of their work (Manolias & Hyatt-Williams, 1993). Traumatic reactions to killing have also been reported in London Underground train drivers who have inadvertently killed or injured members of the public during the course of their work, mostly people who committed suicide by jumping in front of trains (Farmer et al., 1992). In this study six out of seven drivers (85.7 per cent) who developed PTSD reported recurrent and distressing recollections of the event, with another one-third of drivers, who did not reach full diagnostic criteria for PTSD, also reporting intrusive memories of the event.

Table 21.1   Studies of crime-related PTSD and/or intrusive memories

Study or report	n^1	Population	Violent act[2]	Memory detail[3]	Purpose of study / report
Harry & Resnick (1985)	3	Mixed prisoners/ patients	Men who killed female partners	No	To report PTSD in murderers related to the killing
Curle (1990)	20/82	High security hospital male patients	Males who killed	No	To describe psychological responses to killing
Hambridge (1990)	1/3	Medium security patient	Man killed wife by strangulation	No	To describe grief following homicide
Thomas et al. (1994)	1	Medium secure patient	Mother killed 2 children by asphyxiation	No	To describe traumatic response to child murder
Kruppa et al. (1995)	33/44	High secure hospital patients	Mixed	No	To describe PTSD from all causes in perpetrators of violence
Pollock (1999)	66/80	Referrals to psychologist	Homicide	No	To describe PTSD from all causes, e.g. violence
Rogers et al. (2000)	1	Medium secure patient	Woman who killed employee by stabbing	No	To describe a single case study of behavioural treatment of PTSD
Spitzer et al. (2001)	5/34	Maximum secure patients	Mixed	No	To describe PTSD from all causes in forensic inpatients
Gray et al. (2003)	9/27	Mentally disordered offenders in medium secure units	Sexual or violent offence	No	To measure frequency of PTSD arising from a violent or sexual offence in primarily mentally ill population
Papanastassiou et al. (2004)	11/19	Medium secure patients	Conviction for homicide	No	To investigate the prevalence of PTSD related to the offence in a sample of homicide perpetrators
Evans et al. (2007)	105	Young offenders	Murder, Attempted murder, GBH	Yes	To describe memories of violent offending and investigate causes of intrusive memories
Evans et al. (2007)	105	Young offenders	Murder, Attempted murder, GBH	Yes	To investigate the cognitive and emotional correlates of intrusive memories related to violence
Crisford et al. (2008)	45	Regional and local secure unit patients		No	To investigate trauma symptomatology related to a violent offence in a sample of mentally disordered offenders

[1] The number of subjects in the study. Those represented by n/x gives the number out of the total sample that had intrusive memories.
[2] The trauma as identified by the study.
[3] In terms of phenomenology, describing the detailed qualities, characteristics and content of the intrusive memory.

The studies of soldiers and police officers obviously involve a different social context because the injuries to the victims do not result in legal culpability for the perpetrator of the injuries. However, they do support the hypothesis that individuals involved in causing injury to others can find the experience traumatic (Kruppa, 1991) and may experience distressing intrusive memories for the event.

Case reports on detained patients

The report generally held to be the first description of a traumatic response in perpetrators arising directly from their violence was an account of the development of PTSD in three men after they had committed homicides (Harry & Resnick, 1986). A range of symptoms were described which convinced the authors that the killings themselves constituted the traumatic event, including recurrent and intrusive recollections, nightmares, flashbacks, guilt, thoughts triggered by external stimuli, and avoidance of activities which prompted recall of the killing.

The authors attempted to synthesise historical factors for the cases, and considered the legal and clinical issues arising from the post-traumatic responses. Historical factors in common across the three case reports included young adult age, minimal criminal history, chaotic childhood; the killing (real or symbolically) of a woman with whom they had an emotional relationship; the absence of intoxication with alcohol or drugs as a factor; and the experience of extreme emotional distress. They also note that two of the men killed during dissociative episodes and one during an acute psychotic episode.

The authors noted that people who kill or seriously injure others in ways which are socially accepted, for example combat soldiers or police officers, are not exposed to the additional problems which people convicted of murder have to face, including social disapproval, the likelihood that those facing a serious charge will not be free to discuss the event, publicity, and estrangement from family and friends.

The authors went further to consider the clinical and legal implications of the diagnosis of PTSD arising from an act of murder. Clinical concerns included diagnostic confusion, provision of appropriate treatment, reduction in associated suicide risk, and rehabilitation. The legal issues included competency to stand trial, which could be impaired, for example, by impaired concentration; assessment of criminal responsibility; and release decisions of insanity acquittees.

Two further reports reinforced the potential for traumatic responses to killing. In one small case series, assessments of three patients in a regional secure unit in the UK who had killed led to the diagnoses of major depressive episode in two cases and PTSD in the third (Hambridge, 1990). The cases placed emphasis on abnormal grieving processes. The patient who developed PTSD was a 28-year-old man who had previously been convicted of the manslaughter his wife after he had killed her by strangulation when he was suffering from depression. He developed features of PTSD in relation to the killing, including recurrent distressing dreams about the offence, avoidance of thoughts and feelings about the offence, memory gaps for the offence, extreme distress triggered by contact with his young son, blunted affect and feelings of detachment from others. He also had angry outbursts, problems concentrating, and sleep disturbance. The main

idea of the article was that patients in regional secure units on the basis of convictions for manslaughter on the grounds of diminished responsibility were likely to have a heavy loading of risk factors for complicated grief reactions, and that in some cases PTSD could further complicate the grief reaction.

Similarly, Thomas et al. (1994) reported details of a complicated grief reaction in a mother who killed her children in a psychotic state. She had gradually developed a depressive illness culminating in persecutory delusions and delusions of reference, in addition to biological symptoms of depression. She strangled her two children and attempted to kill herself with a knife in the belief that this would prevent her and her children from being sexually abused by men coming to her home. Her course of illness was complicated, with serious relapses of psychosis and depression. A feature of her clinical presentation was intrusive phenomena including flashbacks of the index offence and recurrent nightmares, especially after exposure to any situation that reminded her of her children or her death. The authors noted that guilt and self-blame were a feature of both abnormal grief but also PTSD, which had occurred in relation to her offence. They also noted that her PTSD symptoms seemed to be related to her psychotic illness as well. Overall, the case report highlighted the impact on the recovery of someone who had killed of abnormal grief and PTSD symptoms, with the homicide being considered a particularly powerful figure of PTSD symptoms. The negative life events for the perpetrator arising from the killing, including the loss of her children and husband, and her subsequent depression, were conceptualised as making the perpetrator feel out of control and helpless, thus blurring the distinction between victim and perpetrator (Thomas et al., 1994).

Rogers et al. (2000) provided the first case report of treatment of PTSD arising from a violent offence (Rogers et al., 2000). They described the treatment of PTSD in a 51-year-old woman detained under a restriction order in a UK medium secure unit after killing her female employer by stabbing and being found guilty of manslaughter on the grounds of diminished responsibility. At the time of the offence the patient suffered from a depressive illness but not PTSD, which emerged over four years after the offence in the form of avoidance of knives and intrusive thoughts and nightmares about her offence, flashbacks and panic symptoms when exposed to reminders of her offence, and a range of avoidance behaviours. No history of previous trauma was identified. The treatment intervention involved graded exposure of a 16-week period to imaginal and live non-knife exposure, imaginal knife exposure, and real knife exposure. Clinical and statistically significant improvements in her PTSD and depression symptoms were maintained at 30-month follow-up.

The authors also highlighted some conceptual issues in treatment of violent offenders, in particular a sense of guilt, self-blame and alienation which may arise from killing a known person with whom the offender had a degree of emotional attachment; the likely proximity of the killing; and the court process confirming the public sanction of the behaviour. These aspects are in contrast to the experience of individuals who kill in combat situations in police work, for example, and these differences are reinforced by training and preparation of soldiers and police for their tasks and the support available afterwards.

The potential role of arousal symptoms in the context of PTSD complicating comorbid illnesses such as schizophrenia or depression was identified as a possible treatment target to improve the efficacy of interventions for the other major mental illness.

One interesting possibility is the observation that the onset of PTSD appears to have been significantly delayed following the index offence until specific work focusing on the index offence was introduced as a clinical intervention. This raises the possibility that therapeutic interventions might make individuals more susceptible to post-traumatic responses.

Forensic patient studies

The Broadmoor Hospital Study

The earliest systematic inquiry into traumatic responses to violent acts in perpetrators was an unpublished thesis which directly addressed the existence of intrusive memories and other clinical signs taken as evidence of traumatic or stress responses of violent offending, in male homicide patients detained in a maximum security hospital in the UK (Curle, 1989). The study design involved a case-note review and patient interviews to detect current or past symptoms thought to indicate a stress response to the killing and their attributions in relation to the killing. Symptoms indicative of stress were reported by more than three-quarters of the 128 patients in the casenote review. More specifically with respect to intrusions, 20 out of the 82 (24 per cent) patients interviewed reported current intrusions and 28 (34 per cent) reported past intrusions related to their act of killing. A strength of this study was that it focused on the psychological responses of patients at the phenomenological

level rather than exclusively at the diagnostic level, albeit that only the presence of symptoms and not the phenomenological characteristics or content of intrusive memories was reported.

However, while making a substantial contribution to our understanding of the traumatic and psychological responses to having perpetrated serious violence, there were several methodological limitations in the design of this study which limit the degree to which the main findings can be extrapolated. First, from a phenomenological perspective, it appears that intrusive memories of the killing also included ruminations for the event (the patient's concern about harming others, committing suicide or being the victim of violence themselves), which are not strictly intrusive memories of the event. Second, only limited phenomenological detail was obtained. No descriptions of the intrusions were given and no inter-rater reliability checks were performed, a point related to the decision not to tape-record subject responses. Third, the population of Special Hospital patients who had killed is a highly selected one and generalisability of the data to non-patients, patients detained in less secure conditions, or perpetrators who committed violence but did not kill their victim(s) is unclear. Fourth, the median length of time from the killing to the casenote study was 11.9 years, with time to the actual research interviews even longer. Although the problem of retrospective designs in such studies is unavoidable, the very long time period from index offence to interview creates concern. Finally, the participants in the study were patients who would almost certainly have been exposed to some form of therapeutic intervention, either medication or psychotherapy, which may well have affected their memories of the index offence.

Despite these limitations, the Broadmoor Hospital study represented a significant advance in terms of establishing the prevalence of intrusive memories related to perpetration of serious violence, albeit in a highly selected sample.

The Rampton Hospital Study

An investigation into the prevalence of PTSD in male and female inpatients detained in Rampton Hospital, a UK maximum secure facility, within the legal category of psychopathic disorder found both high lifetime (14/44; 32 per cent) and current (9/44; 22 per cent) PTSD diagnoses (Kruppa et al., 1995). The sample of 44 patients (10 per cent of the overall hospital population) included 11 of the 22 females detained in the hospital within the psychopathic legal category (although all were considered) and 33 of the 50 most recent male admissions within the psychopathic category. All but one male had been admitted to hospital on the basis of a violent offence. Although the overall rate was based on PTSD arising from all sources of trauma, in a significant proportion of the sample (33/44; 75 per cent) the index offence was identified as a 'traumatic event', defined as an event resulting in 'some PTSD symptomatology'; and in half of the cases in which PTSD was diagnosed, the traumatic event was the index offence.

One interesting aspect of this study involved a comparison between the symptom clusters associated with the index offence as opposed to non-offence traumatic events. Scores relating to hyperarousal and hypervigilance arising from non-offence-related trauma were higher than those arising from the index offence. One explanation for this might be that because violent offenders were the instigators of the offence, they might have less need to be vigilant or in a chronically aroused state. Alternatively, it may be that the Special Hospital environment provided frequent reminders of the offence, which presumably might lead to a degree of psychological adjustment.

It was also suggested that different types of traumatic event could lead to different types of symptom profiles. For example, previous work with Vietnam Veterans had found that those associated with the perpetration of abusive violence were more likely to experience denial symptoms as opposed to those who witnessed abusive violence, who were more likely to report re-experiencing symptoms (Laufer et al., 1984). It may be that perpetrators of violent crimes, who are violent in a context without tacit social approval as opposed to those who are violent in military combat situations, may develop specific psychological symptoms.

The authors identified some methodological considerations of their study. They noted that caution should be exercised in terms of accepting self-report data from an offender-patient population who may be motivated to report their index offence as traumatic to provide evidence that their rehabilitation is progressing. They also highlight the diagnostic issues in terms of applying the PTSD criteria (DSM-III-R) to the perpetrator of a traumatic event as opposed to the passive victim. In addition, the Rampton Special Hospital study, as for the Broadmoor Special Hospital study, involved participants reporting PTSD symptoms over relatively long periods of time since the relevant violent offence (a mean of over 5½ years for females; unstated for males),

which raises issues about the potential confounding influences of therapeutic interventions and memory changes over time.

The authors also offered some thoughts about the origins of post-traumatic reactions in perpetrators of violent crime, suggesting that this might relate to that subgroup that experience the precipitating event as unpredictable and uncontrollable, critical aspects of the traumatic event in victims of violent crime who develop PTSD (Foa et al., 1989). Although violent offenders might be expected to offer loss of control as a 'convenient rationalisation' for their behaviour, there may be a group of violent offenders who experience genuine reduced volitional control and who may be at greater risk of developing PTSD symptoms. Given that the distinguishing feature of PTSD is that the traumatic event was of such monumental significance that previously held ideas about safety are dismantled, this type of experience could lead to a state of chronic fear arising from situations previously perceived as safe.

This report also described the apparent conundrum with respect to whether or not to treat PTSD symptoms in violent offenders arising from their index offence. On the one hand, the symptoms might be thought of as a useful reminder of the violent behaviour, suggesting that treatment of these symptoms might not be prudent. On the other hand, allowing potentially treatable symptoms to persist might undermine rehabilitation and allow pathways to violence, for example by exaggerated irritability and violent outbursts, to persist.

The German High Secure Hospitals Study

Similar conclusions were drawn from an investigation of the rate of traumatic events and PTSD symptoms in two maximum secure hospitals in Pomerania, north-eastern Germany (Spitzer et al., 2001). The participants in Germany comprised a case series of 53 patients (51 men and 2 women) out of the combined hospital population of 115 inpatients, with 93 per cent of those meeting the inclusion criteria providing informed consent to participate in the study. The criteria for admission to the hospitals involved two sections of the German Penal Code applicable in cases of diminished responsibility for the offence due to mental illness, involving a profound disturbance of consciousness, mental retardation or another serious mental abnormality, and for substance abuse disorders. The majority of participants suffered from personality disorders and substance use disorders, and 22 (40 per cent) were diagnosed with both. Only one participant was diagnosed with schizophrenia. They were admitted to the maximum secure hospitals following violent, sexual or other, e.g. arson, offences, and the sample was thought to be broadly representative of the maximum secure population in terms of diagnostic and offending profiles.

Using an established measure (The Clinician-Administered PTSD Scale [CAPS; Blake *et al.*, 1995]), the lifetime prevalence of PTSD was found to be 36 per cent (19/53), with current PTSD found in 9 (17 per cent) participants. The majority of the participants (34; 64 per cent) reported at least one DSM-IV defined trauma, with the most common trauma involving childhood physical abuse. The study also found that 8 individuals (15 per cent) had current partial PTSD and 12 (23 per cent) had lifetime partial PTSD. The investigators also found that patients with current PTSD endorsed a broad range of psychiatric symptoms as measured by the Dissociative Experiences Scale (DES; Bernstein & Putnam, 1986) and the Symptom Checklist-90 (SCL-90; Derogatis, 1983). The authors emphasise the importance of detecting PTSD symptoms because of the established association with dissociative symptoms, with the possibility of difficulty with therapeutic interventions arising from persistent dissociation if these symptoms are not identified and managed.

The proportion of patients who reported being exposed to a traumatic event did not exceed the rates found in the general population, although this may have been limited by selection bias with more seriously traumatised individuals avoiding study participation, an elevated threshold for the perception of an event as traumatic, and failure of recall. However, the lifetime and current prevalence rates for PTSD were significantly higher than those found in major epidemiological studies of the general population (Breslau *et al.*, 1997, 1998; Kessler *et al.*, 1995), comparable with higher rates in offender and patient populations.

Finally, for current purposes, it is of interest that the second most common traumatic event (5 patients; 9 per cent) after childhood physical abuse was the patient's own criminal offence, which included serious violence including homicide, and sexual abuse. Unfortunately, no more specific details about symptoms were provided.

As for all hospital studies, the issue of selection bias must be borne in mind when interpreting the prevalence rates. In this German sample, the participants were overwhelmingly diagnosed with personality disorder rather than mental illness. It is likely that patients with personality disorder have higher rates of childhood abusive experiences and this may translate into higher

rates of subsequent PTSD. Nevertheless, a consistent pattern is evident in terms of a significant proportion of patients in high secure hospital settings presenting with a history of trauma, and, more specifically, PTSD or PTSD symptoms relating to their index offence.

UK Medium Secure Hospitals Study
A further prevalence study of PTSD which focused specifically on traumatic responses relating to the index offence was based on assessment of 37 patients (32 males, 5 females) detained in UK medium secure hospitals. Admissions to these regional secure units are based upon the combination of serious criminal offending and serious mental disorder, including both mental illness and personality disorder (Gray *et al.*, 2003). The mean time to assessment from their index offence was just short of four years. The majority of patients suffered from major mental illness, including schizophrenia (24; 65 per cent), bipolar disorder (4; 11 per cent) and depression (4; 11 per cent), while 5 (14 per cent) had personality disorder. The index offences included murder and other violent non-sexual offences, rape, paedophilia, arson and kidnapping.

Methodological concerns arising from this study design included the absence of details about how the participants were selected other than the general inclusion criteria of being detained in a regional secure unit, although it was stated that 37 of the 46 people approached (80 per cent) agreed to take part in the study. Over a quarter (10; 27 per cent) of the participants indicated that they were unable to talk about their index offence, and information, as for other participants, was obtained from depositions. Further, 10 individuals (27 per cent) were too distressed to participate in the semi-structured interview.

One-third of the sample (9; 33 per cent) met DSM-III-R diagnostic criteria for PTSD related to the individual's index offence, with the symptoms distributed evenly across intrusive, avoidant and hyperarousal symptom clusters.

This study went beyond previous work by placing greater attention on an analysis of the nature of the index offence. First, the author's hypothesis that those who killed would have higher scores on the Impact of Events Scale (IES; Horowitz *et al.*, 1979) than those who committed non-lethal violence was not supported for total IES score or avoidant symptoms, but was for intrusive symptoms. Second, the hypothesis that violent acts would more likely be traumatic (as measured by greater IES symptoms) than sexual offences (rape and paedophilia combined), on the basis of sexual offences involving elements of desirability and planning, was just outside the standard 5 per cent level of statistical significance. Third, no difference in PTSD symptoms was found between perpetrators on the basis of whether their victim was considered close, an acquaintance or a stranger. Fourth, the data indicated that intrusive symptoms had a tendency to decline over time since the offence, as opposed to avoidant symptoms, which did not exhibit this pattern of decline. Fifth, they found that those individuals who currently believed that the victim did not deserve the assault had higher scores for intrusive and avoidant symptoms than those who did believe the assault was deserved. Finally, regression analysis showed that two factors – whether the offender's mental disorder involved depression or bipolar illness (i.e. an affective component) and whether the individual still believed that the victim deserved the assault – accounted for a significant amount of the variance of PTSD symptoms.

The authors concluded that their results showed that mentally disordered offenders had very high rates of PTSD (one-third of the sample), which they took to indicate that offenders who commit violent acts in the context of altered mental states are vulnerable to the development of PTSD as a consequence of their offence. In contrast to the suggestions of Harry and Resnick (1986), they did not find evidence to support the idea that young perpetrators, or those who assaulted people with whom they had a close relationship, were more vulnerable to the development of PTSD symptoms. They also suggest that impulsivity is the mediating factor which leads to a stronger post-traumatic response in those convicted of violent as opposed to sexual offences.

Some findings highlighted areas for clinical consideration. For example, the finding that intrusive symptoms showed only a small tendency to reduce in frequency over time, while avoidant symptoms did not show this tendency at all, supports the idea that post-traumatic responses that do not decrease spontaneously over the first few weeks following the precipitating event can be very long-standing. This raises the possibility that violent offenders may be susceptible to prolonged traumatic responses because their offence has a different set of consequences than for victims of violent offenders, including long-term incarceration, prolonged legal processes, and placement in a therapeutic milieu where repeated reminders and interventions focused specifically at the index offence are likely to occur. The finding

that those with an affective component to their mental illness had higher IES scores highlights the possibility that PTSD and depressive illness may have a tendency to exacerbate one another, although this cross-sectional study did not involve a design capable of teasing out the main direction of influence.

A further possibility is that the finding that those individuals who judged their victim not to be deserving of the assault had greater IES symptoms suggests that shame and guilt might increase vulnerability to the development of PTSD symptoms, although this was not measured in this study.

Finally, the authors reinforce the concern expressed by Thomas et al. (1994) that PTSD may, by definition, contribute significant stress symptoms, thus exacerbating the mental illness of the offender and making them less receptive to treatment interventions or increase the likelihood of relapse. Therefore, the identification of prominent PTSD symptoms is an important clinical task in forensic settings, particularly for individuals who appear to be unresponsive to therapeutic interventions.

A similar study based on a sample of patients of a UK regional secure unit investigated the rate of PTSD related to an index offence of homicide in a final sample of 19 patients (16 males, 3 female) who had a primary diagnosis of mental illness (as opposed to personality disorder) (Papanastassiou et al., 2004). Each of the participants identified their index offence as a traumatic event as defined by CAPS criteria. The majority of the sample had committed their index offence within four years of the assessment, with two significant outliers (7 and 20 years respectively). The majority of victims of the index offence were known to the offender (12/19 or 63 per cent family member; 2/19 or 11 per cent friend). More than a third of the sample (7/19 or 37 per cent) had experienced early adverse events, including early separation from parents or sexual or physical abuse. The main finding was that 11/19 (58 per cent) of the patients met diagnostic criteria for full PTSD in relation to their index offence at some point since the event, with 8 (42 per cent) meeting current PTSD criteria. A further 4 participants (21 per cent) met diagnostic criteria for partial lifetime PTSD (defined as having at least one symptom in each of the intrusive, avoidant and hyperarousal clusters as determined by the CAPS interview), and 3 (16 per cent) had a current partial PTSD symptom profile. The majority (16, 84 per cent) of the participants expressed guilt in relation to their index offence using the CAPS item.

With respect to possible aetiological factors, all 12 participants who killed a family member developed either the full (8 individuals) or partial (4 individuals) PTSD syndrome. There was a significant relationship between guilt as measured by the CAPS and PTSD symptoms. Interestingly, the presence of early adverse events was associated with reduced likelihood of developing PTSD in relation to the index offence, which the authors suggest may be linked to the fact that this study involved perpetrators rather than victims of serious violence. No relationship was found between previous violent offending and the development of PTSD symptoms, although a hypothesised relationship between an absence of previous violent offending and PTSD arising from the index offence of killing may have been masked by the small sample size.

The authors noted that the rate of PTSD in their sample was higher than that found in the study by Spitzer *et al.* (2001) which was based on mentally disordered patients, and Pollock (1999) (see below) which was based on a non-mentally-ill prison population, even though they restricted their investigation to PTSD arising specifically from the index offence of homicide.

Two reasons why patients have developed PTSD symptoms in relation to their index offence are offered: the presence of major mental illness other than PTSD and the fact that they are perpetrators rather than victims. Negative consequences of overlooking PTSD in a forensic patient population include increased risk of self-harm or suicide and of violence to others, and an undermining of therapeutic interventions directed towards understanding and adjusting to the index offence.

A recent study also focused on the development of PTSD symptoms in patients from a regional secure and local secure unit in the UK (Crisford *et al.*, 2008) who had been convicted of a violent or sexual offence, but with an emphasis not on determining prevalence but on measuring the association between guilty cognitions and levels of offence-related PTSD. The basis for inclusion for the study was nomination by the treating psychiatrist. A response rate of 58 per cent ($n = 53/91$) was obtained, although a further 8 patients were excluded because of low IQ scores, providing a final sample of 45 participants, of whom 2 were female. Although the study focused on offence-related PTSD, the participants had the opportunity to nominate a previous offence if it was more distressing than the offence for which they were currently detained; 5 participants identified a previous offence. The severity of each offence was determined using a rating scale with five categories, using the mean of three ratings. Although descriptions of each level of severity were not provided, tests of inter-rater reliability were reported as good. The psychological measures used in the study included the Detailed Assessment of Posttraumatic Stress (DAPS; Briere, 2001), the 'Guilt' scale component of the Revised Gudjonsson Blame Attribution Inventory (GBAI; Gudjonsson & Singh, 1989), the guilt cognitions scale of the Trauma-Related Guilt Inventory (TRGI; Kubany, 2004), and the Positive and Negative Affect Scale (the PANAS; Watson *et al.*, 1988).

The time to assessment from the interview had a broad range from 1 to 28 years, with a mean time of 6.5 years. The sample was divided into those with a diagnosis of personality disorder ($n = 11$, 24 per cent) and those without, although over half of those in the personality disorder group were also diagnosed with a major mental illness. The majority of the sample (31, 69 per cent) was deemed to have been psychotic at the time of the offence.

In terms of the main findings, 40 per cent ($n = 18$) of the sample met diagnostic criteria for offence-related PTSD as determined by scores on the DAPS. The main hypothesis, that there will be an association between levels of guilt and levels of offence-related PTSD symptoms, was supported with both measures of guilt. A hierarchical regression analysis including the variables of negative affect, offence severity, ethnicity, and trauma history was undertaken, which showed that the measure of guilt explained an additional 11 per cent of variance in predicting trauma symptomatology, further supporting the main hypothesis.

Analysis also showed that individuals who had offended against unknown victims had higher levels of guilt than those who offended against known victims. The authors suggest that this may be due to the fact that, in contrast to previous research, there were more sex offenders in the group with unknown victims than in the group with known victims.

However, more severe violence was not found to be related to higher levels of guilt cognitions relating to the index offence (although it was related to PTSD symptoms). Similarly, no significant association was found between the level of offence-related PTSD symptoms and time since the offence, past trauma exposure, relationship to the victim, or psychosis or substance use at the time of the index offence.

The strengths of their study highlighted by the authors included the measurement of a wide range of variables, which allow for the control of factors potentially associated with PTSD such as negative affect to reduce possible confounding, and the use of a recently developed measure of guilt cognitions, as opposed to clinical judgement. The strengths were balanced against limitations, including the methods used to gather information about the presence of psychosis and substance use at the time of the index offence, the possibility that the investigators were leading in their questioning about the traumatic nature of previous offences, and the possibility that providing the participants with a choice of past offences may have actually allowed them an opportunity to avoid talking about a genuinely distressing event. The mix of sex offenders with violent offenders also hampered interpretation of results.

Additional limitations were the selection bias involved in psychiatrists nominating potential candidates for the research, compounded by the lack of an explicit account of the information given to clinicians on which they based these nominations; and the dubious conflation of those with comorbid psychosis and personality disorder into a single personality disorder group for analysis.

In discussing the clinical implications of their research, the authors highlight the need for clinicians to be aware of the possibility of PTSD symptoms in relation to violent offending and the potential for these symptoms to complicate the therapeutic interaction, for example by undermining engagement with offence-related work and treatment to reduce the risk of reoffending. They also raise the possibility that successful interventions which lead to improved insight into their offences may predispose the patients to guilt and possible PTSD symptoms. Finally, they observe the need for PTSD to be considered in legal assessments involving possible mitigation and disposal considerations.

Studies using prison populations

A larger case series of 80 homicide offenders detained largely in a prison setting and referred for assessment by a clinical psychologist repeated earlier findings of significant rates of PTSD arising from the index offence (Pollock, 1999). Over half of the offenders (52 per cent) met DSM-III diagnostic criteria for current PTSD, although this included those individuals with PTSD arising from both their index offence and other traumatic events. However, 82 per cent of this subgroup experienced their index offence as a traumatic event and a majority (70 per cent) denied other traumatic events which could account for their symptoms.

An interesting aspect of this study was the division of the sample into those who enacted *instrumental* violence (goal directed, non-affective and pre-meditated violence against a stranger without perceived provocation) and *reactive* violence (non-goal directed, unplanned and angry, aroused violence typically with perceived provocation against a known victim), as 95 per cent of the sample with a PTSD related to their index offence were judged to have performed an act of reactive violence. Further, primary psychopaths defined in terms of Blackburn's personality typology (Blackburn, 1971, 1982, 1993) of violent offenders exhibited less offence-related PTSD than non-psychopaths.

This study reinforces the general proposition that some violent offenders experience their index offence as a traumatic event leading to PTSD, although generalisation of these findings is undermined by the selection bias (issues raised by referrals to a clinician are likely to be weighted towards those experiencing psychological problems), and concerns that half of the sample were also diagnosed as being psychopathic in nature, raising concerns about the reliability of their data, given their propensity towards lying.

A recent study based on a representative sample of 105 young offenders convicted of grievous bodily harm, attempted murder and murder reported the detailed phenomenological characteristics of intrusive memories, ruminations, and symptoms of PTSD related to their violent crime, and the cognitive and emotional factors associated with whether the perpetrators of violent crime developed intrusive memories of their offence (Evans et al., 2007a, 2007b). The mean time from the assault to the assessment was about 23 months. Almost half (48; 46 per cent) of the participants described significant intrusive memories of the assault and 38 (36 per cent) reported ruminations related to the assault. Six participants (6 per cent) met diagnostic criteria for PTSD using the PTSD Symptoms Scale – Interview Version (PSS-I; E.B. Foa & Tolin, 2000).

The phenomenological properties of the intrusive memories were similar to those reported by victims of violence, being involuntarily triggered, highly distressing, uncontrollable, comprised mainly of brief sensory fragments, particularly visual recollections, and repetitive and stereotyped (Ehlers & Steil, 1995; Mellman & Davis, 1985; van der Kolk & Fisler, 1995). For example, one individual experienced distressing memories of his offence that were triggered by having hot showers, which reminded him of the warm, wet feel of his victim's blood spurting onto his face during the index offence.

The sensory fragments did not appear to be random, with the majority (67 per cent) representing the first moments when the meaning of the course of events changed dramatically for the worse, such that it became threatening for the violent offender. These findings suggest that intrusive memories are comprised of central elements of the assault, similar to the concept of 'weapon focus' as described in victims of robberies (Kramer et al., 1990). This was understood to be consistent with the 'warning signal hypothesis' (Ehlers et al., 2002) from the perspective of the perpetrator because, unlike for victims, the moments which carried greatest significance for offenders were those moments with greatest negative consequences, for example probable legal implications. Examples included the sight of the victim not moving or the sight or smell of blood. This hypothesis is consistent with theoretical approaches to PTSD suggesting that intrusive cognitions induce a sense of serious current threat (Ehlers & Clark, 2000).

Qualitative analysis of the content of the intrusive memories showed that the majority of memories comprised visual images classified within two categories: images of the wounded victim (40 per cent) and images of the actual assault (41 per cent). Other categories included images of the weapon, precipitants, elements of the aftermath, and the offender being assaulted. Further qualitative analysis of the subjective meaning of these intrusive memories showed that almost 80 per cent of the intrusive memories were classified in one of four main categories: a moral breach; the victim not deserving what happened; shock or disbelief at what the perpetrator had done; and a sudden realisation of the seriousness of the injury to the victim. The authors suggest that the process of eliciting phenomenological details of the memory an offender has of their act of violence, including intrusive memory fragments, might provide indirect evidence of a negative affective component to the appraisal of their actions, and hence, more persuasive evidence for regret and remorse than simple self-report. The participants sometimes acknowledged that they had never been asked about the phenomenological characteristics of their memories of their violent behaviour and therefore the line of questioning was relatively engaging. When they were asked directly about their interpretation of why specific visual fragments seemed to form the basis of their intrusive memories (as opposed to other parts of the course of events), the participants were often able to provide relatively specific information about their attitude towards their violent actions, which may have relevance for risk assessment purposes.

Over one-third of the sample (38; 36 per cent) described experiencing ruminations of their offence, which were subjectively distressing and involuntary. They appeared to differ from intrusive memories because the content of the ruminations typically changed rather than being stereotyped. Reminiscent of trauma victims, the perpetrators of violence tended to ruminate with circular patterns of thought, including 'what if' questions related to the assault and its consequences, involving dwelling on how things might have been different if only they had acted differently at one particular moment in time (Michael, 2000). A distinction has been made by some researchers between intrusive memories of a traumatic event and intrusive thoughts *about* the event (Ehlers et al., 2002; Halligan et al., 2003). The reported content of ruminations supports the argument that they are best described as intrusive *thoughts* rather than intrusive *memories* (Hackmann et al., 2004; Ehlers et al., in press; Reynolds & Brewin, 1998, 1999). In particular, the content of the ruminations was consistent with research indicating that trauma victims tend to focus in a repetitive, circular fashion on contingencies related to the assault and its consequences, such as 'why' they did something or how things might have turned out differently if they had acted in a different way at the time (Michael, 2000). Ruminations were significantly correlated with PTSD symptom severity. Interestingly, in the 60 per cent of participants who experienced both intrusions and ruminations, ruminative thinking was frequently triggered by intrusive memories, but not vice versa.

This study also extended previous work reviewed above which reported that a minority of violent offenders may develop PTSD in relation to their violent crime, by investigating emotional and cognitive factors which are associated in an act of violence being transformed into a trauma for the perpetrator in the form of intrusive memories, the hallmark of PTSD (Evans et al., 2007a; Horowitz, 1976). In general terms, empirical findings in studies of trauma victims, which placed importance on overwhelming emotions at the time of the offence, the nature of cognitive appraisals of offence, disrupted cognitive processing and the development of intrusive memories of the violence, generalised to violent offenders.

With respect to the role of emotions experienced during the assault, perpetrators of violence with intrusions showed greater intensity of negative emotions during the trauma than the no-intrusion group, which more detailed analysis revealed to be attributable to a greater sense of helplessness and fear. The finding that participants with intrusive memories reported experiencing greater helplessness and fear during the assault than those without intrusions corresponded neatly with Criterion A2 of the DSM-IV criteria for PTSD. This finding helps raise awareness of the complexity of emotional responses experienced by perpetrators; it is easy to assume that anger or bravado might dominate, but this study provides empirical support for a broader range of emotions during the violent sequence of actions. The authors acknowledge that helplessness might have a different meaning for perpetrators of violence rather than victims.

In line with previous research with victims of trauma (e.g. Halligan *et al.*, 2003), disrupted cognitive processing at the time of the event was associated with PTSD symptoms. Dissociation during the event also correlated with intrusive memories. These findings replicate earlier work with victims of violence which provide empirical evidence that compromised information processing during an event can be associated with PTSD. The strongest evidence is for dissociation (Ozer *et al.*, 2003), a complex concept incorporating several components such as derealisation, depersonalisation, time distortion, and amnesia. Two other forms of disrupted cognitive processing, data-driven processing (sensory information processed rather than conceptual information) and lack of self-referent processing (a failure to relate new information to a sense of self and other personal memories), have also been shown to be associated with the development of PTSD in victims of violence (Ehlers & Clark, 2000; Murray *et al.*, 2002; Rosario *et al.*, in press).

It has been argued that disrupted information processing can lead to deficits in the autobiographical memories for a traumatic event, which is supported by the finding of measures of memory disorganisation being related to PTSD symptoms and intrusions in victims of violence. Evans *et al.* (2007a) showed that more disorganised narratives of the assault were associated with PTSD symptoms and intrusive memories.

Previous research with victims of violence, including torture, has demonstrated that excessively negative appraisals of traumatic events can be associated with intrusive memories (Dunmore *et al.*, 1999, 2001; Ehlers & Clark, 2000; E. Foa & Riggs, 1993; Halligan *et al.*, 2003; Resick & Schnicke, 1993). In this study on perpetrators of violence, a series of negative appraisals about the event and its aftermath were associated with intrusions and PTSD symptom severity, including negative view of self, negative interpretation of symptoms (of PTSD), a sense of permanent change, and self-blame. The nature of cognitive appraisals of an event and its aftermath is related to their potential role in the maintenance of intrusive memories of the violence. It is not uncommon for individuals to experience intrusive memories following a traumatic event but they persist for only a minority of individuals (Baum & Hall, 1993), which may be attributable to the appraisals that are made by the individual (Ehlers & Steil, 1995).

In contrast, antisocial beliefs appeared to be protective against the development of intrusions, which would be consistent with 'discrepancy' theories of PTSD, which suggest that intrusions arise from profound inconsistency between deeply held beliefs and an individual's actions.

Evans *et al.* (2007b) used a hierarchical logistic regression analysis to test whether the emotional and cognitive factors explained the presence of intrusions over and above that attributable to demographic factors. All blocks of variables significantly increased the amount of variance explained over and above demographic factors, including antisocial beliefs (5.4 per cent), emotions at the time of the offence (fear and helplessness – 10 per cent), measures of cognitive processing and memory disorganisation (10 per cent), and appraisals of the assault and its aftermath (16 per cent), leading to a total of 60 per cent of the predicted variance.

The authors identified some limitations of their study, including its cross-sectional nature; the delay in interviewing the perpetrators; the dependence on self-report; the examination of a large number of emotional and cognitive variables, raising the possibility of chance findings; the possibility that the nature of cognitive appraisals in perpetrators might have subtle differences compared to victims of violence (for example, permanent change might be associated with shame for a different reason than for victims); and the issue that the study focused on intrusive memories. It remains an open question as to whether the findings translate to the development of PTSD in perpetrators.

Despite these concerns, the study not only replicated previous studies which found that a significant proportion of violent perpetrators experience intrusive memories for their assaultive behaviour and a minority developed PTSD in relation to their crime, but also provided empirical support for the hypothesis that intrusive memories in victims and in perpetrators are explained by similar cognitive and emotional mechanisms.

Clinical and Legal Implications

The series of papers which have provided the basis for the empirical review often concluded by referring to potential clinical or legal implications, or both, of the finding of PTSD symptoms or frank PTSD in violent offenders. The findings have been consistent enough to warrant clinicians routinely considering traumatic responses in forensic evaluations and treatment interventions.

The main concern expressed in terms of legal implications focused on assessments of fitness to plead, which could potentially be undermined by PTSD symptoms. Intrusive phenomena can cause distraction; avoidance behaviours can lead to inadequate instruction of legal representatives; and hyperarousal symptoms can lead to distractibility and difficulty following the course of a trial.

The role of PTSD might also be relevant in terms of representing a mitigating factor at sentencing, although it would be important to be clear about whether preceding PTSD was felt to have contributed to further offending, or whether PTSD arose from the latest offence.

There are several clinical implications of violent offenders developing PTSD symptoms. First, they may complicate the diagnostic picture, leading to an inadequate formulation. For example, PTSD is typically comorbid with other mental disorders, placing importance on a systematic approach to diagnosis. Alternatively, PTSD may mimic other disorders.

Second, PTSD could undermine therapeutic interventions of both a psychotherapeutic and pharmacological nature. The clinical finding of 'treatment resistance' in mentally disordered offenders suggests consideration of PTSD symptoms, just as one would reconsider any evidence for an affective component to a clinical presentation.

Third, crime-related PTSD may warrant treatment itself, although this is potentially a controversial area. The clinical team will need to balance competing ethical concerns about providing effective treatment for the individual mentally disordered offender and the rights of the public. It is plausible that risk could be potentially reduced by appropriate treatment (say, for example, by reduction of irritability, angry outbursts and hypervigilance).

A fourth and more exploratory consideration was raised by Evans et al. (2007a), who raised the possibility that the presence or absence of intrusive phenomena might present a source of rich clinical data in terms of risk assessment. They suggested that the clinical process of uncovering, for example, intrusive memories of the violent offence, followed by a detailed discussion about the content and subjective meaning of the intrusive memory (typically a memory fragment), could be highly informative about the attitudes of the individual towards their own violent behaviour. Although the absence of intrusive memories would not be conclusive, inquiry about the nature of an individual's memories of their index offence has the potential to offer a stronger phenomenological basis on which to judge apparent claims of regret and remorse. Therefore, more specific inquiry about the phenomenological detail – intrusive sensory fragments as opposed to an assumption that memory is fully intact – could pay clinical dividends.

Conclusions

Notwithstanding the debate involving both support (Bradley & Chesterman, 1995) and opposition (Breslau et al., 1998; Green et al., 1987) to the idea that the stressor criterion for PTSD can be met by perpetrators of serious violence such as homicide, there is a growing body of consistent evidence showing that many violent offenders do experience intrusive memories and even PTSD-type syndromes in relation to their violent crime. Initially this was based on case reports but subsequent studies focused on determining the prevalence of PTSD arising for committing a violent crime in various hospital and prison populations. Recent studies have adopted a more detailed and systematic approach (for example, by incorporating inter-rater reliability checks on measurement) of the phenomenology of the traumatic responses, and the emotional and cognitive mechanisms associated with the presence of intrusive memories and PTSD.

Although the empirical base is limited, it has also now gone beyond being clinically trivial and the consistency of the findings of PTSD symptoms and full PTSD warrants routine consideration. Little is known about the extent to which traumatic responses to violent offending are part of standard clinical assessment or training.

Some interesting possibilities arise as candidates for studies which would move our understanding forward in this area. These include closer examination of the variation in symptom profiles in perpetrators as opposed to victims of violence; longitudinal studies which would have greater power to tease out the causal mechanisms underpinning the development of traumatic responses to being violent; and closer examination of the relationship between intrusive memories of being violent and other forms of psychopathology, such as amnesia (Evans *et al.*, in press).

Considerable clarity of thought will be required by clinicians as the focus moves towards possible treatment interventions. The complex ethical dilemmas involved in the treatment of violent offenders, especially in a situation whereby they appear to be suffering from a traumatic response from seriously harming another individual, will most likely invoke a range of responses from mental health professionals.

Note

1   The clinical features of PTSD following traumatic events include: (1) re-experiencing symptoms, such as intrusive memories, thoughts or images, and nightmares; (2) avoidance symptoms such as emotional numbing where the individual is unable to experience a range of emotions, amnesia for all or part of the event, behavioural avoidance where individuals go to great lengths to avoid stimuli which will remind them of the trauma, and cognitive avoidance such as the use of distracting techniques to get rid of unwanted thoughts; and (3) arousal symptoms such as an exaggerated startle response, irritability, and hypervigilance for trauma-related information (American Psychiatric Association, 1994).

References

American Psychiatric Association (1994). *Diagnostic and statistical manual of mental disorders* (4th edn). Washington, DC: APA.

Baum, A. & Hall, M. (1993). Control and intrusive memories as possible determinants of chronic stress. *Psychosomatic Medicine*, 55, 274–286.

Bernstein, E. & Putnam, F. (1986). Development, reliability, and validity of a dissociation scale. *Journal of Nervous and Mental Disease*, 174, 727–735.

Blackburn, R. (1971). Personality types among abnormal homicides. *British Journal of Criminology*, 14, 14–31.

Blackburn, R. (1982). *The Special Hospitals Assessment of Personality and Socialisation (SHAPS)*. Liverpool: Park Lane Hospital.

Blackburn, R. (1993). *The psychology of criminal conduct*. Chichester: Wiley.

Blake, D.D., Weathers, F.W., Nagy, L.M., Kaloupek, D.G., Gusman, F.D. & Charney, D. S. (1995). The development of a Clinician-Administered PTSD Scale. *Journal of Traumatic Stress*, 8, 75–90.

Bradley, C. & Chesterman, P. (1995). A case report of post-traumatic stress symptoms in a perpetrator. *Journal of Psychiatric Case Reports*, 1, 43–47.

Breslau, N., Davis, G. C. & Peterson, E. (1997). Psychiatric sequelae of posttraumatic stress disorder in women. *Archives of General Psychiatry*, 54, 81–87.

Breslau, N., Kessler, R.C., Chilcoat, H., Schultz, L., Davis, G.C. & Andreski, P. (1998). Posttraumatic stress disorder: The stressor criterion. *Journal of Nervous and Mental Disease*, 175(5), 255–264.

Brewin, C., Dalgleish, T. & Joseph, S. (1996). A dual representation theory of posttraumatic stress disorder. *Psychological Review*, 103, 670–686.

Briere, J. (2001). *Detailed assessment of posttraumatic stress*. Odessa, FL: Psychological Assessment Resources.

Briere, J. & Conte, J. (1993). Self-reported abuse in adults molested as children. *Journal of Traumatic Stress*, 6(1), 328–332.

Christianson, S.A. (1992). Emotional stress and eyewitness testimony: A critical review. *Psychological Bulletin*, 112, 284–309.

Crisford, H., Dare, H. & Evangeli, M. (2008). Offence-related posttraumatic stress disorder (PTSD) symptomatology and guilt in mentally disordered violent and sexual offenders. *The Journal of Forensic Psychiatry and Psychology*, 19(1), 86–107.

Curle, C.E. (1989). *An investigation of reaction to having killed amongst male homicide patients resident in a maximum security hospital*. Unpublished PhD thesis, University of London, London.

De Silva, P. & Marks, M. (1999). Intrusive thinking in posttraumatic stress disorder. In W. Yule (Ed.), *Post-traumatic stress disorder: Concepts and therapy* (pp.161–175). New York: Wiley.

Derogatis, L. (1983). *Symptom Checklist-90-R: Administration, scoring, and procedures manual*. Baltimore: Clinical Psychometric Research.

Dunmore, E., Clark, D.M. & Ehlers, A. (1999). Cognitive factors involved in the onset and maintenance of posttraumatic stress disorder (PTSD) after physical and sexual assault. *Behaviour Research and Therapy*, 37, 809–829.

Dunmore, E., Clark, D.M. & Ehlers, A. (2001). A prospective investigation of the role of cognitive factors in persistent Posttraumatic Stress Disorder (PTSD) after physical or sexual assault. *Behaviour Research and Therapy*, 39, 1063–1084.

Easterbrook, J.A. (1959). The effect of emotion on cue utilisation and the organisation of behaviour. *Psychological Review*, 66, 183–201.

Ehlers, A. & Clark, D.M. (2000). A cognitive model of posttraumatic stress disorder. *Behaviour Research and Therapy*, 38, 319–345.

Ehlers, A., Hackmann, A. & Michael, T. (in press). Intrusive reexperiencing in posttraumatic stress disorder: Phenomenology, theory and therapy. *Memory*.

Ehlers, A., Hackmann, A., Steil, R., Clohessy, S., Wenninger, K. & Winter, H. (2002). The nature of intrusive memories after trauma: The warning signal hypothesis. *Behaviour Research and Therapy, 40*, 1021–1028.

Ehlers, A. & Steil, R. (1995). Maintenance of intrusive memories in posttraumatic stress disorder: A cognitive approach. *Behavioural and Cognitive Psychotherapy, 23*, 217–249.

Evans, C., Ehlers, A., Mezey, G. & Clark, D.M. (2007a). Intrusive memories and ruminations related to violent crime in young offenders: Phenomenological characteristics. *Journal of Traumatic Stress, 20*(2), 183–196.

Evans, C., Ehlers, A., Mezey, G. & Clark, D.M. (2007b). Intrusive memories in perpetrators of violent crime: The role of cognitive processing, memory and appraisals. *Journal of Consulting and Clinical Psychology, 75*(1), 134–144.

Evans, C., Mezey, G. & Ehlers, A. (in press). Amnesia for violent crime among young offenders. *The Journal of Forensic Psychiatry and Psychology*.

Falsetti, S.A., Monnier, J., Davis, J.L. & Resnick, H.S. (2002). Intrusive thoughts in posttraumatic stress disorder. *Journal of Cognitive Psychotherapy: An International Quarterly, 16*, 127–143.

Farmer, R., Tranah, T., O'Donnel, I. & Catalan, J. (1992). Railway suicide: The psychological effects on drivers. *Psychological medicine, 22*, 407–414.

Foa, E. & Riggs, M. (1993). Post-traumatic stress disorder in rape victims. In J. Oldham, M. Riba & A. Tasman (Eds.) *Annual review of psychiatry* (vol. 12, pp.273–303). Washington, DC: American Psychiatric Association.

Foa, E.B. & Rothbaum, B.O. (1998). *Treating the trauma of rape: Cognitive behaviour therapy for PTSD*. New York: Guilford Press.

Foa, E.B., Steketee, G. & Rothbaum, B.O. (1989). Behavioral/cognitive conceptualisations of post-traumatic stress disorder. *Behaviour Therapy, 20*, 155–176.

Foa, E.B. & Tolin, D.F. (2000). Comparison of the PTSD Symptom Scale-Interview version and the Clinician-Administered PTSD scale. *Journal of Traumatic Stress, 13*, 181–191.

Foy, D.W., Carroll, E.M. & Donahoe, C.P. (1987). Etiological factors in the development of PTSD in clinical samples of Vietnam combat veterans. *Journal of Clinical Psychology, 43*(1), 17–27.

Foy, D.W., Sipprelle, R., Reuger, D.B. & Carroll, E.M. (1984). Etiology of posttraumatic stress disorder in Vietnam Veterans: Analysis of premilitary, military, and combat exposure influences. *Journal of Consulting and Clinical Psychology, 52*, 79–87.

Gallers, J., Foy, D.W. & Donahoe, C.P. (Eds.) (1985). *Combat-related posttraumatic stress disorder: An empirical investigation*. Los Angeles.

Gray, N.S., Carman, N., Rogers, P., MacCulloch, M.J., Hayward, P. & Snowden, R. (2003). Post-traumatic stress disorder caused in mentally disordered offenders by the committing of a serious violent or sexual offence. *Journal of Forensic Psychiatry and Psychology, 14*, 27–43.

Green, B., Lindy, J. & Grace, M. (1987). The stressor criterion and posttraumatic stress disorder. *Journal of Nervous and Mental Disease, 175*(5), 269–272.

Gudjonsson, G.H. & Singh, K.K. (1989). The Revised Gudjonsson Blame Attribution Inventory. *Personality and Individual Differences, 10*, 66–70.

Hackmann, A., Ehlers, A., Speckens, A. & Clark, D.M. (2004). Characteristics and content of intrusive memories in PTSD and their changes with treatment. *Journal of Traumatic Stress, 17*, 231–240.

Halligan, S.L., Michael, T., Clark, D.M. & Ehlers, A. (2003). Posttraumatic stress disorder following assault: The role of cognitive processing, trauma memory and appraisals. *Journal of Consulting and Clinical Psychology, 71*, 419–431.

Hambridge, J.A. (1990). The grief process in those admitted to Regional Secure Units following homicide. *Journal of Forensic Sciences, 35*, 1149–1154.

Harry, B. & Resnick, P.J. (1986). Posttraumatic stress disorder in murderers. *Journal of Forensic Sciences, 31*, 609–613.

Horowitz, M.J. (1976). *Stress response syndromes* (1st edn). New York: Jason Aronson.

Horowitz, M.J., Winlner, N. & Alvarez, W. (1979). Impact of Event Scale: A subjective measure of stress. *Psychosomatic Medicine, 41*, 209–218.

Joseph, S., Williams, R. & Yule, W. (1997). *Understanding post-traumatic stress. A psychosocial perspective on PTSD and treatment*. Chichester: Wiley.

Kessler, R.C., Sonnega, A., Bromet, E., Hughes, M. & Nelson, C.B. (1995). Posttraumatic stress disorder in the National Comorbidity Survey. *Archives of General Psychiatry, 52*, 1948–1060.

King, D.W., King, L.A., Gudanowski, D.M. & Vreven, D.L. (1995). Alternative representations of war zone stressors: Relationships to posttraumatic stress disorder in male and female Vietnam veterans. *Journal of Abnormal Psychology, 104*, 184–196.

Kramer, T.H., Buckhout, R. & Euginio, P. (1990). Weapon focus, arousal, and eyewitness testimony. *Law and Human Behaviour, 14*, 167–184.

Kruppa, I. (1991). Perpetrators suffer trauma too. *The Psychologist, 4*, 401–403.

Kruppa, I., Hickey, N. & Hubbard, C. (1995). The prevalence of post traumatic stress disorder in a special hospital population of legal psychopaths. *Psychology, Crime and Law, 2*, 131–141.

Krystal, J.H., Southwick, S.M. & Charney, D.S. (1995). Post traumatic stress disorder: Psychobiological mechanisms of traumatic remembrance. In D.L. Schacter (Ed.) *Memory distortion: How minds, brains and societies reconstruct the past* (pp.150–172). Cambridge, MA: Harvard University Press.

Kubany, E. (2004). *The Trauma-Related Guilt Inventory (TRGI): Assessing and treating PTSD: Manual*. Los Angeles: Western Psychological Services.

Laufer, R., Gallops, U. & Frey-Wouters, E. (1984). War stress and trauma: The Vietnam experience. *Journal of Health and Social behaviour, 25*, 65–85.

Manolias, M.B. & Hyatt-Willimams, A. (1993). Effects of post-shooting experiences on police-authorised firearms officers in the United Kingdom. In J.P. Wilson & B. Raphael (Eds.) *International handbook of traumatic stress syndromes*. New York: Plenum Press.

McNally, R.J. (1988). Experimental approaches to cognitive abnormality in posttraumatic stress disorder. *Clinical Psychology Review, 18*, 971–982.

McNally, R.J. (2003). *Remembering trauma*. Cambridge, MA: The Belknap Press/Harvard University Press.

Mellman, T.A. & Davis, G.C. (1985). Combat-related flashbacks in posttraumatic stress disorder: Phenomenology and similarity to panic attacks. *Journal of Clinical Psychiatry, 46*, 379–382.

Michael, T. (2000). *The nature of trauma memory and intrusive cognitions on posttraumatic stress disorder*. Oxford: University of Oxford.

Murray, J., Ehlers, A. & Mayou, R.A. (2002). Dissociation and posttraumatic stress disorder: Two prospective studies of motor vehicle accident survivors. *British Journal of Psychiatry, 180*, 363–368.

Ozer, E., Best, S., Lipsey, T. & Weiss, S. (2003). Predictors of posttraumtic stress disorder and symptoms in adults: A meta-analysis. *Psychological Bulletin, 129*, 52–73.

Papanastassiou, M., Waldron, G., Boyle, J. & Chesterman, L. (2004). Post-traumatic stress disorder in mentally ill perpetrators of homicide. *Journal of Forensic Psychiatry and Psychology, 15*, 66–75.

Pollock, P. (1999). When the killer suffers: Post-traumatic stress reactions following homicide. *Legal and Criminological Psychology, 4*, 185–202.

Resick, P. & Schnicke, M. (1993). *Cognitive processing therapy for rape victims: A treatment manual*. Newbury Park, CA: Sage.

Reynolds, M. & Brewin, C.R. (1998). Intrusive cognitions, coping strategies and emotional responses in depression, post-traumatic stress disorder and a non-clinical population. *Behaviour Research and Therapy, 36*, 135–147.

Reynolds, M. & Brewin, C.R. (1999). Intrusive memories in depression and posttraumatic stress disorder. *Behaviour Research and Therapy, 37*, 201–215.

Rogers, P., Gray, N.S., Williams, T. & Kitchiner, N. (2000). Behavioral treatment of PTSD in a perpetrator of manslaughter: A single case study. *Journal of Traumatic Stress, 13*, 511–519.

Rosario, M., Williams, R. & Ehlers, A. (in press). Cognitive processing during motor vehicle accidents predicts posttraumatic stress disorder.

Solkoff, N., Gray, P. & Keill, S. (1986). Which Vietnam veterans develop posttraumatic stress disorders? *Journal of Clinical Psychology, 42*, 687–698.

Spitzer, C., Dudek, M., Liss, H., Orlob, S., Gillner, M. & Freyberger, H.J. (2001). Post-traumatic stress disorder in forensic inpatients. *Journal of Forensic Psychiatry, 12*, 63–77.

Thomas, C., Adshead, G. & Mezey, G. (1994). Case report: Traumatic responses to child murder. *Journal of Forensic Psychiatry, 5*, 168–176.

Tulving, E. (2002). Episodic memory. *Annual Review of Psychology, 53*, 1–25.

van der Kolk, B. A. & Fisler, R. (1995). Dissociation and the fragmentary nature of traumatic memories: Overview and exploratory study. *Journal of Traumatic Stress, 8*, 505–525.

van der Kolk, B.A. & van der Hart, O. (1991). The intrusive past: The flexibility of memory and the engraving of trauma. *American Imago, 48*, 425–454.

Watson, D., Clark, L. & Tellegen, A. (1988). Development and validation of brief measures of positive and negative affect: The PANAS scales. *Journal of Personality and Social Psychology, 54*, 1063–1070.

Wheeler, M. (2000). Episodic memory and autonoetic awareness. In E. Tulving & F. Craik (Eds.), *The Oxford handbook of memory* (pp.597–608). Oxford: Oxford University Press.

22

Substance Use Disorders

Michael Gossop

Consumption Behaviours, Problems, and Dependence

Substance use disorders can be thought of in terms of consumption behaviours, problems, and dependence. These dimensions are conceptually distinct and separate: in reality, they tend to be related (sometime closely) in a number of ways.

The behavioural parameters of drug taking[1] include such issues as substance type, and frequency and quantity of drug use. Certain drugs are regularly identified as leading to dependence and other drug problems. Heroin is most frequently identified as a 'main drug' by drug users in UK treatment services. Other problematic drugs include crack cocaine, amphetamines and benzodiazepines. Alcohol is one of the most widely used psychoactive drugs and it is also associated with many problems. Alcohol use disorders are common in the general population and even more prevalent among offenders in the criminal justice system.

Problematic substance use often involves the concurrent or sequential use of different substances. Reasons for multiple drug use include: *drug enhancement* (through combined psychoactive effects); *modification of effect* (to counteract the adverse or unwanted effects of one or more drugs); *substitution* (if the preferred drug is not available); and *social* (influence of the social setting and the behaviour of other drug users).

Routes of drug administration include: oral (tablets, liquids), intranasal/snorting/sniffing (e.g. cocaine powder, heroin powder), smoking (cannabis, opium), inhalation (chasing the dragon/heroin, volatile substances), and injection (intravenous, intramuscular, subcutaneous/skin popping). Route of administration influences the dependence liability of the drug, risk of overdose, and the risk of infections and other health problems.

Initially, drugs are used for many reasons, but the decision to use drugs represents a voluntary choice. With the development of dependence, the relationship between the user and their drug is altered. The person become increasingly preoccupied by the drug and feels some degree of compulsion to use it. The initial reasons for drinking or taking drugs may or may not still be present, but the development of dependence introduces new factors which increase the likelihood, intensity and persistence of drug taking. Even when the user wants to cut down or to give up using altogether, they experience great difficulty in giving up the habit. They may have withdrawal reactions and become unwell when they stop taking the drug, and they become preoccupied with thoughts about it. Despite their wishes to stop using, they frequently fail in their efforts to do so.

The cognitive, behavioural and physiological components of the dependence syndrome include:

i)   a feeling of compulsion to take drugs;
ii) a desire to stop taking drugs;
iii) a relatively stereotyped pattern of drug taking;
iv) signs of neuroadaption (tolerance and withdrawal symptoms);
v)   the salience of drug-taking behaviour relative to other priorities and the tendency to return to drug taking after a period of abstinence.

A central characteristic of dependence is the psychological desire for drugs. Of the various elements of dependence, the sense of compulsion is an essential ingredient.

The two psychiatric classification systems (ICD and DSM) have regarded dependence as a categorical disorder (is this person dependent/addicted?). A contrasting approach to assessment regards dependence as being distributed along a dimension (how severely dependent/addicted is this person?). The dimensional view is more in keeping with current understanding of disorders as learned behaviours.

Progression from occasional to dependent use of drugs is not inevitable. Nonetheless, many users find drug effects rewarding and continue to use, sometimes with increasing frequency and regularity, until they are taking drugs every day and several times a day. When this happens, the amounts usually increase, and often they experience social, psychological and physical problems associated with their drug taking (increased financial costs, legal and criminal problems, infections and ill health).

Drugs and Crime

Drug-related crime imposes substantial economic and psychological costs upon society and upon the victims of crime, and it has high priority in public opinion, media, and political views of the problem. Many studies have found high levels of criminal activity among drug-misusing populations and UK police estimates have suggested that about half of all recorded crime may be drug related.

A number of relationships may link substance use disorders and crime. No single relationship applies to all cases, and the direction of effect may differ. Many drug misusers have been involved in crime before they started taking drugs, and crime and drug use often share common psychological and social lifestyle factors. High levels of crime and drug use often coexist in economically disadvantaged and socially deprived neighbourhoods.

Different drugs are associated with different problems. Although only about 5 per cent of illicit drug users take heroin, approximately 20 per cent of the total economic costs of illicit drug use have been linked to heroin use (Harwood et al., 1988). An important association between illicit drug dependence and crime concerns the need to support the drug habit. The regular use of illicit drugs places an excessive economic burden upon the user which, in most cases, cannot be met by normal means. The main options for supporting a drug habit tend to be crime, drug dealing, and prostitution. The onset of addiction is associated with increased levels of criminal behaviour which continue during periods of addiction (Ball et al., 1983). Acquisitive crimes involving theft are among the most frequent ways of obtaining money for drugs. One of the most frequent offences is shoplifting (Stewart et al., 2000).

Crime and addiction do not inevitably go together. Half of the patients recruited to NTORS[2] had not committed any acquisitive crimes during the three months prior to treatment, and, of those who were involved in crime, the majority were relatively low-rate offenders. The majority of acquisitive crimes were committed by a minority of the drug users, with 10 per cent of them committing 76 per cent of the crimes (Stewart et al., 2000). Those who were more heavily involved in crime were more severely dependent on heroin and/or cocaine. Drug-selling offences are common among illicit drug users. However, as with acquisitive crimes, the majority of drug users were not involved in selling drugs. Less than one-third reported selling drugs, and for most of those, this was an infrequent activity. Half of the drug sellers reported purchasing drugs for their own use, and dealers tended to use the same drug that they sold, especially with regard to heroin and crack cocaine (Reuter et al., 1990). Gains are associated both with being able to buy drugs more cheaply if bought in bulk, and through the ability to cream off a percentage of the drug by passing on costs to lower level buyers.

Unlike heroin or crack cocaine, where drug use is often linked to acquisitive crime, the relationship between alcohol and crime is less clear. One link is that between alcohol and violent crime. This is more often related to binge drinking and intoxication than to alcohol use per se, and the association tends to be complex, being mediated by individual propensity for violence and by social and contextual events. Exact figures are difficult to estimate and are disputed, but high estimates suggest that either the offender or victim has consumed alcohol in 65 per cent of homicides, 75 per cent of stabbings, 70 per cent of assaults and half of all domestic assaults (IAS, 2007).

The high rates of criminal behaviour among drug users are reflected in high rates of contact with the criminal justice system. Large numbers of drug users are incarcerated in prisons and this leads to its own problems. Drug users tend to have fewer educational qualifications, lower rates of employment, more housing difficulties, poorer physical health, as well as more behavioural, psychological and psychiatric problems than other, non-drug-using prisoners. Where drug-dependent offenders are incarcerated, the likelihood of illicit drug use within prisons increases. Among offenders who were using heroin at the time of imprisonment, more than half were found to persist with heroin use while in prison, and the probability of heroin use in prison was greatest among those who were dependent on heroin (Strang et al., 2006). More than a fifth of those who used heroin inside prison used the drug by injection.

The societal costs of drug abuse in the UK cannot be calculated precisely but they are known to be massive. Every year the problems associated with drug abuse and its consequences cost the country many billions of pounds. The costs include expenditure on prevention, treatment and rehabilitation programmes. Further human and social costs are associated with impaired health, damaged relationships and lowered productivity, as well as the distress caused to others by drug-related crime.

Assessment of Substance Use Disorders

Clinical assessment should provide information to determine suitability for treatment, to evaluate patient needs and to devise a treatment plan. Assessment is not an impersonal and routine procedure to be completed before the more interesting and important business of treatment: it is an important first stage of the therapeutic process.

Assessment has a pragmatic function. It should identify the presenting problems, and the reasons why the person is making contact. Basic assessment issues are: What types of substances are being used, by which routes of administration and with what sorts of associated problems? Does the user want to give up all drugs? Or do they just want to stop taking one drug that is seen as causing particular problems?

The assessment of severity of dependence is important and will influence treatment decisions. Questions need to be asked concerning the obstacles to maintaining change after giving up drugs. Assessment should identify the antecedents (environmental, emotional and cognitive) of episodes of addictive behaviour, and the consequences that maintain the behaviour.

Limitations in treatment resources may tempt staff to select patients who are believed to be more likely to respond well to treatment. It is extremely difficult to predict who

will respond well or fail to respond to treatment. 'Clinical judgement' provides a poor basis for such predictions (Gossop & Connell, 1983). It has also proved difficult to identify treatment non-responders on the basis of pre-treatment patient characteristics, behaviours and problems (Belding et al., 1998).

In a clinical setting, the interview is the main source of information during assessment. This is heavily reliant upon self-reported problems and behaviours, typically obtained through semi-structured interviews which may or may not also include some use of structured instruments. Commonly used assessment instruments include the AUDIT: this is a short (10 item) questionnaire that provides a composite measure of alcohol consumption, problems and dependence during the previous year (Saunders et al., 1993). The Severity of Dependence Scale (SDS) is a short (5 item) scale that assesses the psychological components of dependence and which can be used to assess dependence upon any drug, including alcohol (Gossop et al., 1995). The Short Opiate Withdrawal Scale (SOWS) is a self-completion questionnaire for the assessment of the opiate withdrawal syndrome (Gossop, 1990). This scale assesses 10 commonly reported symptoms. It is quick and easy to administer, and provides clinically useful information which is relevant to the planning and delivery of treatment programmes.

In a criminal justice setting, the validity of self-reported substance use may be compromised, and greater reliance may be placed upon 'objective' or independent sources of information. Biochemical methods which can be used are analysis of blood, breath, saliva, urine, sweat and hair samples for direct metabolites of abused substances, or for indirect evidence of biological changes related to drug use. The choice of screening method will be influenced by the pharmacokinetics of the drugs which are being investigated, and will depend also on the questions being asked. Biological testing may be useful to monitor and maintain drug-free therapeutic prison wings.

Self-reported drug misuse can have high validity which correlates well with objective measures (Weiss et al., 1998) and self-report remains an essential tool. In many circumstances it is the most practical way to obtain information, and in some circumstances it is the only possible way of obtaining information (as with internal states). Self-report and laboratory tests can also be used interactively. Rates of agreement between self-reported drug use and urinalysis increased when urine was taken for testing prior to interview (Hamid et al., 1999).

Management of Detoxification

Withdrawal from drugs, or 'detoxification,'[3] represents an intermediate treatment goal, and a preliminary phase of abstinence-orientated treatments. Detoxification is not, in itself, a treatment for drug dependence. Detoxification alone leads to little or no improvement compared to no-treatment conditions. Nonetheless, the importance of the treatment and management of withdrawal should not be underestimated. Drug withdrawal can be painful and unpleasant and it should be managed with as little discomfort as possible for the patient.

The main criteria by which the effectiveness of detoxification should be judged are: symptom severity, duration of withdrawal, and completion rates (achieving a drug-free state at the end of the detoxification programme). A detoxification treatment may be fully effective in terms of these criteria but still not touch upon the psychosocial and other factors associated with relapse. The majority of the factors which put the ex-user at risk of relapse are different from, and separate from, withdrawal symptoms and their treatment.

Heroin (and other opiates)

Heroin withdrawal symptoms include: vomiting, diarrhoea, stomach cramps, hot and cold flushes, muscular aches, yawning, sneezing and insomnia. About 8 hours after heroin is discontinued the addict will start to feel uncomfortable. After about 12–15 hours, withdrawal symptoms increase in severity and are at their most intense between 24 and 72 hours. Thereafter, the symptoms gradually lessen in intensity, though it may be a week or more before the person feels well again.

One of the most widely used opiate detoxification methods involves gradually reducing doses of oral methadone. Methadone is often regarded as the most effective pharmacotherapeutic agent currently used for detoxification (Kreek, 2000). Typically, detoxification takes place with gradually reducing doses of methadone over periods of 10–28 days (Gossop et al., 1989).

Centrally acting alpha-2 adrenergic agonists such as clonidine and lofexidine have also been used. Clonidine produces a rapid reduction of withdrawal symptoms (Gossop, 1988), but it may require additional medication to modify residual symptoms. The hypotensive effects of clonidine may restrict the manner in which it can be used, since treatment requires relatively close medical supervision. Lofexidine has comparable efficacy to clonidine, but fewer side effects, particularly with regard to

postural hypotension (Buntwal et al., 2000). Detoxification with lofexidine can also be achieved over periods as short as five days (Bearn et al., 1998).

Stimulants

Some drug users become dependent upon stimulants in the sense that they have impaired capacity to control their use of these drugs. It is unclear whether cocaine and amphetamines have a true withdrawal syndrome, though abstinence after regular use of amphetamines can lead to disrupted sleep patterns, with a reduction in sleep time accompanied by daytime drowsiness and night-time wakefulness (Gossop et al., 1982). There are no pharmacotherapies of proven value for the effective treatment of stimulant withdrawal. Non-pharmacological detoxification treatments for stimulants, including auricular (ear) acupuncture, are sometimes used, though with little evidence to support their effectiveness.

Alcohol

Alcohol dependence has a well-defined withdrawal syndrome. Mild or moderate degrees of dependence may lead to only moderate discomfort during withdrawal. This may require low levels of medication and in some cases, no medication may be required. In other cases, alcohol detoxification may require medication with a benzodiazepine for a few days, though detoxification regimes of more than 7–10 days are rarely necessary for uncomplicated alcohol withdrawal.

Trembling is a common alcohol withdrawal symptom, with increasing tremor appearing 12–24 hours after the last drink, often accompanied by restlessness, agitation and insomnia. The most severe form of alcohol withdrawal is Delirium Tremens. This may develop 2–5 days after alcohol abstinence. Its onset is often abrupt, but may be preceded by nightmares, restlessness and agitation, then by panic, confusion and hallucinations. Delerium Tremens usually subsides in 2–3 days but has a significant morbidity and mortality due to injuries sustained during periods of confusion, and from dehydration, hypothermia, and pneumonia.

Multiple drug detoxification

Drug users may be dependent upon several drugs. Common multiple dependencies which require detoxification involve combinations of opiates, benzodiazepines and alcohol. Where drug users require multiple detoxification, treatment is most appropriately provided in a setting with resources and facilities for intensive clinical supervision and the medically safe treatment of complicated withdrawal states.

The management of withdrawal in custody

The treatment of withdrawal symptoms presents few clinical problems when conducted in a medical setting. Providing detoxification for drug addicts in police custody may be more problematic. The accuracy of self-reported drug use may be compromised in this setting. Police doctors often stay with the suspect for only a few minutes and the next doctor to attend may be a different one. In most cases, resources or facilities do not allow the medical and physical state of the addict to be observed by trained staff.

When addicts are taken into police custody, some treatment intervention may be required to prevent the onset of acute withdrawal. There is often uncertainty and disagreement among police surgeons about how to respond to drug withdrawal syndromes. Police doctors may have conflicting views about methadone prescribing, coupled with negative attitudes towards drug addicts and a lack of knowledge of current drug-misuse treatment practice.

The management of drug-dependent suspects in police custody presents a dilemma. If untreated, they will develop withdrawal symptoms. If given drugs, they may become intoxicated. Both of these states may impair the suspect's capacity to respond appropriately to a police interview and this may subsequently be relevant to the acceptability of statements and confessions in court.

Treatment

(i) Motivation and coercion

Drug users give various reasons for seeking treatment. In addition to drug problems, the person may have physical or psychological problems (a serious infection, depression), or social pressure (from a partner or employer). Facing an imminent court case or having been convicted can be powerful reasons for seeking treatment. Although the person may be aware of the need to change, they are often ambivalent both about drugs and about treatment.

Many drug users in US treatment programmes are directly referred by the criminal justice system (Hubbard et al., 1989). However, direct referral is a relatively insen-

sitive measure of the influence of the criminal justice system and many more users are facing some form of legal pressure such as parole or probation.

It has been suggested that legal pressures or mandatory referrals from the criminal justice system can be used productively. However, the results of research studies are inconsistent. Some studies found comparable outcomes among coerced and non-coerced groups (Anglin, 1988; De Leon, 1988). Other studies found that coercion may lead to worse outcomes (Friedman et al., 1982). The heroin users in NTORS who were facing pressure from the criminal justice system had worse heroin use outcomes at follow-up (Gossop et al., 2002b).

Motivation and treatment readiness are complex, and include readiness for personal change, and readiness to engage with the treatment programme and with specific intervention activities. Readiness also includes patient attributes, skills/resources, confidence/self-efficacy, as well as motivation. Many treatments presume a commitment to change. Motivational interviewing (MI) assumes that the drug user is characterised by ambivalence about their drug-taking behaviour, and sees itself as 'an approach designed to help clients build commitment and reach a decision to change' (Miller & Rollnick, 1991).

Motivational interviewing is seen primarily as a counselling *style* rather than a technique. Motivation is regarded as the product of an interpersonal process in which the therapist has considerable influence on the subsequent attributions and behaviour of the patient. Motivational interviewing is used to help explore and resolve ambivalence about change. Its aim is to increase levels of cognitive dissonance until sufficient motivation is generated for the patient to consider options and interventions for change. Reflective listening is used selectively to elicit self-motivational statements which can orientate the patient towards change. The therapist assists the patient in identification of appropriate goals and in the implementation of strategies to achieve these changes. Motivational interviewing has been found to be a useful tool in many stages of treatment but it has been particularly useful in helping people who are still at an early stage of committing themselves to treatment or to changing their behaviour.

Drug users who received MI were more likely to attend treatment sessions (Carroll et al., 2001), to remain in treatment and to show more commitment to treatment goals, more compliance with treatment requirements, and to remain abstinent after treatment (Baker et al., 2001). Among drug misusers who received court orders to undergo treatment, those who received MI were more likely to attend treatment sessions and to complete the programme (Lincourt *et al.*, 2002).

(ii) Treatment interventions

Cognitive-behavioural treatments

Basic assumptions underlying the various cognitive-behavioural treatments are that: substance use disorders are mediated by cognitive and behavioural processes; these disorders and their associated cognitive-behavioural processes are, to a large extent, learned and can be modified; treatment should facilitate the acquisition of coping skills for resisting drug taking and for reducing drug-related problems (Liese & Najavits, 1997). Such treatments vary in the precedence given to the development of cognitive or behavioural skills.

One treatment which is based on the principles of social-learning theory is a self-management programme designed to enhance the habit-change process. Relapse Prevention (RP) teaches individuals who are trying to change their behaviour how to anticipate and cope with the problem of relapse. It is similar to other cognitive-behavioural treatments and combines behavioural skill training, cognitive interventions, and lifestyle change procedures (Marlatt & Gordon, 1985).

The key components of treatment are the identification of high-risk situations which increase the risk of relapse, and the development and strengthening of effective coping responses. High-risk situations may be situations, events, objects, cognitions or mood states associated with drug use. Most lapses are related to negative emotional states, social pressure and interpersonal conflicts (Bradley *et al.*, 1989).

Relapse is often linked to contact with other drug users. The majority of lapses among heroin addicts occur in the company of drug takers or in a social context related to drug taking (Gossop *et al.*, 1989). More than three-quarters of the opiate addicts in an outpatient treatment programme met other drug users during the previous week: nearly two-thirds had been offered drugs on at least one occasion during the previous week, and 14 per cent had been offered drugs every day (Unnithan *et al.*, 1992). Under such circumstances, the likelihood of a lapse to drug taking is greatly increased for even the most strongly motivated patient.

The provision of treatment within a Relapse Prevention framework involves an individualised assessment of high-risk situations. Patients are taught to recognise high-risk situations and to avoid or to cope with

these risks. RP requires the development of specific coping strategies to deal with risk situations. These may include skills training and the development or strengthening of coping strategies that address issues of lifestyle imbalance and antecedents of relapse.

Positive expectancies and self-efficacy beliefs engender feelings of hope and optimism which facilitate treatment effectiveness. Efficacy expectations reflect the individual's sense of personal control and influence whether they initiate coping behaviour, what degree of effort is devoted to that behaviour, and how long it is maintained in the face of obstacles. Self-efficacy refers to the person's expectations about their capacity to cope with specific high-risk situations. It is concerned with perceived ability to perform a coping response, and not with the general ability to exercise willpower to resist temptation.

Self-efficacy beliefs may apply to the development of addictive behaviour, choice of treatment goals, and the maintenance of behaviour change during recovery (Annis & Davis, 1988). Treatment should take account of cognitive appraisals of past successes and failures in relation to drug-taking situations. Where a coping response is successfully performed, self-efficacy beliefs will be strengthened, and repeated experiences of success will reduce the risk of future lapses or relapse in such situations.

Conversely, where an individual fails to cope with a high-risk situation, their beliefs about their own capacity are undermined and the probability of relapse increases. Loss of confidence may be particularly pronounced among those who rely upon willpower alone to deal with risk situations, since there is nothing they can 'do' to cope. This reinforces the sense of failure, helplessness and lack of control. Addicts who saw relapse episodes as being more amenable to their personal control were more likely to avoid a relapse to opiate use after treatment (Bradley *et al.* 1992).

Relapse Prevention procedures may be applied to anticipate and prevent a relapse or to help the individual recover from a 'lapse' before it escalates into a full-blown relapse. In principle, RP procedures can be used regardless of the theoretical orientation of the therapist or the intervention methods used during the initial treatment phase. Once a heroin addict has stopped using drugs, for example, RP can be used to support continued abstinence, regardless of the methods used to initiate abstinence (e.g. attending 12-step meetings, psychotherapy, or voluntary cessation) (Marlatt & Gordon, 1985).

Twelve-step treatments and therapeutic communities
Twelve-step treatments and therapeutic communities
(TCs) differ in several respects but they also share many
common features. They share a common focus upon
abstinence as the overriding goal of treatment. They see
recovery from addiction as requiring a profound
restructuring of thinking, personality and lifestyle, and
involving more than just giving up drug taking.

Narcotics Anonymous (NA) is a direct descendant of
Alcoholics Anonymous. Both AA and NA have flourished in many countries throughout the world. AA/NA
has a philosophy of mutual help, group affiliation and
identification. Reliance upon the fellowship is seen as
one of the primary therapeutic agents which sets AA/
NA apart from other forms of treatment. Group meetings are one of the best-known aspects of AA/NA.
Meetings may be 'open' or 'closed'. When individuals
join AA/NA, they are usually encouraged to attend
more than one meeting a week, and a target of attending 90 meetings in 90 days is often set (DuPont &
McGovern, 1994).

AA/NA offers a number of social and psychological
support systems for the recovering addict. The peer
group can support efforts to achieve and maintain abstinence, and provides a structure for the member's free
time (Brown *et al.*, 2001). Twelve-step programmes provide a form of cognitive restructuring therapy and can
help to tackle the faulty beliefs and maladaptive cognitions which need to be changed in recovery.

The 12 steps are the essential principles and ingredients of the recovery process. Progression through the
steps is seen as essential for achieving and maintaining
abstinence. The steps emphasise two general themes:
spirituality/belief in a 'higher power' (which is defined
by each individual), and pragmatism (belief in doing
'whatever works' for the individual, meaning doing
whatever it takes in order to avoid returning to substance use).

AA/NA sees addiction as an illness that permeates
all aspects of the individual's life, and which can only
be controlled by lifelong abstinence. The 'disease concept' of addiction has provoked opposition on the
grounds that it may serve 'to absolve the alcoholic [or
drug addict] from moral responsibility for his actions'
(Heather & Robertson, 1989). This view is strongly
rebutted by AA/NA which emphasises the need for
addicts to take responsibility for their own behaviour
and to participate actively in their own recovery
(Wells, 1994).

AA/NA has also been criticised for its 'religious'
orientation. Six of the 12 steps make some reference to
God, and prayer and meditation are seen as important
parts of the recovery process. However, members of the
fellowship are encouraged to interpret the 'higher
power' based upon their own personal understanding.
Examples of this may include the power of the group,
the power of nature, love, truth or honesty (Wells,
1994). Attitudes towards the 12 steps vary greatly.
Addicts tend to show more willingness to accept
'Personal Responsibility' steps than those related to a
'Higher Power' (Best *et al.*, 2001).

Therapeutic communities are used both within and
outside the criminal justice system. As with AA/NA, the
basic goal for problem drug users in TCs requires them
to undergo a complete change in lifestyle, involving
abstinence from drugs, avoidance of antisocial behaviour, the development of prosocial skills, and personal
honesty. The essential element of the TC approach is the
community. This provides both the context and method
in the change process, and the community element distinguishes the TC from other treatment or rehabilitative
approaches to substance abuse and related disorders.

Treatment length varies from short-term with aftercare, to long-term programmes of more than one year's
duration. At one time, treatments were much longer,
and some are still provided over extended periods. TCs
usually divide their programme into three phases of
induction/orientation, treatment and re-entry (Kennard,
1998). Induction/orientation may last for a few weeks or
up to two months. The core, treatment phase involves
the resident living, working, and relating to others
exclusively in the community, and progressing through
the community hierarchy. In the re-entry phase, the
resident has passes to go out while still living in the
community. Some TCs also operate 'half-way' houses
with patients living in semi-independent accommodation after completing the main programme.

Three important psychological principles underlying
the processes of change within TCs are social role training, vicarious learning and efficacy training (De Leon,
2000). The resident positions within the TC hierarchy
provide experience of work roles, and as individuals
learn their various social roles in the community, they
undergo a wide range of social and psychological
changes. Role training builds new behaviours, skills, and
attitudes that are socially and psychologically supportive to the individual in their recovery. Peers and staff
provide role models for appropriate behaviours and

attitudes. Meeting community expectations in performance, responsibility, self-examination and autonomy leads to increased self-efficacy and self-esteem.

Drug maintenance treatments

Maintenance treatments for opiate dependence are widely used throughout the world. About 600,000 people in Europe are currently receiving maintenance treatment: of these, more than 400,000 are receiving methadone treatment.

Methadone maintenance is a long-term treatment for opiate dependence which involves the prescription of daily doses of (usually oral) methadone. When the patient has reached a stable, non-euphoric state, counselling, environmental changes and other social services can help shift their orientation and lifestyle away from drug seeking and related crime towards more socially acceptable behaviours.

Methadone maintenance has been extensively studied in different countries, with different treatment groups, and over a period of four decades. It is the most thoroughly evaluated form of treatment for drug dependence. A meta-analysis of methadone maintenance studies reported consistent associations between maintenance treatment and reductions in illicit opiate use, HIV risk behaviours and drug and property crimes (Marsch, 1998).

Opiate-dependent individuals have been found to show reduced illicit drug use and criminal behaviour when maintained on methadone compared to no treatment or simple detoxification conditions. Methadone patients who are retained in treatment longer have better outcomes than clients with shorter treatment courses, and better outcomes have been found when patients are maintained on higher (50–100 mg) rather than lower doses (Ward *et al.*, 1998). Methadone maintenance treatment has been found to have one of its strongest effects in terms of reducing drug-related criminal behaviours (Marsch, 1998).

Maintenance treatments are used in both specialist (e.g. addiction services) and non-specialist (e.g. GP) settings. Maintenance treatments are also increasingly used in criminal justice settings, though its use in such settings continues to be controversial. One reason for the reluctance to provide maintenance treatment in prisons is because of the fear of diversion of an opioid drug within the prison. This risk of diversion can be greatly reduced, if not eliminated, by means of appropriately supervised consumption of medication. This requires that the treatment be provided with adequate resources and facilities.

In a randomised clinical trial, methadone maintenance treatment in prison was found to be superior to a counselling-only intervention in leading to greater treatment entry in the community after release from prison and to reduced opiate use (confirmed by urine testing) after release (Kinlock *et al.*, 2007). Methadone maintenance treatment in prison has also been found to lead to reduced injecting risk behaviour in prison (Dolan *et al.*, 1998).

Buprenorphine is a mixed agonist-antagonist, unlike full opiate agonists such as heroin or methadone. It is readily absorbed through the mouth and it has been administered both as a solution and as tablets. Although methadone remains the dominant maintenance medication in the UK (83 per cent of all prescriptions in 2005), the prescription of buprenorphine is increasing (Strang *et al.*, 2007).

Research studies have demonstrated the efficacy of buprenorphine for maintenance and detoxification treatments. Buprenorphine and methadone have broadly comparable efficacy (Marsch *et al.*, 2005). Buprenorphine can be as effective as methadone in retaining patients in treatment (Mattick *et al.* (1998) and in leading to reductions in heroin use and to abstinence from heroin (Johnson *et al.*, 2000).

Buprenorphine and methadone are often used in different treatment settings and this is an issue of potential importance to the provision of maintenance treatment in the prison setting. Whereas the prescription of methadone has often been restricted to specialist clinics, buprenorphine has been more widely used in primary care settings.

Buprenorphine's partial agonist effects may be of particular relevance to the use of maintenance treatment in prisons. Buprenorphine produces less severe respiratory depression than full-agonist opioids and the death rate for buprenorphine is lower than for methadone (Auriacombe 2001).

(iii) Effectiveness of treatment

Major national outcome studies have consistently shown improvements in problem behaviours after treatment. US studies showed that treatment leads to reductions in use of heroin and other illicit drugs (Hubbard *et al.*, 1989). Also, predatory crime was reduced during treatment, and remained lower than baseline levels after treatment.

In the UK, NTORS found improvements in a wide range of problem behaviours after treatment, including reductions in use of heroin and other illicit drugs, improvements in psychological health and reductions in crime. Frequency of heroin use after one year, for example, was reduced to about half of the intake levels, and remained at this lower level throughout the five-year follow-up period (Gossop et al., 2003).

There were also substantial reductions in criminal behaviour. Acquisitive crimes were reduced to one-third of intake levels, and the rate of involvement in crime was reduced to about half of intake levels (Gossop et al., 2000). The number of shoplifting offences was reduced to about one-third of intake levels, and burglary offences were reduced to less than one-quarter of intake levels. Changes in offending behaviour were linked to reductions in drug use after treatment, and especially to reduced heroin use. The greatest reductions in criminal activity occurred among the most highly active offenders (Gossop et al., 2000), where crimes were reduced to 13 per cent of intake levels. This represents a huge reduction in criminal behaviour.

The economic costs imposed upon society by drug addicts are largely due to criminality. Treatment has been found to be cost-effective and cost-beneficial, with the costs of treatment being recouped during treatment, and further cost-benefits accrued as a result of reduced post-treatment drug use (Harwood et al., 1988). There are a range of economic benefits from treatment for drug dependence, based solely on costs of crime. Even without the numerous other benefits in addition to reductions in crime, the financial resources expended in treating drug-dependent patients provided a return that justified the cost of treatment. The provision of treatment yielded an immediate cost saving in terms of the reduced victim costs of crime, as well as cost savings within the criminal justice system. The true cost savings to society are likely to be even greater than these crime-focused estimates (Godfrey et al., 2001).

Treatment within prisons can also reduce post-release drug use and reoffending (Knight et al., 1997; Wexler et al., 1990). In many respects, the issues involved in providing effective treatment in prison are similar to those for treating addicts in a standard clinical setting. Good results have been found for participation in residential programmes. Studies of therapeutic community programmes within prisons found that programme participation, time spent in treatment, programme completion and the provision of aftercare were all associated with improved outcomes (Martin et al., 1999).

Studies of the treatment needs of drug misusers in prison suggest that inmates need a range of treatment modalities, and that the provision of correctional treatment is often inadequate relative to need (Belenko & Peugh, 2005). About one-third of male and more than half of female US prison inmates were estimated to need long-term residential treatment.

One response to the lack of treatments in US correctional services involved the expansion of community-based alternatives such as drug courts or diversion programmes (Hser et al., 2003). Drug Treatment and Testing Orders (DTTOs), based upon the US drug courts, were introduced in the UK in 1998. These sought to provide treatment in the community for drug-misusing offenders. The drug user is required to attend a treatment programme for between six months and three years, and to provide urine specimens for testing. An evaluation of DTTOs found that reconviction rates were high (80 per cent), and completion rates were low, with only 30 per cent of the sample completing their programmes (Hough et al., 2003). Studies from other countries have found poor outcomes among drug users processed through drug courts (Belenko et al., 1994; Vermeulen & Walburg, 1998).

The importance of aftercare is widely accepted and studies have demonstrated the importance of aftercare support for offenders (Martin et al., 1999). Relapse Prevention can also provide an aftercare programme for substance abusers after completion of an intensive treatment intervention (Brown et al., 2002). The period immediately after leaving a residential setting (hospital or prison) is one of massively high risk of relapse and the best possible support should be provided during this period. Unfortunately, few services have sufficient resources to provide adequate aftercare, and generally, little is done during this critical period.

Because of its self-supporting nature, AA/NA provides a form of aftercare at no cost to existing services, and offender programmes can make use of AA/NA as an aftercare resource merely by recommending participation and encouraging attendance at meetings.

Further Complications

Psychiatric comorbidity

The co-occurrence of substance use and psychiatric problems creates particular difficulties for intervention. Anxiety and depression are common among individuals with substance use disorders. Psychiatric disorders and drug misuse can coexist with varying degrees of association or independence. Some disorders may be due to intoxication, or withdrawal states. In some cases, anxiety and depressive symptoms are associated with drug use and will remit with abstinence (Gossop et al., 2006).

Stimulant psychosis may occur after high-dose and/or prolonged use of stimulants. Stimulant psychosis has some similarities with schizophrenia, but unlike schizophrenia, the onset of stimulant psychosis is rapid and is often accompanied by an agitated or manic mood state. When stimulant use is discontinued, a stimulant psychosis would be expected to clear within days. The continuation of psychotic symptoms after the drug has ceased to be excreted (usually within a maximum of seven days) should be regarded not as stimulant psychoses but as of possible schizophrenic aetiology.

Some individuals use drugs or alcohol to self-medicate psychological problems. Drug use and psychiatric disorders may also coexist by chance since both disorders are relatively common. Even in these circumstances, psychiatric problems are likely to influence the course and outcome of substance use disorders, and may require a specially tailored treatment approach.

The presence of comorbid psychiatric disorders among substance misusers is generally associated with a poorer treatment prognosis, as is the severity of psychiatric disorders (Ward et al., 1998). The provision of appropriate treatment for underlying psychiatric or psychological disorders leads to improved treatment outcomes (Rounsaville & Kleber, 1985).

Staff in criminal justice settings may need enhanced training to improve their ability to detect, assess, and respond to those with comorbid or dual diagnosis disorders. One of the most difficult challenges is where substance-abusing offenders suffer from schizophrenia or other serious mental illnesses. In such cases, the complexities of providing an effective treatment response within the criminal justice system are likely to be beyond all but the most specialised services.

Suicide

Substance use disorders are strongly associated with suicide. Suicidal ideation and suicide attempts are relatively common among substance misusers. Post-mortem studies have consistently reported that at least one-third of those whose death was due to suicide met criteria for alcohol abuse or dependence. Early onset of substance use problems is associated with increased risk of suicide, and in young people the risk of suicidal behaviours is increased among those with substance misuse problems (Hallfors et al., 2004). Substance use disorders are also associated with a greater frequency of suicide attempts, greater seriousness of intention and greater suicidal ideation.

The prison environment may itself increase suicide risk, and the number of suicides in prison has increased in recent years. One-third of suicides within prison occur during the first week after reception (Shaw et al., 2004). Known risk factors include psychiatric disorders and substance use disorders. Suicide risk after intake to prison is particularly high among women prisoners and remand prisoners. Pre-existing risk of suicide may be increased where the treatment of withdrawal symptoms is not done effectively after admission to prison.

In most prisoners who commit suicide there is evidence of suicide risk at reception screening (Shaw et al., 2004). In this respect, many suicides could be regarded as being, at least in principle, preventable. However, it is extremely difficult to attempt to predict suicidal behaviour in individual cases.

Physical comorbidity

Many substance abusers have poor physical health. Drug abuse can adversely affect a range of organ systems, and damage to health may be both direct and indirect. Alcohol can also cause damage to nearly every tissue and body system, with the possibility of consequent disability or disease. Between 20 and 40 per cent of admissions to general hospital wards may be alcohol related (Lieber, 1995).

The majority of drug- or alcohol-dependent patients tend to have at least one physical health problem at admission to treatment, and many have multiple health problems. Physical health problems are more commonly found among the alcohol-dependent patients. The most common health problems among alcohol-dependent patients are cardiovascular, neurological, and gastrointestinal and liver disorders. Special arrangements may be required in prisons for the clinical management of these health problems.

Drug-dependent patients often suffer from respiratory disorders and from chronic liver disease due to viral hepatitis. Hepatitis C infection is extremely prevalent among drug injectors. A study of London heroin users found a seropositivity rate of 86 per cent for HCV (Best et al., 1999). Although drug users are generally

352 MICHAEL GOSSOP

aware of the risk of hepatitis, their beliefs about their own viral status are frequently inaccurate. This may lead to continued injection risk behaviours both within and outside prisons.

The health risk behaviours of drug users have been the focus for various preventive activities. Dissemination of information about the transmission of blood-borne infections is one of the least controversial prevention responses. This has been widely used and in some circumstances may be effective. Needle and syringe exchange schemes have been more controversial, though these have now been established in many countries throughout the world. Some services provide needles and syringes but make no requirement for the return of used equipment. In other services, needles and syringes are provided on an exchange basis. All services make arrangements for the safe disposal of returned used needles and syringes.

There has often been extreme resistance to providing access to sterile injecting equipment within criminal justice settings. However, it is known that illicit drugs can often be obtained within prisons, and that such drugs may be used by injection (Strang et al., 2006). Where drugs are injected by multiple users who have access only to shared injection equipment, this creates a situation of maximum risk for the potential transmission of blood-borne diseases.

Overdose

Despite the greater attention that is generally given to HIV/AIDS, drug overdose is a more frequent cause of death among drug misusers. Although fatal and non-fatal overdoses are commonly attributed to the use of opiates, these are seldom due simply to the use of opiates. The risk of overdose is strongly linked to, and increased by, polydrug use. Both fatal and non-fatal overdoses which are attributed to heroin are more likely to involve the combined use of opiates and alcohol or other sedatives. The mortality rate of the drug users in the NTORS cohort was 1.2 per cent: this is about six times higher than in the general population: deaths were mainly due to overdose (Gossop et al., 2002a).

The achievement of a drug-free state is not a risk-neutral event. Among patients who have been detoxified in residential programmes, an initial lapse to opiate use often occurs soon after leaving the programme, and the first few weeks after discharge are a critical period (Gossop et al., 1989). The same problem arises when detoxified drug addicts are released from prison. The

risk of drug-related death is seven times higher immediately after release (specifically during the first fortnight) than at any subsequent time (Bird & Hutchinson, 2003). Prison services need to be aware of the potential overdose risk among previously addicted prisoners who have been withdrawn from opiates and have lost their tolerance to the effects of opiates.

Notes

1 To avoid having to keep referring to drugs or alcohol, the chapter uses terms such as 'drugs', 'drug use' and 'substance use' to include both drugs and alcohol. Where the text refers to specific drugs, including alcohol, these are mentioned by name.
2 The National Treatment Outcome Research Study (NTORS) is a five-year prospective, national study of more than 1000 drug-dependent patients in addiction treatment services across England.
3 The term 'detoxification' is widely used and it is retained here to avoid the cumbersome if more accurate phrase, 'treatment of withdrawal symptoms'.

Further Reading

Tonry, M. & Wilson, J.Q. (1990). *Drugs and crime*. Chicago, IL: University of Chicago Press.
This edited volume presents a collection of essays which review the various complex interrelationships between drug taking and crime. It includes chapters which examine these issues from the perspectives of drug-law enforcement, prevention, and treatment as the basic components of public policy strategies. Despite its focus upon problems in the USA, it provides a useful overview of many of the key issues within a single volume.

Gossop, M., Trakada, K., Stewart, D. & Witton, J. (2005). Reductions in criminal convictions after addiction treatment: Five year follow-up. *Drug and Alcohol Dependence*, 79, 295–302.
As part of the National Treatment Outcome Research Study (NTORS), changes in criminal convictions were investigated among 1075 drug-misusing clients admitted to 54 drug misuse treatment services across England. Convictions data during the year prior to treatment, and at one year, two years and five years after treatment intake, were collected from the Home Office Offenders' Index, a national database of all convictions in adult and youth courts. During the year prior to treatment, 34 per cent of the sample had been convicted of at least one offence. Conviction rates at all follow-up points were significantly lower than at intake. Reductions in convictions were

found for acquisitive, drug-selling, and violent crimes. These reductions in crime were linked to reductions in regular heroin use and represent substantial changes in behaviour. As well as the personal, social and clinical significance of these behavioural changes, the reduced criminality also provides substantial economic benefits to society.

Bird, S.M. & Hutchinson, S.J. (2003). Male drugs-related deaths in the fortnight after release from prison: Scotland, 1996–99. *Addiction, 98*, 185–190.

This study investigated the death rate among 15–35-year-old males released after a period of at least 14 days' imprisonment in Scottish prisons. The findings showed that drug-related mortality in this group was seven times higher in the two weeks after release than at other times at liberty. Mortality from other causes, including suicide, during the post-release period was also significantly increased, and this may also be partly related to use of drugs. The authors conclude that investment in, and evaluation of, prison-based interventions for drug abusers is needed to reduce the risk of death during the immediate post-release period.

References

Anglin, M.D. (1988). A social policy analysis of compulsory treatment for opiate dependence. *Journal of Drug Issues, 18*, 527–545.

Annis, H. & Davis, C. (1988). Self-efficacy and the prevention of alcoholic relapse. In T. Baker & D. Cannon (Eds.) *Addictive disorders: Psychological research on assessment and treatment.* New York: Praeger.

Auriacombe, M. (2001). Deaths attributable to methadone vs buprenorphine in France. *Journal of the American Medical Association, 285*, 45.

Baker, A., Boggs, T. & Lewin, T. (2001). Randomized controlled trial of brief cognitive behavioural interventions among regular users of amphetamine. *Addiction, 96*, 1279–1287.

Ball, J., Shaffer, J. & Nurco, D. (1983). The day to day criminality of heroin addicts in Baltimore: A study in the continuity of offence rates. *Drug and Alcohol Dependence, 12*, 119–142.

Bearn, J., Gossop, M. & Strang, J. (1998). Accelerated lofexidine treatment regimen compared with conventional lofexidine and methadone treatment for in-patient opiate detoxification. *Drug and Alcohol Dependence, 50*, 227–232.

Belding, M., McLellan, A.T., Zanis, D. & Incmikoski, R. (1998). Characterising 'nonresponsive' patients. *Journal of Substance Abuse Treatment, 15*, 485–492.

Belenko, S., Fagan, J.A. & Dumanovsky, T. (1994). Effects of legal sanctions on recidivism in special drug courts. *Justice System Journal, 17*(1), 53–81.

Belenko, S. & Peugh, J. (2005). Estimating drug treatment needs among state prison inmates. *Drug and Alcohol Dependence, 77*, 269–281.

Best, D., Harris, J., Gossop, M., Manning, V., Man, L-H., Marshall, J. *et al.* (2001). Are the Twelve Steps more acceptable to drug users than to drinkers? A comparison of experiences of and attitudes to Alcoholics Anonymous (AA) and Narcotics Anonymous (NA) among 200 substance misusers attending inpatient detoxification. *European Addiction Research, 7*, 69–77.

Best, D., Noble, A., Finch, E., Gossop, M., Sidwell, C. & Strang, J. (1999). Accuracy of perceptions of hepatitis B and C status: Cross sectional investigation of opiate addicts in treatment. *British Medical Journal, 319*, 290–291.

Bird, S.M. & Hutchinson, S.J. (2003). Male drugs-related deaths in the fortnight after release from prison: Scotland, 1996–99. *Addiction, 98*, 185–190.

Bradley, B., Gossop, M., Brewin, C., Phillips, G. & Green, L. (1992). Attributions and relapse in opiate addicts. *Journal of Consulting and Clinical Psychology, 60*, 470–472.

Bradley, B., Phillips, G., Green, L. & Gossop, M. (1989). Circumstances surrounding the initial lapse to opiate use following detoxification. *British Journal of Psychiatry, 154*, 354–359.

Brown, B., Kinlock, T. & Nurco, D. (2001). Self-help initiatives to reduce the risk of relapse. In F. Tims, C. Leukefeld & J. Platt (Eds.) *Relapse and recovery in addictions.* New Haven, CT: Yale University Press.

Brown, T.G., Seraganian, P., Tremblay, J. & Annis, H. (2002). Process and outcome changes with relapse prevention versus 12-step aftercare programs for substance abusers. *Addiction, 97*, 677–689.

Buntwal, N., Bearn, J., Gossop, M. & Strang, J. (2000). Naltrexone and lofexidine combination treatment compared with conventional lofexidine treatment for in-patient opiate detoxification. *Drug and Alcohol Dependence, 59*, 183–188.

Carroll, K.M., Libby, B., Sheehan, J. & Hyland, N. (2001). Motivational interviewing to enhance treatment initiation in substance abusers: An effectiveness study. *American Journal on Addictions, 10*, 335–339.

De Leon, G. (1988). Legal pressure in therapeutic communities. *Journal of Drug Issues, 18*, 625–640.

De Leon, G. (2000). *The therapeutic community: Theory, model, and method.* New York: Springer.

Dolan, K.A., Wodak, A.D. & Hall, W.D. (1998). A bleach program for inmates in NSW: An HIV prevention strategy. *Australian and New Zealand Journal of Public Health, 22*, 838–840.

DuPont, R. & McGovern, J. (1994). *A bridge to recovery: An introduction to 12-step programs.* Washington, DC: American Psychiatric Association.

Friedman, S.B., Horvat, G.L. & Levinson, R.B. (1982). The Narcotic Addict Rehabilitation Act: Its impact on federal prisons. *Contemporary Drug Problems, 82*, 101–111.

Godfrey, C., Stewart, D. & Gossop, M. (2001). *National Treatment Outcome Research Study: Economic analysis of the two year outcome data.* London: Department of Health.

Gossop, M. (1988). Clonidine and the treatment of the opiate withdrawal syndrome. *Drug and Alcohol Dependence, 21,* 253–259.

Gossop, M. (1990). The development of a Short Opiate Withdrawal Scale (SOWS). *Addictive Behaviors, 15,* 487–490.

Gossop, M., Bradley, B. & Brewis, R. (1982). Amphetamine withdrawal and sleep disturbance. *Drug and Alcohol Dependence, 10,* 177–183.

Gossop, M. & Connell, P. (1983). Drug dependence, who gets treated? *International Journal of the Addictions, 18,* 99–109.

Gossop, M., Darke, S., Griffiths, P., Hando, J., Powis, B., Hall, W. *et al.* (1995). The Severity of Dependence Scale (SDS): Psychometric properties of the SDS in English and Australian samples of heroin, cocaine and amphetamine users. *Addiction, 90,* 607–614.

Gossop, M., Griffiths, P., Bradley, B. & Strang, J. (1989). Opiate withdrawal symptoms in response to 10-day and 21-day methadone withdrawal programmes. *British Journal of Psychiatry, 154,* 360–363.

Gossop, M., Marsden, J. & Stewart, D. (2006). Remission of psychiatric symptoms among drug misusers after drug dependence treatment. *Journal of Nervous and Mental Disease, 194,* 826–832.

Gossop, M., Marsden, J., Stewart, D. & Rolfe, A. (2000). Reductions in acquisitive crime and drug use after treatment of addiction problems: One year follow-up outcomes. *Drug and Alcohol Dependence, 58,* 165–172.

Gossop, M., Marsden, J., Stewart, D. & Treacy, S. (2002a). A prospective study of mortality among drug misusers during a four year period after seeking treatment. *Addiction, 97,* 39–47.

Gossop, M., Marsden, J., Stewart, D. & Kidd, T. (2003). The National Treatment Outcome Research Study (NTORS): 4–5 year follow-up results. *Addiction, 98,* 291–303.

Gossop, M., Stewart, D., Browne, N. & Marsden, J. (2002b). Factors associated with abstinence, lapse or relapse to heroin use after residential treatment: Protective effect of coping responses. *Addiction, 97,* 1259–1267.

Hallfors, D., Waller, M., Ford, C., Halpern, C., Brodish, P. & Iritani, B. (2004). Adolescent depression and suicide risk. *American Journal of Preventive Medicine, 27,* 224–231.

Hamid, R., Deren, S., Beardsley, M. & Tortu, S. (1999). Agreement between urinalysis and self-reported drug use. *Substance Use and Misuse, 34,* 1585–1592.

Harwood, H., Hubbard, R., Collins, J. & Rachal, J. (1988). The costs of crime and the benefits of drug abuse treatment: A cost–benefit analysis using TOPS data. *NIDA Research Monograph No. 86,* 209–235.

Heather, N. & Robertson, I. (1989). *Problem drinking.* Oxford: Oxford University Press.

Hough, M., Clancy, A., McSweeney, T. & Turnbull, P. (2003). *The impact of drug treatment and testing orders on offending: Two year conviction rates.* Findings 184. London: Home Office.

Hser, Y.I., Teruya, C., Evans, E., Longshore, D., Grella, C. & Farabee, D. (2003). Treating drug-abusing offenders: Initial findings from a five-county study on the impact of California's Proposition 36 on the treatment system and patient outcomes. *Evaluation Review, 27,* 479–505.

Hubbard, R.L., Marsden, M.E., Rachal, J.V., Harwood, H.J., Cavanaugh, E.R. & Ginzberg, H.M. (1989). *Drug abuse treatment: A national study of effectiveness.* Chapel Hill, NC: University of North Carolina Press.

Institute of Alcohol Studies (IAS) (2007). *Alcohol and crime.* London: Home Office.

Johnson, R., Chutuape, M., Strain, E., Walsh, S., Stitzer, M. & Bigelow, G. (2000). A comparison of levomethadyl acetate, buprenorphine, and methadone for opioid dependence. *New England Journal of Medicine, 343,* 1290–1297.

Kennard, D. (1998). *An introduction to therapeutic communities.* London: Jessica Kingsley.

Kinlock, T.W., Gordon, M.S., Schwartz, R.P., O'Grady, K., Fitzgerald, T.T. & Wilson, M. (2007). A randomized clinical trial of methadone maintenance for prisoners: Results at 1-month post-release. *Drug and Alcohol Dependence, 91,* 220–227.

Knight, K., Simpson, D., Chatham, L. & Camacho, L. (1997). An assessment of prison-based drug treatment: Texas in-prison therapeutic community program. *Journal of Offender Rehabilitation, 24,* 75–100.

Kreek, M.J. (2000). Methadone-related opioid agonist pharmacotherapy for heroin addiction. History, recent molecular and neurochemical research and future in mainstream medicine. *Annals of the New York Academy of Sciences, 909,* 186–216.

Lieber C.S. (1995). Medical disorders of alcoholism. *New England Journal of Medicine, 333,* 1054–1065.

Liese, B. & Najavits, L. (1997). Cognitive and behavioral therapies. In J. Lowinson, P. Ruiz, R. Millman & J. Langrod (Eds.) *Substance abuse: A comprehensive textbook.* Baltimore, MD: Williams & Wilkins.

Lincourt, P., Kuettel, T. & Bombardier, C. (2002). Motivational interviewing in a group setting with mandated clients: A pilot study. *Addictive Behaviors, 27,* 381–391.

Marlatt, G.A. (1985). Relapse prevention: Theoretical rationale and overview of the model. In G.A. Marlatt & J.R. Gordon (Eds.) *Relapse prevention: Maintenance strategies in the treatment of addictive behavior.* New York: Guilford Press.

Marsch, L.A. (1998). The efficacy of methadone maintenance interventions in reducing illicit opiate use, HIV risk behaviour and criminality: A meta-analysis. *Addiction, 93,* 515–532.

Marsch, L.A., Stephens, M.A., Mudric, T., Strain, E.C., Bigelow, G.E. & Johnson, R.E. (2005). Predictors of outcome in LAAM, buprenorphine, and methadone treatment for opioid dependence. *Experimental and Clinical Psychopharmacology, 13,* 293–302.

Martin, S., Butzin, C., Saum, C. & Inciardi, J. (1999). Three-year outcomes of therapeutic community treatment for drug-involved offenders in Delaware: From prison to work release to aftercare. *The Prison Journal, 79,* 294–320.

Mattick, R., Oliphant, D., Ward, J. & Hall, W. (1998). The effectiveness of other opioid replacement therapies: LAAM, heroin, buprenorphine, naltrexone and injectable maintenance. In J. Ward, R. Mattick & W. Hall (Eds.) *Methadone maintenance treatment and other replacement therapies.* Amsterdam: Harwood.

Miller, W.R. & Rollnick, S. (1991). *Motivational interviewing.* New York: Guilford Press.

Reuter, P., MacCoun, R. & Murphy, P. (1990). *Money from crime: A study of the economics of drug dealing in Washington, D.C.* Santa Monica, CA: RAND.

Rounsaville, B.J. & Kleber, H. (1985). Psychotherapy/counseling for opiate addicts: Strategies for use in different treatment settings. *International Journal of the Addictions, 20,* 869–896.

Saunders, J.B., Aasland, O.G., Babor, T.F., de la Fuente, J.R. & Grant, M. (1993). Development of the Alcohol Use Disorders Identification Test (AUDIT): WHO collaborative project on early detection of persons with harmful alcohol consumption. *Addiction, 88,* 791–804.

Shaw, J., Baker, D., Hunt, I.M., Moloney, A. & Appleby, L. (2004). Suicide by prisoners: National clinical survey. *The British Journal of Psychiatry, 84,* 263–267.

Stewart, D., Gossop, M., Marsden, J. & Rolfe, A. (2000). Drug misuse and acquisitive crime among clients recruited to the National Treatment Outcome Research Study (NTORS). *Criminal Behaviour and Mental Health, 10,* 10–20.

Strang, J., Gossop, M., Heuston, J., Green, J., Whiteley, C. & Maden, T. (2006). Persistence of drug use during imprisonment: Relationship of drug type, recency of use, and severity of dependence to use of heroin, cocaine, and amphetamine in prison. *Addiction, 101,* 1125–1132.

Strang, J., Manning, V., Mayet, S., Ridge, G., Best, D. & Sheridan, J. (2007). Does prescribing for opiate addiction change after national guidelines? Methadone and buprenorphine prescribing to opiate addicts by general practitioners and hospital doctors in England, 1995–2005. *Addiction, 102,* 761–770.

Unnithan, S., Gossop, M. & Strang, J. (1992). Factors associated with relapse among opiate addicts in an outpatient detoxification programme. *British Journal of Psychiatry, 161,* 654–657.

Vermeulen, E.C. & Walburg, J.A. (1998). What happens if a criminal can choose between detention and treatment: Results of a 4-year experiment in the Netherlands. *Alcohol and Alcoholism, 33,* 33–36.

Ward, J., Mattick, R. & Hall, W. (1998). *Methadone maintenance treatment and other opioid replacement therapies.* Amsterdam: Harwood.

Weiss, R.D., Najavits, L.M., Greenfield, S.F., Soto, J.A., Shaw, S.R. & Wyner, D. (1998). Validity of substance use self-reports in dually diagnosed outpatients. *American Journal of Psychiatry, 155,* 127–128.

Wells, B. (1994). Narcotics Anonymous (NA) in Britain. In J. Strang & M. Gossop (Eds.) *Heroin addiction and drug policy: The British system.* Oxford: Oxford University Press.

Wexler, H., Falkin, G. & Lipton, D. (1990). Outcome evaluation of a prison therapeutic community for substance abuse treatment. *Criminal Justice and Behavior, 17,* 71–92.

23

Children Who Physically or Sexually Harm Others

Kevin Browne and Shihning Chou

It is difficult to ascertain the true extent of child and youth offending due to limitations of information sources on these young people. Studies that rely on official records omit those cases not coming to the attention of law enforcement agencies, which is sometimes termed the 'dark figure' of unreported delinquent/criminal behaviour. Self-reports from victims or the general population usually give a much higher figure but may be distorted due to inaccurate memories or deliberate exaggerations. Therefore, attempts have been made to combine multiple sources to increase the accuracies of estimates (Friendship *et al.*, 2002) and this is evident in the recent House of Commons Home Affairs Committee Report on Knife Crime which illustrates the extent of children violently harming others (House of Commons Home Affairs Committee, May 2009).

Extent of Violence Offences by Children

Violence outside the family

The recent murder of 11-year-old Rhys Jones in Liverpool highlighted the killing of children and young people by juvenile and teenage offenders. Indeed, newspapers reports claimed at least 22 young people had been killed by their peers within a year (*The Guardian*, 18 November 2008).

Home Office figures, for the year October 2006 to September 2007, show that there were 68 homicide victims under 16 years of age in England and Wales (Povey *et al.*, 2008). This represented 9 per cent of all homicides

($N = 734$) for that year. A year earlier (2005/06), there were 52 homicide victims less than 16 years. The majority (49 per cent) of these victims were killed by their parents, 13 per cent by acquaintances of a similar age and 16 per cent by strangers (some of a similar age). In 22 per cent of cases, no suspect has been identified within the 12-month period (Povey *et al.*, 2008). In 37 cases, both the victim and offender were under 18 years. It is claimed that homicides involving young people as victims and perpetrators, in England and Wales, are on the increase (Applegate & Davies, 2006), but this increase is gradual and reflects the gradual increase in serious violent crime generally since 1979 (Brookman & Maguire, 2003).

In England and Wales overall, there were 19,253 individuals who had received an immediate custodial sentence for violence against the person (with 3647 on remand) between October 2007 and September 2008 (Ministry of Justice, 2008). This represented a 2 per cent increase (5 per cent on remand) compared to the previous year (2006/07). Thirty-nine per cent of this population (7181 males and 314 females) and 56 per cent on remand (1953 males and 102 females) were aged between 18 and 20 years. Those aged 15–17 years represented 10 per cent of this population (1806 males and 56 females) and 15 per cent of those on remand (520 males and 17 females). In England and Wales, approximately half of those who receive a custodial sentence for violent offences against the person are convicted for 'wounding or other acts endangering life'. Three per cent are classified as homicide, and a further 3 per cent are classified as attempted murder, both having an intentional component.

Francis *et al.* (2004) used the Home Office 'Homicide Index' for England and Wales to investigate 2145 homicides committed between 1995 and 2000. They found that 150 homicides were committed by children aged 10 to 17 (an average of 30 per year) and a further 236 were committed by young people aged between 18 and 20 (mean = 47 per year). In total, 386 homicides were committed by children and young people under 21 years, which represented 18 per cent of the whole sample. However, no further analyses of homicides committed by young people were reported. Overall, Francis *et al.* (2004) identified that the vast majority of cases (98 per cent) involved a single victim, with only 2 per cent of cases having more than one victim (between 2 and 7). By contrast, 20 per cent of cases involve more than one offender (between 2 and 11). Female victims accounted for 32 per cent of cases but accounted for less than 10 per cent of offenders.

Using the same Homicide Index, Soothill *et al.* (2002) concentrated their study on the criminal histories of men under 45 years convicted of murder for the first time between 1995 and 1997. They identified 569 males of whom 386 (68 per cent) had previous convictions. Of those first-time murderers with previous convictions, over half of them (57 per cent) had committed violent offences previously. However, there were few differences in the 'modus operandi' between murderers with previous convictions and those without. Nevertheless, those men who were given a custodial sentence at the last conviction were twice as likely to go on to commit murder, which may simply reflect the seriousness of their last offence on a continuum towards a fatal assault. Indeed, it was found that wounding (endangering life), robbery, kidnapping and arson were associated with a increased risk of a later murder conviction. Whether the findings are applicable to young offenders is unknown, as this study did not look at the specific details associated with young offenders, which represented 20.6 per cent of their sample (117 of 569 cases from the Homicide Index, 1995 to 1997). The age breakdown of young first-time murderers in this study is as follows:

- less than 15 years, 2 offenders (0.4 per cent);
- 15–17 years, 33 offenders (5.8 per cent);
- 18–20 years, 82 offenders (14.4 per cent).

In relation to homicides committed by young people, the Ministry of Justice sentencing statistics for England and Wales shows that 101 young people aged between 10 and 17 and 103 young people aged between 18 and 20 received a sentence of life imprisonment during the three-year period from 1999 to 2002 (between 7 and 8 per cent of these people were female). For the next three-year period (2003 to 2006), 71 young people were given life imprisonment between age 10 and 17 years (3 per cent female) and 179 young people between 18 and 20 (7 per cent female). Often, these cases involved knives and sharp instruments and less often fire arms.

For all ages in England and Wales, firearm offences accounted for 8 per cent of homicides (59 cases) in the year ending June 2007, ten more than the previous year (2005/06). In a quarter of the cases the offender was under 18 years (Home Office, 2008ab; Povey *et al.*, 2008). In over a third of homicides, a knife or sharp instrument was used (Home Office, 2008a, 2008b; Povey *et al.*, 2008). A survey report by Roe and Ashe (2008) stated that 6 per cent of boys aged 14 to 17 years carry a knife. However, the recently published House of Commons Home Affairs Committee Report on Knife Crime claims that 31 per cent of 11- to 16-year-olds in mainstream education surveyed (MORI Youth Survey) report having carried a weapon over the past 12 months. Most commonly, these weapons were penknives (17 per cent) and BB airguns (15 per cent). These proportions increased for delinquent young people excluded from school, with 54 per cent carrying a knife and a further 7 per cent carrying another type of weapon. However, a US national report on juvenile offenders (Snyder & Sickmund, 2006) found that males were significantly more likely than females to report assault with intent to cause serious harm (31 per cent, 21 per cent), belonging to a gang (11 per cent, 6 per cent) and carrying a handgun (25 per cent, 6 per cent) by the age of 17.

Gender differences

Overall, males have always been found to be significantly more likely than females to offend in all age groups, including juveniles, but the age of onset of delinquency is later in females than in males (Junger-Tas *et al.*, 2004). In a cohort study following up 380 boys and 380 girls in Newcastle upon Tyne, 28 per cent of the boys and 5.5 per cent of the girls had appeared in court before 18.5 years of age (Kolvin *et al.*, 1988). Similarly, a Swedish study (Svensson & Ring, 2007) found that in 2005, the proportion of young people who admitted committing a violent offence was 21.6 per cent for males and 8.7 per cent for females.

However, a recent survey reporting the levels and trends of offending and antisocial behaviour among young people living in the general household population in England and Wales (Wilson *et al.*, 2006) found that teenage boys and girls were equally likely to have committed a violent offence between the ages of 10 and 17 (47 per cent males, 49 per cent females). Nevertheless, a gender difference in violent offending was observed for young people aged between 18 and 25 years (44 per cent males, 28 per cent females). Overall, the survey showed that males were more likely to have committed an offence than females (30 per cent and 21 per cent, respectively).

Gangs

In the USA, where youth gang culture is a serious problem, the US national report (Snyder & Sickmund, 2006) found that 8 per cent of 17-year-olds reported belonging to a gang, 16 per cent had sold drugs and 16 per cent carried a gun. In addition, a quarter of these juveniles who offended at ages 16 to 17 continue to offend as adults at ages 18 to 19. Even though the proportion of young people in a gang seems to be a minority, they are responsible for a disproportionately high share of violent and non-violent offences in the USA. Indeed, those who have friends or families in a gang were three times more likely to report engaging in vandalism, a major theft, a serious assault, carrying a gun, selling and using drugs and running away from home. Similar findings were also reported in the US national report on juvenile offending about why they joined a gang. Over half (54 per cent) of Rochester gang members said that they followed the lead of friends or family members who preceded them, only 19 per cent said they joined for protection and 15 per cent said it was for fun or excitement. Furthermore, those who were neither in school nor in employment had a significantly greater risk of engaging in a wide range of gang-related behaviours such as using and selling drugs, committing a major theft or a serious assault, and carrying a gun.

Violence inside the family

Violence by children in the family (sibling and parent abuse) is an underresearched topic and has been shown to be associated with violence by adults in the family (child, spouse and elder abuse). Indeed, it was claimed in the past that children will begin to show violence in the place where it was first encountered, which is often the family home (Agnew & Huguley, 1989), rather than

in the community. Indeed, it is claimed (Gelles, 1997) that sibling physical abuse is the most common form of family violence in the USA, with 4 out of 10 siblings hitting, kicking, biting or throwing objects at their brothers and sisters. In 16 per cent of cases, the sibling is beaten up and nearly 1 per cent are threatened with a knife or gun (Straus *et al.*, 1980). However, it is now well recognised that physically and/or sexually victimised children in the home may also express their frustration and anger at their situation in schools and in the community and act as bullies to other children, leading to conflict with the law (Browne & Falshaw, 1996; Browne & Herbert, 1997). Furthermore, 4 out of 5 children who run away from home and who are at risk of delinquency and crime are often running away from physically and/or sexually abusive families (Browne & Falshaw, 1998).

Those children who remain in violent families often begin to retaliate as they grow older, resulting in parent–teenager conflict. The overall prevalence of teenagers showing violence towards their parents occurs within 5–10 per cent of families (Browne & Hamilton, 1998). In four out of five cases of teenage violence in the family, this conflict is reciprocal, with parents hitting their teenage children and their teenage children hitting back. However, one in five violent teenagers in the family shows violent behaviour to their current caregiver, who has not been violent to them in the past. Nevertheless, these cases are often associated with a violent parent who has left home previously (Browne & Hamilton, 1998).

In rare cases, teenage to parent violence escalates over time to parricide, where the child kills a parent. Heide (1994) claims that there are more than 300 parents killed each year in the USA and she categorises the perpetrators of these homicides into three categories: the severely abused child, the severely mentally ill child and the 'dangerously antisocial' child, with firearms used most often as a method. The most common perpetrator is the severely abused child acting out of desperation, with a high frequency of substance abuse amongst the parent victims. The families in which these homicides occur are often isolated and excluded from mainstream society so that the perpetrator feels that they have little alternative with no one to turn to.

A recent study of juvenile court cases in the USA has shown that juvenile family violent offenders are more likely to be female compared to non-family offenders. Family violent youths are also treated more leniently by the courts and their violence seen as less serious.

Extent of Sexual Offences by Children

Sexual assault outside the family

It has been recognised that at least a third of adult sex offenders began committing sexual assault during their teenage years (Elliott *et al.*, 1995; Masson & Erooga, 1999) and between 50 and 80 per cent of adult sex offenders acknowledge a sexual interest in children during adolescence (Abel *et al.*, 1993). Indeed, teenage male perpetrators aged 20 and younger account for about one-third of all allegations of sexual abuse (Glasgow *et al.*, 1994; Watkins & Bentovim, 1992) and approximately a quarter of those convicted of a sexual offence in the UK (Masson & Erooga, 1999). Likewise, studies of criminal convictions in the USA report that up to 20 per cent of rapes and 30 to 50 per cent of child sexual abuse are committed by juvenile perpetrators (Davis & Leitenberg, 1987). This was confirmed by the Irish prevalence study which found that victims of sexual abuse claimed the perpetrator was a child (under 17 years) in one out of four cases (McGee *et al.*, 2002). Overall, sex offenders account for 1 in 13 of people in prison but only 4 per cent of imprisoned sex offenders in custody are juveniles (Councell & Olagundoye, 2003), as most juvenile sex offenders are referred to youth treatment services in the community.

Until relatively recently, most juvenile sexual offending was considered 'exploratory' behaviour and something that would cease with age in a similar way to non-violent delinquent behaviour (Ryan & Lane, 1997). However, research indicates that juvenile sex offending does not decline over time without appropriate intervention. Gerhold *et al.* (2007) reviewed 12 studies of sexual recidivism in adolescent sex offenders, with an overall sample of 1315 juvenile sex abusers with an average age of 15. The overall average for recidivism in these studies was 14 per cent for sexual offending and 44 per cent for non-sexual offending. However, it was discovered that those studies with longer follow-up periods had a higher percentage of young people sexually reoffending (see Figure 23.1). Indeed, 28 per cent had reoffended within seven years. These studies suggest that without appropriate intervention and referral to youth services for inappropriate sexual behaviour, these teenagers may go on to commit sexual offences as adults.

Sexual assault inside the family

With regard to the family context, the sexual maltreatment of brothers and sisters by their siblings is much

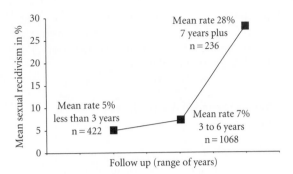

Figure 23.1 Mean rates for sexual recidivism for juvenile sex offenders ($N = 1315$) across 12 studies dependent on length of follow-up. *Source*: Gerhold *et al.* (2007).

more common than once thought. To a certain extent this has been the result of a reappraisal of what was once considered sexual exploration between brothers and sisters, which has been more appropriately described as exploitation where the age difference between the siblings is greater than five years (DeJong, 1989; Finkelhor, 1980), although it has been observed that adolescent incest offenders were less likely to be court ordered for treatment than non-incest offenders (O'Brian, 1991).

In a study of family conflict, 2 per cent of English undergraduate students reported being sexually maltreated by a sibling on at least one occasion (Browne & Hamilton, 1998). Often this sexual maltreatment was associated with physical abuse and bullying, a fact that has been confirmed by a number of American studies for both boys and girls (DeJong, 1989; Johnson, 1988, 1989). Similar to physical and sexual assaults by adults, it is in the context of caregiving or 'child minding' that many of these attacks by adolescent and teenage perpetrators take place (Margolin, 1990).

Indeed, most child sexual offenders begin to take advantage of younger children during their teenage years, with the majority (57 per cent) having been physically and/or sexually assaulted themselves by other teenagers and adults (Elliott *et al.*, 1995). Nevertheless, sibling maltreatment of both a physical and sexual nature has been observed in young children (Cantwell, 1988). For example, Johnson (1988) noted that 46 per cent of a sample of 47 sexually abusive boys were involved in the abuse of their siblings. Similarly, Pierce and Pierce (1987) reported in their study that of the 59 sex offences committed by 37 juvenile offenders, 40 per cent were against sisters and 20 per cent against brothers. The study of physical and sexual maltreatment by brothers and sisters is limited and prevention is only just beginning. It requires a great deal more research given its prevalence and consequences (Laviola, 1989; Mueller & Silverman, 1989).

Characteristics of Antisocial and Violent Children

In the recent UK survey (Wilson *et al.*, 2006), the attributes that showed the strongest association with committing an antisocial offence among 10- to 25-year-olds were: antisocial behaviour, being a victim of personal crime, being drunk once a month or more, having friends/siblings in trouble with the police and taking drugs. It was also found that those who lived with both biological parents had lower lifetime prevalence of breaking law than those who lived in other family types.

It has long been established that poor family environments in childhood and adolescence are associated with antisocial behaviour and delinquency (e.g. Farrington, 1995; Kolvin *et al.*, 1988; Loeber & Dishion, 1983; Moffitt & Caspi, 2001). The largest cohort study on the development delinquency and criminality in the UK (Farrington, 1995) found that convicted delinquents are more likely to have experienced poor parenting, characterised by harsh or erratic parental discipline, neglectful parental attitudes, parental conflicts and lax supervision in their childhood. They are also more likely to have convicted parents or delinquent older siblings. Consequently, convicted delinquents were found to be more likely to have low intelligence, poor concentration, hyperactivity and poor education attainment (Farrington, 1995). An earlier Newcastle study also found that offenders were more likely to have been exposed to poor physical and home care and poor parenting compared to non-offenders. Those who committed their first offence before 15 were more likely to have been exposed to marital instability or parental illness in their preschool years than those who committed their first offence after 15 (Kolvin *et al.*, 1988). A recent Finnish study (Sourander *et al.*, 2006) also found that living in a family other than the two-parent structure, low parental educational level, parent reports of conduct problems and teacher reports of hyperactivity at the age of 8 predicted a high frequency (greater than five) of all types of offences between the ages of 16 and 20. In the USA, McKnight and Loper (2002) investigated risk factors among adolescent girls. Analysis was carried out on 2245 females aged between 10 and 19

years. It was found that experiencing sexual abuse and being brought up by single parents were significant risk factors for delinquency and offending in girls.

Victim to offender

Indeed, childhood victimisation has been also found to be highly prevalent in the background of young offenders (Falshaw & Browne, 1997). A retrospective study of young offenders in secure accommodation found that four out of five (79.2 per cent) had experienced some form of abuse and neglect in their childhood. Of the 79.2 per cent, 8 per cent suffered from single victimisation, 15 per cent experienced repeat victimisation (by the same perpetrator), 8 per cent experienced revictimisation (abuse by different perpetrators) and 69 per cent experienced both repeat victimisation and revictimisation (Hamilton *et al.*, 2002).

The victim to offender pattern seems to be particularly relevant to male child molesters, with 56 to 57 per cent reporting adverse sexual experiences as children in comparison to between 5 and 23 per cent of rapists (Seghorn *et al.*, 1987). A history of sexual abuse in their childhood backgrounds also influences age and gender preferences of male paedophiles and appears to increase the chances of sex offences against boys (Pithers *et al.*, 1988). Retrospective studies have also revealed that 60 to 80 per cent of sex offenders with a history of childhood victimisation began molesting children as adolescents and teenagers (Groth *et al.*, 1982), and it has been estimated that these individuals perpetrate 50 per cent of the sex crimes against boys and up to 20 per cent of offences against girls (Rogers & Terry, 1984). Skuse and colleagues (1998) carried out a retrospective case–control study to investigate risk factors for abused adolescent boys becoming abusers themselves. It was found that experiencing and/or witnessing intrafamilial violence in general and discontinuity of care were significant factors that distinguished those who became abusers and those who did not. Therefore, sexually abusive behaviour towards other children may not be directly related to the sexual abuse they themselves had suffered as a child.

Although poor parenting and abuse/neglect are significant risk factors for delinquency, violence and sex crimes (Falshaw *et al.*, 1996), prospective cohort studies (see Gilbert *et al.*, 2009) show that only a minority of children from abusive and neglectful backgrounds go on to commit offences as juveniles (26 per cent) and as adults (29 per cent), with approximately 1 in 8 sexually abused boys becoming sexual offenders (Salter *et al.*, 2003) and 1 in 6 maltreated children later perpetrating violent offences (Widom, 1989). Nevertheless, children without such adverse experiences are significantly less likely to have a criminal record as juveniles (17 per cent) and as adults (21 per cent).

Therefore, most maltreated children manage to break the cycle of deprivation and crime by the experience of protective factors such as positive interpersonal relationships outside the family (e.g. teachers), good academic achievements, positive attitudes towards authority and effective use of leisure time (Carr & Vandiver, 2001; Hoge *et al.*, 1996).

Factors that facilitate the cycle of violence have also been identified and such risk factors have been shown to distinguish those victims who go on to become offenders (maintainers) from those victims who do not (cycle breakers) (Dixon *et al.*, 2009). It was found that males pose greater risk than females of becoming an abuser and that this risk also depends on the onset, type, frequency, duration and severity of maltreatment suffered as a child. People's responses to disclosure (if any) by the victim also have a strong influence on their risk of offending behaviour. The relationship to perpetrator(s) and the number of perpetrators are also significant, especially when the person has experienced recurrent victimisation. The risk may be further exacerbated by the victim's temperamental personality (Finkelhor, 2008).

Children who kill

Research on adolescents and teenagers who commit homicide has shown that multiple factors are associated with this extreme form of violence (Miyadera, 2005; Myers, 2002). Background factors that may have contributed to the increase of juvenile homicide in the USA, such as a low socio-economic status, harsh parenting, exclusion from school and the availability of weapons, have been explored using case analyses (Heide, 1997, 1998; Hill-Smith *et al.*, 2002; Leary *et al.*, 2003; Schmideberg, 1973). Heide (1997, 1998) identified 15 factors associated with juvenile homicide and divided these factors into five broad categories: situational factors, societal influences, resource availability, personality characteristics and a cumulative effect.

Case analyses of young people who kill, using a clinical perspective, have confirmed the presence of victimisation in the social and family backgrounds of juvenile murderers (Darby *et al.*, 1998; Hill-Smith *et al.*, 2002; Schumaker & Prinz, 2000; Viljoen *et al.*, 2005). Darby

and colleagues' findings (1998) provided preliminary support for the 'lockage phenomenon', which proposes that some children who grow up in chaotic and abusive families may react (as part of post-traumatic stress) by self-harm and suicide or assaults on others and homicide. Some suggest that girls are more likely to internalise their stress and self-harm, whereas boys are more likely to externalise their stress and harm others (Summit, 1983), which offers some explanation for males being responsible for the vast majority of serious violent assaults.

Harries (1990) claims that homicide and assault share a very similar aetiology and differ only in outcome (i.e. a fatal assault). Thus homicide may be a function of violent escalation and preventable. However, Felson and Messner (1996) claim that a proportion of homicides are not just escalated violent assaults that end in a fatal injury by chance. They believe that some offenders plan and intend to kill their victim (for example, out of revenge) and these are characteristically different and more difficult to prevent.

The Development of Antisocial Behaviour in Children

Patterson *et al.* (1989) explained the developmental progression for antisocial behaviour from the social-interactional perspective, in which children's coercive or disruptive behaviours are not effectively dealt with by parents and caregivers. There is a lack of parental supervision or positive reinforcement by caregivers, with inconsistent boundary setting and erratic discipline so that a 'coercive family process' of negative interactions between parent and child becomes the norm (Patterson, 1992). Children may also learn deviant and inappropriate behaviours (such as violent conflict resolution) through direct experience or observation of other family members (Bandura, 1977), and perceive those antisocial behaviours as an effective means of controlling their social environment. Furthermore, the acquisition of deviant behaviours is also enhanced by a lack of encouragement of prosocial skills and good behaviours from the children, which are often ignored by inattentive parents (Snyder, 1977).

On entering school, children with coercive behaviours and poor social skills are likely to meet with peer rejection. Furthermore, growing up in a disruptive and/disorganised family can affect concentration and compliance with educational tasks, which in turn may affect learning and increase the chances of academic under-achievement

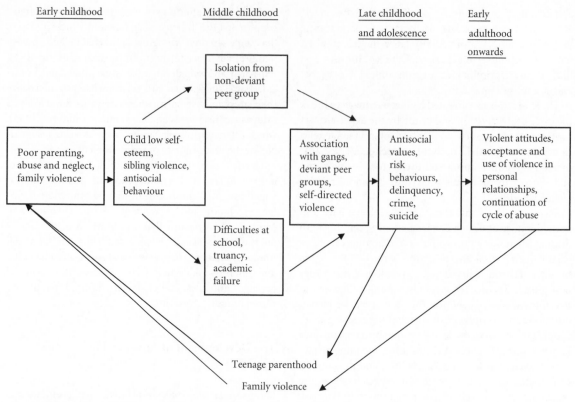

Figure 23.2 The developmental progression from childhood maltreatment to antisocial and violent behaviour. *Source*: by Browne *et al.* (2007b), adapted from Patterson *et al.* (1989).

and low self-esteem. This educational failure increases the likelihood of truancy and gang membership with other truants. In this context, deviant behaviours are valued and exhibited for social approval. The associated increase in self-esteem within the gang reinforces the antisocial behaviour so that it becomes more frequent at the expense of prosocial behaviour. This developmental sequence of events is outlined in Figure 23.2.

Browne and Hamilton-Giachritsis (2005) have also reviewed the evidence showing that young offenders have a preference for violent media entertainment that supports their distorted way of thinking about conflict resolution, for example 'hit first and ask questions afterwards'. This in turn may influence and entrench their attitudes and behaviour and increase the chances and frequency of their committing violent offences. This phenomenon was observed most often for teenagers from violent family backgrounds.

From an attachment perspective, children from 'average' families usually experience sensitive and consistent parenting and learn to perceive their social environment in a positive way. As a consequence, they develop a positive sense of self and positive view of others. By contrast, children from abusive, neglectful or disorganised families are highly likely to have an insecure attachment to their primary carer (Morton & Browne, 1998) as a result of harsh and/or inconsistent parenting. This hinders the development of a positive self-image and these children are more likely to have a negative view of self and a negative view of others, which in turn affects the development of empathy towards others (e.g. Browne & Herbert, 1997).

Need for Early Intervention

It is suggested that early identification of children experiencing poor parenting, abuse and neglect can help in the prevention of antisocial delinquency and crime, if these 'children in need' are supported by intervening with parents in difficulty prior to violence in the family and the development of antisocial behaviour in the child. Figure 23.2 illustrates the developmental progression for antisocial behaviour. The model is based on the theory that growing up in a disorganised/disruptive family or with violent and/or neglectful parents (both sometimes associated with drug and alcohol misuse and/or mental illness and personality disorder in parents) has several negative consequences for the children; for example, the child becomes socially unresponsive, emotionally blunted, passive, apathetic and inattentive (Browne & Herbert, 1997; Patterson *et al.*, 1989).

Following the initiative of the World Health Organization (World Health Organization, 2002, 2006) to address violence from a public health perspective (i.e. in a similar way to tackling individual alcohol and drug misuse), two recent policy briefings (Browne *et al.*, 2007a, 2007b) assert that breaking the intergenerational cycle of violence in families can be achieved by the early assessment of parents' capacity to meet the developmental, health and care needs of their child and an evaluation of risk factors that impinge on the parents' capacity (e.g. poverty and/or social isolation/exclusion). This 'framework for assessment' (Department of Health, 2000) identifies families who are high priority for community health and social services (see Browne *et al.*, 2006; Hamilton & Browne, 2002). Efforts can then be made to promote positive parenting in families before children reach 5 years of age and go to school. Such programmes (e.g. Triple P) have shown effectiveness in improving parenting abilities and parental skills in managing child behaviour and thus reducing undesirable behaviours and conduct disorders in children (Dretzke *et al.*, 2005; Sanders & Cann 2002; Sanders *et al.*, 2007).

It is also important to identify young children with preschool emotional and behaviour problems such as low self-esteem, poor emotional regulation and antisocial behaviour in order to provide support for those children early on, as these children may have been missed earlier or parenting difficulties may have emerged later. Indeed, school programmes that enhance self-esteem in children have been claimed by Briggs and Hawkins (1997) to be a more effective protective mechanism for the prevention of sexual abuse than school programmes specifically addressing this issue (e.g. Elliott, 1994).

In terms of educational provision, the school system needs to include and provide support for children who are failing academically, have behavioural difficulties in school and/or who may be missing school and becoming isolated from their school peers. The underlying causes, such as bullying and victimisation at home, in school or in the community are often ignored or poorly addressed (Stern, 1987). School exclusion and social isolation may push them further towards deviant peer groups and into antisocial or even criminal activities. Incentives need to be provided to those children and adolescents for school completion. Education and counselling regarding positive relationships, reproductive and sexual health, pregnancy and parenthood also will contribute to reducing the risk of intergenerational transmission of violence and maltreatment (Browne *et al.*, 2007b).

For adolescents and their families who are involved in alcohol and drug misuse, antisocial acts or self-harming behaviour either in isolation or in peer groups, positive interventions need to be provided to help them develop more healthy and adaptive strategies in dealing with underlying causes for those problems, such as family conflict in the home (Browne & Herbert, 1997).

For teenagers who have offended, the criminal justice system needs to use appropriate interventions with family and community involvement, for example the use of 'Parenting Orders' (Browne *et al.*, 1998) which aims to change antisocial attitudes and risk behaviours of the child and in some cases the parents. Custodial sentences have been shown to be less effective in creating positive change compared to recent pilot programmes that place young offenders in foster care, where the specially trained foster caregivers offer emotional support and act as role models to the child and possibly the child's parents (Southall, 2007).

Conclusions

Health, education, justice and social service professionals can be more effective in preventing the cycles of violence (both in the home and in the community) by adopting a life-cycle approach, to provide support and services to children and families in need, at different stages in the child's development (Browne *et al.*, 2006; Pinheiro, 2006). Early intervention provides a better prognosis and more cost-effective solutions for the prevention of violence to children and this consequently inhibits the potential for violence that children may develop.

Further Reading

Finkelhor, D. (2008). *Childhood victimization: Violence, crime, and abuse in the lives of young people*. Oxford: Oxford University Press.

Children are the most criminally victimised segment of the population and actually appear before authorities more frequently as victims than as offenders. David Finkelhor presents a comprehensive review about the prevention, treatment and study of juvenile victims. Developmental victimology looks at child victimisation across the lifespan and patterns in victimisation change with age.

Heide, K.M. (1998). *Young killers: The challenge of juvenile homicide*. Thousand Oaks, CA: Sage.

This book provides an assessment of male adolescent murderers and presents cases of several juvenile homicide offenders. It also addresses psychological assessment, treatment issues and prevention strategies aimed at reducing the incidence of juvenile homicide.

Pinheiro, P.S. (Ed.) (2006). *World report on violence against children*. New York: United Nations; United Nations Secretary-General's study on violence against children.

The book is a result of the first global attempt to describe the scale of all forms of violence against children and its impact and calls for a multidisciplinary response. It approaches the issue from the combined perspective of human rights, public health and child protection.

References

Abel, G., Osborn, C. & Twigg, D. (1993). Sexual assault through the life span: Adult offenders with juvenile histories. In H.E. Barbaree, W.L. Marshall & S.M. Hudson (Eds.) *The juvenile sex offender* (pp.104–117). New York: Guilford Press.

Agnew, R. & Huguley, S. (1989). Adolescent violence towards parents. *Journal of Marriage and Family*, 51, 699–711.

Applegate, B.K. & Davies, R.K. (2006). Public views on sentencing juvenile murderers: The impact of offender, offense and perceived maturity. *Youth Violence and Juvenile Justice*, 4(1), 55–74.

Bandura, A. (1977). *Social learning theory*. Englewood Cliffs, NJ: Prentice Hall.

Briggs, F. & Hawkins, R. (1997). *Child protection: A guide for teachers and child care professionals*. Sydney: Allen & Unwin.

Brookman, F. & Maguire, M. (2003). *Reducing homicide: A review of the possibilities*. Home Office Online Report 01/03. London: Home Office.

Browne, K.D., Douglas, J., Hamilton-Giachritsis, C.E. & Hegarty, J. (2006). *A community health approach to the assessment of infants and their parents*. Chichester: Wiley.

Browne, K.D. & Falshaw, L. (1996). Factors related to bullying in secure accommodation. *Child Abuse Review*, 5(1), 123–127.

Browne, K.D. & Falshaw, L. (1998). Street children in the UK: A case of child abuse neglect. *Child Abuse Review*, 7(4), 241–253.

Browne, K.D. & Hamilton, C.E. (1998). Physical violence between young adults and their parents: Associations with a history of child maltreatment. *Journal of Family Violence*, 13(1) 59–79.

Browne, K.D. & Hamilton-Giachritsis, C. (2005). The influence of violent media on children and adolescents: A public-health approach. *Lancet*, 365, 702–710.

Browne, K.D., Hamilton-Giachritsis, C.E. & Vettor, S. (2007a). *Preventing child maltreatment in Europe: A public health approach: Policy briefing*. World Health Organization: Violence and Injury Prevention Programme. Copenhagen: WHO Regional Office for Europe.

Browne, K.D., Hamilton-Giachritsis, C.E. & Vettor, S. (2007b). *The cycles of violence: The relationship between childhood maltreatment and the risk of later becoming a victim or perpetrator of violence: Policy briefing*. World Health Organization: Violence and Injury Prevention Programme. Copenhagen: WHO Regional Office for Europe.

Browne, K.D. & Herbert, M. (1997). *Preventing family violence*. Chichester: Wiley.

Browne, K.D., Lynch, M. & Spicer, D. (1998). The introduction of 'Parenting Orders'. *Child Abuse Review*, 7(5), 297–299.

Cantwell, H.B. (1988). Child sexual abuse: Very young perpetrators. *Child Abuse and Neglect*, 12(4), 579–582.

Carr, M.B. & Vandiver, T.A. (2001). Risk and protective factors among youth offenders. *Adolescence*, 36, 409–426.

Councell, R. & Olagundoye, J. (2003). *The prison population in 2001: A statistical review*. Home Office Research Findings, 195. London: Home Office.

Darby, P.J., Allan, W.D., Kashani, J.H., Hartke, K.L. & Reid, J.C. (1998). Analysis of 112 juveniles who committed homicide: Characteristics and a close look at family abuse. *Journal of Family Violence*, 13(4), 365–375.

Davis, G.E. & Leitenberg, H. (1987). Adolescent sex offenders. *Psychological Bulletin*, 101, 417–427.

DeJong, A.R. (1989). Sexual interactions among siblings and cousins: Experimentation or exploitation? *Child Abuse and Neglect*, 13(2), 271–279.

Department of Health, Department of Education and Employment and the Home Office (2000). *Framework for the assessment of children in need and their families*. London: HMSO.

Dixon, L., Browne, K.D. & Hamilton-Giachritsis, C.E. (2009). Patterns of risk and protective factors in the intergenerational cycle of maltreatment. *Journal of Family Violence*, 24, 111–122.

Dretzke, J., Frew, E., Davenport, C., Barlow, J., Stewart-Brown, S., Sandercock, J. *et al.* (2005). The effectiveness and cost-effectiveness of parent training/education programmes for the treatment of conduct disorder, including oppositional defiant disorder, in children. *Health Technology Assessment, 9*, 1–250.

Elliott, M. (1994). *Kidscape Primary Child Protection Programme*. London: Kidscape.

Elliott, M., Browne, K.D. & Kilcoyne, J. (1995). Child sexual abuse: What offenders tell us. *Child Abuse and Neglect, 19*(5), 579–594.

Falshaw, L. & Browne, K. (1997). Adverse childhood experiences and violent acts of young people in secure accommodation. *Journal of Mental Health, 6*(5), 443–455.

Falshaw, L., Browne, K.D. & Hollin, C. (1996). Victim to offender: A review. *Aggression and Violent Behavior, 1*, 389–404.

Farrington, D.P. (1995). The 12th Jack Tizard Memorial Lecture – The development of offending and antisocial-behavior from childhood – Key findings from the Cambridge Study in Delinquent Development. *Journal of Child Psychology and Psychiatry, 36*, 929–964.

Felson, M. & Messner, S.F. (1996). To kill or not to kill? Lethal outcomes in injurious attacks. *Criminology, 34*, 519–545.

Finkelhor, D. (1980). Sex among siblings: A survey on prevalence, variety and effects. *Archives of Sexual Behaviour, 9*(3), 171–194.

Finkelhor, D. (2008). *Childhood victimization: Violence, crime, and abuse in the lives of young people*. Oxford: Oxford University Press.

Francis, B., Barry, J., Bowater, R., Miller, N., Soothill, K. & Ackerley, E. (2004). *Using homicide data to assist murder investigations*. Home Office Online Report 26/04. London: Home Office. Retrieved 11 September from www.homeoffice.gov.uk/rds/pdfs04/rdsolr2604.pdf

Friendship, C., Beech, A.R. & Browne, K.D. (2002). Reconviction as an outcome measure in research: A methodological note. *British Journal of Criminology, 42*, 442–444.

Gelles, R.J. (1997). *Intimate violence in families* (3rd edn). Thousand Oaks, CA: Sage.

Gerhold, C.K., Browne, K.D. & Beckett, R. (2007). Predicting recidivism in adolescent sexual offenders. *Aggression and Violent Behavior, 12*, 427–438.

Gilbert, R., Spatz-Widom C., Browne, K., Fergusson, D., Webb, E. & Janson, S. (2009). Child maltreatment: Burden and consequences in high-income countries. Lancet Series on Child Maltreatment 1. *The Lancet, 373*, 68–81.

Glasgow, D., Horne, L., Calam, R. & Cox. A. (1994). Evidence, incidence, gender and age in sexual abuse of children perpetrated by children: Towards a developmental analysis of child sexual abuse. *Child Abuse Review, 3*, 196–210.

Groth, A.N., Hobson, W. & Garry, T. (1982). The child sexual molester: Clinical observations. In J. Conte & D. Shore (Eds.) *Social work and child sexual abuse*. New York: Hamworth.

Hamilton, C.E. & Browne, K.D. (2002). Predicting physical maltreatment. In K.D. Browne, H. Hanks, P. Stratton & C.

Hamilton (Eds.) *Early prediction and prevention of child abuse: A handbook* (pp.41–56). Chichester: Wiley.

Hamilton, C.E., Falshaw, L. & Browne, K.D. (2002). The link between recurrent maltreatment and offending behaviour. *International Journal of Offender Therapy and Comparative Criminology, 41*, 75–95.

Harries, K.D. (1990). *Serious violence: Patterns of homicide and assault in America*. Springfield, IL: Charles C. Thomas.

Heide, K.M. (1994). *Why kids kill parents: Child abuse and adolescent homicide*. Thousand Oaks, CA: Sage.

Heide, K.M. (1997). Juvenile homicide in America: How can we stop the killing? *Behavioral Sciences and the Law, 15*, 203–220.

Heide, K.M. (1998). *Young killers: The challenge of juvenile homicide*. Thousand Oaks, CA: Sage.

Hill-Smith, A.J., Hugo, P., Hugues, P., Fonagy, P. & Hartman, D. (2002). Adolescents murderers: Abuse and adversity in Childhood. *Journal of Adolescence, 25*, 221–230.

Hoge, R.D., Andrews, D.A. & Leschied, A.W. (1996). An investigation of risk and protective factors in a sample of youthful offenders. *Journal of Child Psychology and Psychiatry, 37*, 419–424.

Home Office (2008a). *Crime in England and Wales: Quarterly update to June 2008*. Home Office Statistical Bulletin 10/08. London: Home office. Retrieved 11 September 2009 from www.homeoffice.gov.uk/rds/pdfs08/hosb1408.pdf

Home Office (2008b). Crime in England and Wales: Quarterly update to June 2008: Supplementary note on (a) recorded crimes involving firearms and (b) violent and sexual offences involving the use of knives or sharp instruments. *Home Office Statistical Bulletin 10/08*. London: Home Office. Retrieved 11 September 2009 from www.homeoffice.gov.uk/rds/pdfs08/hosb1408supp.pdf

House of Commons, Home Affairs Committee (2009). *Knife crime (7th report 2008–09)*. London: HMSO.

Johnson, T. (1988). Child perpetrators – Children who molest other children: Preliminary findings. *Child Abuse and Neglect, 12*(2), 219–229.

Johnson, T. (1989). Female child perpetrators: Children who molest other children. *Child Abuse and Neglect, 13*(4), 571–585.

Junger-Tas, J., Ribeaud, D. & Cruyff, M.J.L.F. (2004). Juvenile delinquency and gender. *European Journal of Criminology, 1*, 333–375.

Kolvin, I., Miller, F.J., Fleeting, M. & Kolvin, P.A. (1988). Social and parenting factors affecting criminal-offence rates: Findings from the Newcastle Thousand Family Study (1947–1980). *British Journal of Psychiatry, 152*, 80–90.

Laviola, M. (1989). Effects of older brother–younger sister incest: A review of four cases. *Journal of Family Violence, 4*(3), 259–274.

Leary, M., Kowalski, R., Smith, L. & Phillips, S. (2003). Teasing, rejection and violence: Case studies of school shootings. *Aggressive Behavior, 29*, 202–214.

Loeber, R. & Dishion, T.J. (1983). Early predictors of male delinquency: A review. *Psychological Bulletin, 94,* 68–99.

Margolin, L. (1990). Child abuse by adolescents caregivers. *Child Abuse and Neglect, 14*(3), 365–373.

Masson, H. & Erooga, M. (1999). *Children and young people who sexually abuse others.* London: Routledge.

McGee, H., Garavan, R., De Barra, M., Byrne, J. & Conroy, R. (2002). *The Sexual Abuse and Violence in Ireland (SAVI) report.* Dublin: Dublin Rape Crises Centre and Liffey Press.

McKnight, L.R. & Loper, A.B. (2002). The effects of risk and resilience factors in the prediction of delinquency in adolescent girls. *School Psychology International, 23,* 186–198.

Ministry of Justice (2008). *Population in custody monthly tables September 2008 England and Wales.* Ministry of Justice Statistics bulletin. London: Ministry of Justice. Retrieved 11 September 2009 from www.justice.gov.uk/docs/population-in-custody-september08.pdf

Miyadera, T. (2005). *An exploratory study of juvenile homicide in Japan.* Unpublished M.Phil Thesis, University of Birmingham.

Moffitt, T.E. & Caspi, A. (2001). Childhood predictors differentiate life-course persistent and adolescence-limited antisocial pathways among males and females. *Development and Psychopathology, 13,* 355–375.

Morton, N. & Browne, K.D. (1998). Theory and observation of attachment and its relation to child maltreatment: A review. *Child Abuse and Neglect, 22,* 1093–1104.

Mueller, E. & Silverman, N. (1989). Peer relations in maltreated children. In D. Cicchetti & V. Carlson (Eds.) *Child maltreatment: Theory and research on the causes and consequences of child abuse and neglect* (pp.529–578). Cambridge: Cambridge University Press.

Myers, W.C. (2002). *Juvenile sexual homicide.* San Diego, CA: Academic Press.

O'Brian, M. (1991). Taking sibling incest seriously. In M. Parton (Ed.) *Family sexual abuse* (pp.75–92). London: Sage.

Patterson, G.R. (1992). *Coercive family process.* Eugene, OR: Castalia.

Patterson, G.R., DeBaryshe, B.D. & Ramsey, E. (1989). A developmental perspective on antisocial behavior. *American Psychologist, 44,* 329–335.

Pierce, L.H. & Pierce, R.L. (1987). Incestuous victimization by juvenile sex offenders. *Journal of Family Violence, 2,* 351–364.

Pinheiro, P.S. (Ed) (2006). *World report on violence against children.* United Nations, New York; United Nations Secretary-General's Study on violence against Children.

Pithers, W.D., Kashima, K.M., Cumming, G.F. & Beal, L.F. (1988). Relapse prevention: A method of enhancing maintenance of change in sex offenders. In A.C. Salter (Ed). *Treating child sex offenders and victims: A practical guide.* Beverly Hills, CA: Sage.

Povey, D., Coleman, K., Kaiza, P., Hoare, J. & Jansson, K. (2008). *Homicides, firearm offences and intimate violence 2006/07 (Supplementary Volume 2 to Crime in England and Wales 2006/07).* Home Office Statistical Bulletin 01/08. Retrieved 11 September 2009 from www.homeoffice.gov.uk/rds/pdfs07/hosb1107.pdf

Roe, S. & Ashe, J. (2008). *Young people and crime: Findings from the 2006 Offending, Crime and Justice Survey.* Home Office Statistical Bulletin 09/08. London: Home Office. Retrieved 11 September 2009 from www.homeoffice.gov.uk/rds/offending_survey.html.

Rogers, C.M. & Terry, T. (1984). Clinical intervention with boy victims of sexual abuse. In I.R. Stuart & J.G. Greer (Eds.) *Victims of sexual aggression: Men, women and children* (pp.91–103). New York: Van Nostrand Reinhold.

Ryan, G. & Lane, S. (1997). *Juvenile sexual offending: Causes, consequences and corrections.* San Francisco, CA: Jossey-Bass.

Salter, D., McMillan, D., Richards, M., Talbot, T., Hodges, J., Bentovim, A. *et al.* (2003). Development of sexually abusive behaviour in sexually victimized males: A longitudinal study. *Lancet, 361,* 471–476.

Sanders, M. & Cann, W. (2002). Promoting positive parenting as an abuse prevention strategy. In K.D. Browne, H. Hanks, P. Stratton & C. Hamilton (Eds.) *Early prediction and prevention of child abuse: A handbook* (pp.145–164). Chichester: Wiley.

Sanders, M.R., Bor, W. & Morawska, A. (2007). Maintenance of treatment gains: A comparison of enhanced, standard, and self-directed triple P-positive parenting program. *Journal of Abnormal Child Psychology, 35,* 983–998.

Schmideberg, M. (1973). Juvenile murderers. *International Journal of Offender Therapy and Comparative Criminology, 17,* 240.

Schumaker, D.M. & Prinz, R.J. (2000). Children who murder: A review. *Clinical Child and Family Psychology Review, 3*(2), 97–115.

Seghorn, T.K., Prentky, R.A. & Boucher, R.J. (1987). Childhood sexual abuse in the lives of sexually aggressive offenders. *Journal of the American Academy of Child and Adolescent Psychiatry, 26,* 262–267.

Skuse, D., Bentovim, A., Stevenson, J. *et al.* (1998). Risk factors for the development of sexually abusive behaviour in sexually victimised males. *British Medical Journal, 317,* 175–179.

Snyder, H.N. & Sickmund, M. (2006). *Juvenile offenders and victims: 2006 national report.* Washington, DC: US Department of Justice, Office of Justice Program, Office of Juvenile Justice and Delinquency Prevention.

Snyder, J.J. (1977). Reinforcement analysis of interaction in problem and nonproblem families. *Journal of Abnormal Psychology, 86,* 528–535.

Soothill, K., Francis, B., Ackerley, E. & Fligelstone, R. (2002). *Murder and serious sexual assault: What criminal histories can reveal about future serious offending.* Police Research Series, Paper 144. London: Home Office. Retrieved 11 September 2009 from www.homeoffice.gov.uk/rds/prgpdfs/prs144.pdf

Sourander, A., Elonheimo, H., Niemela, S., Nuutila, A.M., Helenius, H., Sillanmaki, L. *et al.* (2006). Childhood predictors of male criminality: A prospective population-based follow-up study from age 8 to late adolescence. *Journal of the American Academy of Child and Adolescent Psychiatry, 45,* 578–586.

Southall, A. (2007). Intensive fostering – one of the first national pilot projects in the UK. Retrieved 11 June 2009 from www.southstaffshealthcare.nhs.uk/services/children/fostering.asp

Straus, M.A., Gelles, R.J. & Steinmetz, S.K. (1980). *Behind closed doors: Violence in the American family.* Garden City, NJ: Doubleday, Anchor Press.

Stern, C. (1987). The recognition of child abuse. In P. Maher (Ed.). *Child abuse: The Educational Perspective.* Oxford: Blackwell.

Summit, R. (1983). The child sexual accommodation syndrome. *Child Abuse and Neglect, 7,* 177–193

Svensson, R. & Ring, J. (2007). Trends in self-reported youth crime and victimization in Sweden, 1995–2005. *Journal of Scandinavian Studies in Criminology and Crime Prevention, 8,* 185–209.

Viljoen, J.L., O'Neill, M.L. & Sidhu, A. (2005). Bullying behaviors in female and male adolescent offenders: Prevalence, types and association with psychosocial adjustment. *Aggressive Behavior, 31,* 1–16.

Watkins, B. & Bentovim, A. (1992). The sexual abuse of male children and adolescents: A review of current research. *Journal of Child Psychology and Psychiatry, 33*(1), 197–248.

Widom, C.S. (1989). The cycle of violence. *Science, 244,* 160–166.

Wilson, D., Sharp, C. & Patterson, A. (2006). *Young people and crime: Findings from the 2005 Offending, Crime and Justice Survey.* London: Home Office.

World Health Organization (2002). *World report on violence and health.* Geneva: WHO.

World Health Organization (2006). *Preventing child maltreatment: A guide to taking action and generating evidence.* Geneva: WHO.

24

Sexually Harmful Adults

Belinda Brooks-Gordon

This chapter provides a critical reflection of sexually harmful adults. First the notion of sexual harm will be considered, then the theories that have been put forward to explain sexually harmful behaviour will be outlined along with the tools that have been developed to assess the risk of sexually harmful behaviour. The treatments that are used in interventions to amend the behaviour of, or rehabilitate, sexually harmful adults will be described, and then an exploration will be undertaken of how, in an era of evidence-based treatment, these interventions are tested for their efficacy.

Sexual harm is also an intensely political issue, so the second part of this chapter provides a critical analysis of some of the main controversies surrounding sexually harmful behaviour. These controversies include (a) the increase over the past two decades in the variety and type of behaviours considered sexually harmful in legislation, (b) the disparity in policy between sexual harm and sexual offending, and (c) how public fear, and the political perception of public fear, can result in the overly mechanist application of tools and policies to manage risk. These three issues will be discussed to show how some contemporary measures to reduce risk may be counterproductive and may actually result in greater risk for the vulnerable and others for whose protection the measures were intended.

Who and What Is a Sexually Harmful Adult?

A sexually harmful adult is someone over the age of 18 years of age whose behaviour to another causes

harm. Such behaviour may be sexual in and of itself or the behaviour may result in sexual behaviour of another. Sexually harmful behaviours can be divided into contact and non-contact behaviours (Craig et al., 2008). Non-contact behaviours include exhibitionism and the viewing of child pornography. Sexually harmful contact behaviours include rape of a male or female, and sexual assault on a minor under 16 years old (often called 'child molestation' and sometimes associated with paedophilia). A sexually harmful adult may be male or female, but research indicates that sexual harm is predominantly a male activity with 80–95 per cent of contact sex offences being committed by men. They may be highly intelligent, socially skilled, or have a low IQ, be learning disabled and not fully understand the consequences of their actions (Cantor et al., 2005).[1]

Prevalence and Incidence[2] of Sexually Harmful Behaviours

While overall police-recorded sexual crimes increased during the past decade from 33,090 to 53,540 incidents, there was a reduction of 7 per cent in police-recorded sexual offences in 2008 on the previous year. So the process has obviously not been one of continuous increase; indeed, any rise in the most serious sexual crimes (including rapes, sexual assaults, and sexual activity with children) halted with a peak in the middle of the last decade and figures have fallen every year since. For example, the most serious sexual crimes numbered 31,334 crimes in 1997, peaking in 2003/04 at 48,732 crimes and falling every year since to the recent figure of 41,460 incidents in the 2007/08 survey (Kershaw *et al.*, 2008), whereas less serious sexual offences (which include soliciting, prostitution offences, and unlawful sexual activity between consenting adults) increased from 1756 in 1997 to a peak of 15,320 in 2004/05 following the creation of many controversial new offences in the Sexual Offences Act 2003 (see Bainham & Brooks-Gordon, 2004). The number of incidents subsequently fell to 12,080 in 2007/08.

Police-recorded crime, however, is subject to the vagaries of reporting whereas victim surveys such as the British Crime Survey are not affected by changes in reporting, police recording or local police activity, and it has been measured in a consistent way since the survey began in 1981. Such surveys show that that a proportion of violent and sexual crimes are not reported. Non-reporting occurs most commonly because victims feel the police could not do anything, or the victim may consider the issue to be a private matter and wish to deal with it themselves. It can be inconvenient to report, or an incident may be reported to other authorities. There may be fear of reprisal or a dislike or fear of the police, especially if there has been previous bad experience with the police or the courts. All of these issues may affect the reporting of sexually harmful behaviour.

While self-report surveys provide a better estimate of hidden crimes such as intimate violence, victim willingness to disclose incidents may depend on the sensitivity of the information, and this can be difficult to disclose face to face. For this reason British Crime Survey (BCS) interviews since 2004/05 have included self-completion modules on intimate violence (for those aged 16 to 59 years of age). Based on the 2006/07 BCS self-completion module on intimate violence, approximately 3 per cent of women and 1 per cent of men had experienced a sexual assault (including attempts) in the previous 12 months. The majority of these were accounted for by less serious sexual assaults. Less than 1 per cent of both men and women reported having experienced a serious sexual assault (Kershaw *et al.*, 2008).

Despite increased public and legal awareness of sexually harmful behaviour, the measures above show that some behaviour goes unreported and therefore undetected and unconvicted. Yet research has focused on the subset of individuals who are reported, detected, arrested and convicted.[3] The evidence base must therefore be interpreted with this bias to the fore (see Crighton & Towl, 2007).

Theories of Sexually Harmful Behaviour

There are five main theories of why adults sexually harm others. According to Palmer (2008) these are: the preconditions model; quadripartite model; the pathways model; interaction model; and the integrated model.

'Four Preconditions' Model (Finkelhor, 1984)

This is a model to explain sexually harmful behaviour towards a child. The model proposes that there are four steps or preconditions that must take place before an adult commits child sexual abuse: 1) motivation – in which there is *sexual arousal* towards a child, *emotional congruence* with a child, and *blockage* whereby the adult's sexual needs are not met by a suitable sexual partner; 2) internal inhibition to cause sexual harm must be overcome – whereby self-regulation against the behaviour is overridden by internal factors such as distorted beliefs about the harm caused, or by the disinhibiting effect of alcohol, drugs or extreme stress; 3) external inhibition must be overcome – such as gaining the trust of the child or their family; 4) resistance of the child must be overcome – through strategies such as force, fear, bribery or other grooming techniques.

Quadripartite Model (Hall & Hirschman, 1992)

This is a model to explain sexually harmful behaviour to a child or adult and it also accounts for the differences between adults who sexually harm children. The theory suggests that sexually harmful behaviour requires the following conditions: 1) deviant physiological sexual arousal (or preference) to a child; 2) distorted beliefs of children as competent sexual partners able to make decisions about sexual activity; 3) emotional disturbance or lack of emotional management or control; and 4) problematic personality traits and/or vulnerability from own adverse early experiences.

Integrated Theory (Marshall & Barbaree, 1990)

This is a general model to explain all sexually harmful behaviour. It aims to explain the background of such behaviour through early attachment and experiences. It suggests that poor early experiences lead to low self-worth, poor emotional regulation, poor problem-solving and inadequate social coping. Such states can all be reinforced by difficult social interactions with peer groups and prospective sexual partners and reinforced by other cultural influences such as the media or social norms. All of these developmental, sociocultural and situational factors make people vulnerable to being psychologically inadequate as well as being susceptible to inappropriate sexual and antisocial behaviour.

Pathways Model (Ward & Siegart, 2002)

This is a theory which combines elements of all the above models into a more complex and comprehensive understanding of sexually harmful behaviour towards children. It is maintained that early life experience, biological factors and cultural influences may lead to vulnerability, which can lead to deviant sexual preferences, intimacy deficits, inappropriate emotions and/or cognitive distortions. These four issues can be dismantled into smaller components which are organised into pathways that lead to the abusive behaviour of a child (see Ward *et al.*, 2006 for further analysis of and a unified theory using these components). It is probably the most influential model of sexually harmful behaviour in research and practice today.

Confluence Model of Sexual Aggression (Malamuth et al., 1993)

This peripheral model is a theory, and one of rape only, which suggests that rape occurs when two paths, sexual promiscuity and hostile masculinity, meet and provide the site for rape to take place. It draws on social learning and feminist theory of a certain type of risk-taking, dominant, competitive male who enjoys power to try to explain the role of sexual behaviour in maintaining self-esteem and peer status. However, this theory remains to be validated using a sample known to have committed sexually harmful behaviours, and is less widely adhered to than the above models.

Evolutionary Theory of Sexual Offending (Thornhill & Palmer, 2000)

Even more controversially, this model dismisses the influence of culture and psychological strategies of power and control to suggest that rape is a result of evolutionary mating strategies. It puts forward a notion that males have evolved with profound sexual desire in order to pass on genes, and this manifests itself in the motivation for sexual activity and the need for multiple partners. Its proponents suggest that rape would only be employed when the conditions are favourable; these

would include lack of psychological or physical resources, social alienation, limited sexual access to females, and unsatisfying sexual relationships (Craig *et al.*, 2008).

There are, of course, questions to be asked of all of these theories and in all cases explanatory power is limited when tested against the circumstances and victims of sexually harmful acts. For example, the Thornhill and Palmer (2000) theory does not explain why men would rape non-procreative beings such as men or children. The confluence model does not explain why female adults carry out sexually harmful behaviour.

Assessing the Risk of Sexually Harmful Adults

The utitility of risk prediction is that it is possible to prevent the circumstances under which a sexually harmful act may occur. These include the ability: 1) to identify high-risk groups from early antecedents of later harmful behaviour, with a view to providing preventative services; 2) to construct aetiological theories in the view that antecedent correlates of behaviour *may* equate to causes, and 3) to derive predictive information for use in criminal justice decision making, for example in placement or release decisions (Blackburn, 1995). A number of psychometric instruments have been devised to determine risk and these divide into actuarial and clinical risk prediction instruments. Actuarial or statistical predictive indices objectively indicate an optimal decision, whereas clinical prediction involves a subjective evaluation of risk based on the client as well as clinical experience of the client group.

Although there continues to be opposition to the use of actuarial risk scales, these scales are in general use in the field of risk assessment and prediction of violent and sexually harmful behaviours and recidivism (Harris *et al.*, 2003).

There are four main actuarial instruments currently in use for sexually harmful behaviour. These include the Violence Risk Appraisal Guide (VRAG; Harris *et al.*, 1998), the Sex Offender Risk Appraisal Guide (SORAG; Quinsey *et al.*, 1998), the Rapid Risk Assessment for Sexual Offense Recidivism (RRASOR; Hanson, 1997), and the STATIC-99 (Hanson & Thornton, 2000).

The VRAG (Harris *et al.*, 1998) was developed for use with men known to have committed a violent offence (whether sexual or not) and to predict any new sexual or violent contact offences. It contains 12 items and the item weights are based on the empirical relationship between the predictor and violent behaviours. Individuals are assigned to one of nine risk categories on the basis of their scores. The Hare Psychopathy Checklist (PCL-R; Hare 1993, 2003) is a major part of the VRAG and is the biggest influence on overall score. The PCL-R scores are based on semi-structured interviews and a review of the file information.[4] It aims to measure characteristics such as impulsivity, irresponsibility and callousness. The SORAG is a modification of the VRAG, with 14 items (10 common to the VRAG), and is designed to predict violent recidivism in men who have already committed sexually harmful contact behaviour. Again the PCL-R score is the most influential.

The RRASOR (Hanson, 1997) was developed for men who have been convicted of at least one sexual offence and is designed specifically to predict sexual recidivism. It has four items: number of prior charges or convictions for sexual offences; age upon release from prison or anticipated opportunity to reoffend in the community; any male victims; or any unrelated victims. Items on the scale are weighted to reflect the magnitude of its relationship with sexual recidivism. The STATIC-99 (Hanson & Thornton, 2000) was developed for men who were known to have committed at least one sexual offence. It is designed to predict either violent recidivism or specifically sexually recidivism. It has ten items, of which four are the same as the RRASOR, and it was constructed by combining the RRASOR with a non-actuarial instrument. On the basis of their score, individuals are allocated to one of seven risk categories.

All the above are actuarial risk scales which are objectively scored and give probabilistic estimates of risk based on the established empirical relationship between their items and the outcome (i.e. sexual harm). Probabilistic estimates suggest the percentage of people with the same score who would be expected to harm sexually within a specified period of opportunity. These scales have good predictive validity and have been cross-validated in new samples of those who sexually harm. The scales contain similar items because they were all empirically derived and their developers drew upon the same sex offender recidivism literature for items (Seto, 2005).

Interventions for Sexually Harmful Adults

Psychological interventions, including behavioural, cognitive-behavioural and psychodynamic therapies, are all used to help change the behaviour of sexually harmful adults. In addition, drug treatment may be given alongside or instead of these therapies. Cognitive-behavioural interventions are the basis of sex offender treatment in prison systems and community programmes in England, Canada, New Zealand and the USA. In the UK National Health Service, however, psychodynamic approaches are common (Grubin, 2002).

Behavioural interventions are associated with traditional classical and operant learning theory and are generally referred to as behaviour modification or behaviour therapy. The hallmark of these interventions is an explicit focus on changes in behaviour by administering a stimulus and measuring its effect upon overt behaviour. Within sex offender treatment this is often used to address deviant sexual interest alongside penile plethysmography (PPG) for 'objective' measurement. Examples include aversion therapy (exposure to deviant material followed by aversive stimulus), covert sensitisation (imagine deviant sexual experience until arousal and then imagine a powerful negative experience), olfactory conditioning (an unpleasant odour is paired with a high-risk sexual situation) and masturbation satiation/orgasmic reconditioning (masturbation to an appropriate sexual fantasy).

A range of interventions falls under the heading of cognitive-behavioural treatment. These interventions have been characterised on a continuum, in the middle of which are interventions seeking to change the individual's internal (cognitive and emotional) functioning as well as their overt behaviour (McGuire, 2000). This best represents cognitive-behavioural treatment as that which has developed from social learning theory. Finally, there are cognitive therapies in which the focus is exclusively on changing some aspect of the individual's cognition. This approach is arguably more likely to have a base in some variant of cognitive theory, such as information processing, than in learning theory. Cognitive-behavioural treatment attempts to change internal processes – thoughts, beliefs, emotions, physiological arousal – alongside changing overt behaviour, such as social skills or coping behaviours. Cognitive behavioural therapy is where the intervention involves: (a) recipients establishing links between their thoughts, feelings and actions with respect to target symptom/s; (b) correction of persons' misperceptions, irrational beliefs and reasoning biases related to target symptom/s; and (c) either or both of the following: (i) recipients monitoring their own thoughts, feelings and behaviours with respect to target symptom/s, and (ii) promotion of alternative ways of coping with target symptom/s.

Psychodynamic psychotherapy involves regular individual therapy sessions with a trained psychotherapist, or a therapist under supervision. Therapy sessions are based on a variety of psychodynamic or psychoanalytic models. Sessions rely on a variety of strategies, including explorative insight-orientated, supportive or directive activity, and applied flexibly with therapists working with transference (the unconscious transfer of feelings to a person which do not befit that person and which actually apply to another (Greenson, 1967)). Psychoanalytic interventions are many and various but usually include regular individual sessions with a trained psychoanalyst three to five times a week working at the infantile sexual relations level of psychoanalytic theory.

Drug treatments administered specifically for sexually harmful behaviour or impulses are sometimes incorrectly referred to as 'chemical castration' or more correctly 'pharmacological diminution of an abnormal sex drive'. These drugs include leuprorelin (Prostap), which switches off the production of testosterone. High testosterone levels are linked with an abnormally high sex drive in paedophiles. Other drugs, such as cyproterone (Androcur), work in a different way, by opposing the action of testosterone in the body instead of interfering with its production. The effect is the same and results in a lowered or absent sex drive and an inability to have sex. Some sexually harmful men are treated with flouxetine (Prozac), an antidepressant that is also prescribed for obsessive compulsive disorders (OCD) along with psychological therapy.

Measuring Interventions

The rise of evidence-based medicine, the philosophical origins of which extend back to mid-19th century Paris, has influenced ways of working with those who sexually harm others. Evidence-based practice is the 'conscientious, explicit, and judicious use of current best evidence in making decisions about the care of individual patients' (Sackett et al., 1996). The practice of evidence-based medicine means integrating individual clinical expertise with the best available external clinical evidence from systematic research. By clinical expertise, Sackett et al. (1996) mean the proficiency and judgement that individual clinicians acquire through clinical experience and clinical practice. They suggest that when asking questions about therapy 'we should try to avoid the non-experimental approaches, since these routinely lead to false positive conclusions about efficacy. Because

the randomised trial, and especially the systematic review of several randomised trials, is so much more likely to inform and so much less likely to mislead us' (p.72). Evidence-based practice is a key feature of psychological interventions and rehabilitative therapies for this group of people within the prison service (Crighton & Towl, 2008).

Past Meta-analyses of Interventions with Sexually Harmful Adults

Hall (1995) carried out a meta-analysis of 12 studies that compared sexual offender treatment with a comparison condition (alternative treatment or no treatment) and provided recidivism data for sexual offences. A small overall effect size was found for institutionalised treatment, and a medium effect size for outpatient samples. Both cognitive-behavioural and hormonal treatments appeared to be superior to behavioural treatments, although a possible criticism of Hall (1995) is that it may have overestimated the effectiveness of treatment because of its use of official recidivism data, which may underestimate actual sexually aggressive behaviour. The results suggested that the effect of treatment with sexual offenders was robust, albeit small, and that treatment was most effective with outpatient participants and when it consisted of hormonal or cognitive-behavioural treatments. A subsequent Cochrane review of randomised controlled trials identified only two relevant studies (total $n = 286$) and no clear effects of relapse prevention/group therapy (White et al., 2000).

In a later meta-analysis Gallagher et al. (1999) quantitatively synthesised the results of 22 studies (25 treatment comparisons) evaluating the effectiveness of different types of treatment for sexual offenders. Like Hall (1995), cognitive-behavioural therapies were considered promising while less support was found for behavioural, chemical, and more general psychosocial therapies. Some of the studies had problematic threats to validity because they involved comparisons between treatment completers and non-completers. This is important, because it is acknowledged amongst practitioners that non-completers are more likely to reoffend.

In Hanson et al. (2002), most of the results were based on matching/incident assignment studies. In incidental assignment studies, comparison groups were selected from offenders in which there were no reasons to expect differences in the treatment group. That analysis showed for the first time a significant difference between recidivism rates for sex offenders who were treated and those who were not, suggested Hanson's team. The study revealed, among the research sample, sexual recidivism rates of 17.3 per cent for untreated offenders, compared with 9.9 per cent for treated offenders. Though that is not a large reduction, the large sample size and widely agreed-upon research methods make it statistically reliable and of practical significance.

Hanson *et al.* (2004) found that examination of individual treatment programmes did not yield any difference in recidivism rates. While the study did not allow conclusions about what was effective or ineffective in the CSOP (Community Sex Offender Program) interventions, the findings do suggest that some 'highly plausible interventions may have little overall effect' and the findings of the review certainly contrast with the positive effects of cognitive-behavioural treatment found in previous reviews (e.g. Gallagher *et al.*, 1999, Hanson *et al.*, 2002). Controversy remains as to the merits of treatment, and the relevant evaluative research on the effectiveness of psychological treatments for sexual offenders is not straightforward (Quinsey *et al.*, 1998). Disappointing results from interventions in England and Wales have been discussed by proponents of treatment who suggest that greater effects might be present yet only detectable using more sensitive psychometric measurement instead of reconviction data (Friendship *et al.*, 2003).

Losel and Schmucker (2005) reported a meta-analysis on controlled outcome evaluations of interventions for sexual offenders. Allowing a wide remit for acceptable studies, the 69 studies containing 80 independent comparisons between 'treated' and 'untreated' offenders. Effects for violent and general recidivism were in a similar range. Medical treatments such as surgical castration or pharmaceutical medication showed larger effect sizes than psychosocial interventions. Of the psychological interventions, cognitive-behavioural approaches had the most robust effect. Overall, Losel and Schmucker found a 6 percentage point reduction in sexual recidivism following treatment, compared to untreated controls.

The largest systematic study was carried out by Brooks-Gordon *et al.* (2006) and also published as a Cochrane review. This study reports a systematic review of randomised control trials reporting the effectiveness of sexual offender treatment programmes. Electronic and hand searches were carried out for randomised control trials published between 1998 and 2003. Searches resulted in nine randomised control trials (RCTs) and

these contained data on interventions for 567 men, 231 of whom were followed up for a decade. Analysis of the nine trials showed that cognitive-behavioural therapy in groups reduced reoffence at one year for child-molesters compared with standard care (*n* = 155). When CBT was compared with a trans-theoretical counselling group therapy, the former may have increased poor attitudes to treatment. The largest trial compared broadly psychodynamic group therapy with no treatment for 231 men guilty of paedophilia, exhibitionism or sexual assault. Rearrest over 10 years was greater for those allocated to group therapy. These findings and the subsequent use of randomised control trials in clinical policy and research are important, because while they may not be popular with those who want to believe that current interventions work for all sexually harmful men forever, they raise important conceptual questions about interventions for sexual harm. For example, do interventions need to be longer term, with community-based relapse prevention (such as Alcoholics Anonymous)? In a parallel study, the same authors (Bilby *et al.*, 2006) also analysed quasi-experimental outcome evaluations and process evaluations in qualitative studies.

Harkins and Beech (2006) review the various research methods of examining treatment effectiveness, and random assignment, risk band analysis and matched control groups are discussed. They conclude that different designs confer different advantages and also have methodological shortcomings. While there are those who feel that only the most scientifically rigorous methodology must be employed if one hopes to draw meaningful conclusions, others feel that less stringent criteria in terms of comparison groups can yield meaningful inferential results. As a means of overcoming some of the shortcomings of recidivism outcome studies discussed, they suggest that the examination of more proximate outcomes, such as change within treatment, provide a useful addition to studies of treatment effectiveness (Harkins & Beech, 2006). The last two meta-analytic reviews reported here represent the two sides of this equation. The strictly defined Brooks-Gordon *et al.* (2006) review conforms to the rigorous Cochrane collaboration methodology to provide a stringent evidence-based measure which meets the so-called 'gold standard'. And the other review, by Losel and Schmucker (2005), takes the wider, more pragmatic remit in which treatment usually takes place in England and Wales.[5]

There are enormous difficulties in carrying out RCTs to evaluate interventions with sexually harmful adults. Randomised controlled trials are often complex and difficult to carry out. It is not ethical to carry out double-blind randomised trials in which neither participant nor clinician knows which group an individual had been allocated to and then wait for the individual to produce sexually harmful behaviour. There is also controversy regarding denial of treatment to this population. Given the belief inherent in policy that treatment works, despite weak evidence, there are human rights and ethical implications should a potentially helpful treatment be withheld within a controlled trial, not to mention implications for future potential victims. It is feasible that such a study could deny a sexually harmful adult an effective treatment, and could also affect the security classification of such a prisoner and decisions regarding parole (Friendship et al., 2002). Prisoners allocated to non-treatment groups could be denied an intervention package that could affect their chances of early release or re-categorisation to a lower security level (Hood et al., 2002). And as Prentky and Schwartz (2006) have pointed out: 'treatment is not likely to be effective for all offenders and that treatment is likely to be effective for some offenders. Essentially, such a conclusion is accurate and, for most of us, obvious. Given the extraordinary variation in sex offenders, it would be only logical that some, but not all, offenders would benefit from treatment. Stated otherwise, treatment undoubtedly will help to restore some offenders to a non-offending lifestyle and will fail to touch other offenders.' It is therefore important to ascertain with as much accuracy as possible whose behaviour is made less harmful by interventions.

Improving the Quality of Treatment Outcome

A collaboration formed to ascertain the quality of sexual offender treatment outcome research recommended that interventions use strong research designs, including random assignment to treatment and comparison conditions. It was also recommended that offenders are matched on risk prior to being assigned to treatment. Random assignment studies are politically unpopular and difficult to implement, but the benefits of these studies are such that researchers should advocate for random assignment studies whenever possible. Researchers using random assignment studies, however, should be prepared for breakdown in the randomisation procedure. Consequently, it was recommended that all participants (treatment and control) should be assessed pre-treatment on risk-relevant variables, and

that researchers are vigilant to problems of treatment integrity, attrition, and crossover (comparison group receiving equivalent services) (Beech et al., 2007).

But many difficulties still hamper researchers wishing to undertake evaluative studies and, as a result, randomised control trials are seldom undertaken in criminal justice settings. In such a situation, the 'next best' evidence has to be considered. Not surprisingly, there are a number of pragmatic trials carried out in quasi-experimental designs. In addition, more sophisticated randomised research designs, which address some of the difficulties associated with traditional randomised control trials such as cluster randomisation, might profitably be explored for the evaluation of programmes.

Cluster Randomisation

Increasingly, 'cluster randomisation' is employed in medical or educational interventions where traditional randomisation trials are not possible. It is a method whereby clusters of individuals rather than independent individuals are randomly allocated to intervention groups. In the case of those who have sexually harmful behaviour, this could be in secure communities or secure accommodation unit clusters. This approach has many advantages. The reasons for adopting this method might be: administrative convenience, to obtain cooperation of investigations, ethical considerations, to enhance participant compliance, to avoid treatment group compliance, and/or to apply the intervention naturally at cluster level. An important property of cluster randomisation trials is that inferences are frequently intended to apply at the individual level while randomisation is at group or cluster level. Thus the unit of randomisation may be different from the unit of analysis.

Analysis and pooling of clustered data, however, does pose some problems. The lack of independence among individuals in the same cluster (i.e. between-cluster variation of different offender characteristics such as motivation could be due to differences in characteristics of the therapist) can create methodological challenges in both design and analysis. Authors must account for intra-class correlation in clustered studies, to avoid 'unit of analysis' error (Divine et al., 1992) which pushes down p values and could lead to overestimating statistical significance and to Type I errors (Bland & Kerry, 1997; Gulliford et al., 1999). In addition, loss of precision can also occur due to: the intervention being applied on a group basis with little or no attention paid to individual study participants; permitting the entry of new participants to a group (cluster) after baseline; entire clusters, rather than individuals, being lost to follow-up; overoptimistic expectations regarding effect size.

Precision can be improved in cluster randomisation trials, argue Donner and Klar (2000), first by establishing a cluster-level eligibility criterion to reduce between-cluster variability, second by increasing the number of clusters randomised, even if only in the control group. Then match or stratify the design by a baseline variable having prognostic importance. Also, obtain baseline measures of other possible prognostic variables, and take repeated assessments over time from the same clusters or from different clusters of subjects. Finally, develop a detailed protocol for ensuring compliance and minimising loss to follow-up. Interpretational difficulties will be present, and the ratio of the total number of participants required using cluster randomisation to the number required using simple randomisation is called the 'design effect'. Thus a cluster randomised trial which has a large design effect will require many more participants than a trial of the same intervention which randomises individuals (Kerry & Bland, 1998).

So far this chapter has explored the theories of sexually harmful behaviour by adults, the ways in which risk is assessed in these adults, and if risk is present, what interventions can be used to address and/or change behaviour. In addition, the first section of the chapter explored how the effectiveness of interventions is measured. While none of these issues is without controversy, there are major controversies around what actually constitutes sexual harm and what steps are legitimate to monitor risk. The next section of this chapter proceeds to discuss these two major issues.

When the 'Sex Offender' Is Not Sexually Harmful

There has been a marked increase over the past two decades in the variety and type of sexual behaviours criminalised in legislation as policy makers have responded to calls for action with unparalleled increases in legislation. This occurred most notably in the Sexual Offences Act 2003 and has continued ever since, most recently in the Criminal Justice and Immigration Act 2008. The review of sexual offences, *Setting the*

Boundaries, took the view that what was wrong in sexual relationships depended upon the principle of *harm* and an assessment of harm done to the individual. However, that which is 'sexual' was defined in the Sexual Offences Act 2003 to be what 'a reasonable person' would consider to be 'sexual' (s.70), and this broad statutory definition is highly problematic.

There is a difference between being sexually harmful and being a sexual offender. For example, in a year when there were 25,000 offenders on the sexual offenders register, only 26 had committed a serious sexual or violent offence (*Daily Telegraph*, 2004). One of the reasons for this is that the number of new sexual offences on the statute book has increased, many of which have little to do with sexual harm and more to do with regulating behaviour or appeasing a perceived public understanding of safety. There were 62,081 recorded sexual offences in England and Wales from 2005 to 2006 (Walker *et al.*, 2006) but not all sexually harmful behaviours will necessarily be recorded as offences, and many sexual offences will not be sexually harmful.

Adult women working in prostitution who are good parents and adults may, because of their working lives in the commercial sex industry, end up with a conviction for prostitution. This conviction now constitutes a sexual offence. Those working in the sex industry who, because they wish to keep their working lives separate from their home lives, or for reasons of safety or company wish to work with other sex workers, prefer to rent rooms or work in a sauna or 'parlour'. Yet those renting out rooms or running parlours (often ex-sex workers or past receptionists, known as 'maids') now fall foul of the laws on brothel-keeping and on conviction are subject to a two-year sentence according to Sentencing Guidelines Council recommendations under laws of brothel-keeping. This too counts as a sexual offence. These two examples show how misleading the statutory categories are.

The ultimate sanction of the criminal law, however, should be used sparingly and only for those behaviours which are demonstrably harmful. There has a been a highly punitive legislative approach resulting in the criminalisation, as opposed to toleration of, sexual diversity (Bainham & Brooks-Gordon, 2004) and this has created a situation whereby what is a sexual offence is not that which is necessarily sexually harmful. And this situation even extends to so-called 'child offences' whereby two young people under the age of 16 years engaged in mutual sexual experimentation are breaking the law.

The Politicisation of Sexual Harm

The electorate and the media expect policy makers to be accountable for the effects of their responses to sexual offending (Hansard, 2002). The politicisation of sexual harm, following a number of high-profile child murders and with politicians aware of global media coverage, added to the statute book new laws in England and Wales and new punitive measures to old laws, in an up-tariffing and redefining of what is sexually harmful. In the USA, such concerns led to Megan's Law in 1996, which allows private and personal information on those registered as sex offenders against children to be made available to the community (Office of the Attorney General, 2004). One of the many examples of political or populist punitiveness in England and Wales came in the Sexual Offences Act which also redefined 'child' as a person under 18 years of age, which would have the effect of criminalising a same-age couple sending pictures to each other over the internet.

In the UK, provisions in the Sexual Offences Act 2003 included substantial increases in sentence length for many sexual offences and increased state control, in terms of notification requirements and supervision, for up to 10 years after a sentence has been spent. Exaggerating the risk of sexual harm is problematic and may increase public fear, and stigmatise and hinder rehabilitation of offenders who have changed their lifestyles, while wasting valuable resources on unnecessary surveillance (Soothill *et al.*, 2000).

Sexual Harm and the Culture of Fear

From 2002, anyone who worked with children in any capacity (even as a volunteer) had to be vetted by the Criminal Records Bureau (CRB). This followed the deaths of Holly Wells and Jessica Chapman who were murdered by the school caretaker Ian Huntley, and suspicion of grown-up behaviour towards children has fostered a climate in which it has become normal for some parents to trust only adults who possess official clearance. In some quarters it is argued that the culture of 'vetting' is damaging relationships with adults and children, and the moral panic over paedophilia has arguably become a panic bordering on hysteria.

The 'War on Terror' has polarised ideas of security vs. liberty; this, a political practice, a speech act, is *one* way of framing, naming and constructing problems. It seeks to mobilise forces behind the idea that 'we' face a threat

that calls for immediate decisions and special measures, argues Loader (2006). Legislative hyperactivity articulates genuine public insecurities about crime, immigration and social disorder. It generates a climate that inhibits, even actively deters, critical scrutiny of the state's claims and practices, and risks fostering a vicious circle of insecurity (atrocity–fear–tough response–atrocity) that ratchets up state powers in ways that become difficult to temper, dismantle and reverse.

In a report called *Licensed to Hug* for the think-tank Civitas, Furedi and Bristow (2008) show how adults have become less inclined to volunteer for mundane activities such as school trips, cricket umpiring or football coaching because they are fearful of being thought predatory or sexually harmful adults. The authors state that the whole notion of harm requires re-examination as 'child protection policies are poisoning the relationship between the generations and damaging the voluntary sector' (Furedi & Bristow, 2008). In addition, parents were sceptical about the efficacy of the vetting procedure and felt it was burdensome and confusing.

Institutionalisation of the vetting of adults with CRB checks

Since October 2009, adults have had to register with the new Independent Safeguarding Authority (ISA), so it is estimated that one in four (or 11.3 million) people will be affected by the scheme. The alleged protective effects of a system of vetting are considered to be largely illusory by Furedi and Bristow (2008), who conclude that the national vetting scheme represents an exercise in impression management rather than offering effective protection. Aside from the fallibility of record-keeping and technical systems, vetting only takes account of what someone has done in the past; it cannot anticipate what they may do in future. The situation de-skills adults, who then also have a diminished sense of responsibility towards children. Adults feel increasingly nervous around children, unwilling to exercise authority or play a positive role. Such intergenerational unease has not made children safer in the past but rather creates conditions for greater harm, as adults lose the nerve or will to look out for any child that is not their own (see also Furedi, 2005). Perversely, it encourages adults to avoid their responsibility to look out for the well-being of children in their community. Thus the policy of attempting to prevent paedophiles coming into contact with children will result in the estrangement of all children from all adults – the very people who would otherwise protect them from paedophiles and other dangers.

While fear and risk were explored in the 1990s through 'ontological insecurity' in a risk society (Bauman, 2000; Beck, 1992). Walklate and Mythen (2008) take this further to argue that the view has developed to the extent that if risk constitutes one side of ontological security, then trust and trust relationships comprise the other. They question the extent to which forensic research has fully accounted for the impacts of global structures and processes that shape human agency on the formation of individual anxieties, and state that not withstanding recent efforts of Gadd and Jefferson (2007), 'fear-of-crime' research 'has not adequately appreciated the full macro climate of this doubt and uncertainty or the way in which it articulates with localised individual experience' (p.215). Governments become embroiled in the politics of fear, and widespread practices and processes result in the paralysis of the 'culture of fear' where not just individuals but whole communities are being scrutinised and surveyed as subject identities are made up through risk discourses, socially determined according to whether they fit the profile of offenders or innocents. A situation then reigns whereby the risk of sexual harm is greater than before.

Conclusions

This chapter has explored sexual harm by outlining firstly the theories that have been developed to understand the behaviour. It proceeded to discuss the interventions currently used to rehabilitate sexually harmful behaviours, and how those treatments have been evaluated and measured, before going on to discuss the difficulties in measurement and evaluation in meta-analytic studies, the ethics of such analysis, and ways of overcoming such pitfalls.

The second part of the chapter shows how sexual harm has become a major challenge for social policy, and the social and political panic around sexual offending and sexual harm is discussed, showing how more laws were introduced to appease perceived public disquiet. The law is now so encompassing that even consensual adult activity in private has become confused in statute with sexual offending. In this way the law fails to equate sexual harm with sexual offending, and the result is confusion, conflict and further strain on stretched resources. The consequence has been to foster a climate

of concern around children that has resulted in fewer activities for them to do, less freedom, and therefore less ability to deal with risk. The resulting culture of fear is, it is argued, a threat to security and safety.

Notes

1 These authors found that although adult males who commit sexual offences scored lower on IQ tests overall than adult males who commit non-sexual offences, IQ differences did not occur across all sexual offender subtypes – the younger the victim age, the lower the sample group's mean IQ. Non-sexual offenders' IQs equated to general population means.

2 The terms prevalence and incidence are not synonymous. How widespread a practice is at a single point in time (its prevalence) and how often it occurs (its incidence) are different entities. A sexually harmful behaviour may be highly prevalent (i.e. be widespread) but have low incidence (i.e. not occur frequently). An example of this is rape by an adult known to the adult victim or so-called 'date-rape'. Other behaviours may not be so prevalent in the population(s) studied but may have high incidence. An example of this might be abuse by teachers of their pupils, whereby the frequency of the abuse happening may be high to one individual but the prevalence of such abuse in the teacher population (and indeed the pupil population) may be low.

3 The bias is greater in research in England and Wales than in the USA where self-referral and diversion schemes operate for individuals who are at risk, or fear they are at risk, of offending (e.g. see Scheela, 1992).

4 Clinical files usually contain some or all the following information: (a) a summary of institutional files, including police records, court records, previous psychological reports, case management reports; (b) notes from semi-structured interview with the miscreant, including information on family background, education, employment, substance use, relationships, mental health, criminal history and future plans; (c) psychological test results; and (d) treatment reports written by the group therapist and the treatment manager.

5 This review may have been unduly weighted by its inclusion of physical/biological interventions such as physical castration and anti-libidinal pharmaceutical treatment.

Further Reading

Ward, T., Polaschek, D.L.L. & Beech, A.R. (2006). *Theories of sexual offending*. Chichester: Wiley.
This text provides a good overview of the theories of sexually harmful behaviours.

Brooks-Gordon, B.M., Bilby, C. & Wells, H. (2006). Sexual offenders: A systematic review on psychological interventions. Part I: Quantitative studies. *Journal of Forensic Psychiatry and Psychology, 17*(3), 442–466.

Bilby, C., Brooks-Gordon, B.M. & Wells, H. (2006). Sexual offenders: A systematic review of psychological interventions. Part II: Qualitative studies. *Journal of Forensic Psychiatry and Psychology, 17*(3), 467–484.

These two studies provide the most comprehensive systematic review of the effectiveness of interventions for sexually harmful adults. The first study is a meta-analysis, followed in the second study by an analysis of lesser data in quasi-experimental studies, and all of the qualitative research on psychological interventions. Between them, these studies provide a comprehensive overview of what is known about the efficacy of treatment at the current time to stringent Cochrane Collaboration standards.

Furedi, F. & Bristow, J. (2008). *Licensed to hug.* London: Civitas.

This study provides a critical look at the culture of fear around sexual harm.

References

Bainham, A. & Brooks-Gordon, B. (2004). Reforming the law on sexual offences. In B.M. Brooks-Gordon, L.R. Gelsthorpe, M.H. Johnson & A. Bainham (Eds.) *Sexuality repositioned: Diversity and the law* (pp.260–296). Oxford: Hart.

Bauman, Z. (2000). *Liquid modernity.* Cambridge: Polity.

Beck, U. (1992). *Risk society.* Cambridge: Polity.

Beech, A., Bourgon, G., Hanson, R.K., Harris, A.J.R., Langton, C., Marques, J. *et al.* (2007). *Sexual offender treatment outcome research: CODC guidelines for evaluation.* Public Safety Canada. Retrieved 9 September 2008 from file:///Sexual per cent20Offender per cent20Treatment per cent20Outcome per cent20Research:per cent20CODC per cent20Guidelines per cent20for per cent20Evaluation.

Bilby, C., Brooks-Gordon, B.M. & Wells, H. (2006). Sexual offenders: A systematic review of psychological interventions. Part II: Qualitative studies. *Journal of Forensic Psychiatry and Psychology, 17*(3), 467–484.

Blackburn, R. (1995). *The psychology of criminal conduct: Theory, research and practice.* Chichester: Wiley.

Bland, J.M. & Kerry, S.M. (1997). Trials randomised in clusters. *British Medical Journal, 315,* 600.

Brooks-Gordon, B.M., Bilby, C. & Wells, H. (2006). Sexual offenders: A systematic review on psychological interventions. Part I: Quantitative studies. *Journal of Forensic Psychiatry and Psychology, 17*(3), 442–466.

Cantor, J.M., Blanchard, R., Robichaud, L.K. & Christensen, B.K. (2005). Quantitative reanalysis of aggregate data on IQ in sexual offenders. *Psychological Bulletin, 131*(4), 555–568.

Craig, L.E., Browne, K.D. & Beech, A.R. (2008). *Assessing risk in sex offenders: A practitioners' guide.* Chichester: Wiley.

Crighton, D. & Towl, G. (2007). Experimental interventions with sex offenders: A brief review of their efficacy. *Evidence-Based Mental Health, 10,* 35–37.

Crighton, D. & Towl, G. (2008). *Psychology in prisons.* Oxford. Blackwell.

Daily Telegraph (2004). Sex offenders register grows by 15 per cent 28 July. Retrieved 11 September 2009 from www.telegraph.co.uk/expat/4193100/Sex-offenders-register-grows-by-15-per-cent.html.

Divine, G.W., Brown, J.T. & Frazer, L.M. (1992). The unit of analysis error in studies about physicians' patient care behavior. *Journal of General Internal Medicine, 7*(6), 623–629.

Donner, A. & Klar, N. (2000). *Design and analysis of cluster randomization trials in health research.* London: Arnold.

Finkelhor, D. (1984). *Child sexual abuse: New theory and research.* New York: Free Press.

Friendship, C., Beech, A.R. & Browne, K.D. (2002). Reconviction as an outcome measure in research: A methodological note. *British Journal of Criminology, 42,* 442–444.

Friendship, C., Falshaw, L. & Beech, A. (2003). Measuring the real impact of accredited offending behaviour programmes. *Legal and Criminological Psychology, 8*(1), 115–127.

Furedi, F. (2005). *Culture of fear.* London: Continuum.

Furedi, F. & Bristow, J. (2008). *Licensed to hug.* London: Civitas.

Gadd, D. & Jefferson, T. (2007). *Psychosocial criminology.* London: Sage.

Gallagher, C.A., Wilson, D.B., Hirschfield, P., Coggeshall, M.B. & MacKenzie, D.L. (1999). A quantitative review of the effects of sex offender treatment of sexual offender. *Corrections Management Quarterly, 3,* 19–29.

Gulliford, M.C., Ukoumunne, O.C. & Chinn, S. (1999). Components of variance and intraclass correlations for the design of community-based surveys and intervention studies: Data from the Health Survey for England 1994. *American Journal of Epidemiology, 149,* 876–883.

Greenson, R.R. (1967). *The technique and practice of psychoanalysis.* New York: International Universities Press.

Grubin, D. (2002). *Expert paper: Sex offender research.* Liverpool: NHS Programme on Forensic Mental Health Research and Development. Retrieved 4 September 2009 from www.dh.gov.uk/assetRoot/04/02/09/04/04020904.pdf.

Hall, G.C.N. (1995). Sexual offender recidivism revisited: A meta-analysis of recent treatment studies. *Journal of Consulting and Clinical Psychology, 63*(5), 802–809.

Hall, G.C.N. & Hirschman, J.R. (1992). Sexual aggression against children: A conceptual perspective of etiology. *Criminal Justice and Behavior, 19,* 8–23.

Hansard (2002, 6 February). Columns 980W and 982W.

Hanson, R.K. (1997). *The development of a brief actuarial risk scale for sexual offense recidivism.* User Report 1997-04. Ottawa: Department of the Solicitor General of Canada.

Hanson, R.K., Broom, I. & Stephenson, M. (2004). Evaluating community sex offender treatment programs: A 12-year follow-up of 724 offenders. *Canadian Journal of Behavioral Science*, 2, 87–96.

Hanson, R.K., Gordon, A., Harris, A.J.R. *et al.* (2002). First report of the Collaborative Outcome Data Project on the effectiveness of treatment for sex offenders. *Sexual Abuse: A Journal of Research and Treatment*, 14, 169–194.

Hanson, R.K. & Thornton, D. (2000). Improving risk assessments for sex offenders: A comparison of three actuarial scales. *Law and Human Behaviour*, 24, 119–136.

Hare, R.D. (1993, 2003). See www.hare.org/.

Harkins, L. & Beech, A. (2006). Measurement of effectiveness of sex offender treatment. *Aggression and Violent Behaviour*, 12(1), 36–44.

Harris, G.T., Rice, M.E., Lalumière, M.L., Boer, D. & Lang, C. (2003). A multisite comparison of actuarial risk instruments for sex offenders. *Psychological Assessment*, 15(3), 413–425.

Harris, G.T., Rice, M.E. & Quinsey, V.L. (1998). Appraisal and management of risk of sexual aggressors. *Psychology, Public Policy, and Law*, 4, 73–115.

Hood, R., Shute, S., Feilzer, M. & Wilcox, A. (2002). Sex offenders emerging from long-term imprisonment: A study of their long-term reconviction rates and of parole board members' judgements of their risk. *British Journal of Criminology*, 42(2), 371–394.

Kershaw, C., Nicholas, S. & Walker, A. (2008). *Crime in England and Wales 2007/08. Findings from the British Crime Survey and police recorded crime*. Home Office Statistical Bulletin. London: Home Office.

Kerry, S.M. & Bland, J.M. (1998). Statistics notes: Sample size in cluster randomization. *British Medical Journal*, 316, 549.

Loader, I. (2006). *Civilizing security. The 2006 John Barry Memorial Lecture*. University of Melbourne, 23 November.

Losel, F. & Schmucker, D. (2005). The effectiveness of treatment of sexual offenders. A comprehensive meta-analysis. *Journal of Experimental Criminology*, I, 117–146.

Malamuth, N.M., Heavey, C.L. & Linz, D. (1993). Predicting men's antisocial behavior against women: The interaction model of sexual aggression. In G.C.N. Hall, R. Hirschman, J.R. Graham & M.S. Zaragoza (Eds.) *Sexual aggression: Issues in etiology, assessment and treatment* (pp.63–97). Washington, DC: Taylor & Francis.

Marshall, W.L. & Barbaree, H.E. (1990). An integrated theory of sexual offending. In W.L Marshall, D.R. Laws & H.E. Barbaree (Eds.) *Handbook of sexual assault; Issues, theories and treatment of the offender* (pp.257–275). New York: Plenum.

McGuire, J. (2000). Defining correctional programs. *Forum on Corrections Research*, 12, 5–9.

Office of the Attorney General (2004). *Megan's law*. Sacramento, CA: Author. Retrieved 11 September 2009 from www.meganslaw.ca.gov/pdf/2004LegReportcomplete.pdf.

Palmer, E.J. (2008). Contemporary psychological contributions to understanding crime. In G. Davies, C. Hollin & R. Bull (Eds.) *Forensic psychology* (pp.29–56). Chichester: Wiley.

Prentky, R. & Schwartz, B. (2006). *Treatment of adult sex offenders*. Harrisburg, PA: VAWnet, a project of the National Resource Center on Domestic Violence/Pennsylvania Coalition Against Domestic Violence. Retrieved 17 July 2008 from www.vawnet.org.

Quinsey, V.L. Harris, G.T., Rice, M.E. & Cormier, C. (1998). *Violent offenders*. Washington, DC: American Psychological Association.

Sackett, D.L., Rosenberg, W.M.C., Gray, J.A.M., Haynes, R.B. & Richardson, W.S. (1996). Evidence based medicine: What it is and what it isn't. *British Medical Journal*. 312, 13 January, 71–72.

Scheela, R. (1992). The remodeling process: A grounded theory study of perceptions of treatment among adult male incest offenders. *Journal of Offender Rehabilitation*, 18(3/4), 167–189.

Seto, M. (2005). *Sex offenders in the community*. Cullompton, Devon: Willan.

Soothill, K., Francis, B., Sanderson, B. & Ackerley, E. (2000). Sex offenders: Specialists, generalists or both? A 32-year criminological study. *British Journal of Criminology*, 40, 56–67.

Thornhill, R. & Palmer, C.T. (2000). *A natural history of rape*. Cambridge, MA: MIT Press.

Walker, A., Kershaw, C. & Nicholas, S. (2006). *Crime in England and Wales 2005/06*. Home Office Statistical Bulletin, 12/06. London: Home Office.

Walklate, S. & Mythen, G. (2008). How scared are we? *British Journal of Criminology*, 48, 209–225.

Ward T., Polaschek, D.L.L & Beech, A.R. (Eds.) (2006). *Theories of sexual offending*. Chichester: Wiley.

Ward, T. & Siegart, R.J. (2002). Toward a comprehensive theory of child sexual abuse: A theory knitting perspective. *Psychology Crime and the Law*, 9, 319–353.

White, P., Bradley, C., Ferriter, M. & Hatzipetrou, L. (2000). Managements for people with disorders of sexual preference and for convicted sexual offenders. In *The Cochrane Library*, 4. Oxford: Update Software. CD000251.

25

Suicide and Self-Injury in Offenders

Jenny Shaw and Naomi Humber

Every year in the UK, hundreds of thousands of offenders pass through the criminal justice system. Social and economic disadvantage, educational and occupational failure, mental illness and substance misuse, combined with the stigma of being associated with the criminal justice system, can often hamper such individuals leading a law-abiding and satisfactory life within society. The demographic, social and clinical characteristics associated with offending closely resemble those associated with suicide and self-injury. The prevalence of self-harm behaviours, including self-injurious behaviour, attempted suicide and suicide, is disproportionately high among offenders compared to the general population.

Recently, policy makers have been urged to improve and expand mental health services, court diversion programmes, community forensic mental health services and reintegration and rehabilitative facilities as preventative measures for reducing rates of suicide and self-injury in offending populations.

Suicide in the General Population

The death rate from suicide and undetermined injury in the general population is approximately 8.5 per 100,000 per year in England and Wales (Department of Health, 2006). Risk factors for suicide in the general population include being young and male (Office of National Statistics, 2003); of a low socio-economic status (Department of Health, 1999); unmarried, widowed or divorced (Charlton et al., 1993); having a history of mental health problems, including psychiatric admissions (Qin & Nordentoft, 2005); previous suicide attempts or acts of self-harm (Appleby et al., 2001); and a history of drug and/or alcohol misuse (Appleby et al., 1999).

The rate of suicide in offending populations is significantly higher than that found in the general community (Pratt et al., 2006; Sattar, 2001; Shaw et al., 2004) and prisoners were one of the key high-risk groups identified in the National Suicide Prevention Strategy for England (Department of Health, 2002)

Background

The assessment and protection of individuals who want to harm themselves is a difficult task in any setting (Young et al., 2006). Within the criminal justice system, practitioners and agencies have a duty of care to protect, and the task of balancing issues of security, punishment and justice with appropriate treatment is undoubtedly complex. This task is particularly difficult as risk factors for suicide are overrepresented in those who come into contact with the system (Sattar, 2001; Shaw et al., 1999).

For example, rates of mental disorder are higher in individuals attending court (Shaw et al., 1999) and prisoners (Birmingham et al., 1996), compared to the general population. Similarly, both unemployment rates (Cox & Pritchard, 1995; Stewart & Stewart, 1993) and the prevalence of alcohol and drug abuse are higher in prisoners and community offenders than in the general population (Gunn et al., 1991; HM Inspectorate of Probation, 2007; Singleton et al., 1998).

Suicide in the Prison Population

The most frequently studied group with respect to suicide within the criminal justice system are prisoners. Growing attention is being paid to suicide in prison in many countries around the world (Wortley, 2002). The prison suicide rate in England and Wales is 114 per 100,000 prisoners in 2007 (Ministry of Justice, 2007). This increased rate compared with the general population is consistent across countries, including the USA (DuRand et al., 1995; Tartaro & Lester, 2005), Australia (Dalton, 1998; Hatty & Walker, 1986), Italy (Tatarelli et al., 1999), Finland (Joukamaa, 1997), Austria (Fruehwald et al., 2002, 2004) and Canada (Wobeser et al., 2002).

Prisoners are a socially excluded population, experiencing various health and social inequalities, with complex needs (Social Exclusion Unit, 2002). The term 'imported vulnerability' was coined by Liebling (1992) to describe the prison population and the social and health inequalities that they bring with them into custody. These social and health inequalities include that, compared to the general population, prisoners are 13 times more likely to be in care as a child; 22 times more likely to be excluded from school; 13 times more likely to be unemployed; and 6 times more likely to be a young parent (Social Exclusion Unit, 2002).

Most studies to date have been descriptive and concerned with the identification of a profile of the high-risk prisoner. Studies have identified characteristics and factors which are overrepresented in prison suicide samples, including remand status (Dooley, 1990a, 1990b), being charged with or convicted of a violent or sexual offence (Dooley 1990a, 1990b), being in the early stages of custody (Shaw et al., 2004), having a history of drug and/or alcohol misuse (Dooley 1990a, 1990b) and psychiatric morbidity (Shaw et al., 2004). The majority of prison suicides occur in local or 'dispersal' prison establishment types (Dooley, 1990a, 1990b) and the most common method of death is by hanging (Shaw et al., 2004).

There are particular subgroups within prison suicides with clusters of particular risk factors. For example, early suicides, or those who die within the first stage of custody, are more likely to be on remand and be drug dependent (Shaw et al., 2004). Those who die within the later stages of custody are sentenced, and more likely to be convicted of a violent crime and serving a life sentence (Dooley 1990a, 1990b; Topp, 1979). There may be grounds for assuming that different specific risk-factor configurations apply to these particular subgroups.

Prison life is markedly different from life in the community, with respect to the social environment and degree of personal control (Wichmann et al., 2000). In addition, there may be pressure from continuous contextual factors, such as staff–prisoner relations. The prison environment can impart unique stresses, which are not the norm in society at large; for example, with an unexpected or long sentence, change of location, overcrowding (Huey & McNulty, 2005), issues of personal safety (Price Waterhouse, 1996), a lack of purposeful activity (Leese et al., 2005), court appearances, refusal of parole (Zamble & Porporino, 1988), disciplinary procedures, bullying (Cox & Morschauer, 1997) and relationship and family problems associated with being in custody. In addition, imprisonment reduces the opportunity to use drugs or alcohol as coping strategies (Liebling & Krarup, 1993). However, features of prison regimes can be protective, with many individuals experiencing stability and obtaining necessary assessment and treatment for the first time (Hek, 2006; Prison Reform Trust, 2006).

Limitations of Prison Suicide Research

The risk factors for suicide in prison have not been definitively isolated. There have been problems with previous suicide research in prison. Problems with previous prisoner suicide research have included that, firstly, research in this area has often been descriptive and retrospective, with no control groups, thus limiting definitive conclusions about risk factors for suicide (Bonner, 1992; Haycock, 1991; Liebling, 1992; Lloyd, 1990). Secondly, prison suicide research often examines static risk markers and this only enables the focus on suicide as a distinct occurrence rather than its investigation as a process (Bonner, 1992). A number of relevant factors, such as marital status, age and a history of drug/alcohol misuse, are characteristic of the prison population as a whole, and these have only limited power in the prediction of suicidal behaviour. Thirdly, caution must be exercised in reviewing the studies of suicide in prison both within and between countries owing to the great variation in methods of data collection, sample size, sociocultural differences, definitions of suicide and the variation in criminal justice practices and populations.

Theoretical and qualitative approaches which allow for the consideration and understanding of suicidal behaviour and completed suicide in prison have been useful (Liebling & Krarup, 1993), but few controlled studies of suicide in prison have been conducted. One case–control study in Austrian jails and prisons between 1975 and 1999 investigated the relevance of psychiatric problems, criminal history and social integration to suicide in prison (Fruehwald *et al.*, 2004). For every suicide, two controls were selected and matched to the suicide by establishment, gender, nationality, age, custodial status and time of admission. Two hundred and twenty cases were matched to 440 controls. The data collection entailed a review of records and the personal files of cases and controls. The most important predictors of suicide were found to be a history of deliberate self-harm, a psychiatric diagnosis, being prescribed psychiatric medication, being in custody for a violent offence and being in a single cell.

However, this study was retrospective in nature and the extent to which it can be generalised to other countries may be limited. The data collection was conducted over 24 years and there must have been changes in policies and procedures within the Austrian prison system over that period. Similarly, there were specific methodological difficulties in that the personal files of controls were found to contain limited amounts of information, particularly when the prisoner had served a relatively short period in custody, resulting in missing data.

Suicide in Community Offenders

Recent research has suggested that the suicide rate is also high among recently released prisoners (Binswanger *et al.*, 2007; Graham 2003; Kariminia *et al.*, 2007; Pratt *et al.*, 2006) and offenders in the community (Pritchard *et al.*, 1997; Sattar, 2001). This increased rate applies to both adult and young offenders (Coffey *et al.*, 2003, 2004).

In England and Wales between 1996 and 1997, suicide rates in ex-prisoners being supervised in the community, offenders serving community sentences and the general population were examined by Sattar (2001). Of approximately 67,000 post-release prisoners, 294 died while under community supervision. Thirteen per cent committed suicide following release from prison. Male offenders under community supervision were at least 10 times more likely to die by suicide than men in the general population. Ten per cent of all ex-prisoner suicides had occurred within the first week of release and 50 per cent by the fourth week. However, this study only included prisoners released under the supervision of the

probation service, thus excluding more than half of released prisoners. A more recent study of self-inflicted deaths within a year of release from prisons in England and Wales revealed a suicide rate of 156 per 100,000 person-years (Pratt *et al.*, 2006). Just over one-fifth of suicides occurred within the 28 days following release. Compared to the general population, suicide in recently released male prisoners was 8 times more likely and 36 times more likely for female prisoners. The authors examined age-specific rate ratios for suicide risk and found that there was a rate ratio of approximately 5 for men younger than 25 years rising to more than 15 in male offenders aged 50 years and older.

Similarly, in New South Wales, Australia, Kariminia *et al.* (2007) corroborated the findings from the UK, by demonstrating a clustering of suicide occurring soon after release from prison, with suicide peaking in men during the first two weeks after release at a rate of 507 per 100,000 person-years, declining to 118 per 100,000 person-years after six months. Interestingly, supporting findings by Pratt *et al.* (2006), the association between time after release and suicide in males was different across age groups. Those males aged 45 years and over had the highest risk in the first two weeks after release from prison. They concluded that the initial period after release from prison is a time of extreme vulnerability, particularly for male offenders and specifically for the elderly.

International studies of the mortality rates and suicide profiles of offenders serving community sentences are limited. In Finland, the suicide rate in offenders within one year of release from prison was almost three times the rate in the general population (Joukamaa, 1998).

Although studies suggest that prisoners post-release are at an increased risk of suicide, little is known about specific individual and service-level risk factors for suicide amongst released prisoners. These risk factors need to be definitively identified before we can introduce intervention programmes and support for offenders. Pritchard *et al.* (1997) conducted a study of male offenders on community probation orders in Dorset, England. They found a suicide rate of over nine times that of the local male general population. However, the sample size was small and within one English county, both of which limit the extent to which the findings can be generalised.

Studies of suicide in community offenders suggest that criminal justice agencies should collaborate with other national service providers within society, such as the National Health Service and social services to ensure support for and/or resettlement of offenders. A shared responsibility to meet the complex needs of the offending population ultimately lies with the prison, probation, health and social services to develop more integrated practices in providing services for this at-risk group.

Suicide in Police Custody

Between 1994 and 1998, the Police Complaints Authority (PCA, 1999) reported 48 suicides, on average 10 deaths per year. Suicide had accounted for one-quarter of all deaths in police custody in this period. Suicides mainly took place in police cells and the most common method of death was by hanging (PCA, 1999). Other studies of deaths in police custody have shown deliberate self-harm to account for one-third of all deaths (Blaauw et al., 1997; Leigh et al., 1998).

There has been little research on suicides in police custody and studies of risk factors are limited.

Committing crime, its investigation and impending punishment can be stressful. Combined with various unmet health and social needs which are inherent in the offending population, of particular interest is how many offenders who have been in contact with the police and then released with a formal caution or bailed into the community engage in acts of self-injury and/or suicidal behaviour.

Some studies have explored contact with the criminal justice system prior to an individual's suicide (Weis et al., 2006) and found that recent criminal involvement was common in offenders who eventually died by suicide (Linsley et al., 2007). As many individuals had police contact within 3 months of their suicide as had contact with mental health services within 12 months (Appleby et al., 2001; Linsley et al., 2007). These findings suggested that those recently released from police custody could be at an increased risk of suicide. This would mirror findings from other studies, as has been demonstrated by studies examining release from other institutions, such as prison and psychiatric hospitals (Appleby et al., 1999; Pratt et al., 2006). However, the studies of police contact prior to suicide have been conducted within one geographical area and a larger sample would be required to ensure the findings were representative and therefore generalisable.

The importance of investigating suicide following release from police custody has been recognised by the Independent Police Complaints Commission (IPCC). The IPCC was notified of 46 suicides between 2004 and 2005 (IPCC, 2005), and 40 suicides between 2005 and 2006 (IPCC, 2006), following release from custody.

However, it is likely that these reported 'release deaths' are a significant underestimate of the actual number following police custody, as there is no comprehensive method of notification of death following release from custody. Due to the limitations which can undermine the validity of these vital statistics, the IPCC is in consultation with the Association of Chief Police Officers (ACPO) in developing a provision of guidelines for forces in order to ensure greater national consistency in the reporting of and the referral of such deaths.

This guidance will suggest that police forces note and record the length of time between the death and the period of police custody, the nature of the police contact and the individual circumstances which preceded the death. This approach is much like that used to investigate deaths following release from other institutions within the criminal justice system.

The collection of this information will enable the IPCC to gain a greater understanding of, and appreciation for, the appropriate care of vulnerable individuals with mental health needs who may be at increased risk of suicide when in contact with the system.

Pre- and Post-Release Planning from Criminal Justice Agencies

Pre- and post-release planning and initiatives for offenders with mental health problems who are going to be, or have been, released from criminal justice agencies are limited. Most offenders who are suffering from a mental illness are released without effective linkages to medication or psychiatric services, both of which are essential for promoting stability in such individuals. There is a lack of pre- and post-release planning for prisoners with identified mental illness (Wolff et al., 2002). Connecting such individuals to community mental health services is critically important (American Psychiatric Association, 2000).

General principles surrounding a duty of care for those who have made initial contact with the criminal justice system would suggest protection against any immediate foreseeable risk of self-injury and/or suicide following a stay in police or prison custody. However, criminal justice agencies currently have no legal duty of care for offenders following release from custody. The duty of care should apply not only to individuals while they are in custody, but immediately beyond that custody. Police and prison services should assess the emotional state of the detainee as they are released back into the community. If there are concerns regarding the detainee's mental state upon release, there should be a concerted effort to ensure that the individual is returned or referred to the appropriate support services in the community.

Concern regarding suicide following release from agencies within the criminal justice system is growing and there is a general acceptance of the need for a multi-agency approach to the development of throughcare services.

Although there have been initiatives to improve the quality of service provision for those with mental health problems inside prison, little attention has been paid to reintegrating mentally ill offenders into the community after discharge. The first months after discharge are crucial for the well-being of prisoners with mental illness. Successful reintegration after discharge requires continuity of care between institutional and community services to make sure that appropriate levels of support and care are given. Intervention studies for those leaving prison with mental illness have been trialled, including one conducted by Shaw and colleagues who adapted the Critical Time Intervention (CTI; Susser et al., 1997) case management programme, previously successfully used to reduce homeless nights in homeless mentally ill males who had been discharged from a shelter. The modified version of CTI has been successfully piloted in selected prison establishments in England and Wales in preparation for a larger study. Adaptations of the post-discharge intervention will further need to identify and address the particular needs of women, young people, and black and minority ethnic (BME) groups.

Risk factors for suicide in offenders who have recently been released from police or prison custody are important to identify. Case–control methods would be necessary to examine the risk factors for those who do not survive following release from police or prison custody. One study currently being conducted by Shaw and colleagues will examine rates of suicide in offenders at different stages of the criminal justice system, from when an offender has been arrested and released into the community through to those being released from prison and into the community. This case–control study will establish risk factors for suicide across the offender pathway and establish periods where suicide risk is heightened.

Self-Injury in Offenders

Self-injury can generally be defined as deliberate injury inflicted by a person upon their body without suicidal intent (Babiker & Arnold, 1997; Thomas et al., 2006). It can also be referred to as deliberate self-harm, intentional self-injury, parasuicide, self-mutilation, self-inflicted violence or self-injurious behaviour. The term includes a spectrum of behaviours where demonstrable injury is self-inflicted. Although, by definition, self-injury is non-fatal, it always has the potential, either intentionally or unintentionally, to be fatal (Cutter et al., 2008; Hawton et al., 1999).

Studies of self-injury in offending populations have been criticised owing to problems in definition and in differentiating self-injurious behaviours from suicidal ones (Crighton & Towl, 2000; Farmer et al., 1996). Interpretation of such studies is often complicated, with wide variation in the definitions adopted, which makes comparisons across different studies difficult.

Individuals engage in self-injurious behaviour for a number of reasons and the aetiology of it is complex (Jeglic et al., 2005). It has been debated whether self-injurious behaviours have different underlying motivations from suicidal behaviour and/or acts (Livingston, 1997). Some have described a continuum, with self-injurious behaviours at one end, suicidal attempts in the middle and suicide completion at the other end (Evans et al. 1995).

Accurate statistics on self-injury in the general population are difficult, as many incidents will go unreported for various reasons and/or may not require hospital treatment (Fox & Hawton, 2004). Recorded figures are usually based on three sources, including general population surveys, hospital admissions and psychiatric samples (Rodham et al., 2005). In the UK, approximately 10 per cent of hospital admissions are as a result of self-injury, with the majority being drug overdoses (BBC News, 2004). Every year this leads to approximately 170,000 hospital attendances and equates to one of the most common reasons for admission to hospital (Kapur, 2005).

Research on self-harm in prison populations is limited (Crighton & Towl, 2000). Studies have suggested that around 30 per cent of all offenders engaged in some form of self-injurious behaviour during their custody (Borrill et al., 2003; Brooker et al., 2002). The most common forms of self-injury in prison are self-cutting, burning and abrasions (Crighton & Towl, 2000; Liebling & Krarup, 1993). The majority of incidents of self-harm in prison have been reported to carry little risk to life (Fleming et al., 1992; Liebling & Krarup, 1993). However, some have suggested that in a closed institution, where access to means of self-harm is limited, prisoners may be increasingly drawn to more lethal means (Crighton & Towl, 2000; Inch et al., 1995).

Nationally, rates of self-injury in prison have risen by almost 40 per cent in the past five years, accelerating well beyond what would be expected from the rising prison population in England and Wales (Howard League for Penal Reform, 2008). In 2003, there were 16,393 incidents of self-injury in prison. In 2007, there were 22,459 incidences, a rise of 37 per cent which is approximately four times the rise in the prison population for the same period. Self-injury rates among female prisoners have risen even further, with a 48 per cent rise in recorded incidents between 2003 and 2007. These figures are only registered incidents of self-injury in prison and a significant number may go unreported.

Self-injurious behaviour is particularly common in the female offender population (Borrill *et al.*, 2003; Home Office, 1990; Turner & Tofler, 1986; Wilkins & Coid, 1991). Research has suggested that 16 per cent of female prisoners self-harm, compared with 3 per cent of male prisoners, with more than half of all recorded incidents of self-harm occurring in the female estate, despite the fact that less than 6 per cent of the prison population is female (Corston Report, Home Office, 2007). A survey of prisoners by the Office of National Statistics reported that 10 per cent of female sentenced prisoners and 7 per cent of male sentenced prisoners reported self-harm during their current prison term (Singleton *et al.*, 1998).

Limited research has been conducted on the prevalence of self-injury in community offenders. As these offenders are not in a restricted setting to enable consistent recording, obtaining statistics on the rates of self-injury in this population is problematic. One local study examined the characteristics of offenders supervised by the West Yorkshire Probation Service (Akhurst *et al.*, 1994). They found a high incidence of deliberate self-harm among these offenders. Of 238 community offenders, almost one-third reported one or more incidents of self-harm, with nearly three-quarters of these incidents believed to be serious attempts at suicide. The profiles of the offenders were found to be very similar to the characteristics commonly associated with suicide, including breakdown in family relationships, mental health problems, alcohol and drug misuse and unemployment. However, there was a low response rate in this study, so the sample is unrepresentative, and it was a local study which limited the extent to which the findings can be generalised more widely.

A similar study by Roberts *et al.* (1995) found that 48 per cent of those on a probation order with a condition of psychiatric treatment attached were viewed as being at risk of self-injury. However, in probationers with no psychiatric supervision condition, 46 per cent were viewed to be similarly at risk. Again, this study was conducted in one locality and a large-scale national study examining the prevalence of self-injury in the community offending population would be required to ensure that a representative sample is obtained for findings to be generalised.

Caution must be noted as studies may vary in their estimates of self-injury, according to whether self-harm motivated by suicidal intent was included (Jackson, 2000).

Risk Factors for Self-Injury in Offenders

Studies in the community have identified certain characteristics and factors which are overrepresented in offenders who self-injure, including being female (HM Inspectorate of Prisons, 1999; Singleton *et al.*, 1998; Social Work Services & Prisons Inspectorate for Scotland, 1998); having previously self-harmed (Dooley, 1990a, 1990b; HM Inspectorate of Prisons, 1999; Inch *et al.*, 1995); having a psychiatric disorder, such as a personality disorder, a conduct disorder or depression (Favazza & Rosenthal, 1993; Mohino *et al.*, 2004; Wessely *et al.*, 1996); having a history of drug and/or alcohol misuse (Wilkins & Coid, 1991); and having had a dysfunctional childhood, including physical and sexual abuse (Liebling, 1991; Wilkins & Coid, 1991). There is substantial overlap between the risk factors for self-injury and suicide and those characteristics common in offending populations (Wessely *et al.*, 1996).

Studies investigating self-injury in such populations would need to employ more rigorous methodology, such as case–control measures to reliably identify how those offenders who self-injure differ from those who do not.

Specific Subgroups of Offenders

An individual's characteristics, circumstances and/or experiences can make them more at risk of self-injury and/or suicide.

Specific subgroups of offenders have been recognised as having different and/or additional needs and therefore risk factors with regards to their own particular characteristics, including, women, BME groups, immigrants and asylum seekers, young offenders and elderly offenders. The profiles of certain groups of offenders and the reasons why they offend vary (Bloom *et al.*, 2003; Care Services Improvement Partnership North West, 2008; Gelsthorpe & McIvor, 2007;

Lewis *et al.*, 2006; Social Work Services & Prisons Inspectorate for Scotland, 1998; Wright *et al.*, 2007). As a consequence, it is important to improve the understanding of health and social care needs of certain offending groups, in order to reduce their risk of self-injury and/or suicide.

There has been little attention given to elderly offenders, who are growing in number within prisons (Codd, 1994; Wahidin, 2004). Given the high risk of suicide found in studies of older recently released prisoners (Kariminia *et al.*, 2007; Pratt *et al.*, 2006), further exploration is required to ascertain need in this particular subgroup of offenders. Similarly female offenders who, although they may constitute a small minority of offenders, are also the subgroup with the fastest growth curve within prison (Rutherford & Taylor, 2004).

There are also those offenders who cross subgroups, such as women from BME groups who may have particularly complex needs, which require an understanding of how one demographic characteristic may mediate the other (Gelsthorpe & McIvor, 2007). These subgroups and their specific characteristics require further exploration in order to adequately assess and meet their needs to ensure the reduction or prevention of self-injury and/or suicide.

Assessing Risk

In order to assess the risk of self-injury and/or suicide, an offender's presenting physical and mental state must be carefully observed by practitioners. Indicators of an increased risk fall into three main categories: an individual's emotional and mental state, their physical state, including behaviour, and their current situation/life events.

Important features of a comprehensive suicide/self-injury risk assessment would include: gathering a full personal history from the offender, including discussing any ideas of suicide/self-injury and any history of suicide attempts or thoughts; the context in which these occurred; assessment of any aggravating features or risk factors present; assessment of the offender's support network and current/impending life events. Indicators of increased risk would include: a history of previous suicide attempts and/or self-injury; current suicidal ideation; current symptoms of depression; cumulative negative life events, such as abuse, unemployment or a breakdown in relationships; charged with or convicted of a particular offence type, such as sexual

offences; a history of drug and/or alcohol abuse; and a history of contact with mental health services.

In the initial contact with an offender, a comprehensive mental health assessment, including risk of self-injury and/or suicide, should be conducted. This should include the collection of information from health, social and criminal justice agencies and also collateral information regarding the individual's history from a relative.

Male offenders, who make up the majority of the offending population, have reported a reluctance to seek help from healthcare professionals for mental health problems because of a distrust of professionals and the stigma associated with a mental illness diagnosis (Howerton *et al.*, 2007). This has particularly been found in young offenders (Harvey, 2005, 2007; HM Inspectorate of Prisons, 1997; Shelton, 2004). It suggests that information sharing and documentation should be of a high standard across all agencies to ensure that accurate and relevant information regarding mental illness and suicide risk is communicated and available to all practitioners.

The criminal justice system should be viewed as a 'continuum of offending agencies', with these agencies requiring integration on a national scale. Developments in information technology, leading to shared electronic offender case notes, should be implemented. 'Offender passports' should be introduced to document self-injury and/or suicide risk assessment, by recording key indicators of risk and also to facilitate the transfer of information between services.

Adequate mental health training, including self-harm and suicide risk assessment, should be provided to all practitioners working with offenders to ensure that they have the appropriate knowledge to support offenders who may be suicidal or at risk of self-injury.

Prevention

Prevention of suicide and self-injury requires an improvement in the general care of all offenders and optimised care of those identified as being at acute risk of suicide. The different agencies have particular strategies, based on setting, but there are some general strategies which can encompass the whole criminal justice system.

It has been recognised that developments and improvements need to occur at all stages of the custodial process, including pre-prison; reception screening; induction or 'first night' centres; primary mental health care; secondary mental health care; acute care within prison; acute care outside prison; throughcare and pre-release; prison transfer and aftercare and prison to community transition (Department of Health & National Institute for Mental Health in England, 2005). This includes the cooperation of agencies and staff in health, social, criminal justice, voluntary sector, housing and education services working together to ensure the effective care and treatment of those individuals with complex problems coming into contact with the system.

Suicide prevention in prison

The Prison Service in England and Wales has adopted two separate approaches to reducing suicide in prison, including whole estate and specific strategies.

A number of changes and developments have been introduced to the estate, including an increase in prisoner peer-support schemes, improved staff skills, knowledge and training with regard to mental health and specifically suicide risk assessment, safer cells, improvements in reception screening procedures, the establishment of 'First Night Centres' and further expansion and development of mental health in-reach services.

Joint working between the Department of Health, the Prison Service and the National Offender Management Service (NOMS) has produced a revised care-planning system for at-risk prisoners (Assessment, Care in Custody and Teamwork or ACCT). The ACCT approach aims to be more proactive, recognising those at high risk of self-harm before an act of self-harm; to develop better targeted assessment of need; to improve accountable case-management; to improve the training of staff and improve information-exchange and teamwork.

Suicide prevention in the community

The supervision of offenders subject to probation on release from prison concentrates more on public protection rather than offender welfare. Ex-prisoners are vulnerable to suicide, but those serving short sentences or on remand receive little or no preparation for release and resettlement into the community (Howard League for Penal Reform/McCarthy, 2002).

Prisoner release support programmes have indicated that the period prior to release from custody can be an important 'window of opportunity' when offenders are motivated to plan for their release (Ross, 2004).

Programmes which encourage resettlement into the community following a custodial sentence require intensive, outreach-based support, with the support agency helping the individual to identify his or her specific needs and facilitating access to support services.

Effective resettlement requires addressing an offender's multiple needs, including not only health and social concerns but also practical issues, such as accommodation and employment. Ensuring the successful resettlement of offenders into the community will involve recognising and addressing the multiple barriers which ex-prisoners face in what is a particularly stressful transitional period. Those at greatest risk are profoundly alienated from society and require substantial reintegration.

Research has highlighted the necessity for shared responsibility between the prison, probation, health and social services both immediately prior to and following release from prison (Pratt et al., 2006).

Within the framework of NOMS, there is currently no suicide prevention strategy or training package on risk assessment for staff working within its agencies.

Suicide prevention in police custody

It is recognised that the police need to assess an individual's risk of self-injury and/or suicide and to know whom to contact when there are concerns.

A number of recommendations have been made with regard to suicide prevention in police custody, including custody officers directly questioning offenders regarding known risk factors for suicide; items of clothing being removed if it is believed that they may be used for self-harm; installing closed circuit television in custody suites; training in dealing with mental health problems; effective communication between disciplines; and handovers to include the provision of all relevant facts and information surrounding detainees (Ingram et al., 1997).

Diversion from the Criminal Justice System

From the point at which an individual is brought into police custody, their mental health and clinical state should be monitored and assessed. While an offender is in custody or at court, there are opportunities to assess defendants, with possible diversion of individuals with suspected mental illness to appropriate agencies. Court diversion schemes may aid the prevention of potential subsequent suicidal behaviour if the correct decision is made regarding an individual at this early stage.

The notion of diverting people suffering from mental disorder from the criminal justice system to treatment within the health service (Home Office, 1990; James & Hamilton, 1991; Joseph & Potter, 1990; Mikhail et al., 2001) is not a new concept in England and Wales. Studies have demonstrated that there is a high incidence of mental illness within the court population (Shaw et al., 1999). However, the development and maintenance of such services as part of a national strategy have proved difficult (NACRO/Smith, 2005). Many individuals requiring such court diversion techniques continue to slip through the net and be routinely processed through the system. This may result in an offender experiencing unnecessary distress, could exacerbate symptoms of their mental illness and thus increase the risk of suicide.

Interventions and Management of Self-Injury

National guidelines have been developed for the management of self-injury in the general population (National Institute for Clinical Excellence (NICE)/National Collaborating Centre for Mental Health, 2004). Service provision for self-harming patients in the general population has remained variable and haphazard (Bennewith et al., 2004). Different interventions and treatments for self-injury have been evaluated, but few have led to clinically significant reductions in such behaviours (Kapur, 2005). Recent studies have provided support for both large trials of low-intensity interventions and smaller trials of longer-term, intensive psychological treatments (Brown et al., 2005; Carter et al., 2005). An alternative to these has been to offer a basic intervention to all those who have self-harmed, using a combination of risk and needs assessment to identify individuals who may benefit from more intensive treatment (Kapur, 2005). Within community populations, brief psychological interventions have been shown to reduce suicidal ideation and self-reported self-harm in patients who had previously engaged in deliberate self-injury (Guthrie et al., 2001a).

Self-injury is more common amongst females than males in both general and offending populations (Corston Report, Home Office, 2007 Favazza, 1989; HM Inspectorate of Prisons, 1999;). The high level of self-injurious behaviours displayed by women in prison is an issue of considerable concern (Milligan & Andrews, 2005). Such behaviours have been linked to a history of sexual and/or physical abuse (Wilkins & Coid, 1991),

with high levels of both childhood abuse and self-injurious behaviours reported by female prisoners (Browne et al., 1999). A 'Women Offenders Repeated Self Harm Intervention Pilot' (WORSHIP) is currently being conducted by Abel and colleagues at a female prison establishment to determine whether a brief psychological intervention can reduce repeated self-injurious behaviour in female prisoners. The study has adapted an intervention used to reduce self-harm and suicide risk in a community sample of women and men (Guthrie et al., 2001b) for use in a women's prison environment. The modified intervention, which is a form of brief talking treatment, is being piloted in a sample of female prisoners who have recently self-harmed. Researchers are establishing the gender-specific needs of women in prison who self-harm, developing an acceptable intervention with the female prisoners and evaluating its effectiveness.

The management, treatment and prevention of self-injury within offending populations require further investigation. Rates of self-injury in offenders may be reduced by examining the views of professionals within the criminal justice agencies towards the behaviour, involving service users in staff training and shifting the focus of service provision from risk to needs assessment (Kapur, 2005).

Conclusions

Suicide and self-injury in offenders are a public health concern which requires concerted effort to explore the prediction of, and vulnerability to, such behaviours in different offending populations.

Studies have demonstrated that the rate of suicide in offending populations is far higher than in the general population in England and Wales and given this high rate, changes in the way that criminal justice, health care, and social services are delivered to this vulnerable population are required.

Although criminal justice authorities have identified this problem, there is a striking lack of integration and communication between the agencies involved to allow its practicable prevention. Transitional periods between different stages and agencies must be managed effectively, involving comprehensive information sharing and communication regarding an offender's risk of suicide. Evidence-based research is needed to determine how we can manage these transitional periods effectively.

Future aims of suicide and self-injury prevention in the offending population will be to identify skills, resources, and strategic and operational arrangements necessary to achieve effective and appropriate risk assessment for 'at risk' individuals and those agencies working with them. Interventions to reduce the incidence of suicide in offending populations should be multidimensional, including health, social and environmental preventative measures to reflect the multidimensional nature of the problem (Snow, 2002).

The identification of those at risk of suicide within the criminal justice system is complex. However, the development of inter-agency cooperation will enhance this identification and, perhaps more importantly, the early identification of these offenders. The more information available on an offender, the better equipped the system is to manage them.

Criminal justice practitioners and agencies can do nothing to change the characteristics of the individuals who enter the system, but they can improve service provision by developing a more informed and comprehensive process, which is subsequently more able to manage such vulnerable people. Adequate information sharing and the formalisation of responsibility for care of offenders within and between offending agencies are a necessity in order to ensure that rates of suicide and self-injury in this population are significantly abated.

Note

1 Inserted by editors.

Further Reading[1]

Shaw, J., Baker, D., Hunt, I.M. et al. (2004). Suicide by prisoners. *The British Journal of Psychiatry, 184*, 263–267.
This paper reports an analysis of 172 self-inflicted deaths in prisoners. A large proportion of such deaths were found to have occurred within 7 days of reception into prison, with hanging or self-strangulation being the most common means of death. A total of 110 (72 per cent; 95 per cent CI 65–79) had a history of mental disorder, with the most common primary diagnosis being drug dependence. The paper concludes with an analysis of approaches to suicide prevention in prisons, suggesting that these should be concentrated in the period immediately following reception into prison, combined with efforts at physical prevention such as removal of ligature points.

Towl, G.J., Snow, L. & McHugh, M.J. (Eds.) (2000). *Suicide in prisons.* Oxford: BPS, Blackwell.
This is the most comprehensive single volume available on suicide in prisons in England and Wales, edited by a panel of experts in the field. The broad and unique scope of the book includes research, policy and practice. There is particular coverage of prevention, a critique of the research, intentional self-injury, risk assessment and management, clinical skills and staff training. Most readers will be likely to find something of interest in this text.

Towl, G.J. & Crighton, D.A. (1998). Suicide in prisons in England and Wales from 1988 to 1995. *Criminal Behaviour and Mental Health, 8*, 184–192.
This research study was the largest-scale study of its kind in the 20th century, with a sample size of 377 case records. The paper includes an interesting discussion of some of the difficult methodological issues in this sensitive area of work. It also includes observations on some of the differences between prisoner suicides and others. The authors highlight the issue of the assumed links between suicide and self-injury as they are reflected in policies and practices in prisons.

References

Akhurst, M., Brown, I. & Wessely, S. (1994). *West Yorkshire Probation and After-care Service, West Yorkshire HA, Association of Chief Officers of Probation. Dying for help: Offenders at risk of suicide.* Leeds: Association of Chief Officers of Probation.

American Psychiatric Association (2000). *Psychiatric services in jails and prisons: A task force report of the American Psychiatric Association.* Washington, DC: American Psychiatric Association.

Appleby, L., Shaw, J., Amos, T. et al. (1999). Suicide within 12 months of contact with mental health services: National clinical survey. *British Medical Journal, 318*, 1235–1239.

Appleby, L., Shaw, J., Sherrat, J., Amos, T. et al. (2001). *Safety first. A five year report of the National Confidential Inquiry into suicide and homicide by people with mental illness.* London: Department of Health.

Babiker, G. & Arnold, A. (1997). *The language of injury: Comprehending self-mutilation.* Leicester: BPS Books.

BBC News (2004). Self-harm. Retrieved 10 September 2009 from http://news.bbc.co.uk/1/hi/health/medical_notes/4067129.stm, British Broadcasting Corporation.

Bennewith, O., Gunnell, D., Peters, T.J. et al. (2004). Variations in the hospital management of self-harm in adults in England: Observational study. *British Medical Journal, 328*, 1108–1109.

Binswanger, I.A., Stern, M.F., Deyo, R.A. et al. (2007). Release from prison – high risk of death for former inmates. *New England Journal of Medicine, 356*, 157–165.

Birmingham, L., Mason, D. & Grubin, D. (1996). Prevalence of mental disorder in remand prisoners: Consecutive case study. *British Medical Journal, 313,* 1521–1524.

Blaauw, E., Kerkhof, A.J.F.M. & Vermunt, R. (1997). Suicides and other deaths in police custody. *Suicide and Life Threatening Behaviour, 27*(2), 153–163.

Bloom, B., Owen, B. & Covington, S. (2003). *Gender-responsive strategies: Research, practice and guiding principles for women offenders.* Washington, DC: US Department of Justice National Institute of Corrections.

Bonner, R.L. (1992). Isolation, seclusion and psychological vulnerability as risk factors for suicide behind bars. In R. Maris *et al.* (Eds.) *Assessment and prediction of suicide.* New York: Guilford Press.

Borrill, J., Burnett, R., Atkins, R. *et al.* (2003). Patterns of self-harm and attempted suicide among white and black/mixed race female prisoners. *Criminal Behaviour and Mental Health, 13,* 229–240.

Brooker, C., Beverley, C., Repper, J. *et al.* (2002). *Mental health services and prisoners: A review for the Department of Health.* London: Department of Health.

Brown, G.K., Ten Have, T., Henriques, G.R. *et al.* (2005). Cognitive therapy for the prevention of suicide attempts: A randomized controlled trial. *Journal of the American Medical Association, 294,* 623–624.

Browne, A., Miller, B. & Maguin, E. (1999). Prevalence and severity of lifetime physical and sexual victimization among incarcerated women. *International Journal of Law and Psychiatry, 22,* 301–322.

Care Services and Improvement Partnership North West (2008). *Commissioning appropriate and responsive services for black and minority ethnic offenders.* North West England: CSIP.

Carter, G.L., Clover, K., Whyte, I.M. *et al.* (2005). Postcards from the Edge project: Randomised controlled trial of an intervention using postcards to reduce repetition of hospital treated deliberate self-poisoning. *British Medical Journal.* doi: 10.1136/bmj.38579.455266.E0.

Charlton, J., Keely, S., Dunnell, K. *et al.* (1993). Trends in suicide deaths in England and Wales. *Population Trends, 69,* 10–16.

Codd, H. (1994). White haired offenders. *New Law Journal, 144*(6672), 1582–1583.

Coffey, C., Veit, F., Wolfe, R. *et al.* (2003). Mortality in young offenders: Retrospective cohort study. *British Medical Journal, 326,* 1064.

Coffey, C., Wolfe, R., Lovett, A. *et al.* (2004). Predicting death in young offenders: A retrospective cohort study. *Medical Journal of Australia, 181,* 473–477.

Cox, J.F. & Morschauer, P.C. (1997). A solution to the problem of jail suicide. *Crisis, 18,* 178–184.

Cox, M. & Pritchard, C. (1995). Troubles come not simply but in battalions. In D. Ward & M. Lacy (Eds.) *Probation: Working for justice* (88–122). London: Whiting and Birch.

Crighton, D. & Towl, G. (2000). International self-injury (ISI). In G. Towl, L. Snow & M. McHugh (Eds.) *Suicide in prisons.* Leicester: BPS Books.

Cutter, D., Jaffe, J. & Segal, J. (2008). Self-injury: Types, causes and treatment. Retrieved 10 September 2009 from www.helpguide.org/mental/self_injury.htm.

Dalton, V. (1998). Prison deaths 1980–1997. National overview and state trends. *Trends and Issues in Crime and Criminal Justice, 81.*

Department of Health (1999). *Saving lives: Our healthier nation.* London: The Stationery Office.

Department of Health (2002). *National suicide prevention strategy for England.* London: Department of Health.

Department of Health (2006). *National Suicide Prevention Strategy.* 3rd Annual Report. April. Reference No: 2006/0144. London: Department of Health.

Department of Health & National Institute for Mental Health in England. (2005). *Offender mental health care pathway.* London: Department of Health.

Dooley, E. (1990a). Prison suicide in England and Wales, 1972–1987. *British Journal of Psychiatry, 156,* 40–45.

Dooley, E. (1990b). Unnatural deaths in prison. *British Journal of Criminology, 30*(2), 229–234.

DuRand, C., Burtka, G., Gederman, E. *et al.* (1995). A quarter century of suicide in a major urban jail: Implications for community psychiatry. *American Journal of Psychiatry, 152*(7), 1077–1080.

Evans, W., Albert, E. & Macari, D. (1995). Suicide ideation, attempts and abuse among incarcerated gang and nongang delinquents. *Child and Adolescent Social Work Journal, 13,* 115–126.

Farmer, K.A., Felthous, A.R. & Holzer, C.E. (1996). Medically serious suicide attempts in a jail with a suicide prevention program. *Journal of Forensic Sciences, 41,* 240–246.

Favazza, A. R. (1989). Why patients mutilate themselves. *Hospital and Community Psychiatry, 40,* 137–145.

Favazza, A.R. & Rosenthal, R.J. (1993). Diagnostic issues in self-mutilation. *Hospital and Community Psychiatry, 44*(2), 134–140.

Fleming, J., McDonald, D. & Biles, D. (1992). Self-inflicted harm in custody. In D. Biles & D. McDonald (Eds.) *Deaths in custody in Australia 1980–1989: The research papers of the Criminology Unit of the Royal Commission into Aboriginal deaths in custody.* Canberra: Australian Institute of Criminology.

Fox, C. & Hawton, K. (2004). *'Sometimes it's nice to see that it is me hurting, instead of somebody else'. Deliberate self-harm in adolescence.* London: Jessica Kingsley.

Fruehwald, S., Frottier, P., Benda, N. *et al.* (2002). Psychological characteristics of jail and prison suicide victims. *Wiener Klinische Wochenschrift, 114,* 691–696.

Fruehwald, S., Frottier, P., Matschnig, T. *et al.* (2004). Suicide in custody: A case–control study, *British Journal of Psychiatry, 185,* 494–498.

Gelsthorpe, L. & McIvor, G. (2007). Difference and diversity in probation. In L. Gelsthorpe & R. Morgan (Eds.) *Handbook of probation*. Portland, OR: Willan.

Graham, A. (2003). Post-prison mortality: Unnatural death among those released from Victorian prisons between January 1990 and December 1990. *Australian and New Zealand Journal of Criminology*, 36, 94–108.

Gunn, J., Maden, A. & Swinton, M. (1991). Treatment needs of prisoners with psychiatric disorder. *British Medical Journal*, 303, 338–341.

Guthrie, E., Kapur, N., Mackway-Jones, K. *et al.* (2001a). Randomised controlled trial of brief psychological intervention after deliberate self poisoning. *British Medical Journal*, 323, 135–138.

Guthrie, E., Moorey, J., Margison, F. *et al.* (2001b). Cost-effectiveness of brief psychodynamic-interpersonal therapy in high utilizers of psychiatric services. *Archives of General Psychiatry*, 56, 519–526.

Harvey, J. (2005). Crossing the boundary: The transitions of young adults. In A. Liebling & S. Maruna (Eds.) *The effects of imprisonment*. Cullompton, Devon: Willan.

Harvey, J. (2007). *Young men in prison: Surviving and adapting to life inside*. Cullompton, Devon: Willan.

Hatty, S. & Walker, J. (1986). *A national study of deaths in Australian prisons*. Canberra: Australian Institute of Criminology.

Hawton, K., Townsend, E., Arensman, E. *et al.* (1999). Psychosocial and pharmacological treatments for deliberate self-harm. *Cochrane Database of Systematic Review*, Issue 4, Article no. CD001764; DOI:10.1002/14651858.

Haycock, J. (1991). Crimes and misdemeanors: A review of recent research on suicides in prison. *Omega*, 23(2), 81–94.

Hek, G. (2006). Unlocking potential: Challenges for primary health care researchers in the prison setting (Editorial). *Primary Health Care Research and Development*, 7, 91–94.

HM Inspectorate of Prisons (1997). *Young prisoners*. October. London: Home Office.

HM Inspectorate of Prisons (1999). Suicide is everyone's concern. London: Home Office.

HM Inspectorate of Probation (2007). *Independent inspection of probation and youth offending work. Annual report 2006/2007*. July. London: Home Office.

Home Office (1990). *Report of a review by HM Chief Inspector of Prisons for England and Wales of suicide and self-harm in prison establishments in England and Wales*. London: HMSO.

Home Office (2007). Baroness Corston. *The Corston Report: A review of women with particular vulnerability in the criminal justice system*. London: Home Office.

Howard League for Penal Reform (2008). *Press Release, 14 April. Prison self-injury rate accelerates at four times the rise in the population*. Retrieved 10 September 2009 from www.howardleague.org/fileadmin/howard_league/user/pdf/Press_2008/self_injury_14_April_2008.pdf

Howard League for Penal Reform (McCarthy, C). (2002). Suicide and self-harm prevention following release from prison. HLM, 22, 1.

Howerton, A., Byng, R., Campbell, J. *et al.* (2007). Understanding help seeking behaviour among male offenders: Qualitative interview study. *British Medical Journal*, 334, 303–307.

Huey, M.P. & McNulty, T. L. (2005). Institutional conditions and prison suicide: Conditional effects of deprivation and overcrowding. *The Prison Journal*, 85(4), 490–514.

Inch, H., Rowlands, P. & Soliman, A. (1995). Deliberate self-harm in a young offenders' institution. *Journal of Forensic Psychiatry*, 6(1), 161–171.

Independent Police Complaints Commission (IPCC) (2005). *Deaths during or following police contact: Statistics for England and Wales 2004–2005*. Tears, R. & Bucke, T. IPCC Research and Statistics Series: Paper 1. London: Author.

Independent Police Complaints Commission (IPCC) (2006). *Deaths during or following police contact: Statistics for England and Wales 2005–2006*. Tears, R. & Menin, S. IPCC Research and Statistics Series: Paper 4. London: Author.

Ingram, A., Johnson, G. & Heyes, I. (1997). *Self-harm and suicide by detained persons: A study*. Preston, UK: Lancashire Constabulary.

Jackson, N. (2000). The prevalence and frequency of deliberate self-harm among male patients in a maximum secure hospital. *Criminal Behaviour and Mental Health*, 10, 21–28.

James, D.V. & Hamilton, L.W. (1991). The Clerkenwell Scheme: Assessing efficacy and cost of a psychiatric liaison service to a magistrates court. *British Medical Journal*, 303, 282–285.

Jeglic, E.L., Vanderhoff, H.A. & Donovick, P.J. (2005). The function of self-harm behaviour in a forensic population. *International Journal of Offender Therapy and Comparative Criminology*, 49(2), 131–142.

Joseph, P.L.A. & Potter, M. (1990). Psychiatric assessment at the magistrates' court. *British Journal of Psychiatry*, 164, 722–724.

Joukamaa, M. (1997). Prison suicide in Finland 1969–1992. *Forensic Science International*, 89(2), 167–174.

Joukamaa, M. (1998). The mortality of released Finnish prisoners: A 7 year follow-up study of the WATTU project. *Forensic Science International*, 96, 11–19.

Kapur, N. (2005). Management of self-harm in adults: Which way now? *British Journal of Psychiatry*, 187, 497–499.

Kariminia, A., Law, M.G., Butler, T.G. *et al.* (2007). Suicide risk among recently released prisoners in New South Wales. *Medical Journal of Australia*, 187, 387–390.

Leese, M., Thomas, S. & Snow, L. (2005). An ecological study of factors associated with rates of self-inflicted death in prisons in England and Wales. *International Journal of Law and Psychiatry*, 29, 355–360.

Leigh, A., Johnson, J. & Ingram, A. (1998). *Deaths in police custody: Learning the lessons*. Police Research Series, Paper 26.

Lewis, S., Raynor, P. & Smith, S. (2006). *Race and probation*. Cullompton, Devon: Willan.

Liebling, A. (1991). *Suicide and self-injury amongst young offenders in custody*. Unpublished PhD dissertation, Cambridge University.

Liebling, A. (1992). *Suicides in prison*. London: Routledge.

Liebling, A. & Krarup, H. (1993). *Suicide attempts and self-injury in male prisons*. Cambridge, UK: Institute of Criminology.

Linsley, K.R., Johnson, N. & Martin, J. (2007). Police contact within 3 months of suicide and associated health service contact. *British Journal of Psychiatry*, 190, 170–171.

Livingston, M. (1997). A review of the literature on self-injurious behaviour amongst prisoners. In G.J. Towl (Ed.) *Suicide and injury in prisons*. Leicester: British Psychological Society, Division of Criminological and Legal Psychology (DCLP).

Lloyd, M. (1990). *Suicide and self-injury in prison: A literature review*. Home Office Research Study No 115. London: HMSO.

Mikhail, S.A., Kinkunmi, A. & Poythress, N. (2001). Mental health courts: A workable proposition? *Psychiatric Bulletin*, 25, 5–7.

Milligan, R. & Andrews, B. (2005). Suicidal and other self-harming behaviour in offender women: The role of shame, anger and childhood abuse. *Legal and Criminological Psychology*, 10, 13–25.

Ministry of Justice (2007). *Deaths in prison custody, 2007*. Retrieved 10 September 2009 from www.justice.gov.uk/news/newsrelease010108a.htm.

Mohino, J.S., Ortega-Monasterio, G.L., Planchat, L.M. *et al.* (2004). Discriminating deliberate self-harm (DSH) in young prison inmates through personality disorder. *Journal of Forensic Sciences*, 49(1), 137–140.

NACRO/Smith, L. (2005). *Findings of the 2004 Survey of Court Diversion/Criminal Justice Mental Health Liaison Schemes for Mentally Disordered Offenders in England and Wales*. London: NACRO.

National Institute for Clinical Excellence (NICE)/National Collaborating Centre for Mental Health (2004). *Self-harm: The short term physical and psychological management and secondary prevention of self-harm in primary and secondary care*. Clinical Guideline 16. London: Gaskell & British Psychological Society.

Office of National Statistics (2003). Singleton, N., Farrell, M. & Meltzer, H. Substance misuse among prisoners in England and Wales. *International Review of Psychiatry*, 15, 150–152.

Police Complaints Authority (PCA) (1999). *Deaths in police custody: Reducing the risks*. London: PCA.

Pratt, D., Piper, M., Appleby, A. *et al.* (2006). Suicide in recently released prisoners: A population-based cohort study. *Lancet*, 368, 119–123.

Price Waterhouse (1996). *National inmate survey. Final report*. Report No. SR-02. Research Branch, Correctional Service of Canada.

Prison Reform Trust (2006). *Bromley briefings: Prison factfile*. November. London: Prison Reform Trust.

Pritchard, C., Cox, M. & Dawson, A. (1997). Suicide and 'violent' death in a six-year cohort of male probationers compared with pattern of mortality in the general population: Evidence of accumulative socio-psychiatric vulnerability. *Journal of Research and Social Health*, 117, 180–185.

Qin, P. & Nordentoft, M. (2005). Suicide risk in relation to psychiatric hospitalisation: Evidence based on longitudinal registers. *Archives of General Psychiatry*, 62, 427–432.

Roberts, C., Hudson, B.L. & Cullen, R. (1995). The supervision of mentally disordered offenders: The work of probation officers and their relationship with psychiatrists in England and Wales. *Criminal Behaviour and Mental Health*, 5, 75–84.

Rodham, K., Hawton, K. & Evans, E. (2005). Deliberate self-harm in adolescents: The importance of gender. *Psychiatric Times*, 22(1), 36–41.

Ross, S. (2004). *Bridging the gap: A release transition support program for Victorian prisoners*. Melbourne: Department of Justice, 2004.

Rutherford, H. & Taylor, P. J. (2004). The transfer of women offenders with mental disorder from prison to hospital. *Journal of Forensic Psychiatry and Psychology*, 15(1), 108–123.

Sattar, G. (2001). *Rates and causes of death among prisoners and offenders under community supervision*. Home Office Research Study, 231. London: Home Office.

Shaw, J., Creed, F., Price, J. *et al.* (1999). Prevalence and detection of serious psychiatric disorder in defendants attending court. *The Lancet*, 353, 1053–1056.

Shaw, J., Baker, D., Hunt, I.M, Moloney, A. & Appleby, L. (2004). Suicide by prisoners: A national clinical survey. *British Journal of Psychiatry*, 184, 263–267.

Shelton, D. (2004). Experiences of detained young offenders in need of mental health care. *Journal of Nursing Scholarship*, 36, 129–133.

Singleton, N., Meltzer, H., Gatward, R. *et al.* (1998). *Psychiatric morbidity among prisoners in England and Wales*. London: HMSO.

Snow, L. (2002). Prisoners' motives for self-injury and attempted suicide. *British Journal of Forensic Practice*, 4, 18–29.

Social Exclusion Unit (2002). *Reducing re-offending by ex-prisoners*. London: SEU.

Social Work Services & Prisons Inspectorate for Scotland. (1998). *Women offenders – a safer way: A review of community disposals and the use of custody for women offenders in Scotland*. Scotland: The Stationery Office.

Stewart, G. & Stewart, J. (1993). *Social circumstances of younger offenders under supervision*. Wakefield: Association of Chief Officer of Probation.

Susser, E., Valencia, E., Conover, S. *et al.* (1997). Preventing recurrent homelessness among mentally ill men: A 'critical time' intervention after discharge from a shelter. *American Journal of Public Health*, 87, 256–262.

Tartaro, C. & Lester, D. (2005). An application of Durkheim's theory of suicide to prison suicide rates in the United States. *Death Studies, 29,* 413–422.

Tatarelli, R., Mancinelli, I., Taggi, F. & Polidori, G. (1999). Suicide in Italian prisons in 1996 and 1997: A descriptive epidemiological study. *International Journal of Offender Therapy and Comparative Criminology, 43*(4), 438–447.

Thomas, J., Leaf, M., Kazmierczak, S. *et al.* (2006). Self-injury in correctional settings: 'Pathology' of prisons or of prisoners? *Reaction Essay, 5*(1), 193–202.

Topp, D. (1979). Suicide in prison. *British Journal of Psychiatry, 134,* 24–27.

Turner, T.H. & Tofler, D.S. (1986). Indicators of psychiatric disorder among women admitted to prison. *British Medical Journal, 292,* 651–653.

Wahidin, A. (2004). *Older women in the criminal justice system: Running out of time.* London: Jessica Kingsley.

Weis, M.A., Bradberry, C., Carter, L.P. *et al.* (2006). An exploration of human services system contacts prior to suicide in South Carolina: An expansion of the South Carolina violent death reporting system. *Injury Prevention, 12,* 17–21.

Wessely, S., Akhurst, R., Brown, I. *et al.* (1996). Deliberate self-harm and the Probation Service: An overlooked public health problem? *Journal of Public Health Medicine, 18*(2), 129–132.

Wichmann, C., Serin, R. & Motiuk, L. (2000). *Predicting suicide attempts among male offenders in federal penitentiaries.* Research Branch, Correctional Service Canada.

Wilkins, J. & Coid, J. (1991). Self-mutilation in female remanded prisoners: I. An indicator of severe psychopathology. *Criminal Behaviour and Mental Health, 1,* 247–267.

Wobeser, W.L., Datema, J., Bechard, B. *et al.* (2002). Causes of death among people in custody in Ontario 1990–1999. *Canadian Medical Association Journal, 167,* 1109–1113.

Wolff, N., Plemmons, D., Veysey, B. *et al.* (2002). Release planning for inmates with mental illness compared with those who have other chronic illnesses. *Psychiatric Services, 53,* 1469–1471.

Wortley, R. (2002). Self-harm. In R. Wortley (Ed.) *Situational prison control* (pp.136–154). Cambridge: Cambridge University Press.

Wright, E.M., Sailsbury, E.J. & Van Voorhis, P. (2007). Predicting the prison misconducts of women offenders: The importance of gender responsive needs. *Journal of Contemporary Criminal Justice, 23*(4), 340.

Young, M.H., Justice, J.V. & Erdberg, P. (2006). Risk of harm: Inmates who harm themselves while in prison psychiatric treatment. *Journal of Forensic Science, 51*(1), 156–162.

Zamble, E. & Porporino, F. (1988). *Coping, behaviour, adaptation in prison inmates.* New York: Springer.

26

Restorative Justice as a Psychological Treatment

Healing Victims, Reintegrating Offenders[1]

Lawrence W. Sherman and Heather Strang

A substantial body of scientific evidence now shows that restorative justice conferencing (RJC) is an effective psychological treatment for offenders and their victims. While there are many varieties of programmes described as 'restorative', only RJC, in which offenders and victims meet in person with family or friends, has been subjected to extensive and rigorous testing. The evidence is particularly strong with respect to violent crimes, even though RJ may be most difficult to arrange in such cases. Results from 12 randomised controlled trials (RCTs) in the UK, Australia and the USA cover adult and youth crime, violent and property crime, offenders in prison as well as in the community, RJC as diversion and as a supplement to ordinary prosecution and sentencing. Outcomes for offenders include reduced frequency of reconviction and cost of crimes committed. Outcomes for victims include reduced post-traumatic stress symptoms, anger, desire for violent revenge, fear and anxiety. Forensic psychologists may be in an ideal position to provide access to RJC for far more victims and offenders than are presently offered opportunities for it in the UK. They may also be able to enhance the evidence base by conducting and reporting small-scale RCTs in their own practices.

1. Introduction

Restorative justice is any response to crime that emphasises repair of existing harm (restoration) over infliction of additional harm (retribution). Such responses have a long history, a contemporary social movement and an uncertain future. Historically, pre-bureaucratic societies made widespread use of restorative justice (RJ) as a means of preventing long and damaging blood feuds between families or tribes (Braithwaite, 2002; Huxley, 1939). While the rise of nation-states and offences against the Crown (Christie, 1977) greatly restricted RJ in favour of retributive punishments, the late 20th century saw a resurgence of restorative practices in a global social movement (United Nations, 2002). It also saw the commissioning of a substantial programme of experimental research to compare RJ conferencing (RJC) to strictly retributive responses. While the RJC test results are generally favourable (Shapland *et al.*, 2008; Sherman & Strang, 2007, forthcoming), the findings are relatively new and not yet widely known or understood. Until they are, it is not clear that victims and offenders will be provided widespread access to RJC even when they request it.

Forensic psychologists may be in a critical position to translate the research results into action. The evidence suggests that it is appropriate to view RJ as a psychological treatment that benefits both offenders and victims. It is therefore appropriate for psychologists to inform their clients about those benefits and how the treatment operates. The evidence suggests that in order to convey a full and complete understanding of RJ, at least one hour of one-on-one discussion is required. Psychologists in forensic settings may be better placed to provide that kind of intensive explanation than many other professionals. If their offender or victim clients elect to undertake RJ in any volume, forensic psychologists may be better placed than most to conduct their own randomised controlled trials (RCTs) of the effects of RJC (or other RJ) on a range of outcomes. Adding more RCTs for specific kinds of offenders at specific points of the justice system could bring far greater precision to the evidence base. It could also help to support the expansion of resources needed to make such treatments more widely available to crime victims and offenders.

This chapter provides an independent overview of the knowledge forensic psychologists need to provide their clients with more access to restorative justice. This knowledge includes when RJ is *not* recommended, given evidence on when RJ is contraindicated due to offence or offender characteristics. It begins by describing the wide range of restorative practices. It then narrows the focus to the one method that has been subjected to randomised controlled trials, and to generally the most extensive field testing: face-to-face RJC meetings of 1–3 hours among victims, their offenders and their respective friends or family members, led by a trained RJ facilitator. After presenting some of the theories of change by which RJC is predicted to affect both victim and offender, the chapter then addresses the practicalities of delivering RJC. These logistical issues set the stage for describing the science and ethics of randomised trials of RJC, followed by summaries of what they show about its effects on offenders and victims. A brief review of other RJ approaches besides conferencing precedes the concluding reflections on the role of forensic psychologists in RJ in general and RJC in particular.

2. Varieties of Restorative Justice

Contemporary usage of the term 'restorative justice' embraces a wide range of definitions. These definitions may be classified on several dimensions. One is the method by which the programme operates. A second is the stage of the criminal process at which it operates, if it is associated with criminal justice. A third is the range of other institutions and settings in which restorative responses to harm – criminal or not – may be organised.

All three of these dimensions fall within the broader definition of RJ adopted by the Home Office in 2003: '… a process whereby all the parties with a stake in a particular offence come together to resolve collectively how to deal with the aftermath of the offence and its implications for the future' (Marshall, 1999). This defi-

nition is arguably so broad that it would include a lynch mob or a gang fight. Yet when added to the essential focus on repair rather than revenge (Strang, 2002), the definition is consistent with more philosophical statements such as the one Desmond Tutu (1999) used to guide the Truth and Reconciliation Commission in South Africa. These ideas about RJ, in fact, have great appeal for the tragic challenges facing post-conflict societies (Strang, forthcoming). The present chapter limits its focus, however, to everyday crime in stable common law democracies, since virtually all of the evidence reviewed comes from the UK, Australia, the USA, New Zealand and Canada.

RJ methods

Several methods are commonly advertised as 'restorative' in nature. These may be arranged on a continuum from 'indirect' to 'direct' restoration of one or more individual victims harmed by an offender, where crimes entailed such victims.

Programmes for offenders who directly harmed no personal victim at all (a so-called 'victimless' crime) are sometimes called restorative, as in the RCTs we conducted in Canberra (Australia) with persons caught driving with legally excessive blood alcohol levels and with under-18 shoplifters caught in large department stores (Sherman & Strang, 2007). In both RCTs the restorative method entailed an RJ conference without a direct victim present, but with frequent participation of a community or store 'representative' in a meeting with the offender, his or her family, friends and a police officer facilitating the discussion.

RJ programmes for offenders who had direct victims may be classified by 'directness' as follows, moving from the least to the most direct method of communication among all parties affected by a crime:

- Orders by judges that offenders must pay restitution or reparations to their victims via the Probation Service, without ever meeting their victims.
- Discussions between professionals and offenders in prison or on probation about how the offenders' crimes hurt their victims, sometimes as a motivation for rehabilitation.
- Videotaped presentations to offenders by victims of other criminals, in which the victims discuss the harm they suffered from crime.

- Group discussions of offenders with live crime victims present, but not their own victims, such as the Sycamore Tree Programme (Prison Fellowship, 2008) and some types of cognitive-behavioural therapy (Landenberger & Lipsey, 2005).
- One-way communication from offenders to their own victims, such as sending letters of apology.
- 'Indirect mediation': two-way communication between offenders and their own victims, conveyed by a 'shuttle' mediator who delivers messages face to face.
- 'Direct mediation': two-way mediation between an offender and a victim, face to face, with a mediator present, possibly supervised by a court or prosecutor, focused on a direct payment of cash or in-kind services by offenders to victims, OR
- 'Restorative Justice Conferencing' (RJC): a face-to-face meeting inviting all persons directly affected by a crime, including one or more offenders who participated in the crime and one or more of the personal victims of the crime, with respective friends or family, hosted by a trained RJC facilitator, focused on offender understanding of the harm that was caused and how it might be repaired across all parties affected by it.

To one side of this continuum we might place the 'family group conference' (FGC): an event, focused on offenders, that victims may attend but sometimes don't (as in New Zealand). The FGC is made up of the young person, his or her youth advocate if one has been arranged, members of the family and whoever they invite, the victim and supporters (or representative of the victim), the police, the youth justice coordinator and sometimes a social worker.

RJC methods are described here in greater detail, given their prevalence in the research literature. Virtually all of the facilitators who led the conferences evaluated in controlled trials have been trained in the same method, often by the same trainers. Two Australian RJ pioneers from New South Wales, Terry O'Connell and John McDonald, developed a conferencing model based in part on traditional Maori practice in New Zealand. One or both of them trained police in Canberra, Indianapolis, London and Northumbria, as well as probation, prison and civilian mediation staff in Thames Valley. They also trained others who became trainers, and who provide training services widely in the UK and abroad. The main elements of the RJC this training calls for are as follows:

- Facilitators should prepare for the conference by one-on-one discussions with as many participants as possible.
- Facilitators should ask questions but not express personal views.
- They should try to engage all persons present in saying something.
- A conference must be held in a closed room with no distractions.
- All participants must be mutually entrained, with one person speaking at a time.
- The structure of the conference should focus on three questions that all present are invited to answer:
  1. What happened?
  2. Who was affected by it and how?
  3. What should be done to try to repair the harm?
- Facilitators can conclude the conference by summarising what was said and preparing a written agreement that may be signed by the offender, and perhaps others present.
- Someone should follow up, over months and years, to ensure that agreements are kept.
- Any use of the outcome agreements in court or for other official purposes should be clarified and accepted by all parties in advance.

Both RJC and other methods vary widely in the extent and kind of any agreement offenders make with the professional involved to try to repair the harm to victims, rehabilitate themselves, or prevent any recurrence. The extent to which these agreements are binding on offenders and subject to penalties for non-completion depends, in turn, on the stage of the criminal justice process in which the RJ occurs.

Stages of criminal process

RJ processes can, in principle, be inserted almost anywhere in the criminal process. In practice, RJC has had the broadest application. Randomised controlled trials on RJC have now been completed both with diversion from prosecution and as a supplement to criminal prosecution and sanctions, as follows:

- An added kind of diversion for offenders under 18 (Northumbria final warnings and Indianapolis).
- A diversion from prosecution in court for both adults and juveniles (Canberra).

- At adjournment for pre-sentence reports in both magistrates' courts (Northumbria) and crown courts (London) in the UK, with results sometimes taken as mitigation in sentencing.
- After sentencing to probation as a means of deciding the treatment plan, sometimes by court order (Thames Valley).
- After sentencing to prison, in anticipation of resettlement on release (Thames Valley).

Other institutions

In addition to governmental criminal justice, RJ and especially RJC have been used increasingly in schools, businesses, medicine, community organisations, and religious courts.

Schools

RJ and RJC are used in primary and secondary schools to deal with matters that might or might not be considered criminal or delinquent, in ways that deflect the cases entirely from the criminal or youth justice process. Fights, bullying, sexual harassment and many other matters have been dealt with in this fashion. Even matters arising from injuries that students cause to teachers or other staff have been dealt with in this way. Unfortunately, no rigorous evaluations or controlled trials are available on the use of RJ in such settings.

Businesses

Conflicts among employees arise in businesses, just as in schools, on matters including race, gender, harassment, religion and bullying. Facilitators trained in RJ methods have been retained to deal with these matters, if only as an attempt to prevent costly civil litigation.

Medicine

Just as some crimes are negligent rather than intentional (as in reckless driving or accidental death), medical injuries give rise to a great sense of injustice and anger. Medical institutions are increasingly attempting to use apologies and restorative practices to resolve these matters in a way that achieves reconciliation of staff with patients and their families.

Community organisations

Conflicts arising in communities over land use, parking, noise, pets, gardens and other matters can sometimes break into violence. Preventive RJ responses to these situations have been used by community organisers, sometimes in conjunction with police.

Religious courts

There is evidence that both Jewish and Muslim (Sharia) religious courts in the UK, as abroad, have been using restorative practices to resolve a wide range of crimes and lesser matters. Rather than bringing these matters to the police or Crown Prosecutors, the victims have chosen to use an authority system in which they or their offenders may have more trust or confidence. Whatever the complex legality of using these arrangements, it is a contemporary example of RJ that provides some victims with access not presently provided by criminal justice.

3. Theories of Change for Victims and Offenders

Placing these methods into theories of change is essential for understanding RJ and interpreting the evidence about it. Many people have been sceptical about a single encounter of several hours having any impact on people's lives, let alone affecting their future offending behaviour. Yet the hypothesis that RJ alone, quite apart from other treatments, can change behaviour is consistent with theories of trauma, reintegration, and interaction ritual.

PTSD for victims and offenders

The best-known effect of an event of short duration is post-traumatic stress disorder (PTSD). In the space of a few seconds, let alone hours, witnessing a traumatic incident can change (and shorten) people's lives. A roadside bomb in Iraq, a jungle firefight in Vietnam, a fire in one's home at night, a suicide bomber in a restaurant – these and other events can happen in an instant, but then inflict lifelong damage to physical as well as mental health (Kubzansky et al., 2007). Charles Dickens' death on 9 June 1870 occurred on the fifth anniversary of the horrifying Staplehurst train crash that he survived – a fact that is often interpreted as more than coincidence, given the sharp decline in his output after suffering the crash at age 53.

The PTSD theory of an RJC turns the brevity of harm on its head. For a victim, it hypothesises that an intensive reversal of the power the offender exercised over the victim during the crime can lead to a sudden amelioration of post-traumatic stress symptoms (PTSS). This theory is not unlike the basis for what Edna Foa and her colleagues have developed as a behaviourist treatment for PTSD suffered by rape victims and others. This treatment, called Prolonged Exposure (PE) Therapy, requires the crime victim to relive the crime experience repeatedly as described in her own voice – often by listening to an audio tape of the client telling the story of the crime. By doing this in safe places without the crime happening again, the client can associate the story of the crime with a feeling and reality of safety as the story is repeated. After 12 to 18 weeks of doing this alone and with a therapist, the evidence suggests substantial drops in PTSS and a high rate of PTSD cure (Rothbaum & Foa, 1999).

By extension, through a far more intensive experience, it can be theorised that an RJC in which the offender apologises will enable the victim to relive the crime in a way that makes the memory 'safe'. And if the victim is able to accept an offender's apology by forgiving the offender, victims may be freed from the burden of vengeful feelings for the rest of their lives (Arendt, 1958).

For an offender, the trauma may lie not in the crime, but in the RJC. One offender who experienced an RJC after a self-reported 5000 crimes describes his reaction in much the same way as PTSD: racing thoughts, nightmares, anxiety and flight reactions. Woolf (2008) reports that he had never been as emotionally distressed by committing a crime, let alone going to prison, as he had been by spending three hours with two of his burglary victims in an RJC. When offenders can no longer deflect the evil of their crimes by techniques of neutralisation (Sykes & Matza, 1957), they may find the 120 to 180 minutes of direct accountability for the harm they cause to be far more painful psychologically than any other experience of criminal sanctions.

Reintegrating offenders

A less punitive theory of offender reform is Braithwaite's (1989) theory of reintegrative shaming, by which social groups can condemn the sin but support the sinner. Using a family model of social control, Braithwaite predicts that RJC experiences will produce more reintegrative shame than formal justice, while the latter will produce more stigmatic shaming and exclusionary messages than RJC. Evidence from our Canberra experiments

suggests that RJC actually produces more of both kinds of shame than prosecution in court (Ahmed *et al.*, 2001). But the evidence of reintegration may be sufficient to confirm the central theoretical premise: that when offenders are invited to rejoin society as fully accepted members once they repair the harm they have caused, it may provide a way to help them stop offending.

Interaction ritual for all participants

Collins (2004) provides a further theory of change for offenders and victims: interaction ritual. This theory predicts that people will become more committed to shared values by experiencing emotionally intense rituals of mutual entrainment, excluding all others from the interaction space who have no moral connection to the ritual. Examples include religious ceremonies, graduations, funerals, weddings and RJC – which Collins explicitly cites as a plausible basis for changing behaviour. The criminal career theory of an offender's 'epiphany' that he should stop committing crime (Sherman, 2003) is consistent with Collins' view that the ritual of an RJC may help to manufacture such an epiphany. Rossner's (2008) analysis of before-and-after differences in rates of offending in Canberra shows that the more often elements of Collins theory were recorded by RJC observers, the greater the decline in the offenders' rate of offending.

Other theoretical perspectives have been suggested for why RJ or RJC might change offender behaviour. What all of them share is the perspective that an RJ experience can be well or badly done. That aspect of the change theories raises the critical importance of delivering the RJ programme, especially an RJC, in a manner consistent with both training and the theories of change.

4. Delivering RJ Conferencing

There are many critical questions in the art and logistics of delivering RJC. Few of them can be answered by science, but the following discussion draws on the best evidence available – including our own experience with over 3000 cases randomly assigned to RJC or control.

Who does RJ best? Police versus others

The question of what kind of person and what kind of professional background is best suited for the actual delivery of RJC has been a controversial one. Debates focus on police versus other service professionals.

Empirical evidence is limited by the few opportunities to compare police delivery to other providers. Yet there has been no shortage of opinion. One opinion, derived in part from observing RJC in several countries, is that police facilitators may be inherently predisposed to be 'on the victim's side' and not impartial, that they will automatically back up their police colleagues' interpretation of the offender's culpability, that offenders will not be inclined to voice complaints about their treatment by arresting police to a police facilitator and that state officials will not be adequately held accountable (Roche, 2003).

These normative criticisms of police delivery are not, however, supported by the empirical evidence available. When we asked juvenile offenders in our RISE experiments in Australia about their experience of that police-run programme they consistently said they rated procedural justice indicators in conferences significantly higher than that experienced in court (www. aic.gov.au/criminal_justice_system/rjustice/rise.aspx). This is despite the fact that juveniles were said to have very bad relations with police in Canberra. They also rated police fairness in their case far higher if they received RJC than if they had not. Nevertheless, it is important to be aware of contraindications of police involvement: for example, the poor response of Aboriginal youth to RJC in Canberra (Sherman & Strang, 2007) may be attributable to historically bad relations between police and Aboriginal communities throughout Australia (Blagg, 1997).

We do not have good evidence either about the advantages and disadvantages of other professional backgrounds for facilitators. Social workers, welfare workers, community organisers and volunteers have all been involved in programme delivery but there is little research available on their effectiveness. It is likely that every kind of background brings its own strengths and weaknesses and that it remains primarily an issue to be resolved by careful attention to training and to supervision.

In our RCTs of RJC in the UK, five of our seven independently evaluated tests had police-run programmes in which the facilitators were sworn police officers. In the two other tests, where the cases involved offenders sentenced either to terms of imprisonment or to community supervision, the facilitators were probation officers, prison officers and community mediators. Across the seven tests there was higher take-up by victims and offenders and faster conclusion of the RJ process in the police-run programmes. However, these

differences may have been a consequence of the different character of post-sentence RJ and of the greater seriousness of the offences. All our facilitators of all Professional backgrounds underwent the same week-long intensive training and all were monitored to ensure they conducted their conferences as they had been trained to do. This was more problematic initially for the mediators whose professional training had been at odds with what was required for conferencing, but they were able to change their style to conform to what was needed under a different theory of practice.

As of this writing, we see no reason to exclude any trained facilitator using the same methods as those which have been found effective in RCTs. There is no clear evidence that background makes a difference. Indeed, an RCT comparing different kinds of professionals would be needed to resolve the debate.

Access, referral, recruitment and consent

Access to suitable cases for RJ, absent a satisfactory routine referral arrangement from criminal justice agencies, remains a crucial operational issue in RJ. The dominant justice paradigm assumes a seamless track from police to prosecution to court, with few opportunities for the consideration of alternative or additional stages of the kind RJC represents. Shapland *et al.* (2004) describes the operational difficulties encountered by the Home Office-funded schemes she evaluated, as they began the process of identifying cases eligible for RJ. In addition, all programmes that did not have police facilitators immediately faced problems from the Data Protection Act in obtaining victim contact details, so police inevitably became involved in the process of identifying and approaching victims.

Operational experience with programmes run on restorative justice principles by the youth offending teams provided lessons about how victims could best be approached for RJ. Miers *et al.* (2001) and Newburn *et al.* (2001) revealed the extremely low levels of victim involvement resulting from lack of attention to prioritising their needs. They also showed that merely writing to victims informing them of the opportunity to meet their offender met with extremely low take-up rates. Our UK RCT's team learned from this and developed a protocol for participant recruitment that proved very successful.

When an ostensibly eligible case was identified by our team, the first step was to make contact with offenders to determine whether they accepted full responsibility for the offence and whether they were willing to meet their victim. This was always a face-to-face meeting, almost always arranged by the facilitator who would conduct the conference (early experimenting with different staff interviewing victims and offenders and passing information on to the conference facilitator was soon abandoned as unfeasible).

For pre-sentence cases, offenders needed to have pleaded guilty in court to the offence (or to have made full admissions in the case of the youth Final Warning studies). For post-sentence cases, ostensibly eligible offenders were asked whether they accepted responsibility for the offence; if they did so, they were accepted into the programme regardless of whether they had pleaded guilty or not guilty in their court case. Those who were serving prison terms were seen in the prison while those serving community sentences were visited at home. Take-up rates by prisoners were high – in the region of 80 per cent – but much lower for offenders in community supervision cases (Shapland *et al.*, 2006).

When offenders had been assessed as eligible and had agreed to participate, facilitators then approached their victims. Initial contact was through a brief letter followed by a phone call asking for a suitable time for a face-to-face visit.

RJ is essentially a voluntary process. Thus consent by all parties is an essential prerequisite to the deliberative dialogue that is key to the process. In our community supervision RCT, judges sentenced eligible offenders to a process of RJ assessment, which at first glance appeared to be a coercive process; however, the purpose of this order was to allow probation staff to discuss RJ with these offenders, to determine whether they admitted their responsibility for the offence and to ask whether they were willing to meet their victim. If they denied responsibility or were unwilling to meet, RJ did not proceed.

Preparation and delivery – in and out of prison

Careful attention to the preparation of both offenders and victims for the RJ process is absolutely essential. At face-to-face meetings in advance of the RJC, sometimes where the offence is serious and emotions raw, the facilitator needs to describe the RJC process in detail. Since the process is not widely known, it is essential that facilitators take the time to answer all questions frankly if consent is to be truly informed. The roles and responsibilities of all participants must be communicated in straightforward language. The desirability of bringing along to the conference family members or friends as supporters needs to be especially emphasised. Indeed, facilitators should talk to the victim's family and friends as well, given that they can often only envisage the risks associated with such an encounter for their loved one unless they too hear directly from RJC facilitators just what is being proposed.

We found that victims were often more reluctant than offenders to consent to an RJC, saying that they still felt too anxious or frightened. Often, victims said that they did not trust themselves to be in the same room with the offender when they still felt so angry. Facilitators responded that the meeting would give them a chance to explain the full consequences of the crime, that they could tell the offender what they thought of him or her, that they could ask questions about the crime that only the offender could answer – why they had been chosen as the victim, whether there was anything they could have done to avoid the crime – and that they could seek appropriate restitution.

Some special preparations are needed for victims whose offenders are in prison, whether on remand awaiting sentence or serving their sentences. Prison procedures need to be explained in detail – where to go upon arrival at the prison, what the security and search arrangements are, who will accompany them to the room set aside for the conference. There must be no surprises for victims, who often are pleased with the opportunity to see the circumstances in which their offender lives.

Aftermath and follow-up

RJ conferences can be emotionally bruising encounters for all participants. Although there have been no reports of actual violence at such meetings anywhere in the world, RJC is sometimes characterised by shouting, tears and powerful feelings. It is the responsibility of the facilitator to allow this level of emotional expression but to ensure that safety is paramount. They should also make sure that by the time the conference finishes all parties have said all they wanted to say. Our conferences were followed by an invitation to all participants to have refreshments together – our facilitators arrived at each prison conference with a suitcase of tea, coffee and biscuits. These often proved to be an extraordinary opportunity for participants to discover what they had in common – worries about their children, shared sporting interests and so on.

A conference can be a cathartic experience for everyone in the room, and participants may leave in a highly emotional state. We were especially conscious of this in the case of imprisoned offenders returning to their cells with little in the way of emotional support available to them. Prison authorities recognised the special vulnerability of these participants and ensured that they were not alone immediately after the conference and that the prison chaplain or Samaritan members were available for them to talk to. The research team also worked to follow up on victims as well as offenders, contacting them within a few days of the conference to ensure that they had not suffered any ill effects from the encounter.

There are also practical issues to follow up after the conference in relation to outcomes agreed between the parties. Despite victims being made well aware of the appropriateness of seeking restitution from the offender, these agreements usually focus instead on strategies that would reduce the likelihood of reoffending by the offender – drug and alcohol programmes, literacy and other skills training, letters of apology, reconnection with families and the like. These undertakings often require follow-up action by facilitators who can liaise with prison and other agencies to connect offenders with programmes that meet their needs. Victims often express their desire to be kept informed of their offender's progress and arrangements need to be made to ensure they are told whether they completed what they agreed to do.

5. Research on Restorative Justice: The Gold Standard

As in any psychological or medical treatment, the key question is whether high-integrity delivery of the treatment can yield a cost-effective benefit with minimal side effects. Answering that question in forensic settings requires a clear understanding of both the science and the ethics of randomised controlled trials (RCTs). It also requires a clear conception of the outcome measures that will determine whether resources will be provided for widening access to RJC.

The science of randomised trials

The purpose of an RCT is to provide an unbiased estimate of the *average* effects of a treatment, as measured by the difference in outcomes between a treatment group and a comparison group (Cook & Campbell,

1979). An RCT does this by holding constant, or controlling, the percentages of risk factors for any outcome in two different groups. Over large and relatively homogeneous samples, those percentages should be roughly equal, leaving the groups almost identical except for the difference in treatment condition.

RCTs focus on average, rather than individual, effects simply because humans vary in their response to medical treatment, criminal sanctions and psychological treatment. Such variability is the primary reason that random assignment of large samples of cases is necessary in the inexact sciences, from agriculture to psychology to medicine, in contrast to more exact sciences such as physics. Some treatments are found effective (on average) in RCTs even though 75 or 80 per cent of persons treated experience no change in their condition. The purpose of an RCT is therefore not to find out what works for everyone with a given problem, but what works for groups of relatively similar individuals.

The purpose of treatment, however, is to provide the most effective means of helping any one individual. This may seem to create a clash between the product of RCTs and the needs of clients, but it does not. RCTs still offer the best means of finding what works for individuals through a continuous process of identifying non-responsive subgroups within samples in which the average effect of treatment is successful (Doll, 1992). For each non-responsive (or negatively responding) subgroup identified within successful average outcomes, a separate RCT can be devised comparing the success-on-average treatment to some new alternative. At minimum, subgroup analysis can help to identify the groups for whom a treatment does not work, as long as sample sizes are large enough.

For these and other reasons, the science of RJC effects can be greatly enhanced by continuing to add RCTs to the evidence base. Since governments may be reluctant to fund further research once an adequate evidence base exists about average effects, it is important for better science – and treatment – that small-scale RCTs continue to be designed, conducted and reported, especially on subgroups with which RJC has yet to be separately tested. Forensic psychologists may be in an ideal position to do this in prison and probation settings, even though it could take several years to accumulate a sample of even 100 cases from the psychologist's own caseload. Yet for psychologists to undertake such RCTs, they will need to satisfy their colleagues, their supervisors and themselves that such RCTs would be ethical.

The ethics of randomised trials

The ethics of RCTs in general depend upon a state of 'equipoise' (Federal Judicial Center, 1981), in which it is equally likely that a given treatment will help or harm an individual. This condition may seem difficult to satisfy once a substantial body of RCT evidence has been accumulated. Even with such evidence in hand, however, there are two further ethical imperatives that may justify further RCTs. One is the identification of a non-responsive or negatively responding subgroup. The other is the need to ration a scarce treatment within a large population that might benefit from it, on the basis of finding those for whom the greatest benefit may be found for the entire society – e.g. future crime victims as well as the offender who is provided with a treatment.

Subgroups of offenders for whom RJC is ineffective or harmful have already been identified within certain samples (see Section 6 below). Even when such subgroups have not been identified, however, there is arguably a state of equipoise for any particular group that has not been directly tested apart from a larger group. With uncertain external validity about the results of a test on men, for example, when applied to women offenders, there is a strong case to be made that separate RCTs should be conducted for women only (since most offenders in RCT samples have been males).

Subgroups of offence types may also have equipoise. Homicide offenders about to be released from prison, for example, have never been tested for RJ, since they were excluded from the Home Office-funded RCTs in the UK. Substantial numbers of homicide offenders leave prison each year, and many may be willing to meet with the surviving family of their victims. If the survivors themselves would consent, there could be substantial benefits – or risks – for both victims and offenders to participate.

Many people find it more ethical to provide treatments without testing than to use random assignment to decide who receives treatment. The Federal Judicial Center (1981) concludes the opposite is true, on two grounds. One is that random assignment eliminates conscious or unconscious biases in selecting some but not all for treatment. The second, more important basis is that it is more unethical to provide an untested treatment (that could cause harm) than to conduct an RCT (where all have an equal chance of being harmed). The common assumption that all treatment is helpful cannot be supported by evidence, especially given the criminogenic effects of RJC on Australian Aboriginals (Sherman

et al., 2006). Only an RCT can disturb the state of equipoise, and many cases that forensic psychologists face daily may not fit into a previous RCT. Hence it may be more ethical to set up even a small RCT than to offer RJ 'off-the-shelf' without a firm evidence base for believing it would be safe and effective to do so.

Outcome measures, costs and benefits

RCTs provide a variety of outcome measures which may not always lead to the same conclusion about the same sample. In RJC tests, for example, the UK results show statistically significant results (in a meta-analysis combining all RCTs) for the *frequency* of reconvictions over a two-year follow-up period (Shapland *et al.*, 2008, and Figure 26.1 below). They do not, however, show significant differences for the *prevalence* of the reconvictions between the RJC and control groups. That is, RJC in these RCTs causes significantly fewer offences, but not significantly fewer offenders. Although both prevalence and frequency of reconvictions are lower for RJC than for controls, the magnitude of the effect is much greater for frequency than for prevalence. However, the reduction in prevalence could have been due to chance, by conventional standards, while the reduction in frequency was highly unlikely (1 in 100 odds) to have been due to chance.

Given such a difference, how should outcome measures be interpreted? One answer is to focus on cost. In criminal justice as in medicine, governments must be concerned about cost-effectiveness. Even effective medicines are excluded from the National Health Service, for example, if they exceed a cost–benefit ratio of £30,000 per added year of quality life. Thus if a treatment can pay for itself in relation to a certain cost standard, it may be eligible for widespread implementation.

Applying the cost–benefit principle to crime, it will generally be preferable to focus on the frequency of offending across an entire group rather than on the likelihood of a single individual desisting from crime. That is because the total cost of more crimes is generally greater than the total cost of fewer crimes, unless the crimes in question vary substantially in cost (such as a few murders in one group and many shop-thefts in another). The Home Office has made such calculations easier by compiling empirical estimates of the average costs of different kinds of crime, which were in fact used by Shapland and her colleagues.

Thus what can be said about RJCs in the largest UK research programme on this treatment is that RJC is effective when judged by the two measures explicitly addressing cost: frequency and cost per crime. It is not effective on the basis of complete desistance from crime, nor on a 10-point ordinal scale of crime severity. For the latter, medical costs and length of prison sentences arguably provide a far more sensitive indicator than a truncated ordinal scale. Conclusions could certainly differ by which criteria one chooses to emphasise and for what reason. Yet if a forensic psychological treatment is to be evaluated from the standpoint of benefit to society, then the cost-focused criteria would seem to be more appropriate.

Once a decision is made to focus on cost, it is important to remember that the UK measurement standards are legalistic and extremely conservative. The convention that only a conviction, and not an arrest or a self-report, can constitute evidence of a crime for *research* purposes creates a bias against detecting treatments as effective. This is especially true for cost measures, where small differences in convictions can indicate large differences in actual offending. In a lifetime self-reported offending study of 411 males born in London in the 1950s, Farrington et al. (2006, p.39) have reported an average of 39 undetected offences for every conviction recorded. The results presented below apply that ratio to differences in convictions in order to estimate the N of undetected crimes prevented per year per RJ conference assigned, at least within the window of the follow-up by Shapland et al. (2008).[2]

6. Effects of RJ Conferencing on Offenders

RJC has many kinds of effects on offenders. We limit the following discussion to RJC effects on future offending behaviour, as indicated by reconvictions or other official records covering 100 per cent of randomly assigned cases in an 'intention-to-treat' analysis (Piantadosi, 1997).

6.a. Overall effects on crime

Using the criterion of frequency of reconviction in two years after the random assignment across the population of eligible RCTs, RJC reduces the frequency of reconvictions across 12 tests overall (forest plot p = .04), with 10 out of all 12 tests reducing reconvictions, including 7 out of all 7 tests in the UK, and 9 out of all 10 tests worldwide with crimes involving personal victims. In the 7 RCTs of RJ conferencing in the UK (Shapland et al., 2008: 27), the overall effect was 27 per cent fewer reconvictions in RJC-assigned cases than in control-assigned

cases, or 209 fewer convictions per year at risk across 374 offenders assigned to RJC. These results, depicted in Figure 2.6 of Shapland et al. (2008) and reproduced here as our Figure 26.1, are statistically significant at the 0.013 level across all 7 tests combined, although not within individual tests.[3]

Using Farrington's undetected offending estimate, RJC may have prevented 8168 crimes among 374 RJC-assigned offenders per year, or an average of 22 offences per year per RJ conference. These results vary in magnitude across the seven reconviction results that Shapland et al. (2008) report, from 5 to almost 50 crimes prevented per RJ conference, depending largely on the base rates of the offenders in the control group as well as the effect size.

Even without the estimated multiplier for undetected offences, the cost–benefit ratio of the investment in RJC is substantial, at an average of 9 pounds of crime costs prevented to 1 pound invested in RJC (Shapland et al., 2008). These results were driven heavily by the sample of persistent London burglars, who comprised a large part of the overall cost – benefit sample (23 per cent of RJC cases) and whose crimes were quite costly – but for whom the return on investment was 14 to 1. None of the 7 RCTs Shapland et al. analysed using Home Office crime cost values showed a negative ratio; all of them did better than paying for themselves in terms of cost of crime to the victim and the criminal justice system combined (separate estimates not available).

6.b. Differences by offence types

While the number of RCTs worldwide is small in relation to the possible subdivisions by offence type, some preliminary insight can be gained from the 12 results to date (which took 15 years to produce). One is that the ten crimes with personal victims did consistently better than the two with only collective victims, despite a large decrease in reconvictions of shoplifters in Canberra. A corresponding *increase* was found in Canberra in convictions for offenders assigned to RJC by diversion from prosecution for driving while intoxicated. This leaves the net effect of collective-victim cases at zero.

More striking is the difference between violent and property crime cases. Taken together in separate meta-analyses (forest plots of standardised mean differences), the five RCTs of violent crime show a statistically significant reduction in reconviction frequency. The RCTs for property crime do not. In the violent crime

RCT	Odds ratio	Lower limit	Upper limit	p-value	Odds ratio and 95% CI
London street crime	0.925	0.433	1.975	0.841	
London burglary	0.825	0.475	1.431	0.493	
Northumbria final warning	0.610	0.372	1.002	0.051	
Northumbria court property	0.694	0.283	1.704	0.425	
Northumbria court assault	0.545	0.185	1.607	0.271	
Thames Valley prison	0.770	0.368	1.612	0.488	
Thames Valley community	0.638	0.261	1.560	0.325	
Fixed	0.715	0.549	0.932	0.013	

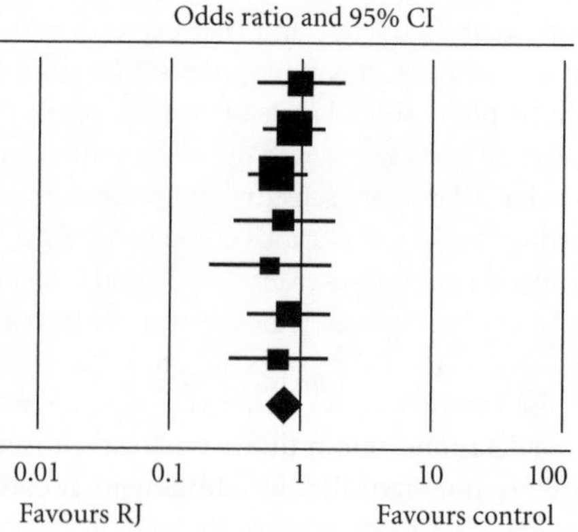

```
        0.01    0.1       1      10     100
        Favours RJ          Favours control
```

Figure 26.1　Odds ratio for the frequency of reconviction within the two years of the RJ period for JRC trials. *Source*: Shapland *et al.* (2008:27).

RCTs, five out of five tests show fewer convictions for RJC than for controls. In the property crime RCTs, one of the four RCTs shows an increase in crime: the Canberra property crime experiment, in which a substantial portion of the offenders were either Aboriginal offenders or chronic offenders or both (see Section 6.c). In both UK property crime RCTs, RJC reduced the frequency of reconvictions. Nonetheless, the evidence to date suggests that RJC works better for violent crime than for property crime, even though in most cases it works for both.

6.c. Differences by offender characteristics

The highly moral and emotional content of the RJC treatment requires a vigilant examination of possible adverse reactions. So far only one clear adverse effect has emerged by offender characteristics, but some evidence of others has also emerged.

Aboriginals

In a separate analysis, the Aboriginal offenders randomly assigned to RJC had such a large increase in arrest frequency compared to controls that we could only conclude that the idea of attending an RJC, as well as doing it, was in combination highly criminogenic. This was not observed, however, for the white offenders. Adding the handful of Aboriginals in the violent crime RCT to a comparison of white and Aboriginal offenders in the two RCTs shows the same interaction of race and treatment, suggesting that the issue is race and not offence type (Sherman & Strang, 2007).

Females

There is also some evidence that RJC works better for females under 18 than for males the same age, at least in violent crimes. Using the criterion of arrest frequency in Northumbria, Sherman and Strang (2007) found this effect in the first year after random assignment. Insufficient numbers of female offenders have been examined for tests using the lower base rates of reconvictions, so it is unclear how general any gender differences in RJC effects may be.

Crime victims as offenders

Measured by arrest differences between RJC-assigned cases and controls, there is preliminary evidence that offenders with previous crime victimisations have an adverse reaction to RJC. Bennett (2008, p.252) reports that London robbery offenders with no previous injury from victimisations against them showed twice as much time to first arrest if they had been assigned to RJC as controls, but the reverse was true for offenders who had been previously injured. It is not clear why this is true, but the difference is statistically significant and the number of crime-free days at stake is large. Among robbery offenders with no previous injury from victimisation, RJC had a statistically significant improvement in crime-free days over the control group: 470 days versus 197. But for robbery offenders with previous injury, the direction (though non-significant) was reversed.

Heroin and cocaine addicts

Bennett (2008, p.212) also found interaction effects between RJC and drug use. Offenders in the London robbery experiment using both heroin and crack cocaine had mean survival to first arrest of 242 days in the RJC group compared to 340 for controls. For those who may have used drugs but not *both* heroin and cocaine, the result was reversed: 447 days mean survival to first arrest for RJC, compared to 355 for controls. Thus RJ may be contraindicated for robbery convicts who use both cocaine and heroin.

6.d. Diversion versus supplementation

A very small sample of four diversion-from-prosecution experiments and eight RJC in-addition-to-prosecution experiments shows, on average, that RJC had no effect when used as diversion, with consistently clear effects when used as supplementation. This finding should be treated with great caution, due to the possibly spurious nature of the finding: it is equally well explained by the difference between a part-time facilitator model in the Australian Federal Police versus a full-time facilitator model in UK police, combined with professional mediators in the prison and probation RCTs in the UK, and a generally more tightly administered process of delivery in the UK than in Canberra.

6.e. Offences brought to justice

One of the most striking benefits of diversion of cases from prosecution, quite apart from reconviction, is the consistently higher rate of offences brought to justice with RJ than without. Sherman and Strang (2007) report that whenever cases are diverted to RJ, whether mediation or RJC, they are more likely to result in offenders being held accountable for their crimes than in the control condition of random assignment to prosecution as normal.

7. Effects of RJ Conferencing on Victims

The effects of RJC on victims are more consistent than for offenders, with larger effect sizes and possibly longer-lasting benefits. Nonetheless, it has proven difficult to attract resources to widen access to RJC based solely on victim benefits. Only the recent evidence on reduced rates of reconvictions seems likely to attract public attention, despite the strong victim preferences for RJC over conventional criminal justice alone.

The evidence base on victim effects comes from two sources. One is the interviews done with victims after

the 7 RCTs in the UK reported by Shapland et al. (2007) as annotated below, as well as by Strang (2002) with the victims of property and violent crime in Canberra and McGarrell et al. (2000) with Indianapolis victims of youth crime. These analyses compare RJC and control groups. In addition, Strang et al. (2006) look at before-and-after differences within the RJC group, as they recall how they felt before the conference compared to how they felt after it was over. The latter evidence is less reliable for causal inference than for exploratory analysis of how RJ works, consistent with the theories of change presented in Section 3 above.

Victim effects are clearly limited in external validity to the kinds of victims who consented to participate, and then by the use of an intention-to-treat model. Victims who do not want RJC exclude themselves, thus creating a selection bias. Victims who drop out after beginning the process may be less satisfied than those who complete it, introducing a further selection bias. The present analysis draws entirely on intention-to-treat studies of consenting victims, thereby excluding one (but not both) forms of bias.

The consent bias is actually quite useful in generalising findings to the kinds of victims who are in fact willing to undertake RJC. The problem with generalising from non-RCT evidence is that programmes vary in the level of effort they put into recruiting cases (see Section 4 above). Where victims have been more diligently recruited (such as by letting them select the date and time of an RJC), the findings may have stronger external validity. That is the case with most of the RCTs summarised below. The two main effects measured across all of them are satisfaction with justice and desire for violent revenge. A third measure may be even more important: reduction of medically significant post-traumatic stress symptoms.

Satisfaction with justice

Victims are consistently more satisfied with RJC than with conventional justice. Strang's (2002) high interview response rate (approximately 90 per cent) with an intention-to-treat design provided the first clear test. When victims were asked whether they were satisfied with the way their case was dealt with by the justice system, there was a statistically significant difference between the court-assigned and the conference-assigned victims (46 vs. 60 per cent). Significantly more of those who actually *experienced* an RJ conference were satisfied, compared with those who cases were dealt with in court (70 vs. 42 per cent, $p < .001$). There was no difference here between property and violence victims in this regard.

Offender apologies appear to play an important role in bringing about emotional restoration of victims. For those Canberra victims assigned to a conference, 72 per cent said their offender had apologised (and 86 per cent of those who actually experienced a conference) compared with 19 per cent of those assigned to court. Furthermore, more conference-assigned victims than court-assigned victims said they felt the apologies they received were sincere (77 vs. 41 per cent).

Strang (2002) also found statistically significant improvements for victims between before-conference and after-conference feelings on all the following dimensions: fear of the offender (especially for violence victims); likelihood of revictimisation; sense of security; anger towards the offender; sympathy for the offender and the offender's supporters; feelings of trust in others; feelings of self-confidence; and anxiety.

The Indianapolis Juvenile Restorative Justice Experiment (McGarrell et al., 2000) was modelled on the Canberra RCTs and produced similar results for crime victims. This study of young (7–14 years) first-time property and minor assault offenders and their victims also found markedly higher levels of satisfaction among victims whose cases were randomly assigned to a conference rather than an array of other court diversions. Furthermore, 97 per cent said they felt involved with the way their case was dealt with, compared with 38 per cent of victims in the control group, and 95 per cent felt they had been able to express their views, compared with 56 per cent of the control group.

Our eight trials of RJC in London, Northumbria and Thames Valley contain a number of measures on victims' experience of RJ derived from interviews from over 200 of the approximately 450 victims involved in RJ in the eight trials during the Sheffield evaluation period (Shapland et al., 2007). Overall they found that about 85 per cent of victims (and 80 per cent of offenders) were satisfied with their experience. In particular, only 12 per cent of victims (and 10 per cent of offenders) expressed any doubt about the outcome agreement reached at the end of the conference and almost all thought it was fair. Looking at various dimensions of satisfaction, the evaluation found that more than 70 per cent of victims in all eight experiments said they found the conference useful and fair and that it had given them a sense of closure about the offence.

Revenge

One additional way RJC may prevent crime is by reducing victim desire for violent revenge against their offenders. In a meta-analysis of eight effect sizes across four RCTs (split by victim gender) in London and Canberra, Sherman et al. (2005) found a statistically significant pattern of moderately large reductions in victim desire for revenge.

Post-traumatic stress

Given the increased risk of coronary heart disease and mortality from low-level but chronic post-traumatic stress symptoms (Kubzansky et al., 2007), it is very important to note that crime victims treated with RJC experience lower levels of PTSS than controls in early and longer-term follow-ups (Angel, 2005). Based on telephone interviews by a psychiatric nurse using the Impact of Events (Revised) scale, the findings on PTSS show about a 40 per cent reduction in the scale values. Unpublished analysis (Angel, personal communication) shows that this is of major benefit to female victims, with much smaller effect sizes for men. All of this evidence is drawn from the two RCTs we completed in the London crown courts, with robbery and burglary.

8. Evidence on Other RJ Options

In general, there is far less evidence on the effects of other RJ options, and what evidence we have suggests that RJC is a substantially more effective treatment. The only options with substantial quasi-experimental evidence in the UK are the direct and indirect mediation projects provided by REMEDI and CONNECT that were evaluated by Shapland et al. (2004, 2006, 2007, 2008). Those reports form the evidence base for the following observations assessing the relative benefits of direct and indirect mediation and comparing both of them to RJ conferencing.

Reconviction

Because these programmes did not have a randomised design, the evaluators established a comparison group in which each individual offender in the RJ group was matched on variables that may affect offending, such as the type of offence, offender's age and gender, etc., with individuals who did not experience any kind of mediation. We need to be cautious about findings based on this design, but they do give us some indication of the effects of mediation.

There was no significant difference in the *prevalence*, *frequency* or *severity* of reconviction in the two years post-treatment for any of the direct or indirect mediation programmes in respect of adults or youths, compared with the matched offenders who did not experience mediation (Shapland *et al.*, 2008). However, this was also true of the individual RCTs of our RJC methods, whereas the latter achieved significance across a far larger sample combining seven RCTs. The very small number of cases in each of the mediation categories of offenders meant that the effect of mediation on reconviction would have needed to be very great for a significant difference to be detected. The biggest difference from the RJC effects is in the cost–benefit ratios of the respective programmes. Unlike their conclusion for the RJC methods, the evaluators concluded that neither the direct nor the indirect mediation programmes could be justified on grounds of cost savings associated with reduced reconvictions and did not provide positive value for money.

Victim benefits

Both victims and offenders said they had found mediation useful, though offenders were more enthusiastic than victims. This was especially the case for indirect mediation where victims complained about not receiving enough information from the offender and about the offender's response. Their dissatisfaction seemed to derive from the lack of opportunity to convey views directly or to see how these views had been received by the offender. Furthermore, Shapland *et al.* (2007) concluded that the indirect process makes it difficult to have outcome agreements between the parties because the quantity and quality of interaction needed to achieve a future-orientated agreement cannot practically be achieved by passing information via a third party. Finally, the evaluators state that RJ is more likely to achieve its full potential by direct mediation than indirect mediation, but that RJ conferencing appears to be even more advantageous because the presence of family and friends is particularly important in their role as supporters of each party both during and after the conference.

9. RJ and Forensic Psychology

To the extent that forensic psychologists may choose which treatments to suggest for offenders, there may be good reason to offer – or at least describe – RJC for many kinds of offenders. This is especially true for violent crimes, where the evidence of reduced reconviction is stronger than for any other crime type.

Opportunities for RJC

Opportunities to suggest RJC – if not other, less evidence-based forms of RJ – may arise in a variety of settings where forensic psychiatry and psychology are found. These include:

- prisoners completing custodial sentences prior to resettlement;
- prisoners who commit violent crimes against other inmates;
- prisoners on community sentences deciding treatment plans;
- young offenders in YOIs;
- private correctional firms and charities providing services to NOMS.

In each of these opportunities, there is likely to be far more work and time involved in delivering RJC than in delivering other 'mass-produced' treatments which may lack RCT-derived evidence. Thus there may be greater confidence that delivering RJC is more likely to be cost-effective in each case than in delivering even a far larger number of cases with an untested treatment.

Arguments against RJC

The difficulties of a forensic psychiatrist or psychologist arranging RJC cannot be underestimated. Coordination with police or probation outside of a prison setting may be difficult to arrange. Victims may live in other parts of the country from a prison or probation setting, and travel costs may need to be provided. Supervisors may object to RJC on these or other grounds.

More often, objections to RJC may be made on the basis of safety or 'revictimisation' of the victims. The evidence summarised in this chapter shows that these concerns are generally unfounded. With appropriate preparation for each RJC event, trained facilitators can generally detect any issues of risk and decide not to proceed. If anything, there is a risk of excluding from RJC offenders who are actually good candidates but are not yet remorseful – because they have not yet been treated. Completion of RJC treatment may be exactly what is indicated, even for offenders who may be unrepentant but are at least willing to accept responsibility.

The role of forensic staff

The larger question about RJC concerns the role of forensic staff. It is not clear that such professionals are ideally suited to facilitate RJC. If they would like to, training in RJC methods is widely available in the UK. Yet it may often be better to broker an RJC delivered by other professionals, people whose only work is to deliver RJC. This may leave forensic staff in the position to deliver hundreds or thousands of RJC events, rather than a mere 20 or 30 per year. By explaining, and perhaps evaluating, RJC on the basis of RCT evidence, they could prevent many crimes and help to heal many lives.

Notes

1 This paper is a product of the Australian National University's Regulatory Institutions Network (RegNet) in the Research School of Pacific and Asian Studies, and the Jerry Lee Program of Randomized Trials in Restorative Justice, a collaboration of ANU's RegNet, the University of Pennsylvania, and the Jerry Lee Centre for Experimental Criminology at the University of Cambridge. Points of view or opinions expressed are those of the authors and not of any of the many governmental and private funding agencies that have supported their research.
2 This does not mean that Shapland et al. actually conducted a self-report survey. They did not. But Farrington's estimate is based on very high response rates, and is unbiased about any differential in criminal justice response between groups. The application of the estimate from an earlier generation of offenders to Shapland's evaluation of our RCTs must be made with some caution, but if anything there is evidence that convictions represent even more offending in recent UK cohorts (Soothill et al., 2008).
3 While it is not clear how the odds ratios were calculated, our own forest plot (Strang et al., forthcoming) using Standardised Mean Difference (SMD) as the effect size statistic shows similar conclusions.

Further Reading

Shapland, J., Atkinson, A., Colledge, E., Dignan, J., Howes, M., Johnstone, J. et al. (2004). Implementing restorative justice schemes (Crime Reduction Programme): A report on the first year. Home Office online report 32/04. London: Home Office. Retrieved 15 September 2009 from www.homeoffice. gov.uk/rds/pdfs04/rdsolr3204.pdf

In 2001 the Home Office funded the development and testing of three RJ programmes (or 'schemes') to be funded under its Crime Reduction Programme. This decision resulted from political and policy interest provoked by an RJ project operated by the Thames Valley Police, focusing on juvenile offenders, which had been running for some years, together with the results of Australian research indicating the potential of RJ as a crime reduction tool, especially for violent crime. The funded programmes were to target mainly adults, as most research evidence worldwide at that time concerned the effects of RJ on juvenile crime. Professor Joanna Shapland and her team at the University of Sheffield were chosen as the independent evaluator of the selected programmes.

This report, the first of four prepared by the Shapland team, discusses the scope and content of the three RJ programmes and their early efforts to get established. All three subscribed to the Home Office definition (Marshall, 1997) of RJ as 'a process whereby parties with a stake in a specific offence collectively resolve how to deal with the aftermath of an offence and its implications for the future'. However, there were variations in the way the programmes operated, with two of the three using both mediation (including direct and indirect mediation) and RJ conferencing, as defined in Section 2 above.

The CONNECT programme, run by trained mediators, worked with adults who had been convicted in London magistrates' courts of a wide range of offences involving personal victims. Participants were offered direct mediation, indirect mediation and RJ conferencing, all of which took place after conviction but before sentencing. At the end of the first year of operation 59 cases had been referred to the programme, in 12 of which there had been indirect or direct mediation.

The REMEDI programme, also run by trained mediators, operated in Yorkshire with both adult and youth offenders who admitted a wide range of property and violent offences. It targeted adults and youths given community sentences, youths given Final Warnings by the police and adults in prison. At the end of the first year 832 cases had been referred, of which 107 had completed direct mediation, most of them involving juvenile offenders.

The third programme, directed by the present authors (Sherman and Strang) for the Justice Research Consortium (JRC) of participating agencies and universities, was designed as a series of randomised controlled trials (RCTs) of face-to-face RJ conferencing only, in London, Northumbria and the Thames Valley. In London, Metropolitan police officers trained as full-time RJC facilitators implemented two experiments with eligible adult offenders who had pleaded guilty in the Crown Courts to burglary or robbery but had not yet been sentenced. In Northumbria studies, police trained as full-time RJC facilitators implemented four experiments: two RCTs of adults who had pleaded guilty in magistrates' courts (one for property crimes involving a personal victim and one for assaults), and two RCTs for juveniles who admitted personal or violent crimes with personal victims and who were to be given Reprimands or Final Warnings by the police (the two youth RCTs were analysed by Shapland's team as a single RCT but randomly assigned in separate blocks for violent and non-violent crimes). The two Thames Valley studies, where a mix of probation officers, prison officers and mediators all worked together as part-time but fully trained RJ conference facilitators, took adult offenders convicted of violent crimes who were either serving custodial sentences for these offences or had been given community sentences. At the end of the first year, London had 271 referrals, 73 of which had been given an RJ conference; Northumbria had 287 referrals with 73 conferences; Thames Valley had 374 referrals with 41 conferences. It was only towards the end of this year, after the programme was well established, that random assignment to RJ conferencing and control groups commenced.

The report discusses difficulties encountered by each of the funded programmes in setting up an RJ programme. The need to operate within the dominant criminal justice paradigm and to negotiate a space within a framework of procedures and values of that culture proved challenging for all of them. As a result, all encountered initial difficulties in obtaining adequate numbers of referrals and considerable effort and ingenuity were entailed in maintaining case flow: in the case of prison, self-referral from prisoners proved an important source. In addition, programmes led by agencies other than the police faced difficulties in obtaining victim contact details, owing to the provisions of the Data Protection Act.

Notwithstanding the difficulties of establishing programmes designed to test such a radical idea as RJ in an environment already fully stretched – among other practitioners for whom the concept was alien to their values and procedures – the report judges the first step a success. Within their first year of operation, the three 'schemes' had managed to process a substantial number of cases to completion and demonstrated the feasibility of establishing viable RJ programmes.

Shapland, J. Atkinson, A., Atkinson, H., Colledge, E., Dignan, J., Howes, M. *et al.* (2006) *Restorative justice in practice: The second report from the evaluation of three schemes*. Sheffield: Sheffield Centre for Criminological Research, University of Sheffield.

The second report of the Sheffield evaluation team on the three Home Office-funded RJ programmes focused on the actual RJ meetings conducted by the programmes and the follow-up of outcomes agreed by the victims and offenders in those meetings. It addressed the extent of participation and the content of the meetings.

By the time the Home Office funding ceased in 2004, the London CONNECT programme had completed 50 RJ events: these had been a mixture of indirect mediations ($N = 37$) in which the mediator had 'shuttled' between the victim and the offender, direct mediations ($N = 11$), and two RJ conferences. In the same period, Yorkshire's REMEDI had provided direct mediation in 35 cases and indirect mediation in 97 cases. The JRC had victim and offender consent to all RJC ($N = 723$) cases that reached the point of randomisation (where both offender and victim had agreed to take part in a conference) of which about half ($N = 342$) resulted in an RJ conference.

Where there was a choice of forms of RJ, as was the case in REMEDI and CONNECT, most participants (around 75 per cent) opted not to meet the other party. However, when no option of indirect mediation was offered, which was the case in the JRC studies, participation rates were as high as in the other two schemes. There was considerable variation in the percentage of cases where victims agreed to participate, with significantly higher numbers agreeing in cases with juvenile offenders than adults. In both the juvenile and adult programmes offender take-up was generally high, except for post-sentence community sentence offenders whose motivation appeared to be less than that of offenders at other points in the justice system.

Shapland *et al.* comment that interviews with participants in direct mediation or RJC showed that even though they had been nervous beforehand, they had been well prepared in terms of their roles and expectations of the RJ meeting. Both offenders and victims tended to emphasise altruistic explanations for taking part, with victims indicating that restitution was not a significant reason for doing so.

The JRC conferences were characterised by high levels of perceived procedural justice (Tyler, 1990), with interview results from offenders and victims rating facilitators as non-dominating and impartial. Shapland *et al.* observed a sample of RJCs in which participants contributed more or less equally to the discussion. Participants also rated RJC as safe encounters, despite the high levels of emotion sometimes expressed, with no assaults and almost no threats. Given the total of over 400 RJ conferences completed by JRC without any safety issues, the evidence strongly suggests the safety of victim–offender meetings. While the Sherman–Strang team did abandon two potential conferences on safety grounds, this was in advance of random assignment and part of a more general eligibility screening for participants' willingness to talk rationally about what happened.

In our JRC conferences, Shapland's team reports that offenders generally admitted a lot of responsibility for the offence. Almost all showed remorse and offered apologies. Victims, who in more than two-thirds of these cases rated themselves as having been considerably affected by the crime, tended in most cases to accept the apologies, though expressed forgiveness was rare. Explicit disapproval of the offence and shaming of the offender occurred in a majority of conferences, but was accompanied by support for the offender in almost all conferences.

Each conference concluded with an outcome agreed by all participants. Both parties and their supporters tended to concentrate on the offender's future and how to stop reoffending, rather than on the victim's needs. Outcomes were usually focused on drug or alcohol problems and remedies, literacy, skills training and employment issues for the offender, with reference to financial reparation for the victim rare. Monitoring of our JRC conferences indicated that almost 90 per cent of offenders completed at least some of their undertakings. Of the remainder, many were unable to complete them because of reasons beyond their control. Participation rates in drug and alcohol programmes were particularly high.

Shapland *et al.* concluded that all three programmes had been generally well implemented in terms of case flow and in following RJ principles, with good relations maintained with criminal justice officials and with high levels of engagement of both victims and offenders.

Shapland, J. Atkinson, A., Atkinson, H., Chapman, B., Dignan, J., Howes, M *et al.* (2007) *Restorative justice: The views of victims and offenders. The third report from the evaluation of three schemes.* London: Ministry of Justice Research Series 3/07.

In their third report, the Sheffield team focuses on the views of victims and offenders who had participated in the three programmes. In our JRC RCTs, two attempts were made to interview participants in both the RJ and the control groups. The first interview was requested within three weeks of the case finalisation to ensure that they had not suffered any ill-effects, and to gain some feedback on their experience. Then 8–10 months after each case was finalised, Shapland's team approached participants in all three programmes in the evaluation study period and asked them to complete either an interview or a questionnaire. The response rate was variable, ranging from 4 to 80 per cent across all the programmes; most were in the range of 40–60 per cent, with slightly higher figures for victims than offenders.

Both victims and offenders in all three programmes said they were pleased with the preparation they had been given and the amount of information they had received about RJ. All were clear that the process was entirely voluntary. Both victims and offenders said they had wanted to take part so as to communicate with each other, to say what they felt about the offence and its effects and to try to solve problems, especially problems behind the offending.

Commenting on the content of the RJ conferences, our JRC victims and offenders told Shapland's team that they were very positive about the experience. Over 85 per cent said the conference went well, that they had felt safe, and that the facilitator had been fair and impartial. Victims said that they especially were glad of the opportunity to explain the effects of the offence, to get answers to their questions directly from the offender and to make their own assessment of the offender. Offenders said the best thing was being able to apologise personally and to explain about the offence, even though they had been very apprehensive beforehand about doing so. Very high percentages of both victims and offenders in all JRC RCTS (almost all in excess of 85 per cent) said that they had been able to say what they wanted and that apologies had been expressed and accepted. Victims were as likely to say that they had accepted apologies in the more serious offences as the less serious; for example 100 per cent of the robbery victims and 86 per cent of

the prison study victims. Overall, 85 per cent of JRC victims and 80 per cent of offenders said that they were satisfied with their conference. Most victims felt that the conference had occurred 'at the right time' after the offence, even though that varied from a matter of a very few weeks to many years, suggesting that there is a broad timeframe in which RJ can be helpful.

RJC in prison. Many of the JRC conferences were held in the prisons where the offenders were either on remand (the London burglary and robbery cases) or serving their sentence (Thames Valley violence cases). Victims almost never indicated that prison had been a problematic location for their conference; they had been well briefed about what they would encounter arriving at the prison (security routines, etc.) and within the prison. Victims often incurred significant travel and other expenses for the prison conferences, but these were met by the programmes. Future programmes would probably need to make provisions for these costs to yield similar take-up rates.

The REMEDI and CONNECT programmes both presented an opportunity to assess the relative benefits of direct and indirect mediation and to compare both of them to RJ conferencing. The evaluators were clear that direct mediation was superior to indirect mediation on important indicators for victims especially, and that RJ conferencing was superior to both of them.

References

Ahmed, E., Harris, N., Braithwaite, J. & Braithwaite, V. (2001). *Shame management through reintegration.* Cambridge: Cambridge University Press.

Angel, C. (2005). *Victims meet their offenders: Testing the impact of restorative justice conferences on victims' post-traumatic stress symptoms.* PhD dissertation, University of Pennsylvania.

Arendt, H. (1958). *The human condition.* Chicago, IL: University of Chicago Press.

Bennett, S. (2008). *Criminal careers and restorative justice.* Phd Dissertation, University of Cambridge.

Blagg, H. (1997). A just measure of shame? Aboriginal youth and conferencing in Australia. *The British Journal of Criminology, 37,* 481–501

Braithwaite, J. (1989). *Crime, shame and reintegration.* Cambridge: Cambridge University Press.

Braithwaite, J. (2002). *Restorative justice and responsive regulation.* Oxford: Oxford University Press.

Christie, N. (1977). Conflicts as property. *British Journal of Criminology, 17,* 1–15.

Collins, R. (2004). *Interaction ritual chains.* Princeton, NJ: Princeton University Press.

Cook, T.D. & Campbell, D.T. (1979). *Quasi-experimentation: Design and analysis for field settings.* Boston, MA: Houghton Mifflin.

Doll, R. (1992). Sir Austin Bradford Hill and the progress of science. *British Medical Journal, 305,* 1521–1526.

Farrington, D.P., Coid, J.W., Harnett, L.M. *et al.* (2006). *Criminal careers up to age 50 and life success up to age 48: New findings from the Cambridge Study in Delinquent Development* (2nd edn). London: Home Office.

Federal Judicial Center (1981). Experimentation in the law: Report of the Federal Judicial Center Advisory Committee on Experimentation in the Law. *Journal of Research in Crime and Delinquency*, 29(1), 34–61.

Huxley, E. (1939). *Red strangers*. London: Chatto and Windus.

Kubzansky, L, Koenen, K., Spiro, A., Vokonas, S. & Sparrow, D. (2007). Prospective study of posttraumatic stress disorder symptoms and coronary heart disease in the Normative Aging Study. *Archives of General Psychiatry*, 64(1), 109–116.

Landenberger, N. & Lipsey, M. (2005). The positive effects of cognitive–behavioral programs for offenders: A meta-analysis of factors associated with effective treatment. *Journal of Experimental Criminology*, 1, 451–476.

Marshall, T. (1999). *Restorative justice: An overview*. London: Home Office.

Marshall, T.F. (1997). Criminal justice conferencing calls for caution. *Mediation* (2 parts).

McGarrell, E., Olivares, K., Crawford, K. & Kroovand, N. (2000). *Returning justice to the community: The Indianapolis restorative justice experiment*. Indianapolis, IN: Hudson Institute.

Miers, D., Maguire, M., Goldie, S., Sharpe, K., Hale, C., Netten, A. *et al.* (2001). *An exploratory evaluation of restorative justice schemes*. Crime Reduction Series, paper 9. London: Home Office.

Newburn, T., Crawford, A., Earle, R., Goldie, S., Hale, C., Masters, G. *et al.* (2001). *The introduction of referral orders into the youth justice system*. HORS 242. London: Home Office.

Piantadosi, S. (1997). *Clinical trials: A methodologic perspective*. New York: Wiley.

Prison Fellowship (2008). *Sycamore Tree Programme*. Retrieved 21 October 2008 from www.prisonfellowship.org.uk/?page=sycamoretree

Roche, D. (2003). *Accountability in restorative justice*. Oxford: Oxford University Press.

Rossner, M. (2008). *Why emotions work: Restorative justice, interaction ritual and the micro potential for emotional transformation*. PhD dissertation, University of Pennsylvania.

Rothbaum, B.O. & Foa, E.B. (1999). Exposure therapy for PTSD. *PTSD Research Quarterly*, The National Center for Post-Traumatic Stress Disorder, White River Junction, VT, 10 (2), 1Y8.

Shapland, J. Atkinson, A., Atkinson, H., Colledge, E., Dignan, J., Howes, M. *et al.* (2006). *Restorative justice in practice. The second report from the evaluation of three schemes*. Sheffield Centre for Criminological Research, University of Sheffield.

Shapland, J. Atkinson, A., Atkinson, H., Chapman, B., Dignan, J., Howes, M. *et al.* (2007). *Restorative justice: The views of victims and offenders. The third report from the evaluation of Three Schemes*. London: Ministry of Justice Research Series 3/07.

Shapland, J. Atkinson, A., Atkinson, H., Dignan, J., Edwards, L., Hibbert, J. *et al.* (2008). *Does restorative justice affect reconviction? The fourth report from the evaluation of three schemes*. London: Ministry of Justice Research Series 10/08.

Shapland, J., Atkinson, A., Colledge, E., Dignan, J., Howes, M., Johnstone, J. *et al.* (2004). *Implementing restorative justice schemes (Crime Reduction Programme): A report on the first year*. Home Office online report 32/04, London, Home Office. Retrieved 15 September 2009 from www.homeoffice.gov.uk/rds/pdfs04/rdsolr3204.pdf

Sherman, L.W. (2003). Reason for emotion: Reinventing justice with theories, innovations and research. The 2002 ASC Presidential Address. *Criminology*, 41, 1–38.

Sherman, L. & Strang, H. (2007). *Restorative justice: The evidence*. London: Smith Institute.

Sherman, L., Strang, H., Angel, C., Woods, D., Barnes, G., Bennett, S. *et al.* (2005). Effects of face-to-face restorative justice on victims of crime in four randomized controlled trials. *Journal of Experimental Criminology*, 1(3), 367–395.

Sherman, L., Strang, H., Barnes, G. & Woods, D. (2006). *Race and restorative justice*. Paper Presented to the American Society of Criminology, November, 2006.

Soothill, K., Francis, B., Ackerley, E. & Humphreys, L. (2008). Changing patterns of offending behaviour among young adults. *British Journal of Criminology*, 48, 75–95.

Strang, H (2002). *Repair or revenge: Victims and restorative justice*. Oxford: Oxford University Press.

Strang, H. (forthcoming). Exploring the effects of restorative justice on crime victims for victims of conflict in transitional societies. In *International handbook of victimology*. Thousand Oaks, CA: Sage.

Strang, H. & Sherman, L. (forthcoming). *The effects of restorative justice conferencing on crime victims and offenders: A Campbell Collaboration Crime and Justice Group systematic review*. Cambridge: Jerry Lee Centre for Experimental Criminology, Institute of Criminology, University of Cambridge.

Strang, H., Sherman, L., Angel, C., Woods, D., Bennett, S., Newbury-Birch, D. *et al.* (2006). Victim evaluations of face-to-face restorative justice experiences: A quasi-experimental analysis. *Journal of Social Issues*, 62(2), 281–306.

Sykes, G.M. & Matza, D. (1957). Techniques of neutralization: A theory of delinquency. *American Sociological Review*, 22, 664–670.

Tutu, D. (1999). *No future without forgiveness*. New York: Rider, Random House.

Tyler, T. (1990). *Why people obey the law*. New Haven, CT: Yale University Press.

United Nations (2002). *Basic principles on the use of restorative justice programmes in criminal matters*. Commission on Crime Prevention and Criminal Justice, April, Vienna.

Woolf, P. (2008). *The damage done*. London: Bantam Press.

27

Concluding Themes
Psychological Perspectives and Futures

Graham J. Towl

Introduction

As readers will perhaps have noticed in this volume, but also in some of the broader professional developments within the British Psychological Society, the term 'forensic' has come to embrace both criminological and legal psychology in the UK. It is no longer viewed, as a term, as narrowly, or some would say as technically accurately, as in the past. It would, of course, no longer be accurate, in any meaningful manner in the modern world of forensic psychology. In this volume alone there is a real breadth of territory covered, which justifies the claim that forensic psychology is becoming a clearly defined branch of applied psychology. The discipline has developed from modest beginnings to emerge as one of the most popular areas of applied psychology with prospective students. The growth is reflected not just in the academic literature but also in the expanding numbers of those in the professional forensic psychological communities. But the field is perhaps at different stages of development in different areas. Some areas are well developed, others much less so. Some areas enjoy the benefits of much empirical evidence, others are considerably less well epistemologically or empirically endowed.

Three pervasive contextual themes emerge from the current state of the field. First, there is a large and expanding set of financial interests in the area. The forensic psychological field of courts, probation, prisons, special hospitals, police stations, secure units and related settings is potentially a large market which can accommodate a range of product lines, including psychometric test

sales, licensing, administration, interpretation and staff training. Second, the managerialist-based approaches have impacted upon much of forensic psychological policy and practice. Third, and most important, has been the need to further develop the professional and ethical basis of much of the forensic field.

Three key psychological perspectives are evident from much of what is contained within this book. First, there are some contested perspectives within (and beyond) the forensic psychological field. We have seen the heavy reliance among many in the field in aping medical perspectives with an uncritical reverence of psychiatric taxonomies. Second, there appears to be wider agreement on the need to adopt a rigorously scientific approach to forensic work. Third, much may be gleaned from both laboratory and field-based experiments in applying the methods and knowledge base of experimental psychology to the applied forensic psychological knowledge, policy and practice base.

Contextual Themes

Perhaps one of the biggest areas of financial interests in the forensic field is in the domain of psychometric testing. Psychometrics is big business. The forensic field is a booming and big market. Both private companies and individual psychologists have benefited financially from this. It is an industry that is keen to expand its markets, market share and shareholder value. Some psychometric tests and 'tools' have been sometimes aggressively marketed in the forensic field. It is important to consider such matters when looking at the merits and demerits of particular approaches to working with offenders. One fundamental question which is often missed in the everyday business of both research and practice is who benefits from the use of a test or assessment? It is a basic but very important question. It is not unknown for psychologists to recommend particular training or testing from which they may receive a financial benefit. This means that there is a clear conflict of interest in such cases. One useful potential parallel is between the psychometrics industry and the drugs industry. The drugs industry is much more tightly regulated. The quality of the research requirements for the release of new drugs is much more stringent than for psychometric tests. This perhaps reflects, to some degree, the power and influence of such businesses. It is a power and influence that few psychologists appear to question, never mind challenge. This can be due to a lack of awareness, complacency, lack of concern or be linked to their individual interests in maintaining the current, sometimes ethically challenging, state of affairs. There are some further parallels that may be noted. For example, we may look at the area of the marketing of drugs and also the marketing of psychometric tests. Both present as having a firm scientific basis. Both may attempt to secure favourable quotes for marketing purposes from those in positions of authority. This may be seen to give the particular product some additional 'product authority'. Additionally, there can be an ethically unacceptable use of language in the marketing of the products. For example, the term 'reliability' in terms of test construction has a particular usage and meaning. It is a meaning which is fundamentally different from its everyday usage. In everyday parlance the term reliability would refer to that which may be relied upon. In the psychometric testing industry the term is used in the technical sense to refer to consistency. In technical terms a test may have high reliability but low validity. Thus it could be marketed, with apparent legitimacy, as having high reliability. However, this would not mean that it could be relied upon in the everyday sense, very far from it. Such uses of language can be fundamentally misleading. Of course, any literature on individual tests needs to be carefully written to convey technical information but also clear in the way that language is being used so as not to lead to ambiguity and confusion. If psychologists find themselves recommending particular tests then it would seem a bare minimum in terms of ethical expectations that they would declare an interest in the administration of the test should they be gaining any financial benefit directly or indirectly from its usage.

Moving on from markets to managerialism, business is the common denominator between these two influential themes underpinning many of the environments that forensic psychologists populate. Successive governments over recent years have sought to import the methods and language of the private sector into the public sector. One purported purpose of this approach has been to introduce private-sector-based efficiencies into the public sector. The idea is that public sector organisations are inefficient and private sector organisations are efficient. Putting aside whether or not such assertions stand even the most perfunctory scrutiny, the language of business has been imported into much of the public sector. Thus senior managers in probation and prisons will refer to their 'business plans' despite having no business to plan, but rather a probation service or prison to run. There is nothing wrong, and in my view, much right, with being 'business like' in the approach to running public services. But prisons, probation, courts and hospitals are not 'businesses' and if such importation is taken too literally, and too far, there can be some rather perverse inefficiencies which result. Some business terms sit uneasily in such an environment; for example, would probation or prison officers be content with serving offenders as customers? Probably not.

Why is this of importance within forensic psychology or to forensic psychologists? It is important because the commitment to managerialism means an unprecedented receptivity to measurement and manualisation. What is counted becomes what counts. Resources are then allocated accordingly, which is a recipe for the potentially wasteful use of public resources. Probably one of the most powerful and costly illustrations of this has been in relation to so-called 'offending behaviour programmes'. These are discrete interventions with a narrow focus rather than 'programmes' as an integrated set of interventions as more generally understood. 'Success' for such interventions within probation and prisons is measured in terms of the number of people attending the courses. This is, of course, a very limited measure, but nonetheless very easily measurable. And this is part of the problem with managerialist approaches. The 'programmes' themselves have become tainted with some of the fundamental problems of managerialism in public services. Such approaches produce perverse incentives amongst the staff and offenders. Even working within such limited models of measurement, alternative more accurate and apposite measures have been suggested and not implemented (see Crighton & Towl, 2008).

There is a popular myth within some of the forensic psychology community that such programmes in probation and prisons thrived simply and chiefly because of the emerging evidence base. This is, at very best, a rather partial truth. Although there was some encouraging international evidence, some of which was replicated on a small scale in the UK, in subsequent years, overwhelmingly there has been a subsequent failure to demonstrate the efficacy of the courses. In financial terms the courses have provided the public with very poor value for money indeed, yet they continue to be invested in. This is remarkable in times of renewed pressures on the public purse. The largest-scale UK studies have failed to demonstrate a convincing reduction in reconviction treatment effect in cognitive-skills-based courses or in the domain of sex offender treatment. There has never been a successful robust demonstration of the reduction of sexual reconviction rates in the entire, now fairly lengthy, history of sex offender treatment in prisons in England and Wales. So the argument that such courses are delivered on the grounds of the evidence are not persuasive. They are more plausibly delivered because of political imperatives.

Interestingly, some of the user community are not fooled by the claims of the efficacy of the courses. Psychologists do have a professional interest in their continuation, in the short term perhaps. But in the long term this cannot be good for the professional reputation of the discipline. In prisons 'programmes', despite initial promise, have become enmeshed in the broader managerial malaise of running prisons. They are less to do with 'treatment' in any psychologically meaningful sense and more to do with structured activities and institutionalised legitimacy for all concerned. They provide legitimacy for prisoners because the narrative is that they are 'addressing their offending'. They provide legitimacy for psychologists and other staff because they are engaging in the genuinely challenging task of working with offenders to reduce the risk of their reoffending. The Parole Board and its members are likely also to express approval that the offender is undertaking such work in view of their commitment to public protection. This is despite the mainstay of UK evidence. The over-reliance upon supportive international studies will have a limited shelf life. We are already well past the 'best before' dates of this family of offender 'treatment' industry products. Undoubtedly though, new products will be brought to this lucrative marketplace.

This brings us rather neatly into the domain of professional and ethical issues. It can be extremely challenging in everyday practice to focus on what are the most important professional and ethical issues to address. This is perhaps especially so with 'systems based' problems. Thus an individual may do their level best to act professionally and ethically but in a potentially less than ethical organisational environment. This can be very difficult emotionally and intellectually. There are few easy answers. Difficult choices sometimes need to be made. This can require a great deal of moral, professional and personal courage. Some of the most difficult ethical decisions for professionals can arise when doing the right things means that there will be a personal and professional cost to such assertive behaviour. This is one reason why it is so important for, particularly fully qualified, staff to ensure that all under their supervision and management are enabled to raise concerns and challenge any existing practices. It has been previously observed that psychologists are by no means immune to the processes of institutionalisation. In environments characterised by vast differences in power we need to be especially mindful of our professional responsibilities to protect the vulnerable and, where appropriate, challenge the powerful. This includes raising concerns with colleagues about their professional practices if there are concerns. Ethical issues within the profession tend to focus on the behaviour of individuals or sometimes groups, but comparatively rarely are the broader contextual issues considered. The impact of managerialism and the growing psychometrics and offender courses industry surely warrant closer professional and ethical scrutiny. Such developments have significant impacts on the immediate environments within which many psychologists in the forensic field function.

But the single most significant milestone in the history of the professional regulation of psychologists came into force in July 2009 with the advent of statutory regulation of practitioner psychologists through the Health Professions Council (HPC). This is a very positive development, with an independent regulation system for psychologists. Peer-based regulatory systems tend to lack credibility, with the spectre of professional self-interest looming in the minds of others. It is far more robust and ethical to have a system which draws from a broader and more truly independent set of perspectives in areas such as, for example, misconduct. Many practitioner psychologists will find this reassuring, but more importantly, so will members of the public. The detail of the new arrangements will of course be important. But the principle most surely will be right; it is better to be regulated by a set of independent others than by one's, sometimes close, peers. This allows for more robustness and transparency of processes, which is important. These are exciting times and statutory regulation will be viewed as a historical turning point in psychological practice in the UK.

Psychological Perspectives

There are some contested accounts within the field of mental health, and this is also so for forensic mental health, about the utility and empirical integrity of psychiatric taxonomies. Some of the discussion and debates are reflected in the chapters of this book. Arguably, one problem has been not solely with the taxonomies themselves but with the uses to which they have sometimes been put. It is as if some psychologists assume that there is more scientific rigour to their development than there is. The uncritical usage of such imported psychiatric terminology is perhaps all too common. Sometimes the collections of descriptions that make up the taxonomies are taken to be explanations in themselves, rather than simply a constellation of observed signs. Readers can make up their own minds, but such considerations do require critical thinking rather than mere professional compliance with the products of the psychiatric industry standards.

Much of the forensic field adopts a rigorously scientific approach to the consideration of research methods. And it is important that as the knowledge base develops, such rigour is built upon. Much has been learned about the developmental trajectories towards criminality. There remains a need for further rigorous, independent and scientifically robust randomised control trials (RCTs) and also longitudinal research. As illustrated in some of the chapters of this book, there has been a growth of work in the area of witness testimony, including research on children as witnesses. The court decision-making processes have also been the subject of scholarly study. There has also been some excellent work undertaken on risk assessment.

But one area where there has been rather more of a mix of research quality has been in the domain of the evaluation of interventions aimed at reducing the risk of reoffending. First, there is a dearth of randomised controlled trials. Second, there is an overreliance upon self-report and related psychometric measures in the evaluation of courses in prisons and probation aimed at reducing the risk of reoffending.

The quality of some of the evaluation research is poor to barely satisfactory. The field has been curiously resistive of the development of RCTs. This perhaps reflects a lack of confidence in the robustness of the interventions themselves. It is unlikely to be fundamentally a financial issue given the very generous amounts of the public purse that have gone into some of these experimental treatments. There have been some ethical concerns raised about the use of RCTs. The primary ethical concern appears to be associated with denying treatment to some who may need it and if they don't get it may go on to harm others. This would perhaps be more persuasive if we knew that the treatments themselves actually worked. We don't know that; that is what we would be seeking to find out. The ethical objection arguably only holds if we have a treatment that works. It could be that some treatments simply teach the participants the appropriate language that they need to learn and use to secure positive reports in support of, e.g. their parole. Some offenders may well take this approach to their courses. But if we think that some of the courses are potentially powerful tools for behavioural change, we need to consider that the change may occur in either direction. That is, for some participants the results may be that they have an increased risk of reoffending as a result of participating in the course. Of course, the hope and expectation is that this will not happen and that change will be positive change. But not all change is positive. In practical terms, one of the implications of this is that we need to be very careful as to how we match prospective participants to courses. This is an ethical issue which, unfortunately, may sometimes be compromised in the name of the managerialist imperative to achieve 'targets' for 'completions' on courses in probation and prisons. As noted above, psychologists have a clear ethical responsibility to challenge such practices if and when they occur.

Elsewhere in this book and chapter the issue of the growth of the psychometric testing industry in moving into forensic markets has been mentioned. There has been a marked overreliance upon these for claims in support of the efficacy of 'offending behaviour' courses in prisons and probation in the UK. One major problem with this, putting the industry interests aside, is that they at best provide us with data that we can make some inferences about. There will, of course, sometimes be some powerful response biases to self-report data, arguably amplified in the forensic context. Again this is an area where industry and professional interests appear sometimes to have been allowed to take precedence over alternative, more rigorously scientific evaluation methods. Of course, this is only an illustrative example of one area of forensic endeavour where a less than rigorous approach has sometimes been taken to evaluation. Similar problems of a lack of methodological rigour apply in, for example, the currently fashionable area of offender profiling; this is touched upon in some detail in an earlier chapter in the book.

The third psychological perspective to be considered is the exciting potential of the wider application of the knowledge base and methods of experimental psychology to forensic psychological study and practice. There are some areas of forensic research where this is already the routine way of working. For example, in looking at witness testimony an understanding of memory research is routinely drawn upon. It is clear that both psychological laboratory and field-based studies of memory may have utility in improving forensic understanding. Such models and methods need perhaps to be more widely applied within the forensic field. In forensic assessments such as interviews for risk assessments we may be heavily reliant upon the patients' reports of previous events. A fuller understanding of the working of memory could perhaps help inform judgements made in assessment report writing. It would perhaps be helpful to see the more widespread uses and applications of models of human behaviour gleaned from experimental psychology applied to the forensic knowledge base. There are numerous opportunities for both laboratory and field-based studies. Opportunities abound in the exciting yet challenging field of forensic psychology.

Futures

With a period of transnational financial recession the pressure on the public purse in the UK is likely to be greater than was previously the case, especially in the more recent boom years of governmental expenditure on public services, including hospitals, prisons and probation services. Senior managers in these domains have enjoyed the benefits of bigger budgets. A different style of management now may be needed. Although the managerialism referred to above is unlikely to disappear, there may well be some refinements of the approach. Large-scale services are likely to have some areas of significant waste, so some large savings could probably be made without a loss of the quality or quantity of service provision.

In terms of the application of the academic discipline of psychology and psychological models there is a need to adopt a more rigorous and empirically consistent approach to the development of some areas of the work. We have seen how, for example, psychologically based courses run with offenders in probation and prisons may well benefit from independent review in terms of the evidence base. The same may be said, as alluded to earlier, for some areas of offender profiling work. Risk assessment is an area that has taken some great strides in recent years, but here again, policy makers and practitioners need to be better informed by the evidence. And this is a central contribution that psychologists can make to the criminal and civil justice systems – we can bring a level of empirical rigour drawing upon a psychological evidence base and perspective. However, this is an area which needs more work within the forensic psychology community. That is, the challenge of how we may lever benefits from the broader experimental psychology knowledge base for the benefit of improving forensic psychological understanding and practice. This is a process already well developed in some areas of forensic psychology, as amply illustrated in this volume. In terms of the stage of development of the discipline, forensic psychology has come of age in recent years and we now need to fulfil our initial promise. It is perhaps serendipitous that the advent of statutory regulation has come upon us at this key developmental stage of our discipline. A future that is self-critical and self-reflective, driven by an evidence-based ethically underpinned approach, will be a bright future.

Reference

Crighton, D.A. & Towl, G.J. (2008). *Psychology in prisons* (2nd edn). Oxford: BPS Blackwell.

Index